W9-AFE-975

Principles of Accounting

Principles of Accounting

Belverd E. Needles, Jr.
Ph.D., C.P.A., C.M.A.
Professor of Accounting
Director, School of Accountancy
DePaul University

Henry R. Anderson
Ph.D., C.P.A., C.M.A.
Professor of Accounting
Dean, School of Business Administration and Economics
California State University, Fullerton

James C. Caldwell
Ph.D., C.P.A.
Manager of Professional Education Service
Arthur Andersen & Co.
Dallas/Fort Worth

Houghton Mifflin Company Boston
Dallas Geneva, Illinois Hopewell, New Jersey Palo Alto London

To Marian Needles, and to Jennifer and Jeff
To Sue Anderson, and to Deborah, Howard, Harold, and Hugh
To Bonnie Caldwell, and to Stephanie, Susan, and Sharon

Cover photograph by David Wade

Printed in the U.S.A.

Library of Congress Catalog Card Number: 80-80503

ISBN: 0-395-29527-0

Contents

Part Six Basic Concepts of Manufacturing Accounting

Preface

Principles of Accounting is a comprehensive first course in accounting for students who have had no previous training in accounting or business. It is designed for both majors and nonmajors and is intended for use in the traditional two-semester and two- or three-quarter sequences. The textbook is part of a well-integrated package consisting of Study Guide; Working Papers (4 sets); Practice Sets I, II, and III; Computer-Assisted Practice Set; Instructor's Solutions Manual; Practice Sets Solutions Manuals; Transparencies (approximately 825); Test Bank; Computer-Assisted Test Bank; Achievement Tests; and Check List of Key Figures.

We wrote this book because we believe that the first course in accounting should emphasize concepts and practices that will be useful to students throughout their careers, whether they are accounting majors or not. The learning method of this book combines doing with understanding. Concepts take on meaning when applied, and practices are most easily understood if related to a conceptual foundation.

These beliefs are reflected in the principal objectives and features of the package: (1) its design for the student's first exposure to accounting; (2) its authoritative and practical basis; (3) its contemporary emphasis; (4) its class-tested and accurate learning materials; and (5) its completeness as a flexible learning system.

Design for the Student's First Exposure to Accounting

The text's intended audience has influenced the organization of the book in several ways. First, we have carefully planned the timing of new concepts and techniques to facilitate learning. We try for a pace that enables the student to grasp and retain the material. For example, we have delayed the presentation of adjusting entries, recognized as one of the most difficult topics for beginning students, until Chapter 4. Second, we have taken special care, particularly in the early part of the book, to limit the number of difficult concepts or practices in each chapter. To aid comprehension of adjusting entries in Chapter 4, for instance, we have devoted most of the chapter to this activity. Third, the book presents accounting as one of the most important and fascinating professions in our society, one in which men and women can participate either as producers or as consumers of accounting information. Finally, the focus throughout is on understanding rather than on mere memorization.

To facilitate student learning, we use the sole proprietorship in the first half of the book to illustrate basic accounting concepts and techniques, but at important points in Chapters 1 and 7 we point out the relationship of proprietorship accounting to corporation accounting. In Chapter 7, for example, we introduce students to corporate financial statements by presenting excerpts from the annual report of McDonald's Corporation and point out the differences between proprietorship and corporation statements.

Authoritative and Practical Basis

We have tried to present accounting as practiced, but at the same time we explain each accounting practice in relation to underlying concepts. Throughout we define accounting terms and concepts according to current pronouncements of the AICPA, APB, FASB, CASB, and other official bodies. As the basis for our discussions, we frequently cite APB Opinions and FASB Statements. We assess various interpretations of accounting situations and controversies in terms of how well they relate to the standards that accounting information must meet, as found in the Accounting Principles Board's *Statement No. 4*, "Basic Concepts and Accounting Principles Underlying Financial Statements of Business Enterprises." Recent FASB Statements of Financial Accounting Concepts (numbers 1 and 2) and Statements of Financial Accounting Standards (numbers 33 and 37) are incorporated into the text.

Contemporary Emphasis

Another of our objectives has been to present the contemporary business world and the real-life complexities of accounting in a clear, concise, easy-to-understand manner. Accounting is treated throughout as an information system that helps people in making economic decisions. Chapter 1 emphasizes this role of accounting in business and society. It describes the use of accounting by all segments of society and discusses the impact of the AICPA, APB, FASB, CASB, SEC, and IRS on generally accepted accounting principles. Inflation accounting and international accounting are only two examples of contemporary topics given emphasis in the book. The inflation accounting section of Chapter 14 is intended to alert the student to some basic ways of dealing with a current problem. The section of Chapter 20 that is devoted to international accounting should help schools to meet the new accreditation standard of the American Assembly of Collegiate Schools of Business requiring that introductory courses cover the global aspect of business. Both of these topics, as well as others, may be supplemented by readings from the Study Guide that accompanies this text.

Class-Tested and Accurate Learning Materials

We have thoroughly class-tested the text, exercises, problems, and other learning materials in this book. In addition, other accounting instructors have used and verified the accuracy of the text, Study Guide, and Practice Sets in classes at Chicago State University and Mesa Community College.

Complete and Flexible Learning System

Organization

The organization of the book in seven parts is designed for schools using either a semester or a quarter sequence. Those using the two-semester or two-quarter sequence may cover three parts during the first term and four parts during the second. Those using the three-quarter sequence may cover two parts in each of the first two quarters and three parts in the last quarter. For schools emphasizing managerial rather than financial accounting, we have included more chapters on managerial accounting in the last two parts than does the typical introductory accounting book. If a shorter course is required, all or parts of Chapters 5, 8, 12, 14, 20, and 21 may be omitted or covered briefly without hindering comprehension of later chapters. For instructors who want to introduce students to the present and future value of money, an appendix with accounting examples and exercises is provided at the end of the text.

Textbook Features

Learning Objectives Action-oriented objectives beginning each chapter indicate in precise terms what the students should be able to do when they complete the chapter. The end-of-chapter review clearly relates each objective to the content of the chapter. The end-of-chapter questions, exercises, and problems test students' mastery of the objectives.

Accounting Practice Features To demonstrate the real-world applications of accounting procedures, many chapters contain graphs or tables illustrating the actual practice of business in relation to the topics of the chapter.

Illustrations The text contains many illustrations to enhance visual understanding of the material. Color is used to highlight important points.

Key Terms and Glossary Throughout the book, key accounting terms are emphasized with bold type and clearly defined in context. These terms are also conveniently arranged in a comprehensive glossary for easy reference.

Chapter Review A unique feature of the text is a special review section comprising (1) a Review of Learning Objectives, which summarizes the main points of the chapter in relation to the objectives; (2) a Self-Test in Chapters 1 through 5, consisting of multiple-choice items that review the basic conceptual material of these crucial early chapters, and end-of-chapter answers that provide immediate feedback on students' progress; and (3) in the more challenging chapters, a Review Problem with complete solution to demonstrate the chapter's major procedures before students tackle the exercises and problems.

Questions Discussion questions based on the major points covered are included at the end of each chapter. These questions usually focus on major concepts and terms.

Classroom Exercises Classroom Exercises provide practice in applying concepts taught in the chapter and are very effective in illustrating lecture points. Each exercise focuses on a single aspect of the chapter.

A and B Problems We have included two sets of problems to provide maximum flexibility in homework assignments. In general, the problems are arranged in order of difficulty, with Problems A-1 or B-1 for each chapter being the simplest, and the last in the series the most comprehensive. A and B problems have been matched by topic, so that A-1 and B-1, for example, are equivalent in content and level of difficulty. Where B problems have been deleted from the text, we have transferred them to both the Working Papers and the Instructor's Solutions Manual. Difficulty ratings, time estimates, and solutions are available to the instructor.

Technical Appendixes As an additional aid to learning, we have provided appendixes that contain information on using present and future value, as well as compound interest and present value tables.

Supplementary Learning Aids

The supplementary learning aids provide a variety of useful tools for the student. They consist of the Study Guide, Working Papers (4 sets), Practice Sets I, II, and III; and a Computer-Assisted Practice Set.

Study Guide This learning aid is a chapter-by-chapter guide to assist the student in understanding the chapter content. Each chapter begins with a summary, in numbered paragraph form, of the major concepts and applications in the chapter. Next, to test the student's basic knowledge of the chapter content, we provide a matching test of the most important key words and concepts, a completion test, a true-false test of important relationships, and a multiple-choice test. Finally, students are asked to apply their knowledge in short exercises. The answers to all tests and exercises are provided at the end of the guide. The Study Guide also contains readings selected from professional journals and the popular press that illustrate career opportunities, the societal impact of accounting, and difficult concepts covered in the text.

Working Papers and Selected Review Problems The working papers are designed to reduce pencil pushing by students to a minimum. Each problem has an appropriate form, certain information is preprinted, and in some cases, part of the answer is entered to provide a model for the student. Fully worked review problems are included for many chapters. Working Papers, Volumes IB and IIB, contain additional B problems.

Practice Set I: College Words and Sounds Store This practice set is designed to present a realistic set of records for a small merchandising concern over a two-month period. The transactions and records presented are typical of a small book and record store.

Practice Set II: Video-Games, Inc. This practice set demonstrates the corporate form of a wholesale sales business. In its early stages it also shows the changeover from partnership to corporation.

Practice Set III: Aluma-Cylinder Company, Inc. This practice set is a comprehensive simulation of a job order cost accounting system for a manufacturing firm. It covers a three-month period.

Computer-Assisted Practice Set: Berger Automotive Company This is a computer-assisted, interactive practice set that covers a twelve-month period. It requires no programming experience on the part of the student or the instructor and actually can be done manually if the instructor wishes. This practice set covers financial accounting and deals with an auto service proprietorship that grows into a corporation. Although the practice set stresses transaction analysis, it also demonstrates the computer's ability to speed the flow of accounting data. The practice set requires only forty to ninety minutes a week and can be handled as a laboratory or as a test.

Instructor's Aids

Instructor's Solutions Manual The Instructor's Solutions Manual contains solutions to all questions, exercises, and problems in the text. We rate each problem as easy, medium, or difficult and suggest the time in minutes that an average student will need to solve it. A chart summarizes the time and difficulty of the exercises and problems. Other features of the Instructor's Solutions Manual are complete chapter outlines, additional B problems, review problems and their solutions, self-tests and their answers for Chapters 6 through 29, answers to the achievement tests, and charts showing how each learning objective in the text is met by specific exercises and problems.

Test Bank and Achievement Tests Comprehensive and flexible sets of testing materials are available for the instructor. We have written all test items ourselves.

The Test Bank, which is available either in printed form or as a computer program, offers a variety of testing material for each chapter. Short exercises and problems are included as well as true-false and multiple-choice items. Overall, the Test Bank totals more than a thousand items.

There are also fourteen preprinted Achievement Tests, each with an A or B version. Each test covers two or three chapters. As in the Test Bank, short exercises and problems are included along with briefer questions. Points are assigned to each item, giving a total score of 100 points for each.

Transparencies More than 825 transparencies, which are free to adopters, provide instructional charts and diagrams as well as solutions to all A and B problems.

Check List of Key Figures This is available in quantity to instructors.

Acknowledgments

An introductory accounting text is a long and demanding project that cannot really succeed without the help of one's colleagues. We are grateful to a large number of professors and other professional colleagues for their constructive comments that have led to improvements in the text. Unfortunately, space does not permit us to mention all of those who have contributed to this volume. Some of those who have been supportive and who have had an impact on our efforts are: Albert Arsenault (Hillsborough Community College), Larry Bailey (Temple University), D. Dale Bandy (California State University, Fullerton), Harold E. Caylor (Lakeland Community College), Kenneth L. Fox (Kansas State University), Alan P. Johnson (California State University, Hayward), Charles Lawrence (Purdue University), W. Morley Lemon (McMaster University), Robert J. McCarter (CPA), Earl L. Smith (Oscar Rose Junior College), and Gary Sundem (University of Washington, Seattle).

We would particularly like to thank Hobart W. Adams (University of Akron) and Joseph Goodman (Chicago State University) for their accuracy checks of various manuscript drafts and Lee Wilson (Mesa Community College) for both his class-test activities and his substantive comments. Ms. Carol A. Gordon (Controller, Western Design Corporation, Costa Mesa, California) was very instrumental in developing problem material as well as in providing input for Practice Set III. Without the help of these and others, this book would not be possible.

B.E.N. H.R.A. J.C.C.

Elements in the Needles/Anderson/Caldwell Principles of Accounting Package

Materials available to assist students in their mastery of the text:

Study Guide and Introductory Readings, by Belverd E. Needles, Jr., and Edward H. Julius

Working Papers IA (for Problem Set A, Chapters 1–15)
Working Papers IIA (for Problem Set A, Chapters 15–29)
Working Papers IB (for Problem Set B, Chapters 1–15)
Working Papers IIB (for Problem Set B, Chapters 15–29)

Practice Set I: College Words and Sounds Store, by Belverd E. Needles, Jr.
Practice Set II: Video-Games, Inc., by Belverd E. Needles, Jr.
Practice Set III: Aluma-Cylinder Company, Inc., by Henry R. Anderson and Carol A. Gordon

Computer-Assisted Practice Set: Berger Automotive Company (for Chapters 3 through 21), by C. P. Carter and Douglas Platt

Materials available to assist instructors:

Instructor's Solutions Manual
Achievement Tests
Test Bank
Computerized Test Bank
Check List of Key Figures
Transparencies
Solutions Manual for Practice Sets
Solutions Manual for Computerized Practice Set

Part One

The Basic Accounting Model

Accounting is an information system for measuring, processing, and communicating information that is useful in making economic decisions.

Part I presents the fundamental concepts and techniques of the basic accounting system, including accounting for a complete cycle of business activities for a service enterprise.

Chapter 1 explores the nature and environment of accounting, with special emphasis on the users of accounting information, the roles of accountants in society, and the organizations that influence accounting practice.

Chapter 2 introduces the four basic financial statements, the concept of accounting measurement, and the effects of business transactions on financial position.

Chapter 3 continues the discussion of accounting measurement by focusing on the problems of recognition, valuation, and classification and how they are solved in the recording of business transactions.

In Chapter 4, the accounting concept of business income is defined, and the role of adjusting entries in its measurement is discussed and demonstrated.

Chapter 5 completes the accounting system with a presentation of the work sheet and closing entries.

Learning Objectives

Chapter One

Accounting in Business and Society

1. *Describe the role of accounting in making informed business and economic decisions.*
2. *Define accounting.*
3. *Recognize the many users of accounting information in society.*
4. *Recognize accounting as a profession with a wide career choice.*
5. *Describe the three basic forms of business organization.*
6. *Relate accounting theory and practice to generally accepted accounting principles (GAAP).*
7. *Recognize the organizations that influence generally accepted accounting principles.*

Your introductory accounting course begins with a general view of the accounting discipline and profession. In this chapter you will learn about the essential roles that accountants play in society and about the organizations where they work. As a result of studying this chapter, you should be able to meet the learning objectives listed on the left.

Every individual or group in society must make economic decisions about the future. For example, the manager of a company needs to know which products have been unsuccessful. With this information, the manager can decide whether to stop selling them or to do something that will increase their appeal to customers. Other individuals will want to find out if a firm is financially sound before accepting a job or investing money in the company. Similarly, nonprofit organizations require financial information. Federal, state, and local government units, for example, need financial information to levy taxes. Other nonprofit institutions such as churches and charities require meaningful and easily understood economic information before planning various social programs. Because of their financial expertise, accountants are often asked to search through the available financial data for clues that will serve as guides to the future.

Accounting and Decision Making

The primary reason for studying accounting is to acquire the knowledge and skills to participate in important economic decisions. The information accountants furnish provides the basis for such decisions both within and outside the business enterprise.

Thus accounting information

> is a tool and, like most tools, cannot be of much direct help to those who are unable or unwilling to use it or who misuse it. Its use can be learned, however, and [accounting] should provide information that can be used by all—nonprofessionals as well as professionals—who are willing to learn to use it properly.[1]

Objective 1
Describe the role of accounting in making informed business and economic decisions

The first step in this learning process is to understand how decisions are made and some of the ways in which accountants can contribute to the process.

To make a wise decision and carry it out effectively, the decision maker must answer the following questions:

What is the goal to be achieved? (Step 1)
What different ways are available to reach the goal? (Step 2)
Which alternative provides the best way to achieve the goal? (Step 3)
What action should be taken? (Step 4)
Was the goal achieved? (Step 5)

Figure 1-1 shows the steps that an individual or an institution follows in making a decision.

When the decision involves business and economic questions, accounting information is essential to the decision system because it provides quantitative information for three functions: planning, control, and evaluation. Figure 1-2 illustrates the role of accounting information in a decision system.

Planning is the process of formulating a course of action. It includes setting a goal, finding alternative ways of accomplishing the goal, and deciding which alternative is the best course of action. At this stage, the accountant should be able to present a clear statement of the financial alternatives. Accounting information dealing with projections of income and budgets of cash requirements would also be important in planning for the future.

Figure 1-1
A Decision System

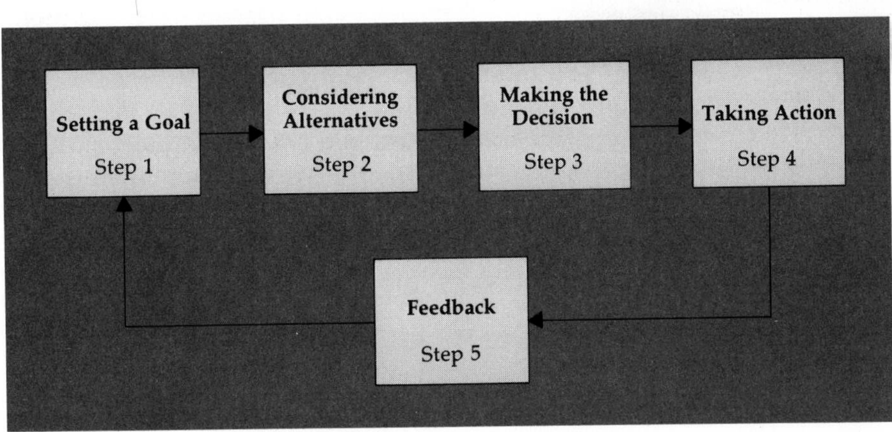

1. "Objectives of Financial Reporting by Business Enterprises," *Statement of Financial Accounting Concepts No. 1* (Stamford, Conn.: Financial Accounting Standards Board, 1978), p. 17.

Figure 1-2
A Decision System and Accounting Information

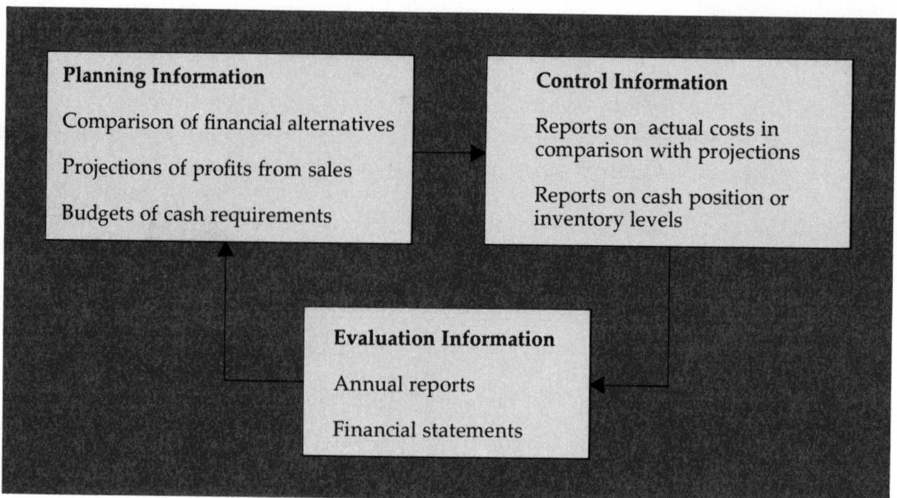

Control is the process of seeing that plans are actually carried out. In other words, do actions conform to plans? At this point, the accountant would be expected to provide information on actual costs, for example, in comparison with projections made earlier.

Evaluation, which encompasses the whole decision system, is the process of scrutinizing the decision system for the purpose of improving it. It asks the question, Was the original goal accomplished (feedback)? If not, the failure could have occurred because of poor planning or control, or perhaps because the wrong goal was chosen. Evaluation information may be contained in annual reports and other financial statements based on accounting information.

Modern Accounting

Objective 2
Define accounting

Early definitions of accounting tended to focus on the traditional record-keeping functions of the accountant. In 1941, for example, the American Institute of Certified Public Accountants (AICPA) defined accounting as "the art of recording, classifying, and summarizing in a significant manner and in terms of money, transactions and events which are, in part at least, of a financial character, and interpreting the results thereof."[2] The modern definition of accounting, however, is much broader. Recently the AICPA stated that the function of accountancy is "to provide quantitative information, primarily financial in nature, about economic entities that is

2. Committee on Accounting Terminology, *Accounting Terminology Bulletin Number 2* (New York: American Institute of Certified Public Accountants, 1953), p. 9.

Figure 1-3
The Role of Accounting in Business Decisions

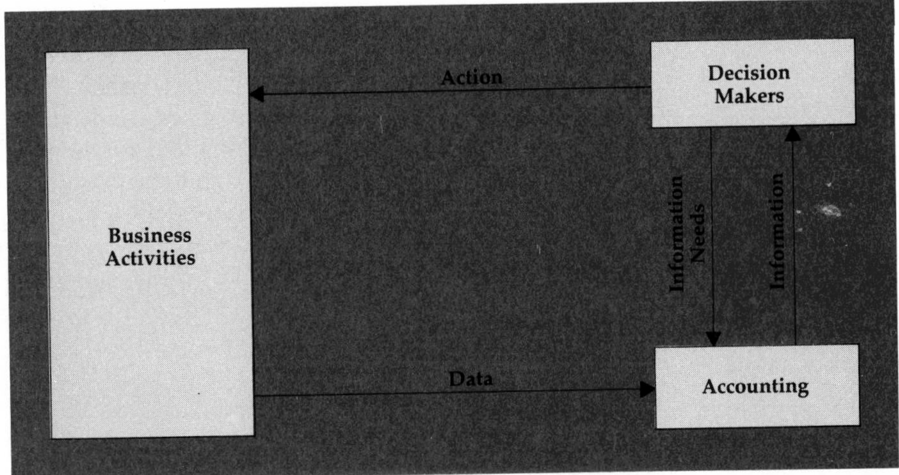

intended to be useful in making economic decisions."[3] (An economic entity is a unit such as a business that has an independent existence.)

The modern accountant, therefore, is concerned not only with record keeping but also with a whole range of activities involving planning and problem solving; control and attention directing; and evaluation, review, and auditing. The new focus of accounting is on the ultimate needs of users of accounting information, whether these users are internal or external to the business enterprise. Thus **accounting** "is not an end in itself"[4] but must be viewed as an information system that measures, processes, and communicates economic information about an identifiable entity. This information permits users to make "reasoned choices among alternative uses of scarce resources in the conduct of business and economic activities."[5]

The modern view of accounting is shown in Figure 1-3. In this view, accounting is seen as a service activity. It is a link between business activities and decision makers. In one sense, accounting is the eyes and ears of the decision makers and contributes largely to their success or failure. For this reason, the information needs of the decision makers must be a major input to accounting.

It is important to clarify the relationships of accounting to bookkeeping, the computer, and management information systems to avoid certain misconceptions about the nature of accounting.

Bookkeeping: An Accounting Process

People often fail to understand the difference between accounting and bookkeeping. **Bookkeeping,** which is a process of accounting, is the means of recording transactions and keeping records. Mechanical and

3. "Basic Concepts and Accounting Principles Underlying Financial Statements of Business Enterprises," *Statement of the Accounting Principles Board, No. 4* (New York: American Institute of Certified Public Accountants, 1970), p. 6.
4. *Statement of Financial Accounting Concepts No. 1,* p. 5.
5. Ibid.

repetitive, bookkeeping represents only a small, simple part of accounting. Accounting, on the other hand, includes the design of an information system that meets user needs, as described earlier. The ultimate objective of accounting is the analysis, interpretation, and use of information. Accountants look for significant relationships in the figures they produce. They are interested in finding trends and studying the effects of different alternatives. Accounting includes systems design, budgeting, cost analysis, auditing, income tax preparation or planning, and computer programming. To become a reasonably proficient bookkeeper takes several months to one year; to become a professional accountant takes years of education and experience.

The Computer: An Accounting Tool

The **computer** is an electronic tool that can collect, organize, and communicate vast amounts of information with great speed. It has revolutionized business activity during the past three decades. For example, given properly designed instructions, the computer enables credit card operations such as Master Card and VISA to record the charges and payments of millions of card holders with ease. It also allows an individual to reserve a seat on almost any airplane in the world months in advance. Using the computer, management can monitor and constantly control giant refineries and accomplish many other complicated tasks.

Accountants have been among the earliest and most enthusiastic users of computers. Before the age of computers, the millions of transactions of large organizations had to be recorded by hand. It often took months to produce financial reports that now take days or hours. Although it may appear that the computer is doing the accountant's job, it is in fact only a tool that is instructed to do the routine bookkeeping operations. Because it is important that the user of accounting information and the new accountant understand the processes underlying accounting, most examples in this book are treated from the standpoint of manual accounting. You should remember, however, that in practice most large accounting operations are now computerized.

Accounting and Management Information Systems

Most businesses use a large amount of information that is not financial in nature. Their marketing departments, for example, are interested in the style or packaging of competitors' products. Personnel departments keep health and employment records of employees. With the widespread use of the computer, many of these diverse information needs are being organized into what might be called a **management information system** (MIS). The management information system consists of the interconnected subsystems that provide the information necessary to operate a business. The accounting information system is the most important subsystem because it plays the primary role of managing the flow of economic data to all parts of a business and to interested parties outside the business. Accounting is the financial hub of the management information system; it gives both management and outsiders a comprehensive view of the business organization.

Decision Makers: The Users of Accounting

Objective 3 Recognize the many users of accounting information in society

We all use accounting and accounting information more than we commonly realize. Here are some questions we might ask about everyday activities that involve accounting:

In going to school How much money will it take to get through the next school year? Will there be enough money for rent, food, and transportation next month? What is the correct way to balance a bank statement and checkbook?
In buying a house Is the price too high? How should the financial statement for the mortgage company be completed? How is the interest on a loan computed? Is it better to rent or to buy?
In taking a job Is the company financially sound? What is its future? What are its most successful products? Are they the most profitable? What are the company's benefit plans and retirement programs?
In making an investment Is this a good company to invest in? What is the risk? What is the possible return? What is the company's profit record? Is the company in a good cash position? What are the chances of increased dividends?

These are just a few of the many important uses of accounting. As a member of various groups in management and society, the student of business and accounting will use accounting daily as an aid in making difficult decisions.

The users of accounting can be divided roughly into three groups: (1) those who manage a business, (2) those outside a business enterprise who have direct financial interest in the business, and (3) those individuals, groups, or agencies that have an indirect financial interest in the business. These groups are shown in Figure 1-4 (next page).

Management

Management is the group of people in a business with overall responsibility for achieving the company's goals. Business enterprises have many goals. These goals include providing quality goods and services at low cost, creating new and improved products, increasing the number of jobs available, improving the environment, and accomplishing many other social tasks. To achieve any of these goals, of course, the company must be successful. Success and survival in a rigorous, competitive economic environment require that management concentrate much of its effort on two primary objectives: profitability and liquidity. Profitability is the

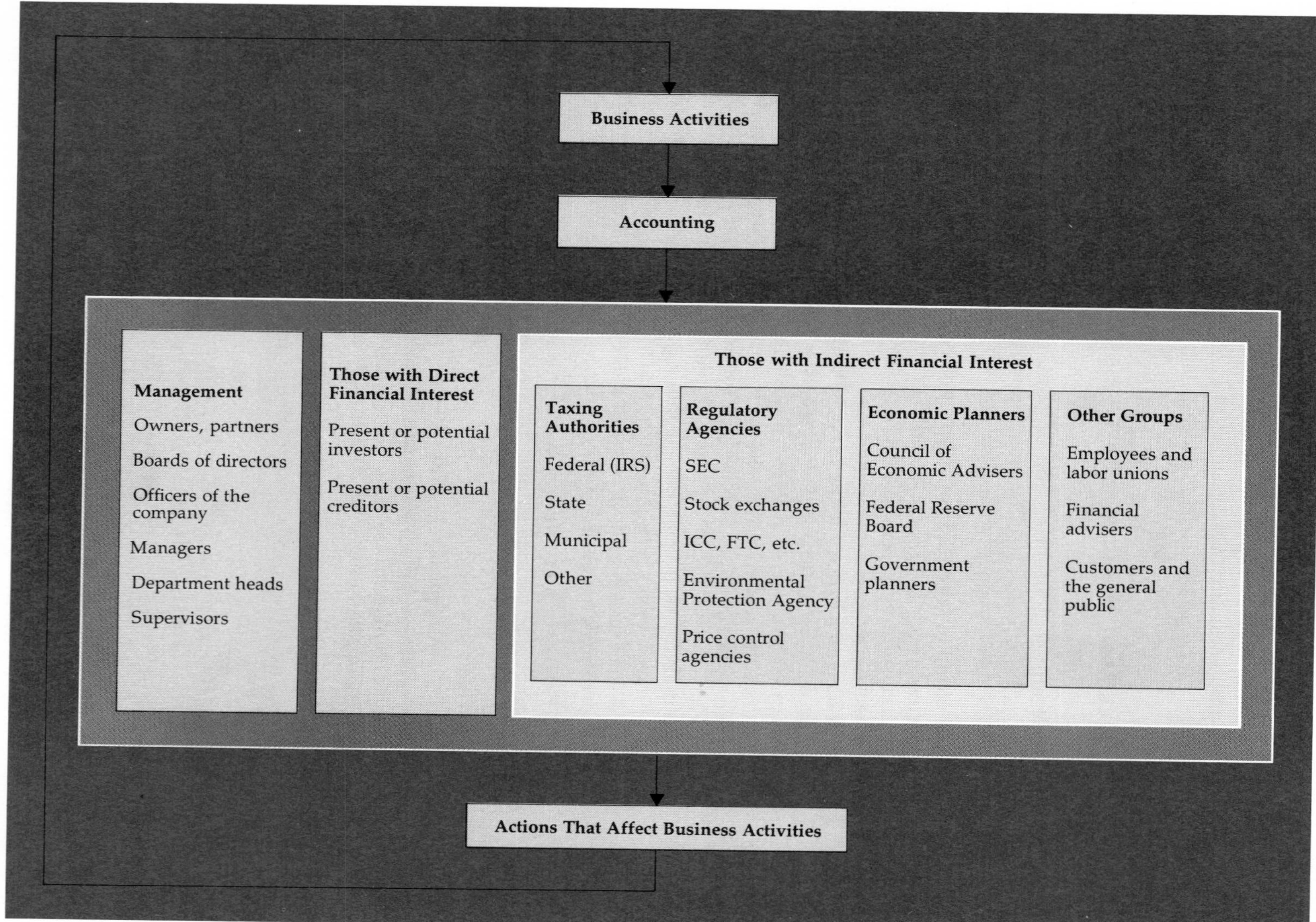
Business Activities
Accounting
Management
Owners, partners
Boards of directors
Officers of the company
Managers
Department heads
Supervisors
Those with Direct Financial Interest
Present or potential investors
Present or potential creditors
Those with Indirect Financial Interest
Taxing Authorities
Federal (IRS)
State
Municipal
Other
Regulatory Agencies
SEC
Stock exchanges
ICC, FTC, etc.
Environmental Protection Agency
Price control agencies
Economic Planners
Council of Economic Advisers
Federal Reserve Board
Government planners
Other Groups
Employees and labor unions
Financial advisers
Customers and the general public
Actions That Affect Business Activities

◀ Figure 1-4 The Users of Accounting

ability to make a profit sufficient to attract and hold investment capital. Liquidity means having enough funds on hand to pay debts when they fall due.

Management at all levels is responsible for a company's successful operation. In a small business, the greatest responsibility is often with the owner, who also manages the company's operations. In a large corporation, there will be many people charged with meeting the company's goals, from the board of directors and officers of the firm to the managers, department heads, and supervisors.

Managers must constantly decide what to do, how to do it, and whether the results conform to the original plans. Successful managers consistently make the right decisions on the basis of timely and valid information. Many of these decisions are based on the flow of accounting data and their analysis. As a consequence, management is one of the most important users of accounting information, and a primary function of accounting is to provide management with information that is relevant and useful.

In carrying out its responsibilities, the management of a company relies on accounting for four kinds of information: (1) status information, (2) planning information, (3) control information, and (4) evaluation information. For example, here are some questions a manager might ask:

How much profit did the company make during the last quarter? Which products, regions, or salespeople were successful in meeting budgeted profits? Where did costs exceed the budget?

Is the return to the owners adequate? How can it be improved?

Does the company have enough cash? What are the projected cash needs in six months? How much money has to be borrowed to build a new factory?

Are inventory levels (amounts of goods or supplies on hand) adequate?

Have collections of receivables (money owed to the company) improved?

What products are most profitable? Should some product lines or divisions be dropped or strengthened? What is the cost of manufacturing each product? How many units must be sold to break even (make up the amount spent in producing the units)? What combination of products should be sold?

Management routinely receives status information through all the financial statements, tax returns, and regulatory reports prepared for the company. These reports, which keep management informed as to the status of the company, are basically scorekeeping in nature. They monitor the overall performance of the company in meeting the goals of profitability, liquidity, and so forth. Although information can be taken from them and used in a variety of ways, these reports normally do not focus on specific operating uses. For the analysis of alternatives for planning and decision making, accounting provides many special reports such as comparisons of financial alternatives, recommendations for investments in new equipment, projections of profits for new sales campaigns, and budgets of cash requirements for the next year. After decisions are made, various managerial controls must be developed to ensure that operations proceed according to plans. To assist management in controlling operations, accountants prepare reports that direct management's attention to problem areas. For example, special accounting reports tell management if costs and production are in line with projections, if projected cash supply is dangerously low, or if inventory levels are too high. Finally, evaluation information enables management to review the progress of the entire management process. For example, reports that highlight key ratios and trends of sales, costs, and profits over a period of time are helpful in evaluating a company's progress.

Direct Financial Interest

A principal function of accounting is to measure and report information about how the business has performed. Most businesses publish periodically a set of general-purpose financial statements that report on their success in meeting objectives of profitability and liquidity. Although these statements represent what has happened in the past, they are important guides to future success. In today's society, there are many people outside the company who carefully study these financial reports.

Present or Potential Investors Those who are considering investment in a company are interested in the past success of the business and its potential for profits in the future. A thorough study of the company's financial statements will help potential investors assess the prospects for a profitable investment. After investing in a company, investors must continually review their commitment. Is the company performing as expected? Are profits satisfactory? Are interest payments and other distributions protected by an adequate supply of cash (cash flow)? Is the company investing in projects that can be expected to be profitable? Are the methods of financing growth and expansion sound? These investor questions and many more can be answered by a study of the periodic financial statements.

Present or Potential Creditors Most companies must borrow money for both long- and short-term operating needs. The creditors, who lend the money, are interested primarily in whether the company will have the cash to pay the interest charges and repay the debt at the appropriate time. They will study the liquidity and cash flow as well as the profitability of the company. Banks, finance companies, mortgage companies, securities firms, insurance firms, individuals, and others who lend money expect to analyze a company's financial position before making a loan to that company.

Indirect Financial Interest

Society as a whole, through its government officials and public groups, has in recent years become one of the biggest and most important users of accounting information. Some of the users who need accounting information to make decisions on public issues include (1) taxing authorities, (2) regulatory agencies, (3) economic planners, and (4) other groups.

Taxing Authorities Our governments are financed through the payment of taxes. Under federal, state, and local laws, companies and individuals pay many kinds of taxes including federal, state, and municipal income taxes, social security and other payroll taxes, excise taxes, and sales taxes. Each tax requires special tax returns and often a complex system of records as well. Proper compliance is usually a matter of law and can be very complicated. The Internal Revenue Code of the federal government, for instance, contains thousands of provisions relating to the preparation of operating financial statements.

Regulatory Agencies Most companies must report to one or more regulatory agencies at the federal, state, and local levels. All public corporations, for example, must report periodically to the Securities and Exchange Commission (SEC), which was set up by Congress to protect the public and which therefore regulates the issuing, buying, and selling of stocks in the United States. Companies that are listed on stock exchanges, such as the New York Stock Exchange, must also meet the special reporting requirements of the exchange.

In addition, the Interstate Commerce Commission (ICC) regulates industries such as trucking and railroads, and the Federal Aviation Administration (FAA) regulates airlines. All public utilities such as electric, gas, and telephone companies are regulated and must justify their rates with accounting reports.

Several new and broader requirements must also be met today. The Environmental Protection Agency (EPA) is concerned with the cost of reducing environmental pollution as well as the speed with which environmental pollution is decreased. The various price control agencies of the federal government often require that all price increases be justified on the basis of cost increases. Accounting reports are obviously an important element in these negotiations.

Economic Planners Since the 1930s, the government's wish to take a more active part in planning and forecasting economic activity has led to greater use of accounting and accounting information. A system of accounting called national income accounting has been developed for the whole economy. This system deals with the total production, inventories, income, dividends, taxes, and so forth of our entire economy. Planners who are members of the President's Council of Economic Advisers or are affiliated with the Federal Reserve System use this information to formulate economic policies and evaluate economic programs. Economic planners are concerned with such questions as these: What will the total profits be next year? What was the total national productivity last year? Should the money supply be increased or decreased? Are interest rates too high? What will the rate of inflation be?

Other Groups Employees, consumers, and the general public all have an interest in the financial statements of business organizations. Employees and labor unions study the financial statements of corporations as part of their preparation for bargaining in labor negotiations. The amount and computation of profits and costs are often significant factors in these negotiations.

Those who advise investors and creditors also have an indirect interest in the financial performance and prospects of a business. Included in this category are financial analysts and advisers, brokers, underwriters, lawyers, economists, and the financial press.

Consumers' groups, customers, and the general public have become more inquisitive about the financing and profits of corporations as they have become concerned with the effects of corporations on inflation, the environment, social problems, and the quality of life. For example, consumers' groups that are concerned about higher prices for food or energy may examine the financial reports of food retailers and wholesalers or oil companies.

The Accounting Profession

Objective 4 Recognize accounting as a profession with a wide career choice

Specially trained individuals measure, process, and communicate economic information to all users of accounting information. These men and women make up the accounting profession. The accounting function is as old as the need to exchange things of value and keep track of the wealth. The commercial and trading revolution of the Renaissance was a great impetus to accounting, as was the Industrial Revolution later. The great growth of industry and government in the twentieth century has expanded the need for accountants even further.

Today, accounting provides interesting, challenging, well-paid, and socially satisfying careers. The profession of accounting can be divided into four broad fields: (1) management accounting, (2) public accounting, (3) government and other nonprofit accounting, and (4) accounting education.

Management Accounting

An accountant employed by a business enterprise is said to be in **management accounting**. A small business may have only one or a few people doing accounting, whereas a medium-size or large company may have hundreds of accountants working under the supervision of a chief accounting officer called a controller, treasurer, or financial vice president. Other positions that may be held by accountants at lower managerial levels are assistant controller, chief accountant, internal auditor, plant accountant, systems analyst, financial accountant, and cost accountant.

Because of their broad and intimate view of all aspects of a company's operations, management accountants often have a significant impact on management decision making. According to most recent surveys, more top-level corporation executives have backgrounds in accounting and fi-

Major Academic Disciplines Representing 10 Percent or More of Top-Level Executive Positions

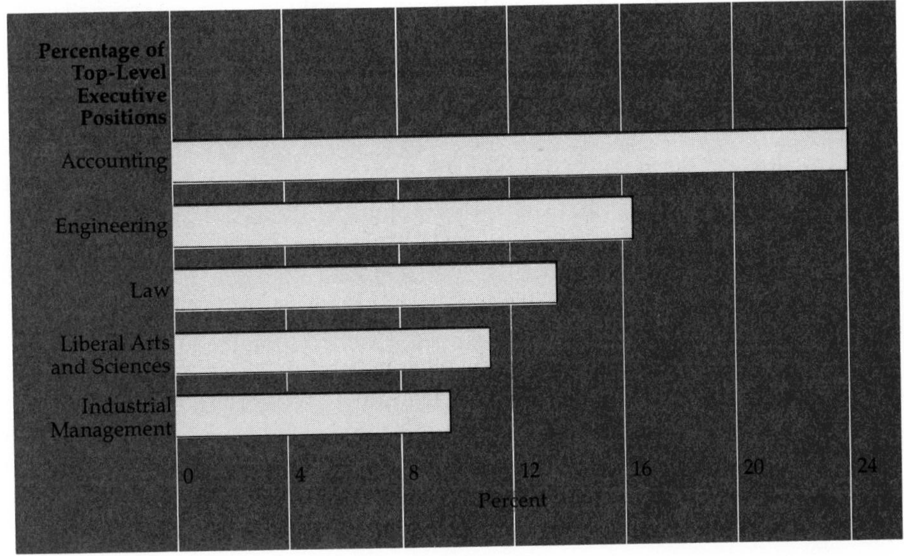

Source: Richard C. Bradish, "Accountants in Top Management," *Journal of Accountancy,* June 1970, p. 51. (Executive positions include chairman of the board, president, vice president, controller and secretary.)

nance than in any other field (see the accompanying graph). Just a few of the prominent companies whose president or chairman of the board is (or has been) an accountant are American Airlines, Chrysler, General Foods, International Business Machines, Caterpillar Tractor, General Motors, Kennecott Copper, Ford, General Electric, General Telephone and Electronics, Consolidated Edison, International Telephone and Telegraph, and 3-M.

It is the management accountants' task to provide management with the information needed for making intelligent decisions. They also establish a system of internal control to increase efficiency and prevent fraud in the company. They aid in profit planning, budgeting, and cost control. They must see that the company has adequate records, prepares proper financial reports, and complies with government taxation and regulation requirements. Management accountants should also be familiar with the latest developments and uses of computers in systems design.

Accountants provide many special reports for management decision making. This function requires the gathering of both historical and projected data. It is important for accountants to present the financial consequences of alternative courses of action so that the best one can be selected. Examples of these special reports include evaluations of proposed new products, analyses of alternative plant sites, a proposed advertising campaign, a long-term financing proposal, and a recommendation that a product, department, or service be dropped.

Management accountants may certify their professional competence and educational attainment in this field by qualifying for the Certificate in Management Accounting (CMA) administered by the Institute of Management Accounting of the National Association of Accountants. The

CMA program requires candidates to pass a series of uniform examinations and meet educational and professional standards.

Some specific activities in which management accountants may engage are described in the next few paragraphs.

General Accounting General accounting applies to overall record keeping, preparation of financial statements and reports, and control of all business activities such as sales, expenses, receivables, inventories, and payment of bills. Much of the material in this book falls into the area of general accounting.

Cost Accounting Cost accounting refers to the determination and control of costs. The cost accountant is concerned with the costs of manufacturing products as well as with the expenses of selling and distributing the products. It is important that the cost accountant collect, assemble, and interpret data in a way that helps management to assess current operations and plan for the future.

Budgeting Budgeting involves the planning of the financial aspects of operations. Budgets are necessary to management both in planning a course of action and in evaluating results. Many companies consider budgeting one of the most important duties of the accountant.

Tax Accounting The planning of business operations so as to minimize the effect of taxes on profits while complying with the tax laws is a very important function. The success of many financial transactions depends on the tax accountant's ability to handle the intricacies of the tax laws.

Information Systems Design Every enterprise requires an information system designed specifically for its requirements. This system includes forms, records, flow charts, manuals, controls, and reports. The design of systems has become more complex because the computer has made possible the expansion of systems design to include all aspects of the business, not just the financial records. Accountants who are specialists in systems design develop the systems and put them into effect.

Internal Auditing Most large companies have accountants who specialize in seeing that management's policies and procedures are complied with. They are also interested in safeguarding the company's assets. These accountants are called internal auditors. Accountants who make a career in this field may qualify for the Certificate in Internal Auditing administered by the Institute of Internal Auditors.

Public Accounting

The field of **public accounting** offers services in auditing, taxes, and management consulting to the public for a fee. In the short period since about 1900, the public accounting profession in this country has achieved stature comparable to that of the older professions of law and medicine. Certified public accountants (CPAs) are licensed by all states for the same reason that lawyers and doctors are—to protect the public by ensuring a high quality of professional service.

To receive a certificate and become a CPA, one must meet rigorous requirements. These requirements vary from state to state but have certain characteristics in common. An applicant must be a person of integrity and have at least a high school education. Most states require a college degree, with a major in accounting.

Further, the applicant must pass a difficult and comprehensive three-day examination in accounting practice, accounting theory, auditing, and business law. Although the examination is uniform in all states, some states require an additional examination in an area such as economics. The examination is prepared by the American Institute of Certified Public Accountants and is given twice a year. It is constantly updated to include the latest developments in the accounting profession.

Most states also require from one to five years' experience in the office of a certified public accountant or acceptable equivalent experience. In some cases, additional education can be substituted for one or more years of accounting experience.

In some states, the practice of accounting is not limited to certified public accountants. In these states, persons can set themselves up as public accountants (or PAs) simply by doing so or by paying a small fee. PAs have not met the requirements of the CPA.

Certified public accountants offer their services to the public for a fee, just as doctors or lawyers do. Accounting firms are made up of partners, who must be CPAs, and staff accountants, many of whom are CPAs and hope to become partners someday. Accounting firms vary in size from large international firms (see the accompanying table) with hundreds of partners and thousands of employees, to small one- or two-person firms.

Accounting's "Big Eight" Certified Public Accounting Firms

Firm	Home Office	Some Major Clients
Arthur Andersen & Co.	Chicago	ITT, Texaco, United Airlines
Arthur Young & Co.	New York	Mobil, RCA, Esmark
Coopers & Lybrand	New York	AT&T, Ford, Firestone
Deloitte, Haskins & Sells	New York	General Motors, Procter & Gamble
Ernst & Whinney	Cleveland	McDonnell Douglas, Coca-Cola
Peat, Marwick, Mitchell & Co.	New York	General Electric, Xerox
Price Waterhouse & Co.	New York	IBM, Exxon, DuPont
Touche Ross & Co.	New York	Chrysler, Boeing, Sears

The work of the public accountant is varied, complex, and interesting. A CPA might commonly be involved in the following activities:

1. Setting up or revising an accounting system for a business
2. Preparing plans for an audit
3. Discussing with a client the information obtained in an audit
4. Helping to prepare papers for registration of a stock issue with the Securities and Exchange Commission
5. Helping a manufacturer develop a computerized cost accounting system that would give the required information for a government contract
6. Assisting a client in obtaining a bank loan
7. Attending a committee of the state professional society to discuss the proper solution of a new accounting problem
8. Planning a system of internal control to prevent fraud or embezzlement
9. Testifying in court as an expert witness
10. Preparing a client's tax return or discussing his or her problems with a representative of the Internal Revenue Service (IRS)
11. Preparing a monthly financial statement for a small business
12. Advising a client about his or her needs for working capital over the coming year
13. Reviewing the financial report of a local community service organization

Most accounting firms organize themselves into three principal areas of specialization: (1) auditing, (2) tax services, and (3) management advisory services.

Auditing The principal and most distinctive function of a certified public accountant is auditing, which is the process of examining and testing financial statements. Society relies heavily on the auditing function—which is also called the attest function—for credible financial reports. All public corporations and many companies that apply for sizable loans must have their financial statements and records audited by an independent certified public accountant.

The purpose of an audit is to express the auditor's independent professional opinion on whether the company's financial reports fairly reflect its financial position and operating results. Auditors make any checks and tests of the accounting records and controls that seem necessary to satisfy themselves as to the adequacy of the financial statements. In addition to such routine procedures as proving cash balances, observing physical inventories, and verifying the amounts owed by customers, auditors must determine whether there are adequate controls and whether the records are kept in accordance with accepted accounting practices. In the end, they must rely on their own professional judgment to reach an opinion about financial reports. Their professional reputation is at stake because banks, investors, and creditors depend on the financial statements bearing their opinions in buying and selling the company's securities, making loans, and granting credit.

Tax Services The tax services offered by public accountants include not only the preparation of tax returns and assurance of compliance with tax laws but also the planning of business decisions to reduce the impact of taxes in the future. Accounting work in taxation requires considerable knowledge and skill regardless of the size of the business. Few business decisions are without tax consequences.

Management Advisory Services A growing and important segment of most public accounting firms' practice is management advisory services, or consulting. On the basis of their intimate knowledge of a business's operations, auditors can make significant suggestions for improvements and, as a matter of course, usually do. Traditionally, these recommendations have related to the areas of accounting records, budgeting, and cost accounting. But in recent years they have expanded into marketing, organizational planning, personnel and recruiting, production, systems, and many other operating areas. The wide use of computers has led to the offering of services in systems design and control and to the use of mathematical and statistical decision models. All these diverse services combined make up management advisory services. A recent brochure of the AICPA mentions the following specific examples of services in this category: long-range planning, executive compensation planning, work simplification, job evaluation, plant layout, materials handling, analysis of shop methods, pricing policies and market analysis, financing, planning for estate taxes (and estate planning), handling of reorganizations and mergers, installation of pension and profit-sharing plans, and renegotiation or termination of government contracts. Even this long list does not include all the services rendered by the management advisory divisions of CPA firms.

Government and Other Nonprofit Accounting

Among the important employers of accountants are government, social agencies, and other nonprofit enterprises.

Government Accounting Accounting for the government does not involve accounting for profit. However, accounting is indispensable to the government, which controls vast amounts of money. Agencies and departments at all levels of government hire accountants to prepare reports so that elected and appointed officials can responsibly carry out their duties. Millions of income, payroll, and sales tax returns must be checked and audited. In the federal government, the Federal Bureau of Investigation (FBI) and the Internal Revenue Service (IRS) use thousands of accountants. The General Accounting Office (GAO) audits government activities for Congress, using many auditors and other accounting specialists all over the world. Federal agencies such as the Securities and Exchange Commission, Interstate Commerce Commission, and Federal Communications Commission (FCC) and state agencies such as those concerned with public utilities regulation or revenue collection use accountants in many capacities in their regulation of business.

Social Accounting In this age of accountability, accountants are being called on more and more to use a new concept called social accounting. Social accounting helps evaluate the impact of government and other human service programs by attempting to answer questions about their cost and effectiveness. Some examples of these programs are welfare programs, housing subsidies, public education, and pollution control. Accountants working in these areas are looking for new ways to apply accounting techniques to pressing social problems. The correct analysis of such problems is one of the accounting profession's greatest challenges, because many of the things that must be evaluated cannot be measured in dollars and cents. For example, how can accounting processes and information aid in assessing the effectiveness of a new criminal justice system or the social benefits of an arts program for inner-city children?

Other Nonprofit Accounting There are many nonbusiness and nonindustrial enterprises besides the government that do not operate for profit but still employ many accountants. Some of these are hospitals, colleges, universities, and foundations. These institutions, like the government, are interested in compliance with the law and efficient use of public resources. They account for over 25 percent of the gross output of our economy. Obviously, the role of accountants in helping these organizations use their resources wisely is significant to our society.

Accounting Education

Training new accountants is a challenging and rewarding career, and instructors of accounting are currently in great demand. Accounting instructors at the secondary level must have a college degree with a concentration in accounting and must meet state teacher certification requirements. Entry-level requirements for teaching at the college level include the master's degree. A doctorate is usually required at the university level. In many schools, holding the CPA or CMA certificate will help an instructor to advance professionally.

Forms of Business Organization

Objective 5
Describe the three basic forms of business organization

Accountants need to understand the three basic forms of business organization: sole proprietorships, partnerships, and corporations. Accountants recognize each form as an economic unit separate from its owners, although legally only the corporation is considered separate from its owners. Other legal differences among the three forms are summarized in Table 1-1 and discussed briefly below. In this book, we first show accounting for the proprietorship because it is the simplest form of accounting. At critical points, however, we call attention to its essential differences from accounting for corporations and partnerships. Later, in Part

Table 1-1 Comparative Features of the Forms of Business Organization

	Sole Proprietorship	Partnership	Corporation
1. Legal status	Not a separate legal entity	Not a separate legal entity	Separate legal entity
2. Risk of ownership	Owner's personal resources at stake	Partners' resources at stake	Limited to investment in corporation
3. Duration or life	Limited by desire or death of owner	Limited by desire or death of each partner	Indefinite, possibly unlimited
4. Transferability of ownership	Sale by owner establishes new company	Changes in any partner's interest requires new partnership	Transferable by sale of stock
5. Accounting treatment	Separate economic unit	Separate economic unit	Separate economic unit

IV, we deal specifically with partnership accounting and corporation accounting.

Sole Proprietorships

A **sole proprietorship** is a business formed by one person. This business form gives the individual a means of controlling the business apart from his or her personal interests. Legally, however, the proprietorship is the same economic unit as the individual. The individual receives all profits or losses and is liable for all obligations of the proprietorship. Proprietorships represent the largest number of businesses in the United States, but typically they are the smallest in size. The life of a proprietorship ends when the owner wishes it to or at the owner's death or incapacity.

Partnerships

A **partnership** is similar in most respects to a proprietorship except that more than one owner is involved. A partnership is not a legal economic unit separate from the owners but an unincorporated association that brings together the talents and resources of two or more people. The partners share profits and losses of the partnership according to an agreed-upon formula. Generally, any partner can bind the partnership to another party, and the personal resources of each can be called on to pay obligations of the partnership if necessary. In some cases, one or more partners may limit their liability, but at least one partner must have unlimited liability. A partnership must be dissolved if the ownership changes, as when a partner leaves or dies. If the business continues, a new proprietorship or partnership must be formed.

Corporations

A corporation is an economic unit that is legally separate from its owners. The owners, whose ownership is represented by shares or stocks in the corporation, do not directly control the operations of the corporation. Instead they elect a board of directors who run the corporation for the benefit of the stockholders. In exchange for limited involvement in the corporation's actual operations, stockholders enjoy limited liability; they are liable only for the amount paid for their shares. If they wish, stockholders can sell their shares to other individuals without affecting corporate operations. Because of this limited liability, stockholders will be willing to invest in riskier, but potentially profitable, activities. Moreover, because ownership can be transferred without dissolving the corporation, the life of the corporation is unlimited and not subject to the whims or health of a proprietor or partner.

Corporations have several important advantages over proprietorships and partnerships (see Chapter 16) that make them very efficient in amassing capital for the formation and growth of very large companies. Although corporations are fewer in number than proprietorships and partnerships, they contribute much more to the national economy in monetary terms (see the accompanying chart). For example, in 1980 General Motors generated more revenues than all but thirteen of the world's countries.

Number and Receipts of U.S. Proprietorships, Partnerships, and Corporations, 1975

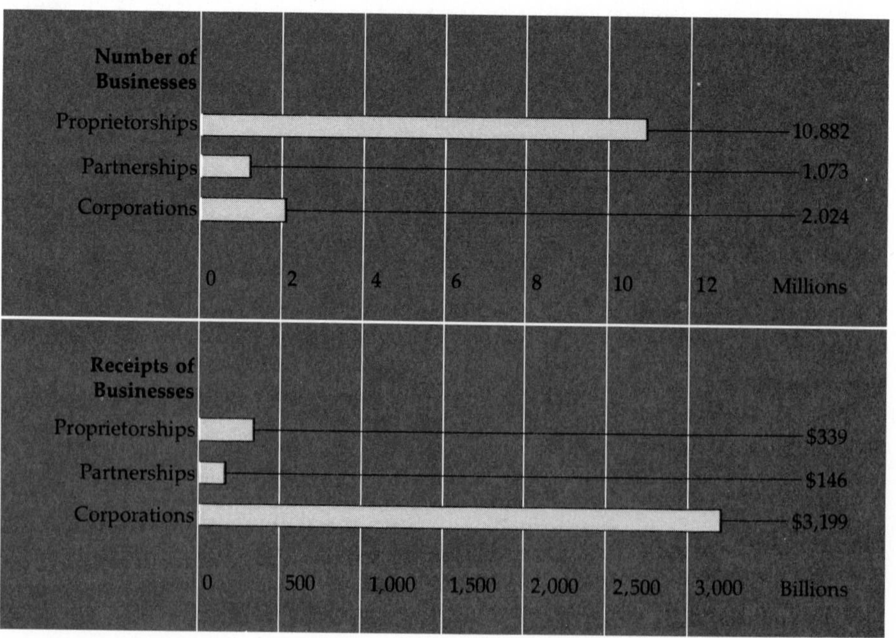

Accounting Theory and Practice

Objective 6 Relate accounting theory and practice to generally accepted accounting principles (GAAP)

Accounting is usually defined in terms of practice, or actions. In accordance with our earlier definition of accounting as an information system that measures, processes, and communicates information, **accounting practice** consists of the procedures used to carry out those functions. Accounting actions, however, must be the logical result of a reasoning process. In other words, a framework of **accounting theory** must underlie the actions or practice of accountants. Accounting theory answers the question, Why?; accounting practice answers the question, How?

In this book, we have attempted to present accounting practice as it exists today. In addition, we have tried to explain the reasons or theory on which the practice is based. The two—theory and practice—are part and parcel of the study of accounting. The student should realize that accounting is a discipline that is constantly growing, changing, and improving. Just as in medicine, where years of research may be necessary before a new surgical technique or lifesaving drug can be introduced into medical practice, research and new discoveries in accounting often take years to become common practice. Thus the student may occasionally encounter practices that seem inconsistent. In some cases, we have pointed toward new directions in accounting. The classroom instructor may mention certain weaknesses in current theory or practice. To help you understand how theory and practice have been and are developed, the following paragraphs examine the concept of generally accepted accounting principles and the organizations that influence them.

Generally Accepted Accounting Principles

The term **generally accepted accounting principles (GAAP)** is used widely and with several meanings in accounting literature. Perhaps the best definition is the following: "Generally accepted accounting principles encompass the conventions, rules, and procedures necessary to define accepted accounting practice at a particular time."[6] In other words, it is the consensus on the theory and practice of accounting at a particular time. Obviously, these "principles" are not like the immutable laws of nature found in chemistry or physics. They are developed by accountants and businesses to serve the needs of decision makers and can be changed as better methods are developed or as circumstances change.

Organizations Concerned with Accounting Practice

By definition, GAAP have wide authoritative support among practicing accountants and other organizations concerned with accounting practice. The more important of these organizations are the American Institute of

6. *Statement of the Accounting Principles Board, No. 4,* p. 54.

Objective 7 Recognize the organizations that influence generally accepted accounting principles

Certified Public Accountants, the Financial Accounting Standards Board (FASB), the Securities and Exchange Commission, the Internal Revenue Service, and the Cost Accounting Standards Board (CASB). In addition, there are state societies of CPAs and international organizations.

American Institute of Certified Public Accountants As discussed earlier, the **American Institute of Certified Public Accountants (AICPA)** is the professional association of CPAs and as such has been concerned with accounting practice longer than most organizations. From 1938 to 1958 the AICPA's Committee on Accounting Procedures issued a series of pronouncements dealing with accounting principles, procedures, and terminology. In 1959 the AICPA organized the Accounting Principles Board (APB) to replace the Committee on Accounting Procedures. The APB published a number of APB Opinions, which are also pronouncements on accounting practice. APB Opinions carry so much weight as authoritative documents that since December 31, 1965, departures from them in accounting practice must be reported along with a company's financial statements.

Financial Accounting Standards Board Although the APB Opinions are still in effect and will be referred to often in this book, the responsibility for developing and issuing rules on accounting practice was transferred in 1973 to a new body called the Financial Accounting Foundation and, in particular, to an arm of the foundation called the **Financial Accounting Standards Board (FASB).** This group is separate from the AICPA and issues pronouncements called Statements of Financial Accounting Standards. The foundation is governed by a board of trustees that includes the president of the AICPA and eight others elected by the AICPA. To ensure a variety of viewpoints, two of the trustees must be financial executives; one, a financial analyst; one, an accounting educator; and the remainder, CPAs in public practice.

Securities and Exchange Commission An important reason for disbanding the APB and establishing the FASB was that, although the APB had substantial influence over accounting practice, there were those both within and outside the government who felt the APB moved too slowly and was influenced too much by the clients of the accountants who served on the board. The **Securities and Exchange Commission (SEC)** is an agency of the federal government that has the legal power to set and enforce accounting practices for firms reporting to it and, as such, has tremendous influence on accounting practice. As the APB proved ineffective in solving some of the major abuses in accounting practice, the SEC began to play a larger and more aggressive role in establishing rules of accounting. The FASB represents a major effort on the part of accountants to maintain control over their profession and to limit the SEC to its traditional role, that of allowing the accounting profession to regulate itself. It appears certain that during the next decade the SEC will continue to apply pressure on the accounting profession to improve its accounting practice. The success or failure of the FASB will be important in determining the extent of the SEC's influence on accounting in the future.

Internal Revenue Service The U.S. tax laws govern the assessment and collection of revenue for operating the government. Because a major source of the government's revenue is the income tax, the law specifies the rules for determining taxable income. These rules are interpreted and enforced by the **Internal Revenue Service (IRS).** In some cases, these rules may be in conflict with good accounting practice, but they are a significant influence on practice. Income tax is a major cost of most profitable businesses and must be reflected in the records. Businesses must use certain accounting practices simply because they are required by the tax law. Sometimes companies follow an accounting practice specified in the tax law to take advantage of provisions that are financially beneficial to them. Cases where the tax law may affect accounting practice are noted throughout this book.

Cost Accounting Standards Board The **Cost Accounting Standards Board (CASB)** is another government agency that affects accounting practice, particularly in the area of cost accounting. The CASB, which was created by Congress in 1970, establishes cost accounting standards to be used by defense contractors in negotiated contracts. These standards are often applied to nondefense contracts.

State Societies of CPAs There are other organizations of accountants besides the AICPA. Each state has its own society of CPAs. In the larger states, such as New York, Illinois, Texas, and California, these societies are very active in the development of accounting practice.

International Organizations Worldwide cooperation in the development of accounting principles has made significant strides in recent years. The International Accounting Standards Committee (IASC) has approved more than ten international standards; these have been translated into six languages. In 1977, the International Federation of Accountants (IFAC), consisting of sixty-three professional accountancy bodies from forty-nine countries, was established to promote international agreement on accounting issues.

Other Organizations Concerned with Accounting The National Association of Accountants (NAA) is composed primarily of industrial accountants. This organization is engaged in education and research, with an emphasis on cost accounting and accounting for management decisions. The Financial Executives Institute (FEI) is made up of individuals who occupy the highest financial positions in large businesses; it is concerned primarily with standards and research in financial accounting.

The American Accounting Association (AAA) was founded in 1935, succeeding the American Association of University Instructors in Accounting, which was established in 1916. This organization has an academic and theoretical orientation. Its members have contributed significantly to the theoretical development of accounting.

Chapter Review

Review of Learning Objectives

1. Describe the role of accounting in making informed business and economic decisions.

Accounting is not an end in itself but a tool to be used to provide information that is useful in making reasoned choices among alternative uses of scarce resources in the conduct of business and economic activities.

2. Define accounting.

Accounting is an information system that measures, processes, and communicates economic information about an identifiable entity for the purpose of making economic decisions.

3. Recognize the many users of accounting information in society.

Accounting plays a significant role in society by providing information to managers of all institutions and to those with direct financial interest in those institutions such as present or potential investors or creditors. Accounting information is also important to those with indirect financial interest such as taxing authorities, regulatory agencies, economic planners, and other groups.

4. Recognize accounting as a profession with a wide career choice.

The people who provide accounting information to users make up the accounting profession. They may be management accountants, public accountants, or government or other nonprofit accountants. Each type of accounting work is an important specialization and represents a challenging career.

5. Describe the three basic forms of business organization.

The three basic forms of business organization are sole proprietorships, partnerships, and corporations. Sole proprietorships, which are formed by one individual, and partnerships, which are formed by more than one individual, are not separate economic units from the legal standpoint. In accounting, however, they are treated separately. Corporations, whose ownership is represented by shares, or stocks, are separate entities for both legal and accounting purposes.

6. Relate accounting theory and practice to generally accepted accounting principles (GAAP).

Accounting theory is the underlying rationale or reasoning behind accounting practice. Acceptable accounting practice at a particular time consists of those conventions, rules, and procedures that make up generally accepted accounting principles.

7. Recognize the organizations that influence generally accepted accounting principles.

Among the organizations that influence the formulation of GAAP are the American Institute of Certified Public Accountants, the Financial Accounting Standards Board, the Securities and Exchange Commission, the Internal Revenue Service, and the Cost Accounting Standards Board. Other organizations with an interest in accounting are the National Association of Accountants, the Financial Executives Institute, and the American Accounting Association.

Self-Test

Test your knowledge of the chapter by choosing the best answer for each item below.

1. Which of the following is an important reason for studying accounting?
   a. The information provided by accounting and accountants is useful in making many economic decisions.
   b. Accounting plays an important role in society.
   c. The study of accounting could lead to a challenging career.
   d. All of the above are important reasons.
2. Accounting is the same as
   a. bookkeeping.
   b. computer systems.
   c. management information systems.
   d. None of the above.
3. Which of the following groups uses accounting information for planning a company's profitability and liquidity?
   a. Management
   b. Investors
   c. Creditors
   d. Economic planners
4. Which of the following groups is most interested in using accounting information to determine a company's ability to pay back a loan?
   a. Management
   b. Investors
   c. Creditors
   d. Regulatory agencies
5. An accountant who provides services to the public for a fee is engaged in
   a. management accounting.
   b. public accounting.
   c. government accounting.
   d. nonprofit accounting.
6. Which of the following is not a type of management accounting?
   a. General accounting
   b. Cost accounting
   c. Auditing
   d. Budgeting
7. The most distinctive service offered by a certified public accountant is
   a. general accounting.
   b. auditing.
   c. tax services.
   d. management advisory services.
8. Which of the following forms of organization is not treated as a separate economic unit in accounting?
   a. Sole proprietorship
   b. Committee
   c. Partnership
   d. Corporation
9. Generally accepted accounting principles
   a. define accounting practice at a point in time.
   b. are similar in nature to the principles of chemistry or physics.
   c. are rarely changed.
   d. are not affected by changes in the ways businesses operate.
10. The organization that has the most influence on generally accepted accounting principles is the
    a. American Institute of Certified Public Accountants.
    b. Financial Accounting Standards Board.
    c. Securities and Exchange Commission.
    d. Internal Revenue Service.

Answers to Self-Test are at the end of this chapter.

Chapter Assignments

Questions

1. Explain how decisions are made.
2. What role does accounting play in the decision system?
3. What decision makers use accounting information?
4. What is the new focus of accounting?
5. Distinguish among these terms: accounting, bookkeeping, and management information systems.
6. What objectives does management seek to achieve by using accounting information?
7. Why are investors and creditors interested in the financial statements of a company?
8. Why has society as a whole become one of the biggest users of accounting information?
9. What groups besides businesses, investors, and creditors use accounting information?
10. What are some of the fields encompassed by the accounting profession?
11. What are some activities the management accountant might participate in?
12. How is public accounting different from management accounting?
13. Describe in general terms the requirements that an individual must meet to become a CPA.
14. What does a CPA do?
15. In what important ways do sole proprietorships, partnerships, and corporations differ?
16. What is the relationship between accounting theory and practice?
17. What are generally accepted accounting principles?
18. What are the AICPA, FASB, SEC, IRS, and CASB, and how do they influence accounting practice?

Classroom Exercises

Exercise 1-1 Role of Computer, Bookkeeper, and Accountant

Jane, James, and Jeff opened a clothing store earlier this year called The 3 Js. They began by opening a checking account in the name of the business, renting a store, and buying some clothes to sell. They paid for the purchases and expenses out of the checking account and deposited cash in the account when they sold the clothes. At this point, they are arguing over how their business is doing and how much each of them should be paid. They also realize that they are supposed to make certain tax reports and payments, but they know very little about them. The following statements are excerpts from their conversation:

Jane: If we just had a computer, we wouldn't have had this argument.
James: No, what we need is a bookkeeper.
Jeff: I don't know, but maybe we need an accountant.

Distinguish among computer, bookkeeper, and accountant and comment on how each might help the operations of The 3 Js.

Exercise 1-2
Users of Accounting Information

Public companies report each year on their success or failure in making a profit. Suppose that the following item appeared in the newspaper:

New York. Transnational Airlines reported yesterday that its net income for the year just ended represented a 200 percent increase over the previous year. . . .

Explain why each of the following individuals or groups may be interested in seeing the accounting reports that support the above statement.

1. The management of Transnational Airlines
2. The stockholders of Transnational Airlines
3. The creditors of Transnational Airlines
4. Potential stockholders of Transnational Airlines
5. The Internal Revenue Service
6. The Securities and Exchange Commission
7. The airline employees' union
8. A consumers' group called the Public Cause
9. An economic adviser to the president

Exercise 1-3
Accountants in Industry

A U.S. senator has been quoted as saying that in recent years more top management positions in industry are being filled by accountants because their experience enables them to take an overall perspective on large, worldwide enterprises and therefore they are better able to control such businesses.[7]

1. What positions in industry that are typically held by accountants can you name that would justify this statement?
2. Do you believe that accountants would be able to handle top government positions?
3. In what ways might an accountant be unsuited or inadequately trained for a top position?

Exercise 1-4
Role of Certified Public Accountant

Clarence Martin, a senior in college, was finishing his last term with a major in history when his father suffered a heart attack and died. Now Clarence finds himself the sole owner of a small manufacturing company that his father founded many years ago. Because he has not made any plans for a career, he decides to try running the family business. However, he is not sure how to start. One of his friends who attends a business school suggests that he might begin by talking to a certified public accountant.

1. Why do you think his friend made this suggestion?
2. In what ways could the certified public accountant be of help?

7. Paraphrased from quotation in Ralph W. Estes, *Accounting and Society* (Los Angeles: Melville, 1973), p. 102.

Exercise 1-5 Forms of Business

Since Sara Martinez began a small women's dress business in a local shopping mall two years ago, her sales have increased each year. She operates her business as a sole proprietorship. Next to her store is a women's shoe and accessory business operated by George Henderson. George has suggested that he and Sara form a partnership and combine the two businesses into a larger, more complete business. Sara believes this is a good idea but wonders if it would be better to form a corporation instead of a partnership.

1. Distinguish among the sole proprietorship, partnership, and corporation as forms of business.
2. What advantages and disadvantages does the partnership have?
3. What advantages and disadvantages does the corporation have?
4. What form of business do you think would be better for Sara and George?

Exercise 1-6 Contrasting Accounting Careers in Private and Public Accounting

Samuel Jones and Martha Thomas are both senior accounting students at the university. Samuel has decided to go to work as an accounting trainee for General Electric, a worldwide electronics company. Martha has accepted a position as a junior accountant for Ernst and Whinney, a worldwide accounting firm.

1. If Samuel is successful at General Electric, what kinds of jobs might he hold there throughout his career?
2. If Martha is successful at Ernst and Whinney, what kinds of activities might she be involved in throughout her career?

Exercise 1-7 Role of Accounting

Accounting can be viewed as (1) an intellectual discipline, (2) a profession, or (3) a social force. In what sense is it each of these?

Answers to Self-Test

1. d	3. a	5. b	7. b	9. a
2. d	4. c	6. c	8. b	10. b

Chapter Two

Accounting as an Information System

Learning Objectives

1. *Describe accounting as an information system.*
2. *Identify the qualitative characteristics of accounting information.*
3. *Identify the four basic financial statements.*
4. *Discuss the concept of accounting measurement.*
5. *Recognize the importance of separate entity, business transactions, and the unit of measure in accounting measurement.*
6. *Demonstrate the effects of simple transactions on financial position.*

This chapter gives you an overview of accounting as an information system for business decisions. First you need to understand the qualitative characteristics of accounting information. Then you are introduced to the basic financial statements, which communicate accounting information. Finally, after learning what accounting actually measures, you will study the effects of certain transactions on a company's financial position. As a result of studying this chapter, you should be able to meet the learning objectives listed on the left.

In Chapter 1, accounting was defined as an information system that measures, processes, and communicates economic information. This information about an identifiable entity provides the basis for reasoned decisions. Figure 2-1, which is an expanded version of Figure 1-3, shows accounting in the context of an information system. First, accounting records data on business activities for future use. Second, through data processing, the data are stored until needed, then processed in such a way as to become useful information. Third, the information is communicated through reports to decision makers who can use it. One might say that data about business activities are the input to the accounting system, and useful information for decision makers is the output.

This chapter looks first at the standards that accounting information must meet in order to be useful. It then examines the basic financial statements that are the most common instruments of accounting communication. The next part of the chapter introduces the study of accounting measurement, which forms a foundation for the more detailed explanation in Chapter 3. The chapter ends with an extended example showing the effects of business transactions on the financial position of a business entity.

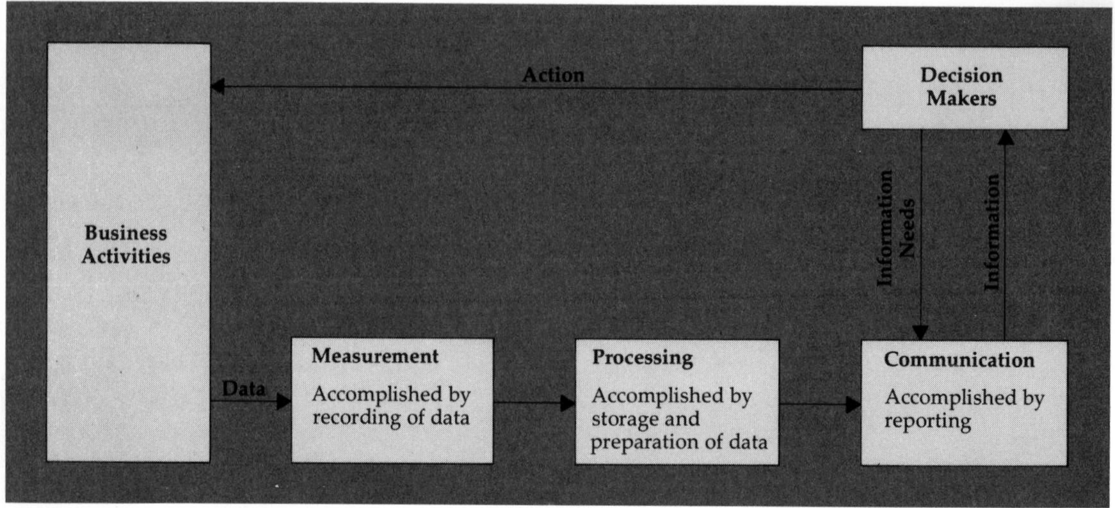

Figure 2-1 Accounting as an Information System for Business Decisions

Qualitative Characteristics of Accounting Information[1]

Although the goal of accounting information is to provide the basic data that diverse users need to make informed judgments, the burden of using information falls partly on the decision maker. The decision maker not only must judge what information to use and how to use it but also must understand the information. Understandability depends as much on the decision maker's ability to use the information as on the information itself.

Objective 1 Describe accounting as an information system (see page 29)

Objective 2 Identify the qualitative characteristics of accounting information

The accountant is concerned with the usefulness of accounting information in decision making. The Financial Accounting Standards Board has determined that, to be useful, accounting information must contain two primary qualitative characteristics. These primary qualitative characteristics, or standards of quality, which are criteria for judging the information accountants provide to decision makers, are relevance and reliability.

Relevance means that the information is capable of making a difference to the outcome of a decision. Information can affect decisions by improving decision makers' ability to predict or by providing feedback about the accuracy of earlier expectations. Closely related to relevance is timeliness. Timeliness relates to the arrival of accounting information to the user in time to make a decision. If information is not available when needed, it has no value for future action and is not relevant.

To be useful, information must be reliable as well as relevant. Reliability depends on representative faithfulness and verifiability. Representative faithfulness is the agreement of the information with what it is meant to represent. Accounting information purports to represent economic resources and obligations of a business and the events affecting those resources and obligations. Verifiability is related to the credibility of

1. The discussion in this section is based on *Statement of Financial Accounting Concepts No. 2*, "Qualitative Characteristics of Accounting Information" (Stamford, Conn.: Financial Accounting Standards Board, 1980).

accounting information and means that the information can be confirmed or duplicated by independent parties using the same measurement techniques.

Adding to the usefulness of accounting information is the characteristic of comparability. Information about an enterprise gains in usefulness if it can be compared with similar information about the same enterprise over several time periods or about another enterprise for the same time period. **Comparability** means that the information is presented in such a way that the decision maker can recognize similarities, differences, and trends. Consistent use of accounting measures and procedures is important in achieving comparability. A decision maker's ability to use accounting information depends greatly on the ability to compare that information with other information and arrive at a meaningful conclusion. Comparability will receive more attention in later chapters.

Judgment is important in the use of accounting information because these standards are not absolute. Reliability, relevance, and comparability are interrelated , and often impinge on one another. For example, comparability may suffer when an accounting method is changed to gain relevance, or relevance may suffer when a certain method is used because it is the most reliable. There may also be practical limits. For example, the cost of meeting a standard may exceed the benefits to be gained from using the information.

Limitations of Accounting Information

It is easy for a student in the first accounting course to get the idea that accounting is 100 percent accurate. This notion is reinforced by the fact that all the problems in this textbook and other introductory textbooks can be solved, the numbers all add up, what is supposed to equal something else does, and so forth. Accounting seems very much like mathematics in its perfection. In this course, we present the basics of accounting in a simple form at first to promote better understanding. In practice, however, accounting information is not simple or perfect and rarely satisfies all the above standards. The FASB emphasizes this fact in the following:

> The information provided by financial reporting often results from approximate, rather than exact, measures. The measures commonly involve numerous estimates, classifications, summarizations, judgments, and allocations. The outcome of economic activity in a dynamic economy is uncertain and results from combinations of many factors. Thus, despite the aura of precision that may seem to surround financial reporting in general and financial statements in particular, with few exceptions the measures are approximations, which may be based on rules and conventions, rather than exact amounts.[2]

The standards therefore represent an ideal. The gap between the ideal and the actual provides much of the interest and controversy in accounting mentioned in Chapter 1. It is also a primary reason why many people find enormous satisfaction in an accounting career. Improvements are constantly being made in the theory and practice of accounting, but great

2. "Objectives of Financial Reporting by Business Enterprises," *Statement of Financial Accounting Concepts No. 1* (Stamford, Conn.: Financial Accounting Standards Board, 1978), p. 9.

challenges still remain. The student who is alert will recognize many of these challenges in the following chapters.

Full Disclosure

One way in which accountants have tackled the problem of the limitations of accounting is through the concept of full disclosure. **Full disclosure** means revealing all important facts that might affect the decisions of an informed user of accounting information. Full disclosure is related to all the qualitative characteristics, but especially to the need for relevant, reliable, and comparable information. In general, full disclosure requires that accounting information contain whatever explanation is necessary to prevent it from being misleading. Thus, if the information is not complete, the accountant should say in what way it is not complete; if the information cannot be verified, the accountant should indicate this limitation; if the information is not neutral but is biased in some way, this fact should also be mentioned.

The principle of full disclosure has been influenced by users of accounting information in recent years. To protect the investor, independent auditors, the stock exchanges, and the SEC have all greatly increased their demands for disclosure by publicly owned companies. The SEC has been particularly aggressive in the enforcement of full disclosure. As a result, more and better information about corporations is available to the public than ever before.

Accounting Communication Through Financial Statements

Financial statements are a central feature of accounting. They are the primary means of communicating important accounting information to users. It is helpful to think of these statements as models of the business enterprise, because they are attempts to portray the business in financial terms. As is true of all models, however, financial statements are not perfect reflections of the real thing but the accountant's best effort to represent what is real. As mentioned before, financial statements have their limitations as accounting information; but used wisely and with an awareness of these limitations, they can be very important to the wide variety of users mentioned in Chapter 1.

The Accounting View of Business Activities

An age-old task of accounting is to measure the progress of a company in achieving its objective of making a profit. In a sense this task is easy. Suppose that the entire life of a business could be viewed at once. It would then be possible to find the difference between the owner's original investment in the business (plus any additional investments during the life of the business) and the owner's investment at the end of the business

Figure 2-2
Earnings During the Life of a Business

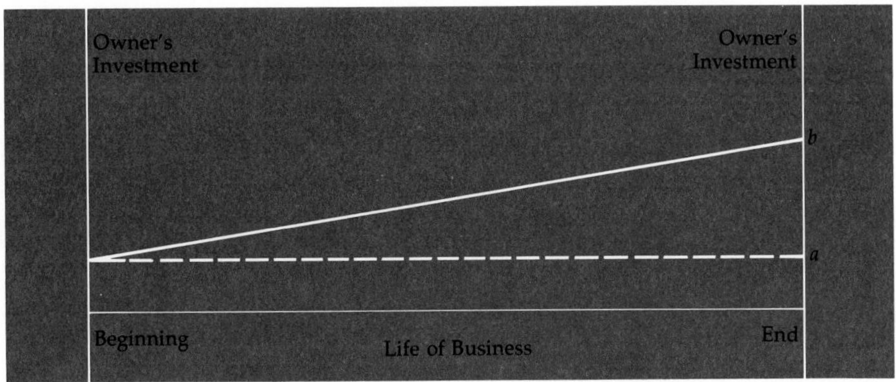

a = original plus additional investments by owners
b = ending owner's investment plus withdrawals of investments

$b - a$ = earnings during the life of the business

(plus any withdrawals of investments during the life of the business). This difference would represent the profit or loss during the life of the business, as illustrated in Figure 2-2. Let us take the example of a boy selling balloons at a parade. If he starts with two dollars in the morning (original investment), invests both dollars in balloons, sells all the balloons, and ends up with four dollars that night, his short-lived business has a profit of two dollars.

Unfortunately, it is not possible to wait until a business ceases to exist before determining its financial success. All public corporations are required to publish their earnings for each year, and many companies calculate earnings quarterly or monthly. Because it is impossible to sell the business each time earnings are calculated, the accounting profession has developed methods for measuring a company's ongoing success. These methods include dividing the life of a business into arbitrary but equal spans of time (such as a month or a year). Using various measurement techniques, a firm determines its financial position at the start and end of the period and the result of its profit-seeking activities during that time. Thus Figure 2-3 becomes a much more realistic version of Figure 2-2

Figure 2-3
Realistic Growth of Owner's Investment During the Life of a Business

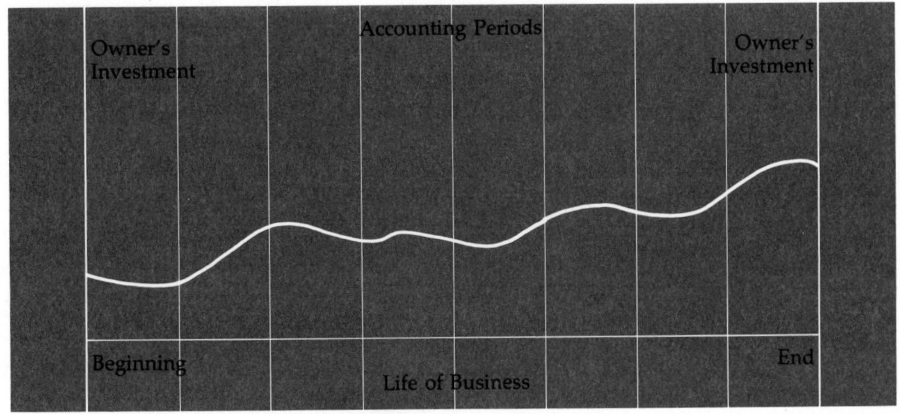

Figure 2-4 Relationship of the Balance Sheet, Income Statement, and Statement of Changes in Financial Position

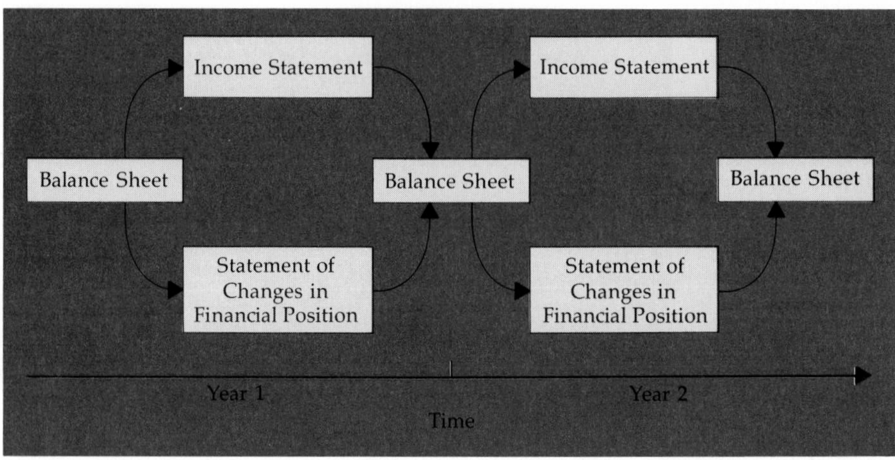

because the life of the business is divided into accounting periods; also, as in a real business, the earnings are not steady from beginning to end.

Objective 3 Identify the four basic financial statements

Four principal financial statements are used to communicate the required information about a business. One is the balance sheet, showing the financial position at either the beginning or the end of the accounting period. Another is the income statement, which reports on the activities or earnings of a business during the period. A third statement, called the statement of owner's equity (or capital statement), is related to a specific part of the balance sheet. A fourth and relatively new financial statement, called the statement of changes in financial position, is considered a major financial statement today. It is used to summarize all changes in financial position during the year, including those represented by the income statement. Figure 2-4 illustrates the relationship to the balance sheet of the income statement and of the statement of changes in financial position. Illustrated in the following sections are typical statements for proprietorships. Statements for partnerships and corporations, which are similar, are illustrated in later chapters.

The Balance Sheet

The purpose of a **balance sheet** is to show the financial position of a business on a particular date. For this reason, it is often called the statement of financial position. The balance sheet presents a view of the business as a collection of resources or assets belonging to the company that is equal to the sources of or claims against those assets. The sources consist of liabilities (debts of the company) and the owner's equity (the owner's interest in the company). Figure 2-5 reflects the financial position of Martin Laundry, the company used as an example.

Observe that the balance sheet for Martin Laundry gives (1) the name of the company; (2) the name of the statement, "Balance Sheet"; (3) the date of the balance sheet; and (4) separate sections for assets, liabilities, and owner's equity. The components of the balance sheet will be explained in more detail later in this chapter.

Figure 2-5
Financial Position of Martin Laundry

Martin Laundry
Balance Sheet
December 31, 19xx

Assets		**Liabilities**	
Cash	$ 1,000	Accounts Payable	$ 2,500
Accounts Receivable	1,300		
Land	500	**Owner's Equity**	
Building	10,000		
Equipment	10,000	John Martin, Capital	20,300
	$22,800		$22,800

The Income Statement

The income statement is a financial statement that shows the amount of income earned by a business over a period of time. Many people consider it the most important financial report because its purpose is to measure whether or not the business achieved or failed to achieve its primary objective of earning an acceptable income. Figure 2-6 is an example of an income statement for Martin Laundry.

Figure 2-6
Income Statement for Martin Laundry

Martin Laundry
Income Statement
For the Year Ended December 31, 19xx

Revenues		
Dry Cleaning	$25,700	
Wash and Dry	6,300	
Total Revenues		$32,000
Expenses		
Salaries Expense	$12,000	
Rent Expense	2,400	
Utilities Expense	3,600	
Telephone Expense	600	
Advertising Expense	4,400	
Total Expenses		23,000
Net Income		$9,000

Figure 2-7
Statement of Owner's Equity for Martin Laundry

Martin Laundry Statement of Owner's Equity For the Year Ended December 31, 19xx		
John Martin, Capital, Jan. 1, 19xx		$17,300
Add: Investment by John Martin	$4,000	
Net Income for the year	9,000	13,000
Subtotal		$30,300
Deduct withdrawals during the year		10,000
John Martin, Capital, Dec. 31, 19xx		$20,300

Note that the income statement sets forth (1) the name of the company, (2) the name of the statement, "Income Statement," (3) the period of time covered by the statement, and (4) separate categories for revenues and expenses. The net income (profit) or net loss represents the difference between the revenues and expenses.

The Statement of Owner's Equity

The statement of owner's equity relates the income statement to the balance sheet by showing how the owner's capital investment changed during the year. Figure 2-7 is the statement of owner's equity for Martin Laundry.

Note that the statement sets forth (1) the name of the company, (2) the name of the statement, "Statement of Owner's Equity," (3) the period of time covered by the statement, and (4) the beginning balance of the owner's capital account and how new investments by the owner, net income for the year, and withdrawals by the owner combine to give the ending balance of the owner's capital on the balance sheet date.

The Statement of Changes in Financial Position

During the past three decades, it has become clear that the income statement is deficient in one major respect. It shows the changes in financial position due only to those operations that produced an operating income or loss. Many significant events, especially those related to investing and financing activities, can occur during an accounting period and not appear on the income statement. For example, the owners may put more money into the business or take it out; buildings, equipment, or other assets may be bought or sold; or new liabilities can be incurred or old ones paid off. Consequently, the statement of changes in financial position is now widely used to show all changes in financial position that occur during an accounting period, especially the investing and financing activities

Figure 2-8
Statement of Changes in Financial Position for Martin Laundry

Martin Laundry Statement of Changes in Financial Position For the Year Ended December 31, 19xx		
Sources of Financial Resources		
Net Income	$ 9,000	
Investment by John Martin	4,000	
Sale of Equipment	3,000	
Total Sources		$16,000
Uses of Financial Resources		
Purchase of Equipment	$ 5,000	
Withdrawal by John Martin	10,000	
Total Uses		15,000
Increase in Financial Resources		$ 1,000

of a business. Figure 2-8 is an example of such a statement for Martin Laundry.

Observe that the statement of changes in financial position shows (1) the name of the company, (2) the title of the statement, "Statement of Changes in Financial Position," (3) the period of time covered by the statement, and (4) separate sections for the sources and uses of financial resources (the term *financial resources* will be defined more precisely in later chapters). The construction and use of the statement of changes in financial position are discussed in detail in Chapter 19.

Relationship of the Four Statements

Accounting attempts to sum up in a meaningful and useful way the financial history of a business, no matter how large and complex, in four relatively simple financial statements—an amazing feat. Two of the statements—the income statement and the statement of changes in financial position—deal with the activities of the business system over time. One statement—the balance sheet—shows the state of the system at a particular point in time. Another statement—the statement of owner's equity—ties the balance sheet and income statement together over a period of time. Much of the rest of this book deals with how to develop, use, and interpret these four statements.

Accounting Measurement

The accountant must answer four basic questions in order to make an accounting measurement:

1. What is to be measured?
2. When should the measurement occur?
3. What value should be placed on the measurement?
4. How is the measurement to be classified?

Objective 4 Discuss the concept of accounting measurement

The first question is answered in this chapter, and the last three questions are answered in Chapter 3. All the questions deal with fundamental underlying assumptions and generally accepted accounting principles, and their answers establish what accounting is and what it is not. Accountants in industry, professional associations, public accounting, government, and academic circles debate the answers to these questions constantly. As explained earlier, the answers change as new knowledge and new experience and practice require, but today's accounting practice rests on a number of widely accepted concepts and conventions mentioned in this and the following chapters.

What Is to Be Measured?

Objective 5 Recognize the importance of separate entity, business transactions, and the unit of measure in accounting measurement

The world contains an unlimited number of things to measure. For example, consider a machine that makes bottle caps. How many measurements of this machine could be made? They might include size, location, weight, cost, and many others. Some attributes of this machine are relevant to accounting; some are not. Every system must define what it measures, and accounting is no exception. Basically, financial accounting is concerned with measuring business transactions of specific business entities in terms of money measures. The concepts of separate entity, business transaction, and money measure are discussed below.

The Concept of Separate Entity

For accounting purposes, a business is treated as a separate entity that is distinct not only from its creditors and customers but also from its owner or owners. It should have a completely separate set of records. Its balance sheet refers only to its own financial affairs. The business owns assets and owes creditors and owners in the amount of their claims.

For example, the Jones Florist Company should have a bank account that is separate from the account of Kay Jones, the owner. Kay Jones may own a home, a car, and other property, and she may have personal debts, but these are not the Jones Florist Company's assets or debts. Kay Jones may own another business such as a stationery shop. If so, she should have a completely separate set of records for each business.

As we saw in Chapter 1, business organizations can take three principal forms: sole proprietorship, partnership, or corporation. Whichever form is used, it should be viewed for accounting purposes as a separate entity, and all its records and reports should be developed from this viewpoint.

Business Transactions as the Object of Measurement

Business transactions are economic events that affect the financial position of a business entity. Business entities may have hundreds or even thousands of transactions every day. These are the raw material of accounting reports.

A transaction may involve an exchange of value (such as a purchase, sale, payment, collection, or borrowing) between two or more independent parties. A transaction may also involve a nonexchange economic event that has the same effect as an exchange transaction. Some examples of nonexchange transactions are disaster losses (such as fire, flood, explosion, and theft), physical wear and tear on machinery and equipment, and day-by-day accumulation of interest.

In any case, to be recorded the transaction must relate directly to the business entity. For example, a customer buys a shovel from Ace Hardware but must buy a hoe from a competing store because Ace is out of hoes. The transaction for selling the shovel must be recorded in Ace's records. However, the purchase of a hoe from a competitor is not recorded in Ace's records because, even though it indirectly affects Ace economically, it does not directly involve an exchange of value between Ace and the customer.

Money Measure

All business transactions are recorded in terms of money; this concept is termed the money measure. In the United States, the basic unit of money measure is dollars. Of course, information of a nonfinancial nature may be recorded, but it is only through the recording of dollar amounts that the diverse transactions and activities of a business are measured. Money is the only factor common to all business transactions, and thus it is the only practical unit of measure that can produce homogeneity of the financial data.

Accounting therefore treats all dollars alike, just as we treat such standard measures as the gallon, mile, or pound in a similar way. The dollar, however, is far inferior to these standards as a unit of measure because of the instability of the purchasing power of the dollar over time. When the prices of goods and services in our economy (general price level) change over time, the value of the dollar changes. Because of inflation during the last three decades, the dollar today is worth considerably less than the dollar in 1945. Proposals for adjusting recorded dollar amounts to reflect changes in the value of the dollar are being advocated by many accountants. But at present the assumption of stability is accepted by accountants for practical reasons and should be recognized by users as a possible limitation of financial reports.[3] The issue of the changing value of the dollar is discussed in more detail in a later chapter.

3. The first major official deviation from the assumption of stability occurred in March 1976, when the Securities and Exchange Commission issued *Accounting Series Release No. 190,* which required over 1,000 large companies to disclose replacement cost information about certain assets for fiscal years ending after December 25, 1976. The FASB now requires supplemental disclosure of the effects of the changing value of the dollar and other current data by certain companies (see Chapter 14).

The Effects of Transactions on Financial Position

Objective 6 Demonstrate the effects of simple transactions on financial position

Because business transactions are economic events that affect the financial position of a business entity, a logical question might be, How do transactions affect financial position? In the remaining sections of this chapter, we define financial position more precisely than previously by using an equation, and we show how simple, but representative, transactions affect this equation.

Financial Position and the Accounting Equation

As mentioned previously, **financial position** refers to the collection of resources belonging to a company and the sources of these resources or claims on them at a particular point in time. Financial position is shown by a balance sheet, so called because it has two sides or parts that must always be in balance. This balance can be expressed as an equation as follows:

assets = liabilities + owner's equity

This equation is known as the **balance sheet equation**, or the accounting equation.

Assets

Assets are economic resources owned by a business that are expected to benefit future operations. Assets include monetary items such as cash and receivables (money owed to the company) from customers as well as nonmonetary physical items such as inventories (goods held for sale), land, buildings, and equipment. Assets may also include nonphysical rights such as those granted by patent, trademark, or copyright,

Liabilities

Liabilities are the debts of the business. They include amounts owed to creditors for goods or services bought on credit (called accounts payable), borrowed money such as notes payable, salaries and wages owed to employees, and taxes owed to the government.

As debts, liabilities are a claim recognized by law in that the law gives to creditors the right to force the sale of a company's assets to pay debts if the company has failed to pay. Creditors have priority over owners and are entitled to payment in full before the owners receive anything, even if payment of the debt exhausts all assets of the business.

For purposes of analysis, liabilities are sometimes considered a part of equity because, in addition to being a claim against assets, they are also a source of the assets of the company. They are a source of assets because they represent funds loaned to the company by creditors for the purchase of assets.

Owner's Equity

The owner's equity represents the resources invested in the business by the owner. It is also known as the residual equity, because it is what would be left over if all the liabilities were paid. Transposing the balance sheet equation, we can state it as follows:

$$\text{assets} - \text{liabilities} = \text{owner's equity}$$

For example, Keane Realty has assets of $42,000 and liabilities of $10,000; therefore, the owner's equity must equal $32,000. If Keane Realty repays $2,000 of the liabilities, assets will decrease to $40,000 and liabilities will decrease to $8,000, but the owner's equity would still be $32,000. Thus it can be reasoned that any transaction affecting only assets and/or liabilities will not affect owner's equity. As will be shown below, owner's equity is affected by four types of transactions:

Type of Transaction	Effect on Owner's Equity
1. Owner's investments	Increase
2. Owner's withdrawals	Decrease
3. Revenues	Increase
4. Expenses	Decrease

Some Illustrations

Let us now examine the effect of some of the most common business transactions on the balance sheet equation. Assume that James Keane is opening a real estate agency called Keane Realty. To conduct his business, he participates in the transactions described in the following numbered paragraphs. For simplicity, we have left out the dates that are usually part of the heading of all financial statements.

1. Investment by Owner James begins his new business by depositing $32,000 in a bank account in the name of Keane Realty. The first balance sheet of the new company would indicate the cash asset as well as the investment (capital) of the owner.

(1)

Keane Realty
Balance Sheet

Assets		**Liabilities**	
Cash	$32,000	(none)	
		Owner's Equity	
		James Keane, Capital	$32,000
	$32,000		$32,000

2. ***Purchase of an Asset for Cash*** James finds an appropriate location and purchases a lot for $7,000 and a building for $22,000 by issuing a check to the previous owner. This transaction does not change the total assets or the owner's equity, but it does involve a shift in the composition of the assets of the company—increasing Land and Building and decreasing Cash.

(2)

Keane Realty
Balance Sheet

Assets		**Liabilities**	
Cash	$ 3,000	(none)	
Land	7,000	**Owner's Equity**	
Building	22,000		
		James Keane, Capital	$32,000
	$32,000		$32,000

3. ***Purchase of an Asset on Credit*** James was able to buy the equipment for his office building for $10,000, with a promise to pay for it at the rate of $2,000 per month. This transaction increases both assets (Equipment) and liabilities (Accounts Payable, or debts of the company).

(3)

Keane Realty
Balance Sheet

Assets		**Liabilities**	
Cash	$3,000	Accounts Payable	$10,000
Equipment	10,000	**Owner's Equity**	
Land	7,000		
Building	22,000	James Keane, Capital	32,000
	$42,000		$42,000

4. ***Payment of a Liability*** James paid the first $2,000 owed on the equipment. This transaction reduces both assets (Cash) and liabilities (Accounts Payable).

(4)

Keane Realty
Balance Sheet

Assets		**Liabilities**	
Cash	$ 1,000	Accounts Payable	$ 8,000
Equipment	10,000	**Owner's Equity**	
Land	7,000		
Building	22,000	James Keane, Capital	32,000
	$40,000		$40,000

5. *Sale of Asset for Cash* More equipment was purchased for Keane Realty than was actually needed. Some of the unneeded equipment, which cost $2,000, was sold for $2,000 cash. This transaction affects two assets—it increases Cash and decreases Equipment—but does not change total assets.

(5)

Keane Realty
Balance Sheet

Assets		**Liabilities**	
Cash	$ 3,000	Accounts Payable	$ 8,000
Equipment	8,000	**Owner's Equity**	
Land	7,000		
Building	22,000	James Keane, Capital	32,000
	$40,000		$40,000

6. *Sale of an Asset on Credit* The rest of the unneeded equipment was sold to an office supply company for $1,000. The office supply company agreed to pay one-half within ten days and the other half the next month. This transaction causes only a rearrangement of assets—increasing Accounts Receivable (amounts due to the company from outsiders) and decreasing Equipment.

(6)

Keane Realty
Balance Sheet

Assets		**Liabilities**	
Cash	$ 3,000	Accounts Payable	$ 8,000
Accounts Receivable	1,000		
Equipment	7,000	**Owner's Equity**	
Land	7,000		
Building	22,000	James Keane, Capital	32,000
	$40,000		$40,000

7. *Collection of Accounts Receivable* Keane Realty receives a check from the office supply company in the amount of $500. This transaction affects two assets—increasing Cash and reducing Accounts Receivable.

(7)

Keane Realty
Balance Sheet

Assets		**Liabilities**	
Cash	$ 3,500	Accounts Payable	$ 8,000
Accounts Receivable	500		
Equipment	7,000	**Owner's Equity**	
Land	7,000		
Building	22,000	James Keane, Capital	32,000
	$40,000		$40,000

8. *Revenue* James is successful in selling two houses, and he collects $4,000 in commissions. This transaction increases both assets (Cash) and owner's equity (James Keane, Capital).

(8)

Keane Realty
Balance Sheet

Assets		**Liabilities**	
Cash	$ 7,500	Accounts Payable	$ 8,000
Accounts Receivable	500		
Equipment	7,000		
Land	7,000	**Owner's Equity**	
Building	22,000	James Keane, Capital	36,000
	$44,000		$44,000

9. *Expense* James pays expenses of $1,500 incurred in connection with the sales in the preceding transaction and $500 in wages for a secretary. Expenses have the effect of decreasing owner's equity and assets.

(9)

Keane Realty
Balance Sheet

Assets		**Liabilities**	
Cash	$ 5,500	Accounts Payable	$ 8,000
Accounts Receivable	500		
Equipment	7,000		
Land	7,000	**Owner's Equity**	
Building	22,000	James Keane, Capital	34,000
	$42,000		$42,000

10. *Withdrawal by Owner* James withdraws $1,000 from the bank account of Keane Realty and deposits it in his personal account to pay his own living expenses. Withdrawals have the effect of reducing assets (Cash) and owner's equity (James Keane, Capital).

(10)

Keane Realty
Balance Sheet

Assets		**Liabilities**	
Cash	$ 4,500	Accounts Payable	$ 8,000
Accounts Receivable	500		
Equipment	7,000		
Land	7,000	**Owner's Equity**	
Building	22,000	James Keane, Capital	33,000
	$41,000		$41,000

The balance sheet is simply a detailed presentation of the accounting equation. To emphasize this point, the ten typical transactions just illustrated are summarized in Figure 2-9 to show their individual effect on the accounting equation. The assets section consists of five specific types of assets; there is one type each of liabilities and owner's equity. Transaction 1, an investment by owner, is shown by an increase in Cash and an increase in James Keane, Capital. Transaction 2, a purchase of assets for cash, is shown by an increase in Land and Building and a decrease in Cash. After each transaction, the balancing effect of the balance sheet equation is maintained. Each of the remaining eight transactions is illustrated in a similar manner.

Figure 2-9 Summary of the Effects of Typical Transactions on the Balance Sheet Equation

	Assets					= Liabilities +	Owner's Equity
	Cash	+ Accounts Receivable	+ Equipment	+ Land	+ Building	= Accounts Payable	+ James Keane, Capital
1.	$32,000	$ 0	$ 0	$ 0	$ 0	$ 0	$32,000
2.	– 29,000			+ 7,000	+ 22,000		
	$ 3,000			$7,000	$22,000		$32,000
3.			+ 10,000			+ 10,000	
	$ 3,000		$10,000	$7,000	$22,000	$10,000	$32,000
4.	– 2,000					– 2,000	
	$ 1,000		$10,000	$7,000	$22,000	$ 8,000	$32,000
5.	+ 2,000		– 2,000				
	$ 3,000		$ 8,000	$7,000	$22,000	$ 8,000	$32,000
6.		+ 1,000	– 1,000				
	$ 3,000	$1,000	$ 7,000	$7,000	$22,000	$ 8,000	$32,000
7.	+ 500	– 500					
	$ 3,500	$ 500	$ 7,000	$7,000	$22,000	$ 8,000	$32,000
8.	+ 4,000						+ 4,000
	$ 7,500	$ 500	$ 7,000	$7,000	$22,000	$ 8,000	$36,000
9.	– 2,000						– 2,000
	$ 5,500	$ 500	$ 7,000	$7,000	$22,000	$ 8,000	$34,000
10.	– 1,000						– 1,000
	$ 4,500	$ 500	$ 7,000	$7,000	$22,000	$ 8,000	$33,000
	$41,000					=	$41,000

Chapter Review

Review of Learning Objectives

1. Describe accounting as an information system.
In the context of an information system, accounting first records data from business activities for future use. Second, through data processing, the data are stored until needed, then processed in such a way as to become useful information. Third, information is communicated through reports to decision makers who can use it.

2. Identify the qualitative characteristics of accounting information.
Accounting information should meet the standards of relevance, timeliness, reliability, representative faithfulness, verifiability, and comparability.

3. Identify the four basic financial statements.
The four basic financial statements are the balance sheet, the income statement, the statement of owner's equity, and the statement of changes in financial position.

4. Discuss the concept of accounting measurement.
To make an accounting measurement, the accountant must determine what is to be measured, when the measurement should occur, what value should be placed on the measurement, and how the measurement should be classified.

5. Recognize the importance of separate entity, business transactions, and the unit of measure in accounting measurement.
Generally accepted accounting principles define the objects of accounting measurement as separate entities, business transactions, and money measures. Relating these three concepts, financial accounting measures business transactions of separate business entities in terms of money measures.

6. Demonstrate the effects of simple transactions on financial position.
Business transactions affect financial position by decreasing or increasing assets, liabilities, and/or owner's equity in such a way that the basic balance sheet equation (assets = liabilities + owner's equity) is always in balance.

Self-Test

Test your knowledge of the chapter by choosing the best answer for each item below.

1. Which of the following is not a qualitative characteristic of accounting information?
   a. Relevance
   b. Verifiability
   c. Partiality
   d. Comparability
2. Which of the following statements about accounting information is true?
   a. Accounting is like mathematics in its perfection.
   b. Accounting information is not perfect and rarely satisfies all the standards.
   c. There are few challenges left in accounting.
   d. None of the above is true.
3. Accountants communicate financial information to users primarily through
   a. letters.
   b. memoranda.
   c. financial statements.
   d. financial notes.

4. The balance sheet is related to the income statement in the same way that
   a. a point in time is related to a period of time.
   b. a period of time is related to a point in time.
   c. a point in time is related to another point in time.
   d. a period of time is related to another period of time.
5. Which of the following is a proper way to date an income statement?
   a. December 31, 19xx
   b. For the Year Ended December 31, 19xx
   c. At the Date December 31, 19xx
   d. None of the above
6. Economic events that affect the financial position of a business are called
   a. separate entities.
   b. business transactions.
   c. money measures.
   d. financial actions.
7. A disadvantage of using dollars to measure business transactions is that
   a. dollars are stable measuring units.
   b. dollars are not common to all business transactions.
   c. dollars change in value over time because of inflation and deflation.
   d. dollars are not useful in measuring financial effects.
8. If a company has liabilities of $19,000 and owner's equity of $57,000, the assets of the company are
   a. $38,000.
   b. $76,000.
   c. $57,000.
   d. $19,000.
9. The payment of a liability will
   a. increase both assets and liabilities.
   b. increase assets and decrease liabilities.
   c. decrease assets and increase liabilities.
   d. decrease assets and decrease liabilities.
10. The purchase of an asset for cash will
   a. increase and decrease assets at the same time.
   b. increase assets and increase liabilities.
   c. increase assets and increase owner's equity.
   d. increase assets and decrease liabilities.

Answers to Self-Test are at the end of this chapter.

Review Problem
Effect of Transactions on the Accounting Equation

Tanya M. Martin finished law school in June and immediately set up her law practice. During the first month, she completed the following transactions:

a. Invested in the practice by placing $2,000 in a bank account established for the business.
b. Purchased a law library for $900 cash.
c. Purchased office supplies for $400 on credit.
d. Accepted $500 in cash for completing a contract.
e. Billed clients $950 for services rendered during the month.

f. Paid $200 of the amount owed for office supplies.
g. Received $250 in cash from one client previously billed for services rendered.
h. Paid for rent, utilities, secretarial services, and other expenses during the month in the amount of $1,200.

Required

Show the effect of each of these transactions on the balance sheet equation by completing the accompanying table in a manner similar to Figure 2-9.

Answer to Review Problem

	Assets				=	Liabilities +	Owner's Equity
	Cash +	Accounts Receivable +	Office Supplies +	Law Library	=	Accounts Payable +	Tanya M. Martin, Capital
a.	$2,000	$ 0	$ 0	$ 0		$ 0	$2,000
b.	− 900			+ 900			
	$1,100			$900			$2,000
c.			+ 400			+ 400	
	$1,100		$400	$900		$400	$2,000
d.	+ 500						+ 500
	$1,600		$400	$900		$400	$2,500
e.		+ 950					+ 950
	$1,600	$950	$400	$900		$400	$3,450
f.	− 200					− 200	
	$1,400	$950	$400	$900		$200	$3,450
g.	+ 250	− 250					
	$1,650	$700	$400	$900		$200	$3,450
h.	− 1,200						− 1,200
	$ 450	$700	$400	$900		$200	$2,250
		$2,450			=	$2,450	

Chapter Assignments

Questions

1. Why is accounting considered an information system, and what are the three processes of accounting in this context?
2. What are the two primary characteristics of accounting information? Why?
3. What is the difference between representative faithfulness and verifiability?

4. In what ways can accounting information be comparable?
5. Can timely information and complete information be incompatible? Give an example to illustrate your answer.
6. Must all the standards be met equally? Explain.
7. How do accountants attempt to overcome the limitations of accounting information?
8. Why would the task of accountants be easier if they could wait until the end of the existence of a business?
9. Why is the balance sheet sometimes called the statement of financial position?
10. Contrast the purposes of the balance sheet and the income statement.
11. How do the income statement and the statement of changes in financial position differ?
12. What are the four basic questions pertaining to measurement in accounting? Why are the answers to them important?
13. Why is the concept of separate entity important?
14. What is a business transaction?
15. Why does accounting use money as the unit of measure?
16. In one sentence, relate separate entity, business transaction, and money as a unit of measure.
17. Define assets, liabilities, and owner's equity.
18. What four items affect owner's equity, and how?
19. Arnold Smith's company has assets of $22,000 and liabilities of $10,000. What is the amount of his owner's equity?
20. Give examples of the types of transactions that will (a) increase assets, (b) increase liabilities.
21. A statement for an accounting period that ends in June may have either (1) June 30, 19xx, or (2) For the Year Ended June 30, 19xx, as part of its identification. State which would be appropriate with (a) a balance sheet, and (b) an income statement.

Classroom Exercises

Exercise 2-1 The Accounting Equation

Use the accounting equation to answer each question below, and show your calculations.

1. The assets of Clark Company are $240,000, and the owner's equity is $180,000. What is the amount of the liabilities?
2. The liabilities of Omega Enterprises equal one-third of the total assets. The firm's owner's equity is $40,000. What is the amount of the liabilities?
3. At the beginning of the year, Alpha Company's assets were $90,000, and its owner's equity was $50,000. During the year, assets increased $30,000, and liabilities decreased $5,000. What was the owner's equity at the end of the year?

Exercise 2-2 Effect of Transactions on Accounting Equation

During the month of April, the Main Street Company had the following transactions:

a. Paid salaries for April, $900.
b. Purchased equipment on account, $1,500.
c. Purchased supplies with cash, $50.

d. Additional investment of cash by owner, $2,000.
e. Received payment for services performed, $300.
f. Paid for part of equipment previously purchased on credit, $500.
g. Billed customers for services performed, $800.
h. Withdrew cash from business for personal expenses, $750.
i. Received payment from customers billed previously, $150.
j. Received utility bill, $35.

On a sheet of paper, list the letters **a** through **j**, with columns for Assets, Liabilities, and Owner's Equity. In the columns, indicate whether each transaction caused an increase (+), a decrease (−), or no change (NC) in assets, liabilities, and owner's equity.

Exercise 2-3 Examples of Transactions

For each of the following categories, describe a transaction that will have the required effect on the elements of the accounting equation.

1. Increase one asset and decrease another asset.
2. Decrease an asset and decrease a liability.
3. Increase an asset and increase a liability.
4. Increase an asset and increase owner's equity.
5. Decrease an asset and decrease owner's equity.

Exercise 2-4 Balance Sheet Preparation

Appearing in random order below are the balance sheet balances for Side Street Company as of December 31, 19xx.

Accounts Payable	$20,000	Accounts Receivable	$25,000
Building	40,000	Cash	10,000
William Side, Capital	80,000	Equipment	20,000
Supplies	5,000		

Sort out these balances, and prepare a balance sheet similar to the one in Figure 2-5.

Exercise 2-5 Accounting Equation and Determination of Net Income

The total assets and liabilities at the beginning and end of the year for Johnson Company are listed below.

	Assets	Liabilities
Beginning of the year	$35,000	$15,000
End of the year	50,000	25,000

Determine the net income for the year under each of the following alternatives:

1. The owner made no investments in the business and no withdrawals from the business during the year.
2. The owner made no investments in the business but withdrew $11,000 during the year.
3. The owner made an investment of $5,000 but made no withdrawals during the year.
4. The owner made an investment of $5,000 and withdrew $11,000 during the year.

Exercise 2-6 Balance Sheet Preparation

The balance sheet below for Ajax Service Company contains a number of errors in placements and headings.

Ajax Service Company
Balance Sheet
For the Year Ended December 31, 19xx

Cash	$ 2,000	Accounts Payable	$10,000
Owner's Investment	42,000	Building	35,000
Equipment	8,000	Accounts Receivable	7,000
Assets	$52,000	Liabilities	$52,000

Using the amounts provided for Ajax Service Company, prepare a balance sheet in correct form similar to the one in Figure 2-5.

Problem Set A

Problem 2A-1 Identification of Transactions

Selected transactions for Morgan Company are summarized in equation form in the accompanying table, with each of the eight transactions identified by letter.

	Assets				=	Liabilities	+	Owner's Equity
	Cash	+ Accounts Receivable	+ Building	+ Equipment	=	Accounts Payable	+	Ann Morgan, Capital
	$ 0	$ 0	$ 0	$ 0		$ 0		$ 0
a.	+ 15,000							+ 15,000
	$15,000	0	0	0		0		$15,000
b.	− 13,000		+ 13,000					
	$ 2,000	0	$13,000	0		0		$15,000
c.				+ 4,000		+ 4,000		
	$ 2,000	0	$13,000	$4,000		$4,000		$15,000
d.	+ 3,000							+ 3,000
	$ 5,000	0	$13,000	$4,000		$4,000		$18,000
e.		+ 2,500						+ 2,500
	$ 5,000	$2,500	$13,000	$4,000		$4,000		$20,500
f.	− 1,000					− 1,000		
	$ 4,000	$2,500	$13,000	$4,000		$3,000		$20,500
g.	+ 500	− 500						
	$ 4,500	$2,000	$13,000	$4,000		$3,000		$20,500
h.	− 300							− 300
	$ 4,200	$2,000	$13,000	$4,000		$3,000		$20,200

Required

Write an explanation of the nature of each transaction. (Note: Assume that item **a** is the only contribution or withdrawal of capital by the owner.)

Problem 2A-2
Effect of Transactions on Accounting Equation

Carlos Gomez graduated from law school and started a law practice in his home town. He completed the following transactions soon after starting the practice:

a. Began his practice by depositing $2,000 in a newly created bank account and investing his law library, valued at $750, in the law practice.
b. Purchased used office equipment for $600 cash.
c. Paid one month's rent of $200 on an office.
d. Purchased office supplies on credit for $150.
e. Completed his first contract, for which he was paid $75 cash.
f. Paid his secretary's salary of $150.
g. Completed a will and billed his client for $100.
h. Withdrew $300 from the practice for his first two weeks' living expenses.

Required

1. Arrange the assets, liabilities, and owner's equity accounts in an equation like that in Figure 2-9, using the following account titles: Cash; Accounts Receivable; Office Supplies; Office Equipment; Law Library; Accounts Payable; and Carlos Gomez, Capital.
2. Show by additions and subtractions, as in Figure 2-9, the effects of Gomez's transactions on the balance sheet equation. Show new totals after each transaction.

Problem 2A-3
Identification of Transactions

In the hypothetical situation below, successive balance sheets are prepared for Quick Car Wash after each transaction.

a.

Quick Car Wash
Balance Sheet
May 1, 19xx

Assets		**Owner's Equity**	
Cash	$42,000	Sam Allred, Capital	$42,000

b.

Quick Car Wash
Balance Sheet
May 4, 19xx

Assets		**Liabilities**	
Cash	$22,000	Accounts Payable	$10,000
Land	5,000	**Owner's Equity**	
Building	25,000	Sam Allred, Capital	42,000
	$52,000		$52,000

c.

Quick Car Wash
Balance Sheet
May 8, 19xx

Assets		Liabilities	
Cash	$10,000	Accounts Payable	$10,000
Supplies	2,000		
Land	5,000	**Owner's Equity**	
Building	25,000		
Equipment	10,000	Sam Allred, Capital	42,000
	$52,000		$52,000

d.

Quick Car Wash
Balance Sheet
May 12, 19xx

Assets		Liabilities	
Cash	$ 5,000	Accounts Payable	$ 5,000
Supplies	2,000		
Land	5,000	**Owner's Equity**	
Building	25,000		
Equipment	10,000	Sam Allred, Capital	42,000
	$47,000		$47,000

e.

Quick Car Wash
Balance Sheet
May 15, 19xx

Assets		Liabilities	
Cash	$ 6,800	Accounts Payable	$ 5,000
Accounts Receivable	200		
Supplies	2,000		
Land	5,000	**Owner's Equity**	
Building	25,000		
Equipment	10,000	Sam Allred, Capital	44,000
	$49,000		$49,000

Required

Write an explanation of the transaction that occurred before each new balance sheet. For example, the transaction leading to the first balance sheet could be described as follows: "On May 1, 19xx, Sam Allred made an investment of $42,000 cash in Quick Car Wash."

Problem 2A-4 Preparation of Financial Statements

After one month's operation, the Seashore Racquet Club had the following account balances:

Accounts Payable	$1,200
Accounts Receivable	600
Cash	1,700
Office Equipment	1,100
Office Supplies	300
Office Supplies Expense	150
Pauline Brown, Capital	6,000*
Pauline Brown, Withdrawals	1,000
Rent Expense	1,000
Tennis Court Equipment	2,000
Tennis Court Rental Revenue	2,100
Tennis Lesson Revenue	550
Salaries Expense	1,700
Utilities and Telephone Expense	300

*Represents investment made at beginning of month.

Required

Using Figures 2-5, 2-6, and 2-7 as models, prepare a balance sheet, an income statement, and a statement of owner's equity for Seashore Racquet Club. (Hint: The final balance of the account Pauline Brown, Capital, is $4,500.)

Problem 2A-5 Effect of Transactions on Accounting Equation

Barney Hobbs owns and operates the Repairs-It Shop. At the beginning of the month, the shop had these assets: Cash, $1,650; Accounts Receivable, $950; Repair Supplies, $850; Tools, $1,275; and Truck, $2,800. The shop had debts of $750 for supplies and tools purchased. During a short period of time, the following transactions were completed:

a. Paid one month's rent, $200.
b. Purchased repair supplies with cash, $50.
c. Paid for repair supplies previously purchased on credit, $250.
d. Purchased tools on credit, $175.
e. Completed repair work for O. Blaney and collected $45 for it.
f. Purchased new tools for cash, $100.
g. Completed repair work for John Ryan on credit, $105.
h. Received payment from customer previously billed, $325.
i. Paid for oil and gas used during the month, $75.
j. Paid utility bills for the month, $90.
k. Wrote a check on the shop bank account to pay the rent for Barney Hobbs's home, $150.

Required

1. Arrange the assets, liabilities, and owner's equity accounts in an equation like that in Figure 2-9, using the following account titles: Cash; Accounts Receivable; Repair Supplies; Tools; Truck; Accounts Payable; and Barney Hobbs, Capital.

2. Enter the beginning balances of the assets and liabilities accounts; then compute the balance of Barney Hobbs, Capital, and enter it.
3. Show by additions and subtractions, as in Figure 2-9, the effects of the transactions on the balance sheet equation. Show new totals after each transaction.

Problem Set B

Problem 2B-1 Identification of Transactions

Selected transactions for the Seasons Tea Company are summarized below in equation form, with each of the eight transactions identified by letter.

	Assets				=	Liabilities	+	Owner's Equity
	Cash	+ Accounts Receivable	+ Building	+ Equipment	=	Accounts Payable	+	P. Seasons, Capital
	$ 0	$ 0	$ 0	$ 0		$ 0		$ 0
a.	+ 28,500							+ 28,500
	$28,500	0	0	0		0		$28,500
b.	− 18,000		+ 18,000					
	$10,500	0	$18,000	0		0		$28,500
c.				+ 4,500		+ 4,500		
	$10,500	0	$18,000	$4,500		$4,500		$28,500
d.		+ 600						+ 600
	$10,500	$600	$18,000	$4,500		$4,500		$29,100
e.	+ 1,150							+ 1,150
	$11,650	$600	$18,000	$4,500		$4,500		$30,250
f.	+ 300	− 300						
	$11,950	$300	$18,000	$4,500		$4,500		$30,250
g.	− 2,500					− 2,500		
	$ 9,450	$300	$18,000	$4,500		$2,000		$30,250
h.	− 850							− 850
	$ 8,600	$300	$18,000	$4,500		$2,000		$29,400

Required

Write an explanation of the nature of each transaction. (Assume that item **a** is the only one that involves an investment or withdrawal of capital by P. Seasons.)

Problem 2B-2 Effect of Transactions on Accounting Equation

Karen Marshall, after receiving her certification as a dentist, began her own practice. She completed the following transactions soon after starting the business:

a. Karen began her practice with a $5,000 cash investment, which she deposited in the bank, and a medical library, which cost $400.
b. Paid one month's rent on an office for her practice. Rent is $180 per month.

c. Purchased dental equipment for $3,500 cash.
d. Purchased $300 of dental supplies on credit.
e. Collected revenue of $15 from each of four patients.
f. Billed patient $55 upon completion of his dental work.
g. Paid expenses of $200.
h. Received $40 from patient billed previously.

Required

1. Arrange the assets, liabilities, and owner's equity accounts in an equation like that in Figure 2-9, using the following account titles: Cash; Accounts Receivable; Dental Supplies; Dental Equipment; Medical Library; Accounts Payable; and Karen Marshall, Capital.
2. Show by additions and subtractions, as in Figure 2-9, the effects of the transactions on the balance sheet equation. Show new totals after each transaction.

Problem 2B-3 Identification of Transactions

In the hypothetical situation below, successive balance sheets are prepared for Downtown Parking Company after each transaction.

a.

Downtown Parking Company
Balance Sheet
February 1, 19xx

Assets		Owner's Equity	
Cash	$38,000	Capital	$38,000

b.

Downtown Parking Company
Balance Sheet
February 5, 19xx

Assets		Liabilities	
Cash	$18,000	Accounts Payable	$ 2,500
Land	20,000	**Owner's Equity**	
Equipment	2,500		
		Capital	38,000
	$40,500		$40,500

c.

Downtown Parking Company
Balance Sheet
February 12, 19xx

Assets		**Liabilities**	
Cash	$18,000	Accounts Payable	$ 4,000
Land	20,000	**Owner's Equity**	
Equipment	2,500		
		Capital	36,500
	$40,500		$40,500

d.

Downtown Parking Company
Balance Sheet
February 15, 19xx

Assets		**Liabilities**	
Cash	$18,000	Accounts Payable	$ 4,000
Accounts Receivable	500	**Owner's Equity**	
Land	20,000		
Equipment	2,500	Capital	37,000
	$41,000		$41,000

e.

Downtown Parking Company
Balance Sheet
February 19, 19xx

Assets		**Liabilities**	
Cash	$15,500	Accounts Payable	$ 1,500
Accounts Receivable	500	**Owner's Equity**	
Land	20,000		
Equipment	2,500	Capital	37,000
	$38,500		$38,500

Required

Write an explanation of the transaction that occurred before each new balance sheet. For example, the transaction leading to the first balance sheet could be described as follows: "On February 1, 19xx, the owner invested $38,000 cash in Downtown Parking Company."

Problem 2B-4 Preparation of Financial Statements

After four weeks' operation, the Exclusive Swim Club had the following account balances:

Swim Lesson Revenue	$ 1,900	Building	15,000
Salaries Expense	1,150	Pool Rental Revenue	750
Accounts Receivable	600	Utilities Expense	300
Olive Cartel, Capital	25,000*	Insurance Expense	500
Equipment	5,000	Cash	13,300
Land	10,500	Olive Cartel, Investment During Month	8,000
Supplies	500	Accounts Payable	15,400
Olive Cartel, Withdrawals	4,200		

*Represents the initial investment by Olive Cartel in the business.

Required

Using Figures 2-5, 2-6, and 2-7 as models, prepare a balance sheet, an income statement, and a statement of owner's equity for Exclusive Swim Club. (Hint: The final balance of the account Olive Cartel, Capital, is $29,500.)

Problem 2B-5 Effect of Transactions on Accounting Equation

Dr. Bernard Small, psychiatrist, moved from his home town to set up an office in Minneapolis. After one month, the business had these assets: Cash, $950; Accounts Receivable, $340; Office Supplies, $150; Office Equipment, $750; and Car, $2,500. The debts were $1,300 for purchase of a car and office equipment on credit. During a short period of time, the following transactions were completed:

a. Paid one month's rent, $175.
b. Billed customer $30 for services rendered.
c. Paid $150 on office equipment previously purchased.
d. Paid for office supplies, $50.
e. Paid secretary's salary, $150.
f. Received $400 from patients.
g. Made car payment, $180.
h. Withdrew $250 for living expenses.
i. Paid telephone bill, $35.
j. Received $145 from patients previously billed.
k. Purchased additional office equipment on credit, $150.

Required

1. Arrange the assets, liabilities, and owner's equity accounts in an equation like that in Figure 2-9 using the following account titles: Cash; Accounts Receivable; Office Supplies; Office Equipment; Car; Accounts Payable; and Bernard Small, Capital.
2. Enter the beginning balances of the assets and liabilities; then compute the balance of Bernard Small, Capital, and enter it.
3. Show by additions and subtractions, as in Figure 2-9, the effects of the transactions on the balance sheet equation. Show new totals after each transaction.

Answers to Self-Test

1. c	3. c	5. b	7. c	9. d
2. b	4. a	6. b	8. b	10. a

Learning Objectives

Chapter Three

The Double-Entry System

1. *Explain in simple terms the generally accepted ways of solving the measurement problems of recognition, valuation, and classification.*
2. *Define and use the terms* account *and* ledger.
3. *Recognize commonly used assets, liabilities, and owner's equity accounts.*
4. *Know the rules for debit and credit.*
5. *Apply the procedure for transaction analysis to simple transactions.*
6. *Record transactions in the general journal.*
7. *Explain the relationship of the journal to the ledger.*
8. *Prepare a trial balance and recognize its value and limitations.*

In the preceding chapter you learned the answer to the question, What is to be measured? Chapter 3 opens with a discussion of these questions: When should the measurement occur? What value should be placed on the measurement? and How is the measurement to be classified? Then, as the focus shifts from accounting concepts to actual practice, you begin working with the double-entry system and applying it to the analysis and recording of business transactions. As a result of studying this chapter, you should be able to meet the learning objectives listed on the left.

Measurement Problems

Business transactions have been defined previously as economic events that affect the financial position of a business entity. To measure a business transaction, the accountant must determine when the transaction occurred (the recognition problem), what value should be placed on the transaction (the valuation problem), and how the components of the transaction should be categorized (the classification problem).

These three problems—recognition, valuation, and classification—are at the base of almost every major issue in financial accounting today. They lie at the heart of such complex issues as accounting for pension plans, mergers of giant companies, international transactions, and the effects of inflation. In discussing the three fundamental problems, we follow generally accepted accounting principles and use an approach that promotes the comprehension of the basic ideas of accounting. However, keep in mind that controversy does exist, and some solutions to the problems are not as cut and dried or generally agreed upon as they may appear.

The Recognition Problem

The recognition problem refers to the difficulty of deciding when a business transaction occurs. Often the facts of a situation are known, but there is disagreement as to when the events should be recorded. For instance, consider the problem of when to recognize a simple purchase. A company orders, receives, and pays for an office desk. Which of the following actions constitutes a recordable event?

1. An employee sends a purchase requisition to the purchasing department.
2. The purchasing department sends a purchase order to the supplier.
3. The supplier ships the desk.
4. The company receives the desk.
5. The company receives the bill from the supplier.
6. The company pays the bill.

Objective 1 Explain in simple terms the generally accepted ways of solving the measurement problems of recognition, valuation, and classification

The answer to this question is important, because the amounts in the financial statements are affected by the date on which the purchase is recorded. Accounting tradition provides a guideline or generally accepted accounting principle stating that the transaction will be recognized when the title to the desk passes from supplier to purchaser and an obligation to pay results. Thus, depending on the details of the shipping agreement, the transaction is recognized at the time of either action 3 or action 4. This is the guideline that we will use generally in this book. However, in many small businesses that use simple business systems, the recognition point is the transfer of cash (action 6), because this is the implied point of transfer of title.

Such problems are not always solved easily. Consider, for example, the case of an automobile manufacturer who builds a car. Value is added to the car up to the time it is finished. Should the extent of value added be recognized as the automobile is being produced or at the time it is completed? According to the above guideline, the increase in value is recorded at the time the automobile is sold. Normally, legal title passes from the automobile manufacturer to the dealer at the point of sale.

The Valuation Problem

The valuation problem is perhaps the most controversial issue of accounting. It has to do with the difficulty of assigning a value to a business transaction. Generally accepted accounting principles state that, in general, the appropriate valuation to assign to all business transactions, and therefore to all assets, liabilities, owner's equity, revenues, and expenses acquired by a business, is the original cost (often called historical cost). Cost is defined here as the exchange price associated with a business transaction at the point of recognition. According to this guideline, the purpose of accounting is not to account for "value," which may change after a transaction occurs, but to account for the cost or value at the time of the transaction. For example, the cost of assets is recorded when they are acquired, and their "value" is also held at that level until they are sold, expire, or are consumed. In this context, value in accounting means the cost at the time of the transaction that brought the item into or took it out of the business entity.

For example, a person may offer a building for sale at $120,000. It may be valued for real estate taxes at $75,000, and it may be insured for $90,000. One prospective buyer may offer $100,000 for the building, and another may offer $105,000. At this point, several different, unverifiable opinions of value have been expressed. Finally, the seller and a buyer may settle on a price and complete a sale for $110,000. All these figures are values of one kind or another, but only the last figure is sufficiently reliable to be used in the records. The market value of this building may vary over the years, but it will remain on the new buyer's records at $110,000 until it is sold again. At that point, the accountant would record the new transaction at the new exchange price, and a profit or loss on the sale would be recognized.

The cost guideline is used because it meets the standard of verifiability. Cost is verifiable because it results from the actions of independent buyers and sellers who come to an agreement about price. This exchange price is an objective price that can be verified by evidence created at the time of the transaction. Both the buyer and the seller may have thought they got the better deal, but their opinions are irrelevant in recording cost. The final price of $110,000, verified by agreement of the two parties, is the price at which the transaction is recorded.

There are proposals to substitute other valuation procedures for the cost basis of accounting, just as there are proposals for adjusting figures to reflect price-level changes on the grounds of better compliance with the standard of relevance. One of the most important of these proposals is the requirement in *Statement No. 33* by the Financial Accounting Standards Board that certain large companies present, with their cost-based financial statements, supplementary financial information based both on current values and on changes in price levels. The full impact of this requirement has yet to be assessed. However, the historical or original cost is still the measure most widely accepted by accountants in the United States because it is difficult to assign values to business events not based on verifiable transactions. There are some notable exceptions to this rule; they will be presented at the appropriate points in this book.

The Classification Problem

The **classification problem** refers to the problem of assigning all the transactions in which a business will engage to the appropriate accounts. For example, a company's ability to borrow money may be affected by the way in which some of its debts are categorized. Or a company's income may be affected by whether a purchase of a small item such as a tool is considered an item of repair expense or an item of equipment (asset). Proper classification depends not only on correct analysis of the effect of each transaction on the business enterprise but also on maintenance of a system of accounts that will reflect that effect. The remainder of this chapter explains the classification of accounts and the analysis and recording of transactions.

Accounts

Objective 2
Define and use the terms **account** *and* **ledger**

When large amounts of data are gathered in the measurement of business transactions, a method of storage is required. Business people should be able to retrieve transaction data quickly and in the form desired. In other words, there should be a filing system to sort out all the transactions that occur in a business. Only in this way can financial statements and other reports be prepared quickly and easily. This filing system consists of storage units called accounts. Whether a company keeps records by hand or computer, management must be able to refer to these accounts in order to study the company's financial history and make future plans. A very small company may require only a few dozen accounts, whereas a multinational corporation will have thousands. In any case, there must be a separate account for each asset, liability, and component of owner's equity.

The T Account

An **account** is the basic storage unit for data in accounting. An accounting system has separate accounts for each asset, liability, component of owner's equity, revenue, and expense.

In its simplest form, an account has three parts: (1) a title that describes the asset, liability, or owner's equity account; (2) a left side, which is called the **debit** side; and (3) a right side, which is called the **credit** side. This form of the account, called a **T account** because of its resemblance to the letter *T*, is used to analyze transactions. It appears as follows:

Title of Account	
Left or Debit Side	Right or Credit Side

Thus any entry made on the left side of the account is a debit or debit entry, and any entry made on the right side of the account is a credit or credit entry. The terms *debit* and *credit* are simply the accountant's words for "left" and "right." A more complete version of the account will be presented later in this chapter.

The Account Illustrated

In Chapter 2, Keane Realty had several transactions that involved the receipt or use of cash. (See Figure 2-9 for a summary of the numbered transactions given below.) These transactions can be summarized in the Cash account by recording receipts on the left or debit side of the account and the payments on the right or credit side of the account as follows:

Cash			
(1)	32,000	(2)	29,000
(5)	2,000	(4)	2,000
(7)	500	(9)	2,000
(8)	4,000	(10)	1,000
4,500	38,500		34,000

The cash receipts have been totaled on the left as $38,500, and this total is written in small-size figures so that it will not be confused with an actual debit entry. The cash payments are totaled in a similar way on the right side. These figures are simply working totals called footings. Footings are calculated at the end of the month as an easy way to determine cash on hand. The difference in total dollars between the total debit footings and the total credit footings is called the balance or account balance. If the balance is a debit, it is written on the left side. If it is a credit, it is written on the right. Notice that Keane Realty's Cash account has a debit balance of $4,500 ($38,500 – $34,000). This represents Keane's cash on hand at the end of the month.

Management's Use of Accounts

The accumulation of information in account form is useful to management in running a business. In the example above, for instance, James Keane can keep a running balance of the cash receipts and payments so that he knows how much cash is on hand at any one time. He can plan ahead to have enough funds to pay salaries and various bills when they are due. He can foresee the need to borrow money from the bank by estimating future cash payments and cash receipts. Good planning for future cash needs requires that he have a record of past receipts and expenditures as well as his current cash balance. The Cash account gives him this information.

The Ledger

In a manual accounting system, each account is kept on a separate page or card. These pages or cards are placed together in a book or file. This book or file, which contains all the company's accounts, is called a ledger. Although in a computer system, which most companies have today, the accounts are maintained on magnetic tapes or disks, the accountant, as a matter of convenience, still refers to the group of company accounts as the ledger.

In order to find an account in the ledger easily and to identify accounts when working with the accounting records, an accountant often numbers the accounts. A list of these numbers with the corresponding account names is usually called a **chart of accounts.** A very simple chart of accounts, suitable for the accounts needed in this chapter's example of the Joan Miller Advertising Agency, is as follows:

Assets	
Cash	111
Notes Receivable	113
Accounts Receivable	114
Art Supplies	115
Office Supplies	116
Prepaid Rent	117
Prepaid Insurance	118
Land	141
Buildings	142
Art Equipment	144
Office Equipment	146

Liabilities	
Notes Payable	211
Accounts Payable	212
Unearned Art Fees	213
Wages Payable	214
Bonds Payable	221
Owner's equity	
Joan Miller, Capital	311
Joan Miller, Withdrawals	312
Revenues and Expenses	
Advertising Fees Earned	411
Office Wages	511
Utility Expense	512
Telephone Expense	513

Notice the gaps in the sequence of numbers. These gaps allow for expansion in the number of accounts. Of course, every company develops a chart of accounts for its own needs. Seldom will two companies have exactly the same chart of accounts. A complete presentation of a chart of accounts appears in Chapter 7.

Types of Commonly Used Accounts

Objective 3 Recognize commonly used assets, liabilities, and owner's equity accounts

The specific accounts used by a company depend on the nature of the company's business. A steel company will have large investments in plant and inventory, whereas an advertising agency may have neither. Each company must design its accounts in a way that will reflect the nature of its business and the needs of its management in directing the business. There are, however, accounts that are common to most businesses. Some important ones are described in the following paragraphs. Remember that the total balances of the asset accounts equal the balances of the liability accounts plus the balances of the owner's equity accounts.

Assets A company must keep records of the increases and decreases in each asset that it owns. Some of the more common asset accounts are as follows:

Cash "Cash" is the title of the account used to record increases and decreases in cash. Cash consists of money or any medium of exchange that a bank will accept at face value for deposit. Included are coins, currency, checks, postal and express money orders, certificates of deposit, and money deposited in a bank or banks. The Cash account also includes cash on hand such as that in a cash register or a safe.

Notes Receivable A promissory note is a written promise to pay a definite sum of money at a fixed future date. Amounts due from others in the form of promissory notes are recorded in an account called Notes Receivable.

Accounts Receivable Companies often sell goods and services to customers on the basis of oral or implied promises to pay in the future, such as in thirty days or at the first of the month. These sales are called Credit Sales, or Sales on Account, and the promises to pay are known as Accounts Receivable. Credit sales increase Accounts Receivable, and collections from customers decrease Accounts Receivable. Of course, it is necessary to keep a record of how much each customer owes the company. How these records are kept is explained in Chapter 8.

Prepaid Expenses Companies often pay for goods and services before they receive or use them. These prepaid expenses are considered assets until they are used, at which time they become expenses. There should be a separate account for each prepaid expense. An example of a prepaid expense is Prepaid Insurance. Insurance protection against fire, theft, and other hazards is usually paid in advance for a period of from one to five years. When the premiums are paid, the Prepaid Insurance account is increased. These premiums expire day by day and month by month. At intervals, therefore, usually at the end of the accounting period, the Prepaid Insurance must be reduced by the amount of insurance that has expired. Another commonly found type of prepaid expense is Office Supplies. Stamps, stationery, pencils, pens, paper, and other office supplies are assets when they are purchased and are recorded as an increase in Office Supplies. As the office supplies are used, the account is reduced. Other typical prepaid expenses that are assets when they are purchased and become expenses as they are used are prepaid rent, store supplies, prepaid taxes, and prepaid wages.

Land and Buildings Increases and decreases in land and buildings owned by a business are recorded in accounts called Land and Buildings, respectively. Although a building cannot be separated from the land it occupies, it is important to maintain separate accounts for the land and the building. The reason for doing so is that the building is subject to wear and tear, but the land is not. In succeeding chapters, the subject of depreciation will be introduced. Wear and tear is an important aspect of depreciation.

Equipment A company may own many different types of equipment. Usually there is a separate account for each type of equipment. For instance, changes in amounts representing the value of desks, chairs, office machines, filing cabinets, and typewriters are recorded in an account called Office Equipment. Increases and decreases in counters, cash registers, showcases, shelves, and similar items are recorded in the Store Equipment account. When a company has a factory, it may own lathes, drill presses, and other factory equipment and would record changes in such items in an account titled Machinery and Equipment. Some companies may have use for a Trucks and Automobiles account.

Liabilities Most companies have fewer liability accounts than asset accounts. It is just as important to keep records of what the company owes as it is to keep asset accounts. There are two types of liabilities: short-term and long-term. The distinction between them is introduced in Chapter 7. The following accounts are short-term liabilities:

Notes Payable The account called Notes Payable is the exact opposite of Notes Receivable. It is used to record increases and decreases in promissory notes owed to creditors.

Accounts Payable Similarly, Accounts Payable is the opposite of Accounts Receivable. It represents amounts owed to creditors on the basis of an oral or implied promise to pay. Accounts payable usually arise as the result of the purchase of merchandise, services, supplies, or equipment on credit. When Company B sells an item to Company A, which promises to pay at the beginning of the month, the amount of the transaction is an Accounts Payable on Company A's books and an Accounts Receivable on Company B's books. As with Accounts Receivable, records of amounts owed to individual creditors must be known. Chapter 8 covers the method of accomplishing this task.

Other short-term liabilities Illustrations of other liabilities and liability accounts are Wages Payable, Taxes Payable, Rent Payable, and Interest Payable. Often customers make deposits on, or pay in advance for, goods and services to be delivered in the future. Advance payments of this nature are also recorded as liabilities. They are liabilities because the money must be returned to the customer if the goods or services are not delivered. These kinds of liability accounts are often called Unearned Fees, Customer Deposits, Advances from Customers, or, more commonly, Unearned Revenues.

The most common type of long-term liabilities are bonds or property mortgages. Because a wide variety of bonds and mortgages have been developed for special financing needs, it is difficult to classify them. They may or may not require the backing of certain of the company's assets for security. For example, a mortgage holder may have the right to force the sale of certain assets if the mortgage debt is not paid when due. For now, however, it will suffice to record increases and decreases in long-term debt in an account called Bonds Payable or Mortgage Payable.

Owner's Equity Accounts Many transactions affect the owner's equity in a company. In the previous chapter's illustrations, several transactions affected owner's equity. The effects of all these transactions were shown by the increases or decreases in the single column representing owner's equity (see Figure 2-9). In reality, it is very important for legal and managerial reasons to separate these transactions by type. Among the most important information that management receives for business planning is a detailed breakdown of revenues and expenses. The law requires a separation of capital contributions and withdrawals from revenues and expenses for income tax reporting, financial reporting, and other reasons. Ownership and equity accounts, especially those for partnerships and corporations, are covered in much more detail in Part IV, but for now the following accounts are important to the study of sole proprietorships.

Capital account When someone invests in his or her own company, the amount of the investment is recorded in a capital account. For instance, in Chapter 2 when James Keane invested his personal resources in his firm, he recorded the amount in the owner's equity account titled James Keane, Capital. Any additional investments by James Keane in his firm would be recorded in this account. The capital accounts for corporations are presented in Chapter 7 and discussed in more detail in Part IV.

Withdrawals account A person who invests in a business usually expects to make a profit and to use at least part of the assets earned from profitable operations to pay personal living expenses. Since the income for a business is determined at the end of the accounting period, the owner often finds it necessary to withdraw assets from the business for living expenses long before profits have been determined. It is not legally possible for the owner of a business to pay himself or herself a salary, but it is possible for the owner to withdraw assets for personal uses. As a result, it has become common practice to set up a withdrawals account to record these payments, which are made with the expectation of earning a profit. For example, an account called James Keane, Withdrawals, would be used to record James Keane's withdrawals from his firm. The withdrawals account often goes by several other names in practice. Among these other titles are Personal and Drawing. This account is not used by corporations.

Revenue and expense accounts Revenues increase owner's equity, and expenses decrease owner's equity. The greater the revenues, the more the owner's equity is increased. The greater the expenses, the more the owner's equity is decreased. Obviously, when revenues exceed expenses, the company has earned a profit or net income; when expenses exceed revenues, the company has incurred a loss or net loss. Management's objective, of course, is to earn a profit, and an important function of accounting is to provide management with information that will help in accomplishing this objective. One way this is done is by providing a ledger account for every revenue and expense item. From these accounts management can learn exactly where all revenues come from and where all expenses go. The revenue and expense accounts a particular company has will depend on the type of business and the nature of its operations. Examples of revenue accounts used in this book are Commissions, Fees Earned for Services, and Sales; examples of expense accounts are Wages, Supplies, Rent, and Advertising.

Titles of Accounts

The names of accounts are often confusing to beginning accounting students because some of the words are new or have special technical meanings. It is also true that the same asset, liability, or owner's equity account may be called by different names in different companies. This is not so strange. People too are often called different names by their friends, family, and associates.

Similarly, long-term assets may be known in various contexts as Fixed Assets, Plant and Equipment, Capital Assets, Long-Lived Assets, and so forth. Even the most acceptable names change over a period of time in accounting, and by habit some companies may use names that are out of date. In general, the account title should describe what is recorded in the account. When students encounter an account title they do not recognize, they should examine the context of the name—that is, whether it is classified as asset, liability, owner's equity, revenue, or expense on the financial statement—and look for the kind of transaction that gave rise to the account.

The Double-Entry System: The Basic Method of Accounting

The double-entry system, the backbone of manual accounting, evolved during the Renaissance. The first systematic presentation of double-entry bookkeeping appeared in 1494, two years after Columbus discovered America. It was described in a mathematics book written by Fra Luca Pacioli, a Franciscan monk who was a friend of Leonardo da Vinci. Goethe, the famous German poet and dramatist, referred to double-entry bookkeeping as "one of the finest discoveries of the human intellect." Werner Sombart, an eminent economist-sociologist, expressed the belief that

> double-entry bookkeeping is born of the same spirit as the system of Galileo and Newton. . . . With the same means as these it orders the phenomenon into an elegant system, and it may be called the first cosmos built upon the basis of a mechanistic thought. Double-entry bookkeeping discloses to us the cosmos of the economic world by the same method as later the cosmos of the stellar universe was unveiled by the great investigations of natural philosophy.[1]

What is the significance of the double-entry system for accounting? The double-entry system is based on the principle of duality, which means that all events of economic importance have two aspects—effort and reward, sacrifice and benefit, sources and uses—that offset or balance each other. In the **double-entry system** each transaction must be recorded twice, in such a way that the total debits and total credits equal each other. Because of the way it is designed, the system as a whole is always in balance and therefore always under control. All accounting systems, no matter how sophisticated, are based on this principle of duality.

1. Werner Sombart, *Der Moderne Kapitalismus* (Leipzig: Duncher & Humblot, 1902), p. 119, trans.

Analysis of Transactions

Objective 4
Know the rules for debit and credit

The mechanics of double-entry bookkeeping are such that every transaction affects at least two accounts. In other words, there must be one or more accounts debited and one or more accounts credited, and the total debits must equal the total credits.

Remember that the words *debit* (abbreviated Dr., from the Latin *debere*) and *credit* (abbreviated Cr., from the Latin *credere*) mean only "left" and "right," not "increase" or "decrease." When we consider the accounting equation

assets = liabilities + owner's equity

we can see that if a debit increases assets, then the opposite, a credit, must be used to increase liabilities or owner's equity; conversely, if a credit decreases assets, then a debit must be used to show a decrease in liabilities or owner's equity. These rules exist because assets are on the opposite side of an algebraic equation from liabilities and owner's equity. These rules can be summarized as follows:

Assets		=	Liabilities		+	Owner's Equity	
Debit for Increases	Credit for Decreases		Debit for Decreases	Credit for Increases		Debit for Decreases	Credit for Increases

1. Increases in assets are debited to asset accounts; decreases in assets are credited to asset accounts.
2. Increases in liabilities and owner's equity are credited to liability and owner's equity accounts; decreases in liabilities and owner's equity are debited to liability and owner's equity accounts. (In applying these rules, recall that revenues increase owner's equity and expenses decrease owner's equity.)

We are now in a position to state a procedure for analyzing transactions. This procedure is used to analyze every transaction that occurs. As an example, let us assume that Jones Manufacturing borrows $1,000 from its bank on a promissory note. The analysis procedure is as follows:

1. Analyze the effect of the transaction on assets, liabilities, and owner's equity. In this case, both assets and liabilities were increased.
2. Apply the appropriate double-entry rule. (It will be helpful at this point for the student to memorize the rules presented above.) Increases in assets are recorded by debits. Increases in liabilities are recorded by credits.
3. Make the entry. The increase in assets is recorded by a debit to the Cash account, and the increase in liabilities is recorded by a credit to the Notes Payable account.

Cash	
1,000	

Notes Payable	
	1,000

Dr. Cash $1,000 equals Cr. Notes Payable $1,000

Another form of this entry, which will be explained later in this chapter, is:

Dr. Cash	1,000	
Cr. Notes Payable		1,000

Transaction Analysis Illustrated

Objective 5 Apply the procedure for transaction analysis to simple transactions

The list below contains the transactions for the Joan Miller Advertising Agency for the month of January. We shall use the transactions to illustrate the application of the principle of duality and to show how transactions are recorded in the accounts.

1. On January 1, Joan Miller invested $5,000 in her own advertising agency.
2. Rented an office, paying two months' rent in advance, $400.
3. Purchased art equipment for $2,100 cash.
4. Purchased office equipment from Morgan Equipment for $1,500, paying $750 in cash and agreeing to pay the rest next month.
5. Purchased on credit art supplies for $900 and office supplies for $400 from Taylor Supply Company.
6. Paid $240 for a one-year insurance policy.
7. Hired a secretary and agreed to pay $300 every two weeks.
8. Paid Taylor Supply Company $500 of the amount owed.
9. Performed a service by placing advertisements for an automobile dealer in the newspaper and collected a fee of $700.
10. Paid the secretary two weeks' salary, $300.
11. Accepted $500 as an advance fee for art work to be done for another agency.
12. Performed a service by placing several advertisements for Ward Department Stores and A & A Grocers. The earned fees of $800 and $600, respectively, will be collected next month.
13. Joan Miller withdrew $700 from the business for personal living expenses.
14. Paid the secretary two more weeks' salary, $300.
15. Paid the utility bill, $50.
16. Received a telephone bill, $35.

1. On January 1, Joan Miller invested $5,000 in her own advertising agency.

Cash

(1)	5,000		

Joan Miller, Capital

		(1)	5,000

Transaction: Investment in business.
Analysis: Assets increased. Owner's equity increased.
Rules: Increases in assets are recorded by debits. Increases in owner's equity are recorded by credits.
Entry: Increase in assets is recorded by debit to Cash. Increase in owner's equity is recorded by credit to Joan Miller, Capital.

Dr. Cash	5,000	
Cr. Joan Miller, Capital		5,000

2. Rented an office, paying two months' rent in advance, $400.

Cash

(1)	5,000	(2)	400

Prepaid Rent

(2)	400		

Transaction: Expense paid in advance.
Analysis: Assets increased. Assets decreased.
Rules: Increases in assets are recorded by debits. Decreases in assets are recorded by credits.
Entry: Increase in assets is recorded by debit to Prepaid Rent. Decrease in assets is recorded by credit to Cash.

Dr. Prepaid Rent	400	
Cr. Cash		400

3. Purchased art equipment for $2,100 cash.

Cash

(1)	5,000	(2)	400
		(3)	2,100

Art Equipment

(3)	2,100		

Transaction: Purchase of equipment.
Analysis: Assets increased. Assets decreased.
Rules: Increases in assets are recorded by debits. Decreases in assets are recorded by credits.
Entry: Increase in assets is recorded by debit to Art Equipment. Decrease in assets is recorded by credit to Cash.

Dr. Art Equipment	2,100	
Cr. Cash		2,100

4. Purchased office equipment from Morgan Equipment for $1,500, paying $750 in cash and agreeing to pay the rest next month.

Cash

(1)	5,000	(2)	400
		(3)	2,100
		(4)	750

Office Equipment

(4)	1,500		

Accounts Payable

		(4)	750

Transaction: Purchase of equipment, partial payment.
Analysis: Assets increased. Assets decreased. Liabilities increased.
Rules: Increases in assets are recorded by debits. Decreases in assets are recorded by credits. Increases in liabilities are recorded by credits.
Entry: Increase in assets is recorded by debit to Office Equipment. Decrease in assets is recorded by credit to Cash. Increase in liabilities is recorded by credit to Accounts Payable.

Dr. Office Equipment	1,500	
Cr. Cash		750
Cr. Accounts Payable		750

5. Purchased on credit art supplies for $900 and office supplies for $400 from Taylor Supply Company.

Art Supplies

(5)	900		

Office Supplies

(5)	400		

Accounts Payable

		(4)	750
		(5)	1,300

Transaction: Purchase of supplies on credit.
Analysis: Assets increased. Liabilities increased.
Rules: Increases in assets are recorded by debits. Increases in liabilities are recorded by credits.
Entry: Increase in assets is recorded by debits to Art Supplies and Office Supplies. Increase in liabilities is recorded by credit to Accounts Payable.

Dr. Art Supplies	900	
Dr. Office Supplies	400	
Cr. Accounts Payable		1,300

6. Paid $240 for a one-year insurance policy (see analysis at top of next page).

Cash			
(1)	5,000	(2)	400
		(3)	2,100
		(4)	750
		(6)	240

Prepaid Insurance			
(6)	240		

Transaction: Paid for insurance coverage in advance.
Analysis: Assets increased. Assets decreased.
Rules: Increases in assets are recorded by debits. Decreases in assets are recorded by credits.
Entry: Increase in assets is recorded by debit to Prepaid Insurance. Decrease in assets is recorded by credit to Cash.

Dr. Prepaid Insurance	240	
Cr. Cash		240

7. Hired a secretary and agreed to pay $300 every two weeks. ***Analysis:*** No entry is made because no transaction occurred. There is no liability until the secretary actually works.
8. Paid Taylor Supply Company $500 of the amount owed.

Cash			
(1)	5,000	(2)	400
		(3)	2,100
		(4)	750
		(6)	240
		(8)	500

Accounts Payable			
(8)	500	(4)	750
		(5)	1,300

Transaction: Partial payment on a liability.
Analysis: Assets decreased. Liabilities decreased.
Rules: Decreases in assets are recorded by credits. Decreases in liabilities are recorded by debits.
Entry: Decrease in liabilities is recorded by debit to Accounts Payable. Decrease in assets is recorded by credit to Cash.

Dr. Accounts Payable	500	
Cr. Cash		500

9. Performed a service by placing advertisements for an automobile dealer in the newspaper and collected a fee of $700.

Cash			
(1)	5,000	(2)	400
(9)	700	(3)	2,100
		(4)	750
		(6)	240
		(8)	500

Advertising Fees Earned			
		(9)	700

Transaction: Revenue earned and collected.
Analysis: Assets increased. Owner's equity increased.
Rules: Increases in assets are recorded by debits. Increases in owner's equity are recorded by credits.
Entry: Increase in assets is recorded by debit to Cash. Increase in owner's equity is recorded by credit to Advertising Fees Earned.

Dr. Cash	700	
Cr. Advertising Fees Earned		700

10. Paid the secretary two weeks' salary, $300.

Cash

(1)	5,000	(2)	400
(9)	700	(3)	2,100
		(4)	750
		(6)	240
		(8)	500
		(10)	300

Office Wages

(10)	300		

Transaction: Payment of wages expense.
Analysis: Assets decreased. Owner's equity decreased.
Rules: Decreases in assets are recorded by credits. Decreases in owner's equity are recorded by debits.
Entry: Decrease in owner's equity is recorded by debit to Office Wages. Decrease in assets is recorded by credit to Cash.

Dr. Office Wages	300	
Cr. Cash		300

11. Accepted $500 as an advance fee for art work to be done for another agency.

Cash

(1)	5,000	(2)	400
(9)	700	(3)	2,100
(11)	500	(4)	750
		(6)	240
		(8)	500
		(10)	300

Unearned Art Fees

		(11)	500

Transaction: Accepted payment for services to be performed.
Analysis: Assets increased. Liabilities increased.
Rules: Increases in assets are recorded by debits. Increases in liabilities are recorded by credits.
Entry: Increase in assets is recorded by debit to Cash. Increase in liabilities is recorded by credit to Unearned Art Fees.

Dr. Cash	500	
Cr. Unearned Art Fees		500

12. Performed a service by placing several advertisements for Ward Department Stores and A & A Grocers. The earned fees of $800 and $600, respectively, will be collected next month.

Accounts Receivable

(12)	800		
(12)	600		

Advertising Fees Earned

		(9)	700
		(12)	1,400

Transaction: Revenue earned, to be paid later.
Analysis: Assets increased. Owner's equity increased.
Rules: Increases in assets are recorded by debits. Increases in owner's equity are recorded by credits.
Entry: Increases in assets are recorded by debits to Accounts Receivable. Increase in owner's equity is recorded by credit to Advertising Fees Earned.

Dr. Accounts Receivable	800	
Dr. Accounts Receivable	600	
Cr. Advertising Fees Earned		1,400

13. Joan Miller withdrew $700 from the business for personal living expenses.

Cash

(1)	5,000	(2)	400
(9)	700	(3)	2,100
(11)	500	(4)	750
		(6)	240
		(8)	500
		(10)	300
		(13)	700

Joan Miller, Withdrawals

(13)	700		

Transaction: Withdrawal of assets for personal use.
Analysis: Assets decreased. Owner's equity decreased.
Rules: Decreases in assets are recorded by credits. Decreases in owner's equity are recorded by debits.
Entry: Decrease in owner's equity is recorded by debit to Joan Miller, Withdrawals. Decrease in assets is recorded by credit to Cash.

Dr. Joan Miller, Withdrawals	700	
Cr. Cash		700

14. Paid the secretary two more weeks' salary, $300.
15. Paid the utility bill, $50.

Cash

(1)	5,000	(2)	400
(9)	700	(3)	2,100
(11)	500	(4)	750
		(6)	240
		(8)	500
		(10)	300
		(13)	700
		(14)	300
		(15)	50

Office Wages

(10)	300		
(14)	300		

Utility Expense

(15)	50		

Transaction: Payment of expenses.
Analysis: Assets decreased. Owner's equity decreased.
Rules: Decreases in assets are recorded by credits. Decreases in owner's equity are recorded by debits.
Entry: Decreases in owner's equity are recorded by debits to Office Wages and Utility Expense. Decreases in assets are recorded by credit to Cash.

Dr. Office Wages	300	
Cr. Cash		300
Dr. Utility Expense	50	
Cr. Cash		50

16. Received a telephone bill, $35.

Accounts Payable

(8)	500	(4)	750
		(5)	1,300
		(16)	35

Telephone Expense

(16)	35		

Transaction: Expense incurred, payment deferred.
Analysis: Liabilities increased. Owner's equity decreased.
Rules: Increases in liabilities are recorded by credits. Decreases in owner's equity are recorded by debits.
Entry: Decrease in owner's equity is recorded by debit to Telephone Expense. Increase in liabilities is recorded by credit to Accounts Payable.

Dr. Telephone Expense	35	
Cr. Accounts Payable		35

Summary of Transactions

As one might surmise from the examples, there is a limited number of ways in which transactions can affect the accounting equation. These are as follows:

Effect	Example Transactions
1. Increase both assets and liabilities	(5), (11)
2. Increase both assets and owner's equity	(1), (9), (12)
3. Decrease both assets and liabilities	(8)
4. Decrease both assets and owner's equity	(10), (13), (14), (15)
5. Increase one asset and decrease another	(2), (3), (6)
6. Increase one liability or owner's equity and decrease another liability or owner's equity	(16)
7. No effect	(7)

Transaction 4 is a more complex transaction, which increases one asset (Office Equipment), decreases another asset (Cash), and increases a liability (Accounts Payable). All the foregoing transactions are summarized in Figure 3-1 in their appropriate accounts, and their relation to the accounting equation is indicated.

Recording Transactions

Objective 6 Record transactions in the general journal

Thus far, the analysis of transactions has been illustrated by entering the transactions directly into the T accounts. This method was used because of its simplicity and its usefulness in analyzing the effect of transactions. Advanced accounting students and professional accountants often use T

Figure 3-1
Summary of Illustrative Accounts and Transactions for Joan Miller Advertising Agency

Assets	=	Liabilities	+	Owner's Equity

Assets

Cash	
(1) 5,000	(2) 400
(9) 700	(3) 2,100
(11) 500	(4) 750
	(6) 240
	(8) 500
	(10) 300
	(13) 700
	(14) 300
	(15) 50

Accounts Receivable	
(12) 800	
(12) 600	

Art Supplies	
(5) 900	

Office Supplies	
(5) 400	

Prepaid Rent	
(2) 400	

Prepaid Insurance	
(6) 240	

Art Equipment	
(3) 2,100	

Office Equipment	
(4) 1,500	

Liabilities

Accounts Payable	
(8) 500	(4) 750
	(5) 1,300
	(16) 35

Unearned Art Fees	
	(11) 500

Owner's Equity

Joan Miller, Capital	
	(1) 5,000

Joan Miller, Withdrawals	
(13) 700	

Advertising Fees Earned	
	(9) 700
	(12) 1,400

Office Wages	
(10) 300	
(14) 300	

Utility Expense	
(15) 50	

Telephone Expense	
(16) 35	

accounts to analyze very complicated transactions. However, there are actually three steps to be followed in the recording processes:

1. Analyze the transactions from the source documents.
2. Enter the transactions into the journal (a procedure usually called journalizing).
3. Post the entries to the ledger (a procedure usually called posting).

The Journal

As illustrated in this chapter, transactions can be recorded directly into the accounts. When this method is used, however, it is very difficult to follow individual transactions with the debit recorded in one account and the credit in another. When a large number of transactions is involved, errors in analyzing or recording transactions are very difficult to find. The solution to this problem is to make a chronological record of all transactions by recording them in a **journal**. The journal is sometimes called the book of original entry, because this is where transactions are first recorded. The journal shows the transactions for each day and may contain explanatory information concerning the transactions. The debits and credits of the transactions can then be transferred to the appropriate accounts.

A separate **journal entry** is used to record each transaction, and the process of recording transactions is called **journalizing**.

The General Journal

It is common for a business to have more than one kind of journal. Several types of journals are discussed in Chapter 8. The simplest and most flexible type is the **general journal**, which is used throughout this chapter. The general journal provides for the recording of the following information about each transaction:

1. The date
2. The names of the accounts debited and credited
3. The dollar amounts debited or credited to each account
4. An explanation of the transaction
5. The account identification numbers, if appropriate

Two transactions for the Joan Miller Advertising Agency are recorded in Figure 3-2.

The procedures for recording transactions in the general journal can be summarized as follows:

1. Record the date by writing the year in small figures at the top of the first column, the month on the first line of the first column, and the day in the second column of the first line. For subsequent entries on the same page for the same month and year, the month and year can be omitted.
2. Write the exact names of the accounts debited and credited under the heading "Description." Write the name of the account debited next to the left margin of the first line, and indent the name of the account credited. The explanation is placed on the next line and further indented. It should be brief but sufficient to explain and identify the transaction. A transaction can have more than one debit and/or credit entry; in such a case it is called a **compound entry**. In a compound entry, all debit accounts involved are listed before any credit accounts.

Figure 3-2
The General
Journal

General Journal					Page
Date		Description	Post. Ref.	Debit	Credit
19xx					
Jan.	5	Art Supplies		900	
		Office Supplies		400	
		Accounts Payable			1,300
		Purchase of art and office supplies on credit			
	6	Prepaid Insurance		240	
		Cash			240
		Paid one-year life insurance premium			

3. Write the debit amounts in the appropriate column opposite the accounts to be debited, and write the credit amounts opposite the accounts to be credited.
4. At the time of recording the transactions, nothing is placed in the Post. Ref. (posting reference) column. (This column is sometimes called LP or Folio.) Later, if the company uses account numbers to identify accounts in the ledger, fill in the account numbers to provide a convenient cross-reference from general journal to ledger and to indicate that posting to the ledger has been completed.
5. It is customary to skip a line after each journal entry.

The Ledger Account Form

So far, we have used the T form of account as a simple and direct means of recording transactions. In practice, a somewhat more complicated form of the account is needed to record more information. The **ledger account form**, with four columns, for dollar amounts, is illustrated in Figure 3-3 (next page).

The *account title* and *number* appear at the top of the account form. The *date* of the transaction appears in the first two columns as it does in the journal. The Item column is used only rarely, because an explanation already appears in the journal. The Post. Ref. column is used to note the journal page number where the journal entry for the transaction can be found. The dollar amount of the entry is entered in the appropriate Debit or Credit column, and a new account balance is computed in the final two columns after each entry. The advantage of this form of account over the T account is that the current balance of the account is always easily available.

Figure 3-3
Accounts
Payable Ledger
Account

General Ledger							
Accounts Payable							**Account No. 212**
						Balance	
Date		Item	Post. Ref.	Debit	Credit	Debit	Credit
19xx							
Jan.	4				750		750
	5				1,300		2,050
	10			500			1,550
	30				35		1,585

Relationship Between the Journal and the Ledger

Objective 7
Explain the relationship of the journal to the ledger

After the transactions have been entered in the journal, they must be transferred to the ledger. This process of transferring journal entry information from the journal to the ledger is called **posting**. Posting is usually done not after each journal entry but after several entries have been made—for example, at the end of each day or less frequently depending on the number of transactions.

Posting consists of transferring each amount in the Debit column of the journal into the Debit column of the appropriate account in the ledger and copying each amount in the Credit column of the journal into the Credit column of the appropriate account in the ledger. This procedure is illustrated in Figure 3-4. The steps in posting are as follows:

1. Locate in the ledger the debit account named in the journal entry.
2. Enter in the Debit column of the ledger account the amount of the debit as it appears in the journal.
3. Enter the date of the transaction and, in the Post. Ref. column of the ledger, the journal page number from which the entry comes.
4. Enter in the Post. Ref. column of the journal the account number of the account to which the amount was posted.
5. Repeat the preceding four steps for the credit side of the journal entry.

Note that Step 4 is the last step in the posting process for each debit and credit. In addition to serving as an easy reference between journal entry and ledger account, this entry in the Post. Ref. column of the journal serves as a check, indicating that all steps for the item are completed. For example, when accountants are called away from their desks by telephone calls or other interruptions, they can easily find where they were before the interruption.

Figure 3-4
Posting from the General Journal to the Ledger

General Journal — Page 2

Date		Description	Post. Ref.	Debit	Credit
19xx					
Jan.	30	Telephone Expense	513	35	
		Accounts Payable	212		35
		Received bill for telephone expense			

General Ledger

Accounts Payable — Account No. 212

Date		Item	Post. Ref.	Debit	Credit	Balance Debit	Balance Credit
19xx							
Jan.	4		J1		750		750
	5		J1		1,300		2,050
	10		J1	500			1,550
	30		J2		35		1,585

Telephone Expense — Account No. 513

Date		Item	Post. Ref.	Debit	Credit	Balance Debit	Balance Credit
19xx							
Jan.	30		J2	35		35	

The Trial Balance

The equality of debit and credit balances in the ledger can be tested periodically by preparing a trial balance. Figure 3-5 (next page) contains a trial balance for the Joan Miller Advertising Agency. It was prepared from the accounts in Figure 3-1. Below Figure 3-5 are the steps to follow in preparing a trial balance.

Figure 3-5
Trial Balance

Joan Miller Advertising Agency Trial Balance January 31, 19xx		
Cash	$ 860	
Accounts Receivable	1,400	
Art Supplies	900	
Office Supplies	400	
Prepaid Rent	400	
Prepaid Insurance	240	
Art Equipment	2,100	
Office Equipment	1,500	
Accounts Payable		$1,585
Unearned Art Fees		500
Joan Miller, Capital		5,000
Joan Miller, Withdrawals	700	
Advertising Fees Earned		2,100
Office Wages	600	
Utility Expense	50	
Telephone Expense	35	
	$9,185	$9,185

1. Determine the balance of each account in the ledger.
2. List each account in the ledger that has a balance, with the debit balances in one column and the credit balances in another.
3. Add each column.
4. Compare the totals of each column.

Objective 8
Prepare a trial balance and recognize its value and limitations

The significance of the trial balance is that it proves whether or not the ledger is in balance. "In balance" means that equal debits and credits have been recorded for all transactions.

If the debit and credit columns of the trial balance do not equal each other, it may be the result of one or more of these errors: (1) a debit was entered in an account as a credit, or vice versa, (2) the balance of an account was incorrectly computed, (3) an error was made in carrying the account balance to the trial balance, or (4) the trial balance was incorrectly summed.

The trial balance proof does not mean that transactions were analyzed correctly or recorded in the proper accounts. For example, there would be no way of determining from the trial balance that a debit should have been made in the Art Equipment account rather than the Office Equipment account. In addition, if a transaction that should be recorded is omitted, it will not be detected by a trial balance proof because equal credits and debits will have been omitted. Also, if an error of the same amount is made both as a credit and as a debit, it will not be discovered by the trial balance. The trial balance proves only the equality of the debits and credits in the accounts.

Other than simply adding the columns wrong, the two most common mistakes in preparing a trial balance are (1) recording an account with a debit balance as a credit, or vice versa, and (2) transposing two numbers in an amount when transferring it to the trial balance (for example, transferring $23,459 as $23,549). The first of these mistakes will cause the trial balance to be out of balance by an amount divisible by 2. The second will cause the trial balance to be out of balance by a number divisible by 9. Thus if a trial balance is out of balance and the addition has been verified, determine the amount by which the trial balance is out of balance and divide it first by 2 and then by 9. If the amount is divisible by 2, look in the trial balance for an amount equal to the quotient. If such a number exists, it is likely that this amount is in the wrong column. If the amount is divisible by 9, trace each amount to the ledger account balance, checking carefully for a transposition error. If neither of these techniques identifies the error, it is necessary to recompute the balance of each account in the ledger and retrace each posting from the journal to the ledger.

Some Notes on Bookkeeping Techniques

Ruled lines appear in financial reports before each subtotal or total to indicate that the amounts above are to be added or subtracted. It is common practice to use a double line under a final total.

Dollar signs ($) are required in all financial statements including the balance sheet and income statement and in schedules such as the trial balance. On these statements, a dollar sign should be placed before the first amount in each column and before the first amount in a column following a ruled line. Dollar signs are *not* used in journals or ledgers.

On unruled paper, commas and periods are used in representing dollar amounts, but when columnar paper is used in journals and ledgers, commas and periods are not needed. In this book, because most problems and illustrations are in even dollar amounts, the cents column is usually omitted. When professional accountants deal with even dollars, they will often use a dash in that column to indicate even dollars rather than take the time to write zeros.

Chapter Review

Review of Learning Objectives

1. Explain in simple terms the generally accepted ways of solving the measurement problems of recognition, valuation, and classification.

To measure a business transaction, the accountant must determine when the transaction occurred (the recognition problem), what value should be placed on the transaction (the valuation problem), and how the components of the transaction should be categorized (the classification problem). In general, recognition occurs when title passes, and a transaction is valued at the cost or exchange price when the transaction is recognized. Classification refers to the categorizing of transactions according to a system of accounts.

2. Define and use the terms *account* and *ledger*.
An account is a device for storing data from transactions. There is one account for each asset, liability, and component of owner's equity. The ledger is a book or file consisting of all of a company's accounts arranged according to a chart of accounts.

3. Recognize commonly used assets, liabilities, and owner's equity accounts.
Commonly used asset accounts are Cash, Notes Receivable, Accounts Receivable, Prepaid Expenses, Land, Buildings, and Equipment. Common liability accounts are Notes Payable, Accounts Payable, and Bonds and Mortgages Payable. Common owner's equity accounts are Capital, Withdrawals, Revenue, and Expense.

4. Know the rules for debit and credit.
The rules for debit and credit are (1) increases in assets are debited to asset accounts; decreases in assets are credited to asset accounts; (2) increases in liabilities and owner's equity are credited to liability and owner's equity accounts; decreases in liabilities and owner's equity are debited to liability and owner's equity accounts.

5. Apply the procedure for transaction analysis to simple transactions.
The procedures for analyzing transactions are to (1) analyze the effect of the transaction on assets, liabilities, and owner's equity; (2) apply the appropriate double-entry rule; and (3) make the entry.

6. Record transactions in the general journal.
The general journal is a chronological record of all transactions. The record of a transaction in the general journal contains the date of the transaction, the names of the accounts and dollar amounts debited and credited, an explanation of the journal entries, and the account numbers to which postings have been made.

7. Explain the relationship of the journal to the ledger.
After the transactions have been entered in the journal, they must be posted to the ledger. Posting is done by transferring each amount in the debit column of the journal to the debit column of the appropriate account in the ledger and transferring each amount in the credit column of the journal to the credit column of the appropriate account in the ledger.

8. Prepare a trial balance and recognize its value and limitations.
A trial balance is used to test the equality of the debit and credit balances in the ledger. It is prepared by listing each account with its balance in the appropriate debit or credit column. The two columns are added and compared to test their balance. The major limitation of the trial balance is that the equality of debit and credit balances does not mean that transactions were analyzed correctly or recorded in the proper accounts.

Self-Test

Test your knowledge of the chapter by choosing the best answer for each item below.

1. Deciding whether an expenditure for a desk is properly recorded as store equipment or office equipment is an example of
   a. a recognition problem.
   b. a valuation problem.
   c. a classification problem.
   d. a communication problem.
2. Deciding whether to record a sale when the order for services is received or when the services are performed is an example of
   a. a recognition problem.
   b. a valuation problem.
   c. a classification problem.
   d. a communication problem.
3. Recording an asset at its exchange price is an example of the accounting solution to the
   a. recognition problem.
   b. valuation problem.
   c. classification problem.
   d. communication problem.
4. The left side of an account is referred to as
   a. the balance.
   b. a debit.
   c. a credit.
   d. a footing.
5. Which of the following is a liability account?
   a. Accounts Receivable
   b. Withdrawals
   c. Rent Expense
   d. Accounts Payable
6. A purchase of office equipment on credit requires a credit to
   a. Office Equipment.
   b. Cash.
   c. Accounts Payable.
   d. Equipment Expense.
7. Payment for a two-year insurance policy requires a debit to
   a. Prepaid Insurance.
   b. Insurance Expense.
   c. Cash.
   d. Accounts Payable.
8. An agreement to spend $100 a month on advertising beginning next month requires
   a. a debit to Advertising Expense.
   b. a credit to Cash.
   c. no entry.
   d. a debit to Prepaid Advertising.
9. Transactions are initially recorded in the
   a. trial balance.
   b. T account.
   c. general journal.
   d. ledger.
10. The equality of debits and credits can be tested periodically by preparing a
    a. trial balance.
    b. T account.
    c. general journal.
    d. ledger.

Answers to Self-Test are at the end of this chapter.

Review Problem
Journal Entries, T Accounts, and Trial Balance

After graduation from veterinary school, Lawrence Cox entered private practice by engaging in the transactions listed here and at the top of the next page.

19xx
May 1 Lawrence Cox deposited $2,000 in his business bank account.
3 He paid $300 for two months' rent in advance for an office.

9 He purchased medical supplies for $200 in cash.
12 He purchased $400 of equipment on credit, making a one-fourth down payment.
15 He delivered a calf for a fee of $35.
18 He made a partial payment of $50 on the equipment purchased on May 12.
27 He paid a utility bill for $40.

Required

1. Record the above entries in the general journal.
2. Post the entries from the journal to the T accounts in the ledger.
3. Prepare a trial balance.

Answer to Review Problem

1. Recording journal entries

General Journal **Page 1**

Date		Description	Post. Ref.	Debit	Credit
19xx					
May	1	Cash		2,000	
		Lawrence Cox, Capital			2,000
		Lawrence Cox deposited $2,000 in his business bank account			
	3	Prepaid Rent		300	
		Cash			300
		Paid two months' rent in advance for an office			
	9	Medical Supplies		200	
		Cash			200
		Purchased medical supplies for cash			
	12	Equipment		400	
		Accounts Payable			300
		Cash			100
		Purchased equipment on credit, paying 25 percent down			
	15	Cash		35	
		Veterinary Fees Earned			35
		Collected fee for delivering a calf			

18	Accounts Payable		50	
	Cash			50
	Made partial payment for the equipment purchased on May 12			
27	Utility Expense		40	
	Cash			40
	Paid utility bill			

2. Posting transactions to the T accounts

Cash

5/1	2,000	5/3	300
5/15	35	5/9	200
		5/12	100
		5/18	50
		5/27	40

Accounts Payable

5/18	50	5/12	300

Medical Supplies

5/9	200		

Lawrence Cox, Capital

		5/1	2,000

Prepaid Rent

5/3	300		

Veterinary Fees Earned

		5/15	35

Equipment

5/12	400		

Utility Expense

5/27	40		

3. Completion of trial balance

Lawrence Cox, Veterinarian
Trial Balance
May 31, 19xx

Cash	$1,345	
Medical Supplies	200	
Prepaid Rent	300	
Equipment	400	
Accounts Payable		$ 250
Lawrence Cox, Capital		2,000
Veterinary Fees Earned		35
Utility Expense	40	
	$2,285	$2,285

Chapter Assignments

Questions

1. What three problems underlie most accounting issues?
2. Why is recognition a problem to accountants?
3. A customer asks the owner of a store to save an item for him and swears that he will pick it up and pay for it next week. The owner agrees to hold it. Should this transaction be recorded as a sale? Explain.
4. Why is it practical for the accountant to rely on original cost for evaluation purposes?
5. What is the basic limitation of using original cost in accounting measurements?
6. What is an account, and how is it related to the ledger?
7. "Debits are bad; credits are good." Comment on this statement.
8. Why is the system of recording entries called the double-entry system? What is so special about it?
9. Suppose that a system of double-entry bookkeeping were developed in which credits increased assets and debits decreased assets. How would accounting for liabilities and owner's equity be affected under that system?
10. Give the rules of debits and credits for (a) assets, (b) liabilities, and (c) owner's equity.
11. Why are the rules the same for liabilities and owner's equity?
12. What is the meaning of the statement "The Cash account has a debit balance of $500"?
13. What are the three steps in transaction analysis?
14. Tell whether each of the following accounts is an asset account, a liability account, or an owner's equity account:
    - **a.** Notes Receivable
    - **b.** Land
    - **c.** Withdrawals
    - **d.** Bonds Payable
    - **e.** Prepaid Expense
    - **f.** Expense
    - **g.** Revenue
15. List the following six items in a logical sequence to illustrate the flow of events through the accounting system:
    - **a.** Analysis of transaction
    - **b.** Debits and credits posted from the journal to the ledger
    - **c.** Occurrence of business transaction
    - **d.** Preparation of financial statements
    - **e.** Entry made in a journal
    - **f.** Preparation of trial balance
16. What purposes are served by a trial balance?
17. Can errors be present even though the trial balance balances? Comment.
18. In recording entries in a journal, which is written first, the debit or the credit? How is indentation used in the general journal?
19. What is the relationship between the journal and the ledger?
20. Describe each of the following:
    - **a.** Account
    - **b.** Journal
    - **c.** Ledger
    - **d.** Book of original entry
    - **e.** Post. Ref. column
    - **f.** Journalizing
    - **g.** Posting
    - **h.** Footings
    - **i.** Compound entry
21. Does double-entry accounting refer to entering a transaction in both the journal and the ledger? Comment.
22. Is it possible or desirable to forgo the journal and enter the transaction directly in the ledger? Comment.
23. Under what conditions could an Accounts Payable account have a debit balance?

Classroom Exercises

Exercise 3-1 Transaction Analysis

Analyze each of the following transactions, using the form shown in the example below the list.

a. Hugo Barnes established Barnes Barber Shop by placing $500 in a bank account.
b. Paid two months' rent in advance, $210.
c. Purchased supplies on credit, $30.
d. Received cash for barbering services, $25.
e. Paid for supplies purchased in c.
f. Paid utility bill, $18.

Example

a. The asset Cash was increased. Increases in assets are recorded by debits. Debit Cash $500.

The owner's equity Hugo Barnes, Capital, was increased. Increases in owner's equity are recorded by credits. Credit Owner's Equity $500.

Exercise 3-2 Recording Transactions in T Accounts

Place the following T accounts on a sheet of paper: Cash; Accounts Receivable; Repair Supplies; Repair Equipment; Accounts Payable; Sidney Davis, Capital; Sidney Davis, Withdrawals; Repair Revenue; Salary Expense; Rent Expense. Record the following transactions directly in the T accounts using the letters to identify the transactions.

a. Sidney Davis opened the Appliance Repair Service by investing $1,200 in cash and $400 in repair equipment.
b. Paid $150 for one month's rent.
c. Purchased repair supplies on credit, $200.
d. Purchased additional repair equipment, $150.
e. Paid salary of $225.
f. Paid $100 of amount purchased on credit in **c.**
g. Withdrew $300 from business for living expense.
h. Accepted cash for repairs completed, $430.

Exercise 3-3 Preparation of Trial Balance

After recording the transactions in Exercise 3-2, prepare a trial balance for Appliance Repair Service.

Exercise 3-4 Application of Recognition Point

Ace Body Works uses a large amount of supplies in its business. The following table summarizes selected transaction data for orders of supplies purchased.

Order	Date Shipped	Date Received	Amount
a	May 10	May 15	$700
b	16	22	400
c	23	30	600
d	27	June 2	750
e	June 1	5	500

Determine the total purchases of supplies for May only under each of the following assumptions:

1. Ace Body Works recognizes purchases when orders are shipped.
2. Ace Body Works recognizes purchases when orders are received.

Exercise 3-5
Preparation of Trial Balance

The following accounts of the Morgan Service Company as of January 30, 19xx, are listed in alphabetical order. The amount of Accounts Payable is omitted.

Accounts Payable	?	Equipment	$ 6,000
Accounts Receivable	$ 1,000	John Morgan, Capital	15,380
Building	17,000	Land	2,600
Cash	3,500	Notes Payable	10,000
		Prepaid Insurance	550

Prepare a trial balance with the proper heading and with the accounts listed in the correct sequence. Compute the balance of Accounts Payable.

Exercise 3-6
Effect of Errors on Trial Balance

Which of the following errors would cause a trial balance to have unequal totals? Explain your answers.

a. A payment to a creditor was recorded as a debit to Accounts Payable for $75 and a credit to Cash for $57.
b. A payment of $100 to a creditor for an account payable was debited to Accounts Receivable and credited to Cash.
c. A purchase of office supplies of $280 was recorded as a debit to Office Supplies for $28 and a credit to Cash for $28.
d. A purchase of equipment of $300 was recorded as a debit to Supplies for $300 and a credit to Cash for $300.

Exercise 3-7
Preparation of Ledger Account

A T account showing the cash transactions for a month follows:

Cash

3/1	10,000	3/2	900
3/7	1,200	3/4	200
3/14	4,000	3/8	1,700
3/21	200	3/9	5,000
3/28	4,600	3/23	600

Prepare the account in ledger account form in a manner similar to the example in Figure 3-3.

Exercise 3-8
Recording Transactions in General Journal

On a sheet of notebook paper, draw a general journal form like Figure 3-2. After completing the form, record the following transactions in the journal.

Dec. 14 Purchased an item of equipment for $1,500, paying $500 in a cash down payment.
28 Paid $500 of the amount owed on the equipment.

Exercise 3-9
Posting to Ledger Accounts

On a sheet of notebook paper, draw three ledger account forms like those shown in Figure 3-3. After completing the forms, post the two transactions from the journal in Exercise 3-8.

Exercise 3-10
Correcting Errors in Trial Balance

The following trial balance for Sinclair Services at the end of July does not balance because of a number of errors.

Sinclair Services Trial Balance July 31, 19xx		
Cash	$ 1,630	
Accounts Receivable	2,830	
Supplies	60	
Prepaid Insurance	90	
Equipment	4,200	
Accounts Payable		$ 2,080
R. Sinclair, Capital		5,780
R. Sinclair, Withdrawals		350
Revenues		2,860
Salary Expense	1,300	
Rent Expense	300	
Advertising Expense	170	
Utility Expense	13	
	$10,593	$11,070

The accountant for Sinclair has compared the amounts in the trial balance with the ledger, recomputed the account balances, and compared the postings. He found the following errors:

a. The pencil footing of the credits to cash was overstated by $200.
b. A cash payment of $210 was credited to cash for $120.
c. A debit of $60 to Accounts Receivable was not posted.
d. Supplies purchased for $30 were posted as a credit to Supplies.
e. A debit of $90 to Prepaid Insurance was overlooked and not posted.
f. The pencil footings for the Accounts Payable account were debits of $2,660 and credits of $4,400.
g. A Notes Payable account with a credit balance of $1,200 was not included in the trial balance.
h. The debit balance of R. Sinclair, Withdrawals, was listed in the trial balance as a credit.
i. A $100 debit to R. Sinclair, Withdrawals, was posted as a credit.
j. The Utility Expense of $130 was listed as $13 in the trial balance.

Prepare a corrected trial balance.

Problem Set A

Problem 3A-1
Preparation of Trial Balance

The Marshall Theater shows first-run movies in a downtown location. The following alphabetical list shows the account balances as of October 31, 19xx:

Accounts Payable	$ 350
Accounts Receivable	1,200
Building	42,000
Cash	1,100
Land	6,000

Mortgage Payable	35,000
Office Equipment	1,800
Revenues from Ticket Sales	19,000
Salary Expense	14,000
Supplies Expense	900
Theater Equipment	3,700
Utilities Expense	170
Vernon Moses, Capital	25,000
Vernon Moses, Withdrawals	?

Required

Prepare a trial balance for the Marshall Theater with the proper heading. Indicate the correct amount for Vernon Moses, Withdrawals.

Problem 3A-2 Transaction Analysis, T Accounts, and Trial Balance

Kurt Shield opened a real estate agency called KS Realty Company.

a. He began business by contributing the following assets to the business:

Cash	$ 5,500
Land	1,000
Building	15,000
Automobile	2,400

b. Paid $150 for advertisement announcing the opening of the agency.
c. Purchased office equipment on credit for $1,900 from Business Furniture Company.
d. Earned and collected a commission of $1,200 from the sale of a house.
e. Purchased supplies for $600.
f. Paid one-half of the amount owed Business Furniture Company.
g. Agreed to place $75 advertisement in newspaper.
h. Paid secretary $140.
i. Billed Arnold Smith $1,800 for the commission on selling his house.
j. Paid utility bill, $70.
k. Received bill for advertising, $75.
l. Paid secretary $140.
m. Wrote check on KS Realty Account for personal expenses, $500.
n. Received partial payment from Arnold Smith, $1,200.
o. Sold a house for a commission of $1,000, one-half of which was collected in cash and the other half of which is to be collected next month.
p. Purchased a three-year insurance policy, $480.

Required

1. Set up the following T accounts: Cash; Accounts Receivable; Supplies; Prepaid Insurance; Land; Building; Automobile; Office Equipment; Accounts Payable; Kurt Shield, Capital; Kurt Shield, Withdrawals; Commission Revenue; Office Salary Expense; Advertising Expense; Utility Expense.
2. Record the transactions by entering debits and credits directly in the T accounts, using the transaction letters to identify each debit and credit.
3. Prepare a trial balance using the current date.

Problem 3A-3 Transaction Analysis, T Accounts, and Trial Balance

Arthur Burnside, M.D., completed the following transactions in his medical practice during October 19xx.

Oct.	1	Began practice by investing $2,500.
	2	Received a loan and signed a note to the bank for $10,000.
	4	Purchased equipment on account, $2,800.

5 Purchased medical supplies for cash, $400.
6 Received cash from patients, $800.
7 Billed patients for medical services, $700.
8 Paid salaries:

Nurse	$180
Receptionist	$150

10 Purchased medical supplies on account, $250.
11 Paid two months' rent in advance, $300.
12 Paid two-year insurance policy, $280.
14 Returned for credit $40 of defective medical supplies purchased on October 10.
15 Paid cash to creditors from whom the equipment was purchased, $500.
16 Received cash from customers previously billed, $650.
20 Sold supplies to another doctor as a courtesy at cost, $50.
22 Paid salaries:

Nurse	$180
Receptionist	$150

23 Received bill for monthly laboratory expenses, $375.
26 Paid utilities, $100.
27 Billed patients for medical services, $800.
28 Received cash for services, $800.
29 Transferred $1,000 to Arthur Burnside's personal account.

Required

1. Set up the following T accounts: Cash; Accounts Receivable; Medical Supplies; Prepaid Rent; Prepaid Insurance; Equipment; Accounts Payable; Notes Payable; Arthur Burnside, Capital; Arthur Burnside, Withdrawals; Medical Fees Earned; Nursing Salaries; Office Salaries; Laboratory Expense; Utility Expense.
2. a. Prepare journal entries to record the above transactions in the general journal.
b. Post the entries to the T accounts.
c. Prepare a trial balance as of October 31, 19xx.

Problem 3A-4 Using General Journal, T Accounts, and Trial Balance

The account balances for OK Household Services Company on May 1, 19xx, are presented in the trial balance on page 94.
During May, Mr. Elsworth completed the following transactions:

May 1 Bought supplies for $100 cash.
2 Purchased new equipment for $500 cash.
5 Billed customers for services, $270.
6 Collected $520 from customers billed last month.
8 Transferred to the company from his personal assets a special type of floor-cleaning equipment worth $230.
9 Received cash from customers for services rendered, $290.
12 Paid amount owed on account to creditors.
13 Made a $100 monthly payment on the note payable.
15 Paid wages for first half of month, $480.
16 Paid monthly rent, $140.

19 Gave a customer a $30 allowance on his account in settlement for faulty work.
22 Withdrew $600 from the business for personal expenses.
23 Billed customers for services rendered, $750.
24 Paid utility bill, $80.
25 Paid gas and oil bill for truck, $110.
27 Recorded cash collection from customers for services rendered, $240.

OK Household Services Company
Trial Balance
May 1, 19xx

Cash	$1,490	
Accounts Receivable	780	
Supplies	470	
Prepaid Insurance	360	
Equipment	1,200	
Truck	2,700	
Accounts Payable		$ 380
Notes Payable		1,800
Carl Elsworth, Capital		5,000
Carl Elsworth, Withdrawals	630	
Service Revenue		1,740
Wages Expense	960	
Rent Expense	140	
Truck Expense	120	
Utility Expense	70	
	$8,920	$8,920

Required

1. Open T accounts for the accounts shown in the trial balance.
2. Enter the May 1 trial balance amounts in the T accounts. Write the abbreviation "Bal" before each amount to indicate that it is the balance in the account from the previous month.
3. a. Prepare the journal entries to record the above transactions in the general journal.
   b. Post the entries to the T accounts.
   c. Prepare a trial balance as of May 31, 19xx.

Problem 3A-5 Relationship of General Journal, Ledger Accounts, and Trial Balance

The City Protective Service provides security services for apartment and office buildings in a densely populated metropolitan area on the Gulf Coast. On July 1, 19xx, the company had a trial balance (account numbers) as shown at the top of the next page.

City Protective Service
Trial Balance
July 1, 19xx

Cash (11)	$ 7,200	
Accounts Receivable (12)	2,400	
Equipment (21)	6,500	
Patrol Cars (22)	12,400	
Accounts Payable (31)		$ 1,700
Matthew Potak, Capital (41)		26,800
	$28,500	$28,500

During the month of July, the company completed the following transactions:

July 1 Entered into a contract with Lakeshore Management Company to provide services beginning July 1 to be billed monthly on the 15th of the month, $500 per month.
2 Paid rent for July, $200.
3 Paid $500 on account.
5 Purchased a new patrol car required for the Lakeshore Management contract. The new car cost $3,600. The down payment was $600. A note was signed for the balance.
6 Received $2,000 from customers billed last month.
10 Purchased supplies for $100 and equipment for $350 on credit.
12 Billed customers for one month's service, $2,400.
14 Received $1,250 cash for providing security for a traveling fair.
15 Billed Lakeshore Management for one month's service, $500.
16 Paid wages for one-half month, $1,100.
18 Matthew Potak took a car no longer needed in the business for his personal use. The car is recorded in the records at $900.
20 Paid cash operating expenses (other than wages and car expenses) of $560 during the month.
22 Drivers turned in gas and oil receipts of $375 and were reimbursed.
25 Matthew Potak took $700 for his personal expenses.
28 $1,000 was accepted in advance from Key Realty for services to begin next month.
29 Paid wages for one-half month, $1,100.

Required

1. Open accounts in the ledger account form for the accounts in the trial balance plus the following accounts:

Account No.	Account Name
13	Supplies
32	Notes Payable
33	Revenue Received in Advance
42	Matthew Potak, Withdrawals
51	Revenue
61	Wages Expense

62	Car Expense
63	Rent Expense
64	Other Operating Expense

2. Enter the July 1 account balances in the appropriate ledger account forms from the trial balance.
3. a. Enter the above transactions in the general journal.
   b. Post the entries to the ledger account. Be sure to insert appropriate posting references to journal and ledger as you post.
   c. Prepare a trial balance as of July 31, 19xx.

Problem 3A-6 Recording and Tracing Transactions from General Journal to Ledger Accounts and Trial Balance

Ernest Haas opened a television repair shop in his garage. He was successful and soon moved to a storefront, which he rented. He tried to keep his accounts informally in T accounts, but this system soon grew too complicated and confusing. His T accounts appear as follows:

Cash			11
8/1 (a)	1,700	8/2 (b)	100
8/9 (f)	30	8/6 (d)	250
8/10 (g)	120	8/12 (h)	75
8/13 (i)	15	8/15 (j)	100

Accounts Receivable			12
8/7 (e)	60	8/13 (i)	15

Repair Supplies			13
8/2 (b)	100		
8/4 (c)	75		

Equipment			21
8/1 (a)	300	8/10 (g)	120
8/6 (d)	750		

Accounts Payable			31
8/12 (h)	75	8/4 (c)	75

Notes Payable			32
		8/6 (d)	500

Ernest Haas, Capital			41
		8/1 (a)	2,000

Repair Revenue			51
		8/7 (e)	60
		8/9 (f)	30

Rent Expense			61
8/15 (j)	100		

Required

1. a. Copy the transactions from the T accounts to the general journal, using the dates to identify each transaction in the general ledger.
   b. Post the transactions in four-column ledger account forms. Be sure to insert the appropriate posting references in journal and ledger as you post.
   c. Prepare a trial balance.
2. What are the advantages for Ernest Haas in using the system of general journal and four-column ledger account forms rather than entering transactions directly into T accounts as he had been doing?

Problem Set B

Problem 3B-1 Preparation of Trial Balance

The McGraw Construction Company builds foundations for buildings and parking lots. The following alphabetical list shows the account balances as of April 30, 19xx:

Accounts Payable	$ 2,200
Accounts Receivable	4,730
Cash	?
Construction Supplies	950
Equipment	12,250
Notes Payable	10,000
Office Trailer	1,100
Prepaid Insurance	2,300
Revenue Earned	8,700
Supplies Expense	3,600
Utility Expense	210
Victor McGraw, Capital	20,000
Victor McGraw, Withdrawals	3,900
Wages Expense	4,400

Required

Prepare a trial balance for McGraw Construction Company with the proper heading. Determine the correct balance for the Cash account on April 30, 19xx.

Problem 3B-2 Transaction Analysis, T Accounts, and Trial Balance

Georgetta Miles opened a secretarial school called Business Secretary Training.

a. She contributed the following assets to the business:

Cash	$3,200
Typewriters	450
Office Equipment	600

b. Found a storefront for her business and paid the first month's rent, $130.
c. Paid $95 for advertisement announcing the opening of the school.
d. Enrolled three students in four-week secretarial program and two students in ten-day typing course.
e. Purchased supplies on credit, $165.
f. Billed enrolled students, $650.
g. Paid assistant one week's salary, $110.
h. Purchased a typewriter, $240, and office equipment, $190, on credit.
i. Paid for supplies purchased on credit.
j. Repaired broken typewriter, $20.
k. Billed new students, $220.
l. Transferred $150 to personal checking account.
m. Received payment from customers previously billed, $540.
n. Paid utility bill, $45.
o. Paid assistant one week's salary, $110.
p. Received cash revenue from another new student, $125.

Required

1. Set up the following T accounts: Cash; Accounts Receivable; Supplies; Typewriters; Office Equipment; Accounts Payable; Georgetta Miles, Capital; Georgetta Miles, Withdrawals; Revenue from Business; Rent Expense; Advertising Expense; Salary Expense; Repair Expense; Utility Expense.

2. Record transactions by entering debits and credits directly in the T accounts, using the transaction letters to identify each debit and credit.
3. Prepare a trial balance using the current date.

Problem 3B-3 Transaction Analysis, T Accounts, and Trial Balance

Martin Grove is a house painter. During the month of April, he completed the following transactions:

April	2	Began his business with equipment valued at $310 and placed $2,250 in a business checking account.
	3	Purchased a used truck costing $550. Paid $200 cash and signed a note for the balance.
	4	Purchased supplies on account, $160.
	5	Completed painting two-story house and billed customer, $240.
	7	Received cash for painting two rooms, $75.
	8	Hired assistant to work with him, to be paid $3 an hour.
	10	Purchased supplies, $80.
	11	Received check from customer previously billed, $240.
	12	Paid $200 on insurance policy for 18 months' coverage.
	13	Billed customers, $310.
	14	Paid assistant for 25 hours' work, $75.
	15	Gasoline and oil for truck, $20.
	18	Paid for supplies purchased on April 4.
	20	Purchased new ladder (equipment) for $30 and supplies for $145 on account.
	22	Received telephone bill, $30.
	23	Received collection from customer previously billed, $165.
	24	Transferred $150 to personal checking account.
	25	Received cash for painting five-room apartment, $180.
	27	Paid $100 on note signed for truck.
	29	Paid assistant for 30 hours' work, $90.

Required

1. Set up the following T accounts: Cash; Accounts Receivable; Supplies; Prepaid Insurance; Equipment; Truck; Accounts Payable; Notes Payable; Martin Grove, Capital; Martin Grove, Withdrawals; Painting Fees Earned; Wages Expense; Telephone Expense; Truck Expense.
2. a. Prepare journal entries to record the above transactions in the general journal.
b. Post the entries to the T accounts.
c. Prepare a trial balance for Martin Grove Painting Service as of April 30, 19xx.

Problem 3B-4 Using General Journal, T Accounts, and Trial Balance

The account balances for Frank's Barber Shop at the end of July are presented in the trial balance shown on the next page.

During August, Mr. Flavin completed the following transactions:

Aug.	1	Paid for supplies purchased on credit last month, $110.
	2	Billed customers for services, $180.
	3	Paid rent for August, $90.
	5	Purchased supplies on credit, $75.
	7	Received cash from customers not previously billed, $145.
	8	Purchased new equipment from Stern Manufacturing Company on account, $650.

9 Received telephone bill for last month, $20.
12 Returned a portion of equipment which was defective. Purchase was made August 8, $160.
13 Received payment from customers previously billed, $95.
14 Paid telephone bill received August 9.
16 Took $55 from business for personal use.
19 Paid for supplies purchased on August 5.
20 Billed customers for services, $135.
23 Purchased equipment from a friend who is retiring, $140. Payment was made from personal checking account but equipment will be used in the business.
25 Received payment from customers previously billed, $195.
27 Paid electric bill, $15.
29 Paid $300 on note.

Frank's Barber Shop
Trial Balance
July 31, 19xx

Cash	$1,350	
Accounts Receivable	110	
Supplies	230	
Prepaid Insurance	200	
Equipment	2,200	
Accounts Payable		$ 150
Notes Payable		1,500
Frank Flavin, Capital		2,100
Frank Flavin, Withdrawals	210	
Service Revenue		690
Rent Expense	90	
Utility Expense	50	
	$4,440	$4,440

Required

1. Open T accounts for the accounts shown in the trial balance.
2. Enter the July 31 trial balance amounts in the T accounts. Write the abbreviation "Bal" before each amount to indicate that it is the beginning balance of the account.
3. a. Prepare journal entries to record the above transactions in the general journal.
b. Post the entries to the T accounts.
c. Prepare a trial balance as of August 31, 19xx.

Problem 3B-5 Relationship of General Journal, Ledger Accounts, and Trial Balance

The Children Daycare Services provides baby-sitting and child-care programs. On February 1, 19xx, the company had a trial balance (account numbers) as follows:

Children Daycare Service
Trial Balance
February 1, 19xx

Cash (11)	$ 1,780	
Accounts Receivable (12)	1,600	
Equipment (21)	990	
Buses (22)	7,400	
Accounts Payable (31)		$ 1,470
Notes Payable (32)		7,000
Therese Evans, Capital (41)		3,300
	$11,770	$11,770

During the month of February, the company completed the following transactions:

Feb. 2 Paid one month's rent, $140.
3 Received fees for one month's services, $400.
4 Purchased supplies on account, $85.
5 Reimbursed bus driver for gas expenses, $20.
7 Paid assistants for two weeks' services, $230.
8 Paid $170 on account.
9 Received $1,200 from customers on account.
10 Billed customers who had not yet paid for this month's services, $700.
11 Paid for supplies purchased on February 4.
13 Purchased playground equipment, $1,000.
14 Withdrew $110 for personal expenses.
17 Contributed equipment to business, $90.
19 Paid utility bills, $45.
22 Received fees for one month's services from customers previously billed, $500.
25 Paid assistants for two weeks' services, $320.
27 Purchased gas and oil for bus on account, $35.
28 Paid $290 for a one-year insurance policy.

Required

1. Open accounts in the ledger account form for the accounts in the trial balance plus the following accounts:

Account No.	**Account Name**
13	Supplies
14	Prepaid Insurance
42	Therese Evans, Withdrawals
51	Service Revenue
61	Rent Expense

62	Bus Expense
63	Wages Expense
64	Utility Expense

2. Enter the February 1 account balances in the appropriate ledger account forms from the trial balance.

3. a. Enter the above transactions in the general journal.

b. Post the entries to the ledger account. Be sure to insert the appropriate posting references in journal and ledger as you post.

c. Prepare a trial balance as of February 29, 19xx.

Problem 3B-6 Recording and Tracing Transactions from General Journal to Ledger Accounts and Trial Balance

Robert Noel, a psychologist, opened an office near his home. For the first two weeks he kept his accounts informally in T accounts, but this system became confusing. He has now hired you to advise him on keeping records that are easier to understand. Mr. Noel's T accounts appear as follows:

Cash 11

5/1 (a)	2,580	5/2 (b)	300
5/5 (d)	170	5/7 (e)	140
5/13 (i)	80	5/9 (f)	180
		5/12 (h)	150

Accounts Payable 31

5/12 (h)	150	5/3 (c)	150
		5/14 (j)	90

Accounts Receivable 12

5/10 (g)	165	5/13 (i)	80

Notes Payable 32

		5/2 (b)	1,200

Supplies 13

5/3 (c)	150		
5/14 (j)	90		

Robert Noel, Capital 41

		5/1 (a)	2,800

Prepaid Insurance 14

5/9 (f)	180		

Therapy Revenue 51

		5/5 (d)	170
		5/10 (g)	165

Equipment 21

5/1 (a)	220		
5/2 (b)	1,500		

Rent Expense 61

5/7 (e)	140		

Required

1. a. Copy the transactions from the T accounts to the general journal, using the dates to identify each transaction in the general ledger.

b. Post the transactions in four-column ledger account forms. Be sure to insert the appropriate posting references in journal and ledger as you post.

c. Prepare a trial balance.

2. Explain to Mr. Noel the advantages of using the general journal and the four-column ledger account forms rather than entering transactions in T accounts.

Answers to Self-Test

1. c	3. b	5. d	7. a	9. c
2. a	4. b	6. c	8. c	10. a

Learning Objectives

Chapter Four

Business Income and Adjusting Entries

1. *Define net income and its components, revenue and expenses.*
2. *Recognize the difficulties of income measurement caused by (a) the accounting period problem, (b) the continuity problem, and (c) the matching problem.*
3. *Define accrual accounting and explain two broad ways of accomplishing it.*
4. *State the four principal situations that require adjusting entries.*
5. *Prepare typical adjusting entries.*
6. *Prepare an adjusted trial balance.*
7. *Relate the need for adjusting entries to accounting standards.*
8. *Prepare correcting entries.*

In this chapter you will learn how accountants define business income. The chapter should also help you recognize the problems of assigning income to specific time periods. Then, through a realistic example, you can gain an understanding of the adjustment process necessary for measuring periodic business income. As a result of studying this chapter, you should be able to meet the learning objectives listed on the left.

Profitable operation is essential for a business to succeed or even survive. Consequently, earning a profit is an important goal of most businesses. A major function of accounting, of course, is to measure and report the success or failure of a company in achieving this goal.

Profit has many meanings. One definition is the increase in owner's equity resulting from business operations. However, even this definition can be interpreted differently by economists, lawyers, business people, and the public. Because of the ambiguity of the word *profit,* accountants prefer to use the term *net income,* which can be defined precisely from an accounting point of view. To the accountant, net income equals revenue minus expenses.

The Measurement of Business Income

Business enterprise is continuously engaged in activities aimed at earning income. As we mentioned in Chapter 2, it would be fairly easy to determine the income of a company if we could wait until the business ceased to exist. However, the business environment requires a firm to report income or loss regularly for short and equal periods of time. For example, owners must receive income reports every year, and the government requires the company to pay taxes on annual income. Within the business, management often wants financial statements prepared every month.

Faced with these demands, the accountant measures net income in accordance with generally accepted accounting principles. If the reader of the financial reports is familiar with these principles, he or she can understand how the accountant is defining net income and will be aware of its strengths and weaknesses as a measurement. The following paragraphs present the accounting definition of net income and explain the problems of implementing it.

Net Income

Objective 1 Define net income and its components, revenue and expenses

To the accountant, **net income** is the net increase in owner's equity resulting from the profit-seeking operations of the company. Net income equals the difference between revenue and expenses:

$$\text{net income} = \text{revenue} - \text{expenses}$$

Revenue In accounting, **revenue** is a measure of the asset values received from customers during a specific period of time. It equals the price of goods sold and services rendered during that time. When a business provides a service or delivers a product to a customer, it usually receives either cash or a promise to pay cash in the near future. The promise to pay is classified as either Accounts Receivable or Notes Receivable. The revenue for a given period of time equals the total of cash and receivables from sales for that period.

As illustrated in Chapter 2, revenue is reflected by an increase in owner's equity. Note that liabilities are not usually affected and that there are transactions that increase cash and other assets but are not revenues. For example, borrowing money from a bank increases cash and liabilities but does not result in revenue. The collection of accounts receivable, which increases cash and decreases accounts receivable, does not result in revenue either. Recall that when a sale on credit occurred, an asset called Accounts Receivable was increased, and simultaneously an owner's equity revenue account was increased. Counting the subsequent collection of the receivable as revenue, therefore, would be counting the same sales event twice.

Not all increases in owner's equity result from revenue. The investment in the company by an owner, for example, increases owner's equity but is not a revenue.

Expenses The costs of the goods and services used up in the process of obtaining revenue are **expenses.** Often called the cost of doing business, expenses include the costs of merchandise sold, the costs of activities necessary to carry on the business, and the costs of attracting and serving customers. Examples are salaries, rent, advertising, telephone service, and the depreciation (allocation of the cost) of the building and office equipment.

Expenses are the opposite of revenue in that they result in a decrease in owner's equity. In addition, they result in a decrease in assets or an increase in liabilities. Just as not all cash receipts are revenue, not all cash payments are expenses. For example, the cash payment to reduce a liability would not result in an expense. The liability may have arisen originally from incurring an expense, such as for advertising, that is to be paid later. There may be two additional steps before an expenditure of cash becomes an expense. For example, prepaid expenses or plant assets (such as machinery and equipment) are recorded as assets upon acquisition. Later, as their usefulness expires in the operation of the business, their cost is transformed into expenses. In fact, expenses are sometimes called expired costs. Later in this chapter, we shall explain these concepts and processes in more detail.

Real and Nominal Accounts As we saw in Chapter 2, revenue and expenses can be recorded directly as increases and decreases in owner's equity. In practice, management and others want to know the details of the increases and decreases in owner's equity caused by revenues and expenses. Therefore, separate accounts for each revenue and expense are necessary. Since these accounts are temporary in nature, they are sometimes called **nominal accounts.** Nominal accounts show the accumulation of revenue and expenses during the accounting period. At the end of the period, their account balances are transferred to owner's equity. Thus these nominal accounts start the next accounting period with zero balances and are ready to accumulate the specific revenues and expenses of that period. In contrast, the balance sheet accounts, such as specific assets and liabilities, are called **real accounts** because their balances can extend past the end of an accounting period. The process of transferring the totals from the nominal revenue and expense accounts to the real owner's equity accounts is presented in Chapter 5.

The Accounting Period Problem

Objective 2a Recognize the difficulties of income measurement caused by the accounting period problem

The **accounting period problem** recognizes the difficulty of assigning revenues and expenses to a short period of time such as a month or year. Not all transactions can be easily assigned to specific periods of time. Purchases of buildings and equipment, for example, have an effect that extends over many years of a company's life. How many years the buildings or equipment will be in use and how much of the cost should be assigned to each year is necessarily an estimate. Accountants solve this problem with an assumption about **periodicity,** which is that the net income for any period of time less than the life of the business must be regarded as necessarily tentative but nevertheless is a useful approximation of the net income for the period. Normally the time periods are of equal length to facilitate comparisons. The time period should be identified in the financial statements.

Any twelve-month accounting period used by a company is called its **fiscal year.** Many companies use the calendar year, ending December 31, for their fiscal year. Many other companies find it convenient to choose a fiscal year that ends during a slack season rather than during a busy or peak season. In this case, the fiscal year would correspond to the natural annual cycle of business activity for the company. Still other companies find it convenient to choose the same fiscal year as most government units, which begins July 1 and ends June 30.

The Continuity Problem

Objective 2b Recognize the difficulties of income measurement caused by the continuity problem

Income measurement, as noted above, requires that certain cash transactions and revenue transactions be allocated over several accounting periods. This creates another problem for the accountant, who of course does not know how long the business will last. Many businesses last less than five years and, in any given year, thousands will go bankrupt. This dilemma is called the **continuity problem.** In order to prepare financial statements for an accounting period, the accountant must make an assumption about the ability of the business to continue. Specifically, the accountant assumes that unless there is evidence to the contrary, the business will continue to operate for an indefinite period. This method of dealing with the problem is sometimes called the **going concern** or continuity assumption.

For example, in measuring net income, the accountant must make assumptions regarding the life expectancy of most assets. It is a well-known fact that the value of assets often is much less if a company is not expected to continue in existence than if it is a going concern. However, we have already pointed out in Chapter 3 that the accountant, after recording assets at cost, does not record subsequent changes in their value. Assets become expenses as they are used up. The justification for all of the techniques of income measurement rests on this assumption of continuity.

If accountants have evidence that a company will not continue, of course, then their procedures must change. Sometimes accountants are asked, in bankruptcy cases, to drop the continuity assumption and prepare statements based on the assumption that the firm will go out of business and sell all its assets.

The Matching Problem

Objective 2c Recognize the difficulties of income measurement caused by the matching problem

Revenue and expenses may be accounted for on a cash received and cash paid basis. This is known as the **cash basis of accounting.** In certain circumstances, an individual or business may use the cash basis of accounting for income tax purposes. When this method is used, revenues are reported as earned in the period in which cash is received, and expenses are reported in periods in which cash is paid. Taxable income is therefore calculated as the difference between cash receipts from revenues and cash payments for expenses.

Although the cash basis of accounting is satisfactory for some small businesses and individuals, it obviously is not satisfactory for most businesses. As explained above, revenue can be earned in a period other than when cash is received, and expenses can be incurred in a period other than when cash is paid. If net income is going to be measured adequately, revenue and expenses must be assigned to the appropriate accounting period. The accountant solves this problem by applying the **matching rule:**

Revenue must be assigned to the accounting period in which the goods were sold or the services performed, and expenses must be assigned to the accounting period in which they were used to produce revenue.

Although direct cause-and-effect relationships can seldom be conclusively demonstrated, many costs appear to be related to particular revenue. Therefore, the accountant will recognize such expenses and related revenue in the same accounting period. Examples are the costs of merchandise sold and sales commissions. When a direct means of associating cause and effect does not exist, the accountant attempts to allocate costs in a systematic and rational manner among the accounting periods that benefit from the cost. For example, a building is converted from an asset to an expense by allocating its cost over the years that benefit from its use.

Accrual Accounting

Objective 3 Define accrual accounting and explain two broad ways of accomplishing it

To apply the matching rule stated above, accountants have developed accrual accounting. **Accrual accounting** consists of all the techniques developed by accountants to apply the matching rule. It is accomplished in two general ways: (1) by recognizing revenue when earned and expenses when incurred, and (2) by adjusting the accounts.

Recognizing Revenue When Earned and Expenses When Incurred The first method has already been illustrated several times in Chapter 3. For example, when the Joan Miller Advertising Agency made sales on credit by placing the advertisements for clients (in transaction 12), revenue was immediately recorded by debiting (increasing) Accounts Receivable and crediting the revenue account Advertising Fees Earned at the time of the sale. The credit sale is thus recognized before the collection of cash. Accounts Receivable, in effect, serves as a holding account until the payment is received. Also, when the Joan Miller Advertising Agency received the telephone bill (in transaction 16), the expense was recognized as having been incurred and as contributing to the production of revenue in the current month. The transaction was recorded by debiting Telephone Expense and crediting Accounts Payable. Until the bill is paid, Accounts Payable serves as a holding account. Recognition of the expense is not dependent on payment of cash.

Adjusting the Accounts An accounting period by definition must end on a particular day. On that day, the balance sheet must contain all assets and liabilities as of that day. The income statement must contain all revenue and expenses applicable to the period ending on that day. Although a business is recognized as a continuous process, there must be a cutoff point. Some transactions invariably span the cutoff point, and as a result some of the accounts need adjustment.

For example, consider the end-of-the-period trial balance for the Joan Miller Advertising Agency from Chapter 3 (also shown in Figure 4-1). On January 31, the trial balance contains prepaid rent of $400. At $200 per month, this represented rent paid in advance for the months of January and February. Consequently, at January 31, one-half of the $400, or $200, represents rent expense for January, and the remaining $200 represents the cost of asset services to be used up in February. An adjustment is required to reflect the $200 balance of the Prepaid Rent account on the balance sheet and the $200 rent expense on the income statement. As we shall see, several other accounts of the Joan Miller Advertising Agency do not reflect their proper balances. Like the Prepaid Rent account, they also require adjusting entries.

Figure 4-1 Trial Balance for the Joan Miller Advertising Agency

Joan Miller Advertising Agency
Trial Balance
January 31, 19xx

Cash	$ 860	
Accounts Receivable	1,400	
Art Supplies	900	
Office Supplies	400	
Prepaid Rent	400	
Prepaid Insurance	240	
Art Equipment	2,100	
Office Equipment	1,500	
Accounts Payable		$1,585
Unearned Art Fees		500
Joan Miller, Capital		5,000
Joan Miller, Withdrawals	700	
Advertising Fees Earned		2,100
Office Wages	600	
Utility Expense	50	
Telephone Expense	35	
	$9,185	$9,185

The Adjustment Process

Accountants use **adjusting entries** to apply accrual accounting to transactions that span more than one accounting period. At the end of an accounting period, adjusting entries may be required in the following principal situations:

Objective 4 State the four principal situations that require adjusting entries

1. There are costs recorded that must be apportioned between two or more accounting periods. Examples: the cost of a building, prepaid insurance, supplies.
2. There is revenue recorded that must be apportioned between two or more accounting periods. Example: commissions collected in advance for services to be rendered in future periods.
3. There are unrecorded expenses. Example: wages earned by employees in the current accounting period but after the last pay period in an accounting period.
4. There are unrecorded revenues. Example: commissions earned but not yet collected or billed to customers.

Objective 5 Prepare typical adjusting entries

We will continue to use the illustration of the Joan Miller Advertising Agency to demonstrate the most common types of adjusting entries.

Apportioning Recorded Costs Between Two or More Accounting Periods

Companies often make expenditures that benefit more than one period. These expenditures are usually debited to an asset account. At the end of the accounting period, the appropriate amount that has been used up in the period is transferred from the asset account to an expense account. Two of the more important categories into which these adjustments fall are prepaid expenses and depreciation of plant and equipment.

Prepaid Expenses Some expenses are customarily paid in advance. These expenditures are called **prepaid expenses.** They include such items as rent, insurance, and supplies. At the end of an accounting period, a portion (or all) of these goods or services probably will have been consumed or will have expired. The portion of the expenditure that has benefited current operations is considered an expense of the period. On the other hand, the portion not consumed or expired is considered an asset relevant to the future operations of the company. If adjusting entries for prepaid expenses are not made at the end of the month, both the balance sheet and the income statement will be misstated. First, the assets of the company will be overstated; and second, the expenses of the company will be understated. Consequently, owner's equity on the balance sheet and net income on the income statement will both be overstated. Besides prepaid rent, the Joan Miller Advertising Agency has prepaid expenses of prepaid insurance, art supplies, and office supplies, all of which require adjusting entries.

At the beginning of the month, the Joan Miller Advertising Agency paid two months' rent in advance. This expenditure resulted in an asset consisting of the right to occupy the office for two months. As each day in the month passed, part of the asset period expired and became a cost. By January 31, one-half had expired, and should be treated as an expense. The analysis of this economic event is shown below.

Prepaid Rent (Adjustment a)

Prepaid Rent			
(2)	400	(a)	200

Rent Expense			
(a)	200		

Transaction: Expiration of one month's rent.
Analysis: Assets decreased. Owner's equity decreased.
Rules: Decreases in assets are recorded by credits. Decreases in owner's equity are recorded by debits.
Entries: Decrease in owner's equity is recorded by debit to Rent Expense. Decrease in assets is recorded by credit to Prepaid Rent.

Dr. Rent Expense	200	
Cr. Prepaid Rent		200

The Prepaid Rent account now has a balance of $200, which represents one month's rent paid in advance. The Rent Expense account reflects the $200 expense for the month.

The Joan Miller Advertising Agency also purchased a one-year insurance policy, paying for it in advance. In a manner similar to prepaid rent, prepaid insurance offers protection that expires day by day. By the end of the month, one-twelfth of the protection had expired. The adjustment is analyzed and recorded as shown below.

Prepaid Insurance (Adjustment b)

Prepaid Insurance			
(6)	240	(b)	20

Insurance Expense			
(b)	20		

Transaction: Expiration of one month's insurance.
Analysis: Assets decreased. Owner's equity decreased.
Rules: Decreases in assets are recorded by credits. Decreases in owner's equity are recorded by debits.
Entries: Decrease in owner's equity is recorded by debit to Insurance Expense. Decrease in assets is recorded by credit to Prepaid Insurance.

Dr. Insurance Expense	20	
Cr. Prepaid Insurance		20

The Prepaid Insurance account now has the proper balance of $220, and Insurance Expense reflects the expired cost of $20 for the month.

Early in the month, the Joan Miller Advertising Agency purchased art supplies and office supplies. As Joan Miller did the art work for various clients during the month, the art supplies were consumed. Her secretary also used up office supplies. There is no need to account for these supplies on a daily basis, because the financial statements are not prepared until the end of the month, and the record keeping would involve too much work.

Instead, Joan Miller makes a careful inventory of the art and office supplies at the end of the month. This inventory records the number and cost of those supplies that are still assets of the company—that is, yet to be consumed.

The inventory reveals that art supplies costing $650 and office supplies costing $300 are still on hand. This means that of the art supplies originally purchased for $900, $250 worth were used up or became an expense, and of the office supplies originally costing $400, $100 worth were consumed. These transactions are analyzed and recorded as follows:

Art Supplies and Office Supplies (Adjustments c and d)

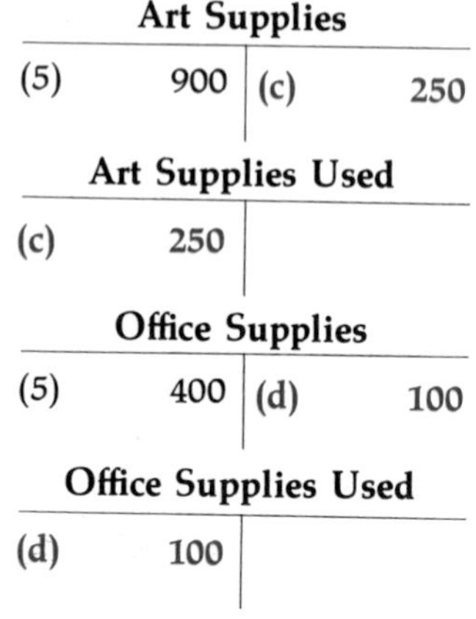

Art Supplies

(5)	900	(c)	250

Art Supplies Used

(c)	250		

Office Supplies

(5)	400	(d)	100

Office Supplies Used

(d)	100		

Transaction: Consumption of supplies.
Analysis: Assets decreased. Owner's equity decreased.
Rules: Decreases in assets are recorded by credits. Decreases in owner's equity are recorded by debits.
Entries: Decreases in owner's equity are recorded by debits to Art Supplies Used and Office Supplies Used. Decreases in assets are recorded by credits to Art Supplies and Office Supplies.

Dr. Art Supplies Used	250	
Cr. Art Supplies		250
Dr. Office Supplies Used	100	
Cr. Office Supplies		100

The asset accounts of Art Supplies and Office Supplies now reflect the proper amounts of $650 and $300, respectively, yet to be consumed. In addition, the amounts of art and office supplies used up during the accounting period are reflected as $250 and $100, respectively.

Depreciation of Plant and Equipment When a company buys a long-lived asset such as a building, equipment, trucks, automobiles, a computer, store fixtures, or office furniture, it is essentially buying or prepaying for the usefulness of that asset for as long as the asset provides a benefit to the company. Proper accounting therefore requires the allocation of the cost of the asset over its estimated useful life. The amount allocated to any one accounting period is called **depreciation** or **depreciation expense.** Depreciation is an expense just like any other cost incurred during an accounting period to secure revenue.

It is often impossible to tell how long an asset will last or how much of the asset is used in any one period. Therefore, depreciation must be estimated. Accountants have developed a variety of methods for estimating depreciation and for dealing with other complex problems concerning it. We will discuss these methods in a later chapter. Only the simplest case is discussed here for illustrative purposes.

Assume that the Joan Miller Advertising Agency estimates the depreciation of art equipment and office equipment for the month as $35 and $25, respectively. These amounts represent the cost allocated to the month, thus reducing the asset accounts and increasing the expense accounts (reducing owner's equity). These transactions can be analyzed as shown below. The use of the contra-asset account called Accumulated Depreciation is described in the next section.

Art Equipment and Office Equipment (Adjustments e and f)

Art Equipment

Debit		Credit	
(3)	2,100		

Accumulated Depreciation, Art Equipment

Debit		Credit	
		(e)	35

Office Equipment

Debit		Credit	
(4)	1,500		

Accumulated Depreciation, Office Equipment

Debit		Credit	
		(f)	25

Depreciation Expense, Art Equipment

Debit		Credit	
(e)	35		

Depreciation Expense, Office Equipment

Debit		Credit	
(f)	25		

Transaction: Recording estimated depreciation.
Analysis: Assets decreased. Owner's equity decreased.
Rules: Decreases in assets are recorded by credits. Decreases in owner's equity are recorded by debits.
Entries: Owner's equity is decreased by debits to Depreciation Expense, Art Equipment, and Depreciation Expense, Office Equipment. Assets are decreased by credits to contra-asset accounts Accumulated Depreciation, Art Equipment, and Accumulated Depreciation, Office Equipment.

Account	Dr.	Cr.
Dr. Depreciation Expense, Art Equipment	35	
Cr. Accumulated Depreciation, Art Equipment		35
Dr. Depreciation Expense, Office Equipment	25	
Cr. Accumulated Depreciation, Office Equipment		25

Accumulated Depreciation—A Contra Account Note that in the analysis of the illustration shown, the asset accounts were not credited directly; instead, new accounts—Accumulated Depreciation, Art Equipment, and Accumulated Depreciation, Office Equipment—were credited. These **accumulated depreciation** accounts are contra-asset accounts used to accumulate the total past depreciation on a specific long-lived asset. They are called **contra accounts** because they represent a balance that is subtracted from the balance of an associated account. In this case, the balance of the Accumulated Depreciation, Art Equipment, represents a deduction from the associated account Art Equipment; likewise, Accumulated Depreciation, Office Equipment, represents a deduction from Office Equipment. After these adjusting entries have been made, the plant and equipment section of the balance sheet for Joan Miller's Advertising Agency appears as shown in Figure 4-2.

The contra account is used for two excellent reasons. First, it recognizes that depreciation is an estimate. Second, the use of the contra account preserves the fact of original cost of the asset and indicates how much of the asset has been allocated to expense as well as the balance left to be depreciated. As the months pass, the amount of the accumulated depreciation will grow, and thus the net amount shown as an asset will be reduced. In six months, for instance, Accumulated Depreciation, Art Equipment, will have a total of $210; when this total is subtracted from Art Equipment, a net amount of $1,890 will remain.

Other names are sometimes used for accumulated depreciation, such as "allowance for depreciation" or the totally unacceptable term "reserve for depreciation." Accumulated depreciation is the newer and better terminology because it is more descriptive.

Apportioning Recorded Revenue Between Two or More Accounting Periods

Just as costs may be paid and recorded before they are used up, revenue may be received before it is earned. When such revenue is received in advance, the company has an obligation to deliver goods or perform serv-

Figure 4-2 Plant and Equipment Section of Balance Sheet

Joan Miller Advertising Agency Partial Balance Sheet January 31, 19xx		
Plant and Equipment		
Art Equipment	$2,100	
Less Accumulated Depreciation	35	$2,065
Office Equipment	$1,500	
Less Accumulated Depreciation	25	1,475
Total Plant and Equipment		$3,540

ices. Consequently, **unearned revenue** is a liability account. For example, publishing companies usually receive payment for magazine subscriptions in advance. These payments must be recorded in a liability account. If the company fails to deliver the magazines for the subscription period, subscribers are entitled to their money back. As the company delivers each issue of the magazine, it earns a portion of the advance payments. This earned portion must be transferred from the Unearned Subscription account to the Subscription Revenue account.

During the month, the Joan Miller Advertising Agency received $500 as an advance for art work to be done for another agency. Assume that, by the end of the month, $200 of the art work was done and accepted by the other agency. This transaction is analyzed as follows:

Unearned Art Fees (Adjustment g)

Unearned Art Fees

(g)	200	(11)	500

Art Fees Earned

		(g)	200

Transaction: Performance of services paid in advance.
Analysis: Liabilities decreased. Owner's equity increased.
Rules: Decreases in liabilities are recorded by debits. Increases in owner's equity are recorded by credits.
Entries: Decrease in liabilities is recorded by debit to Unearned Art Fees. Increase in owner's equity is recorded by credit to Art Fees Earned.

Dr. Unearned Art Fees	200	
Cr. Art Fees Earned		200

The liability account Unearned Art Fees now reflects the amount of work to be performed, or $300; the revenue account Art Fees Earned reflects the amount of services performed during the month, or $200.

Unrecorded or Accrued Expenses

At the end of an accounting period there are usually expenses that have been incurred but not recognized in the accounts. These expenses require adjusting entries. One example is the case of borrowed money. Each day interest accumulates on the debt, and it is necessary to use an adjusting entry at the end of each accounting period to record this accumulated interest, which is an expense to the period, and the corresponding liability to pay the interest. Other comparable expenses are taxes, wages, and salaries. As the expense and the corresponding liability accumulate, they are said to accrue—hence the term **accrued expenses.**

Suppose that the calendar for January appears as shown in the following illustration:

January

Su	M	T	W	Th	F	Sa
	1	2	3	4	5	6
7	8	9	10	11	**12**	13
14	15	16	17	18	19	20
21	22	23	24	25	**26**	27
28	29	30	31			

By the end of business on January 31, the Joan Miller Advertising Agency's secretary will have worked three days (Monday, Tuesday, and Wednesday) beyond the last biweekly pay period, which ended on January 26. The employee has earned the salary for these days, but it is not due to be paid until the regular payday in February. The salary for these three days is rightfully an expense for January, and the liabilities should reflect the fact that the Joan Miller Advertising Agency does owe the secretary for those days. Because the secretary's salary rate is $300 every two weeks or $30 per day ($300 ÷ 10 working days), the expense is $90 ($30 × 3 days). This unrecorded or accrued expense can be analyzed as shown below.

Unrecorded or Accrued Wages (Adjustment h)

Wages Payable

		(h)	90

Office Wages Expense

(10)	300		
(14)	300		
(h)	90		

Transaction: Accrual of unrecorded expense.
Analysis: Liabilities increased. Owner's equity decreased.
Rules: Increases in liabilities are recorded by credits. Decreases in owner's equity are recorded by debits.
Entries: Decrease in owner's equity is recorded by debit to Office Wages Expense. Increase in liabilities is recorded by credit to Wages Payable.

Dr. Office Wages Expense	90	
Cr. Wages Payable		90

The liability of $90 is now correctly reflected in the Wages Payable account. The actual expense incurred for office wages during the month is also correct at $690.

Unrecorded or Accrued Revenue

An **unrecorded** or **accrued revenue** is a revenue for which the service has been performed or the goods have been delivered but that has not been recorded in the accounts. The treatment is very similar to that for unrecorded expenses. Any revenue that has been earned but not recorded during the accounting period requires an adjusting entry that debits an asset account and credits a revenue account. For example, the interest on a loan receivable is earned day by day but may not actually be received until another accounting period. Interest revenue should be credited and interest receivable debited for the interest accrued in the current period.

Assume that the Joan Miller Advertising Agency has placed an advertisement for Marsh Tire Company that appears on January 31, the last day of the month. The fee of $100 for this advertisement, which has been earned but not recorded, is recorded as shown below.

Unrecorded or Accrued Advertising Fees (Adjustment i)

Accounts Receivable

	Debit		Credit
(12)	800		
(12)	600		
(i)	100		

Advertising Fees Earned

	Debit		Credit
		(7)	700
		(12)	1,400
		(i)	100

Transaction: Accrual of unrecorded revenue.
Analysis: Assets increased. Owner's equity increased.
Rules: Increases in assets are recorded by debits. Increases in owner's equity are recorded by credits.
Entries: Increase in assets is recorded by debit to Accounts Receivable. Increase in owner's equity is recorded by credit to Advertising Fees Earned.

	Dr.	Cr.
Dr. Accounts Receivable	100	
Cr. Advertising Fees Earned		100

Both accounts, the asset and the revenue, now show the proper balance: $1,500 in accounts receivable is owed to the company, and $2,200 in advertising fees has been earned by the company during the month.

The Adjusted Trial Balance

In Chapter 3, a trial balance was prepared before any adjusting entries were recorded. It is now desirable to prepare an **adjusted trial balance,** which reflects all the changes in the accounts that have occurred as a result of the adjusting entries. Figure 4-3 shows the trial balance from Chapter 3, along with the adjusting entries and the resulting adjusted trial balance. If the adjusting entries have been posted correctly to the accounts, the adjusted trial balance should have equal debit and credit totals.

Figure 4-3
Determination of the Adjusted Trial Balance

Joan Miller Advertising Agency
Adjusted Trial Balance
January 31, 19xx

Accounts	Trial Balance Debit	Trial Balance Credit	Adjustments Debit		Adjustments Credit		Adjusted Trial Balance Debit	Adjusted Trial Balance Credit
Cash	860						860	
Accounts Receivable	1,400		(i)	100			1,500	
Art Supplies	900				(c)	250	650	
Office Supplies	400				(d)	100	300	
Prepaid Rent	400				(a)	200	200	
Prepaid Insurance	240				(b)	20	220	
Art Equipment	2,100						2,100	
Accumulated Depreciation, Art Equipment					(e)	35		35
Office Equipment	1,500						1,500	
Accumulated Depreciation, Office Equipment					(f)	25		25
Accounts Payable		1,585						1,585
Unearned Art Fees		500	(g)	200				300
Joan Miller, Capital		5,000						5,000
Joan Miller, Withdrawals	700						700	
Advertising Fees Earned		2,100			(i)	100		2,200
Office Wages	600		(h)	90			690	
Utility Expense	50						50	
Telephone Expense	35						35	
	9,185	9,185						
Rent Expense			(a)	200			200	
Insurance Expense			(b)	20			20	
Art Supplies Used			(c)	250			250	
Office Supplies Used			(d)	100			100	
Depreciation Expense, Art Equipment			(e)	35			35	
Depreciation Expense, Office Equipment			(f)	25			25	
Art Fees Earned					(g)	200		200
Wages Payable					(h)	90		90
				1,020		1,020	9,435	9,435

Using the Adjusted Trial Balance to Prepare Financial Statements

Objective 6 Prepare an adjusted trial balance

The adjusted trial balance for the Joan Miller Advertising Agency now shows the correct balances for all the accounts. From this adjusted trial balance, the financial statements can be easily prepared. The income statement can be prepared from the revenue and expense accounts, as shown in Figure 4-4 (next page). In Figure 4-5, the balance sheet has been prepared from the balance sheet accounts, with the exception of net income, which must come from the income statement. Notice that the net income from the income statement is combined with withdrawals on the balance sheet to give the net increase in Joan Miller's capital account of $295.

The Adjustment Process and Accounting Standards

Objective 7 Relate the need for adjusting entries to accounting standards

One might ask, Why worry about adjustments? Doesn't everything come out all right in the end? The primary reason for making adjustments is that they are important to accountants as they try to meet the standards for accounting information. For example, in meeting the standard for relevance, these adjusting entries are necessary to measure income and financial position accurately. The management of a company wants to know how much it has earned during the last month, quarter, or year and what its liabilities and assets are at a certain date. This is an important reason for making the adjusting entries. For example, if the three days' accrued salary for Joan Miller's secretary is not recorded, the income of the agency would be overstated by $90 and the liabilities understated by $90.

Another important reason for the use of adjusting entries is that they make financial statements comparable from one period to the next. Management can see if the company is making progress toward earning a profit or if the company has improved its financial position. For example, if the three days' accrued salary for Joan Miller's secretary is not recorded, not only will the income for January be understated by $90, but the February (the month when payment is made) net income will be understated by $90. This error will make the February earnings, whatever they are, appear worse than they actually are. Look back over all the adjustments for the Joan Miller Advertising Agency for prepaid rent and insurance, art and office supplies, depreciation of office and art equipment, unearned art fees, accrued wages and expenses, and accrued advertising fees. These are all normal and usual adjustments; yet the combined effect of all of them is enormous.

Accountants also insist that adjusting procedures and entries be complete and consistent at the end of every accounting period because there is often more than one acceptable way to apply the matching rule to a given situation. For example, there are several methods of determining the amount of depreciation expense for a given accounting period. Consequently, there is a need for the consistent application of accounting practice from one period to the next so that the financial statements of successive periods will be comparable and understandable. Accounting

Figure 4-4
Relationship of Adjusted Trial Balance to Income Statement

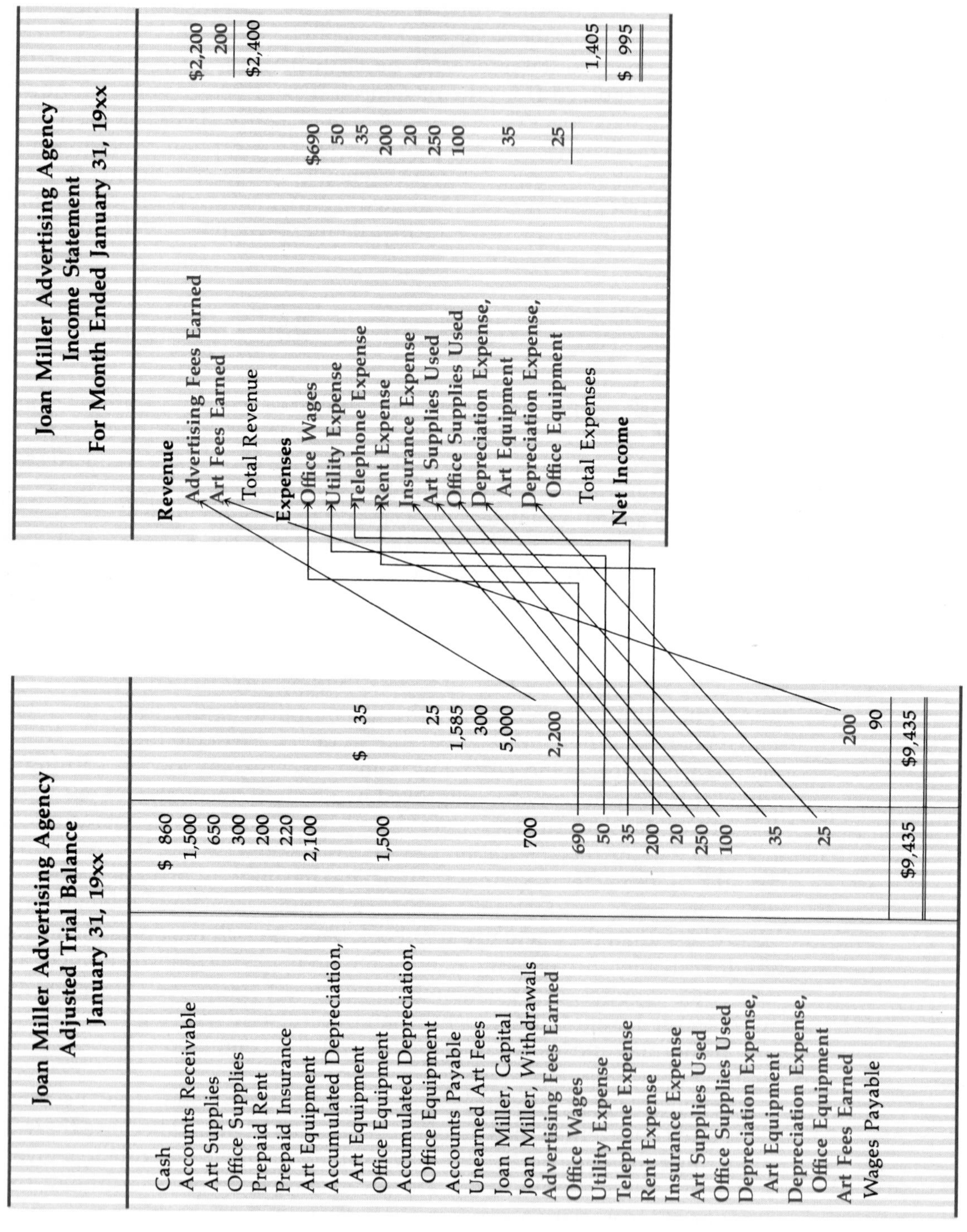

Joan Miller Advertising Agency
Adjusted Trial Balance
January 31, 19xx

Cash	$ 860	
Accounts Receivable	1,500	
Art Supplies	650	
Office Supplies	300	
Prepaid Rent	200	
Prepaid Insurance	220	
Art Equipment	2,100	
Accumulated Depreciation, Art Equipment		$ 35
Office Equipment	1,500	
Accumulated Depreciation, Office Equipment		25
Accounts Payable		1,585
Unearned Art Fees		300
Joan Miller, Capital		5,000
Joan Miller, Withdrawals	700	
Advertising Fees Earned		2,200
Office Wages	690	
Utility Expense	50	
Telephone Expense	35	
Rent Expense	200	
Insurance Expense	20	
Art Supplies Used	250	
Office Supplies Used	100	
Depreciation Expense, Art Equipment	35	
Depreciation Expense, Office Equipment	25	
Art Fees Earned		200
Wages Payable		90
	$9,435	$9,435

Joan Miller Advertising Agency
Income Statement
For Month Ended January 31, 19xx

Revenue		
Advertising Fees Earned		$2,200
Art Fees Earned		200
Total Revenue		$2,400
Expenses		
Office Wages	$690	
Utility Expense	50	
Telephone Expense	35	
Rent Expense	200	
Insurance Expense	20	
Art Supplies Used	250	
Office Supplies Used	100	
Depreciation Expense, Art Equipment	35	
Depreciation Expense, Office Equipment	25	
Total Expenses		1,405
Net Income		$ 995

Figure 4-5
Relationship of Adjusted Trial Balance to Balance Sheet

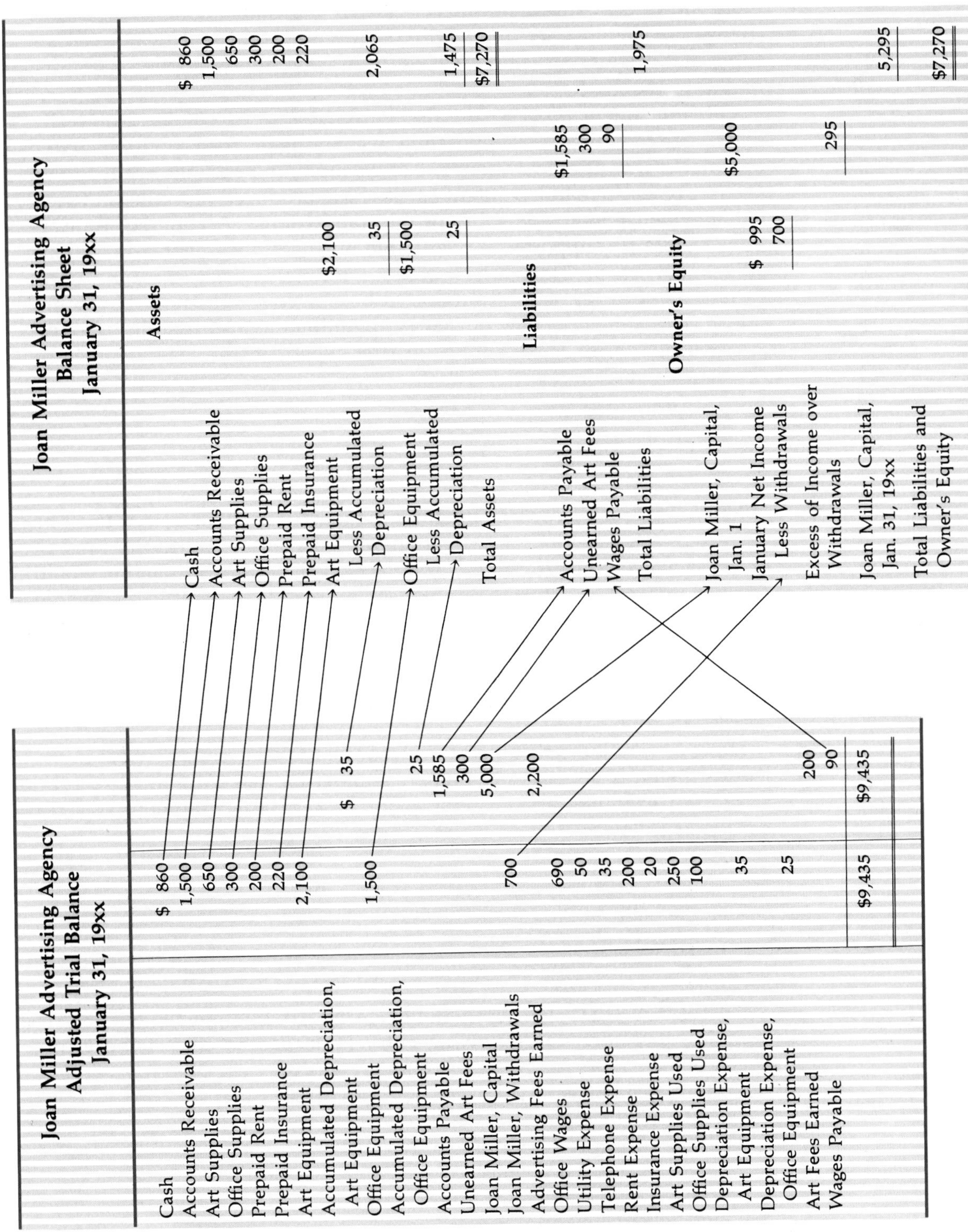

Joan Miller Advertising Agency
Adjusted Trial Balance
January 31, 19xx

Cash	$ 860	
Accounts Receivable	1,500	
Art Supplies	650	
Office Supplies	300	
Prepaid Rent	200	
Prepaid Insurance	220	
Art Equipment	2,100	
Accumulated Depreciation, Art Equipment		$ 35
Office Equipment	1,500	
Accumulated Depreciation, Office Equipment		25
Accounts Payable		1,585
Unearned Art Fees		300
Joan Miller, Capital		5,000
Joan Miller, Withdrawals	700	
Advertising Fees Earned		2,200
Office Wages	690	
Utility Expense	50	
Telephone Expense	35	
Rent Expense	200	
Insurance Expense	20	
Art Supplies Used	250	
Office Supplies Used	100	
Depreciation Expense, Art Equipment	35	
Depreciation Expense, Office Equipment	25	
Art Fees Earned		200
Wages Payable		90
	$9,435	$9,435

Joan Miller Advertising Agency
Balance Sheet
January 31, 19xx

Assets			
Cash			$ 860
Accounts Receivable			1,500
Art Supplies			650
Office Supplies			300
Prepaid Rent			200
Prepaid Insurance			220
Art Equipment	$2,100		
Less Accumulated Depreciation	35		2,065
Office Equipment	$1,500		
Less Accumulated Depreciation	25		1,475
Total Assets			$7,270
Liabilities			
Accounts Payable		$1,585	
Unearned Art Fees		300	
Wages Payable		90	
Total Liabilities			1,975
Owner's Equity			
Joan Miller, Capital, Jan. 1		$5,000	
January Net Income	$ 995		
Less Withdrawals	700		
Excess of Income over Withdrawals		295	
Joan Miller, Capital, Jan. 31, 19xx			5,295
Total Liabilities and Owner's Equity			$7,270

methods can be changed if altered circumstances or other logical reasons require that they be changed. Since a change would violate the comparability standard because of the inconsistent practice, however, the company must indicate in the financial statements the nature and effect of the change. In the absence of such disclosure, the statement reader can assume that accounting methods have been consistently applied from one period to the next.

The adjustment process can also be related to the standard of verifiability. To the fullest extent possible, accounting practice should be based on objective, verifiable evidence. For example, transactions are recorded at cost because two independent parties have produced objective and verifiable evidence as to the value of the transactions. Accounting transactions should be supported by verifiable business documents. In making adjustments, a problem arises because estimates often must be used. Estimates, however, can be supported by objective evidence. For example, in estimating how long buildings or equipment may last, the accountant can rely on objective studies of past experience.

Correcting Errors

Objective 8 Prepare correcting entries

When an error is discovered in either the journal or the ledger, it must be corrected. The method of correction will vary according to the kind of error. However, the error must never be erased, because this action would seem to indicate an effort to conceal something. If an error is discovered in a journal entry before it is posted to the ledger, a line drawn through the incorrect item and the correct item written in will suffice. Similarly, when a posting error involves entering an incorrect amount in the ledger, it is acceptable to draw a line through the incorrect amount and write in the correct amount.

However, if a journal entry has been posted to the wrong account in the ledger, then it is necessary to prepare another journal entry to correct the error. For example, assume that a purchase of art equipment was recorded as follows:

Feb. 20	Art Supplies	100	
	Cash		100
	To record purchase of art equipment		

It is obvious that the debit should be to Art Equipment, not to Art Supplies; therefore, the following entry is needed to correct the error:

Feb. 24	Art Equipment	100	
	Art Supplies		100
	To correct error of Feb. 20, when Art Supplies was debited in error for the purchase of art equipment		

The full explanation provides a record for those who might later question the entry. The Cash account is not involved in the correction, because it was correct originally. The effect of the correction is to reduce Art Supplies by $100 and increase Art Equipment by $100.

Analysis of the Accounts

Throughout Chapters 3 and 4, except in the preceding section, all journal entries have been presented with a full analysis of the transaction. This complete analysis was given to demonstrate the thought process behind each entry. By now, you should be fully aware of the effects of transactions on the balance sheet equation and the rules of debit and credit. Consequently, journal entries will be presented in succeeding chapters in the manner illustrated in the preceding section.

Chapter Review

Review of Learning Objectives

1. Define net income and its components, revenue and expenses.
Net income is the net increase in owner's equity resulting from the profit-seeking operations of a company. Net income equals revenue minus expenses. Revenue is a measure of the asset values received from customers during a specific period of time. Expenses are the costs of goods and services used up in the process of obtaining revenue.

2. Recognize the difficulties of income measurement caused by (a) the accounting period problem, (b) the continuity problem, and (c) the matching problem.
The accounting period problem recognizes the fact that net income measurements for short periods of time are necessarily tentative. The continuity problem recognizes that even though businesses face an uncertain future, accountants must assume that, without evidence to the contrary, a business will continue indefinitely. The matching problem results from the difficulty of assigning revenue and expenses to a period of time and is solved by application of the matching rule.

3. Define accrual accounting and explain two broad ways of accomplishing it.
Accrual accounting consists of all the techniques developed by accountants to apply the matching rule. The two general ways of accomplishing it are (1) by recognizing revenue when earned and expenses when incurred, and (2) by adjusting the accounts.

4. State the four principal situations that require adjusting entries.
Adjusting entries are required (1) when recorded costs are to be apportioned between two or more accounting periods, (2) when recorded revenues are to be apportioned between two or more accounting periods, (3) when unrecorded expenses exist, and (4) when unrecorded revenues exist.

5. Prepare typical adjusting entries.
Some of the more typical adjusting entries involve prepaid expenses such as rent, insurance, and supplies; depreciation of plant and equipment; unearned revenue; accrued expenses; and accrued revenue.

6. Prepare an adjusted trial balance.

An adjusted trial balance is a trial balance that is prepared after adjusting entries have been posted to the accounts in the ledger. Its purpose is to test the balance of the ledger after the adjusting entries are made and before financial statements are prepared.

7. Relate the need for adjusting entries to accounting standards.

Adjusting entries are a means of implementing accrual accounting and thereby aid in producing financial statements that are comparable from period to period and relevant to the needs of users. Although adjusting entries often require estimates, the estimates are usually based on verifiable formulas or facts.

8. Prepare correcting entries.

When a correcting entry is required, it should be made in such a way as to adjust the appropriate accounts to the correct balances. A full explanation should accompany each correcting entry.

Self-Test

Test your knowledge of the chapter by choosing the best answer for each item below.

1. The net increase in owner's equity resulting from business operations is called
   a. net income.
   b. revenue.
   c. expense.
   d. None of the above.
2. The costs of the goods and services used up in the process of obtaining revenue are called
   a. net income.
   b. revenue.
   c. expenses.
   d. None of the above.
3. In general, the accounts in the income statement are known as
   a. real accounts.
   b. nominal accounts.
   c. unearned revenue accounts.
   d. contra-asset accounts.
4. A business may choose a fiscal year that corresponds to
   a. the calendar year.
   b. the natural business year.
   c. any twelve-month period.
   d. Any of the above.
5. Assigning revenues to the accounting period in which the goods were delivered or the services performed and expenses to the accounting period in which they were used to produce revenues is known as the
   a. accounting period problem.
   b. continuity assumption.
   c. matching rule.
   d. None of the above.
6. Adjusting entries are essential to
   a. the matching rule.
   b. accrual accounting.
   c. a proper determination of net income.
   d. All of the above.
7. The adjustment for depreciation is an example of
   a. apportioning costs between two or more periods.
   b. apportioning revenues between two or more periods.
   c. recognizing an accrued expense.
   d. recognizing an unrecorded revenue.
8. Accumulated depreciation is an example of
   a. an expense.
   b. an unrecorded revenue.
   c. a liability.
   d. a contra account.

9. The recording of wages earned but not yet paid is an example of an adjustment that
   a. apportions revenues between two or more periods.
   b. recognizes an accrued expense.
   c. recognizes an unrecorded revenue.
   d. is none of the above.

Answers to Self-Test are at the end of this chapter.

Review Problem
Adjusting Entries, T Accounts, and Adjusted Trial Balance

The unadjusted trial balance for Accurate Answering Service appears as follows on December 31, 19xx:

Accurate Answering Service
Trial Balance
December 31, 19xx

Cash	$2,160	
Accounts Receivable	1,250	
Office Supplies	180	
Prepaid Insurance	240	
Office Equipment	3,400	
Accumulated Depreciation, Office Equipment		$ 600
Accounts Payable		700
Revenue Received in Advance		460
James Neal, Capital		4,470
Answering Service Revenue		2,900
Wages Expense	1,500	
Rent Expense	400	
	$9,130	$9,130

The following information is also available:

a. Insurance that expired during December amounted to $40.
b. Office supplies on hand at the end of December totaled $75.
c. Depreciation for the month of December totaled $100.
d. Accrued wages at the end of December totaled $120.
e. Revenues earned for services performed but not yet billed on December 31 totaled $300.
f. Revenues earned for services performed that were paid in advance totaled $160.

Required

1. Prepare T accounts for the accounts in the trial balance.
2. Determine the required adjusting entries, and record them directly to the T accounts. Open any new T accounts as needed.
3. Prepare an adjusted trial balance.

Answer to Review Problem

1. T accounts set up and amounts from trial balance entered.
2. Adjusting entries recorded.

Cash

	Debit		Credit
Bal.	2,160		

Office Equipment

	Debit		Credit
Bal.	3,400		

Accounts Receivable

	Debit		Credit
Bal.	1,250		
(e)	300		
	1,550		

Accumulated Depreciation, Office Equipment

	Debit		Credit
		Bal.	600
		(c)	100
			700

Office Supplies

	Debit		Credit
Bal.	180	(b)	105
	75		

Accounts Payable

	Debit		Credit
		Bal.	700

Prepaid Insurance

	Debit		Credit
Bal.	240	(a)	40
	200		

Revenue Received in Advance

	Debit		Credit
(f)	160	Bal.	460
			300

James Neal, Capital

	Debit		Credit
		Bal.	4,470

Insurance Expense

	Debit		Credit
(a)	40		

Answering Service Revenue

	Debit		Credit
		Bal.	2,900
		(e)	300
		(f)	160
			3,360

Depreciation Expense

	Debit		Credit
(c)	100		

Wages Expense

	Debit		Credit
Bal.	1,500		
(d)	120		
	1,620		

Office Supplies Expense

	Debit		Credit
(b)	105		

Rent Expense

	Debit		Credit
Bal.	400		

Wages Payable

	Debit		Credit
		(d)	120

3. Adjusted trial balance prepared (top of next page).

Accurate Answering Service
Adjusted Trial Balance
December 31, 19xx

Cash	$2,160	
Accounts Receivable	1,550	
Office Supplies	75	
Prepaid Insurance	200	
Office Equipment	3,400	
Accumulated Depreciation, Office Equipment		$ 700
Accounts Payable		700
Wages Payable		120
Revenue Received in Advance		300
James Neal, Capital		4,470
Answering Service Revenue		3,360
Wages Expense	1,620	
Rent Expense	400	
Insurance Expense	40	
Office Supplies Expense	105	
Depreciation Expense	100	
	$9,650	$9,650

Chapter Assignments

Questions

1. Why does the accountant use the term *net income* instead of *profit?*
2. Define revenue and expense.
3. Why are income statement accounts called nominal accounts?
4. Why does the need for the accounting period cause problems?
5. What is the significance of the continuity assumption?
6. "The matching rule is the most significant concept in accounting." Do you agree with this statement? Explain.
7. What is the difference between the cash and the accrual basis of accounting?
8. In what two ways is accrual accounting accomplished?
9. Why do adjusting entries need to be made?
10. What are the four situations that require adjusting entries? Give an example of each.
11. Explain the statement, "Some assets are expenses that have not expired."
12. What is a contra account? Give an example.
13. What do plant and equipment, office supplies, and prepaid insurance have in common?
14. What is the difference between accumulated depreciation and depreciation expense?
15. Why are contra accounts used in recording depreciation?
16. How does unearned revenue arise? Give an example.
17. Where does an unearned revenue appear on the balance sheet?

18. What accounting problem does a magazine publisher who sells three-year subscriptions have?
19. What is an accrued expense? Give three examples.
20. Under what circumstances might a company have unrecorded revenue? Give an example.
21. Why is the income statement usually the first statement prepared from the trial balance?
22. "Why worry about adjustments? Doesn't it all come out in the wash?" Discuss.
23. What is the difference between a correcting entry and an adjusting entry?

Classroom Exercises

Exercise 4-1 Adjusting Entries for Prepaid Insurance

An examination of the Prepaid Insurance account shows a balance of $1,427 at the end of an accounting period before adjustment.

Prepare journal entries to record the insurance expense for the period under each of the following independent assumptions:

1. An examination of insurance policies shows unexpired insurance that cost $987 at the end of the period.
2. An examination of insurance policies shows insurance that cost $347 has expired during the period.

Exercise 4-2 Supplies Account—Missing Data

Determine the amounts indicated by question marks in the columns below. Consider each column a separate problem.

	a	b	c	d
Supplies on hand July 1	117	214	74	?
Supplies purchased during month	26	?	87	746
Supplies consumed during month	87	486	?	916
Supplies remaining on July 31	?	218	28	494

Exercise 4-3 Adjusting Entry for Accrued Salaries

Handco pays salaries of $25,000 each Friday.

1. Make the adjusting entry required on May 31, assuming that June 1 falls on a Thursday.
2. Make the entry to pay the salaries on June 2.

Exercise 4-4 Adjusting Entries

Prepare year-end adjusting entries for each of the following:

a. Office Supplies had a balance of $185 on January 1. Purchases of supplies during the year amount to $415. A year-end inventory reveals supplies of $75 on hand.
b. Depreciation of office equipment is estimated to be $1,450 for the year.
c. Property taxes for six months, estimated to total $750, have accrued but are unrecorded.
d. Unrecorded interest receivable on U.S. government bonds is $900.
e. The services for revenues received in advance of $300 have now been performed.

Exercise 4-5 Relationship of Expenses to Cash Paid

The income statement for Briggs Company included the following expenses for 19xx.

Rent Expense	$ 2,400
Interest Expense	1,800
Salaries Expense	37,500

Listed below are the related balance sheet account balances at year end for last year and this year:

	Last Year	This Year
Prepaid Rent	—	$ 200
Interest Payable	$ 600	—
Salaries Payable	2,500	5,000

1. Compute cash paid on rent during the year.
2. Compute cash paid on interest during the year.
3. Compute cash paid on salaries during the year.

Exercise 4-6
Accounting for Revenue Received in Advance

Mary Ward, a lawyer, was paid $12,000 on September 1 to represent a client in certain real estate negotiations during the next twelve months.

Give the entries required on September 1 and at the end of the year, December 31. How would this transaction affect the balance sheet and income statement on December 31?

Exercise 4-7
Correction of Errors

A number of errors in journalizing and posting transactions are described below. Prepare the journal entries to correct the errors.

1. Rent payment of $150 for the current month was recorded as a debit to Prepaid Rent and a credit to Cash.
2. A $100 cash payment for equipment repair expense was recorded as a debit to Equipment.
3. Payment of $340 to a creditor was recorded as a debit to Accounts Payable and a credit to Cash in the amount of $430.
4. Payment of the gas and oil bill of $80 for the owner's personal car was recorded as a debit to Delivery Truck Expense and a credit to Cash.
5. A cash payment of $100 for services yet to be performed was debited to Cash and credited to Revenue.

Problem Set A

Problem 4A-1
Preparation of Adjusting Entries

On December 31, at the end of the current accounting period, the following information was available to aid the Sun Company accountants in making adjusting entries.

a. The Office Supplies account showed a beginning balance of $568 and purchases during the year of $1,724. The end-of-year inventory revealed $727 worth of supplies on hand.
b. The Prepaid Insurance account showed the following debit entries at December 31:

Jan. 1 Balance	120
June 1	540
Sept. 1	420

The January 1 balance represents the unexpired portion of a one-year insurance policy purchased the previous year. The June 1 purchase represents a three-year policy, and the September 1 entry is the cost of a one-year policy.
c. Among the liabilities of the company are notes payable in the face amount of $20,000. On December 31, the accrued interest on these notes amounted to $1,000.

d. The company purchased a building on July 1 of the current year for $35,500. The company expects the building to last for twenty-five years but does not expect it to have a salvage value at that time.
e. The company owns some land that it leases for a parking lot. On September 1, the tenant paid one year's rent of $2,400 in advance. The total was credited to Unearned Rent Income.
f. On December 26, the company agreed to rent a truck for $310 a month beginning January 1.
g. On Friday, January 3, the company will pay its weekly employees $760 for the regular five-day pay period, which began on Monday.

Required

Prepare adjusting entries for each item listed above.

Problem 4A-2 Determining Adjusting Entries from Changes in Trial Balance

The schedule below presents the trial balance and adjusted trial balance for the Investor's Advisory Service on December 31.

Investor's Advisory Service
Adjusted Trial Balance
December 31, 19xx

	Trial Balance		Adjusted Trial Balance	
	Debit	Credit	Debit	Credit
Cash	$ 7,500		$ 7,500	
Accounts Receivable	3,750		4,750	
Office Supplies	1,210		120	
Prepaid Rent	600		200	
Office Equipment	4,200		4,200	
Accumulated Depreciation, Office Equipment		$ 700		$ 800
Accounts Payable		2,700		2,850
Notes Payable		5,000		5,000
Interest Payable				250
Unearned Fees		1,350		530
Sara Laakso, Capital		10,910		10,910
Sara Laakso, Withdrawals	10,000		10,000	
Fees Revenue		33,000		34,820
Salary Expense	22,000		22,000	
Utility Expense	2,400		2,550	
Rent Expense	2,000		2,400	
Supplies Expense			1,090	
Depreciation Expense, Office Equipment			100	
Interest Expense			250	
	$53,660	$53,660	$55,160	$55,160

Required

Prepare in journal form, with explanations, the seven adjusting entries that explain the changes in the account balances from the trial balance to the adjusted trial balance.

Problem 4A-3 Determining Adjusting Entries and Tracing Their Effects to Financial Statements

A trial balance for Carlyle Realty at the end of its accounting year is as follows:

Carlyle Realty
Trial Balance
December 31, 19xx

Cash	$ 4,275	
Accounts Receivable	2,325	
Prepaid Insurance	585	
Office Supplies	440	
Office Equipment	2,300	
Accumulated Depreciation, Office Equipment		$ 765
Automobile	3,750	
Accumulated Depreciation, Automobile		750
Accounts Payable		1,700
Unearned Management Fees		1,500
John Carlyle, Capital		9,535
John Carlyle, Withdrawals	12,000	
Sales Commissions Earned		26,700
Office Salaries Expense	10,500	
Advertising Expense	2,525	
Rent Expense	1,650	
Telephone Expense	600	
	$40,950	$40,950

The following information was also available:

a. Supplies on hand, December 31, 19xx, were $135.
b. Insurance still unexpired amounted to $270.
c. Estimated depreciation of office equipment amounted to $375.
d. Depreciation on the automobile was estimated to be 20 percent of its cost.
e. As of December 31, the rent of $150 for December had not been paid.
f. On August 1, the company signed a contract to manage a building for a fee of $125 per month. One year's management fees were collected in advance.

Required

1. Open T accounts for the accounts of the trial balance plus the following: Management Fees Earned; Insurance Expense; Office Supplies Used; Depreciation Expense, Office Equipment; Depreciation Expense, Automobile. Record the balances as shown in the trial balance.
2. Determine adjusting entries, and post them directly to the T accounts.
3. Prepare an adjusted trial balance, an income statement, and a balance sheet.

Problem 4A-4 Determining Adjusting Entries and Tracing Their Effects to Financial Statements

At the end of its accounting period, the trial balance for Sure and Safe Moving and Storage appeared as follows:

Sure and Safe Moving and Storage
Trial Balance
June 30, 19xx

Cash	$ 14,200	
Accounts Receivable	18,600	
Prepaid Insurance	7,900	
Packing Supplies	10,400	
Land	4,000	
Building	80,000	
Accumulated Depreciation, Building		$ 7,500
Trucks	106,000	
Accumulated Depreciation, Trucks		27,500
Accounts Payable		7,650
Unearned Storage Fees		5,400
Mortgage Payable		70,000
Max Percy, Capital		54,740
Max Percy, Withdrawals	18,000	
Revenue from Moving Services		209,000
Storage Fees Earned		26,400
Driver Wages	94,000	
Office Salaries	14,400	
Office Equipment, Rent	3,000	
Gas, Oil, and Repairs	23,450	
Interest Expense	4,200	
Other Expenses	10,040	
	$408,190	$408,190

The following information is also available:

a. A study of insurance policies shows that $3,250 of coverage expired during the year.
b. An inventory of packing supplies shows $1,785 worth on hand.
c. Depreciation for the year on buildings amounts to $2,500 and on trucks $21,000.
d. Accrued interest on mortgage payable amounts to $1,400.
e. Storage fees in the amount of $1,950 of the total collected in advance have been earned by the end of the period.
f. Unrecorded drivers' wages total $1,300.
g. Office salaries are paid on Friday. The weekly payroll for office salaries is $300. June 30 falls on a Tuesday.
h. An estimate of $1,200 was given on June 30 to a customer for a moving job to be done in July.

Required

1. Open T accounts for each account in the trial balance plus the following: Wages and Salaries Payable; Accrued Interest Payable; Insurance Expense; Packing Supplies Expense; Depreciation Expense, Building; Depreciation Expense, Trucks. Record the balances as shown in the trial balance.
2. Determine adjusting entries, and post each directly to the T accounts.
3. Prepare an adjusted trial balance.
4. Prepare an income statement and balance sheet.

Problem 4A-5 Determining Adjusting Entries and Tracing Their Effects to Financial Statements

The Executive Flying Service was developed to provide direct air service between Chicago's Meigs Field, a downtown commuter airport, and Milwaukee. At the end of its second year of operation, its trial balance appeared as follows:

Executive Flying Service
Trial Balance
December 31, 19xx

Cash	$ 26,700	
Accounts Receivable	17,300	
Prepaid Rental Expense	24,000	
Unexpired Insurance	7,200	
Prepaid Maintenance Expense	20,000	
Spare Parts	22,200	
Aircraft	460,000	
Accumulated Depreciation, Aircraft		$ 46,000
Notes Payable		280,000
Manfred Martenez, Capital		236,500
Manfred Martenez, Withdrawals	26,000	
Passenger Revenue Earned		128,000
Gas and Oil Expense	37,500	
Salaries Expense	42,000	
Advertising Expense	7,600	
	$690,500	$690,500

The following information is also available:

a. In order to guarantee space at Meigs Field and at Milwaukee Field, the company paid two years' rent in advance on January 1.
b. An examination of insurance policies showed $4,200 was still unexpired.
c. Normal upkeep of the aircraft is provided under a maintenance contract that calls for a $20,000 deposit. Examination of maintenance invoices shows that $13,000 of the deposit has been used.
d. An inventory of spare parts shows $7,860 on hand.
e. Aircraft are being depreciated at 10 percent a year.
f. A payment of $25,200 for one year's interest on the notes payable is now due.
g. The passenger revenue earned included $4,000 for tickets for January flights purchased in advance by passengers.
h. The advertising expense contains $2,000 for radio commercials, which were paid for last month and will run one-half in December and one-half in January.

Required

1. Open T accounts for the accounts in the trial balance plus these: Prepaid Advertising; Unearned Passenger Revenue; Interest Payable; Rent Expense; Insurance Expense; Spare Parts Expense; Depreciation Expense, Aircraft; Maintenance Expense; Interest Expense. Record the balances as shown in the trial balance.
2. Determine adjusting entries, and post them directly to the T accounts.
3. Prepare an adjusted trial balance, an income statement, and a balance sheet.

Problem 4A-6 Correcting Entries and Adjusting Entries and Tracing Their Effects

The Expert Janitorial Service began business six months ago. Joe Glodnik, the owner, discovered that when the trial balance was prepared, it did not balance.

Expert Janitorial Service
Trial Balance
June 30, 19xx

Cash	$ 495	
Accounts Receivable	856	
Cleaning Supplies	1,336	
Cleaning Equipment	1,740	
Truck	3,600	
Accounts Payable		$ 370
Joe Glodnik, Capital		7,517
Joe Glodnik, Withdrawals	3,000	
Janitorial Revenue		7,420
Wages Expense	2,400	
Rent Expense	700	
Gas, Oil, and Other Truck Expense	340	
Insurance Expense	380	
	$14,847	$15,307

Joe hired an accountant to straighten out the books and to determine whether he had made a profit during his first six months in business. Upon examination of the records and documents, the accountant found the following items of interest:

a. The Accounts Payable balance was incorrectly computed, so that there was an overstatement of $200.
b. A $60 cash purchase of supplies was posted to the Cash account but not to the Cleaning Supplies account.
c. A payment of $100 received for janitorial services was credited to Cash by mistake.
d. Cash of $120 received from a customer was recorded as a debit to Cash and a credit to Accounts Receivable in the amount of $210.
e. A $140 purchase of cleaning supplies was debited to Cleaning Equipment.
f. The cleaning equipment and truck are depreciated at the rate of 20 percent per year (10 percent for each six months).
g. Invoices for gas and oil totaling $40 were unrecorded and are due to be paid.
h. An examination of other gas and oil invoices showed that $90 had been paid and charged to expenses but had actually been for Joe's personal car.

i. During the last week of June, Joe completed some work but has not yet billed customers for $350.
j. Upon examination of the Janitorial Revenue account, it was found that $460 represented a payment in advance for work to be performed next month.
k. On June 30, Joe also owed his one employee $40 for two days' work. This amount would be paid on Friday, three days hence.
l. The Rent Expense account represented a $100 payment made on January 1 toward the last month's rent of a three-year lease plus $100 rent per month for each of the past six months.
m. The insurance expense was the cost of a one-year policy purchased January 1.
n. Supplies on hand were inventoried at $76.

Required

1. Open T accounts for the trial balance accounts plus these: Prepaid Insurance; Prepaid Rent; Accumulated Depreciation, Cleaning Equipment; Accumulated Depreciation, Truck; Wages Payable; Unearned Janitorial Revenue; Supplies Expense; Depreciation Expense, Cleaning Equipment; Depreciation Expense, Truck. Record the balances as shown in the trial balance.
2. Using data from items a through c above, prepare a trial balance that balances, and post the corrections to the T accounts.
3. Using data from items d through n above, prepare adjusting and correcting entries, and post them directly to the T accounts.
4. Prepare an adjusted trial balance, an income statement, and a balance sheet.

Problem Set B

Problem 4B-1 Preparation of Adjusting Entries

On June 30, the end of the current accounting period, the following information was available to aid the Sun Company accountants in making adjusting entries.

a. Among the liabilities of the company is a mortgage payable in the amount of $100,000. On June 30, the accrued interest on this mortgage amounted to $4,500.
b. On Friday, July 2, the company will pay its regular weekly employees $15,600.
c. On June 29, the company completed negotiations and signed a contract to provide services at the rate of $2,000 for the next year to a new client.
d. The Supplies account showed a beginning balance of $1,516 and purchases during the year of $3,667. The end-of-year inventory revealed supplies on hand that cost $1,186.
e. The Prepaid Insurance account showed the following entries at June 30:

Beginning balance	$1,350
January 1	2,800
May 1	3,636

The beginning balance represents the unexpired portion of a one-year policy purchased the previous year. The January 1 entry represents a new one-year policy, and the May 1 entry represents additional coverage in the form of a three-year policy.
f. The table below contains the cost and depreciation rates for buildings and equipment, all of which were purchased before the current year:

Account	Cost	Depreciation
Buildings	$175,000	4%
Equipment	218,000	10%

g. On June 1, the company completed negotiations with another client and accepted a payment of $18,000, which represented one year's services paid in advance. The $18,000 was credited to Services Collected in Advance.

Required

Prepare adjusting entries for each item listed above.

Problem 4B-2 Determining Adjusting Entries from Changes in Trial Balance

The schedule below presents the trial balance and adjusted trial balance for the Management Consulting Company on December 31.

Management Consulting Company
Adjusted Trial Balance
December 31, 19xx

	Trial Balance		Adjusted Trial Balance	
	Debit	Credit	Debit	Credit
Cash	$12,786		$12,786	
Accounts Receivable	14,840		15,440	
Office Supplies	991		86	
Prepaid Rent	1,200		600	
Office Equipment	6,700		6,700	
Accumulated Depreciation, Office Equipment		$ 1,400		$ 2,100
Accounts Payable		1,820		2,020
Notes Payable		10,000		10,000
Interest Payable				600
Accrued Salaries Payable				200
Unearned Fees		2,860		1,410
Marvin Mantona, Capital		19,387		19,387
Marvin Mantona, Withdrawals	15,000		15,000	
Fees Revenue		57,400		59,450
Salary Expense	33,000		33,200	
Utility Expense	1,750		1,950	
Rent Expense	6,600		7,200	
Supplies Expense			905	
Depreciation Expense, Office Equipment			700	
Interest Expense			600	
	$92,867	$92,867	$95,167	$95,167

Required

Prepare in journal form, with explanations, the eight adjusting entries that explain the changes in the account balances from the trial balance to the adjusted trial balance.

Problem 4B-3 Determining Adjusting Entries and Tracing Their Effects to Financial Statements

Having graduated from college with a degree in accounting, Marsha Rilley opened a small tax preparation service to supplement family income. At the end of its second year of operation, the Rilley Tax Service has the following trial balance:

Rilley Tax Service
Trial Balance
December 31, 19xx

Cash	$ 742	
Accounts Receivable	986	
Prepaid Insurance	240	
Office Supplies	782	
Office Equipment	2,100	
Accumulated Depreciation, Office Equipment		$ 210
Copier	1,800	
Accumulated Depreciation, Copier		360
Accounts Payable		635
Unearned Tax Fees		219
Marsha Rilley, Capital		5,394
Marsha Rilley, Withdrawals	9,000	
Fees Revenue		20,400
Office Salaries Expense	8,300	
Advertising Expense	650	
Rent Expense	2,400	
Telephone Expense	218	
	$27,218	$27,218

The following information was also available:

a. Supplies on hand, December 31, 19xx, were $112.
b. Insurance still unexpired amounted to $120.
c. Estimated depreciation of office equipment was $210.
d. Estimated depreciation of copier was $360.
e. The telephone expense for December is $19. This bill has been received but not recorded.
f. The services for all unearned tax fees had been performed by the end of the year.

Required

1. Open T accounts for the accounts of the trial balance plus the following: Insurance Expense; Office Supplies Expense; Depreciation Expense, Office Equipment; Depreciation Expense, Copier. Record the balances as shown in the trial balance.

2. Determine adjusting entries, and post them directly to the T accounts.
3. Prepare an adjusted trial balance, an income statement, and a balance sheet.

Problem 4B-4 Determining Adjusting Entries and Tracing Their Effects to Financial Statements

At the end of its accounting period, the trial balance for Williams Dry Cleaning appeared as follows:

Williams Dry Cleaning
Trial Balance
September 30, 19xx

Cash	$ 1,256	
Accounts Receivable	10,280	
Prepaid Insurance	700	
Cleaning Supplies	2,687	
Land	9,000	
Building	75,000	
Accumulated Depreciation, Building		$ 14,200
Delivery Truck	11,500	
Accumulated Depreciation, Delivery Truck		2,600
Accounts Payable		10,200
Unearned Dry Cleaning Fees		800
Mortgage Payable		60,000
Eldridge Williams, Capital		23,642
Eldridge Williams, Withdrawals	12,000	
Dry Cleaning Revenue		57,200
Laundry Revenue		18,650
Plant Wages	32,560	
Sales and Delivery Wages	18,105	
Cleaning Equipment Rent	3,000	
Delivery Truck Expense	2,187	
Interest Expense	5,500	
Other Expenses	3,517	
	$187,292	$187,292

The following information is also available:

a. A study of insurance policies shows that $170 is unexpired at the end of the year.
b. An inventory of cleaning supplies shows $414 on hand.
c. Estimated depreciation for the year was $4,300 on the building and $1,300 on the delivery truck.
d. Accrued interest on the mortgage payable amounted to $500.
e. On August 1, the company signed a contract with Morgan County Hospital to dry clean, for a fixed monthly charge of $200, the uniforms used by doctors in surgery. The hospital paid for four months in advance.
f. Unrecorded plant wages totaled $982.
g. Sales and delivery wages are paid on Friday. The weekly payroll is $350. September 30 falls on a Thursday.

Required

1. Open T accounts for each account in the trial balance plus the following: Wages Payable; Accrued Interest Payable; Insurance Expense; Cleaning Supplies Used; Depreciation Expense, Building; Depreciation Expense, Delivery Truck. Record the balances as shown in the trial balance.
2. Determine adjusting entries, and post each directly to the T accounts.
3. Prepare an adjusted trial balance.
4. Prepare an income statement and balance sheet.

Problem 4B-5 Determining Adjusting Entries and Tracing Their Effects to Financial Statements

The Metro Livery Service was organized to provide limousine service between the airport and various suburban locations. At the end of its first year of operation, its trial balance appeared as follows:

Metro Livery Service
Trial Balance
June 30, 19xx

Cash	$ 13,414	
Accounts Receivable	19,655	
Prepaid Rental Expense	12,000	
Unexpired Insurance	4,900	
Prepaid Maintenance Expense	12,000	
Spare Parts	11,310	
Limousines	190,000	
Notes Payable		$100,000
Oscar Abello, Capital		78,813
Oscar Abello, Withdrawals	20,000	
Passenger Service Revenue		426,926
Gas and Oil Expense	89,300	
Salaries Expense	206,360	
Advertising Expense	26,800	
	$605,739	$605,739

The following information is also available:

a. In order to obtain space at the airport, Metro paid two years' rent in advance when it began business.
b. An examination of insurance policies reveals that $3,600 expired during the year.
c. To provide regular maintenance for the vehicles, a deposit of $12,000 was made with a local garage. Examination of maintenance invoices reveals that there are $11,277 in charges against the deposit.
d. An inventory of spare parts shows $2,110 on hand.
e. Limousines are to be depreciated at the rate of 12.5 percent a year.
f. A payment of $10,500 for one year's interest on notes payable is now due.

g. Passenger Service Revenue includes $17,815 in tickets that were purchased by employers for use by their executives and that have not been redeemed.
h. The advertising expense includes $1,250 for billboard advertising that will begin in July.

Required

1. Open T accounts for the accounts in the trial balance plus these: Prepaid Advertising; Accumulated Depreciation, Limousines; Unearned Passenger Revenue; Interest Payable; Rent Expense; Insurance Expense; Spare Parts Expense; Depreciation Expense, Limousines; Maintenance Expense; Interest Expense. Record the balances as shown in the trial balance.
2. Determine adjusting entries, and post them directly to the T accounts.
3. Prepare an adjusted trial balance, an income statement, and a balance sheet.

Problem 4B-6 Correcting Entries and Adjusting Entries and Tracing Their Effects

The Reliable Answering Service began business three months ago. Kim Larson, the owner, discovered that when the trial balance below was prepared, it did not balance.

Reliable Answering Service
Trial Balance
March 31, 19xx

Cash	$ 1,907	
Accounts Receivable	3,744	
Office Supplies	746	
Office Equipment	2,117	
Communication Equipment	2,400	
Accounts Payable		$ 1,750
Kim Larson, Capital		5,629
Kim Larson, Withdrawals	2,100	
Answering Service Revenue		9,405
Wages Expense	1,900	
Rent Expense	800	
Office Cleaning Expense	300	
Insurance Expense	720	
	$16,734	$16,784

Kim engaged an accountant to examine the records to determine what errors need to be corrected and what adjustments need to be made in order to compute net income for the first three months of operation. Upon examination of the records and documents, the accountant found the following items of interest:

a. A purchase of communication equipment for $50 was posted as a debit to Accounts Payable by mistake. The Communication Equipment part of the entry was recorded correctly.
b. The balance of Office Supplies was incorrectly computed, so that there was an understatement of $70.

c. A cash receipt of $80 was posted correctly to Answering Service Revenue, but was not posted to the Cash account.
d. Another cash receipt of $96 was recorded as a debit to Cash and a credit to Answering Service Revenue in the amount of $69.
e. A $183 purchase of office equipment was debited to Office Supplies.
f. The office equipment and communication equipment are depreciated at the rate of 16 percent per year (4 percent for each three months).
g. An invoice for office cleaning expenses for $75 was unrecorded and due to be paid.
h. An examination of other office cleaning expenses produced an invoice for $30 that had been paid and charged to expenses but had actually been for cleaning Larson's apartment.
i. At the end of March, several customers for whom services had been provided had not been billed. These services totaled $188.
j. An examination of the Answering Service Revenue account revealed that $881 represented payments for work that had not yet been performed.
k. On March 31, salaries in the amount of $60 had accrued.
l. The Rent Expense account includes a $200 prepayment of the last month's rent of a two-year lease.
m. The Insurance Expense account represents the cost of a one-year policy purchased on January 1.
n. Office supplies on hand were inventoried at $119.

Required

1. Open T accounts for the trial balance accounts plus these: Prepaid Insurance; Prepaid Rent; Accumulated Depreciation, Office Equipment; Accumulated Depreciation, Communication Equipment; Wages Payable; Unearned Answering Service Revenue; Office Supplies Expense; Depreciation Expense, Office Equipment; Depreciation Expense, Communication Equipment. Record the balances as shown in the trial balance.
2. Using data from items a through c above, prepare a trial balance that balances, and post the corrections to the T accounts.
3. Using the data from items d through n above, prepare adjusting and correcting entries, and post them directly to the T accounts.
4. Prepare an adjusted trial balance, an income statement, and a balance sheet.

Answers to Self-Test

1. a	3. b	5. c	7. a	9. b
2. c	4. d	6. d	8. d	

Learning Objectives

Chapter Five

Completing the Accounting Cycle

1. *State all the steps in the accounting cycle.*
2. *Prepare a ten-column work sheet.*
3. *Identify the three principal uses of a work sheet.*
4. *Prepare financial statements from a work sheet.*
5. *Record the adjusting entries from a work sheet.*
6. *Explain the purposes of closing entries.*
7. *Prepare the required closing entries.*
8. *Prepare the post-closing trial balance.*

You will see the accounting cycle completed in this chapter. First you study the uses and preparation of the work sheet, an important tool for accountants. Then, as the final step in the accounting cycle, you learn how to prepare closing entries. As a result of studying this chapter, you should be able to meet the learning objectives listed on the left.

In previous chapters, we focused primarily on the measurement process in accounting. In this chapter, the emphasis is on the accounting system itself and the sequence of steps used by the accountant in completing the accounting cycle. An important part of the accounting system involves the preparation of a work sheet. We present in detail each step in the preparation of the work sheet. This chapter also explains the uses of the work sheet in accomplishing the end-of-period procedures of recording the adjusting entries, preparing financial statements, and closing the accounts in preparation for the next accounting period.

Overview of the Accounting System

The accounting system encompasses the sequence of steps followed in the accounting process, from analyzing transactions to preparing financial statements and closing the accounts. This system is sometimes called the accounting cycle. The purpose of the system, as illustrated in Figure 5-1, is to treat the business transactions as raw material and develop the finished product of accounting—the financial statements—in a systematic way. The steps in this system are summarized on the next page.

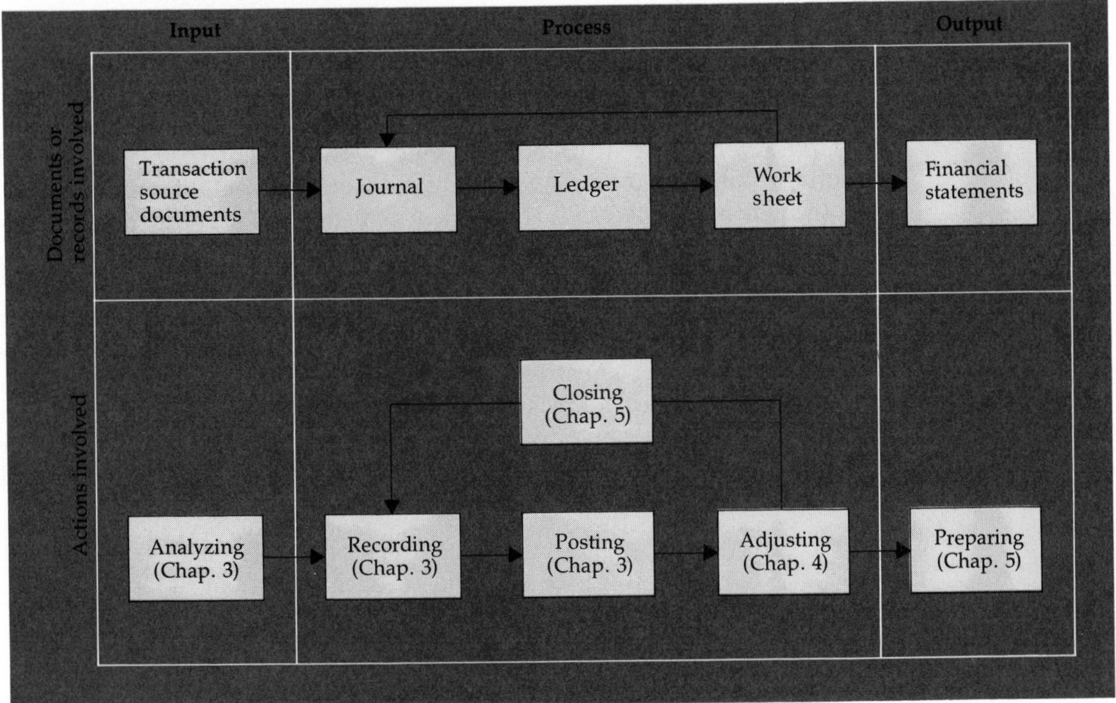

Figure 5-1 An Overview of the Accounting System

1. The transactions are *analyzed* from the *source documents.*
2. The transactions are *recorded* in the *journal.*
3. The entries are *posted* to the *ledger.*
4. The accounts are *adjusted* at the end of the period, usually with the aid of a *work sheet.*
5. *Financial statements* are *prepared* from the work sheet.
6. The accounts are *closed* to conclude the current accounting period and prepare for the beginning of the new accounting period.

Objective 1 State all the steps in the accounting cycle

The first four steps were introduced in Chapters 3 and 4. In this chapter, they are reviewed in conjunction with the use of the work sheet. The use of the work sheet and the final two steps are the major topics of this chapter.

The Work Sheet: A Tool of Accountants

Objective 2 Prepare a ten-column work sheet

The flow of information affecting a business does not arbitrarily stop at the end of an accounting period. In order to prepare the financial reports, accountants must collect relevant data to determine what should and what should not go in the financial reports. For example, accountants must examine insurance policies to see how much prepaid insurance has expired, examine plant and equipment records to determine depreciation, take an inventory of supplies on hand, and calculate the amount of accrued wages. These calculations, together with the other computations, analyses, and preliminary drafts of statements, make up the accountants' **working papers.** Working papers are important for two reasons. First, they aid accountants in organizing their work so that they do not omit important data or steps that affect the accounting statements. Second, they provide evidence of what has been done so that accountants or auditors can retrace their steps and support the basis of the financial statements.

A special kind of working paper is the **work sheet.** The work sheet is used frequently as a preliminary step in the preparation of financial statements. Using a work sheet lessens the possibility of ignoring an adjustment, aids in checking the arithmetical accuracy of the accounts, and facilitates the preparation of financial statements. The work sheet is never published and is rarely seen by management. Nevertheless, it is a useful tool for the accountant.

Steps in Preparing the Work Sheet

In Chapter 4, the adjustments were entered directly in the journal and posted to the ledger, and the financial statements were prepared from the adjusted trial balance. These steps were done rather easily for the Joan Miller Advertising Agency because it is a small company. For larger companies, however, which may require hundreds of adjusting entries, a work sheet is essential. To illustrate the preparation of the work sheet, the Joan Miller Advertising Agency case will be continued.

A commonly used form of work sheet has ten columns with appropriate headings, as shown in Figure 5-2. Observe that the work sheet is identified by a heading that consists of (1) the name of the company, (2) the title "Work Sheet," and (3) the period of time covered.

There are five steps in the preparation of a work sheet, as follows:

1. Enter the account balances in the Trial Balance columns.
2. Enter the adjustments in the Adjustments columns.
3. Enter the account balances as adjusted in the Adjusted Trial Balance columns.
4. Extend the account balances from the Adjusted Trial Balance columns to the Income Statement columns or the Balance Sheet columns.
5. Total the Income Statement columns and the Balance Sheet columns. Enter the net income or net loss in both pairs of columns as a balancing figure, and recompute column totals.

1. Enter the account balances in the Trial Balance columns The titles and balances of the accounts as of January 31 are copied directly from the ledger into the Trial Balance columns, as shown in Figure 5-2.

Recall that the account form in the ledger has two balance columns, one for debit balances and one for credit balances. The usual balance for an account is known as the **normal balance.** Consequently, if increases are

Joan Miller Advertising Agency Work Sheet For the Month Ended January 31, 19xx										
	Trial Balance		Adjustments		Adjusted Trial Balance		Income Statement		Balance Sheet	
Account Name	Debit	Credit	Debit	Credit	Debit	Credit	Debit	Credit	Debit	Credit
Cash	860									
Accounts Receivable	1,400									
Art Supplies	900									
Office Supplies	400									
Prepaid Rent	400									
Prepaid Insurance	240									
Art Equipment	2,100									
Accumulated Depreciation, Art Equipment										
Office Equipment	1,500									
Accumulated Depreciation, Office Equipment										
Accounts Payable		1,585								
Unearned Art Fees		500								
Joan Miller, Capital		5,000								
Joan Miller, Withdrawals	700									
Advertising Fees Earned		2,100								
Office Wages	600									
Utility Expense	50									
Telephone Expense	35									
	9,185	9,185								

Figure 5-2
Entering the Account Balances in the Trial Balance Columns

recorded by debits, the normal balance is a debit balance; if increases are recorded by credits, the normal balance is a credit balance. The table below summarizes the normal account balances of the major account categories.

Account Category	Way of Recording Increases	Normal Balance
Asset	Debits	Debit
Contra-Asset	Credits	Credit
Liability	Credits	Credit
Owner's Equity		
Capital	Credits	Credit
Withdrawals	Debits	Debit
Revenue	Credits	Credit
Expense	Debits	Debit

According to the table, the ledger account for Accounts Payable will typically have a credit balance and can be copied into the Trial Balance columns as a credit balance. When a work sheet is prepared, a separate trial balance is not required.

Occasionally, a transaction will cause an account to have a balance opposite from its normal account balance. Examples are when a customer overpays a bill or when a company overdraws its account at the bank by issuing a check for more money than it has in its balance. If this situation occurs, the abnormal balance should be copied into the Trial Balance columns.

2. Enter the adjustments in the Adjustments columns The required adjustments for the Joan Miller Advertising Agency were explained in Chapter 4. The same adjustments are entered in the Adjustments columns of the work sheet, as shown in Figure 5-3. As each adjustment is entered, a

Figure 5-3 Entries in the Adjustments Columns

Joan Miller Advertising Agency
Work Sheet
For the Month Ended January 31, 19xx

Account Name	Trial Balance		Adjustments		Adjusted Trial Balance		Income Statement		Balance Sheet	
	Debit	Credit	Debit	Credit	Debit	Credit	Debit	Credit	Debit	Credit
Cash	860									
Accounts Receivable	1,400		(i) 100							
Art Supplies	900			(c) 250						
Office Supplies	400			(d) 100						
Prepaid Rent	400			(a) 200						
Prepaid Insurance	240			(b) 20						
Art Equipment	2,100									
Accumulated Depreciation, Art Equipment				(e) 35						
Office Equipment	1,500									
Accumulated Depreciation, Office Equipment				(f) 25						
Accounts Payable		1,585								
Unearned Art Fees		500	(g) 200							
Joan Miller, Capital		5,000								
Joan Miller, Withdrawals	700									
Advertising Fees Earned		2,100		(i) 100						
Office Wages	600		(h) 90							
Utility Expense	50									
Telephone Expense	35									
	9,185	9,185								
Rent Expense			(a) 200							
Insurance Expense			(b) 20							
Art Supplies Used			(c) 250							
Office Supplies Used			(d) 100							
Depreciation Expense, Art Equipment			(e) 35							
Depreciation Expense, Office Equipment			(f) 25							
Art Fees Earned				(g) 200						
Wages Payable				(h) 90						
			1,020	1,020						

letter is used to identify the corresponding debit and credit parts of the entry. A brief explanation of the adjustment and any other data thought necessary should be placed at the bottom of the work sheet and identified by letter. For example, the first adjustment is for recognition of rent expense, which results in a debit to Rent Expense and a credit to Prepaid Rent. This adjustment is identified by a letter **a.**

If the adjustment requires an account that has not already been used in the trial balance, the new account is added below the accounts listed for the trial balance. For example, Rent Expense has been added in Figure 5-3.

When all the adjustments have been completed, the pair of Adjustments columns must be added. This step proves that the debits and credits of the adjustments are equal and tends to reduce error in the preparation of the work sheet.

3. Enter the account balances as adjusted in the Adjusted Trial Balance columns Figure 5-4 (next page) shows the adjusted trial balance, prepared by combining the amount of each account in the original Trial Balance columns with the corresponding amounts in the Adjustments columns and entering the combined amounts on a line-by-line basis in the Adjusted Trial Balance columns. This process, which is called crossfooting, requires horizontal addition and subtraction. It can be contrasted with the addition of items in a vertical column, which is called *footing* the column.

Some examples from Figure 5-4 will illustrate crossfooting. The first line shows Cash with a debit balance of $860. Because there are no adjustments to the Cash account, $860 is entered in the debit column of the Adjusted Trial Balance. The second line is Accounts Receivable, which shows a debit of $1,400 in the Trial Balance columns and a debit of $100 from adjustment **i** in the Adjustments columns. Because both are debits, they are added to produce the total ($1,500) in the debit column of the Adjusted Trial Balance. The next line is Art Supplies, which shows a debit of $900 in the Trial Balance columns and a credit from adjustment **c** in the Adjustments columns. Subtracting $250 from $900 therefore results in a $650 debit balance in the Adjusted Trial Balance. This process is continued through all the accounts, including those added below the accounts listed for the trial balance. The Adjusted Trial Balance columns are then footed to check the arithmetical accuracy of the crossfooting.

4. Extend the account balances from the Adjusted Trial Balance columns to the Income Statement columns or the Balance Sheet columns Every account in the adjusted trial balance is either a balance sheet account or an income statement account. The accounts are sorted, and each account is extended to its proper place as a debit or credit in either the Balance Sheet columns or the Income Statement columns. The result of extending the accounts is shown in Figure 5-5 (page 147). Revenue and expense accounts are extended to the Income Statement columns. Assets and liabilities as well as the capital and withdrawal accounts are then extended to

Joan Miller Advertising Agency
Work Sheet
For the Month Ended January 31, 19xx

Account Name	Trial Balance		Adjustments		Adjusted Trial Balance		Income Statement		Balance Sheet	
	Debit	Credit	Debit	Credit	Debit	Credit	Debit	Credit	Debit	Credit
Cash	860				860					
Accounts Receivable	1,400		(i) 100		1,500					
Art Supplies	900			(c) 250	650					
Office Supplies	400			(d) 100	300					
Prepaid Rent	400			(a) 200	200					
Prepaid Insurance	240			(b) 20	220					
Art Equipment	2,100				2,100					
Accumulated Depreciation, Art Equipment				(e) 35		35				
Office Equipment	1,500				1,500					
Accumulated Depreciation, Office Equipment				(f) 25		25				
Accounts Payable		1,585				1,585				
Unearned Art Fees		500	(g) 200			300				
Joan Miller, Capital		5,000				5,000				
Joan Miller, Withdrawals	700				700					
Advertising Fees Earned		2,100		(i) 100		2,200				
Office Wages	600		(h) 90		690					
Utility Expense	50				50					
Telephone Expense	35				35					
	9,185	9,185								
Rent Expense			(a) 200		200					
Insurance Expense			(b) 20		20					
Art Supplies Used			(c) 250		250					
Office Supplies Used			(d) 100		100					
Depreciation Expense, Art Equipment			(e) 35		35					
Depreciation Expense, Office Equipment			(f) 25		25					
Art Fees Earned				(g) 200		200				
Wages Payable				(h) 90		90				
			1,020	1,020	9,435	9,435				

Figure 5-4 Entries in the Adjusted Trial Balance Columns

the Balance Sheet columns. To avoid overlooking an account, extend the accounts line by line, beginning with the first line (which is Cash) and not omitting any. For instance, the Cash debit balance of $860 is extended to the debit column of the balance sheet; the Accounts Receivable debit balance of $1,500 is extended to the same debit column, and so forth.

5. Total the Income Statement columns and the Balance Sheet columns. Enter the net income or net loss in both pairs of columns as a balancing figure, and recompute column totals This last step, as shown in Figure 5-6 (page 148), is necessary to compute net income or net loss and to prove the arithmetical accuracy of the work sheet.

Joan Miller Advertising Agency
Work Sheet
For the Month Ended January 31, 19xx

Account Name	Trial Balance		Adjustments		Adjusted Trial Balance		Income Statement		Balance Sheet	
	Debit	Credit	Debit	Credit	Debit	Credit	Debit	Credit	Debit	Credit
Cash	860				860				860	
Accounts Receivable	1,400		(i) 100		1,500				1,500	
Art Supplies	900			(c) 250	650				650	
Office Supplies	400			(d) 100	300				300	
Prepaid Rent	400			(a) 200	200				200	
Prepaid Insurance	240			(b) 20	220				220	
Art Equipment	2,100				2,100				2,100	
Accumulated Depreciation, Art Equipment				(e) 35		35				35
Office Equipment	1,500				1,500				1,500	
Accumulated Depreciation, Office Equipment				(f) 25		25				25
Accounts Payable		1,585				1,585				1,585
Unearned Art Fees		500	(g) 200			300				300
Joan Miller, Capital		5,000				5,000				5,000
Joan Miller, Withdrawals	700				700				700	
Advertising Fees Earned		2,100		(i) 100		2,200		2,200		
Office Wages	600		(h) 90		690		690			
Utility Expense	50				50		50			
Telephone Expense	35				35		35			
	9,185	9,185								
Rent Expense			(a) 200		200		200			
Insurance Expense			(b) 20		20		20			
Art Supplies Used			(c) 250		250		250			
Office Supplies Used			(d) 100		100		100			
Depreciation Expense, Art Equipment			(e) 35		35		35			
Depreciation Expense, Office Equipment			(f) 25		25		25			
Art Fees Earned				(g) 200		200		200		
Wages Payable				(h) 90		90				90
			1,020	1,020	9,435	9,435				

Figure 5-5 Entries in the Income Statement and Balance Sheet Columns

Net income or net loss is equal to the difference between the debit and credit columns of the income statement.

Revenue (Income Statement credit column total)	$2,400
Expenses (Income Statement debit column total)	1,405
Net Income	$ 995

In this case, the revenue (credit column) has exceeded the expenses (debit column). Consequently, the company has a net income of $995.

Joan Miller Advertising Agency
Work Sheet
For the Month Ended January 31, 19xx

Account Name	Trial Balance		Adjustments		Adjusted Trial Balance		Income Statement		Balance Sheet	
	Debit	Credit	Debit	Credit	Debit	Credit	Debit	Credit	Debit	Credit
Cash	860				860				860	
Accounts Receivable	1,400		(i) 100		1,500				1,500	
Art Supplies	900			(c) 250	650				650	
Office Supplies	400			(d) 100	300				300	
Prepaid Rent	400			(a) 200	200				200	
Prepaid Insurance	240			(b) 20	220				220	
Art Equipment	2,100				2,100				2,100	
Accumulated Depreciation, Art Equipment				(e) 35		35				35
Office Equipment	1,500				1,500				1,500	
Accumulated Depreciation, Office Equipment				(f) 25		25				25
Accounts Payable		1,585				1,585				1,585
Unearned Art Fees		500	(g) 200			300				300
Joan Miller, Capital		5,000				5,000				5,000
Joan Miller, Withdrawals	700				700				700	
Advertising Fees Earned		2,100		(i) 100		2,200		2,200		
Office Wages	600		(h) 90		690		690			
Utility Expense	50				50		50			
Telephone Expense	35				35		35			
	9,185	9,185								
Rent Expense			(a) 200		200		200			
Insurance Expense			(b) 20		20		20			
Art Supplies Used			(c) 250		250		250			
Office Supplies Used			(d) 100		100		100			
Depreciation Expense, Art Equipment			(e) 35		35		35			
Depreciation Expense, Office Equipment			(f) 25		25		25			
Art Fees Earned				(g) 200		200		200		
Wages Payable				(h) 90		90				90
			1,020	1,020	9,435	9,435	1,405	2,400	8,030	7,035
							995			995
							2,400	2,400	8,030	8,030

Figure 5-6 Entries in the Balance Sheet Columns and Totals

The $995 is entered in the debit side of the Income Statement columns to balance the columns and is entered on the credit side of the Balance Sheet columns. This is done because excess revenue (net income) increases owner's equity, and increases in owner's equity are recorded by credits.

If a net loss has occurred, the opposite rule would apply. The excess of expenses (net loss) would be placed in the credit column of the income statement as a balancing figure and extended to the debit column of the balance sheet, because a net loss causes a decrease in owner's equity, which would be shown by a debit.

As a final check, the four columns are totaled again. If the Income Statement columns and the Balance Sheet columns do not balance, there may be an account extended or sorted to the wrong column, or an error may have been made in adding the columns. Equal totals in the Balance Sheet columns, however, are not absolute proof of accuracy. If an asset has been carried to the debit column of the income statement and if a similar error involving revenues or liabilities has been made, the work sheet will still check out, but the net income figure will be wrong.

Uses of the Work Sheet

Objective 3 Identify the three principal uses of a work sheet

We mentioned earlier that the work sheet is a tool of the accountant. The work sheet has three principal uses: (1) to prepare the financial statements, (2) to record the adjusting entries, and (3) to record the closing entries, which prepare the records for the beginning of the next period.

Preparing the Financial Statements

After completion of the work sheet, it is a simple step to prepare the financial statements because the account balances have been sorted into Income Statement and Balance Sheet columns. The income statement shown in Figure 5-7 is prepared from the accounts in the Income Statement columns in Figure 5-6.

Figure 5-7 Income Statement for the Joan Miller Advertising Agency

Joan Miller Advertising Agency Income Statement For the Month Ended January 31, 19xx		
Revenue		
Advertising Fees Earned		$2,200
Art Fees Earned		200
Total Revenue		$2,400
Expenses		
Office Wages	$690	
Utility Expense	50	
Telephone Expense	35	
Rent Expense	200	
Insurance Expense	20	
Art Supplies Used	250	
Office Supplies Used	100	
Depreciation Expense, Art Equipment	35	
Depreciation Expense, Office Equipment	25	
Total Expenses		1,405
Net Income		$ 995

Figure 5-8
Statement of Owner's Equity for the Joan Miller Advertising Agency

Joan Miller Advertising Agency Statement of Owner's Equity For the Month Ended January 31, 19xx	
Joan Miller, Capital, Jan. 1, 19xx	$5,000
Net Income for January	995
Subtotal	$5,995
Less withdrawals	700
Joan Miller, Capital, Jan. 31, 19xx	$5,295

Objective 4 Prepare financial statements from a work sheet

It is proper to show the changes in owner's equity on the balance sheet as has been done in previous examples. It is, however, common practice to put these changes in a separate financial statement called the statement of owner's equity. When this practice is followed, only the ending balance of owner's equity is shown on the balance sheet.

The statement of owner's equity and the balance sheet of Joan Miller Advertising Agency are presented in Figures 5-8 and 5-9. The account balances are drawn from the Balance Sheet columns of the work sheet shown in Figure 5-6. The totals of the assets and liabilities and owner's equity in the balance sheet do not agree with the totals of the Balance Sheet columns of the work sheet because contra accounts such as Accumulated Depreciation and withdrawals are deducted from the side of the balance sheet opposite the balance of the account.

Recording the Adjusting Entries

Objective 5 Record the adjusting entries from a work sheet

After the financial statements have been prepared, the adjusting entries must be recorded in the journal and posted to the ledger so that the account balances will agree with those on the work sheet and in the financial statements. This is an easy step because the adjusting entries and appropriate explanations appear on the work sheet in the Adjustments columns. These entries are copied into the general journal, as shown in Figure 5-10 (page 152). Quite often, the accountant has documented the adjusting entries on the work sheet (which has not been done in Figures 5-3 to 5-6). When this is the case, he or she may omit explanations.

Recording the Closing Entries

Closing entries, journal entries made at the end of the accounting period, accomplish two objectives. First, at the end of an accounting period, closing entries set the stage for the next accounting period by closing or clearing the expense and revenue accounts of their balances. This step is

Figure 5-9
Balance Sheet for the Joan Miller Advertising Agency

Joan Miller Advertising Agency
Balance Sheet
January 31, 19xx

Assets		
Cash		$ 860
Accounts Receivable		1,500
Office Supplies		300
Art Supplies		650
Prepaid Rent		200
Prepaid Insurance		220
Art Equipment	$2,100	
Less Accumulated Depreciation	35	2,065
Office Equipment	$1,500	
Less Accumulated Depreciation	25	1,475
Total Assets		$7,270
Liabilities		
Accounts Payable	$1,585	
Unearned Art Fees	300	
Wages Payable	90	
Total Liabilities		$1,975
Owner's Equity		
Joan Miller, Capital, Jan. 31		5,295
Total Liabilities and Owner's Equity		$7,270

Objective 6
Explain the purposes of closing entries

necessary because an income statement reports the net income for a single accounting period and reflects the expenses and revenues only for that period. Therefore, the expense and revenue accounts must be closed or cleared of their balances at the end of the period so that the next period may begin with a zero balance in those accounts.

The second objective of closing entries is to summarize a period's revenues and expenses. This is accomplished by transferring the balances of revenues and expenses to the Income Summary account to determine net profit or loss in that account. The balance of the Income Summary will then equal the net income or loss in the income statement. The net income or loss is then transferred to the owner's capital account. This step is necessary because, although expenses and revenues are recorded in expense and revenue accounts, they actually represent decreases and increases in owner's capital. Thus closing entries must transfer the net effect of increases (revenues) and decreases (expenses) to the owner's capital account.

Figure 5-10
Adjustments on Work Sheet Entered in the General Journal

General Journal					Page 1
Date		Description	Post. Ref.	Debit	Credit
Jan.	31	Rent Expense	514	200	
		Prepaid Rent	117		200
		To recognize expiration of one month's rent			
	31	Insurance Expense	515	20	
		Prepaid Insurance	118		20
		To recognize expiration of one month's insurance			
	31	Art Supplies Used	516	250	
		Art Supplies	115		250
		To recognize art supplies used during the month			
	31	Office Supplies Used	517	100	
		Office Supplies	116		100
		To recognize office supplies used during the month			
	31	Depreciation Expense, Art Equipment	518	35	
		Accumulated Depreciation, Art Equipment	145		35
		To record depreciation of art equipment for a month			
	31	Depreciation Expense, Office Equipment	519	25	
		Accumulated Depreciation, Office Equipment	147		25
		To record depreciation of office equipment for a month			
	31	Unearned Art Fees	213	200	
		Art Fees Earned	412		200
		Services paid in advance are performed			
	31	Office Wages Expense	511	90	
		Wages Payable	214		90
		Accrual of unrecorded wages			
	31	Accounts Receivable	114	100	
		Advertising Fees Earned	411		100
		Advertising fees earned but unrecorded			

Closing entries are sometimes referred to as clearing entries because one of their functions is to clear the revenue and expense accounts and leave them with zero balances.

As stated in the previous chapter, revenue and expense accounts are called nominal accounts because they are temporary in nature. Nominal accounts begin each period at zero, accumulate a balance during the period, and return to zero by means of closing entries when the balance is transferred to owner's equity. The accountant uses these accounts to keep track of the increases and decreases in owner's equity in a way that is helpful to management and others interested in the success or progress of the company. However, nominal accounts differ from balance sheet accounts. Balance sheet, or real, accounts often begin with a balance, increase or decrease during the period, and carry the end-of-period balance into the next accounting period.

Required Closing Entries

Closing entries are required for four basic tasks:

Objective 7 Prepare the required closing entries

1. Transferring the revenue account balances to Income Summary
2. Transferring the expense account balances to Income Summary
3. Transferring the Income Summary balance to the capital account
4. Transferring the withdrawals account balance to the capital account

Figure 5-11 (next page) shows owner's equity and nominal (income statement) accounts of Joan Miller Advertising Agency after the work sheet and the financial statements have been prepared and the adjusting entries recorded, but before the closing entries have been recorded. The Income Summary, a new nominal account, is introduced here. This account provides a place to summarize all revenues and expenses in a single net figure before transferring the result to the capital account.

Closing the Revenue Accounts to the Income Summary

Revenue accounts have credit balances before the closing entries are posted. Therefore, an entry debiting each revenue account in the amount of its balance is needed to close the account. The credit portion of the entry is made to the Income Summary account. The compound entry that closes the two revenue accounts for the Joan Miller Advertising Agency is as follows:

Jan. 31	Advertising Fees Earned	411	2,200	
	Art Fees Earned	412	200	
	Income Summary	313		2,400
	To clear revenue accounts			

Figure 5-11
The Accounts Before Closing Entries Are Recorded

Joan Miller, Capital — Account No. 311

Date	Item	Post Ref.	Debit	Credit	Balance Debit	Balance Credit
	Transaction 1			5,000		5,000

Joan Miller, Withdrawals — Account No. 312

Date	Item	Post Ref.	Debit	Credit	Balance Debit	Balance Credit
	Transaction 13		700		700	

Income Summary — Account No. 313

Date	Item	Post Ref.	Debit	Credit	Balance Debit	Balance Credit

Advertising Fees Earned — Account No. 411

Date	Item	Post Ref.	Debit	Credit	Balance Debit	Balance Credit
	Transaction 7			700		700
	12			1,400		2,100
	Adjustment (i)			100		2,200

Art Fees Earned — Account No. 412

Date	Item	Post Ref.	Debit	Credit	Balance Debit	Balance Credit
	Adjustment (g)			200		200

Figure 5-11 (*continued*)

Office Wages — **Account No. 511**

Date	Item	Post Ref.	Debit	Credit	Balance Debit	Balance Credit
	Transaction 10		300		300	
	14		300		600	
	Adjustment (b)		90		690	

Utility Expense — **Account No. 512**

Date	Item	Post Ref.	Debit	Credit	Balance Debit	Balance Credit
	Transaction 15		50		50	

Telephone Expense — **Account No. 513**

Date	Item	Post Ref.	Debit	Credit	Balance Debit	Balance Credit
	Transaction 16		35		35	

Rent Expense — **Account No. 514**

Date	Item	Post Ref.	Debit	Credit	Balance Debit	Balance Credit
	Adjustment (a)		200		200	

Insurance Expense — **Account No. 515**

Date	Item	Post Ref.	Debit	Credit	Balance Debit	Balance Credit
	Adjustment (b)		20		20	

(continued)

Figure 5-11 (*continued*)

Art Supplies Used — **Account No. 516**

Date	Item	Post Ref.	Debit	Credit	Balance Debit	Balance Credit
	Adjustment (c)		250		250	

Office Supplies Used — **Account No. 517**

Date	Item	Post Ref.	Debit	Credit	Balance Debit	Balance Credit
	Adjustment (d)		100		100	

Depreciation Expense, Art Equipment — **Account No. 518**

Date	Item	Post Ref.	Debit	Credit	Balance Debit	Balance Credit
	Adjustment (e)		35		35	

Depreciation Expense, Office Equipment — **Account No. 519**

Date	Item	Post Ref.	Debit	Credit	Balance Debit	Balance Credit
	Adjustment (f)		25		25	

The effect of posting the entry is shown in Figure 5-12. Observe that the dual effect of the entry is to (1) set the balances of the revenue accounts equal to zero, and (2) transfer the balances in total to the credit side of the Income Summary account. Also note that the data for closing the revenue accounts can be found in the credit side of the Income Statement columns in the work sheet illustrated in Figure 5-6.

Advertising Fees Earned

Date	Item	Post. Ref.	Debit	Credit	Balance Debit	Balance Credit
	Trans. 7			700		700
	12			1,400		2,100
	Adj. (i)			100		2,200
Jan. 31			2,200			—

Income Summary

Date	Item	Post. Ref.	Debit	Credit	Balance Debit	Balance Credit
Jan. 31				2,400		2,400

2,200
200
2,400

Art Fees Earned

Date	Item	Post. Ref.	Debit	Credit	Balance Debit	Balance Credit
Jan. 31				200		200
			200			—

Figure 5-12 Posting the Closing Entry of the Revenue Accounts to the Income Summary

Closing the Expense Accounts to the Income Summary

Expense accounts have debit balances before the closing entries are posted. Therefore, a compound entry crediting each expense account for its balance and debiting the Income Summary for the total (which can be found in the debit side of the Income Statement columns) is required:

Jan. 31	Income Summary	313	1,405	
	Office Wages	511		690
	Utility Expense	512		50
	Telephone Expense	513		35
	Rent Expense	514		200
	Insurance Expense	515		20
	Art Supplies Used	516		250
	Office Supplies Used	517		100
	Depreciation Expense, Art Equipment	518		35
	Depreciation Expense, Office Equipment	519		25
	To close the expense accounts			

The effect of posting the closing entry to the ledger accounts is shown in Figure 5-13 (next page). Observe again the dual effect of (1) reducing expense account balances to zero and (2) transferring the total of the account balances to the debit side of the Income Summary account. Observe also that data for closing the expense accounts are on the debit side of the Income Statement columns of the work sheet (Figure 5-6).

Closing the Income Summary to the Capital Account

After the entries closing the revenue and expense accounts have been posted, the balance of the Income Summary account is equal to the net

Office Wages

Date	Item	Post. Ref.	Debit	Credit	Balance Debit	Balance Credit
	Trans. 10		300		300	
	14		300		600	
	Adj. (b)		90		690	
Jan. 31				690	—	

Utility Expense

Date	Item	Post. Ref.	Debit	Credit	Balance Debit	Balance Credit
	Trans. 15		50		50	
Jan. 31				50	—	

Telephone Expense

Date	Item	Post. Ref.	Debit	Credit	Balance Debit	Balance Credit
	Trans. 16		35		35	
Jan. 31				35	—	

Income Summary

Date	Item	Post. Ref.	Debit	Credit	Balance Debit	Balance Credit
Jan. 31				2,400		2,400
31			1,405			995

Rent Expense

Date	Item	Post. Ref.	Debit	Credit	Balance Debit	Balance Credit
	Adj. (a)		200		200	
Jan. 31				200	—	

690
50
35
200
20
250
100
25
35
1,405

Insurance Expense

Date	Item	Post. Ref.	Debit	Credit	Balance Debit	Balance Credit
	Adj. (b)		20		20	
Jan. 31				20	—	

Art Supplies Used

Date	Item	Post. Ref.	Debit	Credit	Balance Debit	Balance Credit
	Adj. (c)		250		250	
Jan. 31				250	—	

Depreciation Expense, Art Equipment

Date	Item	Post. Ref.	Debit	Credit	Balance Debit	Balance Credit
	Adj. (e)		35		35	
Jan. 31				35	—	

Office Supplies Used

Date	Item	Post. Ref.	Debit	Credit	Balance Debit	Balance Credit
	Adj. (d)		100		100	
Jan. 31				100	—	

Depreciation Expense, Office Equipment

Date	Item	Post. Ref.	Debit	Credit	Balance Debit	Balance Credit
	Adj. (f)		25		25	
Jan. 31				25	—	

◀ Figure 5-13 Posting the Closing Entry of the Expense Accounts to the Income Summary

income or loss for the period. A net income will be indicated by a credit balance and a net loss by a debit balance. At this point, the Income Summary balance, regardless of its nature, must be closed to the capital account. For the Joan Miller Advertising Agency the entry is as follows:

Jan. 31	Income Summary	313	995	
	Joan Miller, Capital	311		995
	To close the Income Summary account			

The effect of posting the closing entry is shown in Figure 5-14. Note again the dual effect of (1) closing the Income Summary account balances and (2) transferring the balance, net income in this case, to Joan Miller's capital account.

Closing the Withdrawals Account to the Capital Account

The withdrawals account shows the amount by which capital is reduced during the period by withdrawals of cash or other assets of the business by the owner for personal use. Consequently, the debit balance of the withdrawals account must be closed to the capital account, as follows:

Jan. 31	Joan Miller, Capital	311	700	
	Joan Miller, Withdrawals	312		700
	To close the Withdrawals account			

The effect of posting this closing entry is shown in Figure 5-15 (top of next page). The dual effect of the entry is to (1) close the withdrawals account of its balance and (2) transfer the balance to the capital account.

The Accounts After Closing

After all the steps in the closing process have been completed and the adjusting and closing entries have been posted to the accounts, the stage is set for the next accounting period. The ledger accounts of the Joan Miller

Figure 5-14 Posting the Closing Entry of the Income Summary to the Capital Account

Income Summary

Date	Item	Post. Ref.	Debit	Credit	Balance Debit	Balance Credit
Jan. 31				2,400		2,400
31			1,405			995
31			995			—

Joan Miller, Capital

Date	Item	Post. Ref.	Debit	Credit	Balance Debit	Balance Credit
	Trans. 1			5,000		5,000
Jan. 31				995		5,995

Joan Miller, Withdrawals						
					Balance	
Date	Item	Post. Ref.	Debit	Credit	Debit	Credit
	Trans. 13		700		700	
Jan. 31				700	—	

Joan Miller, Capital						
					Balance	
Date	Item	Post. Ref.	Debit	Credit	Debit	Credit
	Trans. 1			5,000		5,000
Jan. 31				995		5,995
31			700			5,295

Figure 5-15
Posting the Closing Entry of the Withdrawals Account to the Capital Account

Advertising Agency as they appear at this point are shown in Figure 5-16 (below). The revenue, expense, and withdrawals accounts (nominal or temporary accounts) have zero balances. The capital account has been increased or decreased depending on net income or loss and withdrawals. The balance sheet accounts (real accounts) have the appropriate balances, which are carried forward to the next period.

Figure 5-16
The Accounts After Closing Entries Are Posted

Cash						Account No. 111
					Balance	
Date	Item	Post. Ref.	Debit	Credit	Debit	Credit
Various dates	Transaction 1		5,000		5,000	
	2			400	4,600	
	3			2,100	2,500	
	4			750	1,750	
	6			240	1,510	
	8			500	1,010	
	9		700		1,710	
	10			300	1,410	
	11		500		1,910	
	13			700	1,210	
	14			300	910	
	15			50	860	

Accounts Receivable						Account No. 114
					Balance	
Date	Item	Post. Ref.	Debit	Credit	Debit	Credit
	Transaction 12		800		800	
	12		600		1,400	
Jan. 31	Adjustment (i)		100		1,500	

Figure 5-16
(*continued*)

Art Supplies — **Account No. 115**

Date		Item	Post. Ref.	Debit	Credit	Balance	
						Debit	Credit
		Transaction 5		900		900	
Jan.	31	Adjustment (c)			250	650	

Office Supplies — **Account No. 116**

Date		Item	Post. Ref.	Debit	Credit	Balance	
						Debit	Credit
		Transaction 5		400		400	
Jan.	31	Adjustment (d)			100	300	

Prepaid Rent — **Account No. 117**

Date		Item	Post. Ref.	Debit	Credit	Balance	
						Debit	Credit
		Transaction 2		400		400	
Jan.	31	Adjustment (a)			200	200	

Prepaid Insurance — **Account No. 118**

Date		Item	Post. Ref.	Debit	Credit	Balance	
						Debit	Credit
		Transaction 6		240		240	
Jan.	31	Adjustment (b)			20	220	

Art Equipment — **Account No. 144**

Date		Item	Post. Ref.	Debit	Credit	Balance	
						Debit	Credit
		Transaction 3		2,100		2,100	

(*continued*)

Figure 5-16
(*continued*)

Accumulated Depreciation, Art Equipment — **Account No. 145**

Date		Item	Post. Ref.	Debit	Credit	Balance	
						Debit	Credit
Jan.	31	Adjustment (e)			35		35

Office Equipment — **Account No. 146**

Date		Item	Post. Ref.	Debit	Credit	Balance	
						Debit	Credit
		Transaction 4		1,500		1,500	

Accumulated Depreciation, Office Equipment — **Account No. 147**

Date		Item	Post. Ref.	Debit	Credit	Balance	
						Debit	Credit
Jan.	31	Adjustment (f)			25		25

Accounts Payable — **Account No. 212**

Date		Item	Post. Ref.	Debit	Credit	Balance	
						Debit	Credit
		Transaction 4			750		750
		5			1,300		2,050
		8		500			1,550
		16			35		1,585

Unearned Art Fees — **Account No. 213**

Date		Item	Post. Ref.	Debit	Credit	Balance	
						Debit	Credit
		Transaction 11			500		500
Jan.	31	Adjustment (g)		200			300

Figure 5-16
(*continued*)

Wages Payable						**Account No. 214**	
						Balance	
Date		Item	Post. Ref.	Debit	Credit	Debit	Credit
Jan.	31	Adjustment (h)			90		90

Joan Miller, Capital						**Account No. 311**	
						Balance	
Date		Item	Post. Ref.	Debit	Credit	Debit	Credit
Jan.	1	Transaction 1			5,000		5,000
Jan.	31	Closing entry			995		5,995
	31	Closing entry		700			5,295

Joan Miller, Withdrawals						**Account No. 312**	
						Balance	
Date		Item	Post. Ref.	Debit	Credit	Debit	Credit
		Transaction 13		700		700	
Jan.	31	Closing entry			700	—	

Income Summary						**Account No. 313**	
						Balance	
Date		Item	Post. Ref.	Debit	Credit	Debit	Credit
Jan.	31	Closing entry			2,400		2,400
	31	Closing entry		1,405			995
	31	Closing entry			995		—

(continued)

Figure 5-16
(*continued*)

Advertising Fees Earned — **Account No. 411**

Date		Item	Post. Ref.	Debit	Credit	Balance Debit	Balance Credit
		Transaction 9			700		700
		12			1,400		2,100
Jan.	31	Adjustment (i)			100		2,200
	31	Closing entry		2,200			—

Art Fees Earned — **Account No. 412**

Date		Item	Post. Ref.	Debit	Credit	Balance Debit	Balance Credit
Jan.	31	Adjustment (g)			200		200
	31	Closing entry		200			—

Office Wages Expense — **Account No. 511**

Date		Item	Post. Ref.	Debit	Credit	Balance Debit	Balance Credit
		Transaction 10		300		300	
		14		300		600	
Jan.	31	Adjustment (h)		90		690	
	31	Closing entry			690	—	

Utility Expense — **Account No. 512**

Date		Item	Post. Ref.	Debit	Credit	Balance Debit	Balance Credit
		Transaction 15		50		50	
Jan.	31	Closing entry			50	—	

Figure 5-16
(*continued*)

Telephone Expense — **Account No. 513**

Date		Item	Post. Ref.	Debit	Credit	Balance Debit	Balance Credit
		Transaction 16		35		35	
Jan.	31	Closing entry			35	–	

Rent Expense — **Account No. 514**

Date		Item	Post. Ref.	Debit	Credit	Balance Debit	Balance Credit
Jan.	31	Adjustment (a)		200		200	
	31	Closing entry			200	–	

Insurance Expense — **Account No. 515**

Date		Item	Post. Ref.	Debit	Credit	Balance Debit	Balance Credit
Jan.	31	Adjustment (b)		20		20	
	31	Closing entry			20	–	

Art Supplies Used — **Account No. 516**

Date		Item	Post. Ref.	Debit	Credit	Balance Debit	Balance Credit
Jan.	31	Adjustment (c)		250		250	
	31	Closing entry			250	–	

Office Supplies Used — **Account No. 517**

Date		Item	Post. Ref.	Debit	Credit	Balance Debit	Balance Credit
Jan.	31	Adjustment (d)		100		100	
	31	Closing entry			100	–	

(*continued*)

Figure 5-16
(continued)

Depreciation Expense, Art Equipment						Account No. 518	
						Balance	
Date		Item	Post. Ref.	Debit	Credit	Debit	Credit
Jan.	31	Adjustment (e)		35		35	
	31	Closing entry			35	—	

Depreciation Expense, Office Equipment						Account No. 519	
						Balance	
Date		Item	Post. Ref.	Debit	Credit	Debit	Credit
Jan.	31	Adjustment (f)		25		25	
	31	Closing entry			25	—	

The Post-Closing Trial Balance

Objective 8
Prepare the post-closing trial balance

Because it is possible to make an error in posting the adjustments and closing entries to the ledger accounts, it is necessary to retest the equality of the accounts by preparing a new trial balance. This final trial balance, called a **post-closing trial balance,** for the Joan Miller Advertising Agency is shown in Figure 5-17. Notice that only balance sheet accounts have balances. At this point, as previously explained, the income statement accounts have all been closed.

Chapter Review

Review of Learning Objectives

1. State all the steps in the accounting cycle.
The steps in the accounting cycle are to (1) analyze the transactions from the source documents, (2) record the transactions in the journal, (3) post the entries to the ledger, (4) adjust the accounts at the end of the period, (5) prepare the financial statements, and (6) close the accounts.

2. Prepare a ten-column work sheet.
A work sheet is prepared by first entering the account balances in the Trial Balance columns, the adjustments in the Adjustments columns, and the adjusted account balances in the Adjusted Trial Balance columns. Then the amounts from the Adjusted Trial Balance columns are extended to the Income Statement or Balance Sheet columns as appropriate. Next, the Income Statement and Balance Sheet columns are totaled. Finally, net income or net loss is determined from the

Figure 5-17
Post-Closing Trial Balance

Joan Miller Advertising Agency Post-Closing Trial Balance January 31, 19xx		
Cash	$ 860	
Accounts Receivable	1,500	
Art Supplies	650	
Office Supplies	300	
Prepaid Rent	200	
Prepaid Insurance	220	
Art Equipment	2,100	
Accumulated Depreciation, Art Equipment		$ 35
Office Equipment	1,500	
Accumulated Depreciation, Office Equipment		25
Accounts Payable		1,585
Wages Payable		90
Unearned Art Fees		300
Joan Miller, Capital		5,295
	$7,330	$7,330

Income Statement columns and extended to the Balance Sheet columns. The statement columns should now be in balance.

3. Identify the three principal uses of a work sheet.
A work sheet is useful in (1) preparing the financial statements, (2) recording the adjusting entries, and (3) recording the closing entries.

4. Prepare financial statements from a work sheet.
The balance sheet and income statements can be prepared directly from the Balance Sheet and Income Statement columns of a completed work sheet. It is common practice to prepare a separate statement of owner's equity from the work sheet. When this is done, the balance sheet contains only the ending balance of owner's equity.

5. Prepare the adjusting entries from a work sheet.
Adjusting entries can be recorded in the journal directly from the Adjustments columns of the work sheet. If adequate explanations for the adjusting entries appear on the work sheet, it is not necessary to include explanations for the entries in the journal.

6. Explain the purposes of closing entries.
Closing entries have two objectives. First, they clear the balances from the revenue and expense accounts in preparation for the next accounting period. Second, they summarize a period's revenues and expenses in the Income Summary so that the net income or net loss for the period may be transferred as a total to owner's equity.

7. Prepare the required closing entries.

Closing entries are prepared by first transferring the revenue and expense account balances to the Income Summary. Then the balance of the Income Summary account is transferred to the capital account. Finally, the balance of the withdrawals account is transferred to the capital account.

8. Prepare the post-closing trial balance.

As a final check on the balance of the ledger, a post-closing trial balance is prepared after the closing entries have been posted to the ledger accounts.

Self-Test

Test your knowledge of the chapter by choosing the best answer for each item below.

1. Which of the following sequences of actions describes the proper sequence in the accounting cycle?
   a. Post, enter, analyze, prepare, close, adjust
   b. Analyze, enter, post, adjust, prepare, close
   c. Prepare, enter, post, adjust, analyze, close
   d. Enter, post, close, prepare, adjust, analyze
2. The work sheet is a type of
   a. ledger.
   b. journal.
   c. working paper.
   d. financial statement.
3. The normal account balances for Equipment and Accumulated Depreciation, Equipment, are
   a. debit and credit, respectively.
   b. credit and debit, respectively.
   c. debits.
   d. credits.
4. The work sheet is useful in
   a. preparing financial statements.
   b. recording adjusting entries.
   c. recording closing entries.
   d. All of the above.
5. An important purpose of closing entries is
   a. to adjust the accounts in the ledger.
   b. to set balance sheet accounts to zero in order to begin the next period.
   c. to set income statement accounts to zero in order to begin the next period.
   d. None of the above.
6. In preparing closing entries, it is helpful to refer first to
   a. the Adjustments columns of the work sheet.
   b. the Adjusted Trial Balance columns of the work sheet.
   c. the Income Statement columns of the work sheet.
   d. the general journal.
7. After all closing entries have been posted, the balance of the income summary will be
   a. a debit if a net income has been earned.
   b. a debit if a net loss has been incurred.
   c. a credit if a net loss has been incurred.
   d. zero.
8. The post-closing trial balance will
   a. contain only income statement accounts.
   b. contain only balance sheet accounts.
   c. contain both income statement and balance sheet accounts.
   d. be prepared before closing entries are posted to the ledger.

Answers to Self-Test are at the end of this chapter.

Review Problem
Completion of Work Sheet, Preparation of Financial Statements, Adjusting Entries, and Closing Entries

This chapter contains an extended example of the preparation of a work sheet and the last two steps of the accounting cycle for the Joan Miller Advertising Agency. Instead of studying a demonstration problem, the student should carefully review and retrace the steps through the illustrations in the chapter.

Required

1. In Figure 5-6, what is the source of the trial balance figures?
2. Trace the entries in the Adjustments column of Figure 5-6 to the journal entries in Figure 5-10.
3. Trace the journal entries in Figure 5-10 to the ledger accounts in Figure 5-11.
4. Trace the amounts in the Income Statement and Balance Sheet columns of Figure 5-6 to the income statement in Figure 5-7, the statement of owner's equity in Figure 5-8, and the balance sheet in Figure 5-9.
5. Trace the amounts in the Income Statement columns and the withdrawals account balance of Figure 5-6 to the closing entries on pages 153–157.
6. Trace the closing entries on pages 153–157 to the ledger accounts in Figure 5-16.
7. Trace the balances of the ledger accounts in Figure 5-16 to the post-closing trial balance in Figure 5-17.

Chapter Assignments

Questions

1. Arrange the following activities in proper order by placing the numbers 1 through 6 in the blanks:

____ **a.** The transactions are entered in the journal.
____ **b.** Financial statements are prepared.
____ **c.** The transactions are analyzed from the source documents.
____ **d.** A work sheet is prepared.
____ **e.** Closing entries are prepared.
____ **f.** The transactions are posted to the ledger.

2. Why are working papers important to the accountant?
3. Why are work sheets never published and rarely seen by management?
4. Is the work sheet a substitute for the financial statements? Discuss.
5. At the end of the accounting period, does the posting of adjusting entries to the ledger precede or follow the preparation of the work sheet?
6. What is the normal balance of the following accounts, in terms of debit and credit: Cash; Accounts Payable; Prepaid Rent; Sam Jones, Capital; Commission Revenue; Sam Jones, Withdrawals; Rent Expense; Accumulated Depreciation, Office Equipment; Office Equipment
7. What is the probable cause of a credit balance in the Cash account?

8. Should the Adjusted Trial Balance columns of the work sheet be totaled before or after the adjusted amounts are carried to the Income Statement and Balance Sheet columns? Discuss.
9. What sequence should be followed in extending the Adjusted Trial Balance columns to the Income Statement and Balance Sheet columns? Discuss.
10. Do the totals of the Balance Sheet columns of the work sheet usually agree with the totals on the balance sheet? Explain.
11. Do the Income Statement columns and Balance Sheet columns balance after the adjusted amounts from the Adjusted Trial Balance columns are extended?
12. What is the purpose of the Income Summary account?
13. Are adjusting entries posted to the ledger accounts at the same time as the closing entries? Explain.
14. What is the difference between adjusting and closing entries?
15. What are the four basic tasks of closing entries?
16. Which of the following accounts will not have a balance after closing entries are prepared and posted? Insurance Expense; Accounts Receivable; Commission Revenue; Prepaid Insurance; Withdrawals; Supplies; Supplies Expense; Capital
17. What is the significance of the post-closing trial balance?
18. Which of the following accounts will appear on the post-closing trial balance? Insurance Expense; Accounts Receivable; Commission Revenue; Prepaid Insurance; Withdrawals; Supplies; Supplies Expense; Capital

Classroom Exercises

Exercise 5-1 Preparation of Trial Balance

The following alphabetically arranged accounts and balances represent the account balances for the Carr Real Estate Agency. All accounts have normal balances.

Accounts Payable	$ 2,170
Accounts Receivable	1,750
Accumulated Depreciation, Office Equipment	450
Advertising Expense	600
Carr, Capital	10,210
Carr, Withdrawals	9,000
Cash	2,545
Office Equipment	3,000
Prepaid Insurance	560
Rent Expense	2,400
Revenue from Commissions	19,300
Supplies	275
Wages Expense	12,000

Prepare a trial balance by listing the accounts on a sheet of accounting paper in the same order, with the balances in the appropriate debit or credit column.

Exercise 5-2 Preparation of Adjusting Entries from Work Sheet Columns

The items listed at the top of page 171 are from the Adjustments columns of a work sheet as of December 31.

Prepare adjusting journal entries from the information.

	Adjustments			
	Debit		Credit	
Prepaid Insurance			(a)	120
Office Supplies			(b)	315
Accumulated Depreciation, Office Equipment			(c)	700
Accumulated Depreciation, Store Equipment			(d)	1,100
Office Salaries Expense	(e)	120		
Store Salaries Expense	(e)	240		
Insurance Expense	(a)	120		
Office Supplies Expense	(b)	315		
Depreciation Expense, Office Equipment	(c)	700		
Depreciation Expense, Store Equipment	(d)	1,100		
Salaries Payable			(e)	360
		2,595		2,595

Exercise 5-3
Preparation of Closing Entries from Work Sheet

The following items are from the Income Statement columns of the work sheet of the John Ring Repair Store on December 31.

	Income Statement	
	Debit	Credit
Repair Revenue		24,240
Wages Expense	7,840	
Rent Expense	1,200	
Supplies Used	4,260	
Insurance Expense	915	
Depreciation Expense, Repair Equipment	1,345	
	15,560	24,240
Net Income	8,680	
	24,240	24,240

Prepare entries to close revenue, expense, Income Summary, and withdrawal accounts. Mr. Ring withdrew $10,000 during the year.

Exercise 5-4
Preparing a Statement of Owner's Equity

The capital, withdrawal, and Income Summary accounts for Jake's Barber Shop for the year ended December 31, after recording of closing entries, are presented in T account form at the top of the next page.

Jake Brown, Capital	
12/31 12,000	1/1 26,000
	12/31 13,000

Jake Brown, Withdrawals	
4/1 4,000	12/31 12,000
7/1 4,000	
10/1 4,000	

Income Summary	
12/31 39,000	12/31 52,000
12/31 13,000	

Prepare a statement of owner's equity for Jake's Barber Shop.

Exercise 5-5 Completion of Work Sheet

The following list of alphabetically arranged accounts and balances represents a trial balance in highly simplified form.

Trial Balance Accounts and Balances

Accounts Payable	$ 3	Office Equipment	$ 6
Accounts Receivable	5	Prepaid Insurance	2
Accumulated Depreciation, Office Equipment	1	Service Revenue	20
Cash	4	Supplies	4
Joe Hobgood, Capital	12	Unearned Revenue	3
Joe Hobgood, Withdrawals	6	Utilities Expense	2
		Wages Expense	10

1. On accounting paper, prepare a work sheet form, entering the trial balance accounts in the same order in which they appear above. (Arrange the balances in the correct debit or credit column.)

2. Complete the work sheet using the following information:

   a. Expired insurance, $1.

   b. Of the unearned revenue, $2 has been earned by the balance sheet date.

   c. Estimated depreciation on office equipment, $1.

   d. Accrued wages, $1.

   e. Unused supplies on hand, $1.

Exercise 5-6 Deriving Adjusting Entries from Trial Balance and Income Statement Columns

Presented below is a partial work sheet in which the Trial Balance and Income Statement columns have been completed. All amounts are in dollars.

Accounts	Trial Balance		Income Statement	
Cash	$ 5			
Accounts Receivable	10			
Supplies	11			
Prepaid Insurance	8			
Building	25			
Accumulated Depreciation		$ 8		
Accounts Payable		4		
Unearned Revenue		2		
R. J., Capital		32		
Revenue		40		$42
Wages Expense	27		$30	
	$86	$86		
Insurance Expense			4	
Supplies Used			8	
Depreciation Expense			2	
			$44	$42
Net Loss				2
			$44	$44

1. Determine the adjusting entries that have been made. Assume that no adjustments are made to Accounts Receivable or Accounts Payable.
2. Prepare a balance sheet.

Problem Set A

Problem 5A-1 Completion of Work Sheet

Bal Harbor Marina rents one hundred slips in a large dock to owners of small boats in the area. The trial balance of Bal Harbor Marina on December 31, the end of the current fiscal year, is presented below.

Bal Harbor Marina
Trial Balance
December 31, 19xx

Cash	$ 1,360	
Accounts Receivable	2,440	
Supplies	516	
Prepaid Insurance	742	
Dock	30,600	
Accumulated Depreciation, Dock		$ 5,000
Accounts Payable		1,100
Jane Derek, Capital		31,023
Jane Derek, Withdrawals	12,000	
Ship Rentals		19,400
Wages Expense	7,400	
Insurance Expense	915	
Utility Expense	550	
	$56,523	$56,523

Required

1. Enter the trial balance amounts in the Trial Balance columns of a work sheet, and complete the work sheet using the following information:
   a. Expired insurance, $346.
   b. Inventory of unused supplies still on hand, $76.
   c. Estimated depreciation of dock, $2,000.
   d. Unrecorded utility expense owed at the end of year, $50.
2. From the work sheet, prepare an income statement and a balance sheet.
3. From the work sheet, record the adjusting entries and closing entries in the general journal.

Problem 5A-2 Preparation of Work Sheet, Adjusting Entries, and Closing Entries

Ernie Freeman opened his investment advisory service on June 1, 19xx. Some customers paid for counseling services after they were rendered, and others paid in advance for one year of service. After six months of operation Ernie wanted to know how he stood. The trial balance on November 30 appears at the top of the next page.

Freeman Investment Advisory Service
Trial Balance
November 30, 19xx

Cash	$ 475	
Prepaid Rent	1,200	
Office Supplies	275	
Office Equipment	2,500	
Accounts Payable		$ 1,675
Unearned Revenue		1,215
Ernie Freeman, Capital		4,000
Ernie Freeman, Withdrawals	2,400	
Advisory Revenue		3,380
Telephone and Utility Expense	420	
Wages Expense	3,000	
	$10,270	$10,270

Required

1. Enter the trial balance amounts in the Trial Balance columns of a work sheet and complete the work sheet using the following information:
   a. One year's rent paid in advance when Ernie began business.
   b. Inventory of unused supplies, $50.
   c. One-half year's depreciation on office equipment, $200.
   d. Service rendered that had been paid for in advance, $575.
   e. Investment advisory services rendered during the month but not yet billed, $180.
   f. Salaries earned by employees but not yet paid, $125.
2. From the work sheet, prepare an income statement and a balance sheet.
3. From the work sheet, prepare adjusting and closing entries.
4. What is your evaluation of Ernie's first six months in business?

Problem 5A-3 Completion of Work Sheet, Preparation of Financial Statements, Adjusting Entries, and Closing Entries

The trial balance on page 175 was taken from the ledger of Martin Moving and Storage Company on December 31, the end of the company's accounting period.

Required

1. Enter the trial balance amounts in the Trial Balance columns of a work sheet and complete the work sheet using the following information:
   a. Expired insurance, $970.
   b. Inventory of unused moving supplies, $450.
   c. Inventory of unused office supplies, $70.
   d. Estimated depreciation, building, $4,800.
   e. Estimated depreciation, trucks, $5,150.
   f. Estimated depreciation, office equipment, $900.
   g. The company credits the storage fees of customers who pay in advance to the Unearned Storage Fees accounts; of the amount credited to this account during the year, $1,850 has been earned by December 31.
   h. There are $265 worth of accrued storage fees earned but unrecorded and uncollected at the end of the accounting period.

i. Of the $85,800 in the Moving Services Revenue account, $5,000 represents an advance payment by Acme Real Estate Agency for a move by that company to new offices during the next accounting period.

j. There are $640 worth of accrued but unpaid truck drivers' wages at the end of the year.

2. Prepare an income statement and a balance sheet.
3. Prepare adjusting and closing entries from the work sheet.

Martin Moving and Storage Company
Trial Balance
December 31, 19xx

Cash	$ 2,685	
Accounts Receivable	9,415	
Prepaid Insurance	1,780	
Moving Supplies	4,900	
Office Supplies	820	
Land	5,000	
Building	52,000	
Accumulated Depreciation, Building		$ 17,800
Trucks	34,600	
Accumulated Depreciation, Trucks		10,300
Office Equipment	5,300	
Accumulated Depreciation, Office Equipment		3,600
Accounts Payable		2,460
Unearned Storage Fees		2,780
Mortgage Payable		24,000
M. Martin, Capital		42,910
M. Martin, Withdrawals	15,000	
Moving Services Revenue		85,800
Storage Fees Earned		9,600
Truck Drivers' Wages	42,600	
Office Salaries Expense	14,800	
Gas, Oil, and Truck Repairs	10,350	
	$199,250	$199,250

Problem 5A-4 The Complete Accounting Cycle—Two Months

On July 1, 19xx, Stan Beale opened Beale TV Repair Shop and during the month completed the following transactions:

July	1	Deposited $2,000 of his savings in a bank account in the name of the company.
	1	Paid the rent for a store for one month, $150.
	1	Paid the premium on a one-year insurance policy, $240.
	2	Purchased repair equipment from Equipment Company for $2,800 on the basis of $400 down payment and $200 per month for one year. The first payment is due August 1.

5 Purchased repair supplies from Supply Company for $275 on credit.
8 Purchased an advertisement in a local newspaper for $40.
15 Cash TV repair revenue for the first half of the month, $200.
21 Paid $150 of the amount owed to Supply Company.
25 Stan Beale withdrew $300 from the company bank account to pay living expenses.
31 Cash TV repair revenue for the second half of July, $450.

Required for July

1. Open the following accounts: Cash (111); Prepaid Insurance (117); Repair Supplies (119); Repair Equipment (144); Accumulated Depreciation, Repair Equipment (145); Accounts Payable (212); Stan Beale, Capital (311); Stan Beale, Withdrawals (312); Income Summary (313); TV Repair Revenue (411); Store Rent (511); Advertising Expense (512); Insurance Expense (513); Repair Supplies Expense (514); Depreciation Expense, Repair Equipment (515).
2. Prepare and post journal entries to record the July transactions.
3. Prepare a trial balance in the Trial Balance columns of a work sheet, and complete the work sheet using the following information:
   a. One month's insurance has expired.
   b. Remaining inventory of unused repair supplies, $105.
   c. Estimated depreciation on repair equipment, $40.
4. From the work sheet, prepare an income statement and a balance sheet for July.
5. From the work sheet, prepare and post adjusting and closing entries.
6. Prepare a post-closing trial balance.

During August Stan Beale completed the following transactions for the Beale TV Repair Shop:

Aug. 1 Paid the monthly rent, $150.
1 Made monthly payment to Equipment Company, $200.
6 Purchased additional repair supplies on credit from Supply Company, $575.
15 Cash TV repair revenue for the first half of the month, $575.
20 Purchased an additional advertisement in local newspaper, $40.
23 Paid Supply Company on account, $400.
25 Withdrew $300 from the company for living expenses.
31 Cash TV repair revenue for the last half of the month, $545.

Required for August

7. Prepare and post journal entries to record August transactions.
8. Prepare a trial balance in the Trial Balance columns of a work sheet and complete the work sheet based on the following information:
   a. One month's insurance has expired.
   b. Inventory of unused repair supplies, $275.
   c. Estimated depreciation on repair equipment, $40.
9. From the work sheet, prepare an August income statement and balance sheet.
10. From the work sheet, prepare and post adjusting and closing entries.
11. Prepare a post-closing trial balance.

Problem 5A-5 Preparation of Work Sheet from Limited Data

Mark Adams started work as an accountant with the Pleasant Valley Golf Course on June 30, the end of the accounting period. His boss tells him that he must have an income statement and a balance sheet by 9:00 A.M. the next day in order to secure a renewal of the bank loan. Mark takes home the general ledger and supporting data for adjusting entries. At 3:00 A.M., after completing the statements, he lights a cigarette and falls asleep. A few minutes later he awakes to find the papers on fire. He quickly puts out the fire but is horrified to discover that except for the general ledger and the income statement everything else, including the work sheet, supporting data, and balance sheet, is completely destroyed. He decides that he should be able to reconstruct the balance sheet and adjusting entries from the general ledger and the income statement, even though he had not yet recorded and posted the adjusting and closing entries. The information available is as follows:

General Ledger

Account	Debit	Credit
Cash	Bal. 7,200	
Unexpired Insurance	Bal. 3,400	
Prepaid Advertising	Bal. 1,700	
Supplies	Bal. 2,400	
Land	Bal. 245,000	
Equipment	Bal. 52,000	
Accumulated Depreciation, Equipment		Bal. 12,800
Bank Note Payable		Bal. 100,000
Unearned Revenue, Locker Fees		Bal. 4,200
Matthew Arb, Capital		Bal. 157,050
Matthew Arb, Withdrawals	Bal. 18,000	
Revenue from Greens Fees		Bal. 224,500
Advertising Expense	Bal. 14,750	
Water and Utility Expense	Bal. 20,600	
Wages Expense	Bal. 114,000	
Maintenance Expense	Bal. 17,200	
Miscellaneous Expense	Bal. 2,300	

Pleasant Valley Golf Course
Income Statement
For the Year Ended June 30, 19xx

Revenue		
Revenue from Greens Fees	$224,500	
Revenue from Locker Fees	3,200	
Total Revenues		$227,700
Expenses		
Wages Expense	$117,000	
Maintenance Expense	17,200	
Depreciation Expense, Equipment	4,000	
Water and Utility Expense	21,600	
Supplies Expense	2,000	
Advertising Expense	13,250	
Property Taxes Expense	7,500	
Miscellaneous Expense	2,300	
Total Expenses		184,850
Net Income		$ 42,850

Required

1. Using the information above, fill in the Trial Balance and Income Statement columns of a work sheet.
2. Reconstruct the adjusting entries and complete the work sheet. Then record the adjusting entries in the general journal with explanations.
3. Prepare the balance sheet.

Problem Set B

Problem 5B-1 Completion of Work Sheet

Service Trailer Rental owns thirty small trailers, which are rented by the day for local moving jobs. The trial balance of Service Trailer Rental on June 30, 19xx, the end of the current fiscal year, appears on the next page.

Required

1. Enter the trial balance amounts in the Trial Balance columns of a work sheet, and complete the work sheet using the following information:
   a. Expired insurance, $360.
   b. Inventory of unused supplies still on hand, $119.
   c. Estimated depreciation of trailers, $2,400.
   d. Wages earned but unpaid and unrecorded on June 30, $200.
2. From the work sheet, prepare an income statement and a balance sheet.
3. From the work sheet, record adjusting entries and closing entries in the general journal.

Service Trailer Rental
Trial Balance
June 30, 19xx

Cash	$ 346	
Accounts Receivable	972	
Supplies	385	
Prepaid Insurance	720	
Trailers	12,000	
Accumulated Depreciation, Trailers		$ 4,800
Accounts Payable		271
Carla Perez, Capital		5,694
Carla Perez, Withdrawals	7,200	
Trailer Rentals		45,200
Wages Expense	23,200	
Insurance Expense	360	
Other Expenses	10,782	
	$55,965	$55,965

Problem 5B-2 Preparation of Work Sheet, Adjusting Entries, and Closing Entries

Michael Flaherty began his law practice immediately after graduation from law school. In order to help him get started, several clients paid him retainers (payment in advance) for future services. Other clients paid when service was provided. After one year in practice, the law firm had the trial balance shown below.

Michael Flaherty, Attorney
Trial Balance
December 31, 19xx

Cash	$ 1,375	
Accounts Receivable	2,109	
Office Supplies	382	
Office Equipment	3,755	
Accounts Payable		$ 796
Unearned Retainers		5,000
Michael Flaherty, Capital		4,000
Michael Flaherty, Withdrawals	6,000	
Legal Fees		16,200
Rent Expense	1,800	
Utility Expense	717	
Wages Expense	9,858	
	$25,996	$25,996

Required

1. Enter the trial balance amounts in the Trial Balance columns of a work sheet, and complete the work sheet using the following information:
   a. Inventory of unused supplies, $91.
   b. Estimated depreciation on equipment, $600.
   c. Services rendered during the month but not yet billed, $650.
   d. Services rendered to clients who paid in advance that should be applied against retainers, $2,900.
   e. Salaries earned by employees but not yet paid, $60.
2. From the work sheet, prepare an income statement and a balance sheet.
3. From the work sheet, prepare adjusting and closing entries.
4. How would you evaluate the first year of Michael's law practice?

Problem 5B-3 Completion of Work Sheet, Preparation of Financial Statements, Adjusting Entries, and Closing Entries

At the end of the current fiscal year, the trial balance of the Majestic Theater appeared as follows:

Majestic Theater
Trial Balance
September 30, 19xx

Cash	$ 12,200	
Accounts Receivable	8,472	
Prepaid Insurance	9,800	
Office Supplies	280	
Cleaning Supplies	1,795	
Land	10,000	
Building	200,000	
Accumulated Depreciation, Building		$ 18,500
Theater Furnishings	185,000	
Accumulated Depreciation, Theater Furnishings		32,500
Office Equipment	15,800	
Accumulated Depreciation, Office Equipment		7,780
Accounts Payable		22,643
Gift Books Liability		20,950
Mortgage Payable		150,000
Ken Bedford, Capital		156,324
Ken Bedford, Withdrawals	30,000	
Ticket Sales		200,000
Theater Rental		25,000
Usher Wages	92,000	
Office Wages	12,000	
Utilities Expense	56,350	
	$633,697	$633,697

Required

1. Enter the trial balance amounts in the Trial Balance columns of a work sheet and complete the work sheet using the following information:
   a. Expired insurance, $8,900.
   b. Inventory of unused office supplies, $88.
   c. Inventory of unused cleaning supplies, $173.
   d. Estimated depreciation on building, $5,000.
   e. Estimated depreciation on theater furnishings, $18,000.
   f. Estimated depreciation on office equipment, $1,580.
   g. The company credits all gift books sold during the year to a Gift Books Liability account. On September 30, it was estimated that $18,500 worth of the gift books had been redeemed.
   h. Included in the Theater Rental account is a $2,400 item that represents an advance payment by a religious group for rental of the theater each Sunday morning for the next three months.
   i. There are $410 worth of accrued but unpaid usher wages at the end of the year.
2. Prepare an income statement and a balance sheet.
3. Prepare adjusting and closing entries from the work sheet.

Problem 5B-4 The Complete Accounting Cycle—Two Months

During the first month of operation, the Thompson Bicycle Repair Store completed the following transactions:

May	1	Began business by depositing $3,000 in a bank account in the name of the company.
	1	Paid the premium on a one-year insurance policy, $360.
	1	Paid one month's rent, $320.
	2	Purchased repair equipment from Bike Company for $1,900. The terms were $300 down payment and $100 per month for sixteen months. The first payment is due June 1.
	5	Purchased repair supplies from Bergen Company for $195 on credit.
	14	Paid utility expense for the month of May, $77.
	15	Cash bicycle repair revenue for the first half of May, $431.
	20	Paid $100 of the amount owed to Bergen Company.
	29	Owner withdrew $400 from the company for personal living expenses.
	31	Cash bicycle repair revenue for the last half of May, $566.

Required for May

1. Open the following accounts: Cash (111); Prepaid Insurance (117); Repair Supplies (119); Repair Equipment (144); Accumulated Depreciation, Repair Equipment (145); Accounts Payable (212); Joe Thompson, Capital (311); Joe Thompson, Withdrawals (312); Income Summary (313); Bicycle Repair Revenue (411); Store Rent (511); Utility Expense (512); Insurance Expense (513); Repair Supplies Expense (514); Depreciation Expense, Repair Equipment (515).
2. Prepare and post journal entries to record the May transactions.
3. Prepare a trial balance in the Trial Balance columns of a work sheet, and complete the work sheet using the following information:
   a. One month's insurance has expired.
   b. Inventory of unused repair supplies, $86.
   c. Estimated depreciation on repair equipment, $25.
4. From the work sheet, prepare an income statement and a balance sheet for May.
5. From the work sheet, prepare and post adjusting and closing entries.
6. Prepare a post-closing trial balance.

During June, Thompson Bicycle Repair Store engaged in the following transactions:

June 1 Paid the monthly rent, $320.
1 Made the monthly payment to Bike Company, $100.
9 Purchased additional repair supplies on credit from Bergen Company, $447.
15 Cash bicycle repair revenue for the first half of June, $525.
18 Paid utility expense for June, $83.
19 Paid Bergen Company on account, $200.
28 Withdrew $400 from the company for personal living expenses.
30 Cash bicycle repair revenue for the last half of June, $436.

Required for June

7. Prepare and post journal entries to record June transactions.

8. Prepare a trial balance in the Trial Balance columns of a work sheet, and complete the work sheet based on the following information:

a. One month's insurance has expired.

b. Inventory of unused repair supplies, $191.

c. Estimated depreciation on repair equipment, $25.

9. From the work sheet, prepare a June income statement and balance sheet.

10. From the work sheet, prepare and post adjusting and closing entries.

11. Prepare a post-closing trial balance.

Problem 5B-5 Preparation of Work Sheet from Limited Data

Presented below and opposite are the income statement and trial balance for Center Bowling Lanes for the year ending December 31, 19xx:

Center Bowling Lanes
Income Statement
For the Year Ended December 31, 19xx

Revenue		$615,817
Expenses		
Wages Expense	$381,076	
Advertising Expense	15,200	
Utility Expense	42,900	
Depreciation Expense, Building	4,800	
Depreciation Expense, Equipment	11,000	
Supplies Expense	1,148	
Maintenance Expense	81,300	
Insurance Expense	1,500	
Property Tax Expense	10,000	
Miscellaneous Expense	10,200	
Total Expenses		559,124
Net Income		$ 56,693

Center Bowling Lanes
Trial Balance
December 31, 19xx

Cash	$ 12,741	
Accounts Receivable	7,388	
Supplies	1,304	
Unexpired Insurance	1,800	
Prepaid Advertising	900	
Land	5,000	
Building	100,000	
Accumulated Depreciation, Building		$ 19,000
Equipment	125,000	
Accumulated Depreciation, Equipment		22,000
Accounts Payable		14,317
Notes Payable		70,000
Unearned Revenue		2,300
Cora Dunham, Capital		60,813
Cora Dunham, Withdrawals	24,000	
Revenue		614,817
Wages Expense	377,114	
Advertising Expense	14,300	
Utility Expense	42,200	
Maintenance Expense	81,300	
Miscellaneous Expense	10,200	
	$803,247	$803,247

Required

1. Using the information given, fill in the Trial Balance and Income Statement columns of a work sheet.
2. Reconstruct the adjusting entries and complete the work sheet. Assume that there is no adjustment to Accounts Receivable. Then record the adjusting entries in the general journal with explanations.
3. Prepare the balance sheet.

Answers to Self-Test

1. b	3. a	5. c	7. d
2. c	4. d	6. c	8. b

Part Two

Extensions of the Basic Accounting Model

Accounting, as we have seen, is an information system that measures, processes, and communicates information for decision making. Part I presented the fundamental theoretical and technical aspects of the basic accounting system.

In Part II, the basic accounting system is extended to more complex applications.

Chapter 6 expands the discussion to accounting for merchandising operations as opposed to service operations.

Chapter 7 demonstrates the increased usefulness of classified and general-purpose external financial statements over simple statements in communicating information to statement users.

Chapter 8 addresses the goal of processing large volumes of transactions in an efficient and time-saving manner.

Chapter 9 first describes the basic principles of internal control and then applies these principles to cash transactions.

Chapter Six

Accounting for Merchandising Operations

Learning Objectives

1. *Identify the components of income statements for merchandising concerns.*
2. *Journalize transactions involving revenue for merchandising concerns.*
3. *Calculate cost of goods sold.*
4. *Differentiate the perpetual inventory method from the periodic inventory method.*
5. *Journalize transactions involving purchases of merchandise.*
6. *Prepare a work sheet for a merchandising concern.*
7. *Prepare closing entries for a merchandising concern.*

In the preceding chapters, you studied the accounting records and reports for the simplest type of enterprise—the service company. In this chapter, you will study a more complex type of business—the merchandising company. This chapter focuses on the special buying and selling transactions of merchandising concerns and their effects on the income statement. As a result of studying this chapter, you should be able to meet the learning objectives listed on the left.

Service companies such as advertising agencies or law firms perform a service for a fee or commission, and net income is measured as the difference between fees or commissions earned and expenses. In determining net income, a very simple income statement is all that is required.

In contrast, there are many more companies that attempt to make a profit by buying and selling merchandise. Merchandising companies, whether wholesale or retail, do use the same basic accounting methods as service companies, but the process of purchasing and selling merchandise requires some additional accounts and concepts. This process also results in a more complicated income statement than that for a service business.

Income Statement for a Merchandising Concern

As shown in Figure 6-1, the income statement for a merchandising concern consists of three major parts: (1) revenue from sales, (2) cost of goods sold, and (3) operating expenses. It differs from the income statement for the service firm mainly in the cost of goods sold section.

Figure 6-1 Condensed Income Statement for a Merchandising Concern

Wilson Greeting Card Shop Condensed Income Statement For the Month Ended April 30, 19xx	
Revenue from Sales	$12,000
Cost of Goods Sold	7,200
Gross Profit from Sales	$ 4,800
Operating Expenses	4,000
Net Income	$ 800

Objective 1 Identify the components of income statements for merchandising concerns

The cost of goods sold section tells how much the merchant paid for the merchandise that was sold. The merchandiser must sell merchandise for more than cost to pay **operating expenses**—those expenses other than cost of goods sold that are incurred in the operation of a business—and have adequate profit left over. The difference between revenue from sales and cost of goods sold is known as **gross profit from sales,** or simply **gross profit.** The owner must pay operating expenses from gross profit from sales. The remainder is net income.

All three parts of the merchandising income statement are important to a firm's management. Management is interested both in the percentage of gross profit on sales and in the amount of gross profit (40 percent and $4,800, respectively, for the Wilson Greeting Card Shop). This information is helpful in planning business operations. For instance, management may attempt to stimulate sales by reducing the selling price. This strategy results in a reduction in the percentage of gross profit. It will work if total sales are increased enough to increase total gross profit (thereby increasing net income). On the other hand, management may increase operating expenses (advertising expense, for example) in an effort to increase sales and the amount of gross profit. If the increase in gross profit is greater than the increase in advertising, net income will improve.

Revenue from Sales

Revenue from sales requires the computation of net sales, as presented in Figure 6-2. It consists of gross proceeds from sales of merchandise less sales returns and allowances and sales discounts.

If a business is to succeed or even survive, the revenue from sales must be sufficient to cover three items: (1) cost of goods sold, (2) operating expenses, and (3) net income.

Figure 6-2
Partial Income Statement—Revenue from Sales

Hardwick Auto Parts Company Partial Income Statement For the Year Ended December 31, 19xx		
Revenue from Sales		
Gross Sales		$246,350
Less: Sales Returns and Allowances	$2,750	
Sales Discounts	4,275	7,025
Net Sales		$239,325

Objective 2
Journalize transactions involving revenue for merchandising concerns

When revenue from a company's sales is reported in the financial media, it is often compared with revenue from sales for the same period of the previous year. Management, investors, and others often consider the amount and trend of sales important indicators of a firm's progress. Increasing sales suggest growth, whereas decreasing sales indicate the possibility of decreased earnings and other financial problems in the future.

Gross Sales

Under accrual accounting, revenue from the sale of merchandise is usually considered to be earned in the accounting period in which the merchandise is delivered to the customer. Gross sales consist of total sales for cash and total sales on credit for a given accounting period. Because the customer may not pay immediately, the cash for the sale may be collected in a subsequent period, but this does not affect the recording of sales. Consequently, there is likely to be considerable difference between revenue earned and cash sales.

The journal entry to record a sale of merchandise for cash is as follows:

Sept. 16	Cash	1,286	
	Sales		1,286
	To record the sale of merchandise for cash		

The Sales account is used exclusively for recording sales of merchandise. If the sale of merchandise is made on credit, the entry is as follows:

Sept. 16	Accounts Receivable	746	
	Sales		746
	To record the sale of merchandise on credit		

Sales Returns and Allowances

If a customer receives a defective or otherwise unsatisfactory product, the business will usually try to accommodate the customer. The business may allow the customer to return the item for a cash refund, or it may give the customer an allowance off the sales price. A good accounting system will provide management with information about sales returns and allowances because such transactions may mean dissatisfied customers. Each return or allowance is recorded in the general journal as a debit to an account called **Sales Returns and Allowances.** An example of this transaction follows:

Sept. 17	Sales Returns and Allowances	76	
	Accounts Receivable (or Cash)		76
	To record return or allowance on unsatisfactory merchandise		

Sales Returns and Allowances is a contra account and, accordingly, is deducted from gross sales in the income statement (see Figure 6-2).

Sales Discounts

When goods are sold on credit, both parties should always have a definite understanding as to the amount and time of payment. These terms are usually printed on the sales invoice and constitute part of the sales agreement. Customary terms differ from industry to industry. In some industries, payment is expected in a short period of time such as ten days or thirty days. In these cases, the invoice may be marked "n/10" or "n/30," meaning that the net amount of the invoice is due ten days or thirty days, respectively, after the invoice date. If the invoice is due ten days after the end of the month, it may carry the designation "n/10 eom."

In some industries it is common to give discounts for early payment, called **sales discounts.** This practice increases the seller's liquidity by reducing the amount of money tied up in accounts receivable. These terms may be stated on the invoice as 2/10, n/30 or 2/10, n/60. Terms of **2/10, n/30** mean that the debtor may take a 2 percent discount if he or she pays the invoice within ten days after the invoice date. Otherwise, the debtor may wait until thirty days after the invoice date and pay the full amount of the invoice without the discount.

Because it is not usually possible to know at the time of sale whether the customer will take advantage of the discount by paying within the discount period, sales discounts are recorded only at the time the customer pays. For example, assume that Hardwick Auto Parts sells merchandise to a customer on September 20 in the amount of $300 on terms of 2/10, n/60. At the time of sale the entry would be:

Sept. 20	Accounts Receivable	300	
	Sales		300
	To record sale of merchandise on credit		

The customer may take advantage of the sales discount any time on or before September 30. If he or she pays on September 29, the entry is:

Sept. 29	Cash	294	
	Sales Discounts	6	
	Accounts Receivable		300
	To record payment for Sept. 20 sale; discount taken		

At the end of the accounting period, the Sales Discounts account has accumulated all the sales discounts for the period. Because sales discounts reduce revenue from sales, they are usually considered a contra account and deducted from gross sales in the income statement (see Figure 6-2).

Cost of Goods Sold

Objective 3
Calculate cost of goods sold

Cost of goods sold is an important concept. Every merchandising business has goods on hand that it holds for sale to customers. The amount of goods on hand at any one time is known as **merchandise inventory.** The total of goods available for sale during the year is the sum of two factors—merchandise inventory at the beginning of the year plus net purchases during the year.

If a company were to sell all the goods available for sale during a given accounting period or year, the cost of goods sold would then equal goods available for sale. In most cases, however, the business will have goods still unsold and on hand at the end of the year. To find the actual **cost of goods sold,** therefore, we must subtract the merchandise inventory at the end of the year from the goods available for sale.

As a summary, consider this example:

Merchandise Inventory at the beginning of the year	$ 4,000
Add Net Cost of Purchases	53,000
Goods Available for Sale	$57,000
Less Merchandise Inventory at the end of the year	6,000
Cost of Goods Sold	$51,000

In this case, goods costing $57,000 could have been sold because this company started with $4,000 in merchandise inventory at the beginning of the year and purchased $53,000 in goods during the year. At the end of the year, $6,000 in goods were left unsold and should appear as merchandise inventory on the balance sheet. When the merchandise inventory is subtracted from the total available goods, the resulting cost of goods sold is $51,000 and should appear on the income statement.

To understand fully the concept of the cost of goods sold, it is necessary to examine merchandise inventory and net cost of purchases.

Merchandise Inventory

The inventory of a merchandising concern consists of the goods on hand and available for sale to customers. For a grocery store, inventory would include meats, vegetables, canned goods, and the other items a store of this type might have for sale. For a service station, it includes gasoline, oil, and automobile parts. Merchandising concerns purchase their inventories from wholesalers, manufacturers, and other suppliers.

The merchandise inventory on hand at the beginning of the accounting period is called the **beginning inventory.** Conversely, the merchandise inventory on hand at the end of the accounting period is called the **ending inventory.** As we have seen, beginning and ending inventories are used in determining cost of goods sold in the income statement. Ending inventory appears in the balance sheet as an asset.

Measuring Merchandise Inventory Merchandise inventory is a key factor in determining cost of goods sold for the accounting period. Because merchandise inventory represents unsold goods available for sale, there must be a method for determining both the quantity and the cost of goods on hand. The two basic methods of accounting for merchandise inventory are the perpetual inventory method and the periodic inventory method.

Objective 4 Differentiate the perpetual inventory method from the periodic inventory method

A business enterprise that sells items of high unit value such as appliances or automobiles is usually able to account for the cost of each item as it is bought and sold. This system is known as the **perpetual inventory method.** Under the perpetual inventory method, records are kept of the cost of each item in inventory. As each item is sold, its cost is deducted from the inventory and debited to the Cost of Goods Sold account. The total cost of goods sold is determined by adding the costs of the individual items sold, and the merchandise inventory is computed by totaling the costs of goods still on hand.

However, companies that sell items of low value and high volume would find it difficult to keep track of the cost of every single item sold. Instead they rely on the **periodic inventory method.** Using this method, the company waits until the end of the accounting period to count the physical inventory. This actual count of the physical inventory is used along with various accounting records to determine the cost of goods sold for the entire period. A grocery store, for example, which may sell thousands of items every hour, will use the periodic inventory method. It is not practical to record the cost of every item at the time each is sold. Most drugstores, automobile parts stores, department stores, discount companies, and bookstores fall into this category. These companies count the inventory "periodically," usually at the end of the accounting period.

The periodic inventory method for determining cost of goods sold is described in this chapter. The perpetual inventory method is discussed further in Chapters 11 and 23.

The Periodic Inventory Method Most companies rely on an actual count of goods on hand at the end of an accounting period to determine ending inventory and, indirectly, the cost of goods sold. This procedure for determining the merchandise inventory, the periodic inventory method, can be summarized as follows:

1. Make a physical count of the merchandise on hand at the end of the accounting period.
2. Multiply the quantity of each type of merchandise by the appropriate unit cost.
3. Add the resulting costs of each type of merchandise.

The cost of ending merchandise inventory is deducted from goods available for sale in the income statement to determine the cost of goods sold section. The ending inventory of one period is the beginning inventory of the next period. Entries are made in the closing process at the end of the period—to remove the beginning inventory (the last period's ending inventory) and to enter the ending inventory of the current period. These entries are the only ones made to the Inventory account during the period. Consequently, only on the balance sheet date does the Inventory account represent the actual amount on hand. As soon as purchases or sales are made, the inventory figure becomes a historical amount and remains so until the new inventory is entered at the end of the next accounting period.

Taking the Physical Inventory Making a physical count of all merchandise on hand at the end of an accounting period is referred to as **taking a physical inventory.** It can be a difficult task, since it is easy to omit items or count them twice.

Merchandise inventory includes all salable goods owned by the concern regardless of where they are located. It includes all goods on shelves, in storerooms, in warehouses, and in trucks en route between warehouses and stores. It includes goods in transit from suppliers if title to the goods has passed. Ending inventory does not include merchandise sold to customers but not delivered or goods that cannot be sold because they are damaged or obsolete. If the damaged or obsolete goods can be sold at a reduced price, they may be included at the reduced value.

The actual count is usually taken after the close of business on the last day of the fiscal year. Many companies end their fiscal year in a slow season to facilitate the taking of physical inventory. Retail department stores often end their fiscal year in January or February, for example. After hours, at night or on the weekend, the employees count and record all items on numbered inventory tickets or sheets. They follow established procedures to ensure that no items are missed. When the inventory tickets or sheets are completed, they are forwarded to the accounting office.

The accounting office checks to see that all numbered tickets and sheets are accounted for, and copies the information onto inventory ledgers. The appropriate unit costs are then supplied and the computations made.

Net Cost of Purchases

Under the periodic inventory method, the net cost of purchases consists of gross purchases less purchases discounts and purchases returns and allowances plus any freight charges on the purchases.

Objective 5 Journalize transactions involving purchases of merchandise.

Purchases When the periodic inventory method is used, all purchases of merchandise for resale are debited to the Purchases account, as illustrated below:

Nov. 12	Purchases	1,500	
	Accounts Payable		1,500
	To record purchases of merchandise, terms 2/10, n/30		

The Purchases account, a nominal or temporary account, is used only for merchandise purchased for resale. Its sole purpose is to accumulate the total cost of merchandise purchased during an accounting period. The Purchases account does not indicate whether the merchandise has been sold or is still on hand. Purchases of other assets such as equipment should be recorded in the appropriate asset account.

Purchases Returns and Allowances For various reasons, a company may need to return merchandise acquired for resale. The firm may not have been able to sell the merchandise and may ask to return it to the original supplier. Or the merchandise may be defective or damaged in some way and may have to be returned. In some cases, the supplier may suggest that an allowance be given as an alternative to returning the goods for full credit. In any event, **purchases returns and allowances** form a separate account and should be recorded in the journal as follows:

Nov. 14	Accounts Payable	200	
	Purchases Returns and Allowances		200
	Return of damaged merchandise purchased on November 12		

It is important that a separate account be used to record purchases returns and allowances because management needs the resulting information for decision-making purposes. It can be very costly to return merchandise for credit. There are many costs that cannot be recovered, such as ordering costs, accounting costs, sometimes freight costs, and interest on the money invested in the goods. Sometimes there are lost sales resulting from poor ordering or unusable goods. Excessive returns may call for new purchasing procedures or new suppliers.

Purchases Discounts Merchandise purchases are usually made on credit and commonly involve **purchases discounts** for prompt payment. It is almost always worthwhile for the company to take a discount if offered. For example, the terms 2/10, n/30 offer a 2 percent discount for paying only twenty days early (the period between the tenth and the thirtieth day). This is an effective interest rate of 36 percent (there are 18 twenty-day periods in a year) on an annual basis. Most companies can borrow money for less than this rate. Consequently, management wants to know the amount of discounts, which is a separate account and is recorded as follows when the payment is made:

Nov. 22.	Accounts Payable		1,300	
	Purchases Discounts			26
	Cash			1,274
	Paid the invoice of Nov. 12			
	Purchase Nov. 12	$1,500		
	Less return	200		
	Net purchase	$1,300		
	Discount: 2%	26		
	Cash	$1,274		

If a company is able to make only a partial payment on an invoice, most creditors will allow the company to take the discount applicable to the partial payment.

Good management of cash resources calls for both taking the discount and waiting as long as possible to pay. In order to accomplish these two objectives, some companies file invoices by their due date as they get them. Each day, the invoices due on that day are pulled from the file and paid. In this manner, the company utilizes cash as long as possible and also takes the advantageous discounts.

Freight In In some industries, it is customary for the supplier to pay transportation costs, charging a higher price to include them. In other industries, it is customary for the purchaser to pay transportation charges on merchandise. These charges, called freight in or transportation in, should logically be included as an addition to purchases. As with the account above, they should be accumulated in the Freight In account so that management can monitor this cost. The entry is as follows:

Nov. 12	Freight In	134	
	Cash		134
	Paid freight charges on merchandise purchased		

Specialized terms designate whether the supplier or the purchaser pays the freight or transportation charges. FOB shipping point means that the supplier will place the merchandise "free on board" at the point of origin, and the buyer is responsible for paying the charges from that point. In addition, the title to the merchandise passes to the buyer at that point. If you have purchased a car, you know that if the sale agreement says "FOB Detroit," you must pay the freight from that point to where you are.

On the other hand, FOB destination means that the supplier is bearing the transportation costs to the destination. The supplier may prepay the amount, or the buyer may pay the charges and deduct them from the invoice. In this case, title remains with the supplier until the merchandise reaches its destination.

The effects of these specialized shipping terms are summarized below.

Shipping Term	Where Title Passes	Who Pays Transportation Charges
FOB shipping point	At origin	Buyer
FOB destination	At destination	Seller

It is important not to confuse freight-in costs with freight-out costs. If you, as seller, agree to pay transportation charges on goods you have sold, this expense is a cost of selling merchandise, not a cost of purchasing merchandise.

Cost of Goods Sold Summarized

The components of the cost of goods sold section of the income statement should now be clear. A comprehensive version of this section showing net cost of purchases and the beginning and ending inventories is presented in Figure 6-3.

Inventory Losses

Many companies have substantial losses from spoilage, shoplifting, and employee pilferage. Under the periodic inventory method, these costs are automatically included in the cost of goods sold. For example, assume

Figure 6-3
Partial Income Statement—Cost of Goods Sold

Hardwick Auto Parts Company
Partial Income Statement
For the Year Ended December, 31, 19xx

Cost of Goods Sold				
Merchandise Inventory, Jan. 1, 19xx			$ 52,800	
Purchases		$126,400		
Less: Purchases Returns and Allowances	$5,640			
Purchases Discounts	2,136	7,776		
Net Purchases		$118,624		
Add Freight In		8,236		
Net Cost of Purchases			126,860	
Cost of Goods Available for Sale			$179,660	
Less Merchandise Inventory, Dec. 31, 19xx			48,300	
Cost of Goods Sold				$131,360

Hardwick Auto Parts Company
Work Sheet
For the Year Ended December 31, 19xx

Account Name	Trial Balance Debit	Trial Balance Credit	Adjustments Debit	Adjustments Credit	Adjusted Trial Balance Debit	Adjusted Trial Balance Credit	Income Statement Debit	Income Statement Credit	Balance Sheet Debit	Balance Sheet Credit
Cash	10,360				10,360				10,360	
Notes Receivable	10,000				10,000				10,000	
Accounts Receivable	42,400				42,400				42,400	
Merchandise Inventory	52,800				52,800		52,800	48,300	48,300	
Prepaid Insurance	17,400			(a) 5,800	11,600				11,600	
Store Supplies	2,600			(b) 1,540	1,060				1,060	
Office Supplies	1,840			(c) 1,204	636				636	
100 Shares, Consolidated Parts	5,000				5,000				5,000	
Land	4,500				4,500				4,500	
Building	20,260				20,260				20,260	
Accumulated Depreciation, Building		5,650		(d) 2,600		8,250				8,250
Delivery Equipment	18,400				18,400				18,400	
Accumulated Depreciation, Delivery Equipment		4,250		(e) 5,200		9,450				9,450
Office Equipment	8,600				8,600				8,600	
Accumulated Depreciation, Office Equipment		2,800		(f) 2,200		5,000				5,000
Trademark	500				500				500	
Notes Payable		15,000				15,000				15,000
Accounts Payable		25,683				25,683				25,683
Salaries Payable		2,000				2,000				2,000
Mortgage Payable		17,800				17,800				17,800
Joseph Hardwick, Capital		100,552				100,552				100,552
Joseph Hardwick, Withdrawals	20,000				20,000				20,000	
Sales		246,350				246,350		246,350		
Sales Returns and Allowances	2,750				2,750		2,750			
Sales Discounts	4,275				4,275		4,275			
Purchases	126,400				126,400		126,400			
Purchases Returns and Allowances		5,640				5,640		5,640		
Purchases Discounts		2,136				2,136		2,136		
Freight In	8,236				8,236		8,236			
Sales Salaries	22,500				22,500		22,500			
Rent Expense, Store Fixtures	5,600				5,600		5,600			
Freight Out	5,740				5,740		5,740			
Advertising Expense	10,000				10,000		10,000			
Office Salaries	26,900				26,900		26,900			
Dividend Income		400				400		400		
Interest Expense	1,200				1,200		1,200			
	428,261	428,261								
Expired Insurance, Selling			(a) 1,600		1,600		1,600			
Expired Insurance, General			(a) 4,200		4,200		4,200			
Store Supplies Used			(b) 1,540		1,540		1,540			
Office Supplies Used			(c) 1,204		1,204		1,204			
Depreciation Expense, Building			(d) 2,600		2,600		2,600			
Depreciation Expense, Delivery Equipment			(e) 5,200		5,200		5,200			
Depreciation Expense, Office Equipment			(f) 2,200		2,200		2,200			
			18,544	18,544	438,261	438,261	284,945	302,826	201,616	183,735
Net Income							17,881			17,881
							302,826	302,826	201,616	201,616

◀ Figure 6-4
Work Sheet for Hardwick Auto Parts Company

that a company lost $1,250 during an accounting period because merchandise had been stolen or spoiled. Consequently, when the physical inventory is taken, the missing items will not be in stock and cannot be counted. Because the ending inventory will not contain these items, the amount subtracted from goods available for sale is less than it would be if the goods were in stock. Cost of goods sold, therefore, is greater by a similar amount.

Work Sheet of a Merchandising Concern

Objective 6
Prepare a work sheet for a merchandising concern

In Chapter 5, the work sheet was presented as a useful tool in preparing adjusting entries, closing entries, and financial statements. To illustrate the accounts unique to the merchandising company, the complete work sheet for Hardwick Auto Parts Company is presented in Figure 6-4. These new accounts are indicated in color in the illustration.

Trial Balance, Adjustments, and Adjusted Trial Balance Columns

In Figure 6-4, the account balances at the end of the year have been entered in the Trial Balance columns. The only adjustments necessary for Hardwick Auto Parts Company are those for expired insurance, supplies used, and depreciation expense. The Adjusted Trial Balance columns are then completed by extending each item in the Trial Balance and Adjustments columns. Up to this point, every step has been done exactly as it would be for a service company.

Income Statement Columns

The difference between the work sheet for a merchandising company and that for a service company, as shown in Chapter 5, is that the cost of goods sold accounts must be brought together in the Income Statement columns. Note that in the work sheet for Hardwick Auto Parts the amounts associated with Sales, Sales Returns and Allowances, Sales Discounts, Purchases, Purchases Returns and Allowances, Purchases Discounts, and Freight In have been extended to the appropriate Income Statement columns. Because these are either revenue or expense accounts, it is obvious that they should appear in those columns.

The extension that may not be obvious is in the Inventory row. Remember that the beginning inventory must be added and the ending inventory subtracted in computing the cost of goods sold in the income statement.

Extending the beginning inventory balance of $52,800 (which is already in the trial balance) to the debit column of the income statement has the effect, illustrated in Figure 6-3, of adding the beginning inventory to net cost of purchases. Inserting the ending inventory balance of $48,300 (which is determined by the physical inventory and is not in the trial balance) to the credit column of the income statement has the effect of subtracting the ending inventory from goods available for sale, as shown in Figure 6-3.

Completing the Work Sheet

The ending inventory is also inserted in the debit column of the balance sheet because it represents the cost of merchandise on hand as a result of the physical inventory at the end of the year. If this is not done, the work sheet will be out of balance.

The work sheet can now be completed in the usual way by sorting the accounts, determining the net income, carrying net income to the balance sheet, and totaling the Balance Sheet columns as a final check. After financial statements are prepared, adjusting and closing entries should be recorded in the general journal and posted to the ledger.

Adjusting Entries

The adjusting entries are now entered in the general journal just as they are for a service company. There is no difference in this technique between a service company and a merchandising company.

Closing Entries

Objective 7 Prepare closing entries for a merchandising concern

Under the periodic inventory system, it is necessary at the end of the period to remove the beginning inventory balance and enter the ending balance for this year in the Merchandise Inventory account. This is done as part of the process of closing entries. The closing entries for Hardwick Auto Parts Company are displayed in Figure 6-5. Note the effect of the closing entries on the Merchandise Inventory account:

1. Before the closing entries, the amount of the beginning inventory appears in the Merchandise Inventory account as a $52,800 debit balance.
2. After the first closing entry, which clears the previous balance, it contains a zero balance.
3. After the second closing entry, which records the new balance, the Merchandise Inventory account has a debit balance of $48,300.

Merchandise Inventory — **Account No. 116**

Date		Item	Post. Ref.	Debit	Credit	Balance Debit	Balance Credit
Jan.	1	Balance				52,800	
Dec.	31				52,800	—	
	31			48,300		48,300	

Figure 6-5 Closing Entries for a Merchandising Concern

General Journal — **Page 1**

Date		Description	Post. Ref.	Debit	Credit
Dec.	31	Income Summary		284,945	
		Merchandise Inventory			52,800
		Sales Returns and Allowances			2,750
		Sales Discounts			4,275
		Purchases			126,400
		Freight In			8,236
		Sales Salaries			22,500
		Rent Expense, Store Fixtures			5,600
		Freight Out			5,740
		Advertising Expense			10,000
		Office Salaries			26,900
		Interest Expense			1,200
		Expired Insurance, Selling			1,600
		Expired Insurance, General			4,200
		Store Supplies Used			1,540
		Office Supplies Used			1,204
		Depreciation Expense, Building			2,600
		Depreciation Expense, Delivery Equipment			5,200
		Depreciation Expense, Office Equipment			2,200
		To close temporary proprietorship accounts having debit balances and to remove beginning inventory			
	31	Merchandise Inventory		48,300	
		Sales		246,350	
		Purchases Returns and Allowances		5,640	
		Purchases Discounts		2,136	
		Dividend Income		400	
		Income Summary			302,826
		To close temporary proprietorship accounts having credit balances and to establish the ending merchandise inventory			
	31	Income Summary		17,881	
		Joseph Hardwick, Capital			17,881
		To close the Income Summary sheet			
	31	Joseph Hardwick, Capital		20,000	
		Joseph Hardwick, Withdrawals			20,000
		To close the Withdrawals account			

Chapter Review

Review of Learning Objectives

1. Identify the components of income statements for merchandising concerns.
The merchandising company differs from the service company in that it attempts to earn a profit by buying and selling merchandise rather than by offering services. The income statement for a merchandising company has three major parts: (1) revenue from sales, (2) cost of goods sold, and (3) operating expenses. The cost of goods sold section is necessary for the computation of gross profit made on the merchandise that has been sold. Merchandisers must sell their merchandise for more than cost to pay operating expenses and have an adequate profit left over.

2. Journalize transactions involving revenue from merchandising concerns.
Revenue from sales consists of gross sales less sales returns and allowances and sales discounts. The amount of the sales discount can be determined from the terms of the sale. Revenue transactions for merchandising firms may be summarized as follows:

Transaction	Related Accounting Entries: Debit	Related Accounting Entries: Credit
Sell merchandise to customer.	Cash (or Accounts Receivable)	Sales
Collect for merchandise sold on credit.	Cash (and Sales Discounts, if applicable)	Accounts Receivable
Permit customers to return merchandise, or grant them a reduction from original price.	Sales Returns and Allowances	Cash (or Accounts Receivable)

3. Calculate cost of goods sold.
To compute cost of goods sold, add beginning merchandise inventory to the net cost of purchases to determine goods available for sale and then subtract ending merchandise inventory from the total.

The net cost of purchases is calculated by subtracting purchases discounts and purchases returns and allowances from gross purchases and then adding any freight-in charges on the purchases. The Purchases account is used only for merchandise purchased for resale. Its sole purpose is to accumulate the total cost of merchandise purchased during an accounting period.

4. Differentiate the perpetual inventory method from the periodic inventory method.
Merchandise inventory may be determined by one of two alternative methods. (1) Under the perpetual inventory method, the balance of the inventory account is kept up to date throughout the year or as items are bought and sold. (2) Under the periodic inventory method, the company waits until the end of the accounting period to take the physical inventory. Merchandise inventory includes all salable goods owned by the concern regardless of where they are located.

5. Journalize transactions involving purchases of merchandise.
The transactions involving purchases may be summarized as follows:

Transaction	Related Accounting Entries: Debit	Related Accounting Entries: Credit
Purchase merchandise for resale.	Purchases	Cash (or Accounts Payable)
Incur transportation charges on merchandise purchased for resale.	Freight In	Cash (or Accounts Payable)
Return unsatisfactory merchandise to supplier, or obtain a reduction from original price.	Cash (or Accounts Payable)	Purchases Returns and Allowances
Pay for merchandise purchased on credit.	Accounts Payable	Cash (and Purchases Discounts, if applicable)

6. Prepare a work sheet for a merchandising concern.
The major difference between preparing a work sheet for a merchandising concern and preparing one for a service company is that there are additional entries for the merchandiser. The accounts necessary to compute cost of goods sold appear in the Income Statement columns. The beginning inventory appears as a debit in the Income Statement columns, and the ending inventory appears as a credit in the Income Statement columns and a debit in the Balance Sheet columns.

7. Prepare closing entries for a merchandising concern.
Closing entries for a merchandising concern are similar to those for a service business except for the treatment of the Merchandise Inventory account. The procedures and entries can be summarized as follows:

Inventory Procedures at End of Period	Related Accounting Entries: Debit	Related Accounting Entries: Credit
Transfer the balance of the beginning inventory to the Income Summary account.	Income Summary	Inventory
Take a physical inventory of goods on hand at the end of the period, and price these goods at cost.	Inventory	Income Summary

Review Problem

Review Figures 6-2 and 6-3, showing the components of the income statement for a merchandising company, and then study Figure 6-4, illustrating the work sheet, before you do the exercises and problems. For additional help, see the review problem in the working papers.

Chapter Assignments

Questions

1. What is the source of revenue for a merchandising concern?
2. Define gross profit from sales.
3. McGuire Nursery had a cost of goods sold during its first year of $64,000 and a gross profit equal to 40 percent of sales. What was the dollar amount of the company's sales?
4. Could McGuire Nursery (in question 3) have a net loss for the year? Explain.
5. Why is it advisable to maintain an account for sales returns and allowances when the same result could be obtained by debiting each return or allowance to the Sales account?
6. What is a sales discount? If the terms are 2/10, n/30, what is the length of the credit period? What is the length of the discount period?
7. What two related transactions are reflected in the T accounts below?

Cash

(b)	980		

Accounts Receivable

(a)	1,000	(b)	1,000

Sales

		(a)	1,000

Sales Discounts

(b)	20		

8. How much is the cash discount on a sale of $2,250 with terms of 2/10, n/60, on which a credit memo for $250 is issued prior to payment?
9. What is the normal balance of the Sales Discounts account? Is it an asset, liability, expense, or contra revenue account?
10. During the current year, Zain Corporation purchased $100,000 in merchandise. Compute the cost of goods sold under each of the following conditions.

	Beginning Inventory	Ending Inventory
a.	—	—
b.	—	$30,000
c.	$30,000	—
d.	28,000	35,000
e.	35,000	28,000

11. Compute cost of goods sold, given the following account balances: Beginning Inventory, $30,000; Purchases, $160,000; Purchases Returns and Allowances, $4,000; Purchases Discounts, $1,600; Freight In, $3,000; Ending Inventory, $25,000.

12. In counting the ending inventory, a clerk counts a $200 item of inventory twice. What effect does this error have on the balance sheet and income statement?
13. Carpenter Hardware purchased the following items: (a) a delivery truck, (b) two dozen hammers, (c) supplies for office workers, (d) a broom for the janitor. Which item should be debited to the Purchases account?
14. What three related transactions are reflected in the T accounts below?

Cash

		(c)	441

Accounts Payable

(b)	50	(a)	500
(c)	450		

Purchases

(a)	500		

Purchases Returns and Allowances

		(b)	50

Purchases Discounts

(c)	9		

15. Is freight in an operating expense? Explain.
16. Prices and terms are quoted from two companies and fifty units of product, as follows: Supplier A—50 at $20 per unit, FOB shipping point; Supplier B—50 at $21 per unit, FOB destination. Which supplier has quoted the best deal? Explain.
17. Does the beginning or ending inventory appear in the trial balance prepared at the end of the year by a company that uses the periodic inventory method?
18. In which columns of the work sheet for a merchandising company does the ending inventory appear?
19. Under the periodic inventory method, how is the amount of inventory at the end of the year determined?
20. Describe the closing entries as they relate to beginning and ending inventory.

Classroom Exercises

Exercise 6-1 Purchases and Sales Involving Discounts

The Miller Company purchased $2,400 of merchandise, terms 2/10, n/30, from the Morgan Company and paid for the merchandise within the discount period.

Give the entries (1) by the Miller Company to record purchase and payment and (2) by the Morgan Company to record the sale and receipt.

Exercise 6-2 Computation of Net Sales

During 19xx, the Illinois Corporation had total sales on credit of $180,000. Of this amount, $120,000 was collected during the year. In addition, the corporation had cash sales of $60,000. Furthermore, customers returned merchandise for credit of $4,000, and cash discounts of $2,000 were allowed. How much would net sales be for the Illinois Corporation for 19xx?

Exercise 6-3 Income Statement Components—Missing Data

Compute the dollar amount of each item indicated by a letter in the table at the top of the next page. Treat each horizontal row of numbers as a separate problem.

Sales	Beginning Inventory	Net Purchases	Ending Inventory	Cost of Goods Sold	Gross Profit	Expenses	Net Income or (Loss)
75,000	a	35,000	10,000	b	40,000	c	10,000
d	12,000	e	18,000	94,000	60,000	40,000	20,000
210,000	22,000	167,000	f	g	50,000	h	(1,000)

Exercise 6-4 Gross Profit Computation—Missing Data

Determine the amount of gross purchases by preparing a partial income statement showing the calculation of gross profit, from the following data: Purchases Discounts, $2,500; Freight In, $11,000; Cost of Goods Sold, $175,000; Sales, $255,000; Beginning Inventory, $15,000; Purchases Returns and Allowances, $4,000; Ending Inventory, $10,000.

Exercise 6-5 Preparation of Income Statement from Work Sheet

The Income Statement columns of the December 31, 19xx, work sheet for Grey Falls General Store appear below. From the information given, prepare a 19xx income statement for the company.

Account Name	Income Statement Debit	Income Statement Credit
Merchandise Inventory	26,000	22,000
Sales		284,000
Sales Returns and Allowances	11,000	
Sales Discounts	4,200	
Purchases	117,300	
Purchases Returns and Allowances		1,800
Purchases Discounts		2,200
Freight In	5,600	
Selling Expenses	48,500	
General and Administrative Expenses	37,200	
	249,800	310,000
Net Income	60,200	
	310,000	310,000

Exercise 6-6 Preparation of Closing Entries

Prepare closing entries from the information given in Exercise 6-5, assuming that Grey Falls General Store is owned by Sam Johnson and that he made withdrawals of $20,000 during the year.

Exercise 6-7 Preparation of Work Sheet

A simplified list of trial balance accounts and their balances follow in alphabetical order: Accounts Payable, $3; Accounts Receivable, $5; Accumulated Depreciation, Store Equipment, $6; Cash, $10; Freight In, $2; General Expense, $15; Merchandise Inventory (Beginning), $8; Prepaid Insurance, $2; Purchases, $35; Purchases Returns and Allowances, $2; Sales, $75; Sales Discounts, $3; Selling Expenses, $22; Store Equipment, $30; Store Supplies, $9; Wendel Wiggins, Capital, $67; Wendel Wiggins, Withdrawals, $12.

Prepare a work sheet form on accounting paper, and copy the trial balance accounts and amounts onto it in the same order as they appear above. Complete the work sheet, using the following information: (a) estimated depreciation on store equipment, $3; (b) ending inventory of store supplies, $2; (c) expired insurance, $1; (d) ending merchandise inventory, $7.

Problem Set A

Problem 6A-1 Merchandising Transactions

Prepare general journal entries to record the following transactions:

July 1 Purchased merchandise on credit from XYZ Company; terms 2/10, n/30, $1,500.

1 Paid Green Freight Company $75 for freight charges on merchandise received.

3 Sold merchandise on credit to John Jones, terms 2/10, n/60, $1,000.

7 Purchased merchandise on credit from ABC Company, terms 1/10, n/30, $2,000.

7 Paid Green Freight Company $85 for freight charges.

8 Purchased office supplies on credit from D & F Supplies, terms 2/10, n/30, $800.

10 Sold merchandise on credit to Harriet Maxey, terms 2/10, n/30, $800.

11 Paid XYZ Company for purchase of July 1.

12 Returned for credit $200 of damaged merchandise received from ABC Company on July 7.

13 Received check from John Jones for his purchase of July 3.

17 Paid ABC Company balance of amount owed from transactions of July 7 and 12.

20 Received payment in full from Harriet Maxey for sale of July 10.

23 Paid D & F Supplies for purchase of July 8.

31 Sold merchandise for cash, $500.

Problem 6A-2 Work Sheet, Income Statement, Closing Entries for Merchandising Company

The trial balance at the top of the next page was taken from the ledger of Montana Sporting Goods Company at the end of its annual accounting period:

Required

1. Enter the trial balance on a work sheet, and complete the work sheet using the following information: (a) ending merchandise inventory, $42,600; (b) ending store supplies inventory, $275; (c) expired insurance, $1,200; (d) estimated depreciation on store equipment, $2,500; (e) accrued sales salaries payable, $325; (f) accrued utilities expense, $50.

2. Prepare an income statement.

3. From the work sheet, prepare closing entries.

4. Open a Merchandise Inventory account, and enter the $35,700 beginning balance. Then post the portions of the closing entries that affect this account.

Cash	$ 2,525	
Accounts Receivable	12,415	
Merchandise Inventory	35,700	
Store Supplies	1,900	
Prepaid Insurance	2,400	
Store Equipment	25,650	
Accumulated Depreciation, Store Equipment		$ 12,150
Accounts Payable		19,475
Monty Montana, Capital		80,675
Monty Montana, Withdrawals	12,000	
Sales		185,625
Sales Returns and Allowances	2,345	
Sales Discounts	1,895	
Purchases	125,200	
Purchases Returns and Allowances		1,575
Purchases Discounts		2,450
Freight In	5,200	
Sales Salaries	32,300	
Rent Expense	24,000	
Other Selling Expense	16,455	
Utilities Expense	1,965	
	$301,950	$301,950

Problem 6A-3 Journalizing Transactions of a Merchandising Company

Prepare general journal entries to record the following transactions:

Aug. 1 Sold merchandise on credit to A. Barlow, terms 2/10, n/60, $400.
2 Purchased merchandise on credit from Spirit Manufacturing Company, terms 2/10, n/30, FOB shipping point, $3,200.
3 Received freight bill for shipment received on August 2, $225.
4 Sold merchandise for cash, $275.
5 Sold merchandise on credit to C. Davis, terms 2/10, n/60, $600.
6 Purchased merchandise from Time Corporation, terms 1/10, n/30, FOB destination, $1,545.
7 Sold merchandise on credit to E. Ferber, terms 2/10, n/20, $1,100.
8 Purchased merchandise from Spirit Manufacturing Company, terms 2/10, n/30, FOB shipping point, $4,100.
9 Received freight bill for shipment of August 8, $365.
10 Received check from A. Barlow for payment in full for sale of August 1.
11 Returned for credit merchandise of the August 6 shipment, which was the wrong size and color, $145.
12 Paid Spirit Manufacturing Company for purchase of August 2.
13 E. Ferber returned some of merchandise sold to him on August 7 for credit, $100.
15 Received payment from C. Davis for one-half of his purchase on August 5. A discount is allowed on partial payment.
16 Paid Time Corporation balance due on account from transactions on August 6 and 11.
17 In checking purchase of August 8 from Spirit Manufacturing Company, accounting department found an overcharge of $200.

18 Paid Spirit Manufacturing Company for correct balance of August 8 purchase.
20 Paid freight company for freight charges during August.
22 Purchased on credit cleaning supplies from Bruce Wholesale, terms n/5, $125.
27 Received payment in full from E. Ferber for transactions on August 7 and 13.
30 Received payment for balance of amount owed from C. Davis from transactions of August 5 and 15.

Problem 6A-4 Work Sheet, Income Statement, and Closing Entries for Merchandising Concern

A trial balance for Sanford Grocery appears below.

Sanford Grocery
Trial Balance
December 31, 19xx

Cash	$ 3,560	
Accounts Receivable	4,215	
Merchandise Inventory	62,500	
Store Supplies	4,780	
Prepaid Insurance	3,600	
Store Equipment	101,200	
Accumulated Depreciation, Store Equipment		$ 27,400
Accounts Payable		35,780
Sandy Sanford, Capital		84,225
Sandy Sanford, Withdrawals	18,000	
Sales		656,400
Sales Returns and Allowances	5,400	
Purchases	468,250	
Purchases Returns and Allowances		8,250
Purchases Discounts		7,900
Freight In	3,200	
Rent Expense	26,000	
Store Salaries	75,500	
Advertising Expense	37,770	
Utility Expense	5,980	
	$819,955	$819,955

Required

1. Copy the trial balance amounts into the Trial Balance columns of a work sheet, and complete the work sheet using the following information: (a) ending merchandise inventory, $56,780; (b) ending store supplies inventory, $580; (c) expired insurance, $1,800; (d) estimated depreciation on store equipment, $10,600; (e) during current year, rent paid through January of next year; amount debited to rent expense and applicable to January of next year, $1,200; (f) accrued store salaries, $250.

2. Prepare a detailed income statement for the grocery store.
3. Prepare closing entries.

Problem 6A-5 Work Sheet, Income Statement, and Closing Entries for Merchandising Concern

A trial balance for R & R Hardware Company appears below.

R & R Hardware Company
Trial Balance
June 30, 19xx

Cash	$ 2,376	
Accounts Receivable	14,647	
Merchandise Inventory	37,842	
Store Equipment	22,200	
Accumulated Depreciation, Store Equipment		$ 14,600
Delivery Truck	7,800	
Accumulated Depreciation, Delivery Truck		1,000
Accounts Payable		9,800
Rick Rhodes, Capital		75,890
Rick Rhodes, Withdrawals	15,000	
Sales		169,300
Sales Returns and Allowances	2,300	
Sales Discounts	980	
Purchases	101,386	
Purchases Returns and Allowances		2,333
Purchases Discounts		2,144
Freight In	786	
Rent Expense	1,800	
Salaries	52,600	
Store Supplies Expense	3,300	
Insurance Expense	1,500	
Advertising Expense	8,200	
Utilities Expense	2,350	
	$275,067	$275,067

Required

1. Copy the trial balance amounts into the Trial Balance columns of a work sheet, and complete the work sheet using the following information: (a) ending merchandise inventory, $42,660; (b) physical inventory revealed $300 of store supplies on hand; (c) estimated depreciation: store equipment, $2,000; delivery truck, $1,000; (d) accrued salaries, $560; (e) examination of the Insurance Expense account indicated that $500 is applicable to next year.
2. Prepare a detailed income statement for the hardware store.
3. Prepare closing entries.
4. Open the Merchandise Inventory account by entering the beginning merchandise inventory, and post closing entries that apply to the account.

Problem 6A-6 Work Sheet, Income Statement, and Closing Entries for Merchandising Concern

A trial balance for May's Fashion Shop is shown below.

May's Fashion Shop
Trial Balance
August 31, 19xx

Cash	$ 2,100	
Accounts Receivable	32,400	
Merchandise Inventory	34,200	
Prepaid Rent	400	
Store Supplies	3,100	
Office Supplies	1,250	
Store Equipment	20,700	
Accumulated Depreciation, Store Equipment		$ 2,100
Office Equipment	4,700	
Accumulated Depreciation, Office Equipment		1,200
Accounts Payable		17,300
Notes Payable		30,000
May Arnold, Capital		55,810
May Arnold, Withdrawals	12,000	
Sales		142,000
Sales Returns and Allowances	2,000	
Purchases	61,400	
Purchases Returns and Allowances		1,400
Purchases Discounts		1,200
Freight In	2,300	
Store Salaries	32,400	
Office Salaries	12,800	
Advertising Expense	24,300	
Rent Expense	2,200	
Insurance Expense	1,200	
Utility Expense	1,560	
	$251,010	$251,010

Required

1. Copy the trial balance into the Trial Balance columns of a work sheet, and complete the work sheet using the following information: (a) ending merchandise inventory, $26,400; (b) ending inventories: store supplies, $220; office supplies, $75; (c) expired rent, $200; (d) estimated depreciation: store equipment, $1,050; office equipment, $800; (e) interest accrued on note payable, $1,500; (f) accrued salaries: store salaries, $225; office salaries, $75.
2. Prepare a detailed income statement for the fashion shop.
3. Prepare closing entries.
4. Open the Merchandise Inventory account by entering the beginning inventory, and post closing entries that apply to the account.

Problem Set B

Problem 6B-1 Merchandising Transactions

Prepare general journal entries to record the following transactions:

Oct. 1 Sold merchandise to Mary O'Brian on credit, terms 2/10, n/30, $400.
2 Purchased merchandise on credit from Trout Company, terms 2/10, n/30, $1,800.
2 Paid Fast Freight $145 for freight charges on merchandise received.
6 Purchased store supplies on credit from Tracy Supply House, terms n/20, $318.
8 Purchased merchandise on credit from RT Company, terms 2/10, n/30, $1,200.
8 Paid Fast Freight $97 for freight charges on merchandise received.
11 Received full payment from Mary O'Brian for her October 1 purchase.
12 Paid Trout Company for purchase of October 2.
13 Sold merchandise on credit to Tom Samson, terms 2/10, n/30, $600.
14 Returned for credit $300 of merchandise received on October 8.
18 Paid RT Company for purchase of October 8.
23 Received full payment from Tom Samson for his October 13 purchase.
26 Paid Tracy Supply House for purchase of October 6.

Problem 6B-2 Work Sheet, Income Statement, and Closing Entries for Merchandising Company

The following trial balance was taken from the ledger of Bittner Book Store at the end of its annual accounting period:

Bittner Book Store
Trial Balance
June 30, 19xx

Cash	$ 3,175	
Accounts Receivable	9,280	
Merchandise Inventory	29,450	
Store Supplies	1,911	
Prepaid Insurance	1,600	
Store Equipment	37,200	
Accumulated Depreciation, Store Equipment		$ 14,700
Accounts Payable		12,300
Ralph Bittner, Capital		41,994
Ralph Bittner, Withdrawals	12,000	
Sales		99,400
Sales Returns and Allowances	987	
Purchases	62,300	
Purchases Returns and Allowances		19,655
Purchases Discounts		1,356
Freight In	2,261	
Sales Salaries	21,350	
Rent Expense	3,600	
Other Selling Expense	2,614	
Utilities Expense	1,677	
	$189,405	$189,405

Required

1. Enter the trial balance on a work sheet, and complete the work sheet using the following information: (a) ending merchandise inventory, $31,772; (b) ending store supplies inventory, $304; (c) unexpired insurance, $200; (d) estimated depreciation on store equipment, $4,300; (e) accrued sales salaries payable, $80; (f) accrued utilities expense, $150.
2. Prepare an income statement.
3. From the work sheet, prepare closing entries.
4. Open a Merchandise Inventory account, and enter the $29,450 beginning balance. Then post the portions of the closing entries that affect this account.

Problem 6B-3 Journalizing Transactions of a Merchandising Company

Prepare general journal entries to record the following transactions:

Jan. 2 Purchased merchandise on credit from TCP Company, terms 2/10, n/30, FOB destination, $5,600.
3 Sold merchandise on credit to S. Moses, terms 1/10, n/30, $1,000.
5 Sold merchandise for cash, $700.
6 Purchased merchandise on credit from Jackson Company, terms 2/10, n/30, FOB shipping point, $4,200.
7 Received freight bill from Midway Express for shipment received on January 6, $570.
9 Sold merchandise on credit to T. Jesse, terms 1/10, n/30, $3,800.
10 Purchased merchandise from TCP Company, terms 2/10, n/30, FOB shipping point, $2,650.
11 Received freight bill from Midway Express for shipment received on January 10, $291.
12 Paid TCP Company for purchase of January 2.
13 Received payment in full for S. Moses's purchase of January 3.
14 Returned faulty merchandise worth $300 to TCP Company for credit against purchase of January 10.
16 Paid Jackson Company one-half of amount owed from purchase of January 6.
17 Sold merchandise to T. Mayer on credit, terms 2/10, n/30, $780.
19 Received payment from T. Jesse for one-half the purchase of January 9.
20 Paid TCP Company in full for amount owed on purchase of January 10 less return on January 14.
22 Gave credit to T. Mayer for returned merchandise, $180.
26 Paid freight company for freight charges during January.
27 Received payment of amount owed by T. Mayer from purchase of January 17 less credit of January 22.
28 Paid Jackson Company for balance of January 6 purchase.

Problem 6B-4 Work Sheet, Income Statement, and Closing Entries for Merchandising Concern

A trial balance for Battershell's Shoe Store appears on the next page.

Required

1. Copy the trial balance amounts into the Trial Balance columns of a work sheet, and complete the work sheet using the following information: (a) ending merchandise inventory, $29,350; (b) ending store supplies inventory, $288; (c) expired insurance, $2,400; (d) estimated depreciation on store equipment, $8,800; (e) advertising expense includes $1,470 for January clearance sale advertisements, which will begin appearing on January 2; (f) accrued store salaries, $320.
2. Prepare a detailed income statement for the shoe store.
3. Prepare closing entries.

Battershell's Shoe Store
Trial Balance
December 31, 19xx

Cash	$ 2,675	
Accounts Receivable	19,307	
Merchandise Inventory	26,500	
Store Supplies	951	
Prepaid Insurance	2,600	
Store Equipment	32,000	
Accumulated Depreciation, Store Equipment		$ 19,500
Accounts Payable		22,366
Ellen Battershell, Capital		63,601
Ellen Battershell, Withdrawals	15,000	
Sales		103,000
Sales Returns and Allowances	2,150	
Purchases	61,115	
Purchases Returns and Allowances		17,310
Purchases Discounts		1,300
Freight In	2,144	
Rent Expense	4,800	
Store Salaries	41,600	
Advertising Expense	14,056	
Utility Expense	2,179	
	$227,077	$227,077

Problem 6B-6 Work Sheet, Income Statement, and Closing Entries for Merchandising Concern

The year-end trial balance for Obie's Camera Store appears on the next page.

Required

1. Copy the trial balance amounts into the Trial Balance columns of a work sheet, and complete the work sheet using the following information: (a) ending merchandise inventory, $182,657; (b) ending inventories: store supplies, $362; office supplies, $412; (c) estimated depreciation: store equipment, $1,800; office equipment, $1,850; (d) interest accrued on notes payable, $2,500; (e) accrued salaries: store salaries, $1,050; office salaries, $100; (f) accrued utility expense, $1,443.
2. Prepare a detailed income statement for the camera store.
3. Prepare closing entries.
4. Open the Merchandise Inventory account by entering the beginning inventory, and post closing entries that apply to the account.

Obie's Camera Store
Trial Balance
June 30, 19xx

Cash	$ 4,657	
Accounts Receivable	34,770	
Merchandise Inventory	176,551	
Prepaid Rent	1,200	
Store Supplies	826	
Office Supplies	1,226	
Store Equipment	26,400	
Accumulated Depreciation, Store Equipment		$ 5,600
Office Equipment	9,350	
Accumulated Depreciation, Office Equipment		3,700
Accounts Payable		56,840
Notes Payable		50,000
Obie Bauer, Capital		155,440
Obie Bauer, Withdrawals	18,000	
Sales		396,457
Sales Returns and Allowances	11,250	
Purchases	218,350	
Purchases Returns and Allowances		26,450
Purchases Discounts		3,788
Freight In	10,078	
Store Salaries	106,500	
Office Salaries	26,400	
Advertising Expense	18,200	
Rent Expense	14,400	
Insurance Expense	2,800	
Utility Expense	17,317	
	$698,275	$698,275

Learning Objectives

Chapter Seven

General-Purpose External Financial Statements

1. *State the objectives of financial reporting.*
2. *Identify and describe the basic components of a classified balance sheet.*
3. *Distinguish between the multistep and single-step types of classified income statements.*
4. *Relate a chart of accounts to classified financial statements.*
5. *Use classified financial statements for the simple evaluation of liquidity and profitability.*
6. *Identify some of the differences in the financial statements of corporations and proprietorships.*

Financial statements are the central feature of financial reporting. In this chapter, you will learn first how the balance sheet and income statement may be divided into special categories and then how to use these categories to evaluate a business. Finally, a series of annotated financial statements will give you a realistic picture of a major corporation's economic activities. As a result of studying this chapter, you should be able to meet the learning objectives listed on the left.

Financial reporting has both internal and external aspects. Internal management has an interest in the resources, obligations, and earnings of the enterprise and in changes in these items. In addition, management is responsible for informing those outside the business about the financial position and performance of the company. Financial statements are the principal means of communicating accounting information to external users. To enhance their reliability, these financial statements are often audited by independent accountants. This chapter focuses on the objectives, form, and evaluation of financial statements in external reporting.

Objectives of Financial Information[1]

The United States has a highly developed exchange economy. In an exchange economy, most goods and services are exchanged for money or claims to money instead of being consumed or bartered by their producers. Most productive activity is carried on through

1. The discussion in this section is based on "Objectives of Financial Reporting by Business Enterprises," *Statement of Financial Accounting Concepts No. 1* (Stamford, Conn.: Financial Accounting Standards Board, November 1978), par. 6–16 and 28–40.

investor-owned business enterprises, including many large corporations that buy, sell, and obtain financing in national and multinational markets. Those who invest in companies are interested primarily in returns from dividends and market prices of their investments, rather than in actually managing the business. Creditors are interested in the ability of business enterprises to repay debt according to the loan terms. Therefore, investors and creditors have a common interest in the ability of an enterprise to generate favorable cash flows. Financial statements are important to both groups in making this judgment.

Objective 1 State the objectives of financial reporting

Business enterprises raise additional capital for production and marketing activities through financial institutions, small groups, and the public at large by issuing equity and debt securities that are widely traded in the market. Financial statements provide valuable information that enables such investors and creditors to judge a company's ability to pay dividends and pay back debts with interest. Thus they help the market allocate scarce resources to enterprises that use them efficiently and away from inefficient enterprises.

The needs of users and the general business environment described above provide the basis for the Financial Accounting Standards Board's three objectives of financial reporting:

1. To furnish information useful in making investment and credit decisions Financial reporting should provide information that is useful to present and potential investors and creditors as well as to other users in making rational investment and credit decisions. The information should be comprehensible to those who have a reasonable understanding of business and economic activities and are willing to study the information carefully.

2. To provide information useful in assessing cash flow prospects Financial reporting should supply information to help present and potential investors and creditors and other users judge the amounts, timing, and uncertainty of prospective cash receipts from dividends or interest and the proceeds from the sale, redemption, or maturity of securities or loans.

3. To provide information about enterprise resources, claims to those resources, and changes in them Financial reporting should provide information about the economic resources of an enterprise, the obligations of the enterprise to transfer resources to other entities and owner's equity, and the effects of transactions or other events that change its resources and claims to those resources.

General-purpose external financial statements are the principal means of periodically communicating the information that has been accumulated and processed in the financial accounting system to investors, creditors, and other users outside the enterprise. For this reason, these statements—the balance sheet, the income statement, the statement of owner's equity, and the statement of changes in financial position—are the most important output of the accounting system. These financial statements are "general purpose" because of their potential use to a wide and diverse audience. They are "external" because these users are outside the enterprise. Because there may be a conflict between management, who must prepare the financial statements, and the investors or creditors, who invest in or lend money to the enterprise, financial statements are often audited by independent accountants to increase confidence in their reliability.

So far in this book, balance sheets have listed the balances of accounts that fell in the categories of assets, liabilities, and owner's equity, and income statements have listed the balances of accounts that fell in the categories of revenues and expenses. Because even a moderate-size company will have hundreds of accounts, merely listing these accounts by broad categories is not very helpful to a statement user. Creating subcategories within the major categories will often increase the usefulness of the financial statements, however. Investors and creditors often analyze and evaluate the relationships among the subcategories. When general-purpose external financial statements are divided into useful subcategories, they are called **classified financial statements.**

Classified Balance Sheet

Objective 2 Identify and describe the basic components of a classified balance sheet

The balance sheet portrays the financial position of a company at a particular time. The classified balance sheet shown in Figure 7-1 contains subdivisions that are typical of most companies in the United States. The subdivisions under owner's equity of course depend on the form of business.

Assets

The assets of a company are often divided into four categories: (1) current assets; (2) investments; (3) property, plant, and equipment; and (4) intangible assets. Some companies include a fifth category called other assets if there are miscellaneous assets that do not fall into any of the other categories. These categories are listed in the order of their presumed liquidity (the ease with which an asset can be converted into cash). For example, current assets are considered to be more liquid than property, plant, and equipment.

Current Assets The Accounting Principles Board has set up guidelines for defining **current assets:**

> Current assets are defined as . . . cash or other assets that are reasonably expected to be realized in cash or sold during a normal operating cycle of a business or within one year if the operating cycle is shorter than one year.[2]

The normal operating cycle of a company is the average time required to go from cash to cash. Cash is used to purchase merchandise inventory,

2. Accounting Principles Board, *Statement of the Accounting Principles Board, No. 4* (New York: American Institute of Certified Public Accountants, 1970), par. 198.

Figure 7-1
Classified Balance Sheet for Hardwick Auto Parts Company

Know for final exam

Hardwick Auto Parts Company
Balance Sheet
December 31, 19xx

Assets			
Current Assets			
Cash		$10,360	
Temporary Investments		2,000	
Notes Receivable		8,000	
Accounts Receivable		42,400	
Merchandise Inventory		48,300	
Prepaid Insurance		11,600	
Store Supplies		1,060	
Office Supplies		636	
Total Current Assets			$124,356
Investments			
Land Held for Future Use			5,000
Property, Plant, and Equipment			
Land		$ 4,500	
Building	$20,650		
Less Accumulated Depreciation	8,640	12,010	
Delivery Equipment	$18,400		
Less Accumulated Depreciation	9,450	8,950	
Office Equipment	$ 8,600		
Less Accumulated Depreciation	5,000	3,600	
Total Property, Plant, and Equipment			$ 29,060
Intangible Assets			
Trademark			500
Total Assets			$158,916
Liabilities			
Current Liabilities			
Notes Payable	$15,000		
Accounts Payable	25,683		
Salaries Payable	2,000		
Total Current Liabilities		$42,683	
Long-Term Liabilities			
Mortgage Payable		17,800	
Total Liabilities			$ 60,483
Owner's Equity			
Joseph Hardwick, Capital			98,433
Total Liabilities and Owner's Equity			$158,916

which is sold for cash or for a promise of cash (a receivable) if the sale is made on account (for credit). If the sales are on account, the resulting receivables must be collected before the cycle is completed.

The normal operating cycle for most companies is less than one year, but there are exceptions. Tobacco companies, for example, must cure the tobacco for two or three years before their inventory is salable. The tobacco inventory is still considered a current asset because it will be sold within the normal operating cycle. Another example is a company that sells on the installment basis. The collection payments for a television set or stove may be as long as twenty-four or thirty-six months, but these receivables are still considered current assets.

Cash is obviously a current asset. Temporary investments, accounts and notes receivable, and inventory are also current assets because they are expected to be converted to cash within the next year or during the normal operating cycle of most firms. They are listed in the order of the ease of their conversion into cash.

Prepaid expenses, such as rent and insurance paid for in advance, and inventories of various supplies acquired for use rather than for sale should also be classified as current assets. These kinds of property are current in the sense that, if they had not previously been purchased, a current outlay of cash would be needed to obtain them. They are an exception to the current asset definition presented earlier.[3]

In determining whether or not an asset is current or noncurrent, the notion of "reasonable expectation" is important. For example, temporary investments represent an account used for temporary or short-term investments of idle cash or cash not immediately required for operating purposes. As a need for cash arises, these securities will be sold to meet this need. Investments in securities that management does not anticipate selling within the next year and that do not involve the temporary use of idle cash should be shown in the investments category of a classified balance sheet.

In addition, since it is not probable that all the accounts receivable will ultimately be collected, an Allowance for Uncollectible (or Doubtful) Accounts should be established. This allowance is shown as a deduction from Accounts Receivable. The resulting net Accounts Receivable represents the cash reasonably expected to be collected. Temporary Investments and the Allowance for Uncollectible Accounts are discussed in Chapter 10.

Investments The investments category includes assets, generally of a long-term nature, that are not used in the normal operation of a business and that management does not intend to convert to cash within the next year. Items included in this category are securities held for long-run investment, land held for future use, plant or equipment not used in the business, and special funds such as a fund established to pay off a debt or

3. *Accounting Research and Terminology Bulletin*, First Edition (New York: American Institute of Certified Public Accountants, 1961), p. 20.

buy a building. Also included in this category are substantial investments of a permanent nature in another company for the purpose of controlling that company.

Property, Plant, and Equipment The **property, plant, and equipment** category includes assets of a long-term nature that are used in the continuing operation of the business. They represent a place to operate (land and buildings) and equipment to produce, sell, deliver, and service its products. For this reason, they are often called operating assets or sometimes fixed assets, tangible assets, or long-lived assets. We have seen in previous chapters that, through depreciation, the cost of these assets (except land) is spread over the periods they benefit. Prior depreciation is represented by the accumulated depreciation accounts. The exact order in which property, plant, and equipment are listed is not uniform in practice. Assets not used in the regular course of business should be listed in the investments category, as noted above. Chapters 13 and 14 are devoted largely to property, plant, and equipment.

Intangible Assets The category of **intangible assets** includes assets of a long-term nature that have no physical substance but have a value based on rights or privileges accruing to the owner. Examples are patents, copyrights, goodwill, franchises, and trademarks. These assets are recorded at cost, which is spread over the expected life of the right or privilege. These assets are discussed in more detail in Chapter 14.

Liabilities

Liabilities are divided into two categories: current liabilities and long-term liabilities.

Current Liabilities The category called **current liabilities** is made up of obligations due within the normal operating cycle of the business or within a year, whichever is longer. They are usually paid from current assets or by incurring new short-term liabilities. In this category are notes payable, accounts payable, wages payable, taxes payable, and customer advances (unearned revenues). Current liabilities are discussed in more detail in Chapter 12.

Long-Term Liabilities Debts of a business entity that fall due more than one year ahead, beyond the normal operating cycle, or are to be paid out of noncurrent assets are **long-term liabilities**. Mortgages payable, long-term notes, bonds payable, employee pension obligations, and long-term lease liabilities typically fall in this category.

Owner's Equity

The terms *owner's equity, proprietorship, capital,* and *net worth* are used interchangeably. They represent the ownership interest in the company. The first three terms are considered better usage than *net worth* because assets are recorded at original cost rather than at current value; thus the ownership section will not represent "worth."

The accounting treatment of assets and liabilities is not usually affected by the form of business organization. However, the owner's equity section of the balance sheet will be different depending on whether the business is organized as a sole proprietorship, a partnership, or a corporation.

Sole Proprietorship The owner's equity section of a sole proprietorship appears as shown in the balance sheet for Hardwick Auto Parts Company (Figure 7-1). In previous chapters, the increases and decreases in owner's equity resulting from earnings, investments, and withdrawals appeared in this section of the balance sheets. In practice, it is common to prepare a statement called the statement of owner's equity (Figure 7-4) to show these transactions.

Partnership The owners' equity section of the balance sheet for a partnership is called partners' equity and is similar to that of the sole proprietorship. An example of this section follows:

Partners' Equity

A. J. Martin, Capital	$21,666	
R. C. Moore, Capital	35,724	
Total Partners' Capital		$57,390

Corporation Corporations are by law separate and legal entities. The owners are the stockholders. The stockholders' equity section of a balance sheet consists of two parts: contributed or paid-in capital and retained earnings. An illustration follows:

Stockholders' Equity

Contributed Capital		
Common Stock—$10 par value, 5,000 shares authorized, issued, and outstanding	$50,000	
Amounts Contributed in Excess of Par Value	10,000	
Total Contributed Capital		$60,000
Retained Earnings		37,500
Total Stockholders' Equity		$97,500

Recall that owners' equity accounts represent sources of and claims on assets. Of course, these claims are not on any particular asset but rather a cross-section of all assets. It follows, then, that contributed and earned capital accounts of a corporation measure stockholders' claims on corporate property and also represent sources of corporate property. Contributed or paid-in capital accounts reveal the amounts of assets invested by stockholders themselves. Usually, contributed capital is represented on corporate balance sheets by two amounts: (1) the face or par amount of issued stock, and (2) amounts contributed in excess of the face or par amount per share. In the preceding illustration, stockholders evidently invested amounts equal to par amount of outstanding stock (5,000 × $10) plus an additional $10,000.

The **Retained Earnings** account is sometimes called Earned Capital because it represents the amount of assets earned during profitable operations and plowed back into, or reinvested in, corporate operations. Distributions of assets to shareholders, called dividends, reduce the Retained Earnings account balance just as withdrawals of assets by the owner of a business reduce his or her capital account balance. Thus the Retained Earnings account balance also shows the amount of earned assets that have not been distributed to shareholders.

Classified Income Statement

The income statement for a period represents the revenues earned, expenses incurred, gains, losses, and net income (or net loss) recognized during the period. The information presented in this statement is usually considered the most important information provided by financial accounting because profit-directed activity is a paramount concern to those interested in the enterprise. There are two common forms of the income statement, the multistep form and the single-step form.

Objective 3 Distinguish between the multistep and single-step types of classified income statements

Each of these forms of the income statement has advantages and disadvantages. Currently, about an equal number of large United States companies use each type. The **multistep form,** which arrives at net income in steps, provides more detail but may overwhelm the reader. The **single-step form,** which arrives at net income in a single step, has the advantage of simplicity but perhaps gives too little information. Figure 7-2 shows a multistep income statement for Hardwick Auto Parts Company, and Figure 7-3 shows the same statement in single-step form.

In Chapter 6, the discussion of accounting for merchandising concerns covered in detail the major sections of revenue and cost of goods sold of the multistep form. Note that revenue minus cost of goods sold equals gross profit from sales. In a successful operation, this amount is sufficiently larger than operating expenses, income taxes, and other deductions to leave a satisfactory net income. Several of the items in the multistep statement have not been discussed so far. These are operating expenses, income from operations, and financing revenues and expenses. Income tax expense and earnings per share information do not appear on the income statement of Hardwick Auto Parts Company because they apply to corporation accounting.

Operating Expenses

The operating expenses category consists of selling expenses and general and administrative expenses. Selling expenses include all expenses of

Figure 7-2 Multistep Income Statement for Hardwick Auto Parts Company

Hardwick Auto Parts Company
Income Statement
For the Year Ended December 31, 19xx

Revenue			
Net Sales			$239,325
Cost of Goods Sold			
Merchandise Inventory, Jan. 1, 19xx		$ 52,800	
Net Purchases	$118,624		
Freight In	8,236	126,860	
Goods Available for Sale		$179,660	
Merchandise Inventory, Dec. 31, 19xx		48,300	
Cost of Goods Sold			131,360
Gross Profit from Sales			$107,965
Operating Expenses			
Selling Expenses			
Sales Salaries	$ 22,500		
Rent Expense, Store Fixture	5,600		
Freight Out	5,740		
Advertising Expense	10,000		
Expired Insurance, Selling	1,600		
Store Supplies Used	1,540		
Depreciation Expense, Building	2,600		
Depreciation Expense, Delivery Equipment	5,200		
Total Selling Expenses		$ 54,780	
General and Administrative Expenses			
Office Salaries	$ 26,900		
Expired Insurance, General	4,200		
Office Supplies Used	1,204		
Depreciation Expense, Office Equipment	2,200		
Total General and Administrative Expenses		34,504	
Total Operating Expenses			$ 89,284
Income from Operations			$ 18,681
Financing Revenues and Expenses			
Dividend Income		$ 400	
Less Interest Expense		1,200	
Excess Expense over Revenue			800
Net Income			$ 17,881

Figure 7-3 Single-Step Income Statement for Hardwick Auto Parts Company

Hardwick Auto Parts Company Income Statement For the Year Ended December 31, 19xx		
Revenues		
Net Sales	$239,325	
Dividend Income	400	
Total Revenues		$239,725
Operating Costs		
Cost of Goods Sold	$131,360	
Selling Expenses	54,780	
General and Administrative Expenses	34,504	
Interest Expense	1,200	
Total Operating Costs		221,844
Net Income		$ 17,881

storing and preparing goods for sale; displaying, advertising, and otherwise promoting sales; actually making sales; and delivering the goods purchased if the cost of delivery is paid by the seller. General and administrative expenses include expenditures related to the general office, accounting, personnel, credit and collections, and other general expenses.

If the sales and administrative expense categories found on multistep income statements are to reflect operating costs accurately, expenses applicable to both categories should be split up and included in the proper category to reflect this fact. For example, Hardwick Auto Parts Company has allocated insurance expense between the sales and administrative categories.

Income from Operations

The excess of gross profit from sales over operating expenses equals **income from operations.** If operating expenses should exceed gross profit, the excess is called net loss from operations.

Financing Revenues and Expenses

The financing revenues and expenses section of the multistep income statement is a distinct category. It receives special emphasis because these kinds of revenue and expense usually arise from various nonoperating aspects of business activity. **Financing revenues and expenses** include revenues from investments, such as dividends and interest from security holdings and savings accounts, and interest earned on credit or notes extended to customers. Included also are interest expense and other expenses incurred as a result of borrowing money or of credit being extended to the company. Interest expense is considered a nonoperating expense because it represents a charge for using creditors' funds and therefore is a financial rather than an operating expense. If the company has other items of revenue and expense unrelated to normal business operations, they too are classified in this section of the income statement.

Other Financial Statements

Two additional statements considered necessary to an understanding of a firm's financial operations are the statement of owner's equity and the statement of changes in financial position.

The statement of owner's equity for Hardwick Auto Parts Company is shown in Figure 7-4. The statement of retained earnings for a corporation is very similar. In place of the beginning and ending balances of capital are the beginning and ending balances of retained earnings. Substituted for withdrawals are dividends paid to stockholders. Net income is added in a similar manner in the statement of retained earnings. Later in this chapter, we present the retained earnings statement of a major corporation. Chapters 16–18 deal with the special problems of the equity section of the balance sheet for corporations.

A simple version of the statement of changes in financial position was shown in Chapter 2. A more complicated one appears in Figure 7-8, near the end of this chapter. This important statement is discussed in detail in Chapter 19.

Chart of Accounts

Classified financial statements are constructed, of course, from the ledger accounts. Thus the ledger accounts are arranged in the same order as in

Figure 7-4
Statement of Owner's Equity for Hardwick Auto Parts Company

Hardwick Auto Parts Company
Statement of Owner's Equity
December 31, 19xx

Harry Hardwick, Capital, Jan. 1, 19xx		$100,552	
Net Income for the year	$17,881		
Withdrawals	20,000		
Excess of earnings over withdrawals		(2,119)	
Harry Hardwick, Capital, Dec. 31, 19xx			$98,433

Objective 4 Relate a chart of accounts to classified financial statements

the financial statements. Furthermore, because it is necessary to find accounts quickly for posting and for management purposes, most companies have a systematic numbering scheme for identifying the accounts in the ledger, called the **chart of accounts.** The account number tells both the location of the account and its financial statement classification. Each company develops a chart of accounts that is most appropriate for its operations, and it would be only a coincidence if two companies had the same numbering scheme. A common three-digit numbering system that would be appropriate for a merchandising firm will be used in our example.

The first digit refers to the major financial statement classification. An account number beginning with the digit 1 is an asset, an account number beginning with the digit 2 is a liability, and so forth. In our example, 111 to 199 are assigned to asset accounts, 211 to 299 to liability accounts, 311 to 399 to owner's equity accounts, 411 to 499 to sales or revenue accounts, 511 to 599 to cost of goods sold accounts, 611 to 699 to operating expense accounts, and 711 to 799 to other revenue and expense accounts.

The second digit refers to the subclassification of each major statement category. For example, under the asset accounts (111–199), subdivisions 111 to 129 are current assets accounts (second digits of 1 and 2), 131 to 139 are investment accounts (second digit of 3), 141 to 159 are property, plant, and equipment asset accounts (second digits of 4 and 5), and 161 to 179 are intangible asset accounts (second digits of 6 and 7).

The third digit refers to the specific account. On the basis of this numbering scheme, the chart of accounts for Hardwick Auto Parts Company would appear as in Table 7-1 (next page).

Using Classified Financial Statements

Objective 5 Use classified financial statements for the simple evaluation of liquidity and profitability

A major reason for classifying financial statements is to aid in the evaluation of a business. Although the analysis and interpretation of financial statements is the subject of Chapter 21, it is helpful at this point to indicate briefly how classified financial statements can be used to show meaningful relationships. Recall from earlier in this chapter that the objectives of financial reporting, according to the Financial Accounting Standards Board, are to provide information useful in making investment and credit decisions, in assessing cash flow prospects, and in aiding the understanding of enterprise resources and obligations and changes in them. These objectives are related to two of the more important goals of management (explained in Chapter 1)—those of (1) maintaining adequate liquidity and (2) achieving satisfactory profitability—because the decisions made by investors and creditors are based largely on their assessment of the firm's potential liquidity and profitability. The following analysis focuses on these two management goals.

Table 7-1 Hardwick Auto Parts Company Chart of Accounts

Account	No.	Account	No.
Cash	111	Sales	411
Temporary Investments	112	Sales Returns and Allowances	412
Notes Receivable	113	Sales Discounts	413
Accounts Receivable	114	Purchases	511
Merchandise Inventory	116	Purchases Returns and Allowances	512
Prepaid Insurance	117	Purchases Discounts	513
Store Supplies	118	Freight In	514
Office Supplies	119	Sales Salaries	611
Investments	131	Rent Expense, Store Fixtures	612
Land	141	Freight Out	613
Building	142	Advertising Expense	614
Accumulated Depreciation, Building	143	Expired Insurance, Selling	615
Delivery Equipment	144	Office Supplies Used	616
Accumulated Depreciation, Delivery Equipment	145	Depreciation Expense, Building	617
Office Equipment	146	Depreciation Expense, Delivery Equipment	618
Accumulated Depreciation, Office Equipment	147	Office Salaries	631
Trademark	161	Expired Insurance, General	632
Notes Payable	211	Office Supplies Used	633
Accounts Payable	212	Depreciation Expense, Office Equipment	634
Salaries Payable	213	Dividend Income	711
Mortgage Payable	221	Interest Expense	721
Joseph Hardwick, Capital	311		
Joseph Hardwick, Withdrawals	312		

Evaluation of Liquidity

Liquidity means having enough funds on hand to (1) pay a company's bills when they are due and (2) provide for unanticipated needs for cash. Two common measures of liquidity are working capital and the current ratio.

Working Capital The first measure, **working capital,** is the amount by which total current assets exceed total current liabilities. This is an important measure of liquidity, because current liabilities are debts to be paid within one year and current assets are assets to be realized in cash within one year. By definition, current liabilities will be paid out by current assets, and therefore the excess of current assets over current liabilities represents a pool of funds available to continue business operations. It represents the funds or working capital available to purchase inventory, obtain credit, and finance expanded sales. Lack of working capital can lead to the failure of a company. For Hardwick Auto Parts Company, the working capital is computed as follows:

Current Assets	$124,356
Less Current Liabilities	42,683
Working Capital	$ 81,673

As indicated previously, changes in working capital from one period to the next are subjected to close scrutiny in the statement of changes in financial position.

Current Ratio The second measure of liquidity, current ratio, is closely related to working capital and is considered by many bondholders and other kinds of creditors to be a good indicator of a company's ability to pay its bills and to repay outstanding loans. The current ratio is the ratio of current assets to current liabilities. For Hardwick Auto Parts Company, it would be computed as follows:

$$\text{current ratio} = \frac{\text{current assets}}{\text{current liabilities}} = \frac{\$124{,}356}{\$42{,}683} = 2.9$$

Intelligent evaluation of the current ratio of a company necessitates a comparison of this year's ratio with those of previous years and with similar measures in successful companies in the same industry. If other factors were acceptable, however, most analysts would consider a ratio of 3:1—that is, $3 of current assets for each $1 of current liabilities—to be a satisfactory measure of financial liquidity.

Evaluation of Profitability

Equally important as paying one's bills on time is the objective of **profitability**—the ability to earn a satisfactory level of profits. As an objective, profitability competes with liquidity for managerial attention because liquid assets, while important, are not the best profit-producing resources. Cash, for example, means purchasing power, but a satisfactory profit will result only if purchasing power is used to buy profit-producing (and less liquid) assets such as inventory and long-term assets.

Among the common measures that relate to a company's ability to make a profit are (1) profit margin, (2) return on assets, (3) capital structure, and (4) return on owner's investment. To evaluate a company meaningfully, one must relate a company's profit performance to its past and its prospects as well as to the norms (averages) of other firms competing in the same industry.

Profit Margin The **profit margin** indicates the percentage of each sales dollar that results in net income. It is calculated by dividing net income by sales. For Hardwick Auto Parts Company, it is as follows:

$$\text{profit margin} = \frac{\text{net income}}{\text{sales}} = \frac{\$17{,}881}{\$239{,}325} = .075\ (7.5\%)$$

On each dollar of sales, Hardwick Auto Parts Company made 7.5¢. A difference of 1 or 2 percent in a company's profit margin may mean the difference between a fair year and a very profitable one.

Return on Assets The profit margin does not take into consideration the assets necessary to produce the income. The **return on assets** ratio overcomes this deficiency by relating net income to total assets. This ratio reflects the relationship between an income statement measure and a balance sheet measure. For Hardwick Auto Parts Company, it is computed as follows:

$$\text{return on assets} = \frac{\text{net income}}{\text{total assets}} = \frac{\$17{,}881}{\$158{,}916} = .11 \text{ (or 11\%)}$$

This measure shows how efficiently a company is using all its assets. It also indicates the income-generating strength of a firm's resources. Thus, for each dollar invested, Hardwick Auto Parts Company's assets generated 11¢ of income.

Capital Structure Another useful measure indicates how much of the total assets is financed by creditors in the form of liabilities. The **capital structure** is the proportion of the company financed by creditors as opposed to owners. One way of measuring capital structure is to calculate the ratio of total liabilities to total assets. Capital structure is sometimes expressed as the ratio of debt to owner's investment and called the debt to equity ratio. We have chosen to use the total liabilities to total assets measure. The capital structure ratio does not fit neatly into either the liquidity or profitability category. It has obvious importance to liquidity analysis because it relates to debt and its repayment. However, it is relevant to profitability for two reasons. First, creditors are interested in the proportion of the business that is debt financed because the more debt a company has, the more profit it must earn to protect the payment of interest to the creditors. Second, owners are interested in the proportion of the business that is debt financed because the amount of interest that must be paid affects the amount of profit that is left to provide a return on owners' investment (see next ratio below).[4] The capital structure ratio also reveals how much expansion is made possible by borrowing additional long-term funds. For Hardwick Auto Parts Company, 38 percent of its assets are financed by creditors:

$$\text{capital structure} = \frac{\text{total liabilities}}{\text{total assets}} = \frac{\$60{,}483}{\$158{,}976} = .38 \text{ (or 38\%)}$$

Because almost 40 percent of Hardwick Auto Parts Company is financed by creditors, roughly 60 percent is financed by Harry Hardwick's capital.

4. For a more detailed discussion of this topic, see *Statement of Financial Accounting Standards No. 34*, "Capitalization of Interest Costs" (Stamford, Conn.; Financial Accounting Standards Board, 1979).

Return on Owner Investment Obviously, Harry Hardwick is concerned about how much he as the owner earned on his investment in the business. This ratio requires that an income statement item be related to a balance sheet item (owner's equity). His **return on owner investment** is measured by the ratio of net income to owner's equity as follows:

$$\text{return on owner investment} = \frac{\text{net income}}{\text{owner's equity}}$$

$$= \frac{\$17{,}881}{\$98{,}443} = .18 \text{ (or 18\%)}$$

Thus Hardwick Auto Parts Company has earned 18¢ for every dollar invested by the owner, Harry Hardwick.

Financial Statements of a Major Corporation

Objective 6 Identify some of the differences in the financial statements of corporations and proprietorships

Thus far, very simple financial statements have been presented for sole proprietorships. Statements for corporations, however, are quite complicated and have many additional features. Figures 7-5 to 7-9 present the financial statements of a well-known firm, McDonald's Corporation. These statements are filed annually with the Securities and Exchange Commission. They are also a part of the company's annual report, which is printed and distributed each year to stockholders or others who request copies. The published annual report usually includes a number of features in addition to the financial statements. Among these are the president's letter to the stockholders, a list of the principal officers of the corporation, descriptions and pictures of the products and operations, and other items of interest.

Here, the focus is on the financial statements and the important features accompanying them. Each feature of the financial statements discussed is keyed to a numbered text paragraph. As beginning accounting students, you are not expected to understand everything in the report, but you should be able to relate these statements to the simpler ones for the Hardwick Auto Parts Company.

Consolidated Balance Sheet (Figure 7-5)

1. The word *consolidated* used in the title of each statement means that McDonald's Corporation owns other smaller companies that are combined with it for financial reporting purposes.

2. The financial statements contain data for 1979 and 1978, shown in adjacent columns, to aid in the evaluation of the company from year to year. Financial statements presented in this fashion are called **comparative financial statements.** This form of reporting is in accordance with generally accepted accounting principles. For McDonald's, the fiscal year ends on December 31.

3. McDonald's has a typical set of current assets.

McDonald's Corporation consolidated balance sheet

			(1)	(2)
Assets			*December 31, 1979* *(In thousands of dollars)*	*and* *1978*
Current assets		Cash	*$ 47,081*	$ 24,472
		Certificates of deposit	*64,201*	57,130
		Short-term investments, at cost, which approximates market	*29,408*	74,990
	(3)	Accounts receivable	*48,369*	44,144
		Notes receivable	*8,206*	4,953
		Inventories, at cost, which is not in excess of market	*17,798*	14,332
		Prepaid expenses and other current assets	*31,667*	23,437
		Total current assets	*246,730*	243,458
Other assets and deferred charges		Notes receivable due after one year	*48,968*	33,948
	(4)	Investments in and advances to affiliates	*14,145*	9,405
		Miscellaneous	*29,377*	25,282
		Total other assets and deferred charges	*92,490*	68,635
Property and equipment		Property and equipment, at cost	*2,331,870*	1,908,596
	(5)	Less accumulated depreciation and amortization	*386,933*	310,823
		Net property and equipment	*1,944,937*	1,597,773
Intangible assets, net	(6)		*69,849*	43,623
		Total assets	*$2,354,006*	$1,953,489

Liabilities and stockholders' equity			*December 31, 1979* *(In thousands of dollars)*	*and* *1978*
Current liabilities		Notes payable	*$ 33,735*	$ 27,506
		Accounts payable	*127,906*	112,743
	(7)	Income taxes	*27,222*	33,001
		Other accrued liabilities	*41,201*	35,101
		Current maturities of long-term debt	*44,243*	43,656
		Total current liabilities	*274,307*	252,007
Long-term debt		Long-term debt	*875,809*	688,658
		Obligations under capital leases	*90,314*	94,123
(8)		Total long-term debt	*966,123*	782,781
Security deposits by franchisees			*54,633*	50,215
Deferred income taxes			*106,777*	72,149
Stockholders' equity		Common stock, no par value— Authorized—100,000,000 shares Issued—40,605,771 shares in 1979 and 40,599,305 shares in 1978	*4,515*	4,515
	(9)	Additional paid-in capital	*93,508*	92,484
		Retained earnings	*871,918*	703,826
			969,941	800,825
		Less treasury stock, at cost—407,080 shares in 1979 and 94,033 shares in 1978	*17,775*	4,488
		Total stockholders' equity	*952,166*	796,337
		Total liabilities and stockholders' equity	*$2,354,006*	$1,953,489

Courtesy of McDonald's Corporation.

◀ Figure 7-5 Balance Sheet for McDonald's Corporation and Subsidiaries

4. In place of the investments category, McDonald's has a catchall group of other assets and deferred charges. Deferred charges are a type of long-term prepaid expense. Also, note that in this section the notes receivable were excluded from current assets because they were due after one year.

5. McDonald's has a large investment in various types of property and equipment used in its business. McDonald's indicates the composition of owned property and equipment in a note to the financial statements.

6. Included in the total intangible assets is the payment of $1,839,000 made in 1961 for the now-famous McDonald's trademark and trade names.

7. The current liabilities section contains, among other typical current liabilities, the amount of long-term debt that must be paid within one year.

8. The section of the McDonald's balance sheet between current liabilities and stockholders' equity is rather complicated. It includes long-term debt and obligations under capital leases. Security deposits by franchisees are liabilities because they may have to be repaid at the end of the leases. The concept of deferred income taxes is difficult for beginning students. In general, deferred income taxes represent income tax expenses that will not have to be paid until sometime in the future. The topic of deferred income taxes is covered in Chapter 29.

9. The stockholders' equity section of McDonald's balance sheet contains four items. The first two items are common stock and additional paid-in capital. Together, they indicate the capital contributed by the stockholders. The third item, retained earnings, represents the earnings of the business accumulated over the years less any dividends declared. In the case of McDonald's, the amount of retained earnings in relation to contributed capital is evidence of the company's profitability over the years. The fourth item, treasury stock, represents the cost of those shares of the company's own stock that have been repurchased by the company from the stockholders.

Consolidated Statement of Income (Figure 7-6)

1. The consolidated statement of income is also presented in comparative form. In the actual annual report, five years of data were presented. To simplify this illustration, we have shown only two years.

2. McDonald's uses the single-step form and thus includes all operating and nonoperating items of revenue in one section.

3. The second part of the income statement contains all operating and nonoperating costs and expenses except the provision for income taxes.

4. The **provision for income taxes,** or **income tax expense,** represents the expense for federal and state income tax on McDonald's corporate in-

Figure 7-6
McDonald's
Statement of
Income

McDonald's Corporation consolidated statement of income (1)

		Years ended December 31, 1979	1978
		(In thousands of dollars, except per share data)	
Revenues (2)	**Sales by Company-owned restaurants**	*$1,495,216*	$1,290,621
	Revenues from franchised restaurants	*416,637*	352,928
	Other revenues—net	*26,082*	28,342
	Total revenues	*1,937,935*	1,671,891
Costs and expenses (3)	**Company-owned restaurants—**		
	Food and paper	*602,647*	518,686
	Payroll	*333,818*	289,836
	Rent	*18,628*	16,135
	Depreciation and amortization	*51,177*	43,342
	Other operating expenses	*241,063*	204,544
		1,247,333	1,072,543
	Expenses directly applicable to revenues from franchised restaurants—		
	Rent	*23,725*	19,986
	Depreciation and amortization	*35,276*	27,543
		59,001	47,529
	General, administrative and selling expenses	*214,501*	175,658
	Interest expense— Total interest charges	*82,863*	68,968
	Less amounts capitalized	*10,271*	5,632
		72,592	63,336
	Total costs and expenses	*1,593,427*	1,359,066
Income before provision for income taxes (4)		*344,508*	312,825
Provision for income taxes		*155,900*	150,156
Net income		*$ 188,608*	$ 162,669
Net income per share of common stock (5)		*$4.68*	$4.00
Dividends per share (6)	**Declared**	*$ .51*	$ .32
	Paid	*$ .51*	$ .32

Courtesy of McDonald's Corporation.

come. Federal and state income tax laws do not treat sole proprietorships and partnerships as taxable units. The individuals involved are the tax-paying units, and they pay income tax on their share of the business income. Corporations, however, must report and pay income tax on earnings. For this reason, income tax expense is always shown as a separate item on the income statement of the corporation. The amount of the federal income tax is based on taxable net income as defined by the Internal Revenue Code, which may or may not agree with the income as determined by generally accepted accounting principles. Income taxes for corporations are substantial, often approaching 50 percent of income before taxes, and thus have a significant effect on business decisions. Most other taxes, such as property taxes and employment taxes, are shown among the operating expenses. Income taxes are discussed in more detail in Chapter 29.

5. **Net income per share** of common stock, often called **earnings per share,** is also unique to corporation reporting. Ownership in corporations is represented by shares of stock, and the net income per share is reported immediately below net income on the income statement. It is computed by dividing the net income by the number of shares of stock outstanding. For example, if a company has a net income of $286,000 and has 100,000 shares of stock outstanding, the earnings per share are $2.86. Investors have found the figure useful as a shorthand way of assessing a company's profit-earning success and also in evaluating the earnings in relation to the market price of the stock. McDonald's had earnings per share of $4.00 in 1978 and $4.68 in 1979. Earnings per share are discussed in more detail in Chapter 17.

6. The item called dividends per share is the amount per share distributed to the stockholders during the year. McDonald's raised its dividend per share from $.32 in 1978 to $.51 in 1979.

Consolidated Statement of Retained Earnings (Figure 7-7)

McDonald's consolidated statement of retained earnings is very simple. The only items affecting retained earnings were the addition of net income and the deduction of dividends on common stock. You may want to compare the net income amounts in this statement with those in the income statement (Figure 7-6) and the balances at the end of the year with the balances of retained earnings in the balance sheet (Figure 7-5).

Figure 7-7 McDonald's Statement of Retained Earnings

McDonald's Corporation consolidated statement of retained earnings

		Years ended December 31, 1979	1978
		(In thousands of dollars)	
Balance at beginning of year		$703,826	$554,106
Net income		188,608	162,669
		892,434	716,775
Deduct	Cash dividends on common stock	20,516	12,949
Balance at end of year		$871,918	$703,826

Courtesy of McDonald's Corporation.

Figure 7-8
McDonald's Statement of Changes in Financial Position

McDonald's Corporation
consolidated statement of changes in financial position (1)

			Years ended December 31, 1979	1978
			(In thousands of dollars)	
Source of working capital		Operations— Net income	*$188,608*	$162,669
		Items not involving working capital:		
		Depreciation and amortization	*96,967*	79,831
		Deferred income taxes	*24,178*	13,945
		Other—net	*1,450*	(457)
	(2)	Total from operations	*311,203*	255,988
		Issuance of common stock on exercise of options	*584*	4,719
		Long-term debt additions	*506,937*	312,066
		Property and equipment disposals (gains and losses included in operations)	*18,682*	16,976
		Security deposits by franchisees	*8,059*	7,236
		Other	*24,135*	22,085
		Total source of working capital	*869,600*	619,070
Use of working capital		Property and equipment additions	*437,754*	354,095
		Non-current assets of businesses purchased	*52,399*	7,833
	(3)	Notes receivable due after one year	*30,741*	19,425
		Long-term debt reductions	*321,611*	215,052
		Cash dividends	*20,516*	12,949
		Treasury stock purchases	*13,633*	1,416
		Other	*11,974*	10,110
		Total use of working capital	888,628	620,880
Increase (decrease) in working capital	(4)		*$(19,028)*	$ (1,810)
Changes in elements of working capital		Increase (decrease) in current assets:		
		Cash and certificates of deposit	*$ 29,680*	$ 33,466
		Short-term investments	*(45,582)*	(9,205)
		Accounts and notes receivable	*7,478*	5,995
		Inventories	*3,466*	1,920
	(5)	Prepaid expenses and other current assets	*8,230*	3,212
			3,272	35,388
		Increase (decrease) in current liabilities:		
		Accounts and notes payable	*21,392*	17,085
		Income taxes	*(5,779)*	(2,918)
		Other accrued liabilities	*6,100*	6,191
		Current maturities of long-term debt	*587*	16,840
			22,300	37,198
Increase (decrease) in working capital			*$(19,028)*	$ (1,810)

Courtesy of McDonald's Corporation.

Consolidated Statement of Changes in Financial Position (Figure 7-8)

1. The consolidated statement of changes in financial position for McDonald's is complex, and its specific construction is the subject of Chapter 19. However, it is worthwhile for you to look at the major sections of the report at this point. The statement provides an overview of McDonald's major financing and investing activities during the year.

2. The first major section of the statement of changes in financial position lists all the sources of working capital. One important source was the funds generated by operations ($311,203,000 in 1979). There were various other financing sources, including a large addition to long-term debt ($506,937,000 in 1979). The sources of working capital funds totaled $869,600,000 in 1979.

3. The second major section of the report shows where the funds above were used or invested. Scanning this section, one can see that two important items accounted for most of the use of working capital. These were additions to property and equipment ($437,754,000 in 1979) and long-term debt reductions ($321,611,000 in 1979). The uses of working capital funds totaled $888,628,000 in 1979.

4. It is interesting to note that McDonald's used more working capital than its sources provided in both 1978 ($1,810,000) and 1979 ($19,028,000).

5. The change in working capital is proved by listing the changes in its various components. The changes in working capital can also be proved by referring to the balance sheet (in Figure 7-5) as follows:

Working Capital, 1978 (in thousands)		
Current Assets	$243,458	
Less Current Liabilities	252,007	
Total		($8,549)
Working Capital, 1979 (in thousands)		
Current Assets	$246,730	
Less Current Liabilities	274,307	
Total		($27,577)
Decrease in Working Capital (see Figure 7-8)		($19,028)

This example demonstrates again the purpose of the statement of changes in financial position, which explains the change in working capital through financing and investment actions from one year to the next.

Summary of Significant Accounting Policies

The Accounting Principles Board in its *Opinion No. 22* requires that financial statements include a **summary of significant accounting policies.** In this section, which in most cases immediately follows the last financial statement, a company discloses which generally accepted accounting principles it has followed in preparing the statements. For example, McDonald's statement with regard to one item of revenue recognition is as follows:

> Initial location and license fees are recorded as income when the related restaurant is opened. Expenses associated with site assignment and the issuance of franchise agreements are charged to expense as incurred.
>
> Continuing fees from franchised restaurants are recorded as income on the accrual basis as earned.
>
> Gains on sales of Company-owned restaurant businesses are recorded as income when the sales are consummated and other stipulated conditions are met.

Other significant accounting policies listed by McDonald's relate to consolidation policy, property and equipment, intangible assets, income taxes, debt issuance cost, and foreign currency translation. This list is typical of U.S. corporations.

Notes to the Financial Statements

In accordance with the requirement of full disclosure, it is necessary to add **notes to the financial statements** to help the user interpret some of the most complex items in published financial statements. The extensive notes for McDonald's Corporation are included in a section called financial comments. For example, within the footnote on foreign operations, you can learn the extent of McDonald's expansion into other countries:

> Restaurants are located in the United States and in foreign markets. Of the 5,747 restaurants in operation at December 31, 1979, 890 were operating outside of the United States. Of these foreign restaurants, 335 are located in Canada, and the remaining 555 are located in 25 other international markets.

Other notes relate to restaurant acquisitions and dispositions, number of restaurants in operation, income taxes, property and equipment, intangible assets, debt financing and dividend restrictions, lease of property owned by others, stock options, capital stock and additional paid-in capital, franchise arrangements, net income per share, profit-sharing plan, and replacement cost information. This list is typical of major corporations.

Report of Certified Public Accountants (Figure 7-9)

1. The **accountants' report** (or auditors' report) concerns the credibility of the financial statements. This report by independent public accountants contains the accountants' opinion regarding the fairness of presentation of the financial statements. Using financial statements prepared by management without an independent audit would be like having a judge hear a case in which he or she was personally involved or having a member of an opposing team in a sporting event act as a referee. Management, through

Figure 7-9
Report of Certified Public Accountants

(1) **Auditors' report**

The Board of Directors and Stockholders
McDonald's Corporation

(2) **We have examined the accompanying consolidated balance sheets of McDonald's Corporation and subsidiaries at December 31, 1979 and 1978 and the related consolidated statements of income, retained earnings and changes in financial position for each of the five years in the period ended December 31, 1979. Our examinations were made in accordance with generally accepted auditing standards and, accordingly, included such tests of the accounting records and such other auditing procedures as we considered necessary in the circumstances.**

(3) **In our opinion, the statements mentioned above present fairly the consolidated financial position of McDonald's Corporation and subsidiaries at December 31, 1979 and 1978 and the consolidated results of operations and changes in financial position for each of the five years in the period ended December 31, 1979, in conformity with generally accepted accounting principles applied on a consistent basis during the period.**

ARTHUR YOUNG & COMPANY

Chicago, Illinois
February 7, 1980

Courtesy of McDonald's Corporation.

its internal accounting system, is logically responsible for record keeping because it needs similar information for its own use in operating the business. The certified public accountant, acting independently, adds the necessary credibility to management's figures for interested third parties. Note that the certified public accountant reports to the board of directors and the stockholders rather than to management.

In form and language, most auditors' reports are similar to the one shown in Figure 7-9. Characteristically, such a report is brief, but its language is very important. The report is divided into two parts: scope and opinion.

2. The **scope section** tells that the auditor has examined the consolidated balance sheet and the other financial statements for McDonald's. This section states that the examination was made in accordance with generally accepted auditing standards. These standards require an acceptable level of quality in ten areas established by the American Institute of Certified Public Accountants. The CPAs also use whatever tests and other auditing procedures they think are necessary to satisfy themselves about the representation made in the statements.

3. The **opinion section** states the results of the auditor's examination. The use of the word *opinion* is extremely significant because the auditor does not certify or guarantee that the statements are absolutely correct. To do so would exceed the truth, because many such items, such as depreciation, are based on estimates. Instead, the auditor merely gives an opinion as to whether, overall, the financial statements "present fairly" the financial condition of the company. If in the auditor's opinion they do not

present it fairly, the auditor must explain why and to what extent they do not meet the standards.

Chapter Review

Review of Learning Objectives

1. State the objectives of financial reporting.

The objectives of financial reporting are that financial statements should provide (1) information useful in making investment and credit decisions, (2) information useful in assessing cash flow prospects, and (3) information about enterprise resources, claims to those resources, and changes in them.

2. Identify and describe the basic components of a classified balance sheet.

The classified balance sheet is subdivided as follows:

Assets
- Current Assets
- Investments
- Property, Plant, and Equipment
- Intangible Assets

Liabilities
- Current Liabilities
- Long-Term Liabilities

Owner's Equity
- (category titles depend on form of business)

A current asset is an asset that can reasonably be expected to be realized in cash during the next year or normal operating cycle. In general, assets are listed in the order of the ease of their conversion into cash. A current liability is a liability that can reasonably be expected to be paid during the next year or normal operating cycle. The owners' equity section of a corporation differs from that of a sole proprietorship in that it has subdivisions of contributed capital and retained earnings.

3. Distinguish between the multistep and single-step types of classified income statements.

Classified income statements may be in multistep or single-step form. The multistep form provides more detail but may overwhelm the reader. The single-step form is simpler but may give too little information. On the income statement, operating expenses are usually separated into selling expenses and general and administrative expenses. Also, there is usually a separate section for financing revenues and expenses.

4. Relate a chart of accounts to classified financial statements.

The chart of accounts is a systematic numbering scheme for identifying accounts in the ledger. Each account has a unique number. The initial digits of the account number usually identify the major sections of classified financial statements.

5. Use classified financial statements for the simple evaluation of liquidity and profitability.

One major use of classified financial statements is to evaluate the company's liquidity and profitability. Two simple measures of liquidity are working capital and the current ratio. Four simple measures pertaining to profitability are profit margin, return on assets, capital structure, and return on owner investment.

6. Identify some of the differences in the financial statements of corporations and proprietorships.

The financial statements of corporations are similar to those of sole proprietorships but tend to be more complex. The owners' equity section of a corporation's balance sheet must separate contributed capital from retained earnings. The corporation has a statement of retained earnings instead of a statement of owners' equity. On this statement, a dividends account replaces the withdrawals account. The corporate financial statements issued to the public also have more reporting features, such as federal income tax, earnings per share, a statement of accounting policies, and notes to the financial statements.

Review Problem
Analyzing Liquidity and Profitability Using Ratios

Flavin Shirt Company has faced increased competition from imported shirts in recent years. Presented below is summary information for the past two years:

	19x2	**19x1**
Current Assets	$ 200,000	$ 170,000
Total Assets	840,000	700,000
Current Liabilities	90,000	50,000
Long-Term Liabilities	150,000	50,000
Owner's Equity	600,000	600,000
Sales	1,200,000	1,050,000
Net Income	60,000	80,000

Required

Use liquidity and profitability analysis to document the declining financial position of Flavin Shirt Company.

Answer to Review Problem

Liquidity analysis:

	Current Assets	Current Liabilities	Working Capital	Current Ratio
19x1	$170,000	$50,000	$120,000	3.40
19x2	200,000	90,000	110,000	2.22
Decrease in working capital			$ 10,000	
Decrease in current ratio				1.18

Both working capital and the current ratio declined because, although current assets increased by $30,000 ($200,000 − $170,000), current liabilities increased by the greater amount of $40,000 ($90,000 − $50,000) from 19x1 to 19x2.

Profitability analysis:

	Sales			Total Assets		Owner's Equity	
	Net Income	Sales	Profit Margin	Amount	Return on Assets	Amount	Return on Owner Investment
19x1	$80,000	1,050,000	7.6%	700,000	11.4%	600,000	13.3%
19x2	60,000	1,200,000	5.0%	840,000	7.1%	600,000	10.0%
Increase (Decrease)	(20,000)	150,000	(2.6%)	140,000	(4.3%)	—	(3.3%)

Net income decreased by $20,000 in spite of an increase in sales of $150,000 and an increase in total assets of $140,000. The results were decreases in profit margin from 7.6 percent to 5.0 percent and in return on assets from 11.4 percent to 7.1 percent. The decrease in return on owner investment from 13.3 percent to 10.0 percent was not as much as the decrease in return on assets because the growth in total assets was financed by debt instead of owner's equity, as shown by the capital structure analysis below:

	Total Liabilities	Total Assets	Capital Structure Ratio
19x1	$100,000	$700,000	14.3%
19x2	240,000	840,000	28.6%
Increase	$140,000	$140,000	14.3%

Both total liabilities and total assets increased by $140,000. As a result, the amount of the business financed by debt increased from 14.3 percent to 28.6 percent.

Chapter Assignments

Questions

1. What are the three objectives of financial reporting?
2. What is the purpose of classified financial statements?
3. What are four common categories of assets?
4. What criteria must an asset meet to be classified as current? Under what condition will an asset be considered current even though it will not be realized as cash within a year? What are two examples of assets that fall into this category?
5. In what order should current assets be listed?

6. How does one distinguish a temporary investment in the current asset section from a security in the investments section of the balance sheet?
7. What is an intangible asset? Give at least three examples.
8. Name the two major categories of liabilities.
9. What are the primary differences between the owners' equity section of a sole proprietorship or partnership and the corresponding section for a corporation?
10. Explain the difference between contributed capital and retained earnings.
11. Explain how the multistep form of the income statement differs from the single-step form. What are the relative merits of each?
12. Why are financing revenues and expenses separated from operating revenues and expenses on the multistep income statement?
13. Why is there a need for a chart of accounts?
14. Define liquidity, and name two measures of liquidity.
15. How is the current ratio computed?
16. Which is the more important goal—liquidity or profitability?
17. Name four measures of profitability.
18. Evaluate this statement: "Return on assets is a better measure of profitability than profit margin."
19. What are some of the differences between the income statement for a sole proprietorship and that for a corporation?
20. Explain earnings per share and how this figure appears on the income statement.
21. What is the purpose of the accountant's report?
22. Why are notes to financial statements necessary?

Classroom Exercises

Exercise 7-1 Classification of Accounts—Balance Sheet

The lettered items below represent a classification scheme for a balance sheet, and the numbered items represent accounts. In the blank next to each account, write the letter indicating in which category it belongs.

a. Current assets
b. Investments
c. Property, plant, and equipment
d. Intangible assets
e. Current liabilities
f. Long-term liabilities
g. Owner's equity
h. Not on balance sheet

____ **1.** Patent
____ **2.** Building Held for Sale
____ **3.** Prepaid Rent
____ **4.** Wages Payable
____ **5.** Note Payable in Five Years
____ **6.** Building Used in Operations
____ **7.** Fund Held for Long-Term Debt
____ **8.** Inventory
____ **9.** Prepaid Insurance
____ **10.** Depreciation Expense
____ **11.** Accounts Receivable
____ **12.** Interest Expense
____ **13.** Revenue Received in Advance
____ **14.** Temporary Investments
____ **15.** Accumulated Depreciation
____ **16.** J. Martin, Capital

Exercise 7-2 Classification of Accounts—Income Statement

Using the classification scheme at the top of the next page for a multistep income statement, write in the blank the letter of the category in which each of the numbered accounts belongs.

a. Revenue	**d.** General and administrative expense
b. Cost of goods sold	**e.** Financing revenue or expense
c. Selling expense	**f.** Not on income statement

____ **1.** Purchases
____ **2.** Sales Discounts
____ **3.** Beginning Merchandise Inventory
____ **4.** Dividend Income
____ **5.** Advertising Expense
____ **6.** Office Salaries
____ **7.** Freight Out
____ **8.** Unexpired Insurance
____ **9.** Utility Expense
____ **10.** Sales Salaries
____ **11.** Rent Expense
____ **12.** Purchases Returns
____ **13.** Freight In
____ **14.** Depreciation Expense, Delivery Equipment
____ **15.** Taxes Payable
____ **16.** Interest Expense

Exercise 7-3 Preparation of Single-Step and Multistep Income Statements

The following data pertain to a corporation: Sales, $680,000; Cost of Goods Sold, $370,000; Selling Expense, $160,000; General and Administrative Expense, $100,000; Income Tax Expense, $20,000; Interest Expense, $4,000; Interest Revenue, $3,000; Common Stock Outstanding, 20,000 shares.

1. Prepare a single-step income statement including an earnings per share calculation.
2. Prepare a multistep income statement.

Exercise 7-4 Classified Balance Sheet Preparation

The following data pertain to a corporation: Cash, $3,500; Investment in Six-Month Government Securities, $14,600; Accounts Receivable, $38,000; Inventory, $40,000; Prepaid Rent, $1,200; Investment in Corporate Securities (long-term), $20,000; Land, $8,000; Building, $70,000; Accumulated Depreciation, Building, $14,000; Equipment, $152,000; Accumulated Depreciation, Equipment, $17,000; Copyright, $6,200; Accounts Payable, $32,000; Revenue Received in Advance, $2,800; Bonds Payable, $60,000; Common Stock—$10 par, 10,000 shares issued and outstanding, $100,000; Contributed Capital in Excess of Par Value, $50,000; Retained Earnings, $77,700.

Prepare a classified balance sheet.

Exercise 7-5 Computation of Ratios

The simplified balance sheet and income statement for a sole proprietorship appear as follows:

Balance Sheet
December 31

Assets		**Liabilities**	
Current Assets	$ 90,000	Current Liabilities	$ 30,000
Investments	10,000	Long-Term Liabilities	50,000
Property, Plant, and Equipment	283,000	Total Liabilities	$ 80,000
		Owner's Equity	
Intangible Assets	17,000	J. Travis, Capital	320,000
Total Assets	$400,000	Total Liabilities and Owner's Equity	$400,000

Income Statement	
Revenue from Sales (net)	$800,000
Cost of Goods Sold	480,000
Gross Profit from Sales	$320,000
Operating Expenses	280,000
Net Income	$ 40,000

1. Compute the following liquidity measures: (a) working capital and (b) current ratio.
2. Compute the following profitability measures: (a) profit margin, (b) return on assets, (c) capital structure, using the ratio of total liabilities to total assets, and (d) return on owner investment.

Exercise 7-6 Using McDonald's Corporation Financial Statements

The questions in this exercise pertain to the financial statements of McDonald's Corporation in Figures 7-5 to 7-9 and are designed to help you read published financial statements. (Note: 1979 refers to the year ended December 31, 1979, and 1978 refers to the year ended December 31, 1978.)

1. Consolidated balance sheet: (a) Did the amount of working capital increase or decrease from 1978 to 1979? By how much? (b) Did the current ratio improve from 1978 to 1979? (c) Does the company have long-term investments or intangible assets? (d) Why are there notes receivable listed in both the current asset section and the other asset section? (e) Did the capital structure of McDonald's change from 1978 to 1979? (f) How much is the contributed capital for 1979? How does it compare with retained earnings?
2. Consolidated income statement: (a) Does McDonald's use a multistep or single-step form of income statement? (b) Is it a comparative statement? (c) Did net income increase from 1978 to 1979? (d) How significant are income taxes for McDonald's? (e) Did net income per share increase from 1978 to 1979? (f) Did the profit margin increase from 1978 to 1979? (g) Did the return on assets increase from 1978 to 1979? (h) Did the return on owner investment increase from 1978 to 1979?
3. Consolidated statement of retained earnings: (a) What figure came from the income statement? (b) Why are dividends listed in this statement? (c) What figures from this statement also appear in the balance sheet?
4. Statement of changes in financial position: (a) What was the largest source of resources in 1979? (b) What was the largest use of resources in 1979?
5. Report of the certified public accountants: (a) What was the name of McDonald's independent auditor? (b) Did the accountants think the financial statements presented fairly the financial situation of the company?

Problem Set A

Problem 7A-1 Multistep Income Statement

The Income Statement columns from the work sheet of O'Donald Furniture Company as of December 31, 19xx, appear on the next page. The company is a sole proprietorship.

Account Name	Income Statement Debit	Income Statement Credit
Merchandise Inventory	42,300	37,600
Sales		224,600
Sales Discounts	2,600	
Sales Returns and Allowances	9,400	
Purchases	111,100	
Purchases Discounts		1,900
Purchases Returns and Allowances		4,060
Freight In	8,700	
Sales Salaries	31,080	
Sales Supplies Used	820	
Rent, Selling Space	3,600	
Utilities, Selling Space	1,480	
Advertising	8,400	
Depreciation Expense, Delivery Equipment	2,200	
Office Salaries	14,620	
Office Supplies Used	4,380	
Rent, Office Space	1,200	
Utilities, Office Space	500	
Postage	1,160	
Insurance Expense	1,340	
Miscellaneous Expense	720	
General Management Salaries	21,000	
Interest Expense	2,800	
Interest Income		210
	269,400	268,370
Net Loss		1,030
	269,400	269,400

Required

From the information above, prepare a multistep income statement for O'Donald Furniture Company.

Problem 7A-2 Classified Balance Sheet

The Balance Sheet columns from the work sheet of O'Donald Furniture Company as of December 31, 19xx, appear on the next page. The company is a sole proprietorship.

Required

From the information given, prepare a classified balance sheet for O'Donald Furniture Company.

Account Name	Debit	Credit
Cash	7,200	
Temporary Investments	7,800	
Notes Receivable	2,000	
Accounts Receivable	69,000	
Merchandise Inventory	37,600	
Prepaid Rent	400	
Unexpired Insurance	1,200	
Sales Supplies	320	
Office Supplies	110	
Deposit for Future Advertising	920	
Building, Not in Use	12,400	
Land	5,600	
Delivery Equipment	10,300	
Accumulated Depreciation, Delivery Equipment		6,200
Franchise Fee	1,000	
Accounts Payable		26,860
Salaries Payable		1,300
Interest Payable		210
Long-Term Notes Payable		20,000
Jerry O'Donald, Capital		104,510
Jerry O'Donald, Withdrawals	2,200	
Net Loss	1,030	
	159,080	159,080

Problem 7A-3 Ratio Analysis—Liquidity and Profitability

Clay Products Company has been disappointed with its operating results for the past two years. As accountant for the company, you have the following information available:

	19x2	19x1
Current Assets	$ 40,000	$ 30,000
Total Assets	140,000	100,000
Current Liabilities	20,000	10,000
Long-Term Liabilities	20,000	—
Owner's Equity	100,000	90,000
Sales	252,000	200,000
Net Income	12,000	10,000

Required

1. Compute the following measures of liquidity for 19x1 and 19x2: (a) working capital and (b) current ratio. Comment on the differences between years.
2. Compute the following measures of profitability for 19x1 and 19x2: (a) profit margin, (b) return on assets, (c) capital structure as measured by ratio of total liabilities to total assets, and (d) return on owner investment. Comment on the change in performance from 19x1 to 19x2.

Problem 7A-4 Multistep Income Statement

Barney's Card Shop has been in business for one year. During this time, Barney has kept track of all his revenues and expenses. He feels that his sales have been good, but his profit is not as high as he would like. As a friend, you have agreed to look at his profit statement. Barney gives you the following statement:

Barney's Card Shop
Profit Statement
December 31, 19xx

Revenues		
Sales for the Year	$117,300	
Interest on Savings Account	840	
Rent on Building Not Used in Business	3,300	
Purchases Discounts	1,000	
Total Revenues		$122,440
Expenses		
Salaries, Sales Staff	$ 19,300	
Salaries, Administrative	17,070	
Rent, Fixtures: ⅔ Sales, ⅓ Administration	4,800	
Supplies Used: ¾ Sales, ¼ Administration	840	
Interest on Debt	2,940	
Insurance: ½ Sales, ½ Administration	2,120	
Property Taxes: ⅔ Sales, ⅓ Administration	2,430	
Miscellaneous Expenses: ½ Sales, ½ Administration	1,480	
Sales Discounts	940	
Advertising	10,060	
Withdrawals by Owner	6,000	
Cost of Goods Sold for the Year	41,260	
Depreciation Expense: ⅔ Sales, ⅓ Administration	4,500	
Utility Expense: ⅔ Sales, ⅓ Administration	3,990	
Total Expenses		117,730
Profit		$ 4,710

Required

1. Prepare a multistep income statement in good form for Barney's Card Shop.
2. What incorrect classifications did Barney make?
3. Comment on the usefulness of the multistep form over the single-step form of income statement as applied to Barney's Card Shop. (Hint: What have you learned about Barney's operations from the multistep form?)

Problem 7A-5 Classified Financial Statement Preparation and Evaluation

The following accounts (in alphabetical order) and amounts were taken or calculated from the adjusted trial balance of Jill's Jean Company on June 30, 19xx: Accounts Payable, $16,000; Accounts Receivable, $12,360; Accumulated Depreciation, Building, $15,600; Accumulated Depreciation, Equipment, $7,900; Building, $59,000; Cash, $1,340; Cost of Goods Sold, $106,050; Depreciation Expense, Building, $3,000; Depreciation Expense, Equipment, $3,950; Equipment, $29,500; Interest Expense, $4,170; Interest Income, $220; Inventory, $22,440; Jill Stevens, Capital, $60,190; Land Held for Future Use, $31,100; Land Used in Operations, $11,000; Mortgage Payable, $50,000; Notes Payable (short-term), $6,000; Notes Receivable, $1,400; Operating Expense Excluding Depreciation, $79,250; Revenue Received in Advance, $350; Sales, Net, $213,300; Investment in Xerox Corporation—100 shares (short-term), $5,000.

Required

1. From the information above, prepare (a) an income statement in multistep form and (b) a classified balance sheet.
2. Calculate the following measures of liquidity: (a) working capital and (b) current ratio.
3. Calculate the following measures of profitability: (a) profit margin, (b) return on assets, (c) capital structure, computed by the ratio of total liabilities to total assets, and (d) return on owner investment.

Problem 7A-6 Classified Financial Statement Preparation and Evaluation

Target Corporation sells outdoor sports equipment. At the end of 19xx, the following financial information was available from the income statement: Administrative Expenses, $39,400; Cost of Goods Sold, $175,210; Federal Income Tax Expense, $6,335; Interest Expense, $11,320; Interest Income, $1,400; Sales, Net, $347,300; Selling Expenses, $110,100.

The following information was available from the balance sheet: Accounts Payable, $16,300; Accounts Receivable, $52,400; Accumulated Depreciation, Delivery Equipment, $8,550; Accumulated Depreciation, Store Fixtures, $21,110; Cash, $12,400; Common Stock—$1 par value, 5,000 shares issued and outstanding, $5,000; Contributed Capital in Excess of Par Value, $45,000; Delivery Equipment, $42,900; Inventory, $68,270; Investment in J. Corporation (long-term), $28,000; Investment in U.S. Government Securities (short-term), $19,800; Notes Payable (long-term), $50,000; Notes Payable (short-term), $25,000; Retained Earnings, $126,500; Short-Term Prepaid Expenses, $2,880; Store Fixtures, $70,810.

Required

1. From the information above, prepare the following: (a) an income statement in single-step form (beneath the income statement, show earnings per share), and (b) a classified balance sheet.
2. From the two statements you have prepared, compute the following measures: (a) for liquidity—working capital and current ratio; and (b) for profitability—profit margin, return on assets, capital structure as measured by the ratio of total liabilities to total assets, and return on owner investment.

Problem Set B

Problem 7B-1 Multistep Income Statement

The Income Statement columns from the work sheet of Rosenblatt Hardware Company as of June 30, 19xx, appear on the next page. The company is a sole proprietorship.

Account Name	Income Statement	
	Debit	Credit
Merchandise Inventory	172,500	156,750
Sales		527,770
Sales Discounts	4,110	
Sales Returns and Allowances	9,782	
Purchases	209,060	
Purchases Discounts		1,877
Purchases Returns and Allowances		4,282
Freight In	11,221	
Sales Salaries	102,030	
Sales Supplies	1,642	
Rent, Selling Space	18,000	
Utilities, Selling Space	11,256	
Advertising	21,986	
Depreciation Expense, Fixtures	6,778	
Office Salaries	47,912	
Office Supplies	782	
Rent, Office Space	4,000	
Depreciation Expense, Office Equipment	3,251	
Utilities, Office Space	3,114	
Postage	626	
Insurance Expense	2,700	
Miscellaneous Expense	481	
Interest Expense	3,600	
Interest Income		800
	634,831	691,479
Net Income	56,648	
	691,479	691,479

Required

From the information above, prepare a multistep income statement for Rosenblatt Hardware Company.

Problem 7B-2 Classified Balance Sheet

The Balance Sheet columns from the worksheet of Rosenblatt Hardware Company as of June 30, 19xx, appear on the next page. The company is a sole proprietorship.

Required

From the information given, prepare a classified balance sheet for Rosenblatt Hardware Company.

Account Name	Balance Sheet	
	Debit	Credit
Cash	3,700	
Temporary Investments	11,350	
Notes Receivable	40,500	
Accounts Receivable	76,570	
Merchandise Inventory	156,750	
Prepaid Rent	2,000	
Unexpired Insurance	1,200	
Sales Supplies	426	
Office Supplies	97	
Land, Held for Future Expansion	11,500	
Fixtures	72,400	
Accumulated Depreciation, Fixtures		21,000
Office Equipment	24,100	
Accumulated Depreciation, Office Equipment		10,250
Trademark	4,000	
Accounts Payable		91,245
Salaries Payable		787
Interest Payable		600
Notes Payable (due in three years)		36,000
Bernard Rosenblatt, Capital		215,063
Bernard Rosenblatt, Withdrawals	27,000	
Net Income		56,648
	431,593	431,593

Problem 7B-3 Ratio Analysis—Liquidity and Profitability

A summary of data taken from the income statements and balance sheets for Morales Construction Supply for the past two years appears below.

	19x2	**19x1**
Current Assets	$ 135,000	$ 120,000
Total Assets	1,060,000	780,000
Current Liabilities	90,000	60,000
Long-Term Liabilities	300,000	200,000
Owner's Equity	670,000	520,000
Sales	2,200,000	1,740,000
Net Income	200,000	174,000

Required

1. Compute the following measures of liquidity for 19x1 and 19x2: (a) working capital, and (b) current ratio. Comment on the differences between years.
2. Compute the following measures of profitability for 19x1 and 19x2: (a) profit margin, (b) return on assets, (c) capital structure as measured by ratio of total liabilities to total assets, and (d) return on owner investment. Comment on the change in performance from 19x1 to 19x2.

Problem 7B-4 Multistep Income Statement

During her first year of operation, Linda, who owns Linda's Candy Shop, has kept accurate records of all revenues and expenses. At the end of the year, she prepared the income statement shown below. Although the net income appears to be low in relation to sales, Linda finds the statement difficult to interpret.

Linda's Candy Shop
Income Statement
December 31, 19xx

Revenues		
Sales	$177,300	
Purchases Discounts	2,700	
Purchases Returns and Allowances	6,420	
Interest on Government Bonds	2,000	
Rent Income	4,000	
Total Revenues		$192,420
Expenses		
Salaries Expense	$ 57,000	
Rent Expense	4,000	
Supplies Used	1,500	
Interest Expense	2,900	
Insurance Expense	1,800	
Property Taxes	2,400	
Miscellaneous Expense	900	
Sales Discounts	1,200	
Sales Returns and Allowances	945	
Owner's Withdrawals	8,000	
Cost of Goods Sold	89,551	
Depreciation Expense	3,200	
Utility Expense	2,400	
Total Expenses		175,796
Net Income		$ 16,624

Required

1. To aid Linda in evaluating her company, prepare a multistep income statement for her candy shop. Assume that salaries, supplies, and miscellaneous expense should be divided in the ratio of $\frac{2}{3}$ sales expense and $\frac{1}{3}$ general expense and that rent, insurance, property taxes, depreciation, and utility expenses are allocated $\frac{3}{4}$ to sales expense and $\frac{1}{4}$ to general expense.
2. What incorrect classifications did Linda make?
3. What did you learn about Linda's Candy Shop by using the multistep form of income statement?

Problem 7B-5 Classified Financial Statement Preparation and Evaluation

The following accounts (in alphabetical order) and amounts were taken or calculated from the December 31, 19xx, adjusted trial balance of Perfect Lawn Equipment Center: Accounts Payable, $33,600; Accounts Receivable, $87,400; Accumulated Depreciation, Building, $26,200; Accumulated Depreciation, Equipment, $17,400; Building, $110,000; Cash, $6,250; Cost of Goods Sold, $246,000; Depreciation Expense, Building, $4,500; Depreciation Expense, Equipment, $6,100; Dividend Income, $50; Equipment, $75,600; Investment in General Motors—100 shares (short-term), $6,500; Interest Expense, $12,200; Inventory, $56,150; Land Held for Future Use, $20,000; Land Used in Operations, $29,000; Mortgage Payable, $90,000; Notes Payable (short-term), $25,000; Notes Receivable, $12,000; Operating Expenses Excluding Depreciation, $151,350; Sales, Net, $426,000; Tommy Atkins, Capital, $235,450; Tommy Atkins, Withdrawals, $23,900; Trademark, $6,750.

Required

1. From the information above, prepare (a) an income statement in multistep form, and (b) a classified balance sheet.
2. Calculate the following measures of liquidity: (a) working capital, and (b) current ratio.
3. Calculate the following measures of profitability: (a) profit margin, (b) return on assets, (c) capital structure, computed by ratio of total liabilities to total assets, and (d) return on owner investment.

Chapter Eight

Accounting Systems and Special-Purpose Journals

Learning Objectives

1. *Describe the phases of systems installation and the principles of systems design.*
2. *Explain the objectives and uses of special-purpose journals.*
3. *Construct and use the following types of special-purpose journals: sales journal, purchases journal, cash receipts journal, cash payments journal, and others as needed.*
4. *Explain the purposes and relationships of controlling accounts and subsidiary ledgers.*
5. *Describe the basic features of computer systems and their application to data processing.*

Knowledge of accounting systems for processing information is particularly important today because of the variety of systems in use and the rapidly changing needs of individual businesses. In this chapter, you first study the basic concepts and principles of accounting systems design. You then learn about the major types of data processing, ranging from manual systems to computer systems. Because the concept of special-purpose journals is basic to all accounting systems, this chapter emphasizes the special-purpose journals used in manual data processing. As a result of studying this chapter, you should be able to meet the learning objectives listed on the left.

As you learned earlier, accounting systems gather data from all areas of the business enterprise, transform them into useful information, and communicate the results to management. Thus they are essential to business management. As business has become larger and more complicated, the role and importance of accounting systems have grown. With the development of computers, the concept of a total information system with accounting as its base has evolved. These important developments demand that today's accountant understand all phases of a company's operations as well as the latest developments in systems design and technology.

Accounting Systems Installation

The installation of an accounting system consists of three phases: investigation, design, and implementation. Each of these phases is necessary regardless of whether the system is a new one or an existing system that must be altered. The constant changes in business operations and environment call for continuous review of the current accounting system to ensure that it will always be responsive to management's need for information.

Objective 1 Describe the phases of systems installation and the principles of systems design

The purpose of the **system investigation** phase is to determine the requirements of a new system or to evaluate an existing system. This phase involves studying the information needs of management, seeking the sources of this information, and specifying the procedural and processing needs that will transform the data sources into required output. Included in this phase are a review of organizational structure, and job descriptions of personnel and a study of forms, records, reports, procedures, data processing methods, and controls presently in use. Some companies have procedural manuals that give all of this information in great detail. In existing systems, there is the additional task of determining whether procedures are actually followed. This task is accomplished by tracing test transactions through the system and interviewing and observing people actually doing the work.

The new system or the changes in the current system are formulated in the **system design** phase and are based on the studies made during the investigation phase. For a major system development, the design phase may require accountants as well as computer experts, engineers, personnel managers, and other specialists. The design must take into consideration the personnel who run and interact with the system, the communications media such as documents and records, the operational procedures, the reports to be prepared, and the equipment to be utilized in the system. The interaction of all these components must conform to the principles of systems design discussed below.

If management is satisfied with a new system's design, the next phase, **system implementation**, follows. This phase depends on careful planning and communication to ensure that the new system is understood and accepted, properly installed, and satisfactorily operated. The personnel responsible for the operation of the new system should take an active part in the actual implementation. Implementation involves scheduling all activities of the installation. For large systems, implementation may take months or even years. The personnel for the new system must be selected and trained. The equipment, forms, and records must be purchased. The new system must be tested, and then modified as indicated by the tests. After implementation, it is important to appraise the new system regularly as part of the system investigation process.

Principles of Systems Design

In designing an accounting system, the systems designer must adhere to four general principles of systems design: (1) the cost/benefit principle, (2) the control principle, (3) the compatibility principle, and (4) the flexibility principle.

Cost/Benefit Principle

The most important systems principle, the **cost/benefit principle**, holds that the value or benefits received from a system and its information output must be equal to or greater than its cost. Beyond certain routine functions that an accounting system must perform, such as tax and other reporting requirements, preparation of essential financial statements, and maintenance of adequate internal control, management may want or require other information. To be beneficial, this information must be reliable, timely, and useful to management. These benefits of additional information must be weighed against both the tangible and intangible costs of obtaining the information. Tangible costs include those for personnel, forms, and equipment. Intangible costs include the cost of wrong decisions resulting from lack of good information. For instance, incorrect decisions may result in loss of sales, production stoppages, or inventory losses. In some cases, companies have spent thousands of dollars on expensive computer systems that have not provided sufficient benefits. On the other hand, some managers have failed to realize significant benefits that could be gained from investing in more advanced systems. It is the job of the accountant as systems analyst to weigh the opposing factors of costs and benefits.

Control Principle

The **control principle** requires that an accounting system provide all the features of internal control needed to safeguard assets and ensure the reliability of data. Chapter 9 covers the topic of internal control in detail.

Compatibility Principle

The **compatibility principle** holds that the design of a system must be in harmony with the organizational and human factors of a business. An organization is made up of people working in different activities or organizational units. The organizational factors refer to the nature of the business and how the organizational units of the business are formally interrelated to accomplish the objectives of the business. For example, a company may organize its marketing efforts by region or by product. If a company is organized by region, major reports will summarize revenues and expenses by region. A company organized by product, on the other hand, should have a system designed to accumulate revenue and expenses first by product and then by region. The human factors of business refer not to the formal units of the organization but to individuals in those units and their abilities, behaviors, and personal characteristics. The interest, support, and competence of the people in the organization are vital to systems design. In changing systems or installing new systems, the accountant must deal with the individuals presently performing or supervising existing procedures. These people must understand, accept, and, in many cases, be trained in the new procedures. The new system cannot succeed unless the system and the people in the organization are compatible.

Flexibility Principle

According to the **flexibility principle,** the accounting system should have sufficient flexibility to accommodate growth in the volume of transactions and organizational changes in the business. Businesses rarely stay the same. They expand, develop new products, add new branch offices, sell existing divisions, or make other changes that require adjustments in the accounting system. A carefully designed system will allow substantial growth of a business without major alterations. For example, the chart of accounts should be designed to allow for the addition of classifications such as new asset, liability, owner's equity, revenue, or expense accounts without destroying the significance or usefulness of the accounts.

Data Processing

Data processing is the means by which the accounting system collects data, organizes them into meaningful forms, and issues the resulting information to users. It can be viewed from three perspectives—functional, content, and mechanical—as shown in Figure 8-1. The functional and

Figure 8-1
Data Processing from Three Perspectives

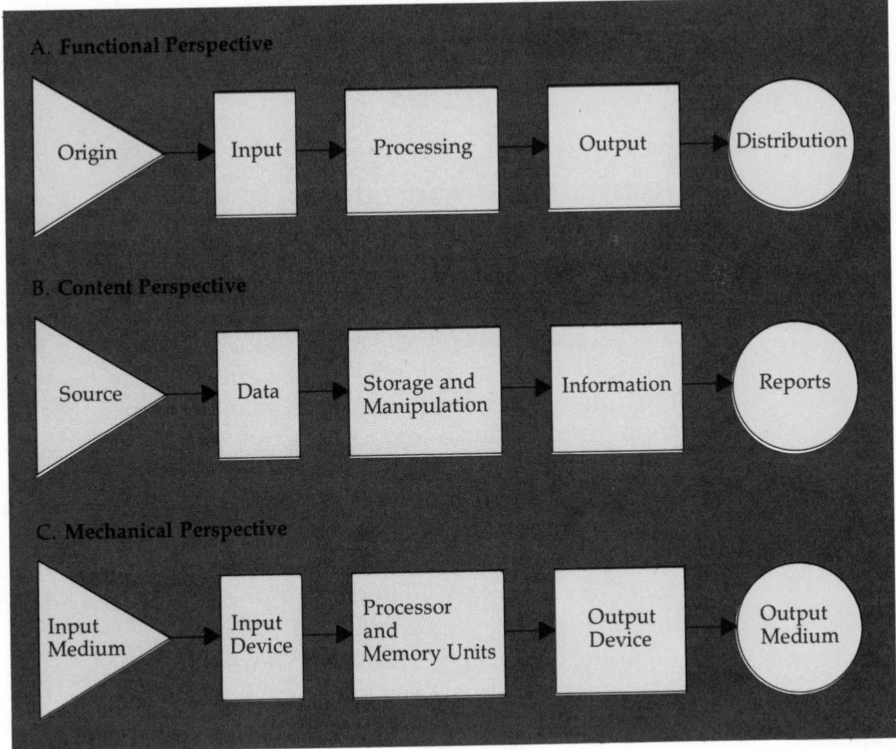

content perspectives are closely related. The functional perspective refers to what is done, and the content perspective refers to the data or material acted upon. The origin of the input is a document of some kind. This document, of course, provides the data content. The processing function organizes the data into meaningful form by manipulating and storing them until they are needed. The output is information made available to users by means of reports. The mechanical perspective refers to the devices used in carrying out data processing. In any data processing system, there must be a medium for originating the data, a device for data input, a processor and memory unit for storing and manipulating the data, a device for output of information, and a medium for distributing the information.

From the mechanical viewpoint, the two extremes of data processing systems are manual systems and computer systems, each of which accomplishes the same basic function. The basic techniques of handling a large volume of data using manual data processing are demonstrated in the next sections of this chapter. The essential features of computer systems and their application to data processing are presented in the latter part of the chapter.

The accountant must be able to work within a wide range of accounting systems, and may also have a voice in choosing the right type of data processing for a business. The first step in acquiring the necessary skill and knowledge is to learn how to use the special-purpose journals to process data manually. This basic knowledge can then be applied to other, more sophisticated, accounting systems.

Manual Data Processing: Journals and Procedures

The system of accounting described so far in this book, presented in Figure 8-2, is a form of manual data processing. This application of the mechanical perspective from Figure 8-1 has been a convenient way to illustrate basic accounting theory and practice in small businesses. The recording procedures are done manually by entering each transaction from a source document, such as an invoice, in the general journal (input device) and posting each debit and credit to the appropriate ledger account (processor and memory device). A work sheet (output device) is then used to aid in preparing financial statements (output devices) to be distributed to users. This system, while useful for illustrating the fundamental concepts of accounting, is limited in practice to only the smallest of companies.

Objective 2 Explain the objectives and uses of special-purpose journals

Larger companies, faced with hundreds or thousands of transactions every week and perhaps every day, must have a more efficient and economical way of recording transactions in the journal and posting entries to the ledger. The easiest and most usual way to do this is to group the company's typical transactions into common categories and develop an input device, called a special-purpose journal, for each. Most business

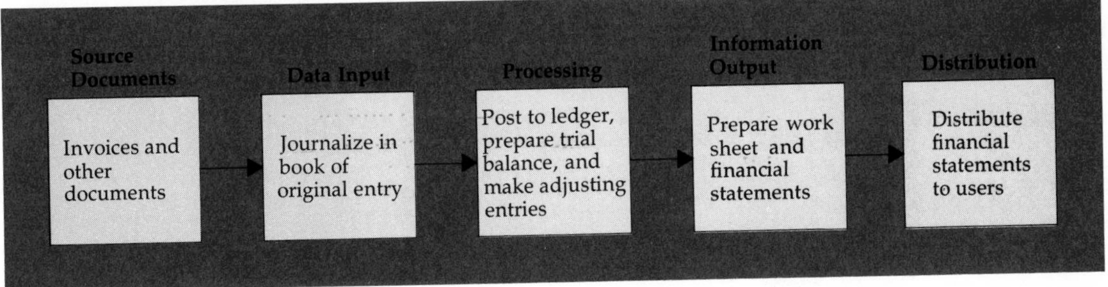

Figure 8-2
Steps and Devices in a Manual Accounting System

transactions, usually 90 to 95 percent, fall into four categories. Each kind of transaction may be recorded in a special-purpose journal as shown below.

Transaction	Special-Purpose Journal	Posting Abbreviation
Sales of merchandise on credit	Sales journal	S
Purchases on credit	Purchases journal	P
Receipts of cash	Cash receipts journal	CR
Disbursements of cash	Cash payments journal	CP

The general journal is retained for recording transactions that do not fall into any of the special categories. For example, purchases or sales returns and adjusting and closing entries are recorded in the general journal. (When transactions are posted from the general journal to the ledger accounts, the posting abbreviation used is J.) It is important to note that use of these five journals greatly reduces the amount of detailed recording work. Also, a division of labor can be achieved if each journal is assigned to a different employee. This division of labor is very important in establishing good internal control, a concept discussed in Chapter 9.

Sales Journal

Special-purpose journals are designed to record particular types of transactions. Thus all transactions in a special-purpose journal result in debits and credits to the same accounts. The sales journal, for example, is designed to handle all credit sales, and only credit sales.

Objective 3 Construct and use the following types of special-purpose journals: sales journal, purchases journal, cash receipts journal, cash payments journal, and others as needed

Figure 8-3 (next page) illustrates a sales journal. Six sales transactions involving five people are recorded in this sales journal. As each sale takes place, several copies of the sales invoice are made. The accounting department of the seller uses one copy to make the entry in the sales journal. From the invoices are copied the date, the customer's name, the invoice number, the amount of the sale, and possibly the credit terms. These data correspond to the columns of the sales journal. If the seller commonly offers different credit terms to different customers, an additional column to indicate the terms can be used. In this case, we assume that each customer has received the same credit terms.

Sales Journal					Page 1
Date		Account Debited	Invoice Number	Post. Ref.	Amount
July	1	Peter Clark	721	✓	750
	5	Georgetta Jones	722	✓	500
	8	Eugene Cumberland	723	✓	335
	12	Maxwell Hertz	724	✓	1,165
	15	Peter Clark	725	✓	1,225
	25	Michael Powers	726	✓	975
					4,950
					(114/411)

Post total at end of month.

Accounts Receivable						114
					Balance	
Date		Post. Ref.	Debit	Credit	Debit	Credit
July	31	S1	4,950		4,950	

Sales						411
					Balance	
Date		Post. Ref.	Debit	Credit	Debit	Credit
July	31	S1		4,950		4,950

Figure 8-3 Sales Journal and Related Ledger Accounts

Note the following time-saving features of the sales journal:

1. Only one line is needed to record each transaction. Each entry consists of a debit to each customer in Accounts Receivable; the corresponding credit to Sales is understood.

2. Account names do not have to be written out, because account names occurring most frequently are used as column headings; thus entry in a column has the effect of debiting or crediting the account.

3. No explanations are necessary, because the function of the special-purpose journal is to record one type of transaction. Only credit sales can be recorded in the sales journal. Sales for cash must be recorded in the cash receipts journal, which is described later in this chapter.

4. Only one amount—the total credit sales for the month—needs to be posted. It is posted twice: once as a debit to Accounts Receivable and once as a credit to Sales. Instead of the six sales entries in the example, there might be hundreds of actual sales transactions in a more realistic situation. Thus one can see the saving in posting time.

Controlling Accounts and Subsidiary Ledgers Every entry in the sales journal represents a debit to a customer's account in Accounts Receivable. In previous chapters, all such transactions have been posted to Accounts Receivable. However, this single Accounts Receivable entry does not readily tell how much each customer bought and paid for or how much each customer owes. In practice, almost all companies that sell to customers on credit keep an individual accounts receivable record for

Objective 4 Explain the purposes and relationships of controlling accounts and subsidiary ledgers

each customer. If the company has 6,000 credit customers, there are 6,000 accounts receivable. To include all these accounts in the ledger with the other assets, liabilities, and owner's equity accounts would make it very bulky. Consequently, most companies take the individual customers' accounts out of the general ledger, which contains the financial statement accounts, and place them in a separate ledger called a **subsidiary ledger.** The customers' accounts are filed alphabetically in this accounts receivable ledger.

When a company puts its individual customers' accounts in an accounts receivable ledger, there is still a need for an Accounts Receivable account in the general ledger to maintain its balance. This Accounts Receivable account in the general ledger is said to control the subsidiary ledger and is called a **controlling** or **control account.** It is a controlling account in the sense that its balance should equal the total of the individual account balances in the subsidiary ledger. This is true because in transactions involving accounts receivable, such as credit sales, there must be postings to the individual subsidiary customer accounts every day and to the controlling account in the general ledger in total each month. If an error has been made in posting, the sum of all customer account balances in the subsidiary accounts receivable ledger will not equal the balance of the Accounts Receivable controlling account in the general ledger. When these amounts do not match, the accountant knows that there is an error and can find and correct it.

The concept of controlling accounts is shown in Figure 8-4 (next page) where boxes are used for the accounts receivable ledger and the general ledger. The principle involved is that the single controlling account in the general ledger takes the place of all the individual accounts in the subsidiary ledger. The trial balance can be prepared using only the general ledger accounts.

Most companies, as we shall see, use an accounts payable subsidiary ledger as well. It is also possible to use a subsidiary ledger for almost any account in the general ledger where management wants a specific account for individual items, such as Notes Receivable, Temporary Investments, and Equipment.

Summary of the Sales Journal Procedure Observe from Figure 8-4 that the procedures for using a sales journal are as follows:

1. Enter each sales invoice in the sales journal on a single line, recording date, customer's name, invoice number, and amount.

2. At the end of each day, post each individual sale to the customer's account in the accounts receivable ledger. As each sale is posted, place a check mark in the Post. Ref. (posting reference) column to indicate that it has been posted. In the Post. Ref. column of each customer account, place an S1 (representing Sales Journal—page 1) to indicate the source of the entry.

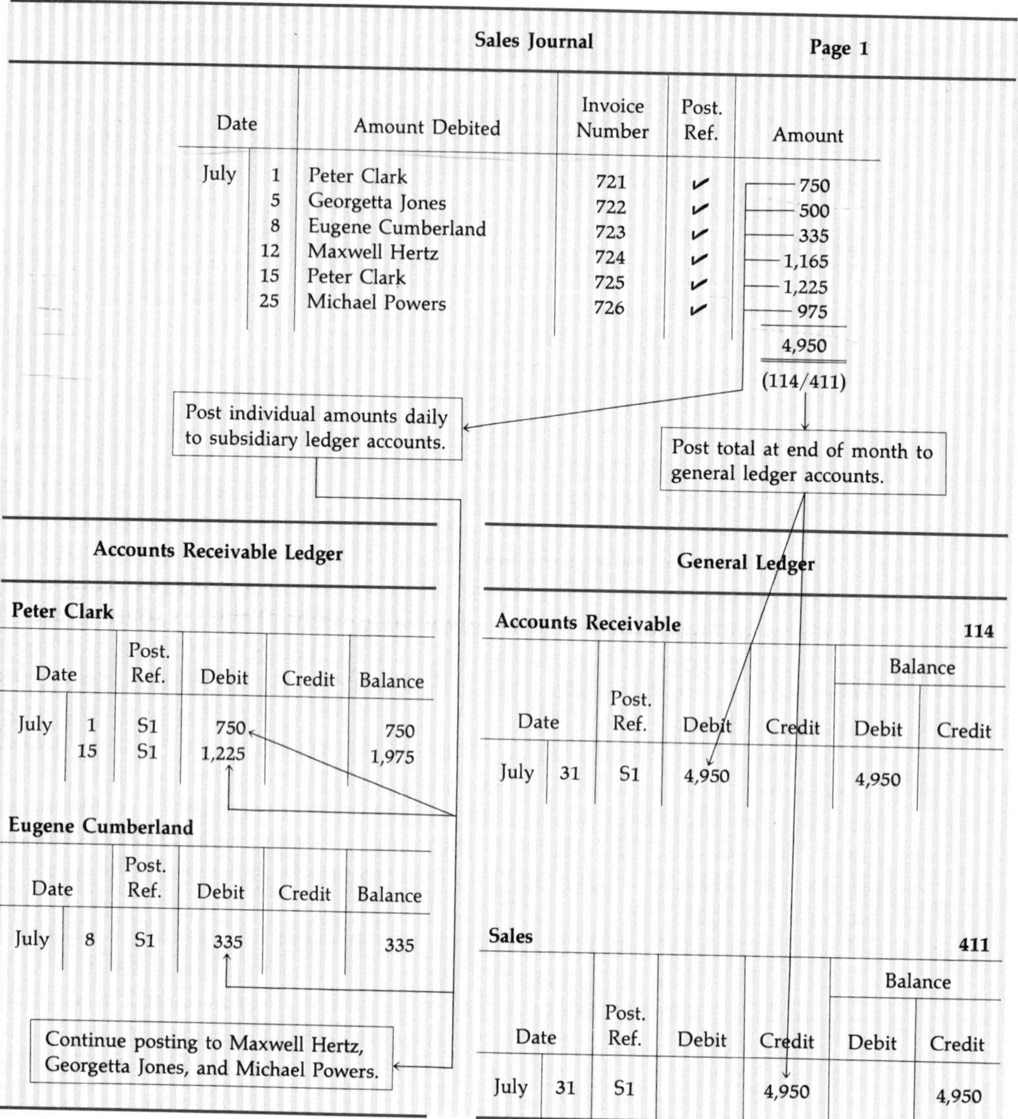

Sales Journal — Page 1

Date		Amount Debited	Invoice Number	Post. Ref.	Amount
July	1	Peter Clark	721	✓	750
	5	Georgetta Jones	722	✓	500
	8	Eugene Cumberland	723	✓	335
	12	Maxwell Hertz	724	✓	1,165
	15	Peter Clark	725	✓	1,225
	25	Michael Powers	726	✓	975
					4,950
					(114/411)

Accounts Receivable Ledger

Peter Clark

Date		Post. Ref.	Debit	Credit	Balance
July	1	S1	750		750
	15	S1	1,225		1,975

Eugene Cumberland

Date		Post. Ref.	Debit	Credit	Balance
July	8	S1	335		335

General Ledger

Accounts Receivable — 114

Date		Post. Ref.	Debit	Credit	Balance Debit	Balance Credit
July	31	S1	4,950		4,950	

Sales — 411

Date		Post. Ref.	Debit	Credit	Balance Debit	Balance Credit
July	31	S1		4,950		4,950

Figure 8-4 Relationship of Sales Journal, General Ledger, and Accounts Receivable Ledger and the Posting Procedure

3. At the end of the month, sum the Amount column to determine the total credit sales, and post the amount to the general ledger accounts (debit Accounts Receivable and credit Sales). Place the numbers of the accounts debited and credited beneath the total in the sales journal to indicate that this step has been completed, and place an S1 in the Post. Ref. column of each account to indicate the source of the entry.

4. Verify the accuracy of the posting by adding the account balances of the accounts receivable ledger and by matching the total with the Accounts Receivable controlling account balance in the general ledger. This step can be accomplished by listing the accounts in a schedule of accounts receivable, as shown in Figure 8-5.

Figure 8-5
Schedule of Accounts Receivable

Mitchell's Used Car Sales Schedule of Accounts Receivable July 31, 19xx	
Peter Clark	$1,975
Eugene Cumberland	335
Maxwell Hertz	1,165
Georgetta Jones	500
Michael Powers	975
Total Accounts Receivable	$4,950

Sales Taxes Other columns, such as a column for credit terms, can be added to the sales journal. The nature of the company's business will determine whether they are needed.

Many cities and states require retailers to collect a sales tax from their customers and periodically remit the total amount of the tax to the state or city. In this case, an additional column is needed in the sales journal. The required entry is illustrated in Figure 8-6. The procedure for posting to the ledger is exactly the same as previously described except that the total of the Sales Taxes Payable column must be posted as a credit to the Sales Taxes Payable account at the end of the month.

Most companies also make cash sales. Cash sales are usually recorded in a column of the cash receipts journal. This procedure is discussed later in the chapter.

Purchases Journal

The techniques associated with the sales journal are very similar to those of the purchases journal. The **purchases journal** is used to record all purchases on credit and may take the form of either a single-column

Figure 8-6
Section of a Sales Journal with a Column for Sales Taxes

Sales Journal — **Page 7**

Date		Account Debited	Invoice Number	Post. Ref.	Debit	Credits	
					Accounts Receivable	Sales Taxes Payable	Sales
Sept.	1	Ralph P. Hake	727		206	6	200

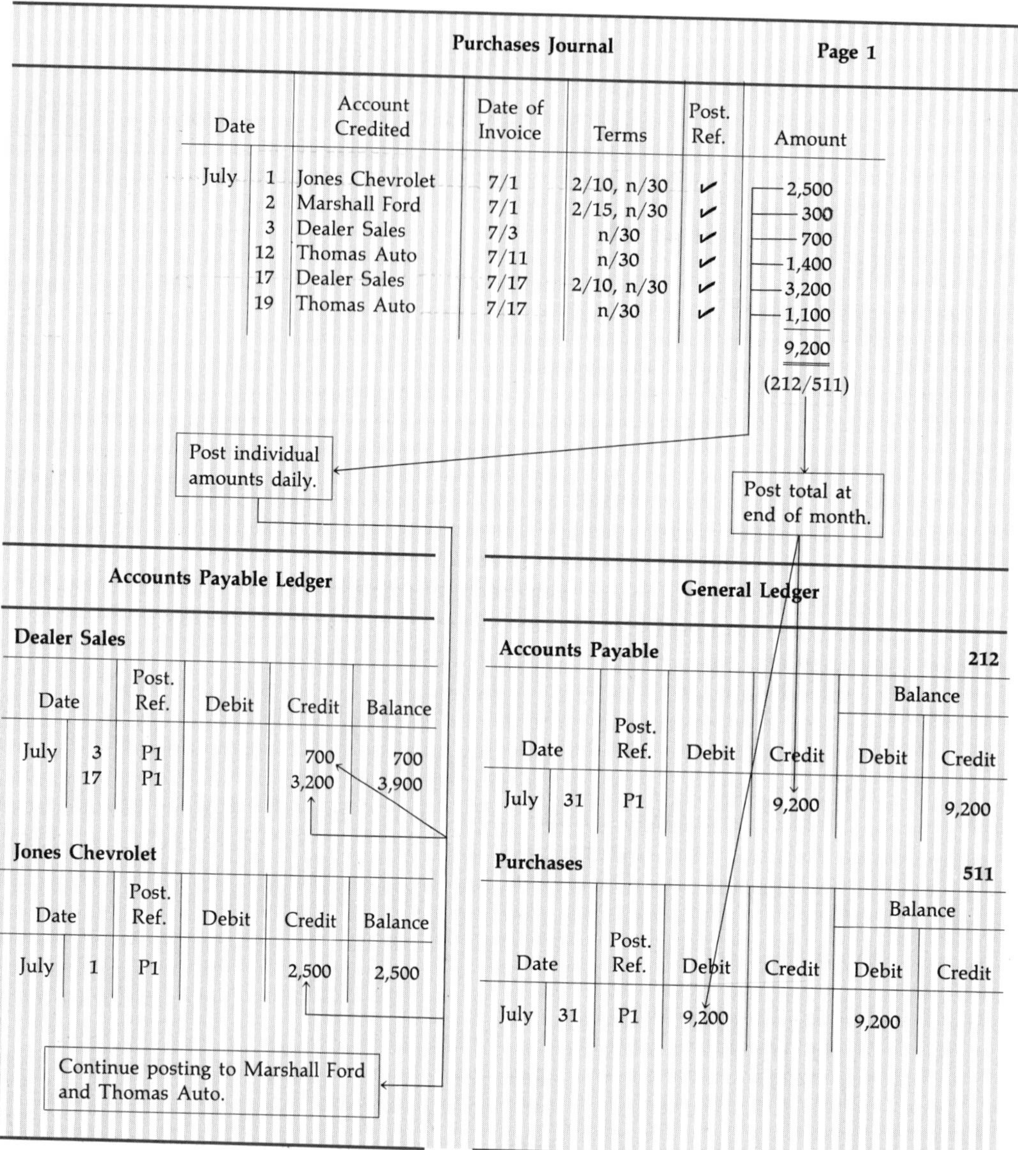

Purchases Journal — Page 1

Date		Account Credited	Date of Invoice	Terms	Post. Ref.	Amount
July	1	Jones Chevrolet	7/1	2/10, n/30	✓	2,500
	2	Marshall Ford	7/1	2/15, n/30	✓	300
	3	Dealer Sales	7/3	n/30	✓	700
	12	Thomas Auto	7/11	n/30	✓	1,400
	17	Dealer Sales	7/17	2/10, n/30	✓	3,200
	19	Thomas Auto	7/17	n/30	✓	1,100
						9,200
						(212/511)

Accounts Payable Ledger

Dealer Sales

Date		Post. Ref.	Debit	Credit	Balance
July	3	P1		700	700
	17	P1		3,200	3,900

Jones Chevrolet

Date		Post. Ref.	Debit	Credit	Balance
July	1	P1		2,500	2,500

General Ledger

Accounts Payable — 212

Date		Post. Ref.	Debit	Credit	Balance Debit	Balance Credit
July	31	P1		9,200		9,200

Purchases — 511

Date		Post. Ref.	Debit	Credit	Balance Debit	Balance Credit
July	31	P1	9,200		9,200	

Figure 8-7 Relationship of Single-Column Purchases Journal to the General Ledger and the Accounts Payable Ledger

journal or a multicolumn journal. In the single-column journal, illustrated in Figure 8-7, only credit purchases of merchandise for resale to customers are recorded. This type of transaction is recorded with a debit to Purchases and a credit to Accounts Payable. When the single-column purchases journal is used, credit purchases of items other than merchandise are recorded in the general journal. Also, cash purchases are recorded, not in the purchases journal, but in the cash payments journal, which is discussed later.

As with Accounts Receivable, the Accounts Payable account in the general ledger is used by most companies as a controlling account. So that the company will know how much it owes each supplier, it maintains an individual account for each supplier in an accounts payable subsidiary ledger. The concepts and techniques described above for the accounts receivable subsidiary ledger and general ledger account apply also to the accounts payable subsidiary ledger and general ledger account. Thus the total of the individual accounts in the accounts payable subsidiary ledger will equal the balance of the Accounts Payable controlling account in the general ledger because of the posting of the individual credit purchases to the individual accounts each day and the total credit purchases to the controlling account each month.

The steps for using a purchases journal, as illustrated in Figure 8-7, are as follows:

1. Enter each purchase invoice in the purchases journal on a single line, recording date, supplier's name, invoice date, terms if applicable, and amount.

2. At the end of each day, post each individual purchase to the supplier's account in the accounts payable subsidiary ledger. As each purchase is posted, place a check in the Post. Ref. column of the purchases journal to indicate that it has been posted, and place a P1 (representing Purchases Journal—page 1) in the Post. Ref. column of each supplier's account to indicate the source of the entry.

3. At the end of the month, compute the total of the credit purchases, and post the amount in the general ledger accounts (Accounts Payable and Purchases). Place the numbers of the accounts debited and credited beneath the total in the purchases journal to indicate that this step has been completed.

4. Verify the accuracy of the posting by adding the balances of the accounts payable ledger accounts and matching the total with the Accounts Payable controlling account balance in the general ledger. This step may be accomplished by preparing a schedule of accounts payable.

The single-column purchases journal may be expanded to record purchases of items other than merchandise by the addition of a separate column for other commonly used debit accounts. For example, the multicolumn purchases journal in Figure 8-8 has columns for Freight In, Store Supplies, and Office Supplies. In this journal, the total credits to Accounts Payable ($9,437) equal the total debits to Purchases, Freight In, Store Supplies, and Office Supplies ($9,200 + $50 + $145 + $42 = $9,437). In a way similar to the procedure already described, the individual transactions in the Accounts Payable column are posted daily to the accounts payable subsidiary ledger, and the totals of each column in the journal are posted monthly to the appropriate general ledger accounts. Credit purchases that require a debit to an account that has no special column (that is, no place to record the debit) in the purchases journal must be recorded in the general journal.

Purchases Journal										Page 1
						Credit	Debits			
Date		Account Credited	Date of Invoice	Terms	Post. Ref.	Accounts Payable	Purchases	Freight In	Store Supplies	Office Supplies
July	1	Jones Chevrolet	7/1	2/10, n/30	✓	2,500	2,500			
	2	Marshall Ford	7/1	2/15, n/30	✓	300	300			
	2	Shelby Car Delivery	7/2	n/30	✓	50		50		
	3	Dealer Sales	7/3	n/30	✓	700	700			
	12	Thomas Auto	7/11	n/30	✓	1,400	1,400			
	17	Dealer Sales	7/17	2/10, n/30	✓	3,200	3,200			
	19	Thomas Auto	7/17	n/30	✓	1,100	1,100			
	25	Osborne Supply	7/21	n/10th	✓	187			145	42
						9,437	9,200	50	145	42
						(212)	(511)	(514)	(132)	(133)

Figure 8-8
A Multicolumn Purchases Journal

Cash Receipts Journal

All transactions involving receipts of cash are recorded in the **cash receipts journal.** Examples of such transactions are cash from cash sales, cash from credit customers in payment of their accounts, and cash from other sources. To be most efficient, the cash receipts journal must be multicolumn. Several columns are necessary because, though all cash receipts are alike in that they require a debit to Cash, they are different in that they require a variety of credit entries. Thus you should be alert to several important differences between the cash receipts journal and the journals previously presented. Among these differences are an Other Accounts column, use of account numbers in the Post. Ref. column, and daily posting of the credits to Other Accounts.

The cash receipts journal illustrated in Figure 8-9 is based on the following selected transactions for July:

July 1 Henry Mitchell invested $20,000 in a used-car business.
5 Sold a used car for $1,200 cash.
8 Collected $500 from Georgetta Jones, less 2 percent sales discount.
13 Sold a used car for $1,400 cash.
16 Collected $750 from Peter Clark.
19 Sold a used car for $1,000 cash.
20 Sold some equipment not used in the business for $500 cash.
24 Signed a note at the bank for a loan of $5,000.
26 Sold a used car for $1,600 cash.
28 Collected $600 from Peter Clark, less 2 percent sales discount.

The cash receipts journal, as illustrated in Figure 8-9, has two debit columns and three credit columns. The two debit columns record Cash and Sales Discounts.

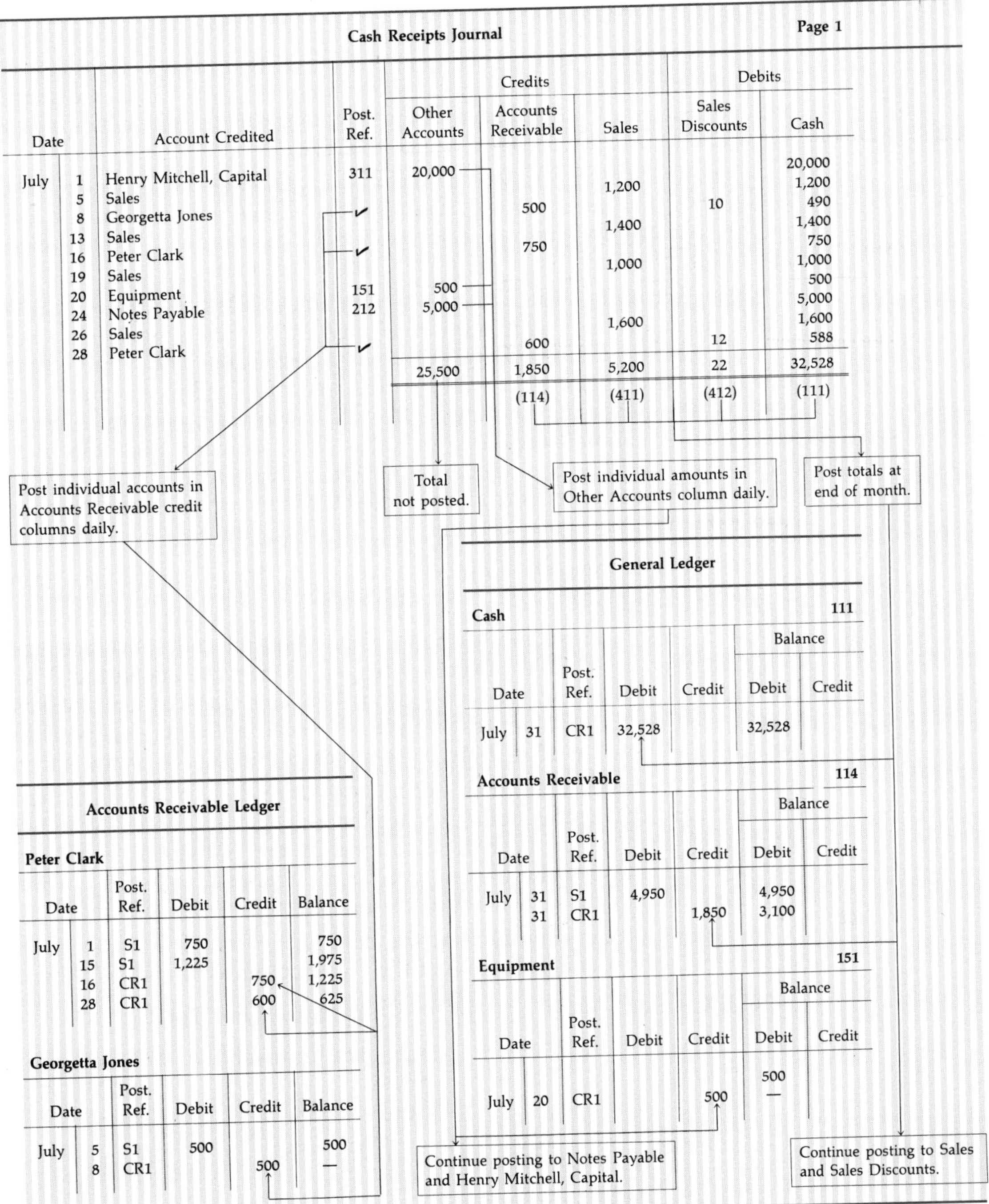

Cash Receipts Journal — Page 1

Date		Account Credited	Post. Ref.	Credits: Other Accounts	Credits: Accounts Receivable	Credits: Sales	Debits: Sales Discounts	Debits: Cash
July	1	Henry Mitchell, Capital	311	20,000				20,000
	5	Sales				1,200		1,200
	8	Georgetta Jones	✓		500		10	490
	13	Sales				1,400		1,400
	16	Peter Clark	✓		750			750
	19	Sales				1,000		1,000
	20	Equipment	151	500				500
	24	Notes Payable	212	5,000				5,000
	26	Sales				1,600		1,600
	28	Peter Clark	✓		600		12	588
				25,500	1,850	5,200	22	32,528
					(114)	(411)	(412)	(111)

General Ledger

Cash — 111

Date		Post. Ref.	Debit	Credit	Balance: Debit	Balance: Credit
July	31	CR1	32,528		32,528	

Accounts Receivable — 114

Date		Post. Ref.	Debit	Credit	Balance: Debit	Balance: Credit
July	31	S1	4,950		4,950	
	31	CR1		1,850	3,100	

Equipment — 151

Date		Post. Ref.	Debit	Credit	Balance: Debit	Balance: Credit
					500	
July	20	CR1		500	—	

Accounts Receivable Ledger

Peter Clark

Date		Post. Ref.	Debit	Credit	Balance
July	1	S1	750		750
	15	S1	1,225		1,975
	16	CR1		750	1,225
	28	CR1		600	625

Georgetta Jones

Date		Post. Ref.	Debit	Credit	Balance
July	5	S1	500		500
	8	CR1		500	—

Figure 8-9 Relationship of the Cash Receipts Journal to the General Ledger and the Accounts Receivable Ledger

1. **Cash** Each entry must have an amount in this column because each transaction must be a receipt of cash.

2. **Sales Discounts** The company in the illustration allows a 2 percent discount for prompt payment. Consequently, it is useful to have a column for sales discounts. Note that in the transactions of July 8 and 28, the debits to Cash and Sales Discounts equal the credit to Accounts Receivable.

The credit columns are the following:

1. **Accounts Receivable** This column is used to record collections on accounts from customers. The customer's name is written in the space entitled Account Credited so that the payment can be entered in his or her account in the accounts receivable ledger.

2. **Sales** This column is used to record all cash sales during the month. Retail firms that normally use cash registers would make an entry at the end of each day for the total sales from each cash register for that day. The debit, of course, is in the Cash Debited column.

3. **Other Accounts** This column is sometimes called Sundry Accounts and is used for the credit portion of any entry that is neither a cash collection from Accounts Receivable nor a cash sale. The name of the account to be credited is indicated in the Account Credited column. For example, the transactions of July 1, 20, and 24 involved credits to accounts other than Accounts Receivable or Sales. If a company finds that it is consistently crediting a certain account in the Other Accounts column, it may be appropriate to add another credit column to the cash receipts journal for that particular account.

The posting of the cash receipts journal, as illustrated in Figure 8-9, can be summarized as follows:

1. Post the Accounts Receivable column daily to each individual account in the accounts receivable subsidiary ledger. A check mark in the Post. Ref. column of the cash receipts journal indicates that the amount has been posted, and a CR1 (representing Cash Receipts Journal—page 1) in the Post. Ref. column of each account indicates the source of the entry.

2. Post the credits in the Other Accounts column daily or at convenient short intervals during the month to the general ledger accounts. Write the account number in the Post. Ref. column as the individual items are posted to indicate that the posting has been done, and write CR1 in the Post. Ref. column of each account to indicate the source of the entry.

3. At the end of the month, total the columns. The sum of the debit column totals must equal the sum of the credit columns totals, as follows:

Debit Column Totals		**Credit Column Totals**	
Cash	$32,528	Accounts Receivable	$ 1,850
Sales Discounts	22	Sales	5,200
		Other Accounts	25,500
Total Debits	$32,550	Total Credits	$32,550

This step is called crossfooting.

4. Post the column totals as follows:
   a. Cash debit column—posted as a debit to the Cash account.
   b. Sales Discounts debit column—posted as a debit to the Sales Discounts account.
   c. Accounts Receivable credit column—posted as a credit to the Accounts Receivable controlling account.

d. Sales credit column—posted as a credit to the Sales account.

e. The account numbers are written below each column as they are posted to indicate that this step has been completed. A CR1 is written in the Post. Ref. column of each account to indicate the source of the entry.

f. Note that the Other Accounts column total is not posted by total because each entry was posted separately. The individual accounts were posted in step 2 above. Accountants sometimes place a check mark at the bottom of the column to show that it is not posted.

Cash Payments Journal

All transactions involving payments of cash are recorded in the **cash payments journal** (also called the cash disbursements journal). Examples of such transactions are cash purchases, payments of obligations resulting from earlier purchases on credit, and other cash payments. As with the cash receipts journal, the cash payments journal must be multicolumn and is similar in design to the cash receipts journal.

The cash payments journal illustrated in Figure 8-10 (next page) is based on the following selected transactions of Mitchell's Used Car Sales for July:

July 2 Purchased merchandise (a used car) from Sondra Tidmore for cash, $400.

6 Paid for newspaper advertising in the *Daily Journal,* $200.

8 Paid one month's land and building rent to Siviglia Agency, $250.

11 Paid Jones Chevrolet for July 1 invoice (previously recorded in purchases journal in Figure 8-7), $2,500, less 2 percent purchase discount earned for payment in ten days or less.

16 Paid Charles Kuntz, a salesman, his salary, $600.

17 Paid Marshall Ford invoice of July 2 (previously recorded in purchases journal in Figure 8-7), $300, less 2 percent discount earned for payment in fifteen days or less.

24 Paid Grabow & Company for two-year insurance policy, $480.

27 Paid Dealer Sales invoice of July 17 (previously recorded in purchases journal in Figure 8-7), $3,200, less 2 percent purchase discount earned for payment in ten days or less.

30 Purchased office equipment for $400 and service equipment for $500 from A & B Equipment Company. Issued one check for the total cost.

The cash payments journal, as illustrated in Figure 8-10, has two credit columns and two debit columns. The credit columns are as follows:

1. **Cash** Each entry must have an amount in this column because each transaction must involve a payment of cash.

2. **Purchases Discounts** When purchases discounts are taken, they are recorded in this column.

Figure 8-10
Cash Payments Journal

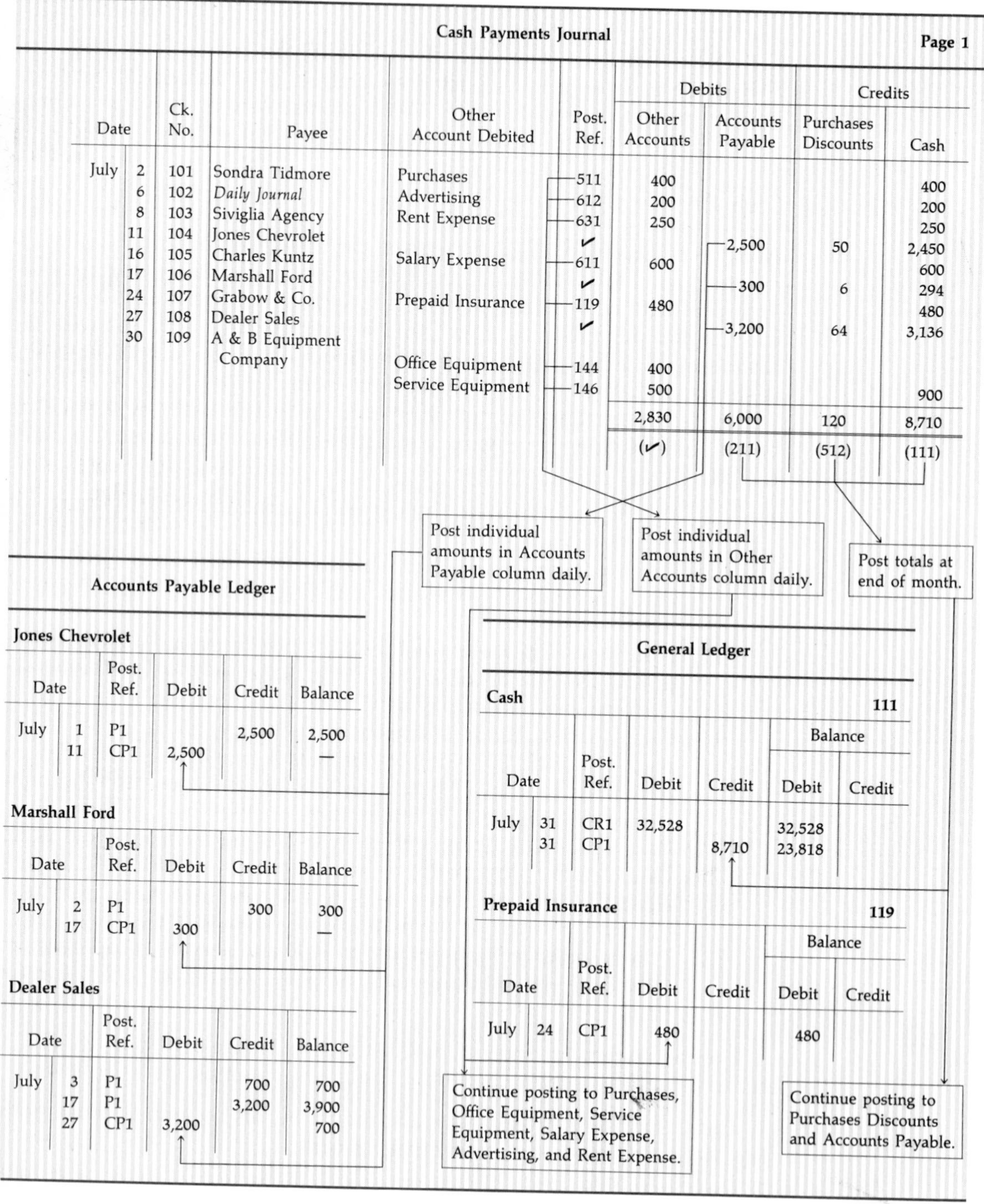

Cash Payments Journal — Page 1

Date		Ck. No.	Payee	Other Account Debited	Post. Ref.	Debits: Other Accounts	Debits: Accounts Payable	Credits: Purchases Discounts	Credits: Cash
July	2	101	Sondra Tidmore	Purchases	511	400			400
	6	102	*Daily Journal*	Advertising	612	200			200
	8	103	Siviglia Agency	Rent Expense	631	250			250
	11	104	Jones Chevrolet		✓		2,500	50	2,450
	16	105	Charles Kuntz	Salary Expense	611	600			600
	17	106	Marshall Ford		✓		300	6	294
	24	107	Grabow & Co.	Prepaid Insurance	119	480			480
	27	108	Dealer Sales		✓		3,200	64	3,136
	30	109	A & B Equipment Company	Office Equipment	144	400			
				Service Equipment	146	500			900
						2,830	6,000	120	8,710
						(✓)	(211)	(512)	(111)

Accounts Payable Ledger

Jones Chevrolet

Date		Post. Ref.	Debit	Credit	Balance
July	1	P1		2,500	2,500
	11	CP1	2,500		—

Marshall Ford

Date		Post. Ref.	Debit	Credit	Balance
July	2	P1		300	300
	17	CP1	300		—

Dealer Sales

Date		Post. Ref.	Debit	Credit	Balance
July	3	P1		700	700
	17	P1		3,200	3,900
	27	CP1	3,200		700

General Ledger

Cash — 111

Date		Post. Ref.	Debit	Credit	Balance: Debit	Balance: Credit
July	31	CR1	32,528		32,528	
	31	CP1		8,710	23,818	

Prepaid Insurance — 119

Date		Post. Ref.	Debit	Credit	Balance: Debit	Balance: Credit
July	24	CP1	480		480	

The debit columns are as follows:

1. **Accounts Payable** This column total is used to record payments to suppliers that have extended credit to the company. The supplier's name is written in the space entitled Payee so that the payment can be entered in his or her account in the accounts payable ledger.

2. **Other Accounts** Cash can be expended for many reasons. Consequently, an Other Accounts or Sundry Accounts column is needed in the cash payments journal. The title of the account to be debited is written in the Other Account Debited column, and the amount is entered in the amount column. If a company finds that a particular account occurs often in the Other Accounts column, it may be desirable to add another debit column to the cash payments journal.

The posting of the cash payments journal, as illustrated in Figure 8-10, can be summarized as follows:

1. The Accounts Payable column should be posted daily to each individual account in the accounts payable subsidiary ledger. A check mark is placed in the Post. Ref. column to indicate that the posting is accomplished.

2. The debits in the Other Accounts debit column should be posted daily or at convenient intervals during the month to the general ledger. The account number is written in the Post. Ref. column as the individual items are posted to indicate that the posting has been completed and a CP1 (representing Cash Payments Journal—page 1) is written in the Post. Ref. column of each account.

3. At the end of the month, the columns are totaled and crossfooted; that is, the sum of the credit column totals must equal the sum of the debit column totals, as follows:

Credit Column Totals		**Debit Column Totals**	
Cash	$8,710	Accounts Payable	$6,000
Purchases Discounts	120	Other Accounts	2,830
Total Credits	$8,830	Total Debits	$8,830

4. The column totals for Cash, Purchases Discounts, and Accounts Payable are posted at the end of the month to their respective accounts in the general ledger. The account numbers are written below each column as they are posted to indicate that this step has been completed, and a CP1 is written in the Post. Ref. column of each account. The total of the Other Accounts column is not posted.

General Journal

Transactions that do not involve sales, purchases, cash receipts, or cash payments should be recorded in the general journal. Usually there are only a few such transactions. Three examples are compound entries that do not fit in a special-purpose journal, a return of merchandise, and an allowance to a supplier for credit. Adjusting and closing entries are also recorded in the general journal. Consider the following transactions:

July 24 Purchased service equipment on credit from A & B Supply for $3,500, paying $500 down and issuing a 90-day note for the balance.

25 Returned one of the used cars purchased from Dealer Sales on July 17 for credit, $700.

26 Agreed to give Maxwell Hertz a $35 allowance on his account because a tire blew out on the car he purchased.

		Post Ref.		
July 24	Service Equipment	146	3,500	
	Cash	111		500
	Notes Payable	211		3,000
	Purchased service equipment from A & B Supply; terms: $500 down payment and 90-day note for balance			
25	Accounts Payable—Dealer Sales	211/✓	700	
	Purchases Returns and Allowances	513		700
	Returned used car for credit; invoice date: 7/3			
26	Sales Returns and Allowances	413	35	
	Accounts Receivable—Maxwell Hertz	114/✓		35
	Allowance given because of faulty tire			

The July 24 entry cannot be made in the cash payments journal (Figure 8-10) because the entry requires credits to both Cash and Notes Payable but the journal allows credits only to Cash and Purchases Discounts. The entries on July 25 and 26 include a debit or a credit to a controlling account (Accounts Payable or Accounts Receivable). The name of the customer or supplier is also indicated. When such an entry is made to a controlling account in the general journal, the entry must be posted twice: once in the controlling account and once in the individual account in the subsidiary ledger. This procedure maintains the equality of the subsidiary ledger to the controlling account. For example, the July 26 transaction is posted by a debit to Sales Returns and Allowances in the general ledger (indicated by the account number 413), by a credit to the Accounts Receivable controlling account in the general ledger (indicated by the account number 114), and by a credit to the Maxwell Hertz account in the accounts receivable subsidiary ledger (indicated by the check mark).

Flexibility of Special-Purpose Journals

The functions of special-purpose journals are to reduce and simplify the work in accounting and to allow for division of labor. These journals should be designed to fit the business in which they are used. As mentioned earlier, if certain accounts show up often in the Other Accounts column of a journal, it is usually wise to add a column for those accounts when a new page of a special-purpose journal is prepared.

In addition, if certain transactions appear regularly in the general journal, it may be appropriate to set up a new special-purpose journal. For example, if Mitchell Used Car Sales finds that it must often give allowances to customers, it may want to set up a special sales returns and allowances journal. Likewise, a purchases returns and allowances journal may be in order. In short, special-purpose journals should be designed to handle the types of transactions a company commonly encounters.

Computer Data Processing[1]

Many small firms are adequately served by manual systems or by simple accounting machines. Larger firms, however, generally rely on the computer.

Objective 5 Describe the basic features of computer systems and their application to data processing

A **computer data processing** system is a type of data processing system in which recording, posting, and other bookkeeping procedures are done with the aid of a computer. This system is made up of hardware, software, procedures, and personnel. All of the equipment needed for the operation of the system is called **hardware.** Data may be fed into the system by optical scanners, card or tape readers, console typewriters, or other input devices. The **central processor** is the actual "computer" of the system. It has three components: (1) the **control unit,** which directs and coordinates all parts of the computer; (2) the **arithmetic/logic unit,** which performs the computations and decision-making junctions; and (3) **storage** (or memory) **units,** which store instructions and other data so they are available when needed. Among the most common output devices are printers, card punches, and cathode ray tubes.

Computer **software** comprises the programs, instructions, and routines for using the hardware. The **program** consists of a sequence of instructions that produce a desired result. It must be written in a language that the computer can understand.

The procedures for a computer system are all the steps taken from data origination to output. Clear, precise procedures are essential to the smooth operation of the system.

The primary personnel in a computer system are the systems analyst, the programmer, and the computer operator. The **systems analyst** designs the system on the basis of information needs. The **programmer** writes the

1. This section was condensed from S. Bernard Rosenblatt, Robert L. Bonnington, and Belverd E. Needles, Jr., *Modern Business,* 2nd ed. (Boston: Houghton Mifflin, 1977), pp. 455–461. Used with permission.

instructions for the computer, and the **computer operator** runs the computer.

The goal of an integrated system is to computerize all the information a company may need, such as purchasing, inventory control, payroll, and production scheduling data. A total system that processes one job at a time in a logical sequence is called **batch processing.** A newer approach is **on-line processing,** in which remote terminals are tied to the central processor, and stored data may be retrieved immediately.

Chapter Review

Review of Learning Objectives

1. Describe the phases of systems installation and the principles of systems design.

The phases of systems installation are system investigation, system design, and system implementation. In designing an accounting system, the system designer should attempt to comply with the four principles of systems design: the cost/benefit principle, the control principle, the compatibility principle, and the flexibility principle.

2. Explain the objectives and uses of special-purpose journals.

The typical manual data processing system consists of several special-purpose journals, each of which is designed to record one type of transaction. Recording all transactions of one type in each journal reduces and simplifies the bookkeeping work and results in the division of labor. The division of labor is important for control purposes.

3. Construct and use the following types of special-purpose journals: sales journal, purchases journal, cash receipts journal, cash payments journal, and others as needed.

A special-purpose journal is constructed by devoting a single column to a particular account (for example, debit cash in the cash receipts journal and credit cash in the cash payments journal). Other columns in such a journal depend on the types of transactions in which the company normally engages. The special-purpose journals also have columns for the transaction dates, explanations or subsidiary account names, and reference columns.

4. Explain the purposes and relationships of controlling accounts and subsidiary ledgers.

Subsidiary ledgers contain the individual accounts of a certain type such as customer accounts (accounts receivable) or supplier accounts (accounts payable). The total of the balances of the subsidiary accounts will equal the total of the controlling or general ledger account because the individual items are posted daily to the subsidiary accounts and the column totals are posted monthly from the special-purpose journal.

5. Describe the basic features of computer systems and their application to data processing.

Computer data processing systems are the most advanced type of data processing systems, in which recording, posting, and other bookkeeping procedures are done with the aid of a computer. The typical computer system consists of hardware, software, procedures, and personnel. The internal processing is specified in the form of programs, which may be designed to allow batch processing (one job at a time) or on-line processing (several jobs at a time).

Review Problem

In this chapter, we suggest that you review the procedures and illustrations given for each of the special-purpose journals before starting the exercises and problems. For additional help, see the review problem in the working papers.

Chapter Assignments

Questions

1. What are the three phases of systems installation?
2. What are the four principles of systems design? Explain the essence of each in a sentence.
3. What is the function of data processing?
4. What are three ways of viewing data processing?
5. How do special-purpose journals save time in entering and posting transactions?
6. Long Transit had 1,700 sales on credit during the current month.
   a. If the company uses a two-column general journal to record sales, how many times will the word *Sales* be written?
   b. How many postings to the Sales account will have to be made?.
   c. If the company uses a sales journal, how many times will the word *Sales* be written?
   d. How many postings to the Sales account will have to be made?
7. What is the purpose of the Accounts Receivable controlling account? What is its relationship to the accounts receivable subsidiary ledger?
8. Why are the cash receipts journal and cash payments journal crossfooted? When is this step performed?
9. A company has the following numbers of accounts with balances: 18 asset accounts, including the Accounts Receivable account but not the individual customer accounts; 200 customer accounts; 8 liability accounts, including the Accounts Payable account but not the individual credit accounts; 100 creditor accounts; 35 owner's equity accounts, including income statement accounts for a total of 361. How many accounts in total would appear in the general ledger?
10. What are the elements of a computer data processing system?
11. What is the difference between hardware and software?
12. Data are the raw material of a computer system. As data pass through the system, in what places or in what components may they be found?
13. What is the purpose of a computer program?
14. What is the difference between batch processing and on-line processing?

Classroom Exercises

Exercise 8-1 Matching Transactions to Special-Purpose Journals

A company uses a one-column sales journal, a one-column purchases journal, a cash receipts journal, a cash payments journal, and a general journal in recording its transactions.

Indicate in which journal each of the following transactions would be recorded: (1) sold merchandise on credit; (2) sold merchandise for cash; (3) gave a customer credit for merchandise purchased on credit and returned; (4) paid a creditor; (5) paid office salaries; (6) customer paid for merchandise previously purchased on credit; (7) recorded adjusting and closing entries; (8) purchased merchandise on credit; (9) purchased sales department supplies on credit; (10) purchased office equipment for cash; (11) returned merchandise purchased on credit; (12) payment of taxes.

Exercise 8-2 Characteristics of Special-Purpose Journals

Santana Corporation uses a sales journal, a purchases journal, a cash receipts journal, a cash payments journal, and a general journal.

1. In which journal would you expect to find the fewest transactions recorded?
2. At the end of the accounting period, to which account or accounts should the total of the purchases journal be posted as a debit and/or credit?
3. At the end of the accounting period, to which account or accounts should the total of the sales journal be posted as a debit and/or credit?
4. What two subsidiary ledgers would probably be associated with the journals listed above? From which journals would postings normally be made to each of the two subsidiary ledgers?
5. In which of the journals are adjusting and closing entries made?

Exercise 8-3 Identifying the Content of a Special-Purpose Journal

Shown below is a page from a special journal.

1. What kind of journal is this?
2. Give an explanation for each of the following transactions: (a) August 27, (b) August 28, (c) August 29, and (d) August 30.
3. Explain the following: (a) the numbers under the bottom lines, (b) the checks entered in the Post. Ref. column, (c) the numbers 215 and 515 in the Post. Ref. column, and (d) the check below the Other Accounts column.

Date			Post. Ref.	Credits			Debits	
				Other Accounts	Accounts Receivable	Sales	Sales Discounts	Cash
		Balance Forward		26,100	10,204	4,282	787	39,799
Aug.	27	Dale McEnroe	✓		500		10	490
	28	Notes Receivable	215	1,000				
		Interest Earned	515	120				1,120
	29	Cash Sale				960		960
	30	Catherine Rawlins	✓		200			200
				27,220	10,904	5,242	797	42,569
				(✓)	(214)	(510)	(511)	(111)

Exercise 8-4 Finding Errors in Special-Purpose Journals

A company records purchases in a one-column purchases journal and records purchases returns in its general journal. During the past month an accounting clerk made each of the errors described below. Explain how each error might be discovered.

1. Correctly recorded an $86 purchase in the purchases journal but posted it to the creditor's account as a $68 purchase.
2. Made an addition error in totaling the Amount column of the purchases journal.

3. Posted a purchases return recorded in the general journal to the Purchases Returns and Allowances account and to the Accounts Payable account but did not post it to the creditor's account.
4. Made an error in determining the balance of a creditor's account.
5. Posted a purchases return to the Accounts Payable account but did not post to the Purchases Returns and Allowances account.

Exercise 8-5 Posting from a Sales Journal

Pandor Corporation began business on September 1. The company maintained a sales journal, which appeared as follows at the end of the month:

Sales Journal — **Page 1**

Date		Account Debited	Invoice Number	Post. Ref.	Amount
Sept.	4	Marshal Thompson	1001	✓	172
	10	Jennifer Carey	1002	✓	317
	15	Juanita Mendez	1003	✓	214
	17	Marshal Thompson	1004	✓	97
	25	Thomas Kernot	1005	✓	433
					1,233
					(112/410)

1. On a sheet of accounting paper, open general ledger accounts for Accounts Receivable (account number 112) and Sales (account number 410) and an accounts receivable subsidiary ledger with a T account for each customer. Make the appropriate postings from the sales journal.
2. Prove the accounts receivable subsidiary ledger by preparing a schedule of accounts receivable.

Exercise 8-6 Multicolumn Purchases Journal

Leet Company uses a multicolumn purchases journal similar to the one illustrated in Figure 8-8. During the month of October, Leet made the following purchases:

Oct. 1 Purchased merchandise from Turbow Company on account for $2,700, invoice dated October 1, terms 2/10, n/30.
2 Received freight bill dated Oct. 1 from Color Freight for above merchandise, $175, terms n/30.
23 Purchased supplies from T & J, Inc., for $120; allocated one-half each to store and office, invoice dated Oct. 20, terms n/30.
27 Purchased merchandise from Jackson Company on account for $987; total included freight in of $87, invoice dated Oct. 25, terms n/30, FOB shipping point.
30 Purchased office supplies from T & J, Inc., $48, invoice dated October 30, terms n/30.

1. Draw a multicolumn purchases journal similar to the one in Figure 8-8.
2. Enter the above transactions in the purchases journal. Then foot and crossfoot the columns.

Problem Set A

Problem 8A-1 Identification of Transactions

Anderson Company uses a general journal, purchases journal, sales journal, cash receipts journal, and cash payments journal similar to those illustrated in the text. On June 30, the T. Taylor account in the accounts receivable subsidiary ledger appeared as follows:

T. Taylor **Account No.**

Date		Item	Post. Ref.	Debit	Credit	Balance
May	31		S4	372		372
June	4		J7		27	345
	10		CR5		100	245
	15		S6	114		359

On June 30, the account of Macey Company in the accounts payable subsidiary ledger appeared as follows:

Macey Company **Account No.**

Date		Item	Post. Ref.	Debit	Credit	Balance
June	16		P7		982	982
	21		J9	106		876
	28		CP8	876		—

Required

1. Write an explanation of each entry affecting T. Taylor's account receivable including the journal from which the entry was posted.
2. Write an explanation of each entry affecting the Macey Company account payable including the journal from which the entry was posted.

Problem 8A-2 Cash Receipts and Cash Payments Journals

The items below detail all cash transactions by Windsor Company for the month of February. The company uses multicolumn cash receipts and cash payments journals similar to those illustrated in the chapter.

Feb. 1 The owner, R. Windsor, invested $30,000 cash in the business.
2 Paid February rent to Harper Agency, $250, with check no. 101.
3 Cash sales, $800.
6 Purchased store equipment, for $2,500, from Sandburg Equipment Company, with check no. 102.
7 Purchased merchandise for cash, $3,250, from Ruben Company, with check no. 103.
8 Paid Hiller Company invoice, $900, less 2 percent, with check no. 104.
9 Paid advertising bill, $175, to *Daily News*, with check no. 105.
10 Cash sales, $1,950.

12 Received $400 on account from J. J. McKewn.
13 Purchased used truck for cash, $1,760, from K & L Auto, with check no. 106.
19 Received $2,090 from Markum Company, in settlement of a $2,000 note plus interest.
20 Received $539 ($550 less $11 cash discount) from Cindy Lewis.
21 Withdrew $1,000 from business for personal use by issuing check no. 107.
23 Paid Deroco Company invoice, $1,250, less 2 percent discount, with check no. 108.
26 Paid Blue Line, Inc., for freight on merchandise received, $80, with check no. 109.
27 Cash sales, $2,400.
28 Paid R. J. Sadler for monthly salary, $700, with check no. 110.

Required

1. Enter the above transactions in the cash receipts and cash payments journals.
2. Foot and rule the journals.

Problem 8A-3 Purchases and General Journals

The items below represent the credit transactions for Morris Supply Company during the month of March. The company uses a multicolumn purchases journal and a general journal similar to those illustrated in the text.

Mar. 2 Purchased merchandise from Streeter Company, $600.
5 Purchased truck from GMR Company, $3,500.
8 Purchased office supplies from Supple Company, $200.
12 Purchased office table from Supple Company, $275.
14 Purchased merchandise, $700, and store supplies, $100, from Tondy Company.
17 Purchased store supplies from Streeter Company, $50, and office supplies from the Paperclip Company, $25.
20 Purchased merchandise from Tondy Company, $736.
24 Purchased merchandise from Streeter Company, $1,226; the invoice included shipping charges of $116.
26 Purchased office supplies from Supple Company, $75.
30 Purchased merchandise from Tondy Company, $145.

Required

1. Enter the above transactions in the purchases journal and the general journal. Assume that all terms are n/30 and that invoice dates are the same as the transaction dates.
2. Foot and rule the purchases journal.
3. Open the following general ledger accounts: Store Supplies (116), Office Supplies (117), Trucks (142), Office Equipment (144), Accounts Payable (211), Purchases (611), and Freight In (612). Open accounts payable subsidiary ledger accounts as needed. Post from the journals to the ledger accounts.

Problem 8A-4 Comprehensive Use of Special-Purpose Journals

Lakeside Discount Auto Supply Company completed the following transactions:

July 1 Received merchandise from Maynard Auto Supply, $1,250, invoice dated June 29, terms 2/10, n/30, FOB shipping point.
2 Issued check no. 116 to Morris Agency for July rent, $1,000.

3 Received merchandise from CSU Manufacturing, $2,700, invoice dated July 1, terms 2/10, n/30, FOB shipping point.
5 Issued check no. 117 to REC Electrical Company for repairs, $280.
6 Received $200 credit memorandum pertaining to July 3 shipment from CSU Manufacturing for unsatisfactory merchandise returned to CSU Manufacturing.
7 Issued check no. 118 to Empire Freight for freight charges on July 1 and July 3 shipment, $92.
8 Sold merchandise to A. Xorn, $500, terms 1/10, n/30, invoice no. 941.
9 Issued check no. 119 to Maynard Auto Supply in full payment less discount.
10 Sold merchandise to B. Yenque for $625, terms 1/10, n/30, invoice no. 942.
11 Issued check no. 120 to CSU Manufacturing for balance of account less discount.
12 Purchased advertising on credit from the *Daily Journal*, $225, terms n/20.
14 Issued credit memorandum to B. Yenque for $25 for merchandise returned.
15 Cash sales for first half of the month, $4,835. (To shorten this problem, cash sales are recorded only twice a month instead of daily, as they would be in actual practice.)
16 Sold merchandise to C. Zax, $350, terms 1/10, n/30, invoice no. 943.
17 Received check from A. Xorn for July 8 purchase less discount.
19 Received check from B. Yenque for balance of account less discount.
20 Received merchandise from Maynard Auto Supply, $1,400, invoice dated July 19, terms 2/10, n/30, FOB shipping point.
21 Received freight bill from R & A Transit, $285, terms n/5.
22 Issued check no. 121 for advertising purchase of July 12.
23 Received merchandise from CSU Manufacturing, $1,800, invoice dated July 22, terms 2/10, n/30, FOB shipping point.
24 Issued check no. 122 for freight charge of July 21.
26 Sold merchandise to A. Xorn, $400, terms 1/10, n/30, invoice no. 944.
27 Received credit memorandum from CSU Manufacturing for defective merchandise received July 23, $150.
28 Issued check no. 123 to Ford Equipment Company for purchase of office equipment, $175.
29 Issued check no. 124 to Maynard Auto Supply for one-half of July 20 purchase less discount.
30 Received check in full from C. Zax, discount not allowed.
31 Cash sales for the last half of month, $5,780.
31 Issued check no. 125, payable to Payroll account for monthly sales salaries, $2,150.

Required

1. Open the following general ledger accounts: Cash (111), Accounts Receivable (112), Office Equipment (141), Accounts Payable (211), Sales (411), Sales Discounts (412), Sales Returns and Allowances (413), Purchases (511), Purchases Discounts (512), Purchases Returns and Allowances (513), Freight In (514), Sales Salaries (521), Advertising Expense (522), Rent Expense (531), and Repairs Expense (532).
2. Open the following accounts receivable subsidiary ledger accounts: A. Xorn, B. Yenque, and C. Zax.
3. Open the following accounts payable subsidiary ledger accounts: CSU Manufacturing, *Daily Journal*, Maynard Auto Supply, and R & A Transit.

4. Prepare a sales journal, a one-column purchases journal, a cash receipts journal, a cash payments journal, and a general journal similar to the ones illustrated in this chapter.
5. Enter the transactions in the journals, and post as appropriate.
6. Foot the journals, and make end-of-month postings.
7. Prepare a trial balance of the general ledger, and prove the control balances of accounts receivable and accounts payable by preparing schedules of accounts receivable and accounts payable.

Problem 8A-5 Comprehensive Use of Special-Purpose Journals

The following transactions were completed by Sanders Sporting Goods Shop during the month of January, its first month of operation:

Jan. 2 Tom Sanders deposited $10,000 in the new company's bank account.
3 Issued check no. 101 to Fox Corporation for one month's rent, $600.
4 Received merchandise from Acme Sports Supply, $3,500, invoice dated January 3, terms 2/10, n/60, FOB shipping point.
5 Received freight bill from Red Line Freight, $482.
6 Issued check no. 102 to Taylor Furniture for store equipment, $3,700.
7 Borrowed $4,000 from bank on a 90-day, 9 percent note.
8 Cash sales for the first week, $991.
10 Sold merchandise to local YMCA, $450, terms 2/10, n/30, invoice no. 1001.
11 Sold merchandise to Charlie Dale, $150, terms n/20, invoice no. 1002.
12 Purchased advertising in *The News,* $75, terms n/15.
13 Issued check no. 103 for purchase of January 4 less discount.
14 Issued a credit memorandum for merchandise returned by Charlie Dale, $15.
15 Cash sales for the second week, $1,746.
17 Received merchandise from Acme Sports Supply, $950, invoice dated January 16, terms 2/10, n/60, FOB shipping point.
18 Received freight bill from Red Line Freight, $131.
19 Received merchandise from Bates Company, $700, invoice dated January 17, terms 1/10, n/60, FOB destination.
20 Received payment in full less discount from local YMCA.
21 Received a credit memorandum from Acme Sports Supply for $50 of merchandise returned.
22 Cash sales for third week, $1,456.
24 Issued check no. 104 for amount owed Red Line Freight.
25 Sold merchandise to local YMCA, $342, terms 2/10, n/30, invoice no. 1003.
26 Issued check no. 105 in payment of amount owed Acme Sports Supply less discount.
27 Sold merchandise to Lynda Heller, $186, terms n/20, invoice no. 1004.
28 Issued check no. 106 for amount owed *The News.*
29 Cash sales for the fourth week, $987.
31 Issued check no. 107 to Payroll account for sales salaries for the month of January, $1,800.

Required

1. Open the following general ledger accounts: Cash (111); Accounts Receivable (112); Store Equipment (141); Accounts Payable (211); Notes Payable (212); Tom

Sanders, Capital (311); Sales (411); Sales Discounts (412); Sales Returns and Allowances (413); Purchases (511); Purchases Discounts (512); Purchases Returns and Allowances (513); Freight In (514); Sales Salaries (611); Advertising Expense (612); and Rent Expense (613).
2. Open the following accounts receivable subsidiary ledger accounts: Charlie Dale, Local YMCA, and Lynda Heller.
3. Open the following accounts payable subsidiary ledger accounts: Acme Sports Supply, Bates Company, Red Line Freight, and *The News*.
4. Prepare a sales journal, a one-column purchases journal, a cash receipts journal, a cash payments journal, and a general journal.
5. Enter the transactions in the journals and post as appropriate.
6. Foot the journals, and make end-of-period postings.
7. Prepare a trial balance of the general ledger, and prove the control balances of Accounts Receivable and Accounts Payable by preparing schedules of accounts receivable and accounts payable.

Problem Set B

Problem 8B-1 Identification of Transactions

The manual accounting system of Clairborne Company contains a general journal, purchases journal, cash receipts journal, and cash payments journal similar to those illustrated in the text.

On May 31, the Sales account in the general ledger appeared as follows:

Sales **Account No.**

Date		Item	Post. Ref.	Debit	Credit	Balance	
						Debit	Credit
May	31		S11		32,617		32,617
	31		CR7		21,207		53,824
	31		J17	53,824			—

On May 31, the J. Simons account in the accounts receivable subsidiary ledger appeared as follows:

J. Simons **Account No.**

Date		Item	Post. Ref.	Debit	Credit	Balance
May	5		S10	1,317		1,317
	9		J14		282	1,035
	15		CR6		500	535

Required

1. Write an explanation of each entry in the Sales account, including the journal from which the entry was posted.
2. Write an explanation of each entry in the J. Simons account receivable, including the journal from which the entry was posted.

Problem 8B-2 Cash Receipts and Cash Payments Journals

Diamond Company is a small retail business that uses a manual data processing system similar to the one illustrated in the chapter. Among its special-purpose journals are multicolumn cash receipts and cash payments journals. All cash transactions for Diamond Company for the month of June are listed below.

June 1 Paid June rent to R. Martin, $400, with check no. 782.
2 Paid T & G Wholesale on account, $850, less a 2 percent discount, with check no. 783.
3 Received $392, net of a 2 percent discount, on account from T. N. Daniels.
4 Cash sales, $1,272.
7 Paid Roadside Freight on account, $299, with check no. 784.
8 The owner, James Diamond, invested an additional $5,000 in the business.
10 Paid James Supply on account, $142, with check no. 785.
11 Cash sales, $1,417.
14 Paid Roadside Freight $155 with check no. 786 for a shipment of merchandise received today.
15 Paid Travis Company on account, $784, net of a 2 percent discount, with check no. 787.
16 Received payment on account from M. Weisel, $60.
19 Cash sales, $987.
20 Received payment on a note receivable of $900 plus $18 interest.
21 Purchased office supplies from James Supply, $54, with check no. 788.
22 Paid a note payable in full to City Bank, $2,050, including $50 interest, with check no. 789.
26 Cash sales, $1,482.
27 Paid $250 less a 2 percent discount to T & G Wholesale, with check no. 790.
29 Paid Tara Morgan, a sales clerk, $550, for her monthly salary, with check no. 791.
30 James Diamond withdrew $600 from the business, using check no. 792.

Required

1. Enter the above transactions in the cash receipts and cash payments journals.
2. Foot and rule the journals.

Problem 8B-3 Purchases and General Journals

Holtzman Lawn Supply Company uses a multicolumn purchases journal and general journal similar to those illustrated in the text. The company also maintains an accounts payable subsidiary ledger. The items below represent the company's credit transactions for the month of October.

Oct. 3 Purchased merchandise from Fertil Fertilizer Company, $1,270.
4 Purchased office supplies of $79 and store supplies of $117 from Company Supply, Inc.
7 Purchased cleaning equipment from Target Company, $928.
10 Purchased display equipment from Company Supply, Inc., $2,350.
14 Purchased lawn mowers from E-Z Lawn Equipment Company, for resale, $4,200; the invoice included transportation charges of $175.
15 Purchased merchandise from Fertil Fertilizer Co., $1,722.

19 Purchased a lawn mower from E-Z Lawn Equipment Company to be used in the business, $475; the invoice included transportation charges of $35.
24 Purchased store supplies from Company Supply, Inc., $27.

Required

1. Enter the above transactions in the purchases journal and the general journal. Assume that all terms are n/30 and that invoice dates are the same as the transaction dates.
2. Foot and rule the purchases journal.
3. Open the following general ledger accounts: Store Supplies (116), Office Supplies (117), Lawn Equipment (142), Display Equipment (144), Cleaning Equipment (146), Accounts Payable (211), Purchases (611), and Freight In (612). Open accounts payable subsidiary ledger accounts as needed. Post from the journals to the ledger accounts.

Problem 8B-5 Comprehensive Use of Special-Purpose Journals

Holtzer Book Store opened its doors for business on September 1. During September the following transactions occurred:

Sept. 1 Hans-Martin Holtzer began business by depositing $17,000 in the new company's bank account.
2 Issued check no. C001 to Campus Rentals for one month's rent, $400.
3 Received a shipment of books from Paperback Books, Inc., $7,840, invoice dated September 2, terms 5/10, n/60, FOB shipping point.
4 Received a bill for freight from Parcel Shippers for previous day's shipment, $395.
5 Received a shipment from Baldwin Books, $5,650, invoice dated September 5, terms 2/10, n/30, FOB shipping point.
6 Issued check no. C002 to TOR Freight, Inc., for transportation charges on previous day's shipment, $287.
8 Issued check no. C003 to Equipment Company for store equipment, $5,200.
9 Sold books to University Center, $782, terms 5/10, n/30, invoice no. I001.
10 Returned books to Paperback Books, Inc., for credit, $380.
11 Issued check no. C004 to WUII for radio commercials, $235.
12 Issued check no. C005 to Paperback Books, Inc., for balance of amount owed less discount.
13 Cash sales for the first two weeks, $1,814.
15 Issued check no. C006 to Baldwin Books, $3,000 less discount.
16 Signed a 90-day, 10 percent note for a bank loan, $10,000.
17 Sold books to Beth Wisher, $130, terms n/30, invoice no. I002.
18 Issued a credit memorandum to University Center for returned books, $62.
19 Received payment in full less discount from University Center.
20 Sold books to Arnold Trigona, $97, terms n/30, invoice no. I003.
22 Received a shipment from Victory Publishing Company, $2,302, invoice dated September 21, terms 5/10, n/60.
23 Returned additional books to Paperback Books, Inc., for credit, $718.
24 Sold books to University Center, $817, terms 5/10, n/30, invoice no. I004.
25 Received a shipment from Paperback Books, Inc., $1,187, invoice dated September 22, terms 5/10, n/60, FOB shipping point.

26 Issued check no. C007 to Parcel Shippers for balance owed on account plus shipping charges of $97 on previous day's shipment.
27 Cash sales for the second two weeks, $3,744.
29 Issued check no. C008 to Payroll account for sales salaries for first four weeks of month, $700.
30 Cash sales for the last two days of month, $277.

Required

1. Open the following general ledger accounts: Cash (111); Accounts Receivable (112); Store Equipment (141); Accounts Payable (211); Notes Payable (212); Hans-Martin Holtzer, Capital (311); Sales (411); Sales Discounts (412); Sales Returns and Allowances (413); Purchases (511); Purchases Discounts (512); Purchases Returns and Allowances (513); Freight In (514); Sales Salaries (611); Advertising Expense (612); and Rent Expense (613).
2. Open the following accounts receivable subsidiary ledger accounts: Arnold Trigona, University Center, and Beth Wisher.
3. Open the following accounts payable subsidiary ledger accounts: Baldwin Books, Paperback Books, Inc.; Parcel Shippers; and Victory Publishing Company.
4. Prepare a sales journal, a one-column purchases journal, a cash receipts journal, a cash payments journal, and a general journal.
5. Enter the transactions in the journals and post as appropriate.
6. Foot the journals, and make end-of-month postings.
7. Prepare a trial balance of the general ledger, and prove the control balances of Accounts Receivable and Accounts Payable by preparing schedules of accounts receivable and accounts payable.

Chapter Nine

Internal Control and Its Application to Cash

Learning Objectives

1. *Define internal accounting control and state its four objectives.*
2. *State five attributes of an effective system of internal control.*
3. *Apply the attributes of internal control to the control of cash receipts and disbursements.*
4. *Prepare a bank reconciliation.*
5. *Describe and record the related entries for a simple petty cash system*
6. *Describe the components of a voucher system.*
7. *State and perform the five steps in operating a voucher system.*

A major objective of the accounting system is maintaining effective control over the transactions and assets of the company. In Chapter 9 you will learn about the primary means of accomplishing this objective. As a result of studying this chapter, you should be able to meet the learning objectives listed on the left.

This chapter consists of five main sections. The first presents the general principles and characteristics of internal control. In the second section, these principles are applied to the control of cash receipts and disbursements. The third and fourth sections explain the role of bank transactions and petty cash procedures in the control of cash. The fifth section describes the voucher system, a common means of controlling cash disbursements.

Internal Control: Basic Principles and Policies

Internal control is defined by the AICPA as

> the plan of organization and all of the co-ordinate methods and measures adopted within a business to safeguard its assets, check the accuracy and reliability of its accounting data, promote operational efficiency, and encourage adherence to prescribed managerial policies.[1]

This is a broad definition. Obviously a system of internal control extends beyond the matters directly related to the accounting

1. *Professional Standards* (New York: American Institute of Certified Public Accountants, July 1, 1977), Vol. I, Sec. AU 320.01.

function. Specifically, this definition involves two kinds of internal controls: internal accounting controls and internal administrative controls.

Objective 1 Define internal accounting control and state its four objectives

Internal accounting controls are the methods and procedures employed primarily to protect assets and ensure the accuracy and reliability of the accounting records. They include, for example, systems of authorization and approval and the separation of record-keeping duties from the duties of operating a department or being the custodian of assets. They are designed to provide reasonable insurance regarding the following:

a. Transactions are executed in accordance with management's general or specific authorization.
b. Transactions are recorded as necessary (1) to permit preparation of financial statements in conformity with generally accepted accounting principles . . . and (2) to maintain accountability for assets.
c. Access to assets is permitted only in accordance with management's authorization.
d. The recorded accountability for assets is compared with the existing assets at reasonable intervals and appropriate action is taken with respect to any differences.[2]

Internal administrative controls are concerned primarily with operational efficiency and adherence to managerial policies. They are related to accounting controls in that they deal with the decision processes leading to management's authorization of transactions. For example, employee training programs, a form of internal administrative control, should teach new employees the proper authorization methods and procedures for handling purchases, sales, and other transactions. Sometimes administrative and accounting controls overlap. For example, sales and cost records classified by departments may be used in making management decisions as well as for accounting control purposes. In the study of internal control, any control, whether administrative or accounting, that relates to transactions involving assets or accounting records is important.

An effective system of internal control will have certain important attributes. These are explained in the paragraphs that follow.

Separation of Duties

Objective 2 State five attributes of an effective system of internal control

The plan of organization should provide for the appropriate separation of functional responsibilities. This means that authorizing transactions, operating a department, handling and processing assets, and keeping the records for the department on assets should not be the responsibility of one person. In other words, an error, either honest or dishonest, cannot occur without being observed by at least one other person.

Sound Accounting System

The system of authorization and the record-keeping procedures should provide reasonable accounting control over assets, liabilities, revenues,

2. Ibid., Sec. AU 320.28.

and expenses. There should be a system of routine and automatic checks and balances in the records and procedures, which should always be done exactly as prescribed. Independent checks should be made, and physical safeguards of assets should be used where possible.

Sound Personnel Policies

Sound practices should be followed in performing the duties and functions of each organizational department. These practices include adequate supervision, rotation of key people in job assignments, insistence that employees take earned vacations, and bonding of personnel who handle cash or inventories. **Bonding** means investigating an employee and insuring the company against any theft by that individual.

Reliable Personnel

Personnel should be qualified to handle responsibilities. This means that employees must be adequately trained and well informed. It is obvious that an accounting system, no matter how well designed, is only as good as the individuals who implement it.

Regular Internal Review

The system should be under regular review. Large companies often maintain a staff of internal auditors who regularly review their company's system of internal control to see that it is functioning properly and that its procedures are being followed.

Limitations of Internal Control

No system of internal control is without certain weaknesses. As long as people must perform control procedures, the internal control system is susceptible to human error. Errors may arise because of misunderstanding of instructions, mistakes of judgment, carelessness, distraction, or fatigue. The separation of duties can be defeated through collusion—that is, when employees secretly agree to deceive the company. Furthermore, procedures designed by management may be ineffective against errors or dishonesty of management. In addition, controls that may have been effective originally may become ineffective because of changes in conditions.[3]

Protection of Assets

Sound internal control procedures are needed in all aspects of business operations, but particularly where assets exist and where they enter or leave the business. When sales are made, for example, cash or other

3. Ibid., Sec. AU 320.34.

assets enter the business, and goods or services leave the business. Procedures must be set up to prevent theft during these transactions. Likewise, purchases and payments of assets and liabilities must be controlled. The majority of these transactions can be safeguarded by adequate purchasing and payroll systems. In addition, assets on hand such as cash, investments, inventory, plant, and equipment must be protected.

Because cash is more susceptible to theft than any other asset, the next section describes the application of internal control procedures to cash receipts and cash disbursements. Internal control systems for other assets and liabilities are discussed at relevant points in later chapters.

Internal Control over Cash

Objective 3 Apply the attributes of internal control to the control of cash receipts and disbursements

A system of internal control when applied effectively to accounting for cash can achieve several important objectives for both accounting and administrative controls. The objectives of accounting controls over cash are:

1. to prevent losses from theft or fraud, and
2. to provide accurate records of cash transactions and balances.

The objectives of administrative controls over cash are:

1. to maintain enough cash to pay liabilities as they are due, plus a reasonable amount for emergencies, and
2. to earn a reasonable return on cash held in excess of the needs of 1 above.

An example of an administrative control is the cash budget, which projects future cash receipts and disbursements. By maintaining adequate cash balances, the company is able to take advantage of discounts on purchases, prepare for borrowing money when necessary, and avoid the embarrassing and possibly damaging effects of not being able to pay bills when they are due. On the other hand, if the company has more cash at a particular time than it needs, this cash can be invested, earning interest, until it is needed.

An example of an accounting control is the separation of duties involving the control of cash. Through this means, theft without detection is impossible except through the collusion of two or more employees. The subdivision of duties is more easily achieved in large businesses than in small ones, where by necessity one person may have to carry out several duties. The effectiveness of internal control over cash will vary depending on the size and nature of the company. Most firms, however, should attempt to use the following procedures:

1. The functions of record keeping and the custodianship of cash should be kept separate.
2. The number of persons who have access to cash should be limited.
3. Persons who are to have responsibility for handling cash should be specifically designated.

4. Banking facilities should be used as much as possible, and the amount of cash on hand should be kept to a minimum.
5. All employees having access to cash should be bonded.
6. Cash on hand should be protected physically by the use of such devices as cash registers, cashiers' cages, and safes.
7. Surprise audits of cash on hand should be made by an individual who does not handle or record cash.
8. All cash receipts should be recorded promptly.
9. All cash receipts should be deposited promptly.
10. All cash disbursements should be paid by check.

Note that each of the above procedures helps to safeguard cash by making it more difficult for any one person to have access to cash and to steal or misuse it undetected. These procedures may be specifically related to the control of cash receipts and cash disbursements.

Control of Cash Receipts

Cash receipts for goods and services may be received by mail or over the counter in the form of checks or currency. Whatever the source, cash receipts should be recorded immediately upon receipt. This is usually done by making an entry in a cash receipts journal. As illustrated in the preceding chapter, this step establishes a written record of the receipt of cash and should prevent errors and make theft more difficult.

Control of Cash Receipts Received Through the Mail Cash that comes in through the mail should be handled by two or more employees. The employee who opens the mail should make a list in triplicate of the money received. This list should contain each sender's name, the purpose for which the money was sent, and the amount. One copy goes with the cash to the cashier, who deposits the money. The second copy goes to the accounting department to be recorded in the cash receipts journal. The person who opens the mail keeps the third copy of the list. Errors can be detected easily because the amount deposited by the cashier must agree with the amount received and the amount recorded in the cash receipts journal.

Control of Cash Received over the Counter Two common means of controlling cash sales are through the use of cash registers and prenumbered sales tickets. Amounts from cash sales should be rung up on a cash register at the time of each sale. The cash register should be placed so that the customer can see the amount recorded. Each cash register should have a locked-in tape on which are printed the day's transactions. At the end of the day, the cashier counts the cash in the cash register and turns it in to the cashier's office. Another employee takes the tape out of the cash register and records the cash receipts for the day in the cash receipts journal. The amount of cash turned in and the amount recorded on the tape should be in agreement; if not, any differences should be accounted for. Large retail chains commonly perform this function by having each cash register tied directly into a computer. Thus each transaction is recorded as it occurs. The separation of duties involving cash receipts, cash deposits, and record keeping is thus achieved, ensuring good internal control.

In some stores, internal control is strengthened further by the use of prenumbered sales tickets and a central cash register or cashier's office, where all sales are rung up and collected by a person who does not participate in the sale. Under this procedure, the salesperson completes a prenumbered sales ticket at the time of sale, giving one copy to the customer and keeping a copy. At the end of the day, all sales tickets must be accounted for, and the sales total computed from the sales tickets should equal the total sales recorded on the cash register.

Cash Over and Short When there are numerous transactions involving cash receipts, small mistakes are bound to occur. For example, cash registers in grocery and retail stores will often have a cash shortage or overage at the end of the day. When the shortages are consistent or large they should, of course, be investigated. If at the end of a day a cash register shows recorded cash sales of $675 but contains only $670 in cash, the following entry would record the sales:

Cash	670	
Cash Over or Short	5	
Sales		675
To record cash sales; a cash shortage of $5 was found		

The **Cash Over or Short** account is debited with shortages and credited with overages. Special columns in the cash receipts journal could be used to record cash over or short in order to call management's attention to irregular activity. If at the end of an accounting period a debit balance appears in Cash Over or Short, it would be reported as a miscellaneous expense in the income statement. A credit balance would be reported as a miscellaneous revenue.

Control of Cash Disbursements

Cash disbursements are very vulnerable to fraud and embezzlement. In a recent and notable case, the treasurer of one of the nation's largest jewelry retailers was charged with having stolen over one-half million dollars by systematically overpaying federal income taxes and pocketing the refund checks as they came back to the company.

To avoid this kind of theft, cash should be disbursed only on the basis of specific authorization that is supported by documents establishing the validity and amount of the claim. In addition, maximum possible use should be made of the principle of separation of duties in the purchase of goods and services and the payments for them. Figure 9-1 (next page) shows how this kind of control can be achieved. In this example, four internal units (the requesting department, the accounting department, the receiving department, and the treasurer) and two external companies (the supplier and the bank) all play a role in the internal control plan. Note

Figure 9-1 Internal Control for Purchasing and Paying for Goods and Services

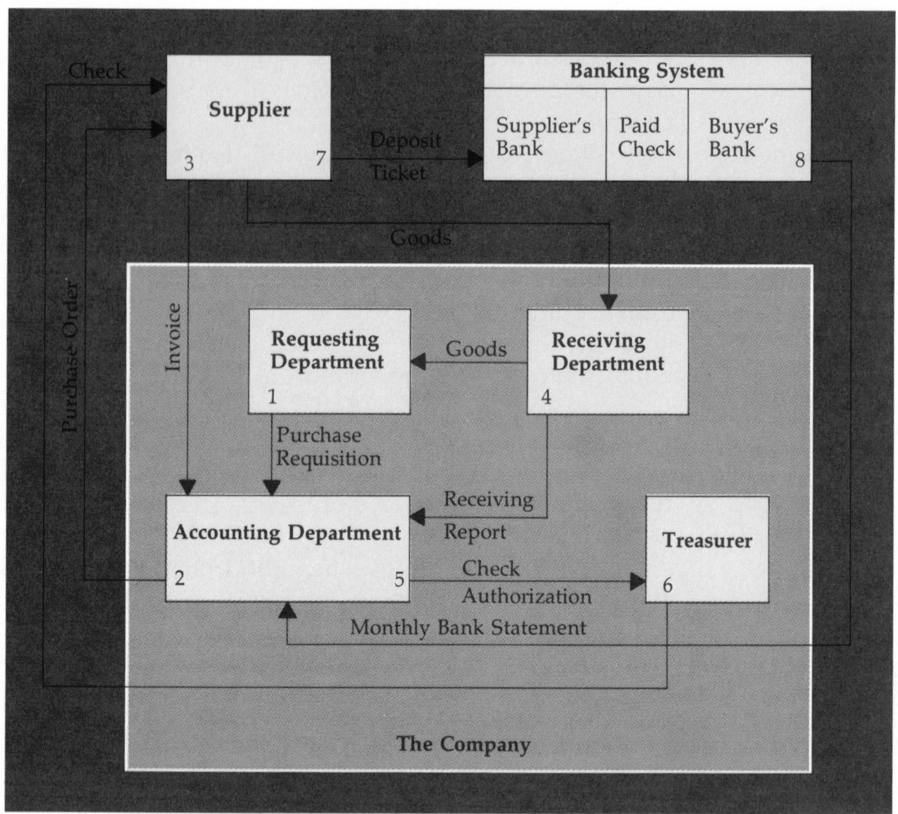

that business documents also play an important role in the plan. The plan is summarized in Table 9-1. Under this plan, every action is documented and subject to verification by at least one other person. For instance, the requesting department cannot work out a kickback scheme with the supplier because the receiving department independently records receipts and the accounting department verifies prices. The receiving department cannot steal goods because the receiving report must equal the invoice; for the same reason, the supplier cannot bill for more than shipped. The accounting department's work is verified by the treasurer, and the treasurer is ultimately checked by the accounting department.

Figures 9-2 through 9-6, which show typical documents used in this plan, serve as a concrete example involving the purchase of twenty boxes of typewriter ribbons. In Figure 9-2 (page 292) the credit office of Martin Maintenance fills out a **purchase requisition** for twenty boxes of typewriter ribbons. The department head approves it and forwards it to the accounting department. The people in the accounting department who carry out the purchasing activity prepare a **purchase order,** as illustrated in Figure 9-3 (page 292). The purchase order is addressed to the vendor (seller) and contains a description of the items ordered; their expected price, terms, and shipping date; and other shipping instructions. Martin will not pay any bill that is not accompanied by a purchase order. Some larger companies have a separate department to perform the purchasing function.

Table 9-1 Internal Control Plan for Cash Disbursements

Business Document	Prepared by	Sent to	Verifications and Related Procedures
1. Purchase requisition	Requesting department	Accounting department	Accounting verifies authorization.
2. Purchase order	Accounting department	Supplier	Supplier sends goods or services in accordance with purchase order.
3. Invoice	Supplier	Accounting department	Accounting receives invoice from supplier.
4. Receiving report	Receiving department	Accounting department	Accounting compares invoice, purchase order, and receiving report. Accounting verifies prices.
5. Check authorization (or voucher)	Accounting department	Treasurer	Accounting staples check authorization to top of invoice, purchase order, and receiving report.
6. Check	Treasurer	Supplier	Treasurer verifies all documents before preparing check.
7. Deposit ticket	Supplier	Supplier's bank	Supplier compares check with invoice. Bank deducts check from buyer's account.
8. Bank statement	Buyer's bank	Accounting department	Accounting compares amount and payee's name on returned check with check authorization.

After receiving the purchase order, the vendor, Henderson Supply Company, ships the goods (in this case delivers them) and sends an **invoice,** or bill (Figure 9-4) (page 293) to Martin Maintenance. The invoice gives the quantity and a description of the goods delivered and the terms of payment. If all goods cannot be shipped immediately, the estimated date for shipment of the remainder is indicated.

When the goods reach the receiving department of Martin Maintenance Company, an employee of this department writes the description, quantity, and condition of the goods on the **receiving report.** The receiving department does not get the purchase order or invoice, so that the people

Figure 9-2
Purchase Requisition

PURCHASE REQUISITION — No. 7077

Martin Maintenance Company

From: Credit Office — Date September 6, 19xx

To: Accounting Department — Suggested Vendor: Henderson Supply Company

Please purchase the following items:

Quantity	Number	Description
20 boxes	X 144	Typewriter ribbons

Reason for Request
Six months' supply for office

Approved BM

To be filled in by Accounting Department

Date ordered 9/8/XX P.O. No. J 102

Figure 9-3
Purchase Order

PURCHASE ORDER — No. J 102

Martin Maintenance Company
8428 Rocky Island Avenue
Chicago, Illinois 60643

To: Henderson Supply Company
2525 25th Street
Mesa, Illinois 61611

Date September 8, 19xx
FOB Destination
Ship by September 12, 19xx
Terms 2/10, n/30

Ship to: Martin Maintenance Company
Above Address

Please ship the following:

Quantity	✓	Number	Description	Price	Per	Amount
20 boxes		X 144	Typewriter ribbons	12.00	box	$240.00

Purchase order number must appear on all shipments and invoices.

Ordered by
Marsha Owen

Figure 9-4
Invoice

INVOICE — No. 0468

Henderson Supply Company
2525 25th Street
Mesa, Illinois 61611

Date September 12, 19xx
Your Order No. J 102
Ship to:
Same

Sold to:

Martin Maintenance Company
8428 Rocky Island Avenue
Chicago, Illinois 60643

Sales Representative: Joe Jacobs

Quantity		Description	Price	Per	Amount
Ordered	Shipped				
20	20	X 144 Typewriter Ribbons	12.00	box	$240.00

FOB Delivered	Terms: 2/10, n/30	Date Shipped: 10/12/xx	Via: Self

in this department will not know what is to be received. In this way, because they do not know if they have received a larger quantity than ordered, they are not tempted to steal the excess.

The receiving report is sent to the accounting department, where it is compared with the purchase order and the invoice. If all is correct, the accounting department completes a **check authorization** and attaches it to the three supporting documents. The check authorization form shown in Figure 9-5 (next page) has a space for each item to be checked off as it is examined. Note that the accounting department has all the documentary evidence for the transaction but does not have access to the assets purchased. Nor does it write the checks for payment. For this reason, the people performing the accounting function cannot gain by falsifying the documents in an effort to conceal a fraud.

Finally, the treasurer again examines all the evidence and issues a **check** (Figure 9-6, next page) for the amount of the invoice less the appropriate discount. In some systems, the accounting department fills out the check so that all the treasurer has to do is inspect and sign it. The check is then sent to the supplier, with remittance advice attached to the bottom. A supplier who is not paid the proper amount will complain, of course, thus providing a form of outside control over the payment. The supplier will deposit the check in the bank, which will return the canceled check with Martin's next monthly bank statement. If the treasurer has made the check for an incorrect amount (or altered a prefilled-in check), it will show up at this point. Looking ahead a little to Figure 9-8, you can see Martin's October bank statement showing that the check for $235.20 was honored on October 12, thus completing the cycle.

Figure 9-5
Check Authorization

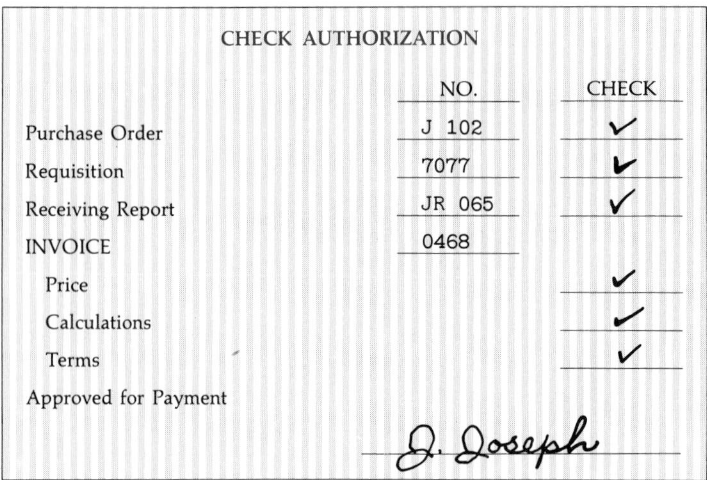

CHECK AUTHORIZATION

	NO.	CHECK
Purchase Order	J 102	✓
Requisition	7077	✓
Receiving Report	JR 065	✓
INVOICE	0468	
Price		✓
Calculations		✓
Terms		✓

Approved for Payment

J. Joseph

Figure 9-6
Check with Attached Remittance Advice

NO. 1787

9/28 19xx

PAY TO
THE ORDER OF Henderson Supply Company $ 235.20

Two hundred thirty-five and 20/100------------------------ Dollars

THE LAKE PARK NATIONAL BANK
Chicago, Illinois

Martin Maintenance Company

by Arthur Martin

Remittance Advice

Date	P.O. No.	DESCRIPTION	AMOUNT
9/28/xx	J 102	20 boxes typewriter ribbons	
		Supplied Inv. No. 0468	$240.00
		Less 2% discount	4.80
		Net	$235.20
		Martin Maintenance Company	

There are many variations of the system just described. This example is offered as a simple system that provides adequate internal control.

Bank Transactions

Banking facilities are an important aid to business in controlling both cash receipts and cash disbursements. Banks are safe depositories of cash, negotiable instruments, and other valuable business documents such as stocks and bonds. The use of checks for disbursements improves control by minimizing the amount of currency on hand and by providing a permanent record of all cash disbursements. Furthermore, banks can serve as agents for a company in a variety of important transactions such as the collection and payment of certain kinds of debts and the exchange of foreign currencies.

Bank Account

The procedure for establishing a bank account varies. In some small towns where the bank personnel are familiar with townspeople's activities, it may be very easy to open an account. In other cases, particularly in large metropolitan areas, the bank may require a financial statement and references.

The evidence used for the bank account is a **signature card.** When a person opens an account, this card must be signed by the depositor in exactly the same way that he or she expects to sign the checks. This signature card is required so that a bank teller can authenticate the depositor's signature on a check. When a corporation opens an account, the board of directors must sign an authorization giving a particular official or officials the right to sign checks. The bank receives a copy of the authorization.

Deposits

When making a deposit, the depositor fills out a **deposit ticket** (usually in duplicate), as illustrated in Figure 9-7 (next page). Space is provided for listing each check and the amounts of coin and currency deposited.

Bank Statement

Once a month the bank will send a statement to the depositor and return the canceled checks that it has paid and charged to the depositor's account. The returned checks are called "canceled" because the bank stamps, or cancels, them to show that they have been paid. The **bank statement** shows the balance at the beginning of the month, the deposits, the checks paid, other debits and credits during the month, and the balance at the end of the month. A bank statement is illustrated in Figure 9-8 (page 297).

Bank Reconciliation

Objective 4 Prepare a bank reconciliation

Rarely will the balance of a company's Cash account exactly equal the cash balance as shown on the bank statement when it is received. Certain transactions shown in the company's records may not be recorded by the bank, and certain bank transactions may not appear in the company's records. Therefore a necessary step in internal control is to prove both the balance of the bank and the balance of cash in the accounting records. The term **bank reconciliation** means accounting for the differences between the balance appearing on the bank statement and the balance of cash according to the depositor's records. This process involves adjusting both balances to the adjusted cash balance.

Figure 9-7
Deposit Ticket

DEPOSIT TICKET

THE LAKE PARK NATIONAL BANK
Chicago, Illinois

Date 10/6/xx

Name Martin Maintenance Company

Address 8428 Rocky Island Avenue

Chicago, Illinois

CASH	CURRENCY	22	00
	COIN	2	50
CHECKS—LIST SINGLY	G. Mason	30	00
	R Enterprises	39	00
	Preston Company	206	50
TOTAL		300	00
Less Cash Received		—	—
NET DEPOSIT		300	00

The most common examples of transactions shown in the company's records but not entered in the bank's records are the following:

1. **Outstanding checks** These are checks issued and recorded by the depositor but not yet presented to the bank for payment.
2. **Deposits in transit** These are deposits mailed or taken to the bank but not received by the bank in time to be recorded before preparation of the monthly statement.

Transactions that may appear on the bank statement but have not yet been recorded by the depositor include:

1. **Service charge (SC)** Banks cannot profitably handle small accounts without making a service charge. Many banks base the service charge on a number of factors, such as the average balance of the account during the month or the number of checks drawn.
2. **NSF (non-sufficient funds) checks** A NSF check is a check deposited by the company that is not paid when the depositor's bank presents it for payment to the maker's bank. The bank charges the depositor's account and returns the check so that the depositor can try to collect the amount

Figure 9-8
Bank Statement

Statement of Account with
THE LAKE PARK NATIONAL BANK
Chicago, Illinois

Martin Maintenance Company
8428 Rocky Island Avenue
Chicago, Illinois 60643

Previous Balance	Checks/Debits—No.	Deposits/Credits—No.	S.C.	Current Balance
$2,645.78	$4,319.33 --15	$5,131.50 --6	$2.50	$3,455.45

CHECKS		DEPOSITS	DATE	BALANCES
			09-30-xx	2,645.78
100.00	250.00	586.00	10-01-xx	2,881.78
56.18			10-04-xx	2,825.60
425.14		1500.00	10-05-xx	3,900.46
17.12		300.00	10-06-xx	4,183.34
1,705.80	235.20		10-12-xx	2,242.34
400.00		1845.50	10-16-xx	3,687.84
29.75	69.00 NSF		10-17-xx	3,589.09
		600.00	10-21-xx	4,189.09
738.50	5.00 DM	300.00 CM	10-24-xx	3,745.59
7.50	152.00		10-25-xx	3,586.09
128.14			10-28-xx	3,457.95
2.50 SC			10-31-xx	3,455.45

Explanation of Symbols:

CM —Credit Memo
DM—Debit Memo
NSF—Not Sufficient Funds
SC —Service Charge
EC —Error Correction
OD —Overdraft

The last amount in this column is your balance.

Please examine; if no errors are reported within ten (10) days, the account will be considered to be correct.

due. If the bank has deducted the NSF check from the bank statement but the depositor has not deducted it from his or her book balance, an adjustment must be made in the bank reconciliation. The depositor usually reclassifies the NSF check from Cash to Accounts Receivable because the depositor must now collect from the person or company that wrote the check.

3. **Miscellaneous charges and credits** Banks also charge for other services such as collection and payment of promissory notes, stopping payment on checks, and printing checks. The bank notifies the depositor of each deduction by including a debit memorandum with the monthly statement. A bank will sometimes serve as an agent in collecting on

promissory notes for the depositor. In such a case, a credit memorandum will be included.

An error by either the bank or the depositor will, of course, require correction.

Steps in Reconciling the Bank Balance The steps to be followed in achieving a bank reconciliation are as follows:

1. Compare the deposits listed on the bank statement with deposits shown in the accounting records. Any deposits in transit should be added to the bank balance. (Any deposits in transit from last month still not listed on the bank statement should be immediately investigated.)
2. Trace returned checks to the bank statement, making sure that all checks are issued by the company, properly charged to the company's account, and properly signed.
3. Arrange the canceled checks returned with the bank statement in numerical order, and compare them with the record of checks issued. List checks issued but not on the bank statement. (Be sure to include any checks still outstanding from last month.) Deduct outstanding checks from the bank balance.
4. Prepare a bank reconciliation similar to the one shown below.
5. Deduct from the balance per books any debit memoranda issued by the bank such as NSF checks and service charges that are not yet recorded on the depositor's records.
6. Add to the balance per books any credit memoranda issued by the bank such as collection of a promissory note that is not yet recorded on the depositor's books.
7. Make journal entries for any items on the bank statement that have not been recorded in the depositor's books.

Illustration of a Bank Reconciliation The October bank statement for Martin Maintenance Company, as shown in Figure 9-8, indicates a balance on October 31 of $3,455.45. We shall assume that Martin Maintenance Company has a cash balance in its records on October 31 of $2,346.77. The purpose of a bank reconciliation is to identify the items that make up this difference and to determine the correct cash balance.

In carrying out the steps outlined above, assume that the following items were found:

1. A deposit in the amount of $276.00 was mailed to the bank on October 31 and was unrecorded by the bank.
2. Five checks issued in October or prior months have not yet been paid by the bank, as follows:

Check No.	Date	Amount
415	Sept. 14	$150.00
576	Oct. 30	40.68
578	Oct. 31	500.00
579	Oct. 31	370.00
580	Oct. 31	130.50

3. The deposit for cash sales of October 6 was incorrectly recorded in Martin's records as $330.00. The bank recorded the deposit on Martin's bank statement correctly as $300.00.

4. Among the returned checks was a credit memorandum showing that the bank had collected a promissory note in the amount of $300.00. A debit memorandum was also enclosed for the $5.00 collection fee. No entry had been made on Martin's records.

5. Also returned with the bank statement was an NSF (non-sufficient funds) check for $69.00. This check had been received from a customer named Arthur Clubb. The NSF check was not reflected in Martin's accounting records.

6. A debit memorandum was enclosed for the regular monthly service charge of $2.50. This charge was not yet recorded by Martin Maintenance Company.

The bank reconciliation for Martin Maintenance Company appears in Figure 9-9. Note that, starting from their separate balances, the book and

Figure 9-9
Bank Reconciliation

Martin Maintenance Company
Bank Reconciliation
October 31, 19xx

Balance per books, October 31		$2,346.77
④ Add notes receivable collected by bank		300.00
		$2,646.77
Less:		
③ Overstatement of deposit of October 6	30.00	
④ Collection fee	5.00	
⑤ NSF check of Arthur Clubb	69.00	
⑥ Service charge	2.50	106.50
Adjusted cash balance, October 31		$2,540.27
Balance per bank, October 31		$3,455.45
① Add deposit of October 31 in transit		276.00
		$3,731.45
② Less outstanding checks:		
No. 451	150.00	
No. 576	40.68	
No. 578	500.00	
No. 579	370.00	
No. 580	130.50	1,191.18
Adjusted cash balance, October 31		$2,540.27

Note: The circled numbers refer to the items listed in the text.

bank amounts are adjusted to the amount of $2,540.27. This adjusted balance is the amount of cash owned by the company on October 31 and thus is the amount that should appear on its October 31 balance sheet.

Adjusting the Records After Reconciliation The adjusted balance of cash differs from both the bank statement and the Martin Maintenance Company's records. The bank balance will automatically become correct when outstanding checks are presented for payment and when the deposit in transit is received and recorded by the bank. Entries are necessary, however, to adjust the company's records to the correct balance. All the items reported by the bank but not yet recorded by the company must be entered into the records by means of the following adjustments:

Oct. 31	Cash	300.00	
	Notes Receivable		300.00
	Note receivable collected by bank		
Oct. 31	Sales	30.00	
	Cash		30.00
	Correction of error in recording a $300.00 deposit as $330.00		
Oct. 31	Accounts Receivable, Arthur Clubb	69.00	
	Cash		69.00
	NSF check of Arthur Clubb returned by bank		
Oct. 31	Bank Service Charges	7.50	
	Cash		7.50
	To record bank service charges ($2.50) and collection fee ($5.00) for October		

Petty Cash Procedures

Objective 5 Describe and record the related entries for a simple petty cash system

Under some circumstances, it is not practical to make all disbursements by check. In most businesses, for example, it is sometimes necessary to make small payments of cash for such things as a few postage stamps, incoming postage or shipping charges due, or minor purchases of supplies.

For situations when it is inconvenient to pay with a check, most companies set up a **petty cash fund.** One of the best methods to use is the **imprest system.** Under this system, a petty cash fund is established for a fixed amount and is periodically reimbursed for the exact amount necessary to bring it back to the fixed amount.

Establishing the Petty Cash Fund

Some companies have a regular cashier, secretary, or receptionist to administer the petty cash fund. A company establishes the petty cash fund by issuing a check for an amount that is intended to cover two to four weeks of small expenditures. The check is cashed, and the money is placed in the petty cash box, drawer, or envelope.

The only entry required when the fund is established is one to record the issuance of the check, as follows:

Oct. 14	Petty Cash	100.00	
	Cash		100.00
	To establish petty cash fund		

Making Disbursements from the Petty Cash Fund

The custodian of the petty cash fund should prepare a **petty cash voucher** for each expenditure, as illustrated in Figure 9-10. On each petty cash voucher is entered the date, amount, and purpose of the expenditure. The voucher is signed by the person receiving the payment.

The custodian of the fund should be informed that surprise audits of the fund will be made occasionally. The cash in the fund plus the sum of the petty cash vouchers should equal the fixed amount of the fund at all times.

Reimbursing the Petty Cash Fund

After a specified time or when the petty cash fund becomes low, it is replenished by a check issued to Petty Cash or to the custodian for the exact amount of the expenditures. From time to time there may be minor discrepancies in the amount of cash left in the fund at the time of reimbursement. In these cases, the amount of the discrepancy should be recorded in Petty Cash Over or Short as a debit if short or as a credit if over.

Assume that after two weeks the petty cash fund established as described above had a cash balance of $14.27 and petty cash vouchers as

Figure 9-10 Petty Cash Voucher

PETTY CASH VOUCHER

No. X 744

Date Oct. 23, 19xx

For Postage due

Charge to Postage

Amount $2.86

W.S. — Approved by

Tom L. — Received by

follows: postage, $25.00; supplies, $30.55; freight in, $30.00. The entry to replenish, or replace, the fund is as follows:

Oct. 28	Postage	25.00	
	Supplies	30.55	
	Freight In	30.00	
	Cash Over or Short	.18	
	Cash		85.73
	To replenish petty cash fund		

Note that the Petty Cash account is debited only when the fund is first established. Expense accounts will be debited each time the fund is replenished. There are usually no further entries to the Petty Cash account unless there is a desire to increase or decrease the original fixed amount of the fund.

The petty cash fund should be replenished at the end of an accounting period to bring it up to its fixed amount and to ensure that the expenses involved will be recorded in the current period's financial statements. If through an oversight the petty cash fund is not replenished at the end of the year, the expenditures must still be shown in the income statement. This is accomplished by an entry debiting the expense accounts and crediting Petty Cash. The result is an unintentional reduction in the petty cash fund.

The Voucher System

Objective 6 Describe the components of a voucher system

A **voucher system** is any system providing documentary evidence of and written authorization for business transactions. Here, a voucher system for a company's expenditures is presented. It consists of records and procedures for systematically accumulating, recording, and paying an organization's expenditures. It is closely related to the control of cash because its objective is to maintain maximum control over expenditures. This system ensures a high degree of internal control by permitting a maximum separation of duties and responsibilities in the following functions:

1. Authorization of expenditures
2. Receipt of goods and services
3. Validation of liability by examination of invoices from suppliers for correctness of prices, extensions, shipping costs, and credit terms
4. Payment of expenditure by check, taking discounts when possible

The voucher system requires that every liability be recorded as soon as it is incurred. A written authorization, called a **voucher,** is prepared for each expenditure, and checks are issued only upon evidence of an approved voucher. No one person has authority both to incur expenses and to issue checks. In large organizations, the duties of authorizing expenditures, verifying receipt of goods and services, checking invoices, recording liabilities, and issuing checks are divided among different employees.

Thus for both accounting and administrative control, every expenditure has been carefully and routinely received and verified before payment. For each transaction, the written approval of key individuals provides a trail of documentary evidence, or **voucher trail.**

Although there is more than one way to design a voucher system, a typical system would consist of (1) vouchers, (2) voucher checks, (3) a voucher register, and (4) a check register.

Vouchers

A voucher is a written authorization for each expenditure, and serves as the basis of an accounting entry. A separate voucher is attached to each incoming invoice and given an identification number. Vouchers are prenumbered consecutively. In the illustration of a cash disbursement system earlier in this chapter, the voucher replaces the check authorization form. The face of a typical voucher, which is shown in Figure 9-11, contains pertinent information about the expenditure. The voucher must be

Figure 9-11 Front and Back of a Typical Voucher Form

FACE OF VOUCHER

Thomas Appliance Company

Payee Livingstone Wholesale — Voucher No. 704
Address Gary, Indiana — Date Due 7/13
Date Paid 7/13
Terms 2/10, n/30 — Check No. 205

Date	Invoice No.	Description	Amount
7/12	XL1066	10 cases Model 70X14	1,200--

Approved M.N. (Controller) — Approved A. Thomas (Treasurer)

BACK OF VOUCHER

Account Debited	Acct. No.	Amount
Purchases	511	1,200.00
Freight In	512	
Rent Expense	631	
Salary Expense	611	
Utility Expense	635	
Total		$1,200.00

Voucher No. 710
Payee Livingstone Wholesale
Address Gary, Indiana

Invoice Amount	1200.00
Less Discount	24.00
Net	1176.00
Date Due	7/13
Date Paid	7/13
Check No.	205

VOUCHER REGISTER									
				Payment		Credit	Debits		
Date		Voucher No.	Payee	Date	Check No.	Vouchers Payable	Purchases	Freight In	Store Supplies
July	1	701	Common Utility	7/6	203	75			
	2	702	Ade Realty	7/2	201	400			
	2	703	Buy Rite Supplies	7/6	202	25			
	3	704	Belmont Products	7/13	205	1,200	1,200		
	6	705	M & M Freight			60		60	
	7	706	Petty Cash	7/7	204	50			
	8	707	Belmont Products	7/18	208	600	600		
	11	708	M & M Freight			30		30	
	11	709	Mack Truck			5,600			
	12	710	Livingstone Wholesale	7/22	209	785	750	35	
	14	711	Payroll	7/14	206	2,200			
	17	712	First National Bank	7/17	207	4,250			
	20	713	Livingstone Wholesale			525	500	25	
	21	714	Belmont Products			400	400		
	24	715	M & M Freight			18		18	
	30	716	Payroll	7/30	210	2,200			
	31	717	Petty Cash	7/31	211	47		17	
	31	718	Maintenance Company	7/31	212	175			
	31	719	Store Supply Company	7/31	213	350			350
						18,990	3,450	185	350
						(211)	(511)	(512)	(116)

Figure 9-12
Voucher
Register

signed by authorized individuals before payment is made. On the reverse side of the voucher is information about the accounts and amounts to be debited and credited. The voucher illustrated identifies the transaction by voucher number and check number and is recorded in the voucher register and check register, as described below.

Voucher Checks

Although regular checks can be used effectively with a voucher system, many organizations use a form of **voucher check** that indicates to the payee the reason for issuing the check. This information may be written either on the check itself or on a detachable stub.

Page 1

Debits								
						Other Accounts		
Office Supplies	Sales Salaries	Office Salaries	Mainte-nance, Selling	Mainte-nance, Office	Utilities	Name	No.	Amount
					75			
						Rent Expense	631	400
25								
						Petty Cash	121	50
						Trucks	148	5,600
	1,400	800						
						Notes Payable	212	4,000
						Interest Exp.	645	250
	1,400	800						
20						Miscel. Exp.	649	10
			100	75				
45	2,800	1,600	100	75	75			10,310
(117)	(611)	(612)	(621)	(622)	(635)			(✓)

Voucher Register

The **voucher register** is the book of original entry in which vouchers are recorded after they have been properly approved. The voucher register replaces the purchases journal illustrated in the preceding chapter. However, a major difference between the two journals is that *all* expenditures, including expenses, payroll, plant, and equipment, as well as purchases of merchandise, are recorded in the voucher register. Recall that only purchases of merchandise were recorded in the single-column purchases journal.

A typical voucher register appears in Figure 9-12. Note that in a voucher system, the Accounts Payable account column is replaced with a new account column entitled Vouchers Payable. For example, the first entry in the voucher register records the receipt of a utility bill. It is recorded as a debit to utility expense and a credit to Vouchers Payable (not

Accounts Payable). Note that the utility bill was later paid by check number 203 on July 6.

Check Register

In a voucher system, the **check register** replaces the cash payments journal in the sense that it is the journal in which the checks are listed as they are written, as shown in Figure 9-13. Study carefully the interrelation of the voucher register and the check register. The incurring of a liability is recorded in the voucher register; its payment is recorded in the check register.

Operation of a Voucher System

There are five steps in the operation of a voucher system, as follows:

Objective 7 State and perform the five steps in operating a voucher system

1. Preparing the voucher
2. Recording the voucher
3. Paying the voucher
4. Posting the voucher and check registers
5. Summarizing unpaid vouchers

Preparing the Voucher A voucher is prepared for each expenditure. All evidence such as purchase orders, invoices, receiving reports, and/or authorization statements should be attached to the voucher when it is submitted for approval.

Figure 9-13
Check Register

Check No.	Date	Payee	Voucher No.	Debit: Vouchers Payable	Credits: Purchases Discounts	Credits: Cash
201	July 2	Ade Realty	702	400		400
202	6	Buy Rite Supplies	703	25		25
203	6	Common Utility	701	75		75
204	7	Petty Cash	706	50		50
205	13	Belmont Products	704	1,200	24	1,176
206	14	Payroll	711	2,200		2,200
207	17	First National Bank	712	4,250		4,250
208	18	Belmont Products	707	600	12	588
209	22	Livingstone Wholesale	710	785	15	770
210	30	Payroll	716	2,200		2,200
211	31	Petty Cash	717	47		47
				11,832	51	11,781
				(211)	(513)	(111)

Many companies pay their employees out of a separate account. In this case, a voucher is prepared to cover the total payroll. The check for this voucher is then deposited in the special Payroll account, and individual payroll checks are drawn on that account.

Recording the Voucher All approved vouchers should be recorded in the voucher register, as shown in Figure 9-12. Vouchers that do not have appropriate approvals or support documents should be investigated immediately.

Paying the Voucher After a voucher has been recorded, it is placed in an unpaid voucher file. Many companies file the vouchers by due date so that checks can be drawn each day to cover all vouchers due on that day. In this way, all discounts for prompt payment can be taken without risk of missing the discount date.

On the date the voucher is due, a check for the correct amount, accompanied by the voucher and supporting documents, is presented to the individual authorized to sign checks. The check is then entered in the check register, as shown in Figure 9-13. The date of payment and the check number are then entered in the voucher register on the line occupied by the corresponding voucher. This procedure facilitates the preparation of a schedule of unpaid vouchers as explained below.

A problem arises in paying a voucher when there has been a purchase return or allowance that applies to the voucher. For example, a part of a shipment of merchandise may be defective and is returned to the supplier for credit. At the time the merchandise is returned or the allowance is given, an entry should be made in the general journal debiting Vouchers Payable and crediting Purchases Returns and Allowances, and a notation should be made on the voucher in the voucher file. At the time of payment, only the net amount of the voucher (original amount less return or allowance and any applicable discount) should be paid and recorded in the check register.

Posting the Voucher and Check Registers Posting of the voucher and check registers is very similar to the posting of the purchases journal and the cash payments journal, respectively, as illustrated in Chapter 8. The only exception is that the Vouchers Payable account is substituted for the Accounts Payable account.

Summarizing Unpaid Vouchers At any particular time, the sum of the vouchers in the unpaid vouchers file equals the credit balance of the Vouchers Payable account. Consequently, an accounts subsidiary ledger as illustrated in Chapter 8 is unnecessary. At the end of each accounting period, the unpaid voucher file should be totaled to prove the balance of the Vouchers Payable account. Figure 9-14 (next page), a schedule of unpaid vouchers, is prepared by listing all unpaid vouchers shown in Figure 9-12. A reconciliation of the voucher register (Figure 9-12) and check register (Figure 9-13) can be accomplished by simple subtraction.

Figure 9-14
Schedule of Unpaid Vouchers

Schedule of Unpaid Vouchers July 31		
Payee	Voucher Number	Amount
M & M Freight	705	$ 60
M & M Freight	708	30
Mack Truck	709	5,600
Livingstone Wholesale	713	525
Belmont Products	714	400
M & M Freight	715	18
Total Unpaid Vouchers		$6,633

Vouchers Payable credit from voucher register	$18,465
Vouchers Payable debit from check register	11,832
Vouchers payable credit balance from schedule of unpaid vouchers	$ 6,633

Although the account title Vouchers Payable sometimes appears on the liability side of the balance sheet, it is preferred practice to use the more widely known term Accounts Payable.

Chapter Review

Review of Learning Objectives

1. Define internal accounting control and state its four objectives.
Internal accounting controls are the methods and procedures employed primarily to protect assets and ensure the accuracy and reliability of the accounting records. The objectives of internal accounting control are to provide reasonable assurance that (1) transactions are executed in accordance with management's general or specific authorization, (2) transactions are recorded to permit preparation of the financial statements in accordance with generally accepted accounting principles and to maintain accountability for assets, (3) access to assets is permitted only in accordance with management's authorization, and (4) recorded accountability is compared with existing assets at reasonable intervals.

2. State five attributes of an effective system of internal control.
Five attributes of an effective system of internal control are (1) separation of duties, (2) a sound accounting system, (3) sound personnel policies, (4) reliable personnel, and (5) regular internal review.

3. Apply the attributes of internal control to the control of cash receipts and disbursements.
Internal control over cash receipts and disbursements is strengthened if the five attributes of effective internal control are applied. First, the functions of authorization, record keeping, and custody should be kept separate. Second, the ac-

counting system should provide for physical protection of cash, prompt recording and depositing of cash receipts, and payment by check only on the basis of documentary support. Third, persons who have access to cash should be specifically designated and their number limited. Fourth, personnel should be trained and bonded. Fifth, the Cash account should be reconciled monthly, and surprise audits of cash on hand should be made by an individual who does not handle or record cash.

4. Prepare a bank reconciliation.
The term *bank reconciliation* means accounting for the differences between the balance appearing on the bank statement and the balance of cash according to the depositor's records. It involves adjusting both balances to the adjusted cash balance. The bank balance is adjusted for outstanding checks and deposits in transit. The depositor's book balance is adjusted for service charges, NSF checks, and miscellaneous charges and credits.

5. Describe and record the related entries for a simple petty cash system.
A petty cash system is established by a debit to Petty Cash and a credit to Cash. It is replenished by debits to various expense accounts and a credit to Cash. Each expenditure should be supported by a petty cash voucher.

6. Describe the components of a voucher system.
A voucher system consists of written authorizations called vouchers; voucher checks; a special journal to record the vouchers, called the voucher register; and a special journal to record the voucher checks, called the check register.

7. State and perform the five steps in operating a voucher system.
The five steps in operating a voucher system are (1) preparing the voucher, (2) recording the voucher, (3) paying the voucher, (4) posting the voucher and check registers, and (5) summarizing unpaid vouchers.

Review Problem

Review the procedures and illustrations for the bank reconciliation, petty cash fund, and voucher system before completing the exercises and problems in this chapter. For additional help, see the review problem in the working papers.

Chapter Assignments

Questions

1. Most people think of internal control as making fraud harder to commit and easier to detect. What are some other important purposes of internal control?
2. What are the attributes of an effective system of internal control?
3. Why is a separation of duties necessary to ensure sound internal control?
4. Should the bookkeeper have responsibility for determining the accounts receivable to be written off? Explain.
5. At Thrifty Variety Store, each sales clerk counts the cash in his or her cash drawer at the end of the day and then removes the cash register tape and prepares the daily cash form, noting any discrepancies. This information is checked by an employee of the cashier's office, who counts the cash, compares the total with the form, and takes the cash to the cashier's office. What is the weakness in this system of internal control?

6. How does a movie theater control cash receipts?
7. What is the difference between internal accounting controls and internal administrative controls?
8. What does a credit balance in the Cash Over or Short account indicate?
9. One of the basic principles of internal control is separation of duties. What does this principle assume about the relationships of employees in a company and the possibility of two or more of them stealing from the company?
10. Why is a bank reconciliation prepared?
11. Assume that each of the numbered items below appeared on a bank reconciliation. Which item would be (a) an addition to the balance on the bank statement? (b) a deduction from the balance on the bank statement? (c) an addition to the balance on the books? (d) a deduction from the balance on the books? Write the correct letter after each numbered item.
(1) Outstanding checks
(2) Deposits in transit
(3) Bank service charge
(4) NSF check returned with statement
(5) Note collected by bank
Which of the above items require an adjusting entry?
12. In a small business, it is sometimes impossible to obtain complete separation of duties. What are three other practices that a small business can follow to achieve the objectives of internal control over cash?
13. Explain how each of the following can contribute to internal control over cash: (a) a bank reconciliation, (b) a petty cash fund, (c) a cash register with printed receipts, (d) printed, prenumbered cash sales receipts, (e) a regular vacation for the cashier, (f) two signatures on checks, and (g) prenumbered checks.
14. At the end of the day, the combined count of cash for all cash registers in a store reveals a cash shortage of $17.20. In what account would this cash shortage be recorded? Would the account be debited or credited?
15. What is the purpose of a petty cash fund, and what is the significance of the total of the fund (the level at which the fund is established)?
16. What account or accounts are debited when a petty cash fund is established? What account or accounts are debited when a petty cash fund is replenished?
17. Should a petty cash fund be replenished as of the last day of the accounting period? Explain.
18. What is the greatest advantage of the voucher system?
19. Before a voucher for the purchase of merchandise is approved for payment, three documents should be compared to verify the amount of the liability. What are the three documents?
20. When the voucher system is used, is there an Accounts Payable controlling account and a subsidiary accounts payable ledger?
21. A company that presently uses a general journal, a sales journal, a cash receipts journal, a cash payments journal, and a purchases journal decides to adopt the voucher system. Which of the five journals would be changed or replaced? What would replace them?
22. What is the correct order for filing (a) unpaid vouchers? (b) paid vouchers?

Classroom Exercises

Exercise 9-1
Petty Cash Entries

The petty cash fund of Swanson Company appeared as follows on December 31, 19xx.

Cash on Hand		$ 76.97
Expense vouchers		
Freight In	$ 8.47	
Postage	20.84	
Flowers for a sick employee	17.50	
Office Supplies	26.22	73.03
Total		$150.00

1. Because there is cash on hand, is there a need to replenish the petty cash fund on December 31? Explain.
2. Prepare in general journal form an entry to replenish the fund.

Exercise 9-2 Bank Reconciliation

Prepare a bank reconciliation from the following information: (a) balance per bank statement as of May 31, $2,944.65; (b) balance per books as of May 31, $1,786.40; (c) deposits in transit, $567.21; (d) outstanding checks, $1,727.96; (e) bank service charge, $2.50.

Exercise 9-3 Bank Reconciliation—Missing Data

Compute the correct amounts to replace each letter in the following table:

Balance per bank statement	a	$8,200	$175	$1,200
Deposits in transit	$ 600	b	50	125
Outstanding checks	1,500	1,000	c	75
Balance per books	2,600	9,400	225	d

Exercise 9-4 Collection of Note by Bank

Maine Corporation received a notice with its bank statement that the bank had collected a note for $1,500.00 plus $7.50 interest from M. Martin and credited Maine Corporation's account for the total less a collection charge of $3.50.

1. Explain the effect that these items have on the bank reconciliation.
2. Prepare a general journal entry to record the information on the books of Maine Corporation.

Exercise 9-5 Voucher System Entries

Tess Company uses a voucher system. The following transactions occurred recently: (a) voucher no. 700 prepared to purchase merchandise from Sour Corp., $600; (b) check no. 401 issued in payment of voucher no. 700; (c) voucher no. 701 prepared to establish petty cash fund of $100; (d) check no. 402 issued in payment of voucher no. 701; (e) voucher no. 702 prepared to replenish the petty cash fund, which contains cash of $30 and the following receipts: supplies, $27; postage, $36; and miscellaneous expense, $7; (f) check no. 403 issued in payment of voucher no. 702.

Record the transactions in general journal form. Indicate beside each transaction in which journal of original entry it would be recorded.

Exercise 9-6 Voucher System Entries

Goodacre Company uses a voucher system. Some related transactions are as follows:

Aug. 1 Voucher no. 352 prepared to purchase office equipment from Monroe Equipment Company, $640, terms n/30.
4 Voucher no. 353 prepared to purchase merchandise from Sawyer Corporation, $1,200, terms 2/10, n/30, FOB shipping point.
5 Voucher no. 354 prepared to pay freight charge to Red Line Freight for August 4 shipment, $175, terms n/10.
14 Issued check no. 846 to pay voucher no. 353.
15 Issued check no. 847 to pay voucher no. 354.
30 Issued check no. 848 to pay voucher no. 352.

Record in journal form each of the transactions. Beside each transaction indicate the journal of original entry in which the transaction would be recorded.

Exercise 9-7 Internal Control Evaluation

Developing a convenient means of providing sales representatives with cash for their incidental expenses, such as entertaining a client at lunch, is a problem many companies face. One company has a plan whereby the sales representatives receive advances in cash from the petty cash fund. Each advance is supported by an authorization from the sales manager. The representative returns the receipt for the expenditure and any unused cash and replaces them in the petty cash fund. The cashier of the petty cash fund is responsible for seeing that the receipt and the cash returned equal the advance. At the time that the petty cash fund is reimbursed, the amount of the representative's expenditure is debited to Direct Sales Expense.

1. What is the weak point of the procedure, and what fundamental principle of internal control has been ignored?
2. What improvement in the procedure can you suggest?

Exercise 9-8 Internal Control Evaluation

An accountant and his assistants are responsible for the following procedures: (a) receipt of all cash; (b) maintenance of the general ledger; (c) maintenance of the accounts receivable ledger; (d) maintenance of the journals for recording sales, cash receipts, and purchases; and (e) preparation of monthly statements to be sent to customers. As a service to customers and employees, the company allows the accountant to cash checks of up to $50 with money from the cash receipts. The accountant may approve the cashing of such a check for current employees and customers. When the deposits are made, the checks are included in place of the cash receipts.

What weakness in internal control exists in this system?

Problem Set A

Problem 9A-1 Petty Cash Transactions

A small company maintains a petty cash fund in its office for small expenditures. The following transactions occurred:

a. The fund was established in the amount of $40.00 on February 1 from the proceeds of check no. 1402, issued for the purpose.
b. On February 28, the petty cash fund had cash of $1.73 and the following receipts on hand: postage, $17.50; supplies, $12.47; delivery service, $6.20; and a rubber stamp, $2.10. Check no. 1473 was drawn to replenish the fund.
c. On March 31, the petty cash fund had cash of $2.53 and the following receipts on hand: postage, $15.60; supplies, $16.42; and delivery service, $3.20. The petty cash custodian could not account for the shortage of $2.25. Check no. 1542 was drawn to replenish the fund.

Required

Prepare in general journal form the entries necessary to record each of the above transactions.

Problem 9A-2 Bank Reconciliation

Use the following information to prepare a bank reconciliation for Bayer Company as of November 30, 19xx:

a. Cash on the books as of November 30 amounted to $27,486.26. Cash on the bank statement for the same date was $34,256.71.
b. A deposit of $3,562.46, representing cash receipts of November 30, did not appear on the bank statement.

c. Outstanding checks totaled $1,823.41.
d. A check for $605.00 returned with the statement was recorded in the check register as $506.00. The check was made in payment for advertising.
e. Bank service charges for November amounted to $6.50.
f. The bank collected for Bayer Company $9,100.00 on a note left for collection. The face value of the note was $9,000.00.
g. An NSF check for $285.00 from a customer, Joe Thompson, was returned with the statement.
h. The bank mistakenly returned a check for $200.00 drawn by Boyer Corporation.

Required

1. Prepare a bank reconciliation for Bayer Company as of November 30, 19xx.
2. Prepare the journal entries necessary to adjust the accounts.
3. State the amount of cash that should appear on the balance sheet as of November 30.

Problem 9A-3 Bank Reconciliation

The following information comes from the records of Leadky Company:

From the Cash Receipts Journal — **Page 7**

Date	Debit Cash
Sept. 1	914
7	1,012
14	3,240
21	2,646
30	1,942
	9,754

From the Cash Payments Journal — **Page 10**

Date	Check Number	Credit Cash
Aug. 28	913	14
Sept. 2	914	283
3	915	416
4	916	27
5	918	5
10	919	5,746
11	920	709
20	921	1,246
21	922	76
		8,522

The bank statement for Leadky Company appears as follows:

LAKE NATIONAL BANK — Statement of Leadky Company, Main and 2nd Streets

Date		Checks and Other Debits		Deposits	Balance
Sept.	1	Balance brought forward			3,785.00
	2	100.00	500.00	914.00	4,099.00
	4	460.00	14.00		3,625.00
	6	416.00			3,209.00
	8	27.00		1,012.00	4,194.00
	12	5.00	15.00 NSF		4,174.00
	14	907.00			3,267.00
	15			3,240.00	6,507.00
	22			2,646.00	9,153.00
	24	5,746.00			3,407.00
	26	76.00		408.00 CM	3,739.00
	30	4.00 SC			3,735.00

Code: CM—Credit Memo NSF—Not Sufficient Funds
DM—Debit Memo SC—Service Charge

The NSF check was received from T. Owens, a customer, for merchandise. The credit memorandum represents a $400 note collected by the bank plus interest. Check number 920 for a purchase of merchandise was incorrectly recorded in the cash payments journal as $709 instead of as the correct amount of $907.

From the General Ledger

Cash **Account No. 111**

Date		Item	Post. Ref.	Debit	Credit	Balance Debit	Balance Credit
Aug.	31	Balance				2,465	
Sept.	30		CR7	9,754		12,219	
	30		CP10		8,522	3,697	

On September 1, there were only the following outstanding checks as reconciling items: number 892 at $100, number 899 at $500, number 911 at $260, and number 912 at $460.

Required

1. Prepare a bank reconciliation as of September 30, 19xx.
2. Prepare adjusting entries in general journal form.
3. What amount should appear on the balance sheet for cash as of September 30, 19xx?

Problem 9A-4
Voucher System Transactions

During the month of October, Kenner Company had the following transactions affecting vouchers payable:

Oct. 1 Prepared voucher no. 471, payable to Jason Company, for merchandise, $900, invoice dated September 30, terms 2/10, n/30, FOB destination.
3 Prepared voucher no. 472, payable to Issacs Corporation, for merchandise, $2,700, invoice dated October 1, terms 2/10, n/30, FOB shipping point.
5 Prepared voucher no. 473, payable to Hawthorne Agency, for one month's rent, $900.
5 Issued check no. 2612 for voucher no. 473.
6 Prepared voucher no. 474, payable to Hagen Corporation, for merchandise, $500, invoice dated October 5, terms 2/10, n/30, FOB shipping point. Hagen Corporation prepaid freight charges of $76 and added them to the invoice, making a total of $576.
8 Prepared voucher no. 475, payable to the *Daily Journal* for advertising, $375.
8 Issued check no. 2613 for voucher no. 475.
10 Issued check no. 2614 for voucher no. 471.
11 Received a credit memorandum from Issacs Corporation for merchandise returned, $300.
11 Issued check no. 2615 for voucher no. 472.
12 Prepared voucher no. 476, payable to First National Bank, for repayment of note, $1,000 plus $30 interest.
12 Issued check no. 2616 for voucher no. 476.
13 Issued check no. 2617 for voucher no. 474.
16 Prepared vouchers no. 477, 478, and 479, payable to Modern Truck Company, for the down payment and subsequent payments on a new truck, terms $1,000 down, $1,500 in 60 days, $1,500 in 120 days.
16 Issued check no. 2618 for voucher no. 477.
21 Prepared voucher no. 480, payable to Issacs Corporation, for merchandise, $1,200, invoice dated October 17, terms 2/10, n/30, FOB shipping point.
22 Prepared voucher no. 481, payable to Hagen Corporation, for merchandise, $1,000, invoice dated October 22, terms 2/10, n/30, FOB shipping point. Hagen Corporation prepaid freight charges of $46 and added them to the invoice, for a total of $1,046.
25 Prepared voucher no. 482, payable to Speedy Freight, for freight in on merchandise received from Issacs Corporation during month, $360, terms n/10th of next month.
27 Issued check no. 2619 for voucher no. 480.
30 Prepared voucher no. 483, payable to Payroll account, for monthly payroll of $7,700 (to be divided between sales salaries of $5,700 and general administrative salaries of $2,000).
30 Issued check no. 2620 for voucher no. 483.
31 Prepared voucher no. 484, payable to Mesa Power and Light, for monthly utility expenses, $287.

Required

1. Prepare a voucher register, a check register, and a general journal similar to those illustrated in this chapter, and record the transactions.
2. Prepare a Vouchers Payable account (number 211), and post the appropriate portions of the journal and register entries. Assume that the September 30 balance of Vouchers Payable was zero.

3. Prove the balance of the Vouchers Payable account by preparing a schedule of unpaid vouchers.

Problem 9A-5 Voucher System Transactions

During the month of July, Donner Records had the following transactions affecting vouchers payable:

July 1 Prepared voucher no. 531, payable to Petty Cash, to establish a petty cash fund, $100.
1 Issued check no. 1201 for voucher no. 531.
2 Prepared voucher no. 532, payable to MC Wholesale Records, for a shipment of merchandise, $350, invoice dated July 1, terms 2/10, n/60, FOB shipping point. MC prepaid freight of $20 and added it to the invoice, for a total of $370.
3 Prepared voucher no. 533, payable to Jones Realty, for July's rent, $500.
3 Issued check no. 1202 for voucher no. 533.
5 Prepared voucher no. 534, payable to Columbus Records, for merchandise, $500, invoice dated July 3, terms 2/10, n/60, FOB shipping point.
6 Prepared voucher no. 535, payable to Parcel Express, for freight in on July 5 shipment, $32, terms n/10.
7 Prepared voucher no. 536, payable to Valley Hardware, for office equipment, $200, terms n/30.
8 Received credit memorandum from Columbus Records for damaged records returned, $50.
9 Prepared voucher no. 537, payable to Columbus Records, for merchandise, $650, invoice dated July 8, terms 2/10, n/60, FOB shipping point.
10 Prepared voucher no. 538, payable to Parcel Express, for freight in on July 9, $47, terms n/10.
11 Issued check no. 1203 for voucher no. 532.
12 Prepared voucher no. 539, payable to Joe Donner, for his personal expenses, $500.
12 Issued check no. 1204 for voucher no. 539.
13 Issued check no. 1205 for voucher no. 534.
15 Issued check no. 1206 for voucher no. 535.
17 Prepared vouchers no. 540, 541, 542, and 543, payable to City Furniture, for office furniture having an invoice price of $1,200, terms one-fourth down and one-fourth each month for three months.
17 Issued check no. 1207 for voucher no. 540.
18 Issued check no. 1208 for voucher no. 537.
19 Issued check no. 1209 for voucher no. 538.
20 Prepared voucher no. 544, payable to Hill Supply, $135 ($95 to be charged to Store Supplies and $40 to Office Supplies), terms n/10th of next month.
22 Prepared voucher no. 545, payable to MC Wholesale Records, for merchandise, $165, invoice dated July 19, terms 2/10, n/30, FOB shipping point. Freight prepaid by shipper and included in invoice total, $15.
23 Prepared voucher no. 546, payable to River National Bank, in payment of a $2,000 note plus interest, $50, total $2,050.
23 Issued check no. 1210 for voucher no. 546.
24 Prepared voucher no. 547, payable to AACE Insurance Company, for a one-year policy, $240.
24 Issued check no. 1211 for voucher no. 547.
26 Prepared voucher no. 548, payable to Columbus Records, for merchandise, $300, invoice dated July 25, terms 2/10, n/60, FOB shipping point.
27 Prepared voucher no. 549, payable to Parcel Express, for freight in on shipment of July 26, $19.

28 Prepared voucher no. 550, payable to Payroll account, for monthly salaries, $3,950 (to be divided as follows: sales salaries, $2,200, and office salaries, $1,750).
28 Issued check no. 1212 for voucher no. 550.
29 Issued check no. 1213 for voucher no. 545.
31 Prepared voucher no. 551 to reimburse petty cash fund. A count of the fund revealed cash on hand, $15, and the following receipts: postage, $22; office supplies, $17; collect telegram, $3; flowers for sick employee, $10; delivery service, $27.
31 Issued check no. 1214 for voucher no. 551.

Required

1. Prepare a voucher register, a check register, and a general journal similar to those illustrated in this chapter, and record the transactions.
2. Prepare a Vouchers Payable account (number 211), and post those portions of the journal and register entries that affect this account. Assume the Vouchers Payable account had a zero balance on June 30.
3. Prove the balance of the Vouchers Payable account by preparing a schedule of unpaid vouchers.

Problem 9A-6 Internal Control

Lassiter Company, a small concern, is attempting to organize its accounting department to achieve maximum internal control, subject to the constraint of limited resources. There are three employees (1, 2, and 3) in the accounting department, each of whom has had accounting courses and some accounting experience. The accounting department must accomplish the following functions: (a) maintain the general ledger, (b) maintain the accounts payable ledger, (c) maintain the accounts receivable ledger, (d) prepare checks for signature, (e) maintain the cash payments journal, (f) issue credits on returns and allowances, (g) reconcile the bank account, and (h) handle and deposit cash receipts.

Required

1. Assuming that each employee will do only the jobs assigned, assign the functions to the three employees in such a manner as to obtain the highest degree of internal control possible.
2. Identify four possible unsatisfactory combinations of functions.

Problem Set B

Problem 9B-1 Petty Cash Transactions

The Monarch Theater Company established a petty cash fund in its snack bar so that payment can be made for small deliveries upon receipt. The following transactions occurred:

Oct. 1 The fund was established in the amount of $200.00 from the proceeds of a check drawn for that purpose.
31 The petty cash fund has cash of $10.71 and the following receipts on hand: for merchandise received, $110.15; delivery charges, $32.87; laundry service, $42.00; miscellaneous expense, $4.27. A check was drawn to replenish the fund.
Nov. 30 The petty cash fund has cash of $22.50 and the following receipts on hand: merchandise, $98.42; delivery charges, $38.15; laundry service, $42.00; miscellaneous expense, $3.93. The petty cash custodian cannot account for the fact that there is an excess of $5.00 in the fund. A check is drawn to replenish the fund.

Required

Prepare in general journal form the entries necessary to record each of the above transactions.

Problem 9B-2 Bank Reconciliation

Use the following information to prepare a bank reconciliation for Jeff Scott Company as of October 31, 19xx.

a. Cash on the books as of October 31 amounted to $20,997.08. Cash on the bank statement for the same date was $25,675.73.
b. A deposit of $2,610.47, representing cash receipts of October 31, did not appear on the bank statement.
c. Outstanding checks totaled $1,968.40.
d. A check for $960.00 returned with the statement was recorded incorrectly in the check register as $690.00. The check was made for a purchase of merchandise.
e. Bank service charges for October amounted to $12.50.
f. The bank collected for Jeff Scott Company $6,120.00 on a note left for collection. The face value of the note was $6,000.00.
g. An NSF check for $91.78 from a customer, Doug Christian, was returned with the statement.
h. The bank mistakenly charged a check for $425.00 drawn by Jeff Scott on his personal checking account to the company account.

Required

1. Prepare a bank reconciliation for Jeff Scott Company as of October 31, 19xx.
2. Prepare the journal entries necessary to adjust the accounts.
3. State the amount that should appear on the balance sheet as of October 31.

Problem 9B-3 Bank Reconciliation

The following information comes from the records of the Desmond Company:

From the Cash Receipts Journal **Page 22**

Date	Debit Cash
Feb. 1	1,416
8	14,486
15	13,214
22	10,487
28	7,802
	47,405

From the Cash Payments Journal		Page 106
Date	Check Number	Credit Cash
Jan. 26	2076	1,218
30	2077	22
Feb. 6	2078	6
7	2079	19,400
8	2080	2,620
12	2081	9,135
16	2082	14
17	2083	186
18	2084	5,662
		38,263

The bank statement for Desmond Company appears as follows:

FIRST NATIONAL BANK — Statement of Desmond Company, Desmond, MO

Date	Checks and Other Debits		Deposits	Balance
Feb. 1	Balance brought forward			12,416.00
2	510.00	32.00	1,614.00	13,488.00
3	1,218.00	4.00		12,266.00
5	22.00			12,244.00
9			14,486.00	26,730.00
10	19,400.00	1,265.00		6,065.00
11	2,620.00			3,445.00
12			1,654.00 CM	5,099.00
16			13,214.00	18,313.00
17	9,135.00	14.00		9,164.00
18	40.00 NSF			9,124.00
23			10,487.00	19,611.00
24	5,662.00			13,949.00
28	17.00 SC			13,932.00

Code: CM—Credit Memo NSF—Not Sufficient Funds
DM—Debit Memo SC—Service Charge

The NSF check was received from M. Sanders, a customer, for merchandise. The credit memorandum represents a $1,600 note collected by the bank plus interest. The February 1 deposit of $1,416 in cash sales was recorded correctly by the bank at $1,614. On February 1, there were only the following outstanding checks as reconciling items: No. 2056 at $510, No. 2072 at $4, No. 2073 at $35, No. 2074 at $1,265, and No. 2075 at $32.

From the General Ledger

Cash **Account No. 111**

Date		Item	Post. Ref.	Debit	Credit	Balance Debit	Balance Credit
Jan.	31	Balance				10,570	
Feb.	28		CR22	47,405		57,975	
	28		CP106		38,263	19,712	

Required

1. Prepare a bank reconciliation as of February 28, 19xx.
2. Prepare adjusting entries in general journal form.
3. What amount should appear on the balance sheet for cash as of February 28, 19xx?

Problem 9B-4 Voucher System Transactions

During the month of January, J and H Company had the following transactions affecting vouchers payable:

Jan. 2 Prepared voucher no. 7901, payable to Rental Agency, for January rent, $700.
2 Issued check no. 5501 for voucher no. 7901.
3 Prepared voucher no. 7902, payable to Turner Company, for merchandise, $4,200, invoice dated January 2, terms 2/10, n/30, FOB destination.
5 Prepared voucher no. 7903, payable to Jackson Supply House, for supplies, $650, to be allocated $450 to Store Supplies and $200 to Office Supplies, terms n/10.
6 Prepared voucher no. 7904, payable to City Power and Light, for monthly utilities, $314.
6 Issued check no. 5502 for voucher no. 7904.
9 Prepared voucher no. 7905, payable to Overton Company, for merchandise, $1,700, invoice dated January 7, terms 2/10, n/30, FOB shipping point. Overton Company prepaid freight charges of $146 and added them to the invoice, for a total of $1,846.
12 Issued check no. 5503 for voucher no. 7902.
15 Issued check no. 5504 for voucher no. 7903.
16 Prepared voucher no. 7906, payable to Underwood Company, for merchandise, $970, invoice dated January 14, terms 2/10, n/30, FOB shipping point.
16 Prepared voucher no. 7907, payable to Rapid Freight Company, for freight shipment from Underwood Company, $118, terms n/10th of next month.
17 Issued check no. 5505 for voucher no. 7905.
18 Returned $220 in defective merchandise to Underwood Company for credit.
22 Prepared voucher no. 7908, payable to Jackson Supply House, for supplies, $375, to be allocated $200 to Store Supplies and $175 to Office Supplies, terms n/10.

23 Prepared voucher no. 7909, payable to American National Bank, for 90-day note, which is due, $5,000 plus $150 interest.
23 Issued check no. 5506 for voucher no. 7909.
24 Issued check no. 5507 for voucher no. 7906.
26 Prepared voucher no. 7910, payable to Overton Company, for merchandise, $2,100, invoice dated January 24, terms 2/10, n/30, FOB shipping point. Overton Company prepaid freight charges of $206 and added them to the invoice, for a total of $2,306.
27 Prepared voucher no. 7911, payable to Telephone Company, $37. Payments for telephone are considered a utility expense.
27 Issued check no. 5508 for voucher no. 7911.
30 Prepared voucher no. 7912, payable to Payroll account, for monthly payroll, $17,200, to be allocated $13,300 to Sales Salaries and $3,900 to Office Salaries.
30 Issued check no. 5509 for voucher no. 7912.
31 Prepared voucher no. 7913, payable to Maintenance Company, $360, to be allocated two-thirds to Selling Maintenance and one-third to Office Maintenance.

Required

1. Prepare a voucher register, a check register, and a general journal similar to those illustrated in this chapter, and record the transactions.
2. Prepare a Vouchers Payable account (number 211), and post the appropriate portions of the journal and register entries. Assume that the December 31 balance of Vouchers Payable was zero.
3. Prove the balance of the Vouchers Payable account by preparing a schedule of unpaid vouchers.

Problem 9B-6 Internal Control

Wainwright Company, a large merchandising concern that stocks over 85,000 different items in inventory, has just installed a sophisticated computer system for inventory control. The computer's data storage system has random access processing and carries all pertinent data relating to individual items of inventory. The system is equipped with fifteen remote computer terminals, distributed at various locations throughout the warehouse and sales areas. Using these terminals, employees can obtain information from the computer system about the status of any inventory item. To make an inquiry, they use a keyboard, similar to a typewriter's, that forms part of the remote terminal. The answer is relayed back instantaneously on a screen, which is also part of the terminal. As inventory is received, shipped, or transferred, employees update the inventory records in the computer system by means of the remote terminals.

Required

1. What potential weakness in internal control exists in the system?
2. What suggestions do you have for improving the internal control?

Part Three

Measuring and Reporting Assets and Current Liabilities

In Parts I and II, the basic accounting model was first presented and then extended to more complex applications.

Part III considers each of the major types of assets as well as the category of current liabilities and payroll accounting, with particular emphasis on the effect of their measurement on net income and their presentation in the financial statements. It also provides an overview of accounting principles and discusses the effects of inflation on accounting.

Chapter 10 begins with a discussion of monetary assets and then focuses on the two major types of receivables: accounts receivable and notes receivable.

Chapter 11 presents the accounting concepts and techniques associated with inventories.

Chapter 12 deals with current liabilities and payroll accounting.

Chapter 13 discusses property, plant, and equipment, and natural resources, including the concepts and techniques of depreciation and depletion.

Chapter 14 discusses in more detail the application of the matching rule to revenue recognition and to allocation of expired costs; the chapter also presents other accounting conventions. In addition, accounting for price level changes and current values is described and related to the requirements of FASB *Statement No. 33*.

Learning Objectives

Chapter Ten

Accounts and Notes Receivable

1. *Name the most common types of short-term monetary assets.*
2. *Explain why estimated losses from uncollectible accounts are important to income determination.*
3. *Apply the percentage of net sales method and the accounts receivable aging method to accounting for uncollectible accounts.*
4. *Journalize entries involving the allowance method of accounting for uncollectible accounts.*
5. *Recognize types of receivables not classified as accounts receivable and specify their balance sheet presentation.*
6. *Define and describe a promissory note.*
7. *Make calculations involving promissory notes.*
8. *Journalize entries involving notes receivable.*

In this chapter, you learn the basic accounting treatment of accounts and notes receivable. These are short-term monetary assets that arise from the extension of credit. As a result of studying this chapter, you should be able to meet the learning objectives listed on the left.

Short-Term Monetary Assets

Short-term monetary assets consist of cash, temporary investments, accounts receivable, and notes receivable. They are useful because they are readily available for paying current obligations. In contrast, nonmonetary assets are assets used in the productive functions of the enterprise. Examples of nonmonetary assets are inventories; property, plant, and equipment; natural resources; and intangibles.

Of all the short-term monetary assets, cash is the most liquid and the most readily available to pay obligations. In Chapter 9, we discussed the control of cash at length but did not deal with the content of the cash item on the balance sheet. Cash is generally considered to consist of coin and currency on hand, checks and money orders received from customers, and deposits in bank checking accounts. Certificates of deposit and time deposits such as savings accounts are also considered cash because of their ready availability.

At various times during the year, a company may find that it has more cash on hand than it needs to pay current obligations. Because it is unwise to allow this cash to lie idle, the company may invest the excess cash in government securities or other marketable securities so that it earns a return until it is needed. Such investments are considered current assets because they are temporary and intended to be held only until needed to pay a current obligation. Some companies are so successful that they accumulate large amounts of cash from earnings, which they invest in marketable securities. On the balance sheet, these investments are called **temporary investments** or **marketable securities.** For example, General Motors Corporation in a recent year listed cash of $297,100,000 and marketable securities of $2,739,300,000 among its current assets. Marketable investments that management intends to hold for an indefinite period of time longer than one year are properly classified as long-term investments. However, as a practical matter, since management usually stands ready to sell these investments if market conditions indicate that they should be sold, they are generally classified as current assets. Temporary investments are recorded initially at cost. In the *Statement of Financial Accounting Standards No. 12,* the Financial Accounting Standards Board requires that marketable securities be listed in the financial statements at either total cost or the market value determined at the balance sheet date, whichever is lower.[1] Investments in corporate securities including the use of special valuation accounts are discussed in Chapter 20.

Objective 1 Name the most common types of short-term monetary assets

The other two major types of short-term monetary assets are accounts receivable and notes receivable. Both result from credit sales to customers. Because credit is available to individuals, many people can buy valuable things such as automobiles, refrigerators, and other appliances that they could not have afforded without credit. Retail companies such as Sears, Roebuck and Company have made credit available to virtually every responsible person in the United States. We live in a credit card society, where every field of retail trade has expanded by allowing customers the right to make payments a month or more after the date of sale. What is not so apparent is the fact that credit at the wholesale and manufacturing levels has expanded even more than that at the retail level. The purpose of the remainder of this chapter is to show the accounting for accounts and notes receivable, which play a key role in this credit expansion.

Accounting for Accounts Receivable

Accounts receivable are short-term monetary assets that arise from sales on credit to customers at either the wholesale or the retail level. This type of credit is often called **trade credit.**

Credit Policies and Uncollectible Accounts

Companies that make sales on credit naturally do not want to sell to customers who will not pay. Consequently, most companies that sell on

1. *Statement of Financial Accounting Standards No. 12,* "Accounting for Certain Marketable Securities" (Stamford, Conn.: Financial Accounting Standards Board, 1975).

credit at either the retail or the wholesale level develop certain control procedures to increase the likelihood of selling only to customers who will pay when they are supposed to. These procedures usually result in the establishment of a credit department, whose responsibilities include the examination of each individual or company that applies for credit and the approval or disapproval of the sale to that customer on credit. Typically, the credit department will ask for information on the customer's financial resources and debts. In addition, it may check personal references and established credit bureaus, which may have information about the customer. On the basis of this information, the credit department will decide whether to sell on credit to that customer. It may recommend the amount of payment, limit the amount of credit, or ask the customer to put up certain assets as security for the credit.

Regardless of how thorough and efficient its credit control system is, the company will always have some customers who will not pay. The accounts owed by such customers are called **uncollectible accounts**, or bad debts, and are a loss or an expense of selling on credit. One might ask, why does a company sell on credit if it expects that some of its accounts will not be paid? The answer is that by extending credit, the company expects to sell much more than it would if it did not sell on credit and, as a result, to make more profit overall. When a customer does not pay his or her account, it reflects the company's poor judgment in making the sale in the first place. But some uncollectible accounts are expected and are the natural result of management's wish to make a profit on total sales. Management may be so conservative in granting credit that it has no credit sales, or it may have very small losses on credit sales. In such cases, it may be losing profitable business from perfectly good customers it has rejected.

Matching Losses on Uncollectible Accounts with Sales

Objective 2 Explain why estimated losses from uncollectible accounts are important to income determination

A balance must be reached between an acceptable level of credit losses and the potential profit on total credit sales. The loss occurs on an individual uncollectible account at the moment credit is granted and a sale is made to the customer. In accounting for these uncollectible accounts, the basic rule of accounting is the matching rule, as it has been in dealing with other issues in this book. Expenses should be matched against the sales they help to produce. If bad debt losses are incurred in the process of generating sales income, they should be charged against the sales income they helped to generate. Of course, a company does not know at the time of a credit sale that the debt will not be collected. In fact, it may take a year or more to exhaust every possible means of collection. Even though the loss may not be specifically identified until a later accounting period, it is still an expense of the accounting period in which the sale was made. Therefore, losses from the uncollectible accounts must be estimated for the accounting period, and this estimate becomes the expense for the year.

For example, let us assume that Cottage Corporation made most of its sales on credit during its first year of operation. At the end of the year, accounts receivable amounted to $100,000. On this date, the management reviewed the status of the accounts receivable, particularly noting accounts past due. Approximately $6,000 of the $100,000 of accounts reviewed were estimated to be not collectible. Thus the uncollectible accounts expense for the first year of operation amounted to $6,000. The following adjusting entry would be made on December 31 of that year:

Dec. 31	Uncollectible Accounts Expense	6,000	
	Allowance for Uncollectible Accounts		6,000
	To record the estimated uncollectible accounts expense for the year 19xx		

The uncollectible accounts expense created by the debit part of the entry is closed to the Income Summary account in the same manner as the other expense accounts. The **allowance for uncollectible accounts** that was credited in the above journal entry will appear in the balance sheet as a deduction from the face value of accounts receivable. It serves to reduce the accounts receivable to the amount that will be collectible, as shown in Figure 10-1.

Allowance for Uncollectible Accounts

The allowance method of accounting for uncollectible accounts argues that losses from an uncollectible account occur at the moment the sale is made to the customer who will not pay. Because the company does not know until after the sale that the customer will not pay, the amount of the loss must be estimated if it is to be matched against the sales or revenue for the period. It is not possible, of course, to credit the account of any particular customer to reflect the overall estimate of the year's credit

Figure 10-1 Partial Balance Sheet Showing Allowance for Uncollectible Accounts

Cottage Corporation
Partial Balance Sheet
December 19xx

Current Assets		
Cash		$ 10,000
Marketable Securities		15,000
Accounts Receivable	$100,000	
Less Allowance for Uncollectible Accounts	6,000	94,000
Inventory		56,000
Total Current Assets		$175,000

losses. Furthermore, it is not possible to credit the Accounts Receivable controlling account in the general ledger because this would cause the controlling account to be out of balance with the numerous customers' accounts in the subsidiary ledger. Therefore, as described above, a separate account called Allowance for Uncollectible Accounts is used to carry the amount of estimated uncollectible accounts. In Figure 10-1, the allowance for uncollectible accounts is deducted from the gross accounts receivable in the current assets section of the balance sheet. Like the Accumulated Depreciation account illustrated in previous chapters, it is called a contra account.[2]

As shown above, the initial balance of the Allowance for Uncollectible Accounts account is established by an adjusting entry made at the end of the year. As accounts are recognized as uncollectible during the following accounting periods, they are written off by a debit to the Allowance account and a credit to the Accounts Receivable account. In other words, the balance of the Allowance account is reduced as people or companies who owe the company do not pay. The credit balance of the Allowance account at any one time therefore represents the remaining estimated credit sales from previous accounting periods that have not yet been determined to be uncollectible. This credit balance is offset against the total accounts receivable on the balance sheet to provide the amount of accounts receivable expected to be collected.

The Allowance for Uncollectible Accounts will often have other titles such as Allowance for Doubtful Accounts or Allowance for Bad Debts. Occasionally, the obsolete phrase Reserve for Bad Debts will be encountered, but in modern practice it should not be used. Bad Debts Expense is often used as an alternative title for Uncollectible Accounts Expense.

Estimating Uncollectible Accounts Expense

Because it is impossible to know which accounts will be uncollectible at the time financial statements are prepared at the end of the accounting period, it is necessary to give an estimate of the expense for the year that is adequate to cover the expected losses. Obviously estimates can vary widely. If one takes an optimistic view and projects a small loss from uncollectible accounts, the resulting net accounts receivable will be larger than if one takes the pessimistic view. Also, the net income will be larger under the optimistic view because the estimated expense will be smaller. The company's accountant makes an estimate on the basis of past experience, modified by current economic conditions. For example, losses from uncollectible accounts are normally expected to be greater in periods of recession than in periods of economic growth. Ultimately, the decision as to how much is adequate is made by management. This decision will depend on objective information such as the accountant's analyses and

2. Note that although the purpose of the allowance for uncollectible accounts is to reduce the gross accounts receivable to the estimated amount collectible (estimated value), the purpose of the Accumulated Depreciation account is not to reduce the gross plant and equipment accounts to realizable value. The purpose of the Accumulated Depreciation account is to show how much of the cost of the plant and equipment has been allocated as an expense to previous accounting periods.

certain qualitative factors such as how investors, bankers, creditors, and others may view the performance of the company. Regardless of the qualitative considerations, the estimated losses from uncollectible accounts should be realistic.

The accountant has two common methods available for estimating uncollectible accounts expense for an accounting period: the percentage of net sales method and the accounts receivable aging method.

Objective 3 Apply the percentage of net sales method and the accounts receivable aging method to accounting for uncollectible accounts

Percentage of Net Sales Method The percentage of net sales method asks the question, How much of this year's net sales will not be collected? The answer determines the amount of uncollectible accounts expense for the year.

For example, assume that the following balances represent the ending figures for Hassel Company for the year 19x9:

	Dr.	Cr.
Sales		$645,000
Sales Returns and Allowances	$40,000	
Sales Discounts	5,000	
Allowance for Uncollectible Accounts		3,600

Assume that actual losses from uncollectible accounts for the past three years have been as follows:

Year	Net Sales	Losses from Uncollectible Accounts	Percentage
19x6	$ 520,000	$10,200	
19x7	595,000	13,900	
19x8	585,000	9,900	
Total	$1,700,000	$34,000	2%

Management believes that uncollectible accounts will continue to be about 2 percent of net sales. The uncollectible accounts expense for the year 19x9 will therefore be:

$$.02 \times (\$645,000 - \$40,000 - \$5,000) = .02 \times \$600,000 = \$12,000$$

Objective 4 Journalize entries involving the allowance method of accounting for uncollectible accounts

The entry to record this estimate is:

Dec. 31	Uncollectible Accounts Expense	12,000	
	Allowance for Uncollectible Accounts		12,000
	To record uncollectible accounts expense at 2 percent of $600,000 net sales		

The Allowance for Uncollectible Accounts now has a balance of $15,600. This figure consists of the $12,000 estimated uncollectible accounts receivable from 19x8 sales and the $3,600 estimated uncollectible accounts receivable from previous years that have not yet been matched with specific uncollectible and written-off accounts receivable resulting from sales in those years. The reason for the $3,600 figure will become clearer later in this section.

Accounts Receivable Aging Method The accounts receivable aging method asks the question, How much of the year-end balance of accounts receivable will not be collected? The answer determines the amount that the allowance for uncollectible accounts expense should be at the end of the year. The difference between this amount and the actual balance of the Allowance account is the expense for the year. In theory, this method should produce the same result as the percentage of net sales method, but in practice it rarely does. The **aging of accounts receivable** is the process of listing each customer in accounts receivable according to the due date of the account. If a customer is past due on the account, there is a possibility that the account will not or cannot be paid. The further past due an account is, the greater the danger that the customer will not pay. The aging of accounts receivable is useful to management in evaluating its credit and collection policies and alerting it to possible problems of collection. The aging of accounts receivable for Myer Company is shown in Figure 10-2. Each account receivable is classified as being not yet due, or 1–30 days, 31–60 days, 61–90 days, or over 90 days past due. The percentage of total accounts receivable represented by each of these categories is calculated so that management may compare the analysis with previous periods.

Figure 10-2 Analysis of Accounts Receivable by Age

Myer Company
Analysis of Accounts Receivable by Age
December 31, 19xx

Customer	Total	Not Yet Due	1–30 Days Past Due	31–60 Days Past Due	61–90 Days Past Due	Over 90 Days Past Due
A. Arnold	$ 150		$ 150			
M. Benoit	400			$ 400		
J. Connolly	1,000	$ 900	100			
R. DiCarlo	250				$ 250	
Others	42,600	21,000	14,000	3,800	2,200	$1,600
Totals	$44,400	$21,900	$14,250	$4,200	$2,450	$1,600
Percentage	100.0	49.3	32.1	9.5	5.5	3.6

Figure 10-3 Calculation of Estimated Uncollectible Accounts

Myer Company Estimated Uncollectible Accounts			
	Amount	Percentage Considered Uncollectible	Allowance for Uncollectible Accounts
Not yet due	$21,900	1	$ 219
1–30 days	14,250	2	285
31–60 days	4,200	10	420
61–90 days	2,450	30	735
Over 90 days	1,600	50	800
	$44,400		$2,459

The aging of accounts receivable method is useful to the accountant in determining the proper balance of the Allowance for Uncollectible Accounts. The accountant knows from experience that the further past due an account is, the less likely it is to be collected. In Figure 10-3, estimates based on past experience show that only 1 percent of the accounts not yet due and 2 percent of the 1–30 days past due accounts will not be collected. Past experience also indicates that of the 31–60 days, 61–90 days, and over 90 days accounts, 10 percent, 30 percent, and 50 percent, respectively, will not be collected. In total, it is estimated that $2,459 of the $44,400 in accounts receivable will not be collected.

Let us assume that the current credit balance of the Allowance for Uncollectible Accounts for Myer Company is $800. Thus the estimated uncollectible accounts expense for the year is $1,659, which is calculated as follows:

Estimated Uncollectible Accounts	$2,459
Credit Balance—Allowance for Uncollectible Accounts	800[3]
Uncollectible Accounts Expense	$1,659

The uncollectible accounts expense is recorded as follows:

Dec. 31	Uncollectible Accounts Expense	1,659	
	Allowance for Uncollectible Accounts		1,659
	To increase the allowance for uncollectible accounts to the level of expected losses		

3. If the Allowance for Uncollectible Accounts had had a debit balance, the amount of the debit balance would have to be added to the estimated uncollectible accounts to obtain the uncollectible accounts expense.

Comparison of the Two Methods Both of the methods attempt to comply with the matching rule, but do so in a different way. The percentage of net sales method represents an income statement viewpoint. It is based on the proposition that of each dollar of sales a certain proportion will not be collected, and this proportion is the expense for the year. Because this method matches expenses against revenues, it is in accordance with the matching rule. However, this way of determining expense is independent of the current balance of the Allowance for Uncollectible Accounts. The estimated proportion of net sales not expected to be collected is added to the current balance of the Allowance account.

The aging of accounts receivable represents a balance sheet viewpoint and is a more direct valuation method. It is based on the proposition that of each dollar of accounts receivable outstanding, a certain proportion will not be collected, and this proportion should be the balance of the Allowance account at the end of the year. This method is also in accordance with the matching rule because the expense is the difference between what the account is and what it should be. This difference is assumed to be applicable to the current year.

In practice, both methods are often used by the same company. During the year, the estimated uncollectible accounts can be determined more easily by using the percentage of net sales method. At the end of the year, the firm's auditors estimate the balance of the Allowance account by doing an accounts receivable aging in order to compare it with the balance arrived at using the percentage of net sales method. If the two methods produce similar results, the auditor is more confident that the estimates are reasonable.

Writing Off an Uncollectible Account

The Allowance for Uncollectible Accounts exists because it is not known in the accounting period which sale or account will not be collected. When it becomes clear that a specific account will not be collected, the amount should be written off to the Allowance for Uncollectible Accounts. Remember that it was already accounted for as an expense when the allowance was established. For example, assume that R. Deering, who owes the Murray Company $250, is declared bankrupt by a federal court. The entry to write off this account is as follows:

Jan. 15	Allowance for Uncollectible Accounts	250	
	Accounts Receivable, R. Deering		250
	To write off receivable from R. Deering as uncollectible; Deering declared bankruptcy on January 15		

Note that the write-off does not affect the estimated net amount of accounts receivable because there is no expense involved and because the related allowance for uncollectible accounts has already been deducted from the receivables. The write-off simply reduces R. Deering's account to zero and reduces the Allowance for Uncollectible Accounts by a similar amount, as the following table shows:

	Before Write-off	**After Write-off**
Accounts Receivable	$44,400	$44,150
Less Allowance for Uncollectible Accounts	2,458	2,208
Estimated net value of Accounts Receivable	$41,942	$41,942

Differences Between Written-off Accounts and Estimates The total of accounts receivable written off in any given year will rarely equal the allowance for uncollectible accounts because the allowance is based on an estimate of uncollectible accounts expense. The Allowance account will show a credit balance as long as the accounts written off as uncollectible are less than the estimated uncollectible accounts. If the company underestimates the amount of uncollectible receivables, the accounts receivable written off will exceed the amount in the Allowance account and will therefore create a debit balance in the Allowance account. This debit balance will be eliminated at the end of the accounting period by the credit to this account resulting from the new adjusting entry that is made to record the estimated uncollectible accounts expense for the current year.

If the percentage of net sales method is used, the new balance of the Allowance account after the adjusting entry will equal the percentage of sales estimated to be uncollectible minus the debit balance. If the accounts receivable aging method is used, the amount of the adjustment must equal the estimated uncollectible accounts plus the debit balance in the Allowance for Uncollectible Accounts. Obviously, if the estimates are consistently wrong, management should reexamine the company's estimation rates.

Recovery of Accounts Receivable Written Off Sometimes a customer whose account has been written off as uncollectible will later be able to pay the amount in full or in part. When this occurs, it is necessary to make two journal entries: one to reverse the earlier write-off, which was incorrect in the first place; and another to show the collection of the account.

For example, assume that on September 1, R. Deering, after his bankruptcy on January 15 (illustrated above), notified the company that he would be able to pay $100 of his account and enclosed a check for $50. The entries to record this transaction are as follows:

Sept. 1	Accounts Receivable, R. Deering	100	
	Allowance for Uncollectible Accounts		100
	To reinstate the portion of the account of R. Deering now considered collectible, which had been written off January 15		

Sept. 1	Cash	50	
	Accounts Receivable, R. Deering		50
	To record collection from R. Deering		

The collectible portion of R. Deering's account must be restored to his account and credited to the Allowance for Uncollectible Accounts for two reasons. First, as it turned out, it was an error of judgment to write off the full $250 on January 15. Only $150 was actually uncollectible. Second, the Accounts Receivable subsidiary account for R. Deering should reflect his ability to pay part of the money he owed in spite of his bankruptcy. This action will give a clear indication of his credit record for future credit action.

Direct Charge-off Method

Some companies record uncollectible accounts by debiting expenses directly when bad debts are discovered instead of using the Allowance for Uncollectible Accounts and adjusting entries to estimate the amount of uncollectible expense in an accounting period. The **direct charge-off method** is not in accordance with good accounting theory because it makes no attempt to match revenues and expenses. Uncollectible accounts are charged to expenses in the accounting period in which they are discovered rather than in the period of the sale. On the balance sheet the accounts receivable are shown at gross value, not realizable value, because there is no Allowance for Uncollectible Accounts. Both the direct charge-off method and the allowance method of estimating uncollectible accounts expense are acceptable for use in computing taxable income under federal income tax regulations. Only the allowance method is used in this book because it is better from the standpoint of accounting theory.

Credit Balances in Accounts Receivable

Objective 5 Recognize types of receivables not classified as accounts receivable and specify their balance sheet presentation

Sometimes customers overpay their accounts because of mistakes or in anticipation of future purchases. When customer accounts show credit balances in the accounts receivable ledger, the balance of the Accounts Receivable controlling account should not appear on the balance sheet as the amount of the accounts receivable. The total of the customers' accounts with credit balances should be shown as a current liability because the company is liable to these customers for their overpayments. For example, assume that the balances in the Accounts Receivable controlling account are as follows:

165 accounts with debit balances	$182,400
10 accounts with credit balances	4,200
Net balance of 175 customer accounts	$178,200

Because the customer accounts with credit balances are liabilities, the balance sheet presentation should be as follows:

Current Assets		Current Liabilities	
Accounts Receivable	$182,400	Credit Balances in Customer Accounts	$4,200

Sales to and Purchases from the Same Firm

Where a firm has made both sales to and purchases from the same company, two separate accounts should be maintained, and they should not be offset against each other. The receivable accounts should be part of the accounts receivable subsidiary ledger and shown on the balance sheet as accounts receivable. The payable account should be part of the accounts payable subsidiary ledger and shown as accounts payable on the balance sheet.

Installment Accounts Receivable

Installment sales constitute a significant portion of the accounts receivable of many retail companies. Department stores, appliance stores, and retail chains all sell goods that are collected in a series of time payments. Companies such as J. C. Penney and Sears have millions of dollars in these **installment accounts receivable.** Although the payment period may be twenty-four months or more, installment accounts receivable are classified as current assets if such credit policies are customary in the industry. There are special accounting rules that apply to installment sales. Because these rules can be very complicated, the study of such practices is usually deferred until a more advanced accounting course.

Credit Card Sales

Many retailers allow customers to charge their purchases to a third-party company that the customer will pay later. The five most widely used national credit cards are American Express, Carte Blanche, Diners Club, Master Card, and VISA. The customer establishes credit with the lender and receives a plastic card to use in making charge purchases. If the seller accepts the card, an invoice is made at the time of the sale that is imprinted by the charge card and signed by the customer. The seller then sends the invoice to the lender and receives cash. Because the seller does not have to establish the customer's credit, collect from the customer, or tie money up in accounts receivable, the seller receives an economic benefit that is provided by the lender. Consequently, the credit card company does not pay 100 percent of the total amount of the credit card sales invoices. The lender takes a discount of 2 to 5 percent on the credit card sales invoices.

Two alternative procedures are used in accounting for credit card sales, depending on whether the merchant must wait for collection from the credit card company or whether the merchant may deposit the sales invoices in a checking account immediately. The following example illustrates the procedure used in the first case. Assume that, at the end of the day, a restaurant has American Express invoices totaling $1,000. These sales are recorded as follows:

Accounts Receivable, American Express	1,000	
Sales		1,000
Sales made for which American Express cards were accepted		

The seller now mails the American Express invoices to American Express and later receives payment for them at 95 percent of their face value. When cash is received, the entry is as follows:

Cash	950	
Credit Card Discount Expense	50	
Accounts Receivable, American Express		1,000
Receipt of payment from American Express for invoices at 95 percent of face value		

The second case is typical of sales made through bank credit cards such as VISA and Master Card. For example, assume that the restaurant made sales of $1,000 on VISA credit cards and that VISA takes a 5 percent discount on the sales. Assume also that the sales invoices may be deposited in a special VISA bank account in the name of the company in much the same way that checks from cash sales may be deposited. These sales may be recorded as follows:

Cash	950	
Credit Card Discount Expense	50	
Sales		1,000
Sales for which VISA cards were accepted		

Other Accounts Receivable

The title Accounts Receivable on the balance sheet should be reserved for sales made to regular customers in the ordinary course of business. If loans or sales that do not fall in this category are made to employees, officers, and stockholders, they should be shown separately on the balance sheet with an asset title such as Receivables from Employees and Officers.

Accounting for Notes Receivable

A **promissory note** is an unconditional promise to pay a definite sum of money on demand or at a future date. The person who signs the note and thereby promises to pay is called the maker of the note. The person to whom payment is to be made is called the payee. When the note is due in less than a year, the payee should record it as a note receivable in the current asset section of the balance sheet, and the maker should record it as a note payable in the current liability section of the balance sheet.

Objective 6 Define and describe a promissory note

In this chapter, we are concerned primarily with notes received from customers. The nature of the business generally determines how frequently promissory notes are received from customers. In companies that sell on an installment basis, installment contracts instead of promissory notes are generally used. Firms selling durable goods of high value, such as farm machinery and automobiles, will often take promissory notes in payment. One advantage of promissory notes in these situations is that the notes can be resold to banks as a financing method. Almost all companies will occasionally receive a note, and many companies obtain notes receivable in settlement of past-due accounts.

Computations Associated with Promissory Notes

In accounting for promissory notes, several terms are important. These are (1) maturity date, (2) duration of note, (3) interest and interest rate, (4) maturity value, (5) discount, and (6) proceeds from discounting.

Objective 7 Make calculations involving promissory notes

Maturity Date The **maturity date** must either be stated on the promissory note or be determinable from the facts stated on it. Among the most common statements of maturity date are the following:

1. A specific date, such as "November 14, 19xx"
2. A specific number of months after the date of the note, for example, "3 months after date"
3. A specific number of days after the date of the note, for example, "60 days after date"

There is no problem in determining the date when it is stated. When the number of months from date of note is the maturity date, one simply uses the same day of the month as the note in the appropriate month in the future. For example, a note dated January 20 that is due two months from that date would be due on March 20.

When the computation of maturity date is based on a specific number of days, the maturity date must be determined on the basis of the passage of the exact number of days. In computing the maturity, it is important to exclude the date of the note and to include the maturity day. For example, a note dated May 20, and due in 90 days, would be due on August 18, computed as follows:

Days remaining in May (31 − 20)	11
Days in June	30
Days in July	31
Days in August	18
Total days	90

Duration of Note Determining the **duration of note**, or length of time in days, is the opposite problem from determining maturity date. This calculation is important because interest must be calculated on the basis of the exact number of days. There is no problem when the maturity date is based on the number of days from date of note. However, if the maturity date is a specified date or a specified number of months from date, the exact number of days must be determined. Assume that the length of time of a note is from May 10 to August 10. The length of time is 92 days, determined as follows:

Days remaining in May (31 − 10)	21
Days in June	30
Days in July	31
Days in August	10
Total days	92

Interest and Interest Rate The **interest** is the cost of borrowing money or the reward for loaning money, depending on whether one is the borrower or the creditor. The amount of interest is based on three factors: the principal (the amount of money borrowed or loaned), the rate of interest, and the length of time. The formula used in computing interest is as follows:

$$\text{principal} \times \text{rate of interest} \times \text{time} = \text{interest}$$

Interest rates are usually stated on an annual basis. For example, the interest on a $1,000, one-year, 8 percent note is computed as follows: $1,000 × 8/100 × 1 = $80.

If the term of the note were three months instead of a year, the interest charge would be $20, computed as follows: $1,000 × 8/100 × 3/12 = $20.

When the terms of a note are expressed in days, the exact number of days must be used in computing the interest. It is common practice to compute interest on the basis of 360 days per year. Therefore, if the term of the above note were 45 days, the interest would be $10, computed as follows: $1,000 × 8/100 × 45/360 = $10.

Accountants using a 360-day year and 6 percent rate of interest frequently employ a short-cut method of determining the interest, known as the 6 percent method. If the interest rate is 6 percent a year, the interest for 60 days on any amount of money may be determined simply by moving the decimal point two places to the left (6/100 × 60/360 = 1/100 = .01 or 1%). For example, the interest at 6 percent for 60 days on $2,462 is $24.62, and the interest at 6 percent for 60 days on $1,946.25 is $19.46.[4]

4. Proof: $2,462 × 6/100 × 60/360 = $2,462 × 1/100 = $24.62; $1,946.25 × 6/100 × 60/360 = $1,946.25 × 1/100 = $19.46.

The 60-day, 6 percent method can be used for time periods other than 60 days by stating the time period as a fraction of 60 days. For instance, note the following examples of the calculation of interest on a 6 percent, $2,000 note, on which interest for 60 days would be $20:

15 days: 15/60 or 1/4 times the interest for 60 days = 1/4 × $20 = $5.

30 days: 30/60 or 1/2 times the interest for 60 days = 1/2 × $20 = $10.

90 days: 90/60 or 3/2 times the interest for 60 days = 3/2 × $20 = $30.

The 60-day, 6 percent method can also be used to compute the interest when the rate is other than 6 percent by stating the rate as a fraction of 6 percent. Study the following example of the calculation of interest on a 60-day, $6,000 note, on which the interest for 60 days would be $60:

4 percent rate: 4/6 times the interest at 6% = 4/6 × $60 = $40.

8 percent rate: 8/6 times the interest at 6% = 8/6 × $60 = $80.

Maturity Value It is often useful to determine the **maturity value** of a note or the total proceeds of the note at maturity date. Maturity value is the face value of the note plus interest. The maturity value of a 90-day, 8 percent, $1,000 note is computed as follows:

$$\begin{aligned}\text{maturity value} &= \text{principal} + \text{interest}\\ &= \$1{,}000 + (\$1{,}000 \times 8/100 \times 90/360)\\ &= \$1{,}000 + \$20\\ &= \$1{,}020\end{aligned}$$

Occasionally, one will encounter a noninterest-bearing note, in which case the maturity value is the face value or principal amount.

Discount To **discount** a note means to take out the interest in advance. The **discount** is the amount of interest deducted. It is very common for banks to use this method when loaning money on promissory notes. The amount of the discount is computed as follows:

$$\text{discount} = \text{maturity value} \times \text{rate} \times \text{time}$$

For example, assume that a noninterest-bearing $1,000 note due in 90 days is discounted at a 10 percent rate of interest:

$$\text{discount} = \$1{,}000 \times 10/100 \times 90/360 = \$25$$

Proceeds from Discounting When someone borrows money on a note at interest, the amount he or she receives or borrows is the face value or principal. When a note receivable is discounted, the amount the borrower receives is called the **proceeds from discounting** and must be computed as follows:

$$\text{proceeds} = \text{maturity value} - \text{discount}$$

Thus, in the preceding example, the proceeds would be computed as follows:

$$\begin{aligned}\text{proceeds} &= \$1{,}000 - (\$1{,}000 \times 10/100 \times 90/360)\\ &= \$1{,}000 - \$25\\ &= \$975\end{aligned}$$

This calculation is very simple when a noninterest-bearing note is involved as illustrated here. However, the calculation is more complicated when an interest-bearing note is involved, as in the case when an interest-bearing note from a customer is discounted to the bank. In this situation, the maturity value must first be computed under the formula described for computing maturity value. Then the discount must be computed on the basis of the maturity value and, finally, the proceeds are determined by deducting the discount from the maturity value. For example, the proceeds of a \$2,000, 8 percent, 90-day note, discounted on the date it is drawn at the bank at 10 percent, would be \$1,989, determined as follows:

$$\begin{aligned}\text{proceeds} &= \text{maturity value} - \text{discount}\\ \text{maturity value} &= \text{principal} + \text{interest}\\ \text{maturity value} &= \$2{,}000 + (\$2{,}000 \times 8/100 \times 90/360)\\ \text{maturity value} &= \$2{,}000 + \$40\\ \text{maturity value} &= \$2{,}040\\ \text{proceeds} &= \$2{,}040 - (\$2{,}040 \times 10/100 \times 90/360)\\ \text{proceeds} &= \$2{,}040 - \$51\\ \text{proceeds} &= \$1{,}989\end{aligned}$$

In this example, the note was discounted to the bank on the same day it was written. Usually some days will lapse between the date the note is written and the date it is discounted. When this situation occurs, the number of days used in computing the proceeds should be the days remaining until the maturity date of the note because this is the length of time for which the bank is lending the money to the company holding the note. For example, assume the same facts as above except that the company holding the note waits 30 days to discount the note to the bank. In other words, at the date of discounting, there are 60 (90 – 30) days remaining until the maturity date. The proceeds are determined as follows:

$$\begin{aligned}\text{proceeds} &= \text{maturity value} - \text{discount}\\ \text{maturity value} &= \$2{,}040 \text{ (from above)}\\ \text{proceeds} &= \$2{,}040 - (\$2{,}040 \times 10/100 \times 60/360)\\ \text{proceeds} &= \$2{,}040 - \$34\\ \text{proceeds} &= \$2{,}006\end{aligned}$$

The difference in the discount of \$17 (\$51 – \$34) between the two cases is equal to the discount on the 30 days lapsed between writing and discounting the note (\$2,040 × 10/100 × 30/360 = \$17).

Illustrative Accounting Entries

The accounting entries for promissory notes receivable fall into five categories: (1) receipt of a note, (2) collection of a note, (3) recording a dishonored note, (4) discounting a note, and (5) recording adjusting entries.

Objective 8 Journalize entries involving notes receivable

Receipt of a Note Assume that a 6 percent, 30-day note is received from a customer, J. Halsted, in settlement of an existing account receivable of $4,000. The entry for this transaction is as follows:

June 1	Notes Receivable	4,000	
	Accounts Receivable, J. Halsted		4,000
	Received 6 percent, 30-day note in payment of account		

Collection of a Note When the note plus interest is collected 30 days later, the entry is as follows:

July 1	Cash	4,020	
	Notes Receivable		4,000
	Interest Earned		20
	Collected 6 percent, 30-day note from J. Halsted		

Recording a Dishonored Note When the maker of a note cannot or will not pay the note at maturity, the note is said to be dishonored. In the case of a **dishonored note**, an entry should be made by the holder or payee to transfer the amount due from the Notes Receivable account to an account receivable from the debtor. If it is assumed that J. Halsted did not pay his note on July 1 but dishonored it, the following entry would be made:

July 1	Accounts Receivable, J. Halsted	4,020	
	Notes Receivable		4,000
	Interest Earned		20
	To record dishonor by J. Halsted of 6 percent, 30-day note		

The interest earned is recorded because, although J. Halsted did not pay the note, he is still obligated to pay both the principal amount and the interest.

Two things are accomplished by transferring dishonored notes receivable into an accounts receivable account. First, it leaves the Notes Receivable account with only notes that have not matured and are presumably collectible. Second, it establishes a record in the borrower's account receivable that he or she has dishonored a note receivable. This information may be helpful in evaluating whether to extend more credit to this customer in the future.

Discounting a Note Many companies raise money for operations by selling notes receivable from customers to banks or finance companies for cash rather than holding them until maturity. This type of financing is usually called discounting because the bank deducts the interest from the maturity value of the note to determine the proceeds. The holder of the note (usually the payee) signs his or her name on the back of the note (as in endorsing a check) and delivers the note to the bank. The bank expects to collect the maturity value of the note (principal plus interest) on the maturity date. If the maker fails to pay, the endorser is liable to the bank for payment.

For example, assume that we discount at 10 percent a $1,000, 8 percent, 90-day note at the bank for cash 60 days before maturity. The cash to be received (proceeds from discounting) is calculated as the maturity value less the discount, and this transaction can be recorded as follows:

Cash	1,003	
Notes Receivable		1,000
Interest Earned		3
To record discounting of an 8 percent, 90-day note with 60 days left at 10 percent		
Maturity value:		
$1,000 + ($1,000 × 8/100 × 90/360) =	$1,020	
Less discount:		
$1,020 × 10/100 × 60/360 =	17	
Proceeds from discounted note receivable	$1,003	

Before discussing the transaction, there are two things to note about the calculations. First, if the proceeds had been less than the note receivable, the difference would have been recorded as a debit to Interest Expense. For example, if the proceeds had been $997 instead of $1,003, Interest Expense would have been debited for $3, and there would have been no entry to Interest Earned. Second, neither the length of the discounting period nor the discount rate is the same as the term or the rate of interest of the note. This situation is typical.

Regarding the journal entry, notice that the account Notes Receivable is credited. Although this entry removes the note from the records, remember that if the maker cannot or will not pay the bank, the endorser is liable to the bank for the note. In accounting terminology, the endorser is said to be contingently liable to the bank. A **contingent liability** is a potential liability that can develop into a real liability if a possible subsequent event occurs. In this case, the subsequent event would be the nonpayment of the note by the maker.

Before the maturity date of the discounted note, the bank will notify the maker that it is holding the note and that payment should be made directly to the bank. If the maker pays the bank as agreed, then no entry is required in the records of the endorser. If the maker does not pay the note and interest on the due date, the note is said to be *dishonored.* To hold the endorser liable for the note, the bank must notify the endorser that the note is dishonored. The bank will normally notify the endorser by protesting the note. The bank does this by preparing and mailing a notice of protest to the endorser. The **notice of protest** is a sworn statement that the note was presented to the maker for payment and the maker refused to pay. The bank typically charges a **protest fee** for protesting the note, which must be paid when the endorser pays the bank the amount due on the dishonored note.

If the note discounted in the example above is dishonored by the maker on the maturity date, the following entry should be made by the endorser when paying the obligation:

Accounts Receivable, Name of Maker	1,025	
Cash		1,025
To record payment of principal and interest on discounted note (maturity value of $1,020), plus a protest fee of $5 to bank; the note was dishonored by the maker		

Recording Adjusting Entries A promissory note received in one period may not be due until a following accounting period. Because the interest on the note accrues by a small amount each day of the duration of the note, it is necessary, according to the matching rule, to apportion the interest earned to the period in which it belongs. For example, assume that on August 31 a 60-day, 8 percent, $2,000 note was received and that the company prepares financial statements monthly. The following adjusting entry on September 30 is necessary to show how the interest earned for September has accrued:

Sept. 30	Accrued Interest Receivable	13.33	
	Interest Earned		13.33
	To accrue 30 days' interest earned on note receivable $\$2,000 \times 8/100 \times 30/360 = \$13.33$		

The account Accrued Interest Receivable is a current asset on the balance sheet. Upon payment of the note plus interest on October 30, the following entry is made:

Oct. 30	Cash	1,026.67	
	Note Receivable		1,000.00
	Accrued Interest Receivable		13.33
	Interest Earned		13.34
	To record payment of note receivable plus interest		

As can be clearly seen from the above transactions, both September and October receive the benefit of one-half the interest earned.

Chapter Review

Review of Learning Objectives

1. Name the most common types of short-term monetary assets.
Short-term monetary assets are useful for the payment of current obligations. They consist of cash, temporary investments, accounts receivable, and notes receivable.

2. Explain why estimated losses from uncollectible accounts are important to income determination.
Because credit is extended in an effort to increase sales, it is reasonable that bad debts associated with the sales be charged as expenses in the period in which the sale is made. However, because there is a time lag between the time a sale is made on credit and the time the account is deemed uncollectible, the accountant must estimate the amount of bad debts in any given period.

3. Apply the percentage of net sales method and the accounts receivable aging method to accounting for uncollectible accounts.
Uncollectible accounts expense is estimated by either the percentage of net sales method or the accounts receivable aging method. According to the first method, bad debts are judged to be a certain percentage of sales during the period. According to the second method, certain percentages are applied to groups of the accounts receivable that have been arranged by due dates.

4. Journalize entries involving the allowance method of accounting for uncollectible accounts.
When the estimate of uncollectible accounts is made, an Allowance for Uncollectible Accounts is established as a contra account to Accounts Receivable by a debit to expense and a credit to the Allowance account. When an individual account is determined to be uncollectible, it is removed from Accounts Receivable by debiting the Allowance account and crediting Accounts Receivable. Should this account later be collected, the preceding entry should be reversed and the collection recorded in the normal manner.

5. Recognize types of receivables not classified as accounts receivable and specify their balance sheet presentation.
Accounts of customers with credit balances should not be classified as negative accounts receivable but as current liabilities on the balance sheet. Installment accounts receivable are classified as current assets if such credit policies are customary in the industry. Receivables from credit card companies should be classified as current assets. Receivables from employees, officers, stockholders, and others not made in the normal course of business should not be included among accounts receivable. They may be either short- or long-term assets depending on when collection is expected to take place.

6. Define and describe a promissory note.
A promissory note is an unconditional promise to pay a definite sum of money on demand or at a future date. Firms selling durable goods of high value such as farm machinery and automobiles will often take promissory notes, which can be resold to banks as a financing method.

7. Make calculations involving promissory notes.
In accounting for promissory notes, it is important to know how to calculate the following: maturity date, duration of note, interest, maturity value, discount, and proceeds from discounting. Discounting is the act of taking out the interest in advance when making a loan on a note.

8. Journalize entries involving notes receivable.
The accounting entries for promissory notes receivable fall into five categories: receipt of a note, collection of a note, recording a dishonored note, discounting a note, and recording adjusting entries.

Review Problem

Before doing the exercises and problems, review the sample journal entries for uncollectible accounts expense and notes receivable transactions given in this chapter. For additional help, see the review problem in the working papers.

Chapter Assignments

Questions

1. Why does a business need short-term monetary assets? What are some of the more common short-term monetary assets?
2. Why does a company sell on credit if it expects that some of the accounts will not be paid? What role does a credit department play in selling on credit?
3. According to the accountant, at what point in the cycle of selling and collecting does the bad debt loss occur?
4. If management estimates that $5,000 of the year's sales will not be collected, what entry should be made at year end?
5. After adjusting and clearing entries at the end of the year, suppose that the Accounts Receivable balance is $176,000, and the Allowance for Uncollectible Accounts balance is $14,500. (a) What is the estimated realizable value of Accounts Receivable? (b) If the $450 account of a bankrupt customer is written off in the first month of the new year, what will be the resulting estimated realizable value of Accounts Receivable?
6. What is the effect on net income of an optimistic versus a pessimistic view by management of estimated uncollectible accounts?
7. In what ways is the Allowance for Uncollectible Accounts similar to and different from Accumulated Depreciation?
8. What procedure for estimating uncollectible accounts also gives management a view of the status of collections and the overall quality of accounts receivable?
9. What is the underlying logic or reasoning behind the percentage of net sales method and the accounts receivable aging method of estimating uncollectible accounts?
10. Is there a difference among the following terms: allowance for bad debts, allowance for doubtful accounts, allowance for uncollectible accounts?
11. Why should the entry for an account that has been written off as uncollectible be reinstated if the amount owed is subsequently collected?
12. What accounting rule is violated by the direct charge-off method of recognizing uncollectible accounts? Why?
13. Which of the lettered items below should be in Accounts Receivable? For those that do not belong in Accounts Receivable, tell where they do belong on the balance sheet: (a) installment accounts receivable from regular customers, due monthly for three years; (b) debit balances in customers' accounts; (c) receivables from employees; (d) credit balances in customers' accounts; (e) receivables from officers of the company; (f) accounts payable to a company that are less than accounts receivable from the same company.

14. What is a promissory note? Who is the maker? Who is the payee?
15. What are the due dates of the following notes: (a) a three-month note dated August 16, (b) a 90-day note dated August 16, (c) a 60-day note dated March 25?
16. What is the difference between a cash discount and a discount on a note?
17. What is the difference between the interest on a note and the discount on a note?
18. A bank is offering Diane Wedge two alternatives for borrowing $2,000. The first alternative is a $2,000, 6 percent, 60-day note. The second alternative is a $2,000, 60-day, noninterest-bearing note discounted at 6 percent. (a) What entries are required by the bank to record the two loans? (b) What entries are needed by the bank to record the collection of the two loans? (c) Which alternative favors the bank, and why?

Classroom Exercises

Exercise 10-1 Adjusting Entries—Accounts Receivable Aging Method

The general ledger controlling account for accounts receivable of Blakely Enterprises shows a debit balance of $180,000 at the end of the year. An aging method analysis of the individual accounts indicates estimated uncollectible accounts to be $8,400.

Give the general journal entry to record the uncollectible accounts expense under each of the following assumptions: (1) The Allowance for Uncollectible Accounts has a credit balance of $600. (2) The Allowance for Uncollectible Accounts has a debit balance of $600.

Exercise 10-2 Adjusting Entry—Percentage of Net Sales Method

At the end of the year, James Corporation estimated the uncollectible accounts expense to be one-half of 1 percent of net sales of $4,600,000. The current credit balance of the Allowance for Uncollectible Accounts is $7,800.

Prepare the general journal entry to record the uncollectible accounts expense.

Exercise 10-3 Accounts Receivable Transactions

Assuming that the allowance method is being used, prepare journal entries to record the following transactions:

May 17, 19x8	Sold merchandise to Chester Jones for $600.
Sept. 20, 19x8	Received $200 from Chester Jones on account.
June 25, 19x9	Wrote off as uncollectible the balance of the Chester Jones account when he was declared bankrupt.
July 27, 19x9	Unexpectedly received a check for $100 from Chester Jones.

Exercise 10-4 Interest Computations—6 Percent Method

Using the 60-day, 6 percent method, determine the interest on the following notes: (a) $10,360 at 6 percent for 60 days; (b) $6,000 at 6 percent for 90 days; (c) $10,000 at 6 percent for 30 days; (d) $8,000 at 9 percent for 60 days; (e) $12,000 at 12 percent for 120 days; (f) $4,500 at 4 percent for 60 days.

Exercise 10-5 Discounting Notes

In an effort to raise cash, Marshall Company discounted two notes at the bank on September 15. The bank charged a discount rate of 10 percent applied to the maturity value.

Compute the proceeds from discounting of each of the following notes:

Date of Note	Amount	Interest Rate	Life of Note
a. Aug. 1	$ 9,000	9%	120 days
b. July 20	$11,000	12%	90 days

Exercise 10-6 Notes Receivable Transactions

Prepare general journal entries to record the following transactions:

Jan. 16 Sold merchandise to Santan Corporation on account for $14,000, terms n/30.
Feb. 15 Accepted a $14,000, 6 percent, 60-day note from Santan Corporation granting an extension on the previous sales.
Mar. 17 Discounted Santan Corporation note at bank at 9 percent.
Apr. 16 Received notice that Santan dishonored the note. Paid the bank the maturity value of the note plus a protest fee of $12.
May 15 Received payment in full from Santan Corporation.

Exercise 10-7 Credit Card Sales Transactions

Prepare journal entries to record the following transactions for Joy's Gift Shop:

Dec. 4 A tabulation of invoices at the end of day showed $150 in American Express invoices and $200 in Diners Club invoices.
5 Received payment from American Express at 96 percent of face value and from Diners Club at 95 percent of face value.
6 A tabulation of invoices at the end of day showed $100 in VISA invoices, which are deposited in a special bank account at full value less 5 percent discount.

Exercise 10-8 Adjusting Entries—Interest Expense

Prepare journal entries to record the following transactions:

Dec. 1 Received a 90-day, 10 percent note for $4,000 from a customer for a sale of merchandise.
31 Made end-of-year adjustment for accrued interest earned.
Mar. 1 Received payment in full for note and interest.

Problem Set A

Problem 10A-1 Percentage of Net Sales Method

On December 31 of last year, the balance sheet of Fremgen Company had accounts receivable of $314,000 and a credit balance in the Allowance for Uncollectible Accounts of $19,400. During the current year, the company's records included the following selected activities: sales on account, $1,215,000; sales returns and allowances, $75,000; collections from customers, $1,150,000; accounts written off as worthless, $16,000; worthless accounts unexpectedly collected, $2,000. In the past, the company had found that 1.5 percent of net sales would not be collected.

Required

1. Give the summary general journal entries to record each of the five items listed above.
2. Give the general journal entry to record the estimated uncollectible accounts expense for the year.
3. Open ledger accounts for the Accounts Receivable controlling account (112) and Allowance for Uncollectible Accounts (113), enter the beginning balances in these accounts, and post the appropriate parts of the transactions in 1 and 2 to these accounts.

Problem 10A-2 Accounts Receivable Aging Method

Johnson Sales Company uses the accounts receivable aging method to estimate uncollectible accounts. The Accounts Receivable controlling account and the Allowance for Uncollectible Accounts had balances of $172,000 and $12,000, respectively, at the beginning of the year. During the year, the company had sales on account of $946,000, sales returns and allowances of $8,400, worthless accounts written off of $14,150, and collections from customers of $901,460.

At the end of the year (December 31), a junior accountant for the company was preparing an aging analysis of accounts receivable. At the top of page 6 of his report, his totals appeared as follows:

Customer Account	Total	Not Yet Due	1–30 Days Past Due	31–60 Days Past Due	61–90 Days Past Due	Over 90 Days Past Due
Balance forward	$176,250	$97,300	$46,450	$17,860	$8,240	$6,400

He had the following accounts remaining to finish the analysis:

Account	Amount	Due Date
J. Walters	$ 1,740	Jan. 14 (next year)
A. Wang	1,180	Dec. 24
R. Weiss	3,910	Sept. 28
J. Whiteside	4,200	Aug. 16
B. Yancy	750	Dec. 14
N. Yanoff	5,370	Jan. 23 (next year)
T. Zimmer	590	Nov. 5
	$17,740	

The company has found from past experience that the following rates of estimated uncollectible accounts produce an adequate balance for the Allowance of Uncollectible Accounts:

Time Past Due	Percentage Considered Uncollectible
Not yet due	2
1–30 days	4
31–60 days	20
61–90 days	30
Over 90 days	50

Required

1. Complete the aging analysis of accounts receivable.
2. Compute the end-of-year balance (before adjustments) for the Accounts Receivable controlling account and the Allowance for Uncollectible Accounts.
3. Prepare an analysis computing the estimated uncollectible accounts.
4. Prepare a general journal entry to record the estimated uncollectible accounts expense for the year. (Round adjustment to the nearest dollar.)

Problem 10A-3 Notes Receivable Transactions

Mann Manufacturing Company engaged in the following transactions involving promissory notes:

Jan. 14 Sold merchandise to Sohn Sales Company for $14,200, terms n/30.
Feb. 13 Received $4,200 in cash from Sohn Sales and received a 90-day, 8 percent promissory note for the balance of the account.
23 Discounted the note at the bank at 10 percent.
May 14 Because no notice that the note had been dishonored was received, it was assumed that Sohn Sales paid the bank.

15 Received a 60-day, 6 percent note from Gyrl Sales Company in payment of a past-due account, $6,000.
30 Discounted the note at the bank at 9 percent.
July 14 Received notice that Gyrl Sales dishonored the note. Paid the bank the maturity value of the note plus a protest fee of $5.
20 Received a check from Gyrl Sales for payment of the maturity value of the note, the $5 protest fee, and interest at 6 percent for the six days beyond maturity.
25 Sold merchandise to Cusson Sales Company for $18,000, with payment of $3,000 cash down and the remainder on account.
31 Received a $15,000, 45-day, 10 percent promissory note from Cusson Sales for the outstanding account.
Aug. 5 Discounted the note at the bank at 8 percent.
Sept. 14 Received notice that Cusson Sales dishonored the note. Paid the bank the maturity value of the note plus a protest fee of $6.
25 Wrote off the Cusson Sales Company account as uncollectible following news that the company had been declared bankrupt.

Required

Prepare general journal entries to record the above transactions.

Problem 10A-4 Notes Receivable Transactions

Parsons Appliance Company engaged in the following transactions:

Jan. 2 Accepted a $5,400, 90-day, 7 percent note from Sally Harris as an extension on her past-due account.
5 Accepted a $900, 90-day, 6 percent note from Arthur Wisdom in payment of a past-due account receivable.
10 Accepted a $1,800, 90-day, 8 percent note from Joseph Johnson as an extension of a past-due account.
12 Discounted the Sally Harris note at the bank at 8 percent.
25 Discounted the Joseph Johnson note at the bank at 6 percent.
30 Accepted a $2,600, 90-day, 6 percent note from Thomas Akins in lieu of immediate payment of a past-due account.
Apr. 2 Received notice that Sally Harris had dishonored her note. Paid bank maturity value plus protest fee of $6.
5 Arthur Wisdom dishonored his note.
10 Received no notice of dishonor by Joseph Johnson and assumed he paid his obligation to the bank.
22 Received payment from Sally Harris for the total amount owed including maturity value, protest fee, and interest at 10 percent for the twenty days past maturity.
25 Wrote off the Arthur Wisdom account as uncollectible because he could not be located.
26 Delivered the Thomas Akins note to bank for collection.
30 Received notice that Thomas Akins paid his note plus interest in full to the bank. The bank credited the amount to Parsons's account and charged a $5 collection fee.

Required

Prepare general journal entries to record the above transactions.

Problem 10A-5 Short-Term Financing by Discounting Customers' Notes

The Recession Company is faced with a severe cash shortage because of slowing sales and past-due accounts. The financial vice president has studied the situation and has found a number of very large past-due accounts. He makes the following recommendations: (a) that the company seek promissory notes from past-due accounts to encourage the customers to pay on time and to earn interest on the money invested in these accounts, and (b) that the company generate cash by discounting the notes at the bank at the going rate of interest. During the first month of this program, the company was successful, as indicated by the following table:

Company	Amount of Note	Length of Note	Date of Note	Interest Rate	Discount Date	Discount Rate
Adams Manufacturing Company	$ 65,000	60 days	Apr. 5	9%	Apr. 7	10%
Fandet Company	100,000	60 days	Apr. 10	6%	Apr. 13	10%
Mendel Corporation	40,000	60 days	Apr. 15	8%	Apr. 20	9%

Adams Manufacturing and Fandet Company paid their notes on the due dates. Mendel Corporation dishonored its note on the due date.

Required

1. Prepare appropriate general journal entries for April.
2. What was the total cash generated during April by the vice president's plan?
3. Prepare appropriate general journal entries for June.
4. What is your evaluation of the plan? What offsetting factors occur in later months such as June?

Problem Set B

Problem 10B-1 Percentage of Net Sales Method

At the beginning of the current year, McGraft Company had accounts receivable of $642,000 and a credit balance in the Allowance for Uncollectible Accounts of $38,200. During the year, the company's records included the following selected activities: sales on account, $2,341,000; sales returns and allowances, $131,000; collections from customers, $2,302,000; accounts written off as worthless, $37,000; worthless accounts unexpectedly collected, $3,000. The company's experience with credit sales has shown that 2 percent of net sales would not be collected.

Required

1. Give the summary general journal entries required to record each of the five items listed above.
2. Give the general journal entry required to record the estimated uncollectible accounts expense for the year.
3. Open ledger accounts for the Accounts Receivable controlling account (112) and Allowance for Uncollectible Accounts (113), enter the beginning balances in these accounts, and post the appropriate parts of transactions 1 and 2 to these accounts.

Problem 10B-2 Accounts Receivable Aging Method

At the beginning of the current year, Melville Discount Store, a company that uses the accounts receivable aging method to estimate uncollectible accounts, had balances in its Accounts Receivable controlling account and Allowance for Uncollectible Accounts of $227,000 and $21,000, respectively. During the year, the company had sales on account of $1,977,000, sales returns and allowances of

$37,000, worthless accounts written off of $24,500, and collections from customers of $1,785,000.

As part of the end-of-year (January 31) procedures, an aging analysis of accounts receivable is prepared. The analysis is partially complete. The totals carried over to the top of page 5 of the analysis appear below.

Customer Account	Total	Not Yet Due	1–30 Days Past Due	31–60 Days Past Due	61–90 Days Past Due	Over 90 Days Past Due
Balance forward	$332,350	$177,280	$72,300	$42,700	$23,200	$16,870

The following accounts remain to be classified in order to finish the analysis:

Account	Amount	Due Date
S. Werner	$ 4,677	January 15
T. Whetzel	916	February 15 (next fiscal year)
A. Wikoff	3,207	December 20
B. Xeplin	147	October 1
J. Yarrington	2,700	January 4
T. Zahn	3,917	November 15
D. Ziegler	9,586	March 1 (next fiscal year)
	$25,150	

From past experience, the company has found that the following rates of estimated uncollectible accounts produce an adequate balance for the Allowance for Uncollectible Accounts:

Time Past Due	Percentage Considered Uncollectible
Not yet due	2
1–30 days	5
31–60 days	15
61–90 days	25
Over 90 days	50

Required

1. Complete the aging analysis of accounts receivable.
2. Compute the end-of-year balance (before adjustments) for the Accounts Receivable controlling account and the Allowance for Uncollectible Accounts.
3. Prepare an analysis computing the estimated uncollectible accounts.
4. Prepare a general journal entry to record the estimated uncollectible accounts expense for the year. (Round adjustment to the nearest dollar.)

Problem 10B-3 Notes Receivable Transactions

T-Bird Textile Company sells fabrics to fashion production companies. In order to improve its liquidity, T-Bird follows the practice of discounting any promissory note it receives. The company engaged in the following transactions involving promissory notes:

Jan. 20 Sold merchandise to Just Fashions Company for $24,300, terms n/10.
30 Accepted a 90-day, 10 percent promissory note in settlement of the account of Just Fashions.
Feb. 4 Discounted the note from Just Fashions at the bank at 12 percent.

Apr. 30	Because no notice that the note had been dishonored was received, it was assumed that Just Fashions paid the bank.
May 2	Sold merchandise to Everware Company for $24,000, terms n/10.
12	Received $4,000 cash and a 60-day, 11 percent note for $20,000 in settlement of the Everware account.
22	Discounted the note from Everware to the bank at 12 percent.
July 11	Received notice that Everware had dishonored the note. Paid the bank the maturity value of the note plus a protest fee of $10.
Aug. 1	Wrote off the Everware account as uncollectible following news that the company had been declared bankrupt.
24	Received a 120-day, 9 percent note for $32,000 from Southern Suit Company in settlement of an account receivable.
28	Discounted the note from Southern Suit at the bank at 9 percent.
Dec. 22	Received notice that Southern Suit had dishonored the note. Paid the bank the maturity value of the note plus a protest fee of $10.
31	Received payment in full from Southern Suit including 9 percent interest for the nine days since the note was dishonored.

Required

Prepare general journal entries to record the above transactions.

Problem 10B-5 Short-Term Financing by Discounting Customers' Notes

The management of Tico Toy Company believes that the company will be at a competitive advantage if terms of 120 days can be offered to toy distributors. These terms enable the distributors to buy toys for the Christmas season in September and collect for them from the retailers before payment must be made in January. The cash flow of the company is not adequate to allow such generous terms. However, the controller of the company has worked out a plan with the bank to finance the receivables from the sales. The plan calls for the company to receive a 120-day, 9 percent note for each sale to each distributor. Each note will be discounted to the bank at the rate of 12 percent.

During September, Tico Toy made the following sales under the plan:

Company	Amount of Note	Date of Note	Discount Date
K-Way Co.	$219,200	Sept. 4	Sept. 6
Toys-for-All Co.	147,500	Sept. 10	Sept. 18
T & J Co.	182,300	Sept. 21	Sept. 24

During January, K-Way and T & J paid on the due date. Toys-for-All dishonored the note. The note was then paid, along with a protest fee of $15 by Tico Toy. Tico Toy collected in full from Toys-for-All on January 31.

Required

1. Prepare general journal entries to record September transactions on Tico Toy Company records.
2. What was the total cash generated during September from the discounting of notes receivable?
3. Prepare general journal entries to record January transactions on Tico Toy records.
4. What is your evaluation of the plan? What offsetting factors occur in later months such as January?

Learning Objectives

Chapter Eleven

Inventories

1. Define nonmonetary assets and state their relationship to the matching rule.

2. Define merchandise inventory and show how inventory measurement affects income determination.

3. Calculate the pricing of inventory, using the cost basis according to the (a) specific identification method; (b) average-cost method; (c) first-in, first-out method; (d) last-in, first-out method.

4. Recognize the effects of each method on income determination in periods of changing prices.

5. Apply the lower-of-cost-or-market rule to inventory valuation.

6. Estimate the cost of ending inventory by using the (a) retail inventory method and (b) gross profit method.

7. Distinguish between perpetual and periodic inventory systems.

This chapter begins with an overview of nonmonetary assets. The rest of the chapter deals with inventory measurement, emphasizing its importance to income determination and describing the methods of determining, valuing, and estimating inventories. As a result of studying this chapter, you should be able to meet the learning objectives listed on the left.

Nonmonetary Assets

Nonmonetary assets are all assets that are not considered monetary. Whereas monetary assets consist of cash and other assets representing the right to receive a specific amount of cash, nonmonetary assets are unexpired costs that will become expenses in future accounting periods. These assets are recorded at historical cost and are allocated to expense in accordance with the matching rule. It is unlikely that the amount at which they are shown on the balance sheet represents the amount of cash that could be realized from their sale because the allocation process is not an attempt to reflect the changing prices of the assets since their purchase.

Nonmonetary assets are of two types: short-term and long-term. **Short-term nonmonetary assets** are classified as current assets. Typical assets in this category are inventory, supplies, prepaid rent, prepaid insurance, and other prepaid expenses.

Long-term nonmonetary assets must be allocated as expenses to two or more future years because they will have a positive effect on revenues during those years. In other words, they are unexpired costs that will expire over more than one future year. Long-term nonmonetary assets usually fall into the following three categories: (1) property, plant, and equipment; (2) natural resources; and (3) intangibles.

Objective 1
Define nonmonetary assets and state their relationship to the matching rule

The most important accounting problem that arises in connection with all categories of nonmonetary assets is the application of the matching rule. Nonmonetary assets are recorded initially as assets or unexpired costs. According to the matching rule, they must be recorded as expenses in the accounting period that they benefit. We have seen, for example, that a three-year insurance policy is recorded as a debit to Prepaid Insurance and a credit to Cash or Accounts Payable. As time passes, it is necessary to use adjusting entries to charge the expired portion of the policy to expense by debiting Insurance Expense and crediting Prepaid Insurance. To measure income properly, two important determinations must be made with regard to each nonmonetary asset: (1) How much of the asset is used up or has expired during the current accounting period and should be transferred to expense? (2) How much of the asset is still unused or unexpired and should remain on the balance sheet as an asset?

These two amounts are closely related because determination of one (expense) automatically establishes the other (asset). In the case of insurance and other prepaid expenses, these calculations are not very difficult. However, the theoretical and practical problems associated with these measurements for inventories and long-term nonmonetary assets are among the most complex in accounting and have stimulated much debate within and outside the accounting profession. For this reason, the rest of this chapter is devoted to the application of the matching rule to inventories. Chapter 13 covers property, plant, and equipment, as well as natural resources, and part of Chapter 14 covers intangibles.

Inventories and Income Determination

Objective 2
Define merchandise inventory and show how the inventory measurement affects income determination

The principal source of revenue for retail or wholesale businesses is the sale of merchandise. In terms of dollars invested, the inventory of merchandise held for sale is one of the largest assets for a merchandising business. Because merchandise is continuously bought and sold, the cost of goods sold is the largest deduction from sales. In fact, it is often larger than all other expenses combined.

Merchandise inventory consists of all goods owned and held for sale in the regular course of business, including goods in transit if shipped FOB shipping point. Because it will normally be converted into cash within a year's time, merchandise inventory is considered a current asset. It is shown on the balance sheet immediately below Accounts Receivable because it is one step further removed from Cash.

In a manufacturing company, inventories consist of three major types: raw materials, partially completed products (often called work in process), and finished goods. The discussion in this chapter applies to manufacturing as well as to merchandising inventories. However, specific consideration of accounting for manufacturing operations is deferred until Part VI.

Objective of Inventory Measurement

The American Institute of Certified Public Accountants states, "A major objective of accounting for inventories is the proper determination of income through the process of matching appropriate costs against revenues."[1] Note that the objective is to determine the best measure of income, not the most realistic inventory value. As you will see, the two objectives are sometimes incompatible, in which case the objective of income determination takes precedence over a realistic inventory figure for the balance sheet.

Review of Gross Profit and Cost of Goods Sold Computations

Because the computations of gross profit and cost of goods sold were presented much earlier in the text, a review might help to show how the cost assigned to inventory and these computations are related. The gross profit on sales earned during an accounting period is computed by deducting cost of goods sold from the net revenues of the period. Cost of goods sold is measured by deducting ending inventory from cost of goods available for sale.

It is clear that the higher the cost of ending inventory, the lower the cost of goods sold will be and the higher the consequent gross profit. Conversely, the lower the value assigned to ending inventory, the higher the cost of goods sold will be and the lower the gross profit. *In effect, the value assigned to the ending inventory determines what portion of the cost of goods originally available for sale will be deducted from net revenues as cost of goods sold and what portion will be carried to the next period as beginning inventory.* Remember that the amount of goods available for sale includes the beginning inventory (unexpired costs passed from the last period to this period) plus net purchases during this period. The effects of errors in the cost of ending inventory on income are demonstrated in the next section.

Effects of Errors in Inventory Measurement

As seen above, the basic problem of separating goods available for sale into the components of goods sold and goods not sold is that of assigning a cost to the goods not sold or to the ending inventory. However, the determination of an ending inventory cost in effect decides the cost of goods sold, because whatever portion of the cost of goods available for sale is assigned to the ending inventory, the remainder is cost of goods sold.

Consequently, an error made in determining the inventory figure at the end of the period will cause an equal error in gross profit and net income in the income statement. The amount of assets and owner's equity in the balance sheet also will be misstated by the same amount. The consequences of overstatement and understatement of inventory are illustrated in the three simplified examples given below. In each case, beginning

1. American Institute of Certified Public Accountants, *Accounting Research and Terminology Bulletins,* Final Edition (New York: AICPA, 1961), p. 28.

inventory, purchases, and cost of goods available for sale are correctly stated. In the first example, ending inventory has been stated correctly. In the second example, inventory is overstated by $6,000, and in the third example, inventory is understated by $6,000.

Example 1. Ending Inventory Correctly Stated at $10,000

Income Statement for the Year		Cost of Goods Sold for the Year	
Net Sales	$100,000	Beginning Inventory	$12,000
Cost of Goods Sold	60,000 ←	Net Purchases	58,000
Gross Profit	$40,000	Cost of Goods Available for Sale	$70,000
Expenses	30,000		
Net Income	$10,000	Ending Inventory	10,000
		→ Cost of Goods Sold	$60,000

Example 2. Ending Inventory Overstated by $6,000

Income Statement for the Year		Cost of Goods Sold for the Year	
Net Sales	$100,000	Beginning Inventory	$12,000
Cost of Goods Sold	54,000 ←	Net Purchases	58,000
Gross Profit	$46,000	Cost of Goods Available for Sale	$70,000
Expenses	30,000		
Net Income	$16,000	Ending Inventory	16,000
		→ Cost of Goods Sold	$54,000

Example 3. Ending Inventory Understated by $6,000

Income Statement for the Year		Cost of Goods Sold for the Year	
Net Sales	$100,000	Beginning Inventory	$12,000
Cost of Goods Sold	66,000 ←	Net Purchases	58,000
Gross Profit	$34,000	Cost of Goods Available for Sale	$70,000
Expenses	30,000		
Net Income	$4,000	Ending Inventory	4,000
		→ Cost of Goods Sold	$66,000

In these examples, the total goods available for sale amounted to $70,000 in each case. The difference in net income resulted from how this $70,000 was divided among ending inventory and cost of goods sold.

Because the ending inventory in one period becomes the beginning inventory in the following period, it is important to recognize that an error in inventory valuation affects not only the current period but also the income statement for the following period. Using the same figures as examples 1 and 2 above, the income statements for two successive years in Figure 11-1 illustrate this carry-over effect.

Figure 11-1
Effect of Error in Ending Inventory on Current and Succeeding Year

Effect of Error in Inventory
Income Statement
For the Year Ended December 31, 19x8

	Correct Statement of Ending Inventory		Overstatement of Ending Inventory	
Sales		$100,000		$100,000
Cost of Goods Sold				
Beginning Inventory, Dec. 31, 19x7	$12,000		$12,000	
Purchases	58,000		58,000	
Cost of Goods Available for Sale	$70,000		$70,000	
Less Ending Inventory, Dec. 31, 19x8	10,000		16,000	
Cost of Goods Sold		60,000		54,000
Gross Profit on Sales		$ 40,000		$ 46,000
Operating Expenses		30,000		30,000
Net Income		$ 10,000		$ 16,000

Effect on Succeeding Year
Income Statement
For the Year Ended December 31, 19x9

	Correct Statement of Beginning Inventory		Overstatement of Beginning Inventory	
Sales		$130,000		$130,000
Cost of Goods Sold				
Beginning Inventory, Dec. 31, 19x8	$10,000		$16,000	
Purchases	68,000		68,000	
Cost of Goods Available for Sale	$78,000		$84,000	
Less Ending Inventory, Dec. 31, 19x9	13,000		13,000	
Cost of Goods Sold		65,000		71,000
Gross Profit on Sales		$ 65,000		$ 59,000
Operating Expenses		50,000		50,000
Net Income		$ 15,000		$ 9,000

Note that over a period of two years the errors will be offset or counterbalanced with regard to net income. In Figure 11-1, for example, the overstatement of ending inventory in 19x8 caused a $6,000 overstatement of beginning inventory in the following year, resulting in an understatement of income by the same amount. This offsetting effect is shown as follows:

		With Inventory at Dec. 31, 19x8, Overstated	
	With Inventory Correctly Stated	Reported Net Income Will Be	Reported Net Income Will Be Overstated (Understated)
Net Income for 19x8	$10,000	$16,000	$6,000
Net Income for 19x9	15,000	9,000	(6,000)
Total Net Income for Two Years	$25,000	$25,000	—

Because the total income for the two years is the same, there may be a tendency to think that one does not need to worry about inventory errors. This presumption is not correct because many management decisions as well as creditor and investor decisions are made on an annual basis and depend on the accountant's rendering of net income. The accountant has an obligation to make the net income figure as useful as possible.

The effects of errors in inventory on net income can be summarized as follows:

1. When the *ending* inventory is understated, the net income for the period will be understated.
2. When the *ending* inventory is overstated, the net income for the period will be overstated.
3. When the *beginning* inventory is understated, the net income for the period will be overstated.
4. When the *beginning* inventory is overstated, the net income for the period will be understated.

If we assume no income tax effects, a change or error in inventory of one amount results in a change or error in net income of the same amount. Thus the measurement of inventory is an important problem and is the subject of the remainder of this chapter.

Inventory Measurement

The cost assigned to ending inventory depends on two measurements: quantity and price. At least once each year, a business must take an actual physical count of all items of merchandise held for sale. This process is called taking a physical inventory, or simply taking inventory, as described in Chapter 6. Although some companies take inventory at various times during the year, many companies take inventory only at the end of each year. Taking the inventory consists of (1) counting the items on hand, (2) pricing each item, and (3) extending (multiplying) to determine the total.

Merchandise in Transit

Because merchandise inventory includes items owned by the company and held for sale, purchased merchandise in transit should be included in the inventory count if title to the goods has passed. In Chapter 6, we pointed out that the terms of the shipping agreement must be examined to determine if title has passed. If goods were shipped FOB shipping point, then title was passed when the goods were given to the common carrier, and they should be counted in the purchaser's inventory even though they may not have been received by the date of the inventory. If the shipping terms were FOB destination, however, then the goods do not belong to the purchaser until they are actually delivered and thus should not be counted in the inventory if they have not been received.

Sold Merchandise on Hand

At the time a physical inventory is taken, a business will undoubtedly have some orders for goods on hand, and some of these goods may be segregated for delivery. If the sale is consummated and the goods in question now belong to the buyer and await delivery, title is presumed to have passed to the buyer, and the goods should not be counted in inventory. Of course, the sale must also be recorded in revenues.

Pricing the Inventory at Cost

The pricing of inventory is one of the most interesting and most widely debated problems in accounting. As demonstrated above, the value placed on ending inventory can have a dramatic effect on net income for each of two consecutive years. Consequently, the ability of companies to raise money by borrowing and by selling more capital stock as well as the amount of dividends they can pay are affected by the value of the inventory. In addition, because federal income taxes are based on income, the valuation of inventory may have a considerable effect on the amount of income taxes to be paid. Federal income tax authorities have therefore been interested in the effects of various inventory valuation procedures and have specific regulations regarding the acceptability of various methods. As a result, the accountant is sometimes faced with the problem of balancing objectives of proper income determination with those of minimizing income taxes payable.

Although there are a number of acceptable methods of valuing inventories in the accounts and on the financial statements, most are based either on cost or on the lower of cost or market. Both methods are acceptable for income tax purposes. We shall first consider variations of the cost basis of inventory valuation and then turn to the lower-of-cost-or-market method later in the chapter.

Cost Defined

According to the AICPA, "The primary basis of accounting for inventory is cost, which has been defined generally as the price paid or consideration given to acquire an asset. As applied to inventories cost means in principle the sum of the applicable expenditures and charges directly or indirectly incurred in bringing an article to its existing condition and locations."[2]

This definition of **inventory cost** has generally been interpreted in practice to include the following costs: (1) invoice price less cash discounts; (2) freight and transportation in, including insurance in transit; and (3) applicable taxes and tariffs.

Other costs, including those for purchasing, receiving, and storage, should in principle also be included in inventory cost. In practice, however, it is so difficult to allocate these costs to specific inventory items that they are usually considered an expense of the accounting period instead of an inventory cost.

Methods of Pricing Inventory at Cost

The prices of most kinds of merchandise vary during the year, and identical lots of merchandise may have been purchased at different prices. In addition, when identical items are bought and sold, it is often impossible to tell which items have been sold and which are still in inventory. Therefore, it is necessary to make an assumption about the order in which items have been sold. Because the assumed order of sale may or may not approximate the actual order of sale, the assumption is in reality an assumption about the flow of costs rather than the flow of physical inventory.

Thus the term **goods flow** refers to the actual physical movement of goods in the operations of the company, and the term **cost flow** refers to the association of costs with their *assumed* flow within the operations of the

2. Ibid., p. 28.

company. The assumed cost flow may or may not correspond to the actual goods flow. Although this statement may seem strange at first, there is nothing wrong with it. Several assumed cost flows are acceptable under generally accepted accounting principles. In fact, it is sometimes preferable to use an assumed cost flow that bears no relationship to goods flow because it gives a better estimate of income, which, as we mentioned, is the primary objective of inventory valuation.

Accountants usually price inventory by using one of the following generally accepted methods, each based on a different assumption of cost flows: (1) specific identification method; (2) average-cost method; (3) first-in, first-out method (FIFO); and (4) last-in, first-out method (LIFO).

Under the **specific identification method,** the actual cost of a particular item is assigned to the item. However, specific identification is not usually practical, so accountants usually price inventory by using one of the other three generally accepted methods. The **average-cost method** assumes that each item carries an equal cost, which is determined by dividing the total cost of the goods available for sale by the number of units to arrive at an average unit cost. Under the **first-in, first-out (FIFO) method,** it is assumed that the costs of the first items purchased are assigned to the first items sold and the costs of the last items purchased are assigned to the items remaining in inventory. Under the **last-in, first-out (LIFO) method,** it is assumed that the costs of the last items purchased are assigned to the first items sold. As a consequence, the cost of the inventory on hand is composed of the costs of items from the oldest purchases. The inventory cost methods used by six hundred large companies are shown in Figure 11-2.

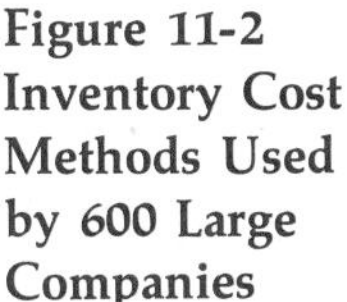

Figure 11-2 Inventory Cost Methods Used by 600 Large Companies

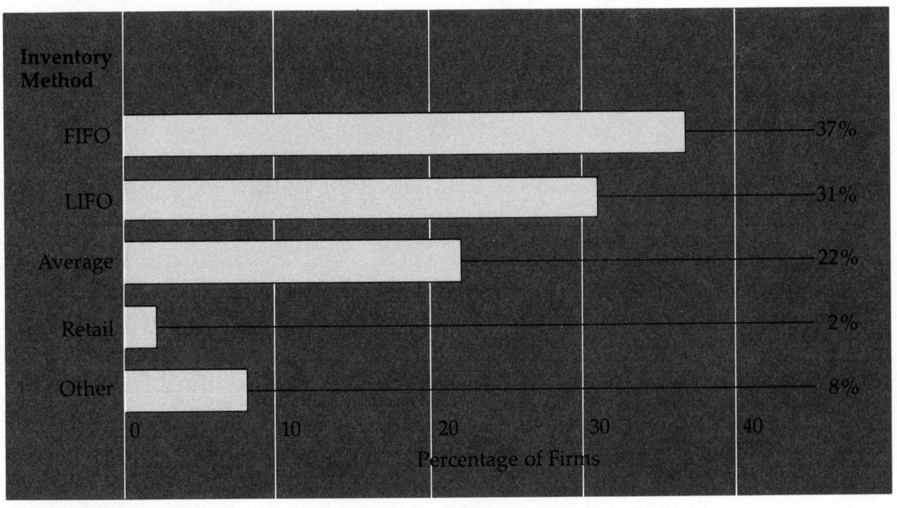

Source: American Institute of Certified Public Accountants, *Accounting Trends and Techniques* (New York: AICPA, 1979).

To illustrate the four methods, the following data for the month of June will be used:

Inventory Data, June 30

June 1	On hand	100 units at $1.00	$100
6	Purchased	100 units at $1.10	110
13	Purchased	100 units at $1.20	120
20	Purchased	100 units at $1.30	130
25	Purchased	100 units at $1.40	140
Totals		500 units	$600
Sales		280 units	
On hand June 30		220 units	

Note that the total available for sale is 500 units, at a total cost of $600. In a nutshell, the problem of inventory pricing is to divide the $600 between the 280 units sold and the 220 units on hand.

Objective 3a Calculate the pricing of inventory, using the cost basis according to the specific identification method

Specific Identification Method If the units in the ending inventory can be identified as coming from specific purchases, they may be priced at the specific prices of these purchases. For instance, assume that the June 30 inventory consisted of 50 units from the inventory on hand June 1, 100 units of the purchase of June 13, and 70 units of the purchase of June 25. The cost to be assigned to the inventory under the specific identification method would be $268, determined as follows:

Inventory, June 30—Specific Identification Method

50 units at $1.00	$ 50
100 units at $1.20	120
70 units at $1.40	98
220 units at a value of	$268

The cost of goods sold during June under the specific identification method is determined as follows:

Cost of Goods Available for Sale	$600
Less June 30 Inventory	268
Cost of Goods Sold	$332

The specific identification method might be used in the purchase and sale of high-priced articles such as automobiles, heavy equipment, and jewelry. However, although this method may appear to have a certain logic to it, it is not actually used much because it has two definite disadvantages. First, it is very difficult and impractical in most cases to keep track of the purchase and sale of individual items. Second, when a company deals in items of an identical nature, it becomes arbitrary which items are sold; thus the company can manipulate income by choosing to sell low- or high-cost items.

Objective 3b Calculate the pricing of inventory, using the cost basis according to the average-cost method

Average-Cost Method Under the average-cost method, it is assumed that the cost of inventory is the average cost of goods on hand at the beginning of the period plus all goods purchased during the period. Average cost is computed by dividing the total cost of goods available for sale by the total units available for sale. The ending inventory in the illustration when the average-cost method is used would be $1.20 per unit, or a total of $264.00, determined as follows:

Inventory, June 30—Average-Cost Method

June 1	Inventory	100 at $1.00	$100
6	Purchased	100 at $1.10	110
13	Purchased	100 at $1.20	120
20	Purchased	100 at $1.30	130
25	Purchased	100 at $1.40	140
Totals		500 units	$600

Average unit cost: $600 ÷ 500 = $1.20
Ending inventory: 220 units @ $1.20 = $264

The cost of goods sold during June under the average-cost method would be as follows:

Cost of Goods Available for Sale	$600
Less June 30 Inventory	264
Cost of Goods Sold	$336

The cost figure obtained for the ending inventory under the average-cost method is influenced by all the prices paid during the year and thus tends to level out the effects that cost increases and decreases during the year have on income. Some criticize the average-cost method because they feel that more recent costs should receive more attention and are more relevant for income measurement and decision making.

Objective 3c Calculate the pricing of inventory, using the cost basis according to the first-in, first-out (FIFO) method

First-In, First-Out (FIFO) Method The first-in, first-out method, usually called FIFO, is based on the assumption that the costs of the first items acquired should be assigned to the first items sold. The costs of the goods on hand at the end of a period are assumed to be from the most recent purchases and the costs assigned to goods that have been sold are assumed to be from the earliest purchases. The FIFO method of determining inventory cost may be adopted by any business, regardless of the actual physical flow of goods, because the assumption is made regarding the flow of costs and not the flow of goods.

For example, in our illustration, the June 30 inventory would be $294 when the FIFO method is used. It is computed as follows:

Inventory, June 30—First-In, First-Out Method

100 units at $1.40 from the purchase of June 25	$140
100 units at $1.30 from the purchase of June 20	130
20 units at $1.20 from the purchase of June 13	24
220 units at a value of	$294

The cost of goods sold during June under the FIFO method would be $306, determined as follows:

Cost of Goods Available for Sale	$600
Less June 30 Inventory	294
Cost of Goods Sold	$306

The effect of the FIFO method is to value the ending inventory at the most recent prices and charge earlier prices against the Cost of Goods Sold account. During periods of consistently rising prices, the FIFO method yields the highest possible amount of net income. One reason for this result is that businesses tend to increase selling prices as prices rise, regardless of the fact that inventories may have been purchased before the price rise. The reverse effect occurs in periods of price decreases. Consequently, a primary criticism of FIFO is that is accentuates the effects of the business cycle on business income.

Last-In, First-Out (LIFO) Method The LIFO method of costing inventories is based on the assumption that the costs of the last items purchased should be assigned to the first to be used or sold and that the cost of the ending inventory consists of the cost of merchandise purchased earlier.

Objective 3d Calculate the pricing of inventory, using the cost basis according to the last-in, first-out (LIFO) method

Under this method, the June 30 inventory would be $234, computed as follows:

Inventory, June 30—Last-In, First-Out Method

100 units at $1.00 from June 1 inventory	$100
100 units at $1.10 from purchase of June 6	110
20 units at $1.20 from purchase of June 13	24
220 units at a value of	$234

The cost of goods sold during June under the LIFO method would be $366, computed as follows:

Cost of Goods Available for Sale	$600
Less June 30 Inventory	234
Cost of Goods Sold	$366

The effect of LIFO is to value inventory at earlier prices and charge the Cost of Goods Sold account with the most recent purchases of goods. This assumption, of course, is not in accord with the actual physical movement of goods in most businesses.

However, there is a strong logical argument to support this method, based on the fact that a certain size inventory is necessary in a going concern. When inventory is sold, it must be replaced with more goods. The proponents of LIFO reason that the fairest determination of income occurs if the current costs of merchandise are matched against current sales prices, regardless of which physical units of merchandise are sold. When prices are moving either upward or downward, LIFO will mean charging the Cost of Goods Sold account with costs closer to the price level at the time the sales of goods are made. As a result, the LIFO method tends to show a smaller net income during inflationary times and a larger net income during deflationary times than other methods of inventory valuation. Thus the peaks and valleys of the business cycle tend to be smoothed out. The important factor from this view is that in inventory valuation the flow of costs and hence income determination is more important than physical movement of goods and balance sheet valuation.

A counterargument may also be made to the LIFO method. Because the inventory valuation on the balance sheet reflects earlier prices, this value is often unrealistic with respect to the current value of the inventory. Thus such balance sheet measures as working capital and current ratio may have limited usefulness.

Comparison of the Alternative Methods of Pricing Inventory

Objective 4 Recognize the effects of each method on income determination in periods of changing prices

Four methods of pricing inventory have now been illustrated: specific identification, average-cost, FIFO, and LIFO. The specific identification method is based on actual costs, whereas the other three methods are based on assumptions regarding the flow of costs. Let us now compare the effects of the four methods on net income using the same data as before and assuming sales during June of $500.

	Specific Identification Method	Average-Cost Method	First-In, First-Out Method	Last-In, First-Out Method
Sales	$500	$500	$500	$500
Cost of Goods Sold				
Beginning Inventory	$100	$100	$100	$100
Purchases	500	500	500	500
Cost of Goods Available for Sale	$600	$600	$600	$600
Less Ending Inventory	268	264	294	234
Cost of Goods Sold	$332	$336	$306	$366
Gross Profit on Sales	$168	$164	$194	$134

Keeping in mind that in the illustration June was a period of rising prices, we can see that LIFO, which charges the most recent and in this case the highest prices to cost of goods sold, resulted in the lowest net income. Conversely, FIFO, which charges the earliest and in this case the lowest prices to Cost of Goods Sold, produced the highest net income. The net income under the average-cost method is between those computed under LIFO and FIFO; thus it is clear that this method has a leveling effect.

During a period of declining prices, the reverse effects would occur. The LIFO method would produce a higher net income than the FIFO method. It is apparent that the method of inventory valuation takes on greatest importance during prolonged periods of price changes in one direction, either up or down.

Evaluating the Inventory Pricing Methods

Each of the four methods of inventory pricing presented above is acceptable for use in published financial statements. Each has its advantages and disadvantages, and none can be considered as best or perfect. The factors that should be considered in choosing an inventory method are the effects of each method on the balance sheet, the income statement, income taxes, and management decisions.

A basic problem in determining the best inventory measure for a particular company is the fact that inventory appears on both the balance sheet and the income statement. As we have seen, the LIFO method is best suited for the income statement because it best matches revenues and cost of goods sold. But it is not the best measure of the current balance sheet value of inventory, particularly when there has been a prolonged period of price rises or decreases. The FIFO method, on the other hand, is best suited to the balance sheet because the ending inventory is closest to current values and thus gives a more realistic view of the current financial assets of a business. Readers of financial statements must be alert to inventory methods and be able to assess their effects.

When prices are changing rapidly, management must base its sales policies on current replacement costs of the goods being sold. The LIFO method most nearly represents the measurement of net income based on these current costs. In addition, as seen in the illustration above, in periods of rising prices LIFO shows a smaller profit. Thus, many businesses use LIFO to reduce the amount of income taxes to be paid.

Many accountants believe that the use of FIFO or average-cost methods in periods of rising prices causes businesses to report fictitious profit, resulting in the payment of excess income taxes. The profit is fictitious because the company must now buy inventory at new higher prices, but some of the funds that should have been used for purchase of replacement inventory went to pay income taxes. During the rapid inflation of 1979 and 1980, billions of dollars reported as profits and paid in income taxes were believed to be the result of poor matching of current costs and revenues under the FIFO and average-cost methods. Consequently, many companies have since switched to the LIFO inventory method.

Valuing the Inventory at the Lower of Cost or Market (LCM)

Objective 5 Apply the lower-of-cost-or-market (LCM) rule to inventory valuation

Although cost is usually the most appropriate basis for valuation of inventory, there are times when inventory may properly be valued at less than its cost. If by reason of physical deterioration, obsolescence, or decline in price level the market value of the inventory falls below the cost, a loss has occurred. This loss may be recognized by writing the inventory down to market. The term market is used here to mean current replacement cost. For a merchandising concern, market is the amount that the concern would pay at the present time for the same goods, purchased from the usual suppliers and in the usual quantities. It may help in applying the lower-of-cost-or-market (LCM) rule by thinking of it as the "lower-of-cost-or-replacement-cost" rule.

Methods of Applying LCM

There are three basic methods of valuing inventories at the lower of cost or market, as follows: (1) the item-by-item method, (2) the major category method, and (3) the total inventory method.

For example, a stereo shop could determine lower of cost or market for each type of speaker, receiver, and turntable (item by item); for all speakers, all receivers, and all turntables (major categories); or for all speakers, receivers, and turntables together (total inventory).

Item-by-Item Method When the item-by-item method is used, cost and market are compared for each item in the inventory. The individual items are then valued at their lower price.

Lower of Cost or Market with Item-by-Item Method

		Per Unit		
	Quantity	Cost	Market	Lower of Cost or Market
Category I				
Item a	200	$1.50	$1.70	$ 300
Item b	100	2.00	1.80	180
Item c	100	2.50	2.60	250
Category II				
Item d	300	5.00	4.50	1,350
Item e	200	4.00	4.10	800
Inventory at the lower of cost or market				$2,880

Major Category Method Under the major category method, the total cost and total market for each category of items are compared. Each category is then valued at its lower price.

Lower of Cost or Market with Major Category Method

	Quantity	Per Unit Cost	Per Unit Market	Total Cost	Total Market	Lower of Cost or Market
Category I						
Item a	200	$1.50	$1.70	$ 300	$ 340	
Item b	100	2.00	1.80	200	180	
Item c	100	2.50	2.60	250	260	
Totals				$ 750	$ 780	$ 750
Category II						
Item d	300	5.00	4.50	$1,500	$1,350	
Item e	200	4.00	4.10	800	820	
Totals				$2,300	$2,170	2,170
Inventory at the lower of cost or market						$2,920

Total Inventory Method Under the total inventory method, the entire inventory is valued at both cost and market, and the lower price is used to value inventory.

Lower of Cost or Market with Total Inventory Method

	Quantity	Per Unit Cost	Per Unit Market	Total Cost	Total Market	Lower of Cost or Market
Category I						
Item a	200	$1.50	$1.70	$ 300	$ 340	
Item b	100	2.00	1.80	200	180	
Item c	100	2.50	2.60	250	260	
Category II						
Item d	300	5.00	4.50	1,500	1,350	
Item e	200	4.00	4.10	800	820	
Totals				$3,050	$2,950	$2,950
Inventory at the lower of cost or market						$2,950

Determination of Market When Using the LCM

The determination of cost in using the lower-of-cost-or-market valuation can be from any of the four methods discussed above. Certain exceptions that must be made for federal income tax purposes are covered below. Market, as already pointed out, means current replacement cost. There may be times, however, when the lower-of-cost-or-market rule should not be strictly followed.

The LCM rule arose in times when bankers and other creditors were the main users of financial statements. They were interested not in income measurement but in stating assets conservatively at a low value to ensure safety. Hence, inventory was sometimes arbitrarily written down because of a price decrease in the wholesale market when prices in the retail market (where the company sold its goods) did not drop. For example, a replacement cost of $5 for an item that originally cost $9 may not reflect market value if the company can sell it for $12. As a consequence, the American Institute of Certified Public Accountants has developed a ceiling and a floor for market value.

The ceiling is the **net realizable value (NRV)**, or the established selling price of the item in the ordinary course of business less reasonable selling costs. This ceiling is established because it is not reasonable to price an item in inventory above what it can be sold for. If the selling cost of the item in the preceding paragraph were $2, the NRV would be $10. Replacement cost should not be stated as greater than this NRV.

The floor is an item's net realizable value minus a normal profit margin. If the item above normally carried a profit margin of 20 percent, its NRV minus a normal profit margin would be $7.60 ($12 selling price − $2 selling costs − $2.40 normal profit). Because the current replacement cost of $5 is less than this floor, the floor value of $7.60 must be used for market in inventory valuation.

Below are three more illustrations of the floor and ceiling rule. Note that replacement cost should be used for market only if it falls between net realizable value (NRV) and net realizable value less a normal profit margin.

Determination of Market in LCM Computations

Item	Replacement Market	Selling Market: NRV	Selling Market: NRV Minus Normal Profit
a	(14)	16	12
b	19	(18)	14
c	20	30	(22)

Note on Inventory Valuation and Federal Income Taxes

The Internal Revenue Service has developed several rules for valuation of inventories for federal income tax purposes. A company has considerable latitude in choosing a method, but once a method is chosen, it must be used consistently from one year to the next. The IRS must approve any changes in inventory valuation method for income tax purposes. This requirement, of course, is also in accordance with the rule of consistency in accounting theory in that changes in inventory method would cause income to fluctuate abnormally and would make successive income statements difficult to interpret. A company can change its inventory method if absolutely necessary as long as it obtains the approval of the IRS and discloses the nature and effect of the change in its financial statements.

If a company uses the LIFO method in reporting income for tax purposes, the IRS requires that the LIFO method also be used in the accounting records. In addition, the IRS will not allow the use of the lower-of-cost-or-market rule if the method of determining cost is the LIFO method. In this case, only the LIFO cost can be used. Another regulation prohibits the use of the total inventory method for determining lower of cost or market.

Valuing the Inventory by Estimation

It is sometimes necessary or desirable to estimate the value of ending inventory. The methods most commonly used for this purpose are the retail method and the gross profit method.

Retail Method of Inventory Estimation

Objective 6a Estimate the cost of ending inventory by using the retail inventory method

The **retail method**, as its name implies, is used in retail merchandising businesses. There are two principal reasons for the use of the retail method. First, management usually requires that financial statements be prepared at least once a month and, as it is time-consuming and expensive to take physical inventory each month, the retail method must be used to estimate inventory valuation. Second, because items in a retail store normally have a price tag, it is common to take the physical inventory at retail from these price tags and reduce the total value to cost through use of the retail method.

When the retail method is used to estimate an end-of-period inventory, the records must show the amount of inventory at the beginning of the period at cost and at retail. The term *at retail* means the amount of the inventory at the marked selling prices of the inventory items. In addition, the records must also show the amount of goods purchased during the period both at cost and at retail. The net sales at retail are, of course, the balance of the Sales account less returns and discounts. A simple example of the retail method is shown below.

The Retail Method of Inventory Valuation	Cost	Retail
Beginning Inventory	$ 40,000	$ 55,000
Net Purchases for the Period	107,000	145,000
Freight In	3,000	
Merchandise Available for Sale	$150,000	$200,000
Ratio of cost to retail price: $\frac{\$150,000}{\$200,000} = 75\%$		
Sales During the Period		160,000
Ending Inventory at Retail		$ 40,000
Ratio of cost to retail		75%
Estimated Cost of Ending Inventory		$ 30,000

Merchandise available for sale is determined both at cost and at retail by listing beginning inventory and net purchases for the period at cost and at the expected selling price of the goods, adding freight in to the cost column, and totaling. The ratio of these two amounts (cost to retail price) provides an estimate of the cost of each dollar of retail sales value. The ending inventory at retail is then determined by deducting sales for the period from the retail price of the goods that were available for sale during the period. The inventory at retail is now converted to cost on the basis of estimated gross profit. Estimated gross profit is determined by finding the ratio of the cost of merchandise available for sale to the retail (selling) price of the merchandise available for sale. The retail method can be more difficult to apply in practice because of certain complications such as changes in the retail price that occur during the year.

Gross Profit Method of Inventory Estimation

Objective 6b Estimate the cost of ending inventory by using the gross profit method

The **gross profit method** assumes that the ratio of gross profit for a business remains relatively stable from year to year. It is used in place of the retail method when records of the retail prices of beginning inventory and purchases are not kept. It is also useful in estimating the amount of inventory lost or destroyed by theft, fire, or other hazards. Insurance companies often use this method to verify loss claims.

The gross profit method is very simple to use and is illustrated at the top of the next page.

The Gross Profit Method of Inventory Valuation		
1. Beginning Inventory at Cost		$ 50,000
Purchases at Cost		290,000
Cost of Goods Available for Sale		$340,000
2. Less Estimated Cost of Goods Sold		
Sales at Selling Price	$400,000	
Less Estimated Gross Margin of 30%	120,000	280,000
3. Estimated Cost of Ending Inventory		$ 60,000

First, compute the cost of goods available for sale in the usual way (beginning inventory plus purchases). Second, estimate the cost of goods sold by deducting the estimated profit margin from sales. Third, deduct the estimated cost of goods sold from the goods available for sale.

Periodic and Perpetual Inventory Systems

Objective 7 Distinguish between perpetual and periodic inventory systems

The system of inventories used so far in this book has been based on periodic physical inventories and is known as the **periodic inventory method.** Under this system, the cost of goods sold is determined by adding the net cost of purchases to beginning inventory and subtracting the ending inventory. A physical inventory must be taken or estimated by the retail method or gross profit method in order to determine inventory at any particular time and at the end of the period to determine cost of goods sold.

Periodic inventory systems are common in retail and wholesale concerns. However, companies that sell goods having a higher unit cost and companies that want to have more control over their inventories may use the perpetual inventory method. Under the **perpetual inventory method,** sales and purchases of individual items are recorded continuously. Thus the cost of goods sold during a period and the inventory may be determined from the accounting records without taking a physical inventory. The availability of computers to keep records of many inventory items at a relatively low cost has increased the use of the perpetual inventory method.

The perpetual inventory system does not separate the Purchases account from the Merchandise Inventory account. In their place is one Merchandise Inventory account that is a controlling account for a subsidiary file of inventory accounts. This mechanism is very similar to that of the Accounts Receivable controlling account and its subsidiary ledger. In the inventory subsidiary file, each item of inventory has a card on which purchases and sales are entered as they occur. Consequently, the inventory of each item is always up to date. A sample perpetual inventory card

Item: Pencil Sharpener, Model D-222									
	Received			Sold			Balance		
Date	Units	Cost	Total	Units	Cost	Total	Units	Cost	Balance
June 1							60	5.00	300.00
4				10	5.00	50.00	50	5.00	250.00
10	100	6.00	600.00				50	5.00	
							100	6.00	850.00
20				30	5.00	150.00	20	5.00	700.00
							100	6.00	

Figure 11-3
Perpetual Inventory Record Card

is shown in Figure 11-3. At any time, this card will show the number of pencil sharpeners on hand, and the total of all the cards is the merchandise inventory.

On June 1, there is a balance of 60 pencil sharpeners that cost $5 each. A sale on June 4 reduces the balance by 10 pencil sharpeners. On June 10, 100 pencil sharpeners are purchased at $6 each. Now the inventory consists of 50 pencil sharpeners purchased at $5 each and 100 pencil sharpeners purchased at $6 each. The method of inventory valuation in Figure 11-2 is first-in, first-out, as can be determined by looking at the June 20 sale. The entire sale of 30 pencil sharpeners is taken from the 50 sharpeners still left from the beginning inventory. If the LIFO method were used, the sale would be deducted from the latest purchase of 100 pencil sharpeners at $6 each. Under LIFO the resulting balance would be $670 [(50 × $5) + (70 × $6)].

Handling Inventory Systems in the Accounts

Under the periodic inventory method, a Purchases account is used to record merchandise when it is purchased. The Inventory account stays at its beginning level until it is adjusted. This adjustment usually takes place when closing entries are made at the end of the accounting period, as illustrated in Chapter 6.

Under the perpetual inventory method, the Merchandise Inventory account is continuously adjusted by entering purchases and sales as they occur and thus is always up to date. This method is summarized as follows:

1. Recording purchases under the perpetual inventory method:

Merchandise Inventory	12,000	
Accounts Payable		12,000
To record purchases of inventory		

2. Recording sales under the perpetual inventory method:

Accounts Receivable	14,000	
Sales		14,000
To record sales		
Cost of Goods Sold	10,000	
Merchandise Inventory		10,000
To record cost of merchandise sold		

Note first that the Purchases account is not used, and second that when a sale is made, the cost of the merchandise for that sale is taken out of the Merchandise Inventory account. At the end of the year, neither adjustments to Merchandise Inventory nor corresponding debits and credits to Income Summary are needed because the Merchandise Inventory account has been continually updated during the year and thus there is no need to establish the ending inventory in the records. The only closing entry required is to close Cost of Goods Sold to Revenue and Expense Summary.

Need for Physical Inventories Under the Perpetual Inventory System

The use of the perpetual inventory system does not eliminate the need for a physical inventory at the end of the accounting year. The perpetual inventory records show what should be on hand, not necessarily what is on hand. There may be losses due to spoilage, pilferage, theft, or other causes. If a loss has occurred, it is reflected in the accounts by a debit to Cost of Goods Sold and a credit to Merchandise Inventory. The individual inventory cards, which may also be the subsidiary ledger, must also be adjusted.

Chapter Review

Review of Learning Objectives

1. Define nonmonetary assets and state their relationship to the matching rule.
Nonmonetary assets are unexpired costs that will become expenses in future accounting periods. Typical nonmonetary assets are inventory; prepaid expenses; property, plant, and equipment; natural resources; and intangible assets. To apply the matching rule to nonmonetary assets, one must determine how much of the asset is used up or expired during the current accounting period and how much of the asset is still unused or unexpired. The former amount is an expense of the period; the latter is an asset.

2. Define merchandise inventory and show how inventory measurement affects income determination.
Merchandise inventory consists of all goods owned and held for sale in the regular course of business. The objective of accounting for inventories is the

proper determination of income. If a misstatement occurs in determining the value of inventory, a corresponding misstatement—dollar for dollar—is made in net income. Furthermore, because the ending inventory of one period is the beginning inventory of the next, the misstatement affects two accounting periods, although the effects are opposite.

3. Calculate the pricing of inventory, using the cost basis according to the specific identification method, the average-cost method, the first-in, first-out (FIFO) method, and the last-in, first-out (LIFO) method.

The value assigned to the ending inventory is the result of two measurements: quantity and price. Quantity is determined by taking a physical inventory. The pricing of inventory is usually based on the assumed cost flow of the goods as they are bought and sold. One of four assumptions is usually made regarding cost flow. These assumptions are represented by four inventory methods. Inventory pricing could be determined by the specific identification method, which associates the actual cost with each item of inventory but is rarely used. The average-cost method assumes that the cost of inventory is the average cost of goods available for sale during the period. The first-in, first-out, (FIFO) method assumes that the costs of the first items acquired should be assigned to the first items sold. The last-in, first-out (LIFO) method assumes that the costs of the last items acquired should be assigned to the first items sold. The method chosen may or may not be equivalent to the actual flow of physical goods.

4. Recognize the effects of each method on income determination in periods of changing prices.

During periods of rising prices, the LIFO method will show the lowest net income; FIFO, the highest; and average cost, in between. The opposite effects occur in periods of falling prices. No generalization can be made regarding the specific identification method.

5. Apply the lower-of-cost-or-market (LCM) rule to inventory valuation.

To the above methods of determining inventory at cost can be applied the lower-of-cost-or-market rule, which states that if the replacement cost (market) of the inventory is lower than cost, the lower figure should be used. The AICPA has stated, however, that the limit on applying this rule is that market should not be used if it is more than the net realizable value or less than net realizable value minus a normal profit margin. The Internal Revenue Service requires that if LIFO is used for tax purposes, it must also be used for book purposes, and that the lower-of-cost-or-market rule cannot be applied to the LIFO method.

6. Estimate the cost of ending inventory using the retail inventory method and the gross profit method.

Two methods of estimating the value of inventory are the retail inventory method and the gross profit method. Under the retail inventory method, inventory is determined at retail prices and is reduced to estimated cost by applying a ratio of cost to retail price. Under the gross profit method, cost of goods sold is estimated by reducing sales by estimated gross margin. The estimated cost of goods sold is then deducted from cost of goods available for sale to estimate the inventory.

7. Distinguish between perpetual and periodic inventory systems.

Under the periodic inventory system, the one used heretofore in this book, inventory is determined by a physical count at the end of the accounting period. Under the perpetual inventory system, the inventory control account is constantly updated as sales and purchases are made during the accounting period.

Review Problem
Periodic and Perpetual Inventory Methods

The table below summarizes the beginning inventory, purchases, and sales of Psi Company's single product during January:

	Inventory			Purchases			
Date	Units	Cost	Total	Units	Cost	Total	Sales Units
Jan. 1	1,400	$19	$26,600				
4							300
8				600	$20	$12,000	
10							1,300
12				900	21	18,900	
15							150
18				500	22	11,000	
24				800	23	18,400	
31							1,350
Totals	1,400		$26,600	2,800		$60,300	3,100

Required

1. Assuming that the company uses the periodic inventory method, compute the cost that should be assigned to ending inventory using (a) a FIFO basis and (b) a LIFO basis.

2. Assuming that the company uses the perpetual inventory method, compute the cost that should be assigned to ending inventory using (a) a FIFO basis and (b) a LIFO basis. (Hint: It is helpful to use a form similar to the perpetual inventory card in Figure 11-2.)

Answer to Review Problem

	Units	Dollars
Beginning Inventory	1,400	$26,600
Purchases	2,800	60,300
Available for Sale	4,200	$86,900
Sales	3,100	
Ending Inventory	1,100	

1. Periodic inventory method
   a. FIFO basis
   Ending inventory consists of

Jan. 24 purchases (800 × $23)	$18,400	
Jan. 18 purchases (300 × $22)	6,600	$25,000

   b. LIFO basis
   Ending inventory consists of

Beginning inventory (1,100 × $19)		$20,900

2. Perpetual inventory method
   a. FIFO basis

Date	Received			Sold			Balance		
	Units	Cost	Total	Units	Cost	Total	Units	Cost	Total
Jan. 1							1,400	$19	$26,600
4				300	$19	$ 5,700	1,100	19	20,900
8	600	$20	$12,000				1,100	19	
							600	20	32,900
10				1,100	19				
				200	20	24,900	400	20	8,000
12	900	21	18,900				400	20	
							900	21	26,900
15				150	20	3,000	250	20	
							900	21	23,900
18	500	22	11,000				250	20	
							900	21	
							500	22	34,900
24	800	23	18,400				250	20	
							900	21	
							500	22	
							800	23	53,300
31				250	20				
				900	21				
				200	22	28,300	300	22	
							800	23	25,000

b. LIFO basis

Date	Received			Sold			Balance		
	Units	Cost	Total	Units	Cost	Total	Units	Cost	Total
Jan. 1							1,400	$19	$26,600
4				300	$19	$ 5,700	1,100	19	20,900
8	600	$20	$12,000				1,100	19	
							600	20	32,900
10				600	20				
				700	19	25,300	400	19	7,600
12	900	21	18,900				400	19	
							900	21	26,500
15				150	21	3,150	400	19	
							750	21	23,300
18	500	22	11,000				400	19	
							750	21	
							500	22	34,300
24	800	23	18,400				400	19	
							750	21	
							500	22	
							800	23	52,750
31				800	23				
				500	22				
				50	21	30,450	700	21	
							400	19	22,300

Chapter Assignments

Questions

1. Why is inventory called a nonmonetary asset, and what measurements of nonmonetary assets must be taken to make a proper income determination? What is the relationship of nonmonetary assets to the matching rule?
2. What is merchandise inventory, and what is the primary objective of inventory measurement?
3. If the merchandise inventory is mistakenly overstated at the end of 19x8, what is the effect on (a) 19x8 net income, (b) 19x8 year-end balance sheet value, (c) 19x9 net income, (d) 19x9 year-end balance sheet value?
4. Fargo Sales Company is very busy at the end of its fiscal year on June 30. There is an order for 130 units of product in the warehouse. Although the shipping department tries, it cannot ship the product by June 30. Should the 130 units be included in the year-end count of inventory?
5. What does the term *taking a physical inventory* mean?
6. What items are included in the cost of inventory?
7. In periods of steadily rising prices, which of the three inventory methods—average-cost, FIFO, or LIFO—will give the (a) highest inventory cost, (b) lowest inventory cost, (c) highest net income, and (d) lowest net income?

8. May a company change its inventory costing method from year to year? Explain.

9. Do FIFO and LIFO result in different quantities of ending inventory?

10. Under which method of cost flow are (a) the earliest costs assigned to inventory, (b) the latest costs assigned to inventory, (c) the average costs assigned to inventory?

11. What are the relative advantages and disadvantages of FIFO and LIFO from management's point of view?

12. In the phrase "lower of cost or market," what is meant by "market"?

13. What methods can be used to determine lower of cost or market?

14. What effects do income taxes have on inventory valuation?

15. What are some reasons why management may want to use the gross profit method of determining inventory?

16. Does using the retail inventory method mean that inventories are measured at retail value on the balance sheet? Explain.

17. Which of the following companies would find a perpetual inventory system practical: a drug store, a grocery store, a restaurant, an automobile dealer, a wholesale auto parts dealer? Why?

18. Which is more expensive to maintain: a perpetual inventory system or a periodic inventory system? Why?

19. What differences occur in recording sales, purchases, and closing entries under the perpetual and periodic inventory systems?

20. Which of the following inventory systems do not require a physical inventory: (a) perpetual, (b) periodic, (c) retail, (d) gross profit?

Classroom Exercises

Exercise 11-1 Inventory Cost Methods

Stan's Service Station had the following purchases and sales of oil during the year:

Jan. 1	Beginning inventory	200 cases at $12 =	$ 2,400
Feb. 25	Purchased	100 cases at $13 =	1,300
June 15	Purchased	400 cases at $14 =	5,600
Aug. 15	Purchased	100 cases at $13 =	1,300
Oct. 15	Purchased	300 cases at $14 =	4,200
Dec. 15	Purchased	200 cases at $15 =	3,000
Totals		1,300 cases	$17,800
Total sales		1,000 cases	
Dec. 31 Ending inventory		300 cases	

Assume that all of the June 15 purchase and 200 cases each from the January 1 beginning inventory, the October 15 purchase, and the December 15 purchase were sold.

Determine the costs that should be assigned to cost of goods sold and ending inventory under each of the following assumptions: (1) Costs are assigned by the specific identification method. (2) Costs are assigned on an average-cost basis. (3) Costs are assigned on a FIFO basis. (4) Costs are assigned on a LIFO basis. What conclusions can you draw from your answers?

Exercise 11-2 Effects of Inventory Errors

Condensed income statements for Viking Company for two years are shown at the top of the next page.

	19x2	19x1
Sales	$88,000	$74,000
Cost of Goods Sold	52,000	38,000
Gross Profit on Sales	$36,000	$36,000
Operating Expenses	18,000	18,000
Net Income	$18,000	$18,000

After the end of 19x2, it was discovered that an error had been made in 19x1 that resulted in an understatement of the ending inventory of 19x1 by $8,000.

Compute the corrected net income for 19x1 and 19x2. What effect will the error have on net income and owner's equity for 19x3?

Exercise 11-3 Inventory Cost Methods

During its first year of operations, Macy Company purchased 5,500 units of a product at $10 per unit. During the second year, it purchased 6,000 units at $12 per unit. During the third year, it purchased 5,000 units at $15 per unit. Macy Company managed to have an ending inventory each year of 1,000 units. The company sells goods at a 100 percent markup over cost.

Prepare comparative cost of goods sold statements that compare the value of ending inventory and cost of goods sold for each of the three years using the following methods: (1) the FIFO method, and (2) the LIFO method. What conclusions can you draw from the resulting data about the relationships between changes in unit price and changes in the value of ending inventory?

Exercise 11-4 Retail Method

Maggie's Fashion Shop had retail sales of $210,000 during the current year. The following additional information was obtained from the accounting records.

	At Cost	At Retail
Beginning Inventory	$ 19,600	$ 32,600
Net Purchases	127,100	217,400
Freight In	4,300	

1. Estimate the company's ending inventory at cost using the retail method.
2. Assume that a physical inventory taken at year end revealed an inventory on hand of $38,000 at retail value. What is the estimated amount of inventory shrinkage (loss due to theft, damage, and so forth) at cost?

Exercise 11-5 Gross Profit Method

Joe Carmel was at home watching Johnny Carson on television when he received a call from the fire department. His business was a total loss from fire. The insurance company asked him to substantiate his inventory loss. Until the date of the fire, Joe's company had sales of $420,000 and purchases of $266,300. Freight in amounted to $13,700, and the beginning inventory was $36,000. It was Joe's custom to price goods in such a way as to have a gross margin of 40 percent on sales.

Compute Joe's estimated inventory loss.

Exercise 11-6 Lower-of-Cost-or-Market Method

Scott Company values its inventory at the lower of cost or market. For each of the following items of inventory, determine the proper per unit valuation for each item.

	Item A	Item B	Item C	Item D
Cost	$12	$26	$35	$20
Net realizable value	18	24	31	22
Net realizable value less a normal profit margin	14	20	25	17
Market (replacement cost)	15	22	24	21

Problem Set A

Problem 11A-1 Inventory Cost Methods

During 19xx, Target Company sold 3,400 units of Product T400 at $120 per unit. Its beginning inventory and purchases during the year were as follows: January 1 inventory, 300 units at $50; February purchases, 400 units at $55; April purchases, 600 units at $60; June purchases, 1,500 units at $55; August purchases, 700 units at $60; October purchases, 300 units at $62; December purchases, 200 units at $65. The company's selling and administrative expenses totaled $170,000, and it uses a periodic inventory method.

Required

1. Prepare a schedule to compute cost of goods available for sale.
2. Prepare an income statement under each of the following assumptions: (a) Costs are assigned to inventory on an average-cost basis. (b) Costs are assigned to inventory on a FIFO basis. (c) Costs are assigned to inventory on a LIFO basis.

Problem 11A-2 Lower-of-Cost-or-Market Method

The physical inventory for Talbot Company appears below.

		Per Unit	
	Quantity	Cost	Market
Category A			
Item A1	70	$25.00	$23.00
Item A2	40	47.00	51.00
Item A3	90	31.00	30.00
Category B			
Item B1	250	17.00	18.40
Item B2	300	15.50	16.00
Item B3	120	12.00	11.00
Category C			
Item C1	850	3.50	3.70
Item C2	910	4.00	3.80
Item C3	250	11.00	9.00

Required

Determine the value of the inventory at lower of cost or market using each of the following methods: (1) the item-by-item method, (2) the major category method, and (3) the total inventory method.

Problem 11A-3 Perpetual Inventory System

The beginning inventory of Product KJP and data on purchases and sales for a two-month period are presented below.

June 1	Inventory	20 units at $40
15	Purchase	60 units at $44
18	Sale	40 units
25	Sale	15 units

July 3	Purchase	30 units at $42
10	Sale	20 units
16	Purchase	60 units at $45
19	Sale	50 units
21	Purchase	20 units at $47
24	Sale	15 units
31	Sale	20 units

Required

1. Assume that the company maintains a perpetual inventory system on a FIFO basis and uses perpetual inventory cards similar to the one illustrated in the text. Follow the example in the text and record the transactions on such a card using two or more lines to show units on hand at each price or units sold when units costing different amounts are on hand or sold.
2. Assume that the company keeps its records on a LIFO basis, and record the transactions on a second record card.
3. Assume that the July 31 sale was made to Arnold Moses on credit for $2,000. Prepare a general journal entry to record the sale and cost of goods sold on a FIFO basis.

Problem 11A-4 Periodic Inventory System

Assume the same data as presented in Problem 11A-3 except that the company uses a periodic inventory system. The company closes its books at the end of each month.

Required

1. Compute the value of the ending inventory at June 30 and July 31 on a FIFO basis.
2. Compute the value of the ending inventory at June 30 and July 31 on a LIFO basis.
3. Prepare a general journal entry to record the sale on July 31 to Arnold Moses on credit for $2,000.

Problem 11A-5 Retail Inventory Method

Tennis, Anyone is a retail sporting goods company that uses the retail inventory method to estimate the cost of ending inventory. To test its controls against shoplifting and employee pilferage, the company makes a practice of taking a physical inventory at retail to compare with the estimate. Data from the accounting records and from a year-end physical inventory are as follows:

	At Cost	At Retail
July 1 Beginning Inventory	$15,214	$ 26,420
Purchases	55,418	101,615
Purchases Returns and Allowances	953	2,485
Freight In	2,140	
Sales		97,340
Sales Returns and Allowances		2,490
July 30 Physical Inventory		15,860

Required

Prepare a schedule to do the following: (1) estimate the dollar amount of the store's year-end inventory using the retail method, (2) use the store's cost ratio to reduce the retail value of the physical inventory to cost, and (3) calculate the estimated amount of inventory shortage at cost and at retail.

Problem 11A-6 Gross Profit Method

Gigantic Tire Company is a wholesale tire dealer that sells mainly to commercial trucking companies. The company maintains an office in the front of a large warehouse where it keeps its inventory. On the night of November 11, the night watchman was overpowered by armed robbers who backed a large truck up to the warehouse and stole several hundred large and expensive tires. Because the company does not maintain perpetual inventory records, the accountant for the company must estimate the amount of the loss.

By noon, the accountant was able to collect the following information: (a) merchandise inventory on October 1, \$117,300; (b) purchases, October 1 through November 11, \$306,270; (c) purchases returns, October 1 through November 11, \$2,220; (d) freight in for the period, \$21,460; (e) sales, October 1 through November 11, \$487,208; (f) sales returns, October 1 through November 11, \$9,788; (g) merchandise inventory still on hand (not stolen), November 11, at cost, \$52,300; (h) average gross profit margin, $33\frac{1}{3}$ percent.

Required

Prepare a schedule showing the amount of inventory that should have been in the warehouse on November 11, and estimate the amount of the loss.

Problem Set B

Problem 11B-1 Inventory Cost Methods

Carle Company merchandises a single product called CC17. The following data represent beginning inventory and purchases of product CC17 during the past year: January 1 inventory, 17,000 units at \$6.00; February purchases, 20,000 units at \$6.50; March purchases, 40,000 units at \$6.20; May purchases, 30,000 units at \$6.30; July purchases, 50,000 units at \$6.40; September purchases, 40,000 units at \$6.30; November purchases, 15,000 units at \$6.60. Sales of product CC17 totaled 192,000 units at \$10 per unit. Selling and administrative expenses totaled \$592,000 for the year.

Required

1. Prepare a schedule to compute cost of goods available for sale.
2. Prepare an income statement under each of the following assumptions: (a) Costs are assigned to inventory on an average-cost basis. (b) Costs are assigned to inventory on a FIFO basis. (c) Costs are assigned to inventory on a LIFO basis.

Problem 11B-2 Lower-of-Cost-or-Market Method

After taking the physical inventory, the accountant for Castle Company prepared the inventory schedule shown at the top of the next page.

	Quantity	Per Unit Cost	Per Unit Market
Product line 1			
Item 11	170	$ 5	$ 5
Item 12	270	4	5
Item 13	210	8	7
Product line 2			
Item 21	110	15	17
Item 22	400	21	20
Item 23	70	18	20
Product line 3			
Item 31	370	26	20
Item 32	310	30	28
Item 33	120	34	39

Required

Determine the value of the inventory at lower of cost or market using each of the following methods: (1) the item-by-item method, (2) the major category method, and (3) the total inventory method.

Problem 11B-3 Perpetual Inventory System

The beginning inventory of Product X19 and data on purchases and sales for a two-month period are presented below.

Apr. 1	Inventory	50 units at $100
10	Purchase	100 units at $110
17	Sale	60 units
25	Sale	30 units
May 2	Purchase	100 units at $108
8	Sale	40 units
14	Purchase	50 units at $112
18	Sale	40 units
22	Purchase	50 units at $115
26	Sale	30 units
31	Sale	70 units

Required

1. Assume that the company maintains a perpetual inventory system on a FIFO basis and uses perpetual inventory cards similar to the one illustrated in the text. Follow the example in the text and record the transactions on such a card using two or more lines to show units on hand at each price or units sold when units costing different amounts are on hand or sold.
2. Assume that the company keeps its records on a LIFO basis, and record the transactions on a second record card.
3. Assume that the May 31 sale was made to Moralles Corporation on credit for $14,000. Prepare a general journal entry to record the sale and cost of goods sold on a LIFO basis.

Problem 11B-4 Periodic Inventory System

Assume the same data as presented in Problem 11B-3 except that the company uses a periodic inventory system. The company closes its books at the end of each month.

Required

1. Compute the value of the ending inventory at April 30 and May 31 on a FIFO basis.
2. Compute the value of the ending inventory at April 30 and May 31 on a LIFO basis.
3. Prepare a general journal entry to record the sale on May 31 to Moralles Corporation on credit for $14,000.

Problem 11B-5 Retail Inventory Method

Mayfair Company operates a large discount store that uses the retail inventory method to estimate the cost of ending inventory. Management suspects that in recent weeks there have been unusually heavy losses from shoplifting or employee pilferage. In order to estimate the amount of the loss, the company has taken a physical inventory and will compare the results with the estimated cost of inventory. Data from the accounting records and from a year-end physical inventory are as follows:

	At Cost	At Retail
September 1 Beginning Inventory	$201,816	$286,400
Purchases	286,832	423,200
Purchases Returns and Allowances	8,172	12,800
Freight In	3,800	
Sales		436,730
Sales Returns and Allowances		3,730
September 30 Physical Inventory		247,000

Required

Prepare a schedule to do the following: (1) estimate the dollar amount of the store's year-end inventory using the retail method, (2) use the store's cost ratio to reduce the retail value of the physical inventory to cost, and (3) calculate the estimated amount of inventory shortage at cost and at retail.

Learning Objectives

Chapter Twelve

Current Liabilities and Payroll Accounting

1. *Define liability and state the ways in which the problems of recognition, valuation, and classification apply to liabilities.*
2. *Identify, compute, and record definitely determinable and estimated current liabilities.*
3. *Identify and compute the liabilities associated with payroll accounting.*
4. *Record transactions associated with payroll accounting.*
5. *Apply internal control to the payroll system.*
6. *Make reversing entries.*

This chapter gives you an overview of the nature and measurement of current liabilities, with examples of many common current liabilities, and introduces you to payroll accounting. As a result of studying this chapter, you should be able to meet the learning objectives listed on the left.

Liabilities are one of the three major sections of the balance sheet and generally represent a company's obligations to nonowners. The two major subdivisions of liabilities are current liabilities and long-term liabilities. This chapter considers the nature and measurement of current liabilities. The discussion of long-term liabilities is postponed until Chapter 18. Because a number of current liabilities arise through the payroll process, the fundamentals of payroll accounting are also presented in this chapter.

Nature and Measurement of Liabilities

Liabilities result from a firm's past transactions and are legal obligations for the future payment of assets or the future performance of services. Note that liabilities consist of more than monetary obligations. For example, revenues received in advance are for services that must be provided to customers. The amount and due date are usually definite or subject to reasonable estimation. The problems of recognition, valuation, and classification apply equally to liabilities and assets.

Recognition of Liabilities

Objective 1 Define liability and state the ways in which the problems of recognition, valuation, and classification apply to liabilities

Timing is important in the recognition of liabilities. Failure to record a liability in an accounting period is usually accompanied by failure to record an expense and results in an understatement of expense and an overstatement of income. Liabilities are recorded when an obligation occurs. This recognition rule is more difficult to apply than it appears on the surface. When there is a transaction that obligates the company to future payments, a liability arises and is recognized, as when merchandise is purchased on credit. However, current liabilities often are not represented by a direct transaction. One of the major reasons for adjusting entries at the end of an accounting period is to recognize unrecorded liabilities. Some examples of these accrued liabilities are salaries payable and interest payable. Other liabilities that can only be estimated, such as taxes payable, also require recognition by adjusting entries.

In contrast, a company may occasionally enter into an agreement for future transactions, such as a salary agreement to pay an executive $50,000 per year for three years or a purchase agreement by a public utility to purchase coal at a certain price over the next five years. These contracts, although they are definite commitments, are not liabilities because they represent future—not past—transactions. No current obligation exists; thus no liability is recognized.

Valuation of Liabilities

Liabilities are usually valued at the amount of money necessary to satisfy the obligation or the fair market value of goods or services to be delivered. For most liabilities the amount is definitely known, but for some it must be estimated. For example, an automobile dealer who sells a car with a one-year warranty is obligated to provide parts and services during the year. The obligation is definite, but the amount must be estimated.

Classification of Liabilities

Current liabilities are debts and obligations that are expected to be satisfied in one year or within the current operating cycle, whichever is longer. Usually they are paid out of current assets or through the incurrence of another short-term liability. The classification of current liabilities corresponds directly to the classification of current assets. In Chapter 7, we noted that two important measures of liquidity are working capital (current assets minus current liabilities) and the current ratio (current assets divided by current liabilities). Liabilities that will not be due during the next year or normal operating cycle are classified as **long-term liabilities.**

Common Categories of Current Liabilities

Current liabilities fall into two principal categories: (1) definitely determinable liabilities and (2) estimated liabilities.

Definitely Determinable Liabilities

Objective 2 Identify, compute, and record definitely determinable and estimated current liabilities

Current liabilities that are determined by contract or by statute and thus can be measured precisely are called **definitely determinable liabilities.** The accounting problems associated with these liabilities are to determine the existence and amount of the liability and to record the liability in the records properly. Some examples of definitely determinable liabilities are trade accounts payable, notes payable, dividends payable, sales and excise taxes payable, current portions of long-term debt, accrued liabilities, payroll liabilities, and deferred revenues.

Trade Accounts Payable Trade accounts payable are short-term obligations to suppliers for goods and services. The amount in the Trade Accounts Payable account is usually supported by an accounts payable subsidiary ledger. Under the voucher system, this account is called Vouchers Payable. Accounting for trade accounts payable has been treated extensively in previous chapters.

Notes Payable Short-term notes payable, which also arise out of the ordinary course of business, are obligations represented by promissory notes. The two primary sources of notes payable are bank loans and payments to suppliers for goods and services. As with notes receivable, presented in Chapter 10, the interest on notes may be stated separately on the face of the note (Case 1 in Figure 12-1), or it may be deducted in advance by discounting (Case 2). For example, in Figure 12-1, Caron Corporation borrows $5,000 on a sixty-day short-term promissory note from the bank at 12 percent interest. The entries to record the note under each alternative are as follows:

Case 1

Aug. 31	Cash	5,000	
	Notes Payable		5,000
	To record 60-day, 12% promissory note with interest stated separately		

Case 2

Aug. 31	Cash	4,900	
	Discount on Notes Payable	100	
	Notes Payable		5,000
	To record 60-day, 12% promissory note with interest included in face amount		

$$\text{Discount} = \$5{,}000 \times \frac{60}{360} \times .12 = \$100$$

Figure 12-1 Two Promissory Notes: One with Interest Stated Separately; One with Interest in Face Amount

Case 1 *Interest Stated Separately*

Chicago, Illinois August 31, 19xx

Sixty days after date I promise to pay to First Federal Bank the sum of $5,000 with interest at the rate of 12% per annum.

Sandra Caron

Caron Corporation

Case 2 *Interest in Face Amount*

Chicago, Illinois August 31, 19xx

Sixty days after date I promise to pay to First Federal Bank the sum of $5,000.

Sandra Caron

Caron Corporation

Note that in Case 1 the money borrowed equaled the face value of the note, whereas in Case 2 the money borrowed ($4,900) was less than the face value ($5,000) of the note. The amount of the discount equals the amount of the interest for sixty days. In order to show the proper liability on the balance sheet, the Discount on Notes Payable is deducted from the Notes Payable as a contra-liability account, as follows:

Partial Balance Sheet

Current Liabilities		
Notes Payable	$5,000	
Less Discount on Notes Payable	100	$4,900

On October 30, when the note is paid, the entry under each alternative is as follows:

Case 1

Oct. 30	Notes Payable	5,000	
	Interest Expense	100	
	Cash		5,100
	Payment of note with interest stated separately		

Case 2

Oct. 30	Notes Payable	5,000	
	Cash		5,000
	Payment of note with interest included in face value		

30	Interest Expense	100	
	Discount on Notes Payable		100
	To record interest expense on matured note		

Dividends Payable Dividends represent a distribution of earnings by a corporation. Because the payment of dividends is solely the decision of the corporation's board of directors, a liability does not exist until the board declares the dividends. There is usually a short time between the date of declaration and the date of payment of dividends. During that short time, the dividends declared are current liabilities of the corporation. Accounting for dividends is treated extensively in Chapter 17.

Sales and Excise Taxes Payable Most states and many cities levy a sales tax on retail transactions. On some products, such as automobile tires, there are federal excise taxes. The merchant who sells goods subject to these taxes must collect the taxes and remit them periodically to the appropriate government agency. The amount of tax collected represents a current liability until it is remitted to the government. For example, assume that a merchant makes a $100 sale that is subject to a 5 percent sales tax and a 10 percent excise tax. Assuming that the sale took place on June 1, the correct entry to record the sale is as follows:

June 1	Cash	115	
	Sales		100
	Sales Tax Payable		5
	Excise Tax Payable		10
	To record sale of merchandise and collection of sales and excise taxes		

The sale is properly recorded at $100, and the tax collections are recorded as liabilities to be remitted at the proper time.

Current Portions of Long-Term Debt If a portion of long-term debt is due within the coming year and is to be paid out of current assets, then the current portion of long-term debt is properly classified as a current liability. For example, suppose that a $500,000 debt is to be paid in installments of $100,000 per year for the next five years. The $100,000 installment due in the current year should be classified as a current liability. The remaining $400,000 should be classified as a long-term liability.

Accrued Liabilities A principal reason for adjusting entries at the end of an accounting period is to recognize and record liabilities that are not already recorded in the accounting records. This applies to any type of liability. For example, in previous chapters, adjustments relating to accrued salaries payable were made. As we will see, accrued liabilities can also apply to estimated liabilities. Here we focus on interest payable, a definitely determinable liability. If a note is interest bearing, there is a daily increase in the interest obligation. At the end of the accounting period, an adjusting entry should be made in accordance with the match-

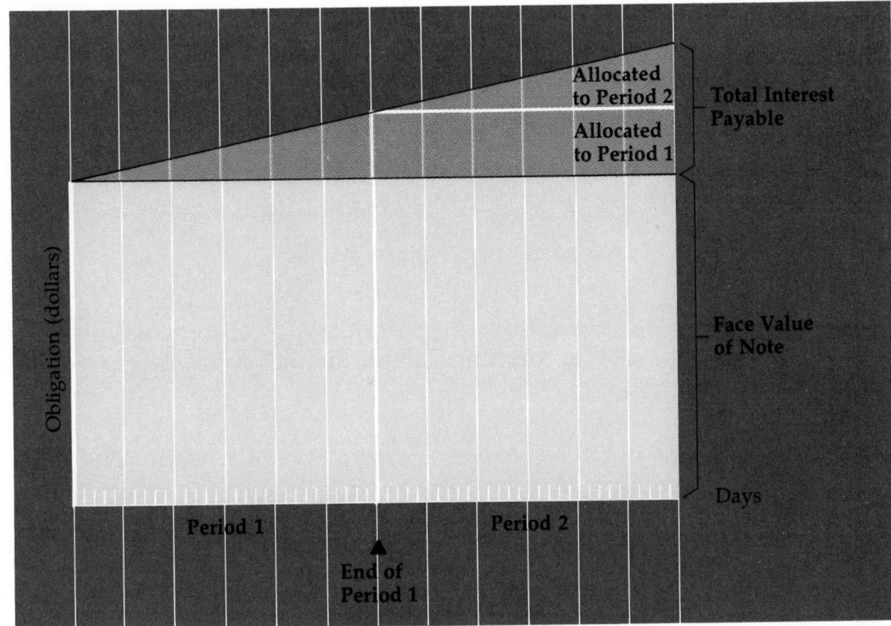

Figure 12-2 Growth in Liability of Interest-bearing Note, with Interest Expense Allocated to Two Accounting Periods

ing rule to record the interest obligation up to that point in time. Figure 12-2 illustrates the increase in this obligation and the allocation of the resulting expense to each accounting period. Thus if we again use the example of the two notes presented earlier in this chapter and assume that the accounting period ends on September 30, or thirty days after the issuance of the sixty-day notes, the adjusting entries for each case would be as follows:

Case 1

Sept. 30	Interest Expense	50	
	Interest Payable		50
	To record interest expense for 30 days on note with interest stated separately		

Case 2

Sept. 30	Interest Expense	50	
	Discount on Notes Payable		50
	To record interest expense for 30 days on note with interest included in face amount		

In Case 2, current liabilities are increased by the credit to Discount on Notes Payable because this credit has the effect of increasing the net amount of Notes Payable from $4,900 on October 30 to $4,950 on September 30. On the latter date, the notes payable would appear on the balance sheet as follows:

Partial Balance Sheet

Current Liabilities		
Notes Payable	$5,000	
Less Discount on Notes Payable	50	$4,950

Payroll Liabilities A number of current liabilities are associated with payroll accounting. These liabilities are discussed in a major section at the end of this chapter.

Deferred Revenues **Deferred revenues** represent obligations for goods or services that the company must deliver in return for an advance payment from a customer. For example, most magazines and other periodicals accept subscriptions paid in advance. The publisher then has a liability that expires when the periodical is delivered. Many businesses such as repair companies, construction companies, and special-order firms ask for a deposit or advance from a customer before they will begin work. These advances are also current liabilities until the goods or services are delivered.

Estimated Liabilities

Estimated liabilities are definite obligations of the firm, the exact amount of which cannot be determined until a later date. In these cases, because there is no doubt as to the existence of the legal obligation, the primary accounting problem is to estimate and record the amount of the liability. Examples of estimated liabilities are income taxes, property taxes, product warranties, and vacation pay.

Income Tax The income of a corporation is taxed by the federal government, most state governments, and some municipalities. The amount of income tax liability depends on the results of operations, and often it is not determined with complete confidence until after the end of the year. In cases of disputes between the corporation and the taxing authority, it may be years before the final tax is established. However, because income taxes are an expense in the year in which income is earned, an adjusting entry is necessary to record the estimated tax liability. An example of this entry follows:

Dec. 31	Federal Income Tax Expense	53,000	
	Federal Income Tax Payable		53,000
	To record estimated federal income tax		

Remember that the income of sole proprietorships and partnerships is not subject to income taxes. Their owners must report their share of the firm's income on their individual tax returns.

Property Taxes Payable Property taxes are taxes levied on real property such as land and buildings and on personal property such as inventory and equipment. Property taxes are the primary source of revenue for state and local governments. Usually they are assessed annually against the property involved. Because the fiscal years of state and local governments and their assessment dates rarely correspond, it is often necessary to estimate the amount of property taxes that applies to each month of the year. Assume, for instance, that a local government has a fiscal year of July 1 to June 30, that its assessment date is November 1 for the fiscal year beginning the previous July 1, and that its payment date is December 15. Assume also that on July 1, Janis Corporation estimates that its property taxes assessment will be $24,000 for the coming year. The adjusting entry to be made on July 31, which would be repeated on August 31, September 30, and October 31, would be as follows:

July 31	Property Taxes Expense	2,000	
	Estimated Property Taxes Payable		2,000
	To record estimated property taxes expense for the month $24,000 ÷ 12 months = $2,000		

On November 1, the firm receives a property taxes bill for $24,720. The estimate made in July was too low. The monthly charge should have been $2,060 per month. Because the difference between the actual and the estimate is small, the company decides to absorb in November the amount undercharged in the previous four months. Therefore, the property taxes expense for November is $2,300 [$2,060 + 4($60)] and is recorded as follows:

Nov. 30	Property Taxes Expense	2,300	
	Estimated Property Taxes Payable		2,300
	To record estimated property taxes		

The Estimated Property Taxes Payable account now has a balance of $10,300. The entry to record payment on December 15 would be as follows:

Dec. 15	Estimated Property Taxes Payable	10,300	
	Prepaid Property Taxes	14,420	
	Cash		24,720
	To record payment of property taxes		

Beginning December 31 and each month thenceforth until June 30, property taxes expense is recorded by a debit to Property Taxes Expense and a credit to Prepaid Property Taxes in the amount of $2,060. The total of these seven entries will reduce the Prepaid Property Taxes account to zero on June 30.

Product Warranty Liability When a firm places a warranty or guarantee on its product at the time of sale, a liability exists for the length of the warranty. The cost of the warranty is properly charged in the period of sale because it is a feature of the product or service sold and thus was one of the reasons the customer made the purchase. On the basis of experience, it should be possible to estimate the amount the warranty will cost in the future. Some products or services will require little warranty service; others may require much. Thus there will be an average cost per product or service. For example, assume that a muffler company guarantees that it will replace any muffler free of charge if it fails any time as long as you own your car. The company makes only a small service charge for replacing the muffler. This is an important selling feature for the firm's mufflers. In the past, 4 percent of the mufflers sold have been returned for replacement under the guarantee. The average cost of a muffler is $25. Assume that during July, 350 mufflers were sold. This accrued liability would be recorded as an adjustment at the end of July as follows:

July 31	Product Warranty Expense	350	
	Estimated Product Warranty Liability		350
	To record estimated product warranty expense, calculated as follows:		

Number of units sold	350
Rate of replacements under warranty	× .04
Estimated units to be replaced	14
Estimated cost per unit	× $25
Estimated liability for product warranty	$350

When a muffler is returned for replacement under the product warranty in a subsequent accounting period, the cost of the muffler is charged against the estimated product warranty liability account. For example, assume that a customer returns on December 5 with a defective muffler and pays a $10 service charge to have the muffler replaced. Assume that this particular muffler cost $20. The entry is as follows:

Dec. 5	Cash	10	
	Estimated Product Warranty Liability	20	
	Service Revenue		10
	Merchandise Inventory		20
	To record replacement of muffler under warranty		

Vacation Pay Liability In most companies, employees earn the right to paid vacation days or weeks as they work during the year. For example, an employee may earn two weeks of paid vacation for each fifty weeks of work. Consequently, she or he is paid fifty-two weeks' salary for fifty weeks' work. Theoretically, the cost of the two weeks' vacation should be allocated as expense over the entire year. Thus vacation pay represents 4 percent (two weeks' vacation divided by fifty weeks) of a worker's compensation. Every week worked earns the employee a small fraction (4 percent) of his or her vacation pay. Not all employees in every company will collect vacation pay because of turnover and rules regarding term of employment.

Assume that a company with the above policy has a weekly payroll of $20,000 and that experience has shown that 75 percent of employees will ultimately collect vacation pay. The consumption of vacation pay expense is as follows: $20,000 × 4 percent × 75 percent = $600.

The entry to record vacation pay expense for a week ended April 20 is as follows:

Apr. 20	Vacation Pay Expense	600	
	Estimated Liability for Vacation Pay		600
	To record estimated vacation pay expense		

At the time that an individual receives his or her vacation pay, an entry is made debiting Estimated Liability for Vacation Pay and crediting Cash or Wages Payable. For example, assume that an employee is paid $550 during a two-week vacation ending August 31, the entry is as follows:

Aug. 31	Estimated Liability for Vacation Pay	550	
	Cash (or Wages Payable)		550
	To record wages of employee on vacation		

Introduction to Payroll Accounting

A major expense of most companies is the cost of labor and related payroll taxes. In some industries such as banking and airlines, payroll costs represent more than 50 percent of the operating costs.

Objective 3 Identify and compute the liabilities associated with payroll accounting

In addition to being important because of the amounts of money involved, payroll accounting is important because the employer must conform to an array of complex laws governing taxes on payrolls. The employer has significant reporting requirements and liabilities for amounts of money withheld from employees' salaries and for taxes on the payroll.

Furthermore, the payroll accounting system is highly sensitive to complaints and to possible fraud. Every employee must be paid on time and receive a detailed explanation of the amount of his or her pay. The payroll system requires strong internal control and efficient processing and distribution of checks, as well as accurate reporting to the government agencies.

This section will focus first on the liabilities and records associated with payroll accounting and then on the control requirements of payroll accounting. The three general types of liabilities associated with payroll accounting are (1) liabilities for employee compensation, (2) liabilities for employee payroll withholdings, and (3) liabilities for employer payroll taxes.

It is important to distinguish between employees and independent contractors. Payroll accounting applies to employees of the firm. Employees are paid a wage or salary by the firm and are under the direct supervision and control of the firm. Independent contractors, on the other hand, are not employees of the firm and hence are not accounted for under the payroll system. They offer services to the firm for a fee but are not under its direct control or supervision. Examples of independent contractors are certified public accountants, advertising agencies, lawyers, and computer service firms.

Liabilities for Employee Compensation

The employer is liable to employees for wages and salaries. The term **wages** refers to compensation for employees at an hourly rate or on a piecework basis. The term **salaries** refers to the compensation for employees who are paid at a monthly or yearly rate. Generally, these are administrative or managerial employees.

In addition to setting minimum wage levels, the federal Fair Labor Standards Act (also called the Wages and Hours Law) regulates overtime pay. Employers who engage in interstate commerce must pay overtime at a minimum of one and one-half times the regular rate for hours worked in excess of forty hours a week or in excess of eight hours a day. Work on Saturdays, Sundays, or holidays may also require overtime pay. Union or other employment contracts may exceed these minimums.

For example, assume that the employment contract of Robert Jones specifies a regular wage of $5 an hour, one and one-half times the regular rate for work over eight hours in any weekday, and twice the regular rate for work on Saturdays, Sundays, or holidays. He works the following schedule during the week of January 18, 19xx:

Day	Total Hours Worked	Regular Time	Overtime
Monday	10	8	2
Tuesday	8	8	0
Wednesday	8	8	0
Thursday	9	8	1
Friday	10	8	2
Saturday	2	0	2
	47	40	7

Jones's wage would be computed as follows:

Regular time	40 hours × $5	=	$200.00
Overtime, weekdays	5 hours × $5 × 1.5	=	37.50
Overtime, weekend	2 hours × $5 × 2	=	20.00
Total wages			$257.50

Liabilities for Employee Payroll Withholdings

The amount paid to employees rarely equals the wages they have earned because the employer is required by law to withhold certain amounts from the employees' wages and send them directly to government agencies to pay taxes owed by the employees. In addition, certain withholdings are made for the employees' benefit and often at their request. In the first category are FICA taxes, federal income taxes, and state income taxes. In the second category are retirement and pension payments, hospitalization insurance premiums, life insurance premiums, union dues, purchases of savings bonds, and charitable contributions. Whatever the reason for the withholding from the employees' wages, the employer is liable for payment to the appropriate agency.

FICA Taxes Beginning with the passage of a national social security program in the 1930s, the federal government has taken more and more responsibility for the well-being of its citizens. The social security program provides retirement and disability benefits, survivor's benefits, and hospitalization and other medical benefits. One of the major extensions of the program provided hospitalization and medical insurance for persons over sixty-five.

This social security program is financed by taxes on employees, employers, and the self-employed. About 90 percent of the people working in the United States fall under the provisions of this program.

The Federal Insurance Contributions Act (FICA) established the tax to pay for this program. The tax applies to *both* employee and employer and is currently based on the following schedule up to 1984:

	1981	**1982**	**1983**	**1984**
Tax rate	6.65%	6.70%	6.70%	6.70%
Maximum wage taxed under present law	$29,700.00	$31,800.00	$33,900.00	$36,000.00
Present maximum tax	$ 1,975.05	$ 2,130.60	$ 2,271.30	$ 2,412.00

The FICA tax applies to the salary of each employee up to a certain level. In 1981, it applies up to the level of $29,700. There is no tax on individual earnings above this amount. Therefore, the maximum tax for the employee or employer or any one person is $1,975.05 ($29,700 × .0665). Both employees and employers must pay this amount. The employer deducts the taxes from the employees' wages and remits this amount to the government along with the employer's portion of the tax. Because of inflation and escalating benefits under the social security system, these provisions are under constant study by Congress; therefore, they are subject to change and should be verified each year.[1] If Robert Jones has earned less than $29,700 this year, the FICA withholding for

1. The tax rate and maximum wage subject to the tax expected to be effective in 1981 will be used in all illustrations and problems.

taxes on his paycheck this week is \$17.12 (\$257.50 × .0665). The employer must pay an equal tax.

Federal Income Tax The largest deduction from most employees' earnings is their estimated liability for federal income taxes. The system of tax collection for federal income taxes is to "pay as you go." The employer is required to withhold funds from employees' paychecks and remit the amount to the Internal Revenue Service.

The amount to be withheld depends on the amount of each employee's earnings and on the number of the employee's exemptions. All employees are required by law to indicate their exemptions by filing a Form W-4 (Employee's Withholding Exemption Certificate). Each employee is entitled to one exemption for himself or herself and one for each dependent. Additional exemptions are possible if the individual is blind or over sixty-five years of age. In our example, Robert Jones has four exemptions—one for himself, one for his wife, and one for each of two children.

The Internal Revenue Service provides employees with tables to aid them in computing the amount of withholdings. For example, Figure 12-3 is a withholding table for married employees who are paid weekly. The withholding from Robert Jones's \$257.50 weekly earnings computed above is \$30.50.

State Income Tax Most states have income taxes, and in most cases the procedures for withholding are similar to those for federal income taxes.

Other Withholdings Some of the other withholdings, such as for a retirement or pension plan, are required of each employee. Others, such as withholdings for insurance premiums or savings plans, may be requested by the employee. The payroll system must allow for treating each employee separately with regard to withholdings and the records of these withholdings. The employer is liable to account for all withholdings and to make proper remittances.

Figure 12-3
Wage-Bracket Table

		Weekly Payroll Period—Employee Married										
And the wages are—		And the number of withholding allowances claimed is—										
At least	But less than	0	1	2	3	4	5	6	7	8	9	10 or more
		The amount of income tax to be withheld shall be—										
\$200	\$210	\$32.00	\$29.20	\$26.30	\$23.60	\$21.30	\$19.00	\$16.70	\$14.40	\$12.10	\$ 9.80	\$ 7.50
210	220	34.40	31.20	28.30	25.40	22.90	20.60	18.30	16.00	13.70	11.40	9.10
220	230	36.80	33.30	30.30	27.40	24.50	22.20	19.90	17.60	15.30	13.00	10.70
230	240	39.20	35.70	32.30	29.40	26.50	23.80	21.50	19.20	16.90	14.60	12.30
240	250	41.60	38.10	34.60	31.40	28.50	25.60	23.10	20.80	18.50	16.20	13.90
250	260	44.00	40.50	37.00	33.60	30.50	27.60	24.70	22.40	20.10	17.80	15.50

Computation of an Employee's Take-Home Pay: An Illustration

Objective 4 Record transactions associated with payroll accounting

To continue with the example of Robert Jones, let us now compute his take-home pay. We know that his total earnings for the week of January 18 are $257.50, that his FICA tax rate at 6.65 percent is $17.12 (he has not earned over $29,700), and that his federal income tax withholding is $30.50. Assume also that his union dues are $2.00, his medical insurance premiums are $7.60, his life insurance premium is $6.00, he places $15.00 per week in savings bonds, and he contributes $1.00 per week to United Charities. His net (take-home) pay is computed as follows:

Gross earnings		$257.50
Deductions		
FICA tax	$17.12	
Federal income tax withheld	30.50	
Union dues	2.00	
Medical insurance	7.60	
Life insurance	6.00	
Savings bonds	15.00	
United Charities contribution	1.00	
Total withheld		79.22
Net (take-home) pay		$178.28

Employee Earnings Record Each employer must maintain a record of earnings and withholdings for each employee. Many companies today use computers to maintain these records, but small companies use manual records. The manual form of **employee earnings record** used for Robert Jones is shown in Figure 12-4 (next page). This form is designed to help the employer comply with legal reporting requirements that each deduction be paid to the proper agency and that the employee receive a report of the deductions made each year. Most columns are self-explanatory. Note, however, the column on the far right, where cumulative earnings (earnings to date) are recorded. This helps the employer comply with the rule of applying FICA taxes only up to the maximum wage level. At the end of the year, the employer reports to the employee on Form W-2, the Wage and Tax Statement, the totals of earnings and deductions for the year so that the employee can complete his or her individual tax return. The employer sends a copy of the W-2 to the Internal Revenue Service. Thus the IRS can check on whether the employee has reported all earned income.

Payroll Register The **payroll register** is a detailed listing of the firm's total payroll that is prepared each payday. A payroll register is presented in Figure 12-5 (next page). Note that the name, hours, earnings, deductions, and net pay of each employee are listed. Compare the January 18 entry in the employee earnings record (Figure 12-4) of Robert Jones with the entry for Robert Jones in the payroll register. Except for the first column, which

Employee Earnings Record

Employee's Name: Robert Jones	Social Security Number: 444-66-9999		
Address: 777 20th Street, Marshall, Michigan 52603	Sex: Male	Employee No.	705
	Single: ___ Married: X	Weekly Pay Rate	$200
Date of Birth: September 20, 1942	Exemptions (W-4): 4	Hourly Rate	$5
Position: Sales Assistant	Date of Employment: July 15, 1972	Date Employment Ended	

1978		Earnings			Deductions							Payment		
Period Ended	Total Hours	Regular	Overtime	Gross	FICA Tax	Federal Income Tax	Union Dues	Medical Insurance	Life Insurance	Savings Bonds	Other: A—United Charities	Net Earnings	Check No.	Cumulative Gross Earnings
Jan. 4	40	200.00	0	200.00	13.30	21.30	2.00	7.60	6.00	15.00	A 1.00	133.80	717	200.00
11	44	200.00	30.00	230.00	15.29	26.50	2.00	7.60	6.00	15.00	A 1.00	156.61	822	430.00
18	47	200.00	57.50	257.50	17.12	30.50	2.00	7.60	6.00	15.00	A 1.00	178.28	926	687.50

Payroll Register

Pay Period: Week ended January 8

		Earnings			Deductions							Payment		Distribution	
Employee	Total Hours	Regular	Overtime	Gross	FICA Tax	Federal Income Tax	Union Dues	Medical Insurance	Life Insurance	Savings Bonds	Other: A—United Charities	Net Earnings	Check No.	Sales Salaries Expense	Office Salaries Expense
Linda Duval	40	160.00		160.00	10.64	20.60		5.80				122.96	923		160.00
John Franks	44	160.00	24.00	184.00	12.24	24.80	2.00	7.60			A 10.00	127.36	924	184.00	
Samuel Goetz	40	400.00		400.00	26.60	67.20		10.40	14.00		A 3.00	278.80	925	400.00	
Robert Jones	47	200.00	57.50	257.50	17.12	30.50	2.00	7.60	6.00	15.00	A 1.00	178.28	926	257.50	
Billie Matthews	40	160.00		160.00	10.64	20.60		5.80				122.96	927		160.00
Rosaire O'Brian	42	200.00	20.00	220.00	14.63	33.30	2.00	5.80				164.27	928	220.00	
James Van Dyke	40	200.00		200.00	13.30	26.30		5.80				154.60	929		200.00
		1,480.00	101.50	1,581.50	105.17	223.30	6.00	48.80	20.00	15.00	14.00	1,149.23		1,061.50	520.00

◀ Figure 12-4
Employee Earnings Record (left)

Figure 12-5
Payroll Register (right)

lists the employee names, and the last column, in which there is a classification of the wage or salary as either sales or office expense, the columns are the same. The columns help employers to record the payroll in the accounting records and to meet legal reporting requirements as mentioned above. The last two columns are necessary for the division of expenses on the income statement into selling and administrative categories.

Recording the Payroll The journal entry for recording the payroll is based on the total of the columns from the payroll register. The journal entry to record the payroll of January 18 is as follows:

Jan. 18	Sales Salaries Expense	1,061.50	
	Office Salaries Expense	520.00	
	FICA Taxes Payable		105.17
	Federal Income Taxes Payable		223.30
	Union Dues Payable		6.00
	Medical Insurance Premiums Payable		48.80
	Life Insurance Premiums Payable		20.00
	Savings Bonds Payable		15.00
	United Charities Payable		14.00
	Salaries Payable		1,149.23
	To record weekly payroll		

Note that each account debited or credited is a total from the payroll register. If the payroll register is considered a special-purpose journal similar to those in Chapter 8, the column can be entered directly in the ledger accounts with the appropriate account numbers indicated at the bottom of each column.

Liabilities for Employer Payroll Taxes

The payroll taxes discussed so far were deducted from the employee's gross earnings, to be paid by the employer. There are three principal taxes on salaries that the employer must also pay: the FICA tax, the federal unemployment insurance tax, and state unemployment compensation taxes. These taxes are considered operating expenses.

FICA Tax The employer must pay FICA (Federal Insurance Contributions Act) tax equal to that paid by the employees. For example, from the payroll register in Figure 12-5, the employer would have to pay FICA taxes of $105.17, equal to that paid by the employees.

Federal Unemployment Insurance Tax The Federal Unemployment Tax Act (FUTA) is another part of the national social security system. It is designed to finance the administration of programs to assist unemployed workers. In this respect, it is different from FICA taxes and state unemployment taxes. This tax is commonly known as unemployment compensation. Unlike the FICA tax, which is levied on both employees and employers, the FUTA is assessed only against employers.

Although the amount of the tax can vary, it amounted recently to 3.4 percent of the first $6,000 earned by each employee. The employer, however, is allowed a credit against this federal tax for unemployment taxes paid to the state. The maximum credit is 2.7 percent of the first $6,000 of each employee's earnings. Most states set their rate at this maximum. Consequently, the FUTA paid is .7 percent (3.4 percent − 2.7 percent).

State Unemployment Insurance Tax Most state unemployment plans provide for unemployment compensation to be paid to unemployed workers. This compensation is paid out of the fund established by the 2.7 percent of the first $6,000 earned by each employee. In some states, employers with favorable employment records may be entitled to pay less than the 2.7 percent.

Recording Payroll Taxes According to Figure 12-5, the gross payroll for the week ended January 18 was $1,581.50. Because it was the first month of the year, all employees had accumulated less than the $29,700 and $6,000 maximum taxable salaries. Therefore, the FICA tax was $105.17 (equal to tax on employees); the FUTA was $11.07 (.007 × $1,581.50); and the state unemployment tax was $42.70 (.027 × $1,581.50). The entry to record this expense and related liability in the general journal is as follows:

Jan. 18	Payroll Taxes Expense	158.94	
	FICA Taxes Payable		105.17
	Federal Unemployment Taxes Payable		11.07
	State Unemployment Taxes Payable		42.70
	To record weekly payroll taxes expense		

Payment of Payroll and Payroll Taxes

After the weekly payroll is recorded, as illustrated earlier, a liability of $1,149.23 exists for salaries payable. How this liability will be paid depends on the system used by the company. Many companies use a special payroll account against which payroll checks are drawn. Under this system, a check must first be drawn on the regular checking account and deposited in the special payroll account before the payroll checks are issued to the employees. If a voucher system is combined with a special payroll account, a voucher for the total salaries payable ($1,149.23) is prepared and recorded in the voucher register as a debit to Payroll Bank Account and a credit to Vouchers Payable.

The combined FICA taxes (both employees' and employer's share) and the federal income taxes must be paid to the Internal Revenue Service at least quarterly. Monthly payments are necessary if more than a certain amount of money is involved. The federal unemployment insurance taxes are remitted yearly if the amount is less than $100. If it is more than $100, quarterly payments are necessary. The payment dates among the states vary. Other payroll deductions must be remitted according to the particular contracts or agreements involved.

Internal Control for Payroll

Objective 5
Apply internal control to the payroll system

Because a great deal of money passes through the payroll system of most companies, it is important to have adequate internal controls over the system. Consider the following possible payroll frauds: An employee who does not exist may be entered on the payroll, and the check may be collected by someone else. Or time cards for employees who no longer work at the company may be turned in. Or an employee may not work all the hours reported.

To avoid these and other payroll frauds, the principles of internal control stated in Chapter 9 should be applied to the payroll system. For example, there should be a separation of duties for the major payroll functions. In brief, these functions may be described as follows:

1. **The personnel function.** All employees hired should have a central employment record that includes, among other things, their wage rate and termination date (if they leave the company).
2. **The timekeeping function.** Employees paid by the hour should be required to punch a time clock on arrival and departure. Salaried employees should prepare time sheets, which are approved by their supervisors.
3. **The accounting function.** A payroll department should prepare checks based on data from the timekeeping function about time worked and from the personnel function on the pay rate and payroll deductions.
4. **The distribution function.** The paychecks from the accounting function should be distributed by an office separate from any of the above functions. Employees should be required to present proper identification and sign their names in order to receive their checks.

Note on Reversing Entries

Objective 6
Make reversing entries

At the end of each accounting period, adjusting entries are made to bring revenues and expenses into conformity with the matching concept. **Reversing entries** are reversals of certain adjusting entries. They are designed to aid the routine bookkeeping process in the *next* accounting period. They are introduced here because a major category of adjustments to which they apply are accrued liabilities. Consider the following accrual of interest payable that might be made at the end of an accounting period:

Dec. 31	Interest Expense	700	
	Accrued Interest Payable		700
	To accrue interest expense at the end of the accounting period		

When the interest is paid, the accountant makes the following entry, using the accounting procedure that should now be familiar to you:

Jan. 20	Interest Expense	100	
	Accrued Interest Payable	700	
	Cash		800
	To record payment of interest		

Note that when the payment is made, the accountant must look in the records to determine how much of the $800 applied to the current accounting period and how much was accrued at the beginning of the period. This procedure may appear easy in this simple example, but consider the problems involved if the company has several notes payable, all due on different dates. Every time a note or interest transaction occurred, the accountant would have to recompute the amounts. The same problems apply to accrued salaries payable, payroll taxes and deductions, and any other accrued liability.

Reversing entries remedy this problem and are performed after closing entries in the accounting cycle. A reversing entry is exactly what its name implies—a reversal of the adjusting entry made by debiting the credits and crediting the debits. For example, consider the following transactions and their effect on the T account for interest expense:

Adjusting (A) entry

(A) Interest Expense	700		**Interest Expense**	
Accrued Interest Payable		700	(A) 700	

Closing (C) entry

(C) Income Summary	700		**Interest Expense**	
Interest Expense		700	(A) 700	(C) 700

Reversing (R) entry

(R) Accrued Interest Payable	700		**Interest Expense**	
Interest Expense		700	(A) 700	(C) 700
				(R) 700

Payment (P) entry

(P) Interest Expense	800		**Interest Expense**	
Cash		800	(A) 700	(C) 700
			(P) 800	(R) 700
			100	

The above transactions registered the following effects on interest expense:

A: Recorded $700 for Interest Expense in the proper accounting period.

C: Cleared the $700 to Income Summary, leaving a zero balance.

R: Set up a credit balance of $700 equal to expense recognized in previous period (also reduced the liability account Accrued Interest Payable to a zero balance).

P: Recorded the amount of payment, $800, as a debit to Interest Expense, automatically leaving a balance of $100, which represents the correct interest expense for the current period.

Making the payment entry was simplified by the reversing entry. Reversing entries apply to any accrued asset or liability. They do not apply to adjusting entries which adjust assets or liabilities that will not be offset by a payment or receipt in the next period. For example, reversing entries do not apply to adjustments for uncollectible accounts expense and depreciation expense. Nor do they apply to the adjustments for supplies, prepaid insurance, prepaid rent, and other prepaid assets if these items are recorded initially as assets. Finally, they do not apply to deferred revenues if these are recorded initially as liabilities.

Chapter Review

Review of Learning Objectives

1. Define liability and state the ways in which the problems of recognition, valuation, and classification apply to liabilities.

Liabilities represent present legal obligations of the firm for future payment of assets or the future performance of services. They result from past transactions and should be recognized when there is a transaction that obligates the company to make future payments. Liabilities are valued at the amount of money necessary to satisfy the obligation or the fair market value of goods or services that must be delivered. Liabilities are classified as current or long-term.

2. Identify, compute, and record definitely determinable and estimated current liabilities.

Two principal categories of current liabilities are definitely determinable liabilities and estimated liabilities. Although definitely determinable liabilities such as accounts payable, notes payable, dividends payable, accrued liabilities, and the current portion of long-term debt can be measured precisely, the accountant must still be careful not to overlook existing liabilities in these categories. Estimated liabilities such as liabilities for income taxes, property taxes, product warranties, and others definitely exist, but the amounts must be estimated and recorded properly.

3. Identify and compute the liabilities associated with payroll accounting.

Labor costs are a large segment of the total cost of most businesses. In addition, three important categories of liabilities are associated with the payroll. The employer is liable for the compensation to the employee, for withholdings from the employee's gross pay, and for the employer portion of payroll taxes. The most common payroll withholdings are the FICA tax, federal and state income taxes, and employee-requested withholdings. The principal employer-paid taxes are

FICA (an amount equal to that of the employee) and federal and state unemployment compensation taxes.

4. Record transactions associated with payroll accounting.
The salary and deductions for each employee are recorded each pay period in the payroll register. From the payroll register the details of each employee's earnings are transferred to the employee's earnings record. The column totals of the payroll register are used to prepare a general journal entry that records the payroll and accompanying liabilities. One further general journal entry is needed to record the employer's share of the FICA taxes and the federal and state unemployment taxes.

5. Apply internal control to the payroll system.
Because of the large amount of money involved and the possibility of fraud, good internal control is important for payroll systems. There should be a separation of duties for the following main payroll functions: the personnel function, the timekeeping function, the accounting function, and the distribution function.

6. Make reversing entries.
Reversing entries are reversals of adjusting entries that adjust assets or liabilities and that will be offset by a payment or receipt in the next period. They facilitate routine bookkeeping procedures.

Review Problem
Notes Payable Transactions and End-of-Period Entries

Rothwell and Shaffer, Inc., whose fiscal year ends June 30, completed the following transactions involving notes payable:

May 11	Purchased a printing press by issuing a 60-day, 9 percent note for $18,000. The face of the note does not include interest.
16	Obtained a $20,000 loan from the bank to finance a temporary increase in receivables by signing a 90-day, 10 percent note. The face value includes interest.
June 30	Made end-of-year adjusting entry to accrue interest expense.
30	Made end-of-year closing entry pertaining to interest expense.
July 1	Made appropriate reversing entry.
10	Paid the note plus interest on the printing press purchase.
Aug. 14	Paid off the note to the bank.

Required

1. Prepare general journal entries for the above transactions.
2. Open general ledger accounts for Notes Payable (212), Discount on Notes Payable (213), Accrued Interest Payable (214), and Interest Expense (721). Post the relevant portions of the entries to these general ledger accounts.

Answer to Review Problem

1. Journal entries prepared (facing page):

General Journal					Page 26
Date		**Description**	**Post. Ref.**	**Debit**	**Credit**
19xx					
May	11	Equipment		18,000	
		Notes Payable	212		18,000
		Purchase of printing press with 60-day, 9 percent note			
	16	Cash		19,500	
		Discount on Notes Payable	213	500	
		Notes Payable	212		20,000
		Loan from bank obtained by signing 90-day, 10 percent note; discount = $20,000 × .1 × 90/360 = $500			
June	30	Interest Expense	721	475	
		Discount on Notes Payable	213		250
		Accrued Interest Payable	214		225
		To accrue interest expense $500 × 45/90 = $250 $18,000 × .09 × 50/360 = $225			
	30	Income Summary		475	
		Interest Expense	721		475
		To close interest expense			
July	1	Discount on Notes Payable	213	250	
		Accrued Interest Payable	214	225	
		Interest Expense	721		475
		To reverse interest expense adjustment			
	10	Notes Payable	212	18,000	
		Interest Expense	721	270	
		Cash			18,270
		Payment of note on equipment $18,000 × .09 × 60/360 = $270			
Aug.	14	Notes Payable	212	20,000	
		Cash			20,000
		Payment of bank loan			
	14	Interest Expense	721	500	
		Discount on Notes Payable	213		500
		To record interest expense on notes payable			

2. Accounts opened and amounts posted:

Notes Payable — **Account No. 212**

Date		Item	Post. Ref.	Debit	Credit	Balance Debit	Balance Credit
May	11		J26		18,000		18,000
	16		J26		20,000		38,000
July	10		J26	18,000			20,000
Aug.	14		J26	20,000			—

Discount on Notes Payable — **Account No. 213**

Date		Item	Post. Ref.	Debit	Credit	Balance Debit	Balance Credit
May	16		J26	500		500	
June	30		J26		250	250	
July	1		J26	250		500	
Aug.	14		J26		500	—	

Accrued Interest Payable — **Account No. 214**

Date		Item	Post. Ref.	Debit	Credit	Balance Debit	Balance Credit
June	30		J26		225		225
July	1		J26	225			—

Interest Expense — **Account No. 721**

Date		Item	Post. Ref.	Debit	Credit	Balance Debit	Balance Credit
June	30		J26	475		475	
	30		J26		475	—	
July	1		J26		475		475
	10		J26	270			205
	14		J26	500		295	

Chapter Assignments

Questions

1. What are liabilities?
2. Why is the timing of liability recognition an important consideration in accounting?
3. At the end of the accounting period, Morris Paving Company had a legal obligation to accept delivery and pay for a load of gravel the following week. Is this legal obligation a liability?
4. Ned Johnson, a star college basketball player, received a contract calling for a salary of $300,000 a year for four years from the Midwest Blazers to play professional basketball. Should this contract be considered a liability and recorded on the books of the basketball team?
5. What is the rule for determining a current liability?
6. Where should the Discount on Notes Payable account appear on the balance sheet?
7. When can a portion of long-term debt be classified as a current liability?
8. Why are deferred revenues classified as liabilities?
9. What is definite about an estimated liability?
10. Why are income taxes payable considered to be estimated liabilities?
11. When does a company incur a liability for a product warranty?
12. Why is payroll accounting important?
13. How does an employee differ from an independent contractor?
14. What are three types of payroll liabilities?
15. Upon whom is the FICA tax levied?
16. What role does the W-4 form play in determining the withholding for estimated federal income taxes?
17. What withholdings might an employee voluntarily request?
18. Why is an employee earnings record necessary, and how does it relate to the W-2 form?
19. How can the payroll register be used as a special-purpose journal?
20. What payroll functions should be separated for good internal control?
21. How can reversing entries aid the bookkeeping process?
22. To what types of adjustments do reversing entries apply? To what types do they not apply?

Classroom Exercises

Exercise 12-1 Interest Expense—Interest Not Included in Face of Note

On the first day of November, Carson Company borrows $10,000 from a bank on a note for sixty days at 10 percent interest.

Assuming that interest is not included in the face amount, prepare the following general journal entries: (1) November 1, recording of note; (2) November 30, accrual of interest expense; (3) November 30, closing entry; (4) December 1, reversing entry; (5) December 30, payment of note plus interest.

Exercise 12-2 Interest Expense—Interest Included in Face of Note

Assuming the same facts as in Exercise 12-1, except that interest *is* included in the face amount of the note, prepare the following general journal entries: (1) November 1, recording of note; (2) November 30, accrual of interest expense; (3) November 30, closing entry; (4) December 1, reversing entry; (5) December 30, payment of note.

Exercise 12-3 Excise and Sales Taxes

Continental Telephone billed its customers for the month of June for a total of $2,280,000, including 9 percent federal excise tax and 5 percent state sales tax.

1. Determine the proper amount of revenue to report for the month.
2. Prepare a general journal entry to record the revenue and related liabilities for the month.

Exercise 12-4 Vacation Pay Liability

Jupiter Corporation currently allows each employee three weeks' paid vacation after working at the company for one year. On the basis of studies of employee turnover and previous experience, management estimates that 80 percent of the employees will qualify for vacation pay this year.

1. Assuming that the February payroll for Jupiter is $200,000, compute the estimated employee benefit for the month.
2. Prepare a general journal entry to record the employee benefit for the month of February.

Exercise 12-5 Payroll Transactions

Bill Matthews earns a salary of $30,000 during the year. FICA taxes are 6.65 percent up to $29,700. Federal unemployment insurance taxes are 3.4 percent of the first $6,000; however, a credit is allowed equal to the state unemployment insurance taxes of 2.7 percent on the first $6,000. During the year, $8,300 was withheld for federal income taxes.

1. Prepare a general journal entry summarizing the payment of $30,000 to Matthews during the year.
2. Prepare a general journal entry summarizing the payment of employer payroll taxes on Matthews's salary for the year.
3. Determine the total cost of employing Matthews for the year.

Exercise 12-6 Net Pay Calculation and Payroll Entries

Janice Watkins is an employee whose overtime pay is regulated by the Fair Labor Standards Act. Her hourly rate is $4.50, and during the week ended May 11 she worked forty-six hours. Janice claims two exemptions, including herself, on her W-4 form. So far this year she has earned $6,300. Each week $8 is deducted from her paycheck for medical insurance.

1. Compute the following items related to the pay for Janice Watkins for the week of May 11: (a) gross pay, (b) FICA taxes (assume a rate of 6.65 percent), (c) federal income tax withholding (use Figure 12-4), and (d) net pay.
2. Prepare a general journal entry to record the wages expense and related liabilities for Janice Watkins for the week ended May 11.

Exercise 12-7 Identification of Reversing Entries

Jaymax Company uses the reversing entry procedure. State which of the following adjusting entries in the company's records require a corresponding reversing entry: (a) a debit to Salary Expense and a credit to Accrued Salaries Payable, (b) a debit to Depreciation Expense and a credit to Accumulated Depreciation, (c) a debit to Accrued Interest Receivable and a credit to Interest income, (d) a debit to Uncollectible Accounts Expense and a credit to Allowance for Uncollectible Accounts.

Exercise 12-8 Product Warranty Liability

Atox Electronics manufactures and sells electronic calculators. Each calculator costs $30 and sells for $50. In addition, each calculator carries a warranty that provides for free replacement if it fails for any reason during the two years following the sale. In the past, 6 percent of the calculators sold had to be replaced under the warranty. During September, Atox sold 12,000 calculators and 650 calculators were replaced under the warranty.

1. Prepare a general journal entry to record the estimated liability for product warranties during the month.
2. Prepare a general journal entry to record the calculators replaced under warranty during the month.

Exercise 12-9 Property Tax Liability

Tristan Corporation accrues estimated liabilities for property taxes. The company's fiscal year ends January 31. The estimated property taxes for the year are $24,000. The bill for property taxes is usually received on April 1 and is due on June 1.

Prepare general journal entries for the following: February 28, accrual of property tax expense; March 31, accrual of property tax expense; April 30, accrual of property tax expense, assuming that the actual bill is $24,600; May 31, accrual of property tax expense; June 1, payment of property taxes; June 30, accrual of property tax expense.

Problem Set A

Problem 12A-1 Payroll Entries

The following payroll totals for the month of March were taken from the payroll register of Thomas Corporation: sales salaries, $13,200; office salaries, $6,450; general salaries, $7,110; FICA taxes withheld, $1,780; income taxes withheld, $4,380; medical insurance deductions, $980; life insurance deductions, $470; salaries subject to unemployment taxes, $18,450.

Required

Prepare general journal entries to record the following: (1) accrual of the monthly payroll, (2) payment of the net payroll, (3) accrual of employer's payroll taxes (assuming an FICA tax equal to the amount for employees, a federal unemployment insurance tax of .7 percent, and a state unemployment tax of 2.7 percent), and (4) payment of all liabilities related to the payroll (assuming that all are settled at the same time).

Problem 12A-2 Product Warranty Liability

Rome Company is engaged in the retail sale of television sets. Each set has a twenty-four-month warranty on parts. If a repair under warranty is required, a charge for the labor is made. Management has found that 20 percent of the sets sold require some warranty work before the twenty-four months pass. Furthermore, the average cost of replacement parts has been $30 per repair. At the beginning of October, the account for the estimated liability for product warranties had a credit balance of $5,340. During October, 30 sets were returned under the warranty. The cost of the parts used in repairing the sets was $856, and $918 was collected as service revenue for the labor involved. Also, during the month, 110 new sets were sold.

Required

1. Prepare general journal entries to record each of the following: (a) the warranty work completed during the month including related revenue; (b) the estimated liability for product warranties for sets sold during the month.
2. Compute the balance of the estimated product warranty liabilities at the end of the month.

Problem 12A-3 Notes Payable Transactions and End-of-Period Entries

Sanford Corporation, whose fiscal year ends April 30, completed the following transactions involving notes payable:

Mar. 11 Signed a 90-day, 9 percent, $20,000 note payable to Madison Bank for a working capital loan. The face value included interest.
21 Obtained a 60-day extension on a $12,000 trade account payable owed to a supplier by signing a 60-day, $12,000 note. Interest is in addition to the face value at the rate of 12 percent.
Apr. 30 Made end-of-year adjusting entry to accrue interest expense.
30 Made end-of-year closing entry pertaining to interest expense.
May 1 Made appropriate reversing entry.
20 Paid off the note plus interest due the supplier.
June 9 Paid amount due bank on 90-day note.

Required

1. Prepare general journal entries for the above transactions.
2. Open general ledger accounts for Notes Payable (212), Discount on Notes Payable (213), Accrued Interest Payable (214), and Interest Expense (721). Post the relevant portions of the entries to these general ledger accounts.

Problem 12A-4 Property Tax and Vacation Pay Liabilities

Continental Corporation prepares monthly financial statements and ends its fiscal year on September 30. In October, your first month as accountant for the company, you find that the company has not previously accrued estimated liabilities. In the past, the company, which has a large property taxes bill, has charged property taxes to the month in which the bill is paid. The tax bill for the previous year was $16,500, and it is estimated that the tax will increase by 12 percent in the coming year. The December tax bill is usually received on December 1, to be paid February 1. You also discover that the company allows employees who have worked for the company for one year to take two weeks' paid vacation each year. The cost of these vacations had been charged to expense in the month of payment. Approximately 70 percent of the employees qualify for this benefit.

You suggest to management that proper accounting treatment for these expenses is to spread their cost over the entire year. Management agrees and asks you to make the proper adjustments.

Required

1. Compute the proper monthly charge to property taxes expense, and prepare general journal entries for the following:

Oct. 31 Accrual of property taxes expense
Nov. 30 Accrual of property taxes expense
Dec. 31 Accrual of property taxes expense, assuming the actual tax bill is $18,960
Jan. 31 Accrual of property taxes expense
Feb. 1 Payment of property taxes
28 Accrual of property taxes expense

2. Assume that for October the total payroll is $106,000 and that $3,700 was paid to employees who were on vacation. (a) Compute the vacation pay expense for October. (b) Prepare a general journal entry to record the accrual of vacation pay expense for October. (c) Prepare a general journal entry to record the wages of employees on vacation in October (ignore payroll deductions and taxes).

Problem 12A-5 FICA and Unemployment Taxes

Hershel Company is subject to a 2.7 percent state unemployment insurance tax and a .7 percent federal unemployment insurance tax after credits. Currently, both federal and state unemployment taxes apply to the first $6,000 earned by each employee. FICA taxes in effect at this time are 6.65 percent for both employee and employer on the first $29,700 earned by each employee during this year.

During the current year, the cumulative earnings for each employee of the company are as follows:

Employee	Cumulative Earnings	Employee	Cumulative Earnings
Boucher, J.	$12,356	Furtado, C.	$ 7,680
Chan, B.	3,216	Lang, R.	3,760
Danbury, B.	15,608	Maloney, C.	19,626
Novak, J.	14,206	Schwartz, J.	13,600
Optin, T.	30,614	Thomas, P.	11,845
Perkins, B.	3,619	Weiss, W.	4,186

Required

1. Prepare and complete a schedule with the following columns: Employee Name, Cumulative Earnings, Earnings Subject to FICA Taxes, Earnings Subject to Unemployment Taxes. Total the columns.
2. Compute the FICA taxes and the federal and state unemployment taxes.

Problem 12A-6 Comprehensive Payroll Register and Related Entries

Seven Services Corporation has seven employees. The salaried employees are paid on the last biweekly payday of each month. Employees paid hourly receive a set rate for regular hours plus one and one-half times their hourly rate for overtime hours, and are paid every two weeks. The employees and company are subject to 6.65 percent FICA taxes on the first $29,700 earned by each employee. The unemployment insurance tax rates are 2.7 percent for the state and .7 percent for the federal government. The unemployment insurance tax applies to the first $6,000 earned by each employee and is levied only on the employer.

The company maintains a supplemental benefit plan that includes medical insurance, life insurance, and additional retirement funds for employees. Under the plan, each employee contributes 5 percent of his or her gross income as a payroll withholding, and the company matches this amount.

Data for the November 30 payroll, the last payday of November, follow:

Employee	Hours		Pay Rate	Cumulative Gross Pay Excluding Current Pay Period	Federal Income Tax to Be Withheld
	Regular	Overtime			
* Aaron, H.	80	10	$ 4.50	$ 2,940.00	$ 50.80
* Bench, J.	Salary		1,380.00	13,800.00	260.40
Fingers, R.	80	6	6.50	3,810.00	74.00
Hunter, C.	80		4.75	7,400.00	30.60
Mays, W.	Salary		950.00	9,500.00	140.80
Ruth, B.	80	12	5.00	8,220.00	66.60
* Thompson, B.	Salary		1,420.00	14,200.00	200.50

*Denotes administrative; the rest are sales.

Required:

1. Prepare a payroll register for the pay period ended November 30. The payroll register should have the following columns:

Employee	Deductions
Total Hours	FICA Tax
Earnings	Federal Income Tax
Regular	Supplemental Benefits Plan
Overtime	Payment
Gross	Distribution
Cumulative	Sales Expense
	Administrative Expense

2. Prepare a general journal entry to record the payroll and related liabilities for deductions for the period ended November 30.
3. Prepare general journal entries to record the expenses and related liabilities for the employer's payroll taxes and contribution to the supplemental benefit plan.

Problem Set B

Problem 12B-1 Payroll Entries

At the end of September, the payroll register for McMurtry Corporation contained the following totals: sales salaries, $27,270; office salaries, $14,680; administrative salaries, $17,240; FICA taxes withheld, $3,936; federal income taxes withheld, $14,914; state income taxes withheld, $2,396; medical insurance deductions, $2,115; life insurance deductions, $1,862; union dues deductions, $216; salaries subject to unemployment taxes, $8,940.

Required

Prepare general journal entries to record the following: (1) accrual of the monthly payroll, (2) payment of the net payroll, (3) accrual of employer's payroll taxes (assuming an FICA tax equal to the amount for employees, a federal unemployment insurance tax of .7 percent, and a state unemployment tax of 2.7 percent), (4) payment of all liabilities related to the payroll (assuming that all are settled at the same time).

Problem 12B-2 Product Warranty Liability

Turner Tire Company guarantees the tires it sells until they wear out. If a tire fails, the customer is charged a percentage of the retail price based on the percentage of the tire that is worn, plus a service charge for putting the tire on the car. In the past, management found that only 2 percent of the tires sold required replacement under warranty, and of those replaced an average 20 percent of the cost is collected under the percentage pricing system. The average tire costs the company $35. At the beginning of July, the account for estimated liability for product warranties had a credit balance of $22,746. During July, 125 tires were returned under the warranty. The cost of the replacement tires was $4,625, of which $1,125 was recovered under the percentage-worn formula. Service revenue amounted to $531. During the month, the company sold 3,525 tires.

Required

1. Prepare general journal entries to record each of the following: (a) the warranty work completed during the month including related revenue; (b) the estimated liability for product warranties for tires sold during the month.
2. Compute the balance of the estimated product warranty liabilities at the end of the month.

Problem 12B-3 Notes Payable Transactions and End-of-Period Entries

DeLaMar Company, whose fiscal year ends September 30, completed the following transactions involving notes payable:

Aug. 16	Purchased a new special-purpose truck by issuing a 90-day, 11 percent note for $14,000. The note is to be paid in full plus interest.
Sept. 10	Borrowed $30,000 from the bank to finance a temporary increase in inventory by signing a 60-day, 10 percent note. The face value includes interest.
30	Made end-of-year adjusting entry to accrue interest expense.
30	Made end-of-year closing entry pertaining to interest expense.
Oct. 1	Made appropriate reversing entry.
Nov. 9	Paid off the note to the bank.
14	Paid off the note plus interest in the truck purchase.

Required

1. Prepare general journal entries for the above transactions.
2. Open general ledger accounts for Notes Payable (212), Discount on Notes Payable (213), Accrued Interest Payable (214), and Interest Expense (721). Post the relevant portions of the entries to these general ledger accounts.

Problem 12B-4 Property Tax and Vacation Pay Liabilities

It is the policy of Grand Junction Company to accrue estimated liabilities for property taxes and for vacation pay. The company's fiscal year ends February 28. It is now March, the first month of the new fiscal year, and data are being gathered for the computation of estimated liabilities. The property taxes for the previous year were $33,000 and are expected to increase by 6 percent in the current year. The bill for property taxes is usually received near May 1, to be paid July 1. In addition, the company allows employees two weeks' paid vacation each year. In the past, 80 percent of the employees qualified for this benefit.

Required

1. Compute the proper monthly charge to property taxes expense, and prepare general journal entries for the following:

Mar. 31	Accrual of property taxes expense
Apr. 30	Accrual of property taxes expense
May 31	Accrual of property taxes expense, assuming the actual tax bill is $34,860
June 30	Accrual of property taxes expense
July 1	Payment of property taxes
31	Accrual of property taxes expense

2. Assume that for March the total payroll was $89,000 and that $1,972 was paid to employees who were on paid vacations. (a) Compute the vacation pay expense for March. (b) Prepare a general journal entry to record the accrual of vacation pay expense for March. (c) Prepare a general journal entry to record the wages of employees on vacation in March (ignore payroll deductions and taxes).

Problem 12B-6 Comprehensive Payroll Register and Related Entries

Sobel Machinery Company has eight employees, two of whom are administrators and are paid a monthly salary. The other six employees are sales personnel who are paid a set rate for regular hours plus two times their hourly rate for overtime hours. Hourly employees are paid once a week. The employees and employer are subject to 6.65 percent FICA taxes on the first $29,700 earned by each employee. The unemployment insurance tax rates are 2.7 percent for the state and .7

percent for the federal government. The unemployment insurance tax applies to the first $6,000 earned by each employee and is levied only on the employer.

Each employee qualifies for a supplemental benefit plan that includes medical insurance, life insurance, and additional retirement funds. Under this plan, each employee contributes 6 percent of his or her gross income as a payroll withholding, and the company matches this amount.

The data for the last pay day of October are as follows:

Employee	Hours Regular	Hours Overtime	Pay Rate	Cumulative Gross Pay Excluding Current Pay Period	Federal Income Tax to Be Withheld
Arden, C.	40	4	$ 8.00	$14,350.00	$ 40.50
Flemming, J.	40		7.75	11,275.00	20.75
Krasprozycki, E.	Salary		1,960.00	17,640.00	410.50
Marcum, D.	40	10	8.50	4,060.00	35.60
Rossi, M.	40	6	8.50	1,962.00	60.50
Stark, M.	40		8.00	7,219.00	23.00
Throop, D.	Salary		1,650.00	14,850.00	240.00
Zinga, A.	40	1	6.00	8,292.00	30.00

Required

1. Prepare a payroll register for the pay period ended October 31. The payroll register should have the following columns:

Employee
Total Hours
Earnings
  Regular
  Overtime
  Gross
  Cumulative
Deductions
  FICA Tax
  Federal Income Tax
  Supplemental Benefits Plan
Payment
Distribution
  Sales Expense
  Administrative Expense

2. Prepare a general journal entry to record the payroll and related liabilities for deductions for the period ended October 31.

3. Prepare general journal entries to record the expenses and related liabilities for the employer's payroll taxes and contribution to the supplemental benefit plan.

Learning Objectives

Chapter Thirteen

Property, Plant, and Equipment

1. *Define types of long-term nonmonetary assets.*
2. *Account for the cost of long-term nonmonetary assets.*
3. *Define depreciation and relate it to depletion and amortization.*
4. *Compute and record periodic depreciation under the (a) straight-line method, (b) production method, and (c) accelerated methods, including (1) sum-of-the-years'-digits method and (2) declining-balance method.*
5. *Apply depreciation methods to problems of partial years, revised rates, items of small unit value, and groups of similar items.*
6. *Account for disposal of depreciable assets.*
7. *Record property, plant, and equipment transactions in the plant asset records.*
8. *Identify the accounting issues associated with natural resources and compute depletion.*

In this chapter, we discuss the accounting treatment of long-term nonmonetary assets. In particular, we consider the major categories of plant assets and natural resources, accounting for their acquisition cost, their use over time through depreciation or depletion, and their disposal. As a result of studying this chapter, you should be able to meet the learning objectives listed on the left.

Long-Term Nonmonetary Assets

Long-term nonmonetary assets (or simply long-term assets) are assets that (1) have a useful life of more than one year, (2) are acquired for use in the operation of the business, and (3) are not intended for resale to customers. These assets are usually classified on the balance sheet as property, plant, and equipment, or some combination of these categories. For many years, it was common to refer to long-term assets as **fixed assets,** but this terminology is no longer in wide use because the word *fixed* implies that they last forever.

Although there is no strict minimum length of time for an asset to be classified as long-term, the most common criterion is that the asset must be capable of repeated use for a period of at least a year. Included in this category is equipment that is used only in peak or emergency periods.

Assets not used in the normal course of business should not be included in this category. Thus land held for speculative reasons or buildings abandoned and no longer used in the ordinary business operations should not be included in the property, plant, and equipment category. Instead, they should be classified as long-term investments.

Finally, if an item is held for resale to customers, it should be classified as inventory—not plant and equipment—no matter how durable it is. For example, a printing press held for sale by a printing press manufacturer would be considered inventory, whereas the same printing press would be plant and equipment for a printing company that buys the press to use in its operations.

Life of Long-Term Nonmonetary Assets

Objective 1 Define types of long-term nonmonetary assets

The primary accounting problem in dealing with short-term nonmonetary assets was to determine how much of the asset benefited the current period and how much should be carried forward as an asset to benefit future periods. This problem was common to inventory and prepaid expenses. Note that exactly the same problem applies to long-term assets because they are long-term unexpired costs.

It is helpful to think of a long-term nonmonetary asset as a bundle of services that are to be used in the operation of the business over a period of years. A delivery truck may provide 100,000 miles of service over its life. A piece of equipment may have the potential to produce 500,000 parts. A building may provide shelter for fifty years. As each of these assets is purchased, the company is paying in advance (prepaying) for 100,000 miles, 500,000 parts, or fifty years of service. In essence, each of these assets is a type of long-term prepaid expense. The accounting problem is to spread the cost of these services over the useful life of the asset. As the services benefit the company over the years, the cost becomes an expense rather than an asset. The expense is called depreciation expense in the case of plant, buildings, and equipment; depletion expense in the case of natural resources; and amortization expense in the case of intangible assets.

Types of Long-Term Nonmonetary Assets

Long-term nonmonetary assets are customarily divided into the following categories:

Asset	Expense
Tangible Assets	
Land	None
Plant, building, and equipment (plant assets)	Depreciation
Natural resources	Depletion
Intangible Assets	Amortization

Tangible assets have physical substance. Land is a tangible asset, and because it has an unlimited life it is the only asset not subject to depreciation or other expense. Plant, buildings, and equipment (referred to hereafter as plant assets) are subject to depreciation. Depreciation refers to periodic allocation of the cost of a tangible long-lived asset over its useful life. The term applies to manmade assets only. Note that accounting for depreciation is an allocation process, not a valuation process. This point is discussed in more detail later.

Natural resources differ from land in that they are purchased for the physical substance that can be taken from them and used up rather than for the value of their location. Natural resources include the ore from mines, the oil and gas from oil and gas fields, and timber from tracts of forest. Natural resources are subject to depletion rather than to depreciation. The term depletion refers to the exhaustion of a natural resource through mining, cutting, pumping, or otherwise using up the resource.

Intangible assets are long-term assets that do not have physical substance and usually refer to legal rights or advantages held. Examples are patents, copyrights, trademarks, franchises, organization costs, leaseholds, leasehold improvements, and goodwill. The process of allocating intangible assets to the periods they benefit is called amortization rather than depreciation or depletion. Although the current assets accounts receivable and prepaid expenses do not have physical substance, they are not considered intangible assets because they are not long-term.

Problems of Accounting for Long-Term Nonmonetary Assets

As with inventories and prepaid expenses, there are two basic accounting problems associated with long-term nonmonetary assets. The first is determining how much of the total cost should be allocated to expense in the current accounting period. The second is determining how much should remain on the balance sheet as an asset to benefit future periods. To solve these problems, four basic questions (illustrated in Figure 13-1) must be answered:

Figure 13-1 Problems of Accounting for Long-Term Assets

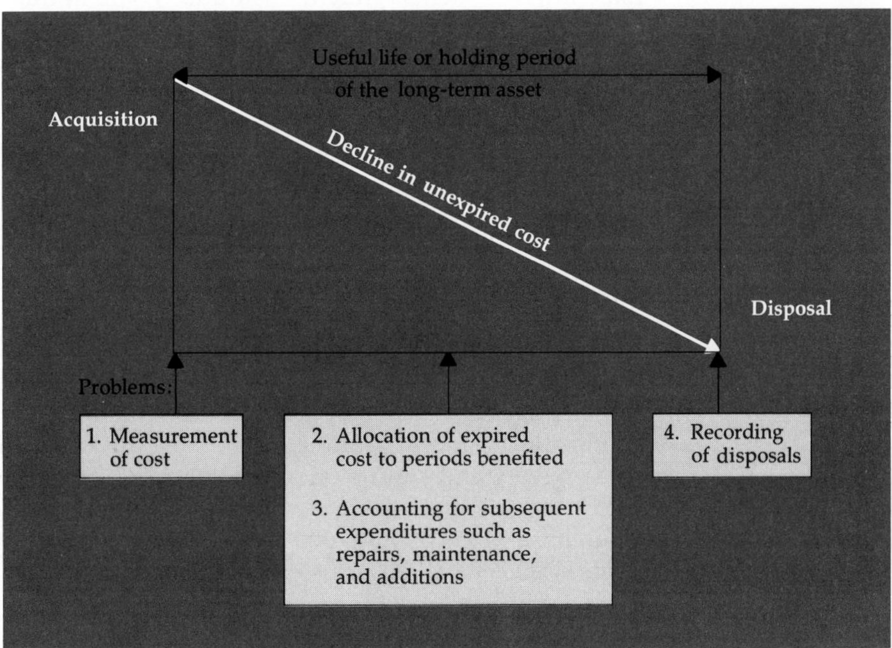

1. How is the cost of the long-term assets determined?
2. How should the expired portion of the cost of the long-term assets be allocated against revenues over time?
3. How should subsequent expenditures such as repairs, maintenance, and additions be treated?
4. How should disposal of long-term assets be recorded?

The rest of this chapter deals with the answers to questions 1, 2, and 4 for plant assets. The discussion of question 3 is deferred until Chapter 14 because expenditures for repairs, maintenance, and additions complicate the basic accounting treatment of long-term assets presented in this chapter. Specific discussion of intangibles is also in Chapter 14.

Acquisition Cost of Property, Plant, and Equipment

Objective 2 Account for the cost of long-term nonmonetary assets

The acquisition cost of property, plant, and equipment includes all expenditures reasonable and necessary to get them in place and ready for use. For example, the cost of installing and testing a machine is a legitimate cost of the machine. However, if the machine is damaged during installation, the cost of repairing the machine is not a cost of the machine.

Cost is easiest to determine when a transaction is made for cash. In this case, the cost of the asset is equal to the cash outlay for the asset plus expenditures for freight, insurance while in transit, installation, and other necessary related costs. If a debt is incurred in the purchase of the asset, the interest charges are not a cost of the asset but are a cost of borrowing the money to buy the asset. They are therefore an expense for the period.

Expenditures such as freight, insurance while in transit, and installation are included in the cost of the asset because these expenditures are necessary for the asset to function. In accordance with the matching rule, therefore, they are allocated to the useful life of the asset rather than charged as an expense in the current period.

Some of the problems of determining the cost of a long-lived asset are demonstrated in the illustrations for land, buildings, equipment, land improvements, and group purchases presented in the next few sections.

Land

In buying land, expenditures in addition to the price of the land often arise that should be debited to the Land account. These include commission to real estate agents; legal fees; accrued taxes paid by the purchaser; cost of draining, clearing, and grading; and assessments for local improvements such as streets and sewage systems.

Let us assume that a company buys a site for a new retail location for a net purchase price of $170,000, pays brokerage fees of $6,000 and legal fees of $2,000, pays $10,000 to have an old building on the site razed, receives $4,000 salvage from the old building, and pays $1,000 to have the site graded. The cost of the land will be $185,000, determined as follows:

Net purchase price		$170,000
Brokerage fees		6,000
Legal fees		2,000
Razing old building	$10,000	
Less salvage	4,000	6,000
Grading		1,000
		$185,000

Sometimes land and buildings will be purchased for a lump sum. Because land is a nondepreciable asset and has an unlimited life, separate ledger accounts must be maintained for land and buildings. Thus the lump-sum purchase price must be apportioned between the land and the building. This is usually accomplished by making an appraisal of the land and building and apportioning the purchase price accordingly.

Building

When an existing building is purchased, its cost includes the purchase price plus all repair and renovation expenses required to put it in usable condition. When a business constructs its own building, the cost includes all reasonable and necessary expenditures, such as those for materials, labor, a proportionate share of overhead and other indirect costs, architectural fees, insurance during construction, legal fees, and building permits. If outside contractors are used in the construction, the net contract price plus additional expenditures necessary to put the building in usable condition are included.

Equipment

The cost of equipment includes all expenditures incurred in purchasing the equipment and preparing it for use. These expenditures include invoice price less cash discounts; freight and transportation, including insurance; excise taxes and tariffs; buying expenses; installation costs; and test runs to ready the equipment for operation.

Land Improvements

Improvements to real estate such as driveways, parking lots, and fences have a limited life and are therefore subject to depreciation. They should be recorded in an account entitled Land Improvements rather than in the Land account.

Group Purchases

Often, a combination or group of long-term assets will be purchased for a lump-sum payment. In this case, the total purchase price must be apportioned among the assets acquired. For example, assume that a building and the land on which it is situated are purchased for a lump-sum payment of $85,000. The apportionment can be made by determining the price of each if purchased separately and applying the appropriate percentages to the lump-sum price. Assume that appraisals yield estimates of $10,000 for the land and $90,000 for the building if purchased separately. In that case, 10 percent, or $8,500, of the lump-sum price would be allocated to the land and 90 percent, or $76,500, would be allocated to the building, as shown below.

	Appraisal	Percentage	Apportionment
Land	$ 10,000	10	$ 8,500
Building	90,000	90	76,500
Totals	$100,000	100	$85,000

Accounting for Depreciation

Depreciation accounting is described by the AICPA as follows:

Objective 3 Define depreciation and relate it to depletion and amortization

> The cost of a productive facility is one of the costs of the services it renders during its useful economic life. Generally accepted accounting principles require that this cost be spread over the expected useful life of the facility in such a way as to allocate it as equitably as possible to the periods during which services are obtained from the use of the facility. This procedure is known as depreciation accounting, a system of accounting which aims to distribute the cost or other basic value of tangible capital assets, less salvage (if any), over the estimated useful life of the unit . . . in a systematic and rational manner. It is a process of allocation, not of valuation.[1]

This description contains several important points. First, all tangible assets except land—that is, plant and equipment assets—eventually wear out or become obsolete. Thus the cost of these assets must be distributed as expenses over the years that they benefit.

Second, the term *depreciation,* as used in accounting, does not mean the physical deterioration of an asset or the decrease in market value of an asset over time. Depreciation means the allocation of the cost of a plant asset to the periods that benefit from the services of the asset. The term is used to describe the gradual conversion of the cost of the asset into an expense.

Third, depreciation is not a process of valuation. Accounting records are kept in accordance with the cost principle and thus are not meant to be indicators of changing price levels. It is possible that, through an advantageous buy and specific market conditions, the market value of a building may rise. Nevertheless, depreciation must continue to be recorded because it is the result of an allocation, not a valuation, process. Eventually the building will wear out or become obsolete regardless of interim fluctuations in market value.

1. *Financial Accounting Standards: Original Pronouncements as of July 1, 1977* (Stamford, Conn.: Financial Accounting Standards Board, 1977), ARB No. 43, Chap. 9, Sec. C, par. 5.

Causes of Limited Useful Life

There are two major causes of the limited useful life of a depreciable asset: physical deterioration and obsolescence.

Physical Deterioration The physical deterioration of tangible assets results from use and from exposure to the elements, such as wind and sun. Periodic repairs and a sound maintenance policy may keep buildings and equipment in good running order or "as good as new" and extract the maximum useful life from them, but every machine or building at some point must be discarded. The need for depreciation is not eliminated by repairs.

Obsolescence The process of becoming out of date is called obsolescence. With fast-changing technology as well as fast-changing demands, machinery and even buildings often become obsolete before they wear out. Most companies consider about five years to be the useful life of a computer because they know that, although it will continue to work, it will be displaced by newer models that are technically better. In some cases, a machine may become inadequate because it cannot handle an expanded volume of activity. Some buildings used in retail businesses become obsolete because of shifts in population. Accountants do not distinguish between physical deterioration and obsolescence because they are interested in the length of the useful life of the asset regardless of what limits that useful life.

Recording Depreciation in the Accounts

When a depreciable asset is purchased, it is debited to an asset account. Depreciation is recorded by debiting Depreciation Expense and crediting Accumulated Depreciation. Accumulated Depreciation is a contra-asset account, and its balance is deducted from the asset account on the balance sheet in a manner similar to the way the Allowance for Uncollectible Accounts is deducted from Accounts Receivable. Furthermore, it is a permanent account that lasts throughout the life of the asset.

For example, assume that a piece of office equipment was purchased on January 1 at a cost of $2,000. During the year, the depreciation was determined to be $400. The entries would be as follows:

Jan. 1	Office Equipment	2,000	
	Cash		2,000
	Purchase of office equipment		
Dec. 31	Depreciation Expense, Office Equipment	400	
	Accumulated Depreciation, Office Equipment		400
	To record depreciation for year		

The income statement would show Depreciation Expense, Office Equipment; the balance sheet would record Accumulated Depreciation, Office Equipment, as follows:

Office Equipment	$2,000	
Less Accumulated Depreciation	400	$1,600

The unexpired portion of the cost of an asset ($1,600 in the illustration) is usually called its book value or carrying value. The latter term is used in this book when referring to long-term nonmonetary assets.

A separate Depreciation Expense account and a separate Accumulated Depreciation account are generally maintained for each group of depreciable assets, such as building, store equipment, office equipment, and delivery equipment, so that proper allocation costs can be made among various business functions, such as manufacturing, selling, and general expenses.

Factors That Affect the Computation of Depreciation

The computation of depreciation for an accounting period is affected by (1) cost, (2) residual value, (3) depreciable cost, and (4) estimated useful life.

Cost As explained above, cost is the net purchase price plus all reasonable and necessary expenditures to get the asset in place and ready for use.

Residual Value The **residual value** of an asset is its estimated net scrap, salvage, or trade-in value as of the estimated date of disposal. Other terms often used are **salvage value** or **disposal value.**

Depreciable Cost The **depreciable cost** of an asset is its cost less its residual value. For example, a truck that costs $12,000 and has a residual value of $3,000 would have a depreciable cost of $9,000.

Estimated Useful Life The **estimated useful life** of an asset is the total number of service units expected from the asset. Service units may be measured in terms of years the asset is expected to be used, units expected to be produced, miles expected to be driven, or similar measures. In determining the estimated useful life of an asset, the accountant should consider all relevant information including (1) past experience with similar assets, (2) the asset's present condition, (3) the company's repair and maintenance policy, (4) current technological and industry trends, and (5) local conditions such as climate.

Methods of Computing Depreciation

Many methods are used to allocate the cost of a plant asset to accounting periods through depreciation. Each of them is appropriate for certain circumstances. The most common methods are (1) the straight-line method, (2) the production method, and (3) two accelerated methods known as the sum-of-the-years'-digits method and the declining-balance method.

Objective 4 Compute and record periodic depreciation under each of four methods

The **straight-line method** is based on the assumption that depreciation depends only on the passage of time. The **production method,** on the other hand, is based on the assumption that depreciation depends solely on how much an asset is used. Consequently, the straight-line method allocates the cost of an asset over its useful life regardless of use and, conversely, the production method ignores the passage of time and bases depreciation on use.

Accelerated methods result in relatively large amounts of depreciation in the early years and reduced amounts in later years. These methods, which are based on the passage of time, presume that many types of plant assets are most efficient when new and thus provide more and better service in the early years of useful life. It is consistent with the matching rule to allocate more depreciation to early years than to later years if the benefits or services received in the early years are greater.

The accelerated methods also recognize that changing technologies make some equipment lose service value rapidly. Thus it is realistic to allocate more to depreciation in current years than in future years. New inventions and products result in obsolescence of equipment purchased earlier, making it necessary to replace equipment sooner than if we had a static technology.

Another argument advanced in favor of accelerated methods is that repair expense is likely to be greater in future years than in current years. Consequently, the total of repair and depreciation expense is relatively constant over a period of years. This result naturally assumes that the services received from the asset are relatively equal from year to year.

Finally, accelerated methods are acceptable for tax purposes. The larger deductions for depreciation in the earlier years reduce the amount of income tax that must be paid in those years, effectively postponing the payment of the income tax until later years, when the depreciation deductions are smaller.

The depreciation methods used by six hundred large companies are illustrated in Figure 13-2 (next page).

Straight-Line Method

Objective 4a Compute and record periodic depreciation under the straight-line method

When the straight-line method is used to allocate depreciation, the depreciable cost of the asset is spread uniformly over the life of the asset. The depreciation expense for each period is calculated by dividing the depreciable cost (cost of the depreciating asset minus its residual value) by the number of accounting periods in the estimated useful life. For example, if a delivery truck costs $10,000 and has an estimated residual value of $1,000 at the end of its estimated useful life of five years, the annual

Figure 13-2 Depreciation Methods Used by 600 Large Companies

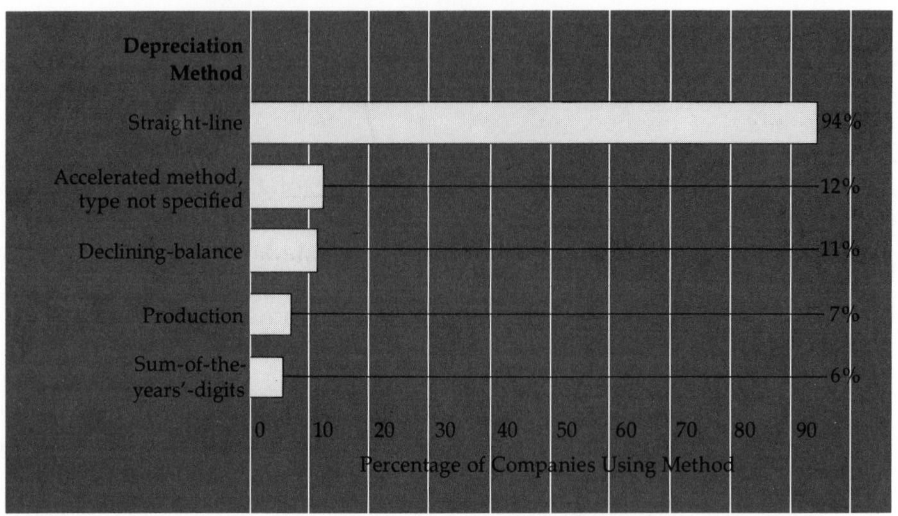

Total percentage exceeds 100 because some companies used different methods for different types of depreciable assets.
Source: American Institute of Certified Public Accountants, *Accounting Trends and Techniques* (New York: AICPA, 1978).

depreciation would be $1,800 under the straight-line method. This calculation is as follows:

$$\frac{\text{cost} - \text{residual value}}{\text{useful life}} = \frac{\$10,000 - \$1,000}{5} = \$1,800$$

The depreciation for the five years would be as follows:

Depreciation Schedule, Straight-Line Method

	Cost	Yearly Depreciation	Accumulated Depreciation	Carrying Value
Date of purchase	$10,000	—	—	$10,000
End of first year	10,000	$1,800	$1,800	8,200
End of second year	10,000	1,800	3,600	6,400
End of third year	10,000	1,800	5,400	4,600
End of fourth year	10,000	1,800	7,200	2,800
End of fifth year	10,000	1,800	9,000	1,000

There are three important points to note from the schedule for the straight-line depreciation method. First, the depreciation is the same each year. Second, the accumulated depreciation increases uniformly. Third, the carrying value decreases uniformly until it reaches the estimated residual value.

Production Method

The production method of depreciation on assets is based on the assumption that depreciation is solely the result of use and that the passage of time plays no role in the depreciation process. If we assume that the delivery truck from the example above has an estimated useful life of 90,000 miles, the depreciation cost per mile would be determined as follows:

Objective 4b Compute and record periodic depreciation under the production method

$$\frac{\text{cost} - \text{residual value}}{\text{estimated units of useful life}} = \frac{\$10{,}000 - \$1{,}000}{90{,}000 \text{ miles}} = \$.10 \text{ per mile}$$

If we assume that the mileage use of the truck was 20,000 miles for the first year, 30,000 miles for the second, 10,000 miles for the third, 20,000 miles for the fourth, and 10,000 miles for the fifth, the depreciation schedule for the delivery truck would appear as follows:

Depreciation Schedule, Production Method

	Cost	Miles	Yearly Deprecia- tion	Accumulated Deprecia- tion	Carrying Value
Date of purchase	$10,000	—	—	—	$10,000
End of first year	10,000	20,000	$2,000	$2,000	8,000
End of second year	10,000	30,000	3,000	5,000	5,000
End of third year	10,000	10,000	1,000	6,000	4,000
End of fourth year	10,000	20,000	2,000	8,000	2,000
End of fifth year	10,000	10,000	1,000	9,000	1,000

Note the direct relation between the amount of depreciation each year and the units of output or use. Also, the accumulated depreciation increases each year in direct relation to units of output or use. Finally, the carrying value decreases each year in direct relation to unit of output or use until it reaches the actual residual value.

Under the production method, the unit of output or use that is used to measure estimated useful life for each asset should be appropriate for that asset. For example, the number of items produced may be appropriate for one machine, whereas the number of hours of use may be a better indicator of depreciation for another.

Sum-of-the-Years'-Digits Method

As noted above, the accelerated methods of computing depreciation assume that an asset depreciates more in its early years than in its later years. Consequently, these methods result in more depreciation being charged to early years and a constantly decreasing amount being charged to subsequent years.

Objective 4c(1) Compute and record periodic depreciation under the sum-of-the-years'-digits method

Under the **sum-of-the-years'-digits method**, the years in the service life of an asset are added. Their sum becomes the denominator of a series of fractions, which are applied against the depreciable cost of the asset in allocating the total depreciation over the estimated useful life. The numerators of the fractions are the individual years in the estimated useful life of the asset in their reverse order.

For the delivery truck used in the previous illustrations, the estimated useful life is five years. The sum of the years' digits is as follows:[2]

$$1 + 2 + 3 + 4 + 5 = 15$$

The annual depreciation is then determined by multiplying each of the following fractions by the depreciable cost ($10,000 – $1,000): $5/15$, $4/15$, $3/15$, $2/15$, $1/15$. The depreciation schedule for the sum-of-the-years'-digits method is as follows:

Depreciation Schedule, Sum-of-the-Years'-Digits Method

	Cost	Yearly Depreciation		Accumulated Depreciation	Carrying Value
Date of purchase	$10,000	—		—	$10,000
End of first year	10,000	($5/15$ × $9,000)	$3,000	$3,000	7,000
End of second year	10,000	($4/15$ × $9,000)	2,400	5,400	4,600
End of third year	10,000	($3/15$ × $9,000)	1,800	7,200	2,800
End of fourth year	10,000	($2/15$ × $9,000)	1,200	8,400	1,600
End of fifth year	10,000	($1/15$ × $9,000)	600	9,000	1,000

From the schedule, note that the depreciation is greatest in the first year and declines each year thereafter. Also, the accumulated depreciation increases by a smaller amount in each succeeding year. Finally, the carrying value decreases each year by the amount of depreciation until it reaches the residual value.

Declining-Balance Method

Objective 4c(2) Compute and record periodic depreciation under the declining-balance method

The **declining-balance method** is based on the same assumption as the sum-of-the-years'-digits method. Both methods result in higher depreciation charges during the early years of a plant asset's life. Although any fixed rate might be used under the method, the most common rate is a percentage equal to twice the straight-line percentage. When twice the straight-line rate (the maximum rate allowable for federal tax purposes) is used, the method is usually referred to as the **double-declining-balance method.**

In our previous example, the delivery truck had an estimated useful life of five years. Consequently, under the straight-line method, the percent-

2. The denominator used in the sum-of-the-years'-digits method can be computed quickly from the following formula:

$$S = \frac{N(N + 1)}{2}$$

where S equals the sum of the digits and N equals the number of years in the estimated useful life. For example, for an asset with an estimated useful life of ten years, the sum of the digits equals 55, calculated as follows:

$$S = \frac{10(10 + 1)}{2} = \frac{110}{2} = 55$$

age depreciation for each year was 20 percent (100 percent ÷ 5 years). Under the double-declining-balance method, the fixed-percentage rate is therefore 40 percent (2 × 20 percent). This fixed rate of 40 percent is applied to the *remaining book value* at the end of each year. The estimated residual value is *not* taken into consideration in computing depreciation except in the last year, when depreciation is limited to the amount necessary to reduce the carrying value to the estimated residual value. The depreciation schedule for this method is shown below.

Depreciation Schedule, Declining-Balance Method

	Cost	Yearly Depreciation		Accumulated Depreciation	Carrying Value
Date of purchase	$10,000	—		—	$10,000
End of first year	10,000	(40% × $10,000)	$4,000	$4,000	6,000
End of second year	10,000	(40% × $6,000)	2,400	6,400	3,600
End of third year	10,000	(40% × $3,600)	1,440	7,840	2,160
End of fourth year	10,000	(40% × $2,160)	864	8,704	1,296
End of fifth year	10,000		296*	9,000	1,000

*Depreciation limited to amount necessary to reduce carrying value to residual value.

Note that the fixed rate is always applied to the carrying value of the previous year. Next, the depreciation is greatest in the first year and declines each year thereafter. Finally, the depreciation in the last year is limited to the amount necessary to reduce carrying value to residual value.

Comparing the Four Methods

To add perspective to the four methods of computing depreciation described above, Figure 13-3 (next page) graphically compares periodic depreciation, accumulated depreciation, and carrying value under the four methods. In the graph representing yearly depreciation, straight-line depreciation is uniform over the five-year period at $1,800, whereas both accelerated depreciation methods (sum-of-the-years'-digits and declining-balance) begin at amounts greater than straight-line ($3,000 and $4,000, respectively), and decrease each year to amounts less than straight-line ($600 and $296, respectively). The production method does not produce a regular pattern of depreciation because of the random fluctuation of the depreciation base from year to year. These yearly depreciation patterns are reflected in the carrying value and accumulated depreciation graphs. For instance, the carrying value for the straight-line method is always greater than that for the accelerated methods, and the accumulated depreciation for the straight-line method is always less than that for the accelerated methods. However, in the latter two graphs, each method starts in the same place (cost of $10,000 or 0) and ends at the same place (residual value of $1,000 or cost minus residual value of $9,000). It is the patterns during the life of the asset that are different.

Figure 13-3 Graphical Comparison of the Four Methods of Determining Depreciation

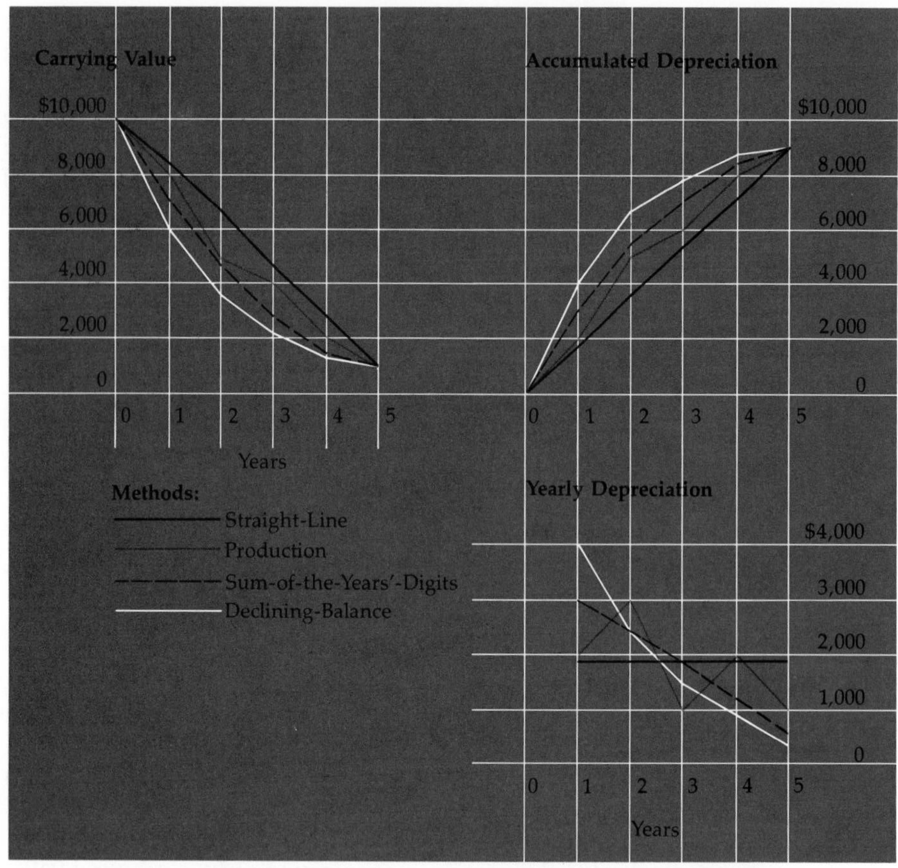

Special Problems of Depreciating Plant Assets

Objective 5 Apply depreciation methods to problems of partial years, revised rates, items of small unit value, and groups of similar items

The illustrations used thus far in this chapter have been simplified to explain the concepts and methods of depreciation. In actual business practice, there is often a need to (1) calculate depreciation for partial years, (2) revise the depreciation rates on the basis of new estimates of the useful life or residual value, (3) develop more practical ways of depreciating items of small unit value, and (4) group items of a similar nature together for the purpose of calculating depreciation. The sections below discuss these situations.

Depreciation for Partial Years

So far, the illustrations of the depreciation methods in this chapter have assumed that the plant assets were purchased and discarded at the beginning or end of the accounting period. However, business people rarely buy assets exactly at the beginning or end of the accounting period. They usually buy the assets when they are needed and sell or discard them when they are no longer usable or needed. The time of the year is normally not a factor in the decision. Consequently, it is often necessary to calculate depreciation for partial years.

For example, assume that a piece of equipment is purchased for $3,500 and that it has an estimated service life of six years, with an estimated residual value of $500 after that length of time. Assume also that it is purchased on September 5 and that the yearly accounting period ends on December 31. Depreciation must be recorded for four months, or four-twelfths of the year. This factor is applied to the calculated depreciation for the entire year. The four months' depreciation under the straight-line method is calculated as follows:

$$\frac{\$3{,}500 - \$500}{6 \text{ years}} \times \frac{4}{12} = \$166.67$$

Typically, the depreciation calculation is rounded off to the nearest whole month. In this case, depreciation was recorded from the beginning of September even though the purchase was made on September 5. If the equipment had been purchased on September 16 or thereafter, depreciation would be charged beginning October 1, as if the equipment were purchased on that date. Some companies round off all partial years to the nearest one-half year for ease of calculation.

When a plant asset is disposed of, the depreciation on this asset must be brought up to the date of disposal. For example, if the asset is not disposed of at the beginning or end of the year, depreciation must be recorded for a partial year, reflecting the time to the date of disposal. The accounting treatment of disposals is covered later in this chapter.

Revision of Depreciation Rates

Because depreciation rates are based on an estimate of the useful life of an asset, the periodic depreciation charge is seldom precisely accurate. Sometimes it is very inadequate or excessive. This situation may result from an underestimate or overestimate of the estimated useful life or perhaps a wrong estimate of the residual value. What action should be taken when it is found, after using a piece of equipment for several years, that the equipment will not last as long as—or will last longer than—originally thought? Sometimes it is necessary to make a revised estimate of the useful life that results in an increase or decrease in the periodic depreciation expense. In such a case, the method for correcting the depreciation program is to spread the undepreciated cost of the asset over the years of the remaining useful life.

Under this method, the annual depreciation expense is increased or decreased so that the subsequent depreciation of the asset will reduce the book value of the asset to residual value at the end of the remaining useful life. To illustrate, let us assume that a delivery truck was purchased for a price of $7,000, with a residual value of $1,000. At the time of the purchase, it was thought that the truck would last six years, and it was depreciated accordingly on the straight-line basis. However, after two years of intensive use, it is determined that the delivery truck will last only two more years and will continue to carry an estimated residual value of $1,000 at the end of the two years. In other words, at the end of the second year, the estimated useful life has been reduced from six years to four years. At that time, the asset account and its related accumulated depreciation account would appear as follows:

Delivery Truck	
Cost 7,000	

Accumulated Depreciation, Delivery Truck	
	Depreciation, year 1 1,000
	Depreciation, year 2 1,000

The remaining depreciable cost is computed as follows:

cost	minus	residual value	minus	depreciation already taken	
$7,000	−	$1,000	−	$2,000	= $4,000

The new annual periodic depreciation charge is computed by dividing the remaining depreciable costs of $4,000 by the remaining useful life of two years. Therefore, the new periodic depreciation charge is $2,000. The annual adjusting entry for depreciation for the next two years would be as follows:

		Debit	Credit
Dec. 31	Depreciation Expense, Delivery Truck	2,000	
	Accumulated Depreciation, Delivery Truck		2,000

This method of revising a depreciation program is used widely in industry and is acceptable in the determination of a taxable income. It is also supported by the Accounting Principles Board of the AICPA in Accounting Principles Board *Opinion No. 9* and *Opinion No. 20.*

Depreciation of Assets of Low Unit Cost

Some classes of plant assets are composed of numerous individual items of low unit cost. In this category are included small tools such as hammers, wrenches, and drills, as well as dyes, molds, patterns, and spare parts. Because of their large numbers, hard usage, breakage, and pilferage, assets such as these are relatively short-lived and require constant replacement. It is impractical to use the usual depreciation methods, and it is often costly to keep records of individual items.

There are two basic methods for accounting for plant assets of low unit cost. The first method is simply to charge the items as expenses when they are purchased. This method assumes that the annual loss on these items from use, depreciation, breakage, and other causes will approximately equal the amount of these items purchased during the year.

The second method used for plant assets of low unit cost is to account for them on an inventory basis. This method is best used when the amounts of items purchased vary greatly from year to year. The inventory basis of accounting for items of small unit value is very similar to the method of accounting for supplies, which you already know. Let us assume that a company account for spare parts on hand at the beginning of the accounting period is represented by a debit balance in the asset account Spare Parts. As spare parts are purchased during the accounting period, their cost is debited to this account. At the end of the period, a physical inventory of usable spare parts on hand in the factory is taken. This inventory amount is subtracted from the end-of-period balance in the Spare Parts account to determine the cost of spare parts lost, broken, and used during this period. This cost, assumed in this case to be $700, is then charged to an expense account as a work sheet adjustment with an adjusting entry as follows:

Dec. 31	Spare Parts Expense	700	
	Spare Parts		700
	To record cost of spare parts used or lost		

Group Depreciation

To say that the estimated useful life of an asset, such as a piece of equipment, is six years means that the average piece of equipment will last six years. In reality, some equipment may last only two or three years, and other equipment may last eight or nine years, or longer. For this reason and also for reasons of convenience, large companies will group items of similar plant assets together for purposes of calculating depreciation. This method is called **group depreciation.**

For example, a large milk company in a metropolitan area may have several hundred delivery trucks, all of a similar nature and with similar estimated useful lives. Rather than compute depreciation on each individual truck, the company accumulates the original cost of all the trucks in one summary account. Depreciation is then computed, not item by item, but for the group in total. The group rate is based on the average estimated life of the whole group. If the total cost of the delivery trucks was $2,400,000 and the average estimated useful life was six years, then under the straight-line method the annual depreciation charge would be $400,000. The declining-balance method may also be used in computing group depreciation.

Group depreciation is used widely in all fields of industry and business, including the utility and telephone industries, which use group depreciation for such assets as power lines, utility poles, and transformers.

Disposal of Depreciable Assets

Objective 6 Account for disposal of depreciable assets

When items of plant assets are no longer useful in a business because they are worn out or obsolete, they may be discarded, sold, or traded in on the purchase of new plant and equipment. Regardless of the method of disposal, it is necessary to bring the depreciation up to the date of disposal and to remove the book or carrying value of the asset from the accounts. This step is accomplished by debiting the Accumulated Depreciation account for the total depreciation to the date of disposal and crediting the asset account for the cost of the asset. (As defined above, the book or carrying value is the original cost of the asset minus the total recorded depreciation, as shown by the Accumulated Depreciation account.)

For example, the entry to record the disposal on January 2 of worthless equipment with a carrying value of $1,000 is as follows:

Jan. 2	Accumulated Depreciation, Store Equipment	1,000	
	Store Equipment		1,000
	Disposal of fully depreciated equipment no longer used in the business		

If an asset lasts longer than its estimated life and as a result is fully depreciated, as often occurs, it should not continue to be depreciated, nor should it be written off until it is actually disposed of. The purpose of depreciation is to spread the depreciable cost of the asset over the future life of the asset. Thus the total accumulated depreciation should never exceed the total depreciable cost. In addition, if the asset is still used in the business, this fact should be evidenced by its cost and accumulated depreciation remaining in the ledger accounts. Proper records will thus be available for maintaining control over plant assets.

Assumptions for the Comprehensive Illustration

For accounting purposes, a plant asset may be disposed of in three ways: (1) discarded, (2) sold for cash, or (3) exchanged for another asset. To illustrate how each of these cases is recorded, assume the following facts. MGC Corporation purchased a machine on January 1, 19x0, for $6,500 and depreciated it on a straight-line basis over an estimated useful life of ten years. The residual value at the end of ten years was estimated to be $500. On January 1, 19x7, the balances of the relevant accounts in the plant ledger appeared as follows:

Machinery		Accumulated Depreciation, Machinery	
6,500			4,200

On September 30, management disposed of the asset. The next few sections illustrate the accounting treatment to record depreciation for the fractional year and under the following assumptions:

1. Discarded the machinery

2. Sold the machinery for cash at (a) carrying value—$1,850, (b) less than carrying value—$1,000, or (c) more than carrying value—$2,000.

3. Exchanged the machinery for similar new machinery, with (a) loss recognized on the exchange (Accounting Principles Board Rule), (b) gain not recognized on the exchange (Accounting Principles Board Rule), or (c) gain or loss not recognized on the exchange (income tax rules).

Depreciation for Fractional Period Prior to Disposal

When items of plant assets are discarded or disposed of in some other way, it is necessary to record depreciation expense up to the date of disposal. This step is necessary because the asset was used until that date and under the matching rule the accounting period should receive the appropriate allocation of depreciation expense.

The depreciation expense for the fractional period prior to disposal is calculated in exactly the same way in which it is calculated for fractional period after purchase.

In the comprehensive illustration stated above, MGC Corporation disposes of the machinery on September 30. The entry to record the depreciation for the first nine months of 19x7 is as follows:

Sept. 30	Depreciation Expense, Machinery	450	
	Accumulated Depreciation, Machinery		450
	To record depreciation for nine months prior to disposal of machinery:		

$$\frac{\$6{,}500 - \$500}{10} \times \frac{9}{12} = \$450$$

The relevant accounts in the plant ledger accounts appear as follows after the entry is posted:

Machinery			Accumulated Depreciation, Machinery	
6,500				4,650

Recording Discarded Plant Assets

Although plant assets are depreciated over their estimated lives, they rarely last exactly as long as their estimated life. If they last longer than their estimated life, they are no longer depreciated. When they are discarded, the original cost equals accumulated depreciation plus residual value, as illustrated in the first section of this discussion above.

In the comprehensive illustration, however, the discarded equipment is not totally depreciated at the time of the disposal. When this situation occurs, a loss should be recorded upon the disposal as follows:

Sept. 30	Accumulated Depreciation, Machinery	4,650	
	Loss on Disposal of Machinery	1,850	
	Machinery		6,500
	Disposal of machine no longer used in the business		

Recording Plant Assets Sold for Cash

The entries to record an asset sold for cash are similar to the one illustrated above except that the receipt of cash should also be recorded. The following entries show how to record the sale of machinery under the three assumptions about the selling price:

Sept. 30	Cash	1,850	
	Accumulated Depreciation, Machinery	4,650	
	Machinery		6,500
	Sale of machinery at carrying value, no gain or loss		
Sept. 30	Cash	1,000	
	Accumulated Depreciation, Machinery	4,650	
	Loss on Sale of Machinery	850	
	Machinery		6,500
	Sale of machinery at less than carrying value, loss of $850 recorded		
Sept. 30	Cash	2,000	
	Accumulated Depreciation, Machinery	4,650	
	Machinery		6,500
	Gain on Sale of Machinery		150
	Sale of machinery at more than carrying value, gain of $150 recorded		

Recording Exchanges of Similar Plant Assets

Of course, business concerns sometimes dispose of plant assets by trading them in on the purchase of similar new plant assets. In such cases, the purchase price is reduced by the amount of a trade-in allowance given for the old plant asset exchanged. If the trade-in allowance is less than the carrying value of the old plant asset, a loss occurs. Conversely, if the trade-in allowance is greater than the carrying value of the old plant asset, a gain occurs. The Accounting Principles Board has ruled that such losses and gains should be handled differently in the accounting records. *Opinion No. 29* states that in exchanges of similar assets, (a) losses should be recognized, and (b) gains should not be recognized.[3]

Loss Recognized on the Exchange To illustrate the first case, let us assume that the firm in our comprehensive example exchanges the machinery for newer, more modern machinery on the following terms:

Price of new machinery	$12,000
Trade-in allowance for old machinery	1,000
Cash payment required	$11,000

In this case, the trade-in allowance ($1,000) is less than the carrying value ($1,850) of the old machinery. Thus there is a loss on the exchange of $850 ($1,850 − $1,000). The following journal entry records this transaction under the assumption that the loss is to be recognized:

Sept. 30	Machinery (new)	12,000	
	Accumulated Depreciation, Machinery	4,650	
	Loss on Exchange of Machinery	850	
	Machinery (old)		6,500
	Cash		11,000
	Exchange of machinery—cost of old machinery and its accumulated depreciation removed from the books and new machinery recorded at list price, loss recognized		

Gain Not Recognized on the Exchange When an exchange of similar assets involving both a trade-in and a cash payment results in a gain, the Accounting Principles Board states that the new asset must be recorded as the sum of the cash paid plus the trade-in allowance. In this way, the gain is not recognized in the records. To illustrate this point, we will continue the comprehensive example by assuming the following terms of the exchange:

Price of new machinery	$12,000
Trade-in allowance for old machinery	3,000
Cash payment required	$ 9,000

3. Accounting Principles Board, *Opinion No. 29,* "Accounting for Nonmonetary Transactions" (New York: American Institute of Certified Public Accountants, 1973), par. 22.

Here, the trade-in allowance ($3,000) exceeds the carrying value ($1,850) of the old machinery by $1,150. Thus there is a gain on the exchange if we assume that the price of the new machinery is not a figure that has been inflated for the purpose of allowing an exorbitant trade-in value. In other words, there is a gain if the trade-in allowance represents the fair market value of the old machinery. Because the gain is not to be recognized in the accounting records, the cost basis of the new machinery must indicate the effect of the unrecorded gain. This cost basis is computed by adding the cash payment to the carrying value of the old asset:

Carrying value of old machinery	$ 1,850
Cash paid	9,000
Cost basis of new machinery	$10,850

The entry to record the transaction is as follows:

Sept. 30	Machinery (new)	10,850	
	Accumulated Depreciation, Machinery	4,650	
	Machinery (old)		6,500
	Cash		9,000
	Exchange of machinery—cost of old machinery and its accumulated depreciation removed from books; machinery recorded at amount to equal carrying value of old machinery plus cash paid, no gain recognized		

The nonrecognition of the gain on the exchange is, in effect, a postponement of the gain. For example, in the illustration above, when the new machinery is eventually discarded or sold, its cost basis will be $10,850 instead of its original price of $12,000. Therefore, any future gain will be increased by $1,150 or future loss reduced by $1,150. If the machinery is not sold, the "unrecognized" gain is reflected in less depreciation each year than if the gain had been recognized. The Accounting Principles Board justifies this position by stating that revenue (that is, the gain) should not be recognized merely because one productive asset is substituted for another but should be recognized in the form of increased net income resulting from the smaller depreciation charges each year over the productive life of the asset.

Gain or Loss Not Recognized on the Exchange (Income Tax Rules) Accounting for exchanges of similar plant assets is further complicated by the fact that the income tax rules agree with the Accounting Principles Board in the nonrecognition of gains but disagree in the treatment of losses. Whereas the Accounting Principles Board requires the recognition of losses on exchanges, the income tax rules state that losses should not be recognized. In other words, for tax purposes the cost basis of an asset acquired in exchange for a similar asset is the total of the cash payment plus the carrying value of the old asset. This rule applies regardless of whether there is a gain or loss on the exchange. Thus in the previous example where a loss was recognized, the new asset was recorded at the purchase price of $12,000 and a loss of $850 was recorded. Under the income tax method, the new asset would be recorded at $12,850 ($11,000 cash payment + $1,850 carrying value), and no loss would be recognized. Thus when a company exchanges similar assets at a loss, two sets of plant asset records must be maintained. One would record depreciation for accounting records on a cost basis of $12,000, and the other would record depreciation for income tax records on a cost basis of $12,850.

Control of Plant Assets

Objective 7
Record property, plant, and equipment transactions in the plant asset records

Most businesses divide their plant assets into functional groups and provide separate asset and accumulated depreciation control accounts for each group. For example, a company will usually have separate controlling accounts for Store Equipment, Office Equipment, and Delivery Truck, with an Accumulated Depreciation controlling account for each of these categories. All transactions affecting any one of the functional groups are recorded in the asset and the Accumulated Depreciation controlling accounts of that group. The purchase, depreciation, exchange, or sale of all delivery equipment will therefore be recorded in one Delivery Equipment account and its related Accumulated Depreciation account. Most businesses must have a subsidiary ledger with a detailed record for each asset, just as they do for each account receivable and account payable, but it is conceivable that a very small business may be able to function without it. Today's complicated income tax regulations require most businesses to substantiate depreciation and gains and losses from sales of assets with such detailed records. Normally a subsidiary ledger is the source of these records.

There are many ways to devise these records. One way is illustrated in Figure 13-4 (next page). In this simple example, the company has only two delivery trucks. The information on the subsidiary records is self-evident. But note that when the two subsidiary records for plant assets 1 and 2 are combined, they equal the balance in the general ledger accounts for both delivery trucks and accumulated depreciation on the delivery trucks. This method of using subsidiary ledgers for plant assets is very similar to the one you have already learned in accounting for accounts receivable and accounts payable. Subsidiary ledgers for plant assets are useful to the accounting department in (1) determining the periodic depreciation expense, (2) recording disposal of individual items, (3) preparing tax returns, and (4) preparing insurance claims in the event of insured losses. Forms may be expanded to provide spaces for accumulating data on the operating efficiency of the assets. Such information as the frequency of breakdowns, the length of time out of service, and the cost of repairs is useful in evaluating equipment.

Figure 13-4 Illustration of Plant Asset Subsidiary Records and Controlling Accounts

Controlling Accounts in General Ledger

Delivery Truck **Account No. 132**

Date		Item	Post. Ref.	Debit	Credit	Balance Debit	Balance Credit
19x5							
Jan.	1		J1	5,400		5,400	
19x6							
Jan.	1		J20	6,200		11,600	

Accumulated Depreciation **Account No. 133**

Date		Item	Post. Ref.	Debit	Credit	Balance Debit	Balance Credit
19x5							
Dec.	31		J19		800		800
19x6							
Dec.	31		J40		800		1,600
	31		J40		900		2,500

Subsidiary Plant Asset and Depreciation Record **Plant Asset No. 1**

Item: Delivery Truck Serial No.: T4862
General Ledger Account: Delivery Truck Purchased from: GMR Corporation
Where Located: Warehouse
Person Responsible for Asset: Delivery foreman
Estimated Life: 6 years Estimated Residual Value: $600.00
Depreciation Method: SL Depreciation per Year: $800.00
Mo.: $66.67

Date	Explanation	Post. Ref.	Asset Record Dr.	Asset Record Cr.	Asset Record Bal.	Depreciation Dr.	Depreciation Cr.	Depreciation Bal.
Jan. 1, 19x5		J1	5,400		5,400			
Dec. 31, 19x5		J19					800	800
Dec. 31, 19x6		J40					800	1,600

Figure 13-4
(*continued*)

Subsidiary Plant Asset and Depreciation Record								**Plant Asset No. 2**
Item: Delivery Truck Serial No.: ST74289								
General Ledger Account: Delivery Truck Purchased from: AMG Corporation								
Where Located: Warehouse								
Person Responsible for Asset: Warehouse foreman								
Estimated Life: 6 years Estimated Residual Value: $800								
Depreciation Method: SL Depreciation per Year: $900								
Mo.: $75								
			Asset Record			Depreciation		
Date	Explanation	Post. Ref.	Dr.	Cr.	Bal.	Dr.	Cr.	Bal.
Jan. 1, 19x6		J20	6,200		6,200			
Dec. 31, 19x6		J40					900	900

Plant assets, of course, represent a significant investment on the part of a company. Most companies identify each plant asset with a number when it is purchased. At least once a year, an inspection and inventory of plant assets is made and compared with the information on the subsidiary records. Such an inventory should disclose changes in use of the plant assets, unusual wear and tear, and loss from theft, damage, or negligence.

Accounting for Natural Resources

Objective 8 Identify the accounting issues associated with natural resources and compute depletion

Natural resources are also known as **wasting assets**. Examples of natural resources are standing timber, oil and gas fields, and mineral deposits. The distinguishing characteristic of these wasting assets is that they are consumed by cutting, pumping, or mining. For example, an oil field is a reservoir of unpumped oil, and a coal mine is a deposit of unmined coal.

Natural resources are shown on the balance sheet as long-term assets with descriptive titles such as Timber Lands, Oil and Gas Reserves, and Mineral Deposits. When the timber is cut, the oil is pumped, or the coal is mined, it becomes an inventory of the product to be sold.

Natural resources are recorded at acquisition cost, which may also include some costs of development. As the resource is consumed through the process of cutting, pumping, or mining, the asset account must be proportionally reduced. The carrying value of oil reserves on the balance sheet, for example, is reduced by a small amount for each barrel of oil pumped. As a result, the original cost of the oil reserves is gradually reduced, and depletion is recognized by the amount of the decrease.

Depletion

The term depletion is used to describe the proportional allocation of the cost of a natural resource to the units removed. The costs are allocated in a way similar to the production method used for depreciation. When a natural resource is purchased or developed, there must be an estimate of the total units that will be available, such as barrels of oil, tons of coal, or board-feet of lumber. The depletion cost per unit is determined by dividing the cost (less residual value, if any) of the natural resource by the estimated number of units available. The amount of the depletion for each accounting period is then computed by multiplying the depletion cost per unit by the number of units pumped, mined, or cut. For example, for a mine having an estimated 1,500,000 tons of coal, a cost of $1,800,000, and an estimated residual value of $300,000, the depletion charge per ton of coal is $1. In addition, if 115,000 tons of coal are mined and sold during the first year, the depletion charge for the year is $115,000. It is recorded as follows:

Dec. 31	Depletion Expense	115,000	
	Accumulated Depletion, Coal Mine		115,000
	To record depletion of coal mine: 115,000 tons mined at $1 per ton		

On the balance sheet, the mine would be presented as follows:

Coal Mine	$1,500,000	
Less Accumulated Depletion	115,000	$1,385,000

A natural resource that is extracted in one year may not be sold until a later year. It is important to note that it is recorded as depletion in the year in which it is extracted. The portion not sold is considered inventory in the current asset section of the balance sheet. For example, if only 100,000 tons of coal in the preceding illustration were actually sold during the accounting period, $100,000 would be debited to Depletion Expense and shown on the income statement, and $15,000 would be debited to Coal Inventory and shown on the balance sheet.

Depreciation of Closely Related Plant Assets

Natural resources often require special on-site buildings and equipment, such as conveyors, roads, trackage, and drilling and pumping devices, in order to extract the resource. If the useful life of these assets is longer than the estimated time it will take to deplete the resource, a special problem arises. Because these long-term assets are often abandoned and have no useful purpose beyond the time when the resources are extracted, they should be depreciated on the same basis as the depletion is computed. For example, if machinery having a useful life of ten years is installed on an oil field that is projected to be depleted in eight years, the machinery should be depreciated over the eight-year period. Each year's depreciation charge should be proportional to the depletion charge. If one-sixth of the oil field's total reserves is pumped in one year, then the depreciation should be one-sixth of the machinery's cost minus the scrap value. If the useful life of a long-term asset is less than the expected life of the depleting asset, the shorter life should be used to compute depreciation.

Development and Exploration Costs in the Oil and Gas Industry

Accounting for the costs of exploration and development of oil and gas resources has been a source of continuing controversy. Until recently, oil and gas companies were free to account for these costs under either of two methods. Under **successful efforts accounting,** successful exploration—for example, the cost of a producing oil well—is a cost of the resource. This cost should be capitalized and depleted over the estimated life of the resource. Conversely, an unsuccessful exploration—for example, the cost of a dry well—is written off immediately as a loss. Because of these immediate write-offs, successful efforts accounting is generally considered the more conservative method and is used by most large oil companies.

Exploration-minded independent oil companies, on the other hand, argue that the cost of the dry wells is a part of the overall cost of the systematic development of the oil field and thus a part of the cost of producing wells. Under this **full-costing** method, all costs including the cost of dry wells are recorded as assets and depleted over the estimated life of the producing resources. This method tends to improve the earnings performance in the early years of companies that use it.

The controversy was apparently resolved when the Financial Accounting Standards Board endorsed successful efforts accounting and prohibited full-cost accounting.[4] However, the controversy began again when the Securities and Exchange Commission—rejecting both of these methods—proposed an entirely and radically new method, called **reserve recognition accounting.**[5] Its basic tenet is that the discovery of oil and gas is the most significant event in exploration, development, and production activities. This being the case, the current value of new proved reserves discovered every year should be recognized immediately, on both the balance sheet and the income statement. This is a simple concept, but it is a radical departure from the successful efforts and full-costing methods, which are both historical cost methods. If the SEC's plan becomes effective, an income statement based on reserve recognition accounting will replace the traditional income statement for oil and gas companies. As a result, a company's net income will depend heavily on the current value of

4. *Statement of Financial Accounting Standards No. 19,* "Financial Accounting and Reporting by Oil and Gas Producing Companies" (Stamford, Conn.: Financial Accounting Standards Board, 1978).
5. Securities and Exchange Commission, *Accounting Series Release No. 253* (Washington: Securities and Exchange Commission, August 1978).

the reserves it discovers each year. The SEC argues that financial statements based on current costs are more relevant than those based on historical costs.[6] Critics point out that reserves are costly to estimate and that the estimates are highly unreliable. The debate is far from settled.

Chapter Review

Review of Learning Objectives

1. Define the types of long-term nonmonetary assets.
Long-term nonmonetary assets are unexpired costs that are used in the operation of the business, are not intended for resale, and have a useful life of more than one year. Long-term assets are either tangible or intangible. In the former category are land, plant assets, and natural resources. In the latter are trademarks, patents, franchises, goodwill, and other rights.

2. Account for the cost of long-term nonmonetary assets.
The acquisition cost of a long-term asset includes all expenditures reasonable and necessary to get it in place and ready for use.

3. Define depreciation and relate it to depletion and amortization.
Except for land, the cost of a long-term asset must be allocated over its useful life. In the case of plant assets, this allocation is called depreciation; for natural resources, it is called depletion; and for intangible assets, it is called amortization.

4. Compute and record periodic depreciation under the (a) straight-line method, (b) production method, and (c) accelerated methods, including (1) sum-of-the-years'-digits method and (2) declining-balance method.
Depreciation is commonly computed by the straight-line method, the production method, or one of the accelerated methods. The two most widely used accelerated methods are the sum-of-the-years'-digits method and the declining-balance method. The straight-line method is related directly to the passage of time, whereas the production method is related directly to use. Accelerated methods, which result in relatively large amounts of depreciation in the early years and reduced amounts in later years, are based on the assumption that plant assets provide greater economic benefit in their early years than in later years.

5. Apply depreciation methods to problems of partial years, revised rates, items of small unit value, and groups of similar items.
In the application of depreciation methods, it may be necessary to calculate depreciation for partial years and to revise depreciation rates. In addition, it may be practical to apply these methods to groups of similar assets and to apply an inventory method to items of small unit value.

6. Account for disposal of depreciable assets.
In the disposal of long-term assets, it is necessary to bring the depreciation up to the date of disposal and to remove the carrying value from the accounts by removing the cost from the asset account and the depreciation to date from the accumulated depreciation account. If a long-term asset is sold at a different price from carrying value, there is a gain or loss that should be recorded and reported in the income statement. In recording exchanges of similar plant assets, a gain or loss may also arise. According to the Accounting Principles Board, losses, but not

6. More on current value versus historical cost is found in Chapter 14.

gains, should be recognized at the time of the exchange. When a gain is not recognized, the new asset is recorded at the carrying value of the old asset plus any cash paid. For income tax purposes, neither gains nor losses are recognized.

7. Record property, plant, and equipment transactions in the plant asset records.
The use of controlling accounts and subsidiary plant ledgers detailing acquisitions, subsequent transactions, depreciation, and disposals is usually necessary to provide adequate control over long-term assets.

8. Identify the accounting issues associated with natural resources and compute depletion.
Natural resources are wasting assets, which are consumed by cutting, pumping, mining, or other forms of extraction. Natural resources are recorded at cost as long-term assets to be allocated as expenses through depletion charges as the resources are depleted. The depletion charge is based on the ratio of the resource extracted to the total estimated resource. A major unresolved issue related to this subject is accounting for oil and gas reserves.

Review Problem

Before doing the examples and exercises, review the sample computations and journal entries for depreciation and disposal of long-term assets in this chapter. For additional help, see the review problem in the working papers.

Chapter Assignments

Questions

1. What are the characteristics of long-term nonmonetary assets?
2. Which of the following items would be classified as plant assets on the balance sheet: (a) a truck held for sale by a truck dealer, (b) an office building that was once the company headquarters but is now to be sold, (c) a typewriter used by a secretary of the company, (d) a machine that is used in the manufacturing operations but is now fully depreciated, (e) pollution-control equipment that does not reduce the cost or improve the efficiency of the factory, (f) a parking lot for company employees?
3. Why is it useful to think of plant assets as a bundle of services?
4. Why is land different from other long-term nonmonetary assets?
5. What in general is included in the cost of a long-term nonmonetary asset?
6. Which of the following expenditures incurred in connection with the purchase of a computer system would be charged to the asset account: (a) purchase price of the equipment, (b) interest on debt incurred to purchase the equipment, (c) freight charges, (d) installation charges, (e) cost of special communications outlets at the computer site, (f) cost of repairing door that was damaged during installation, (g) cost of adjustments to the system during first month of operation?
7. Hale's Grocery obtained bids for the construction of a garage for receiving goods at the back of its store. The lowest bid was $22,000. The company, however decided to build the garage itself and was able to do it for $20,000. The activity was recorded as a debit to Buildings for $22,000 and credits to Notes Payable for $20,000 and Gain on Construction for $2,000. Do you agree with the entry?

8. What do accountants mean by the term *depreciation,* and what is its relationship to depletion and amortization?
9. A firm buys a piece of technical equipment that is expected to last twelve years. What consideration might cause the equipment to be depreciated over a shorter period of time?
10. A company purchased a building five years ago. The market value of the building is now greater than it was when the building was purchased. Should the company stop depreciating the building?
11. Evaluate the following statement: "A parking lot should not be depreciated because adequate repairs will make it last forever."
12. Is the purpose of depreciation to determine the value of equipment? Explain.
13. Contrast the assumptions underlying the straight-line depreciation method with the assumptions underlying the production depreciation method.
14. What is the principal argument supporting accelerated depreciation methods?
15. What does the balance of the Accumulated Depreciation account represent? Does it represent funds available to purchase new plant assets?
16. If a plant asset is sold during the year, why should depreciation be computed for the partial year prior to the date of the sale?
17. What basic procedure should be followed in revising a depreciation rate?
18. Explain why and how plant assets of small unit value can be accounted for on a basis similar to handling supplies inventory.
19. On what basis can depreciation be taken on a group of assets rather than on individual items?
20. If a plant asset is discarded before the end of its useful life, how is the amount of loss measured?
21. When similar assets are exchanged, at what amount is the new asset recorded for federal income tax purposes?
22. When an exchange of similar assets occurs in which there is an unrecorded loss for federal income tax purposes, is the taxpayer ever able to deduct or receive credit for the loss?
23. What records are usually necessary for good control over plant assets?
24. Old Stake Mining Company computes depletion to be $2 per ton. During 19xx, the company mined 400,000 tons of ore and sold 370,000 tons. What amount should be deducted from revenues for depletion expense during the year?
25. Under what circumstances can a mining company depreciate its plant assets over a period of time that is less than their useful lives?

Classroom Exercises

Exercise 13-1 Determining Cost of Long-Term Assets

Harris Manufacturing purchased land adjacent to its factory for the installation of a parking lot. Expenditures incurred by the company were as follows: purchase price, $100,000; broker's fees, $7,000; title search and other fees, $500; demolition of a shack on the property, $2,000; grading, $1,500; parking lots, $15,000; lighting, $10,000; signs, $800.

Determine the amount that should be debited to the Land account.

Exercise 13-2 Depreciation Methods

Martin Oil purchased a delivery truck for $9,100. The company expected the truck to last five years or 200,000 miles, with an estimated residual value of $1,600 at the end of that time. During the second year the truck was driven 60,000 miles.

Compute the depreciation for the second year under each of the following methods: (1) straight-line, (2) production, (3) sum-of-the-years'-digits, and (4) declining-balance, at a rate double the straight-line rate.

Exercise 13-3
Declining-Balance Method

Sanders Company purchased an electric typewriter for $560. The typewriter has an estimated useful life of four years and an estimated residual value of $60.

Compute the depreciation charge for each of the four years using the declining-balance method at a rate double the straight-line rate.

Exercise 13-4
Straight-Line Method—Partial Years

Hatfield Corporation purchased three machines during the year as follows:

February 5	Machine A	$6,000
July 30	Machine B	4,800
October 13	Machine C	7,200

The machines are assumed to last six years and have no estimated residual value. The company's fiscal year corresponds to the calendar year.

Compute the depreciation charge for each machine for the year using the straight-line method.

Exercise 13-5
Revision of Depreciation Rates

Household Delivery Service purchased a special washing machine for cleaning its fleet of trucks. The machine, which cost $36,840, was expected to last ten years, with an estimated residual value of $2,840. After two years of operation (and depreciation charges using the straight-line rate), it became evident that the washing machine would last a total of only seven years. At that time, the estimated residual value would remain the same.

Determine the new depreciation charge for the third year on the basis of the new estimated useful life.

Exercise 13-6
Accounting for Items of Small Unit Value

H & R Auto Service Company maintains a large supply of small tools for servicing automobiles. The company uses the inventory basis for accounting for the tools and assumes that depreciation expense is approximately equal to the cost of tools lost and discarded during the year. At the beginning of the year, the company had an inventory of small tools on hand in the amount of $12,300. During the year, small tools were purchased in the amount of $5,600. At the end of the year (December 31), a physical inventory revealed small tools in the amount of $11,150 on hand.

Prepare a general journal entry to record small tools expense for the year.

Exercise 13-7
Disposal of Plant Assets

A piece of equipment that cost $5,400 and on which $3,000 of accumulated depreciation had been recorded was disposed of on January 3, the first day of business of the current year.

Give general journal entries to record the disposal under each of the following assumptions: (1) It was discarded as having no value. (2) It was sold for $1,000 cash. (3) It was sold for $3,000 cash. (4) The equipment was traded in on similar equipment having a list price of $8,000. A $2,600 trade-in was allowed, and the balance was paid in cash. Follow the Accounting Principles Board Rules. (5) The equipment was traded in on similar equipment having a list price of $8,000. A $1,200 trade-in was allowed, and the balance was paid in cash. Follow the Accounting Principles Board Rules. (6) Same as (5) except that the income tax method was used.

Exercise 13-8
Disposal of Plant Assets

A pickup truck costing $4,900, with accumulated depreciation of $3,600, was traded in on a new model that had a list price of $6,100. A trade-in allowance of $1,000 was given.

1. Compute the carrying value of the old truck.
2. Determine the amount of cash required to purchase the new truck.
3. Compute the amount of loss on the exchange.
4. Determine the cost basis of the new truck for federal income tax purposes.

5. Compute the yearly depreciation on the new truck, for both accounting records and income tax purposes, assuming a useful life of five years, a residual value of $1,600, and straight-line depreciation.

Exercise 13-9 Natural Resource Depletion and Depreciation of Related Plant Assets

Montana Mining Corporation purchased land containing an estimated twelve million tons of ore for a cost of $2,200,000. The land without the ore is estimated to be worth $400,000. The company expects that all the usable ore can be mined in ten years. Buildings costing $200,000, with an estimated useful life of thirty years, were erected on the site. Equipment costing $240,000, with an estimated useful life of eight years, was installed. Because of the remote location, neither the buildings nor the equipment has an estimated residual value. During its first year of operation, the company mined one million tons of ore and at the end of the year had an inventory of 100,000 tons.

1. Compute the depletion charge per ton.
2. Compute the depletion expense that should be charged against revenue for the year.
3. Determine the balance sheet value of the ending ore inventory.
4. Determine the annual depreciation expense for the buildings, using the straight-line method.
5. Determine the annual depreciation expense for the equipment, using the straight-line method.

Problem Set A

Problem 13A-1 Comparison of Depreciation Methods

Jason Sales Company acquired new fixtures for its retail store for $74,000, with an estimated residual value of $5,600 and an estimated useful life of eight years.

Required

1. Compute the annual depreciation for each of the eight years by completing the following table:

	Straight-Line		Sum-of-the-Years'-Digits		Declining-Balance (double straight-line rate)	
End of Year	Carrying Value	Depreciation	Carrying Value	Depreciation	Carrying Value	Depreciation
Date of Purchase						
1						
2						
3						
4						
5						
6						
7						
8						

2. Prepare a pair of graphs similar to the two below, and graph each column from part 1.
3. What conclusions can you draw from the graphs in part 2?

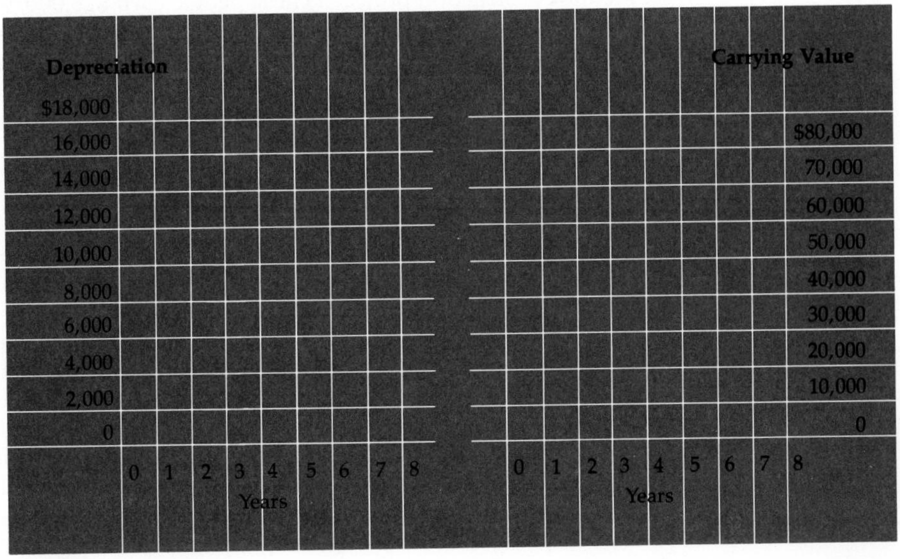

Depreciation
$18,000
16,000
14,000
12,000
10,000
8,000
6,000
4,000
2,000
0
0 1 2 3 4 5 6 7 8
Years

Carrying Value
$80,000
70,000
60,000
50,000
40,000
30,000
20,000
10,000
0
0 1 2 3 4 5 6 7 8
Years

Problem 13A-2 Determining Cost of Plant Assets

Hennings Manufacturing Company began operation on January 1, 19xx. The bookkeeper for this company was inexperienced and debited one account called Lands, Buildings, and Equipment for all expenditures involving long-term assets. The account had a balance at the end of the year of $598,270, made up of the following items:

Cost of land	$ 67,000
Broker's fees for land purchase	4,700
Attorney's fees for land purchase	1,200
Other fees connected with land purchase	650
Cost of draining a small pond from land	3,250
Cost of building up land to prevent further flooding	12,640
Cost of digging basement and foundation for building	7,480
Architect's fee for designing building	27,850
Cost of new building (payment made with $40,000 cash plus U.S. Treasury notes having a face value and book value [cost] of $200,000 on a market value of $198,000 at time of purchase)	240,000
Cost of sidewalks	7,900
Cost of parking lots	15,600
Cost of parking lot lights	7,800
Cost of landscaping	3,800
Cost of machinery	178,400
Cost of delivering machinery	1,800
Cost of repairing parking lot after equipment delivery	500
Cost of installing machinery	12,400
Payment of lawsuit settlement to injured employee	5,000
Cost of repairing windows broken by vandals before building was in use	300
Account balance	$598,270

When the land was purchased, it contained several piles of scrap metal, which were sold for $1,850. This amount was credited to Miscellaneous Income. During construction, the company assigned the factory superintendent and two supervisors to the construction project. These people earn $18,000, $12,000, and $12,000, respectively, per year. They spent six months overseeing the construction of the building, three months supervising the installation of machinery, and three months in their regular factory duties. Their salaries were debited to factory payroll expense.

Required

1. Prepare a schedule with the following headings: Land, Land Improvements, Buildings, Machinery, and Losses. List the items appropriate to these accounts and sort them out into their proper accounts. Negative amounts should be shown in parentheses. Total the columns.
2. Prepare an entry to adjust the accounts based on all the information given, assuming the company's accounts have not been closed at the end of the year.
3. Assume that the factory was in operation for three months during the year. Prepare an adjusting entry to record depreciation expense, assuming that the land improvements are depreciated over fifteen years with no residual value, the buildings are depreciated over twenty-five years with no estimated residual value, and the machinery is depreciated over ten years with the estimated residual value equal to 10 percent of cost. The company uses the straight-line method of depreciation.

Problem 13A-3 Depreciation Methods and Partial Years

During 19x1, Able Company purchased four machines that performed very different operations. Because of their varied functions, the company accountant felt that four different depreciation methods were appropriate. Data on these machines are summarized as follows:

Machine	Date Purchased	Cost	Installation Cost	Estimated Residual Value	Estimated Life	Depreciation Method
1	1/1/x1	$12,800	$1,200	$1,900	10 years	Declining-balance
2	1/1/x1	16,200	400	1,760	7 years	Sum-of-the-years'-digits
3	4/4/x1	7,400	900	1,300	5 years	Straight-line
4	8/25/x1	17,000	2,000	1,000	180,000 units	Production

Required

Assuming that the fiscal year ended December 31, compute the depreciation charges for 19x1, 19x2, and 19x3 by filling in a table with the following column heads:

Machine	Computations	Depreciation		
		19x1	19x2	19x3

Assume that double the straight-line rate is used for the declining-balance method and that production for machine 4 was 24,000 units in 19x1, 46,500 units in 19x2, and 37,800 units in 19x3. Show your computations.

Problem 13A-4 Plant Asset Transactions, Revised Depreciation, and Spare Parts

Johnny Segan's lifelong dream was to operate a small-town newspaper. At the beginning of 19x1, he purchased used newspaper printing equipment for $48,200 and had it moved for $2,700 to a building he owned. It cost him $1,700 to have the equipment installed and $500 to have it cleaned. He paid an experienced repairman $3,000 to get the equipment running and adjusted. He felt that a reasonable useful life for the equipment was three years, with an estimated residual value of $6,000. Because his printing press was old, he purchased $2,100 of spare parts so that it could be fixed at a moment's notice. During the year, he purchased additional spare parts totaling $600 and spent $900 on regular oiling and upkeep of the equipment. At the end of the year, an inventory disclosed $1,650 of spare parts on hand.

During 19x2, it became clear that with regular maintenance the equipment would last five years rather than the three years previously estimated. At the end of five years, the estimated residual value would be $8,600. In 19x2, spare parts of $1,150 were purchased, and the physical inventory revealed $1,540 on hand at the end of the year. Regular maintenance costs were $1,785.

Required

1. Prepare general journal entries for 19x1 to record the purchase of equipment, costs associated with the purchase, the transactions involving spare parts, the upkeep costs, the year-end depreciation charge, and the spare parts expense. The company uses the inventory method of recording spare parts expense and the straight-line method for computing depreciation expense.
2. Prepare general journal entries for 19x2 for spare parts, maintenance, and depreciation expense. The depreciation expense should be based on the new estimates regarding the equipment.

Problem 13A-5 Plant Asset Transactions and Record Cards

Virnon Corporation completed the following transactions for equipment under the control of the shop foreman.

19x1
Jan. 2 Purchased on credit from Ace Supplier a welder, serial number A5106, $590. The machine has an estimated useful life of five years and an estimated residual value of $40. The welder is assigned Plant Asset No. 78-01.
June 27 Purchased on credit from Bates Company an air compressor, serial number BC37, $850. The machine has an estimated useful life of eight years and an estimated residual value of $50. The air compressor is assigned Plant Asset No. 78-02.
Dec. 31 Recorded the 19x1 depreciation on shop equipment using the straight-line method.

19x2
Mar. 24 Purchased on credit from Ace Supplier a welder, serial number A5203, $760. The machine has an estimated useful life of five years and an estimated residual value of $60. The welder is assigned Plant Asset No. 79-01.
Dec. 31 Recorded the 19x2 depreciation on shop equipment using the straight-line method.

19x3
Jan. 2 Sold Plant Asset No. 78-01 for $200.
Dec. 31 Recorded the 19x3 depreciation on shop equipment using the straight-line method.

Required

1. Open ledger accounts for Shop Equipment (141) and Accumulated Depreciation, Shop Equipment (142), and three plant asset record cards.
2. Prepare general journal entries to record the transactions in 19x1, 19x2, and 19x3, and post to the general ledger accounts and plant asset record cards, recording all available information.
3. Prepare a schedule listing the cost and accumulated depreciation to date for each item of shop equipment, and compare with the balances of the shop equipment and related depreciation accounts.

Problem 13A-6 Comprehensive Problem: Initial Recording, Depreciation Methods, and Disposals

Kauffman Manufacturing Company makes metal parts using a special type of machine tool. The company began operating on January 1, 19x1, and terminated operation on December 31, 19x5. Transactions involving four of these machines are presented below.

The company's fiscal year ends December 31. Production on Machine Tool 3 was 6,000 units in 19x3 and 8,000 units in 19x4. The company follows the rules prescribed by the Accounting Principles Board in recording exchanges.

Machine Tool	Acquisition Date	Cost	Estimated Residual Value	Estimated Life	Depreciation Method	Facts Regarding Disposal
1	1/2/x1	$18,900	$2,400	7 years	Sum-of-the-years'-digits	Exchanged on 1/3/x3 for Machine Tool 3; $9,800 trade-in allowed
2	4/4/x2	19,900	2,900	5 years	Straight-line	Sold on 10/1/x5 for $3,000 cash
3	1/3/x3	24,400	3,500	20,000 units	Production	Exchanged on 12/28/x4 for Machine Tool 4; $10,000 trade-in allowed
4	12/28/x4	24,200	4,000	5 years	Declining-balance (double S-L rate)	Sold on 12/31/x6 for $8,000 cash

Required

Prepare in chronological order all general journal entries for the years 19x1 to 19x6 necessary to record the acquisition of each machine tool (assume that each purchase is made for cash), the end-of-year adjustment for depreciation expense for each year, and the disposal of each machine tool.

Problem 13A-7 Comprehensive Natural Resource Entries

Carbon Coal Company purchased property with coal deposits in January 19x1 for $10,700,000. Company geologists estimated that 3,300,000 tons of coal could be extracted from the property and that, when the mining company left, the land would have a residual value of $800,000, net of the costs of restoring the property to pasture land.

At the mining site, the company invested in equipment that cost $2,600,000 and would have a residual value of $500,000 after eight years, and in shelters and other storage buildings that cost $720,000 and would last twenty years with no residual value. Power lines to the site cost $560,000 and would last twelve years.

The geologists estimated that the coal could be removed from the site in six years. When finished with the site, the company would move the equipment to a new mine but would scrap the buildings and power lines. The cost of removing the last two items would approximately equal anything that could be salvaged.

During 19x1, 924,000 tons of coal were mined, of which 870,000 tons were sold at an average price of $6.10 per ton. Operating expenses during the year were $560,000 for labor and $246,000 for other expenses including hauling.

Required

1. Prepare general journal entries to record the purchase of the property and the buildings, equipment, and power lines associated with the mine.
2. Prepare adjusting entries to record depletion and depreciation for the first year (19x1) of operation. Assume that the depreciation rate is equal to the percentage of the total coal mined during the year unless the asset is to be moved. For movable assets, use the straight-line method.
3. Prepare an income statement for 19x1.
4. Prepare a general journal entry, assuming that the coal property, coal inventory, buildings, and power lines, but not the equipment, are sold in January 19x2 for $11 million.

Problem Set B

Problem 13B-1
Comparison of Depreciation Methods

Knebzt Construction Company purchased a new earth-moving tractor for $66,900. The tractor has an estimated residual value of $6,000 and an estimated useful life of six years.

Required

1. Compute the annual depreciation for each of the six years by completing the following table:

	Straight-Line		Sum-of-the-Years'-Digits		Declining-Balance (double straight-line rate)	
End of Year	Carrying Value	Depreciation	Carrying Value	Depreciation	Carrying Value	Depreciation
Date of Purchase						
1						
2						
3						
4						
5						
6						

2. Prepare a pair of graphs similar to the two below, and graph each column from part 1.

Depreciation
$24,000
20,000
16,000
12,000
8,000
4,000
0
0 1 2 3 4 5 6
Years

Carrying Value
$60,000
50,000
40,000
30,000
20,000
10,000
0
0 1 2 3 4 5 6
Years

3. What conclusions can you draw from the graphs in part 2?

Problem 13B-2 Determining Cost of Plant Assets

Jenne Company began operation on January 1 of the current year. At the end of the year, the company's auditor discovered that all expenditures involving long-term assets were debited to an account called Fixed Assets. An analysis of the account, which has a balance at the end of the year of $1,334,901, disclosed that it contained the following items:

Cost of land	$176,200
Surveying costs	1,650
Transfer and other fees	375
Broker's fees	10,572
Attorney's fees associated with land acquisition	3,524
Cost of removing unusable timber from land	25,200
Cost of grading land	2,100
Cost of digging building foundation	17,300
Architect's fee for building and land improvements (80 percent building)	32,400
Cost of building	327,500
Cost of sidewalks	5,700
Cost of parking lots	27,200
Cost of lighting for grounds	40,150
Cost of landscaping	5,900
Cost of machinery	517,000
Shipping cost on machinery	27,650
Cost of installing machinery	88,100
Cost of testing machinery	11,050
Cost of changes in building due to safety regulations required because of machinery	6,270
Cost of repairing building that was damaged in the installation of machinery	4,450

Cost of medical bill for injury received by employee while installing machinery	1,200
Cost of water damage to building during heavy rains prior to opening the plant for operation	3,410
Account balance	$1,334,901

The timber that was cleared from the land was sold to a firewood dealer for $2,000. This amount was credited to Miscellaneous Income. During the construction period, two supervisors devoted their full time to the construction project. These people earn $30,000 and $24,000, respectively. They spent two months on the purchase and preparation of the land, six months on the construction of the building (approximately one-sixth of which was devoted to improvements on the grounds), and two months on installation of machinery. The plant began operation on November 1, and the supervisors returned to their regular duties. Their salaries were debited to Factory Salary Expense.

Required

1. Prepare a schedule with the following column headings: Land, Land Improvements, Buildings, Machinery, and Losses. List the items appropriate to these accounts and sort them out into their proper accounts. Negative amounts should be shown in parentheses. Total the columns.
2. Prepare an entry to adjust the accounts based on all the information given, assuming the company's accounts have not been closed at the end of the year.
3. Assume that the plant was in operation for two months during the year. Prepare an adjusting entry to record depreciation expense, assuming that the land improvements are depreciated over twenty years with no residual value, that the buildings are depreciated over thirty years with no estimated residual value, and that the machinery is depreciated over twelve years with the estimated residual value equal to 10 percent of cost. The company uses the straight-line method.

Problem 13B-3 Depreciation Methods and Partial Years

Vincennes Corporation operates four types of equipment. Because of their varied functions, company accounting policy requires the application of four different depreciation methods to the equipment. Data on this equipment are summarized below.

Equipment	Date Purchased	Cost	Installation Cost	Estimated Residual Value	Estimated Life	Depreciation Method
1	1/1/x1	$ 96,400	$3,600	$10,000	8 years	Double-declining-balance
2	1/1/x1	153,350	5,500	15,000	6 years	Sum-of-the-years'-digits
3	7/1/x1	27,900	2,600	3,000	10 years	Straight-line
4	10/15/x1	48,450	1,350	5,600	20,000 hours	Production

Required

Assuming that the fiscal year ends December 31, compute the depreciation charges for 19x1, 19x2, and 19x3 by filling in a table with the heads shown at top of next page.

Equipment	Computations	Depreciation 19x1	19x2	19x3

Assume that double the straight-line rate is used for the declining-balance method and that production for Equipment 4 was 1,560 hours in 19x1, 3,150 hours in 19x2, and 2,650 hours in 19x3. Show your computations.

Problem 13B-4 Plant Asset Transactions, Revised Depreciation, and Spare Parts

Mary Pontice entered the car-wash business in early 19x1. She was able to purchase used car-wash equipment for $114,250. It cost her $10,400 to have the equipment moved to her building and $3,780 to have it installed. It cost another $960 to clean the equipment and $1,170 to have the equipment adjusted and tested. She estimated that the equipment would have a useful life of ten years and a residual value of $10,000. Additional brushes and other spare parts for the equipment cost $1,165. During the year, more spare parts were purchased at a cost of $980, and regular maintenance of the equipment came to $2,610. At the end of the year, an inventory revealed that $1,035 in spare parts were still on hand.

During 19x2, spare parts of $1,450 were purchased, and the physical inventory disclosed $457 on hand at the end of the year. Regular maintenance costs increased to $4,140 during the year. Soon it became apparent that the equipment would last a total of only six years instead of the originally estimated ten years and the estimated residual value at the end of six years would be only $5,000.

Required

1. Prepare general journal entries for 19x1 to record the purchase of equipment, costs associated with the purchase, the transactions involving spare parts, the upkeep costs, the year-end depreciation charge, and the spare parts expense. The company uses the inventory method of recording spare parts expense and the straight-line method for computing depreciation expense.
2. Prepare general journal entries for 19x2 for spare parts, maintenance, and depreciation expense. The depreciation expense should be based on the new estimates regarding the equipment.

Problem 13B-5 Comprehensive Problem: Initial Recording, Depreciation Methods, and Disposals

Guy Towing Company began operations on January 2, 19x1, when Bert Guy purchased a new towing truck. During its five years of operation, the company owned a total of four towing trucks. The transactions related to these towing trucks are presented at the top of the next page.

Truck 2 was driven 25,000 miles in 19x2, 30,000 miles in 19x3, and 20,000 miles in 19x4. The company's fiscal year ends December 31, and the company follows the practice of recognizing losses but not gains on exchanges at the time of the exchange.

Required

Prepare in chronological order all general journal entries for the years 19x1 to 19x5 necessary to record the acquisition of each truck (assume that each purchase is made for cash), the end-of-year adjustment for depreciation expense for each year, and the disposal of each truck.

Truck	Acquisition Date	Cost	Estimated Residual Value	Estimated Life	Depreciation Method	Facts Regarding Disposal
1	1/2/x1	$18,000	$4,700	4 years	Double-declining-balance	Exchange on 1/3/x3 for truck 3; $3,500 trade-in allowed
2	5/11/x2	20,800	5,500	100,000 miles	Production	Exchange on 5/1/x4 for truck 4; $10,000 trade-in allowed
3	1/3/x3	19,900	4,700	4 years	Sum-of-the-years'-digits	Sold on 12/31/x5 for $6,000 cash
4	5/1/x4	22,175	4,700	4 years	Straight-line	Sold on 11/1/x5 for $12,000 cash

Problem 13B-6 Comprehensive Natural Resource Entries

Joe Billy Waller is a gravel man from New Mexico. On January 3, 19x2, Joe Billy purchased a piece of property with gravel deposits for $3,155,000. He estimated that the gravel deposits contained 4,700,000 cubic yards of gravel. The gravel is used for making roads. After the gravel is gone, the land, which is in the desert, would be worth only about $100,000.

The equipment required to extract the gravel cost $726,000. It has an estimated useful life of six years and an estimated residual value of $34,000. In addition, Joe Billy had to build a small frame building to house the mine office and a small dining hall for the workers. The building cost $76,000 and would have no residual value after its estimated useful life of ten years. It cannot be moved from the mine site. The equipment has an estimated useful life of six years (with no residual value) but could not be moved to another mine site.

Trucks for the project cost $154,000 (estimated life, six years; residual value, $10,000). The trucks, of course, can be used at a different site.

Joe Billy estimated that, in five years, all the gravel would be mined and the mine would be shut down. During 19x2, 1,175,000 cubic yards of gravel were mined. The average selling price during the year was $1.33 per cubic yard, and at the end of the year 125,000 cubic yards remained unsold. Operating expenses were $426,000 for labor and $116,000 for other expenses.

Required

1. Prepare general journal entries to record the purchase of the property and all the buildings and equipment associated with the mine.
2. Prepare adjusting entries to record depletion and depreciation for the first year of operation (19x2). Assume that the depreciation rate is equal to the percentage of the total gravel mined during the year unless the asset is movable. For movable assets, use the straight-line method.
3. Prepare an income statement for 19x2.
4. Prepare a general journal entry, assuming that the mine, gravel inventory, and all buildings and equipment, but not the trucks, are sold on January 1, 19x3, for $3 million cash.

Learning Objectives

Chapter Fourteen

Accounting Principles and Inflation Accounting

1. *Apply the matching rule to revenue recognition.*
2. *Apply the matching rule to the allocation of expired costs as it relates to capital expenditures and revenue expenditures.*
3. *Apply the matching rule to the accounting problems associated with intangible assets, including research and development costs and goodwill.*
4. *Define and describe the use of the conventions of consistency, materiality, conservatism, and full disclosure.*
5. *Identify the two principal types of price changes.*
6. *Using constant dollar accounting, compute purchasing power gains and losses, and restate a balance sheet for changes in the general price level.*
7. *Describe the FASB's approach to accounting for changing prices.*

This chapter has two major purposes. The first is to examine some of the problems that arise in applying the matching concept, including those related to accounting for intangible assets. The second is to discuss the nature of inflation and its effects on financial reporting. As a result of studying this chapter, you should be able to meet the learning objectives listed on the left.

Throughout this book we have emphasized that an important objective of accounting is to determine periodic net income in accordance with the matching rule. Applying the matching rule involves (1) recognizing the revenue earned in a period and (2) allocating the expired costs to the period. The result of these measurements is a matching of revenues and expenses, and the difference between them is the net income or net loss for the period.

Applying the Matching Rule to Revenue Recognition

Revenue is measured by the amount charged for goods sold and services rendered to customers. An important accounting problem associated with revenue is achieving an accurate cutoff at the end of the accounting period—in other words, deciding what revenue should be counted in one accounting period and what revenue should be counted in the next. To determine the point at which revenue should be recognized, two approaches are commonly used: point of sale basis and cash basis.

Point of Sale Basis

From the ordering of merchandise to delivery and collection of cash, a single sale may spread over several weeks or months.

Objective 1
Apply the matching rule to revenue recognition

Previously in this book, we have recognized revenue at the point when title passes to the buyer, which is usually the date of delivery. This is the most commonly used point of recognition in business and is called the **point of sale basis.**

When the sale involves the performance of services, no title transfer exists to mark the recognition point. Theoretically, revenue is earned as the services are being performed. Until the service is performed and the customer accepts the service as satisfactory, however, no claim to the revenue exists. Consequently, although the price and terms of the service may be agreed upon in advance, revenue is not recognized until the work is completed.

Cash Basis

In some circumstances, revenue recognition is postponed until cash is received. On the **cash basis**, revenue is considered to be earned when the cash is collected, regardless of when the sale is made. This method is theoretically justifiable only when there is considerable doubt as to the ultimate collection on a sale. As a practical matter, many individuals who provide services, such as doctors, lawyers, and accountants, use the cash basis because it is simple and eliminates the need to estimate uncollectible accounts. The federal income tax regulations allow individuals who perform services to use the cash basis for reporting their federal income tax liability. This regulation undoubtedly contributes to use of the cash basis by individuals.

Applying the Matching Rule to Allocation of Expired Costs

Objective 2
Apply the matching rule to the allocation of expired costs as it relates to capital expenditures and revenue expenditures

The second major measurement related to the application of the matching rule is the allocation of expired costs to the accounting period. In previous chapters, allocations have been made according to simple rules and procedures to demonstrate the basic procedures of accounting. However, these straightforward practices are not as cut and dried as they appear on the surface, as was also true in the case of revenue recognition. Here we discuss the difficulty of distinguishing between expenditures for assets and expenditures for expenses as well as the arbitrariness of many accounting allocations.

Capital Expenditures and Revenue Expenditures

The term **expenditure** refers to a payment or incurrence of an obligation to make a future payment for an asset, such as a truck, or a service rendered, such as a repair. When the payment or debt is for an asset or a service, it is correctly called an expenditure. A **capital expenditure** is an expenditure for the purchase or expansion of plant assets and is recorded in the asset accounts. An expenditure for repairs, maintenance, fuel, or other items necessary to maintain and operate plant and equipment is called a **revenue expenditure** because it is an immediate charge as an expense against revenue. These are recorded by debits to expense accounts. Revenue expenditures are charged to expense because the benefits from the expenditures will be used up in the current period. They will therefore be deducted from the revenues of the current period in determining the net income. In summary, any expenditure that will benefit several accounting periods is considered a capital expenditure. Any expenditure that will benefit only the current accounting period is referred to as a revenue expenditure.

It is important to observe this careful distinction between capital and revenue expenditures. In accordance with the matching rule, expenditures of whatever type should be charged to the period they benefit. For example, if a purchase of an automobile were mistakenly charged as a revenue expenditure, the expense for the current period would be overstated on the income statement. As a result, current net income would be understated, and in future periods net income would be overstated. If, on the other hand, a revenue expenditure such as the painting of a building were charged to an asset account, the expense of the current period would be understated. Current net income would be correspondingly overstated, and net income of future periods would be understated.

Because it is important, as we have seen, to distinguish between capital and revenue expenditures, many companies adopt policies relating to what constitutes a revenue or a capital expenditure. For example, they may set a minimum dollar amount such as $50 or $100 for a capital expenditure. They may feel that small expenditures are not worth the time and expense of accounting for them. For example, although a wastepaper basket will last longer than one year, the costs of accounting for it as a depreciable asset may exceed its total original cost.

Among the more common types of capital expenditures are the following:

1. **Acquisition of plant and equipment including freight, sales tax, and installation charges** When secondhand property is purchased, the cost of any repairs made to put the property in good operating condition before placing it in use is also considered a capital expenditure and is charged to the asset account.

2. **Additions** Additions are enlargements to the physical layout of a plant asset. If a building is enlarged by adding a new wing, the benefits from the expenditure will be received over a period of years, and the outlay should be debited to the asset account.

3. **Betterments** Betterments are improvements to plant assets that do not add to the physical layout of the asset. Installation of an air-conditioning system is an example of an expenditure for a betterment or improvement that will yield benefits over a period of years and should therefore be charged to the asset account.

4. **Acquisition of intangible assets** See the following discussion.

Among the more common types of revenue expenditures relating to plant equipment are the repairs, maintenance, lubrication, cleaning, and inspection necessary to keep an asset in good working condition.

Repairs fall into two categories: ordinary repairs and extraordinary repairs. **Ordinary repairs** are expenditures that are necessary to maintain an asset in good operating condition. Trucks must have tune-ups, tires and batteries must be replaced regularly, and other ordinary repairs must be made. Offices and halls must be painted regularly and have broken tiles or woodwork replaced. Ordinary repairs consist of any expenditures necessary to maintain a plant asset in its normal state of operation. Such repairs are a current expense.

Extraordinary repairs are repairs of a more significant nature—they affect the estimated residual value or estimated useful life of an asset. For example, a boiler for heating a building may receive a complete overhaul, at a cost of several thousand dollars, which will extend the useful life of the boiler five years.

Typically, extraordinary repairs are recorded by debiting the Accumulated Depreciation account, under the assumption that some of the depreciation previously recorded has now been eliminated. The effect of this reduction in the Accumulated Depreciation account is to increase the book or carrying value of the asset by the cost of the extraordinary repair. Consequently, the new carrying value of the asset should be depreciated over the new estimated useful life. Let us assume that a machine costing $10,000 had no estimated residual value and an original estimated useful life of ten years. After eight years, the accumulated depreciation (straight-line method assumed) would be $8,000, and the carrying value would be $2,000 ($10,000 − $8,000). Assume that, at this point, the machine was given a major overhaul costing $2,000. This expenditure extends the useful life three years beyond the original ten years. The entry for extraordinary repair would be as follows:

Mar. 14	Accumulated Depreciation, Machinery	2,000	
	Cash		2,000
	To record extraordinary repair to machinery		

The annual periodic depreciation for each of the five years remaining in the machine's useful life would be calculated as follows:

Carrying value before extraordinary repairs	$2,000
Extraordinary repairs	2,000
Total	$4,000

$$\text{Annual periodic depreciation} = \frac{\$4{,}000}{5 \text{ years}} = \$800$$

If the machine remains in use for the five years expected after the major overhaul, the annual periodic depreciation charges of $800 will exactly write off the new carrying value, including the cost of extraordinary repairs.

Intangible Assets

Objective 3 Apply the matching rule to the accounting problems associated with intangible assets, including research and development costs and goodwill

The purchase of an intangible asset is a special type of capital expenditure. An intangible asset is long-term but has no physical substance. Its value is derived from the long-term rights or advantages that it represents as a result of ownership and possession. Among the most common examples are patents, copyrights, leaseholds, leasehold improvements, trademarks and brand names, franchises, licenses, formulas, processes, and goodwill. Some current assets, such as accounts receivable and certain prepaid expenses, have no physical nature but are not considered intangible assets because they are short-term. Intangible assets are long-term and nonphysical.

Intangible assets are accounted for at acquisition cost. Some intangible assets such as goodwill or trademarks may have been acquired at little or no cost. Although they may have great value and are essential to profitable operations, they should not appear on the balance sheet unless they have been purchased.

The accounting problems associated with intangible assets are the same as those associated with other long-lived assets. The Accounting Principles Board, in its *Opinion No. 17*, lists these problems as follows:

1. Determining an initial carrying amount
2. Accounting for that amount after acquisition under normal business conditions—that is, through periodic write-off or amortization—in a manner similar to depreciation
3. Accounting for that amount if the value declines substantially and permanently[1]

In addition to these problems, an intangible asset lacks physical qualities and in some cases may be impossible to identify. For these reasons, its value and its useful life may be difficult to estimate.

The Accounting Principles Board has concluded that a company should record as assets the costs of intangible assets acquired from others. However, the company should record as expenses the costs to develop intangible assets. In addition, intangible assets that have a determinable life, such as patents, copyrights, and leaseholds, should be written off through periodic amortization over that useful life in a manner similar to the way plant assets are depreciated. Although some intangible assets, such as goodwill and trademarks, have no measurable limit on their lives, they should also be amortized over a reasonable length of time (not to exceed forty years) because few things, even intangible assets, last forever. Accounting for the various types of intangible assets is summarized in Table 14-1.

Research and Development Costs It is common practice among successful firms to maintain activities, and possibly a specific department, devoted to research and development. These activities include development

1. Adapted from Accounting Principles Board, *Opinion No. 17,* "Intangible Assets" (New York: American Institute of Certified Public Accountants, 1970), par. 2.

Table 14-1 Accounting for Intangible Assets

Type	Description	Special Accounting Problems
Patent	An exclusive right granted by the federal government for a period of 17 years to make a particular product or use a specific process.	The cost of successfully defending a patent in a patent infringement suit is added to the acquisition cost of the patent. Amortize over the useful life, which may be less than the legal life of 17 years.
Copyright	An exclusive right granted by the federal government to the possessor to publish and sell literary, musical, and other artistic materials for a period of the author's life plus 50 years.	Record at acquisition cost, and amortize over the useful life, which is often much shorter than the legal life. For example, the cost of paperback rights to a popular novel would typically be amortized over a useful life of two to four years.
Leasehold	A payment to secure the right to a lease. For example, Company A, which has a 10-year lease to a prime location but does not want to operate in that location, sells the right to Company B. Company B has purchased a leasehold.	Debit Leasehold for the amount of the payment, and amortize it over the remaining life of the lease. Payments to the lessor during the life of the lease should be debited to Lease Expense.
Leasehold improvements	Improvements to leased property that become the property of the lessor at the end of the lease.	Debit Leasehold Improvements for the cost of improvements, and amortize the cost of the improvements over the remaining life of the lease.
Trademark, brand name	A registered symbol or name giving the holder the right to use it to identify a product or service.	Debit the trademark or brand name for the acquisition cost, and amortize it over a reasonable life, not over 40 years.
Franchise, License, Formula, Process	A right to an exclusive territory or to exclusive use of a formula, technique, or design.	Debit the franchise, license, formula, or process for the acquisition cost, and amortize it over a reasonable life, not to exceed 40 years.
Goodwill	The excess of the cost of a group of assets (usually a business) over the market value of the assets individually.	Debit Goodwill for the acquisition cost, and amortize it over a reasonable life, not to exceed 40 years.

of new products, testing of existing and proposed products, and pure research. In the past, it was the practice of some companies to record as an asset those costs of research and development that could be specifically identified with the development of patents, formulas, or other developments. Other costs, such as testing and pure research, were considered expenses of the accounting period and a deduction from income.

The Financial Accounting Standards Board has stated that all research and development costs should be treated as revenue expenditures and charged to expense in the period when incurred.[2] The board argues that it is too difficult to identify specific costs with specific advantageous developments. Furthermore, the costs of maintaining research and development activities are continuous, recurring, and necessary for the successful operation of a business and therefore should be considered current expenses. To support this conclusion, the board cites studies showing that 30 to 90 percent of all new products fail and that three-fourths of new product expenses go to unsuccessful products.

Goodwill The term **goodwill** is widely used by business people, lawyers, and the public to mean various things. One usually thinks of goodwill as meaning the favorable reputation of a business firm. Actually goodwill applies to all the favorable qualities that might cause a company to earn more in future years than is normal in its particular industry. These factors include not only customer satisfaction but also superior management, manufacturing efficiency, monopolistic advantages, location, and good employee relations.

To demonstrate what is meant by above-average earnings, consider the following example:

	Company A	Average of Similar Companies in Same Industry
Net assets other than goodwill	$10,000,000	$10,000,000
Normal rate of return	10%	10%
Normal net income	$ 1,000,000	$ 1,000,000
Actual net income (five-year average)	1,200,000	1,000,000
Earnings above average	$ 200,000	—

There is evidence of goodwill when a purchaser pays more for a business than the fair market value of the assets if purchased separately. Because the purchaser has paid more than the fair market value of the physical assets, intangible assets must exist. If the company being purchased does not have patents, copyrights, leasehold, trademarks, or other intangible assets of value, one must conclude that the excess payment is

2. *Statement of Financial Accounting Standards No. 2*, "Accounting for Research and Development Costs" (Stamford, Conn.: Financial Accounting Standards Board, 1974), par. 12.

for goodwill. The payment above and beyond the fair market value of the tangible assets and other specific intangible assets is properly recorded in the Goodwill account.

In *Opinion No. 17*, the Accounting Principles Board states that the benefits derived from purchased goodwill will eventually disappear. It is difficult for a company to continue superior earnings unless new factors of goodwill replace the old ones. Therefore, goodwill should be amortized or written off by systematic charges to income over a reasonable number of future time periods. The future time periods should in no case exceed forty years.[3]

Goodwill, as mentioned above, should not be recorded unless it is purchased. There are several methods available to the accountant for placing a cost value on goodwill when a business is purchased. Three common methods are as follows:

1. The value of goodwill may be arbitrarily set by the buyer and seller. For example, in a transaction for the sale of a successful business for $260,000, if the buyer and seller agree that net assets other than goodwill are valued at $220,000, goodwill should be recorded at $40,000.

2. Goodwill may be arbitrarily valued at some multiple of the expected earnings in excess of the average. For example, if a company expected to earn $10,000 more per year for the next four years than a similar company in the same industry, goodwill would be valued at $40,000 ($10,000 × 4 years).

3. Goodwill may be measured by capitalizing expected earnings in excess of the average at a rate considered normal in the industry. For example, if (a) a company is expected to earn $6,000 per year more than the average similar company in the industry and (b) the average rate of return in the industry is 12 percent, the goodwill is valued at $50,000 ($6,000 ÷ .12). This is the most theoretically correct way of computing goodwill because it, in effect, answers the question, How many dollars would the company need to invest in assets to earn the $6,000 (12 percent × $50,000) of above-normal earnings that are attributed to goodwill? Note that the higher the average rate of return, the lower the amount of goodwill will be.

Arbitrary Allocation Procedures

At various points in previous chapters, the application of the matching rule has rested on estimates. These estimates are based on allocation procedures, which in turn are based on certain assumptions. For example, here are some of these procedures:

1. For estimating uncollectible accounts expense: percentage-of-net-sales method and accounts receivable aging method.

2. For pricing the ending inventory: average cost method, first-in, first-out (FIFO), and last-in, first-out (LIFO).

3. Accounting Principles Board, *Opinion No. 17*, par. 29.

3. For estimating depreciation expense: straight-line method, production method, sum-of-the-years'-digits method, and declining-balance method.

4. For estimating depletion expense: production (extraction) method.

5. For estimating amortization of intangibles: straight-line method.

All of these procedures are attempts to allocate the costs of assets to the periods in which they contribute to the production of revenue. They are based on a determination of the benefits to the current period (expenses) versus the benefits to future periods (assets). They are estimates and cannot be proved conclusively. In addition, they tend to be arbitrary because it is difficult to justify one method of estimation over another in practice. Consequently, it is important for the accountant as well as the financial statement user to understand the potential impact of alternative accounting procedures on net income and financial position. For example, assume that two companies have similar operations but that one uses FIFO for inventory pricing and straight-line method for determining depreciation and the other uses LIFO for inventory pricing and the sum-of-the-years'-digits (SYD) method for determining depreciation. Their respective income statements might appear as follows:

	FIFO and Straight-Line Company	LIFO and SYD Company
Sales	$500,000	$500,000
Goods Available for Sale	$300,000	$300,000
Less Ending Inventory	60,000	50,000
Cost of Goods Sold	$240,000	$250,000
Gross Profit	$260,000	$250,000
Less:		
Depreciation Expense	$ 40,000	$ 70,000
Other Expenses	170,000	170,000
Total Operating Expenses	$210,000	$240,000
Net Income	$ 50,000	$ 10,000

In actual practice, of course, differences in net income stem from many factors. Nevertheless, the above example is representative of the significant differences that can be caused by using different procedures for allocating costs to accounting periods.

Conventions to Aid Interpretation of Financial Statements

The limitations of financial statements described above derive, to a large extent, from estimates and somewhat arbitrary rules of recognition and allocation. Throughout this book we have pointed out other possible defi-

Objective 4 Define and describe the use of the conventions of consistency, materiality, conservatism, and full disclosure

ciencies of financial statements, such as the failure to recognize the changing value of the dollar and the fact that intangibles, including research and development costs, are treated as assets only if purchased externally, and not if developed within the company. These problems should not be interpreted to mean that financial statements are useless; they are of course essential. However, the people who use them must know how to interpret them. To aid in this interpretation, accountants rely on four conventions when applying accounting procedures: (1) consistency, (2) materiality, (3) conservatism, and (4) full disclosure.

Consistency

The **consistency** convention requires that a particular accounting procedure, once adopted, will not be changed from period to period. Thus users of financial statements may assume that there have been no arbitrary changes in methods that may affect their interpretation of the statements.

If management determines that a particular procedure is not appropriate and should be changed, generally accepted accounting principles require that the fact of the change and its dollar effect be reported in the independent accountant's report:

> The nature of and justification for a change in accounting principle and its effect on income should be disclosed in the financial statements of the period in which the change is made. The justification for the change should explain clearly why the newly adopted accounting principle is preferable.[4]

For example, during the current year, a company disclosed that it had changed from FIFO to LIFO in accounting for inventories because management felt LIFO reflected actual cost flows more realistically.

Materiality

The term **materiality** refers to the relative importance of an item or event. If an item or event is material, it is likely to be relevant to the user of the financial statements. The accountant is often faced with many small items or events that make little difference to users regardless of how they are handled. For example, in Chapter 13, it was suggested that it is more practical to account for small tools on an inventory basis than to depreciate them. Furthermore, small capital expenditures of less than $25 or $50 may be charged as expense rather than recorded as equipment and depreciated.

In general, an item is material if there is a reasonable expectation that knowledge of it would influence the decisions of users of financial statements. The materiality of an item depends on the nature of the item as well as the amount of the item. For example, in a multimillion-dollar

4. Accounting Principles Board, *Opinion No. 20,* "Accounting Changes" (New York: American Institute of Certified Public Accountants, 1971), par. 17.

company an error in recording an item of $5,000 may not be important, but the discovery of a $5,000 bribe or theft may be very significant. Moreover, the accumulation of many small errors may result in a material amount. Accountants must judge the materiality of many items, and the users of financial statements must rely on their judgment.

Conservatism

Accountants attempt to make their decisions on the basis of logic and evidence that will lead to the fairest presentation of the actual situation. In making judgments and estimates, however, accountants are often faced with uncertainties and doubts. In these cases, they rely on the convention of **conservatism.** The conservatism convention means that when accountants face major uncertainties as to which alternative accounting procedure to apply, they tend to exercise caution and choose the procedure that will be least likely to overstate assets and income.

One of the most common applications of the conservatism convention is the use of the lower-of-cost-or-market method in accounting for inventories, discussed in Chapter 11. Under this method, if the market value of inventory is greater than cost, the more conservative cost figure is used. If the market value is less than cost, then the more conservative market value is used.

Conservatism can be a useful tool in uncertain situations, but the abuse of this convention will inevitably produce incorrect and misleading financial statements. For example, if someone incorrectly applied the conservatism convention by charging a long-term asset to expense in the period of purchase, income and assets for the current period would be understated, and income of future periods would be overstated. For this reason, accountants rely on the conservatism convention only as a last resort.

Full Disclosure

The convention of **full disclosure** requires that financial statements and their accompanying footnotes should contain all information relevant to the user's understanding of the situation. This convention has already been referred to in many places in this book. For instance, as mentioned in the section on consistency above, a change from one accounting procedure to another should be disclosed. In general, the form of the financial statements, such as single-step or multistep income statement and classified balance sheet, may affect their usefulness in making certain decisions. Furthermore, some specific items are considered essential to financial statement readers, such as the amount of depreciation expense and income tax expense on the income statement and the amount of the allowance for uncollectible accounts on the balance sheet.

Additional examples of disclosures required by the Financial Accounting Standards Board and other official bodies are the accounting procedures used in preparing the statements, significant changes in accounting estimates, significant events subsequent to the date of the statements, and assets and income of the major segments or divisions of a company. However, there is a point where the statements become so cluttered that they impede rather than aid understanding. Beyond required disclosures, the application of the full-disclosure convention is based, not on definite criteria, but on the judgment of management and the accountants who prepare the statements.

The Nature of Inflation

Americans have been faced with steady inflation for more than a generation and with double-digit inflation for the past several years. In many countries, even greater inflation has become a way of life. One of the most difficult challenges to the accounting profession is to find better ways of dealing with this chronic problem. It is an especially difficult problem because, to deal effectively with inflation, accountants must re-examine several basic tenets of accounting theory. The most important of these tenets are the cost concept and the assumption of a stable measuring unit. To understand how these principles are affected, it is first necessary to examine the nature of inflation.

Objective 5 Identify the two principal types of price changes

In a dynamic society, the price of an electronic calculator may drop 50 percent while at the same time the price of an automobile increases by 20 percent. Each of these price changes relates to inflation, but to the layperson the relationship may be confusing. Part of the confusion arises from the fact that two types of price changes are involved. First, there are changes in **specific price levels,** which reflect the price changes of a specific commodity or item, such as the calculator or automobile mentioned above. Second, there are changes in **general price levels,** which reflect the price changes of a group, or basket, of goods and services. Changes in specific price levels, which may vary widely, contribute to the overall price change as reflected in the general price level. **Inflation,** in the technical sense, refers to change in the general price level.

When the general price level increases, it takes more dollars to buy the same basket of goods than it did previously. As a result, the dollar's **purchasing power**—its ability at a point in time to purchase goods or services—has declined. In the opposite case of **deflation,** when a decrease occurs in the general price level, the purchasing power of the dollar increases because it takes fewer dollars now to purchase the same goods and services as before. In other words, as the general price level changes, the amount of real goods and services that a single dollar can purchase also changes. Therefore, in terms of real goods and services, the dollar is an unstable measuring unit. One might compare this situation to the difficulty of expressing the distance between two cities if the number of feet in a mile were continually changing. In periods when there is little change in the general price level, the unstable dollar does not significantly affect financial statements; in periods of great change, however, the dollars in the financial statements soon become unrealistic measures of the items they are supposed to represent.

Table 14-2
Construction of a Price Index

Commodity	January 1	December 31	Percentage Change in Market Price of Individual Commodities
Hamburger (pound)	$1.19	$1.39	+16.8
Bread (pound loaf)	.49	.59	+20.4
Milk (gallon)	1.83	1.75	−4.4
Lettuce (head)	.39	.79	+102.6
Sugar (5 pounds)	1.19	.79	−33.6
Soap (bar)	.45	.57	+26.7
Tissue (box)	.46	.54	+17.4
	$6.00	$6.42	
Price index (January = 100)	100	107 ($6.42 ÷ $6.00)	

Price Indexes

To show how specific price changes contribute to general price changes, it is helpful to know how a price index is constructed. A **price index** is a series of numbers, one for each period, representing an average price of a group of goods and services, relative to the average price of the same group of goods and services at a beginning date. Consider the figures in Table 14-2. In this example, a price index for a typical grocery basket is computed. During the year, the specific price changes of individual commodities ranged from a decrease of 33.6 percent in the price of sugar to an increase of 102.6 percent in the price of lettuce. Overall, the price index of the basket increased from 100 at the beginning point to 107 at the end of the first year, or 7 percent. One must be careful in interpreting the change in an index number from one year to the next, however. For example, assume that the price index in Table 14-2 increased to 114 by the end of the next year. It would be incorrect to say that prices increased by 7 percent, because on the basis of last year's starting point of 107 the actual percentage change is less. The percentage change from the first year to the second year is 6.54 percent, calculated as follows:

$$\frac{\text{change in index}}{\text{previous year's index}} = \frac{114 - 107}{107} = \frac{7}{107} = 6.54 \text{ percent}$$

General Price Indexes

Agencies of the U.S. government publish several general price indexes. The most widely known general price index is the Consumer Price Index for All Urban Consumers (CPI-U), published by the Bureau of Labor Statistics of the Department of Labor in *Monthly Labor Review.* The Financial Accounting Standards Board uses this index when adjusting financial statements for changes in the general price level because it is readily

Table 14-3
Consumer Price Index for Urban Consumers

Year	Index (1967 = 100)	Year	Index (1967 = 100)
1960	88.7	1973	133.1
1967	100.0	1974	147.7
1968	104.2	1975	161.2
1970	116.3	1976	170.5
1971	121.3	1977	181.5
1972	125.3	1978	195.3

Source: U.S. Department of Labor, *Handbook of Labor Statistics*, 1979.

available, is issued on a monthly basis, and is not revised after its initial publication. Also, it tends to produce a result comparable to other general price indexes.[5]

A partial listing from the CPI-U is reproduced in Table 14-3, with 1967 as a base year. Notice that the purchasing power of the dollar as measured by this index was less than half in 1978 what it was in 1960—that is, the index more than doubled (88.7 to 195.3). This means that it will take more than twice as many dollars to buy the same good or service in 1978 as it did in 1960. For example, assume that it cost $100,000 to buy a building in 1960. A payment of $220,180 would be required in 1978 to equal the payment of $100,000 in 1960. This computation is made as follows:

$$\frac{\text{index of year to which dollars are being converted}}{\text{index of year from which dollars are being converted}} \times \text{dollar amount} = \text{restated amount}$$

$$\frac{\text{1978 index}}{\text{1960 index}} \times \text{cost of building} = \text{restated cost of building}$$

$$\frac{195.3}{88.7} \times \$100{,}000 = \$220{,}180 \text{ (rounded to nearest dollar)}$$

Reporting the Effects of Price Changes

There are two principal methods of accounting for the effects of changing prices on financial statements. One is to restate historical cost financial statements for changes in the general price level (constant dollar accounting). The other is to develop financial statements based on changes in

5. *Statement of Financial Accounting Standards No. 33*, "Financial Reporting and Changing Prices" (Stamford, Conn.: Financial Accounting Standards Board, 1979), par. 39.

specific price levels (current value accounting). These approaches are described below, along with the pros and cons of each.

Constant Dollar Accounting

Objective 6 Using constant dollar accounting, compute purchasing power gains and losses, and restate a balance sheet for changes in the general price level

Constant dollar accounting involves the restatement of historical cost statements for general price level changes. Its objective is to state all amounts in dollars of uniform general purchasing power. As a result, the financial statements are based on a uniform, or constant, monetary measuring unit as of the balance sheet date. The general approach is to convert the number of dollars received or expended at various price levels (corresponding to various balance sheet dates) to an equivalent number of dollars at the price level on the latest balance sheet date.

For instance, according to Table 14-3, a building costing $100,000 in 1960 would be restated as follows at various dates:

Date	1960 Cost	Index	Conversion Factor	Restated Cost
1960	$100,000	88.7		$100,000
1970	$100,000	116.3	$\frac{116.3}{88.7}$	$131,120
1978	$100,000	195.3	$\frac{195.3}{88.7}$	$220,180

When more than one asset is involved, the denominator of the conversion factor for each asset is the index of the year in which the asset was purchased. For example, assume that the business mentioned in the preceding example had another building that cost $200,000 in 1972, in addition to the one that cost $100,000 in 1960. The costs of these two buildings can be restated in terms of common 1978 dollars as follows:

Item	Historical Cost	Conversions (from Table 14-3)	Restatement in Terms of 1978 Dollars
1960 building	$100,000	$\frac{195.3}{88.7}$	$220,180
1972 building	200,000	$\frac{195.3}{125.3}$	311,732
Totals	$300,000		$531,912

Note two important things about this restatement. First, restatement for general price changes is *not* a departure from historical cost, but it is a departure from the accountant's assumption of a stable measuring unit. In this case, the $531,912 is based on an adjustment of historical cost figures of $300,000 to a common or constant 1978 measuring unit. Second, the $531,912 is *not* meant to be a contemporary or market value of the buildings. During the years in question (1960–1978), the specific price level changes and market prices for buildings of the kind used by this company may have differed radically from the general price levels. In summary, general price level restatement, or constant dollar accounting, focuses on changes in the purchasing power of the monetary unit, not on changes in the value of the asset.

It is also important to distinguish monetary from nonmonetary items because changes in the general price level affect them differently. Because monetary items, such as cash, receivables, and all liabilities, represent claims to receive cash or obligations to pay cash, they are stated in terms of current dollars at all times. **Purchasing power gains and losses** occur as a result of holding these items during periods of inflation or deflation because the amounts that must be paid or received are fixed in dollar amounts regardless of any inflation or deflation that might occur. For instance, one who holds cash in a period of inflation will find that the cash purchases fewer goods and services as time passes. Debtors, on the other hand, will be able to retire debts with dollars that are worth less and less in terms of goods and services. On the other side of the transaction, creditors will receive dollars that are worth less. Simply stated, in periods of inflation, owning monetary assets causes a loss in purchasing power, and owing liabilities causes a gain in purchasing power. These results reverse during periods of deflation.

In contrast, holding nonmonetary items, including inventories, investments, plant assets, intangibles, owners' equity, revenues, and expenses, during inflationary or deflationary periods does *not* result in purchasing power gains and losses. Because these items are not tied physically or contractually to a particular dollar amount, they reflect the particular price level in effect when a transaction involving them occurs. In summary, the business does not gain or lose as a result of inflation or deflation from holding or completing transactions involving nonmonetary items.

Purchasing Power Gains and Losses Consider the following data for Town Theater, a simple company with only two monetary items.

	Dec. 31, 19x1	Dec. 31, 19x2	For the Year 19x2
Monetary items			
Cash	$10,000	$20,000	
Notes payable	20,000	20,000	
Ticket receipts			$300,000
Payments for expenses			290,000
General price index	120	144	132 (average)

The purchasing power gain or loss for Town Theater can be calculated in three steps, as illustrated in Figure 14-1 (next page). First, the purchasing power loss from holding monetary assets (cash) is calculated by restating the beginning cash balances. The December 31, 19x1, price index was 120 and the December 31, 19x2, price index was 144; therefore, the cash balance is restated in December 31, 19x2, dollars as follows: $10,000 × 144/120 = $12,000. Next, each increase or decrease in cash is adjusted using the price index existing at the time of the change. Since it is assumed that cash receipts and payments occur uniformly over time, the

Figure 14-1
Calculation of Purchasing Power Gain or Loss

Town Theater
Calculation of Purchasing Power Gain or Loss
For the Year Ended December 31, 19x2

	Recorded Amount	Conversion Factor	Restated Amount	Gain or Loss
Cash				
Beginning balance	$ 10,000	144/120	$ 12,000	
Ticket receipts	300,000	144/132	327,273	
Payments for expenses	(290,000)	144/132	(316,364)	
Ending balance, restated	—		$ 22,909	
Ending balance, actual	$ 20,000		(20,000)	
Purchasing power loss				$2,909
Notes payable				
Beginning balance	$ 10,000	144/120	$ 12,000	
Ending balance, actual	$ 10,000		(10,000)	
Purchasing power gain				(2,000)
Net purchasing power loss				$ 909

average price level (132) for the year 19x2 is used for the denominator in the conversion factor. Thus ticket receipts and payments for expenses are restated as shown in Figure 14-1. The ending balance restated is then calculated by adding the restated figures. Because the ending cash balance is in current dollars and does not need restatement, it is deducted from the restated balance to obtain the purchasing power loss from holding monetary assets ($22,909 − $20,000 = $2,909).

The second step is to calculate the purchasing power gain from owing the note payable of $10,000 for the full year. The beginning balance is adjusted for the change in price level ($10,000 × 144/120 = $12,000), from which is deducted the actual ending balance of $10,000 to obtain the purchasing power gain of $2,000 from owing the monetary liability.

The third step is to calculate the net purchasing power gain or loss by determining the difference of the figures in the first two steps. In this case, Town Theater had a net purchasing power loss of $909.

Balance Sheet Restatement To continue the example of Town Theater, assume that the nonmonetary balance sheet items on December 31, 19x2, are as follows:

Assets		
Theater	$300,000	
Accumulated Depreciation	90,000	$210,000
Stockholders' Equity		
Capital Stock	$150,000	
Retained Earnings	60,000	$210,000

Assume also that the theater was purchased and the capital stock was issued at the same time, when the general price index was 108.

The restated balance sheet is presented in Figure 14-2. It is not necessary to restate monetary items (cash and notes payable) because they have a fixed monetary amount on the balance sheet date. The nonmonetary items are restated by multiplying the dollar amount by the ratio of the current general price index (144) to the general price index when the transaction occurred (108). The retained earnings balance is determined by inserting the amount necessary to make the balance sheet balance, as follows:

Total assets adjusted		$300,000
Less: Note Payable	$ 20,000	
Capital Stock	200,000	220,000
Retained Earnings		$ 80,000

Figure 14-2 Restatement of Balance Sheet

Town Theater
Restatement of Balance Sheet
December 31, 19x2

	Recorded Amount	Conversion Factor	Restated Amount
Cash	$ 20,000	No restatement	$ 20,000
Theater	300,000	144/108	400,000
Accumulated Depreciation	(90,000)	144/108	(120,000)
	$230,000		$300,000
Note Payable	$ 20,000	No restatement	$ 20,000
Capital Stock	150,000	144/108	200,000
Retained Earnings	60,000	(See text)	80,000
	$230,000		$300,000

This retained earnings balance results from balance sheet and income statement effects as well as the purchasing power loss of $909 calculated in the previous section. The details of these effects will be deferred until more advanced courses.

Arguments for and Against Restatement The restatement of financial statements for changes in the general price level is very controversial. Those who favor restated financial statements argue, first, that the annual rate of inflation in the United States is so large that the assumption of a stable measuring unit no longer holds and unadjusted financial statements seriously distort reality. A second argument is that the restatement procedure is based on the traditional historical cost financial statements and is thus as objective, verifiable, and auditable as the traditional statement. Third, amounts that are adjusted for price level, including purchasing power gains and losses, are useful to users.

Critics of statements adjusted for price level argue, first of all, that two sets of financial statements would not be understood by most users. Second, they claim that the measures of general price level are too broad to make purchasing power gains and losses meaningful when applied to an individual firm. A third argument is that changes in the general price level may not correspond to real value changes. Finally, these critics say that financial analysts and bankers do not consider the information provided by such statements useful.

Current Value Accounting

In restating financial statements for changes in general purchasing power in the last section, we relaxed the stable measuring unit assumption but did not abandon historical cost measurement. The building cost that was adjusted from $100,000 to $220,180 because of a change in the general price level from 88.7 to 195.3 may have a current market value of $50,000 or $300,000. The restated figure is not a measure of current value. One of the strongest arguments against restatement is that the resulting financial statements do not reflect specific price changes that have affected a particular company. A lumber company, whose assets consist mostly of lumber inventory, may be much more concerned with changes in the price of lumber than with changes in the general price level. Such a lumber company would have faced the following indexes in 1973 and 1974:[6]

Year	Consumer Price Index—Urban (1967 = 100)	Lumber Index (1967 = 100)
1973	133.1	207.1
1974	147.7	192.5

6. Source: *Statistical Abstract of the United States, 1976.*

Assuming that the company had on average $1,000,000, or three-fourths of its nonmonetary assets, invested in inventory in 1973 and 1974, one could make the following restatements:

Index	Restatement Computation	Restated Amount	Change
General	147.7/133.1 × $1,000,000	$1,109,692	$109,692
Specific	192.5/207.1 × $1,000,000	929,502	(70,498)
Total effect			$180,190

It would be difficult to convince the manager of this lumber company that the lumber inventory should show an increase of $109,692 on the financial statements, when in fact its value in the marketplace dropped by $70,498.

A method of accounting that would recognize the effects of such specific price changes in the financial statements is called **current value accounting.** Current value accounting represents a departure from historical cost accounting. Its advocates propose a three-step transition to current value statements, as follows:

Step 1. Footnote disclosures of the current value of inventories, cost of goods sold, plant assets, and depreciation
Step 2. Statements expressed in current values as supplements to historical cost statements
Step 3. Presentation of only current value statements

A major problem with current value statements is agreement on how to measure current value. There are two main schools of thought. One school recommends that **net realizable value** be used. Net realizable value is an exit value in that it represents what the company could sell its assets for, and is recommended because it is a measure of the company's ability to adapt to the marketplace. The other school of thought recommends **replacement cost.** Replacement cost is an entry value because it represents the cost of buying (or replacing), in the normal course of business, new assets of equivalent operating or productive capacity. This method is recommended because it is more closely related to the concept of maintaining a company's productive capacity as a going concern. This discussion, which is necessarily limited, will focus on replacement cost accounting because of the attention drawn to it by the SEC's requirement for disclosure of replacement costs in 1976[7] and its subsequent repeal of the requirement when the FASB issued *Statement No. 33.*

Arguments for Replacement Cost Disclosure A major argument for replacement cost disclosure is that it is more realistic than historical cost statements. Specific price changes are a fact of life and, if reflected in the financial statements, increase the usefulness of the information presented. A second major argument for replacement cost is that the overall economy is hindered by the unrealistic depreciation rates under historical costing. Because plant assets in most cases would increase significantly if

7. *Accounting Series Release No. 190* (Washington: Securities and Exchange Commission, 1976).

replacement costs were used, depreciation would also increase significantly. Thus these increased costs are more in line with replacing current productive capacity and provide more realistic earnings figures on which to base such things as investment and dividend policies.

Arguments Against Replacement Cost Disclosure On the other side of the argument, critics emphasize that there are no accepted ways of measuring replacement costs, and replacement costs are not based on objective, verifiable transactions that can be audited. Therefore, they contend, the resulting information is of limited usefulness to users.

Critics also claim that through judicious use of current accounting techniques, income measures close to those obtained under replacement cost accounting can be obtained from historical cost statements. For example, by using LIFO inventory, a company in effect charges the most current inventory purchases against income, thus producing gross profit similar to that which would have been obtained by using replacement costs for inventory. Also, by using accelerated depreciation methods, a rapid and increased write-off of plant assets is obtained in the early years, which may help compensate for rises in replacement costs.

The FASB Position

Objective 7 Describe the FASB's approach to accounting for changing prices

Over the years, the Financial Accounting Standards Board has vacillated on the issue of constant dollar versus current value accounting. In 1974, it followed a prior Accounting Principles Board recommendation that all companies include in their annual reports supplemental financial statements expressed in units of general purchasing power.[8] This proposed statement was not acted upon, partially because it was upstaged by the previously mentioned 1976 SEC release on replacement cost disclosure. By 1979, the FASB had reconsidered its position and issued another statement, which requires certain large publicly held companies (those with inventories and property, plant, and equipment of more than $125 million or total assets of more than $1 billion) to disclose supplemental information on both a constant dollar basis and a current value basis.[9] The current value basis used by the FASB is the lower of current cost or net realizable value at the balance sheet date. By current cost, the FASB means the lowest current buying price or production cost of an asset of the same age and in the same condition as the asset owned. Thus the FASB's concept of current value combined the two concepts of net realizable value and replacement cost.

Specifically, the FASB requires supplemental disclosure for the current year, similar to that shown in Figure 14-3 for Westinghouse. In addition,

8. *Proposed Statement of Financial Accounting Standards, Exposure Draft,* "Financial Reporting in Units of General Purchasing Power" (Stamford, Conn.: Financial Accounting Standards Board, 1974); also see Accounting Principles Board, *Statement No. 3* "Financial Statements Restated for General Price Level Changes" (New York: American Institute of Certified Public Accountants, 1969).
9. *Statement of Financial Accounting Standards No. 33,* "Financial Reporting and Changing Prices" (Stamford, Conn.: Financial Accounting Standards Board, 1979).

Supplementary Statement of Income from Continuing Operations Adjusted for Changing Prices (unaudited) (in millions)

	Year Ended December 31, 1979		
	As Reported in the Primary Statements	Adjusted for General Price Changes (Constant Dollar)	Adjusted for Specific Price Changes (Current Cash)
Sales	$7,332.0	$7,332.0	$7,332.0
Cost of sales	5,688.2	5,744.8	5,728.3
Other operating expenses	1,163.7	1,163.7	1,163.7
Depreciation	160.2	238.6	257.3
Interest expense	43.7	43.7	43.7
Other income and minority interest	180.6	180.6	180.6
Income taxes	125.7	125.7	125.7
Income from continuing operations	$ 331.1	$ 196.1	$ 193.9
Loss from decline in purchasing power of net monetary assets		$ 126.0	$ 126.0
Comparison of Price Changes— Inventories and Plant and Equipment Held During the Year*			
Effect of general price changes measured by the consumer price index			$ 387.5
Effect of specific price changes (current cost)			363.6
Amount by which general price increases exceed specific price increases			$ 23.9

*At December 31, 1979 current cost of inventory was $1,758.8 million and current cost of plant and equipment, net of accumulated depreciation was $2,390.3 million.

Figure 14-3 Disclosure for Current Year from Annual Report of Westinghouse Electric Corporation

the FASB requires supplemental disclosure for the most recent five years, similar to the information shown in Figure 14-4 (next page).

There are several important observations to make about these required disclosures. First, they are supplementary to the historical cost financial statements. The FASB believes that most people continue to use historical cost financial statements and that there are four good reasons for keeping them as the primary financial statements, as follows: (1) Historical cost financial statements depend on actual transactions, which determine the change in owners' equity in the long run. (2) Because historical costs are generally the result of arms'-length bargaining, they provide a basis for reliably measuring the results of transactions and are therefore capable of independent verification. (3) Users' understanding of the effect of changing prices may be enhanced if they are able to compare the measurements

Comparison of Selected Supplementary Financial Data Adjusted for Effects of Changing Prices (unaudited)* (in millions)

		1979	1978	1977	1976	1975
Sales	—as reported	$7,332.0	$6,663.3	$6,137.7	$6,145.2	$5,862.7
	in constant dollars	7,332.0	7,413.5	7,351.7	7,835.6	7,906.6
Income from continuing operations	—as reported	331.1	311.3	271.3	223.2	178.6
	in constant dollars	196.1				
	at current cost	193.9				
per common share (in dollars)	—as reported	3.85	3.59	3.10	2.54	2.04
	in constant dollars	2.28				
	at current cost	2.25				
Common stock dividends per share (in dollars)	—as reported	.972	.972	.972	.972	.972
	in constant dollars	.972	1.08	1.16	1.24	1.31
Market price per common share at year-end	—as reported	20⅛	16⅝	18⅛	17⅝	13⅜
	in constant dollars	20⅛	18¾	22⅜	23¼	18½
Net assets at year-end	—as reported	2,250.0	2,423.0	2,293.9	2,138.4	2,001.7
	in constant dollars	3,395.0				
	at current cost	3,659.8				
Average consumer price index		217.4	195.4	181.5	170.5	161.2

*Amounts shown for constant dollars and current cost prior to 1979 are stated in average 1979 dollars based on the average consumer price index, except for market price per common share.

Figure 14-4
Disclosure for Most Recent Five Years from Annual Report of Westinghouse Electric Corporation

in the primary financial statements with measurements reflecting changing prices. (4) Users are accustomed to the present financial statements.

The second observation is that in spite of the importance of historical cost statements, the FASB believes that the supplemental reporting of the effects of changing prices is necessary because this information will aid in the assessment of (1) future cash flows, (2) enterprise performance, (3) the erosion of operating capacity, and (4) the erosion of purchasing power.

Third, the FASB recognizes that many problems remain to be solved in measuring the effect of changing prices. It intends to review the effects of *Statement No. 33* on an ongoing basis and to undertake a comprehensive review of the statement after a period of no more than five years.

Chapter Review

Review of Learning Objectives

1. Apply the matching rule to revenue recognition.

Two bases are used in practice to apply the matching rule to revenue recognition. The point of sale basis is the most common basis and is the one used generally in previous chapters. The cash basis is often used by individuals and recognizes revenue only when cash is received.

2. Apply the matching rule to the allocation of expired costs as it relates to capital expenditures and revenue expenditures.

It is important to distinguish between capital expenditures, which are capitalized, and revenue expenditures, which are charged immediately against income, because the error of classifying one as the other will have a significant effect on net income. Expenditures for plant assets, additions, betterments, and intangible assets are capital expenditures. Extraordinary repairs are also treated as capital expenditures, whereas ordinary repairs are revenue expenditures.

3. Apply the matching rule to the accounting problems associated with intangible assets, including research and development costs and goodwill.

Purchases of intangible assets should be treated as capital expenditures and recorded at acquisition cost, which in turn should be amortized over the useful life of the assets (not to exceed forty years). The FASB requires that research and development costs be treated as revenue expenditures and charged as expense in the period of expenditure. Goodwill is the excess of cost over the market value in the purchase of a business and is usually related to the superior earning potential of the assets. It should be recorded only if purchased and should be amortized over a period not to exceed forty years.

4. Define and describe the use of the conventions of consistency, materiality, conservatism, and full disclosure.

Because accountants' measurements are not exact, certain conventions have come to be applied in current practice to aid the reader in interpreting the financial statements. One of these conventions is consistency, which requires the use of the same accounting procedures from period to period. Second is materiality, which involves the relative importance of an item. Third is conservatism, which entails the use of the procedure that will be least likely to overstate assets and income. Fourth is full disclosure, which means including all relevant information in the financial statements.

5. Identify the two principal types of price changes.

The two principal types of price changes that affect financial statements are specific price changes, which reflect the change in price of an individual commodity or service, and general price changes, which reflect the price changes of a group of goods or services. General price changes result in purchasing power gains or losses.

6. Using constant dollar accounting, compute purchasing power gains and losses, and restate a balance sheet for changes in the general price level.

Holding monetary items during periods of inflation or deflation results in purchasing power gains or losses because monetary items are fixed in terms of current dollars at all times and cannot fluctuate to compensate for the changes in general price level. In contrast, holding nonmonetary items during similar periods does not result in purchasing power gains or losses. Under constant dollar accounting, historical cost statements are restated for general price level changes. Under this method, purchasing power gains or losses are calculated by multiplying the dollar amount by the current price level divided by the price level when the item originated. A balance sheet is restated by adjusting the nonmonetary items for the change in price level since the item's origin. Retained earnings are computed as a balancing figure.

7. Describe the FASB's approach to accounting for changing prices.

Although the FASB believes that historical cost financial statements should be the primary financial statements, it requires that certain large companies provide supplemental information, both for the current year and for a five-year period, on both a constant dollar basis and a current value basis. Current value accounting, which recognizes the effects of specific price level changes in the financial statements, is defined by the FASB to be the lower of current cost or net realizable value. The FASB is encouraging a period of experimentation in reporting the effects of changing prices.

Review Problem
Comprehensive Capital and Revenue Expenditure Entries

The Haywood Haberdashery, Inc., operates several stores featuring men's fashions. The transactions below describe the capital and revenue expenditures that relate to one of the company's stores. All expenditures are made with cash.

The building was purchased on January 1, 1967, for $117,000. At that time the building was repaired and renovated for use as a clothing store at a cost of $63,000. It was estimated that the building would have a useful life of forty years and a residual value after that time of $20,000.

On April 15, 1971, the front windows were replaced because they were cracked, and the roof was repaired because it was leaking. The repairs cost a total of $9,800.

On January 10, 1972, a new addition to the building was completed at a cost of $95,000. The addition did not add to the estimated useful life of the building but did increase the residual value by $10,000.

On August 3, 1975, the building was painted at a cost of $17,500.

On January 7, 1977, a complete overhaul of the heating and cooling system was completed at a cost of $40,000. It was estimated that this work would add ten years to the useful life of the building but would not increase its residual value.

Because of a decline in business, this building was sold on January 1, 1982, for $240,000 in cash.

Required

1. Open ledger accounts for Building (141) and for Accumulated Depreciation, Building (142).
2. Prepare general journal entries for the dates below, and post the portions relating to the two accounts opened in part 1. The dates are (a) January 1, 1967; (b) April 15, 1971; (c) January 10, 1972; (d) August 3, 1975; (e) January 7, 1977; and (f) January 1, 1982.
3. Compute depreciation expense for each year until the date of sale, assuming that the straight-line method is used and that the company's fiscal year ends on December 31. Enter the amounts in the account for Accumulated Depreciation, Building.
4. Prepare a general journal entry to record the sale of the building on January 1, 1982. Post the relevant portions of the entry to the two accounts opened in part 1.

Answer to Review Problem

1. Ledger accounts opened and posted (facing page):

Accumulated Depreciation, Building — **Account No. 142**

Date		Item	Post Ref.	Debit	Credit	Balance Debit	Balance Credit
1967			J		4,000		4,000
1968			J		4,000		8,000
1969			J		4,000		12,000
1970			J		4,000		16,000
1971			J		4,000		20,000
1972			J		7,000		27,000
1973			J		7,000		34,000
1974			J		7,000		41,000
1975			J		7,000		48,000
1976			J		7,000		55,000
1977							
Jan.	10		J	40,000			15,000
Dec.	31		J		5,750		20,750
1978			J		5,750		26,500
1979			J		5,750		32,250
1980			J		5,750		38,000
1981			J		5,750		43,750
1982							
Jan.	1		J	43,750			—

Building — **Account No. 141**

Date		Item	Post Ref.	Debit	Credit	Balance Debit	Balance Credit
1967							
Jan.	1		J	180,000		180,000	
1972							
Jan.	10		J	95,000		275,000	
1982							
Jan.	1		J		275,000		

2 and 4. Journal entries prepared:

General Journal **Page**

Date		Description	Post Ref.	Debit	Credit
1967					
Jan.	1	Building	141	180,000	
		Cash			180,000
		Purchase of building:			
		Cost $117,000			
		Repair and renovation 63,000			
		Total cost $180,000			
1971					
Apr.	15	Repair Expense		9,800	
		Cash			9,800
		Replacement of windows and repair of roof			
1972					
Jan.	10	Building	141	95,000	
		Cash			95,000
		Addition to building			
1975					
Aug.	3	Repair Expense		17,500	
		Cash			17,500
		Painting of building			
1977					
Jan.	7	Accumulated Depreciation, Building	142	40,000	
		Cash			40,000
		Overhaul of heating and cooling system			
1982					
Jan.	1	Cash		240,000	
		Accumulated Depreciation, Building	142	43,750	
		Building	141		275,000
		Gain on Sale of Building			8,750
		Sale of building			

3. Depreciation expense computed:

January 1, 1967, to December 31, 1971—five years

($180,000 − $20,000) ÷ 40 years = $4,000 per year

January 1, 1972, to December 31, 1976—five years

($275,000 − $30,000) ÷ 35 years = $7,000 per year

January 1, 1977, to December 31, 1981—five years
Book value before extraordinary repair:

Building account	$275,000	
Accumulated Depreciation	55,000	$220,000
Extraordinary Repair		40,000
New book value		$260,000
Less salvage value		30,000
Depreciable cost		$230,000
Divide by years remaining in useful life:		
Years remaining before extraordinary item	30	
Years added by extraordinary item	10	40
Depreciation per year		$ 5,750

Chapter Assignments

Questions

1. What are the two principal aspects of applying the matching rule?
2. From the standpoint of matching, why is the point of sale basis of revenue recognition considered better than the cash basis?
3. What is the distinction between revenue expenditures and capital expenditures, and why is this distinction important?
4. What will be the effect on future years' income of charging an addition to a building as repair expense?
5. In what ways do an addition, a betterment, and an extraordinary repair differ?
6. How does an extraordinary repair differ from an ordinary repair? What is the accounting treatment for each?
7. What is the basis of the following statement? "Accounting for net income is a useless measurement because it is based on so many arbitrary estimates."
8. Why are the following concepts important to financial reporting: consistency, materiality, conservatism, and full disclosure? How does each contribute to better financial reporting?
9. Because accounts receivable have no physical substance, can they be considered intangible assets?
10. Under what circumstances can a company have intangible assets that do not appear on the balance sheet?
11. When the Accounting Principles Board indicates that accounting for intangible assets involves the same problem as accounting for tangible assets, what problem is it referring to?
12. How does the Financial Accounting Standards Board recommend that research and development costs be treated?
13. Under what conditions should goodwill be recorded? Should it remain in the records permanently once it is recorded?
14. Why has the assumption of a stable monetary unit been questioned in recent years?
15. Distinguish specific price level changes from general price level changes.
16. "We love debt," says G. James Williams, vice president—finance (of Dow Chemical). "The $3 billion we have in long-term debt is one of the greatest assets

of Dow Chemical Company." For forty years, Williams explained, the company has regarded inflation as a fact of American life, from which springs this corollary: borrow now to repay in cheaper dollars. (Quoted from *Barron's*, October 9, 1978, p. 4) Why does Dow Chemical feel that it is an asset to be a debtor?
17. How does current value accounting differ from constant dollar accounting?
18. What are the FASB requirements for the disclosure of the effects of changing prices?

Classroom Exercises

Exercise 14-1 Balance Sheet Restatement for General Price Changes

The Inflation Company's balance sheet appears as follows:

Inflation Company
Balance Sheet
December 31, 19xx

Cash	$ 50,000	Note Payable	$100,000
Building	210,000	Capital Stock	250,000
Accumulated Depreciation	(15,000)	Retained Earnings	105,000
Equipment	300,000		
Accumulated Depreciation	(90,000)	Total Liabilities and	
Total Assets	$455,000	Stockholder's Equity	$455,000

The following general price level indexes are applicable:

Beginning of year	160	At the time of	
End of year	200	Building purchase	120
Average for year	180	Equipment purchase	150
		Capital stock issue	100

Restate the balance sheet for changes in the general price level.

Exercise 14-2 Amortization of Copyrights and Trademarks

1. Business Publishing Company purchased the copyright to a basic computer textbook for $10,000. The usual life of a textbook is about four years. However, the copyright will remain in effect for another fifty years.

Calculate the annual amortization of the copyright.

2. Tanta Company purchased a trademark from a well-known supermarket for $80,000. The management of the company argued that the trademark value would last forever and might even increase and thus no amortization should be charged.

Calculate the minimum amount of annual amortization that should be charged, according to guidelines of the appropriate Accounting Principles Board opinion.

Exercise 14-3 Computation of Goodwill

Matthew Corporation has assets of $380,000 and liabilities of $100,000. In Matthew Corporation's industry, the typical return is 10 percent of *net* assets. Over the last five years, Matthew Corporation has earned $35,000 per year, with net assets similar to those throughout the industry. Mark Corporation has offered to buy out Matthew Corporation for a cash payment equal to net assets plus five times the excess earnings over industry average.

1. Determine the net assets for Matthew Corporation.
2. Determine by how much Matthew Corporation's earnings exceed the industry average.
3. Calculate how much Mark Corporation is offering for Matthew Corporation.
4. Compute the value of goodwill.

Exercise 14-4 Accounting Concepts and Conventions

Each of the statements below violates a concept or convention in accounting. In each case, state which of the following concepts or conventions is violated: revenue recognition, allocation of expired costs, consistency, materiality, conservatism, or full disclosure.

1. A company changes from the straight-line method of depreciation to the sum-of-the-years'-digits method.
2. The same company does not indicate in the financial statements that the method of depreciation was changed, nor does it specify the effect of the change on net income.
3. Plots of land are sold for 5 percent down, with payments to be made over the next ten years. The entire selling price of the land is recorded as revenue on the date of sale even though this type of sale historically has a high rate of defaults.
4. The cost of an office addition built on the side of a warehouse is charged to repair expense.
5. The asset account for a pickup truck still used in the business is written down to salvage value even though the carrying value under conventional depreciation methods is higher.

Exercise 14-5 Extraordinary Repairs

Hancock Manufacturing Company has an incinerator that originally cost $74,800 and now has accumulated depreciation of $58,300. The incinerator just completed its fifteenth year of service in an estimated useful life of twenty years. At the beginning of the sixteenth year, the company spent $19,300 repairing and modernizing the incinerator to comply with pollution control standards. Consequently, instead of five years, the incinerator is now expected to last ten more years. It will not, however, have more capacity than it did in the past or a residual value at the end of its useful life.

1. Prepare the entry to record the cost of the repairs.
2. Compute the book value of the incinerator after the entry.
3. Prepare the entry to record the depreciation (assuming straight-line method) for the current year.

Exercise 14-6 Effect of Alternative Accounting Methods

At the end of its first year of operations, a company could calculate its ending merchandise inventory, according to three different methods, as follows: FIFO, $62,500; weighted average, $60,000; LIFO, $58,000. If the weighted-average method is used, the net income for the year would be $28,000.

1. Determine the net income if the FIFO method is used.
2. Determine the net income if the LIFO method is used.
3. Which method is most conservative?
4. Will the consistency convention be violated if the LIFO method is chosen?
5. Does the full-disclosure convention require disclosure of the inventory method selected by management in the financial statements?

Exercise 14-7 Calculation of Purchasing Power Gains and Losses

Companies A and B both began operation on January 1 with $50,000 in cash. Company A raised the cash by issuing capital stock, and Company B by issuing a two-year note payable. During the year, both companies had cash receipts of $550,000 and cash payments of $440,000. Also, during the year, the general price level began at 150, ended at 180, and averaged 165.

Calculate the purchasing power gain or loss for each company.

Problem Set A

Problem 14A-1 Accounting Concepts and Conventions

In each of the situations below, generally accepted accounting principles may have been violated.

Required

In each case, state the convention or concept, if any, that has been violated, and explain briefly the nature of the violation. If you believe that the treatment is in accord with generally accepted accounting principles, explain why.

1. Five years ago, Sara Martin opened a clothing store called Sara's Togs. Her business has been very successful, and the name of the store is well known. In recognition of this success, an account called Trademark and Goodwill is opened and debited for $60,000, an amount equal to three years' earnings. The credit is to Sara Martin, Capital.
2. Sampson Company closed its books on December 31, 19x8, before preparing its annual report. On December 30, 19x8, a fire had destroyed one of the company's two factories. Although the company had fire insurance and would not suffer a loss on the building, a significant decrease in sales in 19x9 was expected because of the fire. The fire damage was not reported in the 19x8 financial statements because the operations for that year were not affected by the fire.
3. Grady Drug Company spends a substantial portion of its profits on research and development. During the current year, it developed a new drug, which is expected to produce revenues for at least ten years. The total cost of developing this drug was $2,500,000. This cost was recorded as expense in the year of the expenditure.
4. During the current year, Ruiz Company changed from the sum-of-the-years'-digits depreciation method to the straight-line method. The effect of this change on income in the current year was immaterial.
5. Bailey Manufacturing Company uses the weighted-average method for computing the cost of inventory unless the market value of the inventory is less than the cost, in which case the market value is used. At the end of the current year, the market value is $77,000 and the cost is $80,000. Bailey uses the $77,000 figure to compute net income, and on the balance sheet discloses that it has used the lower of cost or market to compute inventory.
6. Jensen Company has annual sales of $5,000,000. It follows the practice of charging any items costing less than $100 to expense in the year purchased. During the current year, it purchased several chairs at different times for the executive conference rooms at $97 each, including freight. Although the chairs are expected to last for at least ten years, the chairs were charged to expense in accordance with company policy.

Problem 14A-2 Effect of Alternative Accounting Methods

New Products Company began operation this year. At the beginning of the year, the company purchased plant assets of $165,000, with an estimated useful life of ten years and no salvage value.

During the year, the company had sales of $300,000, salary expense of $50,000, and other expenses of $20,000, excluding depreciation. In addition, the company purchased inventory as follows:

January 15	400 units at $100	$ 40,000
March 20	200 units at $102	20,400
June 15	800 units at $104	83,200
September 18	600 units at $103	61,800
December 9	300 units at $105	31,500
Totals	2,300 units	$236,900

At the end of the year, a physical inventory disclosed 500 units still on hand. The managers of New Products know that they have a choice of accounting methods but are not sure what the effect of the methods will be on net income. They have heard of FIFO and LIFO for inventory methods and straight-line and sum-of-the-years'-digits for depreciation methods.

Required

1. Prepare two income statements for New Products Company: one using FIFO basis and straight-line method; the other using LIFO basis and sum-of-the-years'-digits method.
2. Prepare a schedule accounting for the difference in the two net income figures in part 1.

Problem 14A-3 Amortization of Patent and Leasehold Improvements

1. Ecology Enterprises purchased a patent for $117,000 on April 1, 19x6, for a new device to remove harmful particles from smoke. If successful, the device would significantly cut the cost of cleaning the smoke released from industrial plants.

The company immediately began patent infringement suits against four other companies. Ecology Enterprises won these suits and thus has the exclusive right to manufacture the device. The costs of defending the patents were $83,000, all incurred during 19x6. The company manufactured and sold the device during 19x6, 19x7, and 19x8. Although the patent was good for fifteen years beyond the purchase date, the company's management considered eight years to be a reasonable estimated life, given the fast-changing technology in the field.

It became apparent in January 19x9 that the device could not be modified to meet the stricter pollution control standards that the Environmental Protection Agency was enforcing. Consequently, existing orders for the device were canceled.

Required

Prepare general journal entries to record the following: (a) the purchase of the patent, (b) the successful defense of the patent, (c) the amortization expense on December 31, 19x6, and (d) the news of January 19x9.

2. Robert Ashley obtained an eight-year sublease on a two-story building to open an art gallery. To obtain the sublease, he had to pay $5,600 to the current tenant, who had eight years to go on his lease. Robert was willing to pay for the leasehold because of the excellent location of the proposed gallery and the current low rent of only $3,600 per year for the building.

In addition, Robert had to make certain improvements in the building to convert it to a gallery. These included fixtures and lighting, $2,100; carpet, $3,200; a small elevator between floors, \$7,800; and an art vault, \$5,900. He estimated that the carpeting would last eight years and the other improvements would last twenty years, with no estimated residual value.

Required

Prepare general journal entries to record (a) the payment for the sublease; (b) the payments for the fixtures and lighting, carpet, elevator, and vault, none of which can be removed at the end of the lease; (c) the lease payment for the first year; (d) the expense, if any, associated with the sublease; and (e) the expense, if any, associated with the fixtures and lighting, carpet, elevator, and vault.

Problem 14A-4 Calculation of Purchasing Power Gain or Loss and Balance Sheet Restatement

The Downtown Parking Company operates a single parking lot. All receipts are in cash, and expenses are paid in cash. During 19x2, the company had revenues of \$341,000 and expenses of \$242,000. At the end of 19x2, the company's balance sheet appeared as follows:

Downtown Parking Company
Balance Sheet
December 31, 19x2

Assets	
Cash	\$150,000
Land	20,000
Parking Building	300,000
Accumulated Depreciation	(60,000)
Total Assets	\$410,000
Liabilities and Stockholders' Equity	
Note Payable	\$250,000
Capital Stock	70,000
Retained Earnings	90,000
Total Liabilities and Stockholders' Equity	\$410,000

The company was founded on January 1, 19x1, when the land and parking building were purchased and the capital stock was issued. The note has been outstanding during all of 19x2, and the cash balance at the beginning of 19x2 was \$51,000. The general price level during the past two years varied as follows:

January 1, 19x1	200
January 1, 19x2	210
December 31, 19x2	231
Average for 19x2	220

Required

1. Compute the purchasing power gain or loss for Downtown Parking Company for 19x2.
2. Prepare a restated balance sheet at December 31, 19x2.

Problem 14A-5 Comprehensive Capital and Revenue Expenditure Entries

Buy More for Less, Inc., runs a chain of small grocery stores. On June 1, 1965, the company purchased a building on Main Street in a small town outside St. Louis for $224,000. At the time of purchase, it cost $112,000 to repair and renovate the building to make it useful as a grocery store. The building had an estimated useful life of thirty years and an estimated residual value of $30,000.

On August 13, 1969, the roof of the building was repaired at a cost of $2,150.

The store prospered, and on June 10, 1970, a new addition to the building was constructed at a cost of $75,000. The addition increased the estimated residual value of the building by $10,000.

On April 25, 1973, the building was repainted at a cost of $12,650.

Because of structural damage, major repairs costing $45,000 were completed on June 6, 1975. Management felt these repairs would extend the useful life of the building five years but would not increase the residual value.

On June 1, 1976, new managers took over Buy More for Less, Inc., and on December 1, 1977, sold the building on Main Street for $240,000. They received $20,000 cash, land valued at $40,000, and a mortgage for the remainder.

Required

1. Open ledger accounts for Buildings (143) and for Accumulated Depreciation, Buildings (144).
2. Prepare general journal entries for the dates below, and post the relevant portions of the entries to the two accounts opened in part 1. The dates are (a) June 1, 1965; (b) August 13, 1969; (c) June 10, 1970; (d) April 25, 1973; and (e) June 6, 1975.
3. Compute depreciation expense for each year and partial year until the date of sale, assuming that the straight-line method is used and the company's fiscal year ends on May 31. Post the amounts in the account for Accumulated Depreciation, Buildings.
4. Prepare a general journal entry to record the sale of the building on December 1, 1977. Post the relevant portions of the entry to the two accounts opened in part 1.

Problem 14A-6 Purchase of Business with Goodwill Resulting

Bill Whiteside has been looking for a good business to purchase. He found one in Rampy Enterprises, which has earned an average of $44,000 a year for the last five years.

Whiteside proposed that he purchase all the assets, exclusive of cash, of Rampy Enterprises and assume the liabilities of Rampy. He will pay $150,000 cash and give a one-year note for the balance. He is willing to pay for goodwill equal to four times those earnings that exceed the industry average earnings of 10 percent of net tangible assets.

Information from the current balance sheet for Rampy Enterprises follows:

Cash		$ 22,000
Other Current Assets		164,000
Plant Assets		
Land		5,000
Buildings	$124,000	
Less Accumulated Depreciation	42,000	82,000
Equipment	$289,000	
Less Accumulated Depreciation	106,000	183,000
Trademark		22,000
Franchise		17,000
Total Assets		$495,000

Current Liabilities	$ 46,000
Long-Term Note Payable	100,000
Paul Rampy, Capital	349,000
Total Liabilities and Owner's Equity	$495,000

Bill Whiteside and Paul Rampy agree to adjust the Rampy Enterprises books in two ways. First of all, the land, which had been purchased many years before by the Rampy family, was not realistically valued and should have a value of $25,000. Second, the trademark and franchise that had been on the books for many years without being amortized should not be considered to have any value.

Required

1. Prepare a general journal entry to adjust the Rampy Enterprises books in accordance with the agreement.
2. Compute the net tangible assets exclusive of cash.
3. Compute the amount of goodwill to be paid.
4. Prepare a general journal entry in Whiteside's records to show the purchase of Rampy Enterprises.

Problem Set B

Problem 14B-1 Accounting Concepts and Conventions

In each of the situations below, generally accepted accounting principles may have been violated.

Required

In each case, state the convention or concept, if any, that has been violated, and explain briefly the nature of the violation. If you believe that the treatment is in accord with generally accepted accounting principles, explain why.

1. One-Hour Cleaning has a fleet of delivery trucks. The trucks are given a tune-up every six months, and the tires are replaced each year. These trucks last longer as a result of these repairs than they would otherwise. Thus the cost of these repairs is debited to Accumulated Depreciation, thereby lengthening the time over which the cost of the trucks is depreciated.
2. A number of the regular employees of Mattis Company were involved in the construction of Mattis's new office building. Because the salaries of these employees would have been incurred anyway, their cost was charged to expense as incurred.
3. Carter, the auditor of King Corporation, discovered that an official of the company may have authorized the payment of a $1,000 bribe to a local official. Management argued that, because the item was so small in relation to the size of the company ($1,000,000 in sales), the illegal payment should not be disclosed.
4. Elizabeth's Stereo Center built a small addition to the main building to house a new discount record division. Because of uncertainty about whether the record division would succeed or not, a conservative approach was taken by recording the addition as expense.
5. R-B Electronics has used the FIFO inventory method since its origin ten years ago. Because there has been no change in the inventory method, the company does not declare in its financial statements that it uses the FIFO method.

6. After careful study, Jumer Company, which has offices in forty states, has determined that, in the future, the depreciation of its office furniture should be based on an estimated residual value of 5 percent rather than 12 percent, which has been used in the past. The company uses the straight-line method for computing depreciation and plans to make no disclosure of the change in residual value in the financial statements.

Problem 14B-2 Effect of Alternative Accounting Methods

New Trend Company began operations by purchasing $200,000 in equipment that has an estimated useful life of nine years and an estimated residual value of $20,000.

During the year, the company purchased inventory as follows:

January	2,000 units at $25	$ 50,000
March	4,000 units at $24	96,000
May	1,000 units at $27	27,000
July	5,000 units at $27	135,000
September	6,000 units at $28	168,000
November	2,000 units at $29	58,000
December	3,000 units at $28	84,000
Totals	23,000 units	$618,000

The company sold 19,000 units for a total of $840,000 and incurred salary expenses of $170,000 and expenses other than depreciation of $120,000.

New Trend's management is anxious to present its income statement most fairly in its first year of operation and realizes that there are alternative accounting methods available for accounting for inventory and equipment. Management wants to determine the effect of various alternatives on this year's income. Two sets of alternatives are required.

Required

1. Prepare two income statements for New Trend Company: one using FIFO basis for inventory and straight-line method for depreciation; the other using LIFO basis for inventory and sum-of-the-years'-digits method for depreciation.
2. Prepare a schedule accounting for the difference in the two net income figures in part 1.

Problem 14B-4 Calculation of Purchasing Power Gain or Loss and Balance Sheet Restatement

Musical Skating Rink, Inc., began on January 1, 19x1, by issuing capital stock and purchasing a skating rink. Its balance sheet on December 31, 19x2, follows:

Assets	
Cash	$ 30,000
Skating Rink	260,000
Accumulated Depreciation	(39,000)
Total Assets	$251,000
Liabilities and Stockholders' Equity	
Note Payable	$ 10,000
Capital Stock	273,000
Retained Earnings	(32,000)
Total Liabilities and Stockholders' Equity	$251,000

The company operates strictly on a cash basis. On January 2, 19x2, the company had a cash balance of $17,000, including the proceeds from the note payable it issued on that date. During the year, its cash receipts were $162,500, and its payments for expenses were $149,500. The general price level on different dates varied as follows:

January 1, 19x1	100
January 1, 19x2	120
December 31, 19x2	138
Average for 19x2	130

Required

1. Compute the purchasing power gain or loss for Musical Skating Rink, Inc., during 19x2.
2. Prepare a restated balance sheet at December 31, 19x2.

Problem 14B-5 Comprehensive Capital and Revenue Expenditure Entries

Auto Energy, Inc., operates a chain of self-service gasoline stations in several southern states. The transactions below describe the capital and revenue expenditures for one station.

Construction on the station was completed on July 1, 1966, at a cost of $275,000. It was estimated that the station would have a useful life of thirty-five years and a residual value of $30,000.

On September 15, 1970, scheduled painting and minor repairs affecting the appearance of the station were completed at a cost of $3,950.

On July 9, 1971, a new gasoline tank was added at a cost of $80,000. The tank did not add to the useful life of the station, but it did add $7,000 to its estimated residual value.

On October 22, 1974, the driveway of the station was resurfaced at a cost of $1,900.

The cost of major repairs and renovation, which were completed on July 3, 1976, was $55,000. It was estimated that this work would extend the life of the station by five years and would not increase the residual value.

A change in the routing of a major highway led to the sale of the station on January 2, 1979, for $200,000. The company received $20,000 in cash and a note for the balance of the $200,000.

Required

1. Open ledger accounts for Station (143) and for Accumulated Depreciation, Station (144).
2. Prepare general journal entries for the dates below, and record the relevant portions of the two accounts opened in part 1. The dates are (a) July 1, 1966; (b) September 15, 1970; (c) July 9, 1971; (d) October 22, 1974; and (e) July 3, 1976.
3. Compute depreciation expense for each year and partial year until the date of sale, assuming that the straight-line method is used and that the company's fiscal year ends on June 30. Enter the amounts in the account for Accumulated Depreciation, Station.
4. Prepare a general journal entry to record the sale of the station on January 2, 1979. Post the relevant portions of the entry to the two accounts opened in part 1.

Problem 14B-6 Purchase of Business with Goodwill Resulting

R. K. Yaillen, the owner of RKY Enterprises, has reached an agreement for the purchase of the TCT Company from T. C. Trigona.

Information from the balance sheet of TCT Company follows:

Cash		$ 112,400
Other Current Assets		286,600
Plant Assets		
Land		82,000
Buildings	$597,000	
Less Accumulated Depreciation	216,000	381,000
Equipment	$786,000	
Less Accumulated Depreciation	329,000	457,000
Patent		35,000
Total Assets		$1,354,000
Current Liabilities		$ 99,000
Long-Term Mortgage		360,000
T. C. Trigona, Capital		895,000
Total Liabilities and Owner's Equity		$1,354,000

The terms of the agreement were as follows:

a. RKY would purchase the assets other than cash and assume the liabilities of TCT except for an unused building by issuing long-term bonds for the amount of the purchase. The cost of the building was $132,000, and it had $37,000 of accumulated depreciation.

b. TCT would adjust its books to reflect a write-down of $20,000 for obsolete inventory, an increase in the patent account of $15,000, and an increase in current liabilities of $27,000 to acknowledge unrecorded debt.

c. In addition to the amount in part a, RKY would pay TCT for goodwill in the amount of five times the amount by which TCT earnings exceeded the industry average. During the past five years, TCT earned an average of $106,000. The industry average was 9 percent of net assets.

Required

1. Prepare a general journal entry to adjust TCT books in accordance with the agreement.
2. Compute the net assets exclusive of the building not used in the business.
3. Compute the amount of goodwill to be paid.
4. Prepare a general journal entry in RKY's records to show the purchase of TCT.

Part Four

Accounting for Partnerships and Corporations

In the preceding parts of this book, except for the demonstration using financial statements from McDonald's Corporation (Chapter 7), the sole proprietorship has been the primary form of business organization discussed.

In Part IV, introductory accounting concepts and practices pertaining to partnerships and corporations are presented.

Chapter 15 discusses the formation and liquidation of partnerships as well as the problem of income distribution among partners.

Chapter 16 introduces accounting for the corporate form of business, including the issuance of capital stock and other transactions.

Chapter 17 focuses on accounting for retained earnings, a variety of other transactions that affect the stockholders' equity of a corporation, and the components of the corporate income statement.

Chapter 18 introduces the long-term liabilities of corporations and is especially concerned with accounting for bond liabilities. This chapter also has a section on bond investments.

Chapter Fifteen
Accounting for Partnerships

Learning Objectives

1. *Identify the major characteristics of a partnership.*
2. *Identify the advantages and disadvantages of the partnership form of business.*
3. *Record investments of cash and of other assets by the partners in forming a partnership.*
4. *Compute the profit or loss that partners share, based on a stated ratio, the capital investment ratio, and salaries and interest to partners.*
5. *Record a person's admission to or withdrawal from a partnership.*
6. *Compute the distribution of assets to partners when they liquidate their partnership.*

In the first half of this book, we used the sole proprietorship to illustrate the basic principles and practices of accounting. This chapter will focus on accounting for the partnership form of business organization. As a result of studying this chapter, you should be able to meet the learning objectives listed on the left.

The Uniform Partnership Act, which has been adopted by a majority of the states, defines a **partnership** as "an association of two or more persons to carry on as co-owners of a business for profit." Normally, partnerships are formed when owners of small businesses wish to combine capital or managerial talents for some common business purpose.

Partnership Characteristics

We shall examine some of the important characteristics of a partnership by describing voluntary association, partnership agreement, limited life, mutual agency, unlimited liability, co-ownership of partnership property, and the sharing of partnership profits and losses.

Voluntary Association

A partnership is a voluntary association of individuals rather than a legal entity in itself. Therefore, a partner is responsible under the law for his or her partner's business actions within the scope of the partnership. A partner also has unlimited liability for the debts of the partnership. Because of these potential liabilities, an individual must be allowed to choose the people who will join the partnership. A person should select as partners individuals who share his or her business objectives.

Partnership Agreement

Objective 1 Identify the major characteristics of a partnership

A partnership is easy to form. Two or more competent people simply agree to be partners in some common business purpose. This agreement is known as the **partnership agreement** and does not have to be in writing. However, good business practice calls for a written document that clearly states the details of the partnership. The contract should include the name, location, and purpose of the business; the partners and their respective duties; the investments of each partner; the methods for distributing profits and losses; the admission or withdrawal of partners; the withdrawals of assets allowed each partner, and dissolution procedures.

Limited Life

Because a partnership is formed by a contract between partners, it has **limited life:** anything that terminates the contract dissolves the partnership. A partnership is dissolved when (1) a partner withdraws, (2) a partner goes bankrupt, (3) a partner is incapacitated (for example, due to illness), (4) a partner dies, (5) a new partner is admitted, (6) a partner retires, or (7) the partnership ends according to the partnership agreement (for example, when a major project is completed).

Mutual Agency

Each partner is an agent of the partnership within the scope of the business. Because of this **mutual agency** feature, any partner can bind the partnership to a business agreement as long as he or she acts within the scope of normal operations of the business. For example, a partner in a used-car business can bind the partnership through the purchase or sale of used cars. However, this partner cannot bind the partnership to a contract for buying men's clothing or any other goods unrelated to the used-car business. The mutual agency characteristic emphasizes the importance of an individual's selecting business partners who have integrity and business objectives similar to his or her own.

Unlimited Liability

Each partner is personally liable for all the debts of the partnership. If a partnership is in poor financial condition and cannot pay its debts, the creditors must first satisfy their claims from the assets of the partnership. When the assets are not sufficient to pay all debts, the creditors may seek payment from the personal assets of each partner. If a partner's personal assets are depleted before the debts are paid, the creditors may claim additional assets from the remaining partners who are solvent. Each partner could conceivably be required by law to pay all the debts of the partnership; therefore, all the partners have **unlimited liability** for their company's debt.

Co-ownership of Partnership Property

When individuals invest property in a partnership, they give up the right to their separate use of the property. The property becomes an asset of the partnership and is owned jointly by all the partners.

Participation in Partnership Income

Each member of a partnership has the right to share in the firm's profits and the responsibility to share in its losses. The partnership agreement should disclose the method of distributing profits and losses to each partner. If the agreement specifies how profits are to be distributed but does not mention losses, the losses are distributed in the same manner as profits. If the partners fail to include the method of profit and loss distribution in the partnership agreement, the law requires that profits and losses be shared equally.

Summary of the Advantages and Disadvantages of Partnerships

Objective 2 Identify the advantages and disadvantages of the partnership form of business

Partnerships have both advantages and disadvantages. Several of the advantages are the partnership's ease of formation and dissolution, its ability to pool capital resources and individual talents, its lack of a corporate tax burden (because the partnership is not a legal entity, it does not have to pay an income tax but must file an informational return), and the freedom and flexibility it gives to its partners' actions.

Several of the disadvantages of a partnership include its limited life, the ability of one partner to commit the partnership to a contract (mutual agency), the unlimited personal liability of partners, and the difficulties of raising large amounts of capital and of transferring ownership interest.

Accounting for Partners' Equity

Accounting for a partnership is very similar to accounting for a sole proprietorship. A major difference is that the owners' equity of a partnership is called **partners' equity**. In accounting for partners' equity, it is necessary to maintain separate capital and withdrawal accounts for each partner and to divide the profits and losses of the company among the partners. The differences in the capital accounts of a sole proprietorship and a partnership are illustrated below.

Sole Proprietorship

Blake, Capital	
	50,000

Blake, Withdrawals	
12,000	

Partnership

Desmond, Capital		Frank, Capital	
	30,000		40,000

Desmond, Withdrawals		Frank, Withdrawals	
5,000		6,000	

In the partners' equity section of the balance sheet, the balance of each partner's capital account is listed separately, as shown in the partial balance sheet below.

Liabilities and Partners' Equity

Current Liabilities		$28,000
Partners' Equity		
Desmond, Capital	$25,000	
Frank, Capital	34,000	
Total Partners' Equity		59,000
Total Liabilities and Partners' Equity		$87,000

Objective 3 Record investments of cash and of other assets by the partners in forming a partnership

Each partner invests cash, other assets, or a combination of both in the partnership according to the agreement. When other assets are invested, the partners must agree on their value. The value of noncash assets should be their fair market value on the date they are transferred to the partnership. The assets invested by a partner are debited to the proper account, and the total amount is credited to the partner's capital account.

To illustrate the recording of partners' investments, we shall assume that Jerry Adcock and Rose Villa agree to combine their capital and equipment in a partnership for the purpose of operating a jewelry store. Adcock will invest $28,000 cash and $37,000 of furniture and displays, and Villa $40,000 cash and $20,000 of equipment, according to the partnership agreement. The general journal entries that record the initial investments of Adcock and Villa are as follows:

July 1	Cash	28,000	
	Furniture and Displays	37,000	
	Jerry Adcock, Capital		65,000
	To record the initial investment of Jerry Adcock in Adcock and Villa		
July 1	Cash	40,000	
	Equipment	20,000	
	Rose Villa, Capital		60,000
	To record the initial investment of Rose Villa in Adcock and Villa		

The values assigned to the assets in the above illustration would have had to be included in the partnership agreement. These values may differ from those carried on the partners' personal books. For example, the equipment that Rose Villa contributed may have had a value of only $12,000 on her books. However, after she purchased the equipment, its market value increased considerably. Villa's investment should be recognized at the fair market value of the equipment at the time of transfer regardless of book value because it represents the amount of money that Villa has committed to the partnership.

Additional investments are recorded in the same manner. Also, the partnership may assume liabilities in conjunction with investments. To illustrate, we shall assume that after three months Jerry Adcock invests additional equipment with a fair value of $45,000 in the partnership. Related to the equipment is a note payable for $30,000, which the partnership assumes. The entry that records the transaction is as follows:

Oct. 1	Equipment	45,000	
	Notes Payable		30,000
	Jerry Adcock, Capital		15,000
	To record additional investment by Jerry Adcock in Adcock and Villa		

Distribution of Partnership Profits and Losses

Objective 4 Compute the profit or loss that partners share, based on a stated ratio, the capital investment ratio, and salaries and interest to partners

A partnership's profits and losses can be distributed according to any method that the partners specify in the partnership agreement. The agreement should be specific and clear to avoid disputes among the partners over later distributions of profits and losses. However, if the partnership agreement does not mention the distribution of profits and losses, the law requires that they be shared equally by all partners. Also, if the partnership agreement mentions only the distribution of profits, the law requires equal distribution of any losses.

The profits of a partnership are normally composed of three elements: (1) return to the partners for the use of their capital, (2) compensation for services that the partners have rendered, and (3) further economic profit for the business risks the partners have taken. The breakdown of total profit into its three components helps to clarify how much each partner has contributed to the firm.

If all partners are spending the same amount of time, are contributing equal capital, and have similar managerial talents, then an equal sharing of profits and losses would be fair. However, if one partner works full time in the firm whereas another partner devotes only one-fourth of his or her time, then the distribution of profits or losses should reflect this difference. This arrangement would apply to any situation in which the partners contribute unequally to the business.

Several ways for partners to share profits are (1) by stated ratio, (2) by capital investment ratio, and (3) by salaries to the partners and interest on partners' capital, with the remainder according to a stated ratio.

Stated Ratio

One method of distributing profits and losses is to give each partner a stated ratio of the total. If each partner is making an equal contribution to the firm, each may receive the same share of the profits and losses. The equal contribution of the partners may take many forms. For example, each partner may have made an equal investment in the firm. On the other hand, one partner may be devoting more time and talent to the firm, whereas the second partner may make a larger capital investment. Also, if the partners contribute unequally to the firm, unequal stated ratios can be appropriate, such as 60 percent, 30 percent, and 10 percent for a partnership of three persons.

To illustrate this method, we shall assume that Adcock and Villa made a profit last year of $30,000. The partnership agreement states that the percentages of profits and losses distributed to Adcock and Villa will be 60 and 40, respectively. The computation of each partner's share of the profit and the journal entry to show the distribution are as follows:

Adcock ($30,000 × 60%)	$18,000
Villa ($30,000 × 40%)	12,000
Total profits	$30,000

Date	Account	Debit	Credit
June 30	Income Summary	30,000	
	Jerry Adcock, Capital		18,000
	Rose Villa, Capital		12,000
	To distribute the profits for the year to the partners' capital accounts		

Capital Investment Ratio

If the invested capital produces the most income for the partnership business, then profits and losses may be distributed according to capital investment. One method of distributing profits and losses under this condition is to use the ratio of capital balances of each partner at the beginning of the year. Another method is to use the average capital balance of each partner during the year.

To illustrate the first method, we shall assume the following balances for the capital accounts of Adcock and Villa for their first year of operation, which was July 1, 19x1, through June 30, 19x2. The profit for the year was $140,000.

Jerry Adcock, Capital

Debit	Credit
	7/1 65,000

Jerry Adcock, Withdrawals

Debit	Credit
1/1 10,000	

Rose Villa, Capital

Debit	Credit
	7/1 60,000
	2/1 8,000

Rose Villa, Withdrawals

Debit	Credit
11/1 10,000	

Beginning capital balances for Adcock and Villa were as follows:

	Capital	Capital Ratio
Jerry Adcock	$ 65,000	65/125
Rose Villa	60,000	60/125
Total capital	$125,000	

The profit that each partner will receive when distribution is based on beginning capital investment ratios is computed by multiplying the total profit by each partner's capital ratio.

Jerry Adcock	$140,000 × 65/125 =	$ 72,800
Rose Villa	$140,000 × 60/125 =	67,200
Total profit		$140,000

The entry showing distribution of profit is as follows:

June 30	Income Summary	140,000	
	Jerry Adcock, Capital		72,800
	Rose Villa, Capital		67,200
	To distribute the profits for the year to the partners' capital accounts		

If Adcock and Villa use their beginning capital investments to determine the ratio for distributing profits, they do not consider any withdrawals or additional investments made during the year. However, such investments and withdrawals usually change the partners' capital ratio. Therefore, the partnership agreement should specify which capital balances will determine the ratio for distributing profits and losses.

If partners believe their capital balances will fluctuate significantly during the year, they may select their average capital balances as a more equitable means of distributing profits and losses. To illustrate this method, we will assume that, during the first year, Jerry Adcock withdrew $10,000 on January 1, 19x2, and Rose Villa withdrew $10,000 on November 1, 19x1, and invested an additional $8,000 on February 1, 19x2. The profit for the year's operation was $140,000. The calculations for the average capital balances and the distribution of profits are as follows:

Average Capital Balances

Partner	Date	Capital Balance	×	Months Unchanged	=	Total	Average Capital
Adcock	7/x1–12/x1	$65,000	×	6	=	$390,000	
	1/x2–6/x2	55,000	×	6	=	330,000	
				12		$720,000 ÷ 12 =	$ 60,000
Villa	7/x1–10/x1	$60,000	×	4	=	$240,000	
	11/x1–1/x2	50,000	×	3	=	150,000	
	2/x2–6/x2	58,000	×	5	=	290,000	
				12		$680,000 ÷ 12 =	56,667
						Total average capital	$116,667

Average Capital Balance Ratios

$$\text{Adcock} = \frac{\text{Adcock's average capital balance}}{\text{total average capital}} = \frac{\$60{,}000}{\$116{,}667} = 51\%$$

$$\text{Villa} = \frac{\text{Villa'a average capital balance}}{\text{total average capital}} = \frac{\$56{,}667}{\$116{,}667} = 49\%$$

Distribution of Profits

Partner	Profit × Ratio	=	Share of Profit
Adcock	\$140,000 × 51%	=	\$ 71,400
Villa	\$140,000 × 49%	=	68,600
	Total profit		\$140,000

Note that this calculation requires the determination of (1) average capital balances, (2) average capital balance ratios, and (3) each partner's share of profit or loss. To determine a partner's average capital balance, it is necessary to examine the changes that have occurred during the year in the partner's capital balance. These changes result from additional investments and withdrawals. The partner's beginning capital is multiplied by the number of months the balance remains unchanged. After the balance changes, the new balance is multiplied by the number of months it remains unchanged. This process continues until the end of the year. The totals of these computations are added together, then divided by twelve, to determine the average capital balances. Once the average capital balances are determined, the method of computing capital balance ratios for distributing profits and losses is the same as that used for beginning capital balances.

The entry showing how the profit for the year is distributed to the partners' capital accounts is as follows:

		Debit	Credit
June 30	Income Summary	140,000	
	Jerry Adcock, Capital		71,400
	Rose Villa, Capital		68,600
	To distribute the profits for the year to the partners' capital accounts		

Salaries, Interest, and Stated Ratio

Partners seldom contribute equally to a firm. To compensate for these unequal contributions, some partnership agreements will allow for partners' salaries, interest on partners' capital balances, or a combination of both in the distribution of profits. Salaries and interest of this nature are not deducted as expenses before the partnership profit is determined.

They represent a method of arriving at an equitable distribution of the profit or loss.

To illustrate an allowance for partners' salaries, we shall assume that Adcock and Villa agree to the following salaries: $8,000 for Adcock and $7,000 for Villa. Any remaining profits will be divided equally. Each salary is charged to the appropriate partner's withdrawal account. If we assume the same $140,000 profit for the first year, the calculations and journal entry for Adcock and Villa are shown below.

	Income of Partners		Income
	Adcock	Villa	Distributed
Total Income for Distribution			$140,000
Distribution of Salaries			
Adcock	$ 8,000		
Villa		$ 7,000	15,000
Remaining Income After Salaries			$125,000
Equal Distribution of Remaining Income			
Adcock	62,500		
Villa		62,500	125,000
Remaining Income			—
Income of Partners	$70,500	$69,500	

June 30	Income Summary	140,000	
	Jerry Adcock, Capital		70,500
	Rose Villa, Capital		69,500
	To distribute the profits for the year to the partners' capital accounts		

Salaries allow for differences in the services that partners provide to the business. However, they do not consider differences in invested capital. To allow for capital differences, each partner may receive, in addition to salary, a stated interest on his or her invested capital. To illustrate, we shall assume that Adcock and Villa agree to receive 10 percent interest on their beginning capital balances as well as annual salaries of $8,000 for Adcock and $7,000 for Villa. They will share any remaining income equally. The calculations and journal entry for Adcock and Villa, if we assume $140,000 profits, are as follows:

	Income of Partners		Income
	Adcock	Villa	Distributed
Total Income for Distribution			$140,000
Distribution of Salaries			
Adcock	$ 8,000		
Villa		$ 7,000	15,000
Remaining Income After Salaries			$125,000
Distribution of Interest			
Adcock ($65,000 × 10%)	6,500		
Villa ($60,000 × 10%)		6,000	12,500
Remaining Income After Salaries and Interest			$112,500
Equal Distribution of Remaining Income			
Adcock	56,250		
Villa		56,250	112,500
Remaining Income			—
Income of Partners	$70,750	$69,250	

June 30	Income Summary	140,000	
	Jerry Adcock, Capital		70,750
	Rose Villa, Capital		69,250
	To distribute the profits for the year to the partners' capital accounts		

If the partnership agreement allows for paying salaries or interest or both, the partners must receive these amounts even if the profits are insufficient to cover the salaries and interest. This would result in the partners' sharing a negative amount after salaries and interest are paid. The negative amount after payment of salaries and interest must be distributed according to the stated ratio in the partnership agreement. If the agreement does not mention a ratio, the negative amount is distributed equally. To illustrate this situation, we shall assume that the partnership of Adcock and Villa agrees to the following conditions for the distribution of profits and losses:

	Salaries	**Interest**	**Beginning Capital Balance**
Adcock	$70,000	10 percent of beginning	$65,000
Villa	60,000	capital balances	60,000

The income for the first year of operation was $140,000. The computation, and the journal entry that records the distribution of the profit and loss, are shown on the next page.

	Income of Partners		Income
	Adcock	Villa	Distributed
Total Income for Distribution			$140,000
Distribution of Salaries			
Adcock	$70,000		
Villa		$60,000	130,000
Remaining Income After Salaries			$ 10,000
Distribution of Interest			
Adcock ($65,000 × 10%)	6,500		
Villa ($60,000 × 10%)		6,000	12,500
Negative Amount After Distribution of Salaries and Interest			($2,500)
Adcock*	($1,250)		
Villa*		($1,250)	2,500
Remaining Income			—
Income of Partners	$75,250	$64,750	

*Notice that the negative amount was distributed equally because the agreement did not indicate how profits and losses would be distributed after salaries and interest were paid.

June 30	Income Summary	140,000	
	Jerry Adcock, Capital		75,250
	Rose Villa, Capital		64,750
	To distribute the profits for the year to the partners' capital accounts		

On the income statement for the partnership, the distribution of profits or losses is shown below the net income figure. The partial income statement on the next page illustrates this point using the last example.

Dissolution of a Partnership

A partnership is legally dissolved when there is a change in the original association of the partners. Some common reasons for the **dissolution** of a partnership are the admission of a new partner, the withdrawal of a partner, or the death of a partner. When a partnership is dissolved, the partners lose their authority to continue the business as a going concern.

Adcock and Villa
Partial Income Statement
For the Year Ended June 30, 19xx

Net Income		$140,000
Distribution to the partners		
Adcock		
Salary distribution	$70,000	
Interest on beginning capital balance	6,500	
Total	$76,500	
One-half of remaining negative amount	(1,250)	
Share of net income		$ 75,250
Villa		
Salary distribution	$60,000	
Interest on beginning capital balance	6,000	
Total	$66,000	
One-half of remaining negative amount	(1,250)	
Share of net income		64,750
Net Income Distributed		$140,000

This does not mean that the business operation is necessarily ended or interrupted. The remaining partners can act for the partnership in finishing the affairs of the business or in forming a new partnership.

Objective 5 Record a person's admission to or withdrawal from a partnership

Admission of a New Partner

Admission of a new partner will dissolve the old partnership because a new association has been formed. However, the firm cannot admit a new partner without the consent of all the old partners. When a new partner is admitted, a new partnership agreement should describe the new arrangement in detail.

An individual may be admitted into a firm in one of two ways: (1) by purchasing an interest in the partnership from one or more of the original partners, or (2) by investing assets in the partnership.

In the first case, when an individual is admitted to a firm by purchasing an interest from an old partner, each partner must agree to the change. The interest purchased must be transferred from the capital account of the selling partner to the capital account of the new partner.

For example, assume that Jerry Adcock of Adcock and Villa decides to sell his $70,000 interest in the business to Richard Davis for $100,000 on

August 31, 19x3. Rose Villa agrees to the sale. The entry that records the sale would be:

Aug. 31	Jerry Adcock, Capital	70,000	
	Richard Davis, Capital		70,000
	To record the transfer of Jerry Adcock's equity to Richard Davis		

Note that the entry above records the book value of the equity and not the amount paid by Davis. The amount that Davis paid is a personal matter between him and Adcock. Because the amount paid did not affect the assets or liabilities of the firm, it should not be entered into the records.

For another example of a purchase, assume that Richard Davis purchases one-half of Jerry Adcock's $70,000 and one-half of Rose Villa's $80,000 interest in the partnership by paying a total of $100,000 to the two partners on August 31, 19x3. The entry that records this transaction follows:

Aug. 31	Jerry Adcock, Capital	35,000	
	Rose Villa, Capital	40,000	
	Richard Davis, Capital		75,000
	To record the transfer of one-half of Jerry Adcock's and Rose Villa's equity to Richard Davis		

In the second case, when a new partner is admitted by an investment in the partnership, both the assets and the owners' equity of the firm are increased. This is so because, in contrast to the case of buying a partner out, the assets that the new partner invests become partnership assets, and this increase in assets creates a corresponding increase in owners' equity. For example, assume that Richard Davis wished to invest $75,000 for a one-third interest in the partnership of Adcock and Villa. The capital accounts of Adcock and Villa are $70,000 and $80,000, respectively. The assets of the firm are correctly valued. Thus the partners agree to admit Davis to a one-third interest in the firm for a $75,000 investment. Davis's $75,000 investment will equal a one-third interest in the firm after the investment is added to the previously existing capital, as shown below.

Adcock, Capital	$ 70,000
Villa, Capital	80,000
Davis's investment	75,000
Total capital after Davis's investment	$225,000

$$\text{One-third interest} = \frac{\$225{,}000}{3} = \$\ 75{,}000$$

The entry to record this investment is:

Oct. 1	Cash	75,000	
	Richard Davis, Capital		75,000
	To record the admission of Richard Davis to a one-third interest in the company		

Sometimes a partnership is so profitable or otherwise advantageous that a new investor will be willing to pay more than the actual dollar interest that he or she receives in the partnership. An individual may have to pay $100,000 for an $80,000 interest in a partnership. The $20,000 excess of the payment over the interest purchased is considered a **bonus** to the original partners. The bonus should be distributed to the original partners according to their agreement concerning distribution of profits and losses.

As an illustration of the bonus method, assume that the Adcock and Villa Company has operated for several years and that the partners' capital balances and the new profit and loss ratio are as shown below.

Partners	Capital Balances	Profit and Loss Ratio
Adcock	$160,000	55%
Villa	140,000	45%
	$300,000	100%

Richard Davis wishes to join the firm, and he offers to invest $100,000 for a one-fifth interest in the business and profits. The original partners agree to the offer. The computation of the bonus to the original partners is as follows:

Partners' equity in the original partnership		$300,000
Cash investment by Richard Davis		100,000
Partners' equity in the new partnership		$400,000
Partners' equity assigned to Richard Davis ($400,000 × 1/5)		$ 80,000
Bonus to the original partners		
Investment by Richard Davis	$100,000	
Less equity assigned to Richard Davis	80,000	$ 20,000
Distribution of bonus to original partners		
Jerry Adcock ($20,000 × 55%)	$ 11,000	
Rose Villa ($20,000 × 45%)	9,000	$ 20,000

The journal entry that records the admission of Davis to the partnership is as follows:

Dec. 1	Cash	100,000	
	Jerry Adcock, Capital		11,000
	Rose Villa, Capital		9,000
	Richard Davis, Capital		80,000
	To record the sale of one-fifth interest in the firm to Richard Davis and the bonus he paid to the original partners		

In addition, there are several reasons why a partnership might seek a new partner. For example, a firm in financial trouble might seek additional cash from a new partner. Or the original partners, wishing to expand the firm's markets, might require more capital than they can provide. Also, the partners might know a person who would add a unique talent to the firm. Under these conditions, a new partner may be admitted to the partnership with the understanding that part of the original partners' capital will be transferred to the new partner's capital as a bonus.

For example, assume that Adcock and Villa have invited Richard Davis to join the firm. Davis is to invest $60,000 for a one-fourth interest in the company's capital and profits. The capital balances of Adcock and Villa are $160,000 and $140,000, respectively. If Davis is to receive a one-fourth interest in the firm, the interest of the original partners represents a three-fourths interest in the business. The computation of the bonus to Davis follows.

Total equity in partnership		
Adcock, Capital		$160,000
Villa, Capital		140,000
Investment by Richard Davis		60,000
Partners' equity in the new partnership		$360,000
Partners' equity assigned to Richard Davis ($360,000 × 1/4)		$ 90,000
Bonus		
One-fourth interest, Richard Davis	$90,000	
Cash investment by Richard Davis	60,000	$ 30,000
Distribution from original partners		
Jerry Adcock ($30,000 × 55%)	$16,500	
Rose Villa ($30,000 × 45%)	13,500	$ 30,000

The journal entry that records the admission of Davis to the partnership is as follows:

Sept. 1	Cash	60,000	
	Jerry Adcock, Capital	16,500	
	Rose Villa, Capital	13,500	
	Richard Davis, Capital		90,000
	To record the investment of Richard Davis of cash and a bonus		

Withdrawal of a Partner

A partner has the right to withdraw from a partnership whenever he or she chooses. To avoid any controversy when a partner does decide to withdraw or retire from the firm, the partnership agreement should describe the appropriate actions to be taken under these circumstances. The agreement may specify (1) whether or not an audit will be performed by CPAs, (2) how the assets will be reappraised, (3) how a bonus is to be determined, and (4) by what method the withdrawing partner will be paid.

There are several ways in which a partner may withdraw from a partnership. For example, a partner may: (1) sell his or her interest to an outsider with the consent of the remaining partners, (2) sell his or her interest to another partner with the consent of the remaining partners, (3) withdraw assets that are equal to his or her capital balance, (4) withdraw assets that are greater than his or her capital balance (condition that requires withdrawing partner to receive a bonus), (5) withdraw assets that are less than his or her capital balance (condition that requires remaining partners to receive a bonus). These alternatives are illustrated in Figure 15-1.

Figure 15-1 Alternative Ways a Partner May Withdraw

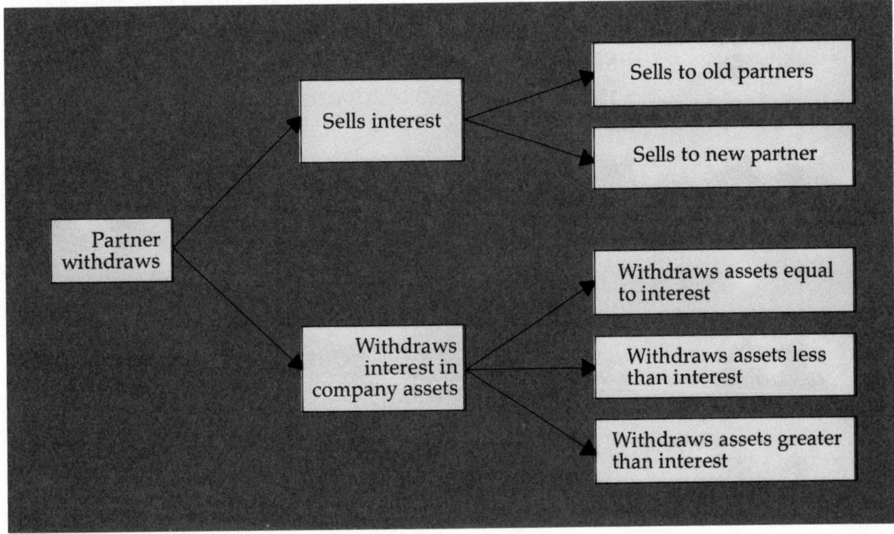

When a partner sells his or her interest to an outsider or to another partner with the consent of the other partners, the transaction is personal and does not change the partnership assets or the owners' equity. For example, we will assume that the capital balances of Adcock, Villa, and Davis are $140,000, $100,000, and $60,000, respectively, for a total of $300,000.

Villa is withdrawing from the partnership and is reviewing two offers for her interest. The offers are to (1) sell her interest to Judy Jones for $120,000, or (2) sell her interest to Davis for $110,000. The remaining partners have agreed to either potential transaction. Because Jones and Davis will pay for Villa's interest from their personal assets, the partnership accounting records will show only the transfer of Villa's interest to Jones or Davis. The entries that record these possible transfers are as follows:

1. If Villa's interest is purchased by Jones: Rose Villa, Capital	100,000	
Judy Jones, Capital		100,000
To record sale of Villa's partnership interest to Jones		
2. If Villa's interest is purchased by Davis: Rose Villa, Capital	100,000	
Richard Davis, Capital		100,000
To record sale of Villa's partnership interest to Davis		

A partnership agreement may state that a withdrawing partner is allowed to remove assets from the firm equal to his or her capital balance. Assume that Richard Davis decides to withdraw from Adcock, Villa, Davis & Company. Davis's capital balance is $60,000, and the partnership agreement states that he may withdraw cash from the firm equal to his capital balance. If there is insufficient cash, he is to accept a promissory note from the new partnership for the balance. The remaining partners of the firm request that Davis take only $50,000 in cash because of a cash shortage at the time of his withdrawal. He agrees to this condition. The journal entry that records Davis's withdrawal is as follows:

Jan. 21	Richard Davis, Capital	60,000	
	Cash		50,000
	Notes Payable, Richard Davis		10,000
	To record the withdrawal of Richard Davis from the partnership		

Partners can establish an alternative arrangement if the partnership agreement states that the assets of the business must be reappraised and any gain or loss distributed to the partners and that the withdrawing partner must remove assets equal to his or her new capital balance. To illustrate this condition, we shall assume that the partnership agreement of Adcock, Villa, Davis & Company calls for an audit and that the assets must be revalued before a partner can withdraw. After the assets are revalued, the withdrawing partner is allowed to remove cash, or cash plus a promissory note, equal to his or her capital balance. Davis, whose current capital balance is $60,000, decides to withdraw from the firm. According to the partnership agreement, an audit and revaluation of the assets are to be performed. The current balances of the Equipment account and the Accumulated Depreciation account are $26,000 and $9,000, respectively. The results of the audit show that the inventory was undervalued by $10,000 and that Equipment should be valued at $30,000 and Accumulated Depreciation at $10,000.

The increase in inventory would have to be recorded and the increase shared by the partners according to their profit and loss ratio. In addition, the Equipment account would be increased by $4,000 and Accumulated Depreciation on the equipment by $1,000, or a net increase of $3,000, which would also be shared by the partners in their profit and loss ratio. Adcock's, Villa's, and Davis's percentages of profits and losses are 40, 40, and 20, respectively. If Davis withdraws $50,000 cash plus a note, the entries that record the revaluation of the assets and Davis's withdrawal are as follows:

Date	Account	Debit	Credit
Mar. 1	Merchandise Inventory	10,000	
	Jerry Adcock, Capital		4,000
	Rose Villa, Capital		4,000
	Richard Davis, Capital		2,000
	To record the revaluation of inventory and to distribute the gain to the partners in their profit and loss ratios		
1	Equipment	4,000	
	Accumulated Depreciation, Equipment		1,000
	Jerry Adcock, Capital		1,200
	Rose Villa, Capital		1,200
	Richard Davis, Capital		600
	To record the revaluation of the equipment and to distribute the gain to the partners in their profit and loss ratios		
1	Richard Davis, Capital	62,600	
	Cash		50,000
	Notes Payable, Richard Davis		12,600
	To record the withdrawal of Richard Davis from the partnership		

Note that any gain or loss on revaluation of the firm's assets is distributed to the partners' capital accounts according to their profit and loss ratio.

A partner may withdraw from a firm and remove assets that are greater than the book value of his or her capital balance. However, the partnership agreement need not require an audit and revaluation of the assets before the partner withdraws. If the firm has been successful, the business will normally be worth more than its book value. A withdrawing partner who recognizes this fact will request more than his or her capital balance upon withdrawal. A withdrawing partner might also receive assets greater than his or her capital if the other partners have asked him or her to withdraw. Rather than revalue the assets and incur the costs of an audit, the remaining partners may agree to give the withdrawing partner a bonus.

When a partner withdraws assets greater than his or her capital balance, the excess may be treated as a bonus. The remaining partners then absorb the bonus according to their profit and loss ratio.

To illustrate, we will assume that the partnership agreement of Adcock, Villa, Davis & Company states that when a partner withdraws at the request of the remaining partners, the withdrawing partner will receive a bonus. Because Adcock and Villa are having difficulty with Davis, they ask him to withdraw from the firm. Adcock and Villa are willing to allow Davis to withdraw $70,000 in cash from the company for his $60,000 interest in the business. Davis agrees to this arrangement and withdraws from the firm. The profit and loss percentages of Adcock, Villa, and Davis are 40, 40, and 20, respectively. The entry that records the withdrawal of Davis follows:

Nov. 16	Richard Davis, Capital	60,000	
	Jerry Adcock, Capital	5,000	
	Rose Villa, Capital	5,000	
	Cash		70,000
	To record the withdrawal of Richard Davis from the partnership		

Sometimes a partner may wish to withdraw from a firm quickly, or at a time when the assets of the firm are overvalued. In such cases, the withdrawing partner may take out assets that represent less than his or her capital balance. A partner who withdraws under these conditions leaves a part of his or her capital in the business. The remaining partners will divide the remaining equity according to their profit and loss ratio. This distribution is considered a bonus to the old partners.

To illustrate, we will assume that Richard Davis of Adcock, Villa, Davis & Company plans to withdraw from the firm. Because he is very eager to leave the partnership, he plans to withdraw assets that represent less than his capital balance. Davis, whose current capital balance is $60,000, and the remaining partners agree that he should withdraw $40,000 when he leaves the firm. Adcock's, Villa's, and Davis's current percentages of profits and losses are 40, 40, and 20, respectively. The computation of the bonus and the entry that records Davis's withdrawal are as follows:

Bonus to old partners	
Davis, Capital	$60,000
Less assets to be withdrawn	40,000
Bonus to old partners	$20,000
Distribution of bonus to old partners	
Adcock ($20,000 × 4/8)	$10,000
Villa ($20,000 × 4/8)	10,000
Total	$20,000

Feb. 16	Richard Davis, Capital	60,000	
	Cash		40,000
	Jerry Adcock, Capital		10,000
	Rose Villa, Capital		10,000
	To record the withdrawal of Davis		

Death of a Partner

When a partner dies, the partnership is dissolved because the original association has changed. The partnership agreement should state the action to be taken upon the death of a partner. Normally the books will be closed and financial statements will be prepared. These actions are necessary to determine the capital balance of each of the partners at the date of the death. The agreement may also indicate whether or not an audit should be conducted, assets appraised, and a bonus recorded, as well as the procedures for settling with the heirs of the deceased partner. The conditions for settling with the heirs may be that the remaining partners purchase the deceased's equity, sell it to outsiders, or deliver certain business assets to the estate.

If the firm intends to continue, a new partnership must be formed.

Liquidation of a Partnership

Objective 6 Compute the distribution of assets to partners when they liquidate their partnership

Liquidation of a partnership is the process of ending a business, which entails selling enough assets to pay the liabilities and distributing any remaining assets among the partners. Unlike the case of dissolution, if a partnership is liquidated, the business will not continue.

The partnership agreement should indicate the procedures to be followed in the case of liquidation. Normally, the books should be adjusted and closed, with the income or loss being distributed to the partners. As the assets of the business are sold, any gain or loss should be distributed among the partners according to the established profit and loss ratio. As cash becomes available, it must be applied first to outside creditors, then to partners' loans, and finally to the partners' capital balances.

Although the process of liquidation may produce a variety of financial results, we shall discuss only the following three: (1) assets sold for a gain,

(2) assets sold for a loss but absorbed by capital balances, and (3) assets sold for a loss when a partner's capital balance is insufficient to absorb the loss. For each alternative we shall assume that the books have been closed for Adcock, Villa, Davis & Company and that the following balance sheet exists prior to liquidation:

Adcock, Villa, Davis & Company
Balance Sheet
February 2, 19xx

Assets		Liabilities and Partners' Equity	
Cash	$ 60,000	Accounts Payable	$120,000
Accounts Receivable	40,000	Adcock, Capital	85,000
Merchandise Inventory	100,000	Villa, Capital	95,000
Plant Assets (net)	200,000	Davis, Capital	100,000
Total Assets	$400,000	Total Liabilities and Partners' Equity	$400,000

The profit and loss percentages of Adcock, Villa, and Davis will be 30, 30, and 40, respectively.

Gain on Sale of Assets

Let us assume that the following transactions occurred in the liquidation of Adcock, Villa, Davis & Company. The accounts receivable were collected for $35,000, and the inventory and plant assets were sold for $110,000 and $200,000, respectively. After the accounts payable were paid off, the partners shared the remaining cash. These transactions are summarized in the statement of liquidation in Figure 15-2. The journal entries that record the transactions are shown here and on the next two pages.

Journal Entries				Explanation on Statement of Liquidation
Feb. 13	Cash	35,000		1
	Gain or Loss from Realization	5,000		
	Accounts Receivable		40,000	
	To record collection of accounts receivable			
14	Cash	110,000		2
	Merchandise Inventory		100,000	
	Gain or Loss from Realization		10,000	
	To record the sale of inventory			

Adcock, Villa, Davis & Company
Statement of Liquidation
February 2–20, 19xx

	Explanation	Cash	Other Assets	Accounts Payable	Adcock, Capital (30%)	Villa, Capital (30%)	Davis, Capital (40%)	Gain (or Loss) from Realization
	Balance 2/2	$ 60,000	$340,000	$120,000	$ 85,000	$ 95,000	$100,000	
1.	Collection of Accounts Receivable	35,000	(40,000)					($5,000)
		$ 95,000	$300,000	$120,000	$ 85,000	$ 95,000	$100,000	$ 5,000
2.	Sale of Inventory	110,000	(100,000)					10,000
		$205,000	$200,000	$120,000	$ 85,000	$ 95,000	$100,000	$ 5,000
3.	Sale of Plant Assets	200,000	(200,000)					
		$405,000	—	$120,000	$ 85,000	$ 95,000	$100,000	$ 5,000
4.	Payment of Liabilities	(120,000)		(120,000)				
		$285,000		—	$ 85,000	$ 95,000	$100,000	$ 5,000
5.	Distribution of Gain or Loss from Realization				1,500	1,500	2,000	(5,000)
		$285,000			$ 86,500	$ 96,500	$102,000	—
6.	Distribution to Partners	(285,000)			(86,500)	(96,500)	(102,000)	
		—			—	—	—	

Figure 15-2
Statement of Liquidation Showing Gain on Sale of Assets

		Debit	Credit	
16	Cash	200,000		3
	Plant Assets		200,000	
	To record the sale of plant assets			
16	Accounts Payable	120,000		4
	Cash		120,000	
	To record the payment of accounts payable			

Date	Account	Debit	Credit	Explanation
20	Gain or Loss from Realization	5,000		5
	Jerry Adcock, Capital		1,500	
	Rose Villa, Capital		1,500	
	Richard Davis, Capital		2,000	
	To record the distribution of the gain on assets ($10,000 gain minus $5,000 loss) to the partners			
20	Jerry Adcock, Capital	86,500		6
	Rose Villa, Capital	96,500		
	Richard Davis, Capital	102,000		
	Cash		285,000	
	To record the distribution of cash to the partners			

Note that cash distributed to the partners is the balance in their respective capital accounts. Cash is *not* distributed according to the partners' profit and loss ratio.

Loss on Sale of Assets

We shall discuss two cases in which there are losses on the sale of the company's assets. In the first case, the losses are small enough to be absorbed by the partners' capital balances. In the second case, one partner's share of the losses is too large for his or her capital balance to absorb.

When a firm's assets are sold at a loss, the partners will share the loss on liquidation according to their profit and loss ratio. As an example of this situation, assume that during the liquidation of Adcock, Villa, Davis & Company, the total cash received from the collection of accounts receivable and the sale of inventory and plant assets was $140,000. The statement of liquidation appears in Figure 15-3, and the journal entries for the transaction are shown below and on the facing page.

Date	Journal Entries	Debit	Credit	Explanation on Statement of Liquidation
Feb. 15	Cash	140,000		1
	Gain or Loss on Realization	200,000		
	Accounts Receivable		40,000	
	Merchandise Inventory		100,000	
	Plant Assets		200,000	
	To record the collection of accounts receivable and the sale of the other assets			
16	Accounts Payable	120,000		2
	Cash		120,000	
	To record the payment of accounts payable			

Adcock, Villa, Davis & Company
Statement of Liquidation
February 2–20, 19xx

	Explanation	Cash	Other Assets	Accounts Payable	Adcock, Capital (30%)	Villa, Capital (30%)	Davis, Capital (40%)	Gain (or Loss) from Realization
	Balance 2/2	$ 60,000	$340,000	$120,000	$ 85,000	$ 95,000	$100,000	
1.	Collection of Accounts Receivable and Sale of Inventory and Plant Assets	140,000	(340,000)					($200,000)
		$200,000	—	$120,000	$ 85,000	$ 95,000	$100,000	($200,000)
2.	Payment of Liabilities	(120,000)		(120,000)				
		$ 80,000		—	$ 85,000	$ 95,000	$100,000	($200,000)
3.	Distribution of Gain or Loss from Realization				(60,000)	(60,000)	(80,000)	200,000
		$80,000			$ 25,000	$ 35,000	$ 20,000	—
4.	Distribution to Partners	(80,000)			(25,000)	(35,000)	(20,000)	
		—			—	—	—	

Figure 15-3
Statement of Liquidation Showing Loss on Sale of Assets

		Debit	Credit	
20	Jerry Adcock, Capital	60,000		3
	Rose Villa, Capital	60,000		
	Richard Davis, Capital	80,000		
	Gain or Loss on Realization		200,000	
	To record the distribution of the loss on assets to the partners			
20	Jerry Adcock, Capital	25,000		4
	Rose Villa, Capital	35,000		
	Richard Davis, Capital	20,000		
	Cash		80,000	
	To record the distribution of cash to the partners			

In some liquidation cases, a partner's share of the losses is greater than his or her capital balance. In this situation, the partner must make up the deficit in his or her capital account from personal assets. For example, assume that after the sale of assets and the payment of liabilities the following conditions exist during the liquidation of Adcock, Villa, Davis & Company:

Assets		
Cash		$30,000
Partners' Equity		
Adcock, Capital	$25,000	
Villa, Capital	20,000	
Davis, Capital	(15,000)	$30,000

Richard Davis must pay $15,000 into the partnership from personal funds to cover his deficit. If we assume that he paid cash to the partnership, the following entry would record his cash contribution:

Feb. 20	Cash	15,000	
	Richard Davis, Capital		15,000
	To record the additional investment of Richard Davis to cover his liquidation losses		

After Davis's payment of $15,000, there is sufficient cash to pay Adcock and Villa their capital balances and thus to complete the liquidation. This transaction is recorded as follows:

Feb. 20	Jerry Adcock, Capital	25,000	
	Rose Villa, Capital	20,000	
	Cash		45,000
	To record the distribution of cash to the partners		

During liquidation, a partner might not have any additional cash to cover his or her obligations to the partnership. When this occurs, the remaining partners must share the loss according to their established profit and loss ratio. This is necessary because all partners have unlimited liability, which is characteristic of a partnership. Assume that Richard Davis cannot pay the $15,000 deficit in his capital account. Adcock and Villa must share the deficit according to the profit and loss ratio. Their percentages are 30 and 30, respectively. Therefore, they will each pay 50 percent of the losses that Davis cannot pay. The new profit and loss ratio for Adcock and Villa is computed as follows:

	Old Ratios	**New Ratios**
Adcock	30%	30/60 = 50%
Villa	30%	30/60 = 50%
	60%	100%

The journal entries that record these transactions are as follows:

Feb. 20	Jerry Adcock, Capital	7,500	
	Rose Villa, Capital	7,500	
	Richard Davis, Capital		15,000
	To record the transfer of Davis's deficit to Adcock and Villa		
Feb. 20	Jerry Adcock, Capital	17,500	
	Rose Villa, Capital	12,500	
	Cash		30,000
	To record the cash distribution to the partners		

Richard Davis's inability to meet his obligations at the time of liquidation does not relieve him of his liabilities to Adcock and Villa. If he is able to pay his liabilities some time in the future, Adcock and Villa may collect the amounts of Davis's deficit that they absorbed.

Chapter Review

Review of Learning Objectives

1. Identify the major characteristics of a partnership.

The partnership form of business organization has several major characteristics that distinguish it from other forms of business. A partnership is a voluntary association of two or more persons who combine their talents and resources for the purpose of making a profit. This joint effort should be supported by a partnership agreement, which specifies the details of operation for the partnership. A partnership is easily dissolved by the admission, withdrawal, or death of a partner, and therefore has a limited life. In addition, each partner acts as an agent of the partnership within the scope of normal operations of the business and is personally liable for the partnership's debts.

2. Identify the advantages and disadvantages of the partnership form of business.

The advantages are ease of formation and dissolution, the opportunity to pool several individuals' talents and resources, the freedom of action each partner enjoys, and no tax burden. The disadvantages are the limited life of the partnership, the unlimited personal liability of the partners, the difficulty of transferring partners' interest and of raising large amounts of capital, and the risk inherent in each partner's being able to bind the partnership to a contract.

3. Record investments of cash and of other assets by the partners in forming a partnership.

Normally a partnership is formed when the partners contribute cash, other assets, or a combination of both to the business in accordance with the partnership agreement. The recording of initial investments entails a charge to the Cash or other asset account and a credit to the investing partner's capital account. The recorded amount of the other assets should be their fair value on the date of transfer to the partnership. In addition, a partnership may assume the investing partner's liabilities. When this occurs, the partner's capital account is credited with the difference between the assets invested and the liabilities assumed.

4. Compute the profit or loss that partners share, based on a stated ratio, the capital investment ratio, and salaries and interest to partners.
The partners should share profits and losses in accordance with the partnership agreement. If the agreement says nothing about the distribution of profit and loss, the partners will share them equally. Some common methods used for distributing profits and losses to partners include the use of stated ratios or capital investment ratios, and the payment of salaries and interest on capital investments. Each method tries to measure the contributions of each partner to the operations of the business. A stated ratio is usually based on the partners' relative contribution of effort to the partnership. If the capital investment ratio is used, the profits (or losses) are divided strictly on the amount of capital provided to the partnership by each partner. The use of salaries and interest on capital investment takes into account both efforts (salary) and capital investment (interest) in dividing profits (or losses) among the partners.

5. Record a person's admission to or withdrawal from a partnership.
An individual is admitted to a partnership by purchasing a partner's interest or by contributing additional assets. When an interest is purchased, the old partner's capital is transferred to the new partner. When the new partner contributes assets to the partnership, it may be necessary to recognize a bonus to be shared or borne by the old partners.

When a partner withdraws from a partnership, the partner either sells his or her interest in the business or withdraws company assets. When assets are withdrawn, the amount can be equal to, greater than, or less than the partner's capital interest. When assets that have a value greater than or less than the partner's interest are withdrawn, a bonus is recognized and distributed among the appropriate partners.

6. Compute the distribution of assets to partners when they liquidate their partnership.
Liquidation of a partnership entails selling the assets necessary to pay the liabilities, then distributing any remaining assets to the partners. Any profit or loss in the sale of the assets is shared by the partners according to their profit and loss ratio. When a partner has a deficit balance in a capital account, that partner must contribute personal assets equal to the deficit. When a partner does not have personal assets to cover a capital deficit, the deficit must be absorbed by the solvent partners according to their profit and loss ratio.

Review Problem
Distribution of Income and Admission of Partner

Jack Holder and Dan Williams reached an agreement in 19x7 to pool their resources for the purpose of forming a partnership to manufacture and sell university T-shirts. In forming the partnership, Holder and Williams contributed $100,000 and $150,000, respectively. They drafted a partnership agreement stating that Holder was to receive an annual salary of $6,000 and Williams was to receive 3 percent interest annually on his original investment in the business. Profits and losses after salary and interest were to be shared by Holder and Williams in a 2:3 ratio.

Required

1. Compute the profit or loss that Holder and Williams share, and prepare the required journal entries, assuming the following profit and loss before salary and interest: 19x7—$27,000 profit; 19x8—$2,000 loss.

2. Assume that Jean Ratcliffe offers Holder and Williams $60,000 for a 15 percent interest in the partnership on January 1, 19x9. Holder and Williams agree to Ratcliffe's offer because they need her resources to expand the business. The capital balances of Holder and Williams are $113,600 and $161,400, respectively, on January 1, 19x9. Record the admission of Ratcliffe to the partnership, assuming that her investment is to represent a 15 percent interest in the total partners' capital and that a bonus is to be given to Holder and Williams in the ratio of 2:3.

Answer to Review Problem

1. Income distribution to partners computed:

	Income of Partner		Income
	Holder	Williams	Distributed
19x7			
Total Income for Distribution			$27,000
Distribution of Salary			
Holder	$ 6,000		6,000
Remaining Income After Salary			$21,000
Distribution of Interest			
Williams ($150,000 × 3%)		4,500	4,500
Remaining Income After Salary and Interest			$16,500
Distribution of Remaining Income			
Holder ($16,500 × 2/5)	6,600		
Williams ($16,500 × 3/5)		9,900	16,500
Remaining Income			—
Income of Partners	$12,600	$14,400	
19x8			
Total Income for Distribution			($2,000)
Distribution of Salary			
Holder	$ 6,000		6,000
Remaining Loss After Salary			($8,000)
Distribution of Interest			
Williams ($150,000 × 3%)		$ 4,500	4,500
Negative Amount After Distribution of Salary and Interest			($12,500)
Distribution of Remaining Loss in Profit/Loss Ratio			
Holder ($12,500 × 2/5)	(5,000)		
Williams ($12,500 × 3/5)		(7,500)	(12,500)
Remaining Income			—
Income of Partners	$ 1,000	($3,000)	

Journal entry—19x7		
Income Summary	27,000	
Jack Holder, Capital		12,600
Dan Williams, Capital		14,400
To record the distribution (based on salary, interest, and stated ratio) of $27,000 profit for 19x7		

Journal entry—19x8		
Dan Williams, Capital	3,000	
Income Summary		2,000
Jack Holder, Capital		1,000
To record the distribution (based on salary, interest, and stated ratio) of $2,000 loss for 19x8		

2. Admission of new partner recorded:

19x9			
Jan. 1	Cash	60,000	
	Jack Holder, Capital		3,900
	Dan Williams, Capital		5,850
	Jean Ratcliffe, Capital		50,250
	To record the $60,000 cash investment by Jean Ratcliffe for a 15 percent interest in the partnership, a bonus being allocated to original partners.		

Computation

Ratcliffe, Capital = (original partners' capital + investment) × 15 percent
= ($113,600 + $161,400 + $60,000) × 15% = $50,250
Bonus = investment − Ratcliffe, Capital
= $60,000 − $50,250 = $9,750

Distribution of bonus:

Holder = $9,750 × 2/5 =	$3,900
Williams = $9,750 × 3/5 =	$5,850
Total bonus	$9,750

Chapter Assignments

Questions

1. Briefly define a partnership, and list several major characteristics of the partnership form of business.
2. What is the meaning of unlimited liability when applied to a partnership?
3. Abe and Bill are partners in a drilling operation. Abe purchased a drilling rig to be used in the partnership's operations. Is this purchase binding on Bill even though he was not involved in it?

4. The partnership agreement for Karla and Jean's partnership does not disclose how they will share profits and losses. How would the profits and losses be shared in this partnership?

5. What are several major advantages of a partnership? What are some possible disadvantages?

6. Edward contributes $10,000 in cash and a building with a book value of $40,000 and fair market vaiue of $50,000 to the Edward and Francis partnership. What is the balance of Edward's capital account in the partnership if the building is recorded at its fair market value?

7. Gayle and Henry share profits and losses in their partnership in a 3:2 ratio. The firm's net income for the current year is $80,000. How would the distribution of income be recorded in the journal?

8. Irene purchases Jane's interest in the Jane and Kane partnership for $62,000. Jane has a $57,000 capital interest in the partnership. How would this transaction be recorded in the partnership books?

9. Larry and Madison each own a $50,000 interest in a partnership. They agree to admit Nancy as a partner by selling her a one-third interest for $80,000. How large a bonus will be distributed to Larry and Madison?

10. Opel and Paul share profits in their partnership in a 2:4 ratio. Opel and Paul receive salaries of $6,000 and $10,000, respectively. How would they share a net income before salaries of $22,000?

11. In the liquidation of a partnership, Robert's capital account showed a $5,000 deficit balance after all the creditors were paid. What obligation does Robert have to the partnership?

12. Describe how a dissolution of a partnership may differ from a liquidation of a partnership.

13. Tom Howard and Sharon Thomas are forming a partnership. What are some of the factors they should consider in deciding how profits might be divided?

Classroom Exercises

Exercise 15-1 Partnership Formation

John Krupp and James McMahon are watch repairmen who wish to form a partnership and open a jewelry store. They have their attorney prepare their partnership agreement, which indicates that assets invested in the partnership will be recorded at their fair market value. The assets contributed by each partner and their fair market value are as follows:

Assets	John Krupp	James McMahon	Total
Cash	$20,000	$15,000	$35,000
Accounts Receivable	26,000	10,000	36,000
Allowance for Uncollectible Accounts	(2,000)	(1,500)	(3,500)
Supplies	500	250	750
Equipment	10,000	5,000	15,000
Accounts Payable	(16,000)	(4,500)	(20,500)

Prepare the journal entry necessary to record the original investments of Krupp and McMahon in the partnership.

Exercise 15-2 Distribution of Profits and Losses

Judy O'Conner and Melvin Melon agreed to form a partnership. O'Conner contributed $100,000 in cash, and Melon contributed assets with a fair market value of $200,000. The partnership was very successful in its initial year and reported profits of $60,000.

Determine how the partners would share the first year's profits, and prepare the journal entry to distribute the profits to the partners under each of the following conditions: (1) O'Conner and Melon failed to include profit and loss ratios in the partnership agreement. (2) O'Conner and Melon agreed to share the profits and losses in a 3:2 ratio. (3) O'Conner and Melon agreed to share the profits and losses in a ratio of original investments. (4) O'Conner and Melon agreed to share the profits and losses by allowing 10 percent interest on original investments and sharing any remainder equally.

Exercise 15-3 Distribution of Income—Salary and Interest

Assume that the partnership agreement of O'Conner and Melon in Exercise 15-2 states that O'Conner and Melon are to receive salaries of $10,000 and $12,000, respectively; that O'Conner is to receive 6 percent on her capital balance at the beginning of the year; and that the remainder of profits and losses are to be shared equally.

Prepare the journal entries for distributing the profit under the following conditions: (1) Profits total $60,000 before deductions for salaries and interest. (2) Profits total $24,000 before deductions for salaries and interest.

Exercise 15-4 Admission of New Partner—Bonus to Old Partners

Wayne, Frank, and Robert have equities in a partnership of $20,000, $20,000, and $30,000, respectively, and share profits and losses in a ratio of 1:1:3. The partners have agreed to admit Peter to the partnership.

Prepare journal entries to record the admission of Peter to the partnership under the following assumptions: (1) Peter invests $30,000 for a one-fifth interest in the partnership, and a bonus is recorded for the old partners. (2) Peter invests $30,000 for a 40 percent interest in the partnership, and a bonus is recorded for Peter.

Exercise 15-5 Partnership Liquidation

Assume the following assets, liabilities, and owners' equity of the Black and Jones partnership on December 31, 19xx:

Assets	=	**Liabilities**	+	**Black, Capital**	+	**Jones, Capital**
$80,000	=	$5,000	+	$45,000	+	$30,000

When the partners agree to liquidate the business, the assets are sold for $60,000, and the liabilities are paid. Black and Jones share profits and losses in a ratio of 3:1.

1. What is the final cash distribution to the partners after liquidation?
2. Prepare journal entries for the sale of assets, payment of liabilities, distribution of loss from realization, and final distribution of cash to Black and Jones.

Exercise 15-6 Withdrawal of Partner

Arthur, DuVal, and Murphy are partners who share profits and losses in the ratio of 3:2:1. Murphy's capital account has a $20,000 balance. Arthur and DuVal have agreed to let Murphy take $25,000 of the company's cash when he retires.

What journal entry must be made on the partnership's books when Murphy retires, assuming that a bonus to Murphy is recognized and absorbed by the remaining partners?

Problem Set A

Problem 15A-1 Partnership Formation and Distribution of Income

Joe Abbott and Jim Barto agreed in January 19x1 to form a partnership to produce and sell printed T-shirts. Abbott contributed $24,000 in cash, and Barto contributed equipment and materials with agreed values of $6,000 and $10,000, respectively, to the new business. The partnership had a profit of $42,000 during 19x1 but was less successful during 19x2, when the profit was only $20,000.

Required

1. Prepare the journal entry to record the investments of both partners.
2. Determine the share of income for each partner in 19x1 and 19x2 under each of the following conditions: (a) the partners agreed to share profits equally. (b) The partners failed to agree on a profit-sharing arrangement. (c) The partners agreed to share profits according to the ratio of their original investments. (d) The partners agreed to share profits by allowing 9 percent on original investment and dividing the remainder equally. (e) The partners agreed to share profits by allowing salaries of $18,000 for Joe and $12,000 for Jim and dividing the remainder equally. (f) The partners agreed to share profits by allowing 9 percent on original investment, paying salaries of $18,000 to Joe and $12,000 to Jim, and dividing the remainder equally.

Problem 15A-2 Distribution of Income—Salaries and Interest

Brad and Karen are partners in a tennis shop. They have agreed that Brad will operate the shop and receive a salary of $12,000 per year. Karen is to receive 4 percent interest on her original capital investment of $80,000. The remaining profits and losses are to be shared by Brad and Karen in a 2:1 ratio.

Required

Determine each partner's share of profits and losses under each of the following conditions. In each case, the profit or loss is stated before distribution of salary and interest. (1) The profit was $24,000. (2) The profit was $14,000. (3) The loss was $2,800.

Problem 15A-3 Admission of a Partner

Pete, Bert, and Larry are partners in the Do-It-Yourself Woodwork Company. Their capital balances as of July 31, 19x7, are as follows:

Pete, Capital		Bert, Capital		Larry, Capital	
	50,000		60,000		40,000

The partners have agreed to admit Terry to the partnership.

Required

Prepare the journal entries to record Terry's admission to the partnership under each of the following conditions: (1) Terry pays Larry $45,000 for one-half of his interest. (2) Terry invests $45,000 cash in the partnership. (3) Terry invests $50,000 cash in the partnership for a 20 percent interest in the business. A bonus is to be recorded for the old partners on the basis of their capital investment balances. (4) Terry invests $50,000 cash in the firm for a 30 percent interest in the business. The old partners give Terry a bonus according to the ratio of their capital investment balances on July 31, 19x7.

Problem 15A-4 Partnership Liquidation

Jones, Peters, and Johnston are partners who share profits and losses in the ratio of 40:30:30, respectively. The partners have agreed to liquidate the partnership. The partnership balance sheet prior to liquidation is as follows:

Cash	$10,000	Accounts Payable	$15,000
Other Assets	85,000	Jones, Capital	30,000
		Peters, Capital	30,000
		Johnson, Capital	20,000
Totals	$95,000		$95,000

On September 10, 19x1, the other assets are sold for $65,000, and the partnership is liquidated.

Required

Prepare the following journal entries: (1) sale of the other assets, (2) payment of the accounts payable, (3) distribution to the partners of gain or loss on liquidation, and (4) distribution to the partners of the remaining cash.

Problem 15A-5 Partnership Liquidation

Stephanie, Susan, and Sharon decide to pool their resources and form a partnership on January 1, 19x1, to produce and sell ceramics. The original investments for Stephanie, Susan, and Sharon were $10,000, $12,000, and equipment with an $8,000 fair market value, respectively.

After operating for three years, the partners decide to liquidate the business as of January 1, 19x4. At that time, the profit and loss ratios to the nearest percent are 34:39:27, respectively, for Stephanie, Susan, and Sharon. The following accounts and balances appear in the company's general ledger as of December 31, 19x3: Cash, $32,000; Accounts Receivable, $30,000; Inventory, $50,000; Equipment, $32,000; Accounts Payable, $10,000; Stephanie, Capital, $45,600; Susan, Capital, $52,000; Sharon, Capital, $36,400.

Required

1. Journalize the following liquidation transactions: (a) Accounts receivable are sold for $20,000. (b) Inventory is sold for $70,000. (c) The gain or loss from realization is distributed to the partners' capital accounts. (d) With the partners' permission, Sharon withdraws the equipment from the business. The partners agree that the withdrawal should be recorded at book value. (e) The accounts payable are paid in full. (f) The final cash is distributed to the partners.
2. Prepare a statement of liquidation.

Problem 15A-6 Comprehensive Partnership Transactions

The events below pertain to a partnership formed by Terry Mendez and Charlie Williams to operate a car rental company.

19x1

Feb. 14 The partnership was formed. Mendez transferred to the partnership $30,000 cash, land worth $20,000, a building worth $120,000, and a mortgage on the building of $60,000. Williams transferred to the partnership $10,000 cash and automobiles worth $40,000.

Dec. 31 During 19x1, the partnership made a profit of only $21,000. The partnership agreement specifies that profits and losses are to be divided by allowing 8 percent interest on beginning capital, paying salaries of $10,000 to Mendez and $15,000 to Williams, and dividing any remainder equally.

19x2

Jan. 1 To improve the prospects for the company, the partners decided to take in a new partner, Linda Kim, who had experience in the car rental business. Kim invested $39,000 for a 25 percent interest in the business. A bonus was transferred in equal amounts from the previous partners' capital accounts to Kim's capital account.

Dec. 31 During 19x2, the company earned a profit of $21,800. The new partnership agreement specifies that profits and losses will be divided by allowing 8 percent on beginning-of-the-year capital balances, paying salaries of $15,000 to Williams and $20,000 to Kim (no salary to Mendez), and dividing the remainder equally.

19x3

Jan. 1 Because it appeared that the business could not support the three partners, the partners decided to dissolve and liquidate the partnership. The asset and liability accounts of the partnership were as follows: Cash, $101,800; Accounts Receivable, $17,000; Land, $20,000; Building (net), $112,000; Automobiles (net), $59,000; Accounts Payable, $22,000; Mortgage Payable, $56,000. The automobiles were sold for $50,000, and the resulting loss was distributed equally to the partners' accounts. The accounts payable were paid. A statement of liquidation was prepared, and the remaining assets and liabilities were distributed. Mendez agreed to accept cash plus the land, buildings, and mortgage payable at book value as payment for his share. Williams accepted cash and the accounts receivable for his share. Kim was paid in cash.

Required

Prepare general journal entries to record all the above facts. Support your computations with schedules, and prepare a statement of liquidation in connection with the January 1, 19x3, entries.

Problem Set B

Problem 15B-1 Partnership Formation and Distribution of Income

On January 1, 19x1, Mary Jaynes and Martha Rosen agreed to form a partnership to establish a health food store in their neighborhood. Jaynes and Rosen invested cash of $60,000 and $40,000, respectively, in the partnership. The business had normal first-year problems, but during the second year the operation was very successful. For 19x1 they reported a $20,000 loss, and for 19x2 a $60,000 profit.

Required

1. Prepare the journal entry to record both partners' investments.
2. Determine Jaynes's and Rosen's share of the profit or loss for each year, assuming each of the following methods of sharing profits and losses: (a) The partners agreed to share profits and losses equally. (b) The partners agreed to share profits and losses in the ratio of 7:3 for Jaynes and Rosen, respectively. (c) The partners agreed to share profits in the ratio of their original investments, but the agreement did not mention losses. (d) The partners agreed to share profits and losses in the ratio of their capital investments at the beginning of the year. (e) The partners agreed to share profits and losses by allowing interest of 10 percent on original investments and dividing the remainder equally. (f) The partners agreed to share profits and losses by allowing interest of 10 percent on original investments, paying salaries of $15,000 to Jaynes and $10,000 to Rosen, and dividing the remainder equally.

Problem 15B-2 Distribution of Income—Salaries and Interest

Mike, James, and Marvin are partners in the I-D Plastic Company. The partnership agreement states that Mike is to receive 6 percent interest on his capital investment at the beginning of the year, James is to receive a salary of $10,000 a year, and Marvin will be paid interest of 5 percent on his average capital balance during the year. Mike, James, and Marvin will share any profit or loss after salaries and interest in a 5:3:2 ratio. Mike's capital investment at the beginning of the year was $60,000, and Marvin's average capital balance for the year was $70,000.

Required

Determine each partner's share of profits and losses under each of the following assumptions: (1) The profit was $117,100. (2) The profit was $14,100. (3) The loss was $9,300.

Problem 15B-3 Admission of Partner

McLeod, Wang, and Cooke are partners in the Noodle Spa. The balances in the capital accounts of McLeod, Wang, and Cooke as of September 30, 19x1, are $20,000, $30,000, and $50,000, respectively. The partners share profits and losses in a ratio of 2:3:5.

Required

Prepare the journal entries under each of the following conditions: (1) Davis pays Cooke $50,000 for four-fifths of Cooke's interest. (2) Davis is to be admitted to the partnership with a one-third interest for a $50,000 cash investment. (3) Davis is to be admitted to the partnership with a one-third interest for a $60,000 cash investment. A bonus is to be distributed to the old partners when Davis is admitted. (4) Davis is to be admitted to the partnership with a one-third interest for a $41,000 cash investment. A bonus is to be given to Davis upon admission.

Problem 15B-5 Partnership Liquidation

The balance sheet of the TET Partnership as of June 30, 19x1, is shown below.

TET Partnership
Balance Sheet
June 30, 19x1

Assets		Liabilities and Partners' Equity	
Cash	$ 500	Accounts Payable	$40,000
Accounts Receivable	10,000	Terry, Capital	6,000
Inventory	22,000	Edward, Capital	15,000
Equipment (net)	38,500	Thomas, Capital	10,000
Total Assets	$71,000	Total Liabilities and Partners' Equity	$71,000

Terry, Edward, and Thomas share profits and losses in the ratio of 5:3:2. Because of tough competition in their industry, the partners have agreed to liquidate the business.

Required

1. Prepare journal entries to liquidate the partnership and distribute any remaining cash, assuming that Terry cannot contribute any additional personal assets to the company during liquidation and that the following transactions occurred during the liquidation: (a) Accounts receivable were sold for 60 percent of their book value. (b) Inventory was sold for $23,000. (c) Equipment was sold for $25,000. (d) Accounts payable were paid in full. (e) Gain or loss from realization was distributed to partners' capital accounts. (f) Terry's deficit was transferred to the remaining partners in their new profit and loss ratio. (g) The remaining cash was distributed to the partners.
2. Prepare a statement of liquidation.

Problem 15B-6 Comprehensive Partnership Transactions

Jessica Turner and Monique Goldman formed a partnership on January 1, 19x1, to operate an employment agency. To begin the partnership, Jessica transferred cash totaling $29,000 and office equipment valued at $21,000 to the partnership. Monique transferred cash of $14,000, land valued at $9,000, and a building valued at $75,000. In addition, the partnership assumed the mortgage of $58,000 on the building.

During the first year, the partnership was unsuccessful and on December 31 reported a loss of $4,000. In the partnership agreement, the women had specified the distribution of profits and losses by allowing interest of 10 percent on beginning capital, salaries of $5,000 to Jessica and $12,000 to Monique, and the remaining amount to be divided in the ratio of 3:2.

On January 1, 19x2, the partners brought into the partnership Jillian Murphy, who was experienced in the employment business. Jillian invested $14,000 in the partnership for a 20 percent interest. The bonus to Jillian was transferred from the original partners' accounts in the ratio of 3:2.

During 19x2, the partnership earned a profit of $27,000. The new partnership agreement required that profits and losses be divided by providing interest of 10 percent on beginning capital balances and salaries of $5,000, $12,000, and $15,000 for Jessica, Monique, and Jillian, respectively. Remaining amounts were to be divided equally.

Because of disagreements among the partners and the lack of sufficient profits, the partners decided to liquidate the partnership on January 1, 19x3. On that date, the assets and liabilities of the partnership were as follows: Cash, $61,000; Accounts Receivable, $38,000; Land, $9,000; Building (net), $70,000; Office Equipment (net), $27,000; Accounts Payable, $27,000; Mortgage Payable, $51,000.

The office equipment was sold for $18,000, and the accounts receivable were valued at $32,000. The resulting losses were distributed equally to the partners' capital accounts, and the accounts payable were paid. Jessica agreed to accept the accounts receivable plus cash in payment for her partnership interest. Monique accepted the land, building, and mortgage payable at book value plus cash for her share in the liquidation. Jillian was paid in cash.

Required

Prepare general journal entries to record all the above facts. Support your computation with schedules, and prepare a statement of liquidation in connection with the January 1, 19x3, entries.

Chapter Sixteen

Corporations: Organization and Operation

Learning Objectives

1. *Define corporation, and state the advantages and disadvantages of the corporate form of business.*
2. *Account for organization costs.*
3. *Describe the basic organization and the key personnel of a corporation.*
4. *Identify and distinguish the components of stockholders' equity.*
5. *Account for the issuance of common and preferred stock for cash and other assets, and for stock subscriptions.*
6. *Calculate book value per share, and distinguish it from market value.*

Although there are fewer corporations than sole proprietorships or partnerships, the corporate form of business dominates the American economy in total dollars of assets and output of goods and services. The major reason for this dominance is that the corporation permits a large accumulation of capital resources. In addition, the corporate form of business is well suited to the modern business trends toward large organizations, international trade, and professional management. As a result of studying this chapter, you should be able to meet the learning objectives listed on the left.

So far, we have discussed accounting practices for the sole proprietorship and partnership forms of business. This chapter will focus on the corporate form of business organization and will introduce accounting for corporate ownership.

The Corporation

A **corporation** is defined as "a body of persons granted a charter legally recognizing them as a separate entity having its own rights, privileges, and liabilities distinct from those of its members."[1] As this definition indicates, the corporation is a legal entity separate from its owners. For this reason, corporate accounting differs from proprietorship and partnership accounting in some respects. Before discussing corporate accounting, however, let us first explore the advantages and disadvantages of this form of business.

1. *The American Heritage Dictionary* (Boston: Houghton Mifflin Company, 1973).

Advantages of a Corporation

The corporate form of a business organization has several advantages over the sole proprietorship and the partnership. Among these advantages are separate legal entity, limited liability, ease of capital generation, ease of transfer of ownership, lack of mutual agency, continuous existence, centralized authority and responsibility, and professional management.

Objective 1 Define corporation, and state the advantages and disadvantages of the corporate form of business

Separate Legal Entity A corporation is a separate legal entity and has basically all the rights of a person except those of voting and marrying. Thus it may buy, sell, or own property, sue and be sued, enter into contracts with all parties, and hire and fire employees.

Limited Liability Because a corporation is a separate legal entity, it is responsible for its own actions and liabilities. Therefore, a corporation's creditors normally cannot look beyond the assets of the company to satisfy their claims. In other words, the creditors can satisfy their claims only against the assets of the corporation, and not against the personal property of the owners of the corporation. Because owners of a corporation are not responsible for the debts of the company, their liability is limited to the amount of their investment. In contrast, the personal property of sole proprietors and partners may be available to creditors.

Ease of Capital Generation It is relatively easy for a corporation to raise money because many individuals can participate in the ownership of the business by investing small amounts of money. Thus a single corporate firm may be owned by many people.

Ease of Transfer of Ownership The ownership of a corporation is represented by a transferable unit called a share of stock. The owner of the share of stock, called a stockholder, can buy and sell shares of stock without affecting the activities of the corporation or needing the approval of other owners.

Lack of Mutual Agency There is no mutual agency with the corporate form of business. If a stockholder, acting as an owner, attempts to enter into a contract for the corporation, the corporation will not be bound by the contract. In contrast, the partnership, where mutual agency exists, can be bound by a partner's actions.

Continuous Existence Another advantage of the corporation being a separate legal entity from its owners is that an owner's death, incapacity, or withdrawal does not affect the life of the corporation. The life of a corporation is set by its charter and regulated by state laws.

Centralized Authority and Responsibility The responsibility and authority for operating the corporation is given to the president of the organization. This power is not divided among the many owners of the business. The president may delegate authority for various segments of the business to others, but he or she has the final responsibility for the business. If the owners are dissatisfied with the performance of the president, they can replace him or her.

Professional Management A corporation is owned by many individuals, who probably do not have the time or expertise to make timely operating decisions for the business. Therefore, management and ownership are separated. This arrangement allows the corporation to hire the best managerial talent available for operating the business.

Disadvantages of a Corporation

The corporate form of business is not without its disadvantages. Among the more important disadvantages are government regulation, taxation, limited liability, and separate ownership and control.

Government Regulation When corporations are created, they must meet the requirements of state laws. Therefore, they are said to be "creatures of the state" and are subject to greater control and regulation by the state than other forms of business. Corporations must file many reports with the states in which they are chartered. In addition, corporations that are publicly held must file reports with the Securities and Exchange Commission and with the stock exchanges. Fulfilling these requirements becomes very costly.

Taxation A major disadvantage of a corporation is **double taxation.** Because the corporation is a separate legal entity, its earnings are subject to federal and state income taxes. These taxes may exceed 50 percent of the corporate earnings. If the corporation's after-tax earnings are then distributed to its stockholders as dividends, these earnings are again taxed as income to the stockholders receiving them. Taxation is different for the sole proprietorship and the partnership, whose earnings are taxed only as personal income to the owners. The taxation of corporations is discussed in Chapter 29.

Limited Liability Earlier, limited liability was cited as an advantage of a corporation. This same feature, however, may limit the ability of a small corporation to borrow funds. Credit of a small corporation is reduced because the stockholders have limited liability and the creditors will have claims only to the assets of the corporation. Under these conditions, the creditors will limit their loans to the level secured by the assets of the corporation.

Separation of Ownership and Control Just as limited liability may prove disadvantageous, so may the separation of ownership and control. Sometimes management makes decisions that do not benefit the corporation as a whole. There may also be a lack of communication, which makes it difficult for stockholders to exercise control over the corporation or even to recognize that management's decisions are disadvantageous.

Formation of a Corporation

To form a corporation in most states, at least three individuals, called incorporators, must sign an application and file it with the proper state official. The application contains the articles of incorporation. If approved by the state, these articles become a contract between the state and the incorporators, called the company charter. Examples of items that may appear in the articles of incorporation are the name and address of the corporation, the purpose of the business to be conducted, the different classes of stocks and their par or stated values, the number of shares of each class of stock authorized, the voting and dividend rights of each class of stock, the name and address of the original subscribers to shares of stock, and the life of the corporation.

After the charter is approved, the company is authorized to do business. First, the incorporators hold a stockholders' meeting to elect a board of directors and pass a set of bylaws to guide the operations of the corporation. Then, the board of directors holds a meeting in order to elect officers of the corporation. Finally, when initial capital is raised through the issuance of shares of stock, the corporation is ready to begin operating.

Organization Costs

Objective 2 Account for organization costs

The costs of forming a corporation are called organization costs. These costs include such items as state incorporation fees, attorneys' fees for drawing up the articles of incorporation, promoters' fees, the cost of printing stock, accountants' fees for services rendered in registering the firm's initial stock, and other expenditures necessary for forming the corporation.

The benefits to be received from these costs should actually span the entire life of the organization. For this reason, the costs should be capitalized as intangible assets and amortized over the years. However, the life of a corporation is normally unknown, so accountants amortize these costs over the early years of a corporation's life. Because the income tax regulations allow organization costs to be amortized over five years or more, most companies amortize these costs over a five-year period. Organization costs normally appear as Other Assets or Intangible Assets on the balance sheet.

To illustrate accounting practice for organization costs, we will assume that a corporation pays a lawyer $5,000 for services rendered in preparing the application for a charter with the state. The entry to record this cost would be as follows:

19x0			
July 1	Organization Costs	5,000	
	Cash		5,000
	To record $5,000 lawyer's fee for services rendered in corporate organization		

If the corporation elects to amortize the organization costs over a five-year period, the entry to record the amortization at the end of the fiscal year on June 30, 19x1, would be:

19x1			
June 30	Amortization of Organization Costs	1,000	
	Organization Costs		1,000
	To record one year's amortization costs: $5,000 ÷ 5 years = $1,000		

Organization of a Corporation

Objective 3 Describe the basic organization and the key personnel of a corporation

The authority to manage the corporation is delegated by the stockholders to the board of directors and by the board of directors to the corporate officers. The stockholders elect the board, which determines company policies and selects the corporate officers, who in turn execute the corporate policies by managing the business.

Stockholders Individual stockholders do not normally participate in the day-to-day management of a corporation. However, a stockholder may serve as a member of the board if elected or as an officer of the company if appointed. In general, stockholders participate in management only through electing the board of directors and voting on particular issues at stockholder meetings. Certain rights accorded to stockholders include the following:

1. They may dispose of their shares of stock at their own discretion.
2. They may vote for directors, thereby indirectly participating in the management of the corporation.
3. They share in the dividends of the corporation when they are declared.
4. They share in the distribution of assets of the corporation in case of liquidation. Stockholders have a residual interest in the assets of the corporation because creditors must be paid in full before stockholders have a right to the assets.
5. They may purchase additional shares of stock when they are issued in proportion to their current holdings. This privilege is known as the **preemptive right** of stockholders. This right merely allows each stockholder to maintain his or her percentage of ownership in the corporation after each additional issuance of stock. For example, Jerry Jones owns 40 percent of the stock of the Laura Cosmetics Company. The company plans to issue an additional 100,000 shares of common stock. Jones has the right to purchase 40 percent of the issue to maintain his percentage of ownership in the company. This right may be waived, however, by vote of the stockholders.

Stockholders will normally meet once a year to elect directors and carry on other business as provided in the company's bylaws. Business transacted at these meetings may include the election of auditors, review of proposed mergers and acquisitions, changes in the charter, stock option plans, and issuance of additional stock and of long-term debt. Each stockholder is entitled to one vote for each share of voting stock that he or she holds. Today, ownership of large corporations is spread over the entire country. As a result, only a few stockholders may be able to attend the annual stockholders' meeting. A stockholder who cannot attend the meeting may vote by proxy. The **proxy** is a legal document, signed by the stockholder, giving another party the authority to vote his or her shares. Normally, this authority is assigned to the current management of the corporation.

Board of Directors The stockholders elect the board of directors and give the board the authority to determine the major business policies of the corporation. The board also has the function of protecting the stockholders and creditors. The directors appoint the administrative officers and delegate to them the authority to carry out the policies determined by the board. Several other specific duties of the board include declaring dividends, authorizing contracts, determining executive salaries, arranging major loans with banks, and engaging and monitoring the work of an independent auditor.

The composition of the board will vary from company to company. In most companies, however, the board will contain several administrative officers of the company and several outsiders. Today, the inclusion of several outside directors is encouraged to ensure the objectivity of the board in evaluating management's performance.

The actions of the board of directors are recorded in the minutes of their meetings. Because many important decisions are made at these meetings, the minutes book is a very important document for the accountant. Many of the decisions serve as a basis for entries in the accounting records. For example, accounting entries must record decisions to issue additional stock, to sell long-term bonds, and to declare dividends.

Management The management of a corporation is appointed by the board of directors to execute the company's policies and carry on day-to-day operations. The management consists of the operating officers, who are normally the president, vice presidents, controller, treasurer, and secretary. The president is the chief officer and is directly responsible to the board for the operations of the company. There may be several vice presidents, each of whom may be responsible for a different operation of the business. For example, there may be a vice president responsible for the production of the company's products and a second vice president responsible for the marketing of the products. The controller, who is normally the chief accountant, has responsibility for maintaining adequate internal control; for preparing accounting records, financial statements, tax returns, and other reports required by the government; and for budgeting. The treasurer is the custodian of company funds and is usually responsible for the planning and control of corporate cash. The secretary maintains minutes for the board of directors and stockholders' meetings, records stock transfers, and represents the company in most contractual and legal matters.

The Components of Stockholders' Equity

Objective 4 Identify and distinguish the components of stockholders' equity

The major difference in accounting for corporations and accounting for sole proprietorships or partnerships involves the owners' equity. The assets and liabilities of a corporation are handled in the same manner as they are for other forms of business. In a corporation's balance sheet, the owners' claims to the business are called **stockholders' equity**, as follows:

Stockholders' Equity

Contributed Capital	
Preferred Stock—$50 par value, 1,000 shares authorized and issued	$ 50,000
Common Stock—$5 par value, 30,000 shares authorized, 20,000 shares issued	100,000
Paid-in Capital in Excess of Par Value, Common	50,000
Total Contributed Capital	$200,000
Retained Earnings	60,000
Total Stockholders' Equity	$260,000

This equity section differs from the balance sheet presentation of a sole proprietorship and partnership in that it is divided into two parts: (1) contributed capital and (2) retained earnings. The **contributed capital** represents the investments made by the stockholders in the corporation. The retained earnings are the earnings of the business that are not distributed to the stockholders but are reinvested in the business.

The contributed capital section of stockholders' equity provides a considerable amount of information about the stock of a corporation. For example, the types of stock, their par value, and the number of shares authorized and issued are disclosed in this section of stockholders' equity. This information in the contributed capital section of stockholders' equity is the subject of the remainder of this chapter. Discussion of retained earnings is deferred until Chapter 17.

Capital Stock

A unit of ownership in a corporation is called a share of stock. A **stock certificate** will be issued to the owner indicating the number of shares of the corporation's stock owned by the stockholder. Stockholders can transfer their ownership at will, but they must endorse their stock certificate and send it to the corporation's secretary. In large corporations listed on the organized stock exchanges, it is difficult to maintain stockholders' records because such companies may have millions of shares of stock, several thousand of which may change ownership every day. Therefore, these corporations often appoint independent registrars and transfer agents to aid in performing the secretary's duties. The registrars and the transfer agents (usually banks and trust companies) are responsible for transferring the corporation's stock, maintaining stockholders' records, preparing a list of stockholders for stockholders' meetings, and paying the dividends. To assist in the initial issue of capital stock, corporations often engage an underwriter. The underwriter is an intermediary between the corporation and the investing public. For a fee—usually the difference between the price the public pays for the stock and the price the corporation receives—the underwriter guarantees the sale of the stock.

Authorization of Stock

When a corporation applies for a charter, the articles of incorporation indicate the maximum number of shares of stock a corporation will be permitted to issue. This number represents **authorized stock.** Most corporations obtain an authorization to issue more shares of stock than are necessary at the time of organization. This action enables the corporation to issue stock in the future to obtain additional capital. For example, if a corporation is planning to expand later, a possible source of capital would be the unissued shares of stock that were authorized in its charter. If all authorized stock is issued immediately, the corporation must change its charter by applying to the state to increase the number of shares of authorized stock. The charter also discloses the par value of the stock that has been authorized. The **par value** is the amount to be printed on each share of stock, and must be recorded in the capital stock accounts. When the corporation is formed, a memorandum entry may be made in the general journal to indicate the number and description of authorized shares.

Outstanding Stock

The **outstanding stock** of a corporation consists of the shares held by the stockholders. For example, a corporation may have been authorized to issue 500,000 shares of stock but chose to issue only 300,000 shares when the company was organized. The 300,000 shares represent the outstanding stock, and the holders of those shares own 100 percent of the corporation. The remaining 200,000 shares of stock are unissued shares and have no rights or privileges associated with them until they are issued. A share of stock may be issued but may not be outstanding because it has been purchased by the corporation or given back to the company by a shareholder. In such a case, a company can have more shares issued than are currently outstanding. The reasons for holding this stock are explained in Chapter 17 under the heading of treasury stock.

Common Stock

A corporation may issue two basic types of stock: common stock and preferred stock. If only one type of stock is issued, it is called **common stock**, and the stockholders have the basic rights indicated earlier. The common stock is the **residual equity** of a company. This term means that all other creditor and preferred stockholder claims to the company's assets rank ahead of those of the common stockholders in case of liquidation. Because the common stock is normally the only stock carrying voting rights, it represents the means of controlling the corporation.

Preferred Stock

The second type of stock, called **preferred stock**, may be issued so that the company can obtain funds from investors who have different investment objectives. Preferred stock has some preference over common stock, usually in the area of dividends. There may be several different classes of preferred stock, each with distinctive characteristics to attract different types of investors. Most preferred stock will have one or more of the following characteristics: preference as to dividends, preference as to assets of the business in liquidation, convertibility or nonconvertibility, callable option, and no voting rights.

Preference as to Dividends If a stock has preference as to dividends, the stockholders are entitled to a dividend before any payment can be made to the common stockholders. The dividend is usually indicated in one of two ways. First, it may be stated as a specific dollar amount per share. For example, a corporation may issue a preferred stock and pay a yearly dividend of $4 per share. Second, the dividend may be expressed as a percentage of par value. For example, a corporation may issue a preferred stock of $100 par value and pay a yearly dividend of 6 percent of par value, which amounts to a $6 annual dividend.

The preferred stockholders have no guarantee of receiving dividends. They will be able to receive a dividend only when the board of directors declares a dividend. In addition, preferred stock may be noncumulative or cumulative. In the case of **noncumulative preferred stock**, if a preferred dividend is not paid in a given year, it lapses and will never have to be paid. However, in any one year the preferred stockholders must be paid their dividend before the common stockholders receive a dividend. In the case of **cumulative preferred stock**, unpaid dividends accumulate over periods of time. Thus if all or a part of a yearly dividend is not paid in the year when it is due, it must be paid in a subsequent year before dividends can be paid to common stockholders. Dividends that are not paid in the year they are due are called **dividends in arrears.** Assume that the preferred stock of a corporation is as follows: preferred stock, 5 percent cumulative, 10,000 shares, $100 par, $1,000,000. If in 19x1 no dividends were paid, at the end of that year there would be preferred dividends of $50,000 in arrears ($1,000,000 × 5% = $50,000). Thus if dividends are paid next year, the preferred stockholders' dividends in arrears plus the 19x2 preferred dividends must be paid before any dividends can be paid in 19x2 on common stock.

As an illustration, let us assume the following facts. On January 1, 19x1, a corporation issued 10,000 shares of $10 par, 6 percent cumulative preferred stock and 50,000 shares of common stock. The first year's operations resulted in income of only $4,000. The board of directors declared a $3,000 cash dividend to the preferred stockholders. The dividend picture at the end of 19x1 appears as follows:

19x1 dividends due preferred stockholders (100,000 × 6%)	$6,000
19x1 dividends declared preferred stockholders	3,000
Preferred stock dividends in arrears	$3,000

In 19x2, the company earned income of $30,000 and wished to pay dividends to both the preferred and the common stockholders. Because the preferred stock is cumulative, the corporation must pay the $3,000 dividends in arrears on the preferred stock plus the current year's dividends before the common stockholders can receive a dividend. For example, assume that the corporation's board of directors declared a $12,000 dividend to be distributed to the preferred and common stockholders. The distribution of the dividend would be as follows:

19x2 declaration of dividends	$12,000
Less 19x1 preferred stock dividends in arrears	3,000
	$ 9,000
Less 19x2 preferred stock dividend ($100,000 × 6%)	6,000
	$ 3,000
Less remainder to common stockholders	3,000
	—

Dividends can be declared only by the board of directors. Once the board declares a dividend, the corporation has a liability that should be recognized. The following entry is made when a dividend is declared:

June 15	Retained Earnings	10,000	
	Dividends Payable		10,000
	To record declaration of a $10,000 cash dividend to preferred stockholders		

Dividends in arrears are not recognized as liabilities of a corporation because a liability does not exist until the board declares a dividend. A corporation cannot guarantee profits; therefore, it cannot guarantee dividends to stockholders. However, if a company has dividends in arrears, they should be disclosed in its financial statements either in the body of the statement or in a footnote. This explanation is necessary to provide adequate information to the users of these financial statements. For example, the following footnote appeared in a steel company's annual report in a recent year:

> On January 1, 19xx, the company was in arrears by $37,851 ($1.25 per share) on dividends to its preferred stockholders. The company must pay all dividends in arrears to preferred stockholders before paying any dividends to common stockholders.

Preferred stock is called **nonparticipating** when its dividend is limited to the stated percentage or dollar amount per share. Preferred stock is called **participating** when the preferred stockholders may receive a larger proportion of the dividends than is indicated by their basic dividend rate. For example, those who owned a 6 percent participating preferred stock with a par value of $100 would be entitled to a $6 dividend per share before the common stockholders received a dividend. The common stockholders would then be entitled to a dividend equal to 6 percent of their stock's par value before any participation takes place. If any additional dividends are declared after the common stockholders receive their 6 percent dividend, the common and preferred stockholders would share the remainder in some stated ratio. For example, assume that a corporation has 1,000 shares of 6 percent, $100 par value fully participating preferred stock and 50,000 shares of $10 par value common stock. The board of directors declares a $42,000 dividend for 19x1, and there are no dividends in arrears. The dividend would be distributed in the way shown below.

Dividend declared	$42,000
Less 19x1 preferred stock dividend ($100,000 × 6%)	6,000
	$36,000
Less 19x1 common stock dividend ($500,000 × 6%)	30,000
Remainder to be shared by preferred and common stockholders	$ 6,000

The $6,000 will be distributed in some stated manner between the preferred and common stockholders. One method is to allocate the remaining dividend according to the relative total par values of the stock as computed at the top of the next page.

Stock	Shares	Par Value	Total Par Value	Allocation Ratio
Preferred	1,000	$100	$100,000	$\frac{100{,}000}{600{,}000} = \frac{1}{6}$
Common	50,000	10	500,000	$\frac{500{,}000}{600{,}000} = \frac{5}{6}$
			$600,000	

Preferred stock:

$$\$6{,}000 \times \frac{1}{6} = \$1{,}000$$

Common stock:

$$\$6{,}000 \times \frac{5}{6} = 5{,}000$$

Dividends allocated $6,000

If no limit is placed on the amount that the preferred stockholders can receive above their stated dividend, the stock is called fully participating preferred stock. If there is a limit on the additional dividends that the preferred stockholders can receive, the stock is called partially participating preferred stock.

Preference as to Assets Many preferred stocks have preference as to the assets of the corporation in the case of liquidation of the business. Thus when the business is terminated, the preferred stockholders are entitled to receive the par value of their stock or a larger stipulated liquidation value per share before the common stockholders receive any share of the corporation's assets. This preference also includes any dividends in arrears owed to the preferred stockholders.

Convertible Preferred Stock A corporation may make its preferred stock more attractive to potential investors by adding a convertible feature. Holders of convertible preferred stock can exchange their shares of preferred stock, if they wish, for shares of the corporation's common stock at a ratio stated in the preferred stock contract. Convertibility is attractive to investors because (1) like all preferred stockholders, owners of convertible stock have greater assurance of regular dividends than do common stockholders, and (2) if the market value of a company's common stock increases, the conversion feature will allow the preferred stockholders to share in this increase. The increased value would occur by parallel increases in the value of the preferred stock or through conversion to common stock.

To illustrate, we will assume that a corporation issued 1,000 shares of 8 percent, $100 par value convertible preferred stock for $100 per share. Each share of stock can be converted into five shares of the company's common stock at any time. The current market value of the common stock is $15 per share. In the past, the dividends on the common stock had been approximately $1 per share per year. The stockholder owning one share of preferred stock currently holds an investment that is worth approximately $100 on the market, and the probability of dividends is higher than with common stock. Assume that in the next several years the corporation's earnings increase and the dividends being paid to common stockholders also increase, to $3 per share. In addition, the market value of a share of common stock increases from $15 to $30. The preferred stockholders can convert each of their preferred shares into five common shares and increase their dividends from $8 on each preferred share to the equivalent of $15 ($3 on each of five common shares). Furthermore, the market value of each share of preferred stock will approximate the $150 value of the five shares of common stock because the share may be converted into the five shares of common stock.

Callable Preferred Stock Most preferred stocks are **callable preferred stocks**—they may be redeemed or retired at the option of the issuing corporation at some particular price stated in the preferred stock contract. The stockholder must surrender a nonconvertible preferred stock to the corporation when requested to do so. If the preferred stock is convertible, the shareholder may either surrender the stock to the corporation or convert it into common stock when the corporation calls the stock. The call price, or redemption price, is usually higher than the par value of the stock. For example, a $100 par value preferred stock might be callable at $102 or $103 per share. When preferred stock is called and surrendered, the stockholder is entitled to (1) the par value of the stock, (2) the call premium, (3) the dividends in arrears, and (4) a prorated portion of the current period's dividend.

There are several reasons why a corporation may call its preferred stock. The first is that the company may wish to force conversion of the preferred stock to common because the cash dividend to be paid on the equivalent common stock is less than the dividend being paid on the preferred shares. Second, it may be possible to replace the outstanding preferred stock on the current market with a preferred stock at a lower dividend rate. Third, the company may simply be profitable enough to retire the preferred stock.

Accounting for Stock Issuance

Objective 5 Account for the issuance of common and preferred stock for cash and other assets, and for stock subscriptions

A share of capital stock is either a par or a no-par stock. If the capital stock is par stock, the corporation charter indicates the par value, and this value must be printed on each share of stock. Par value may be 10¢, $1, $5, $100, or any other amount determined by the organizers of the corporation. The par values of common stocks tend to be lower than those of preferred stocks.

Par value indicates the amount per share that is entered into the corporation's Capital Stock account and constitutes the **legal capital** of the corporation. The legal capital is the minimum amount that can be reported as contributed capital. A corporation may not declare a dividend that would cause stockholders' equity to fall below the legal capital of the firm. Therefore, the par value is a minimum cushion of capital for the protection of creditors. Any amount received in excess of par value from the issuance of stock is recorded as Paid-in Capital in Excess of Par Value and represents a portion of the company's contributed capital.

No-par stock is capital stock that does not have a par value. No-par stock may be issued with or without a stated value. The board of directors of the corporation issuing the no-par stock may place a **stated value** on each share of stock. The stated value can be any value set by the board, but some states do indicate a minimum value per share. The stated value may be set before or after the shares are issued if state law does not specify this point.

When no-par stock is issued, the shares are recorded in the Capital Stock account at the stated value. Any amount received in excess of the stated value is recorded as Paid-in Capital in Excess of Stated Value. The excess of the stated value represents a part of the corporation's contributed capital. However, the stated value is normally considered to be the legal capital of the corporation.

If a company issues a no-par stock without a stated value, then the entire proceeds of the issuance of the stock are recorded in the Capital Stock account. This amount becomes the legal capital of the corporation unless the amount is specified by state law. Because additional shares of the stock may be issued at different prices, the credit to the Capital Stock account will not be uniform per share. In this way it differs from par value stock or no-par stock with a stated value.

There are several reasons for issuing stock without a par value. One is that some investors have confused par value with book or market value of stock and have thus made poor investment decisions. Another reason is that when a par value stock is issued below par, it will normally carry a contingent liability upon the stockholders to creditors of the corporation in the amount of the difference between issue price and par value. This means, in the case of corporate liquidation, that the stockholders who purchased stock below its par value would have to pay the creditors the difference between par value and the purchase price if the company's assets are not sufficient to pay the creditors. Still another reason is that most states will not allow an original issuance of stock below par value and thereby limit a corporation's flexibility in obtaining capital.

Issuance of Par Value Stock

When a par value stock is issued, the Capital Stock account is credited for the par value (legal capital) regardless of whether the proceeds are more or less than the par value. For example, assume that Bradley Corporation is authorized to issue 20,000 shares of $10 par value common stock and actually issues 10,000 shares at $10 per share. The entry to record the issuance of the stock would be as shown on the next page.

		Debit	Credit
Jan. 1	Cash	100,000	
	Capital Stock, Common		100,000
	Issued 10,000 shares of $10 par value common stock for $10 per share		

Cash is debited for $100,000 (10,000 shares × $10), and Capital Stock, Common, is credited for an equal amount because the stock was sold for par value (legal capital). If the stock had been issued for a price greater than par, the proceeds in excess of par would be credited to a capital account entitled Paid-in Capital in Excess of Par Value, Common. For example, assume that the 10,000 shares of Bradley common stock were sold for $12 per share. The entry to record the issuance of the stock would be as follows:

		Debit	Credit
Jan. 1	Cash	120,000	
	Capital Stock, Common		100,000
	Paid-in Capital in Excess of Par Value, Common		20,000
	Issued 10,000 shares of $10 par value common stock for $12 per share		

Cash is debited for the proceeds of $120,000 (10,000 shares × $12), and Capital Stock, Common, is credited at total par value of $100,000 (10,000 shares × $10). Paid-in Capital in Excess of Par Value, Common, is credited for the difference of $20,000 (10,000 shares × $2). The premium paid for the stock is a part of the corporation's contributed capital and will be added to Capital Stock, Common, in the stockholders' equity section of the balance sheet. The stockholders' equity section for Bradley Corporation immediately following the stock issue would appear as follows:

Stockholders' Equity

Contributed Capital	
Capital Stock, Common—$10 par value, 20,000 shares authorized, 10,000 shares issued and outstanding	$100,000
Paid-in Capital in Excess of Par Value, Common	20,000
Total Contributed Capital	$120,000
Retained Earnings	—
Total Stockholders' Equity	$120,000

If a corporation issues stock for less than par, an account entitled Discount on Capital Stock should be debited for the discount. (The issuance of stock at a discount is illegal in many states and rarely occurs.) For example, assume that 10,000 shares of $10 par value common stock are sold for $9 per share, for a total of $90,000. The discount equals $10,000 ($100,000 par value minus $90,000 proceeds) and is recorded as follows:

Jan. 1	Cash	90,000	
	Discount on Capital Stock	10,000	
	Capital Stock, Common		100,000
	Issued 10,000 shares of $10 par value common stock for $9 per share		

If a stock is issued at a discount, a contingent liability equivalent to the discount exists for those stockholders in case of corporate liquidation. This contingency is shown on the balance sheet by deducting the Discount on Common Stock as a contra account from Capital Stock, Common, to arrive at contributed capital, as follows:

Contributed Capital	
Capital Stock, Common—$10 par value, 20,000 shares authorized, 10,000 shares issued and outstanding	$100,000
Discount on Common Stock	(10,000)
Total Contributed Capital	$ 90,000

Issuance of No-Par Stock

As mentioned earlier, stock may be issued without a par value. However, most states require that all or part of the proceeds from the issuance of no-par stock be designated as legal capital not subject to withdrawal, except in liquidation.

For example, we will assume that the Bradley Corporation's capital stock is no-par common and that 10,000 shares are issued on January 1, 19xx, at $15 per share. The $150,000 (10,000 shares at $15) in proceeds would be recorded as shown in this entry:

Jan. 1	Cash	150,000	
	Capital Stock, Common		150,000
	Issued 10,000 shares of no-par common stock at $15 per share		

Since the stock does not have a stated or par value, the entire proceeds of the issue are credited to Capital Stock, No-Par Common, and represent the company's legal capital.

Most states allow the board of directors to establish a stated value on no-par stock, and this value represents the legal capital. Assume that Bradley's board establishes a $10 stated value on its no-par stock. The entry to record the issue of 10,000 shares of no-par common stock for $15 per share would change from that in the previous paragraph to the following:

Jan. 1	Cash	150,000	
	Capital Stock, Common		100,000
	Paid-in Capital in Excess of Stated Value, Common		50,000
	Issued 10,000 shares of no-par common stock with a $10 stated value for $15 per share		

Note that the legal capital credited to Capital Stock, Common, is the stated value as determined by the board of directors and that the account Paid-in Capital in Excess of Stated Value, Common, is credited for $50,000. The $50,000 represents the difference between the proceeds ($150,000) and the total stated value ($100,000). Paid-in Capital in Excess of Stated Value, Common, is presented on the balance sheet in the same way as Paid-in Capital in Excess of Par Value is presented for par value stock.

Issuance of Stock for Noncash Assets

In many stock transactions, stock is issued for assets or services other than cash. As a result, a problem arises as to what dollar amount should be recorded for the exchange. The general rule for such a transaction is to record the transaction at the fair market value of the assets or services received. If the fair market value of the assets or services cannot be determined, the fair market value of the stock issued should be used to record the transaction. Transactions of this nature usually include the exchange of stock for land, buildings, and payment for services of attorneys and promoters.

Where there is an exchange of stock for noncash assets, the board of directors has the right to value the property. For example, when the Bradley Corporation was formed, it issued 100 shares of its $10 par value common stock to its attorney for services rendered. At the time of the issuance, the market value of the stock was not determinable. However, for similar services the attorney would have billed the company for $1,500. The entry to record the noncash transaction follows:

Jan. 1	Organization Costs	1,500	
	Capital Stock, Common		1,000
	Paid-in Capital in Excess of Par Value, Common		500
	Issued 100 shares of $10 par value common stock for attorney's services		

Assume further that the Bradley Corporation exchanged 1,000 shares of its $10 par common stock for a tract of land two years later. At the time of the exchange the stock was selling on the market for $16 per share and the value of the land was indeterminable. The entry to record this exchange would be:

Jan. 1	Land	16,000	
	Capital Stock, Common		10,000
	Paid-in Capital in Excess of Par Value, Common		6,000
	Issued 1,000 shares of $10 par value common stock for a tract of land; market value of the stock $16 per share		

Stock Subscriptions

In some states, corporations may sell stock on a subscription basis. In a **stock subscription**, the investor agrees to pay for the stock on some future date or in installments at an agreed price. When a subscription is received, a contract exists and the corporation acquires an asset Subscriptions Receivable, which represents the amount owed on the stock, and a capital item Capital Stock Subscribed, which represents the par or stated value of the stock not yet fully paid for and issued. The Subscription Receivable account should be identified as either common or preferred stock. The Stock Subscribed account should also be identified as either common or preferred stock. Whether or not the subscriber is entitled to dividends on the subscribed stock depends on the laws of the state in which the corporation is incorporated. In certain states, the stock is considered to be legally issued when a subscription contract is accepted, thereby making the subscriber a legal stockholder. However, in accounting for stock subscriptions, capital stock is not issued and recorded until the subscriptions receivable pertaining to the shares are collected in full and the stock certificate is delivered to the stockholder. Likewise, it may be assumed that dividends are not paid on common stock subscribed until it is fully paid for and the certificates issued.

To illustrate stock subscriptions, we will assume that on January 1, 19xx, the Bradley Corporation received subscriptions for 15,000 shares at $15 per share. The entry to record the subscription would be:

Jan. 1	Subscriptions Receivable, Common	225,000	
	Capital Stock Subscribed, Common		150,000
	Paid-in Capital in Excess of Par Value, Common		75,000
	Received subscriptions for 15,000 shares of $10 par value common stock at $15 per share		

If the full subscription price for 10,000 shares was collected on January 21, 19xx, the entry for the collection of the subscription would be as follows:

Jan. 21	Cash	150,000	
	Subscriptions Receivable, Common		150,000
	Collected subscriptions in full for 10,000 shares of $10 par value common stock at $15 per share		

Because the 10,000 shares are fully paid for, it is appropriate to issue the common stock, as shown here:

Jan. 21	Capital Stock Subscribed, Common	100,000	
	Capital Stock, Common		100,000
	Issued 10,000 shares of $10 par value common stock		

Note that since the paid-in value in excess of par value was recorded in the January 1 entry, there is no need to record it again.

If financial statements are prepared on January 31, 19xx, before the remaining subscriptions are collected, the Subscriptions Receivable account of $75,000 ($225,000 – $150,000) would be classified as a current asset unless there was some reason why it would not be collected in the next year. The balance of $50,000 ($150,000 – $100,000) in the Capital Stock Subscribed account represents the par value of the stock yet to be issued and is a temporary capital account. As such, it is properly disclosed as a part of stockholders' equity under Contributed Capital, as shown in the following illustration:

Stockholders' Equity

Contributed Capital		
Capital Stock, Common—$10 par value, 80,000 shares authorized		
Issued and outstanding, 10,000 shares	$100,000	
Subscribed but not issued, 5,000 shares	50,000	$150,000
Paid-in Capital in Excess of Par Value, Common		75,000
Total Contributed Capital		$225,000

If one-half payment of $37,500 is received on February 5 for the remaining subscriptions receivable, the entry for the collection would be as follows:

Feb. 5	Cash	37,500	
	Subscriptions Receivable, Common		37,500
	Collected one-half payment for subscriptions to 5,000 common shares		

In this case, there is no entry to issue common stock because the subscription pertaining to the stock is not paid in full. If the subscriptions receivable are paid in full on February 20 the entries are as follows:

Feb. 20	Cash	37,500	
	Subscriptions Receivable, Common		37,500
	Collected subscriptions in full for 5,000 shares of $10 par value common stock for $15 per share		

Because the subscriptions are now paid in full, the common stock can be issued as follows:

Feb. 20	Capital Stock Subscribed, Common	50,000	
	Capital Stock, Common		50,000
	Issued 5,000 shares of $10 par value common stock		

Stock Values

Objective 6 Calculate book value per share, and distinguish it from market value

The word *value* is associated with shares of stock in several ways. The terms *par value* and *stated value,* which have already been explained, are each values per share that establish the legal capital of a company. Par value or stated value is arbitrarily set when the stock is authorized and has no relationship to the book value or to the market value.

Book Value

The **book value** of a company's stock represents the total assets of the company less liabilities. Thus it is simply the owners' equity of the company. The book value per share, therefore, represents the equity of the owner of one share of stock in the net assets of the corporation. To obtain the book value per share when the company has only common stock outstanding, divide the total stockholders' equity by the total common shares outstanding plus shares subscribed but not issued. As an illustration, assume the following stockholders' equity of the Bradley Corporation:

Stockholders' Equity

Contributed Capital		
Capital Stock, Common—$10 par value, 20,000 shares authorized, 10,000 shares outstanding	$100,000	
Paid-in Capital in Excess of Par Value, Common	50,000	$150,000
Retained Earnings		50,000
Total Stockholders' Equity		$200,000

The book value per share of common stock is computed by using the following formula:

$$\text{book value per share (BV)} = \frac{\text{total contributed capital} + \text{retained earnings}}{\text{total shares outstanding and subscribed}}$$

$$BV = \frac{\$150{,}000 + \$50{,}000}{10{,}000}$$

$$BV = \frac{\$200{,}000}{10{,}000}$$

$$BV = \$20 \text{ per share}$$

If a company has both preferred and common stock, the determination of book value per share is more complex. The general rule is that the liquidating value (usually equal to par value) of the preferred stock plus any dividends in arrears is deducted from total stockholders' equity to determine the equity pertaining to common stock. For example, assume the following stockholders' equity section:

Stockholders' Equity

Contributed Capital	
Preferred Stock—$100 par value, 9% cumulative and nonparticipating, 2,000 shares authorized, issued, and outstanding	$200,000
Common Stock—$10 par value, 50,000 shares authorized, issued, and outstanding	500,000
Paid-in Capital in Excess of Par Value, Common	200,000
Total Contributed Capital	$900,000
Retained Earnings	100,000
Total Stockholders' Equity	$1,000,000

If we assume no dividends in arrears, the equity pertaining to common stock is determined as follows:

Total stockholders' equity	$1,000,000
Less equity allocated to preferred shareholders	200,000
Equity pertaining to common shareholders	$ 800,000

The book values per share would be as follows:

Preferred Stock: $200,000 ÷ 2,000 shares = $100 per share
Common Stock: $800,000 ÷ 50,000 shares = $16 per share

If we assume the same facts except that two years of preferred stock dividends are in arrears, the stockholders' equity would be allocated as follows:

Total Stockholders' Equity		$1,000,000
Less: Par value of outstanding preferred shares	$200,000	
Dividends in arrears (9% × $200,000 × 2 years)	36,000	
Equity allocated to preferred shareholders		236,000
Equity pertaining to common shareholders		$ 764,000

The book values per share under this assumption are:

Preferred Stock: $236,000 ÷ 2,000 shares = $118 per share
Common Stock: $764,000 ÷ 50,000 shares = $15.28 per share

Undeclared preferred dividends are considered in arrears on the last day of the fiscal year (the date the financial statements are prepared). Also, dividends in arrears do not apply to unissued preferred stock.

Market Value

The book value per share often bears little relationship to the market value per share. The **market value** is the price that investors are willing to pay for a share of stock on the open market. Whereas the book value is based on historical cost, the market value is usually determined by investors' expectations for the particular company and general economic conditions. For example, expectations of the company's future profitability, its perceived riskiness, expected dividends per share, the current financial condition of the company, and the state of the money market will play a role in determining the market value of a corporation's stock.

Chapter Review

Review of Learning Objectives

1. Define corporation, and state the advantages and disadvantages of the corporate form of business.

The corporation is a separate legal entity having its own rights, privileges, and liabilities distinct from its owners. Like other forms of business entities, it has several advantages and disadvantages. The more common advantages are that (a) a corporation is a separate legal entity, (b) stockholders have limited liability, (c) it is easy to generate capital for a corporation, (d) stockholders can buy and sell shares of stock with ease, (e) there is a lack of mutual agency, (f) the corporation has a continuous existence, (g) authority and responsibility are centralized, and (h) it is run by a professional management team. Disadvantages of corporations include (a) a large amount of government regulation, (b) double taxation, (c) limited liability, and (d) the separation of ownership and control.

2. Account for organization costs.

The costs of organizing a corporation are recorded on a historical cost basis. As an intangible asset, organization costs are amortized over a reasonable period of time, usually five years.

3. Describe the basic organization and the key personnel of a corporation.

The stockholders of a corporation elect the board of directors. The board determines company policies and selects the corporate officers, who execute the corporate policies by managing the business. The key personnel in a corporation are the president, secretary, treasurer, controller, and vice presidents for manufacturing, marketing, and finance.

4. Identify and distinguish the components of stockholders' equity.

Stockholders' equity consists of contributed capital and retained earnings. Contributed capital may include more than one type of stock. Two of the most common types of stock are common stock and preferred stock. When only one type of security is issued, it is common stock. The holders of common stock have the right to elect the board of directors and vote on key issues of the corporation. In addition, common stockholders share in the earnings of the corporation, share in the assets of the corporation in case of liquidation, and maintain their percentage ownership.

Preferred stock is issued to investors whose investment objectives differ from those of common stockholders. To attract these investors, corporations give them a preference to certain items. Preferred stockholders' rights normally include the privilege of receiving dividends ahead of common shareholders, the right to assets in liquidation ahead of common shareholders, and convertibility to common stock.

5. Account for the issuance of common and preferred stock for cash and other assets, and for stock subscriptions.

A corporation's stock will normally be issued for cash and other assets, or by subscription. The majority of states require that stock be issued at a minimum value called legal capital. Legal capital is represented by the par or stated value of the stock.

When stock is issued for cash or other assets, the par or stated value of the stock is recorded as common or preferred stock. When the stock is sold at an amount greater than the par or stated value, the excess is recorded as Paid-in Capital in Excess of Par or Stated Value.

Sometimes stock is issued for noncash assets. In these transactions, it is necessary to decide what value to use in recording the issuance of the stock. The general rule is to record the stock at the fair market value of the asset received. If this value cannot be determined, then the fair market value of the stock issued will be used to record the transaction.

When stock is not fully paid for at the time of sale, it is not issued, but the transaction is recorded by debiting Subscriptions Receivable (a current asset) and crediting Capital Stock Subscribed (a stockholders' equity account). When the stock has been fully paid for and is issued, Capital Stock Subscribed is debited and Capital Stock is credited.

6. Calculate book value per share, and distinguish it from market value.

Book value per share is the equity per share and is calculated by dividing stockholders' equity by the number of common shares outstanding. Market value per share is the price investors are willing to pay based on their expectations about the future earning ability of the company.

Review Problem

Before doing the exercises and problems, review the sample journal entries and the stockholders' equity illustrations in this chapter. For additional help, see the review problem in the working papers.

Chapter assignments

Questions

1. What are several advantages of the corporate form of business? Explain.
2. What are several disadvantages of the corporate form of business? Explain.
3. What are organization costs of a corporation?
4. What is the proper accounting treatment of organization costs?
5. What are some of the rights accorded stockholders?
6. What does the preemptive right of stockholders mean?
7. What is the role of a board of directors in a corporation, and how does it differ from the role of management?
8. What are the typical officers in the management of a corporation and their duties?
9. What is the legal capital of a corporation, and what is its significance?
10. How is the value determined for recording stock issued for noncash assets?
11. What are stock subscriptions, and how are Subscriptions Receivable and Common Stock Subscribed classified on the balance sheet?
12. What does it mean for preferred stock to be cumulative, participating, convertible, and/or callable?
13. What are dividends in arrears, and how should they be disclosed in the financial statements?
14. What is the proper classification of the following accounts on the balance sheet? (a) Organization Costs; (b) Capital Stock, Common; (c) Subscriptions Receivable, Preferred; (d) Preferred Stock Subscribed; (e) Paid-in Capital in Excess of Par Value, Preferred Stock; (f) Paid-in Capital in Excess of Stated Value; (g) Discount on Common Stock; (h) Retained Earnings.
15. Would you expect a corporation's book value per share to equal its market value per share? Why or why not?

Classroom Exercises

Exercise 16-1 Journal Entries and Stockholders' Equity

The General Hospital Supply Corporation was organized in 19xx. The company was authorized to issue 100,000 shares of no-par common stock with a stated value at $5 per share, and 20,000 shares of $100 par value, 6 percent noncumulative preferred stock. On March 1 the company sold 50,000 shares of its common stock for $12 per share and 5,000 shares of its preferred stock for $101 per share.

1. Prepare the journal entries to record the sale of the stock.
2. Prepare the company's stockholders' equity section of the balance sheet immediately after the sales.

Exercise 16-2 Stockholders' Equity

The accounts and balances at the top of the next page were taken from the records of Monarch Corporation on December 31, 19xx.

Account Name	Balance Debit	Balance Credit
Common Stock—$10 par value, 60,000 shares authorized, 20,000 shares issued		$200,000
Common Stock Subscribed		20,000
Preferred Stock—$100 par value, 9% cumulative, 10,000 shares authorized, 5,000 shares outstanding		500,000
Paid-in Capital in Excess of Par Value, Common Stock		170,000
Retained Earnings	$12,000	
Subscriptions Receivable, Common	30,000	

Prepare a stockholders' equity section for Monarch Corporation's balance sheet.

Exercise 16-3 Preferred Stock Dividends with Dividends in Arrears

The Brothers Corporation has 10,000 shares of its $100, 8 percent cumulative preferred stock outstanding and 50,000 shares of its $1 par value common stock outstanding. In its first four years of operation, the board of directors of Brothers Corporation paid cash dividends as follows: 19x1, none; 19x2, $140,000; 19x3, $140,000; 19x4, $140,000.

Determine the total cash dividends and dividends per share paid to the preferred and common stockholders during each of the four years.

Exercise 16-4 Journal Entries—Stated Value Stock

The Johnson Engineering Corporation is authorized to issue 200,000 shares of no-par stock. The company recently sold 30,000 shares for $15 per share.

1. Prepare the journal entry to record the sale of the stock if there is no stated value.
2. Prepare the entry if a $5 stated value is authorized by the company's board of directors.

Exercise 16-5 Book Value for Preferred and Common Stock

The stockholders' equity section of the Jim Blue Corporation is shown below.

Stockholders' Equity

Contributed Capital	
Preferred Stock—$100 par value, 6% noncumulative, 10,000 shares authorized, 100 shares issued and outstanding*	$10,000
Common Stock—$5 par value, 100,000 shares authorized, 10,000 shares issued and outstanding	50,000
Paid-in Capital in Excess of Par Value, Common	8,000
Total Contributed Capital	$68,000
Retained Earnings	15,000
Total Stockholders' Equity	$83,000

*One year's dividends are in arrears.

Determine the book value per share for both the preferred and the common stock.

Exercise 16-6 Preferred and Common Stock Dividends

The Bolt Corporation pays dividends at the end of each year. The dividends paid for 19x1, 19x2, and 19x3 were $50,000, $20,000, and $80,000, respectively.

Calculate the total amount of dividends paid each year to the common and preferred stockholders if each of the following capital structures is assumed: (1) 10,000 shares of $100 par, 6 percent noncumulative preferred stock and 30,000 shares of $10 par common stock. (2) 5,000 shares of $100 par, 6 percent cumulative preferred stock and 30,000 shares of $10 par common stock. There were no dividends in arrears at the beginning of 19x1. (3) 5,000 shares of $100 par, 6 percent fully participating noncumulative preferred stock and 30,000 shares of $10 par common stock. (4) Same as 3, except partially participating up to a total of 8 percent.

Exercise 16-7 Organization Costs Journal Entries

The Holiday Truck Company was organized during 19x7. The company incurred the following costs in organizing the company: (1) Attorney's fees, market value of services $2,000, acceptance of 1,500 shares of $1 par common stock. (2) Paid the state $1,000 for incorporation fees. (3) Accountant accepted 1,000 shares of $1 par common stock for services that would normally be billed at $950.

Prepare the journal entries necessary to record these transactions and to amortize organization costs for the first year, assuming that the company elects to write off organization costs over five years.

Exercise 16-8 Issuance of Stock for Noncash Assets

The Ladybug Corporation issued 1,000 shares of its $10 par value common stock for some land. The stock was selling for $12 per share on the day of the transaction.

Prepare the journal entries necessary to record the issuance of the stock for the land under each of the following conditions: (1) the land had a fair market value of $11,000; and (2) management attempted to place a value on the land, but could not determine the value.

Exercise 16-9 Stock Subscriptions

The Brothers Corporation sold 10,000 shares of its $5 par value common stock by subscription for $9 per share on February 15, 19xx. Cash was received in installments from the purchasers: 50 percent on April 1 and 50 percent on June 1.

Prepare the entries necessary to record these transactions.

Problem Set A

Problem 16A-1 Stock Journal Entries and Stockholders' Equity

Kedmark, a new corporation, issued 10,000 shares of its common stock on August 14, 19xx, for $80,000 cash and for building and equipment with fair market values of $40,000 and $20,000, respectively.

Required

1. Record the issuance of the stock, assuming the following conditions: (a) the stock had a par value of $10 per share, (b) the stock had a par value of $15 per share, (c) the stock had no par value, and (d) the stock had no par value, but the stated value of the stock was $12 per share, set by the board of directors.

2. Prepare the stockholders' equity section of Kedmark's balance sheet immediately after the issuance of the stock, assuming that the par value was $10 per share.

Problem 16A-2 Stock Journal Entries and Stockholders' Equity

The Lake Blue Water Recreation Corporation recently received its charter from the state of New Mexico. This charter authorized the company to issue 500,000 shares of $5 par value common stock and 100,000 shares of $100 par value, 6 percent cumulative preferred stock. The company completed the following stock transactions prior to the opening of its recreational facilities.

Feb. 15 Sold 10,000 shares of its common stock for $60,000.
21 Issued 100,000 shares of its common stock for land on Lake Blue Water, which had a fair market value of $510,000.
23 Issued a total of 1,000 shares common stock for services by the company's accountants and lawyers in organizing the company, which were billed to the company as $2,500 and $3,000, respectively.
25 Accepted subscriptions to 10,000 shares of its common stock for $6 per share and 10,000 shares of its preferred stock at $101 per share.
Mar. 10 Collected payment in full for 50 percent of stock subscriptions receivables recorded on February 25.

Required

1. Prepare the journal entries to record the stock transactions of the corporation presented here.
2. Prepare the stockholders' equity section of the corporation's balance sheet as of March 11.

Problem 16A-3 Preferred and Common Stock Dividends

The Trinity Corporation had 100,000 shares of its $10 par value common stock and 8,000 of its $100 par value, 6 percent noncumulative preferred stock outstanding for the years 19x1 through 19x4. The company declared cash dividends of $100,000, $24,000, $60,000, and $150,000 for those years.

Required

1. Compute the total and per share dividends that would be paid to common and preferred stockholders in 19x1, 19x2, 19x3, and 19x4.
2. Perform the same computations, assuming that the preferred stock was cumulative instead of noncumulative.

Problem 16A-4 Preferred and Common Stock Book Values

The Dill Corporation's stockholders' equity as of December 31, 19xx, is presented below.

Stockholders' Equity

Contributed Capital	
Preferred Stock—$100 par value, 6% cumulative, 50,000 shares authorized, 20,000 shares issued and outstanding*	$2,000,000
Paid-in Capital in Excess of Par Value, Preferred	10,000
Common Stock—$10 par value, 1,000,000 shares authorized, 500,000 shares outstanding	5,000,000
Paid-in Capital in Excess of Par Value, Common	100,000
Total Contributed Capital	$7,110,000
Retained Earnings	2,300,000
Total Stockholders' Equity	$9,410,000

*The preferred stock has $60,000 dividends in arrears.

Required

1. Compute the preferred stock book value per share.
2. Compute the common stock book value per share.

Problem 16A-5 Stock Journal Entries and Stockholders' Equity

The W. D. Greene Corporation was organized during 19xx, with authorization to issue 1,000,000 shares of $10 par common stock and 100,000 shares of $100 par value, 9 percent cumulative preferred stock. Stock- and income-related transactions applicable to the first year are as follows:

Jan. 21	Issued 10,000 shares of $10 par value common stock for $110,000.
24	Issued 100 shares of $10 par value common stock to an attorney for services billed at $1,000.
Feb. 14	Accepted subscriptions to 30,000 shares of $10 par value common stock for $12 per share.
Mar. 15	Received full payment on 15,000 shares of the stock subscriptions received on February 14, 19xx. Issued the appropriate number of shares to the stockholders.
June 30	Closed the Income Summary account. Reported income of $30,000 for the first six months of operations during 19xx.
July 20	Collected remaining amount due on the February 14 stock subscriptions and issued the remaining stock.
Nov. 1	Issued 500 shares of $100 par value cumulative preferred stock for $100 per share.
Dec. 20	Accepted subscriptions for 8,000 shares of $10 par value common stock for $14 per share.
31	Closed the Income Summary account. Reported income of $40,000 for the last six months of operations during 19xx.

Required

1. Prepare journal entries to record only the stock transactions in 19xx.
2. Prepare the stockholders' equity section of W. D. Greene Corporation's balance sheet on December 31, 19xx.
3. Compute book value per share of preferred stock and common stock as of December 31, 19xx. For common stock, include common stock subscribed with outstanding stock.

Problem 16A-6 Comprehensive Stockholders' Equity Transactions

The stockholders' equity section of Wollman Corporation's balance sheet is shown below as it appeared on January 1, 19xx.

Stockholders' Equity

Contributed Capital	
Preferred Stock—$40 par value, 8% cumulative, 12,000 shares authorized, 5,000 shares issued and outstanding*	$200,000
Common Stock—$5 stated value, 90,000 shares authorized, 60,000 shares issued and outstanding	300,000
Paid-in Capital in Excess of Stated Value, Common	180,000
Total Contributed Capital	$680,000
Retained Earnings	260,000
Total Stockholders' Equity	$940,000

*One year's dividends are in arrears.

The following selected transactions occurred during the year:

Feb. 15 Sold 1,500 shares of common stock for $7 per share.
Mar. 17 Accepted subscriptions for 18,000 shares of common stock at $9 per share.
Apr. 14 Sold 2,000 shares of common stock for $10 per share.
May 15 Received one-third partial payment on all the subscriptions accepted on March 17.
June 20 Received in full the remaining payment due on one-half the subscriptions accepted on March 17 and issued the stock.
Aug. 10 Issued 1,000 shares of preferred stock in exchange for land valued at $50,000.
Dec. 31 Closed the Income Summary accounts, which showed net income for the year of $75,000.

Required

1. Prepare general journal entries to record the transactions described.
2. Prepare a stockholders' equity section for Wollman Corporation's balance sheet as of December 31.
3. If the board of directors wanted to declare a cash dividend of $80,000 at the end of the year, how much would go to the preferred stockholders and how much to the common stockholders?
4. Assuming no dividends are declared, compute the book value per share of preferred stock and common stock as of December 31. For common stock, include common stock subscribed with outstanding shares.

Problem Set B

Problem 16B-1 Stock Journal Entries and Stockholders' Equity

On July 1, 19xx, Crestmark, a new corporation, issues 15,000 shares of its common stock for a corporate headquarters building. The building has a fair market value of $155,000 and a book value of $130,000.

Required

1. Record the issuance of stock for the building, assuming the following conditions: (a) the par value of the stock is $9 per share, (b) the par value of the stock is $16 per share, (c) the stock is no-par stock, and (d) the stock is no-par stock, but has a stated value of $12 per share.
2. Prepare the stockholders' equity section of Crestmark's balance sheet immediately after the issuance of the stock, assuming that the par value was $9 per share.

Problem 16B-2 Stock Journal Entries and Stockholders' Equity

The Max Rail Company has been authorized by the state of Florida to issue 1,000,000 shares of $1 common stock. The company began issuing its common stock in July of 19xx. During July the company had the following stock transactions:

July 10 Issued 29,000 shares of stock for a building and land with fair market value of $22,000 and $7,000, respectively.
15 Accepted subscriptions to 400,000 shares of its stock for $410,000.
20 Collected full payment on 200,000 shares of the common stock subscribed on July 15. Issued the appropriate shares.
23 Sold 15,000 shares of stock for $15,000 cash.
27 Collected full payment on 100,000 shares of the common stock subscribed on July 15 and issued the shares.

Required

1. Prepare the journal entries to record the stock transactions of the Max Rail Company for the month of July.
2. Prepare the stockholders' equity section of the Max Rail Company's balance sheet as of July 31.

Problem 16B-3 Preferred and Common Stock Dividends

The Mosee Corporation had the following stock outstanding for 19x1 and 19x2:

Preferred stock—$50 par value, 4% cumulative, 10,000 shares authorized, issued, and outstanding
Common stock—$5 par value, 150,000 shares authorized, issued, and outstanding

The company paid $15,000, $15,000, $47,000, and $65,000 in dividends during 19x1, 19x2, 19x3, and 19x4, respectively.

Required

1. Determine the total amounts per share of dividends paid to common stockholders and preferred stockholders in 19x1, 19x2, 19x3, and 19x4.
2. Perform the same computations assuming that the preferred stock is noncumulative and fully participative.

Problem 16B-4 Preferred and Common Stock Book Values

The stockholders' equity section of the Moss Horn Company's balance sheet follows.

Stockholders' Equity

Contributed Capital	
Preferred Stock—$100 par value, 7% cumulative, 10,000 shares authorized, 7,000 shares outstanding*	$ 700,000
Paid-in Capital in Excess of Par Value, Preferred	25,000
Common Stock—$1 par value, 1,000,000 shares authorized, 800,000 shares outstanding	800,000
Total Contributed Capital	$1,525,000
Retained Earnings	2,230,000
Total Stockholders' Equity	$3,755,000

*The preferred stock dividend was not paid last year.

Required

1. Compute the preferred stock book value per share.
2. Compute the common stock book value per share.

Problem 16B-6 Comprehensive Stockholders' Equity Transactions

The stockholders' equity section of Turnip Corporation's balance sheet is shown below as it appeared on June 1, 19xx.

Stockholders' Equity

Contributed Capital	
Preferred Stock—$70 par value, 7.5% cumulative, 10,000 shares authorized, 6,000 shares issued and outstanding*	$ 420,000
Common Stock—$8 stated value, 150,000 shares authorized, 110,000 shares issued and outstanding	880,000
Paid-in Capital in Excess of Stated Value	470,000
Total Contributed Capital	$1,770,000
Retained Earnings	318,000
Total Stockholders' Equity	$2,088,000

*Two years' dividends are in arrears.

The following selected transactions occurred during the year:

June 15 Sold 8,000 shares of common stock at $12 per share.

Aug. 10 Issued 2,000 shares of preferred stock for a plant site. At the time of issue the preferred stock was selling for $80 per share and the plant site was valued by an independent appraiser at $150,000.

Oct. 2 Subscriptions for 8,000 shares of common stock were accepted at $14 per share.

Nov. 10 25 percent partial payment on all the stock subscriptions accepted on October 2 was received.

Dec. 10 The remaining amount due on 4,000 shares of the stock subscribed on October 2 was paid in full and the stock issued.

Dec. 31 The Income Summary account, which showed a loss of $43,000 for the year, was closed to Retained Earnings.

Required

1. Prepare general journal entries to record the transactions described.
2. Prepare a stockholders' equity section for Turnip Corporation's balance sheet as of December 31.
3. If the board of directors wanted to declare a cash dividend on December 31 of $120,000, how much would go to the preferred stockholders and how much to the common stockholders?
4. Assumimg no dividends are declared, compute book value per share for preferred stock and common stock as of December 31. For common stock, include common stock subscribed with outstanding shares.

Learning Objectives

Chapter Seventeen

Corporations: Retained Earnings and Corporate Income Statements

1. Define retained earnings, and prepare a retained earnings statement.

2. Account for cash dividends, stock dividends, and stock splits.

3. Account for treasury stock transactions.

4. Account for the appropriation of retained earnings.

5. Account for the retirement of stock and donations of stock and other assets.

6. Describe the disclosure of discontinued operations, extraordinary items, and accounting changes on the income statement.

7. Compute primary and fully diluted earnings per share.

This chapter continues the study of the stockholders' equity section of corporate financial statements. The discussion covers retained earnings of a corporation, transactions that affect retained earnings, and the retained earnings statement. In addition, the chapter describes some other stockholders' equity transactions and presents an overview of the corporate income statement. As a result of studying this chapter, you should be able to meet the learning objectives listed on the left.

Retained Earnings Transactions

Stockholders' equity, as presented in the previous chapter, is composed of two major items: contributed capital and retained earnings. The **retained earnings** of a firm are the stockholders' equity that comes from retaining assets earned from business operations. They represent accumulated profits of a corporation from the date of its inception minus any losses, dividends to stockholders, or transfers to contributed capital. Figure 17-1 (next page) illustrates a retained earnings statement of Caprock Corporation for 19xx. The beginning balance of retained earnings of $854,000 is increased by net income of $76,000 and decreased by cash dividends of $30,000, resulting in an ending balance of $900,000.

A credit balance in the Retained Earnings account is significant because it indicates the amount of assets that have accumulated from operations but that have not been distributed to the firm's stockholders. Normally these assets are retained in the business for future growth or other business needs. Note, however, that a credit balance in Retained Earnings in no way implies that a

Figure 17-1
A Simplified Retained Earnings Statement

Caprock Corporation Retained Earnings Statement For the Year Ended December 31, 19x1	
Retained Earnings, Jan. 1	$854,000
Net Income, 19x1	76,000
Subtotal	$930,000
Less Common Stock, Cash Dividend	30,000
Retained Earnings, Dec. 31	$900,000

designated set of assets pertains directly to retained earnings. The fact that earnings have been retained means that assets in total have been increased.

Objective 1
Define retained earnings, and prepare a retained earnings statement

Retained Earnings may carry a debit balance. Usually this situation occurs when a company's accumulated losses and distributions to stockholders have exceeded its profits from operations. In such a case, the firm is said to have a **deficit** in retained earnings. The deficit is shown in the stockholders' equity section of the balance sheet as a deduction from contributed capital.

In practice, accountants have used different terms to identify the retained earnings of a firm. One term is *surplus,* which implies the existence of excess assets available for dividends, even though the company may have other business purposes for the assets. Because of this possible misinterpretation, the American Institute of Certified Public Accountants' Committee on Terminology has recommended the use of more appropriate terminology, such as *retained income, retained earnings, accumulated earnings,* or *earnings retained for use in the business.*[1]

The Retained Earnings account is affected by transactions resulting from (1) profits and losses of a company, (2) dividend declarations, (3) certain treasury stock transactions, and (4) prior period adjustments. Following the discussion of these events, we present a comprehensive retained earnings statement.

Profits and Losses of a Corporation

Previous chapters have shown that the profit or loss of a sole proprietorship or partnership is transferred from the Income Summary account to the owners' individual capital accounts. The procedure for a corporation is similar, except that the profit or loss is transferred to the Retained Earnings account rather than to individual capital accounts. The reason for doing so is that the corporation by law must account to its owners—the

1. Committee on Terminology, "Review and Resume," *Accounting Terminology Bulletin No. 1* (New York: American Institute of Certified Public Accountants, 1961), pp. 30–31.

stockholders—for the amount of earnings accumulated and available for distribution as dividends. For example, assume that the Caprock Corporation made a profit of $76,000 in 19x1 and had a loss of $35,000 in 19x2. The entries to transfer the profit or loss to retained earnings follow:

19x1			
Dec. 31	Income Summary	76,000	
	Retained Earnings		76,000
	To transfer the profit for 19x1 to Retained Earnings		
19x2			
Dec. 31	Retained Earnings	35,000	
	Income Summary		35,000
	To transfer the loss for 19x2 to Retained Earnings		

Dividends

Objective 2 Account for cash dividends, stock dividends, and stock splits

A **dividend** is a distribution of assets of a corporation to its stockholders. Each stockholder receives assets, usually cash, in proportion to the number of shares of stock held. The board of directors has sole authority to declare dividends.

Dividends may be paid quarterly, semiannually, annually, or at other times determined by the board. Most states prohibit the board from declaring a dividend that exceeds retained earnings. Where such a dividend is declared, the corporation is essentially returning to the stockholders a portion of their paid-in capital. This is called a **liquidating dividend** and is normally paid when a company is going out of business or is reducing its operations. However, having sufficient retained earnings is not sufficient justification for the distribution of a dividend. If cash or other readily distributable assets are not available for distribution, the board of directors may elect to keep the assets in the business rather than declare a dividend.

There are three important dates associated with dividends. In order of occurrence, these are (1) the date of declaration, (2) the date of record, and (3) the date of payment. The date of declaration is the date the board of directors takes formal action declaring that a dividend will be paid. The date of record is the date on which ownership of the stock of a company and therefore the right to receive a dividend is determined. Those individuals who own the stock on the date of record will be the ones to receive the dividend. The date of payment is the date the dividend will be paid to the stockholders of record.

For example, the board of the Caprock Corporation may declare a dividend of $1.50 per share of common stock on February 21 to those stockholders of record on March 10, payable on March 31. A dividend is recorded as a current liability on the date of declaration (February 21) because the board of directors has legally obligated the corporation to pay the dividend at that time. No entry is required on the date of record (March 10) because this date is used simply to determine the owners of the stock who will receive the dividends. No transaction occurs on that date. On the payment date (March 31), an entry is made to record the distribution of cash and to remove the dividend liability.

Cash Dividends To illustrate the accounting for cash dividends, we will assume that the Caprock Corporation has the following capital structure:

Preferred Stock—$100 par value, 6% cumulative, 1,000 shares authorized and outstanding	$100,000
Common Stock, $5 par value, 100,000 shares authorized and outstanding	500,000

The board of directors has decided that sufficient cash is available to pay a $56,000 cash dividend. The $56,000 will be distributed as a $6,000 annual dividend to the preferred stockholders and a 50¢ per share dividend to the common stockholders. The dividend is declared on February 21, 19xx, to be paid March 31, 19xx, to stockholders of record on March 10, 19xx. The entries to record the declaration and payment of the cash dividend follow:

Date of declaration

Feb. 21	Retained Earnings[2]	56,000	
	Cash Dividends Payable, Common Stock		$50,000
	Cash Dividends Payable, Preferred Stock		6,000
	To record the declaration of a cash dividend, 6% of par value to preferred stockholders and 50¢ per share to common stockholders		
	Preferred dividend ($100,000 × 6%)		$ 6,000
	Common dividend (100,000 shares × $.50)		50,000
	Total dividend		$56,000

Date of record

Mar. 10 No entry necessary

2. Some companies follow the practice of debiting a contra account called Dividends instead of Retained Earnings (see Practice Set III). This practice is common for quarterly and semiannual dividend declarations. The Dividends account is closed to Retained Earnings at the end of the year.

Date of payment

Mar. 31	Cash Dividends Payable, Common Stock	50,000	
	Cash Dividends Payable, Preferred Stock	6,000	
	Cash		56,000
	To record the payment of cash dividends of $56,000		

Note that the obligation to pay the dividend was established on the date of declaration. No entry was required on the date of record, and the liability was liquidated on the date of payment.

Some companies do not pay dividends very often. For one reason, the company may not have any earnings. For another, the company may be growing and thus the assets representing the earnings are kept in the company for business purposes such as expansion of the plant. Investors in such growth companies anticipate a return on their investment in the form of an increased market value of their stock.

Stock Dividends A **stock dividend** is a pro rata distribution of shares of the company's stock to the corporation's stockholders. The distribution does not alter the assets and liabilities of the firm as does a cash dividend. The board of directors may declare a stock dividend because it wants to (1) provide stockholders with some evidence of an increase in their equity in the company without using cash, which would affect the firm's working capital position; (2) reduce the market price of the stock by increasing the number of shares outstanding, although this objective is more often accomplished by stock splits; or (3) allow a nontaxable distribution to stockholders. Stock dividends that meet certain conditions are not considered income, so a tax is not levied on this type of transaction.

When a stock dividend occurs, the total stockholders' equity is not affected. The effect of a stock dividend is to transfer a dollar amount from the Retained Earnings account to the contributed capital section on the date of transfer. The amount to be transferred is the fair market value (usually market price) of the additional shares to be issued. The laws of most states usually identify the minimum to be transferred under a stock dividend, and this minimum is normally the minimum legal capital (par or stated value). However, generally accepted accounting principles state that market value reflects the economic consequence of the stock distribution better than the minimum legal capital does. For this reason, the market price should be used for proper accounting of stock dividends.[3]

To illustrate the accounting for a stock dividend, we shall assume that the Caprock Corporation has the stockholders' equity structure shown at the top of the next page.

3. *Accounting Research and Terminology Bulletin No. 43* (New York: American Institute of Certified Public Accountants, 1961), Chapter 7, Section B, par. 10.

Contributed Capital	
Common Stock—$5 par value, 100,000 shares authorized, 30,000 issued and outstanding	$ 150,000
Paid-in Capital in Excess of Par Value	30,000
Total Contributed Capital	$ 180,000
Retained Earnings	900,000
Total Stockholders' Equity	$1,080,000

Assume further that the board of directors declares a 10 percent stock dividend on February 24, distributable on March 31 to stockholders of record on March 15. The market price of the stock on February 24 was $20 per share. The entries to record the dividend declaration and distribution are as follows:

Date of declaration

Feb. 24	Retained Earnings	60,000	
	Stock Dividends Distributable		15,000
	Paid-in Capital in Excess of Par Value		45,000
	To record the declaration of a 10% stock dividend on common stock, distributable on March 31, to stockholders of record on March 15. 30,000 shares × 10% = 3,000 shares 3,000 shares × $20/share = $60,000		

Date of record

Mar. 15 No entry

Date of distribution

Mar. 31	Stock Dividends Distributable	15,000	
	Common Stock		15,000
	To record the distribution of stock dividend of 3,000 shares		

The effect of the above stock dividend is to transfer the market value of the stock, $60,000, from Retained Earnings to Contributed Capital and to increase the number of shares outstanding by 3,000. Common Stock Distributable is credited for the par value of the stock to be distributed (3,000 × $5 = $15,000). In addition, when the market value is greater than the par value of the stock, Paid-in Capital in Excess of Par Value must be credited for the amount that market value exceeds par value. In this case, total market value of the stock dividend ($60,000) exceeds the total par value ($15,000) by $45,000. No entry is required on the date of record. On the distribution date, the common stock is issued by debiting Stock Dividends Distributable and crediting Common Stock for the par value of the stock ($15,000).

Stock Dividends Distributable is not a liability, because no obligation exists to distribute cash or other assets. The obligation is to distribute additional shares of capital stock. If financial statements are prepared between the date of declaration and the distribution, Stock Dividends Distributable should be disclosed as part of Contributed Capital, as follows:

Contributed Capital	
Common Stock—$5 par value, 100,000 shares authorized, 30,000 issued and outstanding	$ 150,000
Common Stock Dividend Distributable	15,000
Paid-in Capital in Excess of Par Value	75,000
Total Contributed Capital	$ 240,000
Retained Earnings	840,000
Total Stockholders' Equity	$1,080,000

Two points can be made from this example. First, the total stockholders' equity is unchanged before and after the stock dividend. Second, the proportionate ownership in the corporation of any individual stockholder is unchanged before and after the stock dividend. To illustrate these points, we will assume that a hypothetical stockholder owns 1,000 shares before the stock dividend. After the 10 percent stock dividend, this stockholder would own 1,100 shares.

Stockholders' Equity	**Before Dividend**	**After Dividend**
Common Stock	$ 150,000	$ 165,000
Paid-in Capital in Excess of Par Value	30,000	75,000
Total Contributed Capital	$ 180,000	$ 240,000
Retained Earnings	900,000	840,000
Total Stockholders' Equity	$1,080,000	$1,080,000
Shares Outstanding	30,000	33,000
Stockholder's Investment		
Shares owned	1,000	1,100
Percentage of ownership	$3\frac{1}{3}$%	$3\frac{1}{3}$%
Book value of investment ($3\frac{1}{3}$% × $1,080,000)	$36,000	$36,000

Both before and after the stock dividend, the stockholders' equity totals $1,080,000 and the stockholder owns $3\frac{1}{3}$ percent of the company, representing a book value of $36,000.

Some stock dividends are so large that they have a material effect on the price per share of the stock. The AICPA has arbitrarily determined that large stock dividends, those greater than 20 to 25 percent, should be accounted for by transferring the par or stated value of the stock on the date of declaration from Retained Earnings to Contributed Capital.[4] A large

4. Ibid., par. 13.

stock dividend has the effect of reducing the market value of the stock by approximately the same percentage as the dividend. For example, a 30 percent stock dividend would cause the market price of the stock to drop approximately 30 percent. These large stock dividends are accounted for as if they were stock splits.

Stock Splits A **stock split** occurs when a corporation increases the number of outstanding shares of stock and reduces the par or stated value proportionally. A company may plan a stock split when it wishes to reduce the market value per share of its stock and increase the liquidity of the stock. This action is necessary because the market value per share has become so high that it hinders the trading of the company's stock on the market. For example, suppose that the Caprock Corporation has 30,000 shares of $5.00 par value stock outstanding. The market value is $70.00 per share. The corporation plans a 2 for 1 split, which will reduce the par value to $2.50 and increase the number of shares outstanding to 60,000. If a stockholder previously owned 400 shares of the $5.00 par stock, he or she would own 800 shares of the $2.50 par stock after the split. When a stock split occurs, the market value tends to fall in proportion to the increase in outstanding shares of stock. For example, a 2 for 1 stock split would cause the price of the stock to drop by approximately 50 percent to about $35.00. The lower price plus the increase in shares tends to promote the buying and selling of shares.

A stock split does not change the balances in the stockholders' equity section; it changes merely the par value and number of shares outstanding. Therefore, an entry is not necessary for this type of transaction. However, it is appropriate to document the change by making a memorandum entry in the general journal. The change that occurs is illustrated for the Caprock Corporation below.

Before Stock Split

Contributed Capital	
Common Stock—$5 par value, 100,000 shares authorized, 30,000 issued and outstanding	$ 150,000
Paid-in Capital in Excess of Par Value	30,000
Total Contributed Capital	$ 180,000
Retained Earnings	900,000
Total Stockholders' Equity	$1,080,000

After Stock Split

Contributed Capital	
Common Stock—$2.50 par value, 200,000 shares authorized, 60,000 issued and outstanding	$ 150,000
Paid-in Capital in Excess of Par Value	30,000
Total Contributed Capital	$ 180,000
Retained Earnings	900,000
Total Stockholders' Equity	$1,080,000

Treasury Stock Transactions

Objective 3 Account for treasury stock transactions

Treasury stock is capital stock of a company, either common or preferred, that has been issued and reacquired by the issuing company but has not been reissued or retired. The company normally acquires the stock by purchasing the shares on the market or through donations by stockholders. Several reasons why a company purchases its own stock are (1) to have stock available to distribute to employees through stock option plans, (2) to maintain a favorable market for the company's stock, (3) to increase the company's earnings per share, and (4) to have additional shares of the company's stock available for such activities as purchasing other companies.

The effect of a treasury stock purchase is to reduce the assets and stockholders' equity of the company. The treasury stock is capital stock that has been issued but is no longer outstanding. Treasury shares may be held for an indefinite period of time, reissued, or canceled. What this means is that treasury stock is somewhat similar to unissued stock. That is, it has no rights until the stock is reissued. Thus treasury stock does not have voting rights, pre-emptive rights, rights to dividends, or rights to share in assets during liquidation of the company. However, one major difference between unissued shares and treasury shares is that if a share of stock was originally issued at par or greater and fully paid for, and then reacquired as treasury stock, it may be reissued at less than par value without a discount liability attaching to it.

Purchase of Treasury Stock When treasury stock is purchased, it is normally recorded at cost. The transaction reduces both the assets and stockholders' equity of the firm. For example, assume that the Caprock Corporation purchases 1,000 shares of its common stock on the market at a price of $50 per share. The purchase would be recorded as follows:

Sept. 15	Treasury Stock, Common	50,000	
	Cash		50,000
	Acquired 1,000 shares of company's common stock for $50 per share		

Note that the treasury shares were recorded at cost, and any par value, stated value, or original issue price of the stock was ignored.

The stockholders' equity section of Caprock's balance sheet would show the cost of the treasury stock as a deduction from the total of Contributed Capital and Retained Earnings. An example of this disclosure is given at the top of the next page. Note that the number of shares issued has not changed as a result of the treasury stock transaction.

Stockholders' Equity

Contributed Capital	
Common Stock—$5 par value, 100,000 shares authorized, 30,000 shares issued, of which 1,000 are in the treasury	$ 150,000
Paid-in Capital in Excess of Par Value	30,000
Total Contributed Capital	$ 180,000
Retained Earnings	900,000
Total Contributed Capital and Retained Earnings	$1,080,000
Less Treasury Stock, at Cost	50,000
Total Stockholders' Equity	$1,030,000

Reissuance of Treasury Stock The treasury shares may be reissued at cost, above cost, or below cost. When the stock is reissued at cost, the transaction is recorded by reversing the original entry. For example, assume that the 1,000 treasury shares of the Caprock Corporation are sold for $50 per share. The entry to record this transaction is:

Nov. 15	Cash	50,000	
	Treasury Stock, Common		50,000
	Reissued 1,000 shares of treasury stock for $50 per share		

When treasury shares are sold for an amount greater than their cost, the excess of the sales price over cost should be credited to Paid-in Capital, Treasury Stock. No gain should be recorded. For example, suppose that the 1,000 treasury shares of the Caprock Corporation are sold for $60 per share. The entry for the reissue would be:

Nov. 15	Cash	60,000	
	Treasury Stock, Common		50,000
	Paid-in Capital, Treasury Stock Transactions		10,000
	To record the sale of 1,000 shares of treasury stock for $60 per share; cost was $50 per share		

If the treasury shares are reissued below their cost, the difference should be deducted from Paid-in Capital, Treasury Stock. When this account does not exist or is insufficient to cover the excess of cost over reissuance price, Retained Earnings should absorb the excess. No loss should be recorded. For example, assume that on September 15 the Caprock Corporation purchased 1,000 shares of its common stock on the market at a price of $50 per share. The company sold 400 shares of the stock on October 15 for $60 per share and the remaining 600 shares on December 15 for $42 per share. The entries to record these transactions are presented below.

Date	Account	Debit	Credit
Sept. 15	Treasury Stock, Common	50,000	
	Cash		50,000
	To record the purchase of 1,000 shares of treasury stock at $50 per share		
Oct. 15	Cash	24,000	
	Treasury Stock, Common		20,000
	Paid-in Capital, Treasury Stock Transactions		4,000
	To record the sale of 400 shares of treasury stock for $60 per share; cost was $50 per share		
Dec. 15	Cash	25,200	
	Paid-in Capital, Treasury Stock Transactions	4,000	
	Retained Earnings	800	
	Treasury Stock, Common		30,000
	To record sale of 600 shares of treasury stock for $42 per share; cost was $50 per share		

In the December 15 entry, Retained Earnings is credited for $800 because the 600 shares were sold for $4,800 less than cost, an amount that is $800 greater than the $4,000 of paid-in capital generated by the sale of the 400 shares on October 15.

Prior Period Adjustments

Prior period adjustments are events or transactions that relate to earlier accounting periods but were not determinable in the earlier period. The Financial Accounting Standards Board has identified only two items as prior period adjustments: (1) correction of an error in the financial statements of a prior year, and (2) adjustments that result from realization of income tax benefits of preacquisition operating loss carryforward of purchased subsidiaries.[5]

Prior period adjustments are very rare in accounting and occur because of the uncertainty that existed concerning the item in a prior period.

5. *Statement of Financial Accounting Standards No. 16,* "Prior Period Adjustments" (Stamford, Conn.: Financial Accounting Standards Board, June 1977), par. 11.

Figure 17-2
A Retained Earnings Statement

Caprock Corporation **Retained Earnings Statement** **For the Year Ended December 31, 19x2**		
Retained Earnings, Jan. 1, 19x2	$900,000	
Less Prior Period Adjustment, Correction of an Error (Net of Taxes), 19x1	30,000	
Retained Earnings, Jan. 1, 19x2, as Restated		$870,000
Net Income, 19x2		85,000
Subtotal		$955,000
Less:		
Common Stock, Cash Dividend	$ 50,000	
Preferred Stock, Cash Dividend	6,000	
Common Stock, Stock Dividend	60,000	
Sale of Treasury Stock at Less than Cost (Net)	800	$116,800
Retained Earnings, Dec. 31, 19x2		$838,200

The disclosure requirements of prior period adjustments in financial statements were provided by the Accounting Principles Board as follows:

When financial statements for a single period only are presented, this disclosure should indicate the effects of such restatement on the balance of retained earnings at the beginning of the period and on the net income of the immediately preceding period. When financial statements for more than one period are presented, which is ordinarily the preferable procedure, the disclosure should include the effects for each of the periods included in the statements.[6]

As an illustration of a prior period adjustment, assume that the Caprock Corporation discovered in December 19x2 that it had failed to record depreciation on its office equipment in 19x1 and that the effect of the error would be to reduce retained earnings by $30,000 (net of tax effect) for that year. The journal entry to record this prior period adjustment would be as follows:

19x2			
Dec. 31	Retained Earnings	30,000	
	Accumulated Depreciation, Office Equipment		30,000
	To record the correction of an error in depreciation of prior years		

6. Accounting Principles Board, *Opinion No. 9*, "Reporting the Results of Operations" (New York: American Institute of Certified Public Accountants, December 1976), par. 26.

Retained Earnings Statement

The **retained earnings statement** is prepared to provide a summary of the changes in retained earnings during an accounting period. A comprehensive example is shown in Figure 17-2. In this statement, the retained earnings balance on January 1 is first restated for the prior period adjustment related to 19x1. Then the effects of 19x2 transactions are shown. Net income of $85,000 is added to the restated January 1 balance of $870,000 to obtain a subtotal of $955,000. The effects of cash and stock dividends as well as treasury stock transactions are listed. This total of $116,800 is deducted from the subtotal to obtain the December 31 balance of $838,200.

Appropriation of Retained Earnings

Objective 4 Account for the appropriation of retained earnings

In accounting for retained earnings, a corporation may subdivide this account into two classifications: appropriated and unappropriated retained earnings. The purpose of appropriating retained earnings is to separate a portion of the Retained Earnings account on the balance sheet to provide more information to the readers of the company's financial statements. When readers see **appropriated retained earnings** on the balance sheet, they know that a segment of the company's assets are to be used or set aside for purposes other than paying dividends.

Only the board of directors may appropriate retained earnings. Several reasons why retained earnings would be appropriated by the board are as follows:

1. A contractual agreement. For example, bond indentures may place a limitation on the dividends to be paid by the company. The purpose of such action is to protect the working capital position of the firm for paying the bond debt.
2. State law. Many states will not allow dividends or the purchase of treasury stock to impair the capital of a company.
3. Voluntary action by the board of directors. Many times a board will decide to retain assets in the business for future needs. For example, the company may be planning a major plant expansion and may wish to indicate that dividends will be limited in order to accumulate funds for the expansion. Or the company may be facing a large settlement of a lawsuit, with the outcome uncertain at the present time. The company may appropriate retained earnings to indicate the possible future loss of assets resulting from the lawsuit.

There are two ways of communicating retained earnings appropriations to readers of financial statements. First, the appropriation of retained earnings may be shown by a journal entry that transfers the appropriated amounts from Retained Earnings to another stockholders' equity account that is more descriptive, such as Retained Earnings Appropriated for Plant Expansion. Second, the disclosure of appropriated retained earnings may be made by means of a note to the financial statements.

The following situation of the Caprock Corporation will illustrate appropriation of retained earnings by transfer to a more descriptive account. The board of directors recognizes the need to expand the company's plant capacity in the next two years. After considering several alternatives, the board chooses to expand by retaining assets generated by earnings in the amount of $300,000. It takes action on July 1, 19x1, to appropriate retained earnings in this amount. The entry to record the board's action is as follows:

July 1	Retained Earnings	300,000	
	Retained Earnings Appropriated for Plant Expansion		300,000
	To record the appropriation of retained earnings for plant expansion according to action of the board of directors on July 1, 19x1		

This transaction does not affect the total retained earnings or stockholders' equity of the company. It simply subdivides retained earnings into two sections, appropriated and unappropriated. The appropriated portion communicates that assets in that amount are being used or will be used for the purpose indicated. The unappropriated amount represents earnings retained in the business that could be used for dividends and other purposes. The stockholders' equity section of the Caprock Corporation's balance sheet below illustrates this division of retained earnings.

Stockholders' Equity

Contributed Capital		
Common Stock—$5 par value, 100,000 shares authorized, 33,000 shares issued and outstanding		$ 165,000
Paid-in Capital in Excess of Par Value		75,000
Total Contributed Capital		$ 240,000
Retained Earnings		
Retained Earnings Appropriated for Plant Expansion	$300,000	
Unappropriated Retained Earnings	568,200	
Total Retained Earnings		868,200
Total Stockholders' Equity		$1,108,200

The same information concerning retained earnings appropriations could also be presented by means of a note to the financial statement. An illustration of such a note follows:

Retained Earnings (Note 15)	$868,200

Note 15:

Because of plans for expanding the capacity of the clothing division, the board of directors has restricted retained earnings available for dividends by $300,000.

When the conditions for the appropriation no longer exist, the amount of the restriction should be transferred back to Unappropriated Retained Earnings. In fact, the only charge to an appropriated retained earnings account is the one to transfer the balance back to Unappropriated Retained Earnings. To illustrate this situation, we will assume that after two years the Caprock Corporation completed the expansion of its plant capacity for $325,000. Therefore, restriction of $300,000 on retained earnings is no longer needed. The board takes action on July 20, 19x3, to return the appropriated retained earnings to Unappropriated Retained Earnings. The entries to record the plant expansion and the transfer of retained earnings would be as follows:

July 20	Property, Plant, and Equipment	325,000	
	Cash		325,000
	To record the payment for plant expansion of $325,000		
20	Retained Earnings Appropriated for Plant Expansion	300,000	
	Retained Earnings		300,000
	To eliminate appropriated retained earnings for plant expansion, according to the board of directors' action on July 20, 19x3		

Note that the appropriation of retained earnings does not restrict cash in any way. The transaction merely communicates to the readers of the financial statements that a certain amount of earnings will remain in the business for the purpose specified. It is still management's responsibility to ensure the availability of cash or assets necessary to satisfy the restriction.

Other Stockholders' Equity Transactions

Other transactions involving stockholders' equity include the retirement of stock and donations of stock by stockholders and by nonstockholders.

These transactions do not usually affect retained earnings but are concerned with some aspect of stockholders' equity.

Retirement of Stock

Objective 5 Account for the retirement of stock and donations of stock and other assets

A corporation may, with the approval of its stockholders, decide to purchase its stock to retire it. Reasons for this action are similar to those for the purchase of treasury stock except that there are no plans for reissuing the stock.

When stock is retired, all items related to that stock should also be removed from the related capital accounts. When stock is retired for a price that is less than the original contributed capital, the difference is recognized as Paid-in Capital, Retirement of Stock. However, if more is paid to retire the stock than was received when the shares were originally issued, the difference is a reduction in stockholders' equity and is charged to Retained Earnings.

To illustrate the retirement of stock, we will assume that 100 shares of Caprock's common stock are being retired. The stock has a par value of $5 per share and was originally sold for $10 per share. The entries to retire the 100 shares at $10, $12, and $8, respectively, are presented below.

Retirement Price: $10 per share

Mar. 15	Common Stock	500	
	Paid-in Capital in Excess of Par Value	500	
	Cash		1,000
	Retirement of 100 shares of common stock at $10 per share; original issue price $10 per share		

Retirement Price: $12 per share

Mar. 15	Common Stock	500	
	Paid-in Capital in Excess of Par Value	500	
	Retained Earnings	200	
	Cash		1,200
	Retirement of 100 shares of common stock for $12 per share; original issue price $10 per share		

Retirement Price: $8 per share

		Debit	Credit
Mar. 15	Common Stock	500	
	Paid-in Capital in Excess of Par Value	500	
	Cash		800
	Paid-in Capital, Retirement of Common Stock		200
	Retirement of 100 shares of common stock for $8 per share; original issue price $10 per share		

Donation of Stock

When a company is having financial difficulties and the stock is owned by a few people, the stockholders may vote to return a portion of their shares as a gift to the corporation. The stock can then be resold to generate additional working capital for the corporation. Because nothing has been paid for the donated stock, the company's assets, liabilities, and stockholders' equity are not affected. Therefore, donated stock should be recognized when received by a memorandum entry in the general journal. When the stock is resold, the company's assets and equities will be increased as they were with the original issuance of the stock.

Assume the following conditions for the Caprock Corporation. The company has been incurring losses for the last several years. The stockholders vote to donate 1,000 shares of their stock to the corporation for resale. The memorandum entry to record the donation follows:

Apr. 21 Received from the stockholders 1,000 shares of $5 par value common stock as a donation

Although the donation has not affected the assets, liabilities, or stockholders' equity, it must be recognized in some manner. One way would be to open a treasury stock account and to record by memorandum the number of shares received. In addition, the treasury shares are noted in the balance sheet as shown below.

Stockholders' Equity

Contributed Capital	
Common Stock—$5 par value, 100,000 shares authorized, 33,000 shares issued, of which 1,000 shares are in the treasury from stockholder donations	$ 165,000
Paid-in Capital in Excess of Par Value	75,000
Total Contributed Capital	$ 240,000
Retained Earnings	868,200
Total Stockholders' Equity	$1,108,200

Note that treasury stock is not subtracted from stockholders' equity because the treasury shares did not cost the company any money.

To illustrate the resale of donated stock, we will assume that the 1,000 shares are sold for $7 per share. The entry to record this transaction would be:

May 10	Cash	7,000	
	Paid-in Capital, Sale of Donated Stock		7,000
	Sold 1,000 shares of donated stock for $7 per share		

After the sale of the stock, Caprock's stockholders' equity would appear as follows:

Stockholders' Equity

Contributed Capital	
Common Stock—$5 par value, 100,000 shares authorized, 33,000 shares issued and outstanding	$ 165,000
Paid-in Capital in Excess of Par Value	75,000
Paid-in Capital, Sale of Donated Stock	7,000
Total Contributed Capital	$ 247,000
Retained Earnings	868,200
Total Stockholders' Equity	$1,115,200

The sale of the stock has increased contributed capital and total stockholders' equity by $7,000. In addition, if the asset side of the balance sheet were shown, it would also reflect an increase in assets by the same amount.

Donations by Nonstockholders

Sometimes a corporation may receive a gift or donation from someone other than a stockholder. For example, many cities donate plant sites to corporations as an inducement to locate in their area. Such donations increase both the assets and the equity of the corporation. They are recorded at the fair market value of the asset received. For example, assume that as an inducement to locate in that city, Postville donated a plant site with a fair market value of $20,000 to the Caprock Corporation. Caprock would record the donation as follows:

Jan. 21	Land	20,000	
	Paid-in Capital, Donated Plant Site		20,000
	To record the donation of a plant site by the city of Postville; fair value, $20,000		

Many times assets that are donated have some restrictions as to their use. Under these conditions, it is often necessary to explain such restrictions in the notes to the financial statements.

Corporate Income Statements

Objective 6 Describe the disclosure of discontinued operations, extraordinary items, and accounting changes on the income statement

This chapter and the preceding one have shown how certain transactions are reflected in the stockholders' equity section of the corporate balance sheet and in the retained earnings statement. Chapter 19 deals with the statement of changes in financial position. The following sections will briefly describe some of the features of the corporate income statement.

The format of the income statement has not been specified by the accounting profession because flexibility has been considered more important than a standard income statement. Either the single-step or multistep form may be used (see Chapter 7). However, the accounting profession has taken the position that income for a period shall be an all-inclusive amount.[7] This means that income or loss for a period should include all revenues, expenses, gains, and losses of the period, with the exception of prior period adjustments. This approach to the measurement of income has resulted in several items being added to this statement, including discontinued operations, extraordinary items, and accounting changes. In addition, earnings per share figures should be disclosed. Figure 17-3 (next page) illustrates the corporate income statement and the disclosures required.

The phrase *net of taxes* is used in Figure 17-3 and in the discussion below. This phrase means that the effect of applicable taxes (usually income taxes) has been considered when determining the overall effect of the item on the financial statements. For example, if an extraordinary gain of $4,000 results in additional income taxes of $1,000, the net of taxes increase shown on the income statement is $3,000. Similarly, if a loss of $45,000 from disposal of a segment results in a saving in income taxes of $22,000, the net of taxes decrease to be shown in the income statement would be $23,000.

Discontinued Operations

Large companies in the United States usually have many segments. A segment of a business may be a separate major line of business or a separate class of customer. For example, a company that manufactures heavy drilling equipment may also have another line of business, such as mobile homes. These large companies may discontinue or otherwise dispose of particular segments of their business that are not profitable. **Discontinued operations** are segments that are no longer part of the ongoing

7. Ibid., par. 17–19.

Figure 17-3
A Corporate Income Statement

Junction Corporation Income Statement For the Year Ended December 31, 19xx			
Sales (net)			$720,000
Less Cost of Goods Sold			370,000
Gross Profit			$350,000
Operating Expenses			110,000
Income from Continuing Operations Before Taxes			$240,000
Income Tax Expense			119,000
Income from Continuing Operations			$121,000
Discontinued Operations			
Income from Operations of Discontinued Segment (net of taxes $15,000)		$30,000	
Loss on Disposal of Segment (net of tax savings $22,000)		(23,000)	7,000
Income Before Extraordinary Items and Cumulative Effect of Accounting Change			$128,000
Extraordinary Gain (net of taxes $1,000)			3,000
Subtotal			$131,000
Cumulative Effect of a Change in Accounting Principle (net of taxes $5,000)			(6,000)
Net Income			$125,000
Earnings per Common Share:			
Income from Continuing Operations	$ .21		
Income Before Extraordinary Items	.28		
Extraordinary Gain (net of taxes)	.03		
Cumulative Effect of Accounting Change (net of taxes)	(.06)		
Net Income	.25		

operations of the business. Generally accepted accounting principles require that gains and losses from discontinued operations be disclosed separately in the income statement. The reasoning for the separate disclosure requirement is that the income statement will be more useful in evaluating the ongoing activities of the business if results from continuing operations are reported separately from discontinued operations. In Figure 17-3, the disclosure of discontinued operations is composed of two parts. It shows that (1) the income from the segment of business that has been disposed of or will be disposed of to the decision date to discontinue was $30,000 (net of $15,000 taxes) and (2) the loss from disposal of the segment of business was $23,000 (net of $22,000 tax savings).

The computation of the gains or losses is reserved for more advanced accounting courses. The disclosure has been provided, however, to give a complete view of the content of the corporate income statement.

Extraordinary Items

The Accounting Principles Board, in its *Opinion No. 30,* defines **extraordinary items** as "those events or transactions that are distinguished by their unusual nature and the infrequency of their occurrence."[8] As stated in the definition, the major criteria for these items are that they must be unusual and occur very infrequently. Unusual and infrequent occurrences are explained in the opinion as follows:

> Unusual Nature—the underlying event or transaction should possess a high degree of abnormality and be of a type clearly unrelated to, or only incidentally related to, the ordinary and typical activities of the entity, taking into account the environment in which the entity operates.
>
> Infrequency of Occurrence—the underlying event or transaction should be of a type that would not reasonably be expected to recur in the foreseeable future, taking into account the environment in which the entity operates.[9]

Because these items are unusual and infrequent, they should be disclosed separately from continuing operations on the income statement. This disclosure will allow the reader of the statement to identify those gains or losses included in the computation of income that would not be expected to recur in the near future. Examples that may qualify as extraordinary items are (1) uninsured losses from floods, earthquakes, fires, and theft; (2) gains and losses resulting from the enactment of a new law; and (3) expropriation of property by a foreign government. These items should be disclosed in the income statement after discontinued operations. Also, the gain or loss should be shown net of applicable taxes. In Figure 17-3, the extraordinary gain was $3,000 after applicable taxes of $1,000.

8. Accounting Principles Board, *Opinion No. 30,* "Reporting the Results of Operations" (New York: American Institute of Certified Public Accountants, 1973), par. 20.
9. Ibid.

Accounting Changes

Consistency, one of the basic concepts of accounting, means that, for accounting purposes, companies apply the same accounting principles from year to year. However, a company is allowed to make accounting changes if current procedures are incorrect or inappropriate. For example, a change from the straight-line to the sum-of-the-years'-digits method of depreciation may be made if there is adequate justification for the change. Adequate justification usually means that, if the change occurs, the financial statements will better represent the financial activities of the company. A company's desire to decrease the amount of income taxes to be paid is not considered an adequate justification for an accounting change. If justification does exist and an accounting change is made during an accounting period, generally accepted accounting principles require disclosure of the change. The following information must be included in the financial statements:

1. The nature and justification of the accounting change should be disclosed in the notes to the financial statements.
2. The effect of the change on the current period's income and income before extraordinary items should be disclosed in the footnotes.
3. The effect of the change on earnings per share before extraordinary items and net income should be indicated.
4. The cumulative effect of changing the principle should be indicated in the income statement immediately after extraordinary items.[10]

The cumulative effect of an accounting change is the effect that the new accounting principle would have had on net income if it, instead of the old principle, had been applied in past years. For example, assume that the Caprock Corporation has used the straight-line method in depreciating its machinery. The company changes to the sum-of-the-years'-digits method of depreciation this year. The following depreciation charges (net of taxes) were computed by the controller:

Cumulative, 5-year sum-of-the-years'-digits depreciation	$16,000
Less cumulative, 5-year straight-line depreciation	10,000
Cumulative effect of accounting change	$ 6,000

The $6,000 difference (net of applicable income taxes) is the cumulative effect of the change in depreciation methods and must be shown in the current year's income statement as a reduction in income (see Figure 17-3). Further study of accounting changes is deferred to more advanced accounting courses.

Earnings per Share

Readers of financial statements use earnings per share information to evaluate the performance of the company and to compare performance with that of other companies. The Accounting Principles Board recog-

10. Accounting Principles Board, *Opinion No. 20,* "Accounting Changes" (New York: American Institute of Certified Public Accountants, July 1971).

nized the importance of this information in its *Opinion No. 15* by concluding that earnings per share of common stock should be presented on the face of the income statement.[11] As shown in Figure 17-3, the information is normally disclosed immediately below the net income figure. An earnings per share amount is always shown for income from continuing operations, income before extraordinary items and cumulative effect of accounting changes, cumulative effect of accounting changes, and net income. If the statement contains a gain or loss from discontinued operations or a gain or loss on extraordinary items, earnings per share amounts may also be presented for these items.

Objective 7 Compute primary and fully diluted earnings per share

A basic earnings per share amount is found when a company has only common stock and the same number of shares outstanding during the year. For example, assume that in 19x1, Junction Corporation had net income of $25,000, with 100,000 shares of common stock outstanding for the entire year. The earnings per share of common stock would be computed as follows:

$$\begin{aligned}\text{earnings per share} &= \frac{\text{net income}}{\text{shares outstanding}}\\ &= \frac{\$125{,}000}{100{,}000 \text{ shares}}\\ &= \$1.25 \text{ per share}\end{aligned}$$

If, however, the number of shares outstanding changes during the year, it is necessary to compute a weighted-average number of shares outstanding for the year. To illustrate, assume that the Junction Corporation reported the $125,000 of net income as above, but that the common shares outstanding during various periods of the year were as follows: January–March, 100,000 shares; April–September, 120,000 shares; October–December, 130,000 shares. The weighted-average number of common shares outstanding and earnings per share would be computed as shown below:

100,000 shares × ¼ year	25,000
120,000 shares × ½ year	60,000
130,000 shares × ¼ year	32,500
Weighted-average shares outstanding	117,500

$$\begin{aligned}\text{Earnings per share} &= \frac{\$125{,}000}{117{,}500 \text{ shares}}\\ &= \$1.06 \text{ per share}\end{aligned}$$

If a company has nonconvertible preferred stock outstanding, the dividend for this stock must be subtracted from net income before computing earnings per share for common stock. For example, if Junction Corporation has preferred stock on which the annual dividend is $23,500, earnings per share on common stock would be $.86 [($125,000 − $23,500) ÷ 117,500 shares].

11. Accounting Principles Board, *Opinion No. 15,* "Earnings per Share" (New York: American Institute of Certified Public Accountants, May 1969), par. 12.

Companies with a capital structure in which there are no other bonds or stocks that could be converted into common stock are considered to have a **simple capital structure.** The earnings per share for these companies are computed as shown above. Many companies, however, have a **complex capital structure,** which includes convertible stocks and bonds. These convertible securities have the potential of diluting the earnings per share of common stock. Potential dilution means that a person's proportionate share of ownership in the corporation may be reduced by an increase in total shares outstanding through a conversion of stocks or bonds. For example, if a person owns 10,000 shares of a corporation, representing 2 percent of the outstanding shares of 500,000, and holders of convertible bonds convert the bonds into 100,000 shares of stock, the person's holdings of 10,000 shares would represent only 1.67 percent (10,000 ÷ 600,000) of the outstanding shares. In addition, the increased shares outstanding would result in reduced earnings per share and probably a lower market price per share.

If, at the time of issuance, the value of convertible securities is closely related to their conversion value—that is, the value of the stock they could be converted into—they are considered to be **common stock equivalents.** This means that in substance they are equivalent to common stock and should be considered as such in the computation of earnings per share.

When a company has a complex capital structure, a dual presentation of earnings per share is necessary. The company must disclose a **primary earnings per share** and a **fully diluted earnings per share** under the assumption that the stockholders should be aware of the potential effect of dilution of their ownership in the corporation. Computational formulas for these per share amounts are shown below.

$$\text{primary earnings per share} = \frac{\text{net income applicable to common stock}}{\text{weighted-average common shares and common stock equivalents}}$$

$$\text{fully diluted earnings per share} = \frac{\text{net income applicable to common stock}}{\text{weighted-average common stock and common stock equivalents and other potentially dilutive securities}}$$

As an example of the computation of primary and fully diluted earnings per share, assume that the Caprock Corporation had the following capital structure and net income: (1) There are 100,000 shares of $5 par value common stock outstanding for the entire year. (2) There are 10,000 shares of $10 par value cumulative, convertible preferred stock outstanding for the year. Each share is convertible into two shares of common, is a common stock equivalent, and has a dividend rate of $1 per share. (3) There are 5,000 shares of $20 par value cumulative, convertible preferred stock outstanding for the year. Each share is convertible into four shares of common stock. Though not a common stock equivalent at issuance, it is potentially dilutive and has a $2 per share dividend rate. (4) Net income is $280,000. The computation of earnings per share is on the next page.

		Primary	Fully Diluted
Net income		$280,000	$280,000
Less dividend on $20 par value preferred stock (5,000 × $2)		10,000	
Income applicable to common stock		$270,000	$280,000
Common stock for primary earnings per share			
Weighted-average common stock	100,000		
Common stock equivalents—$10 par value preferred stock (10,000 × 2)	20,000	120,000	
Common stock for fully diluted earnings per share			
Common stock for primary	120,000		
Other dilutive securities—$20 par value preferred stock (5,000 × 4)	20,000		140,000
Earnings per share of common stock		$2.25	$2.00

Note that income applicable to common stock for computing primary earnings per share is computed by deducting from net income the dividend on the preferred stock that is not a common stock equivalent.

The earnings per share are presented in the income statement of a company with a complex capital structure and with extraordinary items as follows:

	19x2	19x1
Income Before Extraordinary Items	$780,000	$586,000
Less Extraordinary Loss (net of applicable taxes)	(46,000)	(124,000)
Net Income	$734,000	$462,000
Earnings per Share of Common Stock		
Primary		
Earnings Before Extraordinary Loss	$2.87	$1.99
Extraordinary Loss	(.17)	(.42)
Net Earnings for the Year	$2.70	$1.57
Fully Diluted		
Earnings Before Extraordinary Loss	2.42	1.79
Extraordinary Loss	(.14)	(.39)
Net Earnings for the Year	$2.28	$1.40

Chapter Review

Review of Learning Objectives

1. Define *retained earnings*, and prepare a retained earnings statement.
Retained earnings are the part of stockholders' equity that comes from retaining assets earned in business operations. Prior period adjustments are events or transactions that relate to earlier accounting periods but are not determinable in the earlier period. These adjustments are recorded by adjusting the incorrect account and debiting or crediting the Retained Earnings account. The retained earnings statement is a basic financial statement that summarizes changes in retained earnings during the accounting period. Items appearing on the statement include prior period adjustments, dividends, income or loss, and sale of treasury stock at less than cost.

2. Account for cash dividends, stock dividends, and stock splits.
A dividend is a distribution of assets, usually cash, by a corporation to its stockholders in proportion to the number of shares of stock held by each owner. A summary of the key dates and accounting treatment of cash dividends and stock dividends follows:

Key Date	Cash Dividend	Stock Dividend
Declaration date	Debit Retained Earnings and credit Cash Dividends Payable for the total amount of the dividend.	Debit Retained Earnings for the market value of the stock to be distributed and credit Stock Dividends Distributable (par value) and Paid-in Capital in Excess of Par Value for the excess of market value over the stock's par value.
Record date	No entry.	No entry.
Payment date	Debit Cash Dividends Payable and credit Cash.	Debit Stock Dividends Distributable and credit Common Stock for the par value of the stock that was distributed.

A stock split is usually undertaken to reduce the market value and improve the liquidity of a company's stock. Since there is normally a decrease in the par value of the stock proportionate to the number of additional shares issued, there is no effect on the dollar amounts in the stockholders' equity accounts. The split should be recorded in the general journal by a memorandum entry only.

3. Account for treasury stock transactions.
The treasury stock of a company is stock that has been issued and reacquired but not reissued or retired. A company acquires its own stock for reasons such as creating stock option plans, maintaining a favorable market for the stock, increasing earnings per share, and purchasing other companies. Treasury stock is similar

to unissued stock in that it does not have rights until it is reissued. However, treasury stock can be resold at less than par value without incurring a discount liability. The accounting treatment for treasury stock is summarized below.

Treasury Stock Transaction	Accounting Treatment
Purchase of treasury stock	Debit Treasury Stock and credit Cash for the cost of the shares.
Reissuance of treasury stock at cost	Debit Cash and credit Treasury Stock for the cost of the share.
Reissuance of treasury stock at an amount greater than the cost of the shares	Debit Cash for the reissue price of the shares and credit Treasury Stock for the cost of the shares and Paid-in Capital, Treasury Stock for the excess.
Reissuance of treasury stock at an amount less than the cost of the shares	Debit Cash for the reissue price; debit Paid-in Capital, Treasury Stock for the difference between reissue price and the cost of the shares; and credit Treasury Stock for the cost of the shares.

If Paid-in Capital, Treasury Stock does not exist or is not large enough to cover the difference, Retained Earnings should absorb the difference.

4. Account for the appropriation of retained earnings.

A company may need to retain a portion of its assets in the business for reasons such as plant expansion rather than distribute them to the stockholders' as dividends. Management may communicate the plans to stockholders and other users of the company's financial statements by appropriation of retained earnings, thereby transferring a portion of Retained Earnings to an account such as Retained Earnings Appropriated for Plant Expansion. A more common way to disclose the appropriation is through a note to the financial statements. When the reason for the appropriation no longer exists, the appropriated amount can be returned to the Retained Earnings account or the note removed from the financial statements.

5. Account for the retirement of stock and donations of stock and other assets.

A company may decide to purchase its stock for the purpose of retirement. The reasons for this action are similar to those for purchasing treasury stock except that there are no plans to reissue the stock. When stock is retired, all the contributed capital associated with the retired shares must be removed from the accounts. If stock is retired for less than the original contributed capital, the difference should be recorded as Paid-in Capital, Retirement of Stock. If stock is retired for more than the contributed capital, the difference is a reduction in Retained Earnings.

Stockholders of a company may donate their stock to the company. Because the company does not pay for the shares, the donation should be recorded with a memorandum entry. When the stock is reissued, the company's assets and equity should be increased similarly to the original issuance of the stock. The reissuance is recorded by a debit to the appropriate asset account and a credit to Paid-in Capital, Sale of Donated Stock. Other donated assets should be recorded at fair market value, and a credit should be made to Paid-in Capital, Donated Asset.

6. Describe the disclosure of discontinued operations, extraordinary items, and accounting changes on the income statement.
There are several accounting items that must be disclosed separately from continuing operations and net of income taxes on the income statement because of their unusual nature. These items include a gain or loss on discontinued operations, extraordinary items, and the cumulative effect of accounting changes.

7. Compute primary and fully diluted earnings per share.
Stockholders and other users of financial statements use earnings per share data to evaluate the performance of a company, estimate future earnings, and evaluate their investment opportunities. Therefore, earnings per share data are presented on the face of the income statement. Earnings per share amounts are computed for income from continuing operations, income before extraordinary items and cumulative effects of accounting changes, cumulative effects of accounting changes, and net income. The amounts are computed by dividing the income applicable to common stock by the common shares outstanding for the year. If the number of shares outstanding has varied during the year, then the weighted-average shares outstanding should be used in the computation. When the company has a complex capital structure, a dual presentation of primary and fully diluted earnings per share data must be disclosed on the face of the income statement. Formulas for the computation of primary and fully diluted earnings per share follow.

$$\text{primary earnings per share} = \frac{\text{net income applicable to common stock}}{\text{weighted-average common shares and common stock equivalents}}$$

$$\text{fully diluted earnings per share} = \frac{\text{net income applicable to common stock}}{\text{weighted-average common stock and common stock equivalents and other potential dilutive securities}}$$

Review Problem

Before doing the exercises and problems, review the sample journal entries and stockholders' equity sections given throughout the chapter. For additional help, see the review problem in the working papers.

Chapter Assignments

Questions

1. What are retained earnings, and how do they relate to the assets of a corporation?
2. When does a company have a deficit in retained earnings?
3. What items are identified by generally accepted accounting principles as prior period adjustments?
4. Describe the significance of the following dates as they relate to dividends: (a) date of declaration, (b) date of record, and (c) date of payment.

5. Distinguish between a cash dividend and a stock dividend, and describe the accounting treatment of each.
6. What is the difference between a stock dividend and a stock split? What is the effect of each on the capital structure of a corporation?
7. What is the purpose of appropriating retained earnings?
8. Define treasury stock. Why would a company purchase its own stock?
9. Explain the two major criteria for extraordinary items. How should extraordinary items be disclosed in financial statements?
10. How are earnings per share disclosed in financial statements?
11. When an accounting change occurs, what financial statement disclosures are necessary?
12. What is a common stock equivalent?
13. When does a company have a simple capital structure? a complex capital structure?
14. What is the difference between primary and fully diluted earnings per share?
15. Why should the gain or loss on discontinued operations be disclosed separately on the income statement?

Classroom Exercises

Exercise 17-1 Retained Earnings Statement

The Milton Corporation had a Retained Earnings balance on January 1, 19x2, of $130,000. During 19x2, the company reported a profit of $56,000 after taxes. In addition, the company located a $22,000 error that resulted in an overstatement of prior years' income and that meets the criteria of a prior period adjustment. During 19x2, the company declared cash dividends totaling $8,000.

Prepare the company's retained earnings statement for the year ended December 31, 19x2.

Exercise 17-2 Journal Entries—Cash Dividends and Stock Dividends

The Lafayette Company has 20,000 shares of its $1 par value common stock outstanding.

Record the following transactions as they relate to the company's common stock:

July 1 Declared a 50¢ per share cash dividend on common stock to be paid on July 16 to stockholders of record on July 10.
10 Record date.
16 Paid the cash dividend declared on July 1.
17 Declared a 10 percent stock dividend on common stock to be distributed on August 10. Market value of the stock was $5 per share on this date.
Aug. 10 Distributed the stock dividend declared on July 17.

Exercise 17-3 Stock Split

The General Manufacturing Company currently has 100,000 shares of $1 par value common stock outstanding. The board of directors declared a 2 for 1 stock split on May 15, when the market value of the common stock was $2.50 per share. The Retained Earnings balance on May 15 was $700,000. Paid-in Capital in Excess of Par Value, Common Stock, on this date was $20,000.

Prepare the stockholders' equity section of the company's balance sheet before and after the stock split. What journal entry, if any, would be necessary to record the stock split?

Exercise 17-4 Appropriation of Retained Earnings

The board of directors of the UTC Corporation has approved a major plant expansion during the coming year. The expansion should cost approximately $550,000. The board has taken action to appropriate retained earnings of the company in the amount of $550,000 on July 17, 19x1. On August 20, 19x2, the expansion was completed at a total cost of $525,000 and paid for with cash. Also, on that date, the appropriation of retained earnings was removed.

1. Prepare the necessary journal entries for July 17, 19x1, and August 20, 19x2.
2. If the company had unappropriated retained earnings of $976,000 immediately before the August 20, 19x2, entries, what were the total retained earnings immediately before and after August 20, 19x2?

Exercise 17-5 Treasury Stock Transactions

Prepare the journal entries necessary to record the following stock transactions of the Blend Corporation during 19xx:

May 5 Purchased 200 shares of its own $1 par value common stock for $5.00, the current market price.
17 Sold 75 shares of treasury stock purchased on May 5 for $5.50 per share.
21 Sold 50 shares of treasury stock purchased on May 5 for $5.00 per share.
28 Sold the remaining 75 shares of treasury stock purchased on May 5 for $4.75 per share.

Exercise 17-6 Stock Transactions—Retirement and Donation of Stock

Record the following equity transactions of the Bold Corporation during 19xx:

Mar. 14 Retired 100 shares of $5 par value common stock for $25 per share. Stock was originally sold for $25 per share.
18 Retired 20 shares of $5 par value common stock for $30. Stock was originally sold for $25 per share.
Apr. 26 Retired 100 shares of $5 par value common stock for $22 per share. Stock was originally sold for $25 per share.
May 5 Wilma Mitchell donated to the company 500 shares of her $5 par value common stock.
6 Sold the 500 donated shares for $23 per share.
July 19 John Dooley donated a tract of land to the company as an incentive to move its paint subsidiary to Tullie. Dooley had purchased the land for $15,000, and the current value was $36,000.

Exercise 17-7 Income Statement

Assume that the Outdoor Furniture Company's chief financial officer gave you the following information: Net Sales, $1,500,000; Cost of Goods Sold, $700,000; Extraordinary Gain (applicable income tax on gain of $12,500), $25,000; Loss from Discontinued Operations (applicable income tax benefit of $30,000), $82,000; Selling Expenses, $50,000; Administrative Expenses, $40,000.

From this information, prepare the company's income statement for the year ended June 30, 19xx. (Ignore earnings per share information.)

Exercise 17-8 Earnings per Share

During 19x1, EPS Corporation reported a net income of $1,265,000. On January 1, EPS had 500,000 shares of common stock outstanding. The company issued an additional 300,000 shares of common stock on October 1. In 19x1, the company had a simple capital structure.

On January 1, 19x2, EPS issued 50,000 shares of 8 percent, $100 par value cumulative, convertible preferred stock. Each share of preferred stock is convertible into four shares of common stock. During 19x2, there were no transactions involving common stock, and the company reported net income of $1,820,000.

1. Determine the weighted-average number of common shares outstanding each year.
2. Compute earnings per share for each year, including primary and fully diluted earnings per share, if appropriate, assuming that on the date of issue the preferred stock (a) qualified as a common stock equivalent and (b) did not qualify as a common stock equivalent.

Problem Set A

Problem 17A-1 Treasury Stock Transactions

The Stoneking Gem Company made the following stock transactions during 19xx:

Feb. 12 Purchased 20,000 shares of its common stock on the market at a cost of $10 per share and put it in the treasury.
May 2 Sold 5,000 shares of the treasury stock for $10 per share.
Aug. 4 Sold 6,000 shares of the treasury stock for $11 per share.
Sept. 15 Sold 5,000 shares of the treasury stock for $9 per share.
Nov. 19 Sold the remaining 4,000 shares of the treasury stock for $9 per share.

Required

Record the above transactions in general journal form.

Problem 17A-2 Stock and Retained Earnings Transactions

The following stockholders' equity transactions occurred during 19x7 for the Kemp Corporation.

Jan. 17 Marie Johnson donated a building to the corporation so that it could expand its Shallowater, Alabama, operations. Johnson had paid $60,000 for the building in 19x0, and its market value in 19x7 was $86,000.
Mar. 22 Johnson contributed 10,000 shares of her $1 par value common stock to the corporation. This action was taken so the company could resell the stock to obtain additional working capital. The stock was originally purchased at $12 per share.
Apr. 16 The board of directors voted to appropriate $125,000 of retained earnings for plant expansion. The board determined that the appropriation would not be adequately disclosed by footnote.
May 6 Sold 5,000 of the common stock shares donated by Marie Johnson for $12 per share.
29 Sold the remaining 5,000 of the common shares donated by Johnson for $10 per share.
June 30 Declared a cash dividend of 25¢ per share of common stock. The corporation had 100,000 shares of common stock outstanding.
July 25 Paid the cash dividend declared on June 30.
Dec. 10 Completed and paid for the plant expansion at a cost of $130,000, and the board of directors voted to return the appropriated retained earnings to Unappropriated Retained Earnings.

Required

Prepare general journal entries to record the above transactions.

Problem 17A-3 Dividend Transactions and Stockholders' Equity

The stockholders' equity of the Bressler Manufacturing Company as of December 31, 19x0, was as follows:

Contributed Capital	
Common Stock—$1 par value, 500,000 shares authorized, 400,000 shares issued and outstanding	$400,000
Paid-in Capital in Excess of Par Value	100,000
Total Contributed Capital	$500,000
Retained Earnings	230,000
Total Stockholders' Equity	$730,000

The following transactions were completed during 19x1:

Jan. 9	Declared a cash dividend of 10¢ per share of common stock, to be paid to stockholders of record on February 1. Date of payment is to be February 10.
Feb. 1	Date of record for cash dividend declared January 9.
10	Paid the cash dividend declared on January 9.
June 16	Declared a 5 percent stock dividend to be distributed on July 15. The market value of the stock was $7 per share.
July 15	Distributed the stock dividend declared on June 16.
Oct. 1	The board of directors voted a 2 for 1 stock split.
Dec. 10	Declared a cash dividend of $.05 per share of common stock, to be paid to stockholders of record January 1. Date of payment is to be January 10.
31	Net income for the year of $100,000 is closed to Retained Earnings.

Required

1. Record the above transactions in general journal form.
2. Prepare the stockholders' equity section of the company's balance sheet as of December 31, 19x1.

Problem 17A-4 Corporate Income Statement

Balances from the general ledger of the R. C. Spires Manufacturing Company as of December 31 are presented below.

a. Administrative Expenses	$ 45,000
b. Cost of Goods Sold	300,000
c. Discontinued Operations	
(1) Profit from the Operations of Discontinued Segment (net of tax $60,000)	63,000
(2) Gain on Disposal (net of tax $50,000)	52,000
d. Extraordinary Loss, Expropriation of Plant in Chile (net of taxes $40,000)	46,000
e. Income Tax Applicable to Continuing Operations	95,000
f. Other Operating Expenses	145,000
g. Sales	750,000
h. Sales Commissions Expense	75,000
i. Sales Returns and Allowances	5,000

Required

Prepare the income statement in good form for the company as of December 31, assuming weighted-average common shares of 100,000.

Problem 17A-5 Earnings per Share

The Bartex Tennis Corporation has the following capital structure during 19xx:

a. $5 par value common stock: (1) January–June, 100,000 shares outstanding; (2) July–September, 120,000 shares outstanding; (3) October–December, 140,000 shares outstanding.
b. There are 20,000 shares of $10 par value, cumulative, convertible preferred stock outstanding for the year. The stock is convertible into common stock at a rate of one share of preferred to two shares of common, and is a common stock equivalent. The dividend rate for the peferred stock is $1 per share.
c. There are 10,000 shares of $20 par value, cumulative, convertible preferred stock outstanding for the year. This stock is convertible into common stock at a rate of one share of preferred to three shares of common. The stock is not a common stock equivalent but if converted would dilute the earnings per share of common stock. The dividend rate is $1.25 per share.
d. Net income is $175,000.

Required

1. Compute weighted average number of common stock shares outstanding for 19x7.
2. Compute the earnings per share amounts necessary for proper disclosure for the Bartex Tennis Corporation.

Problem 17A-6 Stockholders' Equity and Retained Earnings Statement

The balance sheet of C. H. Stone Developers presented the following stockholders' equity as of June 30, 19x7:

Contributed Capital	
Preferred Stock—$50 par value, 6% noncumulative, 100,000 shares authorized, 25,000 shares issued and outstanding	$1,250,000
Common Stock—$10 par value, 700,000 shares authorized, 400,000 shares issued and outstanding	4,000,000
Paid-in Capital in Excess of Par Value, Common Stock	600,000
Total Contributed Capital	$5,850,000
Retained Earnings	2,400,000
Total Stockholders' Equity	$8,250,000

The company's activities during the year included the following stockholders' equity transactions: (a) Net income was $650,000. (b) Purchased 20,000 shares of the company's common stock for $15 per share. (c) Sold 15,000 shares of the treasury stock for $16 per share. (d) Received a tract of land, with a market value of $100,000, which was donated to the company. (e) Declared and paid the indicated cash dividend to preferred stockholders for the year. (f) Declared and paid a cash dividend on common stock of 50¢ per share after the treasury stock transactions in b and c were completed. (g) After the above transactions, declared a 2 percent stock dividend on common stock, at which time the common stock was selling for $19 per share. The stock divided had not been distributed at the end of the year. (h) Recorded a prior period adjustment net of tax of $20,000. The adjustment was a correction of a depreciation error in 19x2. The depreciation for buildings was not recorded in 19x2, so depreciation was understated. (i) Accepted near the end of the year subscriptions on 5,000 shares of preferred stock at $54 per share. The subscriptions had not been paid at the end of the year.

Required

1. Prepare journal entries for the above transactions.
2. Prepare a retained earning statement for C. H. Stone Developers for the year ended June 30, 19x8.
3. Prepare the stockholders' equity section of C. H. Stone Developers' balance sheet as of June 30, 19x8.

Problem Set B

Problem 17B-1 Treasury Stock Transactions

The following treasury stock transactions occurred during 19xx for the Cloth Flowers Company: (a) Purchased 15,000 shares of its common stock on the market for $20 per share. (b) Sold 7,000 shares of the treasury stock for $21 per share. (c) Sold 6,000 shares of the treasury stock for $19 per share. (d) Purchased an additional 3,000 shares for $18 per share. (e) Sold all of the treasury stock remaining for $17 per share.

Required

Record these transactions in general journal form.

Problem 17B-2 Stock and Retained Earnings Transactions

A review of the stockholders' equity records of the Stroud Cotton Corporation disclosed the following transactions during 19xx:

Jan. 30	Purchased 5,000 shares of the company's $5 par value common stock for $10. The stock was originally sold for $9. The stock was retired when purchased.
Mar. 5	The board of directors voted to appropriate $265,000 of retained earnings because of a contractual agreement to purchase cotton delinting equipment.
Apr. 16	Received a truck with a market value of $2,500, which was donated by a stockholder.
May 15	The board of directors declared a $20,000 cash dividend to common stockholders.
June 15	Paid the cash dividend.
Aug. 17	Received 500 shares of common stock, originally issued at $8 per share, as a donation from a stockholder. The stock is to be resold.
Sept. 10	Purchased the cotton delinting equipment at a total cost of $285,000, including installation, and removed the appropriation of retained earnings in connection with the purchase contract.
Nov. 5	Sold and reissued the 500 donated shares of common stock at $15.
Dec. 31	Closed Net Income for the year of $65,000 from Income Summary to Retained Earnings.

Required

Record the stockholders' equity transactions of the Stroud Cotton Corporation in general journal form.

Problem 17B-3 Dividend Transactions and Stockholders' Equity

The balance sheet of the Rainwater Apparel Company disclosed the following stockholders' equity as of September 30, 19x1:

Contributed Capital	
Common Stock—$2 par value, 1,000,000 shares authorized, 250,000 shares issued and outstanding	$500,000
Paid-in Capital in Excess of Par Value	60,000
Total Contributed Capital	$560,000
Retained Earnings	400,000
Total Stockholders' Equity	$960,000

The following stockholders' equity transactions were completed during the year in the order presented:

19x1
Dec. 17 Declared a 10 percent stock dividend. The market value per share on the date of declaration was $4.

19x2
Jan. 20 Distributed the stock dividend.
Apr. 14 Declared a 25¢ per share cash dividend. Cash dividend payable May 15 to stockholders of record May 1.
May 15 Paid the cash dividend.
June 17 Split its stock 2 for 1.
Sept. 14 Appropriated retained earnings for plant expansion in the amount of $95,000.
15 Declared a cash dividend of $.10 per share payable October 10 to stockholders of record October 1.
30 Closed Income Summary with a credit balance of $50,000 to Retained Earnings.

Required

1. Record the above transactions in general journal form.
2. Prepare the stockholders' equity section of the company's balance sheet as of September 30, 19x2.

Problem 17B-4 Corporate Income Statement

Information concerning operations of the Tick-Tock Clock Company during 19xx is as follows: (a) Administrative Expenses, $100,000; (b) Cost of Goods Sold, $350,000; (c) Cumulative effect of an accounting change that increased income, change in depreciation methods (net of tax $20,000), $42,000; (d) Extraordinary Item, Loss from Earthquake (net of tax $46,000), ($60,000); (e) Sales (net), $800,000; (f) Selling Expenses, $80,000; (g) Taxes applicable to continuing operations, $135,000.

Required

Prepare the company's income statement for the year ended December 31, 19xx, including earnings per share information, assuming a weighted average of 100,000 common stock shares outstanding during the year.

Problem 17B-6 Stockholders' Equity and Retained Earnings Statement

On January 1, 19xx, the stockholders' equity section of G. I. D. Wholesale Company appeared as shown below.

Contributed Capital	
Common Stock—$4 par value, 100,000 shares authorized, 40,000 shares issued and outstanding	$ 160,000
Paid-in Capital in Excess of Par Value	580,000
Total Contributed Capital	$ 740,000
Retained Earnings	316,000
Total Stockholders' Equity	$1,056,000

Selected transactions involving stockholders' equity are as follows: (a) During January, the board of directors obtained authorization for 20,000 shares of $20 par value preferred stock that carried an indicated dividend rate of $2 per share. The company sold 12,000 shares at $25 per share and issued another 2,000 in exchange for a building valued at $60,000. Also, during January, land valued at $10,000, on which the building was located, was donated to the company. (b) During March, the board of directors also declared a 2 for 1 stock split on the common stock. (c) In April, after the stock split, the company purchased 3,000 shares of common stock for the treasury at an average price of $6 per share; 1,000 of these shares were subsequently sold at an average price of $8 per share. (d) In May, 2,000 shares of the company's common stock were donated to the company through the will of a deceased stockholder. On the date the stock was received, its market value was $10 per share. It was subsequently sold for $13 in June. (e) During July, declared and paid a cash dividend of $2 per share on preferred stock and 20¢ per share on common stock. (f) The board of directors declared a 15 percent stock dividend in November when the common stock was selling for $10. The stock dividend had not been distributed by the end of the year. (g) Stock subscriptions for 4,000 common shares at an average price of $14 per share were received in December. Partial payments amounting to one-half the subscriptions were paid, but none of the stock was fully paid by the end of the year. (h) Also in December a prior period adjustment was made which reduced earnings by $15,000. No income taxes were involved. (i) Net loss for 19x1 was $115,000.

Required

1. Prepare journal entries to record the above transactions.

2. Prepare the company's retained earnings statement for the year ended December 31.

3. Prepare the stockholders' equity section of the company's balance sheet as of December 31.

Learning Objectives

Chapter Eighteen

Corporations: Long-Term Liabilities and Bond Investments

1. Identify and contrast the major characteristics of bonds.

2. Record the issuance of bonds at face value, between interest dates, and at a discount or premium.

3. Amortize bond discount and premium by using the effective interest method, and make year-end adjustments.

4. Account for the retirement and conversion of bonds.

5. Compute sinking fund requirements, and prepare accounting entries associated with sinking fund bonds payable.

6. Explain the basic features of mortgages payable and long-term leases as long-term liabilities.

7. Account for bond investment transactions by a corporation.

This chapter introduces long-term liabilities and investments in bonds by a corporation. We discuss the nature of bonds and the accounting treatment for bonds payable, for other long-term liabilities, and for bond investments. As a result of studying this chapter, you should be able to meet the learning objectives listed on the left.

A corporation has many sources of funds from which to finance operations and expansion. Previous chapters have shown how corporations acquire cash and other assets by engaging in profitable operations, obtaining short-term credit, and issuing stock. Another source of funds for business is the issuance of long-term debt in the form of bonds or notes. When a company issues bonds or notes, it makes a commitment to pay the creditor periodic interest plus the principal of the debt at some future specified date. Notes and bonds are considered long-term if they are due more than one year from the balance sheet date. In practice, long-term notes can range from two to ten years to maturity and long-term bonds from ten to fifty years to maturity.

Nature of Bonds

A **bond** is a security representing money borrowed by a corporation from the investing public. (Other types of bonds are those used by the United States government, state and local governments, and foreign companies and countries to raise money.) Bonds must be repaid at a certain time, and require periodic payments of interest, usually semiannual or twice per year. These bonds must not be confused with stocks. Because stocks are shares of ownership, stockholders are owners. Bondholders, how-

Objective 1 Identify and contrast the major characteristics of bonds

ever, are creditors. Bonds are promises to repay the amount borrowed, called the principal, and a definite rate of interest at specified future dates.

The holder of a bond receives a **bond certificate** as evidence of the company's debt to the bondholder. In most cases, the face value (denomination) of the bond is $1,000 or some multiple thereof. A **bond issue** is the total number of bonds that are issued at the same time. For example, a $1,000,000 bond issue may consist of a thousand $1,000 bonds. Because the issue may be bought and held by many investors, the corporation usually enters into a supplementary agreement, called a **bond indenture.** The bond indenture defines the rights, privileges, and limitations of bondholders. The bond indenture will usually include such items as the maturity date of the bonds, interest payment dates, interest rate, characteristics of the bonds such as convertible or callable features, repayable plans, and restrictions.

The prices of bonds are stated in terms of 100s. If a bond issue is quoted at 103½, this means that a $1,000 bond would cost $1,035 ($1000 × 103½%). When a bond sells at exactly 100, it is said to sell at face or par value. When it sells at above 100, it is said to sell at a premium and when below face value, at a discount. For example, a $1,000 bond quoted at 87.62 is selling at a discount and will cost the buyer $876.20.

A bond indenture can be written to fit the needs of an individual company and its financing needs. As a result, the bonds being issued by corporations in today's financial markets have many different features. Several of the more important features of bonds are described below.

Secured or Unsecured Bonds

Bonds may be either secured or unsecured. Bonds issued on the general credit of the company are **unsecured bonds** (also called **debenture bonds**). **Secured bonds** are those that give the bondholders a pledge of certain assets of the company as a guarantee of repayment. The security identified by a secured bond may be any specific asset of the company or general category such as property, plant, and equipment.

Term or Serial Bonds

When all the bonds of an issue mature at the same time, they are called **term bonds.** For example, a company may issue $1,000,000 worth of bonds, all due twenty years from the date of issuance. If the maturity dates of a bond issue are spread over several maturity dates, they are **serial bonds.** A company may issue serial bonds to ease the problem of accumulating cash for retiring the bonds. An example of serial bonds would be a $1,000,000 issue that called for retiring $200,000 of the principal every five years. This means that after the first $200,000 payment is made, only $800,000 of the bonds would remain outstanding for the next five years. In other words, $1,000,000 is outstanding for the first five years, and $800,000 is outstanding for the second five years.

Registered or Coupon Bonds

Most bonds that are issued today are **registered bonds.** Registered bonds require that the name and address of the bond owner be recorded with the issuing company. The issuing company thus maintains a bond register of the owners and pays interest by check to the bondholders of record on the interest payment date. **Coupon bonds** are normally not registered with the corporation but have interest coupons attached to them. Each coupon identifies the amount of interest due and the payment date. The coupons are detached from the bond on the interest payment dates and deposited in a bank for collection. Thus the interest is paid to the bearer of the coupon.

Accounting for Bonds Payable

Objective 2 Record the issuance of bonds at face value, between interest dates, and at a discount or premium

When the board of directors decides to issue bonds, it normally presents the proposal to the stockholders for their approval. If the stockholders approve the bond issue, the company then prints the bond certificates and draws up a deed of trust. Finally, the bonds are authorized for issuance. It is not necessary to make a journal entry for the authorization of bonds, but most companies prepare a memorandum in the Bonds Payable account describing the issue. The description includes the amount of bonds authorized, interest rate, interest payment dates, and life of the bonds.

Once the bonds are issued, the corporation is obligated to pay the bondholders' interest throughout the life of bonds (usually semiannually) and the principal of the bonds at maturity.

Balance Sheet Disclosure of Bonds

Bonds payable and unamortized discount or premium as appropriate are normally classified on a company's balance sheet as long-term liabilities. However, as explained in Chapter 12, if the maturity date of the bond issue is one year or less and the bonds will be retired by the use of current assets, bonds payable should be classified as current liabilities. If the issue is to be paid with segregated assets or replaced by another bond issue, then they should continue to be classified as long-term liabilities.

Important provisions of the bond indenture are disclosed in the notes to the financial statements, and often include a list of all bond issues, the type of bonds, interest rate, any security associated with the bonds, interest payment dates, maturity date, and effective interest rate.

Bonds Issued at Face Value

As an example of bond issuance, assume that the Vason Corporation has authorized the issuance of $100,000 of 9 percent, five-year bonds on January 1, 19x0. Interest is payable on January 1 and July 1 of each year. Also assume that the bonds are sold on January 1, 19x0, for their face value.

The entry to record the issuance is as follows:

Jan. 1	Cash	100,000	
	Bonds Payable		100,000
	To record the issuance of $100,000 of 9%, 5-year bonds at face value		

As stated above, interest is paid on July 1 and January 1 of each year. Thus the corporation would owe the bondholders $4,500 interest on July 1, 19x0. The interest computation is shown below:

$$\begin{aligned} \text{interest} &= \text{principal} \times \text{rate} \times \text{time} \\ &= \$100{,}000 \times .09 \times \tfrac{1}{2} \text{ year} \\ &= \$4{,}500 \end{aligned}$$

The interest paid to the bondholders on each semiannual interest payment date would be recorded as follows:

July 1	Bond Interest Expense	4,500	
	Cash (or Accrued Interest Payable)		4,500
	To record semiannual interest payment to bondholders of 9%, 5-year bonds		

Sales of Bonds Between Interest Dates

Bonds may be issued on their interest date as in the example above, but many times they are sold between interest dates. The generally accepted method of handling bonds issued in this manner is to collect from the investor the interest that has accrued since the last interest payment date. Then when the next interest period arrives, the corporation pays the investor the interest for the entire period. Thus the interest collected when bonds are sold is returned to the investor on the next interest payment date. If a company were issuing bonds on several different days and did not collect the accrued interest, records would have to be maintained for each bondholder and date of purchase. In such a case, the interest due each bondholder would have to be computed on the basis of different time periods. It becomes clear that large bookkeeping costs would be incurred under this system. On the other hand, if accrued interest is collected when the bonds are sold, then on the interest payment date the corporation can pay the interest due for the entire period, eliminating the extra computations and costs.

For example, assume that the Vason Corporation sold $100,000 of 9 percent, five-year bonds for face value on April 1, 19x0, rather than on January 1, 19x0, the issue date. The entries to record the sale of the bonds and payment of interest on July 1, 19x0, follow:

Apr. 1	Cash	102,250	
	Bond Interest Expense		2,250
	Bonds Payable		100,000
	To record the sale of 9%, 5-year bonds at face value plus 3 months' accrued interest $100,000 × .09 × 3/12 = $2,250		

In this entry, Cash is debited for the amount received, $102,250 (face value of $100,000 plus three months' accrued interest of $2,250). Bond Interest Expense is credited for the $2,250 of accrued interest, and Bonds Payable is credited for face value of $100,000. When the first semiannual payment date arrives, the following entry is made:

July 1	Bond Interest Expense	4,500	
	Cash (or Accrued Interest Payable)		4,500
	To record the payment of semi-annual interest $100,000 × .09% × 1/2 = $4,500		

Note that in this entry the full half-year interest is both debited to Bond Interest Expense and credited to Cash. Also note that the actual interest expense for the six months is $2,250, the net balance of the $4,500 debit to Bond Interest Expense on July 1 minus the $2,250 credit to Bond Interest Expense on April 1. This result can be seen clearly in the posted entries in the ledger account for Bond Interest Expense:

Bond Interest Expense — **Account No. 723**

Date		Item	Post Ref.	Debit	Credit	Balance Debit	Balance Credit
19x0							
Apr.	1				2,250		2,250
July	1			4,500		2,250	

The Effect of the Market Rate of Interest on Bond Prices

The face value of a bond and its face interest rate are fixed. One hundred thousand dollars in bonds at 9 percent will pay $9,000 a year or $4,500 every six months until maturity. However, bonds are bought and sold by investors in the marketplace every day, and, in the market, interest rates vary from day to day. Vason Corporation can receive face value or $100,000 for the bonds, as illustrated above, only if the current market or effective rate of interest is 9 percent for bonds with the same conditions and quality. If the current market rate of interest on this type of bond issue has gone up to 10 percent, Vason could receive only $90,000 ($9,000 ÷ .10) from the bond investor. In other words, given a market rate of interest of 10 percent, the prudent bond investor will pay only $90,000 for an annual interest payment of $9,000. Similarly, if the market rate goes down to 8 percent, Vason Corporation would be able to issue the bonds for $112,500 ($9,000 ÷ .08) because similar bonds will yield only 8 percent.[1]

When issuing bonds, most companies attempt to establish the face interest rate as close as possible to the market interest rate. However, the decision as to what the face interest rate will be must be made in advance to allow time to file with regulatory bodies, publicize the issue, and print the certificates. Thus, there is often a difference in the market or effective rate of interest and the face rate of interest on the issue date. The result is that the issue price of the bond does not equal the principal or face value of the bond. If the issue price is less than the face value of the bonds, the bonds are said to be issued at a **discount**. The discount equals the excess of face value over issue price. If the issue price is more than the face value of the bonds, the bonds are said to be issued at a **premium**. The premium is equal to the excess of the issue price over the face value.

Bonds Issued at a Discount

As an example of issuing bonds at a discount, assume that the Vason Corporation issues its $100,000 of five-year, 9 percent bonds at 96.139. The entry to record the issuance of the bonds at a discount is:

Jan. 1	Cash		96,139	
	Unamortized Bond Discount		3,861	
	Bonds Payable			100,000
	To record the issuance of $100,000 of 9%, 5-year bonds			
	Face Amount of Bonds	$100,000		
	Less Purchase Price of Bonds ($100,000 × .96139)	96,139		
	Unamortized Bond Discount	$ 3,861		

In this entry, Cash is debited for the amount received ($96,139), Bonds Payable is credited for the face amount ($100,000) of the bond liability, and the difference ($3,861) is debited to Unamortized Bond Discount. If a balance sheet is prepared immediately after this issuance of bonds at a discount, the liability for bonds payable is as follows:

Long-Term Liabilities		
9% Bonds Payable, due 1/1/x5	$100,000	
Less Unamortized Bond Discount	3,861	$96,139

1. The calculations in this paragraph are approximate. The calculation of the present value of bonds using time value of money tables can be found in Appendix A.

As can be seen, the Unamortized Bond Discount is deducted from the face amount of the bonds to arrive at the carrying value or present value of the bonds. The bond discount is described as unamortized because it will be amortized (written off) over the life of the bonds. As a result, the carrying value of the bonds will gradually increase. By the time the maturity date of the bonds arrives, the carrying value of the bonds will equal their face value.

Calculation of Total Interest Cost

When bonds are issued at a discount, the effective interest rate paid by the company is greater than the face interest rate on the bonds. The reason for this is that the issuing corporation must pay the bondholder a total amount consisting of the stated interest payments *plus* the amount of the bond discount. In other words, because the company did not receive the full face value of the bonds upon issue, the difference between the issue price and the face value must be added to the interest payments to obtain the actual interest expense. The example below illustrates the total cost to the Vason Corporation of issuing the bonds at a discount and the computation of the effective rate of interest.

Cash to be paid to bondholders	
Face value at maturity	$100,000
Interest payments ($100,000 × .09 × 5 years)	45,000
Total cash to bondholders	$145,000
Cash received from bondholders	96,139
Total interest cost	$ 48,861

Or alternatively,

Interest payments ($100,000 × .09 × 5 years)	$ 45,000
Unamortized Bond Discount	3,861
	$ 48,861

The total interest cost of $48,861 is composed of $45,000 regular interest payments and the $3,861 bond discount. Therefore, the bond discount increases the interest paid on the bonds from the stated to the effective or actual interest rate.

The accounting treatment of the discount requires it to be spread or allocated over the life of the bonds as an increase in the interest expense each period. This process of allocation is called amortization of the bond discount.

Amortizing the Bond Discount

There are two methods of amortizing the discount: the straight-line method and the effective interest method. The straight-line method is the easier of the two and provides for equal amortization of the discount for

Objective 3
Amortize bond discount and premium by using the effective interest method, and make year-end adjustments

each interest period. For example, assume that the interest payment dates for the Vason Corporation's bond issue are January 1 and July 1. The amortization of the bond discount and determination of interest cost is accomplished by the following steps:

1. Total interest payments = interest payments per year × life of bonds
$= 2 \times 5$
$= 10$
2. Amortization of bond discount per interest payment
$$= \frac{\text{bond discount}}{\text{total interest payments}} = \frac{\$3{,}861}{10} = \$386$$
3. Regular cash interest payment
= face value × face interest rate × time
$= \$100{,}000 \times .09 \times \frac{1}{2}$
$= \$4{,}500$
4. Total interest cost per interest date
= interest payment + amortization of bond discount
$= \$4{,}500 + \$386 = \$4{,}886$

The entry to record the interest payment on July 1, 19x0, would be:

July 1	Bond Interest Expense	4,886	
	Unamortized Bond Discount		386
	Cash (or Accrued Interest Payable)		4,500
	To record semiannual interest payment to bondholders and amortized discount on 9%, 5-year bonds		

Note that although bond interest expense is \$4,886, the amount received by the bondholder is the \$4,500 face interest payment. The difference of \$386 is the credit to Unamortized Bond Discount. This credit reduces the debit balance of the Unamortized Bond Discount and thereby increases the carrying value of the bonds payable by \$386 each interest period. When the bond issue matures, the balance of Unamortized Bond Discount will be zero, and the carrying value of the bonds payable will equal \$100,000, exactly equal to the amount due the bondholder.

Although the straight-line method has long been used, it has a conceptual flaw. Because the carrying value increases each interest period and the bond interest expense is the same, the straight-line method results in a decreasing rate of interest over time. Similarly, using the straight-line method to amortize a premium results in an increasing rate of interest over time. For this reason, the APB has ruled that the straight-line method can be used only where it does not result in a material difference from the effective interest method.[2] As will be seen, the effective interest rate method assumes a constant rate of interest over the life of the bond. The rate of interest will be constant if the total interest expense changes

2. Accounting Principles Board, *Opinion No. 21* "Interest on Receivables and Payables" (New York: American Institute of Certified Public Accountants, 1971), par. 15.

slightly each interest period in reaction to the changing carrying value of the bond.

Under the **effective interest method**, the determination of interest and amortization of bond discount for each interest period requires the application of a constant interest rate to the carrying value of the bonds at the beginning of the interest period. The rate used is the market rate (effective rate) at the time the bonds were issued. The amount to be amortized becomes the difference between the interest computed by using the constant rate (effective rate) and the actual interest paid to the bondholders.

As an illustration of the effective interest method, assume the same facts as in the previous example ($100,000 bond issue at 9 percent, five-year maturity, interest paid semiannually). The market or effective rate of interest at the time is 10 percent. The bonds were sold for $96,139, which represents a discount of $3,861. The computation for interest and amortization of the bond discount is shown in Table 18-1.

The following points should help to explain the computations in the table:

Column A: The carrying value of the bonds is the face value of the bonds less unamortized bond discount ($100,000 – $3,861 = $96,139).

Column B: The interest expense to be recorded is the effective interest, which is computed by multiplying the carrying value of the bonds by the effective interest rate for one-half year ($96,139 × .10 × ½ = $4,807).

Table 18-1 Interest and Amortization of Bond Discount— Effective Interest Method

	A	B	C	D	E	F
Semiannual Interest Period	Carrying Value at Beginning of Period	Semiannual Interest Expense at 10% to Be Recorded* (5% × A)	Semiannual Interest to Be Paid to Bondholders (4½% × $100,000)	Amortization of Discount (B – C)	Unamortized Bond Discount at End of Period	Carrying Value at End of Period (A + D)
0					$3,861	
1	$96,139	$4,807	$4,500	$307	3,554	$ 96,446
2	96,446	4,822	4,500	322	3,232	96,768
3	96,768	4,838	4,500	338	2,894	97,106
4	97,106	4,855	4,500	355	2,539	97,461
5	97,461	4,873	4,500	373	2,166	97,834
6	97,834	4,892	4,500	392	1,774	98,226
7	98,226	4,911	4,500	411	1,363	98,637
8	98,637	4,932	4,500	432	931	99,069
9	99,069	4,953	4,500	453	478	99,522
10	99,522	4,978**	4,500	478	—	100,000

*Rounded to nearest dollar.
**Error due to rounding.

Column C: The interest paid in each period is the face value of the bonds multiplied by the interest rate for the bonds multiplied by the interest time period ($100,000 × .09 × ½ = $4,500).

Column D: The discount amortized is the difference between the effective interest expense to be recorded and the interest to be paid on the interest payment date ($4,807 – $4,500 = $307).

Column E: The unamortized bond discount is the balance of bond discount at the beginning of the period ($3,861) less the current period amortization of the discount ($307). The unamortized discount decreases each interest payment period because it is amortized as a portion of interest expense.

Column F: The carrying value of the bonds at the end of the period is the carrying value at the beginning of the period plus the amortization during the period ($96,139 + $307 = $96,446). Notice that the sum of the carrying value and unamortized discount (column E + column F) always equals the face value of the bonds ($96,446 + $3,554 = $100,000).

The entry to record the interest expense is exactly like the one shown when the straight-line method is applied. The only difference is the amounts debited and credited to the various accounts. For example, the entry for July 1, 19x0, using the effective interest method, would be:

July 1	Bond Interest Expense	4,807	
	Unamortized Bond Discount		307
	Cash (or Accrued Interest Payable)		4,500
	To record semiannual interest payment to bondholders and amortized discount on 9%, 5-year bonds		

Note also that an interest and amortization table does not have to be prepared to determine the amortization of discount for any one interest payment period. It is necessary only to multiply the carrying value by the effective interest rate and subtract the interest payment from the result. For example, the amount of discount to be amortized in the seventh interest payment period equals $411 [($98,226 × .05) – $4,500)].

Bonds Issued at a Premium

When bonds have a face interest rate that is above the market rate for similar investments, they will be issued at a price above the face value, or at a premium. For example, assume that the Vason Corporation issued $100,000 of bonds for $104,056. This means that they will be purchased by investors at 104.056 percent of their face value. The entry to record their issuance would be as follows:

Jan. 1	Cash	104,056	
	Unamortized Bond Premium		4,056
	Bonds Payable		100,000
	To record the sale of $100,000 of 9%, 5-year bonds at 104.056		

Immediately following this entry, the balance sheet presentation for bonds payable would appear as follows:

Long-Term Liabilities		
9% Bonds Payable, due 1/1/x5	$100,000	
Unamortized Bond Premium	4,056	$104,056

The carrying value of bonds payable is $104,056, which represents the face value of the bonds plus the unamortized bond premium. The cash received from the issuance of the bonds is also $104,056. This means that the purchasers were willing to pay a premium of $4,056 to obtain these bonds because the face interest on the bonds was greater than the market rate. The $4,056 premium represents funds that will not be paid back to the bondholders at maturity. Therefore, it is amortized over the life of the bonds as a decrease in Bond Interest Expense. Note in the calculation below that, in contrast to the amortization of bond discount, which increased interest expense, the bond premium serves to reduce total interest costs below the amount paid to bondholders.

Cash to be paid to bondholders	
Face value at maturity	$100,000
Interest payments ($100,000 × .09 × 5)	45,000
Total cash paid to bondholders	$145,000
Cash received from bondholders	$104,056
Total interest costs	$ 40,944

Amortizing Bond Premium

When bonds are issued at a premium, the amount of the premium must be spread over the life of the bonds to reduce the interest expense.

As discussed earlier in reference to bond discounts, the effective interest method is the more acceptable method of amortizing bond premium. Using the same facts as above, the amortization of the bond premium using the effective interest method is shown in Table 18-2 (next page). This schedule is essentially the same as that shown in Table 18-1. The difference is that interest expense is being reduced by the amortization of the premium. The entry to record the first interest payment would be:

July 1	Bond Interest Expense	4,162	
	Unamortized Bond Premium	338	
	Cash (or Accrued Interest Payable)		4,500
	To record the semiannual interest payment to bondholders and amortize premium on 9%, 5-year bonds		

Note that the interest expense to be recorded each period decreases because the carrying value to which the effective interest rate is applied decreases each period. Also note that the Unamortized Bond Premium decreases to zero and the carrying value decreases to the face value over the life of the bond.

The amount of premium amortization in any one interest payment period may be determined by subtracting the effective interest expense (product of the carrying value and effective interest rate) from the interest payment. For example, in semiannual interest period 5, the amortization of premium equals $395 [($102,622 × .04) – $4,500].

Bond Issue Costs

Obviously there are costs associated with the issuance of bonds. As noted with regard to capital stock in Chapter 16, most bonds are sold through underwriters who receive a fee for taking care of the details of marketing the issue or for accepting the risk of achieving the selling price. Since bond issue costs benefit the entire life of the bond issue, it is logical to spread these costs over that period. Also, since issue costs decrease the amount of money received by the company for the bond issue, they have the effect of increasing a discount or decreasing a premium on the issue. As a result, bond issue costs may be spread over the life of the bonds

Table 18-2 Interest and Amortization of Bond Premium—Effective Interest Method

	A	B	C	D	E	F
Semiannual Interest Period	Carrying Value at Beginning of Period	Semiannual Interest Expense at 8% to Be Recorded* (4% × A)	Semiannual Interest to Be Paid to Bondholders ($4\frac{1}{2}$% × $100,000)	Amortization of Premium (C – B)	Unamortized Bond Premium at End of Period	Carrying Value at End of Period (A – D)
0					$4,056	
1	$104,056	$4,162	$4,500	$338	3,718	$103,718
2	103,718	4,149	4,500	351	3,367	103,367
3	103,367	4,135	4,500	365	3,002	103,002
4	103,002	4,120	4,500	380	2,622	102,622
5	102,622	4,105	4,500	395	2,227	102,227
6	102,227	4,089	4,500	411	1,816	101,816
7	101,816	4,073	4,500	427	1,389	101,389
8	101,389	4,056	4,500	444	945	100,945
9	100,945	4,038	4,500	462	483	100,483
10	100,483	4,017**	4,500	483	—	100,000

*Rounded to nearest dollar.
**Error due to rounding.

through the amortization of discount or premium. For this reason, it is assumed in the text and problems of this book that all bond issues at either a discount or premium are priced at the net of bond issue costs.

Year-End Accrual for Bond Interest Expense

It is unusual for bond interest payment dates to correspond to a company's fiscal year. As a result, an adjustment is necessary at the end of the accounting period to accrue the interest expense on the bonds from the last payment date to the end of the fiscal year. Further, any discount or premium that may exist with the bonds must also be amortized for the fractional period. Consider the previous example, in which Vason Corporation issued $100,000 in bonds on January 1 at 104.056. Assume that the company's fiscal year ends September 30, 19x0. In the period since the interest payment and amortization of premium on July 1, three months' interest has accrued, and the following adjusting entry must be made:

Sept. 30	Bond Interest Expense	2,074.50	
	Unamortized Bond Premium	175.50	
	Accrued Interest Payable		2,250.00
	To accrue interest on 9% bonds payable for three months and amortize one-half of the premium for second interest payment period		

Because this adjusting entry covers one-half of the second interest period, the Unamortized Bond Premium is debited for $175.50, which is one-half of $351, the amortization of premium for the second period from Table 18-2. Accrued Interest Payable is credited for $2,250 or three months' face interest ($\$100,000 \times .09 \times \frac{1}{4}$). The net debit figure of $2,074.50 ($2,250 − $175.50) represents the Bond Interest Expense for the three-month period.

When the January 1, 19x1, payment date arrives, the entry to pay the bondholders and amortize the premium is as follows:

Jan. 1	Bond Interest Expense	2,074.50	
	Accrued Interest Payable	2,250.00	
	Unamortized Bond Premium	175.50	
	Cash		4,500.00
	To record payment of semiannual interest including that previously accrued and to amortize the premium for the period since the end of the fiscal year		

In this entry, one-half ($2,250) of the amount paid ($4,500) was accrued on September 30. The Unamortized Bond Premium is debited for the remaining amount from Table 18-2 to be amortized for the period

($351.00 − $175.50 = $175.50). The resulting Bond Interest Expense is the amount applicable to the three-month period from September 30 to January 1.

Bond discounts are recorded at year end in the same manner as bond premiums. The difference is that the amortization of bond discounts will increase interest expense instead of decreasing it as a premium does.

Retirement of Bonds

Objective 4 Account for the retirement and conversion of bonds

Most bond issues provide for a call feature, which gives the corporation an option to buy back and retire the bonds at a given price, usually above face value, before maturity. These are known as **callable bonds.** This feature gives the corporation flexibility in financing its operations. If bond interest rates decline, the company can call its bonds and reissue debt at a lower interest rate. The bond indenture will indicate the time period and the prices at which the bonds can be redeemed.

As an illustration of the retirement of bonds with a call provision, assume that Vason Corporation may call or retire the $100,000 bond issue (the one issued at a premium) at 105 and that it elects to do so on July 1, 19x3. Because the bonds were issued on January 1, 19x0, the retirement takes place on the seventh interest payment date. Assume that the entry for the interest payment (which must be made) and the amortization of premium has been made. Then the entry to retire the bonds is as follows:

19x3			
July 1	Bonds Payable	100,000	
	Unamortized Bond Premium	1,389	
	Loss on Retirement of Bonds	3,611	
	Cash		105,000
	To record retirement of 9% bonds at 105		

In this entry, the cash paid is the face value times the call price ($100,000 × 1.05 = $105,000). The Unamortized Bond Premium can be found in column D of Table 18-2. The loss on retirement of bonds occurs because the call price of the bonds is greater than the carrying value ($105,000 − $101,389 = $3,611). The loss is considered an extraordinary item for income statement presentation purposes, as explained in Chapter 17.

Conversion of Bonds into Stock

Bonds that may be exchanged for other securities (usually common stock) of the corporation are called **convertible bonds.** These bonds may be exchanged at the option of the bondholder. The conversion feature may be added to make the bonds more attractive to some investors. The convertible bond has a speculative aspect for the investor because if the market price of the common stock rises, the value of the bond rises. However, if the price of the common stock does not increase, the investor still holds the bond and receives the periodic interest payment as well as the principal at the maturity date.

When bonds are converted into common stock, the basic accounting rule is that the common stock is recorded at the carrying value of the bonds, and the bond liability and associated unamortized discount or premium are written off the books. As a result, no gain or loss is recorded on the transaction. For example, assume that instead of the bonds in the previous example being called on July 1, 19x3, Vason Corporation's stockholders elect to convert all the bonds to $8 par value common stock under a convertible provision of 40 shares of common stock for each $1,000 bond. The resulting entry would be:

19x3			
July 1	Bonds Payable	100,000	
	Unamortized Bond Premium	1,389	
	Common Stock		32,000
	Paid-in Capital in Excess of Par Value		69,389
	To record conversion of 9% bonds payable into common stock at a rate of 40 shares for each $1,000 bond		

The Unamortized Bond Discount is again obtained from Table 18-2. At a rate of 40 shares for each $1,000 bond, 4,000 shares will be issued at a total par value of $32,000 (4,000 × $8). Paid-in Capital in Excess of Par is credited for the difference between the carrying value of the bonds and the par value of the stocks issued ($101,389 − $32,000 = $69,389).

Bond Sinking Fund

Objective 5 Compute sinking fund requirements, and prepare accounting entries associated with sinking fund bonds payable

Many bond issues require that funds be set aside over the life of the issue. This is done to satisfy investors that money will be available to pay the bondholders at maturity. The segregation of assets is called a **bond sinking fund.** The bond indenture will usually specify that the corporation will make periodic deposits over the life of the bonds. The trustee has control of the fund, and is charged with investing the deposits in income-producing securities. It is intended that the deposits plus the earnings on the investment be sufficient to pay the bonds at maturity. Because the assets in the sinking fund cannot be used by the corporation for current operations, the sinking fund is classified as a long-term investment on the balance sheet.

Table 18-3 Growth of Annual Investments in Sinking Fund

	A	B	C	D
End of Year	Fund Balance at Beginning of Year	Deposit	Interest at 8% (8% × A)	Fund Balance at End of Year (A + B + C)
1	$ —	$17,045.64	$ —	$17,045.64
2	17,045.64	17,045.64	1,363.65	35,454.93
3	35,454.93	17,045.64	2,836.39	55,336.96
4	55,336.96	17,045.64	4,426.96	76,809.56
5	76,809.56	17,045.64	6,144.76	99,999.96*

*Off $.04 due to rounding.

When a corporation establishes a sinking fund, it must determine how much cash will be segregated each period to pay the bonds. The amount will depend on the estimated rate of return the investments can earn. As an illustration of the accounting for a bond sinking fund, assume that the Vason Corporation agrees with a trustee to segregate sufficient cash at the end of each year of its bond issue to pay the $100,000 of 9 percent bonds at maturity. The trustee will be able to earn an 8 percent return on the investment of the cash deposited by the company. In order to pay the bonds in five years, the company must deposit $17,045.64 at the end of each year.[3] The investments will grow to a point where the sinking fund is equal to the principal at the maturity date, as shown in Table 18-3.

The entry to record the creation of the sinking fund and the annual deposit would be as follows:

Dec. 31	Bond Sinking Fund	17,045.64	
	Cash		17,045.64
	To record the annual deposit to the bond sinking fund		

Every year the sinking fund trustee invests these funds to obtain the best return possible. The trustee collects interest and dividends and reports them to the corporation. As an illustration, assume that the cash segregated by the Vason Corporation earned the necessary $1,363.65 the second year. The earnings would be recorded as shown in the following entry:

Dec. 31	Bond Sinking Fund	1,363.65	
	Income from Bond Sinking Fund		1,363.65
	To record income from investment in the bond sinking fund		

3. The calculation of this figure using time value of money tables can be found in Appendix A.

The earnings of the sinking fund would appear on the income statement as Other Revenue.

If investments in the sinking fund are sold and result in a gain or loss, the transaction should be recognized by increasing or decreasing the bond sinking fund. For example, if the sale of an investment results in a $1,000 loss, the entry will be:

May 21	Loss on Sale of Sinking Fund Investment	1,000	
	Bond Sinking Fund		1,000
	To record loss on investment in bond sinking fund		

When the bonds mature, the trustee must sell the investments to obtain the cash to pay the bondholders. The actual cash realized is not likely to equal exactly the amount necessary to pay the bondholders because of fluctuations in the amount earned in the fund over the years. When excess cash is available, it should be transferred to Cash. If there is less cash than necessary to retire the bonds, the corporation must provide additional cash. For example, assume that at the bond maturity date the sinking fund contained a total of $999,600. The entry to pay the bonds follows:

Dec. 31	Bonds Payable	1,000,000	
	Bond Sinking Fund		999,600
	Cash		400
	To record the payment of bonds at maturity		

Other Long-Term Liabilities

A company may have long-term liabilities other than notes and bonds. Two of the most common other long-term liabilities are mortgages payable and long-term leases.

Mortgages Payable

Objective 6 Explain the basic features of mortgages payable and long-term leases as long-term liabilities

A **mortgage** is a type of long-term debt secured by real property that is paid in equal monthly installments. Each monthly payment represents partly interest on the debt and partly a reduction in the debt. To illustrate this characteristic, consider Table 18-4 (top of the next page), which shows the first three monthly payments on a $50,000, 12 percent mortgage obtained on June 1 and on which the monthly payments are $800. According to the table, the entry to record the July 1 payment would be as shown on the next page.

Table 18-4 Monthly Payment Schedule on $50,000, 12 Percent Mortgage

	A	B	C	D	E
Payment Date	Unpaid Balance at Beginning of Period	Monthly Payment	Interest for 1 Month at 1% on Unpaid Balance* (1% × A)	Reduction in Debt (B − C)	Unpaid Balance at End of Period (A − D)
June 1					$50,000
July 1	$50,000	$800	$500	$300	49,700
Aug. 1	49,700	800	497	303	49,397
Sept. 1	49,397	800	494	306	49,091

*Rounded to nearest dollar.

July 1	Mortgage Payable	300	
	Mortgage Interest Expense	500	
	Cash		800
	To record monthly payment on mortgage		

Note from the entry and from Table 18-4 that the July 1 payment represents interest expense of $500 ($50,000 × .12 × $\frac{1}{12}$) and a reduction in the debt of $300 ($800 − $500). Because the unpaid balance is reduced by the $300 to $49,700 in July, the interest expense for August is slightly less than it was for July.

Long-Term Leases

Among the ways a company may obtain new operating assets are to borrow the money and purchase the asset, rent the equipment on a short-term lease, or lease the equipment on a long-term lease. The first two methods cause no unusual accounting problems. In the first case, the asset and liability are recorded at the amount paid, and the asset is subject to periodic depreciation. In the second case, the lease, which is short-term or cancelable, is called an **operating lease** because the risks of ownership lie with the lessor. It is proper accounting to treat operating lease payments as an expense and to debit the amount of each monthly payment to Rent Expense.

The third alternative, a long-term lease, is among the fastest-growing ways of financing operating equipment in the U.S. economy. Among its advantages are that it requires no immediate cash payment, the rental payment is deducted in full for tax purposes, and it costs less than a short-term lease. Acquiring the use of a plant asset under a long-term lease does cause some accounting problems, however. Such leases are often noncancelable; they have a length that approximates the useful life of the assets; and they provide for the lessor to purchase the asset at a nominal price at the end of the lease. The lease is, in effect, an installment purchase because the risks of ownership lie with the lessee. The lessee company's available assets have increased and its legal obligations (liabilities) have increased, because it must make a series of payments over the life of the asset. As a result, this "off-the-balance-sheet financing" results in a balance sheet that omits a material asset and a material liability.

Recognizing this problem, the Financial Accounting Standards Board has identified a long-term lease such as the one above as a **capital lease,** in which the terms of the lease make the transaction in essence a purchase/sale on installment. The FASB requires that when a capital lease exists, the lessee must record an asset and a long-term liability equal to the present value at the beginning of the lease of the total lease payments during the lease term.[4] In a manner similar to mortgage payments above, each lease payment becomes partly interest expense and partly a repayment of debt.[5] Further, depreciation expense is calculated on the asset and entered in the records.

Accounting for Bond Investments

Objective 7 Account for bond investment transactions by a corporation

So far, this chapter has discussed bond transactions and disclosures from the issuing corporation's viewpoint. This section of the chapter will examine similar transactions but from the investor's viewpoint. Sometimes a company purchases a bond as a temporary investment to provide a return on idle cash until it is needed for operations. However, a company may purchase a bond as a long-term investment for a variety of reasons. For example, it may hold the bonds of a subsidiary or other company on a long-term basis. The company may invest funds that it is accumulating over a long period of time for a major expenditure such as the purchase of another company or the building of a factory. The classification and valuation problems related to temporary and long-term investments are discussed in Chapters 9 and 20, respectively. Here, we focus on transactions involving purchase of the bonds, amortization of premium and discount and recording receipts for interest, and sale of the bonds. In each case, there are slight differences in the accounting treatments for the same transactions by the issuer.

Purchase of Bonds Between Interest Dates

The purchase price of bonds includes the price of the bonds plus the broker's commission. In addition, when the bonds are purchased between interest dates, the purchaser must pay the interest that has accrued on the

4. "Accounting for Leases," *Statement of Financial Accounting Standards No. 13* (Stamford, Conn.: Financial Accounting Standards Board, 1976), par. 10.
5. A similar example of the calculation of present value using time value of money tables and for recording of capital lease transactions can be found in Appendix A.

bonds since the last interest payment date. On the next payment date, the purchaser will receive a payment for the interest for the entire period. The payment for accrued interest should be recorded in an account called Accrued Interest Receivable.

Assume that on May 1 Vason Corporation purchases twenty $1,000 MGR Corporation bonds that carry a face interest rate of $8\frac{7}{10}$ percent at 88 plus a broker's commission of $400 and accrued interest. The interest payment dates are January 1 and July 1. The following entry records this purchase transaction:

May 1	Investment in Bonds	18,000	
	Accrued Interest Receivable	580	
	Cash		18,580
	To record purchase of MGR Corporation bonds at 88 plus $400 commission and accrued interest $\$20{,}000 \times 8\frac{7}{10}\% \times \frac{1}{3} = \$580$		

Note that the purchase is recorded at cost, as are all purchases of assets. The debit to Investment in Bonds of $18,000 equals the purchase price of $17,600 ($20,000 × .88) plus the commission of $400. Because, in managing its investments, Vason Corporation will buy and sell as seems necessary and will not likely hold the bonds until maturity, the $20,000 face value of the bonds is not entered in the records. This is a very different situation from that of the issuing corporation, which must repay the bonds at maturity date to whoever holds them.

The debit to Accrued Interest Receivable represents four months' interest from January 1 to May 1.

Amortization of Premium or Discount

Accounting Principles Board *Opinion No. 21* requires companies making long-term investments in bonds to amortize the difference between the cost of the investment and its maturity value over the life of the bond. The effective interest method, which results in a constant rate of return over the life of the investment, should be used.[6]

Because the investing company does not use separate accounts for the face value and any related discount or premium, the entry to amortize the premium or discount is made directly to the investment account. The amortization of a premium requires a credit to the investment account to reduce the carrying value gradually to face value. The amortization of a discount requires a debit to the investment account to increase the carrying value gradually to face value.

To continue the example of Vason Corporation's purchase of bonds at a

6. Accounting Principles Board, *Opinion No. 21,* "Interest on Receivables and Payables" (New York: American Institute of Certified Public Accountants, 1971), par. 15.

discount, we assume that the effective interest rate is $10\frac{1}{2}$ percent. Remember that the amount of amortization of a premium or discount is the difference between (1) the face interest rate times the face value and (2) the effective interest rate times the carrying value. On July 1, the first interest date after the purchase, two months will have passed. The amount of discount to be amortized is as follows:

Two months' effective interest:	
$18,000 × $10\frac{1}{2}$% × $\frac{1}{6}$	$315
Two months' face interest:	
$20,000 × $8\frac{7}{10}$% × $\frac{1}{6}$	290
Discount to be amortized	$ 25

The entry to record the receipt of an interest check on July 1 is:

July 1	Cash	870	
	Investment in Bonds	25	
	Interest Earned		315
	Accrued Interest Receivable		580
	To record semiannual interest receipt, some of which was previously accrued, and to amortize discount		

In this entry, Cash is debited for the semiannual interest payment (\$20,000 × $8\frac{7}{10}$% × $\frac{1}{2}$ = \$870), Investment in Bonds is debited for the amortization of discount, and Accrued Interest Receivable is credited for the amount previously paid to the seller on May 1. Note that the Interest Earned of $315 is equal to the effective interest computed in the paragraph immediately preceding.

To continue the example, assume that Vason Corporation's fiscal year corresponds to the calendar year. Although the interest payment will not be received until January, it is necessary to accrue the interest and amortize the discount for the last six months since July 1 in accordance with the matching concept. The entry to record the accrual of interest on December 31 would be as follows:

Dec. 31	Accrued Interest Receivable	870.00	
	Investment in Bonds	76.31	
	Interest Earned		946.31
	To accrue interest earned and amortize discount on bond investment		

The period covered by this entry is six months. Therefore, the amounts to be debited and credited are as shown on the next page.

Six months' effective interest:	
$18,025 × $10\frac{1}{2}$% × $\frac{1}{2}$	$946.31
Six months' face interest:	
$20,000 × $8\frac{7}{10}$% × $\frac{1}{2}$	870.00
Discount to be amortized	$ 76.31

Note that the effective interest rate is applied to the new carrying value of $18,025 after the July 1 entry. The next time that effective interest is calculated, the effective rate would apply to $18,101.31 ($18,025 + $76.31).

Similar calculations are made when a company purchases bonds at premium. The difference is that Investment in Bonds is credited to reduce the carrying value. As a result, interest earned is less than the face interest.

The entry on January 1 to record receipt of the interest payment check would be as follows:

Jan. 1	Cash	870	
	Accrued Interest Receivable		870
	To record receipt of interest on bonds		

Sale of Bonds

The sale of a bond investment is recorded by debiting Cash for the amount received and crediting Investment in Bonds for the carrying value of the investment. Any difference in the proceeds from the sales and the carrying value of the bonds is debited or credited to loss or gain on sale of investments. If the sale is made between interest payment dates, the seller is entitled to the accrued interest from the last interest date, just as the company had to pay the accrued interest when the bonds were purchased. If we assume that Vason Corporation sells the bonds in our continuing example at 94 less commission of $400 on March 1, two entries are required. The first entry is necessary to amortize the discount for two months:

Mar. 1	Investment in Bonds	26.77	
	Interest Earned		26.77
	To amortize 2 months' bond interest		
	Effective interest:		
	$18,101.31 × $10\frac{1}{2}$% × $\frac{1}{6}$ = 316.77		
	Face interest:		
	$20,000 × $8\frac{7}{10}$% × $\frac{1}{6}$ = 290.00		
	Discount to be amortized $26.77		

The second entry is to record the sale:

Mar. 1	Cash	18,690.00	
	Gain on Sale of Investments		271.92
	Investment in Bonds		18,128.08
	Interest Earned		290.00
	To record sale of bonds at 94 less $400 commission plus accrued interest		

The cash received is the selling price of $18,800 ($20,000 × .94) less commission of $400 plus the accrued interest for two months of $290 ($20,000 × $8\frac{7}{10}$% × $\frac{1}{6}$). The gain on sale of investments is the difference between selling price less commission ($18,400) and the carrying value of $18,128.08. The carrying value represents the assigned purchase plus all amortization of discounts:

May 1 purchase	$18,000.00
July 1 amortization	25.00
Dec. 31 amortization	76.31
Mar. 1 amortization	26.77
Carrying value of bond investment	$18,128.08

Chapter Review

Review of Learning Objectives

1. Identify and contrast the major characteristics of bonds.

When bonds are issued, the corporation enters into a contract with the bondholders, called a bond indenture. The bond indenture identifies the major conditions of the bonds. A corporation may issue several types of bonds, each having different characteristics. For example, a bond issue may require security or be unsecured. It may be payable at a single time (term) or at several times (serial). Also, it may be registered in the name of the holder, or the holder may be unidentified and have to return coupons to receive interest payable.

2. Record the issuance of bonds at face value, between interest dates, and at a discount or premium.

When bonds are issued, the bondholder will pay an amount equal to, greater than, or less than the face value of the bond. A bondholder will pay face value for the bonds when the interest rate on the bonds approximates the market rate for similar investments. The issuing corporation records the issuance of bonds as a long-term liability called Bonds Payable equal to the face value of the bonds.

If the bonds are sold on dates between the interest payment dates, the issuing corporation collects from the investor the interest that has accrued since the last interest payment date. When the next interest payment date arrives, the corporation pays the bondholder interest for the entire interest period.

Bonds are purchased at a rate less than the face value of the bonds when the bond interest rate is below the market rate for similar investments. The difference between face value and issue price is called a discount and is debited to Unamortized Bond Discount.

If the interest rate on bonds is greater than the return on similar investments, investors will be willing to pay more than face value for the bonds. The difference between the issue price and face value is called a premium and is credited to Unamortized Bond Premium.

3. Amortize bond discount and premium by using the effective interest method, and make year-end adjustments.

When bonds are sold at a premium or discount, the result is an adjustment of the interest rate on the bonds from the face rate to an effective rate that approximates the market rate when the bonds were issued. Therefore, bond premiums or discounts have the effect of increasing or decreasing the interest paid on the bonds over their life. Under these conditions, it is necessary to amortize the premium or discount over the life of the bonds in a manner that will adjust the interest expense from the stated interest to the effective interest. The effective interest method is the accepted method for amortizing bond discount or premium.

The effective interest method results in a constant rate of interest on the carrying value of the bonds. The determination of interest and the amortization of premiums or discounts require the application of the effective interest rate to the carrying value (face value plus premium or minus discount) of the bonds at the beginning of the interest period. The amount of premium or discount to be amortized is the difference between the interest computed by using the effective rate and that obtained by using the stated rate.

When the end of a corporation's fiscal year does not agree with interest payment dates, the corporation must accrue bond interest expense from the last interest payment date to the end of the company's fiscal year. This results in the inclusion of the interest expense in the year incurred.

4. Account for the retirement and conversion of bonds.

Callable bonds may be retired before maturity at the option of the issuing corporation. The call price is usually an amount greater than the face value of the bonds, and the corporation must usually recognize a loss on the retirement of the bonds.

Convertible bonds have a feature that allows the bondholder to convert the bond to stock of the issuing corporation. In this case, the common stock being issued is recorded at the carrying value of the bonds being converted, and no gain or loss is recognized.

5. Compute sinking fund requirements, and prepare accounting entries associated with sinking fund bonds payable.

Some bond issues require the issuing corporation to segregate assets of the company over the life of the bonds so cash will be available to pay the bonds at maturity. The segregated assets are called a bond sinking fund. The corporation deposits cash in the fund over the life of the bonds. The deposits plus earnings on the deposits are planned so they will be sufficient to pay the face value of the bonds at maturity.

6. Explain the basic features of mortgages payable and long-term leases as long-term liabilities.

A mortgage is a type of long-term debt secured by real property that is paid in equal monthly installments, each of which consists partly of interest expense and partly of debt repayment. When a long-term lease is a capital lease, in which the risks of ownership lie with the lessee, an asset and a long-term liability equal to the present value at the beginning of the lease of the total lease payment during the lease term should be recorded. Like a mortgage payment, each lease payment is partly interest and partly reduction of debt. The recorded asset is subject to depreciation.

7. Account for bond investment transactions by a corporation.

When a company invests in bonds, the bonds are recorded at cost, and no separate premium or discount is recorded. If the investment is long-term, the difference between the cost and face value of the investment is amortized, using the effective interest method.

Review Problem

Before doing the exercises and problems, review the examples of interest and amortization of bond discount and premium, bond retirement, and bond conversion given in the chapter. For additional help, see the review problem in the working papers.

Chapter Assignments

Questions

1. What is the difference between a bond certificate, a bond issue, and a bond indenture?
2. What is the essential difference between the bonds in the case of (a) secured versus debenture bonds, (b) term versus serial bonds, and (c) registered versus coupon bonds?
3. Napier Corporation sold $500,000 of 5 percent bonds on the interest payment date. What would the proceeds from the sale be if the bonds were issued at 95, at 100, at 102?
4. If you were buying a bond on which the face interest rate was less than the market interest rate, would you expect to pay more or less than par value for the bonds? Why?
5. Why does the amortization of a bond discount increase interest expense to an amount above the amount of interest paid? Why does a premium have the opposite effect?
6. When bonds are issued between interest dates, why is it necessary for the issuer to collect an amount equal to accrued interest from the buyer?
7. When the effective interest rate method of amortizing bond discount or premium is used, why does the amount of interest expense change from period to period?
8. Why would a company want to exercise the callable provision of a bond when it can wait longer to pay off the debt?
9. What are the advantages of convertible bonds to the company and to the investor?
10. The long-term investment section of the DeLoach Corporation balance sheet contains an account called Bond Sinking Fund. What is the purpose of this account?
11. What are the two components of a uniform monthly mortgage payment?
12. Under what conditions is a long-term lease called a capital lease? Why would such a lease result in recording both an asset and a liability?
13. Why does the buying company record a bond investment at cost when the issuing company will record the same bond issue at face value and provide a separate account for any discount or premium?

Classroom Exercises

Exercise 18-1 Bond Issue Entries—Issuer and Investor

Turnco is authorized to issue $300,000 in bonds on June 1. The bonds carry a face interest rate of 9 percent, which is to be paid on June 1 and December 1.

1. Prepare journal entries for the issue of the bonds by Turnco under the assumption that (a) the bonds are issued on September 1 at 100, and (b) the bonds are issued on June 1 at 105.
2. Prepare journal entries for the purchase of the bonds by the investor under the assumption that (a) the bonds are issued on September 1 at 100, and (b) the bonds are issued on June 1 at 105.

Exercise 18-2 Journal Entries for Interest Payments

The long-term debt section of the Wong Corporation's balance sheet at the end of its fiscal year, December 31, 1981, is shown below:

Long-Term Liabilities		
Bonds Payable—8%, interest payable 1/1 and 7/1, due 12/31/96	$500,000	
Unamortized Bond Discount	(40,000)	$460,000

Prepare the journal entries relevant to the interest payments on July 1, 1982; December 31, 1982; and January 1, 1983, assuming an effective interest rate of 10 percent.

Exercise 18-3 Sale of Bonds and Interest Payments

The Steam Carpet Company sold $200,000 of its $9\frac{1}{2}$ percent, twenty-year bonds on April 1, 19xx, at 106. The semiannual interest payment dates are April 1 and October 1. The effective interest rate is approximately $8\frac{9}{10}$ percent. The company's fiscal year ends September 30.

Prepare journal entries to record the sale of these bonds on April 1, the accrual of interest and amortization of premium on September 30, and the first interest payment on October 1, using the effective interest method to amortize the premium.

Exercise 18-4 Bond Conversion Journal Entry

The Ellis Corporation has $500,000 of 6 percent convertible bonds outstanding. There is $20,000 of unamortized discount associated with these bonds. The bonds are convertible at the rate of forty shares of $5 par value common stock for each $1,000 bond. On July 1, an interest payment date, bondholders presented $300,000 of the bonds for conversion.

Prepare the journal entry to record the conversion of the bonds.

Exercise 18-5 Bond Retirement Journal Entry

The No-Glo Corporation has outstanding $700,000 of 8 percent bonds callable at 104. On September 1, a semiannual interest payment date, the unamortized bond discount equaled $21,000. On that date, $400,000 of the bonds were called and retired.

Prepare the entry to record the retirement of the bonds on September 1.

Exercise 18-6 Journal Entries for Interest and Amortization of Discount

On March 1, 19x1, the Mojo Corporation issued $600,000 of five-year, 10 percent bonds. The semiannual interest payment dates are March 1 and September 1. Because the market rate of similar investments was 11 percent, the bonds had to be issued at a discount. The discount on the issuance of the bonds was $24,335.

Prepare the journal entries to record the bond issue on March 1, 19x1, and the payments of interest and amortization of the discount on September 1, 19x1 and March 1, 19x2, using the effective interest method. (Ignore year-end accruals.)

Exercise 18-7 Mortgage Payable

Forest Corporation purchased a building by signing a long-term $150,000 mortgage with monthly payments of $2,000. The mortgage carries an interest rate of 12 percent.

1. For the first three months, prepare a monthly payment schedule showing the monthly payment, the interest for the month, the reduction in debt, and the unpaid balance.
2. Prepare a journal entry to record the purchase and the first two monthly payments.

Exercise 18-8 Bond Investment Transactions

On December 1, Barboat Corporation purchased one hundred $1,000 bonds for $1,050,000 plus accrued interest as a long-term investment. The bonds carried a face interest rate of $10\frac{1}{5}$ percent that is paid semiannually on July 1 and January 1.

Prepare journal entries to record the purchase on December 1 and the receipt of the interest check and amortization of premium on January 1, assuming an effective interest rate of $9\frac{1}{2}$ percent.

Problem Set A

Problem 18A-1 Bond Transactions

Kimmark Corporation has $10,000,000 of $10\frac{1}{2}$ percent, twenty-year bonds dated June 1, with interest payment dates of May 30 and November 30. The company's fiscal year ends December 31, and it uses the effective interest method to amortize premium or discount.

Required

1. Prepare general journal entries for August 1, November 30, and December 31, assuming that the bonds are issued at face value plus accrued interest on August 1.
2. Prepare general journal entries for June 1, November 30, and December 31, assuming that the bonds were issued at 103 on June 1, to yield an effective interest rate of $10\frac{1}{10}$ percent.
3. Prepare general journal entries for June 1, November 30, and December 31, assuming that the bonds were issued at 97 on June 1, to yield an effective interest rate of $10\frac{9}{10}$ percent.

Problem 18A-2 Bonds Issued at Discount and Premium

Drebs Corporation found it necessary to raise capital by issuing bonds twice during 19x1. The following transactions describe this financing activity:

19x1	
Jan. 1	Issued $1,000,000 of its own $9\frac{1}{5}$ percent, 10-year bonds dated January 1, 19x1, with interest payable on June 30 and December 31. The bonds were sold at $98\frac{1}{10}$, a price that results in an effective interest rate of $9\frac{1}{2}$ percent.
Apr. 1	Issued $1,000,000 of its own $9\frac{4}{5}$ percent, 10-year bonds dated April 1, 19x1, with interest payable on March 31 and September 30. The bonds were sold at 102, a price that results in an effective interest rate of $9\frac{1}{2}$ percent.
June 30	Paid the semiannual interest on the January 1 issue and amortized the discount, using the effective interest rate method.

Sept. 30 Paid the semiannual interest on the April 1 issue and amortized the premium, using the effective interest rate method.
Dec. 31 Paid the semiannual interest on the January 1 issue and amortized the discount, using the effective interest rate method.
31 Made an adjusting entry to accrue the interest on the April 1 issue and amortize one-half of the premium applicable to the second interest period.

19x2
Mar. 31 Paid the semiannual interest on the April 1 issue and amortized the premium applicable to the second half of the second interest period.

Required

Prepare general journal entries to record the bond transactions.

Problem 18A-3 Bond and Mortgage Transactions Contrasted

Vincent Manufacturing Company is expanding its operations by building and equipping a new plant. It is financing the building and land by issuing a $5,000,000, thirty-year mortgage bond that carries an interest rate of 12 percent and requires monthly payments of $59,000. The company is financing the equipment and working capital for the new plant by issuing $5,000,000, twenty-year bonds that carry a face interest rate of 11 percent, payable semiannually on March 31 and September 30. Transactions during 19x1 and 19x2 related to these two financing issues are as follows:

19x1
Jan. 1 Issued mortgage bonds in exchange for land and building. Land represents 10 percent of total price.
Feb. 1 Made first mortgage payment.
Mar. 1 Made second mortgage payment.
31 Issued bonds for cash at 96, a price that results in an effective interest rate of $11\frac{1}{2}$ percent.
Apr. 1 Made third mortgage payment.
May 1 Made fourth mortgage payment.
June 1 Made fifth mortgage payment.
30 Made year-end adjusting entry to accrue interest on bonds and amortize the discount, using the effective interest method.
July 1 Made sixth mortgage payment.
Aug. 1 Made seventh mortgage payment.
Sept. 1 Made eighth mortgage payment.
30 Made first interest payment on bonds and amortized the discount for the time period since the end of the fiscal year.
Oct. 1 Made ninth mortgage payment.
Nov. 1 Made tenth mortgage payment.

19x2
Mar. 31 Made second interest payment on bonds and amortized the discount for the time period since the last interest payment.

Required

1. Prepare a monthly payment schedule for the mortgage bonds for ten months with the following headings (round amounts to nearest dollar): Payment Date, Unpaid Balance at Beginning of Period, Monthly Payment, Interest for 1 Month at 1% on Unpaid Balance, Reduction in Debt, and Unpaid Balance at End of Period.

2. Prepare the journal entry for each transaction. (Ignore the mortgage payments between December 1, 19x1, and March 1, 19x2.)

Problem 18A-4 Bond Investment Transactions

Draco Corporation follows the practice of purchasing bonds as long-term investments. Draco's long-term bond investment transactions for 19x1 and 19x2 are described below:

19x1

Jan. 1 Purchased on the semiannual interest payment date $200,000 of MGC Company 10 percent bonds at 91, a price that yields an effective interest rate of 12 percent.

Apr. 1 Purchased $100,000 of Metz Corporation 12 percent, twenty-year bonds dated March 1 at face value plus accrued interest.

July 1 Received a check from MGC Company for the semiannual interest and amortized the discount, using the effective interest method.

Sept. 1 Received a check from Metz for the semiannual interest.

Dec. 31 Made a year-end adjusting entry to accrue the interest on the MGC and Metz bonds and to amortize the discount on the MGC bonds, using the effective interest method.

19x2

Jan. 1 Received a check from MGC for the semiannual interest.

Feb. 1 Purchased on the semiannual interest payment date $300,000 of $11\frac{1}{5}$ percent bonds from Xton Corporation at $102\frac{3}{10}$, a price that yields an effective interest rate of $10\frac{9}{10}$ percent.

Mar. 1 Received a check from Metz Corporation for the semiannual interest.

July 1 Received a check from MGC for the semiannual interest and amortized the discount, using the effective interest method.

1 Sold one-half of the MGC bonds at 96.

Aug. 1 Received a check for the semiannual interest from Xton and amortized the premium, using the effective interest method.

Sept. 1 Received a check from Metz for the semiannual interest.

Nov. 1 Sold the Metz bonds at 98 plus the accrued interest.

Dec. 31 Made a year-end adjusting entry to accrue the interest on the remaining MGC and Xton bonds and to amortize the discount and premium, using the effective interest method.

Required

Prepare general journal entries to record the transactions.

Problem 18A-5 Bond Retirements and Conversions

Psi Corporation is authorized to issue $10,000,000 of six-year unsecured convertible bonds. The bonds carry a face interest rate of 9 percent, payable semiannually on June 30 and December 31. Each $1,000 bond is convertible into forty shares of $10 par value common stock. The bonds are callable at 105 any time after June 31, 19x4.

All the bonds are issued on July 1, 19x1, at 95.568, a price that yields effective interest of 10 percent.

On July 1, 19x4, when the common stock was selling for $30 per share, one-half of the bonds outstanding were converted into common stocks.

On January 1, 19x5, the remaining one-half of the bonds were called by the company and retired.

Required

1. Prepare a table similar to Table 18-1 to show the interest and amortization of bond discount for twelve interest payment periods, using the effective interest method (round results to nearest dollar).
2. Prepare general journal entries for the bond issue, interest payments and amortization of bond discounts, bond conversion, and bond retirement on the following dates: July 1, 19x1; December 31, 19x1; June 30, 19x4; July 1, 19x4; December 31, 19x4; and January 1, 19x5.

Problem 18A-6 Bond Issue with a Bond Sinking Fund

Wall Company, Inc., is authorized to issue $10,000,000 of $9\frac{3}{5}$ percent, ten-year sinking fund bonds on January 1, 19x0. Semiannual interest is payable on December 31 and June 30. The company is required to deposit $658,200 with a trustee at the end of each year for the life of the bond issue. It is assumed that the sinking fund investment will earn a return of 9 percent annually. Selected transactions involving this bond issue and its sinking fund are listed below:

19x0
Jan. 1 Sold the entire issue at $97\frac{1}{2}$, a price that yields the buyer a 10 percent annual return.
June 30 Made the first semiannual interest payment and amortized the discount.
Dec. 31 Made the second semiannual interest payment and amortized the discount.
31 Made the first annual sinking fund deposit.

19x1
June 30 Made the third semiannual interest payment and amortized the discount.
Dec. 31 Made the fourth semiannual interest payment and amortized the discount.
31 Made the second annual sinking fund deposit.
31 Received a report from sinking fund trustee indicating that interest earned on the sinking fund was $59,238 for 19x1.

19x9
June 30 Made the nineteenth semiannual interest payment and amortized the discount. (The carrying value of the bond payable on January 1 was $9,962,812.)
Dec. 31 Made the twentieth semiannual interest payment and amortized the discount.
31 Made the final sinking fund deposit.
31 Received a report from the sinking fund trustee indicating that the interest earned on the sinking fund in 19x9 was $774,500.
31 Received from the trustee another report indicating that the bonds had been paid in full and a check for $7,300 representing the amount by which the final sinking fund balance exceeded the bonds payable.

Required

1. Prepare a table showing the growth of annual investments in the sinking fund (round amounts to nearest dollar). The table should have the following headings: End of Year, Fund Balance at Beginning of Year, Deposit, Interest at 9%, and Fund Balance at End of Year.
2. Prepare general journal entries for the above transactions (round amounts to nearest dollar).

Problem Set B

Problem 18B-1 Bond Transactions

Sundant Corporation has $5,000,000 of $9\frac{1}{2}$ percent, twenty-five-year bonds dated March 1, with interest payable on March 1 and September 1. The company's fiscal year ends on November 30, and it uses the effective interest method to amortize premium or discount.

Required

1. Prepare general journal entries for June 1, September 1, and November 30, assuming that the bonds were issued on June 1 at face value plus accrued interest.
2. Prepare general journal entries for March 1, September 1, and November 30, assuming that the bonds were issued at 102.5 on March 1, to yield an effective interest rate of $9\frac{1}{5}$ percent.
3. Prepare general journal entries for March 1, September 1, and November 30, assuming that the bonds were issued at $97\frac{1}{2}$ on March 1, to yield an effective interest rate of $9\frac{4}{5}$ percent.

Problem 18B-2 Bonds Issued at Discount and Premium

Dreyfus Corporation sold bonds twice during 19x2. A summary of the transactions involving these bonds is presented below.

19x2
Jan. 1 Issued $2,000,000 of its own $9\frac{9}{10}$ percent, ten-year bonds dated January 1, 19x2, with interest payable on December 31 and June 30. The bonds were sold at $102\frac{3}{5}$, a price that results in an effective interest rate of $9\frac{2}{5}$ percent.
Mar. 1 Issued $1,000,000 of its own $9\frac{1}{5}$ percent, ten-year bonds dated March 1, 19x2, with interest payable March 1 and September 1. The bonds were sold at $98\frac{1}{5}$, a price that results in an effective interest rate of $9\frac{1}{2}$ percent.
June 30 Paid the semiannual interest on the January 1 issue and amortized the premium, using the effective interest rate method.
Sept. 1 Paid the semiannual interest on the March 1 issue and amortized the discount, using the effective interest rate method.
Dec. 31 Paid the semiannual interest on the January 1 issue and amortized the premium, using the effective interest rate method.
31 Made an end-of-year adjusting entry to accrue the interest on the March 1 issue and amortize two-thirds of the discount applicable to the second interest period.

19x3
Mar. 1 Paid the semiannual interest on the March 1 issue and amortized the remainder of the discount applicable to the second interest period.

Required

Prepare the general journal entries to record the bond transactions.

Problem 18B-3 Bond and Mortgage Transactions Contrasted

Gomez Grocery Stores, Inc., is expanding its operations by buying a chain of four outlets in another city. To finance this purchase of land and buildings, Gomez is issuing $2,000,000 of mortgage bonds that carry an interest rate of 12 percent and require monthly payments of $27,000. To finance the rest of the purchase, Gomez is issuing $2,000,000 of $12\frac{1}{2}$ percent unsecured bonds due in twenty years, with interest payable December 31 and June 30. Transactions relating to these two financing activities are listed on the next page.

Jan. 1 Issued the bonds for cash at 104 to yield an effective rate of 12 percent.
Feb. 1 Issued the mortgage bonds in exchange for land and buildings. The land represents 15 percent of the purchase price.
Mar. 1 Made the first mortgage payment.
31 Made year-end adjusting entry to accrue interest on the bonds and amortize the premium, using the effective interest method.
Apr. 1 Made the second mortgage payment.
May 1 Made the third mortgage payment.
June 1 Made the fourth mortgage payment.
30 Made the first semiannual interest payment on the bonds and amortized the premium for the time period since the end of the fiscal year.
July 1 Made the fifth mortgage payment.
Aug. 1 Made the sixth mortgage payment.
Sept. 1 Made the seventh mortgage payment.
Oct. 1 Made the eighth mortgage payment.
Nov. 1 Made the ninth mortgage payment.
Dec. 1 Made the tenth mortgage payment.
31 Made the second semiannual interest payment on the bonds and amortized the premium for the time period since the last payment.

Required

1. Prepare a monthly payment schedule for the mortgage bonds for ten months with the following headings (round amounts to nearest dollar): Payment Date, Unpaid Balance at Beginning of Period, Monthly Payment, Interest for 1 Month at 1% on Unpaid Balance, Reduction in Debt, and Unpaid Balance at End of Period.
2. Prepare the journal entry for each transaction.

Problem 18B-4 Bond Investment Transactions

The transactions involving long-term bond investments made by Dobler Corporation are described below:

19x1
July 1 Purchased $500,000 of DeLoach Corporation $8\frac{1}{5}$ percent bonds at 88, a price that yields an effective interest rate of $10\frac{7}{10}$ percent. These bonds have semiannual interest payment dates of June 30 and December 31.
Nov. 1 Purchased $300,000 of Kessler Company's $9\frac{4}{5}$ percent bonds, dated August 1, at face value plus accrued interest.
Dec. 31 Received a check from DeLoach for semiannual interest and amortized the discount, using the effective interest method.
31 Made a year-end adjusting entry to accrue the interest on the Kessler bonds.

19x2
Feb. 1 Received a check from Kessler for the semiannual interest.
Apr. 1 Purchased $400,000 of Howell Corporation $12\frac{1}{2}$ percent bonds at 104, a price that yields an effective interest rate of $11\frac{3}{5}$ percent. These bonds pay interest on March 31 and September 30.
June 30 Received a check from DeLoach for the semiannual interest and amortized the discount, using the effective interest method.
Aug. 1 Received a check from Kessler for the semiannual interest.
Sept. 30 Received a check from Howell for the semiannual interest and amortized the premium, using the effective interest method.
Nov. 1 Sold the Kessler bonds at 98 plus accrued interest.

Dec. 31 Received a check from DeLoach for the semiannual interest and amortized the discount, using the effective interest method.
31 Made the year-end adjusting entry to accrue the interest and amortize the premium on the Howell bonds.

19x3
Jan. 1 Sold one-half of the DeLoach bonds at 94.

Required

Prepare general journal entries to record the transactions.

Problem 18B-5 Bond Retirements and Conversions

Jackson Corporation is authorized to issue $6,000,000 of unsecured convertible bonds, due March 31, 19x6. The bonds carry a face interest rate of $11\frac{3}{5}$ percent, payable semiannually on March 31 and September 30. Each $1,000 bond is convertible into twenty-five shares of $20 par value common stock. The bonds are callable at 104 any time after March 31, 19x4.

All the bonds are issued on April 1, 19x1, at 102.261, a price that yields effective interest of 11 percent.

On April 1, 19x4, holders of one-half of the outstanding bonds present their bonds for conversion into common stock.

On October 1, 19x4, Jackson Corporation calls the remaining bonds and retires them.

Required

1. Prepare a table similar to Table 18-2 to show the interest and amortization of bond premium for ten interest payment periods, using the effective interest method (round results to nearest dollar).
2. Prepare general journal entries for the bond issue, interest payments and amortization of bond premium, bond conversion, and bond retirement on the following dates: April 1, 19x1; September 30, 19x1; March 31, 19x4; April 1, 19x4; September 30, 19x4; and October 1, 19x4.

Part Five

Special Reports and Analyses of Accounting Information

Because of the complex nature of business organizations in our society, special reports are needed to communicate important activities and characteristics. In order to understand and evaluate financial statements, it is necessary to learn how to analyze them.

Part V is devoted to important special reports and to the analysis of financial statements.

Chapter 19 presents the statement of changes in financial position, which provides insight into the financing and investing activities of an enterprise. It also presents the cash flow statement.

Chapter 20 attends to the special problems of companies that expand their operations by investing in other companies—a situation often requiring consolidated financial statements—and by operating in foreign markets.

Chapter 21 introduces the fundamental concepts and ratios of financial statement analysis.

Chapter Nineteen

Statement of Changes in Financial Position and Cash Flow Statement

Learning Objectives

1. *Distinguish cash from working capital as a concept of funds.*
2. *Identify the types of transactions that cause changes in working capital.*
3. *Identify common sources and uses of working capital.*
4. *Prepare a statement of changes in financial position work sheet.*
5. *Prepare a statement of changes in financial position and accompanying schedule of changes in working capital.*
6. *Prepare a cash flow statement.*

In previous chapters, you have studied the balance sheet, the income statement, and the statement of retained earnings. In this chapter, you will learn to prepare a fourth major financial statement: the statement of changes in financial position. You will also study the related cash flow statement. As a result of studying this chapter, you should be able to meet the learning objectives listed on the left.

The business enterprise engages in financing and investing activities to earn a profit. The balance sheet reveals the status of these activities at a particular time. Financing activities are represented as liabilities and owners' equity, and investment activities are shown as assets. The income statement reports on the progress of the business enterprise in earning a profit. However, neither of these statements answers the following questions: What new financing and investing activities did the company engage in during the year? How much of the new investment was provided by profitable operations and how much by increased liabilities or owners' equity? Why did the distribution of the assets change during the year? If liabilities were reduced, what was the source of the funds used to reduce the liabilities?

The purpose of the statement of changes in financial position is to answer questions such as those raised above. It shows each source of funds for the business and each use of funds by the business for the year. Although its official name is **statement of changes in financial position,** it is often called simply the statement of changes.

Cash and Working Capital Funds Distinguished

Objective 1 Distinguish cash from working capital as a concept of funds

A source of confusion for the student is that the word *funds* can be defined in more than one way. Most people equate *funds* with *cash.* This is not, however, the way in which most business people or accountants use this term. Instead, they use the term **funds** in the broader sense of working capital, because working capital (current assets minus current liabilities) is closely related to the operating cycle of the business. Cash, on the other hand, is obtained or its use delayed by making sales, issuing short-term notes, or using accounts payable and accrued liabilities. Once obtained, cash is used to pay expenses or to purchase inventory, which in turn is sold for cash or turned into accounts receivable. There is a constant flow from cash to noncash assets and then back to cash. The executive and the accountant tend to think of working capital as a pool of funds to be used in the smooth operation of the business.

As will be seen later in this chapter, of course, accountants can and do prepare cash flow statements. Such statements reveal the sources and uses of a firm's cash and are important tools in the hands of modern financial management. However, the statement of changes in financial position is broader in its perspective because it focuses on changes in working capital. It spans the entire range of a firm's liquid assets, whereas the cash flow statement concentrates on a single asset—cash. In short, the statement of changes in financial position tries to describe all of the changes in a firm's financial position arising during a specified period of time.

Changes in Working Capital

Objective 2 Identify the types of transactions that cause changes in working capital

The process of identifying changes in working capital requires an understanding of the effects of transactions on working capital. These effects are best illustrated by means of a balance sheet consisting of four parts:

A. Current Assets
B. Current Liabilities
C. Noncurrent Assets
D. Noncurrent Liabilities and Owners' Equity

Parts A and B are working capital accounts, and Parts C and D are nonworking capital accounts. A transaction will affect (either increase or decrease) working capital if a part of the transaction involves working capital accounts and a part of it does not. For example, contrast the effects on working capital of borrowing cash by obtaining a short-term bank note and borrowing cash by issuing long-term bonds. In the first transaction, there is no effect on total working capital because both the debit and the credit involve working capital accounts. The debit to Cash (an increase in a working capital account) is offset by the credit to Notes Payable (a decrease in working capital). The net result is no change in total working capital. The second transaction, on the other hand, affects working capital

Figure 19-1
Effect of Transactions on Working Capital

Debit Entry	Credit Entry	
	Current Account	Noncurrent Account
Current Account	No effect	Increase (source)
Noncurrent Account	Decrease (use)	No effect

because the debit is to a working capital account (Cash) and the credit (Bonds Payable) is not. The debit to Cash increases working capital, whereas the credit to Bonds Payable increases a noncurrent liability. The net result is an increase in total working capital. The effects of transactions on working capital are summarized in Figure 19-1.

By applying the decision rules of Figure 19-1 to the four parts of the balance sheet as shown in Figure 19-2, we can distinguish ten types of transactions involving the four parts of the balance sheet (each line with arrows at both ends represents a type of transaction). Note that the horizontal line, consisting of dashes, separates the current from the noncurrent balance sheet accounts. It is labeled the working capital line. Analysis of Figure 19-2 shows six types of transactions (1, 2, 3, 4, 5, 6) that do not cross the working capital line. These transactions, therefore, do not affect the amount of working capital. They may be summarized as follows:

Type of Transaction	Parts of Balance Sheet Affected	Examples
1	A, A	Collected an account receivable
2	A, B	Made a payment on an account payable
3	B, B	Issued a note payable to settle an account payable
4	C, C	Exchanged land for a building; no gain or loss recognized
5	C, D	Acquired a building by issuing a mortgage payable
6	D, D	Declared and issued a stock dividend

Further analysis of Figure 19-2 shows only four types of transactions (7, 8, 9, 10) that cross the working capital line. They are summarized on the next page.

Figure 19-2
Types of Transactions Affecting the Balance Sheet

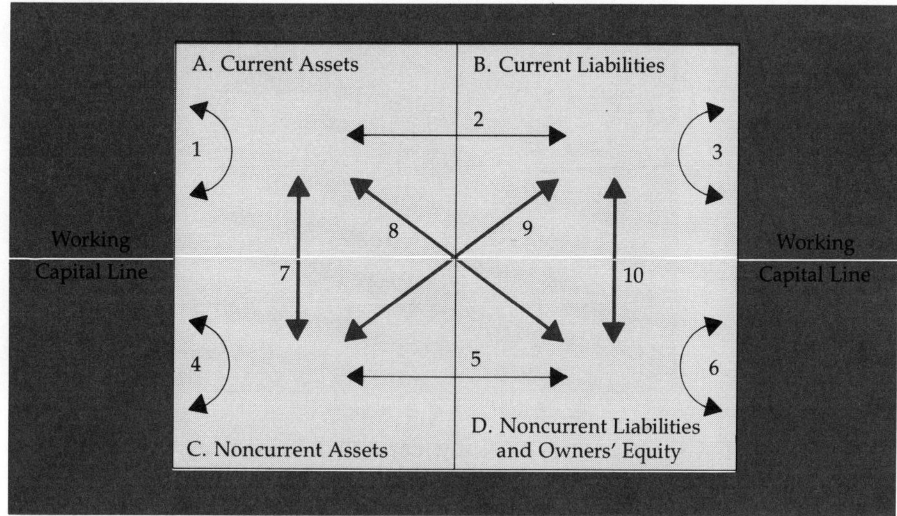

Source: Adapted from Robert J. Brill, "A Visual Aid for Explaining Sources and Applications of Funds," *The Accounting Review,* October 1964, p. 1015. Reprinted by permission of *The Accounting Review.*

Type of Transaction	Parts of Balance Sheet Affected	Examples
7	A, C	Made a sale of long-term asset at book value; purchased computer with cash
8	A, D	Charged a customer for a sale on account; issued common stock for cash
9	B, C	Acquired equipment by issuing a short-term note payable
10	B, D	Purchased advertising on credit; exchanged a long-term note for a short-term note

Because part of each of these transactions is above the working capital line and part is below, each one affects the amount of working capital. The examples of transactions involving income statement accounts may raise a question. Remember that the Sales account and the Advertising Expense account are nominal or temporary owners' equity accounts that ultimately affect Retained Earnings. Therefore, a sale on account affects a working capital account (Accounts Receivable) and a nonworking capital account (Retained Earnings via Sales). A purchase of advertising on credit also affects a working capital account (Accounts Payable) and a nonworking capital account (Retained Earnings via Advertising Expense).

Effects of Transactions on Working Capital

After identifying transactions that affect working capital, it is important to determine the nature of the effects. A transaction that results in a net

Figure 19-3
Common Sources and Uses of Working Capital

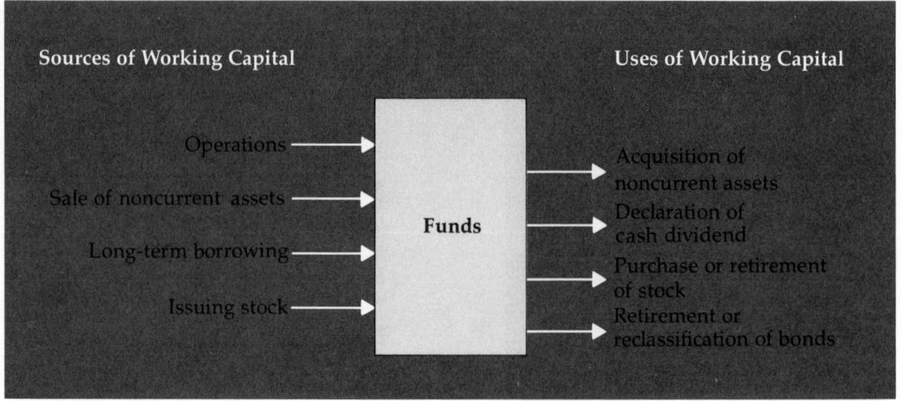

increase in working capital is known as a **source of working capital.** A transaction that results in a net decrease in working capital is known as a **use of working capital.** Common sources and uses of working capital are shown in Figure 19-3. Each source and use will be analyzed below to show its effect on working capital.

Sources of Working Capital

The most common sources of working capital are operations, sale of noncurrent assets, long-term borrowing, and issuance of capital stock.

Objective 3 Identify common sources and uses of working capital

Operations The primary source of working capital is revenues. Similarly, the main use of working capital is expense. Recall that revenues are generally recorded on the accrual basis and represent increases in current assets. The increase in current assets also increases working capital. This occurs, for example, when a merchandising transaction is recorded with a debit to the Accounts Receivable account (part A of the balance sheet) and a credit to the Sales account (part D of the balance sheet).

Expenses are also recorded on the accrual basis and generally represent decreases in working capital. There are, however, expenses that do not affect working capital. A familiar expense that does not bring about a decrease in working capital is depreciation. Recognition of depreciation expense in the accounts requires a debit to a depreciation expense account (part D of the balance sheet) and a credit to an accumulated depreciation account (part C of the balance sheet). Note that the recognition of depreciation expense does not involve a journal entry that crosses the working capital line.

In order to understand income from operations as a source of working capital, it is first necessary to analyze each of the revenue and expense items found on the income statement. For example, each item in the following income statement (column 1) is examined to determine its effect on working capital (column 2).

	(1) Income Statement	(2) Items Affecting Working Capital
Sales	$1,000	$+1,000
Cost of Goods Sold	400	− 400
Gross Profit	$ 600	$ 600
Operating Expenses		
Wages	$ 100	$− 100
Depreciation	100	
Advertising	50	− 50
Other	150	− 150
Total	$ 400	$− 300
Net Income	$ 200	$+ 300

The analysis reveals a $300 net increase in working capital from operations.

Using this approach to determining funds from operations, then, we examine carefully each revenue and expense item shown on an income statement. Once we discover the nonfund items (depreciation in this case), we eliminate them from the income statement and prepare an adjusted income statement in order to determine funds from operations. However, this method is not always feasible. Notice that the income statement above was not very complicated. If a complicated income statement had been used, this approach to determining funds from operations would not have been so easy.

In order to simplify the calculation for determining funds from operations, accountants have devised a short-cut technique. The short cut uses a formula for calculating funds from operations. One form of the formula is:

Net income
Plus: Items decreasing income but not using working capital[1]
Equals: Working capital provided from operations

By using the data from the example in this formula, we arrive at the same $300 funds from operations.

Short-cut technique

Net income	$200
Plus items decreasing income but not using working capital—depreciation	$100
Working capital from operations	$300

Unfortunately, the short-cut technique makes depreciation appear to be a source of working capital. This is clearly not true. Depreciation is only added back to net income to arrive at funds from operations according

1. Items do exist that have the opposite effect—increasing income but not affecting working capital—but consideration of them is deferred to more advanced courses.

to the short-cut formula. The $300 funds provided by operations came from revenues and expenses affecting working capital. Recognition of depreciation is necessary in determining income, but it results only from a bookkeeping entry. As shown earlier, the journal entry recognizes that depreciation does not cross the working capital line and therefore is neither a source nor a use of working capital. Clearly, working capital generated from operations results from revenue and expense items *before* adding or deducting bookkeeping items. As proof of this point, note in the following computations that funds from operations do not change. Net income is reduced from $200 to $100 by deducting the additional $100 in depreciation, but there is no change in funds from operations. The short-cut formula supports this conclusion, as seen in the second computation.

	Income Statement	Items Affecting Working Capital
Sales	$1,000	$+1,000
Cost of Goods Sold	400	− 400
Gross profit	$ 600	$+ 600
Operating Expenses		
Wages	$ 100	$− 100
Depreciation	200	
Advertising	50	− 50
Other	150	− 150
Total	$ 500	$+ 300
Net Profit	$ 100	$+ 300

Short-cut technique

Net profit	$100
Plus items decreasing income but not using working capital—depreciation	200
Working capital from operations	$300

Other expenses that do not involve an outlay of funds and therefore must be added to net income to arrive at working capital provided by operations are amortization expense and depletion of natural resources.

Furthermore, an adjustment is sometimes needed for gains and losses. This situation occurs only if the net income figure used in the statement of changes in financial position contains the gains and losses. Because gains and losses neither use nor provide working capital, an adjustment of the net income figure would be needed. However, if net income from operations (which does not include gains and losses) is used, as we have done in this book, no addition or deduction to net income for gains and losses is required.

Working capital is usually provided by operations. However, if a net operating loss is large enough to exceed the nonworking capital expenses, a decrease in working capital may result. When this condition occurs, the decrease in working capital is placed in the sources as a negative amount.

Sale of Noncurrent Assets When noncurrent assets such as equipment or a long-term investment are sold or exchanged for cash or some other current asset, a company's working capital is increased by the amount of the cash or other current asset received. For example, if a machine is sold for a note receivable of $7,000, the working capital provided by the transaction is $7,000. This is true regardless of the book value and regardless of whether there is a gain or loss. For example, assume that the following transaction reflects the facts:

May 15	Notes Receivable	7,000	
	Accumulated Depreciation, Machinery	8,000	
	Gain on Sale of Machinery		5,000
	Machinery		10,000
	Sale of machinery		

Note that only Notes Receivable is an above-the-line (working capital) account and is debited or increased. The other three accounts involved are below-the-line (noncurrent) accounts. Thus working capital is increased by $7,000. Also note that if the carrying value of the machinery were $9,000 ($17,000 – $8,000) instead of $2,000 ($10,000 – $8,000), with a resulting loss of $2,000 ($9,000 – $7,000), the working capital provided would still be $7,000.

Long-Term Borrowing When a firm borrows cash on a long-term basis, cash (a current asset) and long-term liabilities (noncurrent liabilities) are increased. Because long-term liabilities are not a part of working capital (below the line) and cash is a part of working capital (above the line), the borrowing of cash on a long-term basis is a source of working capital.

Issuance of Capital Stock The issuance of a company's stock for cash or other current assets is another source of funds. The results of such a transaction are to increase current assets (above the line) and owners' equity (below the line). Owners' equity is not a part of working capital, and thus the issuance of capital stock results in a source of working capital.

Uses of Working Capital

Some of the more common uses of working capital are acquisition of noncurrent assets, declaration of a cash dividend, purchase or retirement of stock, and retirement or reclassification of long-term debt.

Purchase of Noncurrent Assets Using current assets to purchase a noncurrent asset increases long-term assets (below the line) and decreases current assets (above the line). For example, assume that the Pipe Corporation purchased a building for $200,000 cash. The entry to record the transaction would be:

Jan. 21	Buildings	200,000	
	Cash		200,000
	Purchase of building		

Note that the debit to Buildings increases a below-the-line nonworking capital account whereas the credit to Cash decreases an above-the-line working capital account. Therefore, a use of working capital of $200,000 results.

Declaration of a Cash Dividend An example of the entry to record the declaration of a cash dividend is as follows:

Oct. 30	Retained Earnings	10,000	
	Cash Dividends Payable		10,000
	Declaration of cash dividend		

Note that the transaction involves both an above-the-line working capital account (Cash Dividends Payable) and a below-the-line nonworking capital account (Retained Earnings). Because an increase in current liabilities reduces working capital, the declaration of a cash dividend is classified as a use of working capital.

Purchase or Retirement of Stock A company may use cash or other current assets to purchase treasury stock or to purchase and retire a portion of its stock. Because such transactions affect both current and noncurrent accounts and reduce current assets, the amount of current assets given up is classified as a use of working capital on the statement of changes in financial position.

Retirement or Reclassification of Long-Term Debt The retirement or reclassification of a long-term debt may result in the use of a firm's working capital. If long-term debt is retired by using current assets, the transaction is similar to the retirement of stock. There is a reduction both in the company's current assets (above the line) and in long-term debt (below the line). The amount of current assets used to retire the long-term debt is classified as a use of working capital.

When a portion of long-term debt comes due for payment during the current year, that portion of the debt must be reclassified as a current liability. This transaction results in an increase in the company's current liabilities (above the line) and in a decrease in long-term debt (below the line). Thus there is a decrease in working capital because of the increase in current liabilities, and the reclassification is treated as a use of working capital.

Exchange Transactions

A company will occasionally exchange a long-term asset for a long-term liability. For example, assume that a $300,000 long-term mortgage is exchanged for $50,000 in land with a $250,000 building on it. The entry to record this transaction would be:

June 1	Land	50,000	
	Building	250,000	
	Mortgage Payable		300,000
	Exchange of mortgage payable for land and building		

This **exchange transaction** involves parts C and D of the balance sheet and does not cross the working capital line. Therefore, it has no direct effect on working capital. It is, however, a significant transaction—one about which a statement user who was examining the financial and investing activities of a business would want to know. For this reason, this exchange transaction may be viewed as two transactions: (1) the issuance of a mortgage payable for $300,000, and (2) the purchase of land for $50,000 and building for $250,000. As a result, the Accounting Principles Board, in its *Opinion No. 19,* requires that an **all financial resources** viewpoint be taken when the statement of changes in financial position is prepared.[2] This means that significant exchange transactions are treated as if they are both a source and use event. In this case, the issuance of the mortgage is shown as a source of working capital and the purchase of the land and buildings is shown as a use of working capital.

Other transactions that should be treated as exchange transactions are exchanges of capital stock for long-term assets and conversions of bonds payable or preferred stock into common stock. Figure 19-4 (next page) illustrates sources and uses of working capital reported by 600 companies.

Preparing the Statement of Changes in Financial Position

Once the transactions identified as affecting working capital—that is, as sources or uses of working capital—are determined, they are presented in the statement of changes in financial position. The primary objective of this statement is to summarize the financing and investing activities of the company, including the extent to which the enterprise has generated

2. Accounting Principles Board, "Reporting Changes in Financial Position," *Opinion No. 19* (New York: American Institute of Certified Public Accountants, 1971), par. 8.

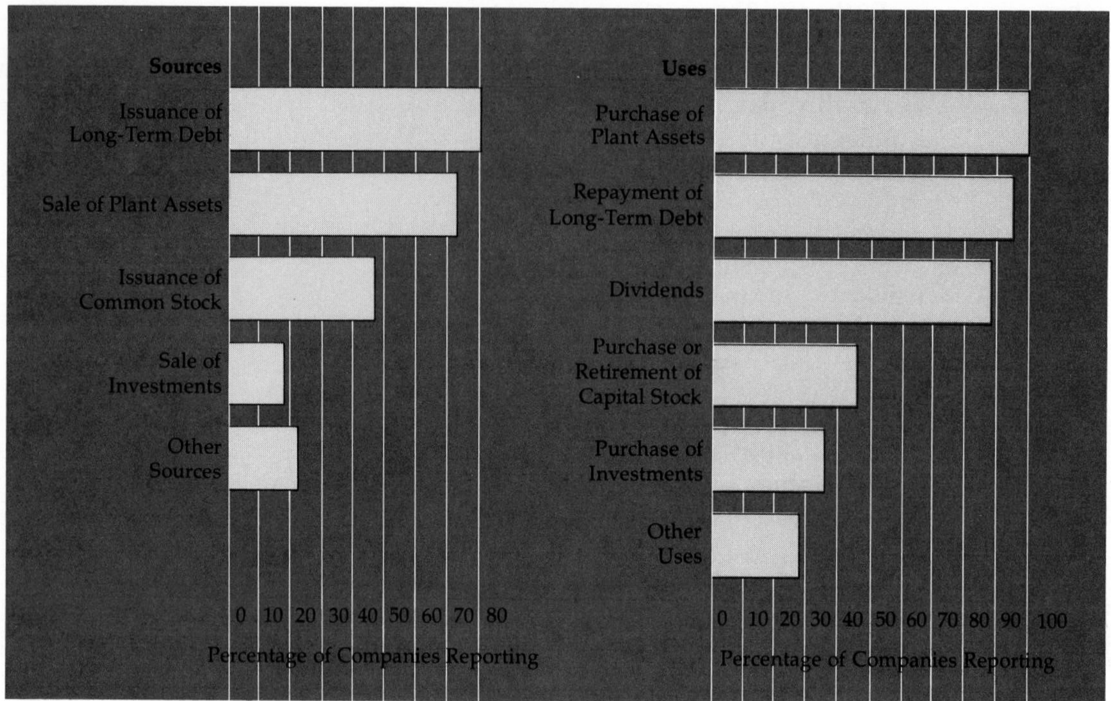

Figure 19-4 Sources of Capital and Uses Other Than Operations Reported by 600 Companies

Source: American Institute of Certified Public Accountants, *Accounting Trends and Techniques* (New York: AICPA, 1979).

working capital from operations during an accounting period. This statement must be prepared whenever an income statement is presented.[3]

The statement of changes in financial position has three major components. They are (1) sources of working capital, including (a) operations and (b) other sources; (2) uses of working capital; and (3) increase (or decrease) in working capital. The financing and investing activities are presented under the appropriate component heading. The statement is accompanied by a schedule of changes in working capital. A completed statement and schedule are shown in Figure 19-8 (pages 656 and 657).

The important steps in preparing a statement of changes in financial position are as follows:

1. Determine the change in working capital for the year.
2. Prepare a work sheet.
3. Analyze the change in each noncurrent account to determine whether it was caused by a transaction that crosses the working capital line. If so, reclassify the change as a source or use of working capital.
4. Prepare the statement of changes in financial position and the supporting schedule of changes in working capital.

The comparative balance sheets of Pipe Corporation are used in Figure 19-5 to illustrate the preparation of the statement of changes in financial position.

3. Ibid., pars. 7 and 14.

Figure 19-5
Comparative
Balance Sheet

Pipe Corporation
Comparative Balance Sheet
December 31, 19x2, and December 31, 19x1

	19x2	19x1
Assets		
Current Assets		
Cash	$ 55,000	$ 30,000
Accounts Receivable (net)	40,000	45,000
Inventories	110,000	100,000
Prepaid Expenses	8,000	10,000
Total Current Assets	$213,000	$185,000
Property, Plant, and Equipment		
Land	$115,000	$115,000
Buildings	450,000	330,000
Accumulated Depreciation, Buildings	(54,000)	(44,000)
Equipment	150,000	60,000
Accumulated Depreciation, Equipment	(28,000)	(24,000)
Total Property, Plant, and Equipment	$633,000	$437,000
Total Assets	$846,000	$622,000
Liabilities		
Current Liabilities		
Accounts Payable	$ 50,000	$ 40,000
Accrued Liabilities	10,000	—
Current Portion of Bonds Payable	5,000	—
Total Current Liabilities	$ 65,000	$ 40,000
Long-Term Liabilities		
Bonds Payable	$345,000	$250,000
Total Liabilities	$410,000	$290,000
Stockholders' Equity		
Common Stock—$5 par value	$275,000	$200,000
Paid-in Capital in Excess of Par Value	25,000	—
Retained Earnings	136,000	132,000
Total Stockholders' Equity	$436,000	$332,000
Total Liabilities and Stockholders' Equity	$846,000	$622,000

Figure 19-6
Computation of Change in Working Capital

Pipe Corporation Summary of Changes in Working Capital For the Year Ended December 31, 19x2		
Current Assets	$213,000	
Current Liabilities	65,000	
Working Capital, December 31, 19x2		$148,000
Current Assets	$185,000	
Current Liabilities	40,000	
Working Capital, December, 31, 19x1		$145,000
Total Increase (Decrease) in Working Capital		$ 3,000

Determining the Changes in Working Capital for the Year

For the first step, compute the change in working capital as shown in Figure 19-6 by comparing the working capital at the end of 19x2 with that at the end of 19x1. Because the total change in working capital for the Pipe Corporation during 19x2 was a $3,000 increase, the sources of working capital should exceed the uses of working capital by $3,000 on the statement of changes in financial position.

Preparing the Work Sheet

Objective 4 Prepare a statement of changes in financial position work sheet

After determining the change in working capital, analyze the noncurrent accounts to determine the causes of the changes in financial position. There are several methods used to gather the relevant data for preparing the statement, but the work sheet approach is used here because it is practical. It is also useful because, when complete, the lower part of the work sheet contains the information necessary to prepare the statement of changes in financial position.

The work sheet for the Pipe Corporation is presented in Figure 19-7. The following steps will serve as guidelines in work sheet preparation. Be sure to relate each step to Figure 19-7.

1. The work sheet should have a Description column (labeled A in Figure 19-7), and additional columns to the right with the following types of headings:
Column B: Account balances for the end of the prior year (19x1)
Column C: Analysis of transactions for the current year (19x2)
Column D: Account balances for the end of the current year (19x2)

Figure 19-7
Sample Work Sheet

Pipe Corporation
Statement of Changes in Financial Position Work Sheet
For the Year Ended December 31, 19x2

A	B	C				D
		Analysis of Transactions for 19x2				
Description	Account Balances, 12/31/x1	Debit		Credit		Account Balances, 12/31/x2
Debits						
Working Capital	145,000	(x)	3,000			148,000
Land	115,000					115,000
Buildings	330,000	(d)	120,000			450,000
Equipment	60,000	(e)	100,000	(c)	10,000	150,000
Total Debits	650,000					863,000
Credits						
Accumulated Depreciation, Buildings	44,000			(b)	10,000	54,000
Accumulated Depreciation, Equipment	24,000	(c)	3,000	(b)	7,000	28,000
Bonds Payable	250,000	(f)	5,000	(e)	100,000	345,000
Common Stock	200,000			(g)	75,000	275,000
Paid-in Capital in Excess of Par Value	—			(g)	25,000	25,000
Retained Earnings	132,000	(h)	10,000	(a)	13,000	136,000
				(c)	1,000	
Total Credits	650,000		241,000		241,000	863,000
Sources of Working Capital						
Operations						
Net Income		(a)	13,000			
Depreciation, Buildings		(b)	10,000			
Depreciation, Equipment		(b)	7,000			
Other Sources						
Sale of Equipment		(c)	8,000			
Issuance of Bonds in Exchange for Equipment		(e)	100,000			
Issuance of Common Stock		(g)	100,000			
Uses of Working Capital						
Purchase of Building				(d)	120,000	
Purchase of Equipment by Exchanging Bonds				(e)	100,000	
Reclassification of Long-Term Debt				(f)	5,000	
Cash Dividend				(h)	10,000	
			238,000		235,000	
Increase in Working Capital, 19x1				(x)	3,000	
Totals			238,000		238,000	

2. Enter working capital on the first line in the Description column, and indicate the amount of working capital at the end of the current and prior years in the appropriate columns ($145,000 and $148,000 in columns B and D). The difference of $3,000 between the columns must be the change in working capital for the current year as computed in Figure 19-6. Label the change with an (x) for later reference in step 7 below.

3. Immediately below the working capital in the Description column, insert all the noncurrent debits that appear on the comparative balance sheet, and enter the amounts in the appropriate columns. Next total the debits for each of the two years. Note that the total debits for 19x1 and 19x2 in the illustration are $650,000 and $863,000, respectively.

4. List the noncurrent accounts with credit balances (including contra-asset accounts) from the comparative balance sheet, enter the amounts in the appropriate column, and total the credits. The total credits for 19x1 and 19x2 in the illustration are $650,000 and $863,000, respectively. The total credits for each year must agree with the total debits.

5. Next drop down several lines on the work sheet and insert the title Sources of Working Capital. Then drop down several more lines and enter a second title, Uses of Working Capital. The reason for this step is that as the changes in noncurrent accounts are analyzed, they can be classified as a source or use. This step will help in preparing the statement of changes in financial position later.

6. Analyze the changes in noncurrent accounts that have occurred during the period. This is the most important step in the preparation of the work sheet because the transactions affecting noncurrent accounts are those that are likely to affect the sources and uses of working capital. For this reason, a separate analysis of each transaction is presented below.

7. Finally, add the debit and credit columns in both the top and bottom portions of the analysis section (column C). The debit and credit columns should balance in the top portion, and they should not balance in the bottom portion. If no errors have been made, the difference in the bottom portion should equal the increase or decrease in working capital. Add this difference to the lower column, and identify it as either an increase or a decrease in working capital. Label the change with an (x) and compare it with the change in working capital, also labeled (x), on the first line of the work sheet. The amounts should be equal.

After completing the work sheet, prepare the statement of changes in financial position. Because all the required information is listed under sources and uses of working capital, it is simply transferred and put in the proper format on the statement.

Analyzing the Changes in Noncurrent Accounts

The most crucial step in the preparation of the statement of changes in financial position, as mentioned earlier, is the analysis of the changes in noncurrent accounts that occurred during the year. To analyze the changes, the following additional information is needed:

a. Net income from operations for the year, $13,000.
b. Depreciation recorded on the building and equipment is $10,000 and $7,000, respectively.
c. Sold equipment that cost $10,000 and had accumulated depreciation of $3,000 for $8,000 cash. The gain is *not* included in net income.
d. Purchased a new building for $120,000 cash.
e. Issued $100,000 of bonds for new equipment.
f. Reclassified $5,000 of bonds payable as current.
g. Issued 15,000 shares of $5 par value common stock for $100,000.
h. Declared a $10,000 cash dividend.

The results of the analysis of the noncurrent accounts for the Pipe Corporation are presented in column C of the work sheet in Figure 19-7. The explanations for these work sheet entries are presented in the following paragraphs. Keep in mind that the objective of each part of the analysis is to explain the change in a noncurrent account. When all changes in noncurrent accounts have been explained and classified, the change in working capital for the year as shown in the first line of the work sheet becomes evident.

a. The Pipe Corporation reported net income for 19x2 of $13,000. Because net income ultimately results in an increase in Retained Earnings (when Income Summary is closed to Retained Earnings at the end of the year), it helps to account for the change in Retained Earnings for the year. Also, as explained previously, net income is considered a source of working capital because it represents the excess of revenues over expenses. Consequently, on the work sheet a credit is made to Retained Earnings for the increase in that account for the year, and a debit is made to Net Income in the lower part of the work sheet under sources of working capital:

(a) Source of Working Capital: Net Income	13,000	
Retained Earnings		13,000

This entry is recorded on the work sheet in the analysis columns as entry **a.**

b. The depreciation expenses for building and equipment were $10,000 and $7,000, respectively. As explained earlier, although depreciation expense is included as a deduction in determining net income, it does not involve an outlay of working capital. The amount of depreciation expense also helps to explain the change in the accumulated depreciation accounts for building and equipment. Thus the work sheet entry would be to credit the accumulated depreciation accounts and to debit the depreciation expense under sources of working capital on the lower part of the work sheet. In this way, depreciation expense is added back to net income:

(b) Increase in Working Capital: Building Depreciation	10,000	
Increase in Working Capital: Equipment Depreciation	7,000	
Accumulated Depreciation, Building		10,000
Accumulated Depreciation, Equipment		7,000

c. Note that although the changes in the Accumulated Depreciation, Buildings have been explained ($44,000 + $10,000 = $54,000), the change in Accumulated Depreciation, Equipment has not been completely explained. In other words, the beginning balance of $24,000 plus the credit of $7,000 does not equal the ending balance of $28,000. Neither has the change in Equipment been explained. Thus we must conclude that other transactions involving the account have occurred. The other information given reveals a sale of equipment that would be recorded as follows:

Cash	8,000	
Accumulated Depreciation, Equipment	3,000	
Gain on Sale of Equipment		1,000
Equipment		10,000
Sale of equipment		

An analysis of this transaction reveals that Cash, a working capital account, has increased by $8,000. The other three accounts are nonworking capital accounts. Since the Gain on Sale of Equipment would have been closed to Retained Earnings, the work sheet entry for the gain is a credit to Retained Earnings. The work sheet entry is as follows:

(c) Source of Working Capital: Sale of Equipment	8,000	
Accumulated Depreciation, Equipment	3,000	
Retained Earnings (Gain)		1,000
Equipment		10,000

With this entry the total change in Accumulated Depreciation, Equipment is accounted for ($24,000 − $3,000 + $7,000 = $28,000).

d. Among the noncurrent asset accounts, the changes in Buildings and Equipment remain to be explained. Turning to the Building account first, we find that the other data given above reveal the purchase of a building for $120,000 cash. The entry to record the purchase is as follows:

Building	120,000	
Cash		120,000

This business transaction reduces working capital by decreasing Cash. The entry on the work sheet is shown as:

(d) Building	120,000	
Use of Working Capital: Purchase of Building		120,000

e. The supplemental information also reveals the issuance of an additional $100,000 of bonds for equipment. This is an exchange transaction that fits the concept of all financial resources. The transaction as shown at the top of the next page does not change working capital because it involves two noncurrent accounts and is a transaction that does not cross the working capital line.

Equipment	100,000	
Bonds Payable		100,000
Issuance of bonds in exchange for equipment		

However, the transaction is viewed as an exchange transaction—that is, as both a source and a use of funds. The transaction is a short cut for issuing bonds for cash, which is the source of working capital, and then purchasing the equipment for cash, which is the use of working capital. To record this transaction properly on the work sheet, it should appear as follows:

(e) Equipment	100,000	
Source of Working Capital: Issuance of Bonds	100,000	
Bonds Payable		100,000
Use of Working Capital: Equipment Purchase		100,000

Note that after this transaction is recorded on the work sheet, the change in Equipment for the year is explained ($60,000 + $100,000 − $10,000 = $150,000). The changes in all noncurrent assets have now been explained.

f. Part of the change in Bonds Payable is yet to be accounted for. Item f reveals that, during the year, $5,000 of Pipe Corporation's long-term debt became current and had to be reclassified as a current liability. The company could then make a formal entry to transfer $5,000 from Bonds Payable to Current Portion of Long-Term Debt as follows:

Bonds Payable	5,000	
Curent Portion of Long-Term Debt		5,000
To reclassify current portion of long-term debt as a current liability		

Part of this transaction is above the line (current liability) and part of it is below the line (noncurrent liability). The increase in Current Portion of Long-Term Debt results in an increase in current liabilities and in a reduction or use of working capital. The work sheet entry to show this use of working capital is presented below:

(f) Bonds Payable	5,000	
Use of Working Capital: Reclassification of Long-Term Debt		5,000

Note that the total change in Bonds Payable in 19x2 has now been accounted for ($250,000 − $5,000 + $100,000 = $345,000).

g. The issuance of an additional 15,000 shares of $5 par value common stock for $100,000 would result in the following entry:

Cash	100,000	
Common Stock		75,000
Paid-in Capital in Excess of Par Value		25,000

When this transaction is analyzed, the increase in Cash causes an increase in working capital, but the increases in the equity accounts do not affect working capital. Thus the transaction results in an increase in working capital. The transaction below is recorded on the work sheet as entry **g.**

(g) Source of Working Capital: Issuance of Stock	**100,000**	
Common Stock		**75,000**
Paid-in Capital in Excess of Par Value		**25,000**

After this work sheet entry is recorded, the year's changes in Common Stock and Premium on Common Stock are accounted for.

h. The remaining account to be analyzed is Retained Earnings. Recall that in work sheet entry **a,** the recording of net income as a source of working capital resulted in a credit to Retained Earnings. The other entry to Retained Earnings during the year was the declaration of a $10,000 cash dividend by the Pipe Corporation. The declaration of a cash dividend results in the following entry:

Retained Earnings	10,000	
Cash Dividends Payable		10,000
Declaration of cash dividend		

This transaction contains one working capital account (Cash Dividends Payable) and one nonworking capital account (Retained Earnings). Because an increase in a current liability results in a decrease in working capital, the entry is recorded on the work sheet as a use of working capital (credit) and a debit to Retained Earnings:

(h) Retained Earnings	**10,000**	
Use of Working Capital, Cash Dividends		**10,000**

The total change in Retained Earnings for the year has now been explained ($132,000 − $10,000 + $13,000 + $1,000 = $136,000).

x. After all the noncurrent transactions have been analyzed, the final step in the work sheet preparation is to total the debit and credit columns for the analysis of transactions for the top half and the bottom half of the work sheet. The two column totals for the top half should be equal. The difference in the two column totals for the bottom half will always equal the change in working capital for the year. Observe that in Figure 19-7 the bottom half of the columns equal total sources of $238,000 and total uses of $235,000. The difference between these two is equal to the increase of $3,000 in working capital for the period. To complete the work sheet, the following entry should be made in the analysis columns:

(x) Working Capital	3,000	
Increase in Working Capital		3,000

Completing the Statement and Supporting Schedule

Objective 5 Prepare a statement of changes in financial position and accompanying schedule of changes in working capital

Note that the transactions placed on the work sheet are *not* entered in the records of the company. The work sheet is merely a tool to assist accountants in preparing the statement of changes in financial position. When the work sheet is completed, it discloses both the sources and the uses of working capital for the period. In addition, the sources and uses are listed according to type. The statement of changes in financial position can then be prepared from the information on the lower portion of the work sheet. The completed statement for the Pipe Corporation is shown in Figure 19-8, on the next two pages. Accompanying the statement of changes in financial position is a schedule of changes in working capital. This schedule, which shows the effect of changes in the individual working capital accounts in the working capital of the company, is a required disclosure.

Preparing the Cash Flow Statement

Objective 6 Prepare a cash flow statement

Up to this point in this chapter, we have focused on the statement of changes in financial position on a working capital basis. By reporting the sources and uses of working capital during a given period, this statement gives management a broad view of the financing and investing activities of the company. However, management must also plan to have sufficient cash available to pay liabilities, dividends, and other obligations. A cash flow statement can provide management with this information. The cash flow statement is also useful to creditors in assessing the liquidity of a company. In other words, it aids in determining whether a company can pay its liabilities and dividends and meet various requirements for business expansion.

The **cash flow statement** reports a company's sources and uses of cash during an accounting period. It may be prepared in the same format as a statement of changes in financial position on a working capital basis. The only difference is that the increase or decrease in cash rather than in working capital is explained. The statement is normally a simple listing of cash receipts (sources) and disbursements (uses), with the difference between the receipts and disbursements disclosed as the increase or decrease in cash for the period. An example of a cash flow statement is presented in Figure 19-11 (page 660).

Figure 19-8
Statement of Changes in Financial Position

Pipe Corporation Statement of Changes in Financial Position For the Year Ended December 31, 19x2			
Sources of Working Capital			
Operations			
Net Income		$ 13,000	
Add Expenses Not Requiring Outlay of Working Capital in the Current Period			
Depreciation, Building	$10,000		
Depreciation, Equipment	7,000	17,000	
Working Capital Provided from Operations			$ 30,000
Other Sources of Working Capital			
Sale of Equipment		$ 8,000	
Issuance of Bonds in Exchange for Equipment		100,000	
Issuance of Common Stock		100,000	208,000
Total Sources of Working Capital			$238,000
Uses of Working Capital			
Purchase of Building		$120,000	
Purchase of Equipment by Exchanging Bonds		100,000	
Reclassification of Long-Term Debt		5,000	
Cash Dividend		10,000	235,000
Increase in Working Capital			$ 3,000

Cash Flow from Operations

The first step in preparing a cash flow statement is to determine the cash flow from operations. To do so, it is necessary to focus on the operating transactions affecting the Cash account.

Cash Receipts from Sales Sales are a source of cash for a company because the sale of goods for cash or on credit results in collection. Cash sales are increases in the cash flow of the company. Credit sales are originally recorded as accounts receivable; when they are collected, there is an inflow of cash to a company. However, one should not assume that total sales are automatically a source of cash, because 100 percent of the accounts receivable are not necessarily collected in the current accounting period. A receivable may prove uncollectible, or it may be collected in a period subsequent to that of the sale. For example, for the $650,000 sales

Figure 19-8
(continued)

Pipe Corporation
Schedule of Changes in Working Capital
For the Year Ended December 31, 19x2

	19x2	19x1	Working Capital Increase	Working Capital Decrease
Current Assets				
Cash	$ 55,000	$ 30,000	$25,000	
Accounts Receivable (Net)	40,000	45,000		$ 5,000
Inventories	110,000	100,000	10,000	
Prepaid Assets	8,000	10,000		2,000
Total Current Assets	$213,000	$185,000		
Current Liabilities				
Accounts Payable	$ 50,000	$ 40,000		10,000
Accrued Liabilities	10,000	—		10,000
Current Portion of Bond Payable	5,000	—		5,000
Total Current Liabilities	$ 65,000	$ 40,000	$35,000	$32,000
Working Capital	$148,000	$145,000		
Increase in Working Capital				3,000
			$35,000	$35,000

in Figure 19-9, assume that $50,000 were cash sales and $600,000 were credit sales. From the balance sheet in Figure 19-5, Accounts Receivable (net) decreased during the year by $5,000—that is, from $45,000 in 19x1 to $40,000 in 19x2. Because credit sales increase Accounts Receivable and collections reduce Accounts Receivable, collections must have exceeded credit sales by $5,000 during the year. The increase in cash from sales during the year then is $655,000 [$50,000 cash sales plus $605,000 ($600,000 + $5,000) collected from accounts receivable].

Cash Payments for Purchases The cost of goods sold amount on the income statement must be adjusted for changes in two balance sheet accounts to arrive at cash payments for purchases. First, cost of goods sold must be adjusted for changes in inventory to arrive at net purchases.

Figure 19-9
Condensed Income Statement

Pipe Corporation Condensed Income Statement For the Year Ended December 31, 19x2	
Net Sales	$650,000
Cost of Goods Sold	520,000
Gross Profit from Sales	$130,000
Operating Expenses	117,000
Net Income from Operations	$ 13,000

Then, net purchases must be adjusted for the change in accounts payable to arrive at cash payments for purchases. These conclusions are logical. If a company is increasing its inventory, net purchases will exceed cost of goods sold, and if a company is increasing its accounts payable, its cash payments for purchases will be less than its net purchases.

Cash Payments for Expenses Just as cost of goods sold does not represent the amount of cash paid for purchases during an accounting period, operating expenses will not correspond to the amount of cash paid. Two adjustments must be made in operating expenses to arrive at cash outflow. The first adjustment is related to the fact that in addition to arising from cash payments, expenses arise from the write-off of prepaid assets and the increase in accrued liabilities. If prepaid assets increase during the year, more cash will have been used than will appear as expense on the income statement. Conversely, if prepaid assets decrease during the year, more expenses will appear on the income statement than cash expended. Also, if accrued liabilities increase during the year, expenses on the income statement will exceed cash expended, and if accrued liabilities decrease during the year, cash expended will exceed reported expenses. Therefore, operating expenses must be adjusted for changes in prepaid assets and accrued liabilities. The second adjustment is related to the fact that certain expenses do not involve a current outlay of cash and must be subtracted from the expense figure on the income statement to arrive at cash payments for expenses. Examples of these expenses are depreciation expense, amortization expense, and depletion expense.

Short-Cut Method Using the logic presented in the three preceding paragraphs, we can convert an income statement from the accrual to the cash basis. However, it is easier to compute cash flow from operations by adjusting net income (which is the net result of sales, cost of goods sold, and operating expenses) for the changes in current assets (other than cash) and current liabilities. This is the same principle as used earlier in the chapter in computing working capital from operations by adding back nonworking capital charges to net income. This short-cut method of computing cash flow from operations is summarized on the next page.

Figure 19-10
Schedule of Cash Flow from Operations

Net Income from Operations			$13,000
Add			
Items reducing income but not using cash			
Depreciation, Equipment	$10,000		
Depreciation, Buildings	7,000	$17,000	
Decreases in current assets other than cash			
Accounts Receivable	$ 5,000		
Prepaid Expenses	2,000	7,000	
Increases in current liabilities			
Accounts Payable	$10,000		
Accrued Liabilities	10,000	20,000	$44,000
Subtotal			$57,000
Deduct			
Increases in current assets other than cash			
Inventories		$10,000	
Decreases in current liabilities		none	10,000
Cash flow from operations			$47,000

Net Income from Operations
Plus: Items reducing income but not using cash
Decreases in current assets other than cash
Increases in current liabilities
Less: Increases in current assets other than cash
Decreases in current liabilities
Equals: Cash Flow from Operations

The changes in the various working capital accounts of Pipe Corporation are found in the schedule of changes in working capital in Figure 19-8. In addition, the company had net income from operations of $13,000 (Figure 19-9) and depreciation $10,000 on equipment and $7,000 on buildings. Cash flow from operations can thus be computed as shown in Figure 19-10.

Completing the Cash Flow Statement

In addition to operations, a company engages in other cash transactions during the year. For example, a company may purchase or sell long-term assets; increase, reduce, or retire long-term debt; issue or purchase capital

Figure 19-11
Cash Flow
Statement

Pipe Corporation Cash Flow Statement For the Year Ended December 31, 19x2		
Sources of Cash		
Operations (see schedule)	$ 47,000	
Sale of Equipment	8,000	
Issuance of Common Stock	100,000	
Total Sources of Cash		$155,000
Uses of Cash		
Purchase of Building	$120,000	
Cash Dividends Paid	10,000	
Total Uses of Cash		130,000
Increase in Cash		$ 25,000

stock; or pay cash dividends. An analysis of previous information in the chapter for Pipe Corporation indicated the following other cash transactions:

a. Sold equipment for $8,000 in cash.
b. Purchased a building for $120,000 in cash.
c. Issued 15,000 shares of $9 par value common stock for $100,000.
d. Paid a $10,000 cash dividend.

Using this information and the computation of cash flow from operations (Figure 19-10), we can prepare a cash flow statement as shown in Figure 19-11. Note that sources of cash provided cash receipts of $155,000 during the year and the uses of cash required cash disbursements of $130,000 during the year. The resultant increase in cash of $25,000 equals the change in cash for the year as shown in the balance sheet in Figure 19-5 and in the schedule in Figure 19-8. If the cash flow from operations had been negative, the amount would have been shown as a use of cash.

Chapter Review

Review of Learning Objectives

1. Distinguish cash from working capital as a concept of funds.
The analysis of cash as a concept of funds is limited to a study of the cash receipts and cash disbursements during the year. This analysis is useful for evaluating a limited aspect of liquidity (cash flow). However, working capital (current assets minus current liabilities) is a broader concept of funds in that its analysis

encompasses the operating cycle and the financing and investing activities of the business.

2. Identify the types of transactions that cause changes in working capital.
Transactions affect working capital if they result in a net increase or net decrease in working capital. The types of transactions that have these effects are those in which part of the transaction involves working capital accounts and part does not. Transactions involving solely working capital accounts and those involving solely noncurrent accounts do not have a net effect on the amount of working capital.

3. Identify common sources and uses of working capital.
Common sources of working capital are operations, sale of noncurrent assets, long-term borrowing, and issuance of common stock. Common uses of working capital are a negative flow from operations, acquisition of noncurrent assets, declaration of cash dividend, purchase or retirement of stock, and retirement or reclassification of long-term debt. Exchange transactions—exchange of one noncurrent asset or liability for another noncurrent asset or liability—result in both a source and a use of working capital.

4. Prepare a statement of changes in financial position work sheet.
A work sheet for the preparation of a statement of changes in financial position is helpful in analyzing the changes that have occurred in each noncurrent account during the year and translating those changes into their effects (as sources and uses) on working capital. To perform this step, the transactions involving noncurrent accounts are reconstructed. The working capital portion of those accounts is identified as a source or use of working capital. The difference between the total debits and credits of this transaction analysis should be equal to the change in working capital.

5. Prepare a statement of changes in financial position and accompanying schedule of changes in working capital.
The statement of changes in financial position is prepared from the information contained in the work sheet. The sources of working capital section should show working capital provided from operations separately from other sources. The other sources should be listed individually. The uses of working capital should also be listed separately. The change in working capital at the bottom of the statement should correspond to the same figure on an accompanying schedule of changes in working capital items. On the schedule, the change in each working capital item is classified by its effect on working capital.

6. Prepare a cash flow statement.
Preparation of a cash flow statement requires, first, that cash flow from operations and, second, that other cash transactions be identified. The cash flow statement explains the change in the balance of cash from the beginning to the end of the year by showing the sources and uses of cash during the year.

Review Problem

Before doing the exercises and problems, review the steps for preparing the statement of changes in financial position in this chapter. For additional help, see the review problem in the working papers.

Chapter Assignments

Questions

1. What are the two concepts of funds that might be applied to the statement of changes in financial position? Which is preferable and why?
2. What is the objective of the statement of changes in financial position?
3. When should a statement of changes in financial position be presented as a major financial statement?
4. What is working capital, and what types of transactions do and do not affect the amount of working capital?
5. What are four or more sources of working capital?
6. What are four or more uses of working capital?
7. Why does the payment of accounts payable from cash not decrease working capital?
8. The Green-Ball Company had a net loss of $25,000 during 19xx, but working capital provided by operations was $5,000. What are some possible conditions that may have caused this situation?
9. What impact does write-off of an uncollectible account against an allowance account have on working capital?
10. Would the following items increase, decrease, or have no effect on working capital: (a) declaration of a cash dividend, (b) declaration of a stock dividend, (c) payment of an account payable with cash, (d) collection of an account receivable in cash?
11. What is an exchange transaction, and what is its impact on the statement of changes in financial position?
12. When a statement of changes in financial position that discloses working capital is prepared, are there any additional disclosure requirements?
13. The Stone Manufacturing Company reclassified $20,000 of its twenty-year, 6 percent bonds as current liabilities. What is the impact of the reclassification on the working capital of the company?
14. In preparing a cash flow statement, why must net income from operations be adjusted for changes in appropriate working capital accounts?

Classroom Exercises

Exercise 19-1 Schedule of Changes in Working Capital

From the comparative balance sheet of the Washington Corporation, prepare a schedule of changes in working capital for the year ended December 31, 19x3.

Washington Corporation
Comparative Balance Sheet
December 31, 19x3, and December 31, 19x2

	19x3	19x2
Assets		
Cash	$ 10,000	$ 6,000
Accounts Receivable (net)	21,000	24,000
Inventory	42,000	36,000
Equipment	60,000	62,000
Other Assets	1,000	1,500
Total Assets	$134,000	$129,500

Liabilities and Stockholders' Equity

Accounts Payable	$ 22,000	$ 17,000
Notes Payable (60 days)	5,000	10,000
Bonds Payable	50,000	50,000
Common Stock	50,000	50,000
Retained Earnings	7,000	2,500
Total Liabilities and Stockholders' Equity	$134,000	$129,500

Exercise 19-2 Effect of Transactions on Working Capital

Analyze the following transactions, and indicate with an X in the appropriate column whether they resulted in a source of funds, a use of funds, or no impact on funds. The concept of funds to use is that of all financial resources.

Transaction	Effect on Working Capital		
	Source	Use	Neither
a. Sold $5,000 of merchandise above cost.			
b. Collected $2,000 of accounts receivable.			
c. Paid $4,000 of accounts payable.			
d. Declared a $10,000 cash dividend.			
e. Issued $100,000 par value common stock to retire at face value $100,000 of the company's long-term bonds.			

Exercise 19-3 Working Capital Provided by Operations

The Green Dome Corporation reported net income for the year ended December 31 as $120,000. At the end of the year, the following adjusting entries were made: (a) recorded depreciation expense, $15,600; (b) accrued interest on notes receivable, $750; (c) accrued interest on bonds payable, $2,000; (d) recorded uncollectible accounts expense, $2,000; (e) amortized prepaid insurance, $400; (f) amortized goodwill, $1,000.

Using the information presented above, determine the increase or decrease in working capital from operations during the year.

Exercise 19-4 Statement of Changes in Financial Position

A comparative balance sheet for the Black Warrior Corporation on September 30, 19x1 and 19x2, appears on the next page.

	19x2	19x1
Assets		
Cash	$ 45,500	$ 12,500
Accounts Receivable (net)	21,000	26,000
Inventory	46,000	51,000
Furniture	65,000	60,000
Accumulated Depreciation, Furniture	(9,000)	(5,000)
Total Assets	$168,500	$144,500
Liabilities and Stockholders' Equity		
Accounts Payable	$ 13,000	$ 14,000
Notes Payable (5 years)	30,000	30,000
Common Stock—$5 par value	95,000	90,000
Retained Earnings	30,500	10,500
Total Liabilities and Stockholders' Equity	$168,500	$144,500

Additional information: (a) issued $5,000 of stock at par value for furniture; (b) depreciation on the furniture during the year, $4,000; (c) cash dividends declared and paid, $5,000; (d) net income, $25,000.

Without using a work sheet, prepare a statement of changes in financial position and an accompanying schedule of changes in working capital.

Exercise 19-5 Cash Flow Statement

The condensed income statement for Black Warrior Corporation for the year ended September 30, 19x2, appears below:

Sales	$120,000
Cost of Goods Sold	80,000
Gross Profit from Sales	$ 40,000
Operating Expenses	15,000
Net Income	$ 25,000

Using the information above and in Exercise 19-4, and without using a work sheet, (1) compute cash flow from operations, and (2) prepare a cash flow statement.

Exercise 19-6 Conversion to Cash Basis Income Statement

The income statement for the Honey Corporation is on the next page.

Additional information: (a) All sales were on credit, and accounts receivable increased by $2,200 during the year. (b) All merchandise purchased was on credit. Inventories remained unchanged, and accounts payable increased by $7,000 during the year. (c) Accrued salaries increased by $500 during the year.

Compute cash flow from operations.

Honey Corporation
Income Statement
For the Year Ended June 30, 19xx

Sales		$50,000
Cost of Goods Sold		30,000
Gross Profit		$20,000
Other Expenses		
Salaries	$15,000	
Depreciation	1,000	
Uncollectible Accounts Expense	1,000	17,000
Net Income		$ 3,000

Problem Set A

Problem 19A-1 Effects of Transactions on Working Capital

In the schedule below, analyze the transactions presented, and place an X in the appropriate column to identify the transaction as increasing, decreasing, or having no effect on total working capital. Exchange transactions are to be treated as affecting working capital.

Transactions	Effect on Working Capital		
	Increase	Decrease	No Effect
a. Incurred a net loss.			
b. Declared a stock dividend.			
c. Paid a cash dividend previously declared.			
d. Collected accounts receivable.			
e. Purchased inventory for cash.			
f. Retired long-term debt for cash.			
g. Reclassified current portion of long-term debt as a current liability.			
h. Issued stock for equipment.			
i. Purchased a three-year insurance policy for cash.			
j. Purchased treasury stock for cash.			
k. Retired a fully depreciated truck (no gain or loss).			

Problem 19A-2 Working Capital and Cash Flow from Operations

The income statement of Wong Record Company is as follows:

Wong Record Company
Income Statement
For the Year Ended June 30, 19xx

Sales		$1,200,000
Cost of Goods Sold		
Beginning Inventory	$ 310,000	
Purchases (net)	760,000	
Goods Available for Sale	$1,070,000	
Ending Inventory	350,000	
Cost of Goods Sold		720,000
Gross Profit from Sales		$ 480,000
Operating Expenses		
Selling and Administrative Salaries	$ 278,000	
Other Selling and Administrative Expenses	156,000	
Total Operating Expenses		434,000
Net Income from Operations		$ 46,000

Additional information: (a) Other selling and administrative expenses include depreciation expense of $26,000, amortization expense of $9,000. (b) At the end of the year, accrued liabilities for salaries were $6,000 less than the previous year, and prepaid expenses were $10,000 more than last year. (c) During the year, accounts receivable (net) increased by $72,000, and accounts payable increased by $57,000.

Required

1. Determine the working capital provided from operations for the Wong Record Company for the year ended June 30, 19xx.
2. Determine the cash flow from operations for the Wong Record Company for the year ended June 30, 19xx.

Problem 19A-3 Statement of Changes in Financial Position

The comparative balance sheet of the Morello Manufacturing Corporation as of September 30, 19x6 and 19x7, is shown at the top of the next page.

Additional information concerning the company and transactions involving the noncurrent accounts that are relevant to preparing a statement of changes in financial position are as follows: (a) Net income for the year was $59,800. (b) Depreciation expense recorded on the income statement was $30,000. (c) Plant was increased in July by $50,000, and the mortgage was increased by the same amount. (d) The company paid $10,000 on the mortgage in September. (e) The notes payable were paid off, but the company borrowed an additional $15,000 under the same conditions in November. (f) A $30,000 dividend was declared and paid in November.

	19x7	19x6
Assets		
Cash	$ 80,000	$ 10,000
Accounts Receivable (net)	50,000	60,000
Finished Goods Inventory	90,000	110,000
Prepaid Insurance	300	500
Property, Plant, and Equipment	326,000	276,000
Accumulated Depreciation, Property, Plant, and Equipment	(100,000)	(70,000)
Total Assets	$446,300	$386,500
Liabilities and Stockholders' Equity		
Accounts Payable	$ 45,000	$ 30,000
Notes Payable (due in 90 days)	15,000	40,000
Mortgage Payable	180,000	140,000
Common Stock—$5 par value	100,000	100,000
Retained Earnings	106,300	76,500
Total Liabilities and Stockholders' Equity	$446,300	$386,500

Required

1. From the information provided, prepare a work sheet and develop the information for a statement of changes in financial position that discloses working capital changes. Exchange transactions are to be disclosed in the statement of changes in financial position.
2. Prepare a statement of changes in financial position and a schedule showing the changes in the individual working capital items.

Problem 19A-4 Statement of Changes in Financial Position

Suppose that the balance sheet account balances for the year ended December 31, 19x2 (see next page), were given to you by Jane Moore of M & M Enterprises.

The following transactions and other information relate to the month of January, 19x3: (a) Net income for the month was $1,200. (b) Depreciation amounts on the building and on furniture and fixtures were $1,000 and $600, respectively. One month's amortization of patent was also recorded in the amount of $100. (c) Issued $10,000 of bonds in exchange for new furniture. (d) Purchased a patent for $7,000. (e) Issued $20,000 of stock at par value for cash. (f) Additional long-term investments were purchased for $17,000. Payment is due to a broker and must be paid in five days.

	As of Dec. 31, 19x2
Assets	
Cash	$ 16,350
Accounts Receivable (net)	35,260
Merchandise Inventory	82,300
Prepaid Assets	2,500
Long-Term Investments	35,000
Building	78,000
Accumulated Depreciation, Building	(15,000)
Furniture and Fixtures	22,000
Accumulated Depreciation, Furniture and Fixtures	(4,000)
Total Assets	$252,410
Liabilities and Stockholders' Equity	
Accounts Payable	$ 35,420
Payable to Broker	17,000
Bonds Payable	80,000
Common Stock	100,000
Retained Earnings	19,990
Total Liabilities and Stockholders' Equity	$252,410

Required

1. Prepare a work sheet for a statement of changes in financial position that explains the change in working capital. Exchange transactions should be disclosed on the statement of changes in financial position. (Hint: The January 31 account balances can be computed when the transactions have been placed properly on the work sheet.)

2. From the work sheet, prepare a statement of changes in financial position.

Problem 19A-5 Comprehensive Statement of Changes in Financial Position

The comparative balance sheet for the No-Glo Wholesale Paint Company for the years ending December 31, 19x2 and 19x3, is presented on the next page.

Additional information available concerning operations and transactions in the noncurrent accounts is as follows: (a) Net income for the year was $24,000. (b) Building and equipment depreciation expense amounts were $20,000 and $10,000, respectively. (c) Intangible assets were written off against net income in the amount of $10,000. (d) The company issued $60,000 of long-term bonds payable at par value. (e) In an exchange transaction, an additional building was purchased for $70,000 by increasing the mortgage payable by the same amount. (f) A cash dividend of $9,000 was declared and paid during the year.

	19x3	19x2
Assets		
Cash	$ 79,400	$ 76,400
Accounts Receivable (net)	174,700	164,700
Marketable Securities	10,000	25,000
Inventory	240,000	200,000
Prepaid Assets	3,700	6,700
Long-Term Investments	110,000	110,000
Land	80,300	80,300
Building	300,000	230,000
Accumulated Depreciation, Building	(60,000)	(40,000)
Equipment	120,000	120,000
Accumulated Depreciation, Equipment	(29,000)	(19,000)
Intangible Assets	5,000	15,000
Total Assets	$1,034,100	$969,100
Liabilities and Stockholders' Equity		
Accounts Payable	$ 117,700	$165,200
Notes Payable (current)	10,000	40,000
Accrued Liabilities	2,700	5,200
Mortgage Payable	270,000	200,000
Bonds Payable	250,000	190,000
Common Stock	300,000	300,000
Paid-in Capital in Excess of Par Value	20,000	20,000
Retained Earnings	63,700	48,700
Total Liabilities and Stockholders' Equity	$1,034,100	$969,100

Required

1. Prepare a work sheet to gather the information for preparing the statement of changes in financial position that discloses working capital.
2. From the work sheet, prepare the statement of changes in financial position and the accompanying schedule of changes in working capital.

Problem 19A-6 Cash Flow Statement

The condensed income statement for the No-Glo Wholesale Paint Company for the year ending December 31, 19x3, is presented at the top of the next page.

Additional information related to No-Glo is presented in Problem 19A-5.

Required

1. Compute cash flow from operations. (Balance sheet information is found in Problem 19A-5.)
2. Prepare a cash flow statement for No-Glo.

Sales		$876,000
Cost of Goods Sold		502,000
Gross Profit from Sales		$374,000
Operating Expenses		
Selling and Administrative Expenses	$310,000	
Depreciation Expenses, Building	20,000	
Depreciation Expense, Equipment	10,000	
Write-off of Intangible Assets	10,000	
Total Operating Expenses		350,000
Net Income from Operations		$ 24,000

Problem Set B

Problem 19B-1 Effect of Transactions on Working Capital

In the schedule below, analyze the transactions presented and place an X in the appropriate column to identify the transaction as increasing, decreasing, or having no effect on working capital. Exchange transactions should be treated as affecting working capital.

Transaction	Effect on Working Capital		
	Increase	Decrease	No Effect
a. Recorded net income.			
b. Declared cash dividend.			
c. Issued stock for cash.			
d. Retired long-term debt by issuing stock.			
e. Paid accounts payable.			
f. Purchased inventory on credit.			
g. Purchased a three-year insurance policy.			
h. Purchased a long-term investment for cash.			
i. Sold marketable securities (at cost).			
j. Sold a machine for its book value (no gain or loss).			
k. Retired fully depreciated equipment.			

Problem 19B-2 Working Capital and Cash Flow from Operations

The income statement for the G & S Hospital Supply Corporation is shown below.

G & S Hospital Supply Corporation
Income Statement
For the Year Ended December 31, 19xx

Sales		$500,000
Cost of Goods Sold		
Beginning Inventory	$220,000	
Purchases (net)	400,000	
Goods Available for Sale	$620,000	
Ending Inventory	250,000	
Cost of Goods Sold		370,000
Gross Profit from Sales		$130,000
Selling and Administrative Expenses		
Selling and Administrative Salaries	$50,000	
Other Selling and Administrative Expenses	11,500	
Depreciation Expense	15,000	
Amortization of Intangible Assets	1,500	78,000
Net Income from Operations		$ 52,000

Additional information: (a) Accounts receivable (net) increased by $18,000, and accounts payable decreased by $26,000 during the year. (b) Accrued salaries payable at the end of the year were $7,000 more than last year. (c) The expired amount of prepaid insurance for the year is $500 and equals the decrease in the Prepaid Insurance account.

Required

1. Determine the working capital provided from operations for the G & S Hospital Supply Corporation for the year.
2. Determine the cash flow from operations for the G & S Hospital Supply Corporation for the year.

Problem 19B-3 Statement of Changes in Financial Position

The comparative balance sheet for the J. C. Carmichael Company as of June 30, 19x1 and 19x2, is presented on the next page.

Additional information concerning the company and transactions involving the noncurrent accounts that are relevant to preparing a statement of changes in financial position are as follows: (a) Net loss for the year was $35,500. (b) Depreciation expense recorded on the income statement was $10,000. (c) A fully depreciated fixture with an original cost of $1,000 was retired in August. (d) Bonds payable in the amount of $50,000 were exchanged for 2,000 shares of common stock.

	19x2	19x1
Assets		
Cash	$ 25,000	$ 25,000
Accounts Receivable (net)	105,000	100,000
Merchandise Inventory	175,000	225,000
Prepaid Rent	1,000	1,500
Furniture and Fixtures	71,000	72,000
Accumulated Depreciation, Furniture and Fixtures	(21,000)	(12,000)
Total Assets	$356,000	$411,500
Liabilities and Stockholders' Equity		
Accounts Payable	$ 92,400	$112,400
Bonds Payable	50,000	100,000
Common Stock—$10 par value	120,000	100,000
Paid-in Capital in Excess of Par Value	90,720	60,720
Retained Earnings	2,880	38,380
Total Liabilities and Stockholders' Equity	$356,000	$411,500

Required

1. From the information above, prepare a work sheet and develop the information for a statement of changes in financial position that discloses working capital changes. Exchange transactions are to be disclosed in the statement of changes in financial position.
2. Prepare a statement of changes in financial position and a schedule showing the changes in the individual working capital items.

Problem 19B-5 Comprehensive Statement of Changes in Financial Position

A comparative balance sheet for the U-Tote Corporation as of June 30, 19x1 and 19x2, is presented at the top of the next page.

The following information was developed by analyzing the company's operations and noncurrent accounts: (a) net loss for the year, $19,000; (b) depreciation expense for buildings and equipment, $15,000 and $3,000; (c) fully depreciated equipment totaling $2,000 was discarded and written off the records; (d) equipment purchases, $1,000; (e) amortization of patent, $2,000; (f) a building was purchased in September for $162,000; cash was paid in the amount of $12,000, and the remainder was paid by issuing a ten-year mortgage note; (g) the company issued 3,000 shares of $10 par value common stock for $50,000 cash; (h) a cash dividend of $18,000 was declared and paid in January.

Required

1. Prepare a work sheet for the statement of changes in financial position that explains the changes in working capital. Exchange transactions should be disclosed on the statement of changes in financial position.
2. Prepare a statement of changes in financial position and a schedule showing the changes in the individual working capital items.

	19x2	19x1
Assets		
Cash	$ 37,060	$ 27,360
Accounts Receivable (net)	102,430	75,430
Inventory	112,890	137,890
Prepaid Assets	—	20,000
Building	162,000	—
Accumulated Depreciation, Building	(15,000)	—
Equipment	33,000	34,000
Accumulated Depreciation, Equipment	(25,000)	(24,000)
Patent	4,000	6,000
Total Assets	$411,380	$276,680
Liabilities and Stockholders' Equity		
Accounts Payable	$ 30,750	$ 56,750
Notes Payable	10,000	—
Accrued Liabilities (current)	—	12,300
Mortgage Payable	150,000	—
Common Stock	180,000	150,000
Paid-in Capital in Excess of Par Value	57,200	37,200
Retained Earnings	(16,570)	20,430
Total Liabilities and Stockholders' Equity	$411,380	$276,680

Problem 19B-6 Cash Flow Statement

In addition to the comparative balance sheet and other information presented for U-Tote Corporation in Problem 19B-5, U-Tote's condensed income statement for the year ended June 30, 19x2, is as follows:

Sales		$259,000
Cost of Goods Sold		140,000
Gross Profit from Sales		$119,000
Operating Expenses		
Selling and Administrative Expenses	$118,000	
Depreciation Expense	18,000	
Patent Amortization	2,000	
Total Operating Expenses		138,000
Net Loss from Operations		($ 19,000)

Required

1. Compute cash flow from operations. (The balance sheets for U-Tote are in problem 19B-5.)
2. Prepare a cash flow statement for U-Tote.

Chapter Twenty

Intercompany Investments and International Accounting

Learning Objectives

1. State the principles of valuation for various types of corporate investments in other firms.
2. Explain when to prepare consolidated financial statements and their uses.
3. Prepare consolidated balance sheets at acquisition date for purchase at (a) book value, and (b) other than book value.
4. Prepare consolidated income statements for intercompany transactions.
5. Contrast the purchase and pooling of interests methods in accounting for business combinations, giving reasons for each.
6. Show how changing exchange rates affect financial reporting.
7. Restate a foreign subsidiary's financial statements in U.S. dollars.
8. Describe progress toward international accounting standards.

Corporations often find it profitable to expand their operations by investing in other companies or by extending their operations to other countries. The purposes of this chapter are to provide an overview of corporate investment in other corporations, with special emphasis on the principles underlying consolidated financial statements, and to discuss some important problems of international accounting. As a result of studying this chapter, you should be able to master the learning objectives that are listed on the left.

When management wants to expand a company's operations, it has several alternatives. The simplest method of expansion is to enlarge the present operation, for example, by installing a new manufacturing process within the existing plant or by adding a new section onto a retail store. If the company wants to appeal to new markets in other geographical locations, new branches or factories may be the answer. Leading companies that have expanded throughout the world are called **multinational**, or **transnational, corporations.**

Expansion requires increasing amounts of capital. Most companies begin as sole proprietorships or small partnerships and follow a trend of development similar to that pictured in Figure 20-1. As the business grows and requires more capital, a corporation may be formed. At this early stage of corporate life, the business may be a **closely held corporation**—one whose stock is owned by only a few individuals and whose securities are not publicly traded. If the company continues to grow and more capital is needed, it may wish to become a **publicly held corporation** by appealing to the public at large for capital. Such a corporation is registered with the Securities and Exchange Commission, and its securities are publicly traded. **Going public** involves meeting the SEC's stringent requirements for protection of the public against fraud in the sale of the securities. If the company is successful, it may be able to spread throughout the world and become a large multinational corporation.

Figure 20-1
A Possible Growth Pattern for a Successful Business

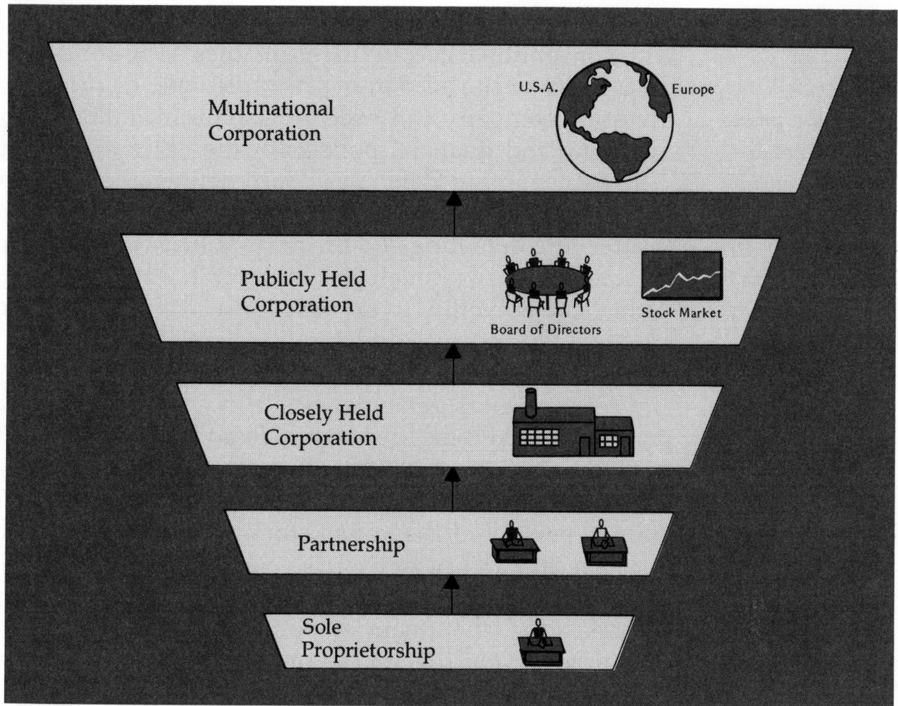

Because a corporation is a legal entity, it has the right to own property and thus may buy the shares of another corporation. In fact, investing in the shares of another corporation's stock is a popular method of expansion. There are many good reasons for expanding by this means. One is that the purchased company may have established customers or operations in an area where the buying company wants to expand. Another is that the purchased company may have access to raw materials needed in the buying company's manufacturing operation. In recent years, for example, some manufacturing companies, utilities, and chemical companies have been purchasing coal and gas companies to assure themselves of a supply of fuel in this age of energy shortages. Still another reason is that a company may need less capital to buy an interest in another company than to start a whole operation independently. In some states and many foreign countries, it is legally easier to buy or invest in a company than to start a new business. Sometimes there are tax advantages to investment in an existing business.

Classification of Long-Term Investments

One corporation may invest in another corporation by purchasing either bonds or stocks. These investments may be either short-term or long-term. In this chapter, we are concerned with long-term investments in stocks.

Objective 1
State the principles of valuation for various types of corporate investments in other firms

All long-term investments in stocks are recorded at cost, in accordance with conventional accounting principles. The subsequent treatment of the investment in the accounting records depends on the extent to which the investing company can exercise significant influence or control over the operating and financial policies of the other company.

The Accounting Principles Board defined the important terms *significant influence* and *control* in its *Opinion No. 18.* **Significant influence** is the ability to affect the operating and financial policies of the company whose shares are owned, even though the investor holds less than 50 percent of the voting stock. Ability to exercise influence may be indicated by representation on the board of directors, participation in policy-making processes, material intercompany transactions, interchange of managerial personnel, and technological dependency. In order to provide some uniformity of practice, the APB decided that unless there is evidence to the contrary, an investment of 20 percent or more of the voting stock should lead to the presumption of significant influence. Conversely, an investment of less than 20 percent of the voting stock would indicate that the investor does not have the ability to exercise significant influence.

Control is defined as the ability of the investing company to determine the operating and financial policies of the other company. Control is considered to exist when the investing company owns more than 50 percent of the voting stock of the company in which it has invested.

From the above definitions, it is possible to classify long-term investments in stock as follows: (1) noninfluential and noncontrolling investment—less than 20 percent ownership, (2) influential but noncontrolling investment—20 percent to 50 percent ownership, and (3) controlling investment—over 50 percent ownership. The accounting treatment for each type of investment is described below.

Noninfluential and Noncontrolling Investment

The **cost method** of accounting for long-term investments applies when less than 20 percent of the voting stock is owned. Under the cost method, the investor records the investment at cost and recognizes income as dividends are received. The Financial Accounting Standards Board requires that long-term investments in stock accounted for under the cost method be valued at the lower of cost or market after acquisition.[1] At the end of each accounting period, the total cost and the total market value of these long-term stock investments must be calculated. If the total market value is less than the total cost, the difference must be credited to a contra-asset account called Allowance to Reduce Long-Term Investments to Market. The offsetting debit is to a contra-owners' equity account called Unrealized Loss on Long-Term Investment. If, at some later date, the market exceeds the valuation reported in the prior period, the Long-Term Investment account is written up to the new market value, but not to exceed the acquisition cost of the investments. When long-term investments in stock

1. *Statement of Financial Accounting Standards No. 12,* "Accounting for Certain Marketable Securities" (Stamford, Conn.: Financial Accounting Standards Board, 1975).

are sold, the difference between the sales price and acquisition cost is recorded and reported as a realized gain or loss on the income statement. Dividend income from such investments is recorded by a debit to Cash and a credit to Dividend Income in the amount received.

For example, assume the following facts about the long-term stock investments of Coleman Corporation:

June 1, 19x0	Paid cash for the following long-term investments: 10,000 shares Durbin Corporation common stock (representing 2 percent of outstanding stock) at $25 per share; 5,000 shares Kotes Corporation common stock (representing 3 percent of outstanding stock) at $15 per share.
Dec. 31, 19x0	Quoted market prices at year end: Durbin common stock, $21; Kotes common stock, $17.
Apr. 1, 19x1	A change in policy required the sale of 2,000 shares of Durbin Corporation common stock at $23.
July 1, 19x1	Received a cash dividend from Kotes Corporation equal to 20¢ per share.
Dec. 31, 19x1	Quoted market prices at year end: Durbin common stock, $24; Kotes common stock, $13.

Entries to record these transactions are shown below.

Investment

19x0			
June 1	Long-Term Investments	325,000	
	Cash		325,000
	To record investments in Durbin common stock (10,000 shares × $25 = $250,000) and Kotes common stock (5,000 shares × $15 = $75,000)		

Year-end adjustment

19x0			
Dec. 31	Unrealized Loss in Long-Term Investment	30,000	
	Allowance to Reduce Long-Term Investments to Market		30,000
	To record reduction of long-term investment portfolio to market, which is less than cost		

Company	Shares	Market Prices	Total Market	Total Cost
Durbin	10,000	$21	$210,000	$250,000
Kotes	5,000	17	85,000	75,000
			$295,000	$325,000

Cost exceeds market by: $325,000 − $295,000 = $30,000

Sale

		Debit	Credit
19x1			
Apr. 1	Cash	46,000	
	Loss on Sale of Investment	4,000	
	Long-Term Investment		50,000
	To record sale of 2,000 shares of Durbin 2,000 × 23 = $46,000 2,000 × 25 = 50,000		

Dividend Received

		Debit	Credit
July 1	Cash	1,000	
	Dividend Income		1,000
	To record receipt of cash dividends from Kotes stocks 5,000 × 20¢ = $1,000		

Year-end Adjustment

		Debit	Credit
Dec. 31	Allowance to Reduce Long-Term Investments to Market	12,000	
	Unrealized Loss in Long-Term Investments		12,000
	To record the adjustment in long-term investment so it is reported at lower of cost or market		

The adjustment equals the previous balance ($30,000 from December 31, 19x0, entry) minus the new balance ($18,000), or $12,000. The new balance of $18,000 is computed as follows:

Company	Shares	Market Prices	Total Market	Cost
Durbin	8,000	$24	$192,000	$200,000
Kotes	5,000	13	65,000	75,000
			$257,000	$275,000

Cost exceeds market by: $275,000 − $257,000 = $18,000

Influential but Noncontrolling Investment

As pointed out above, ownership of 20 percent or more of the voting stock of another company is considered sufficient to influence the operations of another corporation. When this condition exists, the investment in the stock of a controlled company should be accounted for by using the **equity method**. The three main features of this method are as follows:

1. The investor records the original purchase of the stock at cost.

2. The investor records its share of the investee's periodic net income as an increase in the Investment account. The investor must similarly record its share of the investee's periodic loss as a decrease in the Investment account.

3. When the investor receives a cash or property dividend, the appropriate asset account should be increased and the Investment account decreased.

To illustrate the equity method of accounting, we will assume the following facts about an investment by the Vassor Corporation. Vassor Corporation, on January 1 of the current year, acquired 40 percent of the voting common stock of the Block Corporation for $180,000. With this share of ownership, the Vassor Corporation can exert significant influence over the operations of the Block Corporation. During the year, the Block Corporation reports net income of $80,000 and pays cash dividends of $20,000. The entries to record these transactions by the Vassor Corporation are presented below.

Investment

Investment in Block Corporation	180,000	
Cash		180,000
To record investment in Block Corporation common stock		

Recognition of Income

Investment in Block Corporation	32,000	
Income, Block Corporation Investment		32,000
To recognize 40% of income reported by Block Corporation 40% × $80,000 = $32,000		

Receipt of Cash Dividend

Cash	8,000	
Investment in Block Corporation		8,000
To record cash dividend from Block Corporation 40% × $20,000 = $8,000		

Controlling Investment

In some cases, an investor who owns less than 50 percent of the voting stock of a company may exercise such a powerful influence that for all practical purposes the investor "controls" the policies of the other company. Nevertheless, ownership of more than 50 percent of the voting stock is required for accounting recognition. When a controlling interest is owned, a parent and subsidiary relationship is said to exist, and it becomes necessary to consolidate the two financial statements. The investing company is known as the **parent company**, and the other company

Table 20-1 Accounting Treatments of Long-Term Investments

Level of Ownership	Percentage of Ownership	Accounting Treatment
Noninfluential and noncontrolling	Less than 20%	Cost method; value investment subsequent to purchase at lower of cost or market.
Influential but noncontrolling	Between 20% and 50%	Equity method; value investment subsequently at cost plus the investor's share of income (or minus the loss) and minus the dividends received from the other company.
Controlling	More than 50%	Consolidated financial statements are prepared.

is the **subsidiary**. Because both corporations are separate legal entities, each prepares separate financial statements. However, owing to their special relationship, they are viewed for public financial reporting purposes as a single economic entity. Thus they must combine their financial statements into a single set of statements called **consolidated financial statements.**

Accounting for consolidated financial statements is extremely complex. It is usually the subject of an advanced-level course in accounting. However, most large public corporations have subsidiaries and must prepare consolidated financial statements. For this reason, it is important to have a fundamental knowledge of accounting for consolidations.

The accounting treatments appropriate for long-term investment in stock are summarized in Table 20-1.

Consolidated Financial Statements

Objective 2 Explain when to prepare consolidated financial statements and their uses

Most major corporations find it convenient for economic, legal, tax, or other reasons to operate in parent-subsidiary relationships. When we refer to a large corporation such as Ford, RCA, or Texas Instruments, we generally think of the parent company, not of its numerous subsidiaries. When considering investment in one of these firms, however, the investor wants an integrated financial picture of the total economic entity. The basic purpose of consolidated financial statements is to give such a view of the parent and subsidiary firms by treating them as if they were one company. On a consolidated balance sheet, the Inventory account includes the inventory held by the parent and all its subsidiaries. Similarly, on the consolidated income statement, the Sales account is the total revenue from sales by the parent and all its subsidiaries. This overview is very useful to management and stockholders of the parent company in assessing the firm's progress in attaining its objectives. Long-term creditors of the parent also find consolidated statements useful because of their interest in the long-range financial health of the total enterprise.

There are certain situations in which consolidated statements are not used. For example, they are not very useful to creditors and stockholders of the subsidiary companies because their interest in the enterprise is limited to the specific subsidiary. Consolidated statements may also not be useful when the operations of the parent and subsidiary are totally incompatible. For instance, a retailing company that owned a bank would usually not consolidate the financial statements even if it owned more than 50 percent of the bank because the two operations are incompatible. Finally, consolidated statements are sometimes not used when there are certain restrictions on the control of the parent. Subsidiaries in certain foreign countries and subsidiaries that are bankrupt usually would not be consolidated because of such restrictions. The Accounting Principles Board requires that the equity method described earlier be used in accounting for such unconsolidated subsidiaries.[2]

Methods of Accounting for Consolidations

Interests in subsidiary companies may be acquired by paying cash, exchanging shares of the parent's own unissued capital stock for the outstanding shares of the subsidiary's capital stock, issuing long-term bonds or other debt, or negotiating some combination of these forms of payment. For parent-subsidiary relationships that arise in these ways, it is acceptable to use the **purchase method**, which we illustrate below. For simplicity's sake, our illustrations assume payment in cash. In a later section in this chapter, we discuss the special case of establishing a parent-subsidiary relationship through an exchange of stock. In this case, the pooling of interests method is appropriate.

Consolidated Balance Sheet

In the process of preparing consolidated financial statements, similar accounts from the individual statements of parent and subsidiaries are combined. Therefore, it is important that certain **eliminations** be made. These eliminations avoid the duplication of accounts and reflect the financial position and operations from the standpoint of a single entity. Eliminations appear only on work sheets used in preparing consolidated financial statements and are never shown in the accounting records of either the parent or the subsidiary. There are no consolidated journals or ledgers.

2. Accounting Principles Board, *Opinion No. 18,* "The Equity Method for Accounting for Investment in Common Stock" (New York: Accounting Principles Board, 1971).

Duplications are certain amounts that appear on both the parent and subsidiary books as a result of intercompany transactions and that, if combined, would result in a type of double counting. A universal example of this type of duplication is the Investment in Subsidiary account in the parent's balance sheet and the stockholders' equity section of the subsidiary. When the balance sheets of the two entities are combined, these accounts must be eliminated to avoid duplicating these items in the consolidated financial statements.

To illustrate the preparation of a consolidated balance sheet, we will use the following balance sheets for Parent and Subsidiary companies:

Accounts	**Parent Company**	**Subsidiary Company**
Cash	$100,000	$25,000
Other Assets	760,000	60,000
Total Assets	$860,000	$85,000
Liabilities	$ 60,000	$10,000
Capital Stock	600,000	55,000
Retained Earnings	200,000	20,000
Total Liabilities and Stockholders' Equity	$860,000	$85,000

Objective 3a Prepare consolidated balance sheets at acquisition date for purchase at book value

100 Percent Purchase at Book Value Assume that Parent Company purchases 100 percent of Subsidiary Company for an amount exactly equal to the Subsidiary's book value. The book value of Subsidiary Company is $75,000 ($85,000 − $10,000). Parent Company would record the purchase as follows:

Investment in Subsidiary Company	75,000	
Cash		75,000
To record 100 percent purchase of Subsidiary Company at book value		

It is helpful to use a work sheet similar to the one in Figure 20-2 in preparing consolidated financial statements. Note that the balance of Parent Company's Cash account is now $25,000 and that the Investment in Subsidiary Company is shown as an asset in Parent Company's balance sheet, reflecting the purchase of the subsidiary. To prepare a consolidated balance sheet, it is necessary to eliminate the investment in the subsidiary. This procedure is shown by elimination entry 1 in Figure 20-2. This elimination entry accomplishes two things. First, it eliminates the double counting that would occur when the net assets of the two companies are combined. Second, it eliminates the stockholders' equity section of the Subsidiary Company. The theory underlying consolidated financial statements is to view the parent and its subsidiary as a single entity. The

Parent and Subsidiary Companies
Work Sheet for Consolidated Balance Sheet
As of Acquisition Date

Accounts	Balance Sheet Parent Company	Balance Sheet Subsidiary Company	Eliminations		Consolidated Balance Sheet
			Debit	Credit	
Cash	25,000	25,000			50,000
Investment in Subsidiary Company	75,000			(1) 75,000	
Other Assets	760,000	60,000			820,000
Total Assets	860,000	85,000			870,000
Liabilities	60,000	10,000			70,000
Capital Stock—$10 par value	600,000	55,000	(1) 55,000		600,000
Retained Earnings	200,000	20,000	(1) 20,000		200,000
Total Liabilities and Stockholders' Equity	860,000	85,000	75,000	75,000	870,000

(1) Elimination of intercompany investment.

Figure 20-2
Work Sheet for Preparation of Consolidated Balance Sheet

stockholders' equity section of the consolidated balance sheet is the same as the stockholders' equity section of the Parent Company. After eliminating the Investment in Subsidiary Company against the stockholders' equity of the subsidiary, therefore, we can take the information from the right-hand column in Figure 20-2 and present it in the following form:

Parent Company
Consolidated Balance Sheet
As of Acquisition Date

Cash	$ 50,000	Liabilities	$ 70,000
Other Assets	820,000	Capital Stock	600,000
		Retained Earnings	200,000
Total Assets	$870,000	Total Liabilities and Stockholders' Equity	$870,000

Parent and Subsidiary Companies Work Sheet for Consolidated Balance Sheet As of Acquisition Date					
Accounts	Balance Sheet Parent Company	Balance Sheet Subsidiary Company	Eliminations Debit	Eliminations Credit	Consolidated Balance Sheet
Cash	32,500	25,000			57,500
Investment in Subsidiary Company	67,500			(1) 67,500	
Other Assets	760,000	60,000			820,000
Total Assets	860,000	85,000			877,500
Liabilities	60,000	10,000			70,000
Capital Stock—$10 par value	600,000	55,000	(1) 55,000		600,000
Retained Earnings	200,000	20,000	(1) 20,000		200,000
Minority Interest				(1) 7,500	7,500
Total Liabilities and Stockholders' Equity	860,000	85,000	75,000	75,000	877,500

(1) Elimination of intercompany investment. Minority interest equals 10 percent of subsidiary's stockholders' equity.

Figure 20-3 Work Sheet Showing Elimination of Less Than 100 Percent Ownership

Less Than 100 Percent Purchase at Book Value A parent company does not have to purchase 100 percent of a subsidiary to control it. Any purchase of more than 50 percent of the voting stock of the subsidiary company represents legal control. In the consolidated financial statements, therefore, the total assets and liabilities of the subsidiary are combined with the assets and liabilities of the parent. However, it is still necessary to account for the interests of those stockholders of the subsidiary company who own less than 50 percent of the voting stock. These stockholders are called minority stockholders, and their **minority interest** must appear on the consolidated balance sheet at an amount equal to their percentage of ownership times the net assets of the subsidiary.

For example, assume that above Parent Company purchases 90 percent of Subsidiary Company's voting stock at book value of $67,500 (90% × $75,000). The work sheet for the preparation of the consolidated balance sheet appears in Figure 20-3. The elimination is made in the same way as in the example above except that the minority interest must be accounted for. All of the Investment in Subsidiary Company ($67,500) is eliminated against all of Subsidiary's stockholders' equity ($75,000), and the difference ($7,500, or 10% × $75,000) is established as minority interest. The resulting stockholders' equity section of the consolidated balance sheet consists of (1) minority interest and (2) Parent Company's stockholders' equity:

Minority Interest	$ 7,500
Capital Stock	600,000
Retained Earnings	200,000
Total Stockholders' Equity	$807,500

Objective 3b Prepare consolidated balance sheets at acquisition date for purchase at other than book value

Purchase at More Than or Less Than Book Value The purchase price of a business depends on many factors, such as the prevailing market price, the relative strength of the buyer's and seller's negotiating positions, and the prospects for future earnings. Thus it is only by coincidence that the purchase price of a subsidiary will equal the book value of the subsidiary's equity. Usually, the investment in the subsidiary will not equal the book value of the subsidiary's equity. Accounting for the difference is an important problem. For example, a parent company may pay more than the book value of a subsidiary to purchase a controlling interest if the assets of the subsidiary are understated. The recorded historical cost of the subsidiary's assets may not reflect current market values. The parent may also pay more than book value if the subsidiary has something vital to the parent, such as access to a technical process, an innovative product, or a new market. On the other hand, the parent may pay less than book value for its share of the subsidiary's stock if the subsidiary's assets are not worth their original cost. Or the subsidiary may have incurred heavy losses, causing its stock to sell at distress prices.

The Accounting Principles Board has provided the following guidelines for consolidating a purchased subsidiary and its parent:

> First, all identifiable assets acquired . . . and liabilities assumed in a business combination . . . should be assigned a portion of the cost of the acquired company, normally equal to their fair values at date of acquisition.
>
> Second, the excess of the cost of the acquired company over the sum of the amounts assigned to identifiable assets acquired less liabilities assumed should be recorded as goodwill.[3]

To illustrate the application of these principles, we will assume that the Parent Company purchases 100 percent of the Subsidiary Company's voting stock for $92,500, or $17,500 more than book value. Parent Company attributed $10,000 of the $17,500 to the increased value of Subsidiary's other assets and $7,500 of the $17,500 to the overall strength that Subsidiary Company will add to Parent Company's organization. The work sheet for the preparation of the consolidated balance sheet appears in Figure 20-4 (next page).

3. Accounting Principles Board, *Opinion No. 16,* "Business Combinations" (New York: Accounting Principles Board, 1970), p. 318.

Parent and Subsidiary Companies
Work Sheet for Consolidated Balance Sheet
As of Acquisition Date

Accounts	Balance Sheet Parent Company	Balance Sheet Subsidiary Company	Eliminations Debit		Eliminations Credit		Consolidated Balance Sheet
Cash	7,500	25,000					32,500
Investment in Subsidiary Company	92,500				(1)	92,500	
Other Assets	760,000	60,000	(1)	10,000			830,000
Goodwill			(1)	7,500			7,500
Total Assets	860,000	85,000					870,000
Liabilities	60,000	10,000					70,000
Capital Stock—$10 par value	600,000	55,000	(1)	55,000			600,000
Retained Earnings	200,000	20,000	(1)	20,000			200,000
Total Liabilities and Stockholders' Equity	860,000	85,000		92,500		92,500	870,000

(1) Elimination of intercompany investment. Excess of cost over book value ($92,500 – $75,000 = $17,500) allocated $10,000 to Other Assets and $7,500 to Goodwill.

Figure 20-4
Work Sheet Showing Elimination Where Purchase Cost Is Greater Than Book Value

All of the Investment in Subsidiary Company ($92,500) has been eliminated against all of the Subsidiary Company's stockholders' equity ($75,000). The excess of cost over book value ($17,500) has been debited in the amounts of $10,000 to Other Assets and $7,500 to a new account entitled Goodwill, or Goodwill from Consolidation. Goodwill appears as an asset on the consolidated balance sheet and represents the excess of cost of the investment over book value that cannot be allocated to any specifically identifiable asset. Other Assets appears on the consolidated balance sheet at the combined total of $830,000 ($760,000 + $60,000 + $10,000).

When the parent pays less than book value for its investment in the subsidiary, the Accounting Principles Board, in *Opinion No. 16,* requires that the excess of book value over cost of the investment be used to reduce the carrying value of the subsidiary's assets. The presumption is that the subsidiary's assets are not worth the book value. In other words, the APB advises against the use of the concept of negative goodwill except in very special circumstances.

Intercompany Receivables and Payables If either the parent or the subsidiary company owes money to the other, there will be a receivable on the creditor company's individual balance sheet and a payable on the debtor company's individual balance sheet. When a consolidated balance sheet is prepared, both the receivable and the payable should be eliminated because, from the viewpoint of the consolidated entity, neither the asset nor the liability exists. In other words, it does not make sense for an entity to owe money to itself. The elimination entry would be made on the work sheet by debiting the payable and crediting the receivable for the amount of the intercompany loan.

Consolidated Income Statement

Objective 4 Prepare consolidated income statements for intercompany transactions

The consolidated income statement is prepared for a consolidated entity by combining the revenues and expenses of the parent and subsidiary companies. The procedure is the same as in preparing a consolidated balance sheet; that is, intercompany transactions are eliminated to prevent double counting of revenues and expenses. Examples of intercompany transactions that affect the consolidated income statement are (1) sales and purchases of goods and services between parent and subsidiary (purchases for the buying company and sales for the selling company); (2) income and expenses on loans, receivables, or bond indebtedness between parent and subsidiary; and (3) income and expenses from intercompany transactions other than the two preceding transactions.

To illustrate the eliminating entries, we will assume the following transactions between a parent and its 100 percent owned subsidiary. Parent Company made sales of $120,000 in goods to Subsidiary Company, which in turn sold all the goods to others. Subsidiary Company paid Parent Company $2,000 interest on a loan from the parent.

The work sheet in Figure 20-5 (top of next page) shows how to prepare a consolidated income statement. The purpose of the eliminating entries is to treat the two companies as a single entity. Thus it is important to include in Sales only those made to outsiders and to include in Cost of Goods Sold only those purchases from outsiders. This objective is accomplished with the first eliminating entry. This entry eliminates the $120,000 of intercompany sales and purchases by a debit of that amount to Sales and a credit of that amount to Cost of Goods Sold in the work sheet. As a result, only sales to outsiders ($510,000) and purchases from outsiders ($240,000) are included in the Consolidated Income Statement column. The intercompany interest income and expense is eliminated by a debit to Other Revenues and a credit to Other Expenses.

Other Consolidated Financial Statements

Public corporations also prepare consolidated statements of retained earnings and consolidated statements of changes in financial position. For examples of these statements, see Chapter 7.

Parent and Subsidiary Companies Work Sheet for Consolidated Income Statement For the Year 19xx					
Accounts	Income Statement Parent Company	Income Statement Subsidiary Company	Eliminations Debit	Eliminations Credit	Consolidated Income Statement
Sales	430,000	200,000	(1) 120,000		510,000
Other Revenues	60,000	10,000	(2) 2,000		68,000
Total Revenues	490,000	210,000			578,000
Cost of Goods Sold	210,000	150,000		(1) 120,000	240,000
Other Expenses	140,000	50,000		(2) 2,000	188,000
Total Deductions	350,000	200,000			428,000
Net Income	140,000	10,000	122,000	122,000	150,000

(1) Elimination of intercompany sales and purchases.
(2) Elimination of intercompany interest income and interest expense.

Figure 20-5
Work Sheet Showing Eliminations for Preparation of Consolidated Income Statement

Financial Statements Using the Pooling of Interests Method

In each of the cases illustrated earlier, we assumed that the investment in the subsidiary was made by payment in cash. Payment can obviously be made through various combinations of assets, liabilities, or securities. A special case arises when almost all of the acquisition is made through an exchange of stock. For example, assume that Company A acquires Company B by issuing stock held in its treasury for all the outstanding shares of Company B. An important characteristic of this transaction is that all the stockholders in Company B now become stockholders in Company A. One way of accounting for this exchange would be to assign a market value to the stock issued and record that amount as the cost of the investment. In this case, the accounting treatment would be the same as the purchase method already illustrated in this chapter.

However, an alternative way of looking at the transaction is to say that because the stockholders of Company B and the stockholders of Company A are now all stockholders in Company A, they have pooled their interests, instead of one company having sold out to the other. According

Objective 5 Contrast the purchase and pooling of interests methods in accounting for business combinations, giving reasons for each

to this view of the transaction, it is possible to reason that no purchase transaction actually took place. Therefore, the market value of the stock issued is irrelevant. The assets and liabilities of both companies should continue to be valued at historical cost because theoretically they were not sold or purchased. The managements of the two companies have simply combined their resources and operations, and neither "controls" the other. For this reason, the investment account of the acquiring company should be debited at the par or stated value of the capital stock. This method of accounting for an acquisition is called the **pooling of interests method.**

The pooling of interests method has been extremely popular during the last twenty years. However, it was subject to justified criticism during the 1960s because of its abuse in many situations that were clearly not "poolings." The abuses stemmed from the lack of acceptable guidelines as to when the pooling of interests method was appropriate. As a result, companies took advantage of the lower depreciation and amortization charges (and higher income) that resulted from being able to record purchased assets at the low historical costs of the assets of the acquired company. In addition, under the pooling method, the acquiring company was able to include the acquired company's entire earnings for the year of acquisition in its net income for the year, regardless of when in the year the acquisition took place. Thus a company whose stock was priced very high in relation to its earnings could exchange its stock for the stock of a company that was priced very low in relation to its earnings, thereby gaining an instant increase in its earnings per share.

In 1970, the Accounting Principle Board's *Opinion No. 16* laid down rigid limitations on the use of the pooling of interests method, thus reducing the number of abuses. Now this method is used only for acquisitions where 90 percent or more of the transaction is made by an exchange of stock and there is evidence that a real pooling is involved. Table 20-2 (next page) contrasts the purchase method and the pooling of interests method.

To illustrate the pooling of interests method, we will assume that instead of purchasing Subsidiary Company for cash, Parent Company issues 5,000 shares of $10 par value stock, with a current market value of $20 per share, in exchange for all the outstanding shares of Subsidiary Company. Under the pooling of interests method, the market value of the stock is ignored, and Parent Company records the investment as shown below.

Investment in Subsidiary Company	50,000	
Capital Stock		50,000
To record investment in subsidiary under the pooling method		

The work sheet and eliminations needed for the consolidated balance sheet are shown in Figure 20-6 (page 691). The eliminating entry reflects the theory underlying the pooling of interests method. Note that the investment in the Subsidiary Company is eliminated against the capital

	Combination Conditions	Recording of Investment	Treatment of Subsidiary's Retained Earnings at Acquisition	Treatment of Subsidiary's Earnings
Purchase method	Acquires controlling interest of more than 50% of company's voting stock and exchanges cash, other assets, notes, or debt securities for it.	Parent records investment at amount of cash paid or market price of item given or received, whichever is more clearly evident.	Retained earnings of subsidiary are not included in consolidated retained earnings.	Earnings of subsidiary are combined with those of parent only from acquisition date.
Pooling of interests method	Acquires a controlling interest of more than 90% of company's voting stock by exchanging voting stock.	Parent records investment at par or stated value of shares exchanged. Market value of shares is ignored.	Retained earnings of subsidiary are included in consolidated retained earnings.	Earnings of subsidiary for entire year of acquisition are included with parent's earnings for the year and thereafter.

Table 20-2
Purchase Method Versus Pooling of Interests Method

stock of the Subsidiary Company. Because the investment in the Subsidiary Company is less than the capital stock eliminated, the difference is placed in an account called Paid-in Capital in Excess of Par Value. If the investment in Subsidiary Company was greater than the eliminated capital stock, the difference would be made up by debiting existing Paid-in Capital or Retained Earnings. Note that Subsidiary Company's Retained Earnings account was not eliminated. It was combined with Parent Company's retained earnings under the theory that the two companies were always one company.

The pooling of interests treatment can be easily compared with the purchase treatment. Under the purchase method, illustrated earlier in this chapter, the Investment in Subsidiary Company would be recorded at the market value of $100,000 ($20 × 5,000 shares), and Paid-in Capital in Excess of Par Value of $50,000 would be created as shown in the following entry:

Investment in Subsidiary Company	100,000	
Capital Stock—$10 par		50,000
Paid-in Capital in Excess of Par Value		50,000
To record investment in subsidiary under the purchase method		

Parent and Subsidiary Companies Work Sheet for Consolidated Balance Sheet As of Acquisition Date							
Account	Balance Sheet Parent Company	Balance Sheet Subsidiary Company	Eliminations				Consolidated Balance Sheet
			Debit		Credit		
Cash	100,000	25,000					125,000
Investment in Subsidiary Company	50,000				(1)	50,000	
Other Assets	760,000	60,000					820,000
Total Assets	910,000	85,000					945,000
Accounts Payable	60,000	10,000					70,000
Capital Stock—$10 par value	650,000	55,000	(1)	55,000			650,000
Paid-in Capital in Excess of Par Value					(1)	5,000	5,000
Retained Earnings	200,000	20,000					220,000
Total Liabilities and Stockholders' Equity	910,000	85,000		55,000		55,000	945,000

(1) Elimination of intercompany investment.

Figure 20-6 Work Sheet Showing Business Combination on a Pooling of Interests Basis

The balance of the Capital Stock account is now $650,000 ($600,000 + $50,000), and the balance of Paid-in Capital in Excess of Par Value is now $50,000. On the work sheet, the entire stockholders' equity of the subsidiary ($75,000 – capital stock + retained earnings) would be eliminated, and the excess of cost over book value ($25,000 = $100,000 – $75,000) would be debited to Goodwill or to specifically identifiable assets. Consolidated Retained Earnings is equal to the Parent Company's retained earnings of $200,000. The resulting consolidated balance sheet under the two methods may be compared as shown in Figure 20-7 (top of next page).

Figure 20-7
Consolidated Balance Sheets

	Pooling of Interests Method	Purchase Method
Assets		
Cash	$125,000	$125,000
Other Assets	820,000	820,000
Goodwill		25,000
Total Assets	$945,000	$970,000
Liabilities and Stockholders' Equity		
Liabilities	$ 70,000	$ 70,000
Capital Stock—$10 par value	650,000	650,000
Paid-in Capital in Excess of Par Value	5,000	50,000
Retained Earnings	220,000	200,000
Total Liabilities and Stockholders' Equity	$945,000	$970,000

International Accounting

As businesses grow, it is natural for them to look for new sources of supply and new markets in other countries. Today, it is common for businesses, called multinational or transnational corporations, to operate in more than one country, and many of them operate throughout the world. Table 20-3 shows the extent of foreign business for a few multina-

Table 20-3
Extent of Foreign Business for Selected Companies

Company	Country	Total Revenue (Millions)	Foreign Revenue as % of Total
General Motors	U.S.A.	$63,221	22.4
Exxon	U.S.A.	60,335	73.5
British Petroleum	Britain	27,407	81.0
International Business Machines	U.S.A.	21,076	52.4
Nestlé	Switzerland	11,798	98.0
Volkswagenwerk	Germany	13,305	58.0
Xerox	U.S.A.	5,902	47.2
Procter & Gamble	U.S.A.	4,312	56.6

Source: Forbes, June 25, 1979, pp. 56 and 62.

Table 20-4
Partial Listing of Foreign Exchange Rates

Country	Prices in $ U.S.
Britain (pound)	2.20
Canada (dollar)	.85
France (franc)	.23
Italy (lira)	.001
Japan (yen)	.0039
Mexico (peso)	.044
West Germany (mark)	.53

Source: The Wall Street Journal (April 14, 1980).

tional corporations. IBM, for example, has operations in eighty countries and receives about half of its sales and profits from foreign operations. Nestlé, the giant Swiss chocolate and food products company, operates in fifteen countries and receives 98 percent of its sales from foreign operations. The economies of such industrial countries as the United States, Japan, Great Britain, West Germany, and France have spawned large worldwide enterprises. In addition, sophisticated investors no longer restrict their investment activities to their domestic securities markets. Many Americans invest in foreign securities markets, and non-Americans invest heavily in the stock market in the United States.

Objective 6 Show how changing exchange rates affect financial reporting

Such transactions have two major effects on accounting. First, most sales or purchases of goods and services in other countries involve different currencies. Consequently, one currency needs to be translated into another through the use of exchange rates. An **exchange rate** is the value of one currency in terms of another. For example, an English person who purchases goods from a U.S. company and has to pay in U.S. dollars must exchange the British pounds for U.S. dollars before making payment. In effect, the currencies are commodities that can be bought and sold. Table 20-4, illustrating the exchange rates of several currencies in terms of dollars, shows the exchange rate for British pounds as $2.20 per pound on a particular date. Like the price of any commodity, these prices change daily according to supply and demand for the currencies. For example, a year earlier the exchange rate for British pounds was $2.14. Accounting for these price changes in recording foreign transactions and preparing financial statements for foreign subsidiaries is the subject of the next two sections.

The second major effect of international business on accounting is that financial standards differ substantially from country to country, making it difficult for the international investor to compare performances of companies from different countries. Some of the obstacles to achieving better comparability and some of the progress in solving the problem are discussed later in this chapter.

Accounting for Transactions in Foreign Currencies

Among the first activities of an expanding company in the international market are the buying and selling of goods and services. For example, a maker of precision tools may try to expand by selling its product to foreign customers, or it might try to lower its product cost by buying a less expensive component from a source in another country. In previous chapters, all transactions were recorded in dollars, and it was assumed that the dollar is a uniform measure in the same way that inches and centimeters are. In the international marketplace, a transaction may take place in Japanese yen, British pounds, or some other currency. The values of these currencies fluctuate daily in their relation to the dollar.

Foreign Sales When a domestic company sells merchandise abroad, it may bill either in its own country's currency or in the foreign currency. If the billing and the subsequent payment are both in the domestic currency, no accounting problem arises. For example, assume that the precision toolmaker sells $100,000 worth of tools to a British company and bills the British company in dollars. The entry to record the sale and payment is very familiar:

Date of sale:		
Accounts Receivable, British company	100,000	
Sales		100,000
Date of payment:		
Cash	100,000	
Accounts Receivable, British company		100,000

However, if the U.S. company bills the British company in British pounds and accepts payment in pounds, the U.S. company may incur an exchange gain or loss. An exchange gain or loss will occur if the exchange rate of dollars to pounds changes between the date of sale and the date of payment. For example, assume that the sale of $100,000 above was billed as £45,454.55, reflecting an exchange rate of 2.20 (that is, $2.20 per pound) on the sale date, and that by the date of payment, the exchange rate had declined to 2.10. The entries to record the transactions are shown below.

Date of sale:		
Accounts Receivable, British company (£45,454.55)	100,000	
Sales		100,000
Date of payment:		
Cash (£45,454.55 × 2.10)	95,454.55	
Exchange Gain or Loss	4,545.45	
Accounts Receivable, British Company		100,000

The U.S. company has incurred an exchange loss of $4,545.45 because it agreed to accept a fixed number of British pounds in payment, and before the payment was made, the value of each pound declined in value. Had the value of the pound in relation to the dollar increased in value, the U.S. company would have made an exchange gain.

Foreign Purchases Because purchases are the opposite of sales, the same logic applies to them except that the relation of exchange gains and losses to the changes in exchange rates is reversed. For example, assume that the above maker of precision tools purchases $10,000 of a certain component from a Japanese supplier. If the purchase and subsequent payment are made in U.S. dollars, no accounting problem arises.

Date of purchase:		
Purchases	10,000	
Accounts Payable, Japanese company		10,000
Date of payment:		
Accounts Payable, Japanese company	10,000	
Cash		10,000

If the Japanese company bills the U.S. company in yen and is paid in yen, however, the U.S. company will incur an exchange gain or loss if the exchange rate changes between the dates of purchase and payment. For example, assume the same facts as above except that the transaction is in yen and the exchange rates of the dates of purchase and payment are .0040 (that is, $.0040 per yen) and .0038, respectively. The entries are shown below.

Date of purchase:		
Purchases (Y2,500,000 × .004)	10,000	
Accounts Payable, Japanese company		10,000
Date of payment:		
Accounts Payable, Japanese company	10,000	
Exchange Gain or Loss		500
Cash (Y2,500,000 × .0038)		9,500

In this case, the U.S. company received an exchange gain of $500 because it had agreed to pay a fixed Y2,500,000 and between the dates of purchase and payment the exchange value of the yen in relation to the dollar increased.

Realized Versus Unrealized Exchange Gain or Loss The above illustration dealt with completed transactions (in the sense that payment was completed), and the exchange gain or loss was recognized on the date of payment in each case. If financial statements are prepared between the sale or purchase and the subsequent receipt or payment, there will be unrealized gains or losses if the exchange rates have changed. The Financial Accounting Standards Board, in its *Statement No. 8,* requires that "exchange gains and losses shall be included in determining net income for the period in which the rate changes,"[4] including interim (quarterly) periods and regardless of whether the transaction is complete.

This requirement has created much controversy and is currently under review by the FASB. Critics of the requirement charge that it gives undue influence to temporary exchange rate changes, thus producing random fluctuations in earnings that obscure long-run trends. Those who favor the regulation, on the other hand, feel that the use of current exchange rates on the balance sheet date to value receivables and payables is a major step toward economic reality (current values). One proposal being studied by the FASB is to continue to report on the income statement the effects of changes in exchange rates on complex transactions, but to report those from incomplete transactions as a separate component of stockholders' equity.

To demonstrate these effects, we will assume the following facts about the above example involving a U.S. company's purchase of components from a Japanese supplier:

	Date	**Exchange Rate ($ per Yen)**
Date of purchase	Dec. 1	.0040
Balance sheet date	Dec. 31	.0035
Date of payment	Feb. 1	.0038

The only difference is that the complete transaction spanned the balance sheet date and the exchange rate was $.0035 per yen on that date. In summary form, the data and entries can be shown as follows:

	Dec. 1	**Dec. 31**	**Feb. 1**
Sales recorded in U.S. dollars (billed as Y2,500,000)	$10,000	$10,000	$10,000
Dollars to be paid to equal Y2,500,000	10,000	8,750	9,500
Unrealized gain (or loss)	—	$ 1,250	
Realized gain (or loss)			$ 500

Dec. 1	Purchases	10,000	
	Accounts Payable, Japanese company		10,000
Dec. 31	Accounts Payable, Japanese company	1,250	
	Exchange Gain or Loss		1,250
Feb. 1	Accounts Payable, Japanese company	8,750	
	Exchange Gain or Loss	750	
	Cash		9,500

4. *Statement of Financial Accounting Standards No. 8,* "Accounting for the Translation of Foreign Currency Transactions and Foreign Currency Financial Statements" (Stamford, Conn.: Financial Accounting Standards Board, 1975), par. 17.

In this case, the original sale was billed in yen by the Japanese supplier. Following the rules of *Statement No. 8,* an exchange gain of $1,250 is recorded on December 31, and an exchange loss of $750 is recorded on February 1. Although the net effect of these large up-and-down fluctuations is the relatively small net exchange gain over the complete transaction of $500, the effect on each year may be significant.

Translation of Foreign Subsidiary Financial Statements

Expanding companies often make foreign sales and purchases by establishing foreign branches and subsidiaries. We limit the discussion here to foreign subsidiaries because there are special rules that apply to foreign branches that are usually reserved for more advanced courses.

A foreign subsidiary that is more than 50 percent owned and over which the parent company exercises control should be included in the consolidated financial statements. The procedure for consolidation is exactly the same as for consolidating domestic subsidiaries except that the statements of the foreign subsidiary must be translated into U.S. dollars before consolidation. Clearly, it is illogical to combine the assets of one company stated in pesos, for instance, with another stated in dollars.

Objective 7 Restate a foreign subsidiary's financial statements in U.S. dollars

Translation Rates The Financial Accounting Standards Board also included in *Statement No. 8,* the general requirements for translation of accounts in foreign currency financial statements. These rules are summarized below.

Accounts	Translation Rate
Monetary assets—current assets other than inventory and prepaid expenses	Current rate
Inventories and prepaid expenses	Historical rate
Plant assets	Historical rate
Liabilities	Current rate
Owners' equity	Historical rate
Revenues	Average rate
Expenses (except depreciation, which should use the same rate as plant assets)	Average rate

The historical rate is the exchange rate when the transaction occurred. The current rate is the exchange rate on the balance sheet date, and the average rate is the average exchange rate during the period covered by the financial statements.

Example of Translation Assume that Exmar Corporation has a 100 percent owned subsidiary in Mexico called Mexmar Corporation. Before year-end consolidated financial statements can be prepared, the financial statements of Mexmar Corporation must be translated into U.S. dollars. The following translation rates of pesos to dollars are appropriate: historical rate, .06; current rate, .04; average rate, .05.

The balance sheet and income statement of Mexmar Corporation are presented on the next page in both Mexican pesos and U.S. dollars.

Balance Sheet	Pesos	Exchange Rate	U.S. Dollars
Cash	100,000	.04	$ 4,000
Accounts Receivable	250,000	.04	10,000
Inventories	400,000	.06	24,000
Plant Assets (net)	1,500,000	.06	90,000
Total Assets	2,250,000		$128,000
Accounts Payable	150,000	.04	$ 6,000
Bonds Payable	600,000	.04	24,000
Common Stock	500,000	.06	30,000
Retained Earnings	1,000,000	.06	60,000
Exchange Gain			8,000
Total Liabilities and Owners' Equity	2,250,000		$128,000

Income Statement	Pesos	Exchange Rate	U.S. Dollars
Sales	3,000,000	.05	$150,000
Cost of Goods Sold	1,400,000	.05	$ 70,000
Depreciation	200,000	.06	12,000
Other Expenses	1,000,000	.05	50,000
Total Deductions	2,600,000		$132,000
Net Income	400,000		$ 18,000

The exchange gain of $8,000 in the balance sheet is computed by determining the amount necessary to balance the liabilities and stockholders' equity with the assets. Only monetary assets (Cash and Accounts Receivable) and monetary liabilities (Accounts Payable and Bonds Payable) have been translated at the current rate. Thus the exchange gain (or loss) on the balance sheet represents the amount that should be reported on the consolidated income statement in accordance with FASB *Statement No. 8* (see pages 696 and 697).

The Search for Uniformity of International Accounting Standards

Objective 8 Describe progress toward international accounting standards

International investors like to compare the financial position and results of operations of companies from different countries. Currently, however, there are no recognized worldwide standards of accounting. A number of serious problems impede progress in establishing such international standards. One is the failure of accountants and users to consider or agree on the objectives of financial statements. Some other problems involve the differences in the extent to which the accounting profession has developed in various countries, the provisions in the laws regulating companies, and the requirements of government and other regulatory bodies.

Still other difficulties include the failure to consider differences among countries in basic economic factors affecting financial reporting, inconsistencies in practices recommended by the accounting professions in different countries, and the influence of tax laws on financial reporting.[5] In the final area mentioned, for example, a survey for a major accounting firm found widely differing requirements. In nine countries, strict adherence to tax accounting was required; in eleven countries, adherence to tax accounting was required in some areas; and in four countries (including the United States), adherence to tax practice was mostly forbidden.[6]

Some efforts have been made to reach a greater degree of international understanding and uniformity of accounting practice. The Accountants' International Study Group, formed in 1966 and consisting of the AICPA and its counterparts in Canada, England, Wales, Ireland, and Scotland, has issued reports that survey and compare accounting practices in the member countries.

Probably the best hopes for identifying areas of agreement among the wide variety of countries are the International Accounting Standards Committee (IASC) and the International Federation of Accountants (IFAC). The IASC was formed in 1973 with representatives of professional accounting societies from Australia, Canada, France, Germany, Japan, Mexico, the Netherlands, the United Kingdom, and the United States. Approximately twelve other countries participate as associate members. This committee has taken the first steps toward consensus among industrialized countries on the basic accounting issues. The standards issued by the committee are usually followed by large multinational companies that are clients of international accounting firms. The IFAC, formed in 1977 at the 11th International Congress of Accountants, is made up of ninety-nine professional accounting organizations from seventy-one countries. This organization, with a permanent administrative staff in New York City, has as its objective the development of international guidelines for auditing, ethics, education, and management accounting as well as the promotion of research and close relations among all accountants. Much progress is expected from this new body.

Chapter Review

Review of Learning Objectives

1. State the principles of valuation for various types of corporate investments in other firms.

Long-term stock investments fall into three categories. First are noninfluential and noncontrolling investments representing less than 20 percent ownership. To account for these investments, use the cost method, adjusting the investment to

5. *Accounting Standards for Business Enterprises Throughout the World* (Chicago: Arthur Andersen, 1974), pp. 2–3.

6. *Accounting Principles and Reporting Practices: A Survey in 38 Countries* (New York: Price Waterhouse International, 1973), sec. 233.

the lower of cost or market for financial statement purposes. Second are influential but noncontrolling investments representing 20 percent to 50 percent ownership. Use the equity method to account for these investments. Third are controlling interest investments representing more than 50 percent ownership. Account for them by using consolidated financial statement methods.

2. Explain when to prepare consolidated financial statements and their uses. Consolidated financial statements are normally prepared when an investing company has legal and effective control over another company. Control usually exists when the parent company owns more than 50 percent of the voting stock of the subsidiary company. Consolidated financial statements are useful to investors and others because they treat the parent company and its subsidiaries realistically as an integrated economic unit.

3. Prepare consolidated balance sheets at acquisition date for purchase at (a) book value, and (b) other than book value. At the date of acquisition, a work sheet entry is made to eliminate the investment for the parent company's financial statements and the owners' equity section from the subsidiary's financial statements. The assets and liabilities of the two companies are combined. If the parent owns less than 100 percent of the subsidiary, minority interest will appear on the consolidated balance sheet equal to the percentage of the subsidiary not owned by the parent multiplied by the owners' equity of the subsidiary. If the cost of the parent's investment in the subsidiary is greater than the book value of the subsidiary acquired, an amount equal to the excess of cost above book value will appear on the consolidated balance sheet as goodwill. If the cost of the parent's investment in the subsidiary is less than the book value of the subsidiary acquired, the excess of book value over cost should be used to reduce the book value of the assets of the subsidiary.

4. Prepare consolidated income statements for intercompany transactions. When consolidated income statements are prepared, intercompany sales, purchases, interest income, and interest expense must be eliminated in order to avoid double counting of these items.

5. Contrast between the purchase and pooling of interests methods in accounting for business combinations, giving reasons for each. The purchase method is always used when the parent company acquires more than 50 percent but less than 90 percent of the subsidiary company and when the acquisition is not made through an exchange of stock. Under this method, the parent records the investment at the cash or market value of the exchange because it is assumed that the purchase should be recorded in the same way as any new asset of the company. The pooling of interests method is used only in a case where 90 percent or more of the stock of the subsidiary is acquired through an exchange of stock. In this case, the parent company records the investment at the par or stated value of the stock given up, because in theory no real sale has occurred. The two companies have theoretically pooled their operations and management, with neither exercising control over the other. Under this method, the retained earnings of the two companies are combined, whereas under the purchase method, the entire stockholders' equity section of the subsidiary is eliminated.

6. Show how changing exchange rates affect financial reporting.
A domestic company may make sales or purchases abroad in either its own country's currency or the foreign currency. If a transaction (sales or purchase) and its resolution (receipt or payment) are made in the domestic currency, no accounting problem arises. However, if the transaction and its resolution are made in a foreign currency and the exchange rate changes between the time of the transaction and its resolution, an exchange gain or loss will occur and should be recorded.

7. Restate a foreign subsidiary's financial statements in U.S. dollars.
Foreign currencies are converted to U.S. dollars by multiplying the exchange rates by the amount in the foreign subsidiary's financial statements. The translation rates to be used are specified in FASB *Statement No. 8.* In general, monetary assets and liabilities translate at the current rate, other assets and owners' equity at the historical rate, and revenues and expenses at the average rate.

8. Describe progress toward international accounting standards.
There has been some progress toward setting up international accounting standards, especially through the efforts of the International Accounting Standards Committee and the International Federation of Accountants. However, there still are serious inconsistencies in financial reporting among countries that make the comparison of financial statements from different countries difficult.

Review Problem

Before doing the exercises and problems, review especially the preparation of the work sheet for the consolidated balance sheet. For additional help, see the review problem in the working papers.

Chapter Assignments

Questions

1. Why are the concepts of significant influence and control important to a discussion of long-term investments?
2. For each of the following categories of long-term investments, briefly describe the applicable percentage of ownership and accounting treatment: (a) noninfluential and noncontrolling investment, (b) influential but noncontrolling investment, and (c) controlling investment.
3. What is meant by a parent-subsidiary relationship?
4. Are the stockholders of RCA Corporation more interested in the consolidated financial statements of RCA than in the statements of its principal subsidiaries, such as NBC, Hertz Rent-A-Car, or the electronics division? Explain.
5. The annual report for United States Steel Corporation included the following statement in its Summary of Principal Accounting Policies: "*Principles applied in consolidation.*—Majority owned subsidiaries are consolidated, except for leasing and finance companies and those subsidiaries not considered to be material." Why were leasing and finance companies not consolidated?

6. Also from the annual report of United States Steel Corporation is the following statement in the Summary of Principal Accounting Policies: "*Investments.*— Investments in leasing and finance companies are at U.S. Steel's equity in the net assets and advances to such companies. Investments in other companies, in which U.S. Steel has significant influence in management and control, are also on the equity basis." What is the equity basis of accounting for investments, and why does United States Steel use it in this instance?
7. Why may the price paid to acquire a controlling interest in a subsidiary company differ from the book value of the subsidiary?
8. Why should intercompany receivables, payables, sales, and purchases be eliminated in the preparation of consolidated financial statements?
9. The following item appears on a consolidated balance sheet: "Goodwill from Consolidation—$70,000." Explain how this item arose and where you would expect to find it on the consolidated balance sheet.
10. The following item appears on a consolidated balance sheet: "Minority Interest—$50,000." Explain how this item arose and where you would expect to find it on the consolidated balance sheet.
11. Subsidiary Corporation has a book value of $100,000, of which Parent Corporation purchases 100 percent for $115,000. What is the amount of goodwill from consolidation?
12. Subsidiary Corporation, a 100 percent owned subsidiary, has total sales of $500,000, $100,000 of which were made to Parent Corporation. Parent Corporation has total sales of $1,000,000, including sales of all items purchased from Subsidiary Corporation. What is the amount of sales on the consolidated income statement?
13. When is the pooling of interests method for preparing consolidated financial statements appropriate?
14. Par Corporation acquired 100 percent of the voting stock of Sub Corporation, which has a book value of $150,000, by issuing voting stock in Par Corporation, which had a market value of $200,000. What amount would be recorded in the Investment in Subsidiary account in Par Corporation's accounting records under (a) the purchase method and (b) the pooling of interests method? Which method results in goodwill upon consolidation?
15. What is the difference in the treatment of retained earnings of the subsidiary company upon consolidation under the purchase method and the pooling of interests method?
16. What does it mean to say that the exchange rate of a French franc in terms of the U.S. dollar is .20? If a bottle of French perfume costs 200 francs, how much will it cost in dollars?
17. If an American firm does business with a German firm and all their transactions take place in German marks, which firm may incur an exchange gain or loss and why?
18. If you as an investor were trying to evaluate the relative performance of General Motors, Volkswagen(werk), and Toyota Motors from their published financial statements, what problem might you encounter (other than language)?
19. What are some of the obstacles to uniform accounting standards, and what efforts are being made to overcome them?

Classroom Exercises

Exercise 20-1 Long-Term Investments— Cost and Equity Methods

On January 1, Markowitz Corporation purchased, as a long-term investment, 10 percent of the voting stock of Holtz Corporation for $200,000 and 40 percent of the voting stock of March Corporation for $1,000,000. During the year, Holtz

Corporation had earnings of $100,000 and paid dividends of $40,000, and March Corporation had earnings of $300,000 and paid dividends of $200,000. The market value of neither investment declined during the year.

Which of these investments should be accounted for using the cost method? Which should use the equity method? At what amount should each investment be carried on the balance sheet at year end? Give a reason for each choice.

Exercise 20-2 Long-Term Investments—Lower-of-Cost-or-Market Method

Thoma Corporation has the following portfolio of investments at year end:

Company	Percentage of Voting Stock Held	Cost	Year-End Market Value
A Corporation	3	$160,000	$200,000
B Corporation	11	750,000	500,000
C Corporation	4	60,000	90,000
Total		$970,000	$790,000

The Unrealized Loss in Long-Term Investments account and the Allowance to Reduce Long-Term Investments to Market account both currently have a balance of $80,000.

Prepare the year-end adjustment to reflect the above information.

Exercise 20-3 Long-Term Investments—Equity Method

At the beginning of the current year, Caron Corporation acquired 45 percent of the voting stock of Williams Corporation for $2,400,000 in cash, an amount sufficient to exercise significant influence over Williams Corporation activities. During the year, Williams Corporation paid dividends of $400,000 but incurred a net loss of $200,000.

Prepare journal entries to record the above information.

Exercise 20-4 Elimination Entry for a Purchase at Book Value

The Median Manufacturing Company purchased 100 percent of the common stock of the Leigh Manufacturing Company for $125,000. Leigh's stockholders' equity included common stock of $75,000 and retained earnings of $50,000.

Prepare the eliminating entry on the work sheet necessary for consolidating the balance sheets of these two entities as of the acquisition date.

Exercise 20-5 Elimination Entry and Minority Interest

The stockholders' equity section of the LTZ Corporation's balance sheet appeared as follows on December 31:

Common Stock—$5 par value, 40,000 shares authorized and issued	$200,000
Retained Earnings	24,000
Total Stockholders' Equity	$224,000

Assume that Oldley Manufacturing Company owns 90 percent of the voting stock of LTZ and paid $5.60 for each share.

Prepare the entry (including minority interest) to eliminate Oldley's investment and LTZ's stockholders' equity on the work sheet used in preparing the consolidated balance sheet for the two firms.

Exercise 20-6 Consolidated Balance Sheet with Goodwill

On September 1, P Company purchased 100 percent of the voting stock of S Company for $960,000 in cash. The separate condensed balance sheets immediately after the purchase are shown on the next page.

	P Company	S Company
Other Assets	$2,206,000	$1,089,000
Investment in S Company	960,000	—
	$3,166,000	$1,089,000
Liabilities	$ 871,000	$ 189,000
Capital Stock—$1 par value	1,000,000	300,000
Retained Earnings	1,295,000	600,000
	$3,166,000	$1,089,000

Prepare a work sheet for the consolidated balance sheet immediately after P Company acquired control of S Company. Assume that any excess of the cost of the investment in subsidiary over book value acquired is attributable to goodwill from consolidation.

Exercise 20-7 Analyzing the Effects of Elimination Entries

Some of the separate accounts from the balance sheets for X Company and Y Company are shown just after X Company purchased 90 percent of Y Company's voting stock for $810,000 in cash.

	X Company	Y Company
Accounts Receivable	$1,300,000	$400,000
Interest Receivable, Bonds of Y Company	7,200	—
Investment in Y Company	810,000	—
Investment in Y Company Bonds	180,000	—
Accounts Payable	530,000	190,000
Interest Payable, Bonds	32,000	20,000
Bonds Payable	800,000	500,000
Capital Stock	1,000,000	600,000
Retained Earnings	560,000	300,000

The Accounts Receivable and Accounts Payable include the following: Y Company owed X Company $50,000 for services rendered, and X Company owed Y Company $66,000 for purchases of merchandise.

Determine the amount (including minority interest) that would appear in the consolidated balance sheet for each of the above accounts.

Exercise 20-8 Pooling of Interests Method

Mag Corporation acquired 100 percent of Tag Corporation by exchanging 500,000 shares of its $5 par value stock for all the outstanding shares of Tag Corporation. Immediately after the acquisition, the stockholders' equity sections of the two separate companies appeared as follows:

	Mag Corporation	Tag Corporation
Common Stock—$5 par value	$10,000,000	$ 1,000,000
Premium on Common Stock	2,000,000	6,000,000
Retained Earnings	5,000,000	3,000,000
Total Stockholders' Equity	$17,000,000	$10,000,000

Assuming that the pooling of interests method is used, determine the amounts that would appear in the stockholders' equity section of the consolidated balance sheet immediately after acquisition.

Exercise 20-9 Purchase Method

Assuming the same facts as in Exercise 20-8 and that the stock of Mag Corporation has a market value of $20 per share, use the purchase method to prepare the stockholders' equity section as it would appear immediately after acquisition on the consolidated balance sheet.

Exercise 20-10 Recording International Transactions—Fluctuating Exchange Rate

U.S. Corporation purchased a special-purpose machine from German Corporation on credit for 30,000 DM (marks). At the date of purchase, the exchange rate was $.39 per mark. On the date of payment, which was made in marks, the value of the mark had increased to $.41.

Prepare journal entries to record the purchase and payment in the U.S. Corporation's accounting records.

Problem Set A

Problem 20A-1 Long-Term Investments—Equity Method

The S & S Company owns 45 percent of the voting stock of the Dinolfo Company. The investment account for this company on S & S Company's balance sheet had a balance of $150,000 on January 1, 19xx. During 19xx, Dinolfo Company reported the following quarterly earnings and dividends paid:

Quarter	Earnings	Dividends Paid
1	$20,000	$10,000
2	15,000	10,000
3	40,000	10,000
4	(10,000)	10,000
	$65,000	$40,000

S & S Company exercises significant influence over the operations of Dinolfo Company and therefore uses the equity method to account for its investment.

Required

1. Prepare the journal entries that S & S Company must make each quarter in accounting for its investment in Dinolfo Company.
2. Prepare a ledger account for the investment in common stock of Dinolfo Company, enter the beginning balance, and post the relevant portions of the entries made in part 1.

Problem 20A-2 Long-Term Investment Transactions

Sentax Corporation made the following transactions in its long-term investment account over a two-year period:

19x0

Apr. 1 Purchased with cash 20,000 shares of Meta Company stock for $38 per share.

June 1 Purchased with cash 15,000 shares of Nebo Corporation stock for $18.00 per share.

Sept. 1 Received a 50¢ per share dividend from Meta Company.

Nov. 1 Purchased with cash 25,000 shares of Otta Corporation stock for $27.50 per share.

Dec. 31 The market values per share of the shares held in the Long-Term Investment account were as follows: Meta Company, $35.00; Nebo Corporation, $8.00; and Otta Corporation, $30.50.

19x1

Feb. 1 Because of unfavorable prospects for the Nebo Corporation, the Nebo stock was sold for cash at $10.00 per share.

May 1 Purchased with cash 10,000 shares of Patz Corporation for $56.00 per share.
Sept. 1 Received a 50¢ per share dividend from Meta Company.
Dec. 31 The market values per share of the shares held in the Long-Term Investment account were as follows: Meta Company, $40.00; Otta Corporation, $35.00; and Patz Corporation, $50.00.

Required

Prepare the entries to record the transactions above in Sentax Corporation records, assuming that all investments represent less than 20 percent of the voting stock of the company whose stock was acquired.

Problem 20A-3 Consolidated Balance Sheet—Cost Exceeding Book Value

The balance sheets of MD and RD Companies as of December 31, 19xx, are shown below.

	MD Company	RD Company
Assets		
Cash	$ 30,000	$ 20,000
Accounts Receivable	50,000	15,000
Investment in RD Company	150,000	—
Other Assets	50,000	90,000
Total Assets	$280,000	$125,000
Liabilities and Stockholders' Equity		
Liabilities	$ 30,000	$ 15,000
Capital Stock—$10 par value	200,000	100,000
Retained Earnings	50,000	10,000
Total Liabilities and Stockholders' Equity	$280,000	$125,000

Required

Prepare a consolidated balance sheet work sheet for the MD and RD Companies, assuming that the MD Company purchased 100 percent of RD's capital stock immediately prior to the above balance sheet date and that $20,000 of the excess of cost over book value is attributable to RD Company's Other Assets. The rest of the excess is considered to be goodwill.

Problem 20A-4 Preparation of Consolidated Income Statement

The Parent Company has owned 100 percent of the Sub Company since 19x0. The income statements of these two companies for the year ended December 31, 19x1, are shown at the top of the next page.

Additional information: (a) The Sub Company purchased $300,000 of inventory from the Parent Company, all of which had been sold to Sub Company customers by the end of the year. (b) The Sub Company leased its building from the Parent Company for $50,000 per year.

	Parent Company	Sub Company
Sales	$1,500,000	$600,000
Cost of Goods Sold	750,000	400,000
Gross Profit	$ 750,000	$200,000
Less: Selling Expenses	$ 250,000	$ 50,000
General and Administrative Expenses	300,000	100,000
Total Operating Expenses	$ 550,000	$150,000
Net Income from Operations	$ 200,000	$ 50,000
Other Income	50,000	—
Net Income	$ 250,000	$ 50,000

Required

Prepare a consolidated income statement work sheet for the two companies for the year ended December 31, 19x1.

Problem 20A-5 Consolidated Balance Sheet—Less Than 100 Percent Ownership

In a cash transaction, Atex Company purchased 80 percent of the outstanding stock of Bay Company on June 30, 19xx. Immediately after the acquisition, the separate balance sheets of the companies appeared as follows:

	Atex Company	Bay Company
Assets		
Cash	$ 80,000	$ 12,000
Accounts Receivable	130,000	60,000
Inventory	200,000	130,000
Investment in Bay Company	169,600	—
Plant and Equipment (net)	300,000	220,000
Other Assets	10,000	40,000
Total Assets	$889,600	$462,000
Liabilities and Stockholders' Equity		
Accounts Payable	$170,000	$100,000
Long-Term Debt	200,000	150,000
Capital Stock—$5 par value	400,000	200,000
Retained Earnings	119,600	12,000
Total Liabilities and Stockholders' Equity	$889,600	$462,000

Additional information: (a) Bay Company's other assets represent a long-term investment in Atex Company's long-term debt. (b) Atex Company owes Bay Company $15,000 for services rendered.

Required

Prepare a work sheet as of the acquisition date for the preparation of a consolidated balance sheet.

Problem 20A-6 Pooling of Interests Method Versus Purchase Method

The condensed balance sheets of Tennis Corporation and Squash Corporation are presented below. Tennis Corporation intends to merge with Squash Corporation by exchanging 100,000 shares of its stock for all the shares of Squash Corporation. The market value of each share of Tennis Corporation is $27 on the date of acquisition.

	Tennis Corporation	Squash Corporation
Assets	$8,440,000	$4,020,000
Liabilities	$2,260,000	$1,400,000
Stockholders' Equity		
Common Stock—$10 par value	400,000	300,000
Paid-in Capital in Excess of Par Value	2,200,000	1,600,000
Retained Earnings	3,580,000	720,000
	$8,440,000	$4,020,000

Required

1. Prepare general journal entries to record the investment (issue of common stock) by Tennis Corporation assuming that (a) the pooling of interests method is used, and (b) the purchase method is used.
2. Prepare a consolidated balance sheet work sheet as of the date of acquisition using (a) the pooling of interests method, and (b) the purchase method (assuming that excess of cost over book value is goodwill).
3. Comment on the differences in the results achieved in parts 1 and 2.

Problem 20A-7 Conversion of Balance Sheet Using Exchange Rates

The balance sheet of Southern Leather Company, a 100 percent owned subsidiary of Northern Distributors, is on the next page. The subsidiary is located in Mexico City, and the statement is shown in pesos. As you prepare the consolidated financial statements for Northern Distributors, convert Southern Leather's balance sheet from pesos to U.S. dollars. The historical exchange rate is $.07 per peso, the current rate is $.05 per peso, and the average rate is $.06 per peso.

Required

Convert the balance sheet of Southern Leather Company to U.S. dollars for consolidation purposes.

Southern Leather Company Balance Sheet (in pesos) December 31, 19xx	
Assets	
Cash	10,000
Accounts Receivable	80,000
Inventory	160,000
Property, Plant, and Equipment (net)	250,000
Total Assets	500,000
Liabilities and Stockholders' Equity	
Accounts Payable	25,000
Salaries Payable	20,000
Common Stock	400,000
Retained Earnings	55,000
Total Liabilities and Stockholders' Equity	500,000

Problem Set B

Problem 20B-2 Long-Term Investment Transactions

The Safeturf Company on January 2, 19x0, made several long-term investments in the voting stock of various companies. It purchased 10,000 shares of Apex at $2.00 a share, 15,000 shares of U.D.I. at $3.00 a share, and 6,000 shares of Graphics at $4.50 a share. Each investment represents less than 20 percent of the voting stock of the company. The transactions of Safeturf in securities during 19x0 are as follows:

May 15 Purchased with cash 6,000 shares of Durex stock for $3.00 per share. This investment is less than 20 percent of the Durex voting stock.
July 16 Sold the 10,000 shares of Apex stock for $1.80 per share.
Sept. 30 Purchased with cash 5,000 additional shares of U.D.I. for $3.20 per share.
Dec. 31 The market values per share of the stock in the Long-Term Investment account were as follows: U.D.I., $3.25; Graphics, $4.00; and Durex, $2.00.

Safeturf's transactions in securities during 19x1 are as follows:

Feb. 1 Received a cash dividend from U.D.I. of 10¢ per share.
July 15 Sold for cash the 6,000 Graphics shares owned for $4.00 per share.
Aug. 1 Received a cash dividend of 10¢ per share from U.D.I.
Sept. 10 Purchased 3,000 shares of Techco for $7.00 per share.
Dec. 31 The market values per share of the stock in the Long-Term Investment account were as follows: U.D.I., $3.25; Durex, $2.50; and Techco, $6.50.

Required

Prepare the journal entries to record the transactions of Safeturf Company in its long-term investments during 19x0 and 19x1.

Problem 20B-3 Consolidated Balance Sheet—Cost Exceeding Book Value

The balance sheets of Bobbins and Mentel Corporations as of December 31, 19xx, are shown below.

	Bobbins Corporation	Mentel Corporation
Assets		
Cash	$ 600,000	$ 120,000
Accounts Receivable	700,000	600,000
Inventory	250,000	600,000
Investment in Mentel Corporation	750,000	—
Property, Plant, and Equipment	1,350,000	850,000
Other Assets	20,000	50,000
Total Assets	$3,670,000	$2,220,000
Liabilities and Stockholders' Equity		
Accounts Payable	$ 750,000	$ 500,000
Salaries Payable	300,000	270,000
Bonds Payable	300,000	800,000
Common Stock	1,500,000	500,000
Retained Earnings	820,000	150,000
Total Liabilities and Stockholders' Equity	$3,670,000	$2,220,000

Required

Prepare a consolidated balance sheet work sheet for the two companies, assuming that Bobbins purchased 100 percent of the common stock of Mentel for $750,000 immediately prior to December 31, 19xx, and that $60,000 of the excess of cost over book value is attributable to the increased value of Mentel Corporation's inventory. The rest of the excess is considered goodwill.

Problem 20B-4 Preparation of Consolidated Income Statement

The Toni Corporation has owned 100 percent of the U-Fix-It Corporation since 19x0. The income statements of these two companies for 19x2 follow:

	Toni Corporation	U-Fix-It Corporation
Sales	$2,650,000	$900,000
Cost of Goods Sold	1,000,000	500,000
Gross Profit	$1,650,000	$400,000
Less: Selling Expenses	$ 800,000	$150,000
General and Administrative Expenses	200,000	50,000
Total Operating Expenses	$1,000,000	$200,000
Net Income from Operations	$ 650,000	$200,000
Other Income	18,000	—
Net Income	$ 668,000	$200,000

Additional information: (a) U-Fix-It Corporation sold $200,000 of its goods to Toni Corporation, all of which had been sold to Toni's customers by December 31, 19x2. (b) U-Fix-It Corporation purchased $100,000 of inventory items from the Toni Corporation, all of which had been sold as of December 31, 19x2. (c) The U-Fix-It Corporation rents delivery trucks from Toni Corporation at the rate of $1,500 per month.

Required

Prepare a consolidated income statement work sheet for these companies for the year ended December 31, 19x2.

Problem 20B-5 Consolidated Balance Sheet—Less Than 100 Percent Ownership

The National Computer Corporation purchased 70 percent of the outstanding voting stock of the B. J. Electronics Company for $718,200 in cash. The balance sheets of the two companies immediately after acquisition were as follows:

	National Computer Corporation	B. J. Electronics Corporation
Assets		
Cash	$ 150,000	$ 60,000
Accounts Receivable	360,000	200,000
Inventory	1,600,000	700,000
Investment in B. J. Electronics	718,200	—
Property, Plant, and Equipment (net)	2,500,000	1,000,000
Other Assets	100,000	40,000
Total Assets	$5,428,200	$2,000,000
Liabilities and Stockholders' Equity		
Accounts Payable	$ 400,000	$ 150,000
Salaries Payable	50,000	20,000
Taxes Payable	20,000	4,000
Bonds Payable	1,300,000	800,000
Common Stock	2,500,000	900,000
Retained Earnings	1,158,200	126,000
Total Liabilities and Stockholders' Equity	$5,428,200	$2,000,000

Additional information: (a) The Other Assets account on the B. J. Electronics balance sheet represents an investment in National Computer's Bonds Payable. (b) $60,000 of the Accounts Receivable of National Computer Corporation represent receivables due from B. J. Electronics.

Required

Prepare a work sheet as of the acquisition date for the preparation of a consolidated balance sheet.

Problem 20B-7 Conversion of Balance Sheet Using Exchange Rates

States Corporation owns 100 percent of Canadian Corporation, located in Ontario, Canada. To prepare consolidated financial statements for States Corporation and its subsidiary, the financial statements of Canadian Corporation must be converted from Canadian dollars into U.S. dollars. Canadian Corporation's balance sheet is presented below.

Canadian Corporation
Balance Sheet
(in Canadian dollars)
December 31, 19xx

Assets	
Cash	$ 1,350,000
Accounts Receivable	4,650,000
Inventory	10,100,000
Property, Plant, and Equipment	25,600,000
Total Assets	$41,700,000
Liabilities and Stockholders' Equity	
Accounts Payable	$ 8,700,000
Taxes Payable	1,800,000
Common Stock	15,000,000
Retained Earnings	16,200,000
Total Liabilities and Stockholders' Equity	$41,700,000

The historical exchange rate is U.S. $.92 per Canadian dollar, the current rate is U.S. $.88 per Canadian dollar, and the average rate is U.S. $.90 per Canadian dollar.

Required

Convert the balance sheet of Canadian Corporation to U.S. dollars for consolidation purposes.

Learning Objectives

Chapter Twenty-One

Financial Statement Analysis

1. *Describe and discuss the objectives of financial statement analysis.*
2. *Describe and discuss the standards for financial statement analysis.*
3. *State the sources of information for financial statement analysis.*
4. *Apply horizontal analysis, trend analysis, and vertical analysis to financial statements.*
5. *Apply ratio analysis to financial statements in the study of an enterprise's liquidity, profitability, long-run solvency, and market tests.*

This chapter presents a number of techniques designed to highlight significant relationships in the financial statements for decision-making purposes. This collection of techniques is called financial statement analysis. As a result of studying this chapter, you should be able to meet the learning objectives listed on the left.

Effective decision making requires the ability to sort out relevant information from a mass of detail and to make adjustments for changing conditions. Often, financial statements in a company's annual report run ten or more pages, including footnotes and other necessary disclosures. If the financial statements are to be useful in making decisions, decision makers must be able to extract information that shows significant relationships and facilitates comparisons from year to year and from company to company. The assorted techniques that together are called **financial statement analysis** accomplish this objective.

Objectives of Financial Statement Analysis

The users of financial statements belong to two broad categories: internal and external. Management is the main internal user. The techniques of financial analysis are, of course, relevant to management's operation of the enterprise. However, because management has the advantage of inside access to operating information, other techniques (discussed in Chapters 22–29) are also available. Thus the focus here is primarily on the external use of financial analysis.

Creditors make loans in the form of trade accounts, notes, or bonds, on which they receive interest. They expect the loans to be repaid in accordance with the terms of the loan. Investors purchase capital stock, from which they hope to receive dividends and an increase in value. Both groups face risks. The creditor faces the risk that the debtor will default on the loan. The investor faces the risk that dividends will be reduced or omitted or that the price of the stock will decrease. In each case, the objective is to achieve a return that compensates for the risk taken. In general, the greater the risk incurred, the greater the return required as compensation.

Objective 1 Describe and discuss the objectives of financial statement analysis

Any one loan or any one investment can turn out badly. As a result, most creditors and investors commit their funds to a **portfolio** or group of loans or investments. The portfolio enables them to average both the return and the risk. Nevertheless, the portfolio is made up of a number of loans or stocks, on which individual decisions must be made. It is in making these individual decisions that financial statement analysis is most useful. Creditors and investors use financial statement analysis in two general ways: (1) in assessing past performance and current position, and (2) in assessing future potential and the risk associated with the potential.

Assessment of Past Performance and Current Position

Past performance is often a good indicator of future performance. Therefore, an investor or creditor is interested in the trend of past sales, expenses, net income, cash flow, and return on investment as a means of evaluating management's past performance and as a possible indicator of future performance. In addition, an analysis of current position will tell where the business stands today. For example, it will tell what assets the business owns and what liabilities must be paid, what the cash position is, how much debt the company has in relation to equity, and how reasonable the inventories and receivables are. Knowledge of past performance and current position is often important in achieving the second general objective of financial analysis.

Assessment of Future Potential and Related Risk

The past and present information is useful only to the extent that it bears on decisions about the future. An investor assesses the potential earning ability of a company because that ability will affect the value of the investment (market price of the company's stock) and the amount of dividends the company will pay. A creditor assesses the potential debt-paying ability of the company. The potentials of some companies are easier to predict than others and therefore have less risk associated with them. The riskiness of the investment or loan depends on how easy it is to predict future profitability or liquidity. If an investor can predict with confidence that a company's earnings per share will be between $2.50 and $2.60 next year, this is a less risky investment than if the earnings per share are expected to fall between $2.00 and $3.00 per share. For example, the potential associated with an investment in an established and stable electric utility, or a loan to it, is relatively easy to predict on the basis of the company's past performance and current position. The potential associated with a small minicomputer manufacturer, on the other hand, may be much more difficult to predict. Therefore, the investment or loan to the electric utility is less risky than the investment or loan to the small computer company. Typically, in return for assuming the greater risk, the investor in the minicomputer company will demand a higher expected return (increase in market price plus dividends) than the investor in the utility company. Also, a creditor of the minicomputer company will require a higher interest rate and possibly more assurance of repayment (a secured loan, for instance) than a creditor to the utility company. The higher interest rate is compensation to the creditor for assuming a higher risk.

Standards for Financial Statement Analysis

Objective 2 Describe and discuss the standards for financial statement analysis

In using financial statement analysis, decision makers must judge whether the relationships that they have found are favorable or unfavorable. Three standards of comparison that are commonly used are (1) rule-of-thumb measures, (2) past performance of the company, and (3) industry norms.

Rule-of-Thumb Measures

Many financial analysts and lenders use "ideal" or rule-of-thumb measures for key financial ratios. For example, it has long been thought that a current ratio of 3:1 was ideal or satisfactory. The credit-rating firm of Dun and Bradstreet, in its *Key Business Ratios,* provides these guidelines:

Current debt to tangible net worth. Ordinarily, a business begins to pile up trouble when this relationship exceeds 80%.

Inventory to net working capital. Ordinarily, this relationship should not exceed 80%.

Although such measures may suggest areas that need further investigation, there is no proof that they are the best for any one company. For example, a company with a larger than 3:1 current ratio may have a poor credit policy (resulting in accounts receivable being too large), excessive or obsolete inventory, or poor cash management. Conversely, another company may have a less than 3:1 ratio that resulted from excellent management in these three areas. Therefore, rule-of-thumb measures must be used with great caution.

Past Performance of the Company

An improvement over the rule-of-thumb method is the comparison of financial measures or ratios of the same company over a period of time. This standard will at least give the analyst some basis for judging whether

	Sales (in millions)						Operating Income	
	To Unaffiliated Customers		Between Segments		Total			
	1978	1977	1978	1977	1978	1977	1978	1977
Steel manufacturing	$ 8,535.8	$7,352.0	$ 453.0	$ 383.6	$ 8,988.8	$ 7,735.6	$ 33.4	$ (45.0)
Chemicals	763.1	664.5	44.7	35.4	807.8	699.9	21.0	32.7
Resource development	271.1	242.1	124.9	143.4	396.0	385.5	25.1	26.3
Fabricating & engineering and other	1,305.7	1,215.4	230.6	243.9	1,536.3	1,459.3	80.2	80.5
Domestic transportation & utility subsidiaries	173.8	135.9	374.7	310.4	548.5	446.3	119.9	71.3
Adjustments and eliminations	—	—	(1,227.9)	(1,116.7)	(1,227.9)	(1,116.7)	6.5	9.7
Total consolidated	$11,049.5	$9,609.9	$ —	$ —	$11,049.5	$ 9,609.9	$286.1	$175.5

	Identifiable Assets		Wear and Exhaustion		Capital Expenditures	
	1978	1977	1978	1977	1978	1977
Steel manufacturing	$ 5,869.2	$5,616.3	$ 319.9	$ 268.4	$ 398.2	$ 604.9
Chemicals	457.3	353.6	23.6	17.5	100.0	67.5
Resource development	1,085.7	1,057.8	41.3	38.0	54.1	65.0
Fabricating & engineering and other	896.7	769.3	32.0	32.1	30.8	33.4
Domestic transportation & utility subsidiaries	713.1	630.2	19.5	16.4	84.7	93.9
Corporate assets and adjustments	1,514.3	1,487.2	(.7)	(.4)	—	—
Total consolidated	$10,536.3	$9,914.4	$ 435.6	$ 372.0	$ 667.8	$ 864.7

◀ Figure 21-1 Segment Reporting from the Annual Report of United States Steel Corporation

the measure or ratio is improving or worsening. It may also be helpful in disclosing possible future trends. However, since trends do reverse at times, such projections must be made with care. Another disadvantage is that the past may not be a good measure of adequacy. For example, even if return on total investment improved from 3 percent last year to 4 percent this year, the 4 percent return may not be adequate.

Industry Norms

One way of compensating for the limitations of using past performance as a standard is to use industry norms. This standard will tell how the company being analyzed compares with other companies in the same industry. For example, if other companies in the same industry as the company in the previous paragraph have an average rate of return on total investment of 8 percent, then the 3 percent and 4 percent returns are probably inadequate. Industry norms can also be used to evaluate trends. For example, assume that because of an unfavorable change in the economy, a company's profit margin dropped from 12 to 10 percent. A finding that other companies in the same industry had an average drop in profit margin from 12 to 4 percent would indicate that the company being analyzed performed relatively well.

There are three limitations to using industry norms as standards. First, although two companies may appear to be in the same industry, they may not be strictly comparable. For example, consider two companies that are said to be in the oil industry. One may be involved primarily in marketing oil products it buys from other producers through service stations, whereas the other may be an international company that discovers, produces, refines, and markets its own oil products. The operations of these companies are not comparable.

Second, most companies today operate in more than one industry, and some **diversified companies,** often called **conglomerates,** operate in many unrelated industries. The individual segments of a diversified company typically have differing rates of profitability and degrees of risk. In using the consolidated financial statements of these companies for financial analysis, it is often impossible to use industry norms as standards because there are no other companies that are closely enough related. One partial solution to this problem is the requirement by the Financial Accounting Standards Board in *Statement No. 14* that diversified companies report revenue, income from operations, and identifiable assets for each of their operating segments. Segment information may be reported for operations in different industries, in foreign markets, or to major customers depending on specific criteria.[1] An example for industry segments is given in Figure 21-1, an excerpt from U.S. Steel's annual report.

1. *Statement of Financial Accounting Standards No. 14,* "Financial Reporting for Segments of a Business Enterprise" (Stamford, Conn.: Financial Accounting Standards Board, 1976).

Third, companies comparable in operating and industry respects may employ different accounting procedures. For example, inventories may be valued by using different methods or different depreciation methods may be used for similar assets. Nevertheless, industry norms probably offer the best available standards for judging a company's performance, if they are used with care.

Sources of Information

Objective 3 State the sources of information for financial statement analysis

The external analyst is often limited to publicly available information about a company. The major sources of information about publicly held corporations are published reports, SEC reports, business periodicals, and credit and investment advisory services.

Published Reports

The information contained in the annual report of a publicly held corporation is an important source of financial information. Briefly, the major sections of this annual report consist of (1) management's analysis of the past year's operations, (2) the financial statements, (3) the footnotes to the financial statements, (4) the principal accounting procedures used by the company, (5) the auditor's report, and (6) a summary of operations for a five- or ten-year period. In addition, most companies publish **interim financial statements** on a quarterly basis. These reports contain limited information in the form of condensed financial statements, which are subject to a limited review, not a complete audit by the independent auditor. The interim statements are watched closely by the financial community for early signals of significant changes in a company's earnings trend.[2]

SEC Reports

Publicly held corporations are required to file annual reports, quarterly reports, and current reports with the Securities and Exchange Commission (SEC). All such reports are available to the public for a nominal charge. The SEC prescribes a standard format for the annual report (Form 10-K), and this report is more comprehensive than the published annual report. Form 10-K is, therefore, an important source of information. It is available, free of charge, to stockholders of the company. The quarterly report (Form 10-Q) is an important source of short-run financial performance. The current report (Form 8-K), which must be filed within ten days of the occurrence of certain specified significant events, is often the first indicator of crucial developments affecting the company's financial performance in the future.

2. Accounting Principles Board, *Opinion No. 28,* "Interim Financial Reporting" (New York: American Institute of Certified Public Accountants, 1973); and *Statement of Financial Accounting Standards No. 3,* "Reporting Change in Interim Financial Statements" (Stamford, Conn.: Financial Accounting Standards Board, 1974).

Business Periodicals and Credit and Investment Advisory Services

Financial analysts must keep informed on current events in the financial world. Probably the best source of financial news is the *Wall Street Journal,* which is published daily and is the most complete financial journal. Other financial magazines, published either weekly or biweekly, are *Forbes, Barrons, Fortune,* and the *Commercial and Financial Chronicle.* For detailed information about the financial history of companies, the publications of such services as Moody's Investors Services and Standard and Poor's Industrial Surveys are useful. Data on industry norms, average ratios and relationships, and credit ratings are available from such agencies as Dun and Bradstreet, Inc. Dun and Bradstreet publishes, among other useful services, an annual analysis using 14 ratios of 125 industry groups classified as retailing, wholesaling, manufacturing, and construction in its *Key Business Ratios.* Another important source of industry data is the *Annual Statement Studies,* published by Robert Morris Associates, which contain detailed data and ratios for 223 industry classifications. In addition, various private services are available to the analyst for an annual fee.

Tools and Techniques of Financial Analysis

Few numbers when considered alone are very meaningful. It is their relationship to other numbers or their change from one period to another that is important. The tools and techniques of financial analysis are designed to show relationships and changes. Among the more widely used of these techniques are horizontal analysis, trend analysis, vertical analysis, and ratio analysis.

Horizontal Analysis

Objective 4 Apply horizontal analysis, trend analysis, and vertical analysis to financial statements.

Generally accepted accounting principles require the presentation of comparative financial statements that contain the current year's and past year's financial information. A common starting point for examining such statements is **horizontal analysis,** which involves the computation of dollar amount changes and percentage changes from year to year. The percentage change must be calculated to show how the size of the change relates to the size of the amounts involved. A change of $1 million in sales is not so drastic as a change of $1 million in net income, because sales is a larger amount than net income. Figures 21-2 and 21-3 (next two pages) contain the comparative balance sheet and income statement, respectively, for U.S. Steel, with the dollar and percentage changes computed. The percentage change is computed as follows:

$$\text{percentage change} = 100\left(\frac{\text{amount of change}}{\text{base-year amount}}\right)$$

United States Steel Corporation
Consolidated Balance Sheet
December 31, 1978 and 1977

	(In millions)		Increase (Decrease)	
	1978	1977	Amount	Percentage
Assets				
Current Assets				
Cash	$ 377.6	$ 273.4	$ 104.2	38.1
Marketable securities, at cost (approximates market)	338.4	425.5	(87.1)	(20.5)
Receivables, less allowance for doubtful accounts of $15.2 and $13.0	1,433.9	1,086.6	347.3	32.0
Inventories	1,257.0	1,254.8	2.2	.0
Total Current Assets	$ 3,406.9	$3,040.3	$ 366.6	12.1
Long-term receivables and other investments, less estimated losses of $32.3 and $31.0	748.1	745.3	2.8	.1
Property, plant, and equipment, less accumulated depreciation of $7,208.6 and $6,817.3	5,975.0	5,724.2	250.8	4.4
Operating parts and supplies	113.8	116.9	(3.1)	(2.7)
Costs applicable to future periods	292.5	287.7	4.8	1.7
Total Assets	$10,536.3	$9,914.4	$ 621.9	6.3
Liabilities				
Current Liabilities:				
Notes payable	$ 163.8	$ 167.9	$ (4.1)	(2.4)
Accounts payable	827.7	651.1	176.6	27.1
Payroll and benefits payable	638.0	558.8	79.2	14.2
Accrued taxes	339.1	230.4	108.7	47.2
Long-term debt due within one year	74.5	82.1	(7.6)	(9.3)
Total Current Liabilities	$ 2,043.1	$1,690.3	$ 352.8	20.9
Long-term debt, less unamortized discount	2,194.5	2,300.2	(105.7)	(4.6)
Deferred income taxes	416.8	445.8	(29.0)	(6.5)
Deferred credits and other liabilities	100.9	86.4	14.5	16.8
Preferred stock of consolidated subsidiary	500.0	250.0	250.0	100.0
Total Liabilities	$ 5,255.3	$4,772.7	$ 482.6	10.1
Ownership				
Common stock (par value $1 per share, authorized 150,000,000 shares) outstanding 85,567,163 shares and 84,169,399 shares, stated at $20 per share	$ 1,711.3	$1,683.4	$ 27.9	1.7
Capital in excess of stated value	70.0	61.1	8.9	14.6
Net unrealized loss on marketable equity securities	(19.1)	(15.5)	(3.6)	23.2
Income reinvested in business	3,518.8	3,412.7	106.1	3.1
Total Ownership	$ 5,281.0	$5,141.7	$ 139.3	2.7
Total Liabilities and Ownership	$10,536.3	$9,914.4	$ 621.9	6.3

◀ Figure 21-2 Comparative Balance Sheet with Horizontal Analysis

The **base year** in any set of data is always the first year to be considered. For example, from 1977 to 1978, U.S. Steel's cash increased by $104.2 million, from $273.4 million to $377.6 million, or by 38.1 percent, computed as follows:

$$\text{percentage increase} = 100\left(\frac{\$104.2\text{ million}}{\$273.4\text{ million}}\right) = 38.1\%$$

Care must be taken in the analysis of percentage change. For example, in analyzing the changes in current assets in Figure 21-2, one may place approximately equal weight on the 38.1 percent increase in Cash and the 32.0 percent increase in Receivables when, in dollar amount, Receivables increased by over three times as much as Cash ($347.3 million versus

Figure 21-3 Comparative Income Statements with Horizontal Analysis

United States Steel Corporation
Consolidated Statements of Income and Income Reinvested in Business
For the Years Ended December 31, 1978 and 1977

	(In millions)		Increase (Decrease)	
	1978	1977	Amount	Percentage
Sales	$11,049.5	$9,609.9	$1,439.6	15.0
Operating Costs				
Cost of sales (excludes items shown below)	$ 9,046.4	$7,944.5	$1,101.9	13.9
Selling, general and administrative expenses	372.4	349.5	22.9	6.6
Pensions, insurance and other employee benefits	693.6	572.1	121.5	21.2
Wear and exhaustion of facilities	435.6	372.0	63.6	17.1
State, local, and miscellaneous taxes	215.4	196.3	19.1	9.7
Total operating costs	$10,763.4	$9,434.4	$1,329.0	14.1
Operating Income	$ 286.1	$ 175.5	$ 110.6	63.0
Interest, dividends, and other income	155.3	81.2	74.1	91.3
Interest and other financing costs	(191.4)	(154.8)	(36.6)	23.6
Income Before Taxes on Income	$ 250.0	$ 101.9	$ 148.1	145.3
Provision (credit) for estimated United States and foreign income taxes				
Current	$ 6.7	$ (98.3)	$ 105.0	106.8
Deferred	1.3	62.3	(61.0)	(97.9)
Net estimated taxes on income	$ 8.0	$ (36.0)	$ 44.0	122.2
Net Income	$ 242.0	$ 137.9	$ 104.1	75.5
Income Per Common Share [in dollars]				
Primary	$ 2.85	$ 1.66	$ 1.19	71.7
Fully diluted	$ 2.78	$ 1.66	$ 1.12	67.5

$104.2). Note also that the increase in Cash is substantially offset by a decrease in Marketable Securities. Dollar amounts and percentage increases must be considered together. In Figure 21-2, this fact is demonstrated by the $352.8 million or 20.9 percent increase in total current liabilities versus a $482.6 million or 10.1 percent increase in total liabilities. Also, the company is relying more heavily on short-term financing. This is indicated by the fact that current liabilities increased by 20.9 percent ($352.8 million) and long-term liabilities decreased by 4.6 percent ($105.7 million).

In the income statement (Figure 21-3), the most significant changes are the 15.0 percent increase in Sales compared with the smaller 14.1 percent increase in Operating Costs. When combined, these figures result in a 145.3 percent increase in Income Before Taxes on Income and a 75.5 percent increase in Net Income. Among the costs, the most significant increase (21.2 percent) is in Pensions, Insurance and Other Employee Benefits because this increase was greater than the increase in other costs.

Trend Analysis

A variation of horizontal analysis is **trend analysis,** in which percentage changes are calculated for several successive years instead of between two years. Trend analysis is important because, with its longer-run perspective, it may point to basic changes in the nature of the business. Besides comparative financial statements, most companies provide a summary of operations and data on other key indicators for five or more years. Selected items from U.S. Steel's summary of operations together with trend analysis are presented in Figure 21-4. Trend analysis uses an **index number** to show changes in related items over a period of time. Index numbers are constructed by setting one year, the base year, equal to 100 percent. Other years are measured in relation to that amount. For example, the 1978 index of 120.2 for sales was computed as follows:

$$\text{index} = 100\left(\frac{\text{index year amount}}{\text{base year amount}}\right) = 100\left(\frac{\$11{,}049.5}{\$9{,}190.1}\right) = 120.2$$

An index number of 120.2 means that 1978 sales are 120.2 percent or 1.202 times 1974 sales. An examination of the trend analysis in Figure 21-4 reveals that erratic Sales (varying from 88.9 to 120.2) have resulted in erratic Net Income (varying from 100.0 to 21.9) and Per Common Share—Income (varying from 100.0 to 21.4). The trends in Sales and Income have generally been in opposite directions (in 1978 Sales were 120.2 and Net Income was 38.4). The company has tried to offset this variability by steadily increasing dividends from 1974 to 1977 (100.0 to 149.7) but could not continue this policy in 1978, when the dividend index dropped to 108.8.

Vertical Analysis

Vertical analysis uses percentages to show the relationship of the component parts to the total in a single statement. Vertical analysis is done by

Figure 21-4
Trend Analysis

United States Steel Corporation
Summary of Operations
Selected Data

	Dollars in Millions (except per share)				
	1974	1975	1976	1977	1978
Sales	$9,190.1	$8,171.3	$8,707.8	$9,609.9	$11,049.5
Net Income	630.3	559.6	410.3	137.9	242.0
Per Common Share—					
Income	7.76	6.89	5.03	1.66	2.85
Dividends	1.47	1.87	2.12	2.20	1.60

Trend Analysis

	1974	1975	1976	1977	1978
Sales	100.0	88.9	94.8	104.5	120.2
Net Income	100.0	88.8	65.1	21.9	38.4
Per Common Share—					
Income	100.0	88.8	64.8	21.4	36.8
Dividends	100.0	127.2	144.2	149.7	108.8

setting a total figure in the statement (total assets or total liabilities and stockholders' equity in the case of the balance sheet, and revenues or sales in the case of the income statement) equal to 100 percent and computing the percentage of each component of that figure. The resulting statement of percentages is termed a **common-size statement.** Common-size balance sheets and income statements for U.S. Steel Corporation are shown in Figures 21-5 and 21-6 (next two pages). Typically, current assets and current liabilities are given only in total because ratio analysis considers their components in some detail. Vertical analysis is useful for assessing the relative importance of various components in the operation of the business. It is also useful for pointing out significant changes in the components from one year to the next when comparative common-size statements are presented. For example, although the composition of assets (in Figure 21-5) remained relatively stable from 1977 to 1978, the proportion of the total liabilities and stockholders' equity devoted to liabilities increased from 48.1 percent to 49.9 percent. Also, consistent with the horizontal analysis of the balance sheet (Figure 21-2), the increased reliance on short-term financing was reflected in the increased proportion of current liabilities (17.0 percent to 19.4 percent) and decreased proportion of long-term liabilities (23.2 percent to 20.8 percent). Similarly, the common-size

Figure 21-5
Common-Size
Balance Sheet

United States Steel Corporation
Common-Size Balance Sheet
December 31, 1978 and 1977

	1978	1977
Assets		
Current Assets	32.3%	30.7%
Long-Term Receivables and Other Investments	7.1	7.5
Property, Plant, and Equipment, less Accumulated Depreciation	56.7	57.7
Operating Parts and Supplies	1.1	1.2
Costs Applicable to Future Periods	2.8	2.9
Total Assets	100.0%	100.0%
Liabilities		
Current Liabilities	19.4%	17.0%
Long-Term Debt, less Unamortized Discount	20.8	23.2
Deferred Income Taxes	4.0	4.5
Deferred Credits and Other Liabilities	1.0	.9
Preferred Stock of Consolidated Subsidiary	4.7	2.5
Total Liabilities	49.9%	48.1%
Stockholders' Equity		
Common Stock	16.2%	17.0%
Capital in Excess of Stated Value	.7	.6
Net Unrealized Loss on Marketable Equity Securities	(.2)	(.1)
Income Reinvested in Business	33.4	34.4
Total Stockholders' Equity	50.1	51.9
Total Liabilities and Stockholders' Equity	100.0%	100.0%

income statement (Figure 21-6) confirms the importance of the decrease in Cost of Sales from 82.7 percent to 81.9 percent of total sales as the primary cause of the increase in income (from 1.4 percent to 2.2 percent of total sales).

Common-size statements are often used to make comparisons between firms. They enable an analyst to compare the operating and financing characteristics of two companies of different sizes in the same industry. For example, the analyst may want to compare the percentage of total assets financed by debt or the percentage of general administrative and selling expenses to sales and revenues of U.S. Steel to other steel companies. Common-size statements would show these relationships.

Figure 21-6
Common-Size
Income
Statement

United States Steel Corporation
Common-Size Statement of Income
For the Years Ended December 31, 1978 and 1977

	1978	1977
Sales	100.0%	100.0%
Operating Costs		
Cost of Sales	81.9%	82.7%
Selling, General and Administrative Expenses	3.4	3.6
Pensions, Insurance, and Other Employee Benefits	6.3	6.0
Wear and Exhaustion of Facilities	3.9	3.9
State, Local, and Miscellaneous Taxes	1.9	2.0
Total Operating Costs	97.4%	98.2%
Operating Income	2.6%	1.8%
Interest, Dividends, and Other Income	1.4	.8
Interest and Other Financing Costs	(1.7)	(1.6)
Income Before Taxes on Income	2.3	1.0
Net Estimated Taxes on Income	.1	(.4)
Net Income	2.2%	1.4%

Ratio Analysis

Objective 5 Apply ratio analysis to financial statements in the study of an enterprise's liquidity, profitability, long-run solvency, and market tests

Ratio analysis is an important means of stating the relationship between two numbers. To be useful, a ratio must represent a meaningful relationship, but use of ratios is not a substitute for evaluation of the underlying data. Ratios are guides or short cuts that are useful in evaluating the financial position and operations of a company and in comparing them to previous years or to other companies. Their primary purpose is to point out areas for further investigation.

Ratios may be stated in several ways. For example, the ratio of net income of $100,000 to sales of $1,000,000 may be stated as (1) net income is 1/10 or 10 percent of sales, (2) the ratio of sales to net income is 10 to 1 (10:1) or 10 times net income, or (3) for every dollar of sales, the company has an average net income of 10 cents.

Survey of Commonly Used Ratios

In the following sections, ratio analysis is applied to four objectives: the evaluation of (1) liquidity, (2) profitability, (3) long-run solvency, and (4) market strength. Chapter 7 addressed the first two objectives in an introductory manner. Here we expand the evaluation to include additional ratios related to these objectives and to introduce the ratios related to two new objectives. Data for the analyses come from the financial statements of U.S. Steel Corporation presented in Figures 21-2 and 21-3. Additional data are presented as needed.

Evaluation of Liquidity

The objective of liquidity is to have enough funds on hand to pay a company's bills when they are due and to provide for unexpected needs for cash. The ratios that relate to this objective all involve working capital or some component of it because it is out of working capital that debts are paid as they mature. Some common ratios associated with the evaluation of liquidity are the current ratio, the quick ratio, receivable turnover, and inventory turnover.

Current Ratio The **current ratio**, which expresses as a ratio the relationship of current assets to current liabilities, is widely used as a broad indicator of a firm's liquidity position and short-term debt-paying ability. This ratio for U.S. Steel for 1978 and 1977 is computed as follows:

Current Ratio	1978	1977
$\frac{\text{current assets}}{\text{current liabilities}}$	$\frac{\$3,406.9}{\$2,043.1} = 1.67$	$\frac{\$3,040.3}{\$1,690.3} = 1.80$

The current ratio for U.S. Steel shows a small decrease from 1977 to 1978.

Quick Ratio One defect of the current ratio is that it does not consider the composition of current assets. They may appear to be sufficient in quantity, but they may lack proper balance. Clearly, a dollar of cash or even accounts receivable is more readily available to meet obligations than is a dollar of most kinds of inventory. The **quick ratio** is designed to overcome this shortcoming by measuring short-term liquidity, that is, the relationship of the more liquid current assets (cash, marketable securities, and receivables) to current liabilities. This ratio for U.S. Steel Corporation for 1978 and 1977 is computed as follows:

Quick Ratio	1978	1977
$\frac{\text{cash + marketable securities + receivables}}{\text{current liabilities}}$	$\frac{\$377.6 + \$338.4 + \$1,433.9}{\$2,043.1}$	$\frac{\$273.4 + \$425.5 + \$1,086.6}{\$1,690.3}$
	$= \frac{\$2,149.9}{\$2,043.1} = 1.05$	$= \frac{\$1,785.5}{\$1,690.3} = 1.06$

This ratio shows little change from 1977 to 1978.

Receivable Turnover The ability of a company to collect for credit sales in a timely manner affects the company's liquidity. The **receivable turnover** ratio focuses on the relative size of a company's accounts receivable and its credit and collection policies. This ratio shows how many times, on the average, the receivables were converted into cash during the period. Turnover ratios usually consist of one balance sheet account and one income statement account. For U.S. Steel the ratio is as follows:

Receivable Turnover[3]	**1978**	**1977**
$\dfrac{\text{sales}}{\text{accounts receivable}}$	$\dfrac{\$11{,}049.5}{\$1{,}433.9} = 7.7$	$\dfrac{\$9{,}609.9}{\$1{,}086.6} = 8.9$

The higher the turnover ratio the better, because the company is converting receivables into cash at a faster pace with a higher turnover. The speed at which receivables are turned over depends on the company's credit terms. Since a company's credit terms are usually stated in days, such as 2/10, n/60, it is helpful to convert the receivable turnover to **average days' sales uncollected.** This is done by dividing the length of the accounting period (usually 365 days) by the receivable turnover (as computed above) as follows:

Average Days' Sales Uncollected	**1978**	**1977**
$\dfrac{\text{days in year}}{\text{receivable turnover}}$	$\dfrac{365}{7.7} = 47.4$ days	$\dfrac{365}{8.9} = 41.0$ days

In the case of U.S. Steel, the receivable turnover decreased from 8.9 to 7.7, and the average days' sales uncollected increased from 41.0 to 47.4 days. These changes mean that the company must wait longer to collect credit sales and must invest more in receivables per unit of sales. The changes could be caused by a general decrease in the economy (reducing the ability of customers to pay on time) or by a change in credit policy or both.

Inventory Turnover Inventory is two steps removed from cash (sale and collection), and **inventory turnover,** which measures the relative size of inventory, affects the amount of cash available to pay maturing debts. Obviously, inventory should be maintained at an optimum level to support production and sales. In general, however, a smaller, faster-moving inventory means that the company has less cash tied up in inventory and that there is less chance for the inventory to become obsolete. A build-up in inventory may mean that a recession or some other factor is preventing sales from keeping pace with purchasing and production. The computation of inventory turnover for 1978 and 1977 at U.S. Steel follows:

Inventory Turnover[4]	**1978**	**1977**
$\dfrac{\text{cost of goods sold}}{\text{inventory}}$	$\dfrac{\$9{,}046.4}{\$1{,}257.0} = 7.2$	$\dfrac{\$7{,}944.5}{\$1{,}254.8} = 6.3$

3. If the data are available, this ratio should theoretically be composed of net credit sales and average accounts receivable.
4. Theoretically, the denominator should be average inventory, if available. The practice of adding beginning and ending inventory and dividing by 2 produces the true average only by chance.

The increase in receivables and the decrease in receivable turnover found in the previous paragraph have been partially offset by a small favorable increase in inventory turnover from 6.3 to 7.2.

Evaluation of Profitability

A company's long-run survival depends on its ability to earn a satisfactory profit. Investors become and remain stockholders because they believe that the dividends and capital gains they will receive will exceed the returns on other investments of comparable risk. An evaluation of a company's past earning power may provide insight for the investor's decision. Furthermore, as pointed out in Chapter 7, a company's ability to earn a profit ultimately affects its liquidity position. Therefore, the evaluation of profitability is relevant to both investors and creditors. In evaluating the profitability of U.S. Steel, we examine five ratios: profit margin, asset turnover, return on assets, return on owners' investment, and earnings per share. All of these ratios except asset turnover and earnings per share were introduced in Chapter 7.

Profit Margin Profit margin indicates the percentage of each revenue dollar that results in net income. It is computed for U.S. Steel as follows:

Profit Margin[5]	**1978**	**1977**
$\frac{\text{net income}}{\text{revenues}}$	$\frac{\$242.0}{\$11{,}049.5} = 2.2\%$	$\frac{\$137.9}{\$9{,}609.9} = 1.4\%$

This ratio confirms what was apparent from the common-size income statement: that the profit margin increased from 1977 (1.4 percent) to 1978 (2.2 percent). The analysis of the common-size income statement (Figure 21-6) showed that this increase was mainly due to a decrease in the Cost of Sales as a percentage of total sales.

Asset Turnover Asset turnover is a measure of how efficiently assets are used to produce sales. It represents the number of dollars in sales produced by each dollar invested in assets. In other words, it represents the number of times in the period that assets were "turned over" in sales. The higher the asset turnover, the more concentrated is the use of assets. For U.S. Steel, the asset turnovers for 1978 and 1977 are as follows:

Asset Turnover	**1978**	**1977**
$\frac{\text{revenues}}{\text{total assets}}$	$\frac{\$11{,}049.5}{\$10{,}536.3} = 1.05$	$\frac{\$9{,}609.9}{\$9{,}914.4} = .97$

The steel industry requires a large investment in assets for each dollar of sales compared to other industries. A retailer may have an asset turnover

5. In comparing companies in an industry, some analysts use net income before income taxes as the numerator to eliminate the effect of differing tax rates among the individual firms.

of between 4.0 and 6.0. In the case of U.S. Steel, however, the turnover was only .97 in 1977 and 1.05 in 1978. This means that U.S. Steel achieves sales of about one dollar for each dollar of assets. The slight increase, however, does represent an improvement in productivity.

Return on Assets The best overall measure of the earning power or profitability of a company is **return on assets,** which measures the amount earned on each dollar of assets invested. The return on assets for 1978 and 1977 for U.S. Steel is as follows:

Return on Assets[6]	**1978**	**1977**
$\frac{\text{net income}}{\text{total assets}}$	$\frac{\$242.0}{\$10{,}536.3} = 2.3\%$	$\frac{\$137.9}{\$9{,}914.4} = 1.4\%$

U.S. Steel's return on assets increased from 1.4 percent in 1977 to 2.3 percent in 1978, a favorable change, but still quite low by most standards.

One reason why return on assets is a good measure of profitability is that it combines the effects of profit margin and asset turnover. The 1978 and 1977 results of U.S. Steel can be analyzed as follows:

	Profit Margin		**Asset Turnover**		**Return on Assets**
Ratios:	$\frac{\text{net income}}{\text{sales}}$	×	$\frac{\text{sales}}{\text{total assets}}$	=	$\frac{\text{net income}}{\text{total assets}}$
1977	1.4	×	.97	=	1.36
1978	2.2	×	1.05	=	2.31

From this analysis, it is clear that the increase in return on assets in 1978 can be attributed to increases in both profit margin and asset turnover. The steel industry in general, and U.S. Steel in particular, is plagued by both a low profit margin and a low asset turnover in contrast to some industries (see McDonald's Corporation in Chapter 7).

Return on Owners' Investment An important measure of profitability from the stockholders' standpoint is **return on owners' investment.** This ratio measures how much was earned for each dollar invested by owners. For U.S. Steel, this ratio for 1978 and 1977 is computed as follows:

Return on Owners' Investment	**1978**	**1977**
$\frac{\text{net income}}{\text{owners' equity}}$	$\frac{\$242.0}{\$5{,}281.0} = 4.6\%$	$\frac{\$137.9}{\$5{,}141.7} = 2.7\%$

As might be expected from the analysis of other profitability ratios above, this ratio also increased from 1977 to 1978.

A natural question is, Why is there a difference between return on assets and return on owners' investment? The answer lies in the company's use of **leverage,** or debt financing. If the company had no debt, the

6. Some authorities would add interest expense to net income in the numerator because they view interest expense as a cost of acquiring capital, not a cost of operations.

two ratios would equal each other. If the company has debt, however, it is said to be leveraged because it has a fixed interest cost on the debt that, if the company has a return on assets greater than its interest cost, will allow the additional amount earned to increase the return on the owners' investment. U.S. Steel is considered a highly leveraged company because about one-half of its capital is provided by debt, a percentage that increased in 1978. (We will discuss the debt to equity ratio later.)

Earnings per Share One of the most widely quoted measures of profitability is earnings per share of common stock. As a test of profitability, this ratio is relevant only to the common stockholders. Figure 21-3 shows that the primary earnings per share for U.S. Steel rose from $1.66 to $2.85, reflecting the increase in net income from 1977 to 1978. Fully diluted income per common share is also presented. These disclosures are required in financial statements; their calculation was presented in Chapter 17.

Evaluation of Long-Run Solvency

Long-run solvency relates to the ability of a company to survive over many years. The purpose of long-run solvency analysis is to point out early that a company is on the road to bankruptcy. Studies have shown that accounting ratios can indicate as much as five years in advance that a company may fail.[7] Declining profitability and liquidity ratios are key indicators of such dire possibilities. Two other ratios that analysts commonly consider as indicators of long-run solvency are the debt to equity ratio and the interest coverage ratio.

Debt to Equity Ratio The existence of debt in a company's capital structure is considered risky because the company has a legal obligation to make interest payments on time and to pay the principal at the maturity date, regardless of the level of the company's earnings. If the payments are not made, the company may be forced into bankruptcy. In contrast, dividends and other distributions to equity holders are made only when the board of directors declares them. The **debt to equity ratio** measures the relationship of the company's assets provided by creditors to the amount provided by stockholders. The larger the debt to equity ratio, the more fixed obligations the company has and thus the riskier the situation. This ratio is closely related to the capital structure ratio (debt to total assets) presented in Chapter 7 and to the common-size balance sheet in Figure 21-5. It is computed as follows:

Debt to Equity Ratio	1978	1977
$\dfrac{\text{total liabilities}}{\text{owners' equity}}$	$\dfrac{\$5{,}255.3}{\$5{,}281.0} = 1.00$	$\dfrac{\$4{,}772.7}{\$5{,}141.7} = .93$

7. William H. Beaver, "Alternative Accounting Measures as Indicators of Failure," *Accounting Review* (January 1968); and Edward Altman, "Financial Ratios, Discriminant Analysis and the Prediction of Corporate Bankruptcy," *Journal of Finance* (September 1968).

From 1977 to 1978, the debt to equity ratio for U.S. Steel increased from .93 to 1.00. This finding is consistent with the analysis of the common-size balance sheet (Figure 21-5), showing that the total debt of the company increased as a percentage of total assets in 1978. Obviously, this is a situation that bears watching in future years.

Interest Coverage Ratio One question that usually arises at this point is, If debt is bad, why have any? The answer is that, as with many ratios, it is a matter of balance. In spite of its riskiness, debt is a flexible means of financing certain business operations. Also, because it usually carries a fixed interest charge, it limits the cost of financing. Thus if the company is able to earn a return on the assets greater than the cost of the interest, the company makes an overall profit.[8] However, the company runs the risk of not earning a return on assets equal to the interest cost of financing those assets, thereby incurring an overall loss. One measure of the degree of protection creditors have from a default on interest payments is the **interest coverage ratio**, computed as follows:

Interest Coverage Ratio

$$\frac{\text{net income before taxes} + \text{interest expense}}{\text{interest expense}}$$

1978	**1977**
$\frac{\$250.0 + \$191.4}{\$191.4}$	$\frac{\$101.9 + \$154.8}{\$154.8}$
= 2.31	= 1.66

In computing this ratio, net income before taxes is used because interest expense is tax deductible. In U.S. Steel's case, the increase in earnings improved this ratio from 1.66 to 2.31 in spite of an increase in interest expense. However, a coverage ratio of 2.31 does not leave much margin and would be considered low by most analysts. Continuance of these low coverage ratios in future years would be cause for concern.

Market Test Ratios

The market price of a company's shares of stock is of interest to the analyst because it represents what investors as a whole think of a company at a point in time. Market price is the price at which people are willing to buy and sell the stock, and it provides information about how investors view the potential return and risk associated with owning the company's stock. This information cannot be obtained by simply considering the market price of the stock by itself because companies have different numbers of outstanding shares and different amounts of underlying earnings and dividends. The market price must be related to the

8. In addition, as seen in Chapter 14, there are advantages to being a debtor in periods of inflation because the debt, which is fixed in dollar amount, may be repaid with cheaper dollars.

earnings per share, dividends per share, and prices of other companies' shares to extract the necessary information. This is done through the price/earnings ratio, the dividends yield, and market risk.

Price/Earnings Ratio The **price/earnings (P/E) ratio** measures the ratio of the current market price of the stock to the earnings per share. Assuming a current market price of $25 and using the 1978 earnings per share for U.S. Steel from Figure 21-3 of $2.85, we can compute the price/earnings ratio as follows:

$$\frac{\text{market price}}{\text{earnings per share}} = \frac{\$25}{\$2.85} = 8.8 \text{ times}$$

This ratio, which changes from day to day and from quarter to quarter as market price and earnings change, tells how much the investing public as a whole is willing to pay for $1 of U.S. Steel's earnings per share. At this time, U.S. Steel's P/E ratio is 8.8 times the underlying earnings for that share of stock.

This is a very useful and widely used ratio because it places companies on a comparable basis. When a company's P/E ratio is higher than the P/E ratios for other companies, it usually means that investors feel that the company's earnings are going to increase at a faster rate than those of the other companies. Conversely, a relatively low P/E ratio usually means a more negative assessment by investors. In this example, a P/E ratio of 8.8 for U.S. Steel is typical for companies in the steel industry.

Dividends Yield The **dividends yield** is a measure of the current return to an investor in the stock. It is computed by dividing the current annual dividend by the current market price of the stock. Assuming the same $25 per share and using the 1978 dividends of $1.60 per share for U.S. Steel from Figure 21-4, we can compute the dividends yield as follows:

$$\frac{\text{dividends}}{\text{market price}} = \frac{\$1.60}{\$25} = 6.4\%$$

Thus an investor who owns U.S. Steel stock at $25 had a return from dividends in 1978 of 6.4 percent. The dividends yield is only one part of the investor's total return from investing in U.S. Steel. The investor must add or subtract from the dividends yield the percentage change (either positive or negative) in the market value of the stock.

Market Risk Earlier we pointed out that in addition to assessing the potential return from an investment, the investor must also assess the risk associated with the investment. Many factors may be considered when assessing risk, including the nature of the business, the quality of the business, the track record of the company, and so forth. One measure of risk that has gained increased attention among analysts in recent years is market risk. **Market risk** is the volatility of or fluctuation in the price of a stock in relation to the volatility of or fluctuation in the prices of other stocks. The computation of market risk is complex—using computers and sophisticated statistical techniques such as regression analysis—but the idea is simple. Consider the following data about the changes in the prices of the stocks of Company A and Company B and the average change in price of all stocks in the market:

Average Percentage Change in Price of All Stocks	Percentage Change in Price of Company A's Stock	Percentage Change in Price of Company B's Stock
+10	+15	+5
−10	−15	−5

In this example, when the average price of all stocks increased by 10 percent, Company A's price increased 15 percent and Company B's increased only 5 percent. When the average price of all stocks decreased by 10 percent, Company A's price decreased 15 percent and Company B's decreased only 5 percent. Thus relative to all stocks, Company A's stock is more volatile than Company B's stock. If the prices of stocks go down, the risk of loss is greater in the case of Company A than in the case of Company B. If the market goes up, however, the potential for gain is greater in the case of Company A than in the case of Company B.

Market risk can be approximated by dividing the percentage change in price of the particular stock by the average percentage change in the price of all stocks, as follows:

$$\text{Company A} \quad \frac{\text{specific change}}{\text{average change}} = \frac{15}{10} = 1.5$$

$$\text{Company B} \quad \frac{\text{specific change}}{\text{average change}} = \frac{5}{10} = .5$$

These measures mean that an investor can generally expect the value of an investment in Company A to increase or decrease 1.5 times as much as the average increase or decrease in the price of all stocks and an investment in Company B to increase or decrease only .5 times as much as a hypothetical investment in all stocks.

Analysts call this measure of market risk **beta** (β), after the mathematical symbol used in the formula for calculating the relationships of the stock prices. The actual betas used by analysts are based on several years of data and are continually updated. These calculations require the use of computers and are usually obtained from investment services.

The market risk or beta for U.S. Steel in a recent year was 1.01. This means that, other things being equal, a person who invests in the stocks of U.S. Steel can expect its volatility or risk to be about the same as the stock market as a whole (which has a beta of 1.0). This makes sense when one considers that U.S. Steel is a mature company and the largest steel producer, with output closely related to the ups and downs in the economy as a whole.

If the investor's objective is to assume less risk than that of the market as a whole, other companies in the steel industry can be considered. The second largest steel company is Bethlehem Steel, but it can be eliminated because its beta of 1.30 makes it riskier than U.S. Steel. National Steel, the third largest steel processor, has been more stable over the years than its competitors, with a beta of only .85. It is a less risky stock in that there is less potential for loss in a "down" market, but there is also less potential for gain in an "up" market. The beta for National Steel is very low and compares favorably with that of a major regulated utility like American Telephone and Telegraph, which has a beta of .75.

Typically, growth stocks and speculative stocks are riskier than stocks in the market as a whole. For example, McDonald's, a prime example of a growth company, has had a beta of above 1.50 in the past and a recent beta of 1.20. It has rewarded investors' patience over the years but has been much more volatile and thus riskier than the average stock, which would have a beta of 1.00.

Investment decisions are not made on the basis of market risk alone, of course. First, other risk factors such as those indicated by the other ratios and analyses discussed in this chapter as well as by the industry, national, and world economic outlooks must be considered. Second, the expected return must be considered. Further, most investors try to own a portfolio of stocks whose average beta corresponds to the degree of risk they are willing to assume in relation to the average expected return of their portfolio.

Chapter Review

Review of Learning Objectives

1. Describe and discuss the objectives of financial statement analysis.
Creditors and investors use financial statement analysis to assess the past performance and current position of a company, as well as its future potential and the risk associated with this potential. Creditors use the information gained from analysis to help them make loans that will be repaid with interest. Investors use the information to help them make investments that provide a return commensurate with the risk.

2. Describe and discuss the standards for financial statement analysis.
Three commonly used standards for financial statement analysis are rule-of-thumb measures, past performance of the company, and industry norms. Rule-of-thumb measures are weak because of the lack of evidence that they can be applied widely. The past performance of a company can provide a guideline for measuring improvement but is not helpful in judging performance relative to other companies. Although the use of industry norms overcomes this last problem, its disadvantage is the lack of comparability of firms, even in the same industry.

3. State the sources of information for financial statement analysis.
The major sources of information about publicly held corporations are published reports such as annual reports and interim financial statements, SEC reports, business periodicals, and credit and investment advisory services.

4. Apply horizontal analysis, trend analysis, and vertical analysis to financial statements.

Horizontal analysis involves the computation of dollar amount changes and percentage changes from year to year. Trend analysis is an extension of horizontal analysis in that percentage changes are calculated for several years. The changes are usually computed by setting a base year equal to 100 and calculating the measures for subsequent years as a percentage of that base year. Vertical analysis uses percentages to show the relationship of the component parts to the total in a single statement. The resulting statements in percentages are called common-size statements.

5. Apply ratio analysis to financial statements in the study of an enterprise's liquidity, profitability, long-run solvency, and market tests.

The table below summarizes the basic information on ratio analysis.

Ratio	Components	Use or Meaning
Liquidity Ratios		
Current ratio	$\frac{\text{current assets}}{\text{current liabilities}}$	Measure of short-term debt-paying ability
Quick ratio	$\frac{\text{cash + marketable securities + receivables}}{\text{current liabilities}}$	Measure of short-term liquidity
Receivable turnover	$\frac{\text{sales}}{\text{accounts receivable}}$	Measure of relative size of accounts receivable balance and effectiveness of credit policies
Average days' sales uncollected	$\frac{\text{days in year}}{\text{receivable turnover}}$	Measure of time it takes to collect an average receivable
Inventory turnover	$\frac{\text{cost of goods sold}}{\text{inventory}}$	Measure of relative size of inventory
Profitability Ratios		
Profit margin	$\frac{\text{net income}}{\text{revenues}}$	Income produced by each dollar of sales
Asset turnover	$\frac{\text{revenues}}{\text{total assets}}$	Measure of how efficiently assets are used to produce sales
Return on assets	$\frac{\text{net income}}{\text{total assets}}$	Overall measure of earning power or profitability of all assets employed in the business
Return on owners' investment	$\frac{\text{net income}}{\text{owners' equity}}$	Profitabilty of owners' investment
Earnings per share	$\frac{\text{net income}}{\text{outstanding shares}}$	Means of placing earnings on a common basis for comparisons

(continued)

Ratio	Components	Use or Meaning
Long-Term Solvency Ratios		
Debt to equity	total liabilities / owners' equity	Measure of relationship of debt financing to equity financing
Interest coverage	net income before taxes + interest expense / interest expense	Measure of protection of creditors from a default on interest payments
Market Test Ratios		
Price/earnings (P/E)	market price / earnings per share	Measure of amount the market will pay for a dollar of earnings
Dividends yield	dividends / market price	Measure of current return to investor
Market risk	specific change in market price / average change in market price	Measure of volatility of the market price of a stock in relation to that of other stocks

Review Problem

Before doing the exercises and problems, review especially the examples of ratio analysis given in the chapter. For additional help, see the review problem in the working papers.

Chapter Assignments

Questions

1. What differences and similarities exist in the objectives of investors and creditors in using financial statement analysis?
2. What role does risk play in making loans and investments?
3. What standards are commonly used to evaluate ratios, and what are their relative merits?
4. Where may an investor look to find information about a company in which an investment is contemplated?
5. Why would one want to do both horizontal and trend analyses of a company's financial statements?
6. What is the difference between horizontal and vertical analysis?
7. What does the following sentence mean: "Based on 1967 equaling 100, net income increased from 240 in 1980 to 260 in 1981"?
8. What is the purpose of ratio analysis?

9. Why would a financial analyst compare the ratios of Steelco, a steel company, to the ratios of other companies in the steel industry? What might cause such a comparison to be invalid?

10. In a period of high interest rates, why are receivable and inventory turnovers especially important?

11. The following statements were made on page 35 of the November 6, 1978, *Fortune* Magazine: "Supermarket executives are beginning to look back with some nostalgia on the days when the standard profit margin was 1 percent of sales. Last year the industry overall margin came to a thin 0.72 percent." How could a supermarket earn a satisfactory return on assets with such a small profit margin?

12. Circo Company has a return on assets of 12 percent and a debt to equity ratio of .5. Would you expect return on owners' equity to be more or less than 12 percent?

13. Under what circumstances would a current ratio of 3:1 be good? Under what circumstances would it be bad?

14. Company A and Company B both have net incomes of $1,000,000. Is it possible to say that these companies are equally successful? Why or why not?

15. The market price of Company J's stock is the same as Company Q's stock. How might one determine whether investors are equally confident about the future of these companies?

16. Why is it riskier to own a stock whose market price is more changeable than the market price of other stocks?

17. "By almost any standard, Chicago-based Helene Curtis rates as one of America's worst-managed personal care companies. In recent years its return on equity has hovered between 10% and 13%, well below the industry average of 18% to 19%. Net profit margins of 2% to 3% are half that of competitors. . . . As a result, while leading names like Revlon and Avon are trading at three and four times book value, Curtis' trades at less than two-thirds book value."* Considering that many companies are happy with a return on equity (owners' investment) of 10% and 13%, why is this analysis so critical of Curtis's performance? Assuming that Curtis could double its profit margin, what other information would you need in order to project the resulting return on owners' investment? Why does the writer feel that it is obvious that Revlon's and Avon's stocks are trading for more than Curtis's?

Classroom Exercises

Exercise 21-1 Trend Analysis

Prepare a trend analysis of the data below, using 19x1 as a base year, and tell whether the situation shown by the trends is favorable or unfavorable. (Round your answers to one decimal point.)

	19x1	19x2	19x3	19x4	19x5
Sales	$11,000	$11,440	$12,100	$11,990	$12,650
Cost of Goods Sold	7,000	7,350	7,770	7,700	8,540
General and Administrative Expenses	2,400	2,448	2,544	2,592	2,640
Operating Income	1,600	1,642	1,786	1,698	1,470

* *Forbes*, November 13, 1978, p. 154.

Exercise 21-2 Horizontal Analysis

Compute amount and percentage changes for the balance sheet below, and comment on the changes from 19x1 to 19x2. (Round the percentage changes to one decimal point.)

Keough Company
Comparative Balance Sheets
December 31, 19x1 and 19x2

	19x2	19x1
Assets		
Current Assets	$ 19,200	$ 12,800
Property, Plant, and Equipment (net)	108,864	97,200
Total Assets	$128,064	$110,000
Liabilities and Stockholders' Equity		
Current Liabilities	$ 11,200	$ 3,200
Long-Term Liabilities	35,000	40,000
Stockholders' Equity	81,864	66,800
Total Liabilities and Owners' Equity	$128,064	$110,000

Exercise 21-3 Vertical Analysis

Express the comparative income statements below as common-size statements, and comment on the changes from 19x1 to 19x2.

Keough Company
Comparative Income Statement
For the Years Ended December 31, 19x1 and 19x2

	19x2	19x1
Sales	$212,000	$184,000
Cost of Goods Sold	127,200	119,600
Gross Profit from Sales	$ 84,800	$ 64,400
Selling Expenses	$ 53,000	$ 36,800
General Expenses	25,440	18,400
Total Operating Expenses	$ 78,440	$ 55,200
Net Operating Income	$ 6,360	$ 9,200

Exercise 21-4 Liquidity Analysis

Partial comparative balance sheet and income statement information for Jay Company appears below.

	19x2	19x1
Cash	$ 3,400	$ 2,600
Marketable Securities	1,800	4,300
Accounts Receivable (net)	11,200	8,900
Inventory	13,600	12,400
Total Current Assets	$30,000	$28,200
Current Liabilities	$10,000	$ 7,050
Sales	$80,640	$55,180
Cost of Goods Sold	54,400	50,840
Gross Profit from Sales	$26,240	$ 4,340

Compute the current ratio, quick ratio, receivable turnover, average days' sales uncollected, and inventory turnover for each year, and comment on the change in liquidity position from 19x1 to 19x2. (Round the ratios to two decimal places.)

Exercise 21-5 Profitability Analysis

Simic Company had total assets of $340,000 in 19x1 and $380,000 in 19x2 and a debt to equity ratio of .5 in both years. In 19x1, the company made a net income of $38,556 on revenues of $612,000. In 19x2, the company made a net income of $49,476 on revenues of $798,000. Compute the profit margin, asset turnover, return on assets, and return on owners' investment for each year, and comment on the apparent cause of the increase or decrease in profitability. (Round the percentages and other ratios to one decimal place.)

Exercise 21-6 Long-Term Solvency and Market Test Ratios

An investor is considering investments in the long-term bonds and common stock of Companies X and Y. Both companies operate in the same industry, but Company X has a beta of 1.0 and Company B has a beta of 1.2. In addition, both companies pay a dividend per share of $2, and the yield of both companies' long-term bonds is 10 percent. Other data for the two companies are presented below.

	Company X	Company Y
Total Assets	$1,200,000	$540,000
Total Liabilities	540,000	297,000
Net Income Before Taxes	144,000	64,800
Interest Expense	48,600	26,730
Earnings per Share	1.60	2.50
Market Price on Common Stock	20	$23\frac{3}{4}$

Compute debt to equity ratios, interest coverage ratios, price/earnings (P/E) ratios, and dividend yield ratios, and comment on the results. (Round computations to one decimal point.)

Problem Set A

Problem 21A-1 Analyzing the Effects of Transactions on Ratios

Florence Corporation engaged in the transactions listed in the first column of the table at the top of the next page. Opposite each transaction is a ratio and spaces to mark with an X the effect of each transaction on the ratio.

	Transaction	Ratio	Effect: Increase	Decrease	None
a.	Sold merchandise on account.	Current ratio			
b.	Sold merchandise on account.	Inventory turnover			
c.	Collected on account receivable.	Quick ratio			
d.	Write-off on account receivable.	Receivable turnover			
e.	Paid on account payable.	Current ratio			
f.	Declaration of cash dividend.	Return on owners' investment			
g.	Paid advertising expense.	Profit margin			
h.	Issued stock dividend.	Debt to equity			
i.	Issued bond payable.	Asset turnover			
j.	Accrued interest expense.	Current ratio			
k.	Paid previously declared cash dividend.	Dividends yield			
l.	Purchased treasury stock.	Return on assets			

Required

Place an X in the appropriate column to show whether the transaction increased, decreased, or had no effect on the indicated ratio.

Problem 21A-2 Trend Analysis The condensed comparative income statement and additional selected data for MacQuily Corporation appear as follows:

	19x1	19x2	19x3	19x4	19x5
Sales	$784,200	$850,857	$972,840	$892,680	$1,061,500
Cost of Goods Sold	435,600	472,800	589,200	545,820	702,670
Gross Profit from Sales	$348,600	$378,057	$383,640	$346,860	$ 358,830
Operating Expenses	182,100	212,100	227,300	247,050	305,600
Net Income	$166,500	$165,957	$156,340	$ 99,810	$ 53,230

Additional selected data:

	19x1	19x2	19x3	19x4	19x5
Total Assets	$1,342,900	$1,486,200	$1,522,700	$1,552,700	$1,558,200
Total Liabilities	387,900	401,500	452,600	478,700	525,600
Earnings per Share	1.25	1.24	1.20	.80	.52
Dividends per Share	.70	.70	.70	.50	.30

Required

1. Prepare a trend analysis for MacQuily Corporation using 19x1 as the base year. (Round percentages to one decimal point.)
2. Comment on favorable and unfavorable trends shown in the analysis.

Problem 21A-3 Horizontal and Vertical Analysis

The condensed comparative income statement and comparative balance sheet of Master Corporation follow. All figures are given in thousands of dollars.

	19x2	19x1
Sales	$812,800	$786,600
Cost of Goods Sold	522,200	502,100
Gross Profit from Sales	$290,600	$284,500
Operating Expenses		
Selling Expenses	$119,200	$129,500
Administrative Expenses	111,800	105,800
Interest Expense	16,400	9,800
Income Taxes	15,600	14,200
Total Operating Expenses	$263,000	$259,300
Net Income	$ 27,600	$ 25,200

	19x2	19x1
Assets		
Cash	$ 20,300	$ 10,200
Accounts Receivable (net)	58,900	57,300
Inventory	143,700	148,700
Property, Plant, and Equipment (net)	187,500	180,000
Total Assets	$410,400	$396,200
Liabilities and Stockholders' Equity		
Accounts Payable	$ 66,900	$119,300
Notes Payable	50,000	100,000
Bonds Payable	100,000	—
Common Stock	100,000	100,000
Retained Earnings	93,500	76,900
Total Liabilities and Stockholders' Equity	$410,400	$396,200

Required

1. Prepare a schedule showing amount and percentage changes from 19x1 to 19x2 for the corporate income statement and balance sheet. (Round percentages to one decimal point.)
2. Prepare a common-size income statement and balance sheet for 19x1 and 19x2. (Round percentages to one decimal point.)
3. Comment on the results found in parts 1 and 2 by identifying favorable and unfavorable changes in components and composition.

Problem 21A-4 Ratio Analysis

Additional data for Master Corporation in 19x1 and 19x2 appear below. This information should be used along with the data in Problem 21A-3.

	19x2	19x1
Dividends Paid	$14,600,000.00	$ 8,600,000.00
Number of Common Shares	20,000,000.00	20,000,000.00
Market Price per Share	$9.00	$15.00
Beta	1.40	1.25

Required

1. Conduct a liquidity analysis by calculating for each year the (a) current ratio, (b) quick ratio, (c) receivable turnover, (d) average days' sales uncollected, and (e) inventory turnover. Indicate whether each ratio had a favorable (F) or unfavorable (U) change from 19x1 to 19x2.
2. Conduct a profitability analysis by calculating for each year the (a) profit margin, (b) asset turnover, (c) return on assets, (d) return on owners' investment, and (e) earnings per share. Indicate whether each ratio had a favorable (F) or unfavorable (U) change from 19x1 to 19x2.
3. Conduct a long-term solvency analysis by calculating for each year the (a) debt to equity ratio and (b) interest coverage ratio. Indicate whether each ratio had a favorable (F) or unfavorable (U) change from 19x1 to 19x2.
4. Conduct a market test analysis by calculating for each year the (a) price/earnings ratio, (b) dividends yield, and (c) market risk. Note the market beta measures, and indicate whether each ratio had a favorable (F) or unfavorable (U) change from 19x1 to 19x2.

Note: Round all answers to one decimal point, and consider changes of .1 or less to be neither favorable nor unfavorable.

Problem 21A-5 Comprehensive Ratio Analysis of Two Companies

Marcus Livers is considering an investment in the common stock of a chain of retail department stores. He has narrowed his choice to two retail companies, Saver Corporation and Good Deal Corporation, whose balance sheets and income statements are presented on the next page.

	Saver Corporation	Good Deal Corporation
Assets		
Cash	$ 40,000	$ 96,200
Marketable Securities (at cost)	101,700	42,300
Accounts Receivable (net)	276,400	492,700
Inventory	314,900	626,700
Prepaid Expenses	27,200	57,000
Property, Plant, and Equipment (net)	1,456,800	3,276,000
Intangibles and Other Assets	276,600	72,400
Total Assets	$2,493,600	$ 4,663,300
Liabilities and Stockholders' Equity		
Accounts Payable	$ 172,000	$ 286,300
Notes Payable	75,000	200,000
Accrued Liabilities	25,100	36,700
Bonds Payable	1,000,000	1,000,000
Common Stock—$10 par value	500,000	300,000
Paid-in Capital in Excess of Par Value	304,900	1,784,300
Retained Earnings	416,600	1,056,000
Total Liabilities and Stockholders' Equity	$2,493,600	$ 4,663,300

	Saver Corporation	Good Deal Corporation
Sales	$6,280,000	$12,605,000
Cost of Goods Sold	3,071,000	7,417,000
Gross Profit from Sales	$3,209,000	$ 5,188,000
Operating Expenses		
Selling Expenses	$2,411,300	$ 3,554,100
Administrative Expenses	493,000	1,217,000
Interest Expense	97,000	114,000
Income Tax Expense	100,000	150,000
Total Operating Expenses	$3,101,300	$ 5,035,100
Net Income	$ 107,700	$ 152,900

During the year, Saver Corporation paid a total of $25,000 in dividends. The market price per share of its stock is currently $30. In comparison, Good Deal Corporation paid a total of $57,000 in dividends during the year, and the current market price per share of its stock is $38. An investment service indicated that the beta associated with Saver's stock is 1.20 and that associated with Good Deal's stock is .95.

Required

Conduct a comprehensive ratio analysis of each company, and compare the results. This analysis should be done in the following steps:

1. Prepare an analysis of liquidity by calculating for each company the (a) current ratio, (b) quick ratio, (c) receivable turnover, (d) average days' sales uncollected, and (e) inventory turnover.
2. Prepare an analysis of profitability by calculating for each company the (a) profit margin, (b) asset turnover, (c) return on assets, (d) return on owners' investment, and (e) earnings per share.
3. Prepare an analysis of long-run solvency by calculating for each company the (a) debt to equity ratio and (b) interest coverage ratio.
4. Prepare an analysis of market tests by calculating for each company the (a) price/earnings ratio, (b) dividends yield, and (c) market risk.
5. Compare the analysis of each company by inserting the ratio calculations from parts 1 through 4 in a table with the following column heads: Ratio Name, Saver Corporation, Good Deal Corporation, Company with More Favorable Ratio. Indicate in the right-hand column which company had the more favorable ratio in each case. (If the ratios are within .1 of each other, consider them neutral.)

Problem 21A-6 Preparation of Statements from Ratios and Incomplete Data

Presented below and on the next page are the income statement and balance sheet of Jonray Corporation with most of the amounts missing.

Jonray Corporation
Income Statement
For the Year Ended December 31, 19x1
(in thousands of dollars)

Sales		$9,000
Cost of Goods Sold		?
Gross Profit from Sales		?
Operating Expenses		
Selling Expenses	$?	
Administrative Expenses	117	
Interest Expense	81	
Income Tax Expense	310	
Total Operating Expenses		?
Net Income		$?

Jonray Corporation
Balance Sheet
December 31, 19x1
(in thousands of dollars)

Assets		
Cash	$?	
Accounts Receivable (net)	?	
Inventories	?	
Total Current Assets		?
Property, Plant, and Equipment (net)		2,700
Total Assets		$?
Liabilities and Stockholders' Equity		
Current Liabilities	$?	
Bond Payable, 9% interest	?	
Total Liabilities		$?
Capital Stock—$10 par value	$1,500	
Paid-in Capital in Excess of Par Value	1,300	
Retained Earnings	2,000	
Total Stockholders' Equity		$4,800
Total Liabilities and Stockholders' Equity		$?

Additional information: (a) the only interest expense is on long-term debt; (b) the debt to equity ratio is .5; (c) the current ratio is 3:1, and the quick ratio is 2:1; (d) the receivable turnover is 4.5, and the inventory turnover is 4.0; (e) the return on assets is 10 percent.

Required

Complete the financial statements using the information presented. Show supporting computations.

Problem Set B

Problem 21B-1 Analyzing the Effects of Transactions on Ratios

Mayfair Corporation engaged in the transactions listed in the first column of the table at the top of the next page. Opposite each transaction is a ratio and spaces to mark with an X the effect of each transaction on the ratio.

Transaction		Ratio	Effect: Increase	Effect: Decrease	Effect: None
a.	Issued common stock.	Asset turnover			
b.	Declared cash dividend.	Current ratio			
c.	Sold treasury stock.	Return on owners' investment			
d.	Borrowed cash by issuing a note payable.	Debt to equity			
e.	Paid salary expense.	Inventory turnover			
f.	Purchased merchandise for cash.	Current ratio			
g.	Sold equipment for cash.	Receivable turnover			
h.	Sold merchandise on account.	Quick ratio			
i.	Paid current portion of long-term debt.	Return on assets			
j.	Accepted a sales discount.	Profit margin			
k.	Purchased marketable securities for cash.	Quick ratio			
l.	Declared a 5% stock dividend.	Current ratio			

Required

Place an X in the appropriate column to show whether the transaction increased, decreased, or had no effect on the indicated ratio.

Problem 21B-3 Horizontal and Vertical Analysis

The condensed comparative statements of Poisant Corporation appear as follows:

Poisant Corporation
Comparative Income Statement
For the Years Ended December 31, 19x1 and 19x2

	19x2	19x1
Sales	$791,200	$742,600
Cost of Goods Sold	454,100	396,200
Gross Profit from Sales	$337,100	$346,400
Operating Expenses		
Selling Expenses	$130,100	$104,600
Administrative Expenses	140,300	115,500
Interest Expense	25,000	20,000
Income Taxes	14,000	35,000
Total Operating Expenses	$309,400	$275,100
Net Income	$ 27,700	$ 71,300

Poisant Corporation
Comparative Balance Sheet
December 31, 19x1 and 19x2

	19x2	19x1
Assets		
Cash	$ 31,100	$ 27,200
Accounts Receivable (net)	72,500	42,700
Inventory	122,600	107,800
Property, Plant, and Equipment	577,700	507,500
Total Assets	$803,900	$685,200
Liabilities and Stockholders' Equity		
Accounts Payable	$104,700	$ 72,300
Notes Payable	50,000	50,000
Bonds Payable	200,000	150,000
Common Stock	300,000	300,000
Retained Earnings	149,200	112,900
Total Liabilities and Stockholders' Equity	$803,900	$685,200

Required

1. Prepare a schedule showing amount and percentage changes from 19x1 to 19x2 for the comparative income statement and balance sheet.
2. Prepare a common-size income statement and balance sheet for 19x1 and 19x2.
3. Comment on the results found in parts 1 and 2 by identifying favorable and unfavorable changes in components and composition.

Problem 21B-4
Ratio Analysis

Additional data for Poisant Corporation in 19x1 and 19x2 appear below. These data should be used in conjunction with the data in Problem 21B-3.

	19x2	19x1
Dividends Paid	$35,000	$35,000
Number of Common Shares	30,000	30,000
Market Price per Share	40	60
Beta	1.00	.90

Required

1. Prepare a liquidity analysis by calculating for each year the (a) current ratio, (b) quick ratio, (c) receivable turnover, (d) average days' sales uncollected, and (e) inventory turnover. Indicate whether each ratio improved or not from 19x1 to 19x2 by using an F for favorable or U for unfavorable.
2. Prepare a profitability analysis by calculating for each year the (a) profit margin, (b) asset turnover, (c) return on assets, (d) return on owners' investment, and (e) earnings per share. Indicate whether each ratio had a favorable (F) or unfavorable (U) change from 19x1 to 19x2.

3. Prepare a long-term solvency analysis by calculating for each year the (a) debt to equity ratio and (b) interest coverage ratio. Indicate whether each ratio had a favorable (F) or unfavorable (U) change from 19x1 to 19x2.
4. Conduct a market test analysis by calculating for each year the (a) price/earnings ratio, (b) dividends yield, and (c) market risk. Note the market risk measure, and indicate whether each ratio had a favorable (F) or unfavorable (U) change from 19x1 to 19x2.

Note: Round all answers to one decimal point, and consider changes of .1 or less to be neither favorable nor unfavorable.

Problem 21B-5 Comprehensive Ratio Analysis of Two Companies

Frances Simunec has decided to invest some of her savings in common stock. She feels that the chemical industry has good growth prospects and has narrowed her choice to two companies in that industry. As a final step in making the choice, she decided to make a comprehensive ratio analysis of two companies, Chemco and Chemicals, Inc. Balance sheet and income statement data for the two companies appear below and on the next page.

	Chemco	Chemicals, Inc.
Assets		
Cash	$ 126,100	$ 514,300
Marketable Securities (at cost)	117,500	1,200,000
Accounts Receivable (net)	456,700	2,600,000
Inventories	1,880,000	4,956,000
Prepaid Expenses	72,600	156,600
Property, Plant, and Equipment (net)	5,342,200	19,356,000
Intangibles and Other Assets	217,000	580,000
Total Assets	$8,212,100	$29,362,900
Liabilities and Stockholders' Equity		
Accounts Payable	$ 517,400	$ 2,342,000
Notes Payable	1,000,000	2,000,000
Income Taxes Payable	85,200	117,900
Bonds Payable	2,000,000	15,000,000
Common Stock—$1 par value	350,000	1,000,000
Paid-in Capital in Excess of Par Value	1,747,300	5,433,300
Retained Earnings	2,512,200	3,469,700
Total Liabilities and Stockholders' Equity	$8,212,100	$29,362,900

	Chemco	Chemicals, Inc.
Sales	$9,486,200	$27,287,300
Cost of Goods Sold	5,812,200	18,372,400
Gross Profit from Sales	$3,674,000	$ 8,914,900
Operating Expenses		
Selling Expenses	$1,194,000	$ 1,955,700
Administrative Expenses	1,217,400	4,126,000
Interest Expense	270,000	1,360,000
Income Tax Expense	450,000	600,000
Total Operating Expenses	$3,131,400	$ 8,041,700
Net Income	$ 542,600	$ 873,200

During the year, Chemco paid a total of $140,000 in dividends, and the current market price per share of its stock is $20. Chemicals, Inc., paid a total of $600,000 in dividends during the year, and the current market price per share of its stock is $9. An investment service reports that the beta associated with Chemco's stock is 1.05 and that associated with Chemicals, Inc., is .8.

Required

Conduct a comprehensive ratio analysis of each company, and compare the results. This analysis should be done in the following steps:

1. Prepare an analysis of liquidity by calculating for each company the (a) current ratio, (b) quick ratio, (c) receivable turnover, (d) average days' sales uncollected, and (e) inventory turnover.
2. Prepare an analysis of profitability by calculating for each company the (a) profit margin, (b) asset turnover, (c) return on assets, (d) return on owners' investment, and (e) earnings per share.
3. Prepare an analysis of long-run solvency by calculating for each company the (a) debt to equity ratio and (b) interest coverage ratio.
4. Prepare an analysis of market tests by calculating for each company the (a) price/earnings ratio, (b) dividends yield, and (c) market risk.
5. Compare the analysis of each company by inserting the ratio calculations from parts 1 through 4 in a table with the following column heads: Ratio Name; Chemco; Chemicals, Inc.; Company with More Favorable Ratio. In the right-hand column of the table indicate which company had the more favorable ratio in each case. (If the ratios are within .1 of each other, consider them neutral.)

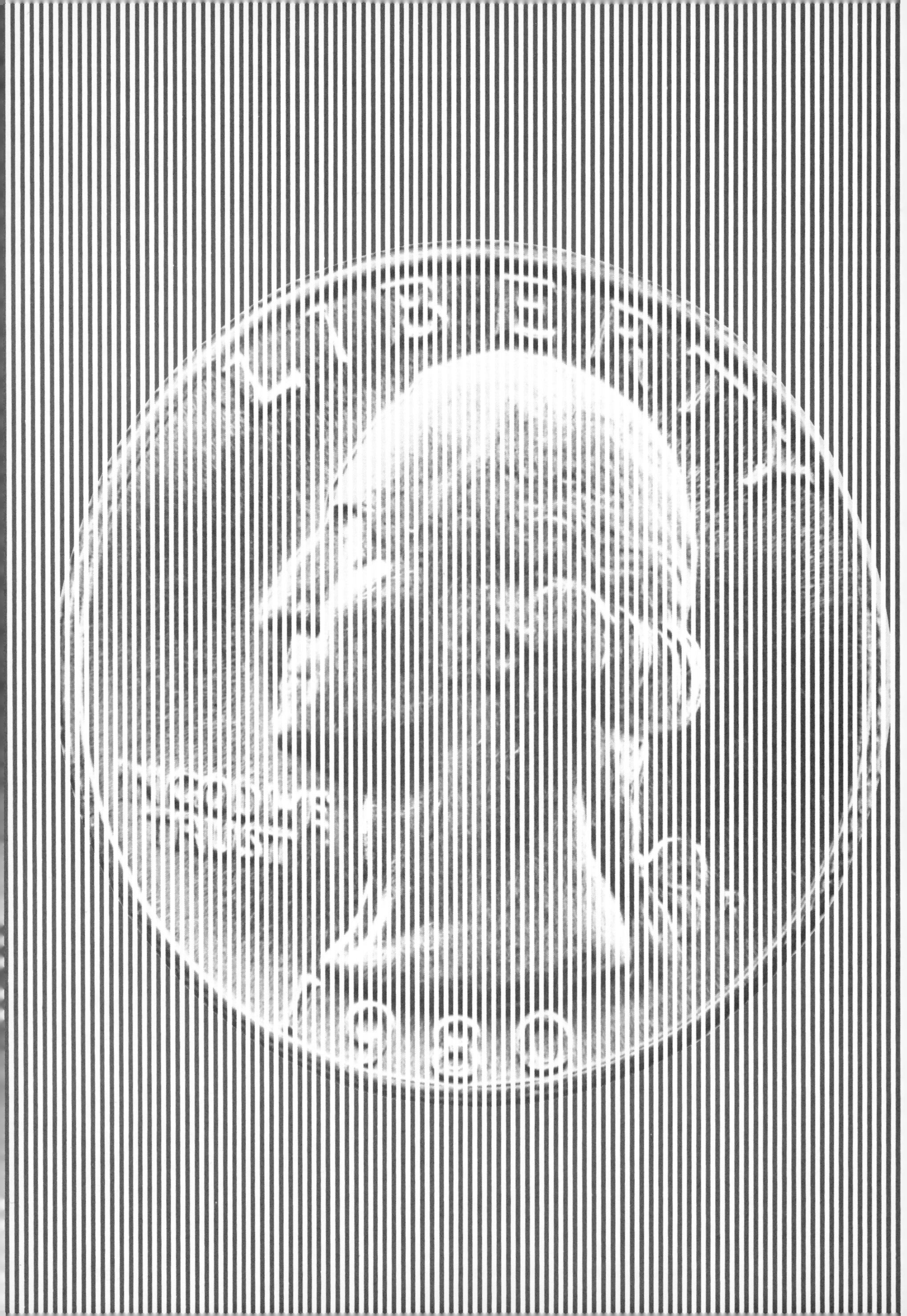

LIBERTY
IN GOD WE TRUST
1980

Part Six

Basic Concepts of Management Accounting

The first five parts of this book dealt primarily with the measurement and reporting problems pertaining to general-purpose financial statements used by people outside the business entity, such as bankers and stockholders. The basic concepts and practices of internal or management accounting are introduced in the final two parts of this text.

The focus in Part VI is on the development and accumulation of manufacturing cost information for use in analyzing operating performance and in reporting the results of operations to management.

Chapter 22 introduces the basic terminology used in accounting for manufacturing operations and is especially concerned with the importance of cost classification and cost assignment.

Chapter 23 centers on the flow of costs through the accounting records of a manufacturing company. In addition, financial statements of a manufacturing operation are developed and work sheet preparation is explained.

Chapters 24 and 25 involve two approaches to product costing. After defining the concept of absorption costing and describing the development and use of predetermined overhead rates, Chapter 24 focuses on product costing within the job order cost accounting system. Chapter 25 analyzes product costing in a process cost accounting environment.

Learning Objectives

Chapter Twenty-Two

Manufacturing Accounting: Cost Elements and Cost Assignment

1. *Identify differences in accounting for manufacturing and merchandising companies.*
2. *Differentiate among the three manufacturing cost elements: direct materials costs, direct labor costs, and manufacturing (factory) overhead costs.*
3. *Identify the source documents used in manufacturing cost accumulation.*
4. *Compute a predetermined overhead rate and a product unit cost.*
5. *State the role of cost objectives in the cost allocation process.*
6. *Assign costs of supporting service functions to production departments.*
7. *Allocate common manufacturing costs to joint products.*

This chapter introduces accounting for manufacturing operations. It emphasizes basic terminology, the elements of manufacturing accounting, cost classification, and joint cost assignment. As a result of studying this chapter, you should be able to master the learning objectives listed on the left.

Accumulating, interpreting, and reporting financial information is important for manufacturing and service-related[1] companies as well as for those classified as merchandising firms. Manufacturing companies are unique because they *produce* a product that is sold to other companies and individuals. Merchandising companies, on the other hand, *purchase* a salable product from someone for the purpose of resale. For a merchandising company, determining the costs of products and inventory values involves simply finding the purchase price of the item in question (plus shipping and handling costs in some cases). A manufacturing company, however, must accumulate a series of production-related costs to arrive at the final cost of the manufactured product.

The financial statements of a manufacturing company look very similar to those of a merchandising company. Each uses balance sheets with assets, liabilities, and owners' equity sections. Revenue and expenses are reported in the income statement. Nevertheless, there are differences in the reporting formats for the two types of companies, which will be explained later.

In addition to the normal financial accounting structure described in earlier chapters, manufacturing companies must also maintain a cost accounting system. This system centers on the costs incurred in manufacturing a specific product. To account for production costs and to assign these costs to products, certain accounting principles and procedures have been developed. The cost accounting system is designed to handle all product-related

1. Service-related organizations such as hospitals, accounting firms, and banks are interested in service costs much as the manufacturing firm is interested in product costs. Thus many of these same internal accounting procedures are used by service-related enterprises.

costs. These costs are assigned to products and are used to determine end-of-period inventory values and the costs of goods sold in the financial statements. Product cost information is important to the accuracy of the company's financial statements. This chapter introduces the basic types of manufacturing costs and the principles of cost assignment to products. Two basic cost allocation problems—assigning supporting service function costs and assigning joint or common production costs—conclude this introduction to manufacturing accounting.

Merchandising Versus Manufacturing Operations

Objective 1 Identify differences in accounting for manufacturing and merchandising companies

Because much of this text has focused on the merchandising organization, it is important here to explain the differences in accounting for manufacturing firms and merchandising firms. Cost accumulation accounting procedures are used by many types of business entities but are particularly important to manufacturing companies. Figures 22-1 and 22-2 show how the computation of cost of goods sold differs between the two types of companies.

A merchandising company normally buys a product that is ready for resale when it is received. Nothing needs to be done to the product to make it salable except to prepare a special package or display to make it more marketable. As shown in Figure 22-1 (next page), the total of the beginning merchandise inventory and purchases during the period is the basis for computing both the cost of goods sold and the ending merchandise inventory balances. Costs assigned to unsold items make up the ending inventory balance. The difference between cost of goods available for sale and the ending inventory amount represents the cost of goods sold during the period. The following example demonstrates this computation:

Beginning merchandise inventory	$ 2,000
Plus total purchases of salable goods	8,000
Cost of goods available for sale	$10,000
Less ending merchandise inventory	(2,700)
Cost of goods sold	$ 7,300

This example and Figure 22-1 illustrate the simplicity of computing the cost of goods sold for a merchandising company. The only cash expenditure occurs when the salable goods are purchased for cash. Any items unsold at year end make up the ending inventory balance. The remainder of the purchase costs (plus any balance in beginning merchandise inventory) are reported as Cost of Goods Sold.

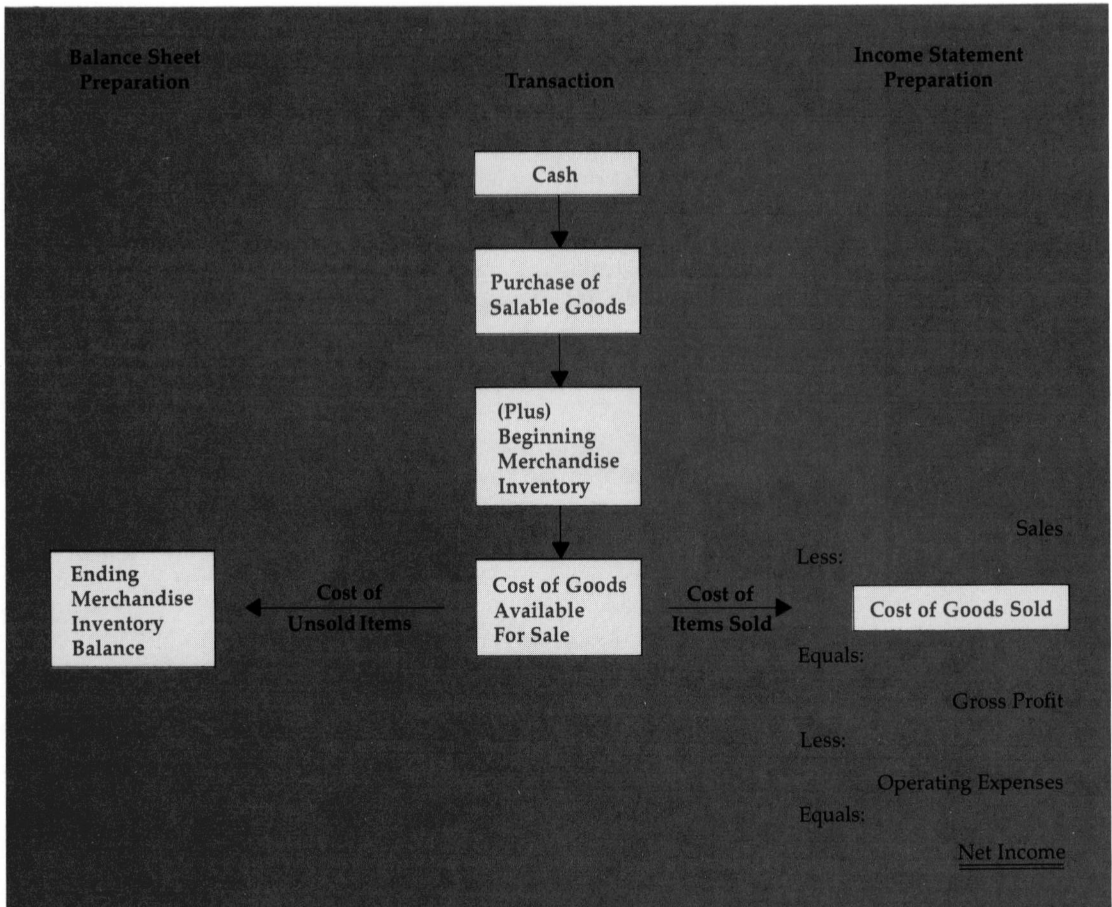

Figure 22-1
Cost of Goods Sold: A Merchandising Company

Computing the cost of goods sold for a manufacturing company is more complex. As illustrated in Figure 22-2,[2] instead of one inventory account, a manufacturer maintains three different types of inventory accounts: Raw Materials Inventory, Work in Process Inventory, and Finished Goods Inventory. Purchased raw materials that are unused during the production process comprise the year-end Raw Materials Inventory balance. The cost of raw materials used plus the costs of labor services and factory overhead (utility costs, depreciation of factory machinery and building, and so forth) are transferred to the Work in Process Inventory account when the raw material, resource, or service is used in the production process.

The three categories of costs discussed above are referred to normally as material, labor, and overhead costs (often abbreviated as M, L, and

2. To make the illustration easier to understand, beginning inventory balances have not been included in Figure 22-2. Beginning balances will be introduced in a later chapter.

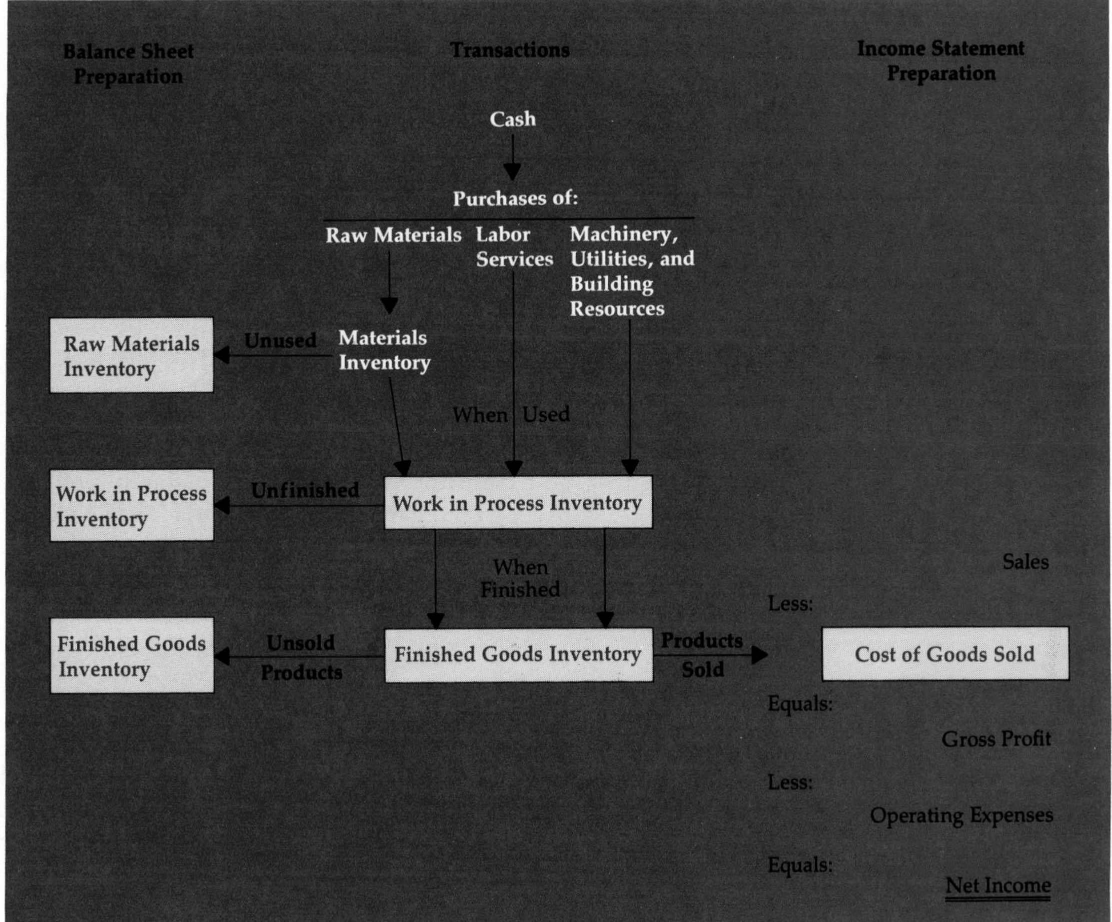

Figure 22-2
Cost of Goods Sold: A Manufacturing Company

OH). These costs are accumulated in the Work in Process Inventory account during an accounting period. When a specific batch or order is completed, all manufacturing costs assigned to the completed units are transferred to the Finished Goods Inventory account. Costs remaining in the Work in Process Inventory account represent costs assigned to partially completed units. These costs comprise the ending balance in the Work in Process Inventory account.

Finished goods inventory is accounted for much like the Merchandise Inventory account illustrated in Figure 22-1. Costs of completed goods are entered into the Finished Goods Inventory account. As shown in Figure 22-2, costs attached to unsold items at year end make up the ending balance in the Finished Goods Inventory account. All costs associated with units sold are accumulated and reported on the income statement as Cost of Goods Sold. To clarify the flow of costs, the following section will analyze the three manufacturing cost elements—raw materials, direct labor, and factory or manufacturing overhead.

Manufacturing Cost Elements

Objective 2 Differentiate among the three manufacturing cost elements: direct materials costs, direct labor costs, and manufacturing (factory) overhead costs

Manufacturing costs can be classified in many different ways. Some costs can be identified with and traced directly to one product or a specific batch of products, whereas other costs cannot be traced directly to products. In compiling information for business decisions, a particular cost may be important to one type of decision analysis and ignored in another. When we change from an external financial reporting approach (preparing financial statements for external users like stockholders) to an internal or management accounting approach, some costs take on different characteristics. In fact, manufacturing costs can be reclassified in many different ways depending on the final goal of a particular cost analysis.

Throughout Chapters 22–28, we explore cost reclassification and define new terms. However, the most common and basic cost classification scheme associated with cost accounting is the grouping of manufacturing costs into three elements: direct (raw) materials costs, direct labor costs, or indirect manufacturing costs (factory overhead). **Direct costs** are traceable to specific products, whereas **indirect costs** must be assigned to products by some allocation method. Direct and indirect costs will be discussed further as the three elements of manufacturing cost are analyzed.

Direct Materials Costs

All manufactured products require basic raw material ingredients. The ingredient may be iron ore for producing steel, sheet steel for producing automobiles, or flour for producing bread. Each of these examples illustrates the link between a basic raw material and a final product.

Direct materials are raw materials that become an integral part of the finished product and are conveniently and economically traceable to specific units of productive output. Therefore, such raw materials costs are direct costs. In some cases, even though a raw material becomes an integral part of a finished product, the expense of actually tracing the cost to a specific product is excessive. Examples of this type of raw material include nails in furniture, bolts in automobiles, or rivets in airplanes. These less significant raw materials and other production supplies that cannot be conveniently or economically assigned to specific products are identified and accounted for as **indirect materials**. Indirect materials costs are included as part of manufacturing (or factory) overhead costs and are discussed later in this chapter.

Objective 3 Identify the source documents used in manufacturing cost accumulation

Direct Materials Purchases Direct materials represent a sizable expenditure each year and require special attention in the purchasing function. A firm must be careful to ensure the purchase of proper quantities and the receipt of quality goods. An efficient system to account for direct material purchases uses several important documents to help safeguard this function. These documents were described in Chapter 9. The **purchase requisition** (or **purchase request**) is used to begin the raw materials purchasing function. This document originates in the production department and identifies the items to be purchased, states the quantities required, and must be approved by a qualified manager or supervisor.

From the information on the purchase requisition, the purchasing department prepares a formal **purchase order.** After multiple copies are made, sufficient copies are forwarded to the vendor or supplier, and the remaining copies are kept for internal use. Upon receipt of the ordered goods, a **receiving report** is prepared and matched with the descriptions and quantities listed on the purchase order. Usually, raw materials are inspected upon receipt to identify inferior quality or damaged goods. The purchasing function is complete when the company receives an invoice from the vendor and approves it for payment.

Direct Material Usage Controlling raw material costs does not end with the receipt and inspection of purchased goods. The raw materials must be stored in a safe place, counted periodically, and issued into production only with the approval of a production supervisor. It is important to keep raw material storage areas clean and orderly, and to lock up valuable items. Periodic physical counts are necessary to identify the number of units on hand and to test the inventory accounting system. Raw materials should be issued to production only when an approved **materials requisition** form is presented to the storeroom clerk. The materials requisition form, shown in Figure 22-3 (next page), is essential to the control of raw materials. In addition to providing the supervisor's approval signature, the materials requisition identifies the types and quantities of goods needed and received.

Direct Labor Costs

Personnel connected with the manufacturing process include machine operators, maintenance people, managers and supervisors, support personnel, and other people performing the materials handling, inspection, and storage functions. Because all these people are connected in some way with the production process, their wages and salaries must be accounted for as production costs of the product. However, it is difficult to trace many of these costs directly to individual products.

To help overcome this problem, the wages of machine operators and other workers involved in actually shaping the product are classified as direct labor costs. **Direct labor** costs encompass all labor costs for specific work performed on products that are conveniently and economically traceable to end products. Labor costs for production-related activities that cannot be associated with, or are not conveniently and economically traceable to, end products are called **indirect labor** costs. Like indirect materials costs, indirect labor costs such as machine helpers, supervisory people, and other support personnel are accounted for as manufacturing (or factory) overhead costs.

Labor Documentation Labor time records are important to both the employee and the company. The employee is concerned about being paid at the correct rate for all hours worked. The company does not wish to

Figure 22-3
The Materials Requisition Form

Gillies Manufacturing Company
Boston, Massachusetts

Materials Requisition

No. 49621

Charge to Job No. ______________

Requested by ______________ Date ______________

Department ______________

Part Number	Description	Quantity Requested	Quantity Issued	Unit Cost	Total Cost

Issued by ______________ Date Received ______________

Approved by ______________

Received by ______________

underpay or overpay its employees. In addition, company management is interested in keeping a record of hours worked on particular products or batches of products manufactured during the period. For these reasons, accounting for wages and salaries requires careful attention.

The basic time record is called an employee time card. On this document, either the supervisor or a time clock records the daily starting and finishing times of each employee. Usually, a company will use another set of labor cards to help verify the time recorded on the time cards and to keep track of labor costs per job or batch of goods produced. These documents, called job cards, contain a record of the time spent by an employee on a particular job. Each eight-hour period recorded on a time card may be supported by several job cards. Special job cards also record machine downtime due to machine repair or product design changes. Job cards verify the productive effort of the employee and help control labor time per job.

Gross Versus Net Payroll The topic of accounting for direct and indirect labor costs often causes misunderstanding. People sometimes confuse gross payroll with net payroll. For internal cost accounting purposes, gross wages and salaries are used. **Net payroll** is the amount paid to the employee after all payroll deductions have been subtracted from gross wages. Payroll deductions, such as for federal income taxes and social security taxes, are expenditures of the employee that the employer withholds and pays to the government. The total of all payroll and payroll-related expenditures made by the employer in connection with wages and salaries constitutes total labor cost. **Gross payroll** is a measure of the total wages and salaries earned by employees and is used to determine total manufacturing costs. The following analysis illustrates the difference between gross and net payroll.

Gross wages earned		
40 hours at $10/hour		$400.00
Less deductions		
Federal income taxes withheld	$82.50	
FICA taxes withheld	26.00	
U.S. government savings bond	37.50	
Union dues	12.50	
Insurance premiums	21.00	
Total deductions		179.50
Net wages paid (amount of check)		$220.50

The employee receives the net wages paid of $220.50, but the company actually pays a total of $400.00 in wages and deductions. The amounts withheld from the employee's gross wages are paid by the company to the various taxing agencies, unions, and insurance companies. Gross payroll in this case is $400.00.

Labor-related Costs Other labor-related manufacturing costs fall into two categories: employee fringe benefits and employer payroll taxes. Fringe benefits are considered part of an employee's compensation package. When labor unions negotiate new labor contracts, increased fringe benefits are as important to the final settlement as are wage increases. Fringe benefits include paid vacations, holiday and sick pay, contributions to an employee pension plan, life and medical insurance premium payments, performance bonuses and profit sharing, and recreational facilities maintained for employee use. Most of these costs vary in direct proportion to labor costs.

In addition to the payroll taxes paid by the employee, there are also payroll-related taxes borne by the employer. For every dollar of social security (FICA) tax withheld from the paycheck, the employer usually pays a comparable amount. State and federal unemployment compensation taxes are also assessed against the employer. Like wages and salaries, labor-related costs are incurred because the company purchases the labor services of its employees. Agreements between management and labor, as well as government regulations, are the source of some labor-related costs. Company management may spend additional dollars on a voluntary basis for the benefit of its employees.

Most labor-related costs are incurred in direct proportion to wages and salaries earned by the employees. To the extent practicable, labor-related costs that are a function of direct labor costs and that can be traced conveniently to such costs should be accounted for as a part of direct labor. All other labor-related costs should be classified as manufacturing (factory) overhead. However, because of the size and complexity of most payroll systems, labor-related costs are not traced to individual employee payroll dollars. Such costs are associated normally with wages and salaries by means of a predetermined rate based on past experience. For instance, a company may incur twelve cents of labor-related costs for every dollar of wages and salaries earned by employees. In this case, labor-related costs average 12 percent of labor costs. Therefore, if direct labor totaled $6,000 for a period of time, total direct labor cost would be $6,720 ($6,000 plus 12 percent or $720 of labor-related costs). Total indirect labor cost would be computed in the same manner.

Manufacturing Overhead

The third manufacturing cost element serves as a catch-all for manufacturing costs that cannot be classified as direct materials or direct labor costs. **Manufacturing (factory) overhead** costs are a diverse collection of production-related costs that are not practically or conveniently traceable to end products. This same collection of costs has also been called factory overhead, factory burden, and indirect manufacturing costs. Examples of the major classifications of manufacturing overhead costs are listed below:

Indirect materials and supplies: nails, rivets, lubricants, small tools.

Indirect labor costs: lift truck driver's wages, maintenance and inspection labor, engineering labor, machine helpers.

Other indirect factory costs: building maintenance, machinery and tool maintenance, property taxes, property insurance, pension costs, depreciation on plant and equipment.

Although this list is not all-inclusive, it includes many common overhead costs and illustrates the diverse types of indirect manufacturing costs that make up the total factory overhead cost category.

Overhead Cost Behavior Cost behavior is an important concept in the field of management accounting. Manufacturing costs tend either to vary with productive volume or to remain constant within specific ranges of output. **Variable manufacturing costs** increase or decrease in direct proportion to the number of units produced. Examples include direct materials costs; direct labor costs; indirect materials and supply costs; heat, light, and power costs; and small-tool costs.

Production costs that remain relatively constant during the accounting period are called **fixed manufacturing costs.** Even with changes in productive output, these costs tend to remain the same. Examples of fixed manufacturing costs include fire insurance premiums, factory rent, supervisory salaries, and depreciation on machinery. Some costs are semivariable because part of the cost is fixed and part varies with usage. Telephone charges (basic charge plus long-distance charges) and utility bills generally fall into this cost behavior category. Cost behavior will be explored further in Chapter 26. In connection with manufacturing overhead costs, cost behavior is used in designing the process of assigning these indirect costs to units of output.

Overhead Cost Assignment A cost is classified as a manufacturing overhead cost because it is not directly traceable to an end product. Yet a product's total cost is made up of direct materials, direct labor, and manufacturing overhead costs. Somehow manufacturing overhead costs must be identified with and assigned to specific products or jobs. Because direct materials and direct labor costs are traceable to products, their cost assignment to units of output is relatively easy. Manufacturing overhead costs, however, require an assignment method to assist in the cost allocation process.

Cost Allocation: Predetermined Overhead Rate One possible method of assigning overhead costs to products is to accumulate all manufacturing overhead costs at the end of a period of time, divide this amount by the number of products manufactured, and assign the resulting amount to each product. This method involves little guesswork and results in a fairly accurate allocation of overhead costs to products. However, this approach to cost allocation has some major disadvantages. First, it assumes the production of identical products. Because some products actually require more time and materials than others, it is possible that more manufacturing overhead costs should be assigned to them. The second disadvantage is that cost of goods sold and ending inventory costs cannot be computed until the end of the accounting period. Therefore, cost analysis is very difficult during the accounting period. Third, such a method does not help to determine a product's price. To be an effective pricing tool, cost input must be known before the order for a product is received, not after the item has already been produced.

The most common approach to overhead cost assignment is to develop and use a predetermined overhead rate. Such a rate is an overhead cost factor used to assign factory overhead costs to specific units or jobs. It is based on *estimated* overhead costs and production volume for the period. The rate is computed in three steps:

Objective 4 Compute a predetermined overhead rate and a product unit cost

1. Using cost behavior analysis, estimate all overhead costs for the coming accounting period.

2. Select an allocation basis that attempts to relate overhead costs to the products produced. The most common allocation bases include direct labor hours, direct labor dollars, machine hours, and units of output. The allocation basis selected becomes the denominator of the fraction used to compute the predetermined overhead rate. The rate, in turn, is expressed in terms of this basis: that is, $2 per direct labor hour or 60 percent of direct labor cost.

3. Divide the total estimated overhead costs computed in step 1 by the total basis (hours, dollars, or units) anticipated for the period. The result is a predetermined overhead rate. The analysis below will help to explain this concept. For illustrative purposes, assume that estimated overhead costs are $450,000 and management anticipates that 25,000 direct labor hours will be worked during the period.

$$\begin{aligned}\text{predetermined overhead rate per direct labor hour} &= \frac{\text{total estimated overhead costs}}{\text{total direct labor hours}} \\ &= \frac{\$450{,}000}{25{,}000 \text{ hours}} \\ &= \$18 \text{ per direct labor hour}\end{aligned}$$

Overhead costs are then applied to individual products on the basis of the number of labor hours required to produce each unit. For example, if it takes one-half hour of direct labor to produce one unit, that unit will be assigned $9 of manufacturing overhead cost. This amount would be added to the direct materials and direct labor costs already assigned to the product to arrive at the total unit cost.

Unit Cost Determination

Direct materials, direct labor, and factory overhead costs represent total manufacturing costs for a period of time or for a batch of products. Product unit cost for each job completed is computed by dividing total material, labor, and factory overhead costs for a partial period by total units produced. For example, assume that Harold Products, Inc., produced 3,000 units of output for Job 12K. Costs for Job 12K included the following: raw materials, $3,000; direct labor, $5,400; and factory overhead, $2,700. The company's unit cost for Job 12K would be computed as follows:

Raw materials ($3,000 ÷ 3,000 units)	$1.00
Direct labor ($5,400 ÷ 3,000 units)	1.80
Factory overhead ($2,700 ÷ 3,000 units)	.90
Total unit cost	$3.70

The unit cost described above was computed at the completion of the job, and in this case all of the information was known. What about pricing situations that need such information during the month? Estimates of unit cost figures must be used. Assume that accounting personnel developed the following data for another product: $2.50 per unit for raw materials, $4.50 per unit for direct labor, and 50 percent of direct labor cost for factory overhead.

Based on the knowledge of a predetermined overhead rate of 50 percent of direct labor cost, the unit cost would be:

Raw materials	$2.50
Direct labor	4.50
Factory overhead (50% of $4.50)	2.25
Total unit cost	$9.25

This $9.25 unit cost is based on an estimate of factory overhead costs but is still useful for product pricing and job costing purposes.

Product and Period Costs

Product costs and *period costs* are commonly used terms in cost accounting analyses. These terms are linked closely with the manufacturing cost elements, combining the three elements under a single classification. Direct materials, direct labor, and manufacturing overhead costs all become part of a product's unit manufacturing cost. These three manufacturing cost elements collectively are called **product costs.** Product costs are those costs associated with the production of a product and are therefore inventoriable. Such costs, when converted into a product's unit cost, are used to establish values for ending Work in Process and Finished Goods Inventory balances on year-end financial statements.

Product costs are also unexpired costs because, as inventory balances, they are considered assets of the company. Assets represent unused resources of an organization. **Period costs (expenses)** are expired costs of an accounting period and represent dollars attached to resources used during the period. Any cost or expense item on an income statement is a period cost. Product costs become period costs when they are attached to units sold during the period. Operating expenses such as selling and administrative expenses are always classified as period costs. Period costs are always linked to services consumed during a period and are never used to determine product unit cost or to establish ending inventory balances.

Cost Assignment

Cost assignment is very important to every phase of manufacturing accounting, including the determination of the unit cost of a product. Some manufacturing costs (direct costs) are traceable and assignable to products, but other costs (indirect costs) must be assigned by using some form of allocation method. The need for cost assignment goes beyond the determination of product costs. Every report that a company's accountants prepare requires some form of cost assignment. Depreciation expense, for example, is a result of cost assignment. The amount of depreciation expense shown on the income statement represents the expired portion of the cost of an asset that is being assigned to the current time period.

In accounting for manufacturing costs, each cost must be assigned to products, departments, jobs (contracts), divisions, or other cost objectives before various types of reports or analyses can be prepared. Without proper cost assignment techniques, management (cost) accountants could not perform their duties. The management accountant has three major tasks in preparing internal accounting documents: (1) to determine product unit costs, (2) to develop cost budgets and cost controls for management, and (3) to prepare reports to explore and support management decisions. Each task depends on proper cost assignment.

A major section of this introductory chapter is devoted to the concept of cost assignment because of its importance to the work of the management accountant. This concept underlies almost all manufacturing accounting procedures. Once you have mastered the concept of cost assignment, the study of accounting for manufacturing operations is easier.

Allocation of Manufacturing Costs

Objective 5 State the role of cost objectives in the cost allocation process

All manufacturing costs can be traced or assigned to corporate divisions, or to departments, or to units of productive output. Direct costs, such as the cost of raw materials, are traceable to specific cost objectives. Many manufacturing costs, however, are indirect costs and are incurred for the benefit of more than one product, department, or division of a company. Such costs should be distributed to those segments or products that benefited from incurring the cost. For example, electricity cost is incurred for the benefit of all departments or divisions of a company. This cost must be allocated to all work performed during a week or month, because assigning all of it to one department would be wrong. This benefit theory and the procedures and methods used in cost distribution processes are the fundamentals of cost assignment.

The cost assignment process is depicted in Figure 22-4. All three cost elements are included. Costs of lumber and the cabinetmaker's wages are direct costs of the product. Factory overhead costs include depreciation of the table saw, clean-up and janitorial services, and nails. All factory overhead costs are indirect costs of the product and must be systematically assigned using an allocation method. In the illustration, the cost objective is the product. Different cost classifications and cost assignment procedures are used when a different cost objective is being analyzed.

Several terms are unique to the concept of cost assignment and should be discussed further. For instance, the terms *cost allocation* and *cost assignment* are often used interchangeably, although *cost allocation* is the more popular of the two terms. For our purposes, cost allocation is the process

Figure 22-4 Cabinet Making: Assigning Manufacturing Costs to the Product

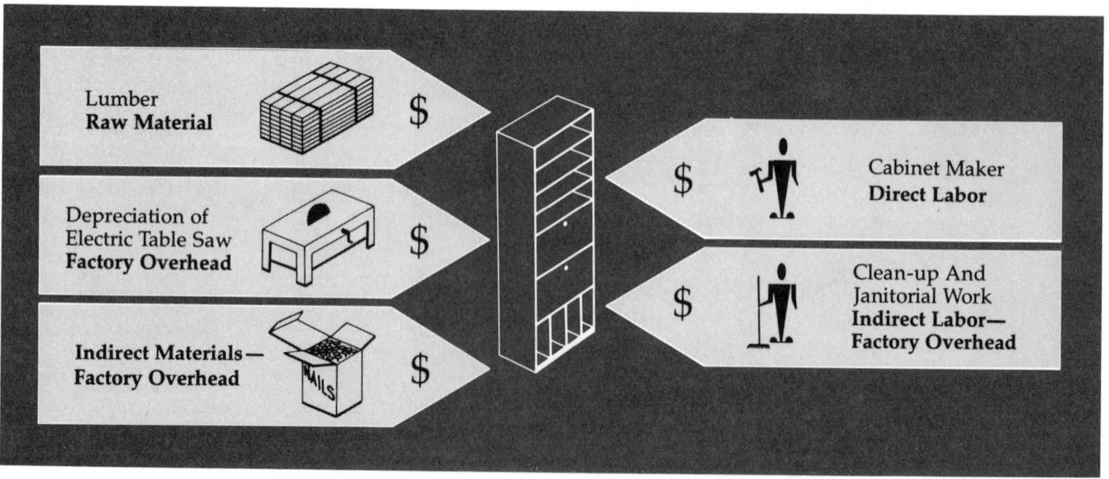

of assigning a specific cost to a specific cost objective.[3] Understanding such terms as *cost center, cost objective, direct cost,* and *indirect cost* is also vital to the study of cost allocation.

Cost Center A cost center is any organizational segment or area of activity for which it is desirable to accumulate costs. Examples of cost centers include the company as a whole, corporate divisions, specific operating plants, departments, and even specific machines or work areas. Once a cost center has been selected, methods can be devised to apportion or assign costs accurately to that cost center. No cost center report can be prepared until all cost assignment procedures have been identified and implemented.

Cost Objectives A cost objective is the destination of an assigned cost.[4] If the purpose of a certain cost analysis is to evaluate the operating performance of a division or department, the cost objective would be the particular cost center being evaluated. But if product costing is the motive for accumulating costs, a specific product, an order, or an entire contract could be the cost objective. The important point is that cost classification and cost assignment methods differ depending on the particular cost objective being analyzed.

Direct and Indirect Costs We may expand the definitions of direct and indirect costs that were used earlier in relation to product costing by describing a direct cost as any cost that is conveniently and economically traceable to a specific cost objective. Raw materials costs and direct labor costs are normally considered direct costs. However, the number of costs classified as direct increases as the size of the cost objective increases. If the cost objective is a large division of a company, then electricity costs, maintenance expenditures, and special tooling costs of the division may be classified as direct costs. Those costs considered to be direct costs will vary with individual cost objectives. An indirect cost is any cost that cannot be conveniently or economically assigned and therefore is not traceable to a specific cost objective. In a particular cost accumulation analysis, any relevant production cost not classified as a direct cost is an indirect cost. These terms and the concept of varying sizes of cost objectives will be illustrated in the next section.

To summarize, allocation of production costs involves assigning direct and indirect manufacturing costs to specific cost objectives. A cost may be a direct cost to one cost objective (a large division) and an indirect cost to another cost objective (a product). In either case, all manufacturing costs are assigned to the specific cost objectives being analyzed.

3. Cost Accounting Standard 402, promulgated by the Cost Accounting Standards Board in 1972, defined the term *allocate* as follows: "To assign an item of cost, or group of items of cost, to one or more cost objectives. This term includes both direct assignment of cost and the reassignment of a share from an indirect cost pool."

4. Cost Accounting Standard 402, promulgated by the Cost Accounting Standards Board in 1972, defined the term *cost objective* as follows: "A function, organizational subdivision, contract, or other work unit for which cost data are desired and for which provision is made to accumulate and measure the cost to processes, products, jobs, capitalized projects, etc."

The Role of Cost Assignment in Corporate Reporting

Accounting reports are prepared for all levels of management, from the president down to the department manager or supervisor. The president is responsible for all costs of the company, whereas the department manager is responsible for only those costs relating to that specific department. Reports must be prepared for all cost centers including the company as a whole, each division, and all departments within each division. The same costs shown in departmental reports will be reclassified and will appear in divisional and corporate-wide reports.

As cost centers or cost objectives change, so does the degree of traceability of costs. Here is where cost assignment comes into the picture. The different types of reports discussed above can be prepared only with the aid of cost assignment techniques. As costs are reclassified and assigned to smaller cost centers or cost objectives, they become more difficult to trace. For instance, more costs are accounted for as indirect when emphasis shifts from divisional to departmental reporting. When the size of the cost objective is reduced to focus on a specific product, only direct materials and direct labor costs are directly traceable. All other manufacturing costs are classified as indirect costs and must be allocated to individual products. Classification and assignment of indirect costs require allocation procedures because they are not traceable directly to a cost objective.

An example will illustrate traceability of costs and the role of cost classification in assigning costs to cost objectives. Table 22-1 shows how three manufacturing costs change in traceability as cost objectives change. Raw materials costs, which are directly traceable to any level of cost objective, are appropriately referred to as direct materials costs. As shown, raw materials are a direct cost at the divisional, departmental, and product levels. All 40,000 pounds of sugar were issued to Division A and are, therefore, directly traceable to that division. Because only one-half (20,000 pounds) of the division's sugar was used by Department XZ, only that amount can be traced directly to that department. At the product level, every unit of Product AB requires one-half pound of sugar. The cost of that one-half pound of sugar is a direct cost traceable to the product. Depreciation of Factory Building G can be traced directly to Division A, but for any smaller cost objectives it becomes an indirect cost. Building depreciation expense must be shared by the various cost centers operating within it. Such costs must be allocated on a systematic or arbitrary basis to departmental or product cost objectives. Depreciation costs of Machine 201 can be traced directly to either Divison A or Department XZ. For product costing purposes, however, depreciation on machinery is considered an indirect manufacturing cost and accounted for as a factory overhead cost. Factory overhead is then allocated to the products produced in Department XZ. The principles of cost classification and traceability shown above underlie the preparation of all internal accounting reports.

Costs	Cost Objectives: Division A	Department XZ	Product AB
Raw Materials	*Direct cost:* 40,000 pounds of sugar issued from inventory that is made up entirely of Division A raw materials.	*Direct cost:* 20,000 of the 40,000 pounds of sugar issued from inventory were used by Department XZ (directly traceable).	*Direct cost:* Every unit of Product AB requires one-half pound of sugar.
Depreciation of Factory Building G	*Direct cost:* Factory Building G is used entirely by Division A. Therefore, all depreciation charges from usage of Factory Building G are directly traceable to Division A.	*Indirect cost:* Department XZ is one of four departments in Factory Building G. Depreciation of Factory Building G is allocated to the four departments according to square footage used by each department.	*Indirect cost:* Depreciation of Factory Building G is an indirect product cost. It is allocated to individual products as part of factory overhead charges applied to products using direct labor hours as a base.
Depreciation of Machine 201	*Direct cost:* Machine 201 is located within Department XZ and used exclusively by Division A (directly traceable).	*Direct cost:* Machine 201 is used only by Department XZ. Therefore, its depreciation charges are directly traceable to Department XZ.	*Indirect cost:* Depreciation of Machine 201 is not directly traceable to individual products it produces. Such depreciation charges are accounted for as part of factory overhead costs.

Table 22-1 Cost Classification and Traceability

Assigning Costs of Supporting Service Functions

Objective 6 Assign costs of supporting service functions to production departments

Every company and manufacturing process requires the assistance of several supporting service functions or departments. A supporting service function is an operating unit or department that is necessary for the overall operation of the company but the function of which is not directly involved in the production process. Examples of supporting service functions include the repairs and maintenance department, production scheduling department, raw materials storage function, central power department, inspection department, and materials handling function. Labor costs and various indirect operating costs are accumulated for each service function. The costs incurred by these supporting service departments are

Table 22-2 Cost Allocation Bases for Assigning Costs of Supporting Service Functions

	Possible Allocation Basis	Circumstances That Justify Its Use
1.	Number of service requests	Used when each service performed is of similar time duration or when a record of service requests is maintained and no other basis is available
2.	Labor hours	Used when service labor hours are recorded for each service performed; a very good basis when each service function has differing time requirements
3.	Kilowatt hours used	Used to distribute the costs of a central power department maintained by the company
4.	Number of raw material requisitions	Used to allocate costs of a raw materials storage area

product costs, and they should be treated as indirect manufacturing costs by assigning them to the products through the Factory Overhead account. This type of cost assignment is accomplished in two steps. First, the service function's costs are allocated to the departments or cost centers that benefited from the services rendered. Once this reclassification or cost reapportionment process has been completed, the assigned costs are included in the production department's Factory Overhead account and allocated to the end products.

Allocating factory overhead costs to products is described in later chapters. At this point, we will concentrate on reapportioning supporting service department costs to production departments. A service function must benefit one or more other departments or its existence would not be justified. It is upon this concept of benefit that supporting service department costs are assigned to production departments. Benefit must be measured or demonstrated using some basis that depicts the relationship between actual service performed and the department that received the service.

Table 22-2 gives examples of bases used to allocate costs of supporting service functions and the circumstances that justify their use. The circumstances actually amount to a benefit relationship between the service function and the production departments. When the number of service requests is used, each request represents an equal amount of benefit or service to the receiving department. When labor hours are used, total benefit is measured by the number of labor hours needed to complete the service. Similar relationships justify the use of kilowatt hours or number of requisitions as the allocation basis. An illustrative problem will help you understand the process of reapportioning supporting service department costs. The solution to the problem provides specific details regarding the cost assignment process.

Illustrative Problem—Assigning Service Department Costs

Six production departments take part in the manufacturing process of the Jansson Metal Products Company. The company also uses three supporting service departments, one being the Repairs and Maintenance (R & M) Department. Costs of the R & M Department are assigned to the six production departments on the basis of the number of service requests made during the period. Costs incurred and charged against the R & M Department during February 19xx are as follows:

Supplies and parts	
Small tools	$ 1,850
Lubricants and supplies	940
Replacement parts	2,100
Labor	
Repair and maintenance	3,910
Supervision	1,600
Depreciation	
Equipment	1,290
Machinery	1,620
Other operating costs	2,440
Total costs for February	$15,750

The production departments made the following number of service requests during February: 16 requests by the Cutting Department, 21 by the Extruding Department, 8 by the Shaping Department, 31 by the Threading Department, 24 by the Polishing Department, and 25 by the Finishing Department.

Required

1. Using the number of service requests, prepare a schedule allocating the R & M Department's operating costs for February to the six production departments.
2. Identify and discuss another possible allocation basis for allocating the R & M Department's costs to the six production departments.

Solution to Illustrative Problem

1. The objective of this part of the problem is to determine what portion of the total cost incurred during February should be assigned to each production department. The specific dollar amounts are computed by using a ratio of the benefits that each production department received to total benefits rendered by the R & M Department. Using the number of service requests as the cost assignment basis, you can approach this determination in two ways:

   a. Find the average cost per request and multiply this amount by each department's number of service requests to compute specific allocations. The actual computations are shown on the next page.

$$\frac{\text{total cost}}{\text{total service requests}} = \frac{\$15{,}750}{125} = \$126 \text{ per request}$$

R & M Department cost allocation for February:

To Cutting Department (16 × $126)	$ 2,016
To Extruding Department (21 × $126)	2,646
To Shaping Department (8 × $126)	1,008
To Threading Department (31 × $126)	3,906
To Polishing Department (24 × $126)	3,024
To Finishing Department (25 × $126)	3,150
Total costs allocated	$15,750

b. To compute specific allocations, multiply the ratio of each department's requests to the total number of requests by the total costs to be allocated.

R & M Department cost allocation for February:

To Cutting Department (16/125) ($15,750)	= $ 2,016
To Extruding Department (21/125) ($15,750)	= 2,646
To Shaping Department (8/125) ($15,750)	= 1,008
To Threading Department (31/125) ($15,750)	= 3,906
To Polishing Department (24/125) ($15,750)	= 3,024
To Finishing Department (25/125) ($15,750)	= 3,150
Total costs allocated	$15,750

2. Labor hours used would be another possible allocation basis. If time records are maintained for each service call performed, costs could be allocated by determining the average R & M Department cost per labor hour worked by the department's employees. This factor would then be multiplied by the service labor hours used by each production department to compute specific allocations.

Accounting for Joint Production Costs

Objective 7 Allocate common manufacturing costs to joint products

Joint or common costs present a special need for cost allocation. A joint cost is one that collectively applies or relates to several products or cost objectives and can be assigned to those cost objectives only by means of arbitrary cost allocation. Joint products are not identifiable as specific products during most of the production process. At a particular point in the manufacturing process, called the split-off point, separate products evolve from a common processing unit. Joint products are associated with industries such as petroleum refining, wood processing, and meat packing. In all cases, more than one end product emerges from a common input base. For example, in the beef processing industry, the final cuts of meat (steaks, roasts, hamburger) do not appear until the end of the process. However, the cost of the steer, transportation costs, storage and hanging costs, and labor costs have been incurred to get the side of beef ready for final butchering. How do we assign these joint costs to specific cuts of beef? This type of cost assignment is the objective of accounting for joint

Figure 22-5
Joint Production Cost Allocation

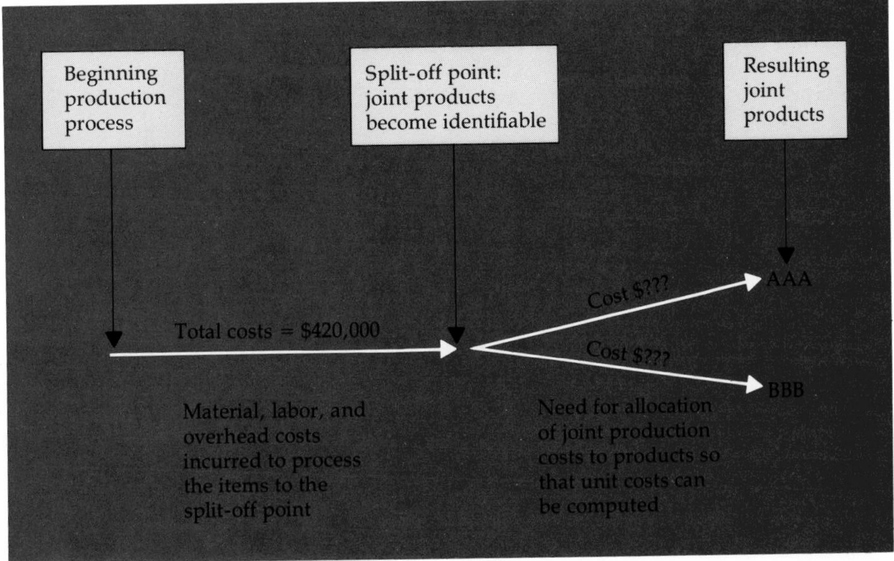

costs. Figure 22-5 illustrates a less complicated joint product production situation and the accounting problem connected with joint or common costs. The problem of assigning or allocating the joint costs of $420,000 to Product AAA and Product BBB produced by the Leo Company can be solved in several ways. We outline the two most commonly used methods in the following paragraphs.

Physical Volume Method One way of allocating joint production costs to specific products is called the **physical volume method.** This approach involves the use of some measure of physical volume (units, pounds, liters, grams) as the basis for joint cost allocation. The illustration below shows the application of the physical volume method to the problem described in Figure 22-5.

Assume that the Leo Company manufactures two grades of paint from a common mixture of substances. During August, 75,000 liters of various ingredients were introduced into the production process. The final output during the same period was 25,000 liters of Product AAA and 50,000 liters of Product BBB. Accounting records show that the total joint production costs incurred during August were $420,000, consisting of $190,000 for raw materials, $145,000 for direct labor, and $85,000 for factory overhead. The joint products are not identifiable until the end of the production process, when Product AAA sells for $9 per liter and Product BBB for $6 per liter.

Using the physical volume method, we take total liters as the allocation basis and assign the joint costs using a ratio of physical volume of each product to total physical volume as shown on the next page.

	Total Liters	Allocation Ratio	Joint Cost Allocation	
Product AAA	25,000	$\frac{25,000}{75,000}$ or $\frac{1}{3}$	$140,000	($420,000 × $\frac{1}{3}$)
Product BBB	50,000	$\frac{50,000}{75,000}$ or $\frac{2}{3}$	$280,000	($420,000 × $\frac{2}{3}$)
Totals	75,000		$420,000	

Because Product AAA generates $225,000 in revenues (25,000 liters at $9 per liter), the net income for this product line will be $85,000, computed by subtracting $140,000 of assigned joint costs from the total revenues of $225,000. Product BBB will sell for a total of $300,000 (50,000 liters at $6 per liter) and will show only a $20,000 profit ($300,000 minus $280,000 of assigned joint costs). The advantage of the physical volume method is its ease of application. However, serious net income distortions often occur because the physical volume of joint products may not be proportionate to the product's revenue-generating ability. In our example, Product BBB's net income suffered because its high-volume content attracted two-thirds of the production costs even though its selling price was much less than that of Product AAA.

Relative Sales Value Method The relative sales value method allocates joint production costs to products in proportion to a product's revenue-producing ability. Extending the Leo Company data to the allocation of joint costs according to the relative sales value method, we would make the analysis below. Sales value at split-off point becomes the basis for determining the joint cost allocation ratios because costs are to be assigned to joint products on the basis of their relative sales value when they first become identifiable as specific products.

	Liters Produced	×	Selling Price	=	Sales Value at Split-off	Allocation Ratio	Joint Cost Allocation
Product AAA	25,000		$9.00		$225,000	$\frac{\$225,000}{\$525,000}$ or $\frac{3}{7}$	$180,000 ($420,000 × $\frac{3}{7}$)
Product BBB	50,000		6.00		300,000	$\frac{\$300,000}{\$525,000}$ or $\frac{4}{7}$	240,000 ($420,000 × $\frac{4}{7}$)
Totals	75,000				$525,000		$420,000

In our example, Product AAA has a relative sales value of $225,000 at split-off, whereas Product BBB's relative sales value totals $300,000. The resulting cost allocation ratios are $\frac{3}{7}$ and $\frac{4}{7}$ for Products AAA and BBB, respectively. Applying these ratios to the total joint cost of $420,000, we assign $180,000 of joint costs to Product AAA and $240,000 to Product BBB.

A comparative income analysis of the two alternative joint cost allocation procedures shows a wide difference in product line gross income.

	Product AAA		Product BBB	
	Physical Volume Method	Relative Sales Value Method	Physical Volume Method	Relative Sales Value Method
Sales	$225,000	$225,000	$300,000	$300,000
Cost of Sales	140,000	180,000	280,000	240,000
Gross Profit	$ 85,000	$ 45,000	$ 20,000	$ 60,000
Gross Profit as Percentage of Sales	37.8%	20%	6.7%	20%

The major advantage of the relative sales value method is that joint costs are allocated according to a product's ability to absorb the cost. Because joint costs are allocated in proportion to the product's revenue-generating ability, equal gross profit percentages will always result when products are valued at the split-off point. This situation will always occur when the relative sales value method is used, because costs are assigned on the basis of a ratio of revenues. Therefore, all revenues and related costs will have the same ratio. As shown above, under the relative sales value method, gross profit as a percentage of sales is 20 percent for both Product AAA and Product BBB.

As mentioned earlier, the assignment of joint production costs is accomplished by using arbitrary allocation methods, such as the physical volume method or the relative sales value method. Arbitrary cost assignment approaches are used when it is difficult to determine how the end products (cost objectives) specifically benefited from the incurrence of the cost. They should be used only where benefit between cost and cost objective cannot be determined. Most of the cost assignment methods used for determining product unit costs are based on a benefit relationship. These methods will be described in later chapters. Even though it is an arbitrary approach, accounting for joint production costs was selected as one of the first cost assignment methods to be illustrated because it is easy to describe and understand.

Chapter Review

Review of Learning Objectives

1. Identify differences in accounting for manufacturing and merchandising companies.

Accounting methods used by a manufacturing company differ significantly from those used by a merchandising company. Management or cost accountants of a manufacturing company must maintain an internal accounting system that classifies and assigns production and production-related costs to the products manufactured. The manufacturing accounting system uses three inventory accounts: Raw Materials Inventory, Work in Process Inventory, and Finished Goods Inventory. Manufacturing costs (product costs) must flow through all three of the inventory accounts, resulting in a more complex internal accounting system.

Merchandise accounting concentrates on the entity as a whole rather than on specific products or processes. Only one account, Merchandise Inventory, is used to record and account for items in inventory. Because the items in merchandise inventory are purchased in salable condition, the cost flow from time of purchase to time of sale involves only three accounts: Cash or Accounts Payable, Purchases, and Cost of Goods Sold.

2. Differentiate among the three manufacturing cost elements: direct materials costs, direct labor costs, and manufacturing (factory) overhead costs.

Direct materials are raw materials that become an integral part of the finished product and are conveniently and economically traceable to specific units of productive output. Direct labor costs encompass all labor costs for specific work performed on products that are conveniently and economically traceable to end products. All other production-related costs are classified and accounted for as manufacturing (factory) overhead costs. Such costs are not practically or conveniently traceable to end products and must be allocated to the products using some cost assignment method. The classification of manufacturing costs into the three elements described above is important for product costing purposes.

3. Identify the source documents used in manufacturing cost accumulation.

The purchase requisition is used to identify the items of raw material needed by the production departments. The purchase order is used to order the items of raw material identified on the purchase requisitions. The receiving report is used to identify items of raw material received from vendors and is matched against purchase orders to make sure that the correct items were received. The materials requisition identifies and verifies issuance of items of raw material into the production process. The time card records the daily starting and finishing times of working hours for each employee. The job card records time spent by each employee on each job. Job cards are matched against the time card to verify productive effort of the employee and to control labor time per job.

4. Compute a predetermined overhead rate and a product unit cost.

A predetermined overhead rate is used to assign overhead costs to products. This rate is usually based on direct labor hours or dollars and is expressed as an amount or ratio of that base. Predetermined overhead rate per direct labor hour is computed by dividing total estimated overhead costs by total direct labor hours. A product unit cost is the sum of the direct materials costs, direct labor costs, and factory overhead costs per unit of productive output.

5. State the role of cost objectives in the cost allocation process.

A cost objective is the destination of an assigned cost. The cost objective varies according to the focus of a particular report and may range from the entire company or a division down to one particular product. Cost allocation is the process of assigning a specific cost to a specific cost objective. Cost objectives provide a target or area of concern for the allocation process.

6. Assign costs of supporting service functions to production departments.

Costs incurred by supporting service departments must be accounted for as indirect manufacturing costs and allocated to production departments using a basis of benefit—a beneficial relationship of cost to cost objective. Several allocation bases exist, each applicable to a certain relationship between the service used and the production department receiving the service.

7. Allocate common manufacturing costs to joint products.
Joint products evolve from a common processing unit and are not identifiable as specific products until the split-off point in the process has occurred. All manufacturing costs incurred prior to the split-off point are common to all joint products. These costs are assigned to individual products by one of two cost assignment methods—the physical volume method or the relative sales value method.

Review Problem

Before proceeding to the questions, exercises, and problems, review the problem-solving approaches for (1) assigning supporting service department costs to production departments, and (2) assigning common production costs to joint products.

Chapter Assignments

Questions

1. Differentiate between a merchandising company and a manufacturing company. Include in your answer a description of inventory cost flows for each type of company.
2. What are the three cost categories included in the concept of product cost?
3. Distinguish between a period cost and a product cost.
4. What is a cost objective, and what is its role in cost accounting?
5. Define a direct cost. What characteristics differentiate a direct cost from an indirect cost?
6. "As the size of the cost center or cost objective is reduced, cost and revenue traceability becomes more limited." Explain this statement.
7. What is a supporting service department? Give examples.
8. Define direct materials.
9. Describe the following: purchase requisition (request), purchase order, and receiving report.
10. Distinguish between direct labor and indirect labor.
11. What are the two categories of labor-related costs? Discuss each category.
12. What characteristics are used to identify a cost as being part of manufacturing overhead?
13. What is meant by cost behavior?
14. Describe the steps used to compute a predetermined overhead rate based on direct labor hours.
15. What is a joint or common manufacturing cost?
16. Describe the physical volume method of allocating joint costs to products. List the advantages and disadvantages of the physical volume method.
17. Should common costs be allocated to a product on the basis of the product's ability to generate revenue? Explain your answer.

Classroom Exercises

Exercise 22-1 Cost Classification

The following is a list of typical costs incurred during the operations of a garment maker: (a) gasoline, oil, etc., for salesperson's automobile; (b) telephone charges; (c) dyes for yardage; (d) seamstresses' regular hourly labor; (e) thread; (f) president's subscription to *The Wall Street Journal;* (g) sales commissions; (h) business forms used in the office; (i) buttons and zippers; (j) depreciation of sewing machines; (k) property taxes, factory; (l) advertising; (m) brand labels; (n) administrative salaries; (o) interest on business loans; (p) starch and fabric conditioners; (q) patterns; (r) hourly workers' vacation pay; (s) roof repair, office; (t) packaging.

1. At the time these costs are incurred, which ones will be classified as period costs and which ones will be treated as product costs?
2. Of those costs identified as product costs, which are direct costs and which are indirect costs?

Exercise 22-2 Service Department Cost Allocation

American Polygraphics, Inc., has six departments that must share the services of a single central computer. Management has decided that the most appropriate basis for cost allocation is the minutes of computer operation used by each of the six departments. A summary of usage by department for June follows: 1,548 minutes for Department A, 2,064 for Department B, 2,580 for Department C, 1,032 for Department D, 516 for Department E, and 2,580 for Department F. The total for all departments was 10,320 minutes. The total cost of operating the computer during the month was $4,650.

Using the information provided, determine the computer expense to be allocated to each department for June.

Exercise 22-3 Overhead Cost Allocation

Overhead costs of Daggett Enterprises, Inc., for the upcoming accounting period, computed by using cost behavior analysis, are expected to amount to $17,500. The allocation basis selected by management for the assignment of overhead costs is direct labor dollars. Total direct labor charges anticipated for 19xx are 640 hours at $7 per hour plus 280 hours at $9 per hour.

1. Compute the predetermined overhead rate, using direct labor dollars as the allocation base.
2. Compute the predetermined overhead rate, using direct labor hours as a base.

Exercise 22-4 Cost Assignment—Allocation Basis

The development of a cost assignment plan is vital to corporate reporting, product costing, and inventory valuation. Examples of costs and related cost objectives are listed below.

Cost	Cost Objective
Materials-handling costs	Product
Plant depreciation costs	Division
Repair and maintenance department costs	One of five production departments served
Corporate president's salary	Division

1. Which costs would be direct costs of the related cost objective and which would be considered indirect costs?
2. For each indirect cost, select a cost allocation basis that provides a logical relationship between the cost and the cost objective. Defend your answers.

Exercise 22-5 Account Classification

For the Cicero Chair Company, identify the product cost category (direct materials, direct labor, or factory overhead) to which each of the following can be economically traced: (a) machinery depreciation, (b) heat, light, and power (factory), (c) paint and varnish, (d) carpenter's regular labor, (e) carpenter's overtime labor costs (half-time premium), (f) monthly janitorial service cost, (g) production supplies, (h) lumber, (i) sheet metal, (j) assorted screws, nuts, and bolts, (k) building maintenance, (l) production supervisor's salary, (m) repairs and maintenance.

Exercise 22-6 Cost Reclassification—Direct Versus Indirect

The classification of a cost as direct or indirect depends on the selection of the cost objective. Depreciation of a factory building is a direct cost when the plant is the cost objective. However, when the cost objective is a product, the cost becomes indirect.

For the costs listed below, indicate for each cost objective whether it would be an indirect cost (I) or a direct cost (D). Be able to defend your answers.

	Cost Objective		
	Division	Department	Product
Direct labor			
Departmental supplies			
Division supervisor's salary			
President's salary			
Department manager's salary			
Raw materials			
Fire insurance on specific machine			
Property taxes, division plant			
Department repairs and maintenance			

Exercise 22-7 Joint Cost Allocation—Physical Volume Method

Molasses and refined sugar are joint products made from a common raw material, the juice extracted from sugar cane. The Ali-Kai Corporation produces both products simultaneously and has elected to use the physical volume method to assign the common or joint costs to products. The allocation base to be used is liters. During February, the Ali-Kai Corporation introduced 620,000 liters of sugar cane juice into the production process. The final products derived from this input were 93,000 liters of molasses and 527,000 liters of refined sugar. The following joint product costs were incurred during the month of February: $1,840 for raw materials, $4,800 for direct labor, and $5,760 for factory overhead. Total joint costs amounted to $12,400.

Assuming no loss through evaporation during the production process, determine the portion of joint production costs to be allocated to each product type using the physical volume method.

Exercise 22-8 Joint Cost Allocation—Relative Sales Value Method

In the processing of pulp for the production of paper, two distinct grades of wood pulp emerge from a common crushing and mixing process. San Clemente Paper Products, Inc., produced 22,000 liters of pulp during January 19xx. Wood raw material inputs cost the company $41,000. Labor and overhead costs for the month were $28,000 and $16,000, respectively. Output for the period was as shown on the next page.

Product	Quantity	Market Value at Split-off
Grade A pulp	14,000 liters	$7.00 per liter
Grade B pulp	8,000 liters	$5.25 per liter

Using the relative sales value method, compute the production costs to be allocated to grade A pulp and to grade B pulp.

Problem Set A

Problem 22A-1 Direct Labor— Cost Flow

A thorough knowledge of direct labor costs is essential to an understanding of the elements and purpose of a cost accounting system.

Required

1. Identify the characteristics of (a) direct labor and (b) indirect labor.
2. List two examples of each cost category listed under part 1.
3. Diagram the flow of all labor costs in a manufacturing environment, and identify the documents used to record these costs and to link them with specific segments of the cost flow diagram.
4. The Hansen Company has just issued the weekly payroll. Ms. Creamer, whose wage rate is $7.25 per hour, worked fifty-two hours (twelve hours overtime at time and a half). Deductions for the current pay period on her paycheck were as follows: $42.05 for federal income tax, $20.00 for state income tax, $28.60 for FICA taxes, $17.50 for bond deduction, $10.00 for union dues, and $13.25 for insurance premium. Compute the amount of gross wages and net wages. Which amount is chargeable to production? Why?

Problem 22A-2 Predetermined Overhead Rate Computation

The Riverside Pottery Company is in need of a predetermined overhead rate to help simplify the complex task of assigning overhead costs to products. Management has decided that the most applicable allocation basis is direct labor hours. Data provided by the records indicate that there will be a 20 percent increase in operating expenses for 19x8 over 19x7. Direct labor hours will be decreased by 20 percent for the same period because of increased competition in the pottery industry. Overhead expenses incurred in 19x7 were as follows: $2,640 for Indirect Labor; $920 for Utilities; $450 for Depreciation, Machinery; $320 for Depreciation, Pottery Factory; $170 for Insurance, Pottery Factory; $1,450 for Supervision; $280 for Small Tools Expense; and $770 for Miscellaneous. During 19x7, 1,750 direct labor hours were worked.

Required

1. Compute a predetermined overhead rate that should have been used for 19x7 based on direct labor hours.
2. After adjusting labor hours and overhead costs on the basis of expected changes for 19x8, compute the predetermined overhead rate for the new year.

Problem 22A-3 Allocation— Cost-Base Relationship

Below are four types of costs that could be incurred and accumulated by a typical manufacturing company. In each case, the total cost for each type must be allocated to a cost objective.

	Type of Cost	Cost Objective
1.	**Materials handling costs** Labor costs of truck drivers, depreciation on trucks and other equipment, fuel costs, operating supplies.	Production Department

2.	**Departmental overhead costs** Each employee runs one machine, and all employees earn similar wages.	Product
3.	**Departmental overhead costs** Each employee runs 20 to 25 machines at the same time.	Product
4.	**Departmental overhead costs** Each employee runs one machine, and there are wide differences in hourly wage rates.	Product

The allocation bases that can be used for assigning the types of costs listed above to cost objectives are (a) direct labor dollars, (b) machine hours, (c) materials costs, (d) direct labor hours, and (e) square footage.

Required

For each of the four cost categories, select the allocation base that has the best beneficial relationship between the cost and the cost objective. Discuss the reasoning used in your selection process.

Problem 22A-4 Unit Cost Computation

Order 8477 has just been completed, and the assistant controller of Niemeyer Corporation is about to compute the order's unit cost. The number of units produced was 14,690. Cost information for Department 12 included 44,070 grams at $.50 per gram for direct material used, 7,345 hours at $6.50 per hour for direct labor, and $4 per direct labor hour for factory overhead rate. Cost information for Department 24 included 14,690 grams at $1.20 per gram for direct materials used, 22,035 hours at $7.00 per hour for direct labor, and $2 per direct labor dollar for factory overhead rate. Cost information for Department 36 included none for direct materials used, 58,760 hours at $6.00 per hour for direct labor, and $1 per direct labor hour for factory overhead rate. All units produced were processed through all three departments. There were no units in the work in process inventory at the end of the period.

Required

1. Compute the unit cost of processing the product through each of the three departments.
2. What is the total unit cost?
3. The entire order was sold to the Kemper Company for $1,057,680. Was the selling price adequate? List the assumptions or computations on which you based your answer. What suggestions would you make to the assistant controller concerning the pricing of future orders?

Problem 22A-5 Joint Cost Allocation

The chemicals used by the Orange County Ink Company to produce three grades of printer's ink are first mixed together in a common production process. After a four-hour mixing process, the solution separates into three distinct grades of ink. Grade AA sells for $25 per liter, grade BB sells for $20 per liter, and grade CC sells for $10 per liter. During September, 48,000 liters of chemical were introduced into the production process. With no loss of materials occurring, the following output was attained for the month: 6,000 liters of grade AA, 18,000 liters of grade BB, and 24,000 liters of grade CC. Cost data for September are: $290,000 for direct materials, $205,000 for direct labor, and $65,000 for factory overhead. Thus total joint costs were $560,000 for the month. Assume that there were no beginning or ending work in process inventories. All three products are salable at the split-off point.

Required

1. Using the physical volume method, compute the amount of joint costs to be assigned to each of the three product groups.
2. Using the relative sales value approach, allocate the joint costs to the three product groups.
3. Prepare an analysis comparing the gross profits (both in total dollars and as percentages of sales) resulting from the two allocation methods for each product group.

Problem 22A-6 Service Department Expense Allocation

Fisher's Appliance Company owns and maintains a company aircraft. The company has six divisions, each operated as an independent unit. For performance evaluation purposes, net income is computed monthly for each division. Before net income can be determined, common corporate expenses must be allocated to the six divisions. Maintenance and depreciation costs associated with the company aircraft are assigned to the various divisions according to the hours of usage.

The aircraft department is a supporting service function, and the costs incurred or charged against it during March are as follows. Depreciation costs were $2,500 for aircraft, $2,100 for building, and $700 for machinery. Labor costs were $2,400 for supervision and $8,000 for maintenance. Materials costs were $650 for small tools, $490 for supplies, and $2,160 for parts. Fuel cost was $6,800. Other operating costs amounted to $1,500. Total costs for March came to $27,300.

Divisional usage of the aircraft for March was as follows: 8.6 hours for TV Division, 10.9 for Refrigerator Division, 0.8 for Stove Division, 42.4 for Oven Division, 19.0 for Dishwasher Division, and 9.3 for Stereo and CB Division.

Required

1. Using hours of usage, prepare a schedule allocating the aircraft department's operating costs for March to the six divisions.
2. Identify and discuss other cost allocation bases that could be used to allocate the aircraft costs to the operating divisions. Discuss the merits and disadvantages of each allocation basis.

Problem Set B

Problem 22B-3 Allocation—Cost-Base Relationship

Below are five types of costs that could be incurred and accounted for by a typical manufacturing corporation. In each case, the total cost in each account must be allocated to a cost objective.

	Type of Cost	Cost Objective
1.	Cost of corporate computer center	Production departments
2.	Depreciation of division factory buildings	Production departments
3.	Tool and die making costs (service department)	Production departments
4.	Raw materials storage costs	Products
5.	Repairs and maintenance department costs	Production departments

A number of allocation bases that could be used to assign the costs listed above to their respective cost objectives are possible. They include (a) direct labor dollars, (b) direct labor hours, (c) machine hours, (d) facility or service usage hours, (e) raw materials costs, (f) square footage, and (g) number of service requests.

Required

For each of the five types of costs, select the allocation base that expresses the best beneficial relationship between the cost and the cost objective. Identify the reasons used to support your answers.

Problem 22B-4 Unit Cost Computation

Niantic Industries has recently finished production of Job CG-28. The corporation's cost accountant is ready to calculate the unit cost for this order. Relevant information for the month ended March 31, 19xx, is as follows: The number of units produced was 38,480. Cost information for Department B-14 included 2,210 liters at $2.00 per liter for direct materials used, 168 hours at $7.50 per hour for direct labor incurred, and $1.60 per direct labor dollar for factory overhead rate. Cost data for Department C-12 included 800 liters at $4.57 per liter for direct materials used, 400 hours at $6.80 per hour for direct labor incurred, and $1.90 per direct labor dollar for factory overhead rate. Cost data for Department D-15 included 1,005 liters at $4.00 per liter for direct materials used, 320 hours at $7.00 per hour for direct labor incurred, and $1.50 per direct labor dollar for factory overhead rate. All units produced are processed through departments B-14, C-12, and D-15. There was no ending work in process inventory as of March 31, 19xx.

Required

1. Compute the unit cost for each of the three separate departments.
2. Compute the total unit cost.
3. Order CG-28 was specially made for the New London Company for a total cash consideration of $30,784. Determine whether the selling price was appropriate. List the assumptions or computations upon which you based your answer. What advice, if any, would you offer the management of Niantic Industries in regard to the sales price of future orders to the New London Company?

Problem 22B-5 Joint Cost Allocation

Three distinct grades of ice cream are produced by the Royal Velvet Ice Cream Company. The initial ingredients for all three grades of ice cream are first blended together. After this blending, a variety of additional ingredients are introduced to produce the three grades that are identifiable at the end of the process. The Extra-Rich blend sells for $2.10 per liter; the Quality blend sells for $1.80 per liter; and the Regular blend sells for $1.50 per liter. During July, 744,000 liters of ingredients were put into production, with the resulting output in July being as follows: 163,680 liters of Extra-Rich blend, 297,600 liters of Quality blend, and 282,720 liters of Regular blend. Joint costs for the period consist of $150,600 for direct materials, $123,000 for direct labor, and $98,400 for factory overhead. Total joint costs for July were $372,000. Assume that there were no beginning or ending inventories and that there was no loss of input during production.

Required

1. Using the physical volume method, compute the joint costs to be allocated to each of the three ice cream blends.
2. Using the relative sales value approach, calculate the amount of joint costs to be assigned to each of the three blends.
3. Prepare a comparative schedule that shows the gross profit at split-off point (both in total dollars and as percentages of sales) resulting from the two allocation methods for the three products.

Problem 22B-6 Service Department Expense Allocation

Deerfield Community Hospital has one respirator that must be shared by the hospital's six departments. In order to evaluate efficiency and to aid in future budgeting, each department's operating income or loss is calculated separately each month. Before these calculations can be made, expenses that are considered "common" expenses must be allocated to each of the departments. Depreciation and maintenance expenses related directly to the respirator are allocated to the departments according to hours of usage.

The costs related to the upkeep of the respirator for the month of October are as follows: Depreciation amounted to $550 on the respirator and $120 on supplemental machinery. Labor costs were $3,000 for the operator and $900 for maintenance. Materials costs were $1,600 for oxygen, $240 for small replacement parts, $480 for supplies, and $310 for other operating costs. Thus total materials costs for October were $7,200.

The respirator usage by department for October is as follows: 86.5 hours for the Oncology Department, 16.3 hours for the Orthopedic Department, 44.1 hours for the Nephrology Department, 36.9 hours for the Geriatric Department, 18.7 hours for the Pediatric Department, and 37.5 hours for the Maternity Department.

Required

1. Prepare an analysis assigning the costs related to the respirator for October to each of the six departments according to hourly usage.
2. Describe and explain other bases of cost allocation that could be used to assign the respirator's operating costs to the six departments. Include in your discussion the advantages and disadvantages of each allocation basis.

Learning Objectives

Chapter Twenty-Three

Manufacturing Accounting: Cost Flow and Reporting

1. *Describe the field of management accounting.*
2. *Describe the nature, contents, and flow of costs through the Raw Materials Inventory, Work in Process Inventory, and Finished Goods Inventory accounts.*
3. *Prepare a statement of cost of goods manufactured.*
4. *Distinguish between the periodic and perpetual inventory methods.*
5. *Prepare the year-end work sheets, closing journal entries, and financial statements for a manufacturing company, using a periodic inventory approach.*

In this chapter, we continue to examine accounting for manufacturing operations, emphasizing the flow of manufacturing costs through Raw Materials, Work in Process, and Finished Goods Inventory accounts. All material, labor, and manufacturing overhead costs eventually become part of the cost of a product and, in turn, part of the Cost of Goods Sold account balance. In addition, we analyze the statement of cost of goods manufactured, briefly discuss the periodic and perpetual inventory methods, and describe and illustrate the preparation of work sheets and financial statements for a manufacturing company. As a result of studying this chapter, you should be able to meet the learning objectives listed on the left.

Management Accounting

Accounting for production- and service-oriented enterprises is an integral part of the discipline known as management accounting. Management accounting is often associated with large, multisegment corporations engaged in manufacturing and assembly operations. These large corporations require more elaborate accounting and reporting systems than do small, one-owner enterprises such as the neighborhood grocer or a shoe merchant. Although large corporations need large *amounts* of information, managers of small and medium-size businesses need certain *types* of vital financial information just as much as do executives of large corporations. The types of data needed to enhance efficient operating conditions are not totally dependent on an organization's size.

Three types of financial information are required for effective management of a manufacturing company: (1) product costing information, (2) data used for planning and control of operations, and (3) special reports and analyses used to support management decisions. The field of **management accounting** consists of specific information gathering and reporting concepts and appropriate accounting techniques and procedures that, when collectively applied to a company's financial and production data, will satisfy management's informational needs. Product costing, the first type of information, uses various cost accounting techniques to accumulate production information, assign specific costs to product batches, and calculate specific product costs. Product costing techniques are discussed in Chapters 24 and 25.

Objective 1 Describe the field of management accounting

Planning and control of cost data, the second category mentioned above, involves concepts and procedures that help management plan production and related cost levels of operation for a future period. Once these anticipated costs are realized, control procedures that systematically compare planned and actual data are used to measure the effectiveness of operations and management. Chapters 26 and 27 focus on these planning and control functions of management accounting.

The third category of informational need concerns management decision making. All management decisions should be supported by analyses of alternative courses of action. The accountant is expected to supply the information used to support the decisions of management. Several approaches used by the accountant are discussed in Chapter 28.

Manufacturing Inventory Accounts

Accounting for inventories is the most difficult area of adjustment in changing from merchandising accounting to manufacturing accounting. Instead of dealing with one account—Merchandise Inventory—you now must use *three* manufacturing inventory accounts: Raw Materials Inventory, Work in Process Inventory, and Finished Goods Inventory.

Objective 2 Describe the nature, contents, and flow of costs through the Raw Materials Inventory, Work in Process Inventory, and Finished Goods Inventory accounts

Raw Materials Inventory

The **Raw Materials Inventory** account, also called the Stores or Materials Inventory Control account, is made up of the balances of raw materials and supplies on hand at a particular time. This account is maintained in much the same manner as the Merchandise Inventory account, the main difference being in the disposal of items in inventory. For the merchandising company, goods taken out of inventory represent those items sold. When a sale is made, an entry is needed to debit Cost of Goods Sold and to credit Merchandise Inventory for the cost of the item. Raw materials, on the other hand, are not purchased for the purpose of resale. They are to be used in manufacturing a product. Therefore, goods taken out of Raw Materials Inventory represent items used in the production process. The cost of an item is transferred to the Work in Process Inventory account (not Cost of Goods Sold) when the item has been requisitioned into production. Figure 23-1 compares the accounting treatment for merchandise inventory with accounting for raw materials inventory, as described above.

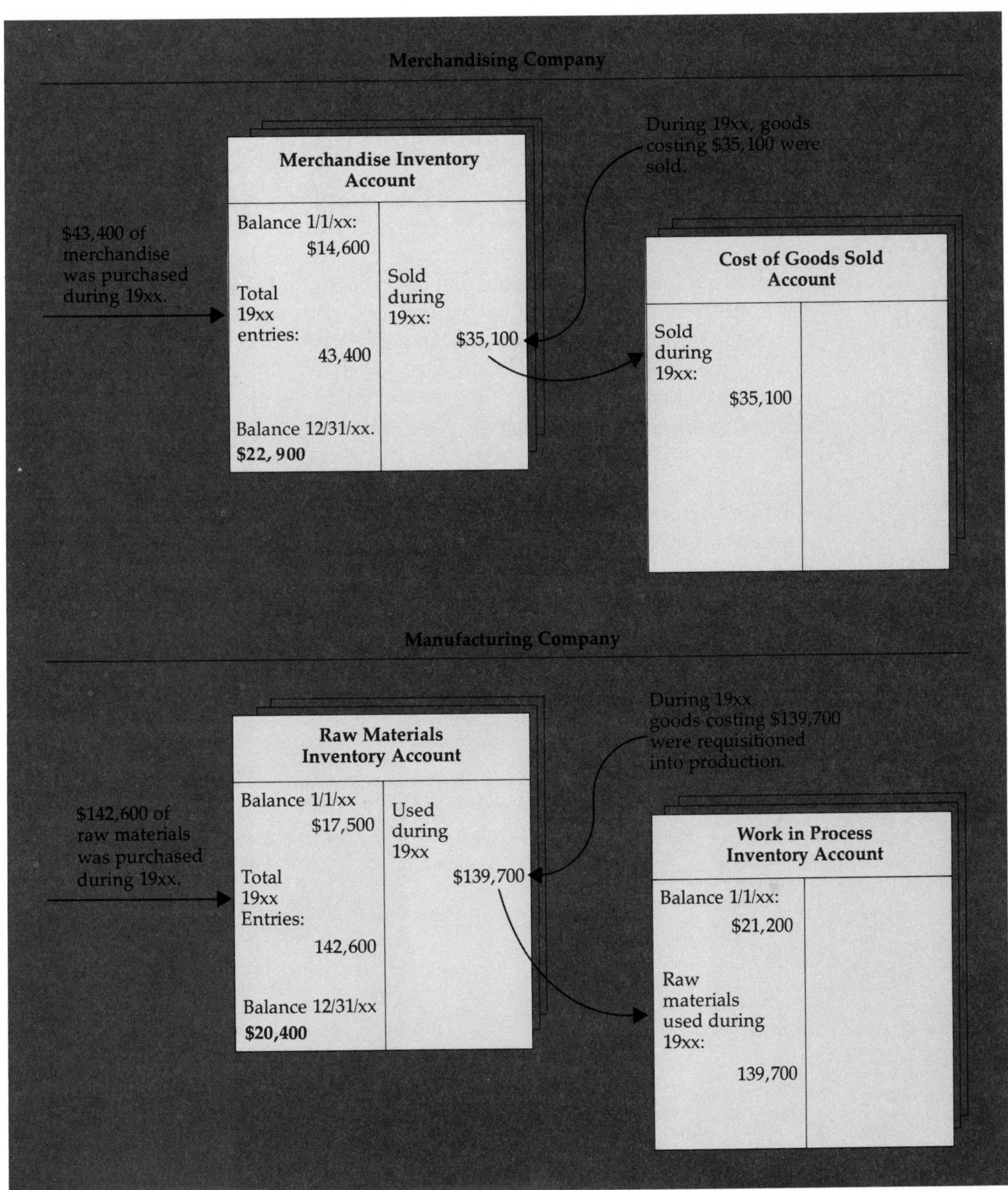

Figure 23-1
Raw Materials Inventory versus Merchandise Inventory Accounting

Work in Process Inventory

All manufacturing costs that are incurred and assigned to products being produced are classified as **Work in Process Inventory** costs. This inventory account has no counterpart in merchandise accounting. Yet a thorough understanding of the concept of Work in Process Inventory is vital to an understanding of manufacturing accounting. Figure 23-2 depicts the various costs that become part of Work in Process Inventory and the way costs are transferred out of the account. Accounting for work in process (products in process) really began in Figure 23-1. The requisitioning of raw materials into production begins the production process. These raw materials must be cut, molded, or in some other way changed to conform to the specifications of a finished product. To accomplish this change, people, machines, and other factory resources (buildings, electricity, supplies, and so on) must be used. All of these costs are manufacturing cost elements, and all of them enter into the accounting for Work in Process Inventory.

Direct labor dollars earned by factory employees are product costs. As these people work on specific products, their labor costs are assigned to those products by including the labor dollars earned as part of the Work in

Figure 23-2 The Work in Process Inventory Account

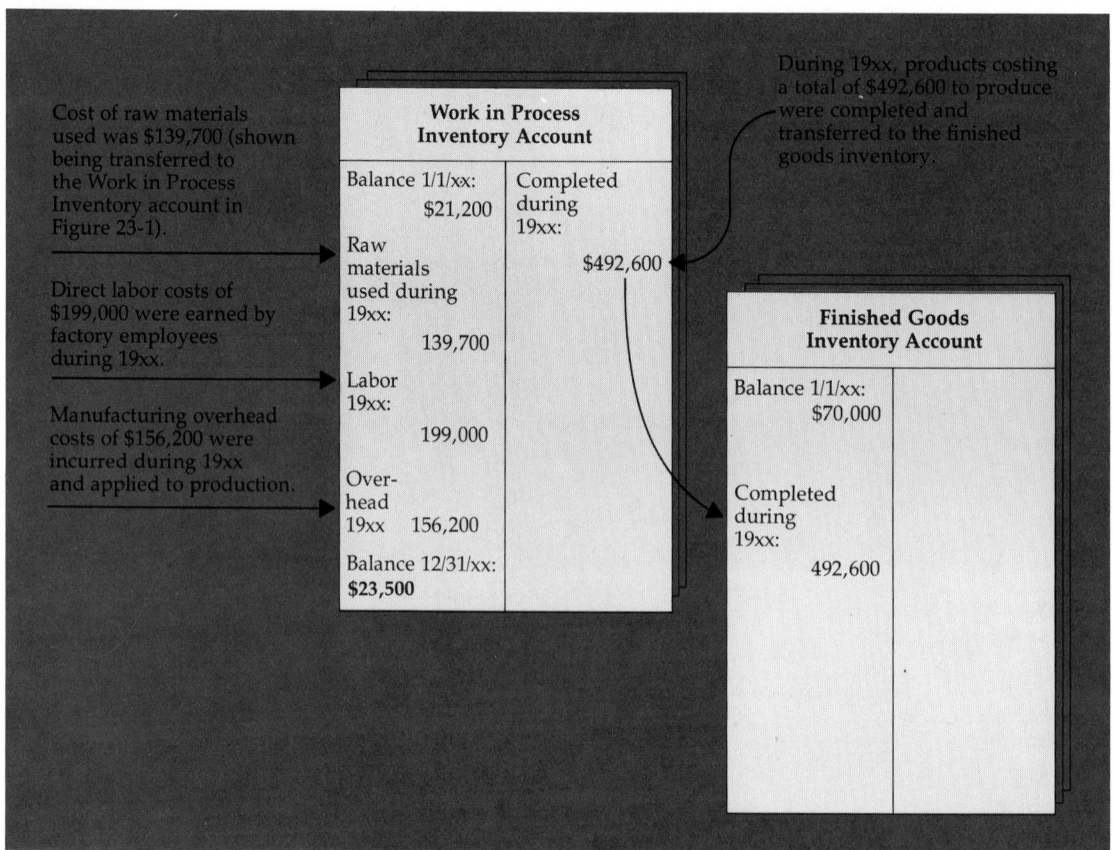

Process Inventory account. Specific product costing is the topic of subsequent chapters. At this point in your learning process, all direct labor costs, earned during a period of time, should be accumulated in the Work in Process Inventory account.

Many types of manufacturing overhead costs are incurred during each accounting period. Because they are considered product costs and must be assigned to specific products, overhead costs are also accumulated in the Work in Process Inventory account. As discussed in Chapter 22, overhead costs are too numerous to account for on an individual basis. To reduce the amount of work needed to assign these costs to products, they are accumulated and accounted for under one account title: Manufacturing Overhead. In addition, these costs may be assigned to products by using a predetermined overhead rate. In our example in Figure 23-2, actual manufacturing overhead costs of $156,200 were charged to the Work in Process Inventory account. The predetermined overhead rate will be discussed in Chapter 24.

As products are completed, they are transferred to the finished goods storage area. These products now have raw materials, direct labor, and manufacturing overhead costs assigned to them. When products are completed, these costs no longer belong to work (products) in process. Therefore, as the completed products are sent to the storage area, their costs are transferred from the Work in Process Inventory account to the Finished Goods Inventory account. After all costs of completed units for the period have been transferred to Finished Goods Inventory, the balance remaining in the Work in Process Inventory account ($23,500 in Figure 23-2) represents costs assigned to products partially completed and still in process at the end of the period.

Finished Goods Inventory

The **Finished Goods Inventory** account also possesses some of the characteristics of the Merchandise Inventory account. We have already discussed how costs are transferred from the Work in Process Inventory account to the Finished Goods Inventory account. At this point, Finished Goods Inventory takes on the characteristics of Merchandise Inventory. Compare the Merchandise Inventory account analysis in Figure 23-1 and accounting for Finished Goods Inventory, shown in Figure 23-3 (next page). The credit sides of both accounts are handled in a similar manner. Both examples show that as goods or products are sold, the costs of those goods are transferred from the Finished Goods Inventory account to the Cost of Goods Sold account. However, the accounting procedures affecting the debit side of the Finished Goods Inventory account differ from those for the Merchandise Inventory account. In a manufacturing firm, salable products are produced rather than purchased. All costs debited to Finished Goods Inventory represent transfers from the Work in Process Inventory account. At the end of an accounting period, the balance in the Finished Goods Inventory account is made up of the costs of products completed but not sold as of that date.

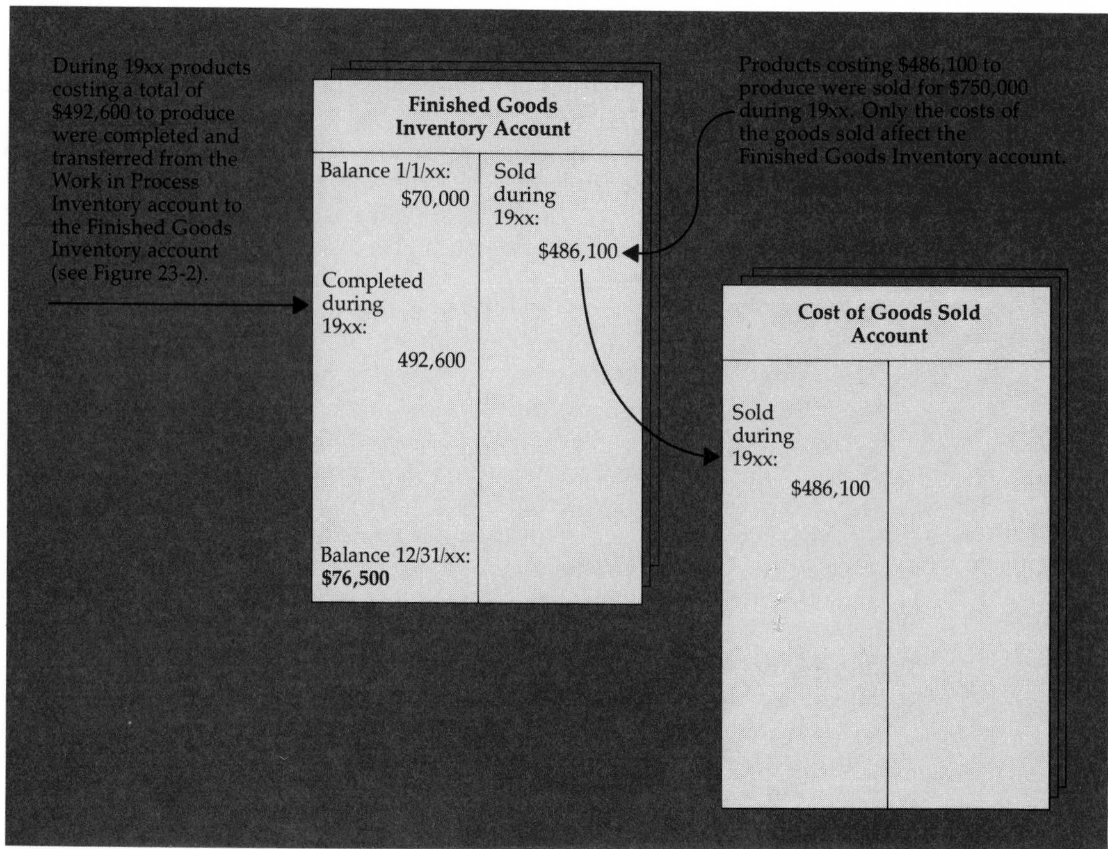

Figure 23-3
Accounting for Finished Goods Inventory

Manufacturing Cost Flow

Product costing, inventory valuation, and financial reporting rely on a defined or structured flow of manufacturing costs. This **manufacturing cost flow** was outlined in our discussion of the three manufacturing inventory accounts. Figure 23-4 summarizes the entire cost flow process as it relates to accounts in the general ledger. At this point, you should not be concerned with the actual journal entries required to make this cost flow operational—these will be the focal point of Chapter 24. For our purposes here, you should concentrate on the concept of manufacturing cost flow. Such a conceptual view is shown in Figure 23-5. The cost flow begins with costs being incurred. Manufacturing costs originate in various ways, including cash payments, incurrence of liabilities, fixed asset depreciation, and the expiration of prepaid expenses. Once these costs have been incurred, they are recorded as being either direct materials, direct labor, or factory overhead costs. As the resources are consumed, the company transfers their costs into the Work in Process Inventory account. When production has been completed, costs assigned to finished units are transferred to the Finished Goods Inventory account. In a similar fashion, costs attached to units sold are transferred to the Cost of Goods Sold account. Before proceeding, compare the cost flow through the general ledger accounts as shown in Figure 23-4 (next two pages) with the conceptual model illustrated in Figure 23-5 (page 792). Both figures depict the same type of cost flow.

The Manufacturing Statements

Financial statements of manufacturing companies differ very little from those of merchandising companies. Depending on the industry, account titles found on the balance sheet (statement of financial position)—such as Cash, Accounts Receivable, Buildings, Machinery, Accounts Payable, and Capital Stock—are identical for most corporations. Even the income statements for the merchandiser and the manufacturer are very similar. However, a closer look reveals that the heading Cost of Goods Manufactured is used in place of Merchandise Purchases and that Merchandise Inventory is replaced by Finished Goods Inventory. Note these differences on the income statement of the Pedersen Company illustrated in Figure 23-6 (page 793). The key to the preparation of an income statement for a manufacturing company is the proper determination of the cost of goods manufactured. This dollar amount is the end result of a special manufacturing statement, the statement of cost of goods manufactured, which is prepared to support the figure that is shown on the income statement.

Statement of Cost of Goods Manufactured

Objective 3 Prepare a statement of cost of goods manufactured

The flow of manufacturing costs, pictured in Figures 23-1 through 23-5, provides the basis for accounting for manufacturing costs. In this process, all manufacturing costs incurred are considered product costs and are used in computing ending inventory balances and the cost of goods sold. The costs flowing from one account to another during the year have been accumulated into one number in the figures to help you understand the basic idea. Actually, hundreds of transactions take place during a year's time, and each transaction influences part of the cost flow process. At the end of the year, the flow of all of the manufacturing costs incurred during the period is summarized in the **statement of cost of goods manufactured,** which yields the dollar amount of costs attached to products completed and transferred to Finished Goods Inventory during that period. The amount computed as cost of goods manufactured should be the same amount as that transferred from the Work in Process Inventory account to the Finished Goods Inventory account during the year.

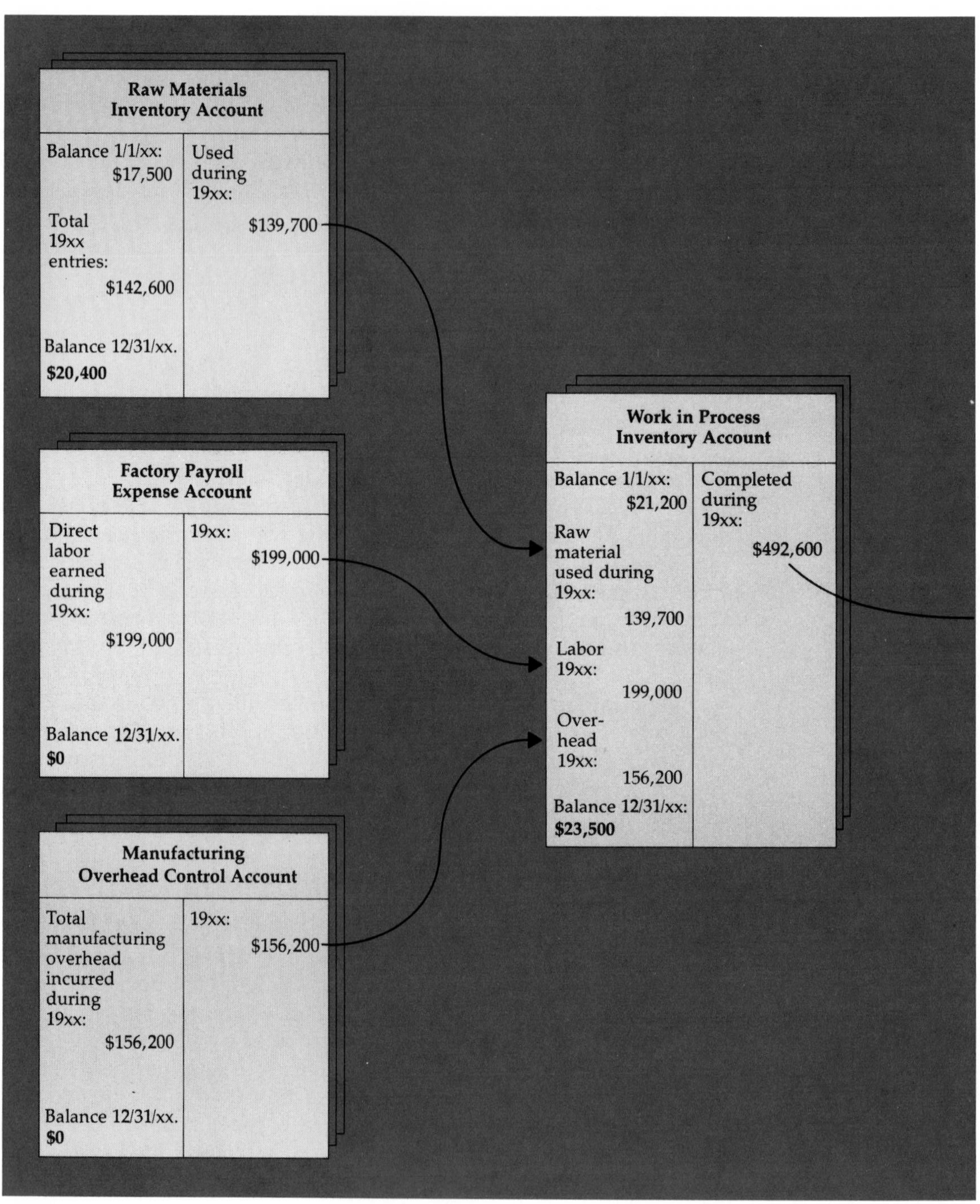

Figure 23-4
Manufacturing
Cost Flow

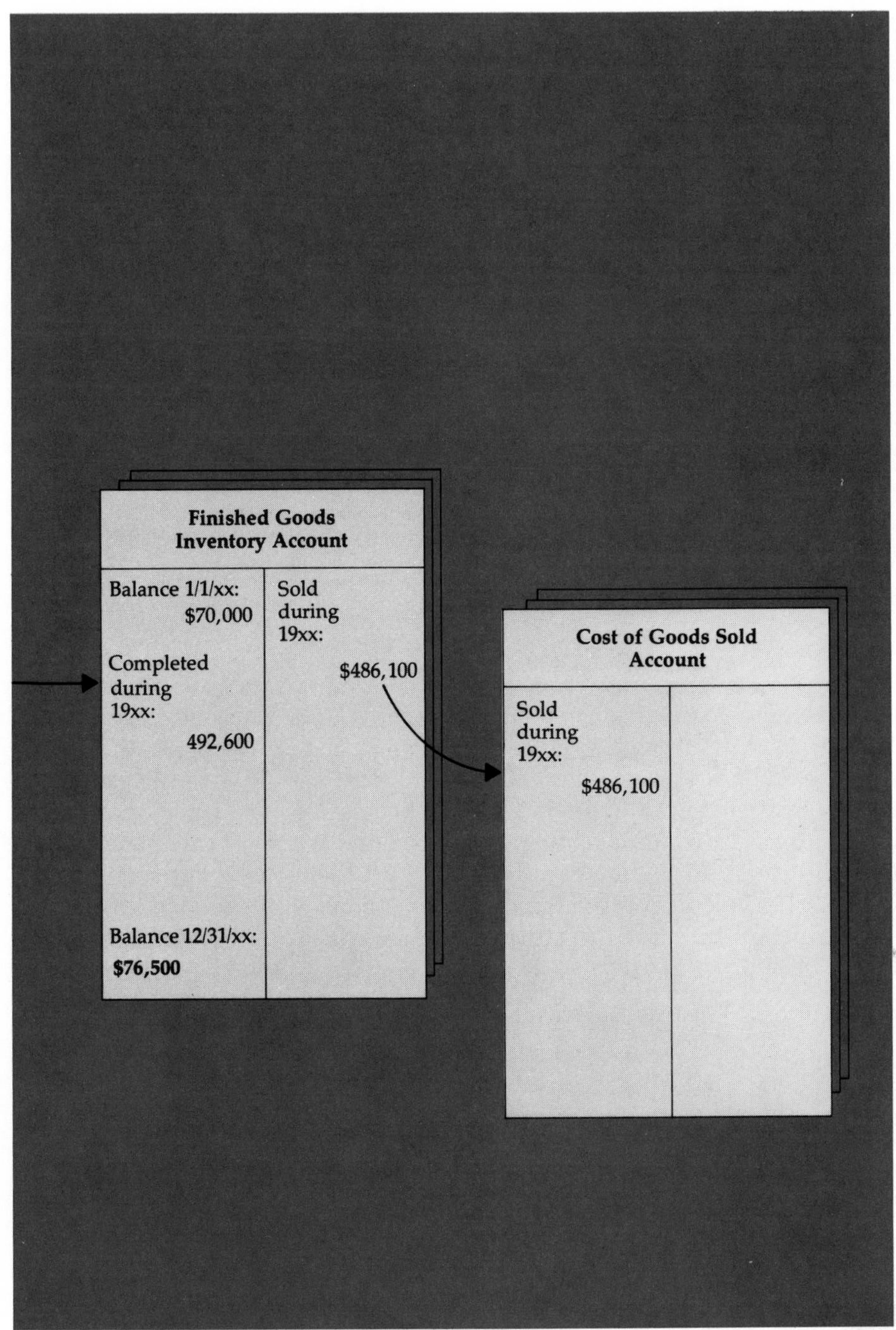

Finished Goods Inventory Account
Balance 1/1/xx: $70,000
Completed during 19xx: 492,600
Balance 12/31/xx: $76,500
Sold during 19xx: $486,100
Cost of Goods Sold Account
Sold during 19xx: $486,100

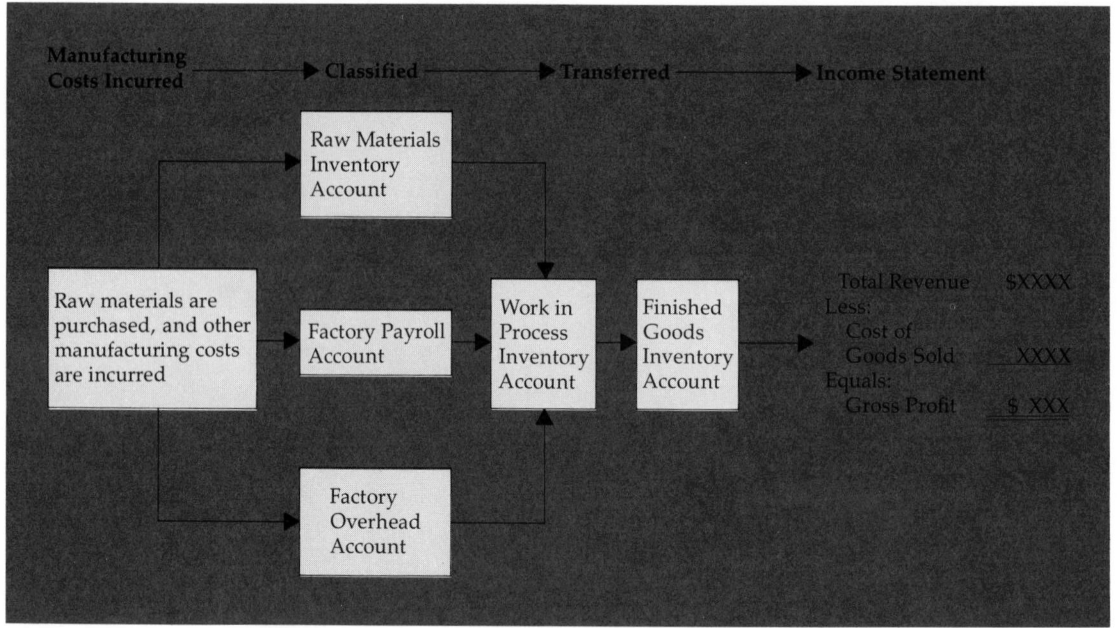

Figure 23-5 Manufacturing Cost Flow: A Conceptual View

The statement of cost of goods manufactured is illustrated in Figure 23-7 (page 794). Although rather complex, it can be pieced together in three steps. The first step is to compute the cost of raw materials used. Add the raw materials purchases for the period to the beginning balance in the Raw Materials Inventory to obtain the cost of raw materials available for use during the year. Then subtract the balance in the ending Raw Materials Inventory from the cost of raw materials available for use. The difference represents the cost of raw materials used during the accounting period.

Computation of Cost of Raw Materials Used

Beginning Balance: Raw Materials Inventory	$ 17,500
Plus Raw Materials Purchases	142,600
Cost of Raw Materials Available for Use	$160,100
Less Ending Balance: Raw Materials Inventory	20,400
Cost of Raw Materials Used	$139,700

Before proceeding to the next step, trace these numbers back to the Raw Materials Inventory account in Figure 23-1 to see the relationship between that account and the statement of cost of goods manufactured.

Determining total manufacturing costs for the year is the second step. As shown in Figure 23-3, compute total manufacturing costs by adding the costs of raw materials used and direct labor to the total of all manufacturing overhead costs incurred during the year. This computation is illustrated below as well as in Figure 23-7.

Figure 23-6
Income Statement for a Manufacturing Company

Pedersen Company
Income Statement
For the Year Ended December 31, 19xx

Net Sales			$750,000
Cost of Goods Sold			
Finished Goods Inventory, Jan. 1, 19xx		$ 70,000	
Cost of Goods Manufactured (Figure 23-7)		492,600	
Total Cost of Finished Goods Available for Sale		$562,600	
Less Finished Goods Inventory, Dec. 31, 19xx		76,500	
Cost of Goods Sold			486,100
Gross Profit from Sales			$263,900
Operating Expenses			
Selling Expenses			
Salaries and Commissions	$46,500		
Advertising	19,500		
Other Selling Expenses	7,400		
Total Selling Expenses		$ 73,400	
General and Administrative Expenses			
Administrative Salaries	$65,000		
Franchise and Property Taxes	72,000		
Other G & A Expenses	11,300		
Total General and Administrative Expenses		148,300	
Total Operating Expenses			221,700
Income from Operations			$ 42,200
Less Interest Expense			4,600
Income Before Income Taxes			$ 37,600
Income Taxes			11,548
Net Income			$ 26,052

Computation of Total Manufacturing Costs

Cost of Raw Materials Used	$139,700
Plus Direct Labor Costs	199,000
Plus Total Manufacturing Overhead Costs	156,200
Total Manufacturing Costs	$494,900

The third step shown in Figure 23-7 transforms total manufacturing costs into total cost of goods manufactured for the year. Add the beginning Work in Process Inventory balance to total manufacturing costs for

Figure 23-7
Statement of Cost of Goods Manufactured

Pedersen Company
Statement of Cost of Goods Manufactured
For the Year Ended December 31, 19xx

Step One	Raw Materials Used		
	Raw Materials Inventory, Jan. 1, 19xx	$ 17,500	
	Raw Materials Purchased	142,600	
	Cost of Raw Materials Available for Use	$160,100	
	Less Raw Materials Inventory, Dec. 31, 19xx	20,400	
	Cost of Raw Materials Used		$139,700
Step Two	Direct Labor		199,000
	Manufacturing Overhead Costs		
	Indirect Labor	$ 46,400	
	Power	25,200	
	Depreciation, Machinery	14,800	
	Depreciation, Building	16,200	
	Small Tools Write-off	2,700	
	Factory Insurance	1,600	
	Supervision	37,900	
	Other Factory Costs	11,400	
	Total Manufacturing Overhead Costs		$156,200
Step Three	Total Manufacturing Costs		$494,900
	Add: Work in Process Inventory, Jan. 1, 19xx		21,200
	Total Cost of Goods in Process During the Year		$516,100
	Less Work in Process Inventory Dec. 31, 19xx		23,500
	Cost of Goods Manufactured		$492,600

the period to arrive at the total cost of goods in process during the year. From this amount, subtract the ending Work in Process Inventory balance for the year to obtain the cost of goods manufactured.

Computation of Cost of Goods Manufactured

Total Manufacturing Costs	$494,900
Plus Beginning Balance: Work in Process Inventory	21,200
Total Cost of Goods in Process During the Year	$516,100
Less Ending Balance: Work in Process Inventory	23,500
Cost of Goods Manufactured	$492,600

The term *total manufacturing costs* must not be confused with cost of goods manufactured. **Total manufacturing costs** represent the total of raw materials used, direct labor, and manufacturing overhead costs incurred and charged to production during an accounting period. **Cost of goods manufactured** represents the total manufacturing costs attached to units of product *completed* during an accounting period. To understand the difference between these two dollar amounts, review the computation shown immediately above. Total manufacturing costs of $494,900, incurred during the current year, are added to the beginning balance in Work in Process Inventory. Costs of $21,200 in the beginning balance, by definition, are costs from a previous period. We are now mixing costs of two different accounting periods to arrive at total cost of goods in process during the year of $516,100. When the costs attached to the ending products still in process ($23,500) are subtracted from the total cost of goods in process during the year, the remainder of $492,600 represents the costs of goods manufactured (completed) during the year. We assume that those items in beginning inventory were completed first. Costs attached to the ending Work in Process Inventory are part of the current period's total manufacturing costs but will not become part of cost of goods manufactured until the next accounting period, when the products are completed.

Cost of Goods Sold

Figures 23-6 and 23-7 demonstrate the relationship between the statement of cost of goods manufactured and the income statement. The total amount of cost of goods manufactured during the period is carried over to the income statement, where it is used to compute cost of goods sold. The cost of goods manufactured is added to the beginning balance of Finished Goods Inventory to obtain the total cost of goods available for sale during the period. Then cost of goods sold is computed by subtracting the ending balance in Finished Goods Inventory (cost of goods completed but unsold) from the total cost of goods available for sale. Cost of goods sold is considered an expense of the period in which the related products were sold.

Computation of Cost of Goods Sold

Beginning Balance: Finished Goods Inventory	$ 70,000
Plus Cost of Goods Manufactured	492,600
Total Cost of Finished Goods Available for Sale	$562,600
Less Ending Balance: Finished Goods Inventory	76,500
Cost of Goods Sold	$486,100

Note that the above computation is very similar to the actual computation of cost of goods sold as shown and highlighted previously in Figure 23-6. The remaining parts of the income statement in Figure 23-6 should be familiar to you from previous discussions in this text.

Periodic Versus Perpetual Inventory Methods

Objective 4 Distinguish between the periodic and perpetual inventory methods

Accounting for manufacturing costs depends on the cost flow assumption found in a particular cost accounting system. The use of either a periodic or a perpetual approach to accounting for inventories dictates a system's cost flow characteristics. In Chapter 11, we discussed the periodic and perpetual inventory methods. Because these methods are relevant to the operation of a cost accounting system, we also include a brief discussion here. A company using the **periodic inventory method** records raw materials purchases in a separate purchases account and assigns manufacturing costs to individual labor accounts and to various overhead cost accounts in the general ledger. Beginning inventory balances in the general ledger remain unchanged during the period. No costs flow through the Raw Materials, Work in Process, and Finished Goods Inventory accounts as illustrated earlier in this chapter. Year-end inventory values are determined by counting the items on hand and placing a cost on these goods. Inventory accounts are then adjusted to reflect the cost of the ending inventories.

Within the records of a company using the **perpetual inventory method**, manufacturing costs flow through inventory accounts as goods and services are purchased and utilized in the production process. Inventory account balances are updated perpetually. Thus it is possible to determine these balances at any point in time. Raw materials purchases are debited to the Raw Materials Inventory account. Direct labor costs are accumulated in a Factory Payroll account and then transferred to the Work in Process Inventory account. Manufacturing overhead items such as heat, light, and power and depreciation expense are accumulated in a Manufacturing Overhead Control account and applied to Work in Process Inventory by using a predetermined overhead rate. As you can see, the perpetual inventory approach was followed in the cost flow discussion earlier in this chapter.

The perpetual inventory method is commonly used within cost accounting systems. More accuracy and better inventory control are the major benefits of this approach. However, a perpetual inventory system is expensive to install and maintain. For this reason, many medium-size and small manufacturing companies use a periodic inventory approach. The rest of this chapter will focus on work sheet and financial statement preparation for a manufacturer using the periodic inventory method. A similar analysis based on the perpetual inventory approach will be developed at the end of Chapter 24.

Work Sheet and Financial Statement Preparation: Illustrative Analysis Using Periodic Inventories

The year-end work sheet analysis for a manufacturing company using a periodic inventory approach is very similar to that for a merchandiser. The only real difference is that the work sheet for a manufacturer contains

Objective 5 Prepare the year-end work sheets, closing journal entries, and financial statements for a manufacturing company, using a periodic inventory approach

two additional columns, for the statement of cost of goods manufactured. In this section of the chapter, we will extend the analysis of the Pedersen Company. Data from the company's records have already been used in this chapter to illustrate cost flow and to describe the calculation of cost of goods manufactured. Pedersen Company's work sheet for the year ending December 31, 19xx, is shown in Figure 23-8 (next two pages). Below is a full explanation of the year-end accounting procedures. Income statement account balances correspond to those used in Figures 23-6 and 23-7.

The Trial Balance Columns

Work sheet analysis begins with the taking of a trial balance. The first two columns in Figure 23-8 represent the trial balance. As its name implies, a trial balance lists all general ledger accounts and account balances to verify that the unadjusted accounts are in balance.

Year-End Adjusting Entries

Account balances in the general ledger at year end represent the cumulative effect of all recorded transactions during the year. However, some account changes result from the passage of time rather than from a transaction. Year-end adjusting entries are prepared so that this type of information can be entered into the accounting records. General journal entries and explanations for the Adjustments column in Figure 23-8 follow.

(a) Depreciation Expense, Machinery and Equipment	14,800	
Accumulated Depreciation, Machinery and Equipment		14,800
To record depreciation of machinery for the period		
(b) Depreciation Expense, Factory Building	16,200	
Accumulated Depreciation, Factory Building		16,200
To record depreciation of factory building for the period		
(c) Small Tools Expense	2,700	
Small Tools		2,700
To write off small tools used		
(d) Factory Insurance Expense	1,600	
Prepaid Insurance		1,600
To charge to expense that portion of prepaid insurance premiums that expired during the period		
(e) Federal Income Tax Expense	11,548	
Federal Income Taxes Payable		11,548
To record federal income taxes for the period		

Figure 23-8 Work Sheet Analysis—Manufacturing Company—Periodic Inventories

Pedersen Company
Work Sheet
For the Year Ended December 31, 19xx

Account Titles	Trial Balance		Adjustments		Adjusted Trial Balance		Statement of Cost of Goods Manufactured		Income Statement		Balance Sheet	
	Debit	Credit	Debit	Credit	Debit	Credit	Debit	Credit	Debit	Credit	Debit	Credit
Cash	24,600				24,600						24,600	
Accounts Receivable	65,000				65,000						65,000	
Allowance for Uncollectible Accounts		1,200				1,200						1,200
Raw Materials Inventory	17,500				17,500		17,500	20,400			20,400	
Work in Process Inventory	21,200				21,200		21,200	23,500			23,500	
Finished Goods Inventory	70,000				70,000				70,000	76,500	76,500	
Prepaid Insurance	4,800			(d) 1,600	3,200						3,200	
Machinery and Equipment	138,500				138,500						138,500	
Accumulated Depreciation, Machinery and Equipment		49,700		(a) 14,800		64,500						64,500
Factory Building	294,800				294,800						294,800	
Accumulated Depreciation, Factory Building		108,000		(b) 16,200		124,200						124,200
Small Tools	9,800			(c) 2,700	7,100						7,100	
Accounts Payable		26,100				26,100						26,100
Notes Payable—$8\frac{1}{2}$%, due in 5 years		100,000				100,000						100,000
Capital Stock—no par value		250,000				250,000						250,000
Retained Earnings, Beginning		50,000				50,000						50,000

Sales		750,000				750,000				750,000		
Raw Material Purchases	142,600				142,600		142,600					
Direct Labor	199,000				199,000		199,000					
Indirect Labor	46,400				46,400		46,400					
Power	25,200				25,200		25,200					
Supervision	37,900				37,900		37,900					
Other Factory Costs	11,400				11,400		11,400					
Sales Salaries and Commissions	46,500				46,500				46,500			
Advertising	19,500				19,500				19,500			
Other Selling Expenses	7,400				7,400				7,400			
Administrative Salaries	65,000				65,000				65,000			
Franchise and Property Taxes	72,000				72,000				72,000			
Other General and Administrative Expenses	11,300				11,300				11,300			
Interest Expense	4,600				4,600				4,600			
	1,335,000	1,335,000										
Depreciation Expense, Machinery and Equipment			(a) 14,800		14,800		14,800					
Depreciation Expense, Factory Building			(b) 16,200		16,200		16,200					
Small Tools Expense			(c) 2,700		2,700		2,700					
Factory Insurance Expense			(d) 1,600		1,600		1,600					
Federal Income Tax Expense			(e) 11,548		11,548				11,548			
Federal Income Taxes Payable				(e) 11,548		11,548						11,548
			46,848	46,848	1,377,548	1,377,548	536,500	43,900				
Cost of Goods Manufactured to Income Statement								492,600	492,600			
							536,500	536,500	800,448	826,500	653,600	627,548
Net Income After Taxes to Balance Sheet									26,052			26,052
									826,500	826,500	653,600	653,600

Accounting for Inventories

The Pedersen Company uses the periodic method of accounting for inventories. Physical counts are made at year end to determine the number and stage of completion of goods on hand. After assigning costs to the year-end inventories, the Pedersen Company had the following ending balances: $20,400 in Raw Materials Inventory, $23,500 in Work in Process Inventory, and $76,500 in Finished Goods Inventory.

As shown in Figure 23-7, the beginning and ending balances of Raw Materials Inventory and Work in Process Inventory are used in computing cost of goods manufactured. These amounts are entered in the Statement of Cost of Goods Manufactured columns in the work sheet (Figure 23-8) for this reason. Beginning balances are carried as debits from the Adjusted Trial Balance columns to the debit column for Statement of Cost of Goods Manufactured. These amounts, in essence, are treated as additional expenses to those incurred during the period. Ending inventory balances are credited because they represent unused costs and are subtracted from total manufacturing costs incurred to arrive at the cost of goods manufactured. The ending inventory balances for Raw Materials and Work in Process are carried over to the Balance Sheet columns as assets (debits).

The same reasoning is used to explain the work sheet treatment of Finished Goods Inventory. Beginning and ending Finished Goods Inventory balances are used to compute cost of goods sold. For this reason, the beginning balance is carried to the Income Statement columns as a debit. The ending balance is credited to the Income Statement columns and debited to the Balance Sheet columns as an asset.

Statement of Cost of Goods Manufactured Columns

In addition to the beginning and ending balances of the Raw Materials Inventory and Work in Process Inventory, all balances of expense accounts pertaining to the manufacturing process are carried from the Adjusted Trial Balance to the Statement of Cost of Goods Manufactured columns. The resulting difference between total debits and total credits in these columns represents the cost of goods manufactured for the year. In Figure 23-8, the amount is $492,600, the same amount computed in Figure 23-7. In our example, the actual statement of cost of goods manufactured was prepared prior to this discussion of the work sheet. Normally, this statement is prepared from data appearing in the Statement of Cost of Goods Manufactured columns on the work sheet. Before proceeding, trace each item in these two columns to the actual statement in Figure 23-7. This action will help you to prepare the statement itself.

Income Statement Columns

On the work sheet, the cost of goods manufactured amount is transferred to the income statement by crediting the Statement of Cost of Goods Manufactured and debiting the Income Statement columns. The remaining amount to be carried over to the Income Statement columns must now be determined. The credit amount for Sales must be extended from the Adjusted Trial Balance columns to the Income Statement columns. Beginning and ending balances of Finished Goods Inventory have already been discussed. Other relevant account balances include Selling Expense accounts, General and Administrative Expense accounts, Interest Expense, and Federal Income Tax Expense. The income statement was also prepared and discussed prior to the development of the work sheet. Ordinarily, this sequence is reversed, and the income statement is prepared from data in these two columns on the work sheet. Trace all amounts from the work sheet columns to the actual income statement in Figure 23-6 to make sure that you understand the relationship between these two documents.

Closing Entries

All account balances used in computing cost of goods manufactured and net income are closed to Retained Earnings at year end. Below are the closing entries and detailed explanations for the Pedersen Company. When the periodic inventory method is used, ending inventory balances are also established during the preparation of closing entries. Ending inventory balances are entered into the records when these entries are posted to the general ledger.

Dec. 31	Manufacturing Summary	536,500	
	Raw Materials Inventory, Jan. 1, 19xx		17,500
	Work in Process Inventory, Jan. 1 19xx		21,200
	Raw Materials Purchases		142,600
	Direct Labor		199,000
	Indirect Labor		46,400
	Power		25,200
	Supervision		37,900
	Other Factory Costs		11,400
	Depreciation Expense, Machinery and Equipment		14,800
	Depreciation Expense, Factory Building		16,200
	Small Tools Expense		2,700
	Factory Insurance Expense		1,600
	To close manufacturing accounts and beginning Raw Materials and Work in Process Inventory balances to Manufacturing Summary		

(*continued*)

	Debit	Credit
31 Raw Materials Inventory, Dec. 31, 19xx	20,400	
Work in Process Inventory, Dec. 31, 19xx	23,500	
Manufacturing Summary		43,900
To establish year-end balances in the Raw Materials and Work in Process Inventory accounts and to remove these costs from the Manufacturing Summary account		
31 Income Summary	800,448	
Finished Goods Inventory, Jan. 1, 19xx		70,000
Sales Salaries and Commissions		46,500
Advertising		19,500
Other Selling Expenses		7,400
Administrative Salaries		65,000
Franchise and Property Taxes		72,000
Other General and Administrative Expenses		11,300
Interest Expense		4,600
Federal Income Tax Expense		11,548
Manufacturing Summary		492,600
To close income statement expenses and beginning Finished Goods Inventory balance to Income Summary		
31 Sales	750,000	
Finished Goods Inventory, Dec. 31, 19xx	76,500	
Income Summary		826,500
To close Sales to Income Summary account and to set up the ending balance in Finished Goods Inventory		
31 Income Summary	26,052	
Retained Earnings		26,052
To close Income Summary account and transfer balance to Retained Earnings		

Balance Sheet Columns

The final two columns in the work sheet analysis represent the year-end balance sheet. All asset, liability, and stockholders' equity account balances are carried from the Adjusted Trial Balance to the Balance Sheet columns. In addition, the year-end net income is credited to the balance sheet. The resulting December 31, 19xx, balance sheet for the Pedersen Company is shown in Figure 23-9. Trace all amounts in the Balance Sheet columns on the work sheet to the actual balance sheet to verify its accuracy.

Figure 23-9
The Balance Sheet

Pedersen Company
Balance Sheet
December 31, 19xx

Assets			
Current Assets			
Cash		$ 24,600	
Accounts Receivable	$ 65,000		
Less Allowance for Uncollectible Accounts	1,200	63,800	
Raw Materials Inventory		20,400	
Work in Process Inventory		23,500	
Finished Goods Inventory		76,500	
Prepaid Insurance		3,200	
Small Tools		7,100	
Total Current Assets			$219,100
Plant and Equipment			
Machinery and Equipment	$138,500		
Less Accumulated Depreciation	64,500	$ 74,000	
Factory Building	$294,800		
Less Accumulated Depreciation	124,200	170,600	
Total Plant and Equipment			244,600
Total Assets			$463,700
Liabilities			
Current Liabilities			
Accounts Payable	$ 26,100		
Income Taxes Payable	11,548		
Total Current Liabilities		$ 37,648	
Long-Term Debt			
Notes Payable		100,000	
Total Liabilities			$137,648
Stockholders' Equity			
Capital Stock		$250,000	
Retained Earnings, Jan. 1, 19xx	$ 50,000		
Net Income for 19xx	26,052		
Retained Earnings, Dec. 31, 19xx		76,052	
Total Stockholders' Equity			326,052
Total Liabilities and Stockholders' Equity			$463,700

Chapter Review

Review of Learning Objectives

1. Describe the field of management accounting.

The field of management accounting consists of specific information gathering and reporting concepts and appropriate accounting techniques and procedures that, when collectively applied to a company's financial and production data, will satisfy certain basic informational needs of management. These needs include (a) product costing information, (b) data used for planning and control of operations, and (c) special reports and analyses used to support management decisions.

2. Describe the nature, contents, and flow of costs through the Raw Materials Inventory, Work in Process Inventory, and Finished Goods Inventory accounts.

The Raw Materials Inventory account is used to record the costs of raw materials received and issued for use in a company's production process. All manufacturing-related costs are recorded in the Work in Process Inventory account as they enter the production process. When products are completed, their costs are transferred out of the Work in Process Inventory account, leaving only costs of in-process items in the account balance. Costs of all completed but unsold products comprise the balance in the Finished Goods Inventory account. Cost flow begins with the incurrence of raw materials, direct labor, and manufacturing overhead costs. Raw materials costs first flow into the Raw Materials Inventory account. When raw materials are requisitioned into production, their costs are transferred from the Raw Materials Inventory account to the Work in Process Inventory account. Direct labor and manufacturing overhead costs are debited also to the Work in Process Inventory account balance as products are being developed. When the products are completed, their costs are transferred from the Work in Process Inventory account to the Finished Goods Inventory account. Costs remain in the Finished Goods Inventory account until the products are sold, at which time their costs are transferred to the Cost of Goods Sold account.

3. Prepare a statement of cost of goods manufactured.

The preparation of a statement of cost of goods manufactured involves three steps. The first is to compute the cost of raw materials used. Total raw materials purchases are added to the beginning balance of Raw Materials Inventory to arrive at the cost of raw materials available for use. From this amount, the ending Raw Materials Inventory balance is subtracted to yield the cost of raw materials used. The second step is to compute the total manufacturing costs for the period. Costs of direct labor and manufacturing overhead are added to the cost of raw materials used to arrive at this amount. The third step is the actual computation of cost of goods manufactured. To total manufacturing costs is added the beginning balance in the Work in Process Inventory account, the sum of which is called total cost of goods in process during the year. By subtracting the ending Work in Process Inventory balance from total cost of goods in process, we can identify the total cost of goods manufactured.

4. Distinguish between the periodic and perpetual inventory methods.

A company using the periodic inventory method records materials purchases in a separate purchases account and assigns manufacturing costs to individual labor accounts and to various overhead cost accounts in the general ledger. Beginning inventory balances remain unchanged during the year because no costs flow through the Raw Materials, Work in Process, and Finished Goods Inventory accounts. These inventory accounts are adjusted at year end to reflect the ending balances. Under the perpetual inventory method, manufacturing costs flow through inventory accounts as goods and services are purchased and utilized in the production process. Inventory balances are updated perpetually, and specific balances can be determined at any time, not only at year end.

5. Prepare the year-end work sheets, closing journal entries, and financial statements for a manufacturing company, using a periodic inventory approach.
Preparation of the work sheet is the key to all year-end accounting procedures. Columns for the trial balance, year-end adjustments, adjusted trial balance, statement of cost of goods manufactured, income statement, and balance sheet are completed. From this information, all year-end financial statements are prepared. Closing entries are developed that (a) close all manufacturing cost account balances to the Manufacturing Summary account, (b) close the beginning balances in the Raw Materials Inventory and Work in Process Inventory accounts to the Manufacturing Summary account and establish ending balances in these inventory accounts, (c) close the Manufacturing Summary account balance and all other revenue and nonmanufacturing expense account balances to the Income Summary account, (d) close the beginning balance in the Finished Goods Inventory account to the Income Summary account and establish the ending Finished Goods Inventory account balance, and (e) close the Income Summary account balance to the Retained Earnings account.

Review Problem

Before doing the exercises and problems, review the three fundamental steps used in computing cost of goods manufactured, focusing on Figure 23-7 in the text. For additional help, see the review problem for this chapter in the working papers.

Chapter Assignments

Questions

1. Describe the field of management accounting using the three categories of informational needs of management.
2. Does the size of a business enterprise dictate the types and/or amount of financial information needed by management? Explain your answer.
3. What is meant by manufacturing cost flow?
4. How does the periodic inventory method differ from the perpetual inventory method?
5. What is the connection between manufacturing cost flow and the perpetual inventory method?
6. Identify and describe the three inventory accounts used by a manufacturing company.
7. Describe the process of computing cost of raw materials used.
8. Differentiate total manufacturing costs from cost of goods manufactured.
9. How is cost of goods manufactured used in computing cost of goods sold?
10. "Computing cost of goods sold for a merchandising company is not as complex as computing the same balance for a manufacturing company." Is this statement true? Explain your answer.
11. What is the purpose of preparing a twelve-column work sheet for a manufacturing company?
12. When a manufacturing company uses the periodic inventory method, what types of accounts are closed to the Manufacturing Summary account? Give specific examples of each type.

Classroom Exercises

Exercise 23-1
Manufacturing Cost Flow

Cost flow within a manufacturing company was illustrated in Figures 23-4 and 23-5 and described in the text.

Using the ideas shown in Figures 23-4 and 23-5 and the concepts expressed in Chapters 22 and 23, describe in detail the flow of raw materials costs through the recording process of a cost accounting system. Include in your answer all general ledger accounts affected and all recording documents used. Prepare your answer in proper chronological fashion.

Exercise 23-2
Cost of Raw Materials Used

Data pertaining to the cost of raw materials for the month ended August 31, 19xx, are as follows: Raw Materials Inventory at August 1, 19xx, $20,700; Raw Materials Inventory at August 31, 19xx, $15,700; purchases of raw materials during August, $18,500.

Compute the cost of raw materials used during August 19xx.

Exercise 23-3
Computing Total Manufacturing Costs

The partial trial balance of Davis Millinery, Inc., is shown below. Inventory accounts still reflect balances at the beginning of the period. Period-end balances are $67,200, $96,400, and $47,600 for Raw Materials Inventory, Work in Process Inventory, and Finished Goods Inventory, respectively.

	Debit	Credit
Accounts Receivable	$147,420	
Raw Materials Inventory	54,800	
Work in Process Inventory	101,200	
Finished Goods Inventory	36,900	
Accounts Payable		$ 79,450
Sales		828,940
Purchases	297,600	
Direct Labor	184,200	
Operating Supplies Expense, Factory	17,700	
Depreciation, Machinery	54,100	
Fire Loss	62,000	
Insurance Expense, Factory	10,700	
Indirect Labor	46,900	
Supervisory Salaries, Factory	32,700	
President's Salary	39,900	
Property Taxes, Factory	9,400	
Other Indirect Manufacturing Expenses	16,500	

From the above information, prepare a schedule (in good form) to compute total manufacturing costs for the period ending May 31, 19xx.

Exercise 23-4
Cost of Goods Manufactured

The Precision Firearms Company manufactures nine-millimeter automatic handguns that are sold exclusively to police agencies. The company has just completed operations for June 19xx, and the following figures have been made available:

Values of Inventories	June 1, 19xx	June 30, 19xx
Raw Materials	$ 463,500	$ 621,800
Work in Process	1,255,100	1,089,000
Finished Goods	611,900	808,300

Purchases of raw materials in June amounted to $1,000,000, less $224,800 credit for defective materials returned to the supplier. During June, the company incurred 80,000 direct labor hours at an average rate of $6.50 per hour. Overhead is applied to production at a rate of $4.00 per direct labor hour. The variance between overhead applied and actual overhead incurred is considered immaterial.

Using good form, prepare a statement of cost of goods manufactured from the information provided. (Hint: Assume that applied overhead is the same as actual overhead incurred.)

Exercise 23-5 Concept of Three Types of Inventories

"For manufacturing companies, the concept of inventories must be expanded to include three types: Raw Materials Inventory, Work in Process Inventory, and Finished Goods Inventory."

Briefly explain how the three inventory accounts function and how they interrelate.

Exercise 23-6 Computing Total Manufacturing Costs

The Ceylon Chutney Company has just finished another successful fiscal year. Relevant production data for the period are provided below.

Beginning and ending raw materials inventories were valued at $641,500 and $598,300, respectively. Purchases of raw materials during the fiscal year amounted to $1,040,700. During the twelve-month period, the firm incurred 111,400 hours of direct labor at an average labor rate of $8.00 per hour. Factory overhead was applied to production at the rate of $9.50 per direct labor hour.

From the information given, compute total manufacturing costs for the year. For purposes of this exercise, use applied overhead in place of actual overhead incurred.

Exercise 23-7 Statement of Cost of Goods Manufactured

Information regarding the manufacturing costs incurred by the Sunset Skateboard Company for the month ended May 31, 19xx, is as follows: Purchases of raw materials during May were $39,000. Direct labor amounted to 9,400 hours at $4.75 per hour. Manufacturing overhead costs were: Utilities, $1,870; Supervision, $18,600; Indirect Supplies, $4,000; Depreciation, $3,200; Insurance, $830; Miscellaneous, $500. Inventories at May 1 were: Raw Materials, $48,600; Work in Process, $53,250; Finished Goods, $60,500. Inventories at May 31 were: Raw Materials, $51,100; Work in Process, $47,400; Finished Goods, $62,450.

From the information given, prepare a statement of cost of goods manufactured.

Exercise 23-8 Computing Cost of Goods Sold

Duffy Distilleries, Inc., produces a deluxe line of wines and beverages. During 19xx, the company operated at record levels, with sales totaling $695,000. The accounting department has already determined total manufacturing costs for the period as being $262,250. Operating expenses for the year were $229,740. Assume a 50 percent tax rate. You discover that inventory balances were as follows:

	Jan. 1, 19xx	Dec. 31, 19xx
Raw Materials Inventory	$25,490	$18,810
Work in Process Inventory	57,400	41,980
Finished Goods Inventory	84,820	69,320

From the above information, prepare an income statement for the year ended December 31, 19xx.

Problem Set A

Problem 23A-1 Cost of Goods Manufactured—Three Fundamental Steps

As part of the procedure for preparing year-end financial statements, Joyce Dean, controller of Baylor Enterprises, was asked to present a formal statement of cost of goods manufactured to management. Account balances were as follows: Raw Materials Inventory, Jan. 1, $62,540; Work in Process Inventory, Jan. 1, $81,050; Finished Goods Inventory, Jan. 1, $100,040; Raw Materials Inventory, Dec. 31, $60,820; Work in Process Inventory, Dec. 31, $84,590; Finished Goods Inventory, Dec. 31, $88,880; Direct Labor (4,900 hours at $11.50 per hour), $56,350; Indirect Labor (6,200 hours at $6.90 per hour), $42,780; Heat, Light, and Power, $3,940; Operating Supplies Used, $7,610; Supervision, Factory, $18,400; Repairs Expense, $6,820; Depreciation, Plant and Equipment, $7,915; Property Taxes, Plant and Equipment, $2,185; Insurance, Plant, $690.

During the year, $262,290 of raw materials were purchased.

Required

1. Prepare a schedule showing the calculation of raw materials used during the year.
2. Given the amount of raw materials used, develop an analysis to determine total manufacturing costs for the year.
3. Given the total manufacturing costs for the period, prepare an analysis that derives the cost of goods manufactured during the year.

Problem 23A-2 Manufacturing Cost Flow

One of the unique aspects of a manufacturing accounting system using a perpetual inventory method is that manufacturing costs flow through the inventory accounts.

Required

For each of the costs below, describe (a) the route that it takes to its final destination in the Cost of Goods Sold account, (b) the reasons for its movement from one account to another, (c) whether the cost flow is different under a periodic versus a perpetual inventory approach, and (d) any documents used to signal the time for an account transfer of the cost.

1. Cost of raw materials
2. Direct labor cost
3. Depreciation expense, factory

Problem 23A-3 Statement of Cost of Goods Manufactured

The Canine Food Company has been in business for several years. The information below was taken from its records on June 30, 19x6, the last day of the company's fiscal year. Inventory balances at July 1, 19x5, were as follows: Raw Materials, $85,800; Work in Process, $192,700; Finished Goods, $96,500. Inventory balances at June 30, 19x6, were as follows: Raw Materials, $86,200; Work in Process, $162,490; Finished Goods, $97,400.

Direct materials were purchased during the year for $214,600. Direct labor totaled 8,420 hours at $5.50 per hour plus 4,850 hours at $4.80 per hour for the twelve-month period. Factory overhead costs incurred during the year were as follows: Indirect Labor, $12,830; Employee Fringe Benefits, $4,720; Janitorial and Maintenance Service, $1,640; Plant Security Service, $1,260; Depreciation of Machinery and Equipment, $850; Depreciation of Building, $600; Insurance, $880; Property Taxes, $1,320; Small Tools Used in the Factory, $250; Heat, Light, and Power, $990; Quality Control, Factory, $1,110.

Required

Using the information provided above, prepare a statement of cost of goods manufactured for the fiscal year ended June 30, 19x6.

Problem 23A-4 Preparation of Manufacturing and Income Statements

The Christown Candy Company, which began operations on February 1, manufactures a limited variety of seasonal candies. The following information pertains to the operations of February: There were no beginning inventories at February 1 in Raw Materials, Work in Process, and Finished Goods. Inventories at February 28 were: Raw Materials, $15,500; Work in Process, $11,700; Finished Goods, $8,900.

Purchases of raw materials during the month amounted to $70,200. Factory overhead expenses incurred during February were as follows: Operating Supplies Used, $12,900; Outside Labor, $11,300; Employee Benefits, $7,800; Depreciation, $5,400; Utilities, $4,600; Other, $1,500. Direct Labor totaled $14,100 for the month of February. Net sales for the month were $148,400. General and administrative expenses were $40,200.

Required

1. Prepare a statement of cost of goods manufactured for the month ended February 28.
2. Using good form, prepare an income statement for February. (Assume a federal income tax rate of 50 percent.)

Problem 23A-5 Statement Preparation—Manufacturing Company

The Barker and Hannigan Pharmaceuticals Corporation manufactures a variety of drugs, which are marketed internationally.

Inventories at April 1 were as follows:

Raw Materials	
Natural Minerals	$ 88,700
Basic Organic Compounds	124,300
Catalysts	40,500
Suspension Agents	32,900
Total Raw Materials	$286,400
Work in Process	$108,800
Finished Goods	$211,700

Inventories at April 30 were as follows:

Raw Materials	
Natural Minerals	$ 70,600
Basic Organic Compounds	111,400
Catalysts	28,900
Suspension Agents	42,200
Total Raw Materials	$253,100
Work in Process	$ 97,200
Finished Goods	$214,100

Purchases of raw materials for April were $142,600, and direct labor costs were computed on the basis of 30,000 hours at $6 per hour. Actual factory overhead costs incurred in April were as follows: Operating Supplies, $5,700; Janitorial and Material-handling Labor, $29,100; Employee Benefits, $110,800; Heat, Light, and Power, $54,000; Depreciation, Factory, $14,400; Property Taxes, $8,000; Expired Portion of Insurance Premiums, $12,000. Net sales for April were $1,188,400. General and administrative expenses were $162,000. Income is taxed at a rate of 60 percent.

Required

1. Using good form, prepare a statement of cost of goods manufactured for the month ended April 30.
2. Using your answer in part 1, prepare an income statement for the same period.

Problem 23A-6 Year-End Work Sheet and Financial Statement Analysis

The trial balance of the Welleson Manufacturing Company as of December 31, 19xx, appeared as follows:

	Debit	Credit
Cash	$ 9,500	
Accounts Receivable	12,000	
Raw Materials Inventory, Jan. 1, 19xx	18,450	
Work in Process Inventory, Jan. 1, 19xx	23,400	
Finished Goods Inventory, Jan. 1, 19xx	28,840	
Manufacturing Supplies Inventory, Jan. 1, 19xx	2,700	
Prepaid Factory Insurance	3,400	
Machinery and Equipment	145,600	
Accumulated Depreciation, Machinery and Equipment		$ 14,560
Small Tools	4,720	
Accounts Payable		21,200
Note Payable ($10,000 per year)		40,000
Common Stock		125,000
Retained Earnings, Jan. 1, 19xx		16,110
Sales		375,900
Raw Materials Purchases	72,150	
Direct Labor	80,420	
Factory Supervision	26,960	
Indirect Labor	16,750	
Heat, Light, and Power, Factory	9,310	
Factory Rent	36,000	
Repairs and Maintenance, Factory	12,650	
Property Taxes, Machinery and Equipment	4,500	
Selling Expenses, Control	38,900	
Administrative Expenses, Control	46,520	
	$592,770	$592,770

Year-end adjustment information is as follows: (a) depreciation for 19xx on machinery and equipment, $7,280; (b) factory insurance expired, $1,400; (c) small tools used during 19xx, $1,700; (d) manufacturing supplies consumed, $900; (e) accrued salaries and wages payable, including Direct Labor, $1,200; Indirect Labor, $890; Factory Supervision, $1,400; (f) ending inventory balances for Raw Materials Inventory, $21,490; Work in Process Inventory, $24,210; Finished Goods Inventory, $29,680; (g) estimated federal income taxes, $4,765.

The company uses the periodic inventory method.

Required

1. Prepare a twelve-column work sheet, and enter the trial balance amounts. Formulate year-end adjusting journal entries from the information given, post entries to the work sheet, and compute adjusted trial balance amounts.
2. Extend all amounts to proper columns for the statement of cost of goods manufactured, the income statement, and the balance sheet.
3. Complete the work sheet, and prepare formal financial statements, including a statement of cost of goods manufactured.
4. Prepare closing entries.

Problem Set B

Problem 23B-3 Statement of Cost of Goods Manufactured

Sebastian and Sons, Inc., operates a large vineyard in California that produces a full line of varietal wines. The company, whose fiscal year runs from November 1 through October 31, has just completed a record-breaking year ending October 31, 19x4. Production figures for this period are as follows:

Account	Nov. 1, 19x3	Oct. 31, 19x4
Raw Materials Inventory	$ 4,956,200	$ 5,203,800
Work in Process Inventory	8,371,000	7,764,500
Finished Goods Inventory	11,596,400	11,883,200

Raw materials purchased during the year amounted to $5,500,000. Direct labor hours incurred totaled 342,500, at an average labor rate of $4.20 per hour. The following factory overhead costs were incurred during the year: Depreciation, Plant and Equipment, $985,600; Operating Supplies, $607,300; Property Taxes, Plant and Equipment, $514,200; Material Handlers' Labor, $1,113,700; Small Tools Expense, $82,400; Utilities, $2,036,500; Employee Fringe Benefits, $846,100.

Required

Using proper form, prepare a statement of cost of goods manufactured from the information provided.

Problem 23B-4 Preparation of Manufacturing and Income Statements

The Gordon Cylinder Company manufactures aluminum compressed-gas cylinders, using aluminum ingot as the only direct material. Inventories at Sept. 1 were as follows: Aluminum Ingot, $118,600; Work in Process, $16,100; Finished Goods, $31,000. Inventories at Sept. 30 were: Aluminum Ingot, $114,100; Work in Process, $14,800; Finished Goods, $28,400.

Purchases of aluminum ingot for September amounted to $7,700. Direct labor hours for September were 1,100 at $5 per hour.

Actual manufacturing overhead costs incurred in September were as follows: Nonaluminum Materials, $1,500; Indirect Labor, $1,600; Fringe Benefits, $1,200; Depreciation, $800; Utilities, $700; Insurance, $300; Property Taxes, $500. Net sales of $56,900 were realized in September. General, selling, and administrative expenses were $3,500. Income is taxed at a rate of 50 percent.

Required

1. Using good form, prepare a statement of cost of goods manufactured for the month ended September 30.
2. Prepare an income statement for September.

Problem 23B-5 Statement Preparation—Manufacturing Company

Below is a partial work sheet of the Anaheim Foundry Company for the year ended December 31.

	Statement of Cost of Goods Manufactured		Income Statement	
	Debit	Credit	Debit	Credit
Raw Materials Inventory	36,400	39,200		
Work in Process Inventory	47,100	48,450		
Finished Goods Inventory			62,800	60,660
Sales				942,250
Raw Material Purchases	180,600			
Direct Labor	194,940			
Indirect Labor	62,000			
Power	21,920			
Supervision	39,900			
Depreciation, Factory	18,100			
Depreciation, Machinery	29,450			
Insurance	2,500			
Other Factory Costs	8,740			
Selling Expenses			145,720	
Administrative Expenses			96,980	
Federal and State Income Taxes (50% of income before taxes)			?	

Required

1. Using good form, prepare a statement of cost of goods manufactured for the year ended December 31.
2. Using your answer in part 1, prepare an income statement for the same period.

Problem 23B-6 Year-End Work Sheet and Financial Statement Analysis

Pattillo Metal Fabricators, Inc., manufactures a diversified line of metal pipe. The corporation trial balance as of December 31, 19xx, is shown on the next page.

Year-end adjustment information for Pattillo is as follows: (a) unexpired factory insurance at Dec. 31, 19xx, $2,400; (b) machinery and equipment depreciation for the year, $9,537; (c) manufacturing supplies used during the year, $2,300; (d) accrued salaries and wages payable at Dec. 31, 19xx, including Direct Labor, $9,120; Indirect Labor, $1,760; Plant Supervision, $2,040; (e) ending inventory balances for Raw Materials Inventory, $30,480; Work in Process Inventory, $26,950; Finished Goods Inventory, $40,690; (f) estimated federal income taxes, $60,000.

The company uses the periodic inventory method.

	Debit	Credit
Cash	$ 16,410	
Accounts Receivable	35,020	
Raw Materials Inventory, Jan. 1, 19xx	24,810	
Work in Process Inventory, Jan. 1, 19xx	30,980	
Finished Goods Inventory, Jan. 1, 19xx	42,110	
Manufacturing Supplies Inventory, Jan. 1, 19xx	6,930	
Prepaid Factory Insurance	4,800	
Machinery and Equipment	238,425	
Accumulated Depreciation, Machinery and Equipment		$ 95,370
Accounts Payable		22,220
Notes Payable ($5,000 per year)		60,000
Common Stock		50,000
Retained Earnings, Jan. 1, 19xx		25,170
Sales		697,400
Raw Materials Purchases	171,080	
Direct Labor	122,610	
Plant Supervision	51,000	
Factory Utilities	12,910	
Factory Rent	26,000	
Indirect Labor	32,625	
Repairs Expense	9,220	
Factory Property Taxes	6,910	
Selling Expenses, Control	48,630	
Administrative Expenses, Control	69,690	
	$950,160	$950,160

Required

1. Prepare a twelve-column work sheet, and enter the trial balance amounts. Formulate year-end adjusting journal entries from the information given, post entries to the work sheet, and compute adjusted trial balance amounts.
2. Extend all amounts to proper columns for the statement of cost of goods manufactured, the income statement, and the balance sheet.
3. Complete the work sheet, and prepare formal year-end financial statements, including a statement of cost of goods manufactured.
4. Prepare closing entries.

Chapter Twenty-Four

Product Costing: The Job Order System

Learning Objectives

1. *Distinguish between job order costing and process costing.*
2. *Describe the concept of absorption costing.*
3. *Compute a predetermined overhead rate, and use this rate to apply overhead costs to production.*
4. *Dispose of underapplied or overapplied overhead.*
5. *Explain the relationship between product costing and inventory valuation.*
6. *Describe the cost flow in a job order cost accounting system.*
7. *Journalize transactions within a job order costing system.*
8. *Compute product unit cost for a specific job order.*

Determining a product's unit cost is one of the basic functions of a cost accounting system. Business success is linked with product costing information in several ways. First, unit costs are an important element in determining an adequate, fair, and competitive selling price. Second, product costing information often forms the basis for forecasting and controlling operations and costs. Finally, product costs provide a vehicle for use in arriving at ending inventory balances. As a result of studying this chapter, you should be able to meet the learning objectives listed on the left.

One important reason for installing and maintaining a cost accounting system is to compute the cost of manufacturing an individual product or a batch of products. Such cost accounting systems vary from one company to another. Each system is designed to yield information that company management considers important. Within each system, however, some form of product cost determination is essential. In this chapter, we integrate the basic information on manufacturing accounting discussed in Chapters 22 and 23 into a traditional product costing system: the job order costing system. We also analyze product cost computations for job order situations and link them to units completed and transferred to the finished goods inventory.

However, before a specific product cost accounting system can be discussed, additional background information is needed. In the first part of this chapter, we compare the two most common product costing systems, job order costing and process costing. (Chapter 25 presents the topic of process costing in more detail.) We then explain the concept of absorption costing and analyze predetermined overhead rates and product costing as they relate to inventory valuation. The chapter's appendix presents a work sheet and financial statement preparation analysis that parallels the one discussed in Chapter 23. Here, however, the perpetual rather than the periodic inventory method is used.

Job Order Versus Process Costing

Objective 1 Distinguish between job order costing and process costing

Job order costing and process costing are the two traditional, basic approaches to product cost accounting systems. Actual cost accounting systems may vary, but all are based on one of these product costing concepts and then adjusted to fit a particular industry, company, or operating department. The objective of the two systems is the same: to provide product unit cost information for purposes of product pricing, cost control, inventory valuation, and income statement preparation. End-of-period values for the Cost of Goods Sold, the Work in Process Inventory, and the Finished Goods Inventory accounts are computed by using product unit cost data.

Characteristics of Job Order Costing

A **job order cost system** is a product costing system used in the manufacturing of unique or special-order products in which raw materials, direct labor, and manufacturing overhead costs are assigned to specific job orders or batches of products. In computing unit costs, the total manufacturing costs for each job order are divided by the number of good units produced for that order. Industries that would use a job order system include those producing ships, airplanes, large machines, and special orders.

The primary characteristics of a job order cost system are (1) accumulation of all manufacturing costs and assignment of these costs to specific jobs or batches of product; (2) concern for job completion periods rather than set time periods; and (3) use of one Work in Process Inventory account in the general ledger, with its balance supported by a subsidiary ledger of job order cost sheets for each job still in process at period end.

Characteristics of Process Costing

A **process cost system** is a product costing system used by companies that produce a large number of similar products or have a continuous production flow. In either case, it is more economical to account for product-related costs for a period of time (week or month) than to try to identify them with specific products or job orders. Unit costs are computed by dividing total manufacturing costs assigned to a particular department or work center during a week or month by the number of good units produced during that time period. If a product is routed through four departments, four unit cost amounts are added together to yield the product's total unit cost. Companies producing paint, oil and gas, automobiles, bricks, or soft drinks would use some form of a process costing system.

The main characteristics of a process cost accounting system include (1) the accumulation of manufacturing costs by department or work center, with little concern for specific job orders; (2) emphasis on a weekly or monthly time period rather than on the time it takes to complete a specific order; and (3) the use of several Work in Process Inventory accounts, one for each department or work center in the manufacturing process. Process costing will be discussed in detail in Chapter 25.

Concept of Absorption Costing

Objective 2 Describe the concept of absorption costing

Product costing is possible only when the accounting system being used contains specific guidelines pertaining to the types of manufacturing costs to be included in the analysis. For instance, should all manufacturing overhead costs be considered costs of making the product, or should only the variable manufacturing overhead costs be used in this computation? The most common product costing assumptions are governed by the concept of absorption costing. **Absorption costing** is an approach to product costing that assigns a representative portion of *all* manufacturing costs to individual products. This means that costs of direct materials, direct labor, variable manufacturing overhead, and fixed manufacturing overhead are assigned to products. The product costing systems explained in this text use absorption costing to account for manufacturing costs.

Direct materials and direct labor costs are not difficult to handle for product costing purposes because, by definition, they are both direct costs that are conveniently and economically traceable to products. Manufacturing overhead, on the other hand, is not as easy to account for in tracing costs to products. For example, how much machine depreciation should be assigned to a particular product? How about the assignment of electrical power costs or indirect labor costs? One approach to this cost assignment problem would be to wait until the end of the accounting period, add up all the variable and fixed manufacturing overhead costs incurred, and divide this amount by the number of units produced during the period. This would be an acceptable method of computing a unit cost if (1) all products were of like shape and required the same manufacturing operations, and (2) the determination of product unit costs was not required until the end of the period. Such a situation is seldom found in industry. A company usually manufactures a diverse line of products and often uses product costing information in determining prices to be charged for manufactured goods prior to their actual production. Therefore, when the absorption costing concept makes it necessary to allocate manufacturing overhead costs to products, an overhead cost assignment method using a predetermined overhead rate is vital to any product costing technique.

Predetermined Overhead Rates

Objective 3 Compute a predetermined overhead rate, and use this rate to apply overhead costs to production

We discussed the development of predetermined overhead rates in Chapter 22. These rates are used to apply manufacturing overhead costs to products. Predetermined overhead rates are useful for purposes of product costing, price determination, inventory valuation, and cost control. The essential elements of this procedure include an overhead rate and a basis for application. For example, if Company Q's overhead rate is $2.50 per machine hour, and Job Order 407 requires 17 machine hours, then $42.50 ($2.50 × 17) of overhead costs would be charged to that job order.

The process of applying overhead to products and job orders depends on the use of an accurate predetermined overhead rate. This rate, in turn, depends on two important factors: (1) an accurate projection of future overhead costs, and (2) an accurate projection of the activity used as a basis for allocation. Overhead costs are generally estimated as part of the normal budgeting function. Anticipated overhead costs are accumulated from all departments involved directly or indirectly with the production process. Each department's cost estimates are submitted to and totaled by the cost accounting department. Supporting service department costs have only an indirect connection with products and must, therefore, be reassigned to the production departments. This is done by treating supporting service department costs as part of manufacturing overhead when computing the predetermined overhead rates for the period.

Allocation Activity Base and the Overhead Rate

The entire process of overhead cost allocation, from the initial estimates of overhead costs and activity bases to the process of cost assignment to products using the overhead rate, is illustrated in Figure 24-1. The first phase centers on the computation of the predetermined overhead rate. The process of developing the numerator—total estimated overhead costs—was discussed above. The development of allocation basis estimates—the denominator of the ratio—is crucial to the success of the overhead cost assignment process. If this projection is wrong, either too little or too much overhead will be charged to production during the period. In addition, if there is no causal or beneficial relationship between the cost and the job or product to which it is to be assigned, improper amounts of

Figure 24-1
Overhead Cost
Allocation

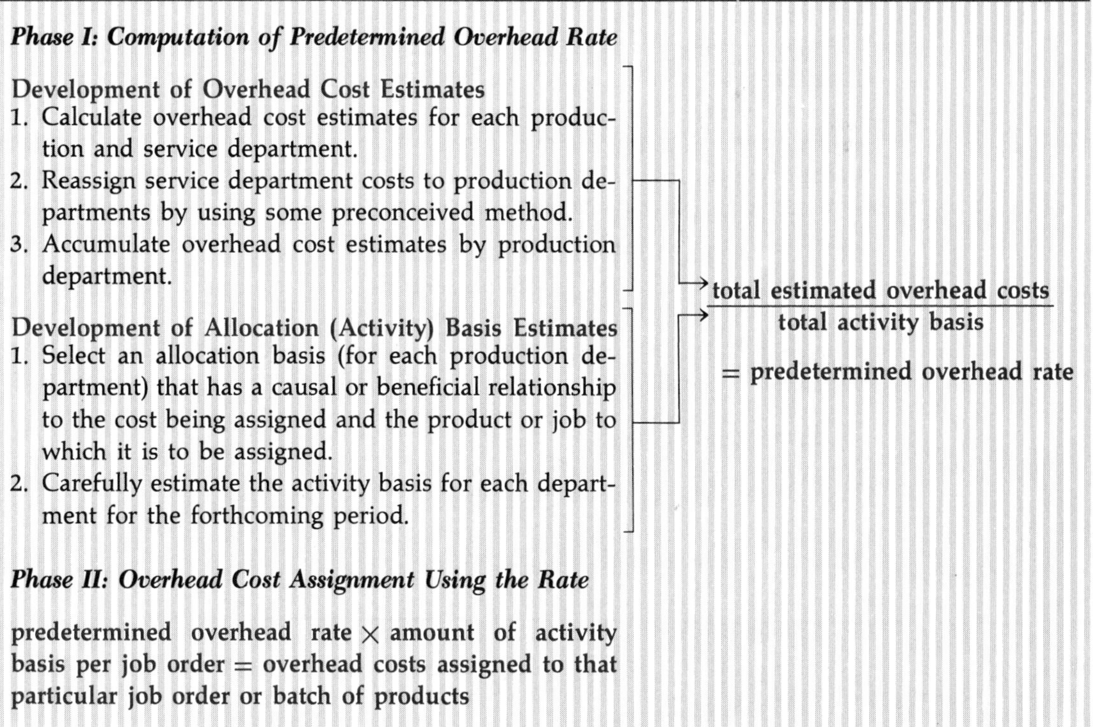

overhead costs will be allocated to individual jobs or products. Thus it is important to select a representative allocation activity basis and to determine carefully the volume of that activity basis for the forthcoming period. The four most common activity bases used for overhead cost assignment are direct labor hours, direct labor dollars, machine hours, and units produced. The second phase shown in Figure 24-1 demonstrates the use of the predetermined overhead rate in computing the amount of overhead costs to be applied to products, jobs, or other measures of work accomplished during the period.

Underapplied or Overapplied Overhead

Objective 4 Dispose of underapplied or overapplied overhead

No matter how much time and effort is put into the estimation of manufacturing overhead costs and the allocation activity base, actual overhead costs and actual production activities will seldom agree with these estimates. Something will happen to cause a difference (or variance) to occur. Differences in either area will cause manufacturing overhead to be **underapplied or overapplied.** That is, the amount of overhead costs applied to products will be more or less than the actual amount of overhead costs incurred. The fact remains that actual overhead costs must be accounted for. If overhead costs applied to products by using a predetermined (estimated) overhead rate do not agree with actual overhead costs incurred, an adjustment is necessary. Estimates used in computing the predetermined overhead rate are usually annual or full-year amounts. Therefore, monthly differences between actual overhead incurred and overhead costs applied are normally not adjusted. In many cases, monthly differences tend to offset one another, leaving only a small adjustment to be made at year end.

An example will illustrate the accounting problems associated with using predetermined overhead rates. Assume that the accounting records of the Fertakis Company revealed the overhead transactions shown below. Also assume that all overhead costs are debited to one general ledger controlling account—the Factory Overhead Control account—instead of individual overhead accounts.

May 25	Paid utility bill for three months, $1,420.
27	Recorded usage of indirect materials and supplies, $940.
June 21	Paid indirect labor wages, $2,190.
Aug. 12	Paid property taxes on factory building, $620.
Sept. 9	Recorded expiration of prepaid insurance premium, $560.
Nov. 27	Recorded depreciation on machinery and equipment for the year, $1,210.

These transactions resulted in the following entries:

May 25	Factory Overhead Control	1,420	
	Cash		1,420
	To record payment of 3-month utility bill		

27	Factory Overhead Control	940	
	Raw Materials (or Supplies) Inventory		940
	To record usage of indirect materials and supplies		
June 21	Factory Overhead Control	2,190	
	Factory Payroll		2,190
	To distribute indirect labor from factory payroll		
Aug. 12	Factory Overhead Control	620	
	Cash		620
	To record payment of property taxes on factory building		
Sept. 9	Factory Overhead Control	560	
	Prepaid Insurance		560
	To record expiration of insurance premiums		
Nov. 27	Factory Overhead Control	1,210	
	Accumulated Depreciation, Machinery and Equipment		1,210
	To record depreciation for the year		

The entries above do account for the incurrence of the actual overhead expenses, but they do not assist in the transfer of the costs to the Work in Process Inventory account. Such a transfer must take place before product unit costs can be computed. Here is where the use of a predetermined overhead rate is appropriate. Assume that the predetermined overhead rate for the period is $2.50 per direct labor hour. The following list of jobs completed during the period shows the related number of direct labor hours required per job and the overhead cost applied to each job.

Job	Direct Labor Hours	×	Rate	=	Overhead Applied
16-2	520		$2.50		$1,300
19-4	718		2.50		1,795
17-3	622		2.50		1,555
18-6	416		2.50		1,040
21-5	384		2.50		960
	2,660				$6,650

A sample of the journal entry used to record the application of overhead costs to jobs worked on during the period appears below. This entry transfers overhead costs to the Work in Process Inventory account and is normally made when payroll is recorded. Because of the relationship of overhead application to labor hours, overhead costs can be applied only after the number of labor hours is known. Weekly or monthly labor data were not available in our example; therefore, overhead is being applied to one entire job.

Mar. 2	Work in Process Inventory	1,300	
	Factory Overhead Applied		1,300
	To record application of overhead costs to Job 16-2		

Similar entries would be prepared for each job worked on during the period. After the posting of all the overhead transactions discussed above, the resulting general ledger account entries and balances are shown below.

Factory Overhead Control (Incurred)

Date	Debit	Credit
5/25	1,420	
5/27	940	
6/21	2,190	
8/12	620	
9/9	560	
11/27	1,210	
6,940		

Factory Overhead Applied

Debit	Job	Credit
	Job 16-2	1,300
	Job 19-4	1,795
	Job 17-3	1,555
	Job 18-6	1,040
	Job 21-5	960
	6,650	

At year end, these records of the Fertakis Company reveal that overhead has been *under*applied by $290 ($6,940 – $6,650). More actual overhead costs were incurred than were applied to products. The use of the predetermined overhead rate (anticipated rate was low) failed to apply all of the overhead costs incurred to the products produced. The $290 must now be added to the production costs of the period.

Two alternative courses of action are available to adjust the overhead account balance situation as described above. First, if the $290 difference is considered small or immaterial, or if most of the items worked on during the year have been sold, the entire amount can be charged to Cost of Goods Sold. This is the most commonly used approach because it is easy to apply. The adjusting entry would be:

Factory Overhead Applied	6,650	
Cost of Goods Sold	290	
Factory Overhead Control		6,940
To close out overhead accounts and to charge underapplied overhead to the Cost of Goods Sold account		

A second alternative is used if the amount of the adjustment needed to reconcile the two overhead accounts is large and the costs of the products worked on during the period are distributed at year end among the Work in Process Inventory, Finished Goods Inventory, and Cost of Goods Sold accounts. For example, assume that at year end the products that the Fertakis Company worked on during the year were located as follows: 30 percent in Work in Process Inventory, 20 percent in Finished Goods Inventory, and 50 percent sold. In such cases, the following entry would be made:

Factory Overhead Applied	6,650	
Cost of Goods Sold (50% of $290)	145	
Work in Process Inventory (30% of $290)	87	
Finished Goods Inventory (20% of $290)	58	
Factory Overhead Control		6,940
To close out overhead accounts and to account for underapplied factory overhead		

The breakdown of the $290 among the three accounts would be based on either the number of units worked on during the period or the direct labor hours incurred and attached to units within the three accounts. The illustrated problem at the end of the chapter provides additional guidance in the area of accounting procedures for underapplied or overapplied overhead.

Product Costing and Inventory Valuation

Objective 5 Explain the relationship between product costing and inventory valuation

One of the main objectives of cost accounting is to supply management with information about manufacturing costs of production. This information is useful for internal decision-making purposes, aids the accountant in controlling costs, and, through inventory valuation, forms the link between financial accounting and management accounting. All manufacturing costs incurred during the period must be accounted for within the year-end financial statements. However, not all of these costs will appear on the income statement. Only those costs assigned to units sold will be reported as part of the income statement. Costs assigned to units sold have "expired," or were used up in producing revenue. Costs assigned to unsold units (ending inventory) are "unexpired," or unused, costs. They are classified as assets and included in either the Work in Process Inventory or the Finished Goods Inventory on the balance sheet. Product unit cost information is necessary to determine end-of-period balances in the Work in Process Inventory and the Finished Goods Inventory as well as to compute the cost of goods sold.

The Job Order Cost System

Objective 6 Describe the cost flow in a job order cost accounting system

A job order cost system is designed to accumulate manufacturing costs for a specific order or batch of products and to aid in the computation of product unit costs. Decisions regarding price determination and production scheduling are based on information generated by a company's cost accounting system. For these reasons, it is necessary to maintain a system that generates timely, accurate product costing data. A job order cost system provides this information and also leads to the computation of the year-end balance in the Cost of Goods Sold account and the valuation of the ending Work in Process Inventory and Finished Goods Inventory.

Incurrence of Materials, Labor, and Factory Overhead Costs

A basic part of a job order cost system is the set of procedures and entries used to record the incurrence of materials, labor, and manufacturing overhead costs. As an aid in controlling these costs, businesses use various documents to support the costs involved in each transaction. The effective use of these procedures and documents promotes accounting accuracy and provides a smooth, efficient flow of cost information through the accounting record system. In addition, it is important to note that all inventory balances in a job order cost system are maintained on a perpetual basis.

Raw Materials The purchase, use, and storage of raw materials is very important to a company. Purchasing is important because if the company fails for some reason to anticipate its needs and does not place a timely purchase order, the manufacturing process will be forced to shut down. Shutting down production results in no products and many unhappy customers, and causes the company to lose sales and profits.

Raw materials usage patterns are important because the company should strive for efficient operations and try to avoid spoilage or excessive use of the materials. Proper raw materials usage can result in large cost savings, thereby enhancing profits and conserving production resources. Adequate storage space and orderly storage procedures are essential. Raw materials must be handled and stored properly to guarantee their satisfactory use in production. Proper records make it possible to find goods easily and minimize the problems resulting from lost or misplaced items.

In recording and controlling raw materials costs, accountants rely heavily on a cost accounting system supported by an integrated series of cost documents including the purchase request, purchase order, receiving report, inventory records, and raw materials requisition. Each of these documents is an important link to accounting for raw materials costs. Direct materials costs are traced to specific jobs or products. Costs of indirect materials and supplies are charged to manufacturing or factory overhead.

Labor Labor services are, in essence, purchased from employees working in the factory. In addition, other types of labor are purchased from people and organizations outside the company. However, the labor cost usually associated with the manufacturing function is that of factory personnel. Labor is one production resource that cannot be stored and used later. Therefore, it is extremely important to account for these costs properly and to identify them with units of productive output. Labor time cards and job cards provide the necessary documentation to record labor cost incurrence. The objective is to be able to trace costs of direct labor to specific jobs or products. Indirect labor costs are routed through the Manufacturing or Factory Overhead account.

Factory Overhead All indirect manufacturing costs are classified as factory overhead. Unlike with raw materials and direct labor, no specialized documents are used in recording overhead costs. Vendors' invoices support most payments. Factory depreciation expenses and usage of prepaid expenses are charged to the Factory Overhead account by use of journal entries. Overhead costs can be accounted for in separate accounts. However, because of their similarity and connection with products, a job order cost system employs a Factory Overhead Control account. All factory overhead costs are debited to this account, but separate subsidiary accounts are still maintained to account for each type of factory overhead cost. These separate accounts make up the **subsidiary ledger** to the Factory Overhead Control account.

Factory overhead costs, by nature, cannot be traced directly to jobs or products. Factory overhead costs are applied to products by means of the predetermined overhead rate. This process was discussed earlier and will be illustrated later in this chapter.

The Work in Process Inventory Account

Job order costing focuses on the flow of costs through the Work in Process Inventory account. All manufacturing costs incurred and charged to production are routed through Work in Process Inventory. Figure 24-2 illustrates cost flow in a job order cost system. Raw materials costs are debited to Work in Process Inventory, whereas indirect materials and supplies are debited to the Factory Overhead Control account. All labor costs traceable to specific jobs are debited to Work in Process Inventory. Indirect labor costs are charged against the Factory Overhead Control account. Individual factory overhead accounts are maintained and, if added together, would equal the Factory Overhead Control account balance. By means of a predetermined overhead rate and an allocation base, such as direct labor dollars or hours, overhead costs are applied to specific jobs by debiting Work in Process Inventory and crediting Factory Overhead Applied.

Attaching costs of raw materials, direct labor, and factory overhead to specific jobs and products is not an automatic process. Even though all manufacturing costs are debited to Work in Process Inventory, a separate accounting procedure is needed to link those costs to specific jobs. A

Figure 24-2
Job Order
Cost Flow

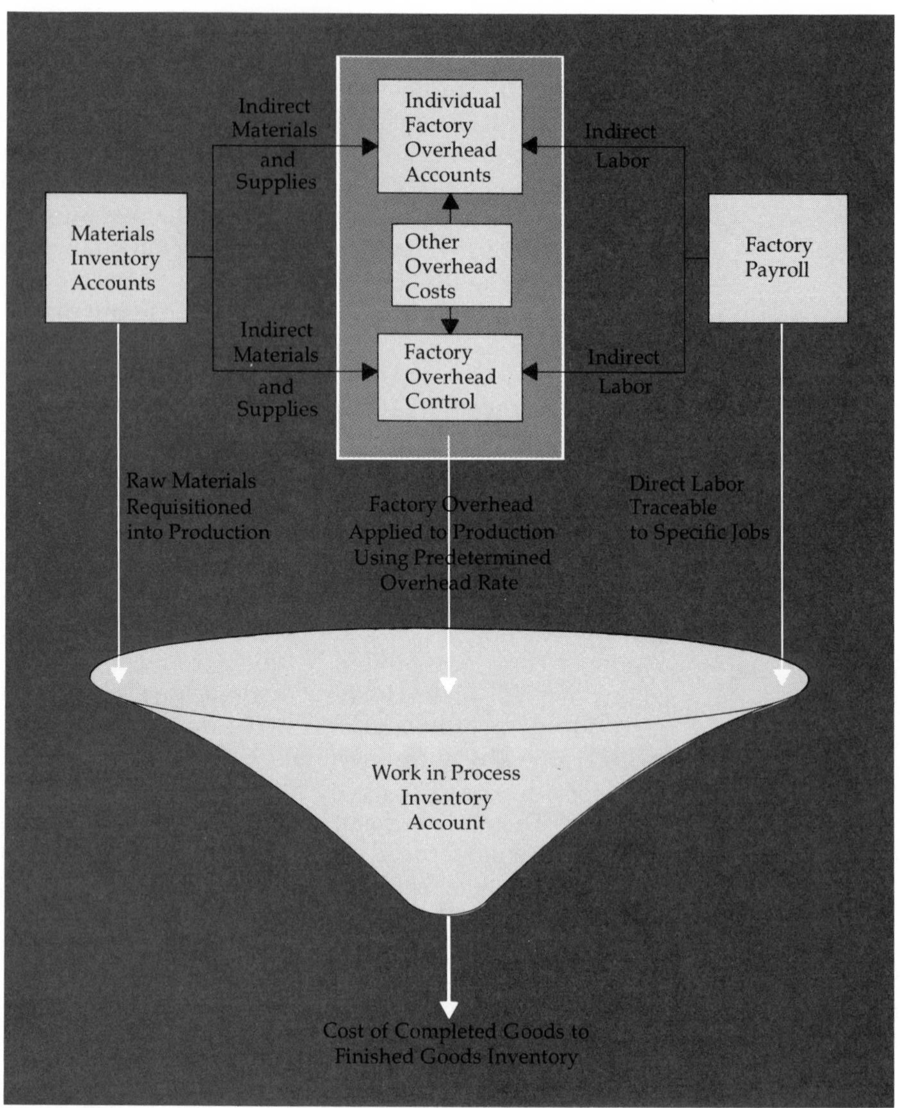

subsidiary ledger consisting of **job order cost cards** is used for this purpose. There is one job cost card for each job being worked on, and all costs of that job are accumulated on it. As costs are debited to Work in Process Inventory, they are reclassified by job and added to the respective job order cost cards.

A typical job order cost card is shown in Figure 24-3. On each card, space is provided for the accumulation of raw materials, direct labor, and factory overhead costs as well as for information concerning the job order number, product specifications, name of customer, date of order, projected completion date, and summary cost data. Job order cost cards for

Figure 24-3
Job Order
Cost Card

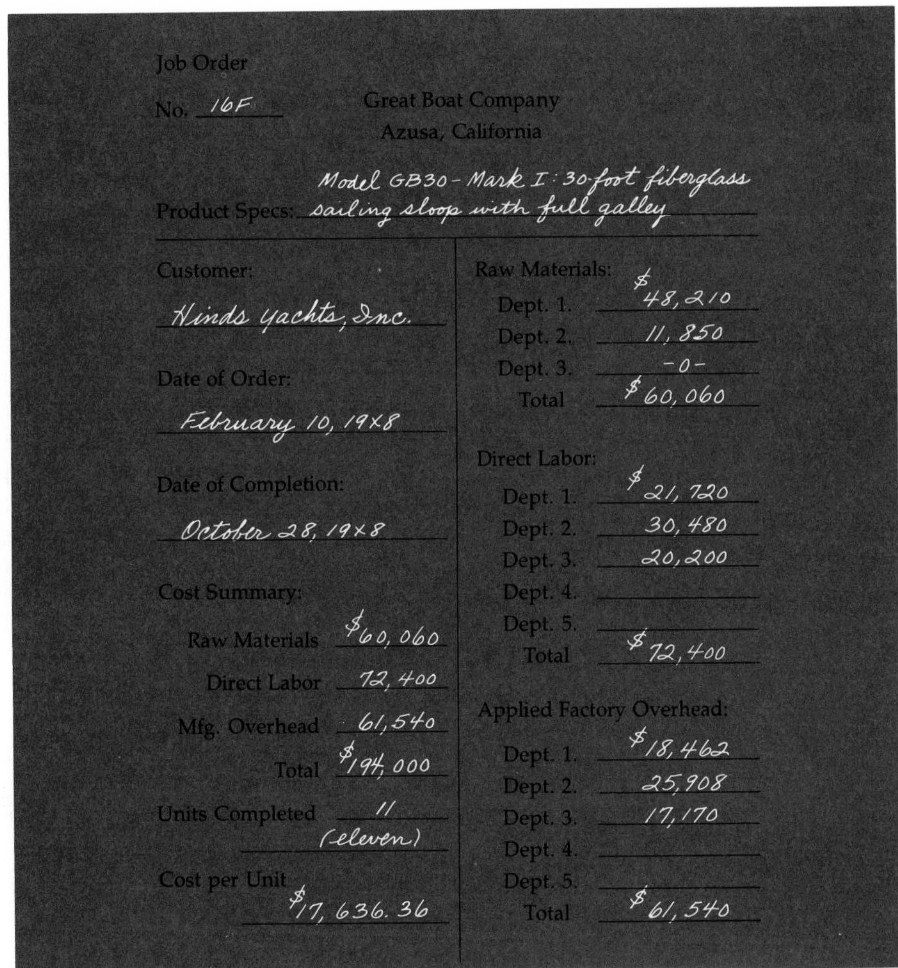

Job Order
No. 16F

Great Boat Company
Azusa, California

Product Specs: Model GB30 - Mark I: 30-foot fiberglass sailing sloop with full galley

Customer: Hinds Yachts, Inc.

Date of Order: February 10, 19X8

Date of Completion: October 28, 19X8

Cost Summary:

Raw Materials	$60,060
Direct Labor	72,400
Mfg. Overhead	61,540
Total	$194,000

Units Completed: 11 (eleven)

Cost per Unit: $17,636.36

Raw Materials:

Dept. 1.	$48,210
Dept. 2.	11,850
Dept. 3.	-0-
Total	$60,060

Direct Labor:

Dept. 1.	$21,720
Dept. 2.	30,480
Dept. 3.	20,200
Dept. 4.	
Dept. 5.	
Total	$72,400

Applied Factory Overhead:

Dept. 1.	$18,462
Dept. 2.	25,908
Dept. 3.	17,170
Dept. 4.	
Dept. 5.	
Total	$61,540

uncompleted jobs make up the subsidiary ledger for the Work in Process Inventory Control account. The ending balance in the Work in Process Inventory Control account is reconciled by comparing it with the total of the costs assigned and shown on the individual job order cost cards.

Accounting for Finished Goods

When a job has been completed, all costs assigned to that particular job order are transferred to Finished Goods Inventory. This is accomplished in the accounting records by debiting the Finished Goods Inventory account and crediting the Work in Process Inventory account. When this entry is made, the job order cost card should be removed from the subsidiary ledger file and used to help update the Finished Goods Inventory records.

Upon shipment, the order is recorded as a sale. In addition to debiting Accounts Receivable and crediting Sales for the entire selling price, it is necessary to account for the goods shipped. The proper procedure is to debit Cost of Goods Sold and to credit Finished Goods Inventory for the cost of the goods shipped.

You must supplement the above description of the job order system with an analysis of transactions and related journal entries if you are to learn the mechanics of operating the system. While studying the journal entry analysis, review the preceding paragraphs. Try to keep the cost flow concept shown in Figure 24-2 in mind.

Journal Entry Analysis

Objective 7 Journalize transactions within a job order costing system

Because emphasis in a job order cost system is on cost flow, it is important to know and understand the journal entries used to record the incurrence of the various costs and the entries that transfer costs from one account to another. In fact, these entries, along with job order cost cards and other subsidiary ledgers for raw materials and finished goods inventories, make up a major part of the job order cost system. In our analysis of the Great Boat Company, as each area is covered, we will first describe the related transaction. We will follow with the journal entry needed to record the transaction. A discussion of the unique features of the transaction or the accounts being used will conclude each section. Figure 24-4 illustrates the entire job order cost flow through the general ledger. Supporting subsidiary ledgers are also shown. As each entry is discussed, trace its number and related debits or credits to Figure 24-4.

Raw Materials Purchased The recording of raw materials purchases will introduce the differences between journal entries used in the perpetual inventory approach and those used when periodic inventories were maintained. For example, a company purchased the following raw materials: Material SX for $28,600 and Material 14Q for $17,000.

Entry 1:	Raw Materials Inventory Control	45,600	
	Accounts Payable (or Cash)		45,600
	To record purchase of $28,600 of Material SX and $17,000 of Material 14Q		

Raw materials purchases are recorded at cost in the Raw Materials Inventory Control account. This procedure differs in several ways from the recording of purchases discussed previously in this text. First, the debit is to an inventory account instead of a purchases account because a perpetual inventory system is being maintained. All costs of raw materials flow through the inventory account. A second difference in our entry above is the use of a **control** or **controlling account.** The term *control* means that the account is an accumulation of several individual account balances. Some companies have hundreds of items in inventory. To maintain a separate account for each item in the general ledger would make the ledger unwieldy and difficult to work with. A control account is used in each area where several similar items are being accounted for and only one cumulative total appears in the general ledger. Each control account is supported by a subsidiary ledger containing all the individual account balances. At the time that entry 1 is posted to the general ledger, the individual accounts in the materials ledger are also updated (see Figure 24-4).

Purchase of Supplies The following transaction and entry involve the purchase of supplies for production: The company purchased $4,100 of operating supplies for the manufacturing process.

		Debit	Credit
Entry 2:	Raw Materials Inventory Control	4,100	
	Accounts Payable (or Cash)		4,100
	To record the purchase of operating supplies		

The procedures used to account for the purchase of supplies are much like those used to record raw materials purchases. Supplies Inventory, in our example, is assumed to be one subsidiary account making up the total Raw Materials Inventory Control account. However, if the supplies inventory is large, a separate general ledger account may be used. If such costs are very small, they can be treated as expenses when incurred and not debited to an inventory account. Whichever method is selected, the accountant should be able to provide reasons to support the approach taken and then follow this approach consistently.

Requisitioning of Raw Materials and Supplies Upon receipt of a properly prepared materials requisition form, the following raw materials and supplies are issued from inventory to production: Material SX for $62,000, Material 14Q for $32,000, and operating supplies for $4,800.

		Debit	Credit
Entry 3:	Work in Process Inventory Control	94,000	
	Factory Overhead Control	4,800	
	Raw Materials Inventory Control		98,800
	To record issuance of $62,000 of Material SX, $32,000 of Material 14Q, and $4,800 of operating supplies into production		

The entry above indicates that $94,000 of direct materials and $4,800 of indirect materials were issued. The debit to the Work in Process Inventory Control account records the cost of raw materials (direct materials) issued to production. Such costs are directly traceable to specific job orders. As the direct materials costs are charged to work in process, amounts traceable to individual jobs are entered on the job order cost cards. As shown in Figure 24-4, $51,900 of raw materials were used on Job 16F, and raw materials costing $42,100 were traceable to Job 23H. Indirect materials costs (supplies) are debited to the Factory Overhead Control account.

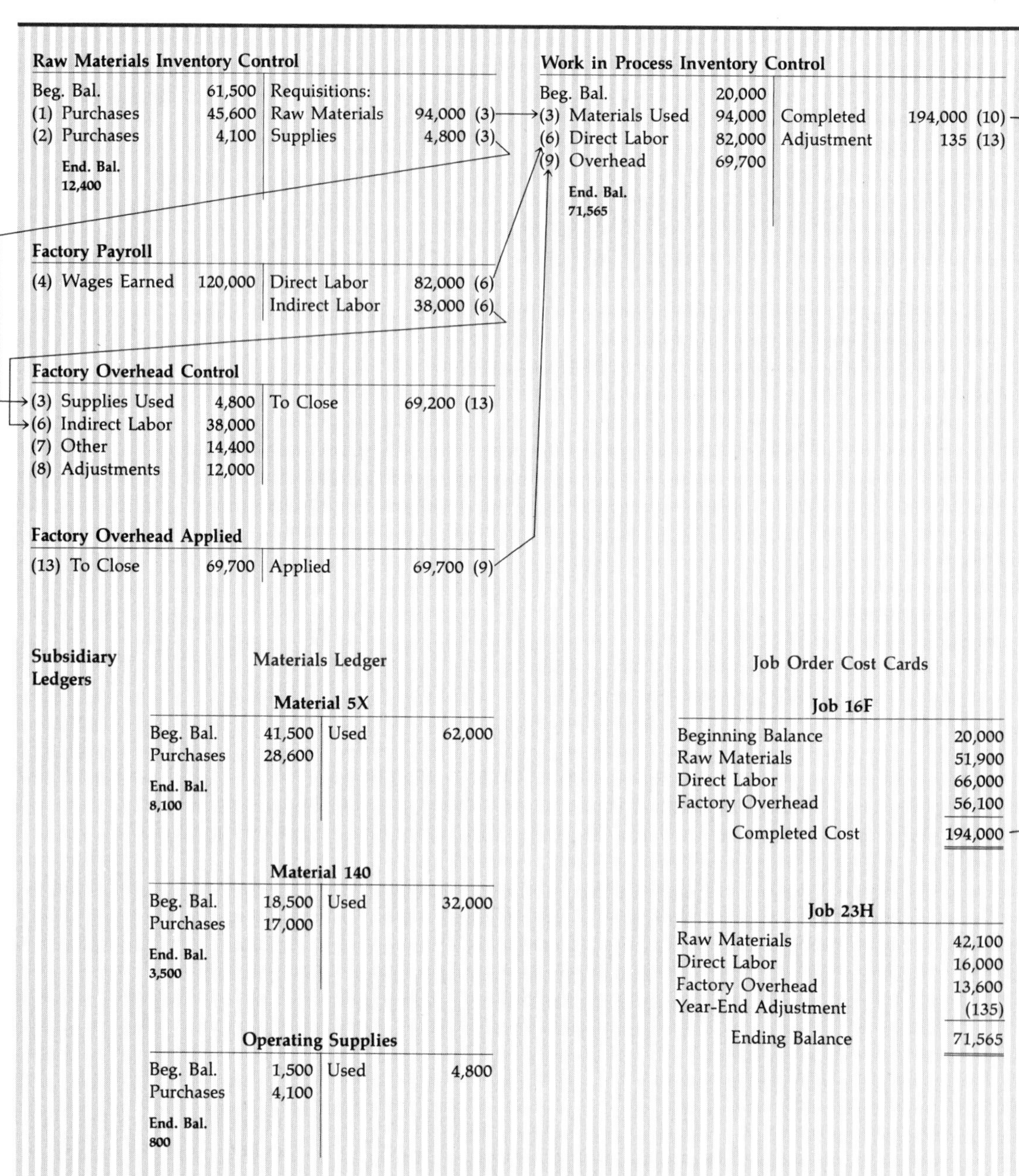

Figure 24-4
The Job Order Cost System

Labor Costs Recording labor costs for a manufacturing company involves three journal entries. Chapter 12 illustrated and discussed journal entries to record payroll for a merchandising company. The procedures for recording payroll for a manufacturing company are more complex, but the same basic payroll documents and transactions apply. In accounting for factory labor costs, however, some new account titles are necessary, and these costs must be assigned to specific products and jobs. The first labor cost entry records the actual payroll liability of the company. Although only $107,640 of net earnings are to be paid to employees, the gross direct

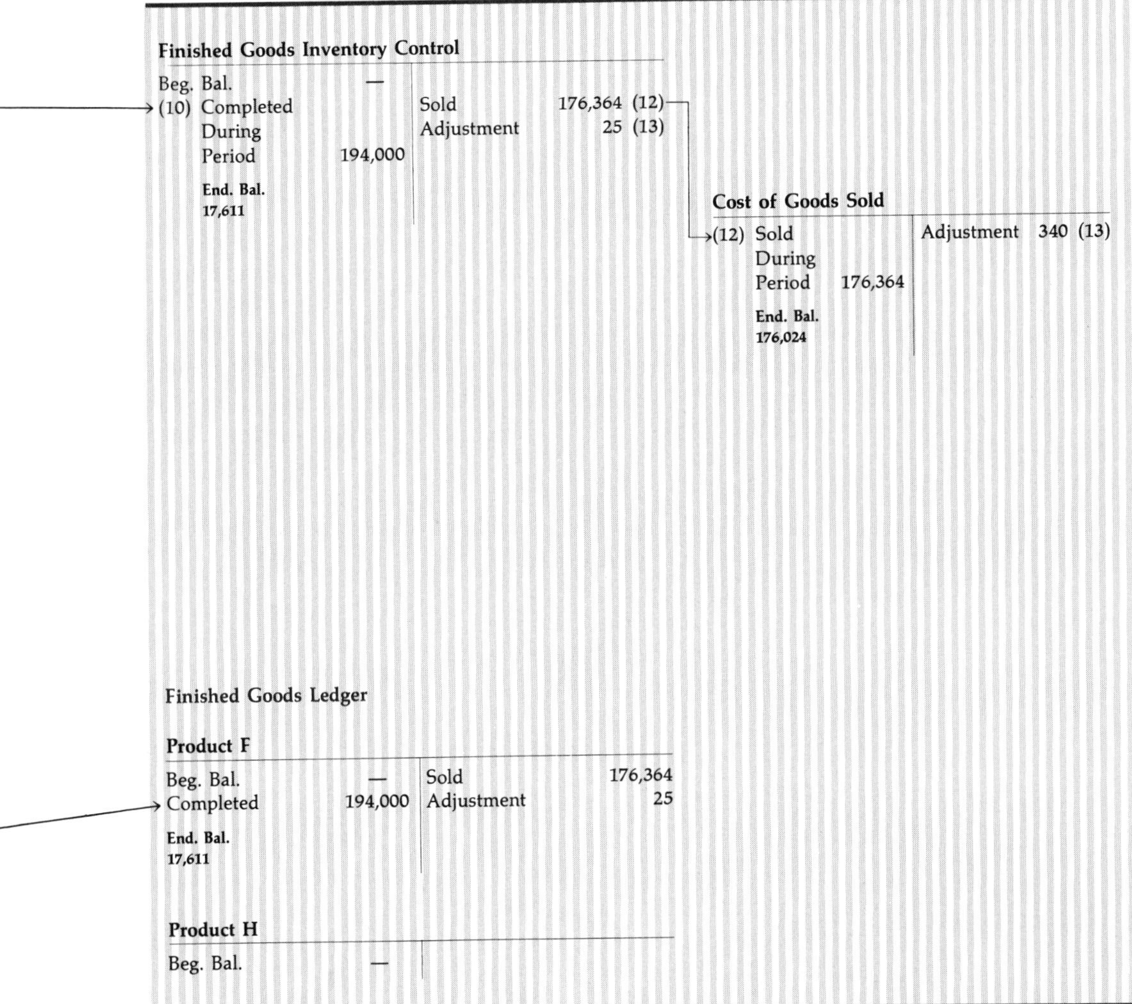

Figure 24-4 (continued)

and indirect labor costs will be used for product and job costing purposes. In this transaction, payroll liability for the period was recorded using the following information: gross direct labor wages, $82,000; gross indirect labor wages, $38,000; gross administrative salaries, $36,000; FICA (social security) taxes withheld, $9,360; federal income taxes withheld, $39,000.

Entry 4:	Factory Payroll	120,000	
	Administrative Salaries Expense	36,000	
	FICA Taxes Payable		9,360
	Federal Income Taxes Payable		39,000
	Wages and Salaries Payable		107,640
	To record payroll liability for the period		

A follow-up entry is now needed to account properly for labor costs.

This entry, Entry 5, will record the payment of the payroll liability established in Entry 4. In this transaction, payroll checks for the period were prepared and distributed to the employees.

Entry 5:	Wages and Salaries Payable	107,640	
	Cash		107,640
	To record payment of payroll		

The total payroll dollars of factory personnel debited initially to the Factory Payroll account must be distributed to the production accounts. In the journal entry for labor distribution, gross direct labor costs are debited to Work in Process Inventory Control, and total indirect wages (including factory supervisory salaries) are debited to Factory Overhead Control. This transaction is the distribution of factory payroll costs to the production accounts.

Entry 6:	Work in Process Inventory Control	82,000	
	Factory Overhead Control	38,000	
	Factory Payroll		120,000
	To record the distribution of factory payroll to production accounts		

In addition, the direct labor costs are accumulated by job and recorded on the individual job order cost cards. This distribution of $66,000 to Job 16F and $16,000 to Job 23H is shown in Figure 24-4.

Other Factory Overhead Costs As factory overhead costs other than indirect materials and labor charges are incurred, they are charged (debited) to the Factory Overhead Control account, and are individually identified in the explanation of the journal entry. Specifically, in this transaction, factory overhead costs including electricity costs of $3,100, maintenance and repair costs of $8,400, insurance costs of $1,300, and property taxes of $1,600 were paid.

Entry 7:	Factory Overhead Control	14,400	
	Cash		14,400
	To record incurrence of the following overhead costs: electricity, $3,100; maintenance and repair, $8,400; insurance expense, $1,300; and property taxes, $1,600		

From the information in the journal entry's explanation, individual subsidiary ledger accounts are updated and maintained. Because of the amount of information already included in Figure 24-4, the subsidiary ledger for the Factory Overhead Control account was not illustrated.

However, the subsidiary ledger would include individual accounts for each type of factory overhead cost and would be accounted for in much the same manner as described for the materials ledger and the job order cost cards.

The next transaction is an adjusting entry required to record depreciation on factory equipment for the period.

Entry 8:	Factory Overhead Control	12,000	
	Accumulated Depreciation, Equipment		12,000
	To record depreciation on factory equipment for the period		

This entry is out of sequence because it usually is prepared as an adjusting entry after all transactions for the period have been recorded. We have illustrated its recording at this point because depreciation of factory equipment is a part of total factory overhead cost. The actual Depreciation Expense account will be part of the overhead subsidiary ledger.

Factory Overhead Applied Factory overhead is applied by using a predetermined overhead rate and an allocation base (direct labor hours, direct labor dollars, machine hours, or units of output). Thus, in this transaction, by using a rate of 85 percent of direct labor dollars, factory overhead costs were applied to production.

Entry 9:	Work in Process Inventory Control	69,700	
	Factory Overhead Applied		69,700
	To apply factory overhead costs to production		

The amount of overhead charged to production is computed by multiplying the overhead rate by the units of the base. In our example, we computed the overhead to be applied by taking 85 percent of the direct labor dollars ($82,000), which gave us $69,700 ($82,000 × .85). This amount was debited to the Work in Process Inventory Control account. Because the overhead application is related to direct labor dollars, the job order cost cards can be updated by using the procedure described above. Job 16F is assigned $56,100 ($66,000 × .85) of overhead costs, and Job 23H receives a charge of $13,600 ($16,000 × .85). These amounts have been posted to the job order cost cards in Figure 24-4.

Accounting for Completed Units As various job orders are completed, their costs are transferred to the Finished Goods Inventory Control account. In this case, goods costing $194,000—Job 16F—were completed and transferred to finished goods inventory.

		Debit	Credit
Entry 10:	Finished Goods Inventory Control	194,000	
	Work in Process Inventory Control		194,000
	To record transfer of completed goods from work in process inventory to finished goods inventory		

Costs summarized on the job order cost card are used to compute unit costs and to determine the amount of the transfer entry. When a job is completed, its job order cost card is pulled from the Work in Process subsidiary ledger and used to help update the Finished Goods ledger.

Accounting for Units Sold The final phase of manufacturing cost flow is the transfer of costs from the Finished Goods Inventory Control account to the Cost of Goods Sold account. At this point, a major portion of Job 16F was shipped to the customer. The selling price for the goods shipped was $260,000, and the cost to manufacture these products totaled $176,364.

		Debit	Credit
Entry 11:	Accounts Receivable	260,000	
	Sales		260,000
	To record sale of portion of Job 16F		
Entry 12:	Cost of Goods Sold	176,364	
	Finished Goods Inventory Control		176,364
	To record the transfer of the cost of the shipped goods from Finished Goods Inventory to Cost of Goods Sold		

Both the entry to record the sale and the entry to establish the cost of the sale are shown above. Entry 12 is made at the same time that the sale is recorded. When the costs of the product sold are transferred out of the Finished Goods Inventory Control account, the finished goods ledger (subsidiary ledger) should also be updated, as shown in Figure 24-4.

Overhead Disposition At the end of an accounting period, the Factory Overhead Control account and the Factory Overhead Applied account must be totaled and an entry made to close these accounts and dispose of any underapplied or overapplied overhead.

		Debit	Credit
Entry 13:	Factory Overhead Applied	69,700	
	Work in Process Inventory Control		135
	Finished Goods Inventory Control		25
	Cost of Goods Sold		340
	Factory Overhead Control		69,200
	To close out factory overhead account balances and to dispose of the overapplied balance		

In this transaction, Factory overhead has been overapplied by $500; therefore, the Factory Overhead Control and Factory Overhead Applied accounts are closed and the difference is apportioned between Work in Process Inventory Control, Finished Goods Inventory Control, Cost of Goods Sold on the basis of each account's balance prior to the adjustment.

The following T account summaries show the current overhead account balances related to the journal entry example above.

Factory Overhead Control			Factory Overhead Applied		
(3)	4,800			(9)	69,700
(6)	38,000				
(7)	14,400				
(8)	12,000				
	69,200				69,700

Overhead has been overapplied by $500 ($69,700 − $69,200). This amount can be either credited to the Cost of Goods Sold account or distributed among the Work in Process Inventory Control, Finished Goods Inventory Control, and Cost of Goods Sold accounts. We have assumed that the amount is significant and is to be distributed to the three accounts on the basis of the ending balances in the respective accounts (see Figure 24-4). The following analysis explains how the distribution amounts were computed:

Account	Ending Balance	Percentage of Each to Total	×	Amount to Be Allocated	=	Allocation of Overapplied Overhead
Work in Process Inventory Control	$ 71,700	27		$500		$135
Finished Goods Inventory Control	14,000	5		500		25
Cost of Goods Sold	180,000	68		500		340
Totals	$265,700	100				$500

After Entry 13 has been posted to the general ledger, the accounts affected will appear similar to those shown in Figure 24-4. In addition, all subsidiary ledgers affected by the overhead adjustment must be updated. In our example, the entire $135 of adjustment to Work in Process was credited to Job 23H. Because Job 16F had been completed, its share of the adjustment was assigned to the Finished Goods Inventory Control and the Cost of Goods Sold accounts.

Computing Product Unit Costs

The process of computing product **unit cost** is relatively simple within a job order costing system. All costs of raw materials, direct labor, and factory overhead for each job are recorded on its job order cost card as the

Objective 8
Compute product unit cost for a specific job order

job progresses. When the job is completed, all costs accumulated on the job order cost card are totaled. The unit cost is then computed by dividing total manufacturing costs for the job by the number of good units produced. Job 16F was completed as part of our journal entry analysis above, and its cost data are summarized on the job order cost card shown in Figure 24-3. Eleven sailing sloops were produced at a total cost of $194,000. As shown, this results in a cost of $17,636 per sloop. Note in Figure 24-4 that only ten of the sloops were shipped to Hinds Yachts, Inc., during the year. One still remains in Finished Goods Inventory Control.

Fully and Partially Completed Products

Within a job order costing system, manufacturing costs are accumulated, classified, and reclassified several times. As products near completion, all manufacturing costs necessary for their production are linked to them. These costs then follow the product as it is transferred first to Finished Goods Inventory Control and then to Cost of Goods Sold. Figure 24-4 illustrates the accounting procedures and cost flows of units worked on during the period. Dollar amounts represent postings from the journal entries discussed above.

At period end, some costs remain in the Work in Process Inventory Control and the Finished Goods Inventory Control accounts. The ending balance of $71,565 in Work in Process Inventory Control represents costs attached to partially completed units in Job 23H. These costs can be traced to the specific job order cost card for partially completed jobs in the subsidiary ledger. Finished Goods Inventory Control also has an ending balance. Of all goods completed during the period, items totaling $17,611 (after the adjustment) from Job 16F were not sold and shipped. They now comprise the ending Finished Goods Inventory Control balance.

Chapter Review

Review of Learning Objectives

1. Distinguish between job order costing and process costing.
Although both job order costing and process costing are basic, traditional approaches to product cost accounting, they have different characteristics. A job order costing system is used in the manufacturing of unique or special-order products in which raw materials, direct labor, and manufacturing overhead costs are assigned to specific job orders or batches of products. In computing unit costs, the total manufacturing cost assigned to each job order is divided by the number of good units produced for that order. A process costing system is used by companies that produce a large number of similar products or have a continuous production flow. In either case, it is more economical to account for product-related costs for a period of time (week or month) rather than to try to identify them with specific products or job orders. Unit costs are computed by dividing total manufacturing costs assigned to a particular department or work center during a week or month by the number of good units produced by that department during that time period.

2. Describe the concept of absorption costing.

Absorption costing is an approach to product costing that assigns a representative portion of *all* manufacturing costs to individual products. This means that costs of direct materials, direct labor, variable manufacturing overhead, and fixed manufacturing overhead are assigned to products.

3. Compute a predetermined overhead rate, and use this rate to apply overhead costs to production.

A predetermined overhead rate is computed by dividing total estimated overhead costs for a period by the total activity basis expected for that same time period. Factory overhead costs are assigned or applied to specific job orders by multiplying the predetermined overhead rate by the amount of the activity base (such as labor hours) used for that particular job order.

4. Dispose of underapplied or overapplied overhead.

If any difference exists between the balances in the Factory Overhead Control and Factory Overhead Applied accounts at year end, there are two alternative courses of action for eliminating that difference. If the difference is small, it should be adjusted to the Cost of Goods Sold account. If the amount of the adjustment is large and if the costs of the products worked on during the period are spread among the Work in Process Inventory, Finished Goods Inventory, and Cost of Goods Sold accounts, the difference should be assigned proportionately to these three accounts.

5. Explain the relationship between product costing and inventory valuation.

Product costing techniques are necessary to attach costs to job orders or units of product worked on during a given time period. At period end when financial statements are prepared, these product costs are used in costing the Work in Process and Finished Goods inventories.

6. Describe the cost flow in a job order cost accounting system.

A job order cost accounting system generally follows the concept of absorption costing and operates by using the perpetual approach to inventory maintenance and valuation. Within these limits, raw materials and supplies costs are first debited to the Raw Materials Inventory Control account, labor costs are debited to the Factory Payroll account, and the various manufacturing overhead costs are debited to the Factory Overhead Control account. As the products are being manufactured, costs of raw materials and direct labor are transferred to the Work in Process Inventory Control account. Factory overhead costs are applied and charged to the Work in Process Inventory Control account by using a predetermined overhead rate. These overhead cost charges are credited to the Factory Overhead Applied account. When products or jobs are completed, the costs assigned to them are transferred to the Finished Goods Inventory Control account. These same costs are transferred to the Cost of Goods Sold account when the products are sold and shipped.

7. Journalize transactions within a job order costing system.

Mastery of a job order costing system requires that the user be able to prepare journal entries for each of the following transactions: (a) purchase of raw materials, (b) purchase of operating supplies, (c) requisition of raw materials and supplies into production, (d) recording of payroll liability, (e) payment of payroll to employees, (f) distribution of factory payroll to production accounts, (g) incurrence of overhead costs paid in cash, (h) recording of noncash overhead costs such as depreciation of factory and equipment, (i) application of factory overhead costs to production, (j) transfer of costs of completed jobs from the Work in Process Inventory Control account to the Finished Goods Inventory Control account, (k) recording of sales of jobs and transfer of costs related to the goods sold from the Finished Goods Inventory Control account to the Cost of Goods Sold account, and (l) disposition of underapplied or overapplied factory overhead.

8. Compute product unit cost for a specific job order.
Product costs in a job order costing system are computed by first totaling all the manufacturing costs accumulated on a particular job order cost card. This amount is then divided by the number of good units produced for that job to find the individual unit cost for the order. Unit cost information is entered on the job order cost card and used for inventory valuation purposes.

Review Problem
Journal Entry Analysis—Job Order System

The McBride Manufacturing Company produces "uniframe" desk and chair assemblies and study carrels for libraries. The firm uses a job order cost system and a current factory overhead application rate of 220 percent of direct labor dollars. The following transactions and events took place during September 19xx:

Sept. 4 Received raw materials costing $9,540. Purchased on account.
7 The production department requisitioned $2,700 of raw materials and $650 of operating supplies.
14 Gross factory payroll of $16,000 was paid to factory personnel. Of this amount, $11,500 represents direct labor and the remaining amount is indirect labor. (Prepare only the entry to distribute factory payroll to production accounts.)
14 Factory overhead costs were applied to production.
16 Received supplies costing $3,500 and raw materials costing $17,000 that were ordered on 9/11/xx and purchased on account. Both items are inventoriable.
20 Requisitioned $9,000 of raw materials and $1,750 of supplies for production.
26 Paid the following overhead costs: heat, light, and power, $1,400; repairs by outside firm, $1,600; and property taxes, $2,700.
28 Gross factory payroll of $15,600 was earned by factory personnel. Of this amount, indirect wages and supervisory salaries totaled $6,400. Prepare only the entry to distribute factory payroll to production accounts.
28 Factory overhead costs were applied to production.
29 Completed units costing $67,500 were transferred to Finished Goods Inventory.
30 Depreciation of plant and equipment for September was $24,000. During the same period, $1,200 of prepaid fire insurance expired.
30 Library carrel units costing $32,750 were shipped to a customer for a total selling price of $53,710.

Required

1. Record the journal entries for all of the above transactions and events.
2. Assume that the beginning balances were $4,700, $6,200, and $9,000 in Raw

Materials Inventory Control, Work in Process Inventory Control, and Finished Goods Inventory Control, respectively. Compute the ending balances in these inventory accounts.

3. Determine the amount of underapplied or overapplied overhead.

4. If 131 carrels were included in the order sold and shipped on September 30, compute the cost and selling price per carrel shipped.

Answer to Review Problem

1. Required journal entries:

			Debit	Credit
Sept.	4	Raw Materials Inventory Control	9,540	
		Accounts Payable		9,540
		To record purchase of raw materials on account		
	7	Work in Process Inventory Control	2,700	
		Factory Overhead Control	650	
		Raw Materials Inventory Control		3,350
		To record requisition of raw materials and supplies into production		
	14	Work in Process Inventory Control	11,500	
		Factory Overhead Control	4,500	
		Factory Payroll		16,000
		To distribute payroll to production accounts		
	14	Work in Process Inventory Control	25,300	
		Factory Overhead Applied		25,300
		To apply factory overhead costs to production ($11,500 × 220%)		
	16	Raw Materials Inventory Control	20,500	
		Accounts Payable		20,500
		To record purchase of $3,500 of operating supplies and $17,000 of raw materials		
	20	Work in Process Inventory Control	9,000	
		Factory Overhead Control	1,750	
		Raw Materials Inventory Control		10,750
		To record requisition of raw materials and supplies into production		
	26	Factory Overhead Control	5,700	
		Cash		5,700
		To record payment of the following overhead costs: heat, light, and power, $1,400; outside repairs, $1,600; property taxes, $2,700		

Date	Account	Debit	Credit
28	Work in Process Inventory Control	9,200	
	Factory Overhead Control	6,400	
	Factory Payroll		15,600
	To distribute payroll to production accounts		
28	Work in Process Inventory Control	20,240	
	Factory Overhead Applied		20,240
	To apply factory overhead costs to production ($9,200 × 220%)		
29	Finished Goods Inventory Control	67,500	
	Work in Process Inventory Control		67,500
	To transfer costs of completed goods to Finished Goods Inventory		
30	Factory Overhead Control	25,200	
	Accumulated Depreciation, Plant and Equipment		24,000
	Prepaid Insurance		1,200
	To charge Factory Overhead Control with expired asset costs		
30	Accounts Receivable	53,710	
	Sales		53,710
	To record sales for November		
30	Cost of Goods Sold	32,750	
	Finished Goods Inventory Control		32,750
	To record transfer of costs from Finished Goods Inventory to Cost of Goods Sold		

2. Ending balances of inventory accounts computed.

Raw Materials Inventory Control

	Debit		Credit
Beg. Bal.	4,700	9/7	3,350
9/4	9,540	9/20	10,750
9/16	20,500		
End. Bal. 20,640			

Work in Process Inventory Control

	Debit		Credit
Beg. Bal.	6,200	9/29	67,500
9/7	2,700		
9/14	11,500		
9/14	25,300		
9/20	9,000		
9/28	9,200		
9/28	20,240		
End. Bal. 16,640			

Finished Goods Inventory Control

Beg. Bal.	9,000	9/30	32,750
9/29	67,500		
End. Bal.			
43,750			

3. Underapplied or overapplied overhead determined.

Factory Overhead Control

9/7	650	
9/14	4,500	
9/20	1,750	
9/26	5,700	
9/28	6,400	
9/30	25,200	
Bal.		
44,200		

Factory Overhead Applied

	9/14	25,300
	9/28	20,240
	Bal.	
	45,540	

Factory overhead is overapplied by $1,340 ($45,540 – $44,200).

4. Cost and selling price per unit computed:

Cost per unit: $32,750 ÷ 131 = $250 per unit
Selling price per unit: $53,710 ÷ 131 = $410 per unit

Chapter Assignments

Questions

1. Identify the common objective of a job order cost system and a process cost system.
2. Explain the concept of absorption costing.
3. Upon what factors does the success of applying overhead to products and job orders depend?
4. What is meant by underapplied or overapplied overhead?
5. Describe two alternative courses of action to adjust for an underapplied or overapplied overhead situation.
6. "Some costs of raw materials, direct labor, and factory overhead used during the period will be reported in the company's income statement, and some will be reported in the company's balance sheet." Discuss the accuracy of this statement.
7. Differentiate between a job order cost system and a process cost system. (Concentrate on the characteristics of each system.)
8. Explain why timely purchasing is a "do or die" function within a company.
9. How does raw materials usage influence the efficiency of operations?
10. "Purchased labor resource services cannot be stored." Discuss this statement.
11. Discuss the role of the Work in Process Inventory account in a job order cost system.
12. What is the purpose of a job order cost card? Identify the types of information recorded on such a card.
13. Define the terms *control account* and *subsidiary ledger*. How are they related?

14. Cost and management accounting are often overshadowed by the more publicized financial accounting sector. Describe the importance of a product costing system to (a) the preparation of financial statements, and (b) profitability.

Classroom Exercises

Exercise 24-1 Concept of Absorption Costing

Using the absorption costing concept, determine product unit cost from these costs incurred during March: $2,500 in Liability Insurance, Factory; $1,900 in Rent Expense, Sales Office; $3,100 in Depreciation Expense, Factory Equipment; $19,650 in Raw Materials Used; $2,480 in Indirect Labor, Factory; $980 in Factory Supplies; $1,410 in Heat, Light, and Power, Factory; $1,600 in Fire Insurance, Factory; $3,250 in Depreciation Expense, Sales Equipment; $2,850 in Rent Expense, Factory; $27,420 in Direct Labor; $2,100 in Manager's Salary, Factory; $4,800 in President's Salary; $7,250 in Sales Commissions; $1,975 in Advertising Expense. The Inspection Department reported that 75,400 units were produced during March.

Exercise 24-2 Overhead Application Rate

Versack Datatrans specializes in the analysis and reporting of complex inventory costing projects. Raw materials costs are minimal, consisting entirely of operating supplies such as data processing cards, inventory sheets, and other recording tools. Labor is the highest single expense item, totaling $392,525 for 120,700 hours of work in 19x4. Factory overhead costs for 19x4 were $766,445, and this amount was applied to specific jobs on the basis of labor hours worked.

In 19x5, the company anticipates a 20 percent increase in overhead costs. The number of hours worked during 19x5 is expected to increase 25 percent.

1. Determine the total amount of factory overhead anticipated by the company in 19x5.
2. Compute the overhead application rate for 19x5. (Round answer to nearest penny.)
3. During April 19x5, the following jobs were completed, with the related hours worked: Job 16A4, 1,490 hours; Job 21C2, 6,220 hours; and Job 17H3, 3,270 hours. Prepare the journal entry required to apply overhead costs to operations for April.

Exercise 24-3 Disposition of Underapplied Overhead (Extension of Exercise 24-2)

At the end of 19x5, Versack Datatrans had compiled a total of 150,250 hours worked. The actual overhead incurred was $924,800 during the year.

1. Determine the total amount of overhead applied to operations during 19x5.
2. Compute the amount of underapplied overhead for the year.
3. Prepare the journal entry to close out the overhead accounts and to dispose of the underapplied overhead amount for 19x5, assuming that the amount is not significant.

Exercise 24-4 Disposition of Overapplied Overhead

The Shields Manufacturing Company ended the year with a total of $1,340 of overapplied overhead. Because management considers this amount to be significant, this favorable difference should be distributed among the three appropriate accounts in proportion to their ending balances. The ending account balances are Raw Materials Inventory Control, $19,540; Work in Process Inventory Control, $16,776; Finished Goods Inventory Control, $43,804; Cost of Goods Sold, $32,620; Factory Overhead Control, $17,450; and Factory Overhead Applied, $18,790.

Using good form, close out the factory overhead accounts, and dispose of the overapplied overhead. Show your work in journal entry form, and support your computations.

Exercise 24-5 Cost System—Industry Linkage

State which of the following types of production activities would normally use a job order costing system, and which would use a process costing system: (a) paint manufacturing, (b) automobile manufacturing, (c) 747 jet aircraft manufacturing, (d) brick manufacturing, (e) manufacturing of large milling machines, (f) liquid detergent manufacturing, (g) production of aluminum compressed-gas cylinders, standard size and capacity, (h) production of aluminum compressed-gas cylinders, special fiberglass-overwrapped design for Mount Everest expedition, (i) manufacture of nails from wire, (j) manufacture of television sets, (k) printing of wedding invitations, (l) limited edition of lithographs, (m) manufacture of flea collars, (n) manufacture of high-speed lathes with special-order thread drills, (o) manufacture of breakfast cereal, (p) manufacture of original evening gown.

Exercise 24-6 Job Order Cost Flow

The three manufacturing cost elements—raw materials, direct labor, and manufacturing overhead—flow through a job order cost system in a structured, orderly fashion. Specific general ledger accounts, subsidiary ledgers, and source documents are used to verify and record the cost information.

In paragraph and in diagrammatic form, describe cost flow in a job order cost accounting system.

Exercise 24-7 Work in Process Account—Journal Entry Analysis

On June 1, there was a $26,430 beginning balance in the Work in Process Inventory account of the Broussard Specialty Company. A summary of the production activity for June is as follows: (a) Raw materials costing $126,200, along with $15,820 of operating supplies, were requisitioned for production. (b) Total factory payroll for June was $167,490, of which $39,990 represented payments for indirect labor. (Assume payroll has been recorded but not distributed to production accounts.) (c) Factory overhead was applied at a rate of 75 percent of direct labor cost.

1. Prepare journal entries to record the materials, labor, and overhead costs for June.
2. Compute the ending balance in the Work in Process Inventory Control account, assuming a transfer of $346,800 to the Finished Goods Inventory Control account during the period.

Exercise 24-8 Journal Entries—Completed Units

A special order of 688 units costing $84,624 was completed on June 16 and the costs were transferred to the Finished Goods Inventory Control account. On June 30, these same goods were shipped to a customer, and the billing for them totaled $113,520.

1. Using good journal entry form, record these June transactions.
2. Compute the unit cost and the unit selling price.

Problem Set A

Problem 24A-1 Ending Inventory Balances

Records of Wallbank Enterprises revealed the following inventory balances on July 1: Raw Materials Inventory Control, $26,700; Work in Process Inventory Control, $18,890; and Finished Goods Inventory Control, $21,400. A summary of transactions and related information for July is given on the next page.

Job order cost cards for jobs in process on July 31 showed the following:

Job	Raw Materials	Direct Labor	Factory Overhead
162	$620	$ 490	$ 588
167	490	600	720
174	980	1,200	1,440
180	510	960	1,152

July's raw materials purchases were $16,400 (July 7), $10,750 (July 20), and $14,900 (July 27). Direct labor costs for July were $29,600 (July 14 payroll) and $32,450 (July 28 payroll).

The predetermined factory overhead rate was 120 percent of direct labor cost. Raw materials requisitioned during July cost $21,550 (July 10) and $23,700 (July 23). Finished goods costing $195,000 were sold during July.

Required

From the information given, prepare an analysis to compute all ending inventory balances. Label all computations, and identify all information used.

Problem 24A-2 Application of Factory Overhead

The Fiorenza Tool and Die Company applies factory overhead costs to production on the basis of direct labor dollars. The firm computes its current predetermined overhead rate by using data from the two preceding operating quarters, adjusted to reflect expectations for the current quarter. During the first ten days of July, the controller used the following information to prepare the overhead rate analysis for the third quarter:

	First Quarter	Second Quarter
Direct labor dollars	$65,200	$ 67,525
Factory overhead costs		
Manufacturing supplies	$19,000	$ 20,900
Materials-handling costs	11,500	12,650
Indirect labor	22,800	25,080
Factory supervision	28,000	30,800
Heat, light, and power	4,800	6,000
Fire insurance	1,600	2,000
Depreciation, plant and equipment	3,400	3,400
Other	6,700	7,370
Total overhead	$97,800	$108,200

For the third quarter of the year, each item of factory overhead costs is expected to increase by the same percentage as was experienced from the first to the second quarter. Direct labor dollars are expected to total $79,920 for the three-month period ending September 30.

Actual operations for the third quarter exceeded the expectations of Fiorenza management. Job orders worked on during the third quarter and related direct labor dollars are as follows: Job 632, $12,400; Job 710, $10,750; Job 698, $9,800; Job 726, $14,650; Job 914, $11,900; Job 852, $8,600; Job 574, $13,100.

Required

1. Compute the overhead rate for the third quarter of the year.
2. Determine the amount of factory overhead applied to production during the three-month period ending September 30.
3. Prepare the journal entry to close the overhead accounts for the third quarter and to dispose of the underapplied or overapplied overhead, assuming that (a) the actual costs were equal to those expected, and (b) the difference between actual and applied costs was considered to be immaterial.

Problem 24A-3 Journal Entry Analysis—Job Order System

The L. Pearce Fabrics Corporation specializes in wind-resistant cloth products for sports enthusiasts. Products are not mass produced because of the varying dimensions and fabric textures required by customer orders. During May, Job Orders I-42, I-48, and K-67 were started and completed. The following events and transactions took place during May:

May 1 Received items contained in purchase order for 17 rolls of fabric costing $3,420, purchased on account, n/30.
2 Operating supplies were received, $450. Invoice price paid in cash.
5 Requisitioned $2,900 of fabric and $250 of operating supplies for production.
8 Paid invoice for materials received May 1.
13 Semimonthly payroll liability was recorded using the following information: gross direct labor wages, $16,300; gross indirect labor wages, $4,900; gross factory supervisory salaries, $7,250; gross administrative salaries, $9,460; FICA (social security) taxes withheld, $2,085; federal income taxes withheld, $11,373.
13 Semimonthly factory payroll costs were distributed to the production accounts. Factory overhead costs are also applied at this time.
15 Payroll checks for the semimonthly pay period ending May 13 were prepared and distributed to the employees.
20 Received raw materials costing $6,810, purchased on account, n/30.
22 Requisitioned new materials costing $5,250 and $100 of operating supplies into production.
26 Paid invoice for materials received May 20.
27 Semimonthly payroll liability was recorded using the following information: gross direct labor wages, $18,100; gross indirect labor wages, $6,050; gross factory supervisory wages, $7,250; gross administrative salaries, $9,460; FICA (social security) taxes withheld, $2,250; federal income taxes withheld, $12,260.
27 Semimonthly factory payroll costs were distributed to the production accounts. Factory overhead costs are also applied at this time.
29 Payroll checks for the semimonthly pay period ending May 27 were prepared and distributed to the employees.
31 Paid and recorded various factory overhead costs. Cash payments were as follows: utility bills, $1,110; small tools, $590; factory rent, $750; others, $200. End-of-month adjustments were for depreciation, equipment, $1,480; and expired insurance (prepaid), $275.
31 Completed jobs costing $68,540 were transferred to Finished Goods Inventory Control.
31 The total selling price of orders sold on account during the month amounted to $104,600. Manufacturing costs of $69,980 were attached to the goods sold during May.

Additional information:

a. Factory overhead is applied to production when payroll is recorded, and a rate of 90 percent of direct labor cost is used.
b. Underapplied or overapplied overhead is closed to Cost of Goods Sold at the end of each month.
c. Inventory balances on May 1 were as follows: Raw Materials Inventory Control, $8,200; Work in Process Inventory Control, none; and Finished Goods Inventory Control, $10,650.

Required

1. Prepare journal entries to record the events and transactions for May.
2. Compute the balance in underapplied or overapplied overhead, and prepare the entry to close the overhead accounts and to dispose of the underapplied or overapplied overhead.
3. Determine the ending inventory balances at May 31.

Problem 24A-4 Job Order Costing—Unknown Quantity Analysis

Fragments of the operating data for Reck Business Forms Company for May and June are shown below. The company uses an overhead rate of 150 percent of direct labor cost.

	May	June
Beginning Raw Materials Inventory Control	(a)	(e)
Beginning Work in Process Inventory Control	$52,650	(f)
Beginning Finished Goods Inventory Control	46,920	$39,800
Direct Labor Charges	22,800	26,200
Factory Overhead Applied	(b)	(g)
Raw Materials Requisitioned	28,250	(h)
Cost of Units Sold	91,650	(i)
Raw Materials Purchased	27,700	29,480
Ending Raw Materials Inventory Control	19,420	16,840
Ending Work in Process Inventory Control	(c)	(j)
Ending Finished Goods Inventory Control	39,800	17,950
Cost of Completed Units	(d)	129,330

Required

From the information given, compute the amount of each lettered unknown. Show your computations.

Problem 24A-5 Job Order Costing—Journal Entry Analysis and T Accounts

Moran Manufacturing Company, which makes patio furniture, began operations in April. The company uses a job order cost system and a current overhead application rate of 180 percent of direct labor dollars. The following transactions and events took place during April:

Apr. 2 Received raw materials totaling $207,250 that were purchased on account.
4 Requisitioned $180,000 of raw materials and $22,000 of operating supplies for production.
14 Factory personnel earned gross payroll of $210,304. Of this amount, $163,000 represented direct labor, and the balance was indirect labor.
15 Overhead costs were applied to production.
17 Received supplies (purchased on account) costing $18,160 and raw materials costing $90,000 from vendor.
18 Requisitioned $75,000 of raw materials and $15,250 of operating supplies into production.

20 Paid the following overhead expenses: insurance premium on plant, $207,500; property taxes, $9,230; maintenance contract, $112,000; and utilities, $3,460.
28 Factory personnel earned gross payroll of $202,620. Of this amount, $157,000 represented direct labor, with the balance being allocated as indirect labor.
29 Overhead costs were applied to production.
30 Completed furniture costing $744,000 was tranferred to Finished Goods Inventory Control.
30 Depreciation of factory building and machinery was $46,000. Miscellaneous factory overhead expenses amounted to $83,411 and were paid on this date.
30 Patio furniture costing $680,000 was shipped to customers on account for a total selling price of $1,426,000.

Required

1. Record the journal entries for all of the above transactions and events. For the payroll entries, concern yourself only with the distribution of factory payroll to the production accounts.
2. Post the entries prepared in part 1 to T accounts, and determine the partial account balances.
3. Determine the amount of underapplied or overapplied overhead at April 30.

Problem 24A-6 Job Order Costing—Comprehensive Journal Entry Analysis

On March 1, the accounting records of the Ripley Manufacturing Company revealed that the inventory control account balances were as follows: $72,700 in Raw Materials, $96,440 in Work in Process, and $63,100 in Finished Goods.

On the same date, subsidiary ledger balances were as follows: the materials ledger had $34,880 for Sheet Steel, $31,610 for Pipe, and $6,210 for Operating Supplies; the job order cost cards revealed $82,640 for Job AA1, $11,200 for Job BB3, and $2,600 for Job DD6; finished goods ledger had no balance for Product AA, $20,500 for Product BB, and $42,600 for Product CC.

The Cost of Goods Sold balance was $190,000. The Factory Payroll, Factory Overhead Control, and Factory Overhead Applied accounts have no balances carried forward from February because these accounts are closed at the end of each month. The company employs an overhead application rate of 90 percent of direct labor cost. During March, the following transactions and events took place:

Mar. 2 Received $46,200 of sheet steel and $29,850 of pipe, purchased on account.
3 Operating supplies totaling $2,940 were requisitioned into production.
8 Paid the following factory overhead costs in cash: electricity bill, $490; gas and oil bill, $520; repairs and maintenance, $850; and outside labor services, $1,710.
10 Requisitioned $28,100 of sheet steel and $14,850 of pipe into production for Job BB3.
10 The following semimonthly payroll liability was recorded: gross direct labor wages (Job AA1, $11,000; Job BB3, $6,500; Job DD6, $4,100), $21,600; gross indirect labor wages, $13,200; gross administrative salaries, $6,750; FICA taxes withheld, $2,493; federal income taxes withheld, $10,803.
10 Factory payroll was distributed to the production accounts.

10 Factory overhead costs were applied to production.
12 Purchased and received $3,250 of operating supplies, on account.
15 Payroll checks for the liability recorded on March 10 were prepared and distributed to the employees.
16 Paid factory rent of $1,400, chargeable to factory overhead.
20 Job AA1 was completed and transferred to Finished Goods Inventory.
22 Requisitioned $16,400 of sheet steel and $11,110 of pipe into production for Job DD6.
24 The following semimonthly payroll liability was recorded: gross direct labor wages (Job BB3, $14,200; Job DD6, $8,200), $22,400; gross indirect labor wages, $14,600; gross administrative salaries, $6,750; FICA taxes withheld, $2,625; federal income taxes withheld, $11,375.
24 Factory payroll was distributed to the production accounts.
24 Factory overhead costs were applied to production.
26 A major portion of Job AA1 was sold and shipped to the customer. Fifty products were shipped at a unit cost of $1,660. The entire shipment sold for $132,800.
29 Payroll checks for the liability recorded on March 24 were prepared and distributed to the employees.
30 Depreciation of machinery of $2,800 for the month was recorded.
30 The Factory Overhead Control and Factory Overhead Applied accounts were closed out and the difference distributed to the Cost of Goods Sold account.

Required

1. Prepare the journal entries for all of the above transactions and events.
2. Prepare T accounts for all of the general ledger and subsidiary ledger accounts relevant to the job order costing system. Post the journal entries prepared in part 1 to these accounts.
3. Check accuracy of ending inventory control account balances by reconciling them with totals of their respective subsidiary ledger accounts.

Problem Set B

Problem 24B-3 Journal Entry Analysis—Job Order System

Ponting Press specializes in printing wedding invitations. Because of the special wording requested by customers, the company operates on a job order cost system. During September, Job Orders 3-1, 3-2, 3-3, and 3-4 were started and finished. The following operating events and transactions took place during September:

Sept. 1 Received ink and high-quality bond paper totaling $232, purchased on account.
3 Received operating supplies totaling $1,423 and paid for them in cash.
4 Requisitioned $946 of raw materials and $225 of operating supplies into production.
7 Paid for goods received on September 1.
14 Semimonthly payroll liability was recorded using the following information: gross direct labor wages, $8,240; gross indirect labor wages, $3,112; gross factory supervisory salaries, $1,500; gross administrative salaries, $4,680; FICA (social security) taxes withheld, $970; federal income taxes withheld, $5,260.

14 Semimonthly factory payroll costs were distributed to the production accounts. Overhead costs are also applied at this time.
16 Payroll checks for the semimonthly pay period ending September 14 were prepared and distributed to the employees.
16 Received additional bond paper costing $1,980, purchased on account.
20 Requisitioned $1,826 of raw materials and $1,380 of operating supplies into production.
26 Paid for materials received on September 16.
28 Semimonthly payroll liability was recorded using the following information: gross direct labor wages, $8,830; gross indirect labor wages, $3,089; gross factory supervisory salaries, $1,500; gross administrative salaries, $4,680; FICA (social security) taxes withheld, $995; federal income taxes withheld, $5,430.
28 Semimonthly factory payroll costs were distributed to the production accounts. Factory overhead costs are also applied at this time.
30 Payroll checks for the semimonthly pay period ending September 28 were prepared and distributed to the employees.
30 The following production-related overhead expenses were paid: group insurance premium for factory personnel, $850; small tools for the plant, $313; monthly rent of factory, $700; utility bill for factory, $477.
30 Month-end adjustments were for the expired portion of prepaid insurance premium for factory, $420; and depreciation, printing equipment, $600.
30 Completed jobs costing $29,822 were transferred to Finished Goods Inventory Control.
30 During September, $66,850 of sales on account were recorded by the Sales Department. These products cost $28,460 to manufacture.

Additional information:

a. Factory overhead is applied to production semimonthly at a rate of 80 percent of direct labor dollars.
b. Underapplied or overapplied overhead is closed to Cost of Goods Sold.
c. Beginning inventory balances were as follows: Raw Materials Inventory Control, $2,482; Work in Process Inventory Control, $4,730; and Finished Goods Inventory Control, $2,150.

Required

1. Prepare all journal entries needed to record the events and transactions that took place in September.
2. Determine whether the overhead was underapplied or overapplied, and prepare the necessary journal entry to close out the overhead accounts and to dispose of the underapplied or overapplied balance.
3. Compute all ending inventory balances at September 30.

Problem 24B-4 Job Order Costing—Unknown Quantity Analysis

Partial operating data for the Truglio Tire Company for October and November are given below. Management has decided on an overhead rate of 120 percent of direct labor dollars.

	October	November
Beginning Raw Materials Inventory Control	(a)	(e)
Beginning Work in Process Inventory Control	$ 89,505	(f)
Beginning Finished Goods Inventory Control	79,764	$ 67,660
Raw Materials Requisitioned	48,025	(g)
Raw Materials Purchased	47,090	50,116

Direct Labor Costs	38,760	44,540
Factory Overhead Applied	(b)	(h)
Cost of Units Completed	(c)	219,861
Cost of Goods Sold	155,805	(i)
Ending Raw Materials Inventory Control	33,014	28,628
Ending Work in Process Inventory Control	(d)	(j)
Ending Finished Goods Inventory Control	67,660	30,515

Required

Using the data provided, compute the amount of each lettered unknown. Show your computations.

Problem 24B-5 Job Order Costing—Journal Entry Analysis and T Accounts

Lawrence Manufacturing, Inc., produces electric shopping carts. These carts are special-order items, and a job order cost accounting system is required. Factory overhead is applied at the rate of 75 percent of direct labor cost. Below is a listing of events and transactions for March.

Mar. 1 Raw materials costing $186,400 were received (purchased on account).

2 Received $28,500 of operating supplies, which were purchased on account.

4 Production personnel requisitioned into production raw materials costing $174,200 and operating supplies costing $22,100.

10 Paid the following overhead costs: utilities, $3,400; factory rent, $2,500; and maintenance charges, $1,800.

15 Payroll was distributed to employees. Gross wages and salaries were as follows: direct labor, $128,000; indirect labor, $42,620; sales commissions, $22,400; and administrative salaries, $28,000.

15 Overhead was applied to production.

19 Operating supplies costing $27,550 and raw materials listed at $200,450, purchased on account, were received by the company.

21 Raw materials costing $192,750 and operating supplies costing $29,400 were requisitioned into production.

26 Production completed during the month was transferred to Finished Goods Inventory Control. Total costs assigned to these jobs were $463,590.

31 The following gross wages and salaries were paid to employees: direct labor, $142,000; indirect labor, $46,240; sales commissions, $21,200; and administrative salaries, $28,000.

31 Overhead was applied to production.

31 Products costing $394,520 were shipped to customers during the month. Total selling price of these goods was $526,800, and these sales should be recorded at month end.

31 The following overhead costs should be recorded: prepaid insurance expired, $3,900; property taxes (payable at year end), $3,200; and depreciation, machinery, $52,500.

Required

1. Record the journal entries for all March transactions and events. For the payroll entries, concern yourself only with the distribution of factory payroll to the production accounts.
2. Post the entries prepared in part 1 to T accounts, and determine the partial account balances.
3. Compute the amount of underapplied or overapplied factory overhead at March 31.

Problem 24B-6 Job Order Costing—Comprehensive Journal Entry Analysis

The Windham Manufacturing Company maintains a job order cost accounting system and is currently using an overhead application rate of 130 percent of direct labor cost.

Accounting records on August 1 showed that the Raw Materials Inventory Control account balance was $83,390 and the materials subsidiary ledger balances were $39,800 for Mixing Fluid, $34,610 for MX Powder, and $8,980 for Operating Supplies. The Work in Process Inventory Control account balance was $95,060 and the subsidiary ledger job order cost card balances were $74,910 for Job 20-4, $13,730 for Job 30-5, and $6,420 for Job 50-6. The Finished Goods Inventory Control account balance was $57,850 and the finished goods subsidiary ledger balances were: none for Product 20, $26,240 for Product 30, and $31,610 for Product 50.

The Factory payroll, Factory Overhead Control, and Factory Overhead Applied accounts have no balances carried forward from July because these accounts are closed at the end of each month. The following transactions and events took place during August:

Aug. 1 Operating supplies totaling $13,650 were requisitioned into production.

4 Received $51,650 of mixing fluid and $32,720 of MX powder, purchased on account.

6 Paid the following factory overhead costs in cash: factory rent, $1,850; heat, light, and power, $1,790; repairs and maintenance, $6,240; and outside contractual services, $8,525.

9 The following semimonthly payroll liability shown below was recorded: gross direct labor wages (Job 20-4, $21,640; Job 30-5, $6,800; Job 50-6, $4,810), $33,250; gross indirect labor wages, $17,420; gross administrative salaries, $8,250; FICA taxes withheld, $3,535; federal income taxes withheld, $15,320.

9 Factory payroll was distributed to the production accounts.

9 Factory overhead costs were applied to production.

12 Purchased and received $14,120 of operating supplies, on account.

13 Requisitioned $35,280 of mixing fluid and $19,960 of MX powder into production for Job 30-5.

14 Payroll checks for the liability recorded on August 9 were prepared and distributed to the employees.

15 Paid property taxes of $4,100, chargeable to factory overhead.

18 Job 20-4 was completed and transferred to Finished Goods Inventory.

20 Requisitioned $21,890 of mixing fluid and $16,770 of MX powder into production for Job 50-6.

23 The following semimonthly payroll liability shown below was recorded: gross direct labor wages (Job 30-5, $19,410; Job 50-6, $11,810), $31,220; gross indirect labor wages, $18,140; gross administrative salaries, $8,250; FICA taxes payable, $3,460; federal income taxes withheld, $14,980.

23 Factory payroll was distributed to the production accounts.

23 Factory overhead costs were applied to production.

26 A major portion of Job 20-4 was sold and shipped to a customer. Four thousand liters were shipped at a cost of $23 per liter. This shipment sold for $139,840.

28 Payroll checks for the liability recorded on August 23 were prepared and distributed to the employees.

30 Depreciation on machinery of $7,940 for the month was recorded.
30 The Factory Overhead Control and the Factory Overhead Applied accounts were closed out, and the difference was distributed to the Cost of Goods Sold account.

Required

1. Prepare the journal entries for all of the above transactions and events.
2. Prepare T accounts for all of the general ledger and subsidiary ledger accounts relevant to the job order costing system. Post the journal entries prepared in part 1 to these accounts.
3. Check accuracy of ending inventory control account balances by reconciling them with totals of their respective subsidiary ledger accounts.

Appendix 24-1
Work Sheet and Financial Statement Preparation: An Illustrative Analysis Using Perpetual Inventories

The purpose of this appendix is to provide an illustrative analysis of work sheet and financial statement preparation when a company employs perpetual inventories. Review this appendix before attempting Practice Set III, *Aluma-Cylinder Company, Inc.*, by Henry R. Anderson and Carol A. Gordon.

Much of the financial information in the Pedersen Company analysis in Chapter 23 has been used in this analysis. However, the numbers and financial results are not identical. The Pedersen Company data were used to establish a comparative type of analysis. Compare the contents of this appendix with the analysis in Chapter 23 to identify differences in the preparation of work sheets and financial statements caused by using either a periodic or a perpetual approach to accounting for inventories.

After all of the normal transactions for December 19xx were posted, the trial balance was as shown on the next page.

Subsidiary ledgers were reconciled with the inventory control accounts in the general ledger, and revealed the following information:

Materials Ledger:	Material AC	$10,100
	Material DG	8,900
	Operating Supplies	1,400
	Total	$20,400
Job Order Cost Cards:	Job 20-045	$20,100
	Job 20-046	3,400
	Total	$23,500
Finished Goods Ledger:	Product 20	$ 2,900
	Product 34	47,700
	Product 61	25,900
	Total	$76,500

Pedersen Company
Trial Balance
December 31, 19xx

	Debit	Credit
Cash	$ 24,600	
Accounts Receivable	65,000	
Allowance for Uncollectible Accounts		$ 1,200
Raw Materials Inventory Control	20,400	
Work in Process Inventory Control	23,500	
Finished Goods Inventory Control	76,500	
Prepaid Insurance	4,800	
Machinery and Equipment	138,500	
Accumulated Depreciation, Machinery and Equipment		49,700
Factory Building	294,800	
Accumulated Depreciation, Factory Building		108,000
Small Tools	9,800	
Accounts Payable		26,100
Wages and Salaries Payable		—
FICA Taxes Payable		—
Federal Income Taxes Payable, Employees		—
Notes Payable, 8½% due in 5 years		100,000
Capital Stock—$10 par value		250,000
Retained Earnings		21,800
Sales		750,000
Cost of Goods Sold	459,600	
Factory Payroll	—	
Factory Overhead Control	120,900	
Factory Overhead Applied		157,900
Sales Salaries and Commissions	46,500	
Advertising	19,500	
Other Selling Expenses	7,400	
Administrative Salaries	65,000	
Franchise and Property Taxes	72,000	
Other General and Administrative Expenses	11,300	
Interest Expense	4,600	
	$1,464,700	$1,464,700

The subsidiary ledger for overhead costs contains the following items supporting the unadjusted balance of Factory Overhead Control at December 31:

Indirect labor	$36,150
Operating supplies	27,600
Heat, light, and power	16,140
Repairs and maintenance	24,620
Plant supervision salaries	16,390
Total	$120,900

Year-end adjusting entries are needed for the following items:

a. Depreciation of machinery and equipment and of the factory building for the year was $14,800 and $16,200, respectively.
b. Small tools costing $2,700 were used during the year.
c. Prepaid insurance of $1,600 expired during 19xx.
d. Accrued payroll data at year end included direct labor wages, $1,450; indirect labor wages, $890; administrative salaries, $1,220; FICA taxes payable, $214; and federal income taxes payable, employees, $925.
e. After adjustments **a** through **d** have been posted to the work sheet, the Overhead Control and Overhead Applied accounts should be closed and any difference debited or credited to Cost of Goods Sold.
f. Interest expense of $1,250 is payable at year end.
g. Federal income tax is 50 percent of pretax net income.

Preparation of Adjusting Journal Entries

From the above data, the following journal entries were prepared:

	Debit	Credit
a. Factory Overhead Control	31,000	
Accumulated Depreciation, Machinery and Equipment		14,800
Accumulated Depreciation, Factory Building		16,200
To record depreciation of machinery and factory building for the period		
b. Factory Overhead Control	2,700	
Small Tools		2,700
To write off small tools used during the period		
c. Factory Overhead Control	1,600	
Prepaid Insurance		1,600
To charge to expense that portion of prepaid insurance premiums that expired during the period		

d. Work in Process Inventory Control (Job 20-046)	1,450	
Factory Overhead Control	890	
Administrative Salaries	1,220	
FICA Taxes Payable		214
Federal Income Taxes Payable, Employees		925
Wages and Salaries Payable		2,421
To record payroll liability for last six days of year and to distribute factory payroll to production accounts		
e. Factory Overhead Applied	157,900	
Factory Overhead Control		157,090
Cost of Goods Sold		810
To close out factory overhead account balances and to dispose of over-applied amount		
f. Interest Expense	1,250	
Interest Payable		1,250
To record interest payable on note at year end		
g. Federal Income Tax Expense	31,220	
Federal Income Taxes Payable, Company		31,220
To record federal taxes on company income for the period		

The Work Sheet

Pedersen Company's work sheet for 19xx is shown in Figure 24A-1 (next two pages). After the above entries are posted, amounts can be extended to the Adjusted Trial Balance, Income Statement, and Balance Sheet columns. Note that no columns have been provided for cost of goods manufactured. When perpetual inventories and a job order cost system are used, all manufacturing costs are assigned to the Work in Process Inventory, Finished Goods Inventory, or Cost of Goods Sold account in the general ledger. Most of the data needed to prepare the statement of cost of goods manufactured are taken from subsidiary ledgers. This dollar amount cannot be determined from accounts shown on the work sheet because it is part of the total cost of goods sold. Net income after taxes for the period is $31,220.

Accounting for Inventories

In the work sheet analysis in Chapter 23, the trial balance contained beginning-of-year balances for the three inventory accounts. A special accounting procedure was followed to close out these balances and establish the year-end balances used to prepare the financial statements. In this example, we are using perpetual inventories. Therefore, the general ledger balances in the three inventory control accounts are always current. There is no need to make special adjustments to these accounts on the work sheet. For purposes of preparing the statement of cost of goods manufactured, inventory balances at January 1, 19xx, were as follows: Raw Materials Inventory Control, $17,500; Work in Process Inventory Control, $21,200; and Finished Goods Inventory Control, $70,000.

Figure 24A-1
Work Sheet Analysis—Manufacturing Company—Perpetual Inventories

Pedersen Company
Work Sheet
For the Year Ended December 31, 19xx

Account Names	Trial Balance		Adjustments		Adjusted Trial Balance		Income Statement		Balance Sheet	
	Debit	Credit	Debit	Credit	Debit	Credit	Debit	Credit	Debit	Credit
Cash	24,600				24,600				24,600	
Accounts Receivable	65,000				65,000				65,000	
Allowance for Uncollectible Accounts		1,200				1,200				1,200
Raw Materials Inventory Control	20,400				20,400				20,400	
Work in Process Inventory Control	23,500		(d) 1,450		24,950				24,950	
Finished Goods Inventory Control	76,500				76,500				76,500	
Prepaid Insurance	4,800			(c) 1,600	3,200				3,200	
Machinery and Equipment	138,500				138,500				138,500	
Accumulated Depreciation, Machinery and Equipment		49,700		(a) 14,800		64,500				64,500
Factory Building	294,800				294,800				294,800	
Accumulated Depreciation, Factory Building		108,000		(a) 16,200		124,200				124,200
Small Tools	9,800			(b) 2,700	7,100				7,100	
Accounts Payable		26,100				26,100				26,100
Wages and Salaries Payable				(d) 2,421		2,421				2,421
FICA Taxes Payable				(d) 214		214				214
Federal Income Taxes Payable, Employees				(d) 925		925				925

Notes Payable, 8½%, due in 5 years		100,000				100,000				100,000
Capital Stock—$10 par value		250,000				250,000				250,000
Retained Earnings		21,800				21,800				21,800
Sales		750,000				750,000		750,000		
Cost of Goods Sold	459,600			(e) 810	458,790		458,790			
Factory Payroll					—					
Factory Overhead Control	120,900		(a) 31,000 (b) 2,700 (c) 1,600 (d) 890	(e) 157,090	—					
Factory Overhead Applied		157,900	(e) 157,900			—				
Sales Salaries and Commissions	46,500				46,500		46,500			
Advertising	19,500				19,500		19,500			
Other Selling Expenses	7,400				7,400		7,400			
Administrative Salaries	65,000		(d) 1,220		66,220		66,220			
Franchise and Property Taxes	72,000				72,000		72,000			
Other General and Administrative Expenses	11,300				11,300		11,300			
Interest Expense	4,600		(f) 1,250		5,850		5,850			
	1,464,700	1,464,700								
Interest Payable				(f) 1,250		1,250				1,250
Federal Income Tax Expense			(g) 31,220		31,220		31,220			
Federal Income Tax Payable, Company				(g) 31,220		31,220				31,220
			229,230	229,230	1,373,830	1,373,830	718,780	750,000	655,050	623,830
Net Income After Taxes to Balance Sheet							31,220			31,220
							750,000	750,000	655,050	655,050

Statement of Cost of Goods Manufactured

Before we can prepare the statement of cost of goods manufactured, some supporting data are needed. Purchases of raw materials and supplies during 19xx totaled $145,075, and $142,175 of these items were issued to production. The issued items included $27,600 of operating supplies charged to Factory Overhead Control. Direct labor for the year, before year-end adjustments, totaled $197,375. When overhead is applied to production by using an overhead rate, the amount applied should be used in preparing the statement of cost of goods manufactured. This statement is shown in Figure 24A-2.

The treatment of the $27,600 of supplies charged to factory overhead requires an explanation here. Operating supplies are a part of Raw Material Inventory Control. If the $27,600 were ignored in the computation of the Cost of Raw Materials Used, the amount would also include supplies used. However, this amount has already been charged to factory overhead and makes up a part of the factory overhead applied to production. Therefore, to avoid including the $27,600 twice, it must be subtracted when computing the amount for Cost of Raw Materials Used.

Income Statement and Balance Sheet

The income statement and balance sheet for the Pedersen Company for 19xx are illustrated in Figures 24A-3 and 24A-4 (next two pages).

Figure 24A-2 Statement of Cost of Goods Manufactured

Pedersen Company
Statement of Cost of Goods Manufactured
For the Year Ended December 31, 19xx

Raw Materials Used		
Raw Materials Inventory Control, Jan. 1, 19xx	$ 17,500	
Raw Materials and Supplies Purchased	145,075	
Cost of Raw Materials Available for Use	$162,575	
Less: Raw Materials Inventory Control, Dec. 31, 19xx	(20,400)	
Supplies Charged to Factory Overhead	(27,600)	
Cost of Raw Materials Used		$114,575
Direct Labor		197,375
Factory Overhead Applied		157,900
Total Manufacturing Costs		$469,850
Plus Work in Process Inventory Control, Jan. 1, 19xx		21,200
Total Costs in Process During the Year		$491,050
Less Work in Process Inventory Control, Dec. 31, 19xx		24,950
Cost of Goods Manufactured		$466,100

Figure 24A-3
Income
Statement

Pedersen Company Income Statement For the Year Ended December 31, 19xx			
Net Sales			$750,000
Cost of Goods Sold			
Beginning Finished Goods Inventory Control		$ 70,000	
Cost of Goods Manufactured (see Figure 24A-2)		466,100	
Total Cost of Finished Goods Available for Sale		$536,100	
Less: Ending Finished Goods Inventory Control		(76,500)	
Overapplied Overhead		(810)	
Cost of Goods Sold			458,790
Gross Profit on Sales			$291,210
Operating Expenses			
Selling Expenses			
Salaries and Commissions	$46,500		
Advertising	19,500		
Other Selling Expenses	7,400		
Total		$ 73,400	
General and Administrative Expenses			
Administrative Salaries	$66,220		
Franchise and Property Taxes	72,000		
Other General and Administrative Expenses	11,300		
Total		149,520	
Total Operating Expenses			222,920
Income from Operations			$ 68,290
Less Interest Expense			5,850
Income Before Income Taxes			$ 62,440
Federal Income Taxes			31,220
Net Income			$ 31,220

Figure 24A-4
Balance Sheet

Pedersen Company
Balance Sheet
December 31, 19xx

Assets			
Current Assets			
Cash		$ 24,600	
Accounts Receivable	$ 65,000		
Less Allowance for Uncollectible Accounts	1,200	63,800	
Raw Materials Inventory Control		20,400	
Work in Process Inventory Control		24,950	
Finished Goods Inventory Control		76,500	
Prepaid Insurance		3,200	
Small Tools		7,100	
Total Current Assets			$220,550
Plant and Equipment			
Machinery and Equipment	$138,500		
Less Accumulated Depreciation	64,500	$ 74,000	
Factory Building	$294,800		
Less Accumulated Depreciation	124,200	170,600	
Total Plant and Equipment			244,600
Total Assets			$465,150
Liabilities			
Current Liabilities			
Accounts Payable	$ 26,100		
Wages and Salaries Payable	2,421		
Withholding Taxes Payable	1,139		
Federal Income Taxes Payable	31,220		
Interest Payable	1,250		
Total Current Liabilities		$ 62,130	
Long-Term Debt			
Notes Payable		100,000	
Total Liabilities			$162,130
Stockholders' Equity			
Capital Stock		$250,000	
Retained Earnings, Jan. 1, 19xx	$ 21,800		
Net Income for 19xx	31,220		
Retained Earnings, Dec. 31, 19xx		53,020	
Total Stockholders' Equity			303,020
Total Liabilities and Stockholders' Equity			$465,150

Closing Entries

Closing entries are much less involved when perpetual inventories and a job order cost system are being used. The Factory Overhead Control and Factory Overhead Applied accounts have already been closed as part of the process of adjusting journal entries. The Factory Payroll account is reduced to a zero balance each time payroll is distributed to the production accounts. Beginning inventory balances do not have to be canceled and ending balances established. Ending balances already exist. Therefore, the only general ledger accounts remaining that must be closed are Sales, Cost of Goods Sold, the operating expenses, Interest Expense, and Federal Income Tax Expense.

Dec. 31	Sales	750,000	
	Income Summary		750,000
	To close Sales to the Income Summary account		
31	Income Summary	718,780	
	Cost of Goods Sold		458,790
	Sales Salaries and Commissions		46,500
	Advertising		19,500
	Other Selling Expenses		7,400
	Administrative Salaries		66,220
	Franchise and Property Taxes		72,000
	Other General and Administrative Expenses		11,300
	Interest Expense		5,850
	Federal Income Tax Expense		31,220
	To close Cost of Goods Sold and expense accounts to Income Summary		
31	Income Summary	31,220	
	Retained Earnings		31,220
	To close Income Summary to Retained Earnings		

Learning Objectives

Chapter Twenty-Five

Product Costing: The Process Cost System

1. *Explain the role of the Work in Process Inventory account in a process cost system.*
2. *Describe product flow and cost flow through a process cost system.*
3. *Compute equivalent production for situations without units in the beginning Work in Process Inventory and also with a beginning inventory balance (schedule of equivalent production).*
4. *Calculate product unit cost for a specific time period (unit cost analysis schedule).*
5. *Prepare a cost summary schedule that assigns costs to units completed and transferred during the period and to ending inventory.*
6. *Formulate the journal entry necessary to transfer costs of completed units out of the Work in Process Inventory account.*

A major objective of any cost system is to formulate product unit costs and to generate ending values for Work in Process and Finished Goods inventories. The processing of continuous product flows (liquids) and long production runs of identical products generally requires the use of a process cost accounting system. With this system, manufacturing costs are averaged over the units produced during a particular period of time rather than traced to specific products or job orders. As a result of studying this chapter, you should be able to meet the learning objectives listed on the left.

The process costing analysis revolves around three schedules: (1) the schedule of equivalent production, (2) the unit cost analysis schedule, and (3) the cost summary schedule. From the information generated by these three schedules, the amount of costs attached to units completed and transferred out of the department can be determined. The final step is to prepare a journal entry that transfers these costs out of the Work in Process Inventory account. Those costs remaining after the transfer are the costs assigned to units still in process at period end. This chapter will analyze the process cost system and explain the technique used to compute product unit costs. It will also illustrate the computation of the period-end balance for the Work in Process Inventory and the costs assigned to units completed and transferred either to the next department or to the Finished Goods Inventory account.

Cost Flow Through Work in Process Inventory Accounts

Accounting for the incurrence of raw materials, direct labor, and factory overhead costs does not change significantly between job order costing and process costing. Under both systems, costs must be recorded and charged eventually to production. Raw materials and supplies must be purchased and requisitioned into production, direct labor wages must be distributed to the employees and charged to production accounts, and various cost items of factory overhead are incurred and applied to production. Journal entries similar to those described in Chapter 24 are used to record these transactions and events. Thus the flow of costs *into* the Work in Process Inventory account is quite similar.

The major difference between job order cost accounting and process cost accounting is in the techniques used to assign costs to products. In a job order system, costs are traced to specific jobs and products; in a process cost system, an averaging technique is used. The basis used in computing unit cost for the process system is made up of all products worked on during a specific time period (a week or a month). Total costs of raw materials, direct labor, and factory overhead that have been accumulated in the Work in Process Inventory account or accounts are divided by the units worked on during the period. However, there are some technical aspects of this procedure that make it more difficult than it first appears. These areas are discussed below.

Work in Process Inventory Accounts

Objective 1 Explain the role of the Work in Process Inventory account in a process cost system

The Work in Process Inventory accounts are the focal point of process costing. Unlike the job order approach, a process cost system is not restricted to one Work in Process account. In fact, process costing uses as many Work in Process Inventory accounts as there are departments or phases in the production process. The process illustrated in Figure 25-1 (next page) has two departments. Finished units of Department 1 become the raw material input of Department 2. As shown in this figure, the three cost elements flow into the Work in Process Inventory account of Department 1. The total unit cost of each product of Department 1 is transferred to Department 2 simultaneously with the transfer of goods. In Department 2, the products transferred in from Department 1 are processed further until they are completed. No additional raw materials are needed in Department 2, but as shown in Figure 25-1, additional labor is used and factory overhead is usually applied as a function of labor cost or hours.

When the completed products are transferred to finished goods inventory from work in process inventory (Department 2), individual product unit cost amounts are made up of five cost inputs, three from Department 1 and two from Department 2. A detailed breakdown is shown below, using *hypothetical* dollar amounts.

Total Unit Cost

Department 1		
Raw materials	$1.40	
Direct labor	1.10	
Factory overhead	.55	
Total, Department 1		$3.05

Figure 25-1
Cost Elements and Process Cost Accounts

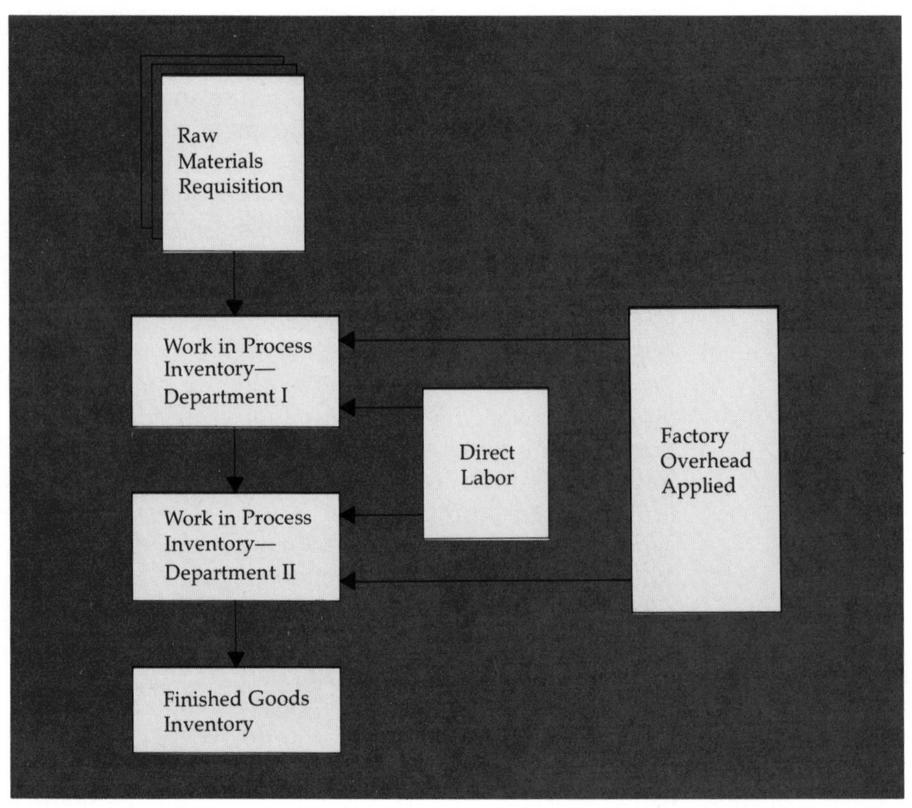

Department 2		
Direct labor	$1.90	
Factory overhead	2.09	
Total, Department 2		3.99
Total unit cost (to Finished Goods Inventory)		$7.04

Production Flow Combinations

Objective 2 Describe product flow and cost flow through a process cost system

There are hundreds of possible combinations of product flows and departmental structures. Two basic structures are illustrated in Figure 25-2. Example 1 shows a *series* of processes or departments. As in Figure 25-1, the completed product of one department here becomes the raw materials input of the next department. The number of departments within a series can vary from two to over a dozen. The important point to remember is that product unit cost is composed of the sum of cost elements used in each of the departments.

Example 2 in Figure 25-2 shows a different type of production flow structure. Again there are three departments. In this example, however, the product does not flow through all departments in a simple 1–2–3

Figure 25-2
Cost Flow for
Process Costing

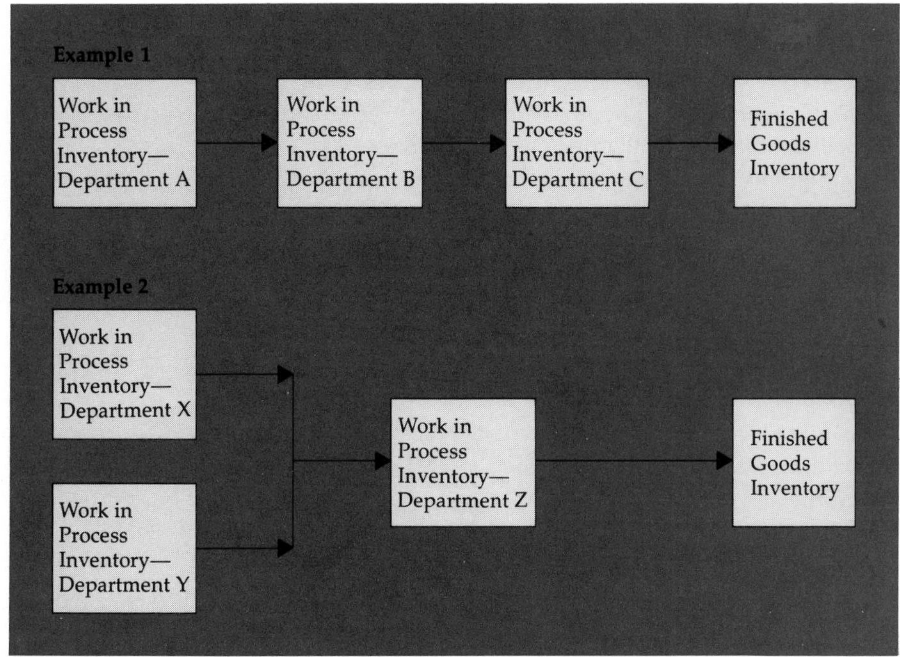

order. Here, two separate products are developed, one in Department X and another in Department Y. Both products are then transferred to Department Z, where they may be assembled, blended together, or mixed with a third raw material input. The possible combinations are again limitless. The unit cost that is transferred to Finished Goods Inventory when the products are completed includes cost elements from Departments X, Y, and Z.

Note that the three-schedule analysis illustrated in the following sections of this chapter must be prepared for *each* department for *each* time period being analyzed. Thus for a company with three production departments and two monthly time periods, it is necessary to prepare six *sets* of the three-schedule analyses.

The Concept of Equivalent Production

Another unique feature of a process cost accounting system is the computation of equivalent units of production during any one accounting period. Remember that in process costing an averaging approach is used to compute product unit costs. All manufacturing costs incurred by a department are divided by the units produced during the period. The important questions are, How many units were produced? Do we count only those units completed during the period? What about partially completed units in beginning work in process inventory? Do we count them even if only a portion of the work necessary to complete them was performed during this period? What about those products in ending work in process inventory? Is it proper to concentrate only on those units started and completed during the period?

Objective 3 Compute equivalent production for situations without units in the beginning Work in Process Inventory and also with a beginning inventory balance (schedule of equivalent production)

The answers to all these questions are linked to the concept of equivalent production. **Equivalent production** (also called **equivalent units**) is a measure of productive output of units for a period of time, expressed in terms of fully completed or equivalent whole units produced; partially completed units are restated in terms of equivalent whole units. The number of equivalent units produced is equal to the sum of (1) total units started and completed during the period, and (2) an amount for partially completed products that represents a restatement of these units in terms of equivalent whole units. A percentage of completion factor is used to compute the number of equivalent whole units. Equivalent production is a key factor in the computation of process unit costs. Figure 25-3 illustrates equivalent unit computation. During February, 4.25 equivalent units were completed. Three automobiles were started and completed during the month. In addition, one-half (.5) of Car A is completed in February and three-quarters (.75) of Car E is completed. Total equivalent units for the period are determined by adding together those units started and completed (3.0) and those units partially completed (.5 and .75). Therefore, equivalent production for February for direct labor and factory overhead is 4.25 units.

As we will show later in this chapter, unit costs are computed for raw materials and conversion costs for each department within the production process. **Conversion costs** are defined as the combined total of direct labor and factory overhead costs incurred by a production department. The equations for calculating the unit cost amounts appear at the top of the next page. (Note the role of equivalent units.)

Figure 25-3 Equivalent Unit Computation

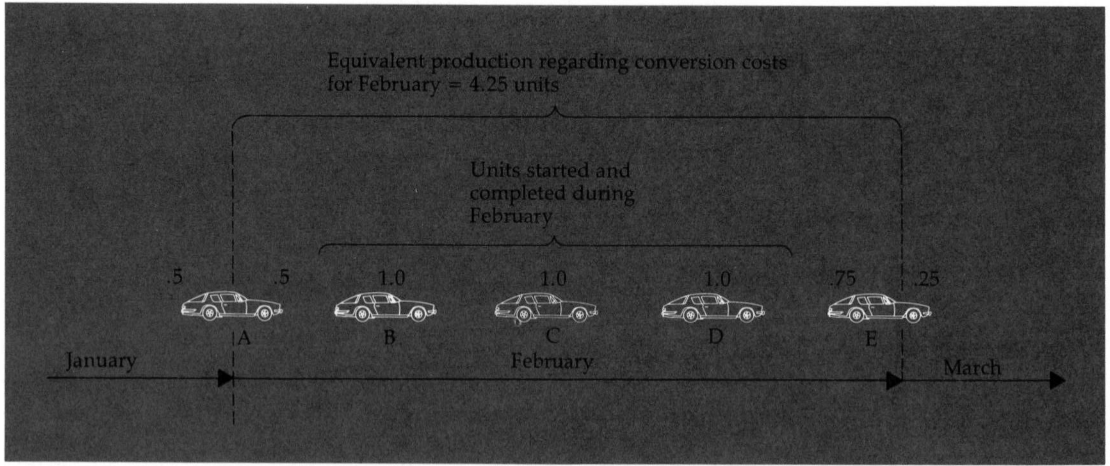

Facts: All raw materials are added to production when the automobile begins to be assembled. All direct labor and factory overhead costs are incurred uniformly as the automobile moves toward completion. Equivalent production for raw materials for February would be 4.0 units. During February, the raw materials for cars B, C, D, and E were introduced into the production process.

$$\text{unit cost for raw materials} = \frac{\text{total raw materials costs}}{\text{equivalent units—materials}}$$

$$\text{unit cost for conversion costs} = \frac{\text{total labor and factory overhead costs}}{\text{equivalent units—conversion costs}}$$

The computation of equivalent units of production for materials usually differs from that for conversion costs. As shown in Figure 25-3, raw materials are usually added at the beginning of the process. Therefore, materials for Car A were added in January and do not influence equivalent units for materials in February. However, raw materials for Car E were *all* added to production in February. To determine the equivalent units of production for materials for February (4.0 units), add 3.0 (units started and completed—Cars B, C, and D) and 1.0 (Car E).

No Beginning Work in Process Inventory

To begin the analysis for computing equivalent production, we will assume that there are no units in beginning work in process inventory. Without any units in beginning inventory, the only remaining possibilities are (1) units started and completed during the period, and (2) units started but not completed. By definition, units started but not completed comprise the ending work in process inventory unit balance. Equivalent product production is computed in parts as follows:

Part 1: Units started and completed = (number of units) × 100 percent
Part 2: Equivalent units in ending work in process inventory = (number of units) × (percentage of completion)

The *sum* of these two amounts represents the equivalent whole units completed during the period. Percentage of completion factors are obtained from supervisors in the production departments.

Earlier we noted that direct labor and factory overhead costs are usually lumped together and called conversion costs in computing unit cost. The reason for doing so is that both types of costs are usually incurred uniformly throughout the production process. Combining them saves one unit cost computation. Materials costs are generally not used uniformly within the process. Such costs are incurred either at the beginning of the process (raw materials input) or at the end of the process (packing materials). Because of this difference, the equivalent unit amount for raw materials will not be the same as that for conversion costs. Separate computations are necessary.

To illustrate the computation of equivalent units where there were no partially completed units in beginning work in process inventory, we will use an example. Assume that the records of Ivar Jansson Clothing, Inc., for January 19xx contain the following information: (a) 47,500 units started during period; (b) 6,200 units partially complete at period end; (c) 60 percent completion of ending work in process inventory; (d) raw materials added at *beginning* of process, and conversion costs incurred *uniformly* throughout process; no units lost or spoiled during month.

Figure 25-4
Equivalent Units—No Beginning Inventory

Ivar Jansson Clothing, Inc.
Schedule of Equivalent Production
For the Month Ended January 31, 19xx

Units—Stage of Completion	Units to Be Accounted For	Equivalent Units	
		Materials	Conversion Costs
Beginning inventory—units completed in this period	—	—	—
Units started and completed in this period	41,300	41,300	41,300
Ending inventory—units started but not completed in this period	6,200		
(Materials—100% complete)		6,200	
(Conversion costs—60% complete)			3,720
Totals	47,500	47,500	45,020

The **schedule of equivalent production,** in which equivalent production is computed for the period for both materials and conversion costs, is shown in Figure 25-4. Because there were no units in beginning work in process inventory, dashes are entered in the appropriate column. All 41,300 units started and completed during the period (47,500 units started less 6,200 units not completed) have received 100 percent of the materials, labor, and overhead effort needed to complete them. Therefore, 41,300 equivalent units are recorded in both the Materials and Conversion Costs columns.

Accounting for equivalent units in ending inventory is a bit more complicated. These 6,200 units have received all raw materials inputs because materials were added to each product as it entered the production process. Therefore, in the Materials column, 6,200 equivalent units are entered. However, conversion costs (direct labor and factory overhead) are added uniformly as the products move through the process. The 6,200 units in ending inventory are only 60 percent complete. Equivalent whole units are determined by multiplying the number of units by the percentage completed. In Figure 25-4, the amount of equivalent units for conversion costs of ending inventory is computed as follows:

$$6{,}200 \text{ units} \times 60\% \text{ completion} = 3{,}720 \text{ equivalent units}$$

As a result of these computations for January, there were 47,500 equivalent units for materials and 45,020 equivalent units for purposes of accounting for conversion costs.

With Beginning Work in Process Inventory

A situation where there is no beginning work in process inventory is very seldom found in industry. By definition, process costing techniques are used in industries where production flows continuously or where there are long runs of identical products. In these situations, because there is always something in process at month end, there are always units in beginning work in process inventory in the following period. Thus we turn our analysis to this situation, expanding the example used above.

During February 19xx, unit production results for Ivar Jansson Clothing, Inc., were as follows: (a) 6,200 units in beginning work in process inventory; (b) 60 percent completion of beginning inventory; (c) 57,500 units started during period; (d) 5,000 units partially completed at period end; and (e) 45 percent completion of ending work in process inventory.

Beginning inventories make the computation of equivalent units somewhat more difficult. Before analyzing the actual computations, we must explain the concept of first-in, first-out (FIFO) product flow. Because process costing is normally associated with a continuous production flow, products in process at the beginning of the period are assumed to be the first products completed during the current period. After the units in beginning work in process inventory are completed, new units introduced into production are worked on and completed. Costs are treated in the same manner, with beginning inventory costs serving as the starting point on the cost summary schedule. Therefore, in making both unit and dollar computations, we assume **FIFO product and cost flows.**[1]

February operations of Ivar Jansson Clothing, Inc., involve both beginning and ending balances in Work in Process Inventory. To compute equivalent units for February, we must be careful to account only for the work done in February. The computation of equivalent units is illustrated in Figure 25-5 (next page). Units in beginning inventory were 60 percent complete as to conversion costs before the period began, and all materials were added to these products in the preceding period (January). Therefore, for these units, no equivalent units of materials were applicable to February, and only 40 percent of the conversion costs were needed during the current month to complete these units. As shown in Figure 25-5, completing the units in beginning inventory required no raw materials and only 2,480 equivalent units of conversion costs (6,200 units times 40 percent, the remaining percentage of completion).

Computations involving units started and completed, as well as ending inventory computations, are similar to those used in the January illustration. Units started and completed receive the full amount of raw materials and conversion costs. Therefore, the resulting equivalent units equal 52,500 (57,500 started minus the 5,000 not completed) for both materials and conversion costs. Ending inventory is 100 percent complete as to

1. Cost accounting courses treat the topic of process costing in more depth and introduce an average costing method that does not assume FIFO cost flow.

Figure 25-5 Equivalent Units—With Beginning Inventory

Ivar Jansson Clothing, Inc.
Schedule of Equivalent Production
For the Month Ended February 29, 19xx

Units—Stage of Completion	Units to Be Accounted For	Equivalent Units: Materials	Equivalent Units: Conversion Costs
Beginning inventory—units completed in this period	6,200		
(Materials—100% complete)		—	
(Conversion costs—60% complete)			2,480
Units started and completed in this period	52,500	52,500	52,500
Ending inventory—units started but not completed in this period	5,000		
(Materials—100% complete)		5,000	
(Conversion costs—45% complete)			2,250
Totals	63,700	57,500	57,230

materials and 45 percent complete as to conversion costs. The end result is that February produced 57,500 equivalent units that used raw materials and 57,230 equivalent units that received conversion costs.

Note that the above illustrations cover only two of the hundreds of possible process costing situations with varying percentages of completion that could arise in the computation of equivalent units. These examples, however, establish the procedures necessary to solve all process costing problems utilizing the FIFO product and cost flows.

Cost Analysis Schedules

Objective 4 Calculate product unit cost for a specific time period (unit cost analysis schedule)

Thus far in the discussions concerning process cost accounting, we have placed primary emphasis on accounting for *units* of productive output. In the schedule of equivalent production, we have computed totals for units to be accounted for and equivalent units for materials and conversion costs. Once the unit information has been sorted out and equivalent unit figures have been generated, we can turn to the dollar information. Accounting for manufacturing costs, cost per equivalent unit, and inventory costing can now be brought into our analysis.

Unit Cost Analysis Schedule

The **unit cost analysis schedule** is a process costing statement used to (1) accumulate all costs charged to the Work in Process Inventory account of each department or production process, and (2) compute cost per equivalent unit for materials and conversion costs. A unit cost analysis schedule is pictured in Figures 25-6 and 25-8, discussed later in this chapter. The schedule has two parts: total cost analysis and computation of equivalent unit costs. The unit cost analysis schedule functions as the accumulation point for all costs of the period, and the Total Costs to Be Accounted For column serves as a check figure for the final distribution of costs to inventories in the third schedule, the cost summary schedule. The costs making up the total costs to be accounted for may become part of ending Work in Process Inventory and remain in the account, or they may be part of the costs of completed goods transferred to the next department or to Finished Goods Inventory. The amount of total costs to be accounted for is made up of costs of materials and conversion costs incurred during the current period plus those costs included in the beginning balance of Work in Process Inventory.

The second part of the unit cost analysis schedule involves the computation of costs per equivalent unit. For both materials and conversion costs, *current period costs* are divided by the respective equivalent unit amounts. Costs attached to units in beginning inventory are *not* included in computing costs per equivalent unit. Under the FIFO cost flow assumption, separate costing analyses are used for each accounting period, and costs of different periods are not averaged. Therefore, costs attached to beginning inventory are isolated and treated separately.

Cost Summary Schedule

Objective 5 Prepare a cost summary schedule that assigns costs to units completed and transferred during the period and to ending inventory

The final phase of the process costing analysis involves the distribution of total costs accumulated during the period to the units in ending Work in Process Inventory or to the units completed and transferred out of the department. This is done through the use of the **cost summary schedule.** Information used in this schedule originates in either the schedule of equivalent production or the unit cost analysis schedule. Using hypothetical amounts, the following analysis illustrates the computation of total costs transferred out of the department during the period.

Units in beginning inventory	
Costs attached to units in beginning inventory	$ 4,460
Costs necessary to complete units in beginning inventory	2,910
Total cost of units in beginning inventory	$ 7,370
Costs of units started and completed during the period	46,880
Total cost of completed units	$54,250

The computation of each of these amounts is illustrated in the next section. All costs remaining in Work in Process Inventory after costs of completed units have been transferred out represent the cost of ending units in process.

To complete the cost schedule analysis, we add together the total cost of completed units transferred and the costs attached to ending Work in Process Inventory and compare their total with the total costs to be accounted for in the unit cost analysis schedule. If the two totals are not equal, there has been a computational error in the analysis.

Illustrative Analysis

To fully explain the form and use of the cost schedules, we will expand the Ivar Jansson Clothing, Inc., example. In addition to the equivalent unit information analyzed earlier, the company disclosed the following cost data:

January, 19xx	
Beginning Work in Process Inventory	—
Cost of raw materials used	$154,375
Conversion costs for the month	258,865
February, 19xx	
Cost of raw materials used	$189,750
Conversion costs for the month	320,488

From the above data, we will compute equivalent unit costs, total costs transferred to Finished Goods Inventory, and the ending balance in Work in Process Inventory for January and February 19xx.

January Cost analysis schedules for January are shown in Figures 25-6 and 25-7. Total costs to be accounted for are $413,240 for January as depicted in the unit cost analysis schedule in Figure 25-6. Dividing the January costs for materials of $154,375 and the conversion costs of $258,865 by the equivalent unit amounts computed in Figure 25-4, we obtain costs per equivalent unit of $3.25 ($154,375 ÷ 47,500) for materials and $5.75 ($258,865 ÷ 45,020) for conversion costs. These per unit amounts are used in the cost summary schedule to compute costs transferred to Finished Goods Inventory and the cost of ending Work in Process Inventory.

The cost summary schedule for January is shown in Figure 25-7. No units were in process at the beginning of January, so no costs are entered for beginning inventory. (Even though there was no beginning inventory for January, the schedule headings are included because the schedule forms shown can be used for any process costing situation.) Units transferred to Finished Goods Inventory in January are made up entirely of units started and completed because there were no units in beginning inventory. These 41,300 units cost $9 each to produce (total cost per equivalent unit), so $371,700 must be transferred to Finished Goods Inventory.

Figure 25-6
Unit Cost Determination— No Beginning Inventories

Total Cost Analysis	Costs from Beginning Inventory		Costs from Current Period		Total Costs to Be Accounted For
Materials	—		$154,375		$154,375
Conversion costs	—		258,865		258,865
Totals	—		$413,240		$413,240
Computation of Equivalent Unit Costs	Current Period Cost	÷	Equivalent Units	=	Cost per Equivalent Unit
Materials	$154,375		47,500		$3.25
Conversion costs	258,865		45,020		5.75
Totals	$413,240				$9.00

Figure 25-7
Ending Inventory Computation— No Beginning Inventories

	Cost of Goods Transferred to Finished Goods Inventory	Cost of Ending Work in Process Inventory
Beginning inventory*		
Costs from preceding period	—	
Costs to complete this period	—	
Units started and completed*		
41,300 units × $9.00 per unit	$371,700	
Ending inventory*		
Materials: 6,200 units × $3.25		$ 20,150
Conversion costs: 3,720 units × $5.75		21,390
Totals	$371,700	$ 41,540
Computational check		
Costs to Finished Goods Inventory		$371,700
Cost of ending Work in Process Inventory		41,540
Total costs to be accounted for (unit cost analysis schedule)		$413,240

*Note: Unit figures come from schedule of equivalent production for January.

Because we debited $413,240 to Work in Process Inventory during January and just transferred $371,700 of that amount to Finished Goods Inventory, the difference of $41,540 remaining in the account is the ending inventory balance. This amount, $41,540, is verified in Figure 25-7. Using the ending inventory amounts from the schedule of equivalent production in Figure 25-4 and the costs per equivalent unit from the cost analysis schedule in Figure 25-6, we make the following computations:

Materials: 6,200 equivalent units × $3.25 per unit	$20,150
Conversion costs: 3,720 equivalent units × $5.75 per unit	21,390
Ending Work in Process Inventory balance	$41,540

The computational check at the bottom of Figure 25-7 verifies that all computations are correct.

February The cost analysis for February is more difficult because it is necessary to consider units and costs in beginning Work in Process Inventory. February operating results are analyzed in Figures 25-8 and 25-9. Total costs to be accounted for in February are $551,778. Included in this amount are the beginning inventory balance of $41,540 (see January computation in Figure 25-7) plus current period costs from February of $189,750 and $320,488 for materials and conversion costs, respectively.

Figure 25-8
Unit Cost Determination—With Beginning Inventories

Ivar Jansson Clothing, Inc.
Unit Cost Analysis Schedule
For the Month Ended February 29, 19xx

Total Cost Analysis	Costs from Beginning Inventory	Costs from Current Period	Total Costs to Be Accounted For
Materials	$20,150	$189,750	$209,900
Conversion costs	21,390	320,488	341,878
Totals	$41,540	$510,238	$551,778

Computation of Equivalent Unit Costs	Current Period Cost	÷	Equivalent Units	=	Cost per Equivalent Unit
Materials	$189,750		57,500		$3.30
Conversion costs	320,488		57,230		5.60
Totals	$510,238				$8.90

Figure 25-9
Ending Inventory Computation— With Beginning Inventories

Ivar Jansson Clothing, Inc.
Cost Summary Schedule
For the Month Ended February 29, 19xx

	Cost of Goods Transferred to Finished Goods Inventory	Cost of Ending Work in Process Inventory
Beginning inventory*		
Costs from preceding period	$ 41,540	
Costs to complete this period		
Materials: none	—	
Conversion costs: 2,480 units × $5.60	13,888	
Subtotal	$ 55,428	
Units started and completed*		
52,500 units × $8.90 per unit	467,250	
Ending inventory*		
Materials: 5,000 units × $3.30		$ 16,500
Conversion costs: 2,250 units × $5.60		12,600
Totals	$522,678	$ 29,100
Computational check		
Costs to Finished Goods Inventory		$522,678
Costs to ending Work in Process Inventory		29,100
Total costs to be accounted for (unit cost analysis schedule)		$551,778

*Note: Unit figures come from schedule of equivalent production.

Even though February has a beginning balance in Work in Process Inventory, the procedure to compute costs per equivalent unit is similar to the technique used in the January analysis. As shown in Figure 25-8, only current period costs are used. February costs of $189,750 for materials and $320,488 for conversion costs are divided by the equivalent unit figures computed in Figure 25-5. February's $8.90 cost per equivalent unit includes $3.30 per unit for raw materials and $5.60 per unit for conversion costs.

The February cost analysis concludes with the preparation of the cost summary schedule, illustrated in Figure 25-9. Costs transferred to Finished Goods Inventory include costs of $41,540 attached to the 6,200 units in beginning inventory from January, the costs of completing the units in beginning inventory, and the costs of producing the 52,500 units started and completed during February. January costs of $41,540 were carried forward to February as the beginning balance in the Work in Process Inventory account (see Figure 25-7). In addition, as shown in Figure 25-5, 2,480 equivalent units of conversion cost effort were required to complete the 6,200 units. Because the equivalent unit conversion cost for February is $5.60, $13,888 of additional costs were required to complete units in beginning inventory. Units started and completed in February (52,500 units) cost $8.90 each to produce. This total of $467,250 is added to the $55,428 cost to produce the 6,200 units in beginning inventory to arrive at the $522,678 of costs transferred to Finished Goods Inventory during February.

The ending Work in Process Inventory balance of $29,100 is made up of $16,500 of materials costs and $12,600 of conversion costs. The extensions of these amounts are shown in Figure 25-9. At the conclusion of the cost summary schedule, the computational check reveals that no calculation errors were made in the February cost analysis.

Journal Entry Analysis

Objective 6 Formulate the journal entry necessary to transfer costs of completed units out of the Work in Process Inventory account

Although the major emphasis in the study of process cost accounting is on the preparation of the schedules for equivalent production, unit cost analysis, and cost summary, none of the schedules provides a direct means for actual cost transfer within the accounting records. All of the computations within these schedules involve the Work in Process Inventory account. The objective of the entire process costing analysis is to compute the dollar totals for goods completed and transferred to Finished Goods Inventory and for partially completed products that remain in the Work in Process Inventory account. However, the three schedules alone do not cause costs to flow through accounts in the general ledger. They only provide the information needed before the accounting for cost flow is possible. Journal entries are required to effect the flow of costs from one account to another.

The culmination of a process costing analysis, then, is the preparation of a journal entry to transfer costs of completed products out of Work in Process Inventory. Remember that all of the entries analyzed in earlier chapters are also necessary in a process costing system. Only one entry is highlighted here, however, because it is involved directly with the cost transfer of completed goods. To transfer the costs of units completed, we debit Finished Goods Inventory (or Work in Process Inventory of a subsequent department) and credit Work in Process Inventory for the amount of the cost transfer computed in the cost summary schedule.

In the example of Ivar Jansson Clothing, Inc., the following entries would be made at the end of each time period:

Jan. 31	Finished Goods Inventory	371,700	
	Work in Process Inventory		371,700
	To transfer cost of units completed in January to Finished Goods Inventory		
Feb. 29	Finished Goods Inventory	522,678	
	Work in Process Inventory		522,678
	To transfer cost of units completed in February to Finished Goods Inventory		

After the entries are posted, the Work in Process Inventory account would appear as follows on February 29, 19xx:

Work in Process Inventory

Balance	—	Transferred to Finished Goods in Jan.	371,700
Jan. materials	154,375		
Jan. conversion costs	258,865		
Balance 1/31/xx 41,540			
Feb. materials	189,750	Transferred to Finished Goods in Feb.	522,678
Feb. conversion costs	320,488		
Balance 2/29/xx 29,100*			

*This amount is confirmed by the cost summary schedule in Figure 25-9.

In the analysis of Ivar Jansson Clothing, Inc., the company employed only *one* production department, and the analysis centered on two consecutive monthly accounting periods. Because only one production department was used, only one Work in Process Inventory account was needed. The following example deals with *two* production departments in a series. The product passes from the first to the second department and then to Finished Goods Inventory and is similar to the situation depicted in Example 1 of Figure 25-2. When the production process requires two departments, the accounting system must maintain two separate Work in Process Inventory accounts, one for each department. This situation does entail more work but does not complicate the computational aspects of the process costing system. The key point to remember is to treat *each* department and related Work in Process Inventory account as a separate analysis. The three schedules must be prepared for *each* department. Departments should be analyzed in the order in which they appear in the series.

Illustrative Problem: Two Production Departments

Jackson Manufacturing Company produces a liquid chemical compound used in converting salt water to fresh water. The production process involves the Mixing Department and the Cooling Department. Every unit produced must be processed by both departments, with cooling as the final operation.

In the Mixing Department, a basic chemical powder, Material BP, is blended with water, heated to 88° Celsius, and mixed actively for two hours. Assume that no evaporation takes place and that Material BP is added at the beginning of the process. Conversion costs are incurred uniformly throughout the process. Operating data for the Mixing Department for April 19xx are as follows:

Beginning Work in Process Inventory		
Units (30% complete)		1,450 liters
Costs:	Raw materials	$13,050
	Conversion costs	$ 1,760
Ending Work in Process Inventory		
All units 60% complete		
April operations		
Units started		55,600 liters
Costs:	Raw materials used	$486,500
	Conversion costs	$278,575
Units completed and transferred to the Cooling Department		54,800 liters

Required

1. Using a good form, prepare (a) a schedule of equivalent production, (b) a unit cost analysis schedule, and (c) a cost summary schedule.
2. From information in the cost summary schedule, prepare the proper journal entry to transfer costs of completed units for April out of the Mixing Department.

Solution

Before completing the three schedules and preparing the journal entry, it is necessary to make a special analysis of the units (liters) worked on during April. In order to complete the schedule of equivalent production, we must first calculate the number of units started and completed and the number of units in ending work in process inventory. These amounts were not stated explicitly in the data given above but can be easily computed.

Units started and completed:

	Units completed and transferred (given)	54,800 liters
Less:	Units in beginning inventory (given)	1,450 liters
Equals:	Units started and completed	53,350 liters

Units in ending inventory:		
	Units started during April (given)	55,600 liters
Less:	Units started and completed (above)	53,350 liters
Equals:	Units in ending inventory	2,250 liters

With the knowledge of the number of units started and completed and the number of units in ending work in process inventory, we can now prepare the three schedules in the cost analysis.

1a. Schedule of Equivalent Production

Units—Stage of Completion	Units to Be Accounted For	Equivalent Units: Materials	Equivalent Units: Conversion Costs
Beginning inventory—portion completed in this period	1,450		
(Materials—100% complete)		—	
(Conversion costs—30% complete)			1,015 (70% of 1,450)
Units started and completed in this period	53,350	53,350	53,350
Ending inventory—units started but not completed in this period	2,250		
(Materials—100% complete)		2,250	
(Conversion costs—60% complete)			1,350 (60% of 2,250)
Totals	57,050	55,600	55,715

1b. Unit Cost Analysis Schedule

Total Cost Analysis	Costs from Beginning Inventory	Costs from Current Period	Total Costs to Be Accounted For
Materials	$13,050	$486,500	$499,550
Conversion costs	1,760	278,575	280,335
Totals	$14,810	$765,075	$779,885

Computation of Equivalent Unit Cost	Current Period Costs	÷	Equivalent Units	=	Cost per Equivalent Unit
Materials	$486,500		55,600		$ 8.75
Conversion costs	278,575		55,715		5.00
Totals	$765,075				$13.75

1c. Cost Summary Schedule

	Cost of Goods Transferred to Cooling Department	Cost of Ending Work in Process Inventory
Beginning inventory		
Costs from preceding period	$ 14,810	
Costs to complete this period		
Materials: none	—	
Conversion costs:		
1,015 units × $5.00	5,075	
Units started and completed		
53,350 units × $13.75 per unit	733,563*	
Ending inventory		
Materials: 2,250 units × $8.75		$19,687*
Conversion costs:		
1,350 units × $5.00		6,750
Totals	$753,448	$26,437

Computational check:	
Costs to Cooling Department	$753,448
Costs in ending Work in Process Inventory	26,437
Total costs to be accounted for (unit cost analysis schedule)	$779,885

*Figures were rounded to avoid decimals.

2. The costs of completed units for April are now ready to be transferred from the Mixing Department to the Cooling Department. The required journal entry would be as follows:

Work in Process—Cooling Department	753,448	
Work in Process—Mixing Department		753,448
To record the transfer of cost of completed units in April from Mixing Department to Cooling Department		

Note that, in the above entry, the $753,448 is being transferred from one Work in Process Inventory account to another. The $753,448 attached to the units transferred into the Cooling Department during April would be accounted for in the same way as raw materials used in the Mixing Department. All other procedures and schedules illustrated in the Mixing Department example would be used again for the Cooling Department. See the review problem at the end of this chapter for the accounting treatment of the Cooling Department.

Chapter Review

Review of Learning Objectives

1. Explain the role of the Work in Process Inventory account in a process cost system.

The Work in Process Inventory account is the focal point of the process cost accounting system. Each production department or operating unit is assigned a Work in Process Inventory account. All costs charged to that department flow into this inventory account. Special analysis, using the three schedules, is required to determine the amount of cost flowing out of the account at period end. All special analyses connected with the process cost accounting system are related to costs in the Work in Process Inventory account.

2. Describe product flow and cost flow through a process cost system.

Because of the nature of products in a process costing environment (liquids or long production runs of identical products), products flow in a FIFO (first in, first out) fashion. Once a product is started into production, it in turn flows to completion. Manufacturing costs are handled in the same manner. Costs of raw materials, direct labor, and factory overhead of the current period are assigned either to units completed during the period or to units still in process at period end. All costs assigned to ending Work in Process Inventory will be accounted for first in the following period.

3. Compute equivalent production for situations without units in the beginning Work in Process Inventory and also with a beginning inventory balance.

Equivalent production is determined with the aid of a schedule of equivalent production. Units worked on during the period are categorized as either being (a) in beginning inventory (started last period) and completed this period, (b) started and completed this period, *or* (c) started this period and still in process at period end. By using percentage of completion data, equivalent units are computed for materials and conversion costs.

4. Calculate product unit cost for a specific time period.

In the unit cost analysis schedule, costs attached to units in beginning inventory and costs of the current period are totaled to yield the total costs to be accounted for. Next, the current period amounts for raw materials and conversion costs are divided by their respective equivalent unit amounts to arrive at product unit costs for the period.

5. Prepare a cost summary schedule that assigns costs to units completed and transferred during the period and to ending inventory.

Costs assigned to units completed and transferred during the period are the first to be calculated by using the cost summary schedule. This is accomplished in two steps: (a) costs needed to complete units in beginning inventory are added to costs assigned from the previous period, and (b) units started and completed during the current period are assigned a full dose of production costs. The total of these two calculations represents costs attached to units completed and transferred during the period. The second portion of the cost summary schedule focuses on computing the cost assigned to units still in process at period end. Unit costs for raw materials and conversion costs are multiplied by the respective equivalent unit amounts for these categories. The total of these two dollar amounts represents the ending Work in Process Inventory balance for the period.

6. Formulate the journal entry necessary to transfer costs of completed units out of the Work in Process Inventory account.

Once the first part of the cost summary schedule has been completed (determining the costs assigned to units completed and transferred during the period), a journal entry can be prepared to transfer these costs out of the Work in Process Inventory account. A credit is made to the inventory account for the entire amount. The corresponding debit can be either to Finished Goods Inventory or to another Work in Process Inventory account, depending on the network of production departments within the process.

Review Problem Costs Transferred In

In addition to reviewing the three-schedule analysis used in process costing, this problem will introduce two new situations common to the process costing area.

1. **Costs transferred in** Accounting for the second in a series of Work in Process Inventory accounts is very similar to accounting for the first department's costs. The only difference is that instead of accounting for current raw materials costs, you are dealing with *costs transferred in* during the period. All procedures used to account for costs transferred in are identical to those used to account for raw materials costs and units. So when accounting for costs and units transferred in, treat them as you would raw materials added at the beginning of the process.
2. **Rounding of numerical answers** Unlike the problems discussed thus far in this chapter, most real-world unit cost computations will not result in even-numbered dollars and cents figures. We introduce the concept of rounding in this problem. Three simple rules will help to overcome the problem of rounding: (a) Round unit cost computations to three decimal places. (b) Round cost summary data to the nearest dollar. (c) On the cost summary schedule, any difference caused by rounding should be added to or subtracted from the amount being transferred out of the department before the journal entry is prepared.

To illustrate the accounting approach for the second in a series of production departments and to show how cost rounding is done, we will expand the example of the Jackson Manufacturing Company's Cooling Department. Operating data for the Cooling Department for April 19xx are shown below. No new raw materials are added in this department. Only additional conversion costs are necessary to accomplish the cooling objective.

Beginning Work in Process Inventory	
Units (40% complete)	2,100 liters
Costs: Transferred in	$29,200
Conversion costs	2,654
Ending Work in Process Inventory	
All units 60% complete	
April operations	
Units transferred in	54,365 liters
Costs: Transferred in	$753,448
Conversion costs	172,130
Units completed and transferred to Finished Goods Inventory	54,450 liters

Required

1. Using good form, prepare (a) a schedule of equivalent production, (b) a unit cost analysis schedule, and (c) a cost summary schedule.
2. From the cost summary schedule data, prepare the journal entry to transfer costs of completed units for April to Finished Goods Inventory.

Answer to Review Problem

Before completing the three-schedule analysis, we again must first analyze the unit information given in the problem to arrive at unit data needed for solution of the problem.

Units started and completed:

	Units completed and transferred (given)	54,450 liters
Less:	Units in beginning inventory (given)	2,100 liters
Equals:	Units started and completed	52,350 liters

Units in ending Work in Process Inventory:

	Units transferred in during April (given)	54,365 liters
Less:	Units started and completed (above)	52,350 liters
Equals:	Units in ending inventory	2,015 liters

With this unit information available, we can now prepare the three schedules.

Jackson Manufacturing Company
Process Cost Analysis—Cooling Department
For the Month Ended April 30, 19xx

1a. Schedule of Equivalent Production

Units—Stage of Completion	Units to Be Accounted For	Equivalent Units: Transferred In	Equivalent Units: Conversion Costs
Beginning inventory—a portion completed in this period	2,100		
(Transferred in—100% complete)		—	
(Conversion costs—40% complete)			1,260
Units started and completed in this period	52,350	52,350	52,350
Ending Inventory—units started but not completed in this period	2,015		
(Transferred in—100% complete)		2,015	
(Conversion costs—60% complete)			1,209
Totals	56,465	54,365	54,819

1b. Unit Cost Analysis Schedule

Total Cost Analysis	Costs from Beginning Inventory	Costs from Current Period	Total Cost to Be Accounted For
Transferred-in costs	$29,200	$753,448	$782,648
Conversion costs	2,654	172,130	174,784
Totals	$31,854	$925,578	$957,432

Computation of Equivalent Unit Cost	Current Period Costs	÷	Equivalent Units	=	Cost per Equivalent Unit
Transferred-in costs	$753,448		54,365		$13.859*
Conversion costs	172,130		54,819		3.140*
Totals	$925,578				$16.999

1c. Cost Summary Schedule

	Cost of Goods Transferred to Finished Goods Inventory	Cost of Ending Work in Process Inventory
Beginning inventory		
Costs from preceding period	$ 31,854	
Costs to complete this period		
Transferred-in costs: none	—	
Conversion costs:		
1,260 units × $3.14	3,956†	
Units started and completed		
52,350 units × $16.999 per unit	889,897†	
Ending Inventory		
Transferred-in costs: 2,015 units × $13.859		$27,926†
Conversion costs: 1,209 units × $3.14		3,796†
Totals	$925,707	$31,722

*Answer is rounded to three decimal places.
†Answer is affected by the use of rounded unit cost amounts.

Computational check:

Costs to Finished Goods Inventory	$925,707
Costs in ending Work in Process Inventory	31,722
Error due to rounding—add to costs transferred to Finished Goods Inventory	3
Total costs to be accounted for (unit cost analysis schedule)	$957,432

2. The costs of completed units for April are now ready to be transferred from the cooling department to Finished Goods Inventory. The proper journal entry is:

Finished Goods Inventory	925,710	
Work in Process—Cooling Department		925,710
To record the transfer of cost of completed units in April from the Cooling Department to Finished Goods Inventory		

Chapter Assignments

Questions

1. What production characteristics lend themselves to the adoption of a process cost system?
2. "For job order costing, *one* Work in Process Inventory account is used; but in process costing, it is not uncommon to find *several* Work in Process Inventory accounts being employed." Explain this statement.
3. Define equivalent units.
4. Why is it necessary to adjust actual unit data to equivalent unit data for product costing purposes in a process cost system?
5. Define *conversion costs,* and give the reason for using this concept in process costing computations.
6. Name the three schedules necessary for the process costing analysis.
7. Why is it easier to compute equivalent units when there are no units in beginning inventory than when there are beginning inventory data?
8. Why is the FIFO cost flow appropriate for product unit costing in a process cost system?
9. In computing equivalent production for conversion costs, units in ending inventory are multiplied by the percentage of completion, whereas in the same computation applied to beginning inventory, the inverse of the percentage of completion or the percentage not completed is used. Why?
10. What are the purposes of the unit cost analysis schedule?
11. Why do we ignore costs attached to beginning inventory when computing unit costs under the FIFO cost flow assumption?
12. What are the two important dollar amounts evolving from the cost summary schedule, and how do they relate to the year-end financial statements?
13. Describe the method for checking the accuracy of the results of the cost summary schedule.
14. What is the significance of the journal entry used to transfer costs of completed products out of the Work in Process Inventory account?

Classroom Exercises

Exercise 25-1 Process Cost Flow Diagram

Raiborn Real-Tone Paint Company uses a process costing system to account for manufacturing costs incurred in its various lines of paint. Production of Quality Brand starts in Department QB1, where raw materials AH and C24 are added to a water base. The solution is heated to 70° Celsius and transferred to Department QB2. There it is mixed for one hour at the same temperature. Then the product is transferred to Department QB3, where it is cooled and packaged in four-liter cans. Direct labor and factory overhead charges are incurred uniformly throughout each part of the process.

Prepare a diagram showing the product flow for the Quality Brand product of the Raiborn Real-Tone Paint Company.

Exercise 25-2 Equivalent Units—No Beginning Inventories

David West Liquids, Inc., began operations on January 2 and installed a process cost accounting system at that time. Bath oil is the main product. During the year, 45,600 liters of raw materials were introduced into the production process. On December 31, 2,800 liters were still in process. Raw materials are added at the beginning of the process, and conversion costs are incurred evenly throughout the process. Ending inventory was 40 percent complete on December 31.

From the above information, prepare a schedule of equivalent production for the year ending December 31.

Exercise 25-3 Product Flow Diagram

Four departments are required to produce Hazel Hand Cream, the main product of Haseman Products, Inc. Department A transforms Raw Material 29 into a paste. A dye is produced in Department B by using Raw Materials 16, 19, and 31. Plastic containers are made from Raw Materials 14 and 21 in Department C. In Department D, the paste is mixed with the dye and Raw Material 9 to produce the hand cream. The completed product is packaged in the plastic containers at the end of Department D's process before being transferred to finished goods inventory. With the exception of the plastic containers in Department D, raw materials are added only at the beginning of each process, but the conversion costs are incurred uniformly throughout each process.

Prepare a product flow diagram of Haseman's production process.

Exercise 25-4 Equivalent Units—Beginning Inventories

Reichardt Enterprises produces Rainwater Shampoo for professional hair stylists. On January 1, 26,400 liters of product were in process, 60 percent complete as to conversion costs and 100 percent complete as to raw materials. During the year, 142,500 liters of raw materials were entered into the production process. Work in process inventory on December 31 is summarized as follows: contents, 7,500 liters; stage of completion, 70 percent of conversion costs and 100 percent of raw material content.

From the information supplied for Reichardt Enterprises, prepare a schedule of equivalent production for the year.

Exercise 25-5 Unit Cost Determination with Beginning Inventories

Drake Kitchenwares, Inc., manufactures durable cookware. Production has just been completed for July. The following production figures are provided:

a. Beginning Work in Process Inventory: materials, $40,200; conversion costs, $46,800.
b. Cost of raw materials used in July was $123,475.
c. Conversion costs for the month were $206,349.
d. During July, 35,190 units were started and completed.
e. A schedule of equivalent production for July, which had aleady been prepared, yielded the following information: conversion costs, 52,910 equivalent units; raw materials, 49,390 equivalent units.

Using the information provided, prepare a unit cost analysis schedule for July, assuming a FIFO cost flow.

Exercise 25-6
Cost Summary Schedule

The Capriotti Family Bakery uses a process cost system for internal record-keeping purposes. Production for August, had the following results:

a. Beginning inventory included costs from the preceding period (materials at $74,000 and conversion costs at $166,000), and costs to complete this period (no cost for materials, but conversion costs of 4,200 equivalent units at $8.30 per unit).
b. Units started and completed totaled 118,600 units at $12.00 per unit.
c. Ending Work in Process Inventory was made up of: materials, 12,000 equivalent units at $3.70 each; and conversion costs, 6,500 equivalent units at $8.30 each.

Using the information provided, compute the cost of goods transferred to Finished Goods Inventory, the cost of ending Work in Process Inventory, and the total costs to be accounted for.

Exercise 25-7
Unit Cost Computation—Beginning Inventories

Graber Fastener Company produced 47,500,000 finished wood screws in 19xx. A special analysis revealed the following equivalent production figures: raw materials, 48,200,000 units; conversion costs, 46,800,000 units. See summary below.

	Raw Materials	**Direct Labor**	**Factory Overhead**
Beginning inventory	$ 26,400	$ 14,100	$ 28,900
Charged to production during the year	1,205,000	561,600	1,404,000
Total costs	$1,231,400	$575,700	$1,432,900

Using the data provided for the Graber Fastener Company and assuming a FIFO cost flow, prepare a unit cost analysis schedule for 19xx.

Exercise 25-8
Cost Transfer—Journal Entry Required

The cost summary schedule below was compiled from data in the records of the Hillman Paste Company for the year ended July 31, 19xx.

	Cost of Goods Transferred to Finished Goods Inventory	Cost of Ending Work in Process Inventory
Beginning inventory		
Costs from preceding period	$ 31,840	
Costs to complete this period		
Materials: none	—	
Conversion costs: 13,140 units at $.90	11,826	
Units started and completed: 84,960 units at $2.10	178,416	
Ending inventory		
Materials: 6,400 units at $1.20		$ 7,680
Conversion costs: 3,200 units at $.90		2,880
Totals	$222,082	$10,560

1. From the information contained in the cost summary schedule, prepare the journal entry required for July 31, 19xx.
2. Reconstruct the company's schedule of equivalent production, assuming that raw materials are added at the beginning of the process and beginning inventories are 70 percent complete as to conversion costs.

Problem Set A

Problem 25A-1 Process Costing —No Beginning Inventories

The Maple Syrup Company produces a complete line of food-topping products. On January 2, 19xx, a new product, Tangerine Syrup, was introduced. Two basic raw materials, tangerine juice and a basic syrup mixture, are added at the beginning of the process. No other liquids are used in the process. Direct labor and factory overhead costs are incurred uniformly throughout the process. The following cost and unit data pertaining to the production of Tangerine Syrup were accumulated during 19xx:

Raw Materials Used	Liters	Cost
Tangerine juice	75,000	$201,000
Basic syrup mixture	150,000	60,000

Additional information: Direct labor cost was $78,810. Factory overhead applied during the period was $236,430. Ending Work in Process Inventory statistics: 12,000 liters, 100 percent complete as to raw materials and 75 percent complete as to conversion costs. Assume that no units were lost due to spoilage or evaporation.

Required

1. Using good form, prepare (a) a schedule of equivalent production, (b) a unit cost analysis schedule, and (c) a cost summary schedule.
2. From the information in the cost summary schedule, prepare the proper journal entry to transfer costs of completed units for 19xx to Finished Goods Inventory.

Problem 25A-2 Process Costing —No Beginning Inventories

The Denniston Chemical Corporation produces compounds used in the synthesis of an antibiotic. It has just completed its first month of operation. The production process involves two operating departments: the Compounding Department, in which direct labor, factory overhead, and all raw materials are added; and the Centrifuging Department, in which only conversion costs are added. Each unit produced needs to be processed by both departments. No significant evaporation occurs in either department. The following operating information was provided by the Accounting Department as of July 31, 19xx: During July 152,400 units were started. Costs of raw materials used were $1,981,200, and conversion costs were $797,160. A total of 88,200 units were completed and transferred to the Centifuging Department. In ending Work in Process Inventory, all units in the Compounding Department at July 31 are 40 percent complete as to conversion costs. All raw materials are added at the beginning of the process.

Required

1. Using good accounting form, prepare the following schedules for the Compounding Department: (a) a schedule of equivalent production, (b) a unit cost analysis schedule, and (c) a cost summary schedule.
2. From information in the cost summary schedule, prepare the necessary journal entry to transfer costs of completed units for July to the Centrifuging Department.

Problem 25A-3 Process Costing —With Beginning Inventories

The main product of the Bukstein Britches Company is a line of corduroy jeans for infants. All operations are performed by a series of automated machines in one process. Corduroy material is introduced at the beginning of the process. Actual processing of the pants is uniform throughout the process.

During August, 462,500 square meters of material were introduced into the process. Average unit cost of this material was $2.80 per square meter. The August labor cost amounted to $229,568, and the actual overhead incurred was $92,775. Work in Process Inventory at August 1 was made up of 3,700 units (pairs of pants), which were 100 percent complete as to raw materials and 80 percent complete as to conversion costs. The Beginning Inventory value was $30,500, with $25,300 representing the cost of raw materials.

The ending Work in Process Inventory of 6,800 units is complete as to raw materials costs, but is only 30 percent complete as to conversion costs. Note that one square meter of corduroy material is used to produce two units of output.

Required

1. Using good form and assuming a FIFO cost flow, prepare (a) a schedule of equivalent production, (b) a unit cost analysis schedule, and (c) a cost summary schedule.
2. From the information in the cost summary schedule, prepare the proper journal entry to transfer costs of completed units in August to Finished Goods Inventory.

Problem 25A-4 Process Costing —With Beginning Inventories

Microphysics, Inc., manufactures fuse assemblies for guided missiles. The painting operation is one of the many production processes involved. Paint is applied to the assemblies at the beginning of the process, and conversion costs are added as the units pass through the Painting Department. After drying and polishing, the assemblies are sent to the Inspection Department. Operations for May have recently been completed.

Beginning Work in Process Inventory for the Painting Department consists of 2,900 units (60 percent complete). Costs of raw materials were $40,600, and conversion costs were $3,520.

During the May operations in the Painting Department, 111,200 units were started. Costs of raw materials used were $1,556,800, and conversion costs were $546,050. There were 109,600 units completed and sent to the Inspection Department.

In ending Work in Process Inventory, all fuse assemblies remaining in the Painting Department as of May 31 were 30 percent complete as to conversion costs.

Required

1. Using good accounting form and assuming a FIFO cost flow, prepare the following for the Painting Department for May: (a) a schedule of equivalent production, (b) a unit cost analysis schedule, and (c) a cost summary schedule.
2. From the information in the cost summary schedule, prepare the journal entry needed to transfer costs of completely painted, dried, and hand-polished fuse assemblies for May to the Inspection Department.

Problem 25A-5 Process Costing —One Process and Two Time Periods

The production of an inexpensive dry red wine is the specialty of the Weirich Winery. Raw materials include a water base, fresh grape juice, sugar, and an aging ingredient, all of which are added at the beginning of the process. The aging ingredient results in a rapid artificial aging process so that the wine may be considered a finished product immediately upon completion of the production process. Data for February and March are shown below.

	February	March
Beginning Work in Process Inventory		
Units	7,100 liters	?
Costs: Raw materials	$5,050	?
Conversion costs	1,920	?
Production during the period		
Units started	194,000 liters	205,000 liters
Current period costs		
Raw materials	$139,680	$149,650
Conversion costs	84,114	101,545
Ending Work in Process Inventory		
Units	12,400 liters	16,900 liters

For all partially completed inventories, all raw materials have been added. The February beginning inventory was 60 percent complete as to conversion costs, and the ending inventory for February was 20 percent complete for these costs. Ending inventory for March was 30 percent complete regarding conversion costs. Costs of labor and factory overhead are incurred uniformly throughout the process. Assume no loss due to spoilage or evaporation.

Required

1. Using good form and assuming a FIFO cost flow, prepare the following schedules for the month of February: (a) a schedule of equivalent production, (b) a unit cost analysis schedule, and (c) a cost summary schedule.
2. From the information in the cost summary schedule, prepare the proper journal entry to transfer costs of completed units in February to Finished Goods Inventory.
3. Repeat the requirements listed in parts 1 and 2 above for the month of March.

Problem 25A-6 Process Costing —With Beginning Inventories and Two Departments

The Cobb Flake Company manufactures breakfast cereals and has been operating successfully for three generations. The production of bean flakes involves several processes, two of which are blending and baking. Raw materials are added at the beginning of the blending process, but no raw materials are added in the baking process. Conversion costs are incurred uniformly throughout both processes. After the baking process is finished, the units of product are sent to the Packaging Department. Production has just been completed for March. The Accounting Department has provided the month's production data as shown below.

Beginning Work in Process Inventories for the Blending Department consisted of 6,200 units (25 percent complete), costs of raw materials were $43,400, and conversion costs were $18,600. Beginning Work in Process Inventories for the Baking Department were 5,800 units (40 percent complete), transferred-in costs were $72,500, and conversion costs were $20,880.

March operations for the Blending Department showed 23,000 units started; costs for raw materials were $161,000, and conversion costs were $130,260. There were 18,400 units completed and transferred to the Baking Department. The Baking Department started with 18,400 units, transferred-in costs were unknown, and conversion costs were $197,400. A total of 22,200 units were completed and transferred to the Packaging Department.

In ending Work in Process Inventories for the Blending Department, all units were 45 percent complete as to conversion costs and for the Baking Department, all units were 60 percent complete as to conversion costs.

Before completing this problem, you may need to refer to the Review Problem.

Required

1. Using proper accounting form and assuming a FIFO cost flow, prepare the following schedules for the Blending Department for March: (a) a schedule of equivalent production, (b) a unit cost analysis schedule, and (c) a cost summary schedule.
2. From the information in the cost summary schedule, prepare the journal entry needed to transfer costs of completed units for March from the Blending Department to the Baking Department.
3. Prepare the same analyses as requested in part 1 above for the Baking Department and an entry to transfer costs of completed units for March from the Baking to the Packaging Department.

Problem Set B

Problem 25B-3 Process Costing —With Beginning Inventories

The Giovanni Wafer Company manufactures high-vitamin-and-calorie wafers used by professional sports organizations for supplying quick energy to players. The company uses a process costing system based on a FIFO cost flow. Production of these thin, white wafers is through a continuous product flow process. The company recently purchased several automated machines so that the wafers can be produced in a single department. The raw materials are all added at the beginning of the process. The costs for the machine operator's labor and production-related overhead are incurred uniformly throughout the processing.

In March, a total of 231,200 liters of raw materials were put into production. The average cost of raw materials was $1.60 per liter. Two liters of raw materials are used to produce one unit of output (one unit = 144 wafers). Labor costs for March were $124,500, and factory overhead incurred was $187,620. Beginning work in process inventory at March 1 contained 56,000 units, 100 percent complete as to raw materials and 40 percent complete as to conversion costs. The total cost of beginning inventory was $244,400, with $177,200 representing the cost of the raw materials. The ending work in process inventory of 48,000 units is fully complete as to raw materials, but is only 30 percent complete as to conversion costs.

Required

1. Using good form and assuming no loss due to spoilage, prepare (a) a schedule of equivalent production, (b) a unit cost analysis schedule, and (c) a cost summary schedule.
2. From the information in the cost summary schedule, prepare the proper journal entry to transfer costs of completed units in March to Finished Goods Inventory.

Problem 25B-4 Process Costing —With Beginning Inventories

Spencer Bottling Company makes and sells several types of soft drinks. Raw materials (sugar solution and artificial flavoring) are added at the beginning of production in the Mixing Department. Direct labor and factory overhead costs are applied to products on a uniform basis. Accounting records revealed the following information for August for the Fruit Punch product. Beginning Work in Process Inventory (60 percent complete) was 2,400 liters, and ending inventory (50 percent complete) was 3,600 liters. Unit production data showed 90,000 liters started, and 88,800 liters completed and transferred to the Bottling Department.

Production cost data were as follows

	Raw Materials	Conversion Costs
Beginning inventory	$ 576	$ 648
Current period costs	22,500	35,664

Required

1. Using good accounting form and assuming a FIFO cost flow, prepare the following schedules for the Mixing Department for August: (a) a schedule of equivalent production, (b) a unit cost analysis schedule, and (c) a cost summary schedule.
2. From the information in the cost summary schedule, prepare the journal entry required to transfer the cost of completed units to the Bottling Department.

Problem 25B-5 Process Costing —One Process and Two Time Periods

The Harvest Honey Company owns thousands of beehives and produces organic honey for sale to health food stores. Before raw honey can be sold, it must pass through several filterings to remove impurities such as pieces of the honeycomb and dust. No materials other than the honey from the hives are used. The production operation is a simple one in which the impure honey is added at the beginning of the process. A series of filterings follow, leading to a pure finished product. Production data for April and May are shown below.

	April	May
Beginning Work in Process Inventory		
Units	28,400 liters	?
Costs: Raw materials	$20,200	?
Conversion costs	7,680	?
Production during the period		
Units started	776,000 liters	820,000 liters
Current period costs:		
Raw materials	$ 465,600	$ 492,000
Conversion costs	1,046,752	1,137,304
Ending Work in Process Inventory		
Units	49,600 liters	67,600 liters

For all incomplete inventories, all raw materials have been added. April beginning inventory was 60 percent complete as to conversion costs, and these same costs for the ending inventory for April were 20 percent complete. Ending inventory for May was 30 percent complete for conversion costs. Costs of labor and factory overhead are incurred throughout the filtering process. Assume that there was no measurable loss from spoilage or evaporation.

Required

1. Using good form and assuming a FIFO cost flow, prepare the following schedules for the month of April: (a) a schedule of equivalent production, (b) a unit cost analysis schedule, and (c) a cost summary schedule.
2. From the information in the cost summary schedule, prepare the proper journal entry to transfer costs of completed units in April to Finished Goods Inventory.
3. Repeat the requirements in parts 1 and 2 above for May.

Problem 25B-6 Process Costing —With Beginning Inventories and Two Departments

Canned fruits and vegetables are the main products of Rickert Foods, Inc. In the preparation of canned peaches, the basic raw materials are introduced at the beginning of the Mixing Department's process. When thoroughly mixed, the solution is transferred to the Cooking Department, where it is heated to 100° Celsius and allowed to simmer for twenty minutes. When cooled, the mixture is transferred to the Canning Department for final processing. Throughout the operations of the Mixing and Cooking Departments, direct labor and factory overhead costs are incurred uniformly. No raw materials are added in the Cooking Department.

Cost data and related operating information for January are shown below.

Production Cost Data

	Raw Materials	Conversion Costs
Mixing Department		
Beginning inventory	$ 13,200	$ 2,400
Current period costs	216,000	91,200
	Transferred-in	**Conversion Costs**
Cooking Department		
Beginning inventory	$ 31,500	$ 6,660
Current period costs	?	335,520

Work in Process Inventories	
Beginning Inventories	
Mixing Department (40% complete)	12,000 liters
Cooking Department (20% complete)	18,000 liters
Ending Inventories	
Mixing Department (70% complete)	16,000 liters
Cooking Department (80% complete)	20,000 liters

Unit Production Data

	Mixing Department	Cooking Department
Units started during January	180,000 liters	176,000 liters
Units transferred out during January	176,000 liters	174,000 liters

Assume that no spoilage or evaporation loss took place during January.

(Before completing this problem, refer to the Review Problem.)

Required

1. Using proper accounting form and assuming a FIFO cost flow, prepare the following schedules for the Mixing Department for January: (a) a schedule of equivalent production, (b) a unit cost analysis schedule, and (c) a cost summary schedule.
2. From the information in the cost summary schedule, prepare the journal entry required to transfer costs of completed units for January from the Mixing to the Cooking Department.
3. Prepare the same schedules for the Cooking Department as were requested in part 1 above. Also prepare a journal entry to transfer costs of completed units from the Cooking to the Canning Department.

1937

Part Seven

Accounting for Management Decision Making

Part VI exposed you to the field of management accounting, focusing on the development of useful manufacturing cost information for product costing and management reporting purposes. Emphasis was placed on the first of three aspects of management accounting: management's need for product costing information.

In Part VII, we analyze the final two aspects of the field of management accounting: management's need for (1) data used for planning and control of operations, and (2) special reports and analyses used to support management decisions.

Chapter 26 introduces cost planning and control, specifically focusing on cost behavior patterns, cost-volume-profit relationships, responsibility accounting, and the nature, purpose, and development of standard costing information.

In Chapter 27, the cost planning and control tools described in Chapter 26 are used to implement the planning and control functions of the budgetary control process.

Chapter 28 deals with ways of developing and providing relevant information, including direct costing, contribution reporting, and incremental analysis. These approaches to information reporting are then applied to operating decisions involving capital expenditure analysis, make or buy alternatives, special product orders, and sales mix analyses.

Chapter 29 concludes this section on accounting for management decision making by illustrating the important role that income taxes play in business decisions.

Learning Objectives

Chapter Twenty-Six

Basic Cost Planning and Control Tools

1. Identify, define, and classify variable costs, semivariable costs, and fixed costs.

2. Compute the break-even point in units of output and in dollars of sales.

3. Project levels of sales that will generate anticipated profit amounts, using cost-volume-profit analysis.

4. Describe the nature of a responsibility accounting system.

5. Describe the nature and purpose of standard costs.

6. Identify the six elements of a standard unit cost, and describe the factors considered in the development of each standard or element.

7. Compute a standard unit cost.

Cost planning and control are vital to the continued existence of a company. A well-developed planning function results in efficient production activities, and cost reduction through control procedures leads to profitable operations. Knowledge of cost behavior patterns, cost-volume-profit relationships, a responsibility accounting system, and standard costing facilitates the cost planning and control functions. As a result of studying this chapter, you should be able to meet the learning objectives listed on the left.

Cost Behavior

Before estimating a future cost or preparing a budget, a manager must be aware of concepts underlying the basic movements or patterns of costs. One such concept is known as cost behavior, the manner in which costs respond to changes in activity or volume. To determine cost behavior, it is necessary to understand the basic cost characteristics and the accounting classifications of costs. This knowledge is used for predicting future costs and analyzing past cost performance.

Variable and Fixed Costs

Almost any cost can be classified as either a variable cost or a fixed cost. Some cost totals increase or decrease in direct proportion to increases or decreases in productive output, whereas others remain constant. Although our discussion will focus on cost behavior as it relates to productive output, we do not mean to imply that costs respond only to productive output measures. Sales commissions vary in direct proportion to sales revenue, and not to output measures such as cost of goods sold or number of units produced.

Objective 1 Identify, define, and classify variable costs, semivariable costs, and fixed costs

Total costs that change in direct proportion to productive output or any other volume measure are called **variable costs.** To illustrate the behavior of a variable cost, we will consider the example of an automobile manufacturer. Each new automobile is equipped with five tires, and each tire costs $38. The following cost analysis is pertinent to cost-planning activities of the automobile manufacturer: the total tire cost (five tires per automobile) is $190 for one automobile, $380 for two, $570 for three, $760 for four, $950 for five, $1,900 for ten, and $19,000 for one hundred. In the manufacturing of automobiles, total tire cost is a variable cost. On a per unit basis, a variable cost remains constant. In the above analysis, tire cost *per automobile* is $190 ($38 × 5) whether one car is produced or one hundred cars.

In our discussion of variable costs, we have assumed that a linear relationship exists between the cost and volume factors. Figure 26-1 depicts a linear variable cost behavior pattern. In this example, each unit of output requires $2.50 of labor cost. Total labor cost accumulates in direct proportion to the increase in units of output. However, not all variable costs behave in this manner. Power costs, for instance, decrease per unit of usage as consumption increases. Although variable in some regards, this cost pattern is more closely associated with semivariable costs, discussed in a later section of this chapter. As an introduction to the topic of cost behavior, we will assume that variable costs have a linear relationship to volume, as shown in Figure 26-1.

Figure 26-1 A Common Cost Behavior Pattern: Variable Cost

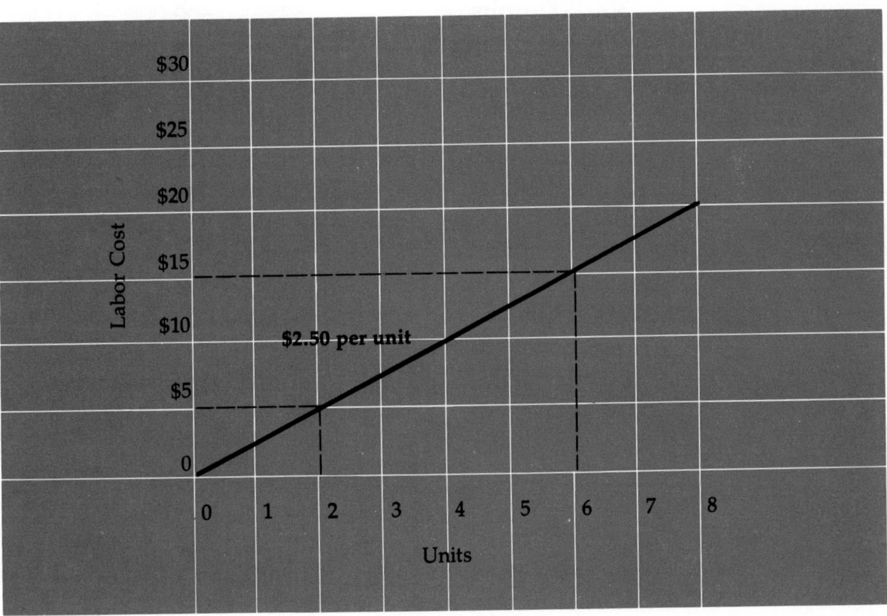

Fixed costs behave in an entirely different manner. Fixed costs remain constant in total within a relevant range of volume or activity. A relevant range of activity represents the potential volume levels within which actual operations are likely to occur. Supervisory salaries are a good example of a fixed cost. Assume that a local manufacturing company needs one supervisor for an eight-hour work shift. Production can range from 0 to 500,000 units per month per shift. The supervisor's salary is $2,000 per month, and the relevant range is 0 to 500,000 units. Total cost behavior is illustrated below.

Number of Products Required	Total Supervisory Salaries per Month
100,000	$2,000
200,000	2,000
300,000	2,000
400,000	2,000
500,000	2,000
600,000	4,000

Note that because a maximum of 500,000 units can be produced per shift, any output over 500,000 units requires an additional work shift and supervisor.

On a per unit basis, fixed costs decrease as volume increases. In the above example, supervisory costs per unit would fluctuate as follows:

Volume of Activity	Cost per Unit
100,000 units	$2,000/100,000 = $.02
200,000 units	$2,000/200,000 = $.01
300,000 units	$2,000/300,000 = $.0067
400,000 units	$2,000/400,000 = $.005
500,000 units	$2,000/500,000 = $.004
600,000 units	$4,000/600,000 = $.0067

The per unit cost increased at the 600,000 unit level because the volume was not within the relevant range and an additional supervisor was hired.

Total fixed costs remain constant at any level of activity within the relevant range. The graphic view of this fixed overhead cost is shown in Figure 26-2. Fixed overhead costs of $2,000 are required for the first 500,000 units of production. The same fixed costs of $2,000 are incurred at any level of output as long as the relevant range is not exceeded. Output over 500,000 units requires an additional supervisor, and the cost level jumps to $4,000.

Semivariable and Mixed Costs

Some costs cannot be classified as being only variable or fixed. A semivariable cost possesses both variable cost and fixed cost behavior characteristics in that part of the cost is fixed and part varies with the volume of output. Telephone expense is an example of a semivariable cost.

Figure 26-2
A Common Cost Behavior Pattern: Fixed Cost

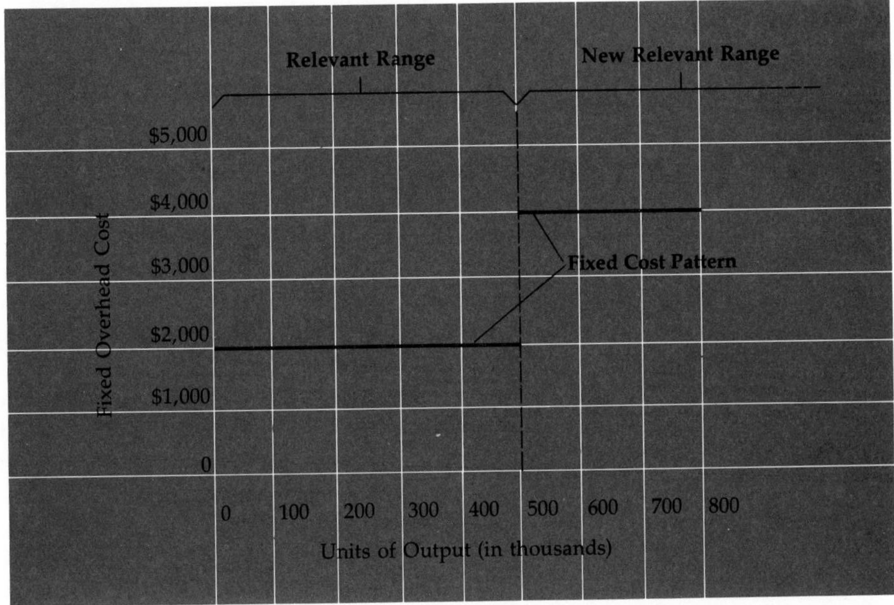

Monthly telephone charges are made up of a minimum service charge for a specific one-party line plus additional charges for extra telephones and for long-distance calls. The minimum service charge and the cost of extra telephones are fixed costs, whereas the long-distance charges are variable in that they vary according to usage.

Mixed costs also have variable and fixed cost behavior characteristics. **Mixed costs** result when more than one type of cost is charged to the same general ledger account. The Repairs and Maintenance account is a good example of an account balance made up of mixed costs. Labor charges to this account may vary in proportion to the amount of repairs required. However, one repair and maintenance worker may be employed on a full-time basis, and additional help hired when needed. In this case, the full-time worker's wages should be treated as a fixed cost. Depreciation costs for repair and maintenance machinery are also a fixed cost, but repair supplies will vary according to usage. For purposes of cost planning and control, semivariable and mixed costs must be divided into their respective variable and fixed cost elements. They can then be merged with other variable and fixed cost groupings for analysis.

Plant Capacity: Definition and Cost Influence

Plant capacity plays an important role in the study of cost behavior and in the budgetary control process. Expressions of plant capacity (productive volume levels) set limits on productive output and related costs when predictions are being formulated. Because variable costs increase or decrease in direct proportion to anticipated volume or output, it is important to understand what is meant by the term *plant capacity.* **Theoretical** or **ideal capacity** is the maximum productive output of a department or a company if all machinery and equipment were operated at optimum speed without any interruptions in production for a given time period. Although theoretical capacity is useful for establishing maximum productive capability, it has little value and no relationship to day-to-day operations. No company operates at ideal capacity. Practical capacity is theoretical capacity reduced by normal and anticipated work stoppages. Productive interruptions arise from machine downtime for retooling, repair and maintenance, or employee work breaks. These interruptions and resulting decrease in output should be included when measuring capacity.

Seldom does a company operate at either ideal or practical capacity levels. Excess capacity, defined as machinery and equipment purchased in excess of needs so that extra capacity is available on a stand-by basis, is often purchased for use when the regular facilities are being repaired. Seasonal sales often influence how much of the plant is in operation. During a slow season, a company may work just one or two shifts instead of around the clock. Because of these circumstances, normal capacity, rather than ideal or practical capacity, is often utilized as the measure of anticipated activity for planning purposes. Normal capacity is the average annual level of operating capacity that is required to satisfy anticipated sales demand. This demand figure is adjusted for seasonal business factors and operating cycles. Therefore, normal capacity is a realistic capacity measure that expresses what *will* be produced rather than what *can* be produced by an operating unit during a specific time period.

The Cost-Volume-Profit Relationship

Cost behavior patterns underlie the study of the relationships among cost, volume, and profit, known as cost-volume-profit analysis (or C-V-P analysis). These relationships are useful for predicting anticipated future operations. A company may use cost-volume-profit analysis as a planning tool when the sales volume is known and management wishes to determine the profit resulting from such an activity level. Another planning approach is to begin with a target profit objective and, through C-V-P analysis, determine the sales volume necessary to support that profit level.

For cost control purposes, C-V-P relationships provide a means for measuring the performance of various departments or other operating segments of the company. At the end of a period, the company analyzes sales volume and related actual costs to compute actual profit. It measures performance by preparing a comparative analysis of the actual costs and the predicted costs. These predicted costs are computed by applying C-V-P analysis to the actual sales volume. The result is a performance report that compares actual costs incurred with costs that should have been incurred at that specific activity level. Such reports provide the basis for the control of costs by management.

C-V-P Analysis: Break-even Point and Profit Planning

Objective 2 Compute the break-even point in units of output and in dollars of sales

Cost-volume-profit analysis is based on the relationships among operating cost, sales volume and revenue, and target net income. In approaching C-V-P analysis, costs must first be classified as being either variable costs (VC) or fixed costs (FC). Sales (S) are computed by multiplying units sold by the selling price per unit; target net income (NI) is projected by management. The formula associated commonly with C-V-P analysis is

$$\text{sales revenue} = \text{variable costs} + \text{fixed costs} + \text{net income}$$

Expressed in symbolic terms, the equation becomes

$$S = VC + FC + NI$$

By moving the variable costs (VC) and fixed costs (FC) over to the left side of the equal sign and changing these signs from positive to negative, this same equation becomes an expression in income statement format:

$$S - VC - FC = NI$$

Break-even Point One approach to planning operations for a period of time is to compute the **break-even point**—that point where total revenue equals total costs incurred and at which a company begins to generate a profit. When emphasis is on a company's or a product's break-even point, only the sales (S), variable cost (VC), and fixed cost (FC) elements are used. There is no net income (NI) when a company breaks even. The objective is to determine the level of activity where sales revenue equals the sum of all variable and fixed costs. Break-even data can be expressed in terms of break-even sales units or sales dollars. The general equations for determining the break-even point would be

$$S = VC + FC \quad \text{or} \quad S - VC - FC = 0$$

An example will illustrate specific applications of the equation to generate break-even units and dollar information. Sterling Products, Inc., manufactures wooden stands for portable television sets. Variable costs are $25 per unit, and fixed costs average $20,000 per year. Each wooden stand sells for $45. Given this information, we can compute the break-even point for this product in sales units and dollars.

Break-even point in sales units (represented by x):

$$\begin{aligned} S &= VC + FC \\ \$45x &= \$25x + \$20{,}000 \\ \$20x &= \$20{,}000 \\ x &= 1{,}000 \text{ units} \end{aligned}$$

Break-even point in sales dollars:

$$\$45/\text{unit} \times 1{,}000 \text{ units} = \$45{,}000$$

Another approach to computing the break-even point is through graphic analysis. This method is less precise, but it does yield meaningful data and is useful for illustrating break-even procedures. Figure 26-3 (next page) illustrates the break-even analysis of Sterling Products.

Figure 26-3
Graphic Break-Even Analysis: Sterling Products, Inc.

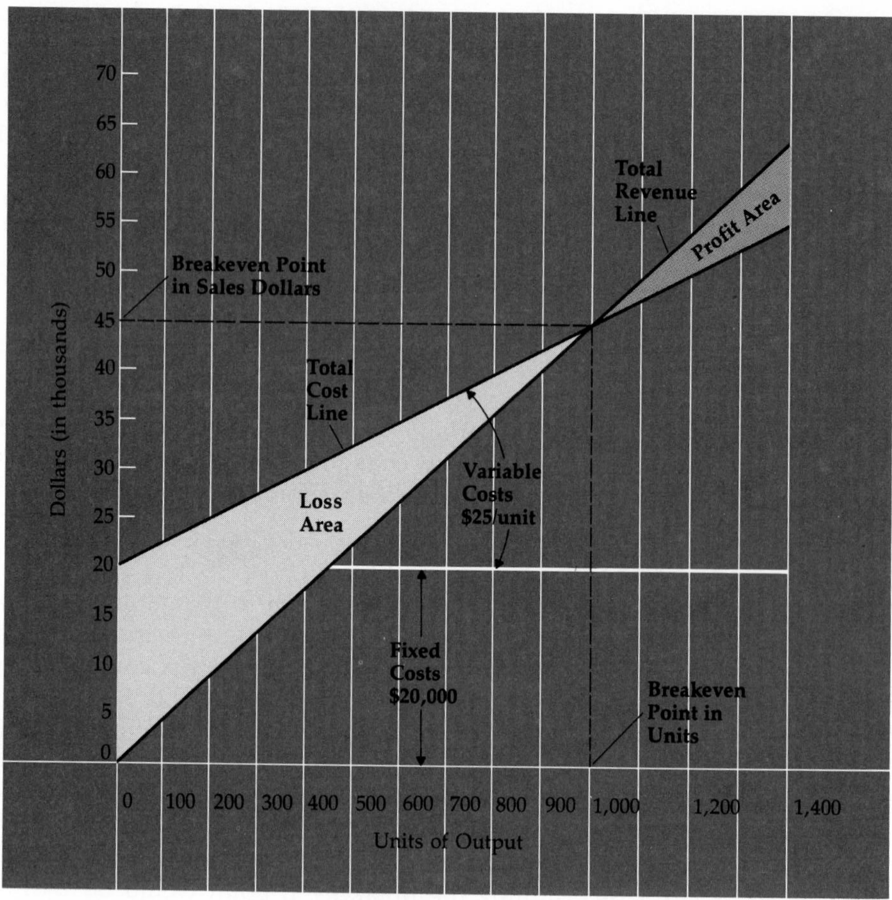

This standard break-even chart has the following elements: (1) horizontal axis in volume or units; (2) vertical axis in dollars; (3) horizontal line representing upper limit of fixed costs ($20,000); (4) total cost line beginning at point where fixed cost line intersects vertical axis and sloping upward to the right (slope is determined by variable costs per unit); (5) total revenue line beginning at origin of vertical and horizontal axes and sloping upward to the right (slope is a function of the selling price per unit). At the point where the total revenue line intersects the total cost line, revenues will equal total costs. The break-even point, expressed in either units or dollars of sales, can be found by extending this point of intersection to the horizontal or vertical axis, respectively. As shown in Figure 26-3, Sterling Products will break even when 1,000 television stands have been manufactured and sold, generating $45,000 in sales.

Profit Planning Break-even procedures can be extended easily to bring profit planning into the analysis. Assume that the Sterling Products president, Myra Miles, has set a $10,000 profit for 19x4 as the goal for management. If all of the previous data remain constant, how many television stands must Sterling Products manufacture and sell to generate the target profit? The answer is computed below (number of units = x).

Objective 3 Project levels of sales that will generate anticipated profit amounts, using cost-volume-profit analysis

$$\begin{aligned} S &= VC + FC + NI \\ \$45x &= \$25x + \$20{,}000 + \$10{,}000 \\ \$20x &= \$30{,}000 \\ x &= 1{,}500 \text{ units} \end{aligned}$$

To check the accuracy of this answer, insert all known data into an equation for an income statement.

$$\begin{aligned} S - VC - FC &= NI \\ (1{,}500 \text{ units} \times \$45) - (1{,}500 \times \$25) - (\$20{,}000) &= NI \\ \$67{,}500 - \$37{,}500 - \$20{,}000 &= \underline{\underline{\$10{,}000}} \end{aligned}$$

Contribution Margin Concept

The analysis of cost-volume-profit relationships is not complete without a discussion of the contribution margin concept. **Contribution margin** is the excess of revenues over all variable costs related to a particular sales volume. The contribution margin concept provides a fresh approach or an additional dimension to C-V-P analysis. A product line's contribution margin represents its net contribution to the absorption of fixed costs and to the generation of a profit from operations. Net income for Sterling Products, Inc., computed by using the contribution approach, is shown below.

	Units Produced and Sold	
	1,000	1,500
Sales revenue ($45 per unit)	$45,000	$67,500
Less variable costs ($25 per unit)	25,000	37,500
Contribution margin	$20,000	$30,000
Less fixed costs	20,000	20,000
Net income	—	$10,000

The introduction of contribution margin into C-V-P analysis changes the make-up of the equations as well as the format of the income statement. The equation would be

$$S - VC = CM - FC = NI$$

Because contribution margin (CM) is the remainder after variable costs have been subtracted from total sales, the break-even point (BE) can be expressed as the point where contribution margin (CM) minus total fixed costs (FC) equals zero. That is, break-even occurs when $CM - FC = 0$.

In terms of units of product, the break-even point equation would be changed as follows:

$$(\text{CM per unit} \times \text{BE units}) - \text{FC} = 0$$

Our objective is to determine an equation that isolates the expression, BE units, and the analysis below indicates how this amount is computed. The equation above can be rearranged mathematically as follows:

1. Move FC to right side of equation:

$$\text{CM/unit} \times \text{BE units} = \text{FC}$$

2. Divide both sides of equation by the expression "CM/unit":

$$\frac{\text{CM/unit} \times \text{BE units}}{\text{CM/unit}} = \frac{\text{FC}}{\text{CM/unit}}$$

3. After canceling terms, the end result would be:

$$\text{BE units} = \frac{\text{FC}}{\text{CM/unit}}$$

For profit-planning purposes, the equation is adjusted to include target net income as follows:

$$\text{target unit sales} = \frac{\text{FC} + \text{NI}}{\text{CM/unit}}$$

To illustrate the use of these equations, we shall refer to the data given earlier for Sterling Products.

$$\text{BE units} = \frac{\text{FC}}{\text{CM/unit}} = \frac{\$20{,}000}{\$45 - \$25} = \frac{\$20{,}000}{\$20} = 1{,}000 \text{ units}$$

$$\text{target unit sales} = \frac{\text{FC} + \text{NI}}{\text{CM/unit}} = \frac{\$20{,}000 + \$10{,}000}{\$20} = \frac{\$30{,}000}{\$20} = 1{,}500 \text{ units}$$

Once mastered, the use of the contribution margin simplifies the break-even and profit-planning computation procedures.

Assumptions Underlying C-V-P Analysis

Cost-volume-profit computations are accurate only under specific assumptions and certain conditions. If one or more of these assumptions and conditions are absent in a particular situation, the results of the analysis may be misleading. These assumptions and conditions are that (1) behavior of variable and fixed costs can be determined accurately, (2) cost and revenue elements have close linear approximations, (3) efficiency and productivity are constant within the relevant range of activity, (4) cost and price variables will remain constant during the planning period, (5) product sales mix will not change during the planning period, and (6) production and sales volume will be approximately equal during the planning period.

Responsibility Accounting

Objective 4 Describe the nature of a responsibility accounting system

Reporting of manufacturing costs requires special report formats and reporting techniques. The objective of the statement of cost of goods manufactured is to translate manufacturing cost data into usable information for inventory valuation, profit measurement, and external reporting purposes. As discussed in Chapter 23, all costs of raw materials, direct labor, and factory overhead are used to compute the cost of goods manufactured. However, management needs more than the statement of cost of goods manufactured to obtain information and costs on many day-to-day activities. Budget preparation, revenue and cost recording, cost control, and managerial performance evaluation require a special information accumulation and reporting system.

Responsibility accounting provides for the classification and comparative reporting of financial data according to specific areas of responsibility within a company. Also called **activity accounting** or **profitability accounting**, a **responsibility accounting system** personalizes accounting reports by classifying and reporting cost and revenue information according to defined responsibility areas of specific managers or management positions. When a company employs a responsibility accounting system, it is still necessary to use normal cost and revenue data accumulation and recording practices, the same debit and credit entries, a general ledger, special journals, and a defined chart of accounts. However, responsibility accounting centers on the reporting—not the recording—of operating cost and revenue data. Once the financial data from daily operations have been recorded, specific costs and revenues can be reclassified and reported for specific areas of managerial responsibility.

Organizational Structure and Reporting

A responsibility accounting system is made up of several reporting centers, one for each area or level of managerial responsibility. The reports for the various centers include only those cost and revenue items that are controllable by the manager of the particular segment being analyzed. If the manager cannot influence the amount of a particular cost or revenue item, that item is not included in the report. Because there is a report for each manager, and because lower-level managers report to higher-level managers, the same costs will appear in several reports. Thus, lower-level operating data are aggregated for reports to higher-level managers.

A look at a corporate organization chart and a series of reports will clarify the functioning of a responsibility accounting system. Figure 26-4 (next page) shows a typical management hierarchy with three vice presidents under the corporate president. We have abbreviated the middle and lower-level management positions in the sales and finance areas to direct attention toward the manufacturing area. The production managers of Divisions A and B report directly to the vice president of manufacturing. Within Division B, the managers of the Stamping Department, Painting Department, and Assembly Department report to the division's production manager.

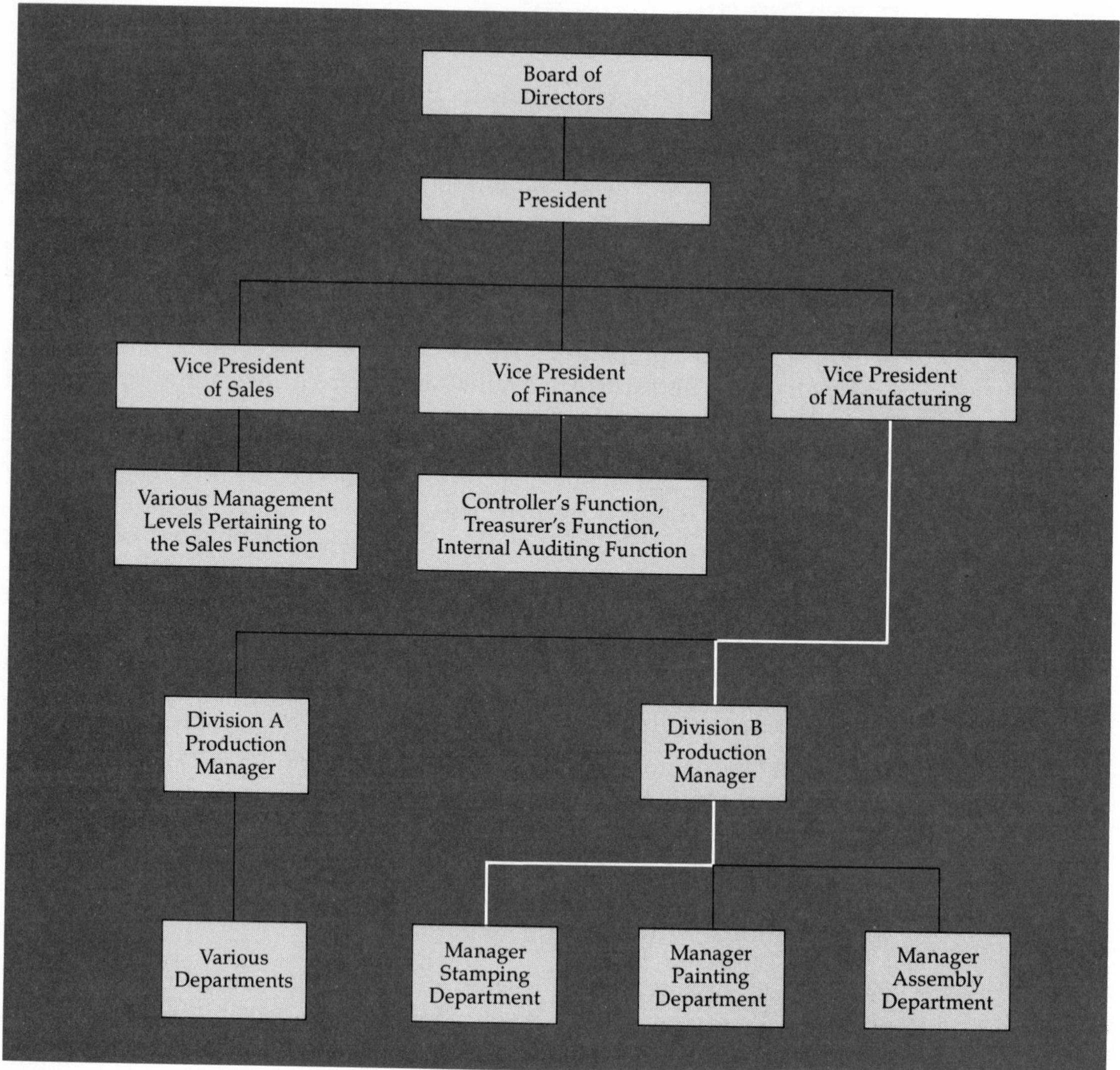

Figure 26-4 Organization Chart Emphasizing the Manufacturing Area

Within a responsibility accounting environment, operating reports prepared for each level of management are tailored to individual needs, emphasizing the cost and revenue items over which each manager has influence and control. As shown in Figure 26-5, the responsibility reporting network is linked together. At the department level, the report gives a detailed listing of cost items controllable by the manager and compares anticipated (or budgeted) costs with actual costs to measure operating performance. The manager who receives the departmental report in Figure 26-5 should be particularly concerned with direct materials cost and maintenance salaries because they are so much over budget.

The production manager of Division B is responsible for the three operating departments plus the controllable divisionwide costs. The production manager's report includes a summary of results from the Stamping Department as well as from all other areas of responsibility. However, at

Figure 26-5
Reporting Within a Responsibility Accounting System

Manufacturing: Vice President — **Monthly Report: November**

Amount Budgeted	Controllable Cost	Actual Amount	Over (Under) Budget
	Central production		
$ 281,400	scheduling	$ 298,100	$16,700
179,600	Office expenses	192,800	13,200
19,800	Operating expenses	26,200	6,400
	Divisions		
339,500	A	348,900	9,400
426,200	B	399,400	(26,800)
$1,246,500	Totals	$1,265,400	$18,900

Division B: Production Manager — **Monthly Report: November**

Amount Budgeted	Controllable Cost	Actual Amount	Over (Under) Budget
	Division expenses		
$101,800	Salaries	$96,600	$ (5,200)
39,600	Utilities	39,900	300
25,600	Insurance	21,650	(3,950)
	Departments		
46,600	Stamping	48,450	1,850
69,900	Painting	64,700	(5,200)
142,700	Assembly	128,100	(14,600)
$426,200	Totals	$399,400	$(26,800)

Stamping Department: Manager — **Monthly Report: November**

Amount Budgeted	Controllable Cost	Actual Amount	Over (Under) Budget
$22,500	Direct materials	$23,900	$1,400
14,900	Factory labor	15,200	300
2,600	Small tools	1,400	(1,200)
5,100	Maintenance salaries	6,000	900
1,000	Supplies	1,200	200
500	Other costs	750	250
$46,600	Totals	$48,450	$1,850

the division level, the report does not present detailed cost items; only departmental totals appear. Even more data aggregation is present in the vice president's report. Only corporate and summarized divisional data representing costs controllable by the vice president are included. Note that the actual supplies cost at the departmental level is a part of the vice president's report (in the $399,400), but like all costs reported at lower levels, specific identity has been lost.

Cost and Revenue Controllability

Management is interested in minimizing costs and maximizing profits. To accomplish this objective, it is necessary to determine the origin of the cost or revenue item and to identify the person responsible for the item. The separable or traceable costs of each company segment become important for control purposes. Traceable costs are specifically identified with a department's operation and are assigned to that department without proration or allocation on some logical or arbitrary basis. From a listing of traceable costs that originate in a particular corporate segment, responsibility accounting focuses on those traceable costs that are controllable by the segment manager.

Controllable costs of a particular segment manager are those costs that result from his or her actions and decisions. If a specific manager can regulate or influence a cost or revenue item, the item is controllable at that level of operation. If managers have the authority to acquire or supervise the use of a particular resource or service, they control the related cost.

Controllability is the key to a successful responsibility accounting system. The cumulative nature of controllability means that every cost incurred by a company is traceable to and controllable by at least one manager or executive. Identification of controllable costs at lower management levels is often difficult. At lower levels, managers seldom have absolute authority to acquire or supervise resource and service use. Such managers have only partial control and influence over particular costs. Because identification of a controllable cost is sometimes difficult, managers should participate in identifying costs for which they will be held accountable in their performance reports. If controllability of cost and revenue items is linked properly to origin and area of responsibility, the result is an efficient, meaningful reporting system for measuring operating performance and for pinpointing operational trouble spots.

Standard Cost Accounting

Standard cost accounting is another tool used by management for cost planning and cost control purposes. When a company employs standard costs, all costs affecting the three inventory accounts and the Cost of Goods Sold account are stated in terms of standard or predetermined costs rather than actual costs incurred. A standard cost system is employed with an existing job order or process costing system and is not a full cost accounting system in itself. Together with cost behavior relationships and the various cost-volume-profit analyses, the incorporation of standard costs in a cost accounting system provides the foundation for the budgetary control process. Standard costs are useful internally for (1) evaluating the performance of workers and management, (2) preparing budgets and forecasts, and (3) helping to develop appropriate selling prices. Because the topic of standard costs is so important and represents such a drastic change in costing concepts, its discussion and explanation will be divided into two parts. In this chapter, we will look at the nature of standard costs, their make-up, how they are developed, their use in product costing, and their journal entry recording. In Chapter 27, we will analyze their primary use as a cost control tool.

Objective 5
Describe the nature and purpose of standard costs

Nature and Purpose of Standard Costs

Standard costs are realistically predetermined costs for raw materials, direct labor, and factory overhead. They are usually expressed as a cost per unit of finished product. Predetermined overhead costs, which have already been discussed, differ from standard costs. Standard costing is a total unit cost concept dealing with all three manufacturing cost elements. It goes beyond the factory overhead cost area. In addition, more care and effort are given to the computation of standard costs.

Predetermined overhead costing and standard costing do share two very important characteristics: (1) both produce forecasted amounts to be used in product costing, and (2) both are formulated by using anticipated costs or budgeted data. But this is where the similarity ends. Cost information supporting final computation of the projected standard costs is based on engineering estimates, forecasted demand, worker input, time and motion studies, and raw materials types and quality. More than the simple projections of trends of past cost performance that are used to develop predetermined overhead rates are required to support standard cost data. However, we do not intend to minimize the role of the predetermined overhead rate. On the contrary, a standard overhead rate provides some of the same data as do predetermined overhead rates. Standard costing is a sophisticated and expensive component to add to a company's cost accounting system. If such an extension of the cost system is not feasible economically, predetermined overhead rates should still be used.

Standard costing is a total cost concept in that standard unit costs are determined for raw materials, direct labor, and factory overhead. In a fully integrated standard cost system, all actual manufacturing cost data are replaced by standard (or predetermined) cost data. Accounts such as Raw Materials Inventory, Work in Process Inventory, Finished Goods Inventory, and Cost of Goods Sold are all stated in terms of standard costs. All debit and credit entries made to these accounts are in terms of standard costs, not actual costs. All inventory balances are computed by using standard unit costs. Separate records of actual costs incurred are maintained for purposes of comparing standard costs (what should have been spent) with actual costs. These comparisons are usually made at the end of each accounting period, whether it is weekly, monthly, or quarterly. If large differences (variances) exist, the cost accountant attempts to determine the causes of these differences. This process, known as variance analysis, is one of the most effective cost control tools, and is discussed in Chapter 27.

Standard costs are introduced into a cost accounting system to help in the budgetary control process. Standard costs are useful for preparing operating budgets, for identifying areas of the production process requiring cost control measures, for determining realistic prices, and basically for simplifying cost accounting procedures for inventories and product costing. Although expensive to install and maintain, a standard cost accounting system can save a company considerable amounts of money through reduction in the amount of wasted resources. Emphasis in this chapter will be on the development of cost standards. Their use in a cost accounting system will be explained in the next chapter.

Development of Standard Costs

Objective 6 Identify the six elements of a standard unit cost and describe the factors considered in the development of each standard or element

A standard unit cost has six computational components: (1) raw materials price standard, (2) raw materials quantity standard, (3) direct labor time standard, (4) direct labor rate standard, (5) standard variable factory overhead rate, and (6) standard fixed factory overhead rate. To explain the development of a standard unit cost, we must identify and analyze each of these components.

Standard Raw Materials Cost The standard raw materials cost is computed by multiplying the raw materials price standard by the raw materials quantity standard. If the price standard for a particular item were $2.75 and a specific job required the use of eight of these items as its standard quantity, the standard raw materials cost for that job would be $22.00 (8 × $2.75).

The raw materials price standard is a carefully derived estimate or projected amount of what a particular type of raw material will cost when purchased during the next accounting period. Care must be taken to anticipate price increases, changes in quantities available, and possible new supplier sources, all of which could influence the price standard. A company's purchasing agent is responsible for the development of price standards for all items of raw materials. In addition, the purchasing agent should follow through with actual purchases at projected standard prices.

The standard usage of raw materials is one of the most difficult standards to forecast. The raw materials quantity standard is an expression of forecasted or expected quantity usage and is influenced by product engineering specifications, quality of raw materials used, age and productivity of the machines being used, and the quality and experience of the machine operators and set-up people. Production managers are usually responsible for establishing and policing raw materials quantity standards. However, many people provide input into their development.

Standard Direct Labor Cost The **standard direct labor cost** for a product or job order is computed by multiplying the direct labor time standard by the direct labor rate standard. Assume that a product is to be produced in 1.5 standard direct labor hours and the standard labor rate is $8.40 per hour. Even if the person actually making the product were paid $7.90 per hour, $12.60 ($8.40 × 1.5) of standard direct labor cost would be charged to the Work in Process Inventory account.

Current time and motion studies of workers and machines and past employee/machine performances provide the basic input for the creation of a **direct labor time standard.** Such standards are hourly expressions (or fractions of an hour) of the time it takes for each department, machine, or process to complete production on one unit or one batch of output. In many cases, standard time per unit will be a small fraction of an hour. Adherence to time standards is the responsibility of the department manager or supervisor. These standards should be revised whenever a machine is replaced or the quality of workers changes.

Labor rates are either set by labor contracts or defined in company personnel policies. **Direct labor rate standards** express the hourly labor cost per function or job classification that is expected to exist during the next accounting period. Rate ranges are established for each class or type of worker, and rates vary within these ranges according to length of service to the company. Because of labor contracts or company personnel policies, standard labor rates are fairly easy to formulate. Problems arise when a worker with a wrong classification performs a specific task. For instance, a machine operator making $9.25 per hour may actually perform the work of a set-up person earning $4.50 per hour. Here, a difference (or variance) from the anticipated standard direct labor rate will result.

Standard Factory Overhead Cost The **standard factory overhead cost** is computed by multiplying the standard variable overhead rate and the standard fixed overhead rate by the appropriate application base. This procedure is very similar to that used for applying factory overhead when using a predetermined overhead rate. The application base is usually standard direct labor hours, but other bases such as standard labor cost, units of output, or standard machine hours can be used.

We have already discussed the procedure for computing a predetermined overhead rate. Standard factory overhead rates differ from predetermined overhead rates in two areas. First, standard factory overhead rates are broken down usually into standard variable and standard fixed factory overhead rates. Second, more time and effort is put into the derivation of standard overhead rates. Procedurally, however, the basic computations are the same in both cases.

In determining standard overhead rates, the most difficult areas are forecasting the total variable and fixed overhead costs and arriving at the proper application base amounts appropriate for both the variable and the fixed components. The **standard variable overhead rate** is computed as follows:

$$\text{standard variable overhead rate} = \frac{\text{total budgeted variable overhead costs}}{\text{application base}}$$

For purposes of the variable rate, the application base is usually the anticipated number of standard direct labor hours to be worked during the next accounting period. As discussed earlier, a different application base can be used if labor hours are not a good barometer of variable factory overhead costs incurred.

The computation of the standard fixed overhead rate is based on a different premise. Fixed overhead costs are incurred to maintain a certain level of productive capacity, commonly referred to as normal capacity. If this level of capacity is used to compute the standard fixed overhead rate, all fixed overhead costs should be applied to units produced at the point in time when normal capacity is reached. If actual output exceeds normal capacity, a favorable situation exists, because more fixed overhead would be applied to production that was actually incurred. An unfavorable condition exists if actual output is less than normal capacity. The computation of the **standard fixed overhead rate** is as follows:

$$\text{standard fixed overhead rate} = \frac{\text{total budgeted fixed overhead costs}}{\text{normal capacity}}$$

The difference (variance) resulting when factory overhead incurred and factory overhead applied are not equal will be discussed further in Chapter 27. Of primary concern here is that two separate computations are necessary to arrive at the standard variable and standard fixed factory overhead rates.

Using Standards for Product Costing

Using standard costs for product costing eliminates the need to compute unit costs on a weekly or monthly basis or by batch of productive output from actual cost data. Once standards are developed for raw materials, direct labor, and factory overhead, a standard unit cost can be computed at any time. These standard manufacturing cost elements become the amounts used to determine the (1) cost of purchased raw materials entered into Raw Materials Inventory, (2) cost of goods requisitioned out of Raw Materials Inventory and into Work in Process Inventory, (3) cost of direct labor charged to Work in Process Inventory, (4) cost of factory overhead applied or charged to Work in Process Inventory, (5) cost of goods completed and transferred to Finished Goods Inventory, and (6) cost of units sold during the period and charged to the Cost of Goods Sold account. In other words, all transactions (entries) affecting the three inventory accounts and Cost of Goods Sold will be expressed in terms of standard costs, no matter what the actual costs incurred. An illustrative problem using standard costs will help to explain this concept.

Illustrative Problem: Use of Standard Costs

Ike Industries, Inc., employs a standard cost system in its Dennison, Texas, division. Recently, the company revised its standards for the automatic pencil product line to reflect current standard costs for the year 19xx. New standards include the following: Raw materials price standards

Objective 7
Compute a standard unit cost

were $7.20 per square foot for casing material and $1.25 for each movement mechanism. Raw materials quantity standards were .25 square foot of casing material per pencil and one movement mechanism per pencil. Direct labor time standards were .01 hour per pencil for the Stamping Department and .05 hour per pencil for the Assembly Department. Direct labor rate standards were $6.00 per hour for the Stamping Department and $7.20 per hour for the Assembly Department. Standard factory overhead rates were $18.00 per direct labor hour for the standard variable overhead rate and $12.00 per direct labor hour for the standard fixed overhead rate.

Required

Compute the standard manufacturing cost of one automatic pencil.

Solution

Standard cost of one pencil computed:

Raw materials costs	
Casing ($7.20/sq ft × .25 sq ft)	$1.80
One movement mechanism	1.25
Direct labor costs	
Stamping department: (.01 hr/pencil × $6.00/hr)	.06
Assembly department: (.05 hr/pencil × $7.20/hr)	.36
Factory overhead	
Variable overhead: (.06 hr/pencil × $18.00/hr)	1.08
Fixed overhead: (.06 hr/pencil × $12.00/hr)	.72
Total standard cost per pencil	$5.27

Journal Entry Analysis

The recording of data in a standard cost accounting system is similar to the recording of actual cost data as discussed in prior chapters. The only major difference is that any amount for raw materials, direct labor, or factory overhead being entered into the Work in Process Inventory account is stated at standard cost. If this is the case, the Work in Process Inventory account is stated entirely at standard cost. Any transfers of units to Finished Goods Inventory and to the Cost of Goods Sold account will automatically be at standard unit cost. When actual costs for raw materials, direct labor, and factory overhead differ from standard cost, the difference is recorded in a variance account. Here we will assume that all costs incurred are at standard cost. Referring back to the Ike Industries, Inc., example, record the following transactions:

Transaction: Purchased 400 square feet of casing material at standard cost.

Entry: Raw Materials Inventory	2,880	
Accounts Payable		2,880
To record purchase of 400 sq ft of casing material at $7.20/sq ft		

(If the purchase price had been higher or lower than the standard price, the same $2,880 standard cost would have been entered into the Raw Materials Inventory account.)

Transaction: Requisitioned 60 square feet of casing material and 240 movement mechanisms into production.

Entry:		Debit	Credit
	Work in Process Inventory	732	
	Raw Materials Inventory		732
	To record requisition of 60 sq ft of casing material (at $7.20/sq ft) and 240 movement mechanisms (at $1.25 each) into production		

Transaction: At period end, 300 pencils were completed and transferred to Finished Goods Inventory.

Entry:		Debit	Credit
	Finished Goods Inventory	1,581	
	Work in Process Inventory		1,581
	To record the transfer of 300 completed units to finished goods inventory (300 pencils × $5.27/pencil)		

The above analysis includes only a few examples of the journal entries used in recording standard cost information. The examples given in the next chapter are more realistic and easier to understand because they are included with the analysis of variances. Our purpose here was simply to show that when a standard cost accounting system is being used, standard costs rather than actual costs flow through the production accounts.

Chapter Review

Review of Learning Objectives

1. Identify, define, and classify variable costs, semivariable costs, and fixed costs.

Variable costs are costs that change in total in direct proportion to productive output. Raw materials and direct labor are examples of variable costs. Semivariable costs possess both variable and fixed cost behavior characteristics in that part of the cost is fixed and part varies with the volume of output. Examples are power costs and telephone charges. Fixed costs remain constant in total within a relevant range of volume or activity. Examples of fixed costs include supervisory salaries and depreciation charges.

2. Compute the break-even point in units of output and in dollars of sales.

The break-even point is that point where total revenue equals total costs incurred. In formula form, break-even occurs when S = VC + FC. In terms of contribution margin, the formula would be

$$\text{BE units} = \frac{\text{FC}}{\text{CM/unit}}$$

Once the number of break-even units is known, it can be multiplied by the product's selling price to get the break-even point in dollars of sales.

3. Project levels of sales that will generate anticipated profit amounts, using cost-volume-profit analysis.

The addition of a factor for projected net income (NI) to the break-even equation makes it possible to plan levels of operation that yield target profits. The formula in terms of contribution margin would be

$$\text{target unit sales} = \frac{\text{FC} + \text{NI}}{\text{CM/unit}}$$

4. Describe the nature of a responsibility accounting system.

Responsibility accounting provides for the classification and comparative reporting of financial data according to specific areas of responsibility within a company. Also called activity or profitability accounting, a responsibility accounting system personalizes accounting reports by classifying and reporting cost and revenue information according to defined responsibility areas of specific managers or management positions. A responsibility accounting system is made up of several reports, one for each area or level of managerial responsibility.

5. Describe the nature and purpose of standard costs.

Standard costs are realistically predetermined costs for raw materials, direct labor, and factory overhead that are usually expressed as a cost per unit of finished product. They are introduced into a cost accounting system to help in the budgetary control process. Standard costs are useful for preparing operating budgets, for identifying areas of the production process requiring cost control measures, for determining realistic prices, and basically for simplifying cost accounting procedures for inventories and product costing.

6. Identify the six elements of a standard unit cost, and describe the factors considered in the development of each standard or element.

The six elements of a standard unit cost are (1) the raw materials price standard, (2) the raw materials quantity standard, (3) the direct labor time standard, (4) the direct labor rate standard, (5) the standard variable factory overhead rate, and (6) the standard fixed factory overhead rate. The raw materials price standard is carefully derived by considering anticipated price increases, changes in quantities available, and possible new supplier sources. An expression of forecasted or expected quantity usage, the raw materials quantity standard is influenced by product engineering specifications, quality of raw materials used, age and productivity of the machines being used, and the quality and experience of the machine operators and set-up people. The direct labor time standard is based on current time and motion studies of workers and machines and past employee/machine performances. Labor union contracts and company personnel policies lead to the development of direct labor rate standards. Standard variable and fixed factory overhead rates are derived from total budgeted or forecasted variable and fixed factory overhead costs divided by an appropriate application base such as standard direct labor hours or normal capacity.

7. Compute a standard unit cost.

A product's total standard unit cost is computed by adding together the following costs: (1) raw materials cost (equals raw materials price standard times raw materials quantity standard), (2) direct labor cost (equals direct labor time standard times direct labor rate standard), and (3) factory overhead cost (equals standard variable and standard fixed factory overhead rate times standard direct labor hours per unit).

Review Problem

Before doing the exercises, review especially the break-even analysis and profit planning examples in the chapter. For additional help, see the review problem in the working papers.

Chapter Assignments

Questions

1. What important characteristic is associated with variable costs?
2. "Fixed costs remain constant in total but decrease per unit as output increases." Explain this statement.
3. Discuss what is meant by the relevant range of activity.
4. Why is a telephone charge considered a semivariable cost?
5. Differentiate between practical capacity and ideal capacity.
6. Why does a company seldom operate at either an ideal or a practical capacity level? What alternative expression of capacity is more relevant and therefore more useful? Why?
7. What is the relationship between cost-volume-profit analysis and the concept of cost behavior?
8. Define the concept of break-even point, and state why such information is useful to management.
9. Describe the use of a corporate organization chart in the process of designing a responsibility accounting system.
10. Define controllable cost and describe its role in a responsibility accounting system.
11. Define contribution margin. What does contribution margin represent?
12. State the equation that determines target unit sales, using the elements of fixed costs, net income, and contribution margin.
13. What are the assumptions and conditions under which cost-volume-profit computations are accurate?
14. What is a standard cost?
15. What similar characteristics do predetermined overhead costing and standard costing share? How do these costing approaches differ?
16. "Standard costing is a total cost concept in that standard unit costs are determined for raw materials, direct labor, and factory overhead." Explain this statement.
17. Identify the six standards used to compute total standard unit cost.
18. What three factors could influence a raw material price standard?
19. "Standard labor cost is a function of efficiency and unionization." Is this a true statement? Defend your answer.
20. What general ledger accounts are affected by the installation of a standard cost system?

Classroom Exercises

Exercise 26-1 Break-even Analysis

Hedlund Manufacturing Company produces head covers for golf clubs. The company expects to generate a profit during the next calendar year. It anticipates that fixed manufacturing costs will be $95,000 and that fixed general and administrative expenses will be $115,100 for the year. Variable manufacturing and selling costs per set of head covers will be $4.75 and $1.25, respectively. Each set will sell for $11.50.

1. Compute the break-even point in sales units.
2. Compute the break-even point in sales dollars.

Exercise 26-2 Determination of Fixed and Variable Costs

From the following list of costs of productive output, indicate which costs are usually considered variable costs and which are accounted for as being fixed costs: (1) packing materials for stereo components, (2) real estate taxes, (3) gasoline for delivery truck, (4) property insurance, (5) depreciation expense of buildings (straight-line method), (6) supplies, (7) indirect materials used, (8) bottles used in the sale of liquids, (9) license fees for company cars, (10) wiring used in producing radios, (11) machine helper's wages, (12) wood used in the production of bookcases, (13) city operating license, (14) employer's share of social security payments, (15) machine operators' wages, (16) cost of required outside inspection on each unit produced. Could any be considered a semivariable cost? Explain.

Exercise 26-3 Profit Planning

Short-term automobile rentals are the specialty of Rockford Auto Loans, Inc. Average variable operating expenses have been $7.00 per day per automobile. The company owns thirty cars. Fixed operating costs for the next year are expected to be $75,050. Average daily rental revenue per automobile is anticipated to be $18.50. Management would like to earn $25,000 during the coming year.

1. Calculate the number of total *daily* rentals that the company must generate during the year to earn the anticipated profit.
2. On the basis of your answer to part 1, compute the number of days on the average that each automobile must be rented.
3. Compute the total rental revenue for the year that is required to earn the $25,000 profit.

Exercise 26-4 Responsibility Accounting

Dave Abramson is supervisor of the Taping Department of Minnesota Packing Company. During August 19xx, departmental activities generated the performance report at the top of the next page.

The divisional superintendent is satisfied with Mr. Abramson's overall departmental performance but has questioned the cost coverages for the following items: (a) Insurance Expense; (b) Depreciation, Equipment; (c) Depreciation, Building; (d) Property Taxes; and (e) General and Administrative Expenses.

1. If you were Mr. Abramson, how would you respond to the superintendent's inquiry?
2. Assume that the Minnesota Packing Company is going to install a responsibility accounting system. Which cost items included in the above report would you exclude if you were using a responsibility accounting format? State the reasons supporting your exclusion of these selected cost items.

Minnesota Packing Company
Performance Report, Taping Department
For the Month Ended August 31, 19xx

	Actual	Budgeted	Difference Over (Under)
Raw Materials Used	$14,590	$15,400	$(810)
Direct Labor	12,645	13,000	(355)
Insurance Expense	890	700	190
Indirect Labor	6,110	6,000	110
Heat, Light, and Power	1,468	1,500	(32)
Depreciation, Equipment	3,740	3,500	240
Depreciation, Building	2,600	2,000	600
Repairs and Maintenance	1,980	2,000	(20)
Property Taxes	1,205	1,000	205
Inventory Storage Costs (allocated portion)	472	500	(28)
General and Administrative Expenses (allocated portion)	2,650	2,000	650
Miscellaneous Departmental Costs	716	800	(84)
	$49,066	$48,400	$666

Exercise 26-5 Contribution Margin Approach to Profit Planning

Maritime Ballistics, Ltd., produces undersea projectiles for nuclear submarines. The management has just been offered a project that will be funded by a government contract. The contract purchase price is $30,000 per unit, but the number of units to be purchased has not yet been negotiated. The company's fixed costs are budgeted at $4,090,000, and the variable costs per unit are $18,500.

Compute the number of units at the stated contract price that the company should agree to produce in order to earn a target net income of $15,000,000.

Exercise 26-6 Standard Unit Cost Analysis

Accountants and engineers of the Danelid Manufacturing Company have developed the following cost, usage, and time standards for the production of a small chain saw, one of the company's main products. Raw materials required are a saw motor casing at $4.75, an operating chain at $3.50, a 3-horsepower motor at $19.90, and a chain housing at $6.25. Direct labor consists of .5 hour from a materials inspector at $5.50 per hour, .5 hour from an assembler at $7.00 per hour, and .25 hour from a product tester at $6.00 per hour. Factory overhead charges are figured at a variable rate of $10.00 per labor hour, and at a fixed rate of $7.40 per labor hour.

Compute the total standard manufacturing cost of one chain saw.

Exercise 26-7 Standard Unit Cost Computation

Heliscope Aerodynamics, Inc., manufactures electronically equipped weather-detecting balloons for university meteorological departments. Recent effects of nationwide inflation have caused the company's management to recompute the standard costs.

New raw material price standards are $620 per set for electronic components and $4 per square meter for heavy-duty canvas. Raw material quantity standards are one set of electronic components per balloon and 95 square meters of heavy-duty canvas per balloon. Direct labor time standards are 14.5 hours per balloon for the Electronics Department and 12.0 hours per balloon for the Assembly Department. Direct labor rate standards are $9.00 an hour for the Electronics Department and $6.50 an hour for the Assembly Department. Standard factory overhead rates are $12.00 per direct labor hour for the standard variable overhead rate and $7.00 per direct labor hour for the standard fixed overhead rate.

Using the production standards provided, compute the standard manufacturing cost of one weather balloon.

Exercise 26-8
Journal Entries Using Standard Costs

Townsend Machine Tool Company employs a standard job order cost system. Current-year standards per unit of output are as follows: Raw materials consist of 2 kilograms at $4.90 per kilogram. Direct labor is 2.5 hours at $6.00 per hour. Factory overhead applied consists of variable costs of $1.50 per direct labor hour and of fixed costs of $2.80 per direct labor hour.

Using the data above, prepare journal entries for the following transactions:

May 9 Purchased 1,200 kilograms of raw materials at standard cost.
June 3 Requisitioned 940 kilograms of raw materials into production.
Aug. 1 Transferred 460 completed units of output to finished goods inventory.

Problem Set A

Problem 26A-1
Break-even Analysis

Selling citrus trees is the specialty of Orange County Nursery, Inc. The company grows its trees on a 200-acre farm outside Villa Park, California. The nursery is considering a new line of deciduous fruit trees, which will be sold only in 57-liter container sizes. Management expects that fixed costs will increase $61,200 per year because of the introduction of the new line of fruit trees. Variable costs are expected to be $28 per tree. Average selling price is anticipated to be $45 per tree.

Required

1. From the above information, compute the number of trees that must be sold per year if the company is to break even on the new line of trees.
2. Determine the new break-even point in unit sales if the selling price were increased by 20 percent.
3. Assuming the original data, determine the break-even point in unit sales if fixed costs were reduced by $6,800.
4. Calculate the break-even point in unit sales if variable costs per tree were reduced to $25, assuming all other original data remained constant.

Problem 26A-2
Break-even Analysis

The manufacture of pipes for sprinkler systems involves a chemical-mixing and substance-molding process. DKA Products, Inc., produces pipes with different diameters, all in 5-meter lengths. The 1.9-centimeter pipe has variable costs per 5-meter section of $.08 for raw materials, $.06 for direct labor, and $.05 for variable manufacturing costs. Total variable costs are thus $.19. Fixed costs assignable to the 1.9-centimeter pipe are expected to be $67,855 for the year. The projected selling price is $.60 per 5-meter section.

Required

1. Compute the break-even point in sales units.
2. Compute the break-even point in sales dollars.
3. Determine the unit break-even point if management could cut fixed costs by $2,255 while maintaining the same selling price.
4. Using the original information, compute the break-even point in units if the selling price were increased to $.70 per unit, fixed costs were decreased by $7,855, and variable costs per unit were reduced by $.02.

Problem 26A-3 Profit Planning

The profit goal as determined by the management of Newport Carburetors, Inc., for the coming 19xx calendar year is $22,000. The company has decided on a new selling price of $35 per carburetor. Variable costs per unit equal $11, and total fixed costs are anticipated to be $80,000.

Required

1. Compute the number of carburetors that the company will have to sell to generate the target profit, and convert this amount to sales dollars.
2. Compute break-even sales in dollars.
3. Explain the dollar differences between break-even sales and the dollar sales necessary to earn the target profit. Use contribution margin as part of your explanation.
4. Present a graphic analysis of the projected sales and profit figures.

Problem 26A-4 Profit Planning—Contribution Margin Approach

Producing college textbooks entails many complex steps, all of which contribute to the cost of published materials. High-quality paper and binding materials also add significantly to the cost as well as to the useful life of a book. Dalberg Publishing Company is taking a very careful look at a new text manuscript. Initial estimates indicate that variable costs per book will be $6.80 and that total fixed costs will be $60,000. The company plans to market the book wholesale at $12.80 per copy.

Required

1. Using the contribution margin approach, compute the number of copies of the book the company must sell to earn a profit of $30,000.
2. Continuing with the same approach, compute the number of copies that must be sold to earn a target profit of $61,000 if fixed costs are cut to $50,000.
3. Assuming the original information, determine the selling price that the company must use to generate $80,700 of profit if 21,000 copies of the book could be sold.
4. The company's marketing director has stated that the most optimistic sales estimate for the book would be 36,000 copies. If the highest possible selling price that the company can charge is $13.20, and if variable costs per unit cannot be reduced below the original estimates, how much more can be spent on fixed advertising costs if the new target profit is $40,000?

Problem 26A-5 Development of Standards: Raw Materials

Bandy-Hardman, Inc., manufactures an electronic gadget called a Taxputer. This device accumulates and stores financial data and computes a person's taxable income on a perpetual input basis. Parts for the assembly of the gadget in 19x6 include the following standard costs: housing at $6.00 per unit, electronic mechanism at $9.50 per unit, and wires, circuits, etc., at $4.50 per unit.

In 19x7, housings are to be bought from two sources: 40 percent at $7.00 from Supplier A and 60 percent at $7.50 from Supplier B. All electronic mechanisms will be purchased from Supplier C at a 30 percent increase over the 19x6 cost. Prices of wire, circuits, and so on, per unit are expected to increase 10 percent over 19x6 amounts.

Required

Consider each of the following cases separately.

1. Compute the total standard materials cost per unit for 19x7.
2. If the company purchased the housings and electronic mechanisms in lots of 1,000, it would receive a 20 percent price reduction from 19x6 prices. Wire, circuits, and so on, will still increase by 10 percent. Determine the resulting standard raw materials unit cost.
3. Substandard housings can be purchased at $5.50, but 20 percent of them will be unusable and cannot be returned. Compute the standard raw materials unit cost if the company followed this procedure, assuming the original facts of the case for the remaining data. The cost of the defective raw materials will be spread over good units produced.

Problem 26A-6 Developing and Using Standard Costs

Hank's Lawn and Garden Company manufactures and sells chemical fertilizers for home and business use. In addition, the company assembles and markets a line of gardening tools and accessories. For these items, the company purchases all of the necessary parts, assembles the parts into a product in the Assembly Department, and transfers the products to the Painting and Packing Department for final processing. One of the main items in this line of tools and accessories is a lawn chemical spreader. Labor and overhead standards for the spreader for the coming year, 19x4, are as follows: Direct labor is .5 hour in the Assembly Department at $7.80 per hour and .2 hour in the Painting and Packing Department at $9.00 per hour. The standard for variable overhead in the factory is 220 percent of all direct labor dollars, and for fixed overhead in the factory is 180 percent of all direct labor dollars.

Raw materials price standards for 19x4 have not yet been developed. Price standards for 19x3 are $1.60 per set of wheels, $3.70 per casing, $2.40 per handle assembly, and $1.20 for paint per spreader. After careful analysis, the following changes are expected in raw materials prices for 19x4: wheels will increase 20 percent per set; 30 percent of the casings will be purchased from Vendor A at $3.80 per unit and 70 percent will be purchased from Vendor B at $4.00 per unit; the handle unit will increase 30 percent in price; and paint prices will go up 10 percent.

Required

1. Compute the total standard raw materials cost per spreader for 19x4.
2. Using your answer in part 1 and the other information given in the problem, compute the 19x4 standard manufacturing cost of one lawn chemical spreader.
3. Using the data compiled in your answers to parts 1 and 2, prepare journal entries for the following transactions:

Jan. 31 Purchased 700 sets of wheels at standard cost on account.
Feb. 20 Requisitioned 450 spreader casings into production.
Mar. 31 Transferred 190 completed spreaders to finished goods inventory.

Problem Set B

Problem 26B-3 Profit Planning

In 19xx, Swad Enterprises is expecting to earn a profit of $86,500. The company manufactures ornamental concrete blocks. Each lot of one hundred blocks requires variable costs of $6.00 for raw materials, $3.50 for direct labor, $2.50 for manufacturing overhead, and $2.00 for selling costs. Total variable costs are thus $14.00 per lot. Fixed costs for 19xx are anticipated to be $381,500. Each hundred-block lot will sell for $40.

Required

1. Determine how many lots of ornamental block the company must sell to earn its target profit, and convert this amount to sales dollars.
2. Compute break-even sales in dollars.
3. Explain the dollar difference between break-even sales and dollar sales necessary to earn the target profit. Use contribution margin as part of your explanation.
4. Present a graphic analysis of the projected sales and profit figures.

Problem 26B-4 Profit Planning—Contribution Margin Approach

Bishopston Industries manufactures portable microwave ovens. The ovens are costly to produce because of the intricate body interiors and the skilled craftsmanship needed in the assembly process. A less expensive, slightly modified version is being considered to reach the lower-income market. The proposed estimates are as follows: variable costs per oven of $90, total fixed costs of $330,000, and a tentative selling price per oven of $260.

Required

1. Using the contribution margin approach, determine the number of portable microwave ovens that the company will need to sell to achieve a desired profit of $80,000.
2. Continuing with the same approach, determine the number of ovens that must be sold to obtain a target profit of $105,000 if fixed costs are increased to $420,000.
3. Assuming the original information, compute the new selling price that the company should use to generate $426,000 of profit if 4,200 ovens can be sold.
4. The marketing vice president has determined that the maximum sales for the new, less expensive oven is 19,800 units. If the highest possible selling price that the company can charge is $290, and if variable costs per unit cannot be reduced below the original estimates, how much more can be spent on fixed advertising costs if the new target profit is $140,000?

Problem 26B-5 Development of Standards: Direct Labor

A planned change in the employee labor rate structure has caused the Coventry Salt Company to develop a new standard direct labor cost for its product. Standard direct labor costs per 100 pounds of salt in 19x4 were .5 hour in the Sodium Preparation Department at $8.40 per hour, .8 hour in the Chloride Mixing Department at $9.00 per hour, and .2 hour in the Cleaning and Packaging Department at $6.50 per hour. Labor rates are expected to increase in 19x5 by 10 percent in the Sodium Preparation Department, 5 percent in the Chloride Mixing Department, and 12 percent in the Cleaning and Packaging Department. New machinery in the Chloride Mixing Department will lower the direct labor time standard by 25 percent per 100 pounds of salt. All other time standards are expected to remain the same.

Required

Consider each of the following cases separately.

1. Compute the standard direct labor cost per 100 pounds of salt in 19x5.
2. Management has a plan to improve productive output by 20 percent in the Sodium Preparation Department. If such results were achieved in 19x5, determine (a) the effect on the direct labor time standard, and (b) the resulting total standard direct labor cost per 100 pounds of salt.
3. Unskilled labor can be hired to staff all departments in 19x5, with the result that all labor rates paid in 19x4 would be cut by 60 percent in the new year. Such a change in labor skill would cause the direct labor time standards to increase by 50 percent over their anticipated 19x5 levels using skilled labor. Compute the standard direct labor cost per 100 pounds of salt if this change occurred.

Problem 26B-6 Developing and Using Standard Costs

Sue's Aquatic Supplies Company manufactures swimming pool equipment and accessories. In the production of swimming pool umbrellas, waterproof canvas is first processed through the cutting department. In the assembly department, the canvas is stretched over the umbrella's ribs on the center pole and opening mechanism. When this task is completed, the umbrella is mounted on a heavy base before being packed for shipment to various distribution warehouses.

The company employs a standard cost accounting system. Direct labor and factory overhead standards for the production of each pool umbrella for 19x6 have been computed as follows: Direct labor consists of .2 hour charged to the Cutting Department at $7.00 per hour and of .8 hour charged to the Assembly Department at $8.50 per hour. Variable overhead in the factory is 140 percent, and fixed overhead in the factory 120 percent, of total direct labor dollars.

During 19x5 the company used the following raw materials standards: Waterproof canvas was $1.30 per square yard for 4 square yards. The standard for a unit consisting of pole, ribs, and opening mechanism was $8.50 per unit. The base was $5.40 per unit.

Quantity standards are expected to remain the same during 19x6. However, the following price changes are anticipated: The cost of waterproof canvas will increase by 40 percent. The pole, ribs, and opening mechanism will be purchased from three vendors: Vendor A will provide 10 percent of the total supply at $8.60 per unit; Vendor B will provide 60 percent at $8.80; and Vendor C will supply 30 percent at $9.00. The cost of each base will increase 20 percent.

Required

1. Compute the total standard raw materials cost per umbrella for 19x6.
2. Using your answer in part 1 and other information given in the problem, compute the 19x6 standard manufacturing cost of one pool umbrella.
3. Using the data compiled in your answers to parts 1 and 2, prepare journal entries for the following transactions:

Jan. 20	Purchased 4,500 square yards of waterproof canvas at standard cost on account.
Feb. 1	Requisitioned 525 pole, rib, and opening mechanism assemblies into production.
Mar. 15	Transferred 350 completed pool umbrellas to finished goods inventory.

Learning Objectives

Chapter Twenty-Seven

Budgetary Control

1. *Define the concept of budgetary control.*
2. *Describe a period budget.*
3. *Identify the components of a master budget and describe their integration.*
4. *Differentiate between cost planning activities and those used for cost control purposes.*
5. *Prepare a flexible budget.*
6. *Compute and evaluate raw materials, direct labor, and factory overhead variances.*

The budgetary control process comprises the cost planning function and the cost control function. The basic elements of effective budgetary control are cost behavior patterns, cost-volume-profit analysis, and standard costing. Cost behavior and C-V-P analysis are linked closely to budget preparation, and standard costing provides the foundation for variance analysis leading to cost control. As a result of studying this chapter, you should be able to meet the learning objectives listed on the left.

Cost planning and control are key functions leading to effective management. The total process of (1) developing plans for a company's anticipated operations, and (2) controlling operations to aid in accomplishing those plans is known as **budgetary control**. Earlier chapters centered on the various accounting tools used in the budgetary control process. This chapter shows the relationship of cost behavior, cost-volume-profit analysis, responsibility accounting, and standard costing to the cost planning and the cost control functions. Emphasis here is on the preparation of period budgets and standard cost variance analysis.

Budgetary Control: The Planning Function

Objective 1 Define the concept of budgetary control

A primary requirement of an accounting system is that it produce relevant, timely information. One way to fulfill this requirement is to build effective budgetary control elements into the accounting system. Budgetary control involves procedures leading to realistic planning of future company activities *and* proper cost control methods to help achieve those plans. The planning element is the first area of concern.

The Need for Planning

A successful business venture does not achieve the benefits of an effective budgetary control system by operating in some haphazard manner from day to day. The company must quantify its goals, define the roles of various individuals, and identify intermediate operating targets. These procedures represent the first steps in the planning process. Companies approach the planning function by projecting operating results for two different time periods. Initially, they must prepare and maintain a long-term plan covering a five- or ten-year time period. Such plans are general in nature, describing probable product line changes, expansion of plant and facilities, machinery replacement, and changes in marketing strategies. Long-term plans are important because they provide broad goals to strive for through yearly operations.

Annual operating plans do not evolve automatically from long-term plans. Although long-term projections provide broad goals, they do not contain specific instructions on how to attain the anticipated results through annual production and sales efforts. Given the five- or ten-year plan, management must translate long-term objectives into specific annual goals. Once the goals have been defined for the forthcoming accounting period, various levels of managers must work out in detail the operations required to attain these annual goals. This task centers on a one-year time period and involves specific targets.

The Period Budget

Objective 2 Describe a period budget

Short-term or one-year plans are usually formulated in a set of period budgets. A **period budget** is a forecast of annual operating results for a segment of a company that represents a quantitative expression of planned activities. Preparation of period budgets involves the entire management team and requires timely information and careful coordination. The period budgeting process converts unit sales and production forecasts into revenue and cost estimates for each of the many operating segments of the company. Everyone involved in this budgeting process should take care to ensure that these forecasts are accurate and realistic.

Budgeting and Responsibility Accounting Period budget preparation relies heavily on several cost accounting tools already discussed. One very important tool in the budgeting process is responsibility accounting and the resulting network of managerial responsibilities and information flows. The orderly generation of information is the key to successful budget preparation. To aid in the establishment of an information system, a responsibility accounting system should be designed to link report generation with various tiers of management.

Where data flow is based on a responsibility accounting system, budget preparation begins by communicating the annual sales and production plans of top management to the various levels of management. Individual segment or department managers are expected to develop detailed operating budgets for their areas of responsibility. This information is then sent up through the managerial hierarchy for comment and adjustment before being assembled by the controller or budget director. After making necessary adjustments and integrating all the individual period budgets into a cohesive overall plan, the controller presents the annual operating budget to management. Such a plan is a composite of individual departmental operating budgets that are based on and reflect the long-range goals of top management.

Budgeting and C-V-P Analysis Knowledge of cost behavior patterns and the use of C-V-P analysis aid in budget preparation. Costs that vary directly with production volume can be computed as soon as a forecast of productive output is available. Variable selling costs can be projected after the announcement of the unit sales target. Fixed costs are a function of volume or capacity and are estimated on the basis of the company's operating capabilities.

Profit planning is possible only after all cost behavior patterns have been identified. As shown in Chapter 26, cost-volume-profit relationships lend themselves to profit planning and budgeting activities. Because cost behavior is a function of sales and production volumes, one can identify the conditions for maximum profit by simulating operating results at various levels of sales and productive output. If the company uses a target profit figure in its planning, C-V-P analysis is necessary to determine the volume required to support the profit expectations.

Budgeting and Standard Costs Budgeting and standard costing are closely related, and each of these cost systems benefits the other. Standard costs are very useful for budget preparation. However, accurate standard costs are computed only after anticipated costs and production volume are carefully projected.

Standard costs are used in product costing, pricing, inventory valuation, and cost control analysis. Their primary function is not budget preparation. To the extent that estimated data are required, however, such budgets or cost projections are made when standards are being revised and updated. Once computed, standard costs should be used in the preparation of the company's operating plans.

The Master Budget

Objective 3 Identify the components of a master budget and describe their integration

A **master budget** is an integrated set of departmental or functional period budgets that have been consolidated into forecasted financial statements for the entire company. Each departmental or functional area's period budget supplies the projected cost and revenue data for that specific part of the company. When combined, these individual budgets represent all transactions of the company for a future accounting period. With this information available, anticipated results of operations can be integrated with the beginning general ledger balances to produce forecasted statements of net income and financial position of the company for the budget time period. This budget preparation cycle has three phases: (1) preparation of detailed operating or period budgets, (2) compilation of data to produce the forecasted income statement, and (3) determination of the resulting financial position and balance sheet.

Detailed Operating Budgets Period budgets are normally prepared for each departmental or functional cost and revenue generating segment. The various functions utilized for budget preparation purposes are the (1) sales budget (units), (2) production budget (units), (3) selling expense budget, (4) raw materials purchase budget, (5) raw materials usage budget, (6) labor hour requirement budget, (7) direct labor dollar budget, (8) factory overhead budget, (9) general and administrative (G&A) expense budget, and (10) capital expenditure budget.

These budgets are interrelated. Following the sales unit forecast, the production budget can be prepared. The selling expense budget is also a function of the sales forecast. Raw materials usage and resulting purchase requirements are related to the production forecast. The production budget also leads to the formulation of the labor and factory overhead budgets. Anticipated general and administrative expenses and capital expenditures are determined usually by top management. Much of this information may be accumulated at the departmental level and incorporated into these functional period budgets. The key factor to remember is that the sales unit forecast provides the catalyst for all of the period budgets. Figure 27-1 (next page) shows how these detailed operating budgets provide the basis for determining the effects of planned operations on the company's financial position.

Forecasted Income Statement Once the detailed operating budgets have been prepared, the controller or budget director can begin to integrate the information. This person compiles a cost of goods sold forecast from data in the raw materials, direct labor, and factory overhead budgets. Revenue information is computed from the unit sales budget. Using the anticipated revenue and cost of goods sold data, and integrating information from the selling expense and general and administrative expense budgets, the controller can prepare the forecasted income statement. This process is shown in Figure 27-1.

Cash Flow Forecast (Cash Budget) Cash flow is one of the most important aspects of the operating cycle of a business. A **cash flow forecast (cash budget)** usually shows the firm's projected ending cash balance and the cash position for each month of the year so that periods of high or low cash availability can be anticipated. Excessively large cash balances mean that funds of the company are not being used to earn an optimal rate of return. Low cash reserves may mean that the company will be unable to meet its current payment obligations. Therefore, to prevent either of these potential problems from occurring, careful cash planning is necessary.

Within the master budget cycle, the cash budget is prepared after all period budgets are final and the forecasted income statement is complete. The cash budget has two primary sections—forecasted cash receipts and forecasted cash disbursements. Sales budgets, cash versus credit sales data, and accounts receivable collection data are used to formulate the

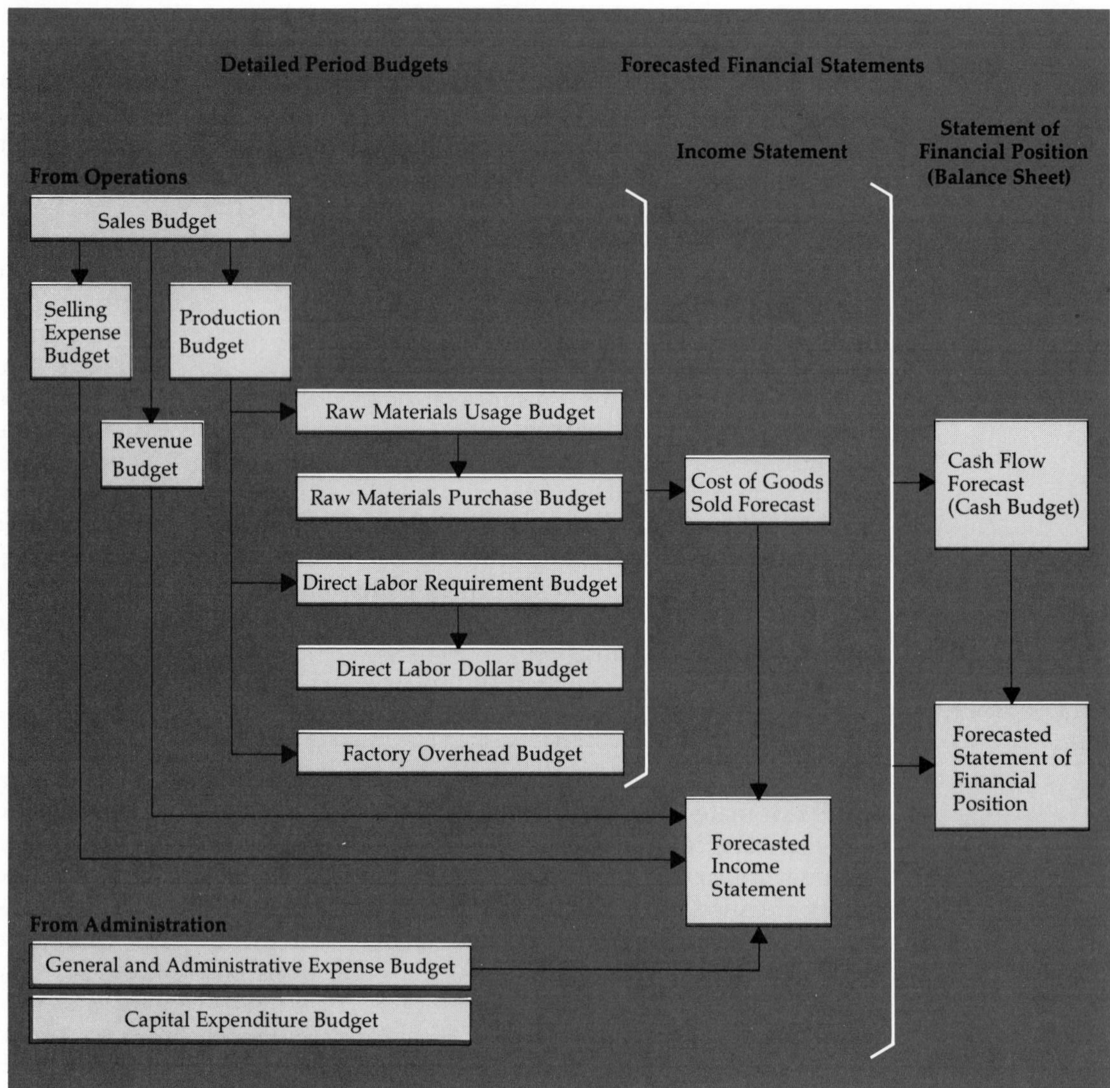

Figure 27-1 Preparation of Master Budget

expected cash receipts for each period. Other sources of cash such as sale of stock or loan receipts also enter the cash receipts planning cycle.

Anticipated cash disbursement data are taken from the various period budgets. The person preparing the cash budget must know how the raw materials, labor, and other goods and services are going to be purchased—that is, either for cash or on account. When dealing with accounts payable, it is important to know the company's payment policies. In addition to the regular operating expenses, cash is also used for purchasing equipment and paying off long-term liabilities. All of this information must be available in order to prepare an accurate cash budget. After the forecasted cash receipts are added to the beginning cash balance for the period to arrive at total cash available, total cash disbursements are subtracted to yield the forecasted cash balance at period end.

Financial Position Forecast The final phase of the master budget process is to prepare a financial position forecast or projected balance sheet for the company, assuming that planned activities actually occurred. As Figure 27-1 shows, all budgeted data are used in this process. The controller compiles a cash flow forecast or cash budget from all planned transactions requiring cash inflow or expenditure. In preparing the forecasted statement of financial position or balance sheet, the controller must know the projected cash balance and must have determined the net income and capital expenditures. In essence, all of the anticipated transactions included in the period budgets must be categorized and posted to the various accounts in the general ledger. The resulting projected financial statements are the final product of the budgeting process. At this point, management must decide to adopt the proposed master budget and be satisfied with planned operating results or else direct the controller to alter the plans and redo parts of the budget assembly process.

Budget Preparation and Implementation

Budget preparation involves timely effort and input by many people. Top management as well as middle and lower-level managers take part in the budgeting process. This process not only requires an efficient coordinator or director but also depends heavily on a clearly defined timetable of events and a set of procedures or instructions. The presence of a responsibility accounting system helps to coordinate the budgeting process. To be effective, a master budget must be as realistic and timely as the forecasting process will allow.

Budget implementation is also the responsibility of the controller or budget director. Two important factors determine whether the implementation process will be successful. The first is proper communication of budget expectations and production and profit targets to all key operating personnel. All persons involved in the operations of the business must know what is expected of them and receive directions on how to attain the goals. Second, and equally important, is support and encouragement by top management. No matter how sophisticated the budgeting process is, it will succeed only if middle and lower-level managers can see that top management is truly interested in the final outcome and willing to reward people for attaining the budget goals.

Illustrative Problem

The period budget preparation process and the make-up of the master budget will differ among companies. Therefore, it is impossible to cover all procedures found in actual practice. The problem below is only one approach to the preparation of period budgets. However, by applying the tools of cost behavior, C-V-P analysis, and responsibility accounting to particular circumstances, one can prepare any type of budget.

Stallman Steelworks, Inc., manufactures cans from 4-foot by 8-foot sheets of aluminum and steel of varying gauges or thicknesses. Can production per sheet of steel varies with the height and diameter of the cans. During 19xx, the company anticipates the following sales and unit changes in inventory:

Can Size	Unit Sales	Unit Change in Finished Goods Inventory
6″ × 3″	1,250,000	100,000 (increase)
8″ × 4″	710,000	8,000 (decrease)
10″ × 5″	700,000	3,400 (decrease)

Raw material requirements for these three products are as follows:

Can Size	Sheet Steel Type	Cans per Sheet	Lids per Sheet
6″ × 3″	No. 16	75	450
8″ × 4″	No. 22	36	216
10″ × 5″	No. 26	27	162

Usage is uniform over a twelve-month period. On the first day of each operating quarter, 25 percent of the annual raw materials requirements will be purchased, starting January 1. Assume no changes in the balances in the Raw Materials Inventory and Work in Process Inventory accounts.

Required

Prepare a raw materials usage budget and a raw materials purchase budget for 19xx. Expected prices for the year are $10.20 per sheet for No. 16, $13.40 per sheet for No. 22, and $16.80 per sheet for No. 26.

Solution

Before preparing the required budgets, we must compute the total number of cans (including lids for tops and bottoms) to be produced per sheet of steel. The following relationships are true for Stallman Steelworks:

6″ × 3″ can	75 cans (plus 150 lids) require $1\frac{1}{3}$ sheets of steel 225 cans (plus 450 lids) require 4 sheets of steel (or) 56.25 cans and necessary lids per sheet of steel
8″ × 4″ can	36 cans (plus 72 lids) require $1\frac{1}{3}$ sheets of steel 108 cans (plus 216 lids) require 4 sheets of steel (or) 27 cans and necessary lids per sheet of steel
10″ × 5″ can	27 cans (plus 54 lids) require $1\frac{1}{3}$ sheets of steel 81 cans (plus 162 lids) require 4 sheets of steel (or) 20.25 cans and necessary lids per sheet of steel

Stallman Steelworks, Inc.
Raw Materials Usage Budget
For the Year Ended December 31, 19xx

	Number of cans
6″ × 3″ Can	
Expected sales	1,250,000
Plus increase in inventory	100,000
Total to be produced	1,350,000

No. 16 sheets to be used:

$$\frac{\text{units to be produced}}{\text{cans per sheet}} = \frac{1{,}350{,}000 \text{ cans}}{56.25 \text{ cans/sheet}} = 24{,}000 \text{ sheets}$$

	Number of cans
8″ × 4″ Can	
Expected sales	710,000
Less decrease in inventory	8,000
Total to be produced	702,000

No. 22 sheets to be used:

$$\frac{\text{units to be produced}}{\text{cans per sheet}} = \frac{702{,}000 \text{ cans}}{27 \text{ cans/sheet}} = 26{,}000 \text{ sheets}$$

	Number of cans
10″ × 5″ Can	
Expected sales	700,000
Less decrease in inventory	3,400
Total to be produced	696,600

No. 26 sheets to be used:

$$\frac{\text{units to be produced}}{\text{cans per sheet}} = \frac{696{,}600 \text{ cans}}{20.25 \text{ cans/sheet}} = 34{,}400 \text{ sheets}$$

Stallman Steelworks, Inc.
Raw Materials Purchase Budget
For the Year Ended December 31, 19xx

Sheet Steel Type	Unit Cost/Sheet	Sheets to Be Purchased Quarterly*	Total Quarterly Purchase Cost	Annual Cost
No. 16	$10.20	6,000	$ 61,200	$ 244,800
No. 22	13.40	6,500	87,100	348,400
No. 26	16.80	8,600	144,480	577,920
Total Purchases Budget				$1,171,120

**Note:* Purchases on January 1, April 1, July 1, and October 1.

Budgetary Control: The Control Function

Objective 4 Differentiate between cost planning activities and those used for cost control purposes

The second part of the budgetary control process is to provide a means of monitoring operations so that operating plans and targets can be achieved. Generally we classify management accounting tools used in this process as performance evaluation techniques. Any procedure that analyzes past performance can be included in this classification. The discussion below will concentrate on analyses of differences (1) between actual costs and budgeted costs, and (2) between actual costs and standard costs. Although performance evaluation is usually associated with cost variances in the manufacturing process, evaluation of the selling and distribution functions of a company is equally important to profitability and operating efficiency.

Evaluating Performance

Performance is evaluated or measured by comparing what did happen with what should have happened. This evaluation process has several interrelated facets, some involving company policies and others relating to human or behavioral factors. Regarding company policies, an effective control program requires defined procedures for (1) preparing plans or operational goals, (2) establishing lines of responsibility for performance, (3) communicating operational plans to key personnel, (4) evaluating each area of responsibility, and (5) if variances exist, allowing those responsible for unplanned performance to give reasons to supervisory personnel for the differences. These policies describe the mechanical aspects of the performance evaluation process.

Company policies are important but, alone, will not lead to effective control of operations. The human aspect is the most important part of corporate goal attainment. People do the planning, people perform the manufacturing operations, and people evaluate or are evaluated.

Some simple rules regarding people must be part of the evaluation process. First, any person who is held responsible for an operating area must have direct input into the planning or goal-setting process. If a manager does not consider an operating target to be realistic or if plans are developed without the participation of department-level personnel, the desire to attain those goals may be lacking. The incentive to perform is a key factor to goal attainment. Second, management must clearly communicate every goal or plan to all relevant personnel, spelling out the exact responsibilities of all people to be evaluated. Failure to communicate is a common cause of inefficient operating performance. The third rule involving human behavior within the evaluation process centers on the importance of informing the responsible individual of the results of his or her performance. Management should praise good performance rather than simply taking it for granted. Silence does not imply good performance; it means bad management. If performance is poor or substandard, the responsible individual should have the opportunity to defend any actions taken. There may be a logical reason for the individual's poor performance. Perhaps the cause is beyond the person's influence or control. In any case, management should take care to integrate allowances for human behavior and company policies into the performance evaluation process.

Flexible Budgets

Objective 5 Prepare a flexible budget

The topic of budgets was emphasized in an earlier section of this chapter focusing on the planning function. Why should we introduce the concept of flexible budgets as a part of the cost control function rather than as a planning tool? We do so because a flexible budget (also called a variable budget) is a cost control tool or device used to help evaluate performance. A **flexible budget** is a summary of anticipated costs prepared for a range of activity levels and is geared to changes in the level of productive output. The budgets discussed in relation to the planning function are considered static or fixed budgets because they were prepared in relation to one level of expected sales and production activity. Period budgets are established usually on the basis of an anticipated or normal level of output.

For budgeting or planning purposes, a set of static budgets based on a single level of output adequately serves management needs. These budgets present a picture of projected operating results consistent with the desires of management and provide a target or goal for managers to use in developing monthly and weekly operating plans. However, these budgets often prove inadequate for purposes of assessing operating results. Figure 27-2 presents data for Seth Industries Inc. Actual costs exceed budgeted costs by $14,300. This amount is 7.2 percent over budgeted costs of $199,900. This overrun is considered significant by most managers. But was there really a cost overrun? As explained in the notes to Figure 27-2, the budgeted amounts are based on productive output of 17,500 units whereas actual costs were incurred to produce 19,100 units.

Before analyzing the performance of the Michigan Division, we must adjust the budgeted data to reflect output of 19,100 units. Therefore, in this example, the static budget for 17,500 units is not useful for performance evaluation purposes. The role of a flexible budget is to provide forecasted data that can be adjusted automatically for changes in the level of output. Figure 27-3 presents a flexible budget for Seth Industries, Inc., with budgeted data for 15,000, 17,500, and 20,000 unit output levels. Of primary importance in this illustration is the flexible budget formula shown at the bottom, which was developed from data in the analysis. The $8.60 variable cost per unit is computed at the upper right of the exhibit, whereas the $49,400 is found in the fixed-cost section of the analysis. Using this formula, we can create a budget for the Michigan Division at virtually any level of output.

In the performance evaluation illustration of Seth Industries, Inc. (Figure 27-2), budgeted data were not comparable and would have to be adjusted to reflect anticipated costs at the 19,100-unit level before the data

Figure 27-2
Performance Analysis: Comparison of Actual and Budgeted Data

Seth Industries, Inc.
Performance Report—Michigan Division
For the Year Ended December 31, 19xx

Cost Item	Budget*	Actual†	Difference Under (Over) Budget
Direct materials	$ 42,000	$ 46,000	$ (4,000)
Direct labor	68,250	75,000	(6,750)
Factory overhead			
Variable			
Indirect materials	10,500	11,500	(1,000)
Indirect labor	14,000	15,250	(1,250)
Utilities	7,000	7,600	(600)
Other	8,750	9,750	(1,000)
Fixed			
Supervisory salaries	19,000	18,500	500
Depreciation	15,000	15,000	—
Utilities	4,500	4,500	—
Other	10,900	11,100	(200)
Totals	$199,900	$214,200	$(14,300)

*Budget based on anticipated productive output of 17,500 units.
†Actual cost data generated by producing 19,100 units.

could be compared with actual dollar amounts. Figure 27-4 (on page 934) depicts a performance report using flexible budget data. Unit variable cost amounts have been multiplied by 19,100 units to arrive at the variable budgeted dollar figures. Fixed overhead information has been carried over from the flexible budget developed in Figure 27-3. As the new performance report indicates, costs exceeded budgeted amounts by only $540 during the year, which is a deviation of only two-tenths of one percent. Using the flexible budget concept, we find that the performance of the Michigan Division is almost on target. Performance has now been measured and analyzed accurately.

Variance Determination

Objective 6 Compute and evaluate raw materials, direct labor, and factory overhead variances

We can evaluate operating performance by comparing actual results with either budgeted results or expectations expressed in standard costs. Budgeted data tend to be less precise than standard cost data, but both provide cost goals or targets for performance evaluation by managers. This section of the chapter will emphasize performance evaluation based on standard costs. The first step in the evaluation process is to find out if a cost variance exists. Variance determination helps to locate areas of oper-

Figure 27-3
Flexible Budget
Preparation

Seth Industries, Inc.
Flexible Budget Analysis—Michigan Division
For the Year Ended December 31, 19xx

Cost Item	Unit Levels of Activity 15,000	17,500	20,000	Variable Cost per Unit
Direct materials	$ 36,000	$ 42,000	$ 48,000	$2.40
Direct labor	58,500	68,250	78,000	3.90
Variable factory overhead				
Indirect materials	9,000	10,500	12,000	.60
Indirect labor	12,000	14,000	16,000	.80
Utilities	6,000	7,000	8,000	.40
Other	7,500	8,750	10,000	.50
Total variable costs	$129,000	$150,500	$172,000	$8.60
Fixed factory overhead				
Supervisory salaries	$ 19,000	$ 19,000	$ 19,000	
Depreciation	15,000	15,000	15,000	
Utilities	4,500	4,500	4,500	
Other	10,900	10,900	10,900	
Total fixed costs	$ 49,400	$ 49,400	$ 49,400	
Total costs	$178,400	$199,900	$221,400	

Flexible budget formula:
(variable cost per unit × number of units produced) + budgeted fixed costs
= ($8.60 × units produced) + $49,400

Note: Activity expressed in units was used as the basis for this analysis. When units are used, direct material and direct labor costs are included in the analysis. Flexible budgets commonly are restricted to overhead costs. In such a situation, direct labor hours are used in place of units produced.

ating efficiency or inefficiency so that corrective measures can be prescribed if necessary. But the key to effective control of operations is not just determining the amount of the variance. Identifying the reason for the variance is a very critical part of the evaluation process. Once the reason is known, steps can be taken to correct the trouble spot.

Management needs a system for analyzing operations to identify areas that are functioning above or below expectations. Many companies are so large that it is virtually impossible to review all areas of operation. Locating and analyzing only the areas of unusually good or bad performance is called **management by exception.** Variance analysis is the primary cost accounting tool that management uses in exception reporting. Techniques

Figure 27-4
Performance Analysis Using Flexible Budget Data

Seth Industries, Inc.
Performance Report—Michigan Division
For the Year Ended December 31, 19xx

Cost Item (Variable Unit Cost)	Budget Based on 19,100 Units Produced	Actual Costs at 19,100-Unit Level	Differences Under (Over) Budget
Direct materials ($2.40)	$ 45,840	$ 46,000	$(160)
Direct labor ($3.90)	74,490	75,000	(510)
Factory overhead			
Variable			
Indirect materials ($.60)	11,460	11,500	(40)
Indirect labor ($.80)	15,280	15,250	30
Utilities ($.40)	7,640	7,600	40
Other ($.50)	9,550	9,750	(200)
Fixed			
Supervisory salaries	19,000	18,500	500
Depreciation	15,000	15,000	—
Utilities	4,500	4,500	—
Other	10,900	11,100	(200)
Totals	$213,660	$214,200	$(540)

are developed to isolate variances (differences) between standard and actual costs for raw materials, direct labor, and factory overhead. If standard costs exceed actual costs, the variance is "favorable" and is identified by placing an (F) behind the amount of the variance. Where actual costs are greater than standard costs, a (U) is used to distinguish it as being "unfavorable." A variance has to exceed, either favorably or unfavorably, a minimum amount or percentage difference before it is considered an exception and is then subjected to careful analysis to determine its cause.

We can compute variances for entire cost categories, such as total raw materials cost, or we can derive variances for each item or component of raw materials used in the production process. The more refined and detailed the analysis, the better the effectiveness for cost control purposes. The remaining discussion and illustration in this chapter involve standard cost variance analysis and focus on simplified cost areas. In practice, the analyses are much more involved, taking into account all facets of the production and distribution functions. However, the techniques illustrated below provide the basis for the more complicated situations.

Raw Materials Variances The raw materials variances are computed by using actual cost data, the raw materials price standard (referred to as standard price), and the raw materials quantity standard (or standard quantity). The standard amounts are compared with actual prices and materials usage to determine whether variances exist. Let us assume, for example, that Marquette Company manufactures leather chairs. Each chair should require 4 yards of leather material (standard quantity), and the standard price of leather is $6.00 per yard. During August, 760 yards of leather material costing $5.90 were purchased and used to produce 180 chairs. The total raw materials cost variance is computed below.

Actual cost		
	actual quantity × actual price =	
	760 yd at $5.90/yd =	$4,484
Standard cost		
	standard quantity × standard price =	
	(180 chairs × 4 yd/chair) at $6.00/yd =	
	720 yd at $6.00/yd =	4,320
Total raw materials cost variance		$ 164(U)

The problem facing management is that part of this variance is caused by raw materials usage and part is caused by price differences. In order to identify the area or people responsible for these variances, the total raw materials cost variance must be broken down into two parts: the raw materials price variance and the raw materials quantity variance.

The **raw materials price variance** is the difference between the actual price and the standard price, multiplied by the actual quantity purchased. For the Marquette Company, it would be computed as follows:

Actual price	$5.90
Less standard price	6.00
Difference	$ .10(F)

price variance = difference in price × actual quantity
= .10(F) × 760 yards
= $76(F)

The **raw materials quantity variance** is the difference between the actual quantity used and the standard quantity that should have been used, multiplied by the standard price.

Actual quantity	760 yd
Less standard quantity (180 chairs × 4 yd/chair)	720 yd
Difference	40 yd(U)

quantity variance = difference in quantity × standard price
= 40(U) yd × $6/yd
= $240(U)

As a check of these answers, the sum of the price variance and the quantity variance should equal the total raw materials cost variance.

Price variance	$ 76(F)
Quantity variance	240(U)
Total raw materials variance	$164(U)

Normally the purchasing agent is responsible for the price variance, whereas the production department supervisors are accountable for quantity variances. In cases like the one above, however, the cheaper raw materials may have caused the excessive usage. Each situation must be evaluated according to the specific circumstances involved and not on general guidelines.

Direct Labor Variances The approach to direct labor variance analysis parallels the approach to raw materials variances. Total direct labor variance is computed by finding the difference between the actual labor cost incurred and the standard labor cost that should have been incurred to generate the good units produced. Expanding the operating data of the Marquette Company, we find that each chair requires 2.4 standard labor hours and the standard labor rate is $8.50 per hour. During August, 450 direct labor hours were required to produce the 180 chairs at an average pay rate of $9.20 per hour. The total direct labor cost variance is computed as shown below.

Actual cost

actual hours × actual rate = 450 hr × $9.20/hr = $4,140

Standard cost

standard hours allowed × standard rate =
(180 chairs × 2.4 hr/chair) × $8.50/hr =
432 hr × $8.50/hr = 3,672

Total direct labor cost variance $ 468(U)

For effective cost control, management must know the portion of the total direct labor cost variance resulting from different labor rates and the portion influenced by varying labor hour usage. This information is obtained by computing the labor rate variance and the labor efficiency variance.

The **direct labor rate variance** is the difference between the actual labor rate and the standard labor rate, multiplied by the actual hours worked.

Actual rate	$9.20
Less standard rate	8.50
Difference	$ .70(U)

rate variance = difference in rate × actual hours
= .70(U) × 450 hours
= $315(U)

The **direct labor efficiency variance** is the difference between actual hours worked and standard hours allowed for the good units produced, multiplied by the standard labor rate.

Actual hours of work	450 hr
Less standard hours allowed (180 chairs × 2.4 hr/chair)	432 hr
Difference	18 hr(U)

$$\begin{aligned}\text{efficiency variance} &= \text{difference in hours} \times \text{standard rate}\\ &= 18\ \text{hr(U)} \times \$8.50/\text{hr}\\ &= \$153\text{(U)}\end{aligned}$$

The following check shows that the variances are correct.

Rate variance	$315(U)
Efficiency variance	153(U)
Total labor variance	$468(U)

Responsibility for direct labor variances can also be defined. Labor rate variances are normally the responsibility of the personnel department. A rate variance often occurs when a person is hired at an incorrect rate or performs the duties of a higher- or lower-paid employee. Labor efficiency variances are traceable to departmental supervisors. As was the case with raw materials variances, an unfavorable labor efficiency variance can occur because an inexperienced, lower-paid person is assigned to a task requiring greater skill. Management must be careful to analyze each situation only after considering the circumstances involved.

Factory Overhead Variances Controlling overhead costs is more difficult than controlling raw materials and direct labor costs because responsibility for overhead cost incurrence is hard to identify. Because variable overhead costs can be linked to operating departments, some control is possible. Most fixed costs, however, are not controlled by specific departmental managers.

Analyses of factory overhead variances range in the degree of sophistication involved. The basic approach is to compute the total overhead variance and then divide this amount into two component parts: the controllable overhead variance and the overhead volume variance. Other, more involved approaches are possible, but we will use this basic format. In our example, the Marquette Company had budgeted standard variable overhead costs of $5.75 per direct labor hour plus $1,300 of fixed overhead costs for August. Normal capacity was set at 400 direct labor hours per month. The company incurred $4,100 of actual overhead costs in August.

Before computing the overhead variances, we must calculate the total overhead rate. The total standard overhead rate consists of two parts: the variable rate of $5.75 per direct labor hour and the standard fixed overhead rate, which is computed by dividing budgeted fixed factory overhead or $1,300 by normal capacity. The standard fixed overhead rate under these circumstances is $3.25 per direct labor hour ($1,300 ÷ 400 hours), and the total standard overhead rate is $9.00 per direct labor hour ($5.75 + $3.25). The total fixed overhead costs divided by normal capacity provide a rate that assigns fixed overhead costs to products on a basis consistent with expected volume or output. The total factory overhead variance (or underapplied or overapplied overhead) for the Marquette Company is computed below.

Actual overhead costs incurred	$4,100
Standard overhead costs applied to good units produced (180 chairs × 2.4 hr/chair) × $9.00/direct labor hour	3,888
Total overhead variance	$ 212(U)

The **controllable overhead variance** is the difference between the actual overhead costs incurred and the factory overhead budgeted for the level of production achieved. Thus the controllable variance for the Marquette Company for August would be:

Actual overhead costs incurred		$4,100
Less budgeted factory overhead (flexible budget) for 180 chairs:		
Variable overhead cost (180 chairs × 2.4 hr/chair) × $5.75/direct labor hour	$2,484	
Budgeted fixed overhead cost	1,300	
Total budgeted factory overhead		3,784
Controllable overhead variance		$ 316(U)

The **overhead volume variance** is the difference between the factory overhead budgeted for the level of production achieved and the overhead applied to production using the standard overhead rate. Continuing with the Marquette Company example, we have:

Budgeted factory overhead (see above)	$3,784
Less factory overhead applied (180 chairs × 2.4 hr/chair) × $9.00/direct labor hour	3,888
Overhead volume variance	$ 104(F)

Checking the computations, we find that the two variances do equal the total overhead variance.

Controllable overhead variance	$316(U)
Overhead volume variance	104(F)
Total overhead variance	$212(U)

The controllable overhead variance measures the difference between the costs actually incurred and the costs that should have been incurred at the level of output attained. In the above example, the company spent more than it should have, so the controllable variance was unfavorable.

Usage of existing facilities and capacity is measured by the overhead volume variance. A volume variance will exist only if more or less capacity than normal is actually utilized. In the example, 400 direct labor hours is the measure of normal usage of facilities. In producing 180 chairs, the company should have used 432 standard direct labor hours (direct hours allowed). Fixed overhead costs are applied on the basis of standard hours allowed. In the example, overhead would be applied on the basis of 432 hours, but the fixed overhead rate was computed by using 400 hours (normal capacity). Thus more fixed costs would be applied to products than were budgeted. Because the products can absorb no more than actual costs incurred, this condition would tend to lower unit cost. When expected capacity usage is exceeded, the result is a favorable overhead volume variance. With less than normal capacity, all fixed overhead costs will not be applied to units produced. It is then necessary to add the amount of underapplied fixed overhead to the cost of the good units produced, thereby increasing their cost. This is an unfavorable condition.

Overhead variance analysis is illustrated in Figure 27-5. All procedures shown are identical to those explained above. To compute the controllable variance, subtract the budgeted overhead amount (using a flexible budget) for the level of performance achieved from actual overhead costs incurred. A positive answer yields an unfavorable variance, because actual costs were greater than those budgeted. The controllable variance is favorable if the difference is negative. Subtracting total overhead applied from overhead budgeted at the level of achieved performance produces the volume variance. As before, a positive answer indicates an unfavorable variance, and a negative answer indicates a favorable variance. The data from the Marquette Company illustration are shown diagrammatically in the lower part of Figure 27-5. Carefully check the solution in the exhibit with that presented earlier.

Performance Reports Using Standard Costs

Performance reports should be tailored to a system of reporting designed to meet responsibility accounting specifications. These reports should be accurate, clearly stated, and limited to those cost items controllable by the manager receiving the report. Figure 27-6 illustrates a performance report using the variance data generated in the Marquette Company problem that pertains only to the production department supervisor. The production supervisor is responsible for raw materials used (and the related raw materials quantity variance), direct labor hours used (and the related direct labor efficiency variance), and the cost areas used in computing the controllable overhead variance. Dollar figures shown in Figure 27-6 have been limited to these amounts. Adequate space should be made available for managers to identify reasons for the variances.

The report shown has been simplified for illustrative purposes. Normally such a report would include several items of raw materials, two or more direct labor classifications, and many items of overhead cost.

Figure 27-5
Overhead
Variance Analysis

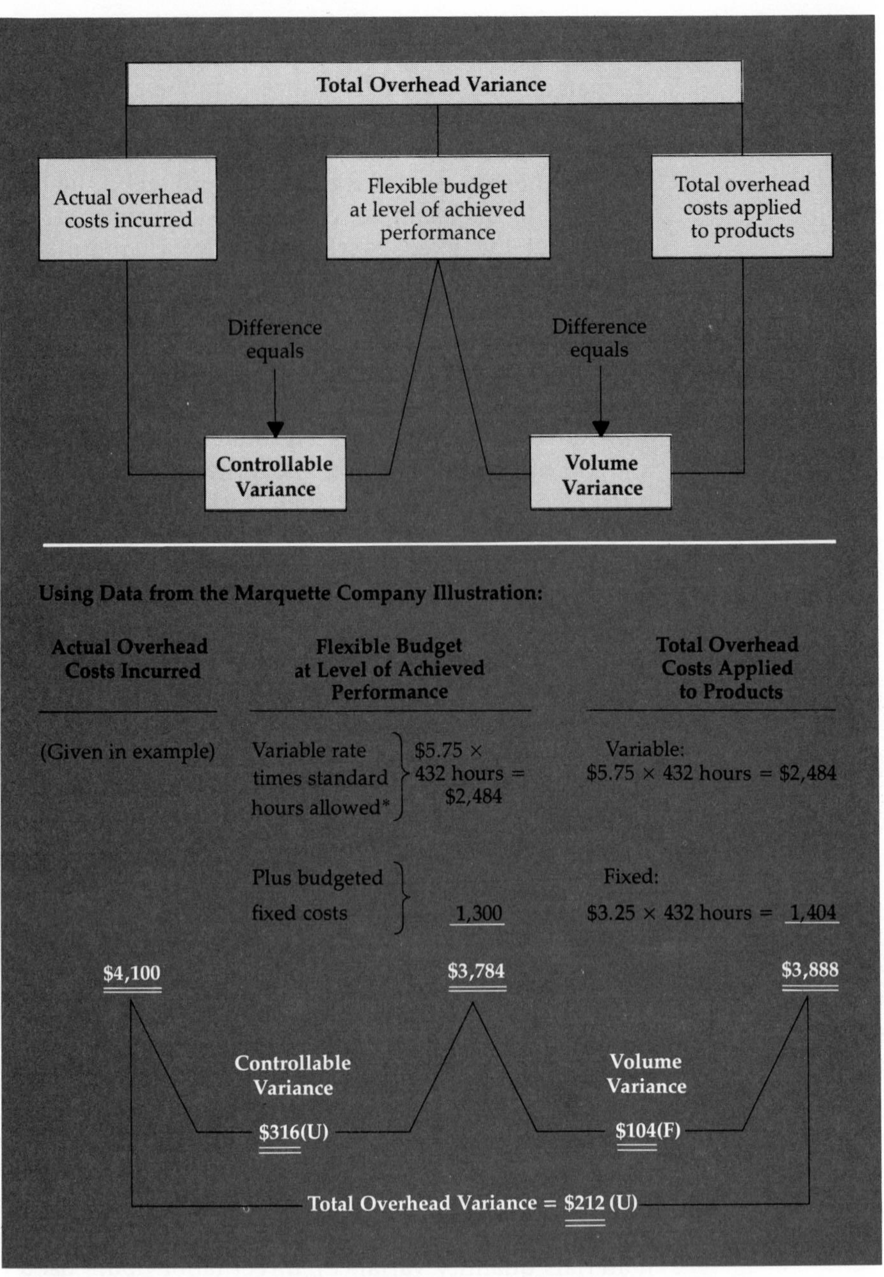

*Standard hours allowed (achieved performance level) is computed by multiplying good units produced times required standard time per unit. Here the computation is as follows:

180 chairs produced × 2.4 hours per chair = 432 standard hours allowed

Figure 27-6
Performance Report Using Variance Analysis

Marquette Company
Production Department Performance Report—Cost Variance Analysis
For the Month Ended August 31, 19xx

400 hours: Normal capacity (direct labor hours)
432 hours: Capacity performance level achieved
180 chairs: Good units produced

Cost Analysis

	Costs		Variance	
	Budgeted	Actual	Amount	Type
Raw materials used (leather)	$ 4,320	$ 4,560	$240(U)	Quantity variance
Direct labor usage	3,672	3,825	153(U)	Efficiency variance
Controllable factory overhead	3,784	4,100	316(U)	Controllable overhead variance
Totals	$11,776	$12,485	$709(U)	

Reasons for Variances

Raw material quantity variance: (1) inferior quality-control inspection and (2) cheaper grade of raw material caused excessive scrap

Direct labor efficiency variance: (1) inferior raw materials and (2) new inexperienced employee

Controllable overhead variance: (1) excessive indirect labor usage, (2) changes in employee overtime, and (3) unexpected price changes

Chapter Review

Review of Learning Objectives

1. Define the concept of budgetary control.
The budgetary control process consists of the cost planning function and the cost control function. Cost planning and control are key functions leading to effective management. Budgetary control is the total process of (1) developing plans for a company's anticipated operations and (2) controlling operations to aid in accomplishing those plans.

2. Describe a period budget.
A period budget is a forecast of annual operating results for a segment or function of a company that represents a quantitative expression of planned activities. The period budgeting process converts unit sales and production forecasts into revenue and cost estimates for each of the many operating segments of the company.

3. Identify the components of a master budget and describe their integration.

A master budget is an integrated set of departmental or functional period budgets that have been consolidated into forecasted financial statements for the entire company. The detailed operating or period budgets are first prepared. These include the sales budget, production budget, selling expense budget, raw materials purchase budget, raw materials usage budget, labor hour requirement budget, direct labor dollar budget, factory overhead budget, general and administrative expense budget, and capital expenditure budget. The budgets are interrelated. The selling expense budget and the production budget are computed from the sales budget data. Raw materials usage, direct labor hour and dollar, and factory overhead budgets are a function of the production budget. Raw materials purchases can be determined only after raw materials usage is identified. General and administrative expenses and proposed capital expenditures are determined by top management. Once these budgets have been prepared, a forecasted income statement, a forecasted cash flow statement (cash budget), and a forecasted balance sheet can be prepared, assuming that all budgeted or anticipated transactions occur.

4. Differentiate between cost planning activities and those used for cost control purposes.

Cost planning activities take place before various transactions occur. They help management to anticipate what should happen in the future. Preparing budgets using cost-volume-profit projections and developing standard costs fall in the category of cost planning activities. Cost control, on the other hand, involves procedures and techniques that are designed to help keep actual costs from exceeding the budgeted or anticipated amounts. Usually this involves some form of comparison of budgeted and actual amounts. In addition, causes for any differences are identified so that such differences will not occur in the future.

5. Prepare a flexible budget.

A flexible budget is a summary of anticipated costs prepared for a range of activity levels and is geared to changes in the level of productive output. Variable and fixed costs are summarized for several levels of capacity or output, with each column yielding a total anticipated cost figure for the respective output level. Once prepared, the flexible budget is used to determine the flexible budget formula. This formula can be applied to any level of productive output and is a key tool in evaluating performance of individuals and departments.

6. Compute and evaluate raw materials, direct labor, and factory overhead variances.

Cost variances or differences between actual and standard manufacturing costs can be computed in the raw materials, direct labor, and factory overhead cost areas. The raw materials price and quantity variances help explain differences between actual and standard raw materials costs. Direct labor cost differences are analyzed through the direct labor rate variance and the direct labor efficiency variance. The controllable overhead variance and the overhead volume variance assist in evaluating differences in overhead costs. Each variance results from specific causes and, therefore, helps pinpoint reasons for the differences between actual and standard costs.

Review Problem

Before doing the exercises and problems, you may want to review the text examples of variance analysis. For additional help, see the review problem in the working papers.

Chapter Assignments

Questions

1. Describe the concept of budgetary control.
2. What is the relationship between budgetary control and standard cost accounting?
3. Distinguish between long-run plans and annual operating plans.
4. What is a period budget?
5. How does responsibility accounting aid period budget preparation?
6. What is a master budget?
7. Why is the preparation of a forecasted cash flow statement or cash budget so important to a company?
8. Identify the three main phases of the budget preparation cycle.
9. Identify and discuss the interrelationships of detailed operating budgets.
10. "Performance is evaluated or measured by comparing what did happen with what should have happened." What is meant by this statement? Relate your comments to the budgetary control process.
11. What is a variance?
12. How can a variance aid management in achieving effective control of operations?
13. What is the formula for computing a raw materials price variance?
14. How would you interpret and explain an unfavorable raw materials price variance?
15. Differences between actual labor cost and standard labor cost are explained by analyzing two variances. Name the two variances. Identify possible causes of each of these two variances.
16. Differentiate between the controllable overhead variance and the overhead volume variance.
17. What is a flexible budget?
18. What are the two parts of a flexible budget formula? Identify the relationships between these parts.
19. If standard hours allowed are more than normal hours, will the period's volume variance be favorable or unfavorable? Explain your answer.
20. What is the formula for computing the direct labor efficiency variance?
21. Can an unfavorable raw material quantity variance be caused, at least in part, by a favorable material price variance? Explain.

Classroom Exercises

Exercise 27-1 Production Budget Preparation

A forecast of unit sales for 19x3 for the Dover Garage Door Company is as follows: January, 30,000; February, 40,000; March, 50,000; April, 60,000; May, 50,000; June, 40,000; July, 30,000; August, 40,000; September, 50,000; October, 60,000; November, 70,000; December, 50,000.

The forecast of unit sales for January 19x4 is 40,000. Beginning finished goods inventory on January 1, 19x3, contained 5,000 doors. Company policy states that minimum inventory is 5,000 units and that the maximum amount of finished goods inventory is one-half of the following month's sales. Maximum productive capacity is 55,000 units per month.

Using the information given above, prepare a monthly production budget stating the number of units to be produced. Keep in mind that the company wishes to have a fairly constant productive output so that a constant work force can be maintained. How many units will be in finished goods inventory on December 31, 19x3?

Exercise 27-2 Raw Materials Purchase Budget Linked to Exercise 27-1

Refer to the data for the Dover Garage Door Company in Exercise 27-1. Prepare a raw materials purchase budget for January, February, and March 19x3, assuming the following breakdown of parts needed:

Hinges	4 sets/door	$ 6.00/set
Door panels	4 panels/door	$17.00/panel
Other hardware	1 lock/door	$11.00/lock
	1 handle/door	$ 2.50/handle
	2 roller tracks/door	$22.00/set of two roller tracks
	8 rollers	$ 1.00/roller

All raw materials are purchased in the month prior to their use in production.

Exercise 27-3 Flexible Budget Preparation

Fixed overhead costs for the Weitzman Company for 19xx are expected to be as follows: depreciation, $42,000; supervisory salaries, $38,000; property taxes and insurance, $12,000; other fixed overhead, $6,000. Total fixed overhead is thus expected to be $98,000. Variable costs per unit are anticipated as follows: raw materials, $2.50; direct labor, $2.75; operating supplies, $.75; indirect labor, $1.00; and other variable overhead costs, $.50.

Using the information given above, prepare a flexible budget for 16,000-unit, 18,000-unit, and 20,000-unit levels of activity. What is the flexible budget formula for 19xx?

Exercise 27-4 Raw Materials Price Variance

The Tamarind Tree Farm uses vermiculite to fortify the soil around trees bearing rare fruit, as the trees are the company's main product. The price standard used is $2.40 per 10-pound sack of vermiculite. During the current year, the actual purchase price averaged $2.65 per sack, according to the company's purchasing agent. The company purchased and used 1,470 sacks of vermiculite during the year.

Using the data given, compute the raw material price variance.

Exercise 27-5 Raw Materials Quantity Variance

The Sturdibuilt Elevator Company manufactures small hydroelectric vertical plungers with a maximum capacity of ten passengers each. One of the raw materials used by the production department is heavy-duty carpeting for the floors of the elevators. The raw materials quantity standard used for the month ended April 30, 19xx, was 6 square yards per elevator. The purchasing agent was able to obtain this carpeting at $8 per square yard, which equaled the price standard. During April, 82 elevators were finished and sold. The production department used 5.6 yards of carpet per elevator.

From the information given, calculate the raw material quantity variance for April 19xx.

Exercise 27-6 Direct Labor Rate and Efficiency Variances

Villa Foundry, Inc., manufactures castings used by other companies in the production of machinery. For the past two years, the largest-selling product has been a casting for an eight-cylinder engine block. Standard direct labor hours per engine block are 1.8 hours. During June, 16,500 engine blocks were produced. Actual direct labor hours and cost for that same time period were 30,000 hours and $222,000, respectively. The current labor contract requires that $7.25 per hour be paid to all direct labor employees.

1. Compute the direct labor rate variance for June for the engine block product line.

2. Using the same data, compute the direct labor efficiency variance for June for the engine block product line. [Check your answer, assuming that total direct labor variance is $6,675(U).]

Exercise 27-7 Factory Overhead Variances

The Svenson Company produces handmade lobster pots, which are sold to distributors throughout New England. The company incurred $6,200 of actual overhead costs in May. Budgeted standard overhead costs were $4 of variable overhead costs per direct labor hour plus $1,250 in fixed overhead costs for May. Normal capacity was set at 1,000 direct labor hours per month. In May, the company was able to produce 400 lobster pots. The efficiency standard is 3 direct labor hours per lobster pot.

Using the information provided, compute the controllable overhead variance, the overhead volume variance, and the total overhead variance for May.

Exercise 27-8 Factory Overhead Variances

Susan Manufacturing Company has been operating for five years. During that time period, a net loss from operations has been incurred each year. Management believes that one trouble spot is in the area of factory overhead.

During 19xx, the company produced 1,200 tables. Each table requires 6.5 standard direct labor hours. Variable overhead costs at standard are $4.50 per direct labor hour. Fixed factory overhead costs for the year should have been $28,000. Normal capacity is 8,000 direct labor hours per year. Actual factory overhead costs for 19xx amounted to $66,000.

Analyze the company's factory overhead costs by computing the controllable overhead variance and the overhead volume variance.

Problem Set A

Problem 27A-1 Budget Preparation

One of the products manufactured by Neilsson Corporation is a heavy-duty construction nail. Because of modern technology, many of the production steps have been combined through the use of laborsaving equipment. Below is the cost and production information relevant to this specific construction nail.

Raw materials needed are steel wire (5,000-foot coil at $29 per coil; 20,000 nails per coil), and packing material (bulkpack at $.10 per 1,000 nails). Direct labor for the cut-blank-head operation is figured at $9.60 per direct labor hour, and 5 minutes are required per 1,000 nails; for the point-polish-pack operation the rate should be $9.00 per direct labor hour, and 1 minute is required per 1,000 nails. Factory overhead for the cut-blank-head operation is figured at a rate of 80 percent of the department's direct labor dollars, and for the point-polish-pack operation at a rate of 60 percent of the department's direct labor dollars.

For the three-month period ending March 31, 19xx, management is anticipating the following monthly unit production figures: 3,600,000 nails in January, 4,800,000 nails in February, and 6,000,000 nails in March.

Required

1. For the three-month period ending March 31, 19xx, prepare *monthly* production cost information for the manufacture of the construction nails, showing a detailed breakdown of all costs involved and computation methods used.
2. Prepare a quarterly production cost budget for the construction nails. Show monthly cost data and combined totals for the quarter for each cost category.

Problem 27A-2 Budget Performance Analysis (Linked to Problem 27A-1)

The budget information for the production of a heavy-duty construction nail by the Neilsson Corporation was developed as part of Problem 27A-1. The actual output for the three-month period ending March 31, 19xx, was 3,800,000 nails in January, 5,200,000 nails in February, and 6,000,000 nails in March. The following costs were incurred:

	January	February	March
Steel wire	$5,500	$7,550	$8,700
Packing material	390	540	590
Cut-blank-head			
Direct labor	3,100	4,100	4,800
Factory overhead	2,500	3,270	3,900
Point-polish-pack			
Direct labor	580	820	900
Factory overhead	350	500	450

Required

Using the information in Problem 27A-1 and the above data, prepare a performance report for the three-month period comparing actual results with those budgeted. Hint: A flexible budget approach should be used because estimated production and actual production differed.

Problem 27A-3 Raw Materials and Direct Labor Variances

Law Library, Ltd., manufactures premium-quality reference books for attorneys. According to company standards, 1 square meter of leather fabric at $6.60 per square meter would be required for each book. In September, the firm produced 2,400 law books, consuming 3,000 square meters of fabric. The total price for this fabric was $20,250. The budgeted direct labor for the 2,400 books was 1,200 hours, or .5 hour per book, representing a total standard direct labor cost of $6,000. The actual direct labor required to manufacture the books was 1,680 hours at $4.50 per hour.

Required

Using the data provided, compute the raw materials price and quantity variances and the direct labor rate and efficiency variances. Show check figures to verify your answer.

Problem 27A-4 Materials and Labor Variances

John Woo & Co., Ltd., specializes in tailor-made suits, produced from imported fabrics. An average-size suit requires 3 meters of suit fabric and 1 meter of lining material. The standard price of suit fabric was set at $28 per meter, with lining material having a standard cost of $18 per meter.

Labor is classified under three separate functions: cutting, tailoring, and cleaning. The standard times and labor rates per suit for 19xx were as follows:

	Labor Time Standard	Labor Rate Standard
Cutting	.5 hr	$6/hr
Tailoring	5.0 hr	$9/hr
Cleaning	.2 hr	$4/hr

During 19xx, the company produced 2,900 suits. Actual operating data are shown below.

Materials usage and cost		**Total Cost**
Suit fabric	9,000 meters	$247,500
Lining material	2,850 meters	$ 54,150
Direct labor usage and cost		
Cutting	1,500 hours	$ 9,000
Tailoring	14,500 hours	131,950
Cleaning	600 hours	2,550

Required

1. Compute the materials price and quantity variances for both the fabric and the lining material.
2. Compute the labor rate and efficiency variances for the cutting, tailoring, and cleaning functions.

Problem 27A-5 Raw Materials, Direct Labor, and Overhead Variances

A forged socket wrench is the product made by Socket Systems, Inc. Each socket wrench should use 1 kilogram of liquid steel at a standard cost of $1.90 per kilogram. Each wrench requires .4 standard direct labor hour at a standard rate of $7.50 per hour. The standard variable overhead rate is $4.20 per direct labor hour, and normal capacity was set at a monthly level of 30,000 hours of direct labor. Fixed overhead costs of $75,600 were budgeted for June.

In June, the firm actually produced 80,000 socket wrenches, consuming 84,000 kilograms of liquid steel at a total cost of $151,200. A total of 25,200 direct labor hours were used at an expense of $201,600. Total overhead expenses incurred came to $181,360.

Required

Using the figures above, compute (1) raw materials price variance, (2) raw materials quantity variance, (3) direct labor rate variance, (4) direct labor efficiency variance, (5) controllable overhead variance, and (6) overhead volume variance.

Problem 27A-6 Comprehensive Variance Analysis

Roland Specialty Products Company produces various lines of gardening tools. The company's long-handled spade is considered a superior product. A stamping operation is required to cut and shape the blade of the spade and the neck portion of the assembly. The firm purchases wooden handles in lots of 1,000 from a local woodworking shop. Quantity, time, and cost standards for this product are listed below.

Raw materials needed are sheet metal (1 $\times$ 2 meter sheets at $10.80 per sheet; 18 blades and 18 necks should be produced from each sheet), and wooden handles at $380 per 1,000 handles. Direct labor is expected to include stamping blade and neck sets (180 sets per hour at a labor rate of $9.00 per hour), and assembly (60 units per person per hour at a labor rate of $8.40 per hour). Factory overhead for stamping will consist of a variable rate of $5.40 per direct labor hour and of a fixed rate of $6.30 per direct labor hour. Factory overhead for assembly will consist of a variable rate of $4.20 per direct labor hour and of a fixed rate of $2.10 per direct labor hour. Normal capacity is 300,600 units per year. Budgeted fixed factory overhead is $10,521 for each of the two departments, stamping and assembly, for the year.

The company manufactured 291,600 spades during the year. Company records revealed the following operating data:

	Usage	Cost
Raw materials		
Sheet metal	16,300 sheets	$11/sheet
Wooden handles	292,200 handles	$390/1,000 handles
Direct labor		
Stamping	1,600 hr	$9.00/hr
Assembly	4,900 hr	$8.50/hr
Factory overhead		
Stamping: Variable	$ 8,600	
Fixed	10,100	
Assembly: Variable	20,500	
Fixed	10,300	

Required

From the above information, compute (1) standard hours allowed for the stamping and assembly departments for the year, (2) raw materials price variances, (3) raw materials quantity variances, (4) direct labor rate variances, (5) direct labor efficiency variances, (6) controllable overhead variances, and (7) overhead volume variances.

Problem Set B

Problem 27B-3 Raw Materials and Direct Labor Variances

As a part of the production of a complete line of golf accessories, the Subpar Corporation manufactures multicolored golf tees. The tees are produced and sold in 1,000-unit lots. The quantity standard for raw materials is 30 kilograms of wood per 1,000-unit batch. The price standard for the wood is \$.28 per kilogram. The standard number of hours allowed for direct labor is .5 hour per 1,000-unit batch. The rate standard for direct labor is \$6.50 per hour.

During January, the company produced 2,500 batches of tees. The actual quantity of raw materials used was 76,000 kilograms of wood at a cost of \$22,800. Direct labor actually required was 1,250 hours at a cost of \$7,500.

Required

From the data given, compute the raw materials price and quantity variances and the direct labor rate and efficiency variances. Verify your solutions.

Problem 27B-4 Materials and Labor Variances

The Sunshine Basket Company manufactures plastic berry baskets for food wholesalers. Each basket requires 1.6 grams of liquid plastic and 1.2 grams of an additive that provides the coloration and hardening agents. The standard prices are \$.004 per gram of liquid plastic and \$.005 per gram of additive.

Labor is divided into three categories: molding, trimming, and packing. The labor time standard per 1,000 boxes and the rate standards are as follows: Molding is expected to take .4 hour per batch, at an hourly rate of \$10. Trimming also takes .4 hour per batch, at an hourly rate of \$8. Packing takes .2 hour, at \$5 per hour.

During 19xx, the company produced 4,225,000 berry baskets. Actual operating data for materials consisted of 6,637,000 grams of liquid plastic, at a total cost of \$33,185; and 5,492,000 grams of additive, which cost \$27,460. Data on direct labor included 1,710 hours for molding, at a total cost of \$16,758; 1,700 hours for trimming, which came to \$13,532; and 848 hours for packing, which cost \$4,240.

Required

1. Compute the raw materials price and quantity variances for both the liquid plastic and the additive.
2. Compute the direct labor rate and efficiency variances for the molding, trimming, and packing processes.

Problem 27B-5 Raw Materials, Direct Labor, and Overhead Variances

Foedish Footwear Company has a Sandal Division that produces a line of all-vinyl thongs. Each pair of thongs requires .4 meter of vinyl material that costs \$1.00 per meter. Standard direct labor hours and cost per pair of thongs are .25 hour and \$1.75 (.25 hour $\times$ \$7.00 per hour), respectively. The division's current standard variable overhead rate is \$.60 per direct labor hour, and the standard fixed overhead rate is \$1.40 per direct labor hour.

In August, the Sandal Division manufactured and sold 30,000 pairs of thongs. During the course of the month, 12,200 meters of vinyl material were consumed, at a total cost of $11,590. The total actual overhead costs for August amounted to $15,800. The total number of direct labor hours worked were 7,450, and August's factory payroll for direct labor was $52,895. Monthly normal capacity for the year has been set at 25,000 pairs of thongs.

Required

From the above data, compute the (1) raw materials price variance, (2) raw materials quantity variance, (3) direct labor rate variance, (4) direct labor efficiency variance, (5) controllable overhead variance, and (6) overhead volume variance.

Problem 27B-6 Comprehensive Variance Analysis

Woodland Products, Inc., produces a variety of camping products on a year-round basis. The best-selling item is a compact portable camping stove made from sheets of rust-free aluminum. Production of this stove requires two main operations: cutting/assembly and coating. The two basic raw materials used are aluminum sheeting and a polyurethane-base coating. Quantity, time, and cost standards for the camping stove are given below.

Raw materials consist of sheet aluminum (two 2 × 3 meter sheets per stove at $1.20 per sheet) and 1.6 liter of coating material per stove at $.80 per liter. Direct labor in the Cutting/Assembly Department is expected to produce 60 stoves per hour at $7.50 per hour. Direct labor in the Coating Department can handle 40 stoves per hour at $6.00 per hour. Factory overhead in the Cutting/Assembly Department is estimated at a variable rate of $6.50 per direct labor hour and a fixed rate of $4.00 per direct labor hour. Factory overhead in the Coating Department is figured at a variable rate of $5.00 per direct labor hour and at a fixed rate of $3.00 per direct labor hour. Normal capacity is 126,000 stoves per year.

The firm actually produced 124,800 units during the year, and the production records contain the following information:

In raw materials, the firm used 274,560 sheets of sheet aluminum at $1.10 per sheet and 174,720 liters of coating at $.95 per liter. Direct labor in the Cutting/Assembly Department came to 2,400 hours at $7.25 per hour; in the Coating Department it came to 3,120 hours at $6.50 per hour. Factory overhead in the Cutting/Assembly Department totaled $15,840 in variable costs and $9,120 in fixed costs. Factory overhead in the Coating Department came to $17,160 in variable costs and $7,800 in fixed costs.

Required

Using the information provided, determine the (1) standard hours allowed for the Cutting/Assembly and the Coating Departments for the year, (2) raw materials price variances, (3) raw materials quantity variances, (4) direct labor rate variances, (5) direct labor efficiency variances, (6) controllable overhead variances, and (7) overhead volume variances.

Learning Objectives

Chapter Twenty-Eight

Management Decisions: Special Analyses and Reports

1. Define and identify relevant decision information.

2. Describe the steps in the management decision cycle.

3. Calculate product costs using direct costing procedures.

4. Prepare an income statement using the contribution reporting format.

5. Develop decision data using the incremental analysis technique.

6. Describe the purpose of a minimum desired rate of return and explain the methods used to arrive at this rate.

7. Evaluate capital expenditure proposals using (a) the accounting rate of return method, (b) the payback method, and (c) the present value method.

8. Prepare decision alternative evaluations for make or buy decisions, special order decisions, and sales mix analyses.

Management relies heavily on the accountant for information that is relevant to decision making. To evaluate decision alternatives, the accountant uses special analyses and reporting techniques. The long-term capital expenditure decision area is the most complex. However, day-to-day operating decisions also require accurate evaluation methods. As a result of studying this chapter, you should be able to meet the learning objectives listed on the left.

Management uses of accounting information include product costing for pricing and inventory valuation, cost analysis for operational planning and control, and special analysis assignments for managerial decision making. This chapter emphasizes the third use—providing cost input for management decisions. Each of the several types of managerial decisions requires specific kinds of cost information. After exploring the management decision cycle and discussing various approaches to decision analysis, we shall describe and analyze several types of special management decisions.

Relevant Information for Management

The management decision process involves analyzing two or more alternative problem-solving actions and selecting the action considered superior under the circumstances. Supplying relevant information to management for each alternative is the responsibility of the management accountant. When members of top management evaluate the various alternatives available for solving a particular problem, they should not have to wade through pages and pages of data to find the projected effects of each alternative on the operations of the business. Many of the estimates or facts may be the same for each alternative. For instance, total sales may not be affected by a cost-savings proposal. If three alternative courses of action are available and total sales are the same for each action, the sales data would not influence the decision. In addition, the accountant may use past or historical data as a basis for preparing cost estimates of various decision alternatives. The cost estimates are relevant to the decision, but the historical data are not. **Relevant decision information** is defined as *future* cost, revenue, or resource usage data used in decision analyses that *differ* among the decision's alternative courses of action. Because a decision must be made on the basis of the alternatives available, information that is similar for those alternatives, or historical costs or events and transactions that have already happened, will not help to distinguish the one superior alternative action. Such information is irrelevant. Relevant information includes only future data that differ among the various alternatives.

Objective 1 Define and identify relevant decision information

Management Decision Cycle

The decision-making process is, by nature, an unstructured area of responsibility. Many decisions are unique and do not lend themselves to strict rules, steps, or timetables. However, there are similar events that accompany each type of management decision analysis. Figure 28-1 illustrates the events that make up the management decision cycle. Following

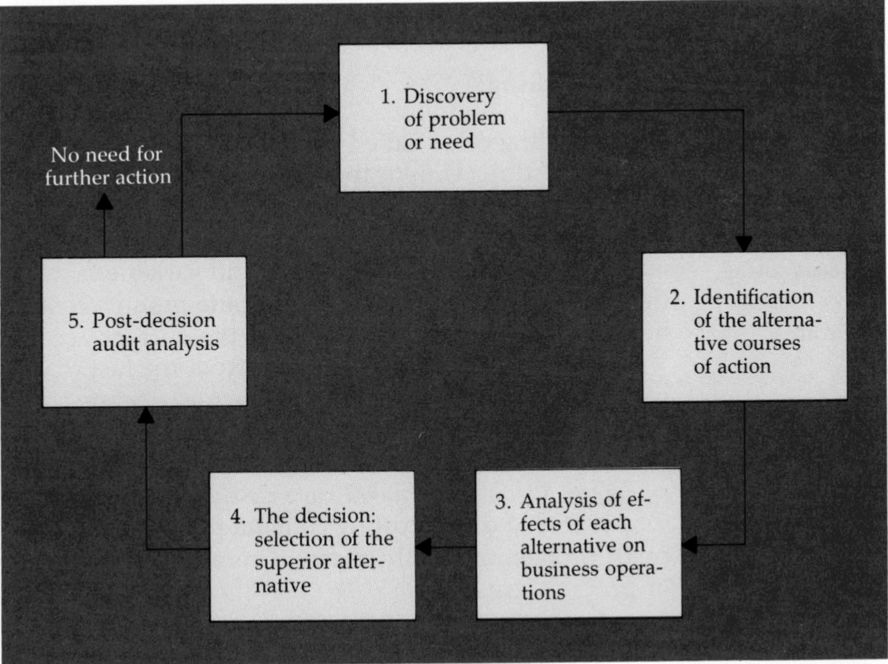

Figure 28-1 The Management Decision Cycle

Objective 2 Describe the steps in the management decision cycle

the detection of a problem area or resource need, the accountant should seek out all alternative courses of action open to management that will solve the problem or satisfy the need. After identifying the alternative actions, the accountant prepares a complete analysis for each action, showing total cost, cost savings, or financial effects on business operations. Each type of decision requires different information. When all the information has been gathered and assembled in a meaningful manner, management can decide on or select the one superior course of action. After the decision alternative has been implemented, the accountant should prepare a post-decision audit analysis to determine the success and accuracy of the decision. If further action is needed, the decision cycle begins again. If not, this particular decision process has been completed.

Accounting Tools and Reports for Decision Analysis

The accountant usually plays the role of data supplier in the managerial decision process. Certain accounting techniques and reporting formats help to accomplish this objective. Management expects decision information to be accurate, timely, refined, and presented in a readable manner. Therefore, the accountant must be concerned not only with the information itself but with a reporting structure as well.

Direct costing and incremental analysis are the two most common decision tools used by the accountant. Each technique aids in identifying information relevant to a particular decision. In addition, each technique provides the accountant with a special decision reporting format.

Direct Costing

Objective 3 Calculate product costs using direct costing procedures

Direct costing (also called variable costing) is primarily an approach to product costing. Unlike absorption costing, which assigns *all* manufacturing costs to products, direct costing employs only the variable manufacturing costs for product costing and inventory valuation purposes. Direct materials costs, direct labor costs, and variable factory overhead costs are the only cost elements used to compute product costs. Fixed factory overhead costs are considered costs of the current accounting period.

Support for direct costing stems from the fact that fixed manufacturing costs will be incurred whether the factory operates or not. For this reason, proponents argue that such costs do not have a direct relationship to the product and should not be used to determine product unit cost. *Fixed manufacturing costs are linked more closely with time than with productive output.* Opponents of direct costing contend that without the fixed manufacturing costs, production would cease. Therefore, such costs are an integral part of product costs.

Whatever side of the argument you are on, two points are certain: (1) direct costing is very useful for internal management decision purposes, and (2) direct costing is *not* recognized as being acceptable for external reporting purposes by either the Internal Revenue Service or the American Institute of Certified Public Accountants. Therefore, a direct costing reporting and product costing approach cannot be used for computing federal income taxes or for reporting the results of operations and financial position to stockholders and others outside the organization.

Product Costing For product costing purposes, direct costing differentiates fixed manufacturing costs from those that vary with output. A point that is often overlooked is that fixed manufacturing costs are also excluded from all inventories. Therefore, inventories resulting from direct costing are lower in value than those computed by means of the absorption costing technique.

An example will help to explain the differences between these two product costing approaches. Granoff Industries, Inc., produces outdoor cooking accessories. During 19xx, the company put a new disposable grill into production. A summary of 19xx cost and production data for the grill follows: Raw materials cost, $59,136; direct labor, $76,384; variable factory overhead, $44,352; and fixed factory overhead, $36,960. There were 24,640 units completed and 22,000 units sold during 19xx. There were no beginning or ending work in process inventories.

Using the above data, we can determine unit cost information as well as ending inventory and cost of goods sold amounts for 19xx under a direct costing approach and under an absorption costing approach. This information is summarized in Figure 28-2. Unit production cost under direct costing is $7.30 per grill, whereas unit cost is $8.80 working with the absorption costing procedures. Ending Finished Goods Inventory balances differ because of the $1.50 difference in unit cost. Because fewer costs remain in inventory at year end with direct costing amounts, it is logical that greater costs will appear on the income statement. As shown in Figure 28-2, $197,560 of current manufacturing costs are considered period costs, to be subtracted from revenue in the direct costing income statement. Only $193,600 are shown as Cost of Goods Sold when absorption costing techniques are used. The difference of $3,960 (2,640 units in inventory × $1.50 fixed costs per unit) is an inventoriable cost under the absorption costing procedure.

Performance Analysis: The Income Statement Direct costing procedures lead to differences in financial reporting as well as in product costing. Combining the concepts of contribution margin and direct costing results in an entirely new income statement format. This new format emphasizes cost variability and segment or product line contributions to profit. Costs are no longer classified as manufacturing versus nonmanufacturing. Instead, attention is focused on separating variable costs from fixed costs.

Objective 4 Prepare an income statement using the contribution reporting format

Expansion of the Granoff Industries example will help to illustrate this point. Assume the following additional information for 19xx: Selling price per grill is $24.50. Variable selling costs per grill are $4.80. Fixed

Figure 28-2
Direct Costing Versus Absorption Costing

Granoff Industries, Inc.
Unit Cost and Ending Inventory Values
For the Year Ended December 31, 19xx

	Direct Costing	Absorption Costing
Unit cost		
Raw materials ($59,136 ÷ 24,640 units)	$2.40	$2.40
Direct labor ($76,384 ÷ 24,640 units)	3.10	3.10
Variable factory overhead ($44,352 ÷ 24,640 units)	1.80	1.80
Fixed factory overhead ($36,960 ÷ 24,640 units)	—	1.50
Total unit cost	$7.30	$8.80
Ending Finished Goods Inventory		
2,640 units at $7.30	$ 19,272	
2,640 units at $8.80		$ 23,232
Cost of Goods Sold for 19xx		
22,000 units at $7.30	$160,600	
22,000 units at $8.80		$193,600
Plus fixed factory overhead	36,960	
Costs appearing on 19xx income statement	$197,560	$193,600
Total costs to be accounted for	$216,832	$216,832

selling expenses are $48,210, and fixed administrative expenses are $82,430. Net income computed under both direct costing and absorption costing procedures is shown in comparative fashion in Figure 28-3. The contribution format is depicted first. Note that the caption "gross profit" is replaced by "contribution margin" and that only variable costs are subtracted from sales to compute the contribution margin. This amount represents what each segment or product line is contributing to the fixed costs and profits of the enterprise. Net income computed by using the conventional statement format is shown in the lower part of Figure 28-3. Note that net income does differ under the two methods. This difference, $3,960, is the same amount discussed earlier—that portion of fixed manufacturing overhead cost that is inventoried when absorption costing procedures are followed.

Contribution Reporting and Decisions Direct costing and the contribution approach to reporting are used extensively in decision analysis. Their most common use is in deciding whether to continue or discontinue a particular segment, division, or product line. Other uses are in the evaluation of new product lines and in sales mix studies. Decisions to determine

Figure 28-3
The Income Statement—Contribution Versus Conventional Formats

Granoff Industries, Inc.
Disposable Grill Division
Income Statement
For the Year Ended December 31, 19xx

Contribution Format Using Direct Costing Procedures

Sales		$539,000
Variable Manufacturing Cost of Goods Produced	$179,872	
Less Ending Inventory	19,272*	
Variable Cost of Goods Sold	$160,600*	
Plus Variable Selling Costs (22,000 units at $4.80)	105,600	266,200
Contribution Margin		$272,800
Less Fixed Costs		
Fixed Manufacturing Costs	$ 36,960	
Fixed Selling Expenses	48,210	
Fixed Administrative Expenses	82,430	167,600
Net Income (before taxes)		$105,200

Conventional Format Using Absorption Costing Procedures

Sales		$539,000
Cost of Goods Sold		
Cost of Goods Manufactured	$216,832*	
Less Ending Inventory	23,232*	193,600*
Gross Profit on Sales		$345,400
Selling Expenses		
Variable	$105,600	
Fixed	48,210	
Administrative Expenses	82,430	236,240
Net Income (before taxes)		$109,160

*Detailed computations are found in Figure 28-2.

the contribution of sales territories also use the contribution approach to income reporting. We will illustrate these uses later in this chapter in discussing specific types of decisions.

Incremental Analysis

Objective 5 Develop decision data using the incremental analysis technique

Another approach often used in decision reporting is to compare different alternatives by looking only at informational differences. This type of reporting structure is called **incremental analysis.** Because only decision data that differ among alternatives are of concern and, for decision purposes, only future data are included, incremental analysis is based on information relevant to the decision at hand. By focusing on the areas of difference among alternatives, incremental analysis helps to highlight the important issues, makes the evaluation easier for the decision maker, and reduces the time needed to select the best course of action.

As an illustration, assume that the Edson Company is evaluating the purchase of one of two machines, P and Q. Management has been able to collect the following annual operating estimates concerning the two machines:

	Machine P	Machine Q
Increase in revenue	$16,200	$19,800
Increase in annual operating costs		
Raw materials	2,800	2,800
Direct labor	4,200	6,100
Variable factory overhead	2,100	3,050
Fixed factory overhead (depreciation included)	5,000	5,000

The most appropriate method of comparing these two decision alternatives is to prepare an analysis that will reveal incremental revenue and incremental cost data regarding the decision. This is shown below.

Edson Company
Incremental Decision Analysis

	Machine P	Difference Resulting if Machine Q Is Selected Instead of Machine P	Machine Q
Increase in revenue	$16,200	$3,600	$19,800
Increase in operating costs			
Raw materials	$ 2,800	—	$ 2,800
Direct labor	4,200	1,900	6,100
Variable factory overhead	2,100	950	3,050
Fixed factory overhead	5,000	—	5,000
Total operating costs	$14,100	$2,850	$16,950
Resulting increase in net income	$ 2,100	$ 750	$ 2,850

If we assume that the purchase price and useful life of the two machines are comparable, the analysis shows that Machine Q will generate $750 more in net income than Machine P. Thus the decision would be to purchase Machine Q.

Special Reports

Decision analysis usually differs for each type of decision facing management. Therefore, a familiarity with the contribution approach to income reporting and with the reports structured around the incremental or relevant cost approach alone will not be adequate for all decision analyses. Often the accountant has to improvise, fitting the decision reporting format to the circumstances of the decision or special informational needs of management.

Qualitative as well as quantitative data are useful in the decision process. When only quantitative data are being considered, most problems of alternative choice can be presented adequately by using either the contribution reporting or the incremental analysis format. However, some decisions involve many alternatives, each of which is the best alternative under defined circumstances. One may be more profitable, but another may further diversify a company's product line. A third alternative may help prevent a massive layoff of personnel in a specific geographical area, thereby bolstering the company's goodwill in that city. Although many other equally qualitative decision alternatives may be available, management must select only one course of action. For situations such as those described above, the accountant must use imagination and prepare the special decision report warranted by the circumstances. There is no defined structure or format for these special decision reports. They are created by skilled, experienced accountants to fit individual situations.

The Capital Expenditure Decision

One of the most important types of decisions facing management is determining when and how much to spend on capital facilities for the company. These decisions are called **capital expenditure decisions** and include decisions for installing new equipment, replacing old equipment, expanding the production area through additions to an existing building, purchasing or constructing a new building, or acquiring an existing company to be merged with present operating facilities. These major monetary decisions require careful analysis by the accountant and usually involve comparative analysis of two or more alternatives.

Capital Budgeting: An Interdisciplinary Problem

The process of identifying a facility need, analyzing alternative courses of action to satisfy that need, preparing the reports for management, selecting the best alternative, and rationing available capital expenditure funds among competing resource needs is collectively known as **capital budgeting**. All too often, one academic business discipline or another claims that capital budgeting is within its particular operating or teaching domain.

The fact is that capital budgeting involves input from every aspect of the business organization. Finance people are expected to supply a target cost of capital or desired rate of return for the decision analysis and an estimate of how much money can be spent on any one project. Without this type of information, a decision cannot be reached. Marketing personnel influence the areas of the enterprise that need plant and facility expansion through predictions of future sales trends. Management people at all levels help to identify facility needs and often prepare preliminary cost estimates of the desired facility or project. These same people assist in implementing capital expenditure decisions by trying to keep actual results within the cost and revenue confines of the predecision analyses.

The accountant gathers and organizes the decision information into a workable, readable format and usually applies one or more proposal evaluation methods to the information gathered for each alternative. The most common capital expenditure proposal evaluation methods include the (1) accounting rate of return method, (2) payback method, and (3) present value method. Once these methods have been applied to the decision alternatives, management can make a selection based on the decision criteria under the circumstances. The remaining sections of this part of the chapter center on the accountant's function of proposal evaluation using these methods and on the final selection process of capital expenditure requests.

Desired Rate of Return on Investment

Objective 6 Describe the purpose of a minimum desired rate of return and explain the methods used to arrive at this rate

Selecting the best capital expenditure alternative is not always the approach taken in the decision-making process. Most companies have an established minimum rate of return, below which the expenditure request is refused automatically. If none of the capital expenditure requests is expected to meet the minimum desired rate of return, all requests will be refused.

Why do companies employ a minimum rate of return cutoff point? The idea is that if a specific expenditure request fails to qualify because it falls below the cutoff rate, the funds can be used more profitably in another area of the company. Supporting poor-return proposals now will eventually lower the entire company's profitability.

Determining a company's minimum desired rate of return is no simple matter. Each of the alternative rates that can be established and used as a cutoff point has superior characteristics. A sample of the alternatives includes (1) cost of capital measures, (2) corporate return on investment, (3) industry average return on investment, and (4) bank interest rate.

Cost of Capital Measures Of all the desired rates of return shown above, cost of capital measures are the most widely used and discussed. The goal is to find the cost of financing the company's activities. However, a company finances its activities through funding obtained from various debt instruments, preferred and common stock issuances, and profitable operations. Each of these financing alternatives has a different cost rate, and each company maintains a different mix of these sources for acquiring the means of financing current and future operations.

To establish a desired cutoff rate of return, management can use cost of debt, cost of preferred stock, cost of equity capital, or cost of retained earnings. In many cases, a company will average these cost results to establish an **average cost of capital** measure. Sophisticated methods are used to compute these financial return measures.[1] Because the purpose here is to identify measures used, we shall present only a brief description of each type of cost of financing.

Cost of debt is the ratio of loan charges to net proceeds of the loan. After-tax considerations and present value of interest charges must be acknowledged, but the rate is essentially the ratio of costs to loan proceeds. **Cost of preferred stock** is the stated dividend rate of the individual stock issue. Tax considerations are not important, because dividends are not a deductible expense as are interest charges. **Cost of equity capital** is the rate of return to the investor that maintains the stock's value in the marketplace. It is not just the dividend rate to the stockholder because the dividend rate can be raised or lowered almost at will by management. This concept is very involved but has sound authoritative financial support.[2] **Cost of retained earnings** is the opportunity cost or dividends forgone by the stockholder. Such a cost is linked closely with the cost of equity capital discussed above. The point is that a firm's cost of capital is very difficult to compute because it represents a weighted average of the costs of the various financing methods. When computed, however, a weighted average cost of capital figure represents the best estimate of a minimum desired rate of return.

Weighted average cost of capital is computed by first determining the cost rate of maintaining each source or class of capital-raising instrument. The second part of the computation is to calculate the percentage or ratio of each source of capital to the total debt and equity financing of the company. Weighted average cost of capital is the sum of the products resulting from multiplying each financing source's percentage or ratio by its cost rate. For example, assume that Alexander Company's financing structure is as follows:

Cost Rate	Source of Capital	Amount	Capital Mix (Percentage of Each to Total)
10%	Debt financing	$150,000	30
8%	Preferred stock	50,000	10
12%	Common stock	200,000	40
14%	Retained earnings	100,000	20
	Totals	$500,000	100

1. See James Van Horne, "Cost of Capital," in *Financial Management and Policy*, 2nd ed. (Englewood Cliffs, N.J.: Prentice-Hall, Inc., 1971), Chapter 4, pp. 89–117.
2. Ibid.

Weighted average cost of capital of 11.4 percent would be computed by the following process:

Source of Capital	Cost Rate	×	Ratios of Capital Mix	=	Portion of Weighted Average Cost of Capital
Debt financing	.10		.30		.030
Preferred stock	.08		.10		.008
Common stock	.12		.40		.048
Retained earnings	.14		.20		.028
Weighted average cost of capital					.114

Other Cutoff Measures If cost of capital information is not available, management can use one of three less accurate but still effective amounts as the minimum desired rate of return. The first is average total corporate return on investment. The reasoning used to support such a measure is that any capital investment that produced a return lower than an amount earned historically by the company would negatively influence future results of operations. A second alternative is to use industry averages of the cost of capital. Most sizable industries supply such information. A last-resort type of measure would be the current bank lending rate. Because most companies are both debt and equity financed, this rate does not reflect an accurate rate of return.

Accounting Rate of Return Method

Objective 7a Evaluate capital expenditure proposals using the accounting rate of return method

Among the methods used to measure the estimated performance of a capital investment, the **accounting rate of return method** is a crude but easy approach to use and understand. With this method, the evaluation of anticipated performance concentrates on two variables: estimated annual after-tax net income from the project and the average investment cost. The basic equation is as follows:

$$\text{accounting rate of return} = \frac{\text{project's average annual after-tax net income}}{\text{average investment cost}}$$

Average annual after-tax net income must be computed from revenue and expense data generated for project evaluation purposes. Average investment in the proposed capital facility is computed as follows:[3]

3. The procedure of adding salvage value to the numerator may not seem logical. However, a fixed asset is never depreciated below its salvage value. Average investment is computed by determining the midpoint of the depreciable portion of the asset and adding back the salvage value. Another way of stating the above formula would be

$$\text{average investment} = \frac{\text{total investment} - \text{salvage value}}{2} + \text{salvage value}$$

which reduces to the formula used above.

$$\text{average investment} = \frac{\text{total investment} + \text{salvage value}}{2}$$

For example, assume that the Kollias Company is interested in purchasing a new bottling machine. Only projects that promise to yield more than a 16 percent return are acceptable to management. Estimates for the proposal included an increase in revenue of \$17,900 per year, operating cost increases of \$8,500 per year (including depreciation), cost of machine at \$51,000, salvage value of machine at \$3,000, and a tax rate of 50 percent. Should the company invest in the machine? To answer the question, we compute the accounting rate of return as follows:

$$\text{accounting rate of return} = \frac{(\$17{,}900 - \$8{,}500) \times .50}{\dfrac{\$51{,}000 + \$3{,}000}{2}}$$

$$= \frac{\$4{,}700}{\$27{,}000} = \underline{\underline{17.4\%}}$$

Because the projected rate of return is higher than the 16 percent minimum desired rate of return, management should seriously consider the investment.

This method is easy to understand and apply. As a result, it is widely used in practice. However, it is important to know the disadvantages of the accounting rate of return method. First, the use of averages tends to equalize all information, thereby producing inaccuracies in annual income and investment data. Second, the method is difficult to use if estimated annual net incomes differ from year to year. Finally, time value of money is not considered in the computations. Thus future and present dollars are treated as being equal.

Cash Flow and the Payback Method

Objective 7b Evaluate capital expenditure proposals using the payback method

Instead of measuring the rate of return on investments, many managers are more interested in the estimated cash flow to be generated by a capital investment. The objective is to determine the minimum length of *time* it may take to recoup the initial amount of the investment. If two investment alternatives are being considered, the choice will be the investment with the shortest cost-recoupment period. This period of time is known as the payback period, and the capital investment evaluation approach is called the payback method.

We compute the payback period as follows:

$$\text{payback period} = \frac{\text{cost of capital investment}}{\text{annual net cash inflow}}$$

To apply the payback method to the proposed capital investment of the Kollias Company discussed earlier, we need some additional information. We need to determine the *net cash flow*. This is accomplished by identifying and eliminating the effects of all the noncash revenue and expense items included in the analysis of net income. In our problem, we will assume that the only noncash expense or revenue item is machine depreciation. To compute this amount, we must know the asset life and the depreciation method. Assume that the Kollias Company uses the straight-line depreciation approach, and the new bottling machine will have a ten-year estimated service life. Payback period for this proposal would be computed as shown below.

$$\begin{aligned}\text{annual depreciation} &= \frac{\text{cost} - \text{salvage value}}{10 \text{ (years)}}\\ &= \frac{\$51{,}000 - \$3{,}000}{10}\\ &= \underline{\underline{\$4{,}800}} \text{ per year}\end{aligned}$$

$$\begin{aligned}\text{payback period} &= \frac{\text{cost of machine}}{\text{cash revenue} - \text{cash expenses} - \text{taxes}}\\ &= \frac{\$51{,}000}{\$17{,}900 - (\$8{,}500 - \$4{,}800) - \$4{,}700}\\ &= \frac{\$51{,}000}{\$9{,}500}\\ &= \underline{\underline{5.368}} \text{ years}\end{aligned}$$

If the company's desired payback period is six years or less, the capital investment proposal would be approved.

Payback has the advantage of being easy to compute and understand, and is widely used for this reason. However, the disadvantages of this approach far outweigh the advantages. First, the method does not measure or pertain to profitability. Second, the present value of cash flows from different periods is not recognized. Finally, emphasis is on getting out of the investment rather than paying attention to the long-run payback of the investment.

Present Value Method[4]

Objective 7c Evaluate capital expenditure proposals using the present value method

Because of opportunities that exist today to do something with investment capital other than purchase fixed assets, management expects a reasonable return from an asset during its economic life. Capital expenditure decision analysis involves the evaluation of data estimates for several time periods in the future. Cash flows from different periods have differing values when measured in current dollars. Therefore, to treat all future income flows alike ignores the time value of money. This disadvantage is common to both the accounting rate of return and payback evaluation methods.

4. This section is based on the concept of present value. Appendixes A and B explain this concept and provide tables of multipliers for computations.

The concept of **discounted cash flow** helps to overcome the disadvantages of the accounting rate of return and payback methods in the evaluation of capital investment alternatives. By using the present value tables found in Appendix B, it is possible to discount future cash flows back to the present for analysis purposes. This approach to capital investment analysis is called the **present value method.** Multipliers used to compute the present value of a future cash flow are found in the present value tables and are determined by connecting (1) the minimum desired rate of return and (2) the life of the asset or length of time for which the amount is being discounted. Each element of cash inflow and cash outflow to be realized over the life of the asset is discounted back to the present. If the present value of all expected future net cash inflows exceeds the amount of the current investment, the expenditure meets the minimum desired rate of return, and the project should be implemented.

Situations of equal versus unequal annual cash flows dictate different approaches to present value determination. If all annual cash flows (inflows less outflows) are the same, the discount factor to be used will come from Table B-4 in Appendix B. This table contains multipliers for the present value of $1 received *each period* for a given number of time periods. One computation will include the cash flows of all time periods involved. If, however, expected cash inflows and outflows differ from one year to the next, each year's amounts have to be discounted back to the present. Discount factors used in this type of analysis are found in Table B-3 in Appendix B. Multipliers in Table B-3 are used to compute the present value of $1 to be received (or expended) at the end of a given number of time periods.

An example will help to show the difference in the present value analysis of expenditures with equal and unequal cash flows. Suppose that the De La Ronde Metal Products Company is evaluating two stamping machine alternatives. The Red Machine has equal expected annual net cash inflows, and the Green Machine has unequal annual amounts. A summary of analysis data follows:

	Red Machine	**Green Machine**
Expected life	5 years	5 years
Estimated net cash inflows		
19x4	$ 4,500	$ 5,500
19x5	4,500	5,000
19x6	4,500	4,000
19x7	4,500	3,500
19x8	4,500	3,500
Purchase price: January 1, 19x4	$15,000	$14,500

The company's minimum desired rate of return is 16 percent. Which—if either—of the two alternatives should be selected?

The evaluation process is illustrated in Figure 28-4. An analysis involving equal annual cash flows is the easier type to prepare. Present value of net cash inflows for the five-year period for the Red Machine is computed by multiplying $4,500 by 3.274. The multiplier, 3.274, is found in Table B-4 in Appendix B. Using the 16 percent minimum desired rate of return and the five-year life of the Red Machine, we find the multiplier in

Figure 28-4
Present Value Analysis: Equal Versus Unequal Cash Flows

De La Ronde Metal Products Company
Capital Expenditure Analysis
19x3

Red Machine		
Present value of net cash inflows 19x4–19x8 ($4,500 × 3.274)		$14,733
Less purchase price of machine		(15,000)
Negative net present value		($ 267)
Green Machine		
Present value of net cash inflows:		
19x4	($5,500 × .862)	$ 4,741
19x5	($5,000 × .743)	3,715
19x6	($4,000 × .641)	2,564
19x7	($3,500 × .552)	1,932
19x8	($3,500 × .476)	1,666
Total		$14,618
Less purchase price of machine		(14,500)
Positive net present value		$ 118

the table at the intersection of these coordinates. Present value of the total cash inflows from the Red Machine is $14,733. When we compare this figure with the $15,000 purchase price, the result is a *negative* net present value of $267.

Analysis of the Green Machine alternative yields different results. As shown in Figure 28-4, unequal net cash inflows cause more work for the analyst. Multipliers in this part of the evaluation process are located by using the same coordinate, 16 percent. However, five different multipliers must be used, one for each year of the life of the asset. Table B-3 in Appendix B is used because each annual amount must be individually discounted back to the present. For the Green Machine, the $14,618 present value of net cash inflows exceeds the $14,500 purchase price of the machine, resulting in a *positive* net present value of $118.

A positive net present value figure means that the return on the asset exceeds the 16 percent minimum desired rate of return. A negative total indicates that the rate of return is below the minimum cutoff point. In the De La Ronde Metal Products example, the decision would be to purchase the Green Machine.

Incorporating the time value of money into the evaluation of capital expenditure proposals is the primary advantage of the present value method. This method also deals primarily with total cash flows resulting from the investment over its useful life, thereby bringing total profitability into the analysis. The major disadvantage of the present value method is that many managers do not trust or understand the procedure. They prefer the payback or the accounting rate of return method because the computations are easier.

Illustrative Problem

A problem applying several evaluation approaches will help clarify the techniques used in capital expenditure decisions. The George Johnson Construction Company deals primarily with the development of large shopping centers. One of the large pieces of earthmoving equipment needs to be replaced. Although various kinds of equipment are on the market, the controller has narrowed the search to two alternatives. The following data have been compiled:

		Cash Flow Estimates		
		Cash Revenues	Cash Expenses	Net Cash Inflow
Model Y	Year 1	$300,000	$180,000	$120,000
	Year 2	300,000	180,000	120,000
	Year 3	300,000	180,000	120,000
	Year 4	300,000	180,000	120,000
Model Z	Year 1	$400,000	$180,000	$220,000
	Year 2	390,000	200,000	190,000
	Year 3	380,000	220,000	160,000
	Year 4	370,000	240,000	130,000

Purchase prices and estimated life and salvage values for each model are shown below. The company uses the straight-line depreciation method.

	Model Y	**Model Z**
Purchase price	$400,000	$500,000
Salvage value	$ 80,000	$140,000
Useful life	4 years	4 years

The company considers 14 percent to be its minimum desired rate of return and its desired payback period to be 2.5 years or less.

Required

1. Analyze the two alternatives and determine which model the George Johnson Construction Company should purchase. In your analysis, include (a) the accounting rate of return method, (b) the payback period method, and (c) the present value method.

2. Prepare an incremental analysis of the two alternatives using the present value evaluation approach.

Solution

1a. The accounting rate of return method yields the following figures on average income and investment:

		Increase in Net Income		
		Net Cash Inflow	− Depreciation =	Net Income
Model Y	Year 1	$120,000	$ 80,000	$ 40,000
	Year 2	120,000	80,000	40,000
	Year 3	120,000	80,000	40,000
	Year 4	120,000	80,000	40,000
	Totals	$480,000	$320,000	$160,000
Model Z	Year 1	$220,000	$ 90,000	$130,000
	Year 2	190,000	90,000	100,000
	Year 3	160,000	90,000	70,000
	Year 4	130,000	90,000	40,000
	Totals	$700,000	$360,000	$340,000

$$\text{accounting rate of return} = \frac{\text{model's average annual net income}}{\text{average investment cost}}$$

$$\text{Model Y} = \frac{\$160{,}000 \div 4}{(\$400{,}000 + \$80{,}000) \div 2} = \frac{\$40{,}000}{\$240{,}000} = \underline{\underline{16.67\%}}$$

$$\text{Model Z} = \frac{\$340{,}000 \div 4}{(\$500{,}000 + \$140{,}000) \div 2} = \frac{\$85{,}000}{\$320{,}000} = \underline{\underline{26.56\%}}$$

1b. Payback period figures are shown below.

$$\text{Model Y:} \quad \frac{\text{total cash investment}}{\text{annual net cash inflow}} = \frac{\$400{,}000}{\$120{,}000} = \underline{\underline{3.33}} \text{ years}$$

Model Z: Unequal cash flows require an analysis of yearly amounts.

Total cash investment		$500,000
Less cash flow recovery		
Year 1	$220,000	
Year 2	190,000	
Year 3 (9/16 of $160,000)	90,000	(500,000)
Uncovered investment		—

Payback period = $2\frac{9}{16}$ years or $\underline{\underline{2.5625}}$ years

1c. Present value method (minimum desired return = 14 percent) yields the information on the next page.

In comparative form, the decision analysis boils down to:

	Model Y	**Model Z**
Accounting rate of return	16.67%	26.56%
Payback method	3.33 years	2.5625 years
Net present value	($2,960)	$106,890

	Year	Net Cash Inflows	×	Present Value Multipliers (14%)	=	Present Value
Model Y:	1–4	$120,000		2.914		$349,680
	4	80,000 (salvage)		.592		47,360
	Total present value					$397,040
	Cost of initial investment					(400,000)
	Negative net present value					($ 2,960)
Model Z:	1	$220,000		.877		$192,940
	2	190,000		.769		146,110
	3	160,000		.675		108,000
	4	130,000		.592		76,960
	4	140,000 (salvage)		.592		82,880
	Total present value					$606,890
	Cost of initial investment					(500,000)
	Positive net present value					$106,890

For all of the approaches, the decision points to Model Z. Of some interest is the information on rate of return and net present value for Model Y. When the accounting rate of return method is used, Model Y is shown as producing a 16.67 percent return, which is above the minimum desired rate of return. However, the same information applied to the present value method generates a negative present value, which means that the actual rate of return is below the minimum 14 percent figure. This is a good example of how the accounting rate of return can be misleading when applied to more than one time period.

2. Incremental analysis, using the present value approach, produces the following information:

Year		Net Cash Inflows: Model Z	Net Cash Inflows: Model Y	Difference Z − Y	Present Value Multipliers (14%)	Present Value
1		$220,000	$120,000	$100,000	.877	$ 87,700
2		190,000	120,000	70,000	.769	53,830
3		160,000	120,000	40,000	.675	27,000
4		130,000	120,000	10,000	.592	5,920
4	(salvage)	140,000	80,000	60,000	.592	35,520
Totals		$840,000	$560,000	$280,000		
Net present value of incremental cash flows (for Model Z)						$209,970
Initial capital expenditures:						
		$500,000	$400,000	$100,000		(100,000)
Net present value (in favor of Model Z)						$109,970

The comparative advantage of investing in Model Z is measured in this incremental analysis.

Other Operating Decisions of Management

Management relies on the accountant to supply relevant information for many types of decisions other than those involving capital expenditures. We discuss the data relevant to the special order decision, the make or buy decision, and the sales mix analysis below.

Make or Buy Decisions

Objective 8 Prepare decision alternative evaluations for make or buy decisions, special order decisions, and sales mix analyses.

One common group of decision analyses centers on component parts in a product assembly operation. In this area, management is faced continually with the decision as to whether to make or to buy some or all of the parts. The objective of the make or buy decision is to identify those cost and revenue elements relevant to this type of decision. Below is the information to be considered.

To Make	To Buy
Need for expensive machinery	Purchase price of item
Other variable costs of making the item	Rent or net cash flow to be generated from vacated space in factory
Repair and maintenance expenses	Salvage value of machinery

To illustrate a make or buy decision, we present the case of the Timmerman Electronics Company. The firm has been purchasing a small transistor casing from an outside supplier for the past five years at a cost of $1.25 per casing. However, the supplier has just informed Timmerman Electronics that the price will be increased by 20 percent effective immediately. The company has idle machinery that could be used to produce the casings. In addition, management has been able to determine that the costs of producing the casings would be $84 per 100 casings for raw materials, six minutes labor per casing at $4 per direct labor hour, and variable factory overhead of $2 per direct labor hour. Fixed factory overhead would include $4,000 of depreciation per year and $6,000 of other fixed costs. Annual production and usage would be 20,000 casings. The space and machinery to be utilized would not be usable if the part were purchased. Should Timmerman Electronics Company make or buy the casings?

From the information given, the company should make the casings. An incremental cost analysis of the two decision alternatives is presented in Figure 28-5. All costs connected with the decision are shown in the analysis. Because the machinery has already been purchased and it and the required factory space have no other usage, the fixed factory overhead costs are the same for both decision alternatives and are, therefore, irrelevant to the decision. The costs of making the needed casings (excluding the fixed overhead costs) total $28,800. Total costs to purchase 20,000

Figure 28-5 Incremental Analysis: Make or Buy Decision

Timmerman Electronics Company
Incremental Decision Analysis
Current Year—Annual Usage

	Make	Difference in Favor of Make	Buy
Raw materials (20,000 ÷ 100 × $84)	$16,800	$(16,800)	—
Direct labor (20,000 ÷ 10 × $4)	8,000	(8,000)	—
Variable factory overhead (20,000 ÷ 10 × $2)	4,000	(4,000)	—
Fixed factory overhead			
Depreciation*	4,000	—	4,000
Other*	6,000	—	6,000
To purchase completed casings 20,000 × $1.50	—	30,000	30,000
Totals	$28,800	$ 1,200	$30,000

*Irrelevant because these amounts are the same for both decision alternatives. Amounts have not been included in totals.

casings will be $30,000 with the increased purchase price. It is clear, then, that $1,200 will be saved if the casings are made within the company.

Using incremental analysis is a good approach to the make or buy type of decision. This decision format enables the analyst to use all decision data available and quickly identifies those items irrelevant to the final decision.

Special Product Orders

Management is often confronted with **special order decisions,** requiring acceptance or rejection of special product orders. These orders are normally for large numbers of similar or identical products to be sold at prices below those listed in advertisements. Management would not have anticipated such orders and so would not have included them in any annual cost or sales estimates. Usually, these orders are one-time events and should not be included in estimates of subsequent years' operations. (Because standard-type products are sold to the public at stated prices, legal advice concerning federal price discrimination statutes should be obtained before accepting special orders.)

An example of such a case will illustrate the analysis required. Moustafa Sporting Goods, Inc., manufactures a complete line of sporting equipment. Amer Enterprises operates a large chain of discount stores and has approached the Moustafa company with a special order. The order calls for 30,000 deluxe baseballs to be shipped with bulk packaging of 500 baseballs per box. Amer is willing to pay $2.45 per baseball.

The following data were developed by the Moustafa accounting department: annual expected production, 400,000 baseballs; current year's production, 410,000 baseballs; maximum production capacity, 450,000 baseballs.

Unit cost data		
Raw materials	$.60	
Direct labor	.90	
Factory overhead		
Variable	.50	
Fixed ($100,000 ÷ 400,000)	.25	
Packaging per unit	.30	
Advertising ($60,000 ÷ 400,000)	.15	
Other fixed selling and administrative costs ($120,000 ÷ 400,000)	.30	
Total	$3.00	
Unit selling price		$4.00
Total estimated bulk packaging costs (30,000 baseballs: 500 per box)		$2,500

Should Moustafa Sporting Goods, Inc., accept the Amer offer?

A profitability analysis reveals that the special order from Amer Enterprises should be accepted. Figure 28-6 contains a comparative analysis structured on the contribution reporting format. Net income before taxes is computed for the Baseball Division for operations both with and without the Amer order.

The only costs affected by the order are for raw materials, direct labor, variable factory overhead, and packaging. Materials, labor, and overhead costs are shown for sales of 410,000 and 440,000 baseballs, respectively. Sales data were computed using these same unit amounts. Packaging costs increase, but only by the additional bulk packaging costs. All other costs remain the same under each situation. The net result of accepting the special order is an $11,000 increase in contribution margin (and net income before taxes). This amount can be verified by the following computation:

$$\begin{aligned} \text{net gain} &= [(\text{selling price} - \text{variable mfg. costs}) \times \text{units}] - \text{bulk pack. costs} \\ &= [(\$2.45 - \$2.00)30{,}000] - \$2{,}500 \\ &= \$13{,}500 - \$2{,}500 = \underline{\underline{\$11{,}000}} \end{aligned}$$

For special order analysis, both the comparative contribution reporting approach and incremental analysis can be used. In the above example, we selected contribution reporting because of the misleading fixed cost data given in the problem. Contribution reporting highlights the influence of variable cost changes on contribution margin and net income.

Figure 28-6
Contribution Reporting: Special Product Order

Moustafa Sporting Goods, Inc.
Comparative Decision Analysis
Special Product Order—Baseball Division

	Without Amer Order	With Amer Order
Sales	$1,640,000	$1,713,500
Less variable costs		
Raw materials	$ 246,000	$ 264,000
Direct labor	369,000	396,000
Variable factory overhead	205,000	220,000
Packaging costs	123,000	125,500
Total variable costs	$ 943,000	$1,005,500
Contribution margin	$ 697,000	$ 708,000
Less fixed costs		
Factory overhead	$ 100,000	$ 100,000
Advertising	60,000	60,000
Selling and administrative	120,000	120,000
Total fixed costs	$ 280,000	$ 280,000
Net income before taxes	$ 417,000	$ 428,000

Sales Mix Analysis

Profit analysis and maximization are possible only when the profitability of all product lines is known. The question is, Which product or products contribute the most to company profitability in relation to the amount of capital assets or other scarce resources required to produce the item(s)? To answer this question, the accountant must measure the contribution margin of each product. The next step is to determine a set of ratios of contribution margin to the required capital equipment or other scarce resources. Once this step is completed, management should request a marketing study to establish the upper limits of demand on those products that are most profitable. If product profitability can be computed and market demand exists for these products, management should shift production emphasis to the more profitable products.

Many decision categories can be related to the approach described in this section. Sales mix analysis means determining the most profitable combination of product sales when a company produces more than one product. Closely associated with sales mix analysis is the product line profitability study designed to identify those products losing money for the company. The same decision approach is used with the objective of eliminating the unprofitable product lines. A third decision area is that of corporate segment analysis. The contribution margin approach is again used, with the goal being the isolation of production costs in order to identify unprofitable segments. If corrective action is not possible, management should eliminate the noncontributing segments. Although not all these decision areas will be discussed, it is important to remember that the same decision approach to be used for sales mix analysis is applicable to product line profitability studies and corporate segment analyses.

An example of this type of analysis will aid understanding. The management of Joe Mori and Sons, Inc., is in the process of analyzing its sales mix. The company manufactures three products—C, S, and U—using the same production equipment for all products. The total productive capacity is being utilized. Below are the product line statistics.

	Product C	**Product S**	**Product U**
Current production and sales (units)	20,000	30,000	18,000
Machine hours per product	2	1	2.5
Selling price per unit	$24.00	$18.00	$32.00
Unit variable manufacturing costs	$12.50	$10.00	$18.75
Unit variable selling costs	$ 6.50	$ 5.00	$ 6.25

Should the company sell more of one product and restrict production of another?

Because total productive capacity is being used, the only way to expand the production of one product is to reduce the production of another product. The sales mix analysis of Joe Mori and Sons, Inc., is illustrated in Figure 28-7. Although contribution reporting is employed here, contribu-

Figure 28-7 Contribution Reporting: Sales Mix Analysis

Joe Mori and Sons, Inc.
Sales Mix Analysis
Contribution Reporting Format

	Product C	Product S	Product U
Sales price	$24.00	$18.00	$32.00
Variable costs			
Manufacturing	$12.50	$10.00	$18.75
Selling	6.50	5.00	6.25
Total	$19.00	$15.00	$25.00
Contribution margin (A)	$ 5.00	$ 3.00	$ 7.00
Machine hours required per unit (B)	2	1	2.5
Contribution margin per machine hour (A ÷ B)	$ 2.50	$ 3.00	$ 2.80

tion margin per product is not the important figure for a decision regarding shifts in sales mix. In the analysis, Product U has the highest contribution margin. However, as all products use the same machinery and all machine hours are being utilized, machine hours become the scarce resource.

The analysis in Figure 28-7 goes one step beyond the computation of contribution margin per unit. A sales mix decision such as this one should use two decision variables: contribution margin per unit and machine hours required per unit. For instance, Product C requires two machine hours to generate $5 of contribution margin, whereas Product S would generate $6 of contribution margin using the same two machine hours. For this reason, we computed contribution margin per machine hour. On the basis of this information, management can readily see that it should produce and sell as much of Product S as possible. Next, it should push Product U. If any productive capacity remains, it should produce Product C.

Chapter Review

Review of Learning Objectives

1. Define and identify relevant decision information.

Any future cost, revenue, or resource usage item used in decision analyses that differs among the decision's alternative courses of action is considered relevant decision information. Recognition of relevant data comes from development of a comparative analysis of the decision alternatives.

2. Describe the steps in the management decision cycle.

The decision cycle begins with the discovery of a problem or resource need. Then, the various alternative courses of action to solve the problem are identified. Next, a complete analysis to determine the effects of each alternative on business operations is prepared. With this supportive data, the decision maker selects the superior alternative. Following the implementation of the decision, the accountant is expected to conduct a post-audit to determine if the decision was correct or if additional needs have arisen.

3. Calculate product costs using direct costing procedures.

Direct costing employs only variable manufacturing costs for product costing and inventory valuation purposes. Direct materials costs, direct labor costs, and variable factory overhead costs are the only cost elements used to compute product costs. Fixed factory overhead costs are considered costs of the current period.

4. Prepare an income statement using the contribution reporting format.

Unlike the conventional income reporting format, which depends on the absorption costing concept, the contribution format is based on direct costing procedures. Variable costs of goods sold and variable selling expenses are subtracted from sales to arrive at contribution margin. All fixed costs, including those from manufacturing, selling, and administration, are subtracted from contribution margin to determine net income (before taxes).

5. Develop decision data using the incremental analysis technique.

Incremental analysis implies a decision reporting structure in which the various decision alternatives are exposed and information differences are examined. When all revenue and cost data are examined in this way, the data relevant to the decision are highlighted since they are the ones where differences exist. Revenue and cost items that are identical under the various alternatives are not relevant to the decision.

6. Describe the purpose of a minimum desired rate of return, and explain the methods used to arrive at this rate.

The purpose of establishing a minimum desired rate of return is to create a decision point below which the related capital expenditure request is refused automatically. By means of such an approach to decision making, many unprofitable requests are turned away or discouraged without a great deal of wasted executive time. The types of minimum desired rates of return include cost of capital, corporate return on investment, industry average return on investment, and bank interest rates. Weighted average cost of capital and average return on investment are the most widely used approaches to determining a minimum desired rate of return.

7. Evaluate capital expenditure proposals using the accounting rate of return method, the payback method, and the present value method.

When evaluating two or more capital expenditure proposals using the accounting rate of return method, the alternative that yields the highest ratio of net income after taxes to average cost of investment is selected. When using the payback method to evaluate capital expenditure proposal, primary emphasis is placed on the shortest time period required to recoup in cash the original amount of the investment. The present value method relies heavily on the time value of money concept. Present values of future cash inflows are examined to see if they exceed the current cost of the capital expenditure being evaluated.

8. Prepare decision alternative evaluations for make or buy decisions, special order decisions, and sales mix analyses.

Make or buy decision analysis assists management in determining whether to purchase a component part to an assembly or to make the part inside the company. This analysis centers on an incremental view of the costs of each alternative. Special order decisions relate to unused capacity and the determination of a minimum acceptable selling price of a product. Fixed costs are usually irrelevant to the decision because they have been covered by regular operations. Contribution margin is a key decision yardstick. Sales mix analysis means determining the most profitable combination of product sales when a company produces more than one product using a common scarce resource. A similar approach can be used for decisions involving the identification of profitable sales territories or profitable corporate segments. Comparative analyses using the contribution reporting format are important in these studies.

Review Problem

Before doing the exercises and problems, review the example involving a capital expenditure decision analysis and the examples of direct costing, contribution reporting, incremental analysis, make or buy decisions, special product order decisions, and sales mix analysis.

Chapter Assignments

Questions

1. What is meant by the term *relevant decision information?* What are the two pertinent characteristics of such information?
2. Describe and discuss the five steps of the management decision cycle.
3. Describe the concept of direct costing. How does direct costing differ from absorption costing?
4. Is direct costing used for financial reporting purposes? Defend your answer.
5. What is the connection between direct costing and the contribution approach to reporting?
6. What are the purposes or uses of incremental analysis?
7. Discuss and illustrate some of the qualitative inputs into decision analysis.
8. What is a capital expenditure? Define capital budgeting. Give illustrations of various types of capital expenditure decisions.
9. What is a crude but easy method for evaluating capital expenditures? List the advantages and disadvantages of this method.
10. What is the formula used for determining payback period? Is this decision measure accurate? Defend your answer.
11. "To treat all future income flows alike ignores the time value of money." Discuss this statement.
12. What is the objective of utilizing the concept of discounted cash flows?
13. How does one determine the data relevant to make or buy decision analysis?
14. Identify and discuss information relevant to special product orders.
15. What question must be answered in an attempt to maximize product line profitability? Give some examples of approaches to the solution of this question.

Classroom Exercises

Exercise 28-1 Relevant Data and Incremental Analysis

Mr. Roush, business manager for Marine Industries must select a new typewriter for his secretary. Rental of Model H, which is similar to the type currently being used, is $300 per year. Model G is a deluxe typewriter that rents for $400 per year, but it will require a new desk for the secretary. The annual desk rental charge is $150. The secretary's salary of $400 per month will not change. If Model G is purchased, $130 in training costs will be incurred. Model G has greater capacity and is expected to save $410 per year in part-time secretarial wages. Upkeep and operating costs will not differ between the two models.

1. Identify the relevant data in this problem.
2. Prepare an incremental analysis for the business manager to aid him in his decision.

Exercise 28-2 Direct Costing: Unit Cost Computation

Magnetrac Enterprises produces a full line of energy-tracking devices. These devices are capable of detecting and tracking all forms of thermochemical energy-emitting space vehicles. The following cost data are provided: Raw materials cost $485,000 for four units. Direct labor for assembly is 640 hours per unit at $11.50 per hour. Variable factory overhead is $15.00 per direct labor hour, and fixed factory overhead is $792,000 per month (based on an average production of 128 units per month). Packaging materials come to $7,200 for four units, and packaging labor is 11.5 hours per unit at $8.20 per hour. Advertising and marketing cost $89,600 per month, and other fixed selling and administrative costs are $87,680 per month.

1. From the cost data above, determine the unit cost using both the direct costing and the absorption costing methods.

2. Assuming that the current month's ending inventory is twelve units, determine the inventory valuation under both direct and absorption costing methods.

Exercise 28-3 Income Statement—Contribution Reporting Format

The income statement in the conventional reporting format for Smith Products, Inc., for the year ended December 31, 19xx, appeared as follows:

Sales		$296,400
Cost of Goods Sold		
Cost of Goods Available for Sale	$125,290	
Less Ending Inventory	12,540	112,750
Gross Profit on Sales		$183,650
Less Operating Expenses		
Selling Expenses		
Variable	$ 49,820	
Fixed	26,980	
Administrative Expenses	37,410	114,210
Net Income Before Taxes		$ 69,440

Fixed manufacturing costs of $18,600 and $1,850 are included in Cost of Goods Available for Sale and Ending Inventory, respectively. Total fixed manufacturing costs for 19xx were $18,540. There were no beginning or ending Work in Process inventories.

From the above information, prepare an income statement for Smith Products, Inc., for the year ended December 31, 19xx, using the contribution reporting format.

Exercise 28-4 Capital Expenditure Decision—Accounting Rate of Return Method

Protectra Limited manufactures metal hard hats for on-site construction workers. Recently management has sought to increase productivity to meet the growing demand from the real estate industry. The company is currently considering a new stamping machine. Management has decided that only projects that will yield a 20 percent return will be accepted. The following projections for the proposal are given: The new machine will cost $95,000; revenue will increase $45,600 per year; the salvage value of the new machine will be $5,000; and operating cost increases (including depreciation) will be $34,600.

Using the accounting rate of return method, decide whether the company should invest in the machine. (Show all computations to support your decision.)

Exercise 28-5 Capital Expenditure Decision—Payback Method

Vibramedia, Inc., manufacturers of stereo speakers, is considering the addition of a new injection molding machine. This machine can produce component parts that the company currently purchases from outsiders. The machine has an estimated life of fourteen years and will cost $82,000. Gross cash revenue from the machine will be approximately $165,000 per year, and related cash expenses should total $126,750. Taxes on income are estimated at $16,000 per year. The payback period as stipulated by management should be four years or less.

On the basis of the data provided, determine whether the company should invest in this new machine, using the payback method. Show the computations that were used to support your answer.

Exercise 28-6 Capital Expenditure Decision—Present Value Method

The Dennis Manufacturing Company is contemplating the purchase of an automatic extruding machine. This piece of equipment would have a useful life of five years, would cost $33,250, and would increase annual net cash inflows by $9,630. Assume that there is no salvage value at the end of the five years. The company's minimum desired rate of return is 14 percent.

Prepare an analysis using the present value method to determine whether or not the company should purchase the machine.

Exercise 28-7 Minimum Desired Rate of Return

The controller of Shirley Corporation is trying to establish a minimum desired rate of return and would like to use a weighted average cost of capital. Current data concerning the corporation's financing structure are as follows: debt financing, 40 percent; preferred stock, 20 percent; common stock, 30 percent; retained earnings, 10 percent. After-tax cost of debt is 4 percent. Dividend rates on the preferred and common stock issues are 6 and 10 percent, respectively. Cost of retained earnings is 12 percent.

Compute the weighted average cost of capital.

Exercise 28-8 Make or Buy Decision

One of the parts for a radio assembly being produced by Sprigg Audio Systems, Inc., is being purchased currently for $85 per 100 parts. Management is studying the possibility of manufacturing these parts. Cost and production data are as follows. Annual production (usage) is 50,000 units. Fixed costs (all of which remain unchanged whether the part is made or purchased), are $13,000. Variable costs consist of $.35 per unit for raw materials, $.20 per unit for direct labor, and $.28 per unit for manufacturing overhead.

Using an incremental decision analysis format, determine whether the company should make the part or continue to purchase it from an outside vendor.

Exercise 28-9 Special Order Decision

Shades of Old, Inc., produces antique-looking lampshades. Management has just received a request for a special design order and must decide whether or not to accept it. The special order calls for 12,000 shades to be shipped in a total of twelve bulk pack cartons. Shipping costs of $800 per carton will replace normal packing and shipping costs. The purchasing company is offering to pay $16 per shade plus shipping expenses.

The following information has been provided by the accounting department: Annual expected production is 150,000 shades, and the current year's production (before special order) is 160,000 shades. Maximum production capacity is 180,000 shades. Unit cost data include $4.20 for raw materials, $6.00 for direct labor, variable factory overhead of $3.80, and fixed factory overhead ($375,000 ÷ 150,000) of $2.50. Packaging per unit comes to $1.50, and advertising ($30,000 ÷ 150,000) is $.20 per unit. Other fixed administrative costs ($120,000 ÷ 150,000) are $.80 per unit. Total cost per unit is thus $19.00, with per unit selling price set at $26.00. Total estimated bulk packaging costs ($800 per carton × 12 cartons) are $9,600.

Determine whether this special order should be accepted. Assume that only the bulk packaging costs are incurred as additional costs to those listed above.

Exercise 28-10 Sales Mix Analysis

DBA Associates is analyzing its sales mix to determine whether it is maximizing profits. The company produces three similar items: Alpha, Tau, and Omega. All three of these products are made with the same equipment, and maximum productive capacity measured in machine hours is currently being utilized. Product line statistics are as follows:

	Alpha	Tau	Omega
Current production and sales (units)	70,000	105,000	63,000
Machine hours per unit	7	3.5	8.75
Selling price per unit	$84.00	$63.00	$112.00
Unit variable manufacturing costs	$43.75	$35.00	$ 65.62
Unit variable selling costs	$22.75	$17.50	$ 21.88

Determine whether the existing sales mix is the most profitable one possible. If your answer is no, offer your suggestion to improve the sales mix.

Problem Set A

Problem 28A-1 Direct Costing/ Contribution Approach to Income Statement

On December 31, 19xx, Harvey Industries completed its first full year of operation. A summary of cost and production data for 19xx follows: $132,990 for raw materials, $81,510 for direct labor, $60,060 for variable factory overhead, $47,190 for fixed factory overhead, 42,900 units completed, 41,600 units sold, selling price per unit of $22, variable selling expenses per unit of $7, fixed selling expenses of $62,550, and fixed administrative expenses of $98,900. There were no beginning or ending work in process inventories and no beginning finished goods inventory.

Required

1. Compute the unit cost and ending Finished Goods Inventory value using (a) direct costing procedures, and (b) absorption costing procedures.
2. Prepare the year-end income statement for Harvey Industries using the (a) contribution format based on direct costing data, and (b) conventional format based on absorption costing data.

Problem 28A-2 Capital Expenditure Decision—Present Value Method

Comfort-Stride, Inc., is considering the purchase and implementation of a new hole-punch machine to speed up the production of its only product, arch support inserts. This new machine has an estimated twenty-year life and will cost $5,000 in cash plus a five-year note of $10,000. The increased annual net cash inflows generated by the increased output should approximate $2,000 per year. The minimum desired rate of return has been determined to be 12 percent.

Required

1. Using the present value method to evaluate this capital expenditure, decide whether the company should purchase the new machine. (Ignore interest factor on $10,000 note.)
2. If the minimum desired rate of return were 10 percent, would your answer in part 1 be altered? Show all computations to support your answers.

Problem 28A-3 Minimum Desired Rate of Return

Capital investment analysis is the main function of Eugene Corman, special assistant to the controller of Shields Manufacturing Company. During the previous twelve-month period, the company's capital mix and respective cost (after tax) were as follows:

	Percentage of Total Financing	Cost of Capital (percent)
Debt financing	30	5
Preferred stock	20	8
Common stock	40	12
Retained earnings	10	12

Plans for the current year call for a shift in total financing of 20 percent from common stock financing to debt financing. In addition, after-tax cost of debt is expected to increase to 6 percent, though the cost of the other types of financing will remain the same.

Mr. Corman has already analyzed several proposed capital expenditures. He anticipates that the return on investment on each capital expenditure would be as follows: 7.5 percent on project A, 8.5 percent on equipment item B, 15.0 percent on product line C, 6.9 percent on project D, 9.0 percent on product line E, 11.9 percent on equipment item F, and 8.0 percent on project G.

Required

1. Compute the weighted average cost of capital for the previous year.
2. Using the anticipated adjustments to cost and capital mix, compute the weighted average cost of capital for the current year.
3. Identify the proposed capital expenditures that should be implemented as the basis of the minimum desired rate of return calculated in part 2.

Problem 28A-4 Make or Buy Decision

The Argosy Basketball Company is presently buying the rubber valves needed to inflate its basketballs. The valves have been purchased at a cost of $86.40 per ten cases; each case holds 144 valves. Management has just been informed that the price of these valves is to increase 50 percent, effective with the next shipment. Argosy has idle machinery that it could easily convert to produce similar rubber valves. The company's cost analyst has proposed the following estimates of the cost to produce the part using the idle machinery: raw materials would cost $2.88 per 144 valves; and direct labor required would be five minutes per 20 valves at $4.80 per hour. Variable factory overhead would be $.03 per valve, and fixed factory overhead, which would be incurred under either decision alternative, would be $1,150 per year for depreciation and $2,850 per year for other expenses. Annual production and usage will be 849,600 valves. Assume that the idle machinery cannot be used economically for any other purpose.

Required

1. Prepare an incremental decision analysis to determine whether the company should continue to purchase the valve at the increased rate, or whether it should begin production of its own valves.
2. Compute unit costs to make and to buy one valve.

Problem 28A-5 Special Order Decision

Fisher Body Builders, Ltd., has approached Miscellaneous Printers, Inc., with a special order to produce 300,000 two-page brochures. Most of the work done by Miscellaneous consists of recurring short-run orders. The order proposed by Fisher will be a one-shot deal, but Miscellaneous Printers does have the capacity to handle the order over a two-month period.

Fisher's management has stated that the company would not be willing to pay more than $36 per thousand brochures. The following cost data were assembled by Miscellaneous's controller for this decision analysis: raw materials (paper) would be $21.50 per thousand brochures, direct labor costs would be $4.90 per thousand brochures, raw materials (ink) would be $2.40 per thousand brochures, and variable production overhead would be $4.20 per thousand brochures. Machine maintenance (fixed) is $1.00 per direct labor dollar, other fixed production overhead amount to $2.40 per direct labor dollar, and packing costs would be $4.30 per thousand brochures. In addition, the allocable share of general and administrative expenses (fixed) would be $5.25 per direct labor dollar.

Required

1. Prepare an analysis to be used by Miscellaneous's management in deciding whether to accept or reject the offer by Fisher Body Builders, Ltd. What decision should be made?
2. What is the lowest possible price that Miscellaneous Printers could quote per thousand and still make a $6,000 profit on the order?

Problem 28A-6 Capital Expenditure Decision—Comprehensive

Thomas Spencer is the director of capital facilities for Pickering Enterprises, an international land development company. Recently, two equipment manufacturers have marketed a new piece of earthmoving equipment called the Payloader. Mr. Spencer is interested in purchasing one of the devices and has compiled the following data concerning the two alternatives:

		Cash Flow Estimates		
		Cash Revenues	Cash Expenses	Net Cash Inflow
Payloader 1	Year 1	$260,000	$200,000	$ 60,000
	Year 2	280,000	190,000	90,000
	Year 3	300,000	180,000	120,000
	Year 4	320,000	170,000	150,000
Payloader 2	Year 1	$280,000	$170,000	$110,000
	Year 2	280,000	170,000	110,000
	Year 3	280,000	170,000	110,000
	Year 4	280,000	170,000	110,000

Pickering Enterprises uses the straight-line method in depreciating its equipment. The anticipated useful life of either piece of equipment is four years. Payloader 1 has a purchase price of $310,000 and a salvage value of $60,000. Payloader 2 costs $300,000 and has a salvage value of $40,000. Mr. Spencer uses a 16 percent minimum desired rate of return and a three-year or less payback period for capital expenditure evaluation purposes.

Required

1. Analyze the two alternatives, and determine which piece of equipment Pickering Enterprises should purchase. Include the following evaluation approaches in

your analysis: (a) accounting rate of return method, (b) payback period method, and (c) present value method.
2. Prepare an incremental analysis of the two alternatives using the present value evaluation approach.

Problem Set B

Problem 28B-3 Sales Mix Analysis

The vice president of finance for Mueller Machine Products, Inc., is evaluating the profitability of the company's four product lines. During the current year, the company will operate at full machine hour capacity. The following production data have been compiled:

Product	Current Year's Production (units)	Total Machine Hours Used
14E	60,000	150,000
27M	100,000	200,000
19S	40,000	40,000
30T	180,000	90,000

Sales and operating cost data are as follows:

	Product 14E	Product 27M	Product 19S	Product 30T
Selling price per unit	$30.00	$40.00	$50.00	$60.00
Unit variable manufacturing cost	$12.00	$30.00	$35.00	$50.00
Unit fixed manufacturing cost	$ 6.00	$ 4.00	$ 3.00	$ 2.00
Unit variable selling costs	$ 3.00	$ 2.00	$ 8.00	$ 5.50
Unit fixed administrative costs	$ 4.00	$ 2.00	$ 4.00	$ 1.50

Required

1. Compute the machine hours needed to produce one unit of each product type.
2. Determine the profitability of each product type.
3. Which product line(s) should be pushed by the company's sales force? Why?

Problem 28B-4 Make or Buy Decision

The Bremen Refrigerator Company is purchasing and installing defrost clocks in its products. The clocks cost $345.60 per case; each case contains thirty-six clocks. The supplier recently gave advance notice that, effective in thirty days, the price will increase by 55 percent. Bremen Refrigerator Company has dormant equipment that could be used to produce similar defrost clocks with only a few alterations to the equipment.

The following cost estimates have been prepared under the assumption that the company could make the product itself. Raw materials would cost $216 per 36 clocks, and direct labor required would be 10 minutes per clock at a labor rate of $9.00 per hour. Variable factory overhead would be $3.50 per clock, and fixed factory overhead (which would be incurred under either decision alternative) would be $86,400 per year for depreciation and $129,600 per year for other expenses. Production and usage are estimated to be 72,000 clocks per year. (Assume that the dormant equipment is not economically suitable for any other purpose.)

Required

1. Prepare an incremental decision analysis to determine whether the defrost clocks should be made within the company or purchased from the existing supplier at the increased rate.
2. Compute the unit cost to make and to buy one clock.

Problem 28B-5 Special Order Decision

On November 15, 19xx, Spoto Sporting Equipment, Inc., received a special order for 6,000 three-wood golf sets. These golf clubs will be marketed in Europe. Swedish Imports, Ltd., the purchasing company, wants the clubs bulk packaged and is willing to pay $68 per set for the clubs.

Mr. Angelo, president of Spoto Sporting Equipment, Inc., has accumulated the following product costing information concerning the set of woods being discussed: raw materials (wood) cost $800 per 100 sets, raw materials (metal) are $1,100 per 100 sets, and raw materials (grips) are $200 per 100 sets. Direct labor is $27 per set. Variable manufacturing costs are $16 per set, and fixed manufacturing costs are 20 percent of direct labor dollars. Variable selling expenses are $14 per set, and variable shipping costs are $9 per set. Fixed general and administrative costs are figured as 30 percent of direct labor dollars. Bulk shipping costs will total $12,000, thereby eliminating both variable selling and variable shipping costs from consideration. The company did not anticipate this order and will attain planned production capacity for the year, leaving sufficient plant capacity for the special order.

Required

1. Prepare an analysis for Mr. Angelo to use in deciding whether to accept or reject the offer by Swedish Imports, Ltd. What decision should be made?
2. What is the lowest possible price that Spoto Sporting Equipment, Inc., could quote per set of woods and still make a $10,000 profit on this order?

Problem 28B-6 Capital Expenditure Decision—Comprehensive

The Danelid Machine Tool Company, based in Rockford, Illinois, is one of the fastest-growing machine tool companies in the industry. According to Mr. Gunnar, the company's production vice president, keeping up with technological changes is what makes the company a leader in the industry.

Mr. Gunnar feels that either one of two new machines introduced recently would fulfill an important need of the company. Either machine has an anticipated useful life of four years. Machine 1 has a purchase price of $140,000 and a salvage value of $20,000. Machine 2 costs $118,000 and has a salvage value of $18,000. The company's controller has developed estimated operating results using each of the machine alternatives, summarized on the next page. The company uses straight-line depreciation for all its machinery. Mr. Gunnar employs a 10 percent minimum desired rate of return and a 3.2-year payback period for capital expenditure evaluation purposes.

Required

1. Analyze the two alternatives, and determine which machine the company should purchase. Include the following evaluation approaches in your analysis: (a) the accounting rate of return method, (b) the payback period method, and (c) the present value method.
2. Prepare an incremental analysis of the two alternatives using the present value evaluation approach.

		Cash Flow Estimates		
		Cash Revenues	Cash Expenses	Net Cash Inflow
Machine 1	Year 1	$100,000	$ 60,000	$40,000
	Year 2	100,000	60,000	40,000
	Year 3	100,000	60,000	40,000
	Year 4	100,000	60,000	40,000
Machine 2	Year 1	$150,000	$100,000	$50,000
	Year 2	150,000	110,000	40,000
	Year 3	150,000	120,000	30,000
	Year 4	150,000	130,000	20,000

Learning Objectives

Chapter Twenty-Nine

Tax Considerations in Business Decisions

1. *Explain and differentiate some basic concepts related to income taxes and accounting.*
2. *Identify the major components used for determining the income tax liability of individuals.*
3. *Identify the major differences between the income tax provisions for corporations and for individuals.*
4. *Identify several ways in which income taxes affect business decisions.*
5. *Prepare journal entries to account for differences between accounting and taxable income.*

The preceding chapters have emphasized the role of accounting information in business decisions. The purpose of this chapter is to demonstrate the importance of tax considerations in those decisions. As a result of studying this chapter, you should be able to meet the learning objectives listed on the left.

The United States Congress first passed a permanent income tax law in 1913, after the sixteenth amendment to the Constitution established the legality of such a tax. Its original purpose was to provide revenue for the U.S. government, and today the income tax is still a major source of revenue. In addition, most states and many cities have an income tax. Because these tax laws are in many cases similar to those in the federal tax system, the discussion in this chapter is limited to the federal income tax.

Although it is still an important purpose of the federal income tax laws to produce revenue, Congress has also used its taxing power as a source of economic policy. Among the economic goals proposed by Congress are the more equitable distribution of income, the stimulation of economic growth, the attainment of full employment, the encouragement of exploration for oil and minerals, the control of inflation, and the attainment of a variety of social changes.

All three branches of the federal government have a part in the federal income tax system. The Internal Revenue Service (IRS), which is an agency of the Treasury Department, administers the system. The basis of the income tax law is the over fifty revenue acts and other laws implementing the tax that have been passed by Congress since 1913. In addition, the IRS issues regulations that interpret the law. It is the federal court system, however, that must uphold these important regulations and that has ultimate authority for interpreting the law.

The income tax has had significant effects on both individuals and businesses. In 1913, an individual who earned $30,000 paid only $300 or $400 in income taxes. Today, an individual who earns the same amount may pay as much as $5,000 or more, and corporations may pay almost half of their income in taxes. Clearly, the income tax is an important cost of doing business today.

Some Basic Concepts Related to Federal Income Taxes

Objective 1
Explain and differentiate some basic concepts related to income taxes and accounting

To understand the nature of federal income taxes, it is important to distinguish between taxable income and accounting income, between tax planning and tax evasion, between cash basis and accrual basis, and among classifications of taxpayers.

Taxable Income and Accounting Income

The government assesses income taxes on **taxable income,** which usually is gross income less various exclusions and deductions specified by the law and the IRS regulations. Taxable income is generally determined by referring to information in the accounting records. However, it is very unlikely that taxable income and accounting income for an entity will be the same, because they have different purposes. The government levies income taxes in order to obtain revenue from taxpayers and to implement economic policies totally unrelated to the measurement of economic income, which is the purpose of accounting. The nature of some of these differences and their accounting treatment in the records and financial statements are the concern of this chapter's final section.

Tax Planning and Tax Evasion

The arrangement of a taxpayer's affairs in such a way as to incur the smallest legal tax is called **tax planning.** For almost every business decision, alternative courses of action are available that will affect taxable income in different ways. For example, the taxpayer may lease or buy a truck, may use straight-line methods or accelerated methods to measure depreciation, or may time an expenditure to be accounted for in one accounting period or another. Once the taxpayer chooses and acts upon an alternative, however, the IRS will usually consider this alternative to be the final one for income tax determination. Therefore, in tax planning it is important to consider tax-saving alternatives before implementing decisions.

It is the natural goal of any taxable entity to pay as small a tax as possible; both the tax law and the IRS hold that no entity should pay more than is legally required. The best way to accomplish this goal is by careful tax planning. It is, however, illegal to evade paying taxes by concealment of actual tax liabilities. This is called **tax evasion.**

Cash Basis and Accrual Basis

In general, taxpayers may use either the cash basis or the accrual basis to determine taxable income. Most individuals use the **cash basis**—the reporting of items of revenue and expense when they are received or paid—because it is the simplest method. Employers usually report their employees' income on a cash basis, and companies that pay dividends and interest on a cash basis must also report them in this way.

Professional and other service enterprises such as those of accountants, attorneys, physicians, travel agents, and insurance agents also typically use the cash basis in determining taxable income. One advantage of this method is that fees charged to clients or customers are not considered to be earned until payment is received. Thus it is possible to defer the taxes on these revenues until the tax year in which they are received. However, the government does not allow a deduction for estimated uncollectible accounts in this case because these losses will simply show up as reduced revenues (cash receipts). Similarly, expenses such as rent, utilities, and salaries are recorded when they are paid. Thus a business can engage in tax planning by carefully timing its expenditures. Nevertheless, this method does not apply to expenditures for buildings and equipment used for business purposes; such items must be depreciated in a manner identical to the accrual basis.

Businesses that engage in production or trading of inventories must not use the cash basis and may use the **accrual basis** of accounting. In other words, they must report revenues from sales in the period in which they sold the goods, regardless of when they received the cash, and they must record purchases in the year of purchase rather than in the year of payment. They must follow the usual accounting for beginning and ending inventories in determining cost of goods sold. However, the tax laws do not require a strict accrual method in the accounting sense for manufacturing and merchandising concerns. Various modified cash and accrual bases are possible as long as they yield reasonable and consistent results from year to year.

Classifications of Taxpayers

The federal tax law recognizes four classes of taxpayers: individuals, corporations, estates, and trusts. Members of each class must file tax returns and pay taxes on taxable income. This chapter discusses only individuals and corporations, leaving estates and trusts to a more advanced course.

Although they are business entities for accounting purposes, sole proprietorships and partnerships are not taxable entities. Instead, a proprietor must include the business income on an individual income tax return; and each partner in a business must include his or her share of the partnership income on an individual return. Each partnership, however, must file an information return showing the results of the partnership's operations and how each partner's share of the income was determined.

In contrast, corporations are taxable entities that must file tax returns and are taxed directly on their earnings. If, after paying its income tax, the corporation distributes some of its earnings to its stockholders, the stockholders must include the dividend income in their gross income. This requirement has led to the assertion that corporate income is subject to double taxation—once when it is earned by the corporation and once when it is paid to the stockholders.

Income Tax for Individuals

Objective 2 Identify the major components used for determining the income tax liability of individuals

It is important to study income tax for individuals for several reasons. First, all individuals who earn taxable income must file a tax return. Second, all individuals who operate sole proprietorships or partnerships must report the income from their businesses on their individual tax returns. Third, much of the basic tax terminology applies to both individuals and corporations.

The Internal Revenue Code establishes the method of calculating taxable income for individuals. The starting place for computing taxable income is the determination of gross income. The next step is to calculate adjusted gross income by subtracting deductions from gross income, a category that includes the expenses of operating a business or profession and certain other expenses related to earning revenues. Then from adjusted gross income one subtracts a second category of deductions, called deductions from adjusted gross income, to arrive at taxable income. This second category consists of (1) nonbusiness expenses and specified personal expenses, and (2) arbitrary allowances known as exemptions. These procedures can be summarized as follows:

Gross income		$xxx
Less deductions from gross income		xxx
Adjusted gross income		$xxx
Less deductions from adjusted gross income		
a. Excess of itemized nonbusiness and specified personal expenses over zero bracket amount	$xxx	
b. Exemptions	xxx	xxx
Taxable income		$xxx

Gross Income

The Internal Revenue Code defines **gross income** as income from all sources, less allowable exclusions. Examples of types of gross income are wages, salaries, bonuses, fees, tips, interest, dividends, pensions, annuities, rents, royalties, alimony, prizes, profits or shares of profits from business, and gains on sale of property or securities. Income from illegal sources also must be included in gross income.

Deductions from Gross Income

The calculation of adjusted gross income is important to the individual because it serves as the basis for certain personal deductions in computing taxable income. The purpose of these **deductions from gross income** is to provide a more equitable base than gross income. For example, some individuals may have a high gross income but may have incurred many business expenditures to achieve that gross income. Thus it is fair to let them deduct the expenditures required in achieving the gross income. Similarly, employees who incur expenses in connection with their jobs should be allowed to deduct these expenditures from gross income. An example is the automobile expenses of salespeople who must furnish their own automobiles. Each of the allowable deductions is subtracted from its related revenues in determining **adjusted gross income.**

Deductions from Adjusted Gross Income

Deductions from adjusted gross income fall into two categories: (1) excess itemized deductions, if any, and (2) exemptions. In the first category, every taxpayer is entitled to deduct the excess of itemized deductions over the zero bracket amount. The **zero bracket amount** is the amount of taxable income on which there is no tax. It is called by this name because taxpayers who earn less than the zero bracket amount pay no taxes. For a single person or unmarried head of household, the zero bracket amount in a recent year was $2,300. For married couples filing jointly, the amount was $3,400. If a taxpayer can prove that he or she spent more than the zero bracket amount on certain specified items, the taxpayer may deduct the total of these items instead of the zero bracket amount. Obviously, it is advantageous to the taxpayer to itemize deductions if possible. The allowable itemized deductions are medical and dental expenses, interest expense, taxes, charitable contributions, casualty losses, and miscellaneous deductions such as professional or union dues.

In addition to itemized deductions or the zero bracket amount, a taxpayer is allowed a second kind of deduction called an **exemption.** For each exemption, the taxpayer may deduct $1,000 from adjusted gross income. A taxpayer is allowed a personal exemption for himself or herself plus one for each dependent. To qualify as a dependent, a person must (1) be closely related to the taxpayer or have lived in the taxpayer's house for the entire year, (2) have received over half of his or her support from the taxpayer during the year; (3) file a joint return with his or her spouse (if married), (4) have had less than $1,000 of gross income during the year, and (5) must be a U.S. citizen or resident or a resident of Canada or Mexico. Additional exemptions are allowed if the taxpayer is over sixty-five years of age or blind. If husband and wife file a joint return, they may combine their exemptions.

Computing Tax Liability

In general, the income tax is a **progressive tax,** which means that the rate becomes larger as the amount of taxable income becomes larger. In other words, the higher a person's taxable income, the larger the proportion of it that goes to pay taxes.[1] Different rate schedules apply to single taxpayers, married taxpayers who file joint returns, married taxpayers who file separate returns, and single taxpayers who qualify as heads of households. Any of these taxpayers can find their **tax liability** by referring to a tax table for their category. Parts of two of these tables are reproduced in Figure 29-1. These tables take into account the zero bracket amount and the deductions for exemptions, and apply to taxpayers whose taxable income is less than $20,000 (except married taxpayers who file joint returns, in which case the limit is $40,000). For example, a single taxpayer with two exemptions earning $7,275 would have a tax liability of $472, as shown in Tax Table A in Figure 29-1a.

Taxpayers whose taxable income exceeds these limits must use the tax rate schedules, two of which are reproduced in Figure 29-2. These schedules take into account the zero bracket amount but not the exemptions. By examining this schedule, one can easily see the progressive nature of the income tax. For example, a single taxpayer with taxable income between $23,500 and $28,800 pays $5,367 plus 39 percent of the amount over $23,500. A single taxpayer with taxable income between $28,800 and $34,100 pays $7,434 plus 44 percent of the amount over $28,800. The 39 percent and the 44 percent in this example are known as the **marginal tax rates** because they apply to the last increment of taxable income. The average tax rate is much lower because the lower levels of income were taxed at lower rates.

Although from Figure 29-2 it is clear that the marginal tax rate can go as high as 70 percent, the law sets the maximum tax on personal service income at 50 percent. A single taxpayer who earns in excess of $41,500 and married taxpayers, filing jointly, who earn in excess of $60,000 can take advantage of this provision. The law also provides a tax break for taxpayers whose income fluctuates widely from year to year. They are allowed to use a formula called **income averaging,** which averages their taxable income over five years.

Capital Gains and Losses

One effective means of tax planning is to arrange transactions involving certain types of assets in such a way that they qualify for special treatment as capital gains and losses. These assets, called **capital assets,** usually include stocks and bonds owned by individuals and, under certain circumstances, buildings, equipment, and land used in businesses. Capital

1. In contrast to a progressive tax rate, a **regressive tax** rate becomes less as one's income rises. An example of a regressive tax is the social security (FICA) tax, which is levied on incomes only up to a certain amount. A **proportional tax** is one in which the rate is the same percentage regardless of income. Examples are most sales taxes and the income taxes of some states, such as Illinois.

Figure 29-1a
Excerpt from
Tax Table A

1979 Tax Table A—SINGLE (Box 1)

(For single persons with tax table income of $20,000 or less who claim 3 or fewer exemptions)

If Form 1040, line 34 is—		And the total number of exemptions claimed on line 7 is—		
Over	But not over	1	2	3
		Your tax is—		
11,100	11,150	1,413	1,203	1,001
11,150	11,200	1,424	1,214	1,010
11,200	11,250	1,434	1,224	1,020
11,250	11,300	1,445	1,235	1,029
11,300	11,350	1,455	1,245	1,039
11,350	11,400	1,466	1,256	1,048
11,400	11,450	1,476	1,266	1,058
11,450	11,500	1,487	1,277	1,067
11,500	11,550	1,497	1,287	1,077
11,550	11,600	1,508	1,298	1,088
11,600	11,650	1,518	1,308	1,098
11,650	11,700	1,529	1,319	1,109
11,700	11,750	1,539	1,329	1,119
11,750	11,800	1,550	1,340	1,130
11,800	11,850	1,561	1,350	1,140
11,850	11,900	1,573	1,361	1,151
11,900	11,950	1,585	1,371	1,161
11,950	12,000	1,597	1,382	1,172
12,000	12,050	1,609	1,392	1,182
12,050	12,100	1,621	1,403	1,193
12,100	12,150	1,633	1,413	1,203
12,150	12,200	1,645	1,424	1,214
12,200	12,250	1,657	1,434	1,224
12,250	12,300	1,669	1,445	1,235
12,300	12,350	1,681	1,455	1,245
12,350	12,400	1,693	1,466	1,256
12,400	12,450	1,705	1,476	1,266
12,450	12,500	1,717	1,487	1,277
12,500	12,550	1,729	1,497	1,287
12,550	12,600	1,741	1,508	1,298
12,600	12,650	1,753	1,518	1,308
12,650	12,700	1,765	1,529	1,319

To find your tax: Read down the left income column until you find your income. Read across to the column headed by the total number of exemptions claimed. The amount shown at the point where the two lines meet is your tax.

Figure 29-1b
Excerpt from
Tax Table B

1979 Tax Table B—MARRIED FILING JOINTLY (Box 2) and QUALIFYING WIDOW(ER)S (Box 5)

(For married persons filing joint returns or qualifying widow(er)s with tax table income of $40,000 or less who claim 9 or fewer exemptions)

If Form 1040, line 34 is—		And the total number of exemptions claimed on line 7 is—							
Over	But not over	2	3	4	5	6	7	8	9
		Your tax is—							
11,200	11,250	923	743	570	410	256	116	0	0
11,250	11,300	932	752	578	418	263	123	0	0
11,300	11,350	941	761	586	426	270	130	0	0
11,350	11,400	950	770	594	434	277	137	0	0
11,400	11,450	959	779	602	442	284	144	4	0
11,450	11,500	968	788	610	450	291	151	11	0
11,500	11,550	977	797	618	458	298	158	18	0
11,550	11,600	986	806	626	466	306	165	25	0
11,600	11,650	995	815	635	474	314	172	32	0
11,650	11,700	1,004	824	644	482	322	179	39	0
11,700	11,750	1,013	833	653	490	330	186	46	0
11,750	11,800	1,022	842	662	498	338	193	53	0
11,800	11,850	1,031	851	671	506	346	200	60	0
11,850	11,900	1,040	860	680	514	354	207	67	0
11,900	11,950	1,049	869	689	522	362	214	74	0
11,950	12,000	1,058	878	698	530	370	221	81	0
12,000	12,050	1,067	887	707	538	378	228	88	0
12,050	12,100	1,076	896	716	546	386	235	95	0
12,100	12,150	1,085	905	725	554	394	242	102	0
12,150	12,200	1,094	914	734	562	402	249	109	0
12,200	12,250	1,103	923	743	570	410	256	116	0
12,250	12,300	1,112	932	752	578	418	263	123	0
12,300	12,350	1,121	941	761	586	426	270	130	0
12,350	12,400	1,130	950	770	594	434	277	137	0
12,400	12,450	1,139	959	779	602	442	284	144	4
12,450	12,500	1,148	968	788	610	450	291	151	11
12,500	12,550	1,157	977	797	618	458	298	158	18
12,550	12,600	1,166	986	806	626	466	306	165	25
12,600	12,650	1,175	995	815	635	474	314	172	32
12,650	12,700	1,184	1,004	824	644	482	322	179	39
12,700	12,750	1,193	1,013	833	653	490	330	186	46
12,750	12,800	1,202	1,022	842	662	498	338	193	53

To find your tax: Read down the left income column until you find your income. Read across to the column headed by the total number of exemptions claimed. The amount shown at the point where the two lines meet is your tax.

assets usually do not include receivables, inventories, certain government obligations, and rights to literary and other artistic works. If the capital assets being sold or exchanged have been held for less than one year, they are classified as short-term; if they have been held for one year or more they are classified as long-term. The combined total of all gains and losses on short-term assets during a tax year is called **net short-term capital gain (or loss)**. The combined total of all gains and losses on long-term capital

Figure 29-2
Excerpt from the
Tax Rate Schedules

1979 Tax Rate Schedules

Note: *Your new zero bracket amount has been built into these Tax Rate Schedules.*

SCHEDULE X—Single Taxpayers

Use this schedule if you checked **Filing Status Box 1** on Form 1040—

If the amount on Schedule TC, Part I, line 3, is:		Enter on Schedule TC, Part I, line 4:	
Not over $2,300........		—0—	
Over—	*But not over—*		*of the amount over—*
$2,300	$3,400	14%	$2,300
$3,400	$4,400	$154+16%	$3,400
$4,400	$6,500	$314+18%	$4,400
$6,500	$8,500	$692+19%	$6,500
$8,500	$10,800	$1,072+21%	$8,500
$10,800	$12,900	$1,555+24%	$10,800
$12,900	$15,000	$2,059+26%	$12,900
$15,000	$18,200	$2,605+30%	$15,000
$18,200	$23,500	$3,565+34%	$18,200
$23,500	$28,80C	$5,367+39%	$23,500
$28,800	$34,100	$7,434+44%	$28,800
$34,100	$41,500	$9,766+49%	$34,100
$41,500	$55,300	$13,392+55%	$41,500
$55,300	$81,800	$20,982+63%	$55,300
$81,800	$108,300	$37,677+68%	$81,800
$108,300	....	$55,697+70%	$108,300

SCHEDULE Y—Married Taxpayers and Qualifying Widows and Widowers

Married Filing Joint Returns and Qualifying Widows and Widowers

Use this schedule if you checked **Filing Status Box 2 or 5** on Form 1040—

If the amount on Schedule TC, Part I, line 3, is:		Enter on Schedule TC, Part I, line 4:	
Not over $3,400........		—0—	
Over—	*But not over—*		*of the amount over—*
$3,400	$5,500	14%	$3,400
$5,500	$7,600	$294+16%	$5,500
$7,600	$11,900	$630+18%	$7,600
$11,900	$16,000	$1,404+21%	$11,900
$16,000	$20,200	$2,265+24%	$16,000
$20,200	$24,600	$3,273+28%	$20,200
$24,600	$29,900	$4,505+32%	$24,600
$29,900	$35,200	$6,201+37%	$29,900
$35,200	$45,800	$8,162+43%	$35,200
$45,800	$60,000	$12,720+49%	$45,800
$60,000	$85,600	$19,678+54%	$60,000
$85,600	$109,400	$33,502+59%	$85,600
$109,400	$162,400	$47,544+64%	$109,400
$162,400	$215,400	$81,464+68%	$162,400
$215,400	....	$117,504+70%	$215,400

assets during a tax year is called net long-term capital gain (or loss). The combined amount of these two figures is called the net capital gain (or loss).

Net Capital Gain The effect of the above classification of assets on the resulting net capital gain is to limit the tax. If a net capital gain is composed of an excess of net long-term gain over short-term loss (if any) of not more than $50,000, 60 percent of this excess is deducted from gross income in arriving at adjusted gross income. Thus the effect is to cut the tax rate by 60 percent on the long-term portion of the net capital gain.

Net Capital Loss When a taxpayer's transactions involving capital assets for a year result in a net capital loss, the deductibility of the loss in any one year is limited. The taxpayer can use the loss to reduce gross income only to the extent of $3,000. Any excess of net capital loss over $3,000 must be carried over to be deducted in future years.

By timing the holding period for capital gains and losses during the year in which the capital transactions take place, an individual can significantly alter the amount of tax he or she pays. For example, if the taxpayer must take a loss in a stock investment, it may be wise to sell the stock just before the end of the twelve-month holding period in order to incur a short-term loss, which is fully deductible. If the taxpayer has a gain, on the other hand, it may be best to wait until just beyond the twelve-month period to sell the stock and recognize the gain because it will receive preferential treatment. Near the end of the tax year, it is sometimes a good idea to sell securities in order to recognize gains and offset losses incurred earlier in the year, or vice versa.

Credits Against the Tax Liability

Tax credits are subtractions from the computed tax liability and should not be confused with deductions that are subtracted from income to determine taxable income. Since tax credits reduce tax liability dollar for dollar, they are more beneficial to the taxpayer than an equal dollar amount of deductions from taxable income. A tax credit is allowed for one-half the contributions made to candidates for public office, subject to a $50 maximum (or $100 if filing jointly). There are also tax credits for the elderly, for dependent care expenses, for a percentage of certain investments, for income taxes paid in foreign countries, for wages paid in work incentive programs, and for jobs given to members of certain groups. Homeowners and renters are entitled to a tax credit for a percentage of their energy-saving expenditures as well.

Withholding and Estimated Tax

For most individuals the tax year ends on December 31, and their return is due three and one-half months later, on April 15. If they are wage earners or salaried employees, their employer is required to withhold an estimated income tax from their pay during the year and remit it to the Internal Revenue Service. The employer reports this withholding to the employee on a form W-2 within thirty days after the end of the year (see Chapter 12 for a discussion of payroll procedures). Taxpayers who have income beyond a certain amount that is not subject to withholding must report a Declaration of Estimated Tax and pay an estimated tax, less any amount expected to be withheld, in four installments during the year. When taxpayers prepare their tax returns, they deduct the amount of estimated tax withheld and the amount paid in installments from the total tax liability to determine the amount they must pay when they file the tax return.

Income Tax for Corporations

Objective 3 Identify the major differences between the income tax provisions for corporations and for individuals

Corporations are separate taxable entities under federal tax laws and therefore must file tax returns and pay taxes. Because taxation of corporations is an extremely complex matter, many accountants and lawyers devote their entire careers to tax practice. In this chapter, we discuss only the major features of corporate tax laws. First we point out some differences between the taxation of individuals and the taxation of corporations. Then we illustrate the format for calculating the corporate tax.

Features of Taxable Income of Corporations

Except for certain classes of corporations such as banks, insurance companies, regulated investment companies, and cooperatives, most corporations determine their taxable income by subtracting allowable business deductions from includable gross income. Corporations are not allowed to use the zero bracket amount, and there is no adjusted gross income step in the calculation of taxable income. Among the many other differences between computing taxable income for corporations and computing that for individuals are the following broadly applicable areas:

1. **Dividends received deduction** Although corporations must include all dividends received on shares of stock in other corporations in gross income, they may subtract 85 percent of such dividends as a special deduction from gross income. This means that the receiving corporation pays taxes on only 15 percent of the dividends.

2. **Net operating loss deduction** This deduction allows corporations to offset losses of one year against the income of other years. In general, they may offset an operating loss of one year against the income of the three preceding years and, if unused losses still remain, against the income of five successive years.

3. **Capital gains and losses** Net capital losses of corporations are not deductible from ordinary income, but are treated in a manner similar to net operating losses described above. That is, corporations may offset such losses against net capital gains in the three preceding years and five successive years. Unlike the treatment of the excess of net long-term capital gains over net short-term capital losses for individuals, corporations may not take a 60 percent deduction from gross income. For corporations, this amount is taxed at a maximum rate of 28 percent.

4. **Charitable contributions** Corporations may deduct charitable contributions from taxable income, but this deduction is limited to 5 percent of an amount equal to taxable income plus the contributions and the special deduction for dividends received (1, above). Contributions in excess of 5 percent in any given year may be carried forward to five subsequent years, subject to the 5 percent limitation in each of those years.

5. **Special credits** In order to encourage expenditures related to the objectives of national policies, Congress allows special tax credits to businesses for certain types of expenditures that are deemed to be in the

Figure 29-3
Tax Rate Schedule for Corporations

Taxable Income		Tax Liability	
Over	But Not Over		Of the Amount Over
—	$25,000	0 + 17%	—
25,000	50,000	$4,250 + 20%	$25,000
50,000	75,000	9,250 + 30%	50,000
75,000	100,000	16,750 + 40%	75,000
100,000	—	26,750 + 46%	100,000

national interest. For example, to encourage new investment, an investment credit equal to 10 percent (in most cases) for property acquired and placed in service during the year is allowed. To reduce unemployment, a credit of 20 percent of the salaries and wages paid to employees in their first twelve months of employment in a work incentive program may be claimed. Additional credits apply to new jobs formed and to expenditures for certain building rehabilitations, pollution control facilities, and vocational rehabilitation programs. Also, certain deductions are allowed for expenditures to remove barriers to the handicapped and elderly.

Corporate Income Tax Basis

Corporations pay income taxes on their taxable income. The current corporate income tax rates are summarized in Figure 29-3. For example, a corporation with a taxable income of $70,000 would have a federal income tax liability of $15,250. The amount is computed by adding $9,250 (the income tax on the first $50,000 of taxable income) to $6,000 (30 percent times the $20,000 earned in excess of $50,000).

Corporate Tax Illustration

Figure 29-4 illustrates the points described in the two preceding sections by showing the computation of tax liability for the Huron Corporation. For this example, assume that the Huron Corporation has a gross profit of $600,000, business expenses of $500,000 including charitable contributions of $30,000, dividends from domestic corporations of $40,000, net long-term capital gains of $65,000, and a net capital loss carry-forward of $15,000 from the previous year.

Income Tax and Business Decisions

Income taxes constitute an important cost of doing business and often have a significant impact on business decisions. Some of the ways of assessing this impact relate to using the marginal tax rate, establishing the business, financing the business, and operating the business.

Figure 29-4
The Computation of Corporate Tax Liability

Huron Corporation
Summary of Federal Income Tax Data
For the Year Ended December 31, 19xx

Gross profit			$600,000
Dividends from domestic corporations			40,000
Net long-term capital gain	$65,000		
Less net capital loss carry-forward	15,000		50,000
			$690,000
Less business expenses	$500,000		
Less charitable contributions	30,000		470,000
Taxable income before deductions			$220,000
Deductions			
Charitable contributions, limited to 5% of $220,000		$11,000	
Dividends received deduction, 85% of $40,000		34,000	45,000
Taxable income			$175,000
Less excess of long-term gain over short-term loss, to be taxed at 28% ($65,000 – $15,000)			50,000
Taxable at regular rates			$125,000
Regular tax			
On first $100,000		$26,750	
On next $25,000 at 46%		11,500	$ 38,250
Tax on excess of long-term gain over short-term loss, $50,000 at 28%			14,000
Total tax liability			$ 52,250

Using the Marginal Tax Rate

Objective 4 Identify several ways in which income taxes affect business decisions

When assessing the impact of income taxes on business deductions, it is important to use the marginal tax rate for the entity rather than the average tax rate. Because contributions are tax deductible for both individuals and corporations, subject to certain limitations, they provide a good illustration. Assume that four taxpayers, two individuals and two corporations, are considering making a $1,000 contribution. Individual A has taxable income of $30,000, Individual B has taxable income of $50,000, Corporation C has taxable income of $30,000, and Corporation D has taxable income of $55,000. If A and B are single taxpayers, their marginal tax rates from Figure 29-2 are 44 percent and 55 percent, respectively. Because the taxable income for Corporation C is between $25,000 and $50,000, its marginal tax rate is 20 percent, and because the taxable income of Corporation D is over $50,000, its marginal tax rate is 30 percent. The contribution, if made, will reduce the tax liabilities of the taxpayers because it reduces taxable income. Thus the after-tax effect of the decision to make the contribution can be determined by multiplying the marginal tax rate by the proposed contribution, as follows:

		A	B	C	D
1.	Proposed contribution	$1,000	$1,000	$1,000	$1,000
2.	Marginal tax rate	44%	55%	20%	30%
3.	Tax saving	$ 440	$ 550	$ 200	$ 300
4.	Net after-tax cost (1 − 3)	$ 560	$ 450	$ 800	$ 700

We can prove this computation by calculating the total tax liability before and after the proposed contribution:

		A	B	C	D
1.	Taxable income before contribution	$30,000	$50,000	$30,000	$55,000
2.	Tax liability assuming no contribution	7,962	18,067	6,000	10,750
3.	Taxable income after contribution	29,000	49,000	29,000	54,000
4.	Tax liability assuming contribution	7,522	17,517	5,800	10,450
5.	Decrease in tax liability (2 − 4) equal to tax saving (3) in first table	440	550	200	300

Thus the taxpayer who has the highest marginal tax rate (B) will have the largest tax saving and the correspondingly lowest after-tax cost. This rule of using the marginal tax rate applies to any business decision that results in a decrease (expense or cost) or increase (revenue) in taxable income. Therefore, it is applicable to most decisions that involve alternative actions.

Establishing the Business

One of the basic decisions a business person must make is whether to operate a sole proprietorship, partnership, or corporation. Because tax rates and provisions differ greatly depending on the form of a business, they are important considerations in making this decision.

As mentioned previously, corporations are taxable entities and are taxed on their income before it can be distributed to shareholders in the form of dividends. On the other hand, because sole proprietorships and partnerships are not taxable entities, the income from these organizations goes to the owners before it is taxed. On the surface, it might appear unlikely that the corporate form of business would ever be used by smaller or family-owned companies because of the double taxation. However, the corporate form has some advantages. For example, a corporation may pay its employees, including stockholders who work in the business, a reasonable salary, which is a tax deductible expense. The corporation does not have to pay dividends and thus can use retained income in the business for expansion rather than have it taxed the second time as dividends to the owners. In a partnership or proprietorship, the owners are taxed on the earnings regardless of whether they take the related money out of the business. If the owners of a small business want to gain some of the legal benefits of incorporation but wish to be taxed as a partnership, they may establish a corporation under subchapter S of the Internal Revenue Code. These **subchapter S corporations** must meet stringent requirements, but have been used successfully by many small businesses.

An example will illustrate how the form of organization affects the tax liability of a small business. Assume that James McGee, a single man, starts a business that he expects will produce $56,000 in business income. He plans to withdraw $28,000 a year from the business. The combined corporate and individual taxes under the corporate and proprietorship form of organization are summarized below.

	Form of Organization	
	Corporation	Proprietorship
Business income	$56,000	$56,000
Salary to James McGee	28,000	—
Taxable income	$28,000	$56,000
Corporation tax [$4,250 + (.20 × $3,000)]	4,850	—
Net income	$23,150	$56,000
Combined corporate and individual tax		
Corporate tax from above	$ 4,850	
Individual tax [assuming combined deductions and exemptions of $7,000 ($4,700 net after zero bracket amount) on both forms]		
On McGee's $28,000 salary	5,299	
On McGee's share of business income		$18,782
Total tax on business income	$10,149	$18,782

In the short run, by choosing the corporate form, McGee has reduced his total tax liability by $8,633, which he may use for the expansion of his business. If at some later date the corporation distributes all or part of the $23,150 net income of the corporation as dividends, the dividends will be taxable income on his individual tax return. If, on the other hand, he never withdraws the retained income and can sell his business for an amount that recognizes these profits as increased value of the business, they will be treated as long-term capital gains and taxed under the preferential treatment discussed previously.

There is a danger, however, in accumulating retained earnings that are too large. An additional income tax may be assessed by the IRS against corporations that accumulate earnings beyond $100,000 with the intent of avoiding the income tax that would be levied on stockholders if such earnings were distributed as dividends. The management of the corporation may have to prove that the excess accumulation is justified by the needs of the business.

Financing the Business

When a corporation is expanding, it acquires new capital by accumulating earnings in the manner described in the preceding section, by issuing additional capital stock, or by issuing debt securities. Although there are many considerations in making this complicated decision, the tax effect can be important. As an illustration of this effect in a very simple case, assume that Vilim Corporation is considering whether to raise additional capital of $1,000,000 by issuing $1,000,000 in 10 percent bonds at par or by issuing 10,000 shares of $100 par value preferred stock with an indicated dividend rate of 8 percent. At first glance, it appears that the preferred stock is cheaper for the company by $20,000 per year [(10% − 8%) × $1,000,000]. But remember that interest payments are tax deductible, whereas dividends on preferred stock must be paid out of income after tax. To compare the two issues with regard to cost, we must put them on the same basis. Either the bond issue must be put on an after-tax basis, or the stock issue must be put on a before-tax basis. To do the former, we must subtract the tax savings from the bond interest cost to obtain the after-tax cost before comparing it to the indicated dividend payout:

Annual interest ($1,000,000 × 10%)	$100,000
Tax savings (assumed marginal tax rate of 46 percent times $100,000)	46,000
After-tax cost	$ 54,000
After-tax dividend cost ($1,000,000 × 8%)	80,000
Advantage of bonds over preferred stock	$ 26,000

To place the dividend on the preferred stock on a before-tax basis, we must divide the dividend payment by the difference between 1.0 and the marginal tax rate before comparing it to the interest payment:

Annual indicated dividend ($1,000,000 × 8%)	$ 80,000.00
Divide by (1.0 − marginal tax rate) (1.0 − .46)	÷ .54
Before-tax cost	$148,148.15
Yearly interest payment ($1,000,000 × 10%)	100,000.00
Advantage of bonds over preferred stock	$ 48,148.15

The two results may be reconciled as follows:

$$\$48,148.15 - (48,148.15 \times .46) = \$26,000.$$

Management must weigh all important factors before making a final decision, but in terms of cost to the corporation it is clear that the bonds require a lower yearly commitment of cash flow. The principle illustrated here is that when comparing the tax effects on two or more alternatives, we should use the same tax basis.

Operating the Business

In operating a business, there are many ways to plan for minimizing the tax liability. We have already mentioned several of these ways. One of the most important is the timing of business transactions. For example, a corporation that is nearing $50,000 of taxable income for the year may want to defer an income-producing transaction until just past the end of the year in order to avoid the higher tax rate, or it may accelerate certain expenditures for the same purpose (for cash basis taxpayers only).

Another important way to minimize tax liability through operating decisions is by the timing of transactions involving capital assets. For example, no capital asset should be sold at a gain less than twelve months from the date of purchase, if at all possible. On the other hand, it is usually advisable to take losses before holding the assets twelve months. If the corporation is holding capital assets that have both gains and losses, it may be possible to sell the assets with losses in one year and deduct them from ordinary income, and to defer selling the assets with gains until the next year, when the capital gains can receive the preferential long-term treatment.

It is always good management to consider taking advantage of provisions of the tax law that allow preferential treatment. For example, the tax law has often been used to encourage investment in areas deemed important for national goals. Because these goals change over the years, the tax law has been used to promote everything from emergency war equipment to pollution control devices. Currently, if one purchases tangible personal (that is, removable) property, such as office equipment, having a useful life of at least six years from the date it is acquired, one may take an additional first-year depreciation equal to 20 percent of the cost in addition to the regular depreciation. Because this provision does not apply to land, buildings, or structural components, a company may consider using modern office furniture with portable partitions built into the desks and filing cabinets rather than installing permanent walls. In addition, special credits are allowed for certain expenditures that reduce unemployment or aid the handicapped.

Earlier we showed how a cash basis taxpayer can shift income from one tax year to another by timing receipts and expenditures. An accrual basis taxpayer cannot do the same by timing cash receipts and payments in the usual case, but there is an accounting method available to companies that sell on the installment plan to achieve the same goal. The tax code allows for the recognition of income for tax purposes according to the installment method. The installment method recognizes revenue (and costs) from installment sales in the period of receipt of cash.

As described in previous chapters, the tax code also allows the use of accelerated depreciation methods in determining the yearly depreciation expense (Chapter 13) and the use of the LIFO method of inventory valuation (which charges the latest and presumably highest costs against income) in determining the cost of goods sold (Chapter 11).

These examples are only illustrative of the many ways in which the provisions of the tax law can affect operating decisions.

Taxes and Financial Reporting

Most small businesses find it convenient to keep their accounting records on the same basis as their tax records. This practice is usually acceptable when there is not a material difference between the tax treatment of an item and the proper accounting treatment of the same item. However, the purpose of accounting is the determination of net income in accordance with generally accepted accounting principles, whereas the purpose of the tax code is to determine taxable income and tax liability. Because there can be significant differences in results, accountants cannot let the tax procedures dictate the method of preparing reports if the result is misleading.

For example, consider the case of Mason Corporation, which has a before-tax accounting income of $100,000 in each of two years. Assume that Mason has an expense item of $30,000, which may be taken as a tax deduction in year 1 but should be deducted for accounting purposes in year 2. The company's accounting and taxable income, and the actual income taxes due (assuming a tax rate of 46%), are as follows:

	Year 1	**Year 2**
Before-tax accounting income	$100,000	$100,000
Taxable income	$ 70,000	$130,000
Income tax rate	×.46	×.46
Actual income taxes due	$ 32,200	$ 59,800

One alternative for Mason Corporation would be simply to report the actual taxes paid on its financial statements, with the following result:

	Year 1	Year 2
Before-tax accounting income	$100,000	$100,000
Actual income taxes paid	32,200	59,800
Net income	$ 67,800	$ 40,200

Income Tax Allocation

Objective 5 Prepare journal entries to account for differences between accounting and taxable income

The astute reader of the above financial statements would surely question such a difference in tax expense when the accounting income is the same for both years. This is a serious problem and one that the Accounting Principles Board addressed in its *Opinion No. 11,* "Accounting for Income Taxes." The APB's solution to the problem is an accounting technique called **income tax allocation.** The objective of income tax allocation is to accrue income taxes on the basis of accounting income whenever there are differences in accounting and taxable income caused by the timing of revenues or expenses. In the example of Mason Corporation above, this means that the income statement for year 1 would report an income tax expense of $46,000 based on the accounting income for that year. The reported income tax expense for year 2 would be the same, and the reported net income for both years would be $54,000, which better reflects the real accounting situation. We record this procedure in the accounting records as follows:

Year 1	Income Tax Expense	46,000	
	Current Income Taxes Payable		32,200
	Deferred Income Tax Liability		13,800
	To record current and deferred income taxes at 46% of accounting income of $100,000		
Year 2	Income Tax Expense	46,000	
	Deferred Income Tax Liability	13,800	
	Current Income Taxes Payable		59,800
	To record current and deferred income tax at 46% of accounting income of $100,000		

If the company uses income tax allocation, the income statements for the two years would appear as shown below.

	Year 1	Year 2
Before-tax accounting income	$100,000	$100,000
Income tax expense	46,000	46,000
Net income	$ 54,000	$ 54,000

The difference in accounting and taxable income may also be the result of differences in methods applied over a series of years. For example, the table below shows some possible alternatives.

	Accounting Method	Tax Method
Sales	Point of sale	Installment
Inventories	Average-cost	FIFO
Depreciation	Straight-line	Accelerated

To illustrate the accounting treatment of such differences, we will continue to use the Mason Corporation as our example. Assume that the firm purchases a truck that costs $25,000 and is expected to have a salvage value of $5,000 after the end of its estimated life of four years. The company's marginal tax rate is 40 percent, and it elects to use the sum-of-the-years'-digits (SYD) method of depreciation for tax purposes. The company uses the straight-line (S-L) depreciation method for accounting purposes. The annual depreciation calculated under each method is:

Year	Straight-Line	Sum-of-the-Years' Digits
1	$ 5,000	$ 8,000 (4/10 × $20,000)
2	5,000	6,000 (3/10 × $20,000)
3	5,000	4,000 (2/10 × $20,000)
4	5,000	2,000 (1/10 × $20,000)
Totals	$20,000	$20,000

Assume further that the company has income before depreciation and taxes in each of the four years of $50,000. The annual income taxes can be computed as shown below.

	Year 1	Year 2	Year 3	Year 4	Totals
Income before depreciation and income taxes	$50,000	$50,000	$50,000	$50,000	$200,000
Depreciation for tax purposes (SYD)	8,000	6,000	4,000	2,000	20,000
Taxable income	$42,000	$44,000	$46,000	$48,000	$180,000
Annual income taxes (40% of taxable income)	$16,800	$17,600	$18,400	$19,200	$ 72,000

If the company were to prepare its financial statements using the actual tax liability for each year, they would appear as follows:

	Year 1	Year 2	Year 3	Year 4	Totals
Income before depreciation and income taxes	$50,000	$50,000	$50,000	$50,000	$200,000
Depreciation for accounting purposes (S-L)	5,000	5,000	5,000	5,000	20,000
Income before taxes	$45,000	$45,000	$45,000	$45,000	$180,000
Income taxes (actual)	16,800	17,600	18,400	19,200	72,000
Net income	$28,200	$27,400	$26,600	$25,800	$108,000

The result is that reported net income decreases year by year even though income before depreciation and income taxes remain the same. Under the income tax allocation procedure, this would not happen. The tax expense deducted on the income statement should be the amount that would have resulted if the method of depreciation used in the accounting records (S-L) had also been used to calculate the income tax expense instead of the tax method (SYD). Therefore, under income tax allocation, the income statements for the four years would appear as follows:

	Year 1	**Year 2**	**Year 3**	**Year 4**	**Totals**
Income before depreciation and income taxes	$50,000	$50,000	$50,000	$50,000	$200,000
Depreciation for accounting purposes (S-L)	5,000	5,000	5,000	5,000	20,000
Income before taxes	$45,000	$45,000	$45,000	$45,000	$180,000
Income taxes (based on S-L)	18,000	18,000	18,000	18,000	90,000
Net income	$27,000	$27,000	$27,000	$27,000	$ 90,000

Note that the total income taxes and the total net income for the four years are the same under both of the above methods of reporting. The differences lie in the reported income taxes and net income for the individual years.

The entries to record income tax expense each year follow the same procedure as illustrated earlier.

Year 1	Income Taxes Expense	18,000	
	Current Income Taxes Payable		16,800
	Deferred Income Taxes		1,200
Year 2	Income Taxes Expense	18,000	
	Current Income Taxes Payable		17,600
	Deferred Income Taxes		400
Year 3	Income Taxes Expense	18,000	
	Deferred Income Taxes	400	
	Current Income Taxes Payable		18,400
Year 4	Income Taxes Expense	18,000	
	Deferred Income Taxes	1,200	
	Current Income Taxes Payable		19,200

Note that in the entries given, the Deferred Income Taxes account has a credit balance for the first three years (total credits to Deferred Income Taxes exceed total debits). Whether or not the Deferred Income Taxes credit balance is classified as a current or long-term liability depends on the classification of the asset or liability that gave rise to the timing difference. For example, if the timing difference was due to different inventory methods, the deferred tax liability would be classified as a current liability. If the difference arose from different depreciation methods or plant assets, it would be a long-term liability.[2] Some insight into the importance of deferred income taxes to financial reporting may be gained from examining the financial statements of six hundred large companies surveyed in a recent year. Of those surveyed, 90 percent reported some type of deferred taxes. Of these, approximately two-thirds reported Deferred Income Taxes with a credit balance in the noncurrent liability section, and about 20 percent reported a debit balance in the current asset section. The rest were some combination of current and noncurrent assets and liabilities.

Tax Effects of Extraordinary Items

When a company has extraordinary gains and losses, they are disclosed in a separate section of the income statement as explained in Chapter 17. These extraordinary gains or losses should be reported at net of income taxes in order not to distort the net operating income figure. For example, assume that a corporation with $80,000 operating income before taxes has a total tax liability of $70,000 based on taxable income, including a capital gain of $100,000, on which a tax of $30,000 is due. The proper presentation is as follows:

Net Operating Income Before Taxes	$ 80,000
Income Taxes (actual taxes are $70,000, of which $30,000 is applicable to extraordinary gain)	40,000
Income Before Extraordinary Item	$ 40,000
Extraordinary Gain, Net of Taxes ($100,000 – $30,000)	70,000
Net Income	$110,000

If all the taxes payable were deducted from net operating income before taxes, both the income before extraordinary items and the extraordinary gain would be distorted.

A company follows the same procedure in the case of an extraordinary loss. For example, assume the same facts as above except that total tax liability is only $10,000 because of a $100,000 extraordinary loss, which results in a $30,000 tax saving:

2. *Statement of Financial Accounting Standards, No. 37,* "Balance Sheet Classification of Deferred Income Taxes" (Stamford, Conn.: Financial Accounting Standards Board, 1980).

Net Operating Income Before Taxes	$80,000
Income Taxes (actual taxes of $10,000 as a result of an extraordinary loss)	40,000
Net Income Before Extraordinary Item	$40,000
Extraordinary Loss, Net of Taxes ($100,000 − $30,000)	70,000
Net Loss	($30,000)

Chapter Review

Review of Learning Objectives

1. Explain and differentiate some basic concepts related to income taxes and accounting.

Income taxes are an important cost of doing business. They are assessed on taxable income, which may differ considerably from accounting income because the two income concepts are used for different purposes. Tax planning, which is the arrangement of a taxpayer's affairs in such a way as to pay the smallest legal tax, is an important part of business operation. Tax evasion is the concealment of actual tax liabilities. Taxpayers, in general, may use either the cash basis or the accrual basis for determining taxable income and often use a combination of both. There are four classes of taxpayers: individuals, corporations, estates, and trusts. Proprietors and partners must report their share of business earnings on their individual returns.

2. Identify the major components used for determining the income tax liability of individuals.

Taxable income for individuals is computed in two steps. The first step is to deduct certain items from gross income to obtain adjusted gross income. The second step is to deduct itemized nonbusiness and specified personal expenses (or the zero bracket amount) and exemptions from adjusted gross income to obtain taxable income. The tax liability is determined by applying the tax rate from the appropriate tax table or tax rate schedule to the taxable income. Gains and losses on capital assets are includable in gross income but are subject to special rules.

3. Identify the major differences between the income tax provisions for corporations and for individuals.

Corporations are taxable entities under federal tax laws and file tax returns. Some special features of corporate tax provisions are: a special dividends received deduction, carry-forwards and carry-backs for net operating loss deduction and net capital losses, and a limit on the deduction for charitable contributions to 5 percent of taxable income. In general, corporations are subject to a tax of 17 percent on their first $25,000 of taxable income, 20 percent on the next $25,000, 30 percent on the next $25,000, 40 percent on the next $25,000, and 46 percent on taxable income over $100,000.

4. Identify several ways in which income taxes affect business decisions.

The marginal tax rate of the taxpayer should be used in assessing the impact of the tax on business decisions. Tax factors may have a significant effect on important business decisions, such as choosing the form of operation for the business, financing the business, and operating the business. In the latter category, the timing and nature of business transactions and the choice of accounting methods have a significant impact on tax liability.

5. Prepare journal entries to account for differences between accounting and taxable income.

When there are material differences between accounting income and taxable income, the income tax allocation procedure should be used. Basically, this procedure accrues income taxes on the basis of accounting income whenever there are differences between accounting and taxable income. The difference between the accrued income taxes and the actual income taxes is debited or credited to an account called Deferred Income Taxes. If a company has extraordinary items to report, it should present them on the income statement at net of taxes. The income taxes deducted from net operating income before taxes should be shown at what they would be without considering the extraordinary items.

Review Problem

Before doing the exercises and problems, review especially the text examples of tax planning. For additional help, see the review problem in the working papers.

Chapter Assignments

Questions

1. What is the difference between tax planning and tax evasion?
2. What are the four classes of taxpayers?
3. J. Vickery's sole proprietorship had a net income of $37,500 during the taxable year. During the same year, Vickery withdrew $24,000 from the business. What income must Vickery report in his individual tax return?
4. Which of the two methods of accounting, cash or accrual, is more commonly used by individual taxpayers?
5. Why is it sometimes claimed that corporate income is subject to double taxation?
6. Figure 29-2 indicates that a single taxpayer with a taxable income (after deduction for exemption) of $20,000 owes $4,177 in federal income taxes. What is this taxpayer's average tax rate and his or her marginal tax rate?
7. If a friend of yours turned down the opportunity to earn an additional $500 of taxable income because it would put him in a higher tax bracket, would you consider this action rational? Why?
8. What are capital assets and why is the concept important to tax accounting?
9. Distinguish between tax deductions and tax credits. What are three examples of tax credits?
10. What are four (or more) ways in which the calculation of taxable income for corporations differs from that for individuals?
11. In evaluating a business decision, should the average tax rate or the marginal tax rate be used? Explain.
12. What advantage would incorporating a small business and paying the president a salary have over maintaining the proprietorship form? What disadvantage is there to this plan?
13. Why may a bond that pays 8 percent interest be a less expensive way to raise money for a company than a preferred stock that pays a 7 percent dividend?

14. What alternative ways of treating transactions in the operation of a business might be used in effective tax planning?
15. "Accounting income should be geared to the concept of taxable income because the public understands the concept of taxable income." Comment on this statement.
16. Why is income tax allocation necessary?

Classroom Exercises

Exercise 29-1 Computation of Tax Liability

From Figures 29-1, 29-2, and 29-3, compute the income tax before-tax credits for each of the following: (1) single individual (one exemption) with taxable income of $6,200, (2) single individual with taxable income of $59,000 (after deduction for exemption), (3) married couple (two exemptions) filing jointly with taxable income of $6,200, (4) married couple filing jointly with taxable income of $59,000 (after deduction for exemptions), (5) corporation with taxable income of $6,200, and (6) corporation with taxable income of $59,000.

Exercise 29-2 Taxable Income/ Tax Liability for Corporations

Calculate the taxable income and the tax liability of Werner Corporation based on the following data: taxable revenues, $565,000; allowable business deductions, $462,000; dividends from other domestic corporations, $18,600; operating loss carry-forward from previous years, $26,200; charitable contributions, $10,000.

Exercise 29-3 Form of Organization Decision

Sylvia Gomez is the owner of a small but profitable business. She is expanding her business and wants to reinvest earnings in the business. Her only income is from the business, from which she withdraws $24,000 per year for personal living expenses. She is single and has no dependents. She is thinking of forming a corporation in order to save on current taxes.

Assuming that her business had a taxable income of $49,000, determine how much more or less she would pay in total taxes under the corporate form, with the withdrawal paid as a salary, than under the sole proprietorship form.

Exercise 29-4 Income Tax Allocation

The Watson Corporation reported the following income before income tax, income tax expense, and net income for 19x8 and 19x9.

	19x8	19x9
Income before income tax	$140,000	$140,000
Income tax expense	35,950	54,350
Net income	$104,050	$ 85,650

In 19x8, Watson deducted an item of $20,000 for income tax purposes. For accounting income purposes, the company did not deduct this item until 19x9. Watson has a marginal tax rate of 40 percent and does not use income tax allocation procedures.

1. Identify the distortions in Watson's income statements due to the failure to use income tax allocation procedures.
2. Show how the three income statement items would appear for both years using income tax allocation procedures.

Exercise 29-5 Effect of Accounting Alternatives on Income Tax

The Wainwright Company, which was in the 40 percent tax bracket, purchased a special-purpose machine for $65,000. This machine has a five-year estimated useful life, at the end of which time it will have a salvage value of $5,000.

Assuming that Wainwright uses straight-line depreciation for accounting purposes and sum-of-the-years'-digits depreciation for income tax purposes, prepare a table with the following column headings (show negative amounts in brackets), and total the columns: Year, Straight-Line Depreciation, Sum-of-the-Years'-Digits Depreciation, Difference in Depreciation, Effect on Income Tax.

Problem Set A

To determine income tax liability in Problem Sets A and B, use the tax rate schedules in Figure 29-2 for individuals and in Figure 29-3 for corporations.

Problem 29A-1 Taxable Income and Tax Liability for Corporations

The following data come from the records of the Yates Corporation: sales, $1,355,440; dividends from other corporations, $87,000; beginning inventory, $52,800; ending inventory, $46,700; net purchases, $782,500; selling expenses, $271,300; general expenses, $96,400; contributions to charities, $27,500; long-term capital gains, $57,250; short-term capital losses, $14,650; operating loss carryforward from previous years, $116,250.

Required

1. Compute taxable income for Yates Corporation.
2. Compute the income tax liability for Yates Corporation, assuming a tax rate of 28 percent on net long-term capital gains.

Problem 29A-2 Form of Organization Decision

John O'Leary is thinking of incorporating his business because he believes such a change will save on current income taxes. During the current year, his business had sales of $650,000, cost of goods sold of $420,000, and operating expenses of $160,000 excluding his withdrawals. He owns stock in domestic corporations that are in the business's name and that pay dividends of $4,000 per year. He withdraws $28,000 on an annual basis for living expenses and feels that this amount would be a reasonable salary. Mr. O'Leary is unmarried and does not itemize deductions.

Required

1. Prepare comparative income statements showing the taxable income of the business organized as a sole proprietorship and as a corporation.
2. Determine the total combined income tax, assuming that (a) the business is not incorporated, and (b) the business is incorporated.

Problem 29A-3 Financing Decision

The Zurns Corporation is in serious need of capital for expansion. Management has determined that it needs $500,000 to finance additions to working capital. During the past year, the company had taxable income of $110,000, on which it paid taxes of $31,350, or 28.5 percent. Its marginal tax rate is 46 percent.

Zurns's management has negotiated a five-year loan from the bank for the full amount needed at an annual interest rate of 13 percent. Two of Zurns's major stockholders, however, have suggested that they can save the company money if they put up the $500,000 in exchange for a new issue of preferred stock that carries an indicated dividend rate of 10 percent. Management is considering this alternative.

Required

1. Prepare a schedule that compares the annual after-tax cost to the corporation of each alternative.
2. Comment on the relative desirability of each alternative.

Problem 29A-4
Tax Planning

Frazer Corporation's tax year ends December 31. It has been a very successful year for the company, and Bill Frazer, president of the company, wants to avoid a large tax liability. On December 1, Susan Acre, the company's accountant, suggests that the firm still has time to do some end-of-the-year tax planning in order to minimize the legal tax that must be paid. Bill agrees and asks for a report as soon as possible.

After a week of studying Frazer Corporation's actual and projected transactions, Susan presents the following data:

Projected taxable income, assuming no change in accounting procedures, is $287,000. (Except for computing cost of goods sold and depreciation, the company used a cash basis for reporting revenues and expenses.)

Items with tax-planning possibilities are as follows: (a) A major customer is scheduled to make a payment on account of $30,000 on December 30. (b) Expenses scheduled to be paid during the first week of January total $23,000. (c) A major piece of equipment was purchased last January for $175,000. It has an estimated useful life of eight years and an estimated salvage value of $25,000. Although the company has always used straight-line depreciation for both accounting and tax purposes, it may elect an accelerated method at a rate double that of the straight-line method. (d) The company has used the FIFO inventory method in the past but can change to the LIFO method. This procedure would reduce income by $42,000. (e) The company has made no charitable contributions during the current year. The maximum allowable deduction for contributions is 5 percent of taxable income before deductions of the contribution.

Required

1. Calculate the adjusted taxable income, assuming that in each case above, Bill Frazer elects to take the action that will reduce current income tax liability.
2. Prepare a schedule showing projected taxable income, income tax liability, and projected income after tax for both alternatives.

Problem 29A-5
Income Tax Allocation

Holstein Corporation has before-tax accounting income of $300,000 in each of two years, 19x1 and 19x2. Included in 19x1 income is a major revenue item of $80,000 that does not have to be reported for tax purposes until 19x2.

Required

1. For each tax year, determine taxable income; actual income tax due, assuming normal corporate tax rates; and net income, assuming no income tax allocation.
2. For each tax year, determine income tax expense and net income, assuming that the income tax allocation procedure is used.
3. Prepare journal entries to record income tax expense and income tax payable for each year, assuming that the income tax allocation procedure is used.

Problem 29A-6
Income Tax Allocation

Jersey Corporation has completed the purchase and installation of a new cotton-spinning machine in its plant at a cost of $595,000, including installation costs. It is estimated that the spinner will have a useful life of five years and a salvage value of $100,000 at the end of that time. Also, the spinner should produce an income before depreciation of $200,000 during each of the five years. The company uses the straight-line method of depreciation for accounting purposes and the sum-of-the-years'-digits method for income tax purposes. In accordance with APB *Opinion No. 11,* the company also uses income tax allocation procedures.

Required

1. Prepare a schedule showing, for each of the five years, net income after deducting sum-of-the-years'-digits depreciation and actual taxes due. The company's marginal tax rate is 46 percent.
2. Prepare a second schedule showing, for each of the five years, net income after deducting straight-line depreciation and actual taxes due.
3. Prepare a third schedule showing net income to be reported to stockholders with straight-line depreciation and allocated income taxes for each of the five years.
4. Prepare journal entries for each year to record income tax expense and income tax payable, using the income tax allocation procedure.
5. Set up a ledger account for Deferred Income Taxes and show therein the entries resulting from the allocation of income taxes.

Problem Set B

Problem 29B-1 Taxable Income and Tax Liability for Corporations

After two years of losses, DDT Corporation became profitable in the current year. In preparation for filing the company's tax return, the DDT accountant found that the company had a gross profit of $268,500 and business expenses of $110,000, including charitable contributions of $12,000. In addition, the company received dividends from other corporations of $27,000 and had a long-term capital gain of $20,000. It also had an operating loss carry-forward of $91,175 from the previous two years.

Required

1. Compute taxable income for DDT Corporation.
2. Compute the income tax liability for DDT Corporation, assuming a tax rate of 28 percent on net long-term capital gains.

Problem 29B-2 Form of Organization Decision

Sara Burnside operates a successful dry cleaning establishment as a sole proprietorship. Her individual income taxes have been high, and she wonders if establishing a corporation would result in a smaller tax liability. During the current year, her company had revenues of $656,000 and operating expenses of $605,000. In addition, the company owned corporate stocks that paid dividends of $5,000. She withdraws $26,000 per year as a salary. On her personal return, she uses the standard deduction, claims an invalid mother as a dependent, and uses the rates for single taxpayers.

Required

1. Prepare comparative income statements showing taxable income of the business organized as a sole proprietorship and as a corporation.
2. Using Figures 29-2 and 29-3, determine the total combined income tax, assuming that (a) the business is not incorporated, and (b) the business is incorporated.

Problem 29B-3 Financing Decision

Dunne Corporation is planning an expansion of its operation from the Midwest to the West Coast. Projections by management indicate a need for new capital of $20 million. This money can be raised by issuing either long-term bonds at an annual interest cost of 9 percent or preferred stock carrying an indicated dividend rate of 8 percent per year. During the past year, Dunne Corporation had a net income of $10 million and paid federal income tax of $4 million, or an average rate of 40 percent. The company's marginal tax rate is 46 percent.

Required

1. Prepare a schedule that compares the after-tax cost to the corporation of each alternative.
2. Comment on the relative desirability of each alternative.

Problem 29B-4 Tax Planning

Action Toys, Inc., is a small manufacturer of mechanical toys. Although the company has been successful in the past, it has recently been pressed for cash. Next year management expects to invest heavily in a new toy based on a current television series. To keep borrowing at a minimum, management is looking for ways to reduce its cash outflow for the current year, which ends December 31, and for next year. The company's accountant suggests that Action Toys plan its transactions and accounting procedures before year end so as to minimize the legal amount of income tax that will have to be paid on this year's income.

After studying the company's actual and projected transactions, the accountant has concluded that taxable income for the year will be $538,000 unless one or more of the following tax-planning opportunities are taken: (a) Equipment purchases during the year were $1,275,000. The projected net income was computed using the straight-line method with an estimated useful life of five years and an estimated salvage value of $125,000. The company may elect to use the double-declining-balance method at twice the straight-line rate for tax purposes. (b) By changing from the average-cost inventory method to the LIFO inventory method, net income would be reduced by $43,000. (c) Projected expenses to be paid in the first week of January are $76,000. (d) Major customers are due to make payments for merchandise of $116,000 during the last week of December. The company reports income for tax purposes on a modified cash basis, which means that revenues and expenses are reported on a cash basis and cost of goods sold and depreciation are reported on the accrual basis.

Required

1. Calculate the adjusted taxable income, assuming that in each case above, the company elects to take the action that will reduce current income tax liability.
2. Prepare a schedule showing projected taxable income, income tax liability, and income after tax for both alternatives.

Problem 29B-5 Income Tax Allocation

Rayette Corporation has before-tax accounting income of $400,000 in each of two years, 19x3 and 19x4. Included in 19x3 income is a major expense item of $100,000 that is not deductible for tax purposes until 19x4.

Required

1. For each tax year, determine taxable income; actual income tax due, assuming normal corporate tax rates; and net income, assuming no income tax allocation.
2. For each tax year, determine income tax expense and net income, assuming that the income tax allocation procedure is used.
3. Prepare journal entries to record income tax expense and income tax payable for each year, assuming that the income tax allocation procedure is used.

Problem 29B-6 Income Tax Allocation

Turnbough Metals has completed the purchase and installation of a computerized lathe at a total cost of $1,210,000. Management estimates that the lathe will produce an income of $380,000 per year for five years, at which time it will have a salvage value of approximately $100,000. The company uses the straight-line method of depreciation for accounting purposes and the sum-of-the-years'-digits method for income tax purposes. In accordance with APB *Opinion No. 11,* the company uses income tax allocation procedures.

Required

1. Prepare a schedule showing, for each of the five years, net income after deducting sum-of-the-years'-digits depreciation and actual taxes due. The company's marginal tax rate is 46 percent.
2. Prepare a second schedule showing, for each of the five years, net income after deducting straight-line depreciation and actual taxes due.
3. Prepare a third schedule showing net income to be reported to stockholders with straight-line depreciation and allocated income taxes for each of the five years.
4. Prepare journal entries for each year to record income tax expense and income tax payable, using the income tax allocation procedure.
5. Set up a ledger account for Deferred Income Taxes and show therein the entries that result from the allocation procedure.

Appendix A

The Use of Future Value and Present Value in Accounting

Learning Objectives

1. *Distinguish simple interest from compound interest.*
2. *Use compound interest tables to compute (a) the future value of a single invested sum at compound interest, and (b) the future value of an ordinary annuity.*
3. *Use present value tables to compute (a) the present value of a single sum due in the future, and (b) the present value of an ordinary annuity.*
4. *Apply the concept of present value to some simple accounting situations.*

Interest is an important cost to the debtor and an important revenue to the creditor. Because interest is a cost associated with time, and "time is money," it is also an important consideration in any business decision. For example, an individual who holds $100 for one year without putting that $100 in a savings account has forgone the interest that could have been earned. Thus there is a cost associated with holding this money equal to the interest that could have been earned. Similarly, a business person who accepts a noninterest-bearing note instead of cash for the sale of merchandise is forgoing the interest that could have been earned on that money. These examples illustrate the point that the timing of the receipt and payment of cash must be considered in making business decisions.

Simple Interest and Compound Interest

Interest is the cost associated with the use of money for a specific period of time. **Simple interest** is the interest cost for one or more periods, if we assume that the amount on which the interest is computed stays the same from period to period. **Compound interest** is the interest cost for two or more periods, if we assume that after each period the interest of that period is added to the amount on which interest is computed in future periods. In other words, compound interest is interest earned on a principal sum that is increased at the end of each period by the interest of that period.

Example: Simple Interest Joe Sanchez accepts an 8 percent, $30,000 note due in 90 days. How much will he receive in total at that time? Remember the formula for calculating simple interest, which was presented in Chapter 12, on notes receivable:

interest = principal × rate × time
interest = $30,000 × 8/100 × 90/360
interest = $600

The total that Sanchez will receive is computed as follows:

$$\begin{aligned} \text{total} &= \text{principal} + \text{interest} \\ \text{total} &= \$30{,}000 + \$600 \\ \text{total} &= \$30{,}600 \end{aligned}$$

Example: Compound Interest Ann Clary deposits $5,000 in a savings account that pays 6 percent interest. She expects to leave the principal and accumulated interest in the account for three years. How much in total will be in her account at the end of three years? Assume that the interest is paid at the end of the year and is added to the principal at that time and that this total in turn earns interest. The amount at the end of three years may be computed as follows:

(1) Year	(2) Principal Amount at Beginning of Year	(3) Annual Amount of Interest (col. 2 × .06)	(4) Accumulated Amount at End of Year (col. 2 + col. 3)
1	$5,000.00	$300.00	$5,300.00
2	5,300.00	318.00	5,618.00
3	5,618.00	337.08	5,955.08

At the end of three years, Clary will have $5,955.08 in her savings account. Note that the annual amount of interest increases each year by the interest rate times the interest of the previous year. For example, between year 1 and year 2, the interest increased by $18 ($318 – $300), which exactly equals .06 times $300.

Future Value of a Single Invested Sum at Compound Interest

Another way to ask the question in the example of compound interest above is, What is the future value of a single sum ($5,000) at compound interest (6 percent) for three years? Future value is the amount that an investment will be worth at a future date if invested at compound interest. A business person often wants to know future value, but the method of computing the future value illustrated above is too time-consuming in practice. Imagine how tedious the calculation would be if the example were ten years instead of three. Fortunately, there are tables that make problems involving compound interest much simpler and quicker to solve. Table A-1, showing the future value of $1 after a given number of time periods, is an example. It is actually part of a larger table, B-1, in Appendix B. Suppose that we want to solve the problem of Clary's savings account above. We simply look down the 6 percent column in Table A-1 until we reach period 3 and find the factor 1.191. This factor when multiplied by $1 gives the future value of that $1 at compound interest of 6 percent for three years (years in this case). Thus we solve the problem:

$$\begin{array}{ccc} \text{principal} \times \text{factor} & = & \text{future value} \\ \$5{,}000 \times 1.191 & = & \$5{,}955 \end{array}$$

Except for a rounding error of $.08, the answer is exactly the same. Another example will illustrate this simple technique again.

Periods	1%	2%	3%	4%	5%	6%	7%	8%	9%	10%	12%	14%	15%
1	1.010	1.020	1.030	1.040	1.050	1.060	1.070	1.080	1.090	1.100	1.120	1.140	1.150
2	1.020	1.040	1.061	1.082	1.103	1.124	1.145	1.166	1.188	1.210	1.254	1.300	1.323
3	1.030	1.061	1.093	1.125	1.158	1.191	1.225	1.260	1.295	1.331	1.405	1.482	1.521
4	1.041	1.082	1.126	1.170	1.216	1.262	1.311	1.360	1.412	1.464	1.574	1.689	1.749
5	1.051	1.104	1.159	1.217	1.276	1.338	1.403	1.469	1.539	1.611	1.762	1.925	2.011
6	1.062	1.126	1.194	1.265	1.340	1.419	1.501	1.587	1.677	1.772	1.974	2.195	2.313
7	1.072	1.149	1.230	1.316	1.407	1.504	1.606	1.714	1.828	1.949	2.211	2.502	2.660
8	1.083	1.172	1.267	1.369	1.477	1.594	1.718	1.851	1.993	2.144	2.476	2.853	3.059
9	1.094	1.195	1.305	1.423	1.551	1.689	1.838	1.999	2.172	2.358	2.773	3.252	3.518
10	1.105	1.219	1.344	1.480	1.629	1.791	1.967	2.159	2.367	2.594	3.106	3.707	4.046

Source: Henry R. Anderson and Mitchell H. Raiborn, *Basic Cost Accounting Concepts* (Boston: Houghton Mifflin, 1977), excerpt from Table 1, p. 552.

Table A-1
Future Value of $1 after a Given Number of Time Periods

Example: Future Value of a Single Invested Sum at Compound Interest Ed Bates invests $3,000, which he believes will return 5 percent interest compounded over a five-year period. How much will Bates have at the end of five years? From Table A-1, the factor for period 5 of the 5 percent column is 1.276. Therefore, we calculate as follows:

$$\begin{array}{l} \text{principal} \times \text{factor} = \text{future value} \\ \$3{,}000 \times 1.276 = \quad \$3{,}828 \end{array}$$

Bates will have $3,828 at the end of five years.

Future Value of an Ordinary Annuity

Another common problem involves an ordinary annuity, which is a series of equal payments made at the end of equal intervals of time, with compound interest on these payments.

Example: Future Value of an Ordinary Annuity Assume that Ben Katz deposits $200 at the end of each of the next three years in a savings account that pays 5 percent interest. How much money will he have in his account at the end of the next three years? One way of computing the amount is shown in the following table:

(1) Year	(2) Beginning Balance	(3) Interest Earned (5% × col. 2)	(4) Periodic Payment	(5) Accumulated at End of Period (col. 2 + col. 3 + col. 4)
1	$ —	$ —	$200	$200.00
2	200.00	10.00	200	410.00
3	410.00	20.50	200	630.50

Katz would have $630.50 in his account at the end of three years, consisting of $600 in periodic payments and $30.50 in interest.

This calculation can also be simplified by using Table A-2. We look down the 5 percent column until we reach period 3 and find the factor 3.153. This factor

Periods	1%	2%	3%	4%	5%	6%	7%	8%	9%	10%	12%	14%	15%
1	1.000	1.000	1.000	1.000	1.000	1.000	1.000	1.000	1.000	1.000	1.000	1.000	1.000
2	2.010	2.020	2.030	2.040	2.050	2.060	2.070	2.080	2.090	2.100	2.120	2.140	2.150
3	3.030	3.060	3.091	3.122	3.153	3.184	3.215	3.246	3.278	3.310	3.374	3.440	3.473
4	4.060	4.122	4.184	4.246	4.310	4.375	4.440	4.506	4.573	4.641	4.779	4.921	4.993
5	5.101	5.204	5.309	5.416	5.526	5.637	5.751	5.867	5.985	6.105	6.353	6.610	6.742
6	6.152	6.308	6.468	6.633	6.802	6.975	7.153	7.336	7.523	7.716	8.115	8.536	8.754
7	7.214	7.434	7.662	7.898	8.142	8.394	8.654	8.923	9.200	9.487	10.09	10.73	11.07
8	8.286	8.583	8.892	9.214	9.549	9.897	10.26	10.64	11.03	11.44	12.30	13.23	13.73
9	9.369	9.755	10.16	10.58	11.03	11.49	11.98	12.49	13.02	13.58	14.78	16.09	16.79
10	10.46	10.95	11.46	12.01	12.58	13.18	13.82	14.49	15.19	15.94	17.55	19.34	20.30

Source: Henry R. Anderson and Mitchell H. Raiborn, *Basic Cost Accounting Concepts* (Boston: Houghton Mifflin, 1977), excerpt from Table 2, p. 553.

Table A-2 Future Value of $1 Paid in Each Period for a Given Number of Time Periods

when multiplied by $1 gives the future value of a series of three $1 payments (years in this case) at compound interest of 5 percent. Thus we solve the problem:

periodic payment × factor = future value
$200 × 3.153 = $630.60

Except for a rounding error of $0.10, this result is the same as the one above.

Present Value

Suppose that you had the choice of receiving $100 today or one year from today. Intuitively, you would choose to receive the $100 today. Why? You know that if you have the $100 today, you can put it in a savings account to earn interest and will have more than $100 a year from today. Therefore, we can say that an amount to be received in the future (future value) is not worth as much today as an amount to be received today (present value) because of the cost associated with the passage of time. In fact, present value and future value are closely related. Present value is the amount that must be invested now at a given rate of interest to produce a given future value.

Example: Present Value Sue Dapper needs $1,000 one year from now. How much should she invest today to achieve that goal if the interest rate is 5 percent? From earlier examples, the following equation may be established:

present value × (1.0 + interest rate) = future value
present value × 1.05 = $1,000
present value = $1,000 ÷ 1.05
present value = $952.38

Thus to achieve a future value of $1,000, a present value of $952.38 must be invested. Interest of 5 percent on $952.38 for one year equals $47.62, and these two amounts added together equal $1,000.

Present Value of a Single Sum Due in the Future

When more than one time period is involved, the calculation of present value is more complicated. Consider the following example.

Example: Present Value of a Single Sum in the Future Don Riley wants to be sure of having $4,000 at the end of three years. How much must he invest today in a 5 percent savings account to achieve this goal? Adapting the above equation, we compute the present value of $4,000 at compound interest of 5 percent for three years in the future.

Year	Amount at End of Year		Divide by		Present Value at Beginning of Year
3	$4,000.00	÷	1.05	=	$3,809.52
2	3,809.52	÷	1.05	=	3,628.12
1	3,628.12	÷	1.05	=	3,455.35

Riley must invest a present value of $3,455.35 to achieve a future value of $4,000 in three years.

This calculation is again made much easier by using the appropriate table. In Table A-3, we look down the 5 percent column until we reach period 3 and find the factor 0.864. This factor when multiplied by $1 gives the present value of that $1 to be received three years from now at 5 percent interest. Thus we solve the problem:

$$\text{future value} \times \text{factor} = \text{present value}$$
$$\$4{,}000 \times 0.864 = \$3{,}456$$

Except for a rounding error of $0.65, this result is the same as the one above.

Present Value of an Ordinary Annuity

It is often necessary to compute the present value of a series of receipts or payments. When we calculate the present value of equal amounts equally spaced over a period of time, we are computing the present value of an ordinary annuity.

Example: Present Value of an Ordinary Annuity Assume that Kathy Foster has sold a piece of property and is to receive $15,000 in three equal annual payments

Table A-3
Present Value of $1 to Be Received at the End of a Given Number of Time Periods

Periods	1%	2%	3%	4%	5%	6%	7%	8%	9%	10%
1	0.990	0.980	0.971	0.962	0.952	0.943	0.935	0.926	0.917	0.909
2	0.980	0.961	0.943	0.925	0.907	0.890	0.873	0.857	0.842	0.826
3	0.971	0.942	0.915	0.889	0.864	0.840	0.816	0.794	0.772	0.751
4	0.961	0.924	0.888	0.855	0.823	0.792	0.763	0.735	0.708	0.683
5	0.951	0.906	0.883	0.822	0.784	0.747	0.713	0.681	0.650	0.621
6	0.942	0.888	0.837	0.790	0.746	0.705	0.666	0.630	0.596	0.564
7	0.933	0.871	0.813	0.760	0.711	0.665	0.623	0.583	0.547	0.513
8	0.923	0.853	0.789	0.731	0.677	0.627	0.582	0.540	0.502	0.467
9	0.914	0.837	0.766	0.703	0.645	0.592	0.544	0.500	0.460	0.424
10	0.905	0.820	0.744	0.676	0.614	0.558	0.508	0.463	0.422	0.386

Source: Henry R. Anderson and Mitchell H. Raiborn, *Basic Cost Accounting Concepts* (Boston: Houghton Mifflin, 1977), excerpt from Table 3, p. 554.

of $5,000, beginning one year from today. What is the present value of this sale, assuming a current interest rate of 5 percent? This present value may be computed by calculating a separate present value for each of the three payments (using Table A-3) and summing the results, as shown below.

Future Receipts (Annuity)				Present Value Factor at 5 percent (from Table A-3)		Present Value
Year 1	Year 2	Year 3				
$5,000			×	0.952	=	$ 4,760
	$5,000		×	0.907	=	4,535
		$5,000	×	0.864	=	4,320
Total Present Value						$13,615

The present value of this sale is $13,615. Thus there is an implied interest cost (given the 5 percent rate) of $1,385 associated with the payment plan that allows the purchaser to pay in three installments.

We can make this calculation by using Table A-4. We look down the 5 percent column until we reach period 3 and find factor 2.723. This factor when multiplied by $1 gives the present value of a series of three $1 payments (spaced one year apart) at compound interest of 5 percent. Thus we solve the problem:

periodic payment × factor = present value
$5,000 × 2.723 = $13,615

This result is the same as the one computed above.

Time Periods

In all the examples above and in most other cases, the compounding period is one year, and the interest rate is stated on an annual basis. However, in each of the four tables the left-hand column refers, not to years, but to periods. This wording is intended to accommodate compounding periods of less than one year. Savings accounts that record interest quarterly and bonds that pay interest semiannually are cases where the compounding period is less than one year. In order to use the tables in such cases, it is necessary to (1) divide the annual interest rate by the number of periods in the year, and (2) multiply the number of periods in one year by the number of years.

Example: Time Periods Assume that a $6,000 note is to be paid in two years and carries an annual interest rate of 8 percent. Compute the maturity (future) value of the note, assuming that the compounding period is semiannual. Before using the table, it is necessary to compute the interest rate that applies to the compounding period and the number of periods. First, the interest rate to use is 4 percent (8% annual rate ÷ 2 periods per year). Second, the number of compounding periods is 4 (2 periods per year × 2 years). From Table A-1, therefore, the maturity value of the note may be computed as follows:

principal × factor = future value
$6,000 × 1.170 = $7,020

The note will be worth $7,020 in two years.

Periods	1%	2%	3%	4%	5%	6%	7%	8%	9%	10%
1	0.990	0.980	0.971	0.962	0.952	0.943	0.935	0.926	0.917	0.909
2	1.970	1.942	1.913	1.886	1.859	1.833	1.808	1.783	1.759	1.736
3	2.941	2.884	2.829	2.775	2.723	2.673	2.624	2.577	2.531	2.487
4	3.902	3.808	3.717	3.630	3.546	3.465	3.387	3.312	3.240	3.170
5	4.853	4.713	4.580	4.452	4.329	4.212	4.100	3.993	3.890	3.791
6	5.795	5.601	5.417	5.242	5.076	4.917	4.767	4.623	4.486	4.355
7	6.728	6.472	6.230	6.002	5.786	5.582	5.389	5.206	5.033	4.868
8	7.652	7.325	7.020	6.733	6.463	6.210	5.971	5.747	5.535	5.335
9	8.566	8.162	7.786	7.435	7.108	6.802	6.515	6.247	5.995	5.759
10	9.471	8.983	8.530	8.111	7.722	7.360	7.024	6.710	6.418	6.145

Source: Henry R. Anderson and Mitchell H. Raiborn, *Basic Cost Accounting Concepts* (Boston: Houghton Mifflin, 1977), excerpt from Table 4, p. 556.

Table A-4
Present Value of $1 Received Each Period for a Given Number of Time Periods

This procedure for determining the interest rate and the number of periods when the compounding period is less than one year may be used with all the tables.

Applications of Present Value to Accounting

The concept of present value is widely applicable in the discipline of accounting. Here, the purpose is to demonstrate its usefulness in some simple applications. In-depth study of present value is deferred to more advanced courses.

Imputing Interest on Non-Interest-Bearing Notes

Clearly there is no such thing as an interest-free debt, regardless of whether the interest rate is explicitly stated. The Accounting Principles Board has declared that when a long-term note does not explicitly state an interest rate (or if the interest rate is unreasonably low), a rate based on the normal interest cost of the company in question should be assigned, or imputed.[1] The next example applies this principle.

Example: Imputing Interest on Noninterest-Bearing Notes On January 1, 19x8, Gato purchases merchandise from Haines by making an $8,000 noninterest-bearing note due in two years. Gato can borrow money from the bank at 9 percent interest. Gato pays the note in full after two years. Prepare journal entries to record these transactions.

Note that the $8,000 note represents partly a payment for merchandise and partly a payment of interest for two years. In recording the purchase and sale, it is necessary to use Table A-3 to determine the present value of the note. The calculation follows.

future value	×	present value factor (9%, 2 years)	=	present value
$8,000	×	0.842	=	$6,736

1. Accounting Principles Board, *Opinion No. 21,* "Interest on Receivables and Payables" (New York: American Institute of Certified Public Accountants, 1971), par. 13.

The imputed interest cost is $1,264 ($8,000 − $6,736). The entries necessary to record the purchase in the Gato records and the sale in the Haines records are shown below.

Gato Journal

Purchases	6,736	
Prepaid Interest	1,264	
Notes Payable		8,000

Haines Journal

Notes Receivable	8,000	
Discount on Notes Receivable		1,264
Sales		6,736

On December 31, 19x8, the adjustments to recognize the interest expenses and interest earned will be:

Gato Journal

Interest Expense	606.24	
Prepaid Interest		606.24

Haines Journal

Discount on Notes Receivable	606.24	
Interest Earned		606.24

The interest is calculated by multiplying the original purchase by the interest for one year ($6,736 × .09 = $606.24). When payment is made on December 31, 19x9, the following entries will be made in the respective journals:

Gato Journal

Interest Expense	657.76	
Notes Payable	8,000.00	
Prepaid Interest		657.76
Cash		8,000.00

Haines Journal

Discount on Notes Receivable	657.76	
Cash	8,000.00	
Interest Earned		657.76
Notes Receivable		8,000.00

The interest entries represent the remaining interest to be expensed or realized ($1,264 − $606.24 = $657.76). This amount approximates (because of rounding errors in the table) the interest for one year on the purchases plus last year's interest (($6,736 + $606.24) × .09 = $660.80).

Valuing an Asset

An asset is recorded because it will provide future benefits to the company that owns it. This future benefit is the basis for the definition of an asset. Usually, the purchase price of the asset represents the present value of these future benefits. It is possible to evaluate a proposed purchase price of an asset by comparing that price with the present value of the asset to the company.

Example: Valuing an Asset Sam Hurst is thinking of buying a new labor-saving machine that will reduce his annual labor cost by $700 per year. The machine will last eight years. The interest rate that Hurst assumes for making managerial decisions is 10 percent. What is the maximum amount (present value) that Hurst should pay for the machine?

The present value of the machine to Hurst is equal to the present value of an ordinary annuity of $700 per year for eight years at compound interest of 10 percent. From Table A-4, we compute the value as follows:

periodic savings × factor = present value
$700 × 5.335 = $3,734.50

Hurst should not pay more than $3,734.50 for the new machine.

Valuing a Bond

Bonds are of interest here because their value is based on the present value of a series of fixed interest payments and the present value of a single payment at maturity. To determine the present value of a bond, therefore, use Tables A-3 and A-4. The amount of interest that a bond pays is fixed over its life. During its life, however, the market rate of interest varies from day to day. Thus the amount that investors are willing to pay for the bond changes as well.

Example: Valuing a Bond Assume that a particular bond has a face value of $10,000 and pays a fixed amount of interest of $450 (9 percent annual rate) every six months. The bond is due in five years. If the market rate of interest today is 8 percent, how much is the present value of the bond?

Because the compounding period is more than once a year, it is necessary to convert the annual rate to 4 percent (8% ÷ two six-month periods per year) and to use ten periods (five years × two six-month periods per year). Using this information, we compute the present value of the bond:

Present value of 10 periodic payments (from Table A-4): $450 × 8.111	=	$ 3,649.95
Present value of a single payment (from Table A-3): $10,000 × 0.676	=	6,760.00
Present value of $10,000 bond	=	$10,409.95

Recording Lease Obligations

A lease is a periodic payment for the right to use an asset or assets. Most leases, known as operating leases, are recorded in a manner similar to the way in which rent expense payments are recorded. There are certain long-term leases, however, that are, in effect, installment purchases of assets. The Financial Accounting Standards Board calls this type of lease a capital lease and says that when such a lease exists, an asset and a corresponding liability should be recorded at the present value of the lease payments. Each lease payment then consists partly of a repayment of debt and partly of the interest payment on the debt.[2]

Example: Recording Lease Obligations Isaacs Company enters into a long-term lease for a machine used in its manufacturing operations. The lease terms call for an annual payment of $4,000 for six years, which approximates the useful life of the machine. At the end of the lease period, the title to the machine passes to Isaacs. This lease is clearly a capital lease and should be recorded according to FASB *Statement No. 13*. The present value of the lease payments may be computed as follows, if Isaacs' usual interest cost is 10 percent:

periodic payment	×	factor (Table A-4) (10%, 6 years)	=	present value
$4,000	×	4.355	=	$17,420

The entry to record the lease contract is:

Leased Asset, Equipment	17,420	
Lease Obligations		17,420

2. *Statement of Financial Accounting Standards No. 13*, "Accounting for Losses" (Stamford, Conn.: Financial Accounting Standards Board, 1976), par. 13.

Each year, Isaacs must record depreciation on the leased asset. If we assume a six-year life and no salvage value, the entry will be:

Depreciation Expense	2,903.33	
Accumulated Depreciation, Leased Equipment		2,903.33

The lease payments are recorded as follows:

Interest Expense (col. 3 below)	xxx	
Lease Obligations (col. 4 below)	xxx	
Cash		4,000

The amount of the interest expense for each year would be computed by multiplying the interest rate (10 percent) by the amount of the remaining lease obligation. The table below shows these calculations.

(1) Year	(2) Lease Payment	(3) Interest (10%) on Unpaid Obligation (col. 5 × 10%)	(4) Reduction of Lease Obligation (col. 2 − col. 3)	(5) Balance Lease Obligation
Beginning				$17,420.00
1	$ 4,000	$1,742.00	$ 2,258.00	15,162.00
2	4,000	1,516.20	2,483.80	12,678.20
3	4,000	1,267.82	2,732.18	9,946.02
4	4,000	994.60	3,005.40	6,940.62
5	4,000	694.06	3,305.94	3,634.68
6	4,000	365.32*	3,634.68	—
	$24,000	$6,580.00	$17,420.00	

*Last year's interest equals lease payment minus remaining balance of lease obligation ($365.32 = $4,000.00 − $3,634.68) and does not exactly equal $363.46 ($3,634.68 × .10) because of cumulative rounding errors.

Other Accounting Applications

There are many other applications of present value to accounting. A few of them are the recording of pension obligations; the determination of premium and discount on debt; accounting for depreciation of plant, property, and equipment; analysis of the purchase price of a business; evaluation of capital expenditure decisions; and generally any problem where time is a factor.

Exercises

Tables B-1 to B-4 in Appendix B may be used to solve these exercises.

Exercise A-1 Future Value Calculations

Naber receives a one-year note that carries a 12 percent annual interest rate on $1,500 for the sale of a used car.

Compute the maturity value under each of the following assumptions: (1) the interest is simple interest, (2) the interest is compounded semiannually, (3) the interest is compounded quarterly, and (4) the interest is compounded monthly.

Exercise A-2 Future Value Calculations

Compute the future value of (1) a single payment of $10,000 at 7 percent for ten years, (2) ten annual payments of $1,000 at 7 percent, (3) a single payment of $3,000 at 9 percent for seven years, and (4) seven annual payments of $3,000 at 9 percent.

Exercise A-3 Present Value Calculations

Compute the present value of (1) a single payment of $12,000 at 6 percent for twelve years, (2) twelve annual payments of $1,000 at 6 percent, (3) a single payment of $2,500 at 9 percent for five years, and (4) five annual payments of $2,500 at 9 percent.

Exercise A-4 Future Value Calculations

If $20,000 is invested today, compute the amount that would accumulate at the end of seven years when the interest is (1) 8 percent annual interest compounded annually, (2) 8 percent annual interest compounded semiannually, and (3) 8 percent annual interest compounded quarterly.

Exercise A-5 Future Value Calculations

Calculate the accumulation of periodic payments of $500 for four years, assuming (1) 10 percent annual interest compounded annually, (2) 10 percent annual interest compounded semiannually, (3) 4 percent annual interest compounded annually, and (4) 16 percent annual interest compounded quarterly.

Exercise A-6 Future Value Applications

a. Two parents have $10,000 to invest for their child's college tuition, which they estimate will cost $20,000 when the child enters college twelve years from now.

Calculate the approximate rate of annual interest that the investment must earn to reach the $20,000 goal in twelve years. (Hint: Make a calculation; then use Table B-1.)

b. Bill Roister is saving to purchase a summer home that will cost about $32,000. He has $20,000 now, on which he can earn 7 percent annual interest.

Calculate the approximate length of time he will have to wait to purchase the summer home. (Hint: Make a calculation; then use Table B-1.)

Exercise A-7 Working Backwards from a Future Value

May Marquez has a debt of $45,000 due in four years. She wants to save money to pay it off by making annual deposits in an investment account that earns 8 percent annual interest.

Calculate the amount she must deposit each year to reach her goal. (Hint: Use Table B-2; then make a calculation.)

Exercise A-8 Present Value of a Lump-Sum Contract

A contract calls for a lump-sum payment of $30,000. Compute the present value of the contract, assuming that (1) the payment is due in five years, and the current interest rate is 9 percent; (2) the payment is due in ten years, and the current interest rate is 9 percent; (3) the payment is due in five years, and the current interest rate is 5 percent; and (4) the payment is due in ten years, and the current interest rate is 5 percent.

Exercise A-9 Present Value of an Annuity Contract

A contract calls for annual payments of $600. Compute the present value of the contract, assuming that (1) the number of payments is seven, and the current interest rate is 6 percent; (2) the number of payments is fourteen, and the current interest rate is 6 percent; (3) the number of payments is seven, and the current interest rate is 8 percent; and (4) the number of payments is fourteen, and the current interest rate is 8 percent.

Exercise A-10 Noninterest-Bearing Note

On January 1, 19x8, Olson purchases a machine from Carter by signing a two-year, noninterest-bearing $16,000 note. Olson currently pays 12 percent interest to borrow money at the bank.

Prepare journal entries in Olson's and Carter's records to (1) record the purchase and the note, (2) adjust the accounts after one year, and (3) record payment of the note after two years (on December 31, 19x9).

Exercise A-11 Valuing an Asset for the Purpose of Making a Purchasing Decision

Kubo owns a service station and has the opportunity to purchase a car wash machine for $15,000. After carefully studying projected costs and revenues, Kubo estimates that the car wash will produce a net cash flow of $2,600 annually and will last for eight years. Kubo feels that an interest rate of 14 percent is adequate for his business.

Calculate the present value of the machine to Kubo. Does the purchase appear to be a correct business decision?

Exercise A-12 Determining an Advance Payment

Ellen Saber is contemplating paying five years' rent in advance. Her annual rent is $4,800. Calculate the single sum that would have to be paid now for the advance rent, if we assume compound interest of 8 percent.

Exercise A-13 Valuing Bonds

Pat Taber is contemplating an investment in two bonds: (a) a $10,000 bond that pays semiannual interest of $330 and is due in fifteen years, and (b) a $10,000 bond that pays semiannual interest of $225 and is due in twenty years. Assume that the market rate of interest for each bond is 8 percent.

Calculate the amount that Taber will have to pay to purchase the bonds. (Calculate the present value of each bond and sum.)

Exercise A-14 Recording Lease Obligations

Ted Usry has leased a new building to house manufacturing operations. The terms of the lease are $22,000 per year for forty years, which is the approximate useful life of the building. Usry's company can obtain a long-term loan at 9 percent interest.

1. Calculate the present value of the lease.
2. Prepare the journal entry to record the lease agreement.
3. Prepare the entry to record depreciation of the building for the first year (assume straight-line method and no salvage value).
4. Prepare the entry to record the lease payment for the first two years.

Appendix B

Compound Interest and Present Value Tables

Table B-1 provides the multipliers necessary to compute the future value of a *single* cash deposit made at the *beginning* of year 1. Three factors must be known before the future value can be computed: (1) time period in years, (2) stated annual rate of interest to be earned, and (3) dollar amount invested or deposited.

Example Determine the future value of $5,000 deposited now that will earn 9 percent interest compounded annually for five years. From Table B-1, the necessary multiplier for five years at 9 percent is 1.539, and the answer is:

$$\$5{,}000(1.539) = \underline{\underline{\$7{,}695}}$$

Situations requiring the use of Table B-2 are similar to those requiring Table B-1 except that Table B-2 is used to compute the future value of a *series* of *equal* annual deposits.

Example What will be the future value at the end of thirty years if $1,000 is deposited each year on January 1, assuming 12 percent interest compounded annually? The required multiplier from Table B-2 is 241.3, and the answer is:

$$\$1{,}000(241.3) = \underline{\underline{\$241{,}300}}$$

Table B-1 Future Value of $1 After a Given Number of Time Periods

Periods	1%	2%	3%	4%	5%	6%	7%	8%	9%	10%	12%	14%	15%
1	1.010	1.020	1.030	1.040	1.050	1.060	1.070	1.080	1.090	1.100	1.120	1.140	1.150
2	1.020	1.040	1.061	1.082	1.103	1.124	1.145	1.166	1.188	1.210	1.254	1.300	1.323
3	1.030	1.061	1.093	1.125	1.158	1.191	1.225	1.260	1.295	1.331	1.405	1.482	1.521
4	1.041	1.082	1.126	1.170	1.216	1.262	1.311	1.360	1.412	1.464	1.574	1.689	1.749
5	1.051	1.104	1.159	1.217	1.276	1.338	1.403	1.469	1.539	1.611	1.762	1.925	2.011
6	1.062	1.126	1.194	1.265	1.340	1.419	1.501	1.587	1.677	1.772	1.974	2.195	2.313
7	1.072	1.149	1.230	1.316	1.407	1.504	1.606	1.714	1.828	1.949	2.211	2.502	2.660
8	1.083	1.172	1.267	1.369	1.477	1.594	1.718	1.851	1.993	2.144	2.476	2.853	3.059
9	1.094	1.195	1.305	1.423	1.551	1.689	1.838	1.999	2.172	2.358	2.773	3.252	3.518
10	1.105	1.219	1.344	1.480	1.629	1.791	1.967	2.159	2.367	2.594	3.106	3.707	4.046
11	1.116	1.243	1.384	1.539	1.710	1.898	2.105	2.332	2.580	2.853	3.479	4.226	4.652
12	1.127	1.268	1.426	1.601	1.796	2.012	2.252	2.518	2.813	3.138	3.896	4.818	5.350
13	1.138	1.294	1.469	1.665	1.886	2.133	2.410	2.720	3.066	3.452	4.363	5.492	6.153
14	1.149	1.319	1.513	1.732	1.980	2.261	2.579	2.937	3.342	3.798	4.887	6.261	7.076
15	1.161	1.346	1.558	1.801	2.079	2.397	2.759	3.172	3.642	4.177	5.474	7.138	8.137
16	1.173	1.373	1.605	1.873	2.183	2.540	2.952	3.426	3.970	4.595	6.130	8.137	9.358
17	1.184	1.400	1.653	1.948	2.292	2.693	3.159	3.700	4.328	5.054	6.866	9.276	10.76
18	1.196	1.428	1.702	2.026	2.407	2.854	3.380	3.996	4.717	5.560	7.690	10.58	12.38
19	1.208	1.457	1.754	2.107	2.527	3.026	3.617	4.316	5.142	6.116	8.613	12.06	14.23
20	1.220	1.486	1.806	2.191	2.653	3.207	3.870	4.661	5.604	6.728	9.646	13.74	16.37
21	1.232	1.516	1.860	2.279	2.786	3.400	4.141	5.034	6.109	7.400	10.80	15.67	18.82
22	1.245	1.546	1.916	2.370	2.925	3.604	4.430	5.437	6.659	8.140	12.10	17.86	21.64
23	1.257	1.577	1.974	2.465	3.072	3.820	4.741	5.871	7.258	8.954	13.55	20.36	24.89
24	1.270	1.608	2.033	2.563	3.225	4.049	5.072	6.341	7.911	9.850	15.18	23.21	28.63
25	1.282	1.641	2.094	2.666	3.386	4.292	5.427	6.848	8.623	10.83	17.00	26.46	32.92
26	1.295	1.673	2.157	2.772	3.556	4.549	5.807	7.396	9.399	11.92	19.04	30.17	37.86
27	1.308	1.707	2.221	2.883	3.733	4.822	6.214	7.988	10.25	13.11	21.32	34.39	43.54
28	1.321	1.741	2.288	2.999	3.920	5.112	6.649	8.627	11.17	14.42	23.88	39.20	50.07
29	1.335	1.776	2.357	3.119	4.116	5.418	7.114	9.317	12.17	15.86	26.75	44.69	57.58
30	1.348	1.811	2.427	3.243	4.322	5.743	7.612	10.06	13.27	17.45	29.96	50.95	66.21
40	1.489	2.208	3.262	4.801	7.040	10.29	14.97	21.72	31.41	45.26	93.05	188.9	267.9
50	1.645	2.692	4.384	7.107	11.47	18.42	29.46	46.90	74.36	117.4	289.0	700.2	1,084

Source: All tables in Appendix B are from Henry R. Anderson and Mitchell H. Raiborn, *Basic Cost Accounting Concepts* (Boston: Houghton Mifflin, 1977), pp. 552–557. Reprinted with permission.

Periods	1%	2%	3%	4%	5%	6%	7%	8%	9%	10%	12%	14%	15%
1	1.000	1.000	1.000	1.000	1.000	1.000	1.000	1.000	1.000	1.000	1.000	1.000	1.000
2	2.010	2.020	2.030	2.040	2.050	2.060	2.070	2.080	2.090	2.100	2.120	2.140	2.150
3	3.030	3.060	3.091	3.122	3.153	3.184	3.215	3.246	3.278	3.310	3.374	3.440	3.473
4	4.060	4.122	4.184	4.246	4.310	4.375	4.440	4.506	4.573	4.641	4.779	4.921	4.993
5	5.101	5.204	5.309	5.416	5.526	5.637	5.751	5.867	5.985	6.105	6.353	6.610	6.742
6	6.152	6.308	6.468	6.633	6.802	6.975	7.153	7.336	7.523	7.716	8.115	8.536	8.754
7	7.214	7.434	7.662	7.898	8.142	8.394	8.654	8.923	9.200	9.487	10.09	10.73	11.07
8	8.286	8.583	8.892	9.214	9.549	9.897	10.26	10.64	11.03	11.44	12.30	13.23	13.73
9	9.369	9.755	10.16	10.58	11.03	11.49	11.98	12.49	13.02	13.58	14.78	16.09	16.79
10	10.46	10.95	11.46	12.01	12.58	13.18	13.82	14.49	15.19	15.94	17.55	19.34	20.30
11	11.57	12.17	12.81	13.49	14.21	14.97	15.78	16.65	17.56	18.53	20.65	23.04	24.35
12	12.68	13.41	14.19	15.03	15.92	16.87	17.89	18.98	20.14	21.38	24.13	27.27	29.00
13	13.81	14.68	15.62	16.63	17.71	18.88	20.14	21.50	22.95	24.52	28.03	32.09	34.35
14	14.95	15.97	17.09	18.29	19.60	21.02	22.55	24.21	26.02	27.98	32.39	37.58	40.50
15	16.10	17.29	18.60	20.02	21.58	23.28	25.13	27.15	29.36	31.77	37.28	43.84	47.58
16	17.26	18.64	20.16	21.82	23.66	25.67	27.89	30.32	33.00	35.95	42.75	50.98	55.72
17	18.43	20.01	21.76	23.70	25.84	28.21	30.84	33.75	36.97	40.54	48.88	59.12	65.08
18	19.61	21.41	23.41	25.65	28.13	30.91	34.00	37.45	41.30	45.60	55.75	68.39	75.84
19	20.81	22.84	25.12	27.67	30.54	33.76	37.38	41.45	46.02	51.16	63.44	78.97	88.21
20	22.02	24.30	26.87	29.78	33.07	36.79	41.00	45.76	51.16	57.28	72.05	91.02	102.4
21	23.24	25.78	28.68	31.97	35.72	39.99	44.87	50.42	56.76	64.00	81.70	104.8	118.8
22	24.47	27.30	30.54	34.25	38.51	43.39	49.01	55.46	62.87	71.40	92.50	120.4	137.6
23	25.72	28.85	32.45	36.62	41.43	47.00	53.44	60.89	69.53	79.54	104.6	138.3	159.3
24	26.97	30.42	34.43	39.08	44.50	50.82	58.18	66.76	76.79	88.50	118.2	158.7	184.2
25	28.24	32.03	36.46	41.65	47.73	54.86	63.25	73.11	84.70	98.35	133.3	181.9	212.8
26	29.53	33.67	38.55	44.31	51.11	59.16	68.68	79.95	93.32	109.2	150.3	208.3	245.7
27	30.82	35.34	40.71	47.08	54.67	63.71	74.48	87.35	102.7	121.1	169.4	238.5	283.6
28	32.13	37.05	42.93	49.97	58.40	68.53	80.70	95.34	113.0	134.2	190.7	272.9	327.1
29	33.45	38.79	45.22	52.97	62.32	73.64	87.35	104.0	124.1	148.6	214.6	312.1	377.2
30	34.78	40.57	47.58	56.08	66.44	79.06	94.46	113.3	136.3	164.5	241.3	356.8	434.7
40	48.89	60.40	75.40	95.03	120.8	154.8	199.6	259.1	337.9	442.6	767.1	1,342	1,779
50	64.46	84.58	112.8	152.7	209.3	290.3	406.5	573.8	815.1	1,164	2,400	4,995	7,218

Table B-2
Future Value of $1 Paid in Each Period For a Given Number of Time Periods

Periods	1%	2%	3%	4%	5%	6%	7%	8%	9%	10%	12%
1	0.990	0.980	0.971	0.962	0.952	0.943	0.935	0.926	0.917	0.909	0.893
2	0.980	0.961	0.943	0.925	0.907	0.890	0.873	0.857	0.842	0.826	0.797
3	0.971	0.942	0.915	0.889	0.864	0.840	0.816	0.794	0.772	0.751	0.712
4	0.961	0.924	0.888	0.855	0.823	0.792	0.763	0.735	0.708	0.683	0.636
5	0.951	0.906	0.883	0.822	0.784	0.747	0.713	0.681	0.650	0.621	0.567
6	0.942	0.888	0.837	0.790	0.746	0.705	0.666	0.630	0.596	0.564	0.507
7	0.933	0.871	0.813	0.760	0.711	0.665	0.623	0.583	0.547	0.513	0.452
8	0.923	0.853	0.789	0.731	0.677	0.627	0.582	0.540	0.502	0.467	0.404
9	0.914	0.837	0.766	0.703	0.645	0.592	0.544	0.500	0.460	0.424	0.361
10	0.905	0.820	0.744	0.676	0.614	0.558	0.508	0.463	0.422	0.386	0.322
11	0.896	0.804	0.722	0.650	0.585	0.527	0.475	0.429	0.388	0.350	0.287
12	0.887	0.788	0.701	0.625	0.557	0.497	0.444	0.397	0.356	0.319	0.257
13	0.879	0.773	0.681	0.601	0.530	0.469	0.415	0.368	0.326	0.290	0.229
14	0.870	0.758	0.661	0.577	0.505	0.442	0.388	0.340	0.299	0.263	0.205
15	0.861	0.743	0.642	0.555	0.481	0.417	0.362	0.315	0.275	0.239	0.183
16	0.853	0.728	0.623	0.534	0.458	0.394	0.339	0.292	0.252	0.218	0.163
17	0.844	0.714	0.605	0.513	0.436	0.371	0.317	0.270	0.231	0.198	0.146
18	0.836	0.700	0.587	0.494	0.416	0.350	0.296	0.250	0.212	0.180	0.130
19	0.828	0.686	0.570	0.475	0.396	0.331	0.277	0.232	0.194	0.164	0.116
20	0.820	0.673	0.554	0.456	0.377	0.312	0.258	0.215	0.178	0.149	0.104
21	0.811	0.660	0.538	0.439	0.359	0.294	0.242	0.199	0.164	0.135	0.093
22	0.803	0.647	0.522	0.422	0.342	0.278	0.226	0.184	0.150	0.123	0.083
23	0.795	0.634	0.507	0.406	0.326	0.262	0.211	0.170	0.138	0.112	0.074
24	0.788	0.622	0.492	0.390	0.310	0.247	0.197	0.158	0.126	0.102	0.066
25	0.780	0.610	0.478	0.375	0.295	0.233	0.184	0.146	0.116	0.092	0.059
26	0.772	0.598	0.464	0.361	0.281	0.220	0.172	0.135	0.106	0.084	0.053
27	0.764	0.586	0.450	0.347	0.268	0.207	0.161	0.125	0.098	0.076	0.047
28	0.757	0.574	0.437	0.333	0.255	0.196	0.150	0.116	0.090	0.069	0.042
29	0.749	0.563	0.424	0.321	0.243	0.185	0.141	0.107	0.082	0.063	0.037
30	0.742	0.552	0.412	0.308	0.231	0.174	0.131	0.099	0.075	0.057	0.033
40	0.672	0.453	0.307	0.208	0.142	0.097	0.067	0.046	0.032	0.022	0.011
50	0.608	0.372	0.228	0.141	0.087	0.054	0.034	0.021	0.013	0.009	0.003

Table B-3
Present Value of $1 to Be Received at the End of a Given Number of Time Periods

14%	15%	16%	18%	20%	25%	30%	35%	40%	45%	50%	Periods
0.877	0.870	0.862	0.847	0.833	0.800	0.769	0.741	0.714	0.690	0.667	1
0.769	0.756	0.743	0.718	0.694	0.640	0.592	0.549	0.510	0.476	0.444	2
0.675	0.658	0.641	0.609	0.579	0.512	0.455	0.406	0.364	0.328	0.296	3
0.592	0.572	0.552	0.516	0.482	0.410	0.350	0.301	0.260	0.226	0.198	4
0.519	0.497	0.476	0.437	0.402	0.328	0.269	0.223	0.186	0.156	0.132	5
0.456	0.432	0.410	0.370	0.335	0.262	0.207	0.165	0.133	0.108	0.088	6
0.400	0.376	0.354	0.314	0.279	0.210	0.159	0.122	0.095	0.074	0.059	7
0.351	0.327	0.305	0.266	0.233	0.168	0.123	0.091	0.068	0.051	0.039	8
0.308	0.284	0.263	0.225	0.194	0.134	0.094	0.067	0.048	0.035	0.026	9
0.270	0.247	0.227	0.191	0.162	0.107	0.073	0.050	0.035	0.024	0.017	10
0.237	0.215	0.195	0.162	0.135	0.086	0.056	0.037	0.025	0.017	0.012	11
0.208	0.187	0.168	0.137	0.112	0.069	0.043	0.027	0.018	0.012	0.008	12
0.182	0.163	0.145	0.116	0.093	0.055	0.033	0.020	0.013	0.008	0.005	13
0.160	0.141	0.125	0.099	0.078	0.044	0.025	0.015	0.009	0.006	0.003	14
0.140	0.123	0.108	0.084	0.065	0.035	0.020	0.011	0.006	0.004	0.002	15
0.123	0.107	0.093	0.071	0.054	0.028	0.015	0.008	0.005	0.003	0.002	16
0.108	0.093	0.080	0.060	0.045	0.023	0.012	0.006	0.003	0.002	0.001	17
0.095	0.081	0.069	0.051	0.038	0.018	0.009	0.005	0.002	0.001	0.001	18
0.083	0.070	0.060	0.043	0.031	0.014	0.007	0.003	0.002	0.001		19
0.073	0.061	0.051	0.037	0.026	0.012	0.005	0.002	0.001	0.001		20
0.064	0.053	0.044	0.031	0.022	0.009	0.004	0.002	0.001			21
0.056	0.046	0.038	0.026	0.018	0.007	0.003	0.001	0.001			22
0.049	0.040	0.033	0.022	0.015	0.006	0.002	0.001				23
0.043	0.035	0.028	0.019	0.013	0.005	0.002	0.001				24
0.038	0.030	0.024	0.016	0.010	0.004	0.001	0.001				25
0.033	0.026	0.021	0.014	0.009	0.003	0.001					26
0.029	0.023	0.018	0.011	0.007	0.002	0.001					27
0.026	0.020	0.016	0.010	0.006	0.002	0.001					28
0.022	0.017	0.014	0.008	0.005	0.002						29
0.020	0.015	0.012	0.007	0.004	0.001						30
0.005	0.004	0.003	0.001	0.001							40
0.001	0.001	0.001									50

Table B-3 is used to compute the value today of a *single* amount of cash to be received sometime in the future. To use Table B-3, you must first know: (1) time period in years until funds will be received, (2) annual rate of interest, and (3) dollar amount to be received at end of time period.

Example What is the present value of $30,000 to be received twenty-five years from now, assuming a 14 percent interest rate? From Table B-3, the required multiplier is 0.038, and the answer is:

$$\$30{,}000(0.038) = \underline{\underline{\$1{,}140}}$$

Periods	1%	2%	3%	4%	5%	6%	7%	8%	9%	10%	12%
1	0.990	0.980	0.971	0.962	0.952	0.943	0.935	0.926	0.917	0.909	0.893
2	1.970	1.942	1.913	1.886	1.859	1.833	1.808	1.783	1.759	1.736	1.690
3	2.941	2.884	2.829	2.775	2.723	2.673	2.624	2.577	2.531	2.487	2.402
4	3.902	3.808	3.717	3.630	3.546	3.465	3.387	3.312	3.240	3.170	3.037
5	4.853	4.713	4.580	4.452	4.329	4.212	4.100	3.993	3.890	3.791	3.605
6	5.795	5.601	5.417	5.242	5.076	4.917	4.767	4.623	4.486	4.355	4.111
7	6.728	6.472	6.230	6.002	5.786	5.582	5.389	5.206	5.033	4.868	4.564
8	7.652	7.325	7.020	6.733	6.463	6.210	5.971	5.747	5.535	5.335	4.968
9	8.566	8.162	7.786	7.435	7.108	6.802	6.515	6.247	5.995	5.759	5.328
10	9.471	8.983	8.530	8.111	7.722	7.360	7.024	6.710	6.418	6.145	5.650
11	10.368	9.787	9.253	8.760	8.306	7.887	7.499	7.139	6.805	6.495	5.938
12	11.255	10.575	9.954	9.385	8.863	8.384	7.943	7.536	7.161	6.814	6.194
13	12.134	11.348	10.635	9.986	9.394	8.853	8.358	7.904	7.487	7.103	6.424
14	13.004	12.106	11.296	10.563	9.899	9.295	8.745	8.244	7.786	7.367	6.628
15	13.865	12.849	11.938	11.118	10.380	9.712	9.108	8.559	8.061	7.606	6.811
16	14.718	13.578	12.561	11.652	10.838	10.106	9.447	8.851	8.313	7.824	6.974
17	15.562	14.292	13.166	12.166	11.274	10.477	9.763	9.122	8.544	8.022	7.120
18	16.398	14.992	13.754	12.659	11.690	10.828	10.059	9.372	8.756	8.201	7.250
19	17.226	15.678	14.324	13.134	12.085	11.158	10.336	9.604	8.950	8.365	7.366
20	18.046	16.351	14.878	13.590	12.462	11.470	10.594	9.818	9.129	8.514	7.469
21	18.857	17.011	15.415	14.029	12.821	11.764	10.836	10.017	9.292	8.649	7.562
22	19.660	17.658	15.937	14.451	13.163	12.042	11.061	10.201	9.442	8.772	7.645
23	20.456	18.292	16.444	14.857	13.489	12.303	11.272	10.371	9.580	8.883	7.718
24	21.243	18.914	16.936	15.247	13.799	12.550	11.469	10.529	9.707	8.985	7.784
25	22.023	19.523	17.413	15.622	14.094	12.783	11.654	10.675	9.823	9.077	7.843
26	22.795	20.121	17.877	15.983	14.375	13.003	11.826	10.810	9.929	9.161	7.896
27	23.560	20.707	18.327	16.330	14.643	13.211	11.987	10.935	10.027	9.237	7.943
28	24.316	21.281	18.764	16.663	14.898	13.406	12.137	11.051	10.116	9.307	7.984
29	25.066	21.844	19.189	16.984	15.141	13.591	12.278	11.158	10.198	9.370	8.022
30	25.808	22.396	19.600	17.292	15.373	13.765	12.409	11.258	10.274	9.427	8.055
40	32.835	27.355	23.115	19.793	17.159	15.046	13.332	11.925	10.757	9.779	8.244
50	39.196	31.424	25.730	21.482	18.256	15.762	13.801	12.234	10.962	9.915	8.305

Table B-4 Present Value of $1 Received Each Period for a Given Number of Time Periods

Table B-4 is used to compute the present value of a *series* of *equal* annual cash flows.

Example Arthur Howard won a contest on January 1, 1980, in which the prize was $30,000, payable in fifteen annual installments of $2,000 every December 31, beginning in 1980. Assuming a 9 percent interest rate, what is the present value of Mr. Howard's prize on January 1, 1980? From Table B-4, the required multiplier is 8.061, and the answer is:

$$\$2{,}000(8.061) = \underline{\underline{\$16{,}122}}$$

Table B-4 applies to *ordinary annuities,* in which the first cash flow occurs one time period beyond the date for which present value is to be computed. An *annuity due* is a series of equal cash flows for N time periods, but the first payment

14%	15%	16%	18%	20%	25%	30%	35%	40%	45%	50%	Periods
0.877	0.870	0.862	0.847	0.833	0.800	0.769	0.741	0.714	0.690	0.667	1
1.647	1.626	1.605	1.566	1.528	1.440	1.361	1.289	1.224	1.165	1.111	2
2.322	2.283	2.246	2.174	2.106	1.952	1.816	1.696	1.589	1.493	1.407	3
2.914	2.855	2.798	2.690	2.589	2.362	2.166	1.997	1.849	1.720	1.605	4
3.433	3.352	3.274	3.127	2.991	2.689	2.436	2.220	2.035	1.876	1.737	5
3.889	3.784	3.685	3.498	3.326	2.951	2.643	2.385	2.168	1.983	1.824	6
4.288	4.160	4.039	3.812	3.605	3.161	2.802	2.508	2.263	2.057	1.883	7
4.639	4.487	4.344	4.078	3.837	3.329	2.925	2.598	2.331	2.109	1.922	8
4.946	4.772	4.607	4.303	4.031	3.463	3.019	2.665	2.379	2.144	1.948	9
5.216	5.019	4.833	4.494	4.192	3.571	3.092	2.715	2.414	2.168	1.965	10
5.453	5.234	5.029	4.656	4.327	3.656	3.147	2.752	2.438	2.185	1.977	11
5.660	5.421	5.197	4.793	4.439	3.725	3.190	2.779	2.456	2.197	1.985	12
5.842	5.583	5.342	4.910	4.533	3.780	3.223	2.799	2.469	2.204	1.990	13
6.002	5.724	5.468	5.008	4.611	3.824	3.249	2.814	2.478	2.210	1.993	14
6.142	5.847	5.575	5.092	4.675	3.859	3.268	2.825	2.484	2.214	1.995	15
6.265	5.954	5.669	5.162	4.730	3.887	3.283	2.834	2.489	2.216	1.997	16
6.373	6.047	5.749	5.222	4.775	3.910	3.295	2.840	2.492	2.218	1.998	17
6.467	6.128	5.818	5.273	4.812	3.928	3.304	2.844	2.494	2.219	1.999	18
6.550	6.198	5.877	5.316	4.844	3.942	3.311	2.848	2.496	2.220	1.999	19
6.623	6.259	5.929	5.353	4.870	3.954	3.316	2.850	2.497	2.221	1.999	20
6.687	6.312	5.973	5.384	4.891	3.963	3.320	2.852	2.498	2.221	2.000	21
6.743	6.359	6.011	5.410	4.909	3.970	3.323	2.853	2.498	2.222	2.000	22
6.792	6.399	6.044	5.432	4.925	3.976	3.325	2.854	2.499	2.222	2.000	23
6.835	6.434	6.073	5.451	4.937	3.981	3.327	2.855	2.499	2.222	2.000	24
6.873	6.464	6.097	5.467	4.948	3.985	3.329	2.856	2.499	2.222	2.000	25
6.906	6.491	6.118	5.480	4.956	3.988	3.330	2.856	2.500	2.222	2.000	26
6.935	6.514	6.136	5.492	4.964	3.990	3.331	2.856	2.500	2.222	2.000	27
6.961	6.534	6.152	5.502	4.970	3.992	3.331	2.857	2.500	2.222	2.000	28
6.983	6.551	6.166	5.510	4.975	3.994	3.332	2.857	2.500	2.222	2.000	29
7.003	6.566	6.177	5.517	4.979	3.995	3.332	2.857	2.500	2.222	2.000	30
7.105	6.642	6.234	5.548	4.997	3.999	3.333	2.857	2.500	2.222	2.000	40
7.133	6.661	6.246	5.554	4.999	4.000	3.333	2.857	2.500	2.222	2.000	50

occurs immediately. The present value of the first payment equals the face value of the cash flow; Table B-4 then is used to measure the present value of $N - 1$ remaining cash flows.

Example Determine the present value on January 1, 1980, of twenty lease payments; each payment of \$10,000 is due on January 1, beginning in 1980. Assume an interest rate of 8 percent:

$$\text{present value} = \text{immediate payment} + \begin{cases}\text{present value of 19} \\ \text{subsequent payments at 8\%}\end{cases}$$

$$= \$10{,}000 + [10{,}000(9.604)]$$

$$= \underline{\underline{\$106{,}040}}$$

Glossary

Note: The number in parentheses after each definition refers to the chapter where the term is first defined.

Absorption costing: an approach to product costing that assigns a representative portion of *all* manufacturing costs to individual products. (24)
Accelerated methods: methods of depreciation that allocate relatively large amounts of the depreciable cost of the asset to earlier years and reduced amounts to later years. (13)
Account: the basic storage unit for data in accounting systems; consists of one for each asset, liability, component of owner's equity, revenue, and expense. (3)
Accountant's report (or auditor's report): a report by an independent public accountant that accompanies the financial statements and contains the accountant's opinion regarding the fairness of presentation of the financial statements. (7)
Account balance: the difference in total dollars between the total debit footing and the total credit footing of an account. (3)
Accounting: an information system that measures, processes, and communicates economic information about an identifiable entity to permit users of the system to make informed judgments and decisions. (1)
Accounting cycle: all steps in the accounting process including analyzing and recording transactions, posting entries, adjusting and closing the accounts, and preparing financial statements; accounting system. (5)
Accounting equation, see Balance sheet equation
Accounting period problem: the difficulty of assigning revenues and expenses to short periods of time such as months or years; related to the periodicity assumption. (4)
Accounting practice: the procedures employed in accounting to measure, process, and communicate information. (1)
Accounting rate of return method: a method used to measure the estimated performance of a capital investment that yields an accounting rate of return computed by dividing the project's average after-tax net income by the average cost of the investment over its estimated life. (28)
Accounting system, see Accounting cycle
Accounting theory: the theoretical framework which underlies the actions or practice of accountants. (1)
Accounts receivable: short-term monetary assets that arise from sales on credit to customers at either the wholesale or the retail level. (10)
Accounts receivable aging method: a method of estimating uncollectible accounts expense based on the assumption that the probability of collecting accounts receivable at the end of the period will depend on the length of time individual accounts are past due. (10)
Accrual accounting: all the techniques developed by accountants to apply the matching rule. (4)
Accrual basis: the reporting of revenues from sales in the period in which they are sold, regardless of when the cash is received, and the reporting of expenses in the period of purchase, regardless of when payment is made. (29)
Accrued expense: an expense that has been incurred but is not recognized in the accounts, necessitating an adjusting entry; unrecorded expense. (4)
Accrued revenue: a revenue for which the service has been performed or the goods have been delivered but that has not been recorded in the accounts; unrecorded revenue. (4)
Accumulated depreciation: a contra-asset account used to accumulate the total past depreciation on a specific long-lived asset. (4)

Addition: an expenditure resulting from an expansion of an existing plant asset. (14)
Adjusted gross income: gross income minus deductions from gross income. (29)
Adjusted trial balance: a trial balance prepared after all adjusting entries have been reflected in the accounts. (4)
Adjusting entry: entry made to apply accrual accounting to transactions that span more than one accounting period. (4)
Aging of accounts receivable: the process of listing each customer in accounts receivable according to the due date of the account. (10)
All financial resources (concept of funds): the concept of funds used in preparation of the statement of changes in financial position when exchange transactions are considered as both a source and a use of working capital. (19)
Allowance for uncollectible accounts: a contra accounts receivable account in which appears the estimated total of the as yet unidentified accounts receivable that will not be collected. (10)
American Institute of Certified Public Accountants (AICPA): the professional association of CPAs. (1)
Amortization: the periodic allocation of the cost of an intangible asset over its useful life. (13)
Appropriated retained earnings: a restriction of retained earnings that indicates that a portion of a company's assets are to be used for purposes other than paying dividends. (17)
Arithmetic/logic unit: the part of the central processor in a computer system that performs the computing and decision-making functions. (8)
Articles of incorporation: a contract between the state and the incorporators forming the corporation. (16)
Asset: an economic resource owned by a business that is expected to benefit future operations. (2)
Asset turnover: a ratio that measures how efficiently assets are used to produce sales. (21)
Auditing: the principal and most distinctive function of a certified public accountant; the process of examining and testing the financial statements of a company in order to render an independent professional opinion as to the fairness of their presentation; also called the attest function. (1)
Auditor's report, see Accountant's report
Authorized stock: the maximum number of shares a corporation may issue without changing its charter with the state. (16)
Average-cost method: an inventory costing method under which each item of goods sold and of inventory is assigned a cost equal to the average cost of all goods purchased. (11)
Average cost of capital: a minimum desired rate of return on capital expenditures computed by finding the average of the cost of debt, cost of preferred stock, cost of capital equity, and cost of retained earnings. (28)
Average days' sales uncollected: a ratio that measures how many days it takes before the average receivable is collected. (21)

Balance sheet: a financial statement that shows the financial position of a business at a particular date. (2)
Balance sheet equation: algebraic expression of financial position; assets = liabilities + owner's equity; also called the accounting equation. (2)
Bank reconciliation: the process of accounting for the differences between the balance appearing on the bank statement and the balance of cash according to the depositor's records. (9)
Bank statement: a monthly statement of the transactions related to a particular bank account. (9)
Base year: the first year to be considered in any set of data. (21)
Batch processing: a type of computer system design in which separate computer jobs such as purchasing, inventory control, payroll, production scheduling, and so forth are processed individually but in a carefully coordinated way. (8)
Beginning inventory: merchandise on hand for sale to customers at the beginning of the accounting period. (6)
Beta: the measure of market risk. (21)
Betterment: an expenditure resulting from an improvement to but not an enlargement of an existing plant asset. (14)
Bond: a security, usually long-term, representing money borrowed by a corporation from the investing public. (18)
Bond certificate: the evidence of a company's debt to the bondholder. (18)
Bond indenture: a supplementary agreement to a bond issue that defines the rights, privileges, and limitations of bondholders. (18)
Bonding: investigating an employee and insuring the company against any theft by that individual. (9)
Bond issue: the total number of bonds that are issued at one time. (18)
Bond sinking fund: a fund established by the segregation of assets over the life of the bond issue to satisfy investors that money will be available to pay the bondholders at maturity. (18)
Bonus: in partnership accounting, an amount that accrues to the original partners when a new partner pays more to the partnership than the interest re-

ceived or that accrues to the new partner when the amount paid to the partnership is less than the interest received. (15)

Bookkeeping: the means by which transactions are recorded and records are kept; a process of accounting. (1)

Book value: total assets of a company less total liabilities; owners' equity. (16)

Break-even point: that point in financial analysis at which total revenue equals total cost incurred and at which a company begins to generate a profit. (26)

Budgetary control: the total process of (1) developing plans for a company's anticipated operations and (2) controlling operations to aid in accomplishing those plans. (27)

Business transaction: an economic event that affects the financial position of a business entity. (2)

Callable bonds: bonds that a corporation has the option of buying back and retiring at a given price, usually above face value, before maturity. (18)

Callable preferred stock: preferred stock that may be redeemed and retired by the corporation at its option. (16)

Capital assets: certain types of assets that qualify for special treatment when gains and losses result from transactions involving the assets. (29)

Capital budgeting: the combined process of identifying a facility need, analyzing alternative courses of action to satisfy that need, preparing the reports for management, selecting the best alternative, and rationing available capital expenditure funds among competing resource needs. (28)

Capital expenditure: an expenditure for the purchase or expansion of plant assets. (14)

Capital expenditure decision: the decision to determine when and how much money to spend on capital facilities for the company. (28)

Capital lease: long-term lease that is in effect an installment purchase of assets; recorded by entering on the books an asset and a corresponding liability at the present value of the lease payments; each lease payment is partly a repayment of debt and partly an interest payment on the debt. (18)

Capital structure: the proportion of a company financed by creditors as opposed to owners. (7)

Carrying value: the unexpired portion of the cost of an asset; sometimes called book value. (13)

Cash basis of accounting: a basis of accounting under which revenues and expenses are accounted for on a cash received and cash paid basis. (4, 14, 29)

Cash disbursements journal, see Cash payments journal

Cash flow forecast: a forecast or budget that shows the firm's projected ending cash balance and the cash position for each month of the year so that periods of high or low cash availability can be anticipated; also called a cash budget. (27)

Cash flow statement: a financial statement that shows a company's sources and uses of cash during an accounting period. (19)

Cash over or short: an account used to record small shortages or overages that result from the handling of cash. (9)

Cash payments journal: a multicolumn special-purpose journal in which disbursements of cash are recorded; also called cash disbursements journal. (8)

Cash receipts journal: a multicolumn special-purpose journal in which transactions involving receipts of cash are recorded. (8)

Central processor: a piece of hardware in which the actual computing in the computer system is done; consists of the control unit, the arithmetic/logic unit, and the storage units. (8)

Certified public accountant (CPA): public accountants who have met stringent licensing requirements. (1)

Chart of accounts: a numbering scheme that assigns a unique number to each account to facilitate finding the account in the ledger. (3, 7)

Check: a negotiable instrument used to pay for goods and services. (9)

Check authorization: a document prepared by the accounting department authorizing the payment of the invoice; supported by a purchase order, invoice, and receiving report. (9)

Check register: a special-purpose journal used in a voucher system to record each expenditure made by check. (9)

Classification problem: the difficulty of assigning all the transactions in which a business engages to the appropriate account or accounts. (3)

Classified financial statements: financial statements divided into useful subcategories. (7)

Clearing entries, see Closing entries

Closely held corporation: a corporation whose stock is owned by a few individuals and whose securities are not publicly traded. (20)

Closing entries: journal entries made at the end of the accounting period that set the stage for the next accounting period by closing the expense and revenue accounts of the balances and transferring the net amount to the owner's capital account or retained earnings; clearing entries. (5)

Common-size statement: a statement in which all components of the statement are shown as a percentage of a total in the statement; results from applying vertical analysis. (21)

Common stock: the stock representing the most basic rights to ownership of a corporation. (16)

Common stock equivalents: convertible securities that, at the time of issuance, have a value that is closely related to their conversion value, that is, the value of the stock into which they could be converted. (17)
Comparability: the qualitative characteristic of accounting information that presents information in such a way that the decision maker can recognize similarities, differences, and trends over time and/or make comparisons with other companies. (2)
Comparative financial statements: financial statements in which data for two or more years are presented in adjacent columnar form. (7)
Compatability principle: a principle of systems design that holds that the design of a system must be in harmony with organizational and human factors of a business. (8)
Complex capital structure: a capital structure with additional securities (convertible stocks and bonds) that can be converted into common stock. (17)
Compound entry: a journal entry that has more than one debit and/or credit entry. (3)
Compound interest: the interest cost for two or more periods, if one assumes that after each period the interest of that period is added to the amount on which interest is computed in future periods. (Appendix A)
Computer: an electronic tool for the rapid collection, organization, and communication of large amounts of information. (1)
Computer data processing: a type of data processing in which recording, posting, and other bookkeeping procedures are done with the aid of a computer. (8)
Computer operator: the person who runs the computer. (8)
Conglomerate: a company that operates in more than one industry; a diversified company. (21)
Conservatism: an accounting convention that means when accountants are faced with major uncertainties as to which alternative accounting procedure to apply, they tend to exercise caution and choose the procedure that is least likely to overstate assets or income. (14)
Consistency: an accounting convention that requires that a particular accounting procedure, once adopted, will not be changed from period to period. (14)
Consolidated financial statements: the combined financial statements of a parent company and its subsidiaries. (20)
Constant dollar accounting: the restatement of historical cost statements for general price level changes with the result that all amounts are stated in dollars of uniform general purchasing power. (14)
Contingent liability: a potential liability that can develop into a real liability if a possible subsequent event occurs. (10)
Continuity problem: the difficulty associated with the indefinite life of business enterprises; related to the going concern assumption. (4)
Contra account: an account whose balance is subtracted from an associated account in the financial statements. (4)
Contributed or paid-in capital: that part of owners' equity representing the amounts of assets invested by stockholders. (7, 16)
Contribution margin: the excess of revenues over all variable costs related to a particular sales volume. (26)
Control: the process of seeing that plans are carried out. (1)
Control (of parent over subsidiary): in connection with long-term investments, the ability of the investing company to determine the operating and financial policies of the investee company. (20)
Controllable costs: those costs that result from a particular manager's actions and decision and over which he or she has full control. (26)
Controllable overhead variance: the difference between actual overhead costs incurred and factory overhead budgeted for the level of production achieved. (27)
Controlling (or control) account: an account in the general ledger that summarizes the total balance of a group of related accounts in a subsidiary ledger. (8, 24)
Control principle: a principle of systems design that holds that an accounting system must provide all the features of internal control needed to safeguard assets and ensure the reliability of data. (8)
Control unit: the part of the central processor in a computer system that directs and coordinates all parts of the computer. (8)
Conversion costs: the combined total of direct labor and factory overhead costs incurred by a production department or other work center. (25)
Convertible bonds: bonds that may be exchanged for other securities of the corporation, usually common stock. (18)
Convertible preferred stock: stock that can be converted into common stock. Bonds may also have this feature. (16)
Copyright: an exclusive right granted by the federal government to the possessor to publish and sell literary, musical, and other artistic materials. (14)
Corporation: a body of persons granted a charter legally recognizing them as a separate entity having its own rights, privileges, and liabilities distinct from those of its members. (1, 16)

Cost: exchange price associated with a business transaction at the point of recognition; original cost; historical cost. (3)

Cost Accounting Standards Board (CASB): an agency of the federal government that establishes cost accounting standards to be used by defense contractors in negotiated contracts. (1)

Cost allocation (assignment): the process of assigning a specific cost or pool of costs to a specific cost objective or cost objectives. (22)

Cost behavior: the manner in which costs respond to changes in activity or volume. (26)

Cost/benefit principle: a principle of systems design that holds that the value or benefits from a system and its information output must be equal to or greater than its cost. (8)

Cost center: any organizational segment or area of activity for which it is desirable to accumulate costs. (22)

Cost flow: the association of costs with their assumed flow within the operations of a company. (11)

Cost method: a method of accounting for long-term investments when the investor has neither significant influence nor control of the investee; the investor records the investment at cost and recognizes dividends as income when they are received. (20)

Cost of debt: the ratio of loan charges to net proceeds of the loan. After-tax considerations and present value of interest charges should be acknowledged in the computation. (28)

Cost of equity capital: the rate of return to the investor that maintains the stock's value in the marketplace. (28)

Cost of goods manufactured: a term used in the statement of cost of goods manufactured that represents the total manufacturing costs attached to units of product completed during an accounting period. (23)

Cost of goods sold: item on income statement that is computed by subtracting the merchandise inventory at the end of the year from the goods available for sale; deducted from revenue to give gross profit. (6)

Cost of preferred stock: the stated dividend rate of the individual stock issue. (28)

Cost of retained earnings: the opportunity cost or dividends forgone by the stockholder. (28)

Cost summary schedule: a process costing schedule in which total manufacturing costs accumulated during the period are distributed to units completed and transferred out of the department or the units in ending Work in Process Inventory. (25)

Cost-volume-profit (C-V-P) analysis: an analysis based on the relationships among operating cost, sales volume and revenue, and target net income; used as a planning device to predict one of the factors when the other two are known. (26)

Coupon bonds: bonds whose owners are not registered with the issuing corporation but that have interest coupons attached. (18)

Credit: the right side of an account. (3)

Crossfooting: horizontal addition and subtraction of rows in adjacent columns. (5)

Cumulative preferred stock: preferred stock on which unpaid dividends accumulate over time and must be satisfied in any given year before a dividend may be paid to common stockholders. (16)

Current assets: cash or other assets that are reasonably expected to be realized in cash or sold during a normal operating cycle of a business or within one year if the operating cycle is shorter than one year. (7)

Current liabilities: obligations due to be paid within the normal operating cycle of the business or within a year, whichever is longer. (7, 12)

Current ratio: a measure of liquidity; current assets divided by current liabilities. (7, 21)

Current value accounting: a method of accounting that would recognize the effects of specific price changes in the financial statements. (14)

Data processing: the means by which the accounting system collects data, organizes them into meaningful forms, and issues the resulting information to users. (8)

Debenture bonds, See Unsecured bonds

Debit: the left side of an account. (3)

Debt to equity ratio: a ratio that measures the relationship of assets provided by creditors to the amount provided by stockholders. (21)

Declining-balance method: an accelerated method of depreciation. (13)

Deductions from gross income: certain personal deductions allowed in computing taxable income. (29)

Deferred revenues: obligations for goods or services that the company must deliver in return for an advance payment from a customer. (12)

Deficit: a debit balance in the Retained Earnings account. (17)

Definitely determinable liability: a liability that is determined by contract or statute and can be measured precisely. (12)

Deflation: a decrease in the general price level. (14)

Depletion: the proportional allocation of the cost of a natural resource to the units removed; the exhaustion of a natural resource through mining, cutting, pumping, or otherwise using up the resource. (13)

Deposits in transit: deposits mailed or taken to the bank but not received by the bank in time to be recorded before preparation of the monthly statement. (9)
Deposit ticket: a document used to make a deposit in a bank. (9)
Depreciable cost: the cost of an asset less its residual value. (13)
Depreciation (depreciation expense): the periodic allocation of the cost of a tangible long-lived asset over its estimated useful life. (4, 13)
Direct charge-off method: a method of accounting for uncollectible accounts by debiting expenses directly when bad debts are discovered instead of using the allowance method; a method that is unacceptable because it violates the matching rule. (10)
Direct cost: a manufacturing cost that is traceable to a specific product or cost objective. (22)
Direct costing: an approach to product costing in which only variable manufacturing costs are assigned to products for product costing and inventory valuation purposes. (28)
Direct labor: all labor costs for specific work performed on products that are conveniently and economically traceable to end products. (22)
Direct labor efficiency variance: the difference between actual hours worked and standard hours allowed for the good units produced, multiplied by the standard labor rate. (27)
Direct labor rate standards: the hourly labor cost per function or job classification that is expected to exist during the next accounting period. (26)
Direct labor rate variance: the difference between the actual labor rate paid and the standard labor rate, multiplied by the actual hours worked. (27)
Direct labor time standard: an hourly expression of the time it takes for each department, machine, or process to complete production on one unit or one batch of output; based on current time and motion studies of workers and machines and past employee/machine performances. (26)
Direct materials: raw materials that become an integral part of the finished product and are conveniently and economically traceable to specific units of productive output. (22)
Discontinued operations: segments of a business that are no longer part of the ongoing operations of the company. (17)
Discount: *verb:* to take out the interest on a promissory note in advance; *noun:* the amount of the interest deducted. (10, 18)
Discounted cash flow: the process of discounting future cash flows back to the present using an anticipated discount rate. (28)
Dishonored note: a promissory note that the maker cannot or will not pay at the maturity date. (10)
Disposal value, see Residual value
Dissolution: a change in the original association of the partners in a partnership resulting from such events as the admission, withdrawal, or death of a partner. (15)
Diversified company, see Conglomerate
Dividend: a distribution of assets of a corporation to its stockholders. (17)
Dividends in arrears: the accumulated unpaid dividends on cumulative preferred stock from prior years. (16)
Dividends yield: a ratio that measures the current return to an investor in a stock. (21)
Double-declining balance method: an accelerated method of depreciation, related to the declining-balance method, under which the fixed rate used in the method is double the straight-line rate; this rate is the maximum allowable for income tax purposes. (13)
Double-entry system: a system of recording business transactions requiring that each transaction have equal debit and credit totals, thereby maintaining a balance within the accounts taken as a whole. (3)
Double taxation: a term referring to the fact that earnings of a corporation are taxed twice, both as the net income of the corporation and as the dividends distributed to the stockholders. (16)
Duration of note: length of time in days between the making of a promissory note and its maturity date. (10)

Earnings per share: item on corporate income statements that shows the net income earned on each share of common stock; net income divided by the weighted average of common shares outstanding; also called net income per share. (7, 17)
Effective interest method: a method of determining the interest and amortization of bond discount or premium for each interest period that requires the application of a constant interest rate to the carrying value of the bonds at the beginning of the period. (18)
Eliminations: adjustments that appear on work sheets in the preparation of consolidated financial statements that are intended to reflect the financial position and operations from the standpoint of a single entity. (20)
Employee earnings record: a record of earnings and withholdings for a single employee. (12)
Ending inventory: merchandise on hand for sale to customers at the end of the accounting period. (6)

Equity method: a method of accounting for long-term investments under which the investor records the initial investment at cost and records its proportionately owned share of subsequent earnings and dividends of the investee as increases or decreases, respectively, in the investment account. (20)
Equivalent units: a measure of productive output of units for a period of time, expressed in terms of fully completed or equivalent whole units produced; partially completed units are restated in terms of equivalent whole units; also called equivalent production. (25)
Estimated liability: a definite obligation of the firm, the exact amount of which cannot be determined until a later date. (12)
Estimated tax: an amount paid in advance by a taxpayer in anticipation of income not subject to withholding. (29)
Estimated useful life: the total number of service units expected from a long-term asset. (13)
Evaluation: the process of scrutinizing the entire decision system for the purpose of improving it. (1)
Excess capacity: machinery and equipment purchased in excess of needs so that extra capacity is available on a stand-by basis during peak usage periods or when other machinery is down for repair. (26)
Exchange rate: the value of one currency in terms of another. (20)
Exchange transaction: when used in connection with the statement of changes in financial position, an exchange of a long-term asset for a long-term liability. (19)
Exemption: a type of deduction from adjusted gross income based on personal characteristics and number of dependents. (29)
Expenditure: a payment or incurrence of an obligation to make a future payment for an asset or service rendered. (14)
Expenses: the costs of the goods and services used up in the process of obtaining revenue; expired cost. (4)
Extraordinary items: events or transactions that are distinguished by their unusual nature and the infrequency of their occurrence. (17)
Extraordinary repairs: repairs that affect the estimated residual value or estimated useful life of an asset. (14)

FIFO product and cost flow: first products to be introduced into a production process are the first products to be completed. Costs attached to those first products are the first costs to be transferred out of the particular production center or department. (25)
Financial Accounting Standards Board (FASB): body that has responsibility for developing and issuing rules on accounting practice; issues Statements of Financial Accounting Standards. (1)
Financial position: the collection of resources belonging to a company and the sources of these resources or claims on them at a particular point in time; shown by a balance sheet. (2)
Financial statement analysis: the collective term used for the techniques that show significant relationships in financial statements and that facilitate comparisons from period to period and among companies. (21)
Financial statements: the means by which accountants communicate to information users; financial reports. (2)
Financing revenues and expenses: revenues from investments and interest expense and other expenses incurred as a result of borrowing money. (7)
Finished goods inventory: an inventory account unique to the manufacturing or production area to which the costs assigned to all completed products are transferred. The balance at period-end represents all manufacturing costs assigned to goods completed but not sold as of that date. (23)
First-in, first-out (FIFO) method: an inventory costing method under which the cost of the first items purchased are assigned to the first items sold and the costs of the last items purchased are assigned to the items remaining in inventory. (11)
Fiscal year: any twelve-month accounting period used by a company. (4)
Fixed assets: another name, no longer in wide use, for long-term nonmonetary assets. (13)
Fixed cost: a cost that remains constant in total within a relevant range of volume or activity. (26)
Fixed manufacturing costs: production-related costs that remain relatively constant in amount during the accounting period and vary little in relation to increases or decreases in production. (22)
Flexibility principle: a principle of systems design that holds that the accounting system should be sufficiently flexible to accommodate growth in the volume of transactions and organizational changes in the business. (8)
Flexible budget: a summary of anticipated costs prepared for a range of different activity levels and geared to changes in the level of productive output. (27)
FOB destination: term relating to transportation charges meaning that the supplier bears the transportation costs to the destination. (6)
FOB shipping point: term relating to transportation charges meaning that the buyer bears the transportation costs from the point of origin. (6)

Footing: a memorandum total of a column of numbers; to foot, to total a column of numbers. (3)
Freight in: transportation charges on merchandise purchased for resale; transportation in. (6)
Full costing: a method of accounting for oil and gas development and exploration under which the costs associated with both successful and unsuccessful explorations are capitalized and depleted over the useful life of the producing resources. (13)
Full disclosure: an accounting convention requiring that financial statements and their accompanying footnotes contain all information relevant to the user's understanding of the situation. (2, 14)
Fully diluted earnings per share: net income applicable to common stock divided by the sum of the weighted-average common stock and common stock equivalents and other potentially dilutive securities. (7, 17) See also Earnings per share.
Funds: equivalent to working capital when used in connection with the statement of changes in financial position. (19)
Future value: the amount that an investment will be worth at a future date if invested at compound interest. (Appendix A)

General journal: the simplest and most flexible type of journal. (3)
Generally accepted accounting principles (GAAP): the conventions, rules, and procedures necessary to define accepted accounting practice at a particular time. (1)
General price level: a price level that reflects the price changes of a group of goods or services. (14)
General-purpose external financial statements: means by which the information accumulated and processed in the financial accounting system is periodically communicated to those persons, especially investors and creditors, who use it outside the enterprise. (7)
Going concern: the assumption that unless there is evidence to the contrary the business will continue to operate for an indefinite period. (4)
Going public: the process by which a corporation offers its shares to the public. (20)
Goods flow: the actual physical movement of inventory goods in the operations of a company. (11)
Goodwill: the excess of the cost of a group of assets (usually a business) over the market value of the assets individually. (14)
Gross income: income from all sources, less allowable exclusions. (29)
Gross payroll: a measure of the total wages or salary earned by an employee before any deductions are subtracted. This amount is also used to determine total manufacturing labor costs. (22)
Gross profit: difference between revenue from sales and cost of goods sold; also called gross profit from sales. (6)
Gross profit method: a method used to estimate the value of inventory. (11)
Gross sales: total sales for cash and on credit for a given accounting period. (6)
Group depreciation: the grouping of items of similar plant assets together for purposes of calculating depreciation. (13)

Hardware: all the equipment needed for the operation of a computer data processing system. (8)
Horizontal analysis: the computation of dollar amount changes and percentage changes from year to year. (21)

Imprest system: a petty cash system in which a petty cash fund is established at a fixed amount of cash and is periodically reimbursed for the exact amount necessary to bring it back to the fixed amount. (9)
Income averaging: a formula that allows taxpayers whose income fluctuates widely to average their income over five years. (29)
Income from operations: the excess of gross profit from sales over operating expenses. (7)
Income statement: a financial statement that shows the amount of income earned by a business over an accounting period. (2)
Income summary: a nominal account used during the closing process in which are summarized all revenues and expenses before the net amount is transferred to the capital account or retained earnings. (5)
Income tax allocation: an accounting method designed to accrue income taxes on the basis of accounting income whenever there are differences in accounting and taxable income. (29)
Income tax expense, see Provision for income taxes
Incremental analysis: a decision analysis format that highlights only relevant decision information or the differences between costs and revenues under two or more alternative courses of action. (28)
Index number: a number constructed by setting the base year equal to 100 percent and calculating other years in relation to the base year. (21)
Indirect cost: a manufacturing cost that is not traceable to a specific product or cost objective and must be assigned by some allocation method. (22)
Indirect labor: labor costs for production-related activities that cannot be associated with, or are not conveniently and economically traceable to, end products and must be assigned by some allocation method. (22)
Indirect materials: less significant raw materials and other production supplies that cannot be convenient-

ly or economically assigned to specific products and must be assigned by some allocation method. (22)
Inflation: an increase in the general price level. (14)
Installment accounts receivable: accounts receivable that are payable in periodic payments. (10)
Intangible assets: long-term assets that have no physical substance but have a value based on rights or privileges accruing to the owner. (7, 13, 14)
Interest: the cost associated with the use of money for a specific period of time. (10, Appendix A)
Interest coverage ratio: a ratio that measures the protection of creditors from a default on interest payments. (21)
Interim financial statements: financial statements prepared on a condensed basis for an accounting period of less than one year. (21)
Internal accounting controls: the controls employed primarily to protect assets and ensure the accuracy and reliability of the accounting records. (9)
Internal administrative controls: controls established to ensure operational efficiency and adherence to managerial policies; related to the decision processes leading to management's authorization of transactions. (9)
Internal control: the plan of organization and all of the coordinate methods and measures adopted within a business to safeguard its assets, check the accuracy and reliability of its accounting data, promote operational efficiency, and encourage adherence to prescribed managerial policies. (9)
Internal Revenue Service (IRS): federal agency that interprets and enforces the U.S. tax laws governing the assessment and collection of revenue for operating the government. (1)
Inventory cost: cost recorded upon purchase of inventory; includes invoice price less cash discounts plus freight and transportation in and applicable insurance, taxes, and tariffs. (11)
Inventory turnover: a ratio that measures the relative size of inventory. (21)
Investments: assets, generally of a long-term nature, that are not used in the normal operation of a business and that management does not intend to convert to cash within the next year. (7)
Invoice: a document prepared by a supplier requesting payment for goods or services provided. (9)
Item-by-item method: a method of applying the lower-of-cost-or-market rule to inventory pricing. (11)

Job card: a labor card supplementing the time card, on which each employee's time on a specific job is recorded; used to support an employee's daily time recorded on the time card and to assign labor costs to specific jobs or batches of product. (22)
Job order cost card: a document maintained for each job or work order in process, upon which all costs of that job are recorded and accumulated as the job order is being worked on. These cards make up the subsidiary ledger of the Work in Process Inventory Control account. (24)
Job order cost system: a product costing system used in the manufacturing of unique or special-order products in which raw materials, direct labor, and manufacturing overhead costs are assigned to specific job orders or batches of products. (24)
Joint cost: a cost that collectively applies or relates to several products or cost objectives and can be assigned to those cost objectives only by means of arbitrary cost allocation. (22)
Journal: a chronological record of all transactions; place where transactions are first recorded. (3)
Journal entry: a separate entry in the journal, that records a single transaction. (3)
Journalizing: the process of recording transactions in a journal. (3)

Last-in, first-out (LIFO) method: an inventory costing method under which the costs of the last items purchased are assigned to the first items sold and the cost of the inventory is composed of the cost of items from the oldest purchases. (11)
Leasehold: a payment made to secure the right to a lease. (14)
Leasehold improvement: an improvement to leased property that becomes the property of the lessor at the end of the lease. (14)
Ledger: a book or file of all of a company's accounts, arranged as in the chart of accounts. (3)
Ledger account form: a form of the account that has four columns, one for debit entries, one for credit entries, and two columns (debit and credit) for showing the balance of the account; used in the general ledger. (3)
Legal capital: the minimum amount that can be reported as contributed capital; usually equal to par value or stated value. (16)
Leverage: the use of debt financing. (21)
Liability: a debt of the business; an amount owed to creditors, employees, government bodies, or others; a claim against assets. (2, 12)
Limited life: the characteristic of a partnership shown when certain events such as the admission, withdrawal, or death of a partner can terminate the partnership. (15)
Liquidating dividend: a dividend that exceeds retained earnings. (17)
Liquidation: the process of ending a business; entails selling assets, paying liabilities, and distributing any remaining assets to the partners. (15)

Liquidity: the position of having enough funds on hand to pay a company's bills when they are due and provide for unanticipated needs for cash. (1, 7)

Long-term liabilities: debts of a business that fall due more than one year ahead, beyond the normal operating cycle, or are to be paid out of noncurrent assets. (7, 12)

Long-term nonmonetary assets: assets that (1) have a useful life of more than one year, (2) are acquired for use in the operation of the business, and (3) are not intended for resale to customers; fixed assets. (11, 13)

Lower-of-cost-or-market rule: a method of inventory pricing under which the inventory is priced at cost or market, whichever is lower. (11)

Major category method: a method of applying the lower-of-cost-or-market method to inventory pricing.

Make or buy decision: a decision commonly faced by management as to whether to make the item, product, or component or to purchase it from outside sources. (28)

Management: the group of people in a business with overall responsibility for achieving the company's goals. (1)

Management accounting: the aspect of accounting that consists of specific information gathering and reporting concepts and accounting procedures that, when applied to a company's financial and production data, will satisfy internal management's needs for product costing information, data used for planning and control of operations, and special reports and analyses used to support management's decisions. (1, 23)

Management advisory services: consulting services offered by public accountants. (1)

Management by exception: a review process whereby management locates and analyzes only the areas of unusually good or bad performance. (27)

Management information system: the interconnected subsystems that provide the information necessary to operate a business. (1)

Manual data processing: a system of data processing in which recording, posting, and other bookkeeping procedures are done by hand. (8)

Manufacturing cost flow: the defined or structured flow of raw materials, direct labor, and manufacturing overhead costs from their incurrence through the inventory accounts and finally to the Cost of Goods Sold account. (23)

Manufacturing (factory) overhead: a diverse collection of production-related costs that are not practically or conveniently traceable to end products and must be assigned by some allocation method. (22)

Marginal tax rates: the tax rate that applies to the last increment of taxable income. (29)

Market: in inventory valuation, the current replacement cost of inventory. (11)

Marketable securities: investment in securities which are readily marketable; temporary investments. (10)

Market risk: the volatility or fluctuation of the price of a stock in relation to the volatility or fluctuation of the prices of other stocks. (21)

Market value: the price investors are willing to pay for a share of stock on the open market. (16)

Master budget: an integrated set of departmental or functional period budgets that have been consolidated into forecasted financial statements for the entire company. (27)

Matching rule: the rule of accounting that revenue must be assigned to the accounting period in which the goods were sold or the services performed, and expenses must be assigned to the accounting period in which they were used to produce revenue; the rule underlying accrual accounting. (4)

Materiality: an accounting convention that refers to the relative importance of an item. (14)

Materials requisition: a document that must be completed and approved before raw materials are issued to production. This form is essential to the control of raw materials and contains such information as the types and quantities of raw materials and supplies needed and the supervisor's approval signature. (22)

Maturity date: the due date of a promissory note. (10)

Maturity value: the total proceeds of a promissory note including principal and interest at the maturity date. (10)

Merchandise inventory: goods on hand and available for sale to customers. (6)

Minority interest: the percentage of ownership attributable to minority stockholders times the net assets of the subsidiary, an amount which appears in the stockholders' equity section of a consolidated balance sheet. (20)

Mixed cost: a cost category that results when more than one type of cost is charged to the same general ledger account. The Repairs and Maintenance account is an example of a mixed cost account. (26)

Money measure: a concept in accounting that requires that business transactions be measured in terms of money. (2)

Mortgage: a type of long-term debt secured by real property that is paid in equal monthly installments. (18)

Multinational corporations: corporations that do business or operate in more than one country; also, transnational corporation. (20)

Multistep form: form of the income statement that arrives at net income in steps. (7)
Mutual agency: the authority of partners to act as agents of the partnership within the scope of normal operations of the business. (15)

Natural resources: long-term assets purchased for the physical substance that can be taken from them and used up rather than for the value of their location. (13)
Net capital gain (or loss): the combined amount of net short-term and net long-term gains or losses. (29)
Net income: the net increase in owner's equity resulting from the profit seeking operations of a company; net income = revenue − expenses. (4)
Net income per share, see Earnings per share
Net long-term capital gain (or loss): the combined total of all gains and losses on long-term capital assets during a tax year. (29)
Net payroll: the amount paid to the employee (cash or check) after all payroll deductions have been subtracted from gross wages. (22)
Net realizable value (NRV): the established selling price of an item in the ordinary course of business less reasonable selling costs. (11, 14)
Net short-term capital gain (or loss): the combined total of all gains and losses on short-term assets during a tax year. (29)
Nominal accounts: temporary accounts showing the accumulation of revenue and expenses only for an accounting period; at the end of the accounting period, these account balances are transferred to owner's equity. (4)
Noncumulative preferred stock: preferred stock on which the dividend may lapse and does not have to be paid if not paid within a given year. (16)
Nonmonetary assets: assets that represent unexpired costs that will become expenses in future accounting periods. (11)
Nonparticipating preferred stock: preferred stock on which the dividend is limited to the indicated amount or rate per share. (16)
No-par stock: capital stock that does not have a par value. (16)
Normal balance: the balance that one would expect an account to have; the usual balance of an account. (5)
Normal capacity: the average annual level of operating capacity that is required to satisfy anticipated sales demand; adjusted to reflect seasonal business factors and operating cycles. (26)
Notes to the financial statements: a section of a corporate annual report that contains notes that aid the user in interpreting some of the items in the financial statements. (7)
Notice of protest: a sworn statement that a promissory note was presented to the maker for payment and the maker refused to pay. (10)
NSF (not sufficient funds) check: a check deposited by the company that is not paid when the depositor's bank presents it for payment to the maker's bank. (9)

Obsolescence: the process of becoming out of date; a contributor, together with physical deterioration, to the limited useful life of tangible assets. (13)
On-line processing: a type of computer system design in which input devices and random-access storage files are tied directly to the computer, enabling transactions to be entered into the records as they occur and data to be retrieved as needed. (8)
Operating expenses: expenses other than cost of goods sold incurred in the operation of a business; especially selling and administrative expenses. (6)
Operating lease: periodic payment for the right to use an asset or assets, recorded in a manner similar to the way in which rent expense payments are recorded. A short-term cancelable lease for which the risks of ownership lie with the lessor. (18)
Opinion section (of accountant's report): the portion of the accountant's report that tells the results of the accountant's audit of the financial statements. (7)
Ordinary annuity: a series of equal payments made at the end of equal intervals of time, with compound interest on these payments. (Appendix A)
Ordinary repairs: expenditures, usually of a recurring nature, that are necessary to maintain an asset in good operating condition. (14)
Organization costs: the costs of forming a corporation. (16)
Outstanding checks: checks issued and recorded by the depositor but not yet presented to the bank for payment. (9)
Outstanding stock: the shares of a corporation's stock held by stockholders. (16)
Overhead volume variance: the difference between the factory overhead budgeted for the level of production achieved and the overhead applied to production using the standard overhead rate. (27)
Owner's equity: the resources invested by the owner of the business; assets − liabilities = owner's equity; also called residual equity. (2)

Parent company: a company that owns a controlling interest in another company. (20)
Participating preferred stock: preferred stock on which stockholders may receive a dividend higher than the indicated rate if common stockholders receive a dividend. (16)
Partners' equity: the owners' equity section of the balance sheet in a partnership. (15)

Partnership: an association of two or more persons to carry on as co-owners a business for profit. (1, 15)
Partnership agreement: the contractual relationship between partners that identifies the details of the partnership; agreement should clarify such things as name of the business, duties of partners, partner investments, profit and loss ratios, and procedures for admission and withdrawal of partners. (15)
Par value: the amount printed on each share of stock, which must be recorded in the capital stock accounts; used in determining the legal capital of a corporation. (16)
Patent: an exclusive right granted by the federal government to make a particular product or use a specific process. (14)
Payback method: a method used to evaluate a capital expenditure proposal that focuses on the cash flow of the project and determines the payback period or the time required to recoup the original investment through cash flow from the item or project. (28)
Payroll register: a detailed listing of a firm's total payroll, prepared each payday. (12)
Percentage of net sales method: a method of estimating uncollectible accounts expense based on the assumption that a certain percentage of total net sales will not be collectible. (10)
Period budget: a forecast of annual operating results for a segment or functional area of a company that represents a quantitative expression of planned activities. (27)
Period costs (expenses): expired costs of an accounting period that represent dollars attached to resources used or consumed during the period; any cost or expense item on an income statement. (22)
Periodic inventory method: a method of accounting for inventory under which the cost of goods sold is determined by adding the net cost of purchases to beginning inventory and subtracting the ending inventory. (6, 11, 23)
Periodicity: the assumption that the measurement of net income for any period less than the life of the business is necessarily tentative, but nevertheless a useful approximation. (4)
Perpetual inventory method: a method of accounting for inventory under which the sales and purchases of individual items of inventory are recorded continuously, therefore allowing cost of goods sold to be determined without taking a physical inventory. (6, 11, 23)
Petty cash fund: a small fund established by a company to make small payments of cash. (9)
Petty cash system, see Imprest system
Petty cash voucher: a document that supports each payment made out of a petty cash fund. (9)
Physical inventory, see Taking a physical inventory
Physical volume method: an approach to the problem of allocating joint production costs to specific products that is based on or uses some measure of physical volume (units, pounds, liters, grams, etc.) as the basis for joint cost allocation. (22)
Planning: the process of formulating a course of action. (1)
Point-of-sale basis: a basis of revenue recognition that recognizes revenue at the point when title passes to the buyer, usually the date of delivery. (14)
Pooling of interests method: a method of accounting for a business combination in which the combining companies are treated as having their net assets pooled instead of one company having sold out to the other. (20)
Portfolio: a group of loans or investments designed to average the return and risks of a creditor or investor. (21)
Post-closing trial balance: a trial balance prepared after all adjusting and closing entries have been posted and immediately before the beginning of the next period as a final check on the balance of the ledger. (5)
Posting: the process of transferring journal entry information from the journal to the ledger. (3)
Practical capacity: theoretical capacity reduced by normal and anticipated work stoppages. (26)
Predetermined overhead rate: an overhead cost factor that is used to assign manufacturing (factory) overhead costs (all indirect manufacturing costs) to specific units, jobs, or cost objectives. (22)
Preemptive right: the right of stockholders to purchase additional shares of stock when they are issued in proportion to their current holdings. (16)
Preferred stock: a type of stock that has some preference over common stock, usually including dividends. (16)
Premium: the amount by which the issue price of a stock or bond exceeds the face value. (18)
Prepaid expenses: expenses paid in advance that do not expire during the current accounting period; an asset account. (4)
Present value: the amount that must be invested now at a given rate of interest to produce a given future value. (Appendix A)
Present value method: a discounted cash flow approach to measure the estimated performance of a capital investment. The value of all future cash flows discounted back to the present (present value) must exceed the initial investment if a positive decision is to be made. (28)
Price/earnings (P/E) ratio: a ratio that measures the relationship of the current market price of a stock to the earnings per share. (21)

Price index: a series of numbers, one for each period, that represents an average price for a group of goods and services, relative to the average price of the same group of goods and services at a beginning date. (14)

Primary earnings per share: net income applicable to common stock divided by the sum of the weighted-average common shares and common stock equivalents. (7, 17) See also Earnings per share.

Prior period adjustments: events or transactions that relate to an earlier accounting period but were not determinable in the earlier period. (17)

Proceeds from discounting: the amount received by the borrower when a promissory note is discounted; proceeds = maturity value − discount. (10)

Process cost system: a product costing system used by companies that produce a large number of similar products or have a continuous production flow where manufacturing costs are accumulated by department or process rather than by batches of products. (24)

Product cost: costs identified as being either raw materials, direct labor, or manufacturing overhead, traceable or assignable to products; they become part of a product's unit manufacturing cost, and are in inventories at period end. (22)

Production method: a method of depreciation that bases the depreciation charge for a period of time solely on the amount of use of the asset during the period of time. (13)

Profit: imprecise term for the earnings of a business enterprise. (4)

Profitability: the ability of a business to earn a satisfactory level of profits and to attract investor capital (1, 7)

Profit margin: a measure of profitability; the percentage of each sales dollar that results in net income; net income divided by sales. (7, 21)

Program: the means by which a computer is instructed; consists of a sequence of instructions that, when carried out, will produce a desired result. (8)

Programmer: the person who writes the programs that instruct the computer based on the specifications of the systems analyst. (8)

Progressive tax: a tax based on a rate structure that increases the rate of tax as the amount of taxable income becomes larger. (29)

Promissory note: an unconditional promise to pay a definite sum of money on demand or at a future date. (10)

Property, plant, and equipment: tangible assets of a long-term nature used in the continuing operation of the business. (7)

Proportional tax rate: a tax in which the rate is the same percentage regardless of the amount of taxable income. (29)

Protest fee: the charge made by a bank for preparing and mailing a notice of protest. (10)

Provision for income taxes: the expense for federal and state income tax shown on the income statement; income tax expense. (7)

Proxy: a legal document, signed by the stockholder, giving another party the authority to vote his or her shares. (16)

Public accounting: the field of accounting that offers services in auditing, taxes, and management advising to the public for a fee. (1)

Publicly held corporation: a corporation registered with the Securities and Exchange Commission; its securities are traded publicly. (20)

Purchase method: a method of preparing consolidated financial statements. (20)

Purchase order: a document prepared by the accounting department authorizing a supplier to ship specified goods or provide specified services. (9, 22)

Purchase requisition (request): a document, used to begin the raw materials purchasing function, that originates in the production department and identifies the items to be purchased, states the quantities required, and must be approved by a qualified manager or supervisor. (9, 22)

Purchases: an account used under the periodic inventory system in which the cost of all merchandise bought for resale is recorded. (6)

Purchases discounts: allowances made for prompt payment for merchandise purchased for resale; a contra purchases account. (6)

Purchases journal: a type of special-purchase journal in which are recorded credit purchases of merchandise (if it is a single-column journal) or credit purchases in general (if it is a multicolumn journal). (8)

Purchases returns and allowances: account used to accumulate cash refunds and other allowances made by suppliers on merchandise originally purchased for resale; a contra purchases account. (6)

Purchasing power: the ability of a dollar at a point in time to purchase goods or services. (14)

Purchasing power gains and losses: gains and losses that occur as a result of holding monetary items during periods of inflation or deflation. (14)

Qualitative characteristics: criteria for judging the information accountants provide to decision makers; the primary criteria are relevance and reliability. (2) See also Standards of quality.

Quick ratio: a ratio that measures the relationship of

the more liquid current assets (cash, marketable securities, and accounts receivable) to current liabilities. (21)

Ratio analysis: a means of stating a meaningful relationship between two numbers. (21)

Raw materials inventory: an inventory account made up of balances of raw materials and supplies on hand at a particular time; also called Stores or Inventory Control account. (23)

Raw materials price standard: a carefully derived estimate or projected amount of what a particular type of raw material will cost when purchased during the next accounting period. (26)

Raw materials price variance: the difference between the actual price paid for raw materials and the standard price, multiplied by the actual quantity purchased. (27)

Raw materials quantity standard: an expression of forecasted or expected quantity usage that is influenced by product engineering specifications, quality of raw materials used, age and productivity of the machines being used, and the quality and experience of the machine operators and set-up people. (26)

Raw materials quantity variance: the difference between the actual quantity of raw materials used and the standard quantity that should have been used, multiplied by the standard price. (27)

Real accounts: balance sheet accounts; accounts whose balances can extend past the end of an accounting period. (4)

Receivable turnover: a ratio that measures the relative size of accounts receivable. (21)

Receiving report: a document prepared when ordered goods are received, the data of which are matched with the descriptions and quantities listed on the purchase order to verify that the goods ordered were actually received. (9, 22)

Recognition problem: the difficulty of deciding when a business transaction occurs; usually determined to be the point in a sale when title is transferred. (3)

Registered bonds: bonds for which the name and address of the bond owner are recorded with the issuing company. (18)

Regressive tax: a tax based on a rate structure that decreases the rate of tax as the amount of taxable income becomes larger. (29)

Relative sales value method: an approach to the problem of allocating joint production costs to specific products that is based on or uses the product's revenue-producing ability (sales value) as the basis for joint cost allocation. (22)

Relevance: standard of quality requiring that accounting information bear directly on the economic decision for which it is to be used; one of the primary qualitative characteristics of accounting information. (2)

Relevant decision information: future cost, revenue, or resource usage data used in decision analyses that differ among the decision's alternative courses of action. (28)

Relevant range: a range of productive activity that represents the potential volume levels within which actual operations are likely to occur. (26)

Reliability: standard of quality requiring that accounting information be faithful to the original data and that it be verifiable; one of the primary qualitative characteristics of accounting information. (2) See also Representative faithfulness and Verifiability.

Replacement cost: an entry value that represents the cost to buy (or replace), in the normal course of business, new assets of equivalent operating or productive capacity. (14)

Representative faithfulness: the agreement of information with what it is supposed to represent. (2)

Reserve recognition accounting: a method of accounting for oil and gas reserves proposed by the Securities and Exchange Commission under which new proved reserves would be recognized immediately in the accounting records at their estimated current value. (13)

Residual equity: the common stock of a corporation. (16)

Residual value: the estimated net scrap, salvage, or trade-in value of a tangible asset at the estimated date of disposal; also called salvage value or disposal value. (13)

Responsibility accounting system: an accounting system that personalizes accounting reports by classifying and reporting cost and revenue information according to defined responsibility areas of specific managers or management positions; also called activity accounting or profitability accounting. (26)

Retail method: a method of estimating inventory at cost in a retail enterprise. (11)

Retained earnings: the stockholders' equity that has arisen from retaining assets from earnings in the business; the accumulated earnings of a corporation from its inception minus any losses, dividends, or transfers to contributed capital. (7, 17)

Retained earnings statement: a statement that provides a summary of the changes in retained earnings during the accounting period. (17)

Return on assets: a measure of profitability that shows how efficiently a company is using all its assets; net income divided by total assets. (7)

Return on owner investment: a measure of profitability related to the amount earned by a business in relation to the owners' investment in the business; net income divided by owners' equity. (7, 17)

Revenue: a measure of the asset values received from customers during a specific period of time; equals the price of goods sold and services rendered during that time. (4)

Revenue expenditure: an expenditure necessary to maintain and operate plant and equipment; charged to expense because the benefits from the expenditure will be used up in the current period. (14)

Reversing entries: entries made after the closing of records for one accounting period that reverse certain adjusting entries; designed to aid in routine bookkeeping the next accounting period. (12)

Salaries: compensation to employees who are paid at a monthly or yearly rate. (12)

Sales discounts: discounts given to customers for early payment for sales made on credit; a contra sales account. (6)

Sales journal: a type of special-purpose journal used to record credit sales. (8)

Sales mix analysis: an analysis to determine the most profitable combination of product sales when a company produces more than one product. (28)

Sales returns and allowances: account used to accumulate amount of cash refund granted to customers or other allowances related to prior sales; a contra sales account. (6)

Salvage value, see Residual value

Schedule of equivalent production: a process costing schedule in which equivalent production is computed for the period for both materials and conversion costs. (25)

Scope section (of accountant's report): the portion of the accountant's report that tells the extent of the accountant's audit of the financial statements. (7)

Secured bonds: bonds that give the bondholders a pledge of certain assets of the company as a guarantee of repayment. (18)

Securities and Exchange Commission (SEC): an agency of the federal government that has the legal power to set and enforce accounting practices for firms reporting to it. (1)

Semivariable cost: a cost that possesses both variable and fixed cost behavior characteristics in that part of the cost is fixed and part varies with the volume of output. (26)

Separate entity: a concept in accounting that requires a business to be treated as separate from its creditors, customers, and owners. (2)

Serial bonds: a bond issue with several different maturity dates. (18)

Service charge: a charge made by banks for various functions they perform for a depositor. (9)

Short-term monetary assets: assets such as cash, temporary investments, accounts receivable, and notes receivable that derive their usefulness from their relative availability for the payment of current obligations; these assets are not used in the productive functions of the enterprise. (10)

Short-term nonmonetary assets: current assets such as inventory, supplies, and prepaid expenses. (11)

Signature card: a card, maintained by a bank, that contains the signatures authorized to sign a depositor's checks. (9)

Significant influence (of investor over investee company): ability of an investor to affect operating and financial policies of an investee company, even though the investor holds less than 50 percent of the voting stock of the investee. (20)

Simple capital structure: a capital structure with no other securities (either stocks or bonds) that can be converted into common stock. (17)

Simple interest: the interest cost for one or more periods, if one assumes that the amount on which the interest is computed stays the same from period to period. (Appendix A)

Single-step form: form of the income statement that arrives at net income in a single step. (7)

Social accounting: field of accounting devoted to the evaluation through cost-benefit analysis of government and other human service programs and projects. (1)

Software: comprises the programs, instructions, and routines that make possible the use of computer hardware. (8)

Sole proprietorship: a business formed by one person. (1)

Source of working capital: a transaction that results in net increase in working capital. (19)

Special order decision: a type of decision faced by management in which a customer wishes to purchase a large number of similar or identical products at prices below those listed in brochures or advertisements. If capacity exists to produce the order while not disturbing the regular production process, the company can consider the order; also called special product order decision. (28)

Special-purpose journal: an input device in an accounting system that is used to record a single type of transaction. (8)

Specific-identification method: an inventory costing method under which the actual cost of specific items is used for determining cost of goods sold. (11)

Specific price level: a price level that reflects the price changes of a specific commodity or item. (14)

Split-off point: a particular point in a manufacturing process where a joint product splits or divides and two or more separate products emerge. (22)

Standard costs: realistically predetermined costs for raw materials, direct labor, and factory overhead that are usually expressed as a cost per unit of finished product. (26)
Standard direct labor cost: a standard cost computed by multiplying the direct labor time standard by the direct labor rate standard. (26)
Standard factory overhead cost: a standard cost computed by multiplying the standard variable overhead rate and the standard fixed overhead rate by the appropriate application base. (26)
Standard fixed overhead rate: an overhead application rate computed by dividing the total budgeted fixed overhead costs by the normal capacity for the period. (26)
Standard raw materials cost: a standard cost computed by multiplying the raw materials price standard by the raw materials quantity standard. (26)
Standards of quality: criteria for judging the information accountants provide to decision makers. (2) See also Qualitative characteristics.
Standard variable overhead rate: an overhead application rate computed by dividing the total budgeted variable overhead costs by the application base being used by the company. (26)
Stated value: a value assigned by the board of directors to no-par stock. (16)
Statement of changes in financial position: a major financial statement that summarizes the financing and investing activities of a business. (2, 19)
Statement of cost of goods manufactured: formal statement summarizing the flow of all manufacturing costs incurred during a period; yields the dollar amount of costs of products completed and transferred to Finished Goods Inventory in that period. (23)
Statement of owner's equity: a financial statement that shows the changes in the owner's capital investment during the year. (2)
Stock certificate: a document issued to a stockholder in a corporation indicating the number of shares of stock owned by the stockholder. (16)
Stock dividend: a pro rata distribution of shares of a corporation's stock to the corporation's stockholders. (17)
Stockholders' equity: the owners' equity section of a corporation's balance sheet. (16)
Stock split: an increase in the number of outstanding shares of stock accompanied by a proportionate reduction in the par or stated value. (17)
Stock subscription: an issuance of stock where the investor agrees to pay for the stock on some future date or in installments at an agreed price. (16)
Storage units: the part of the central processor in a computer system where programs and data are retained until needed. (8)
Straight-line method: a method of depreciation that assumes that depreciation is dependent on the passage of time and that allocates an equal amount of depreciation to each period of time. (13)
Subchapter S corporation: a corporation established by the owners of small businesses to gain some of the legal benefits of incorporation while still being taxed as a partnership. (29)
Subsidiary: a company whose stock is more than 50 percent owned by another company. (20)
Subsidiary ledger: a ledger separate from the general ledger; contains a group of related accounts the total of whose balances equals the balance of a controlling account in the general ledger. (8, 24)
Successful efforts accounting: a method of accounting for oil and gas development and exploration costs under which the costs of successful exploration are capitalized and depleted over the useful life of the producing resources and the costs of unsuccessful explorations are expensed immediately. (13)
Summary of significant accounting policies: section of a corporate annual report that discloses which generally accepted accounting principles the company has followed in preparing the financial statements. (7)
Sum-of-the-years'-digits method: an accelerated method of depreciation. (13)
System design: a phase of system installation whose purpose is to formulate the new system or changes in the existing system. (8)
System implementation: a phase of system installation whose purpose is to put in operating order a new system or change in an existing system. (8)
System investigation: a phase of system installation whose purpose is to determine the requirements of a new system or to evaluate an existing system. (8)
Systems analyst: the person who, in a computer system, carries out the functions of systems investigation and systems design. (8)

T account: a form of an account which has a physical resemblance to the letter T; used to analyze transactions. (3)
Taking a physical inventory: the act of making a physical count of all merchandise on hand at the end of an accounting period. (6)
Tangible assets: long-term assets that have physical substance. (13)
Taxable income: the amount on which income taxes are assessed. (29)
Tax credits: deductions from the computed tax liability. (29)
Tax evasion: the illegal concealment of actual tax liabilities. (29)

Tax liability: the amount of tax that must be paid based on taxable income and the applicable tax table. (29)

Tax planning: the arrangement of a taxpayer's affairs in such a way as to incur the smallest legal tax. (29)

Tax services: services offered by public accountants in tax planning, compliance, and reporting. (1)

Temporary investments (marketable securities): investments intended to be held only until needed to pay a current obligation. (10)

Term bonds: bonds of a bond issue that all mature at the same time. (18)

Theoretical capacity: the maximum productive output of a department or a company if all machinery and equipment were operated at optimum speed without any interruptions in production for a given time period; also called ideal capacity. (26)

Time card: a basic time record document of an employee upon which either the supervisor or a time clock records the daily starting and finishing times of the person. (22)

Timeliness: the qualitative characteristic of Accounting information that reaches the user in time to help in making a decision. (2)

Total inventory method: a method of applying the lower-of-cost-or-market method to inventory pricing. (11)

Total manufacturing costs: a term used in the statement of cost of goods manufactured that represents the total of raw materials used, direct labor, and manufacturing overhead costs incurred and charged to production during an accounting period. (23)

Trade credit: credit to customers at either the wholesale or the retail level. (10)

Trademark: a registered symbol that gives the holder the right to use it to identify a product or service. (14)

Transportation in, see Freight in

Treasury stock: capital stock of a company, either common or preferred, that has been issued and reacquired by the issuing company but has not been reissued or retired. (17)

Trend analysis: the calculation of percentage changes for several successive years; a variation of horizontal analysis. (21)

Trial balance: a listing of accounts in the general ledger with their debit or credit balances in respective columns and a totaling of the columns; used to test the equality of debit and credit balances in the ledger. (3)

2/10, n/30: credit terms enabling the debtor to take a 2 percent discount if the invoice is paid within ten days after the invoice date; otherwise, the debtor must pay the full amount of the invoice within thirty days. (6)

Uncollectible accounts: accounts receivable from customers who cannot or will not pay. (10)

Underapplied or overapplied overhead: the difference resulting when the amount of factory overhead costs applied to products during an accounting period is more or less than the actual amount of factory overhead costs incurred during the same period. (24)

Understandability: the qualitative characteristic of accounting information that is presented in a form and in terms that its user can understand. (2)

Unearned revenue: a revenue received in advance for which the goods will not be delivered or the services performed during the current accounting period; a liability account. (4)

Unit cost: the amount of manufacturing costs incurred in the completion or production of one unit of product; usually computed by dividing total production costs for a job or period of time by the respective number of units produced. (24)

Unit cost analysis schedule: a process costing statement used to (1) accumulate all costs charged to the Work in Process Inventory account of each department or production process, and (2) compute cost per equivalent unit for materials and conversion costs. (25)

Unlimited liability: each partner has a personal liability for all debts of the partnership. (15)

Unsecured bonds: bonds issued on the general credit of a company; debenture bonds. (18)

Use of working capital: a transaction that results in a net decrease in working capital. (19)

Valuation problem: the difficulty of assigning a value to a business transaction; in general, determined to be original, or historical, cost. (3)

Variable cost: a cost that changes in total in direct proportion to productive output or any other volume measure. (26)

Variable manufacturing costs: types of manufacturing costs that increase or decrease in direct proportion to the number of units produced. (22)

Verifiability: the qualitative characteristic of accounting information that can be confirmed or duplicated by independent parties using the same measurement techniques. (2)

Vertical analysis: the calculation of percentages to show the relationship of the component parts of a financial statement to the total in the statement. (21)

Voucher: a written authorization prepared for each expenditure in a voucher system. (9)
Voucher check: a check specifically designed for use in a voucher system. (9)
Voucher register: a special-purpose journal in which vouchers are recorded after they have been properly approved. (9)
Voucher system: any system providing documentary evidence of and written authorization for business transactions, usually associated with expenditures. (9)
Voucher trail: the sequence of written approval by key individuals supporting an expenditure in a voucher system. (9)

Wages: compensation for employees at an hourly rate or on a piecework basis. (12)
Wasting assets: another term for natural resources. (13)
Working capital: the amount by which total current assets exceed total current liabilities. (7)
Working papers: documents prepared and used by the accountant that aid in organizing the accountant's work and provide evidence to support the basis of the financial statements. (5)
Work in process inventory: an inventory account unique to the manufacturing or production area to which all manufacturing costs incurred and assigned to products are charged. The balance at period-end represents all costs assigned to goods partially completed at that particular time. (23)
Work sheet: a type of working paper that is used as a preliminary step and aid to the preparation of financial statements. (5)

Zero bracket amount: an amount of gross income equal to the amount on which no income tax liability would result. (29)

Index

Note: Boldface indicates a key term and the page where it is defined.

now for final exam:
balance sheet (p 217) without aid of text
income statement (p 222) without aid of text